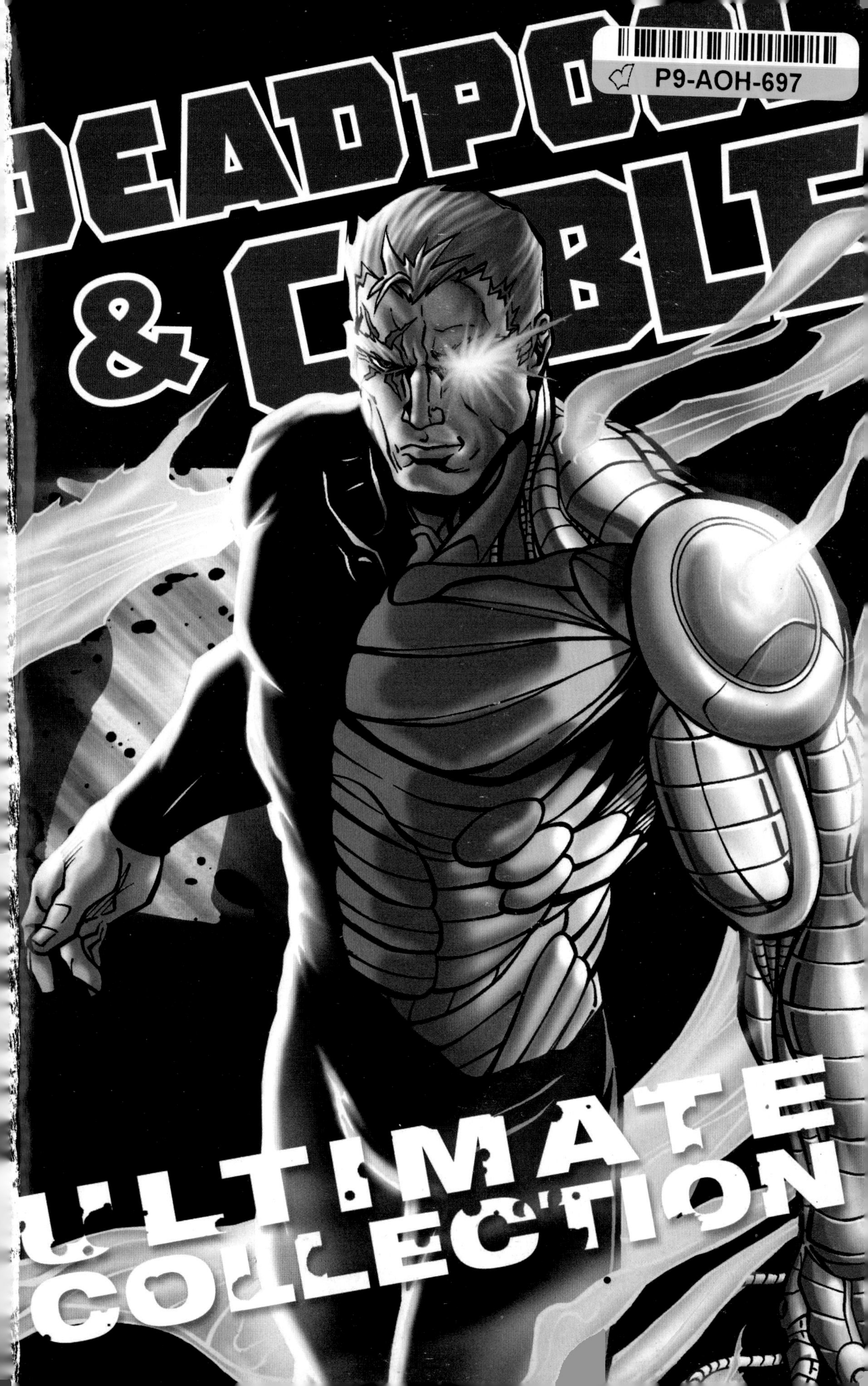
ULTIMATE
COLLECTION

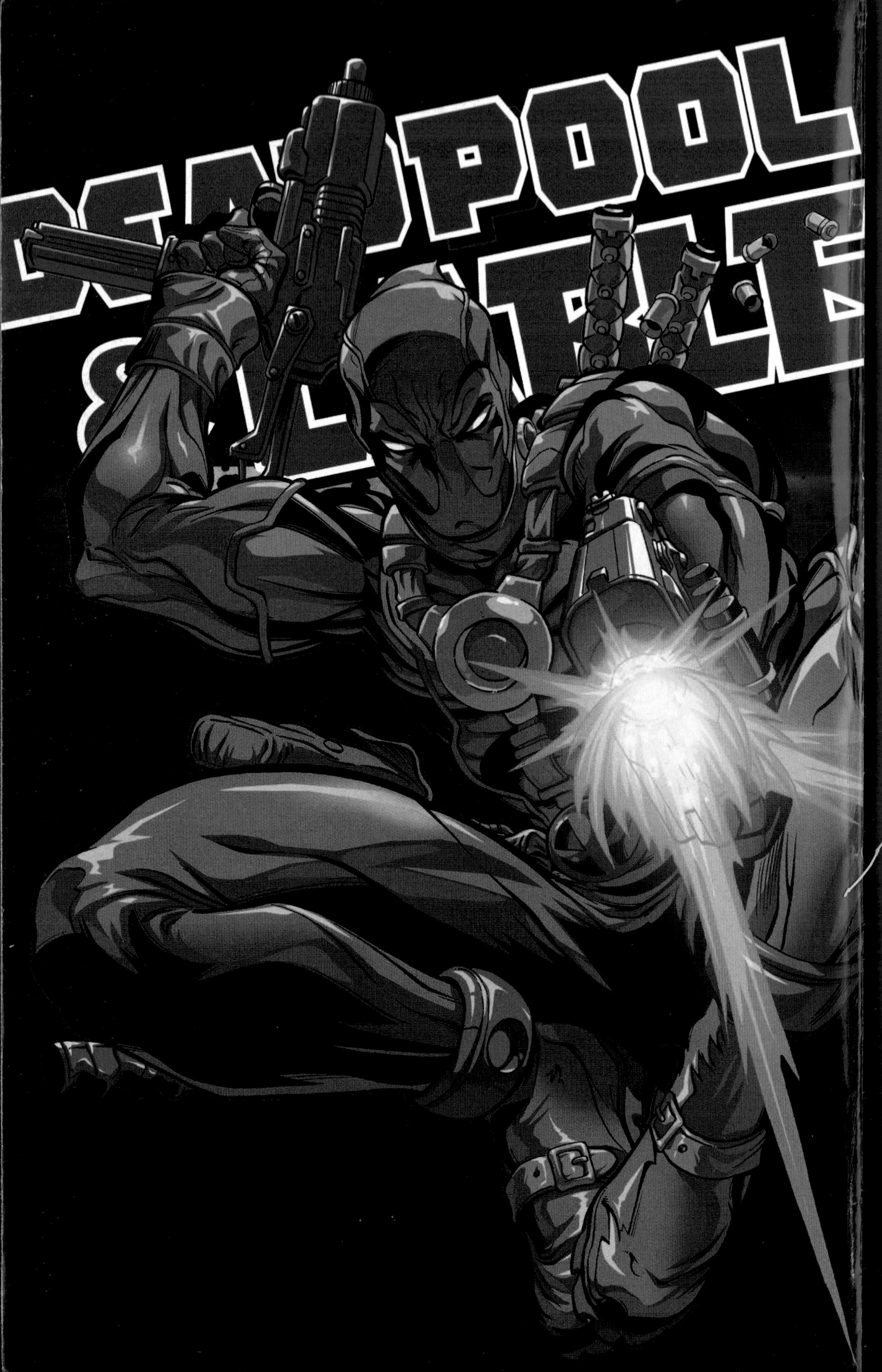

ULTIMATE COLLECTION

WRITER: **FABIAN NICIEZA**

ISSUES #1-2
ARTISTS: **UDON'S MARK BROOKS** & **SHANE LAW**
WITH **CHRIS STEPHENS**

ISSUES #3-18
PENCILER: **PATRICK ZIRCHER**
INKERS: **UDON'S ROB ROSS, ALAN TAM** & **M3TH**
WITH **DEREK FRIDOLFS** (ISSUE #12)
COLORISTS: **UDON'S SHANE LAW** & **KEVIN YAN** AND **GOTHAM STUDIOS**
UDON CHIEF: **ERIK KO**

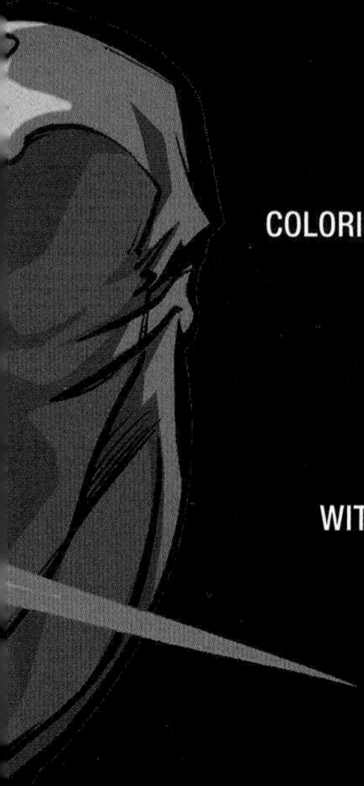

LETTERERS: **VIRTUAL CALLIGRAPHY'S CORY PETIT, RUS WOOTON** & **CHRIS ELIOPOULOS**
COVER ARTISTS: **ROB LIEFELD, MARK BROOKS** & **PATRICK ZIRCHER**
WITH **M3TH, ROB ROSS, SHANE LAW, FRANK D'ARMATA** & **PAUL MOUNTS**
ASSISTANT EDITORS: **ANDY SCHMIDT** & **MOLLY LAZER**
EDITORS: **TOM BREVOORT** & **NICOLE BOOSE**
CONSULTING EDITORS: **JOHN BARBER** & **RALPH MACCHIO**

COLLECTION EDITOR: **CORY LEVINE**
EDITORIAL ASSISTANTS: **JAMES EMMETT** & **JOE HOCHSTEIN**
ASSISTANT EDITORS: **ALEX STARBUCK** & **NELSON RIBEIRO**
EDITORS, SPECIAL PROJECTS: **JENNIFER GRÜNWALD** & **MARK D. BEAZLEY**
SENIOR EDITOR, SPECIAL PROJECTS: **JEFF YOUNGQUIST**
SENIOR VICE PRESIDENT OF SALES: **DAVID GABRIEL**
BOOK DESIGN: **RODOLFO MURAGUCHI**

EDITOR IN CHIEF: **AXEL ALONSO**
CHIEF CREATIVE OFFICER: **JOE QUESADA**
PUBLISHER: **DAN BUCKLEY**
EXECUTIVE PRODUCER: **ALAN FINE**

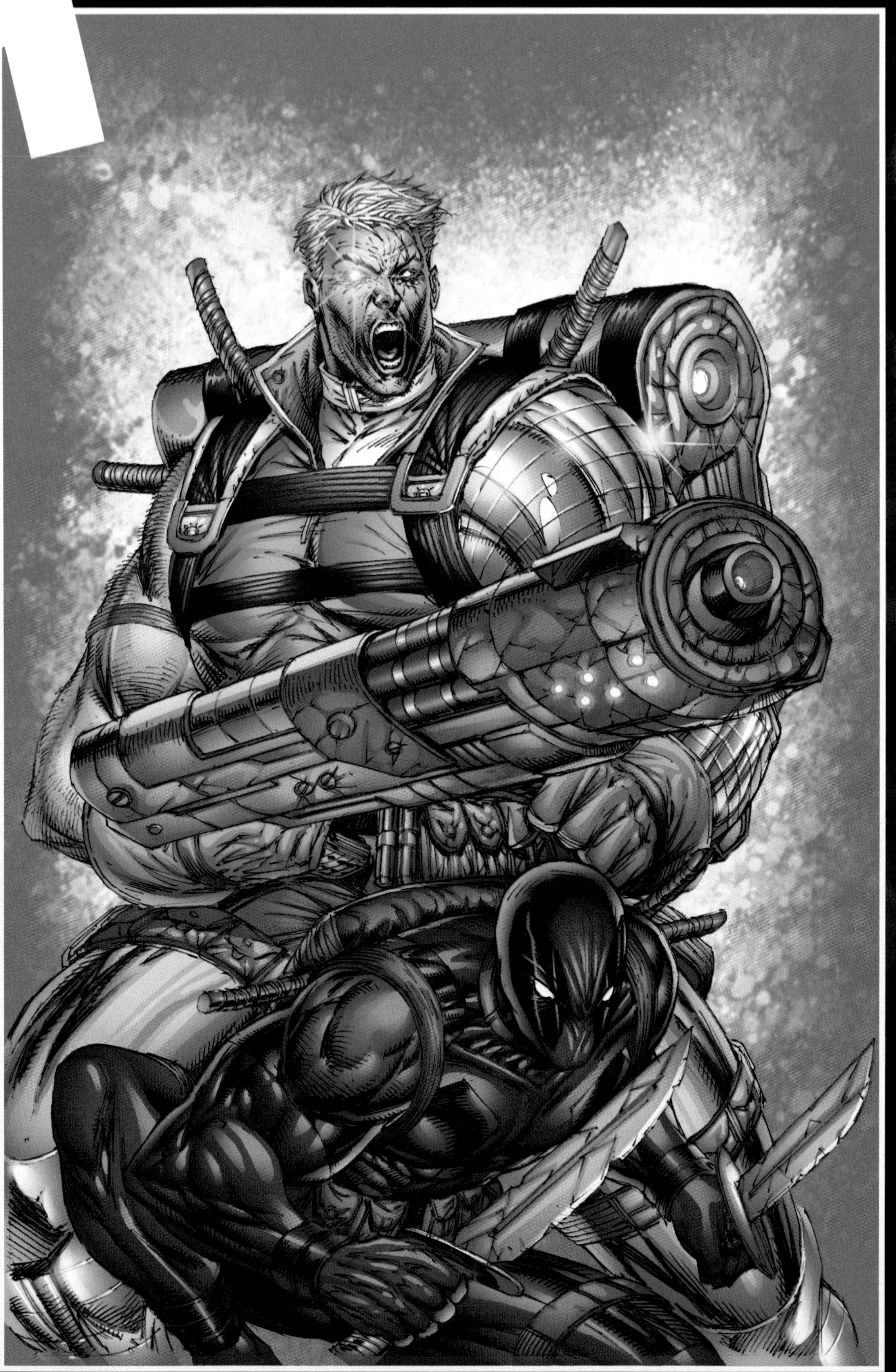

CABLE

NATHAN SUMMERS IS ONE OF THE WORLD'S MIGHTIEST MUTANTS, BUT RECENTLY HIS TELEKINETIC AND TELEPATHIC ABILITIES HAVE SPUN OUT OF CONTROL. NATHAN STRUGGLES, AT WAR WITH HIMSELF AND THE TIMES HE LIVES IN, BECAUSE HE KNOWS THAT THE ONLY WAY TO FORGE A PEACEFUL TOMORROW IS TO FIGHT FOR PEACE TODAY.

DEADPOOL

WADE WILSON IS A GUN-FOR-HIRE. A BY-PRODUCT OF THE MILITARY'S WEAPON X PROGRAM, WILSON WAS GIVEN INCREDIBLE STRENGTH, AGILITY AND HEALING POWERS – BUT AT A PRICE. HIS CELLULAR STRUCTURE IS IN CONSTANT FLUX AND HIS SANITY IS QUESTIONABLE. AN OUTSIDER, ALL WILSON WANTS TO DO IS SWIM IN THE SOCIETAL CESSPOOL. PREFERABLY THE BREASTSTROKE. BUT NO SPEEDOS…

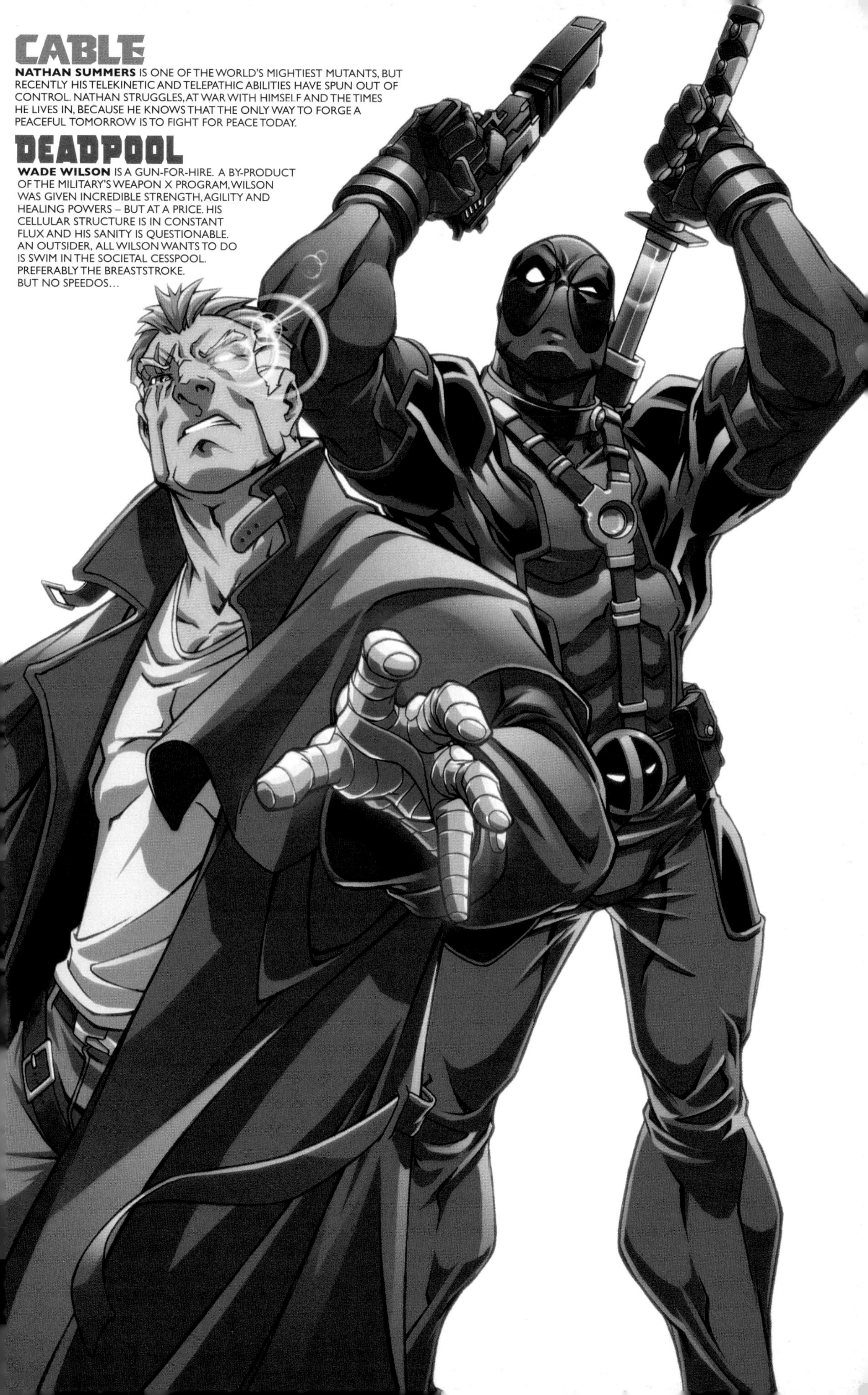

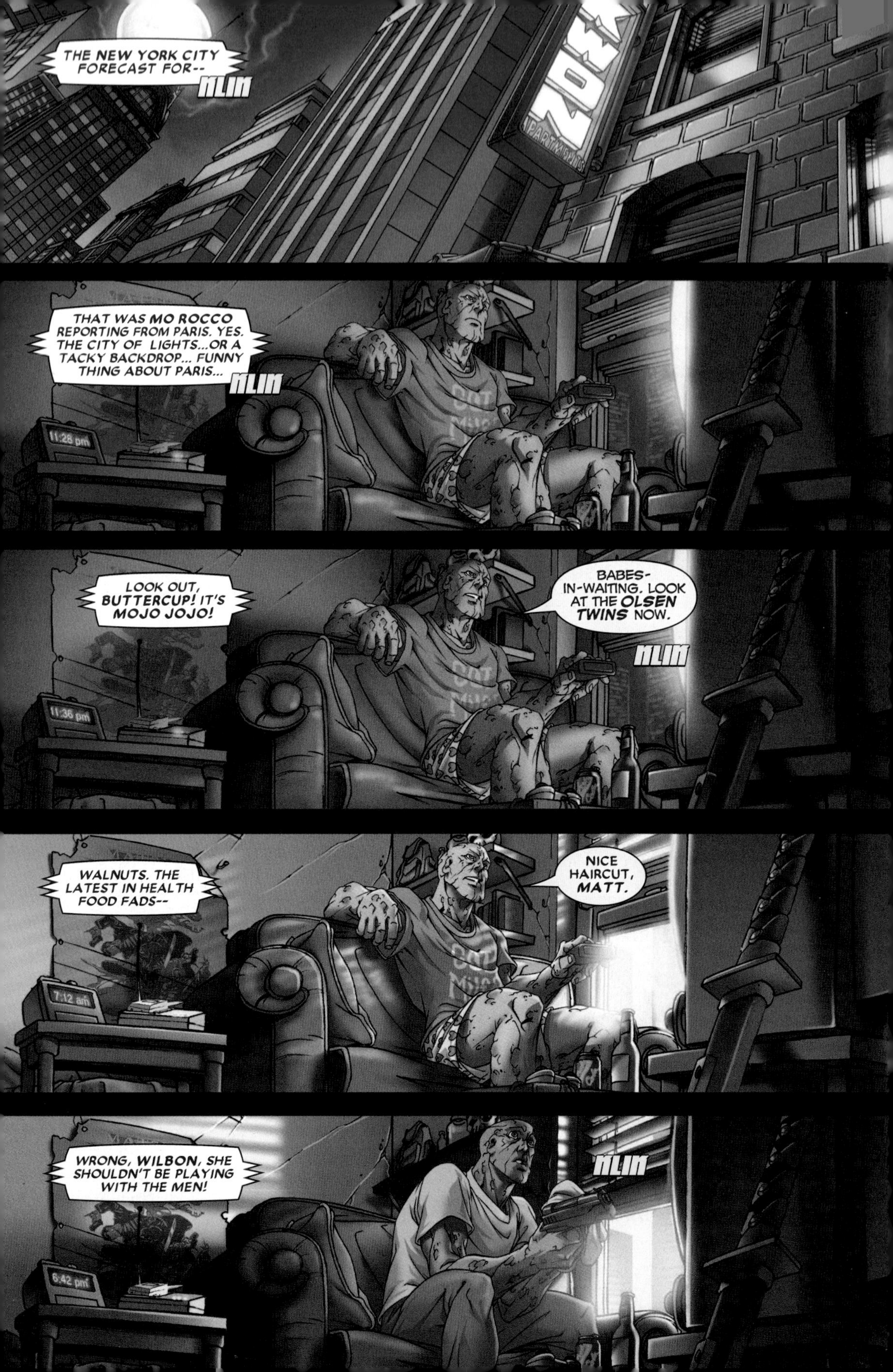
THE NEW YORK CITY FORECAST FOR--
KLIK
THAT WAS MO ROCCO REPORTING FROM PARIS. YES. THE CITY OF LIGHTS...OR A TACKY BACKDROP... FUNNY THING ABOUT PARIS...
KLIK
11:28 pm
LOOK OUT, BUTTERCUP! IT'S MOJO JOJO!
BABES-IN-WAITING. LOOK AT THE OLSEN TWINS NOW.
KLIK
11:36 pm
WALNUTS. THE LATEST IN HEALTH FOOD FADS--
NICE HAIRCUT, MATT.
7:12 am
WRONG, WILBON, SHE SHOULDN'T BE PLAYING WITH THE MEN!
KLIK
6:42 pm

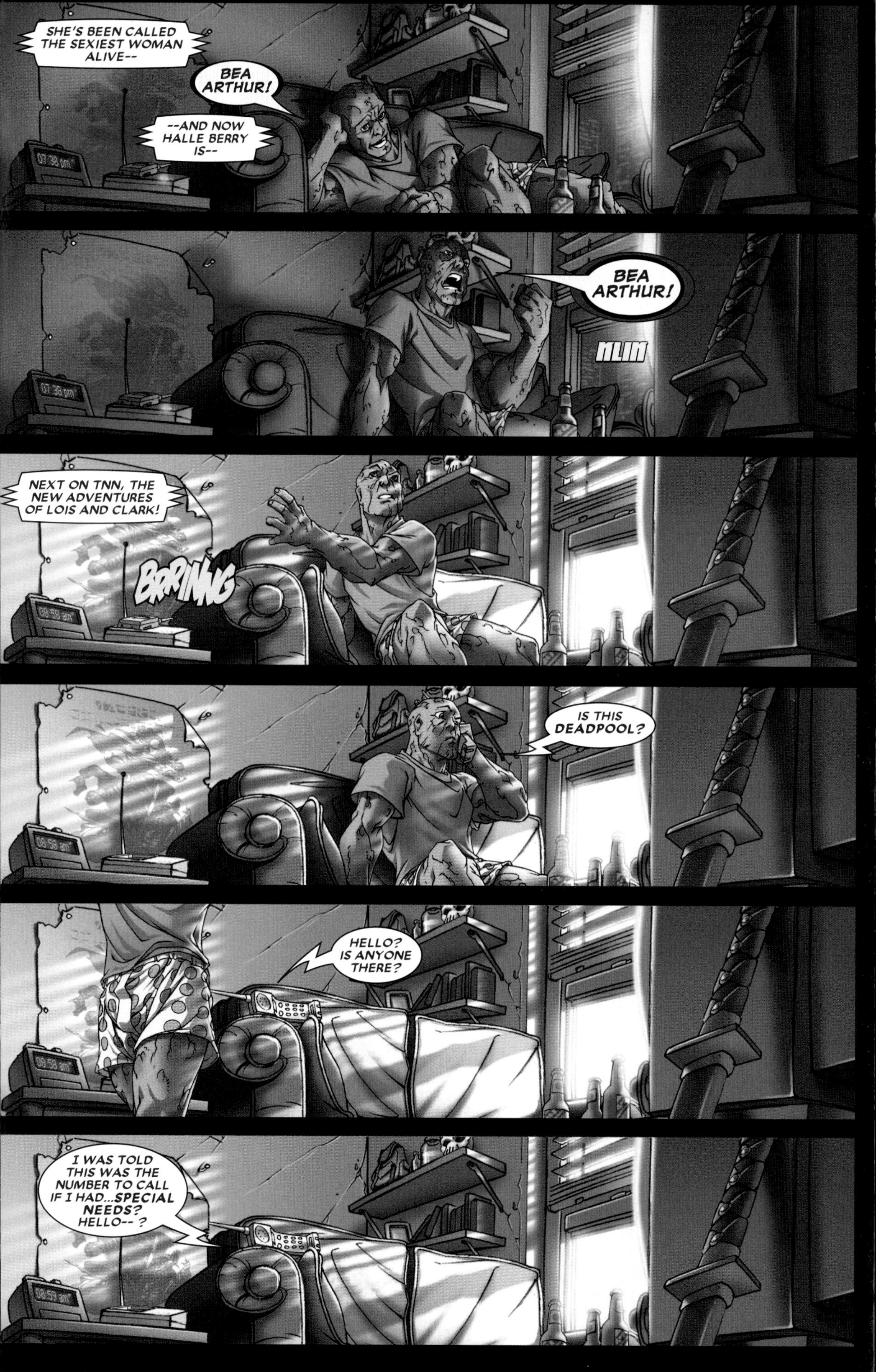

SHE'S BEEN CALLED THE SEXIEST WOMAN ALIVE--
BEA ARTHUR!
--AND NOW HALLE BERRY IS--
BEA ARTHUR!
NLIM
NEXT ON TNN, THE NEW ADVENTURES OF LOIS AND CLARK!
BRRINNG
IS THIS DEADPOOL?
HELLO? IS ANYONE THERE?
I WAS TOLD THIS WAS THE NUMBER TO CALL IF I HAD...SPECIAL NEEDS? HELLO-- ?

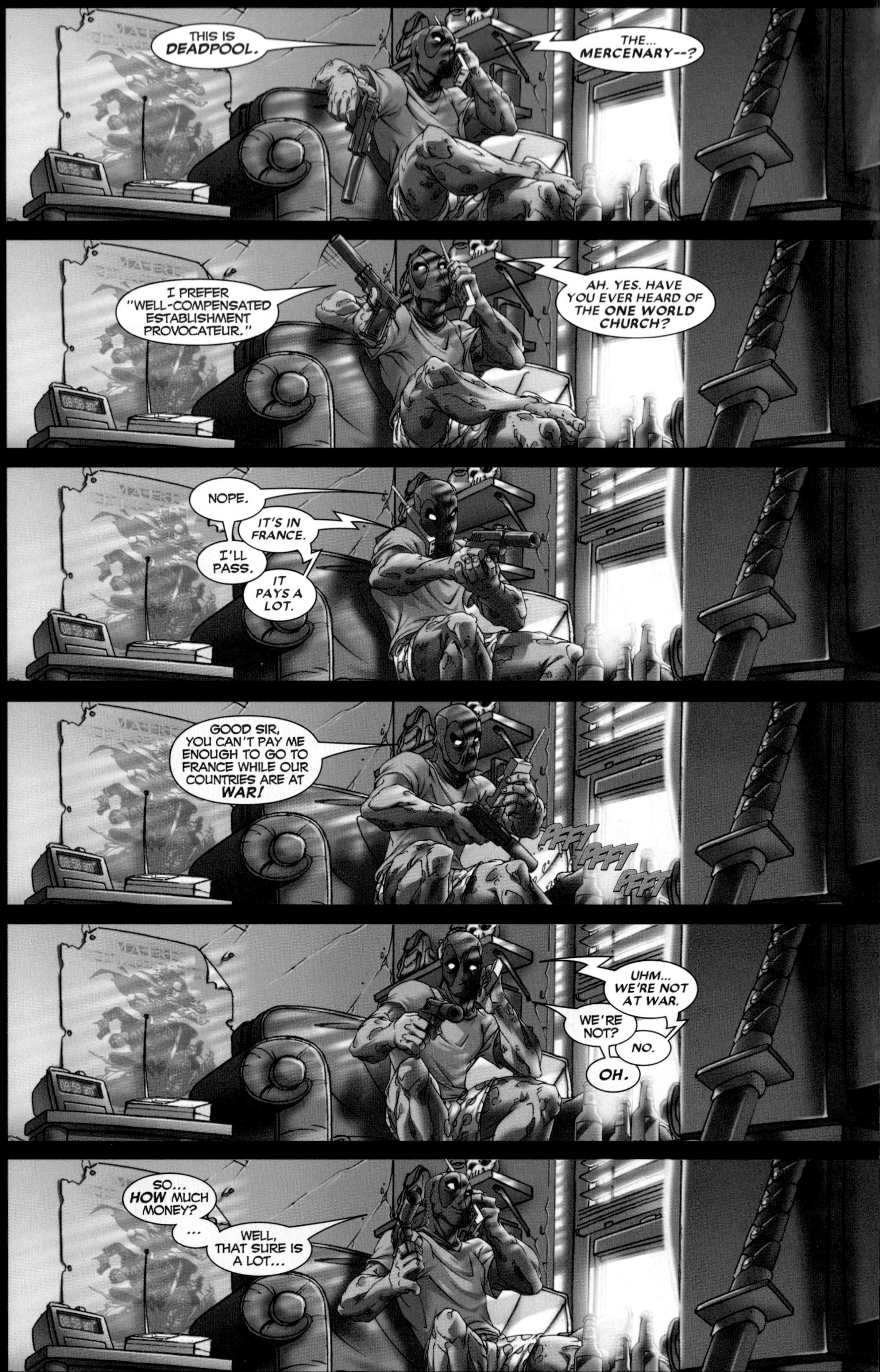
THIS IS DEADPOOL.
THE... MERCENARY--?
I PREFER "WELL-COMPENSATED ESTABLISHMENT PROVOCATEUR."
AH. YES. HAVE YOU EVER HEARD OF THE ONE WORLD CHURCH?
NOPE.
IT'S IN FRANCE.
I'LL PASS.
IT PAYS A LOT.
GOOD SIR, YOU CAN'T PAY ME ENOUGH TO GO TO FRANCE WHILE OUR COUNTRIES ARE AT WAR!
PFFT PFFT PFFT
UHM... WE'RE NOT AT WAR.
WE'RE NOT?
NO.
OH.
SO... HOW MUCH MONEY?
...
WELL, THAT SURE IS A LOT...

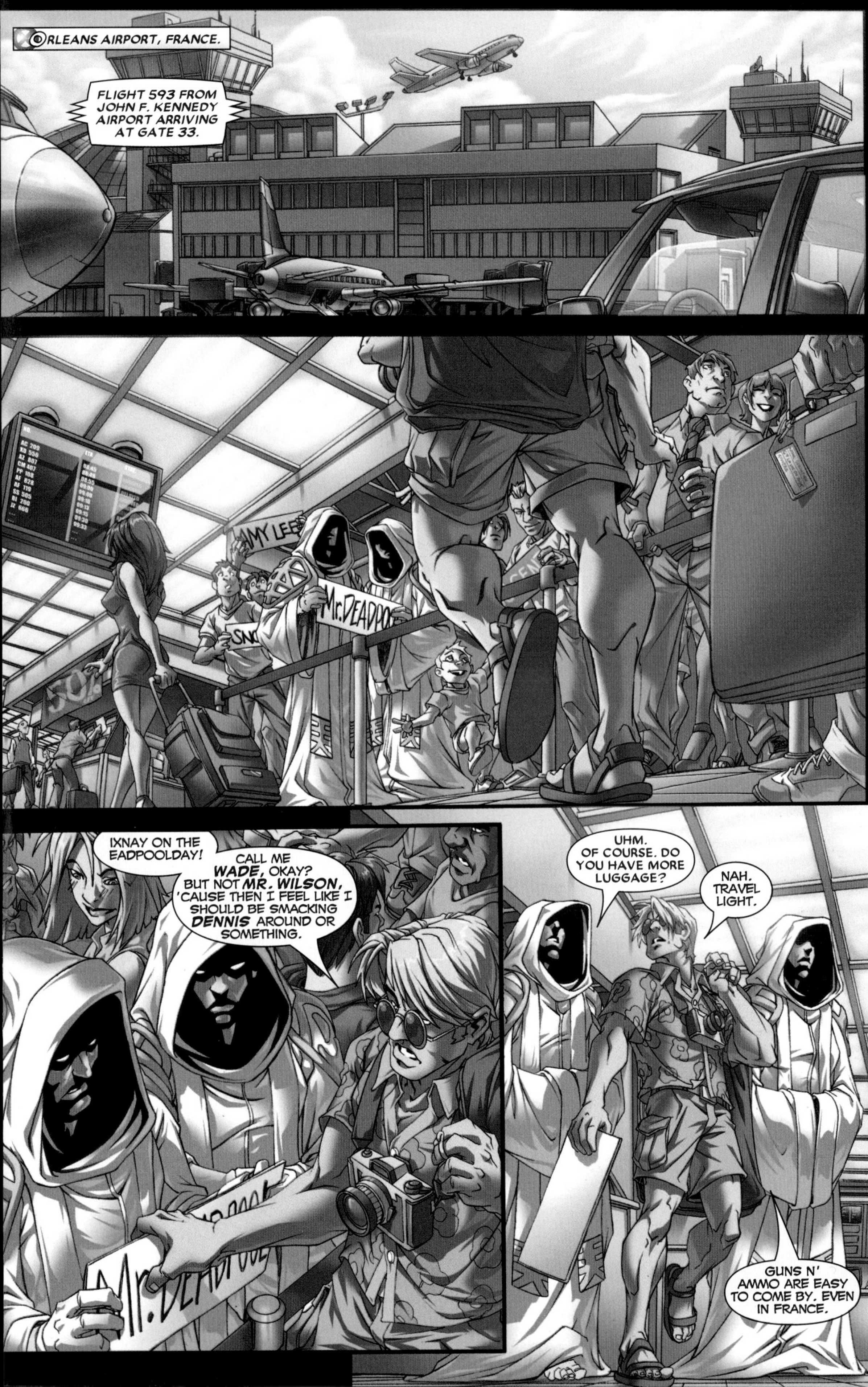
ORLEANS AIRPORT, FRANCE.
FLIGHT 593 FROM JOHN F. KENNEDY AIRPORT ARRIVING AT GATE 33.
AMY LEE
Mr. DEADPOO
IXNAY ON THE EADPOOLDAY!
CALL ME WADE, OKAY? BUT NOT MR. WILSON, 'CAUSE THEN I FEEL LIKE I SHOULD BE SMACKING DENNIS AROUND OR SOMETHING.
UHM. OF COURSE. DO YOU HAVE MORE LUGGAGE?
NAH. TRAVEL LIGHT.
GUNS N' AMMO ARE EASY TO COME BY. EVEN IN FRANCE.

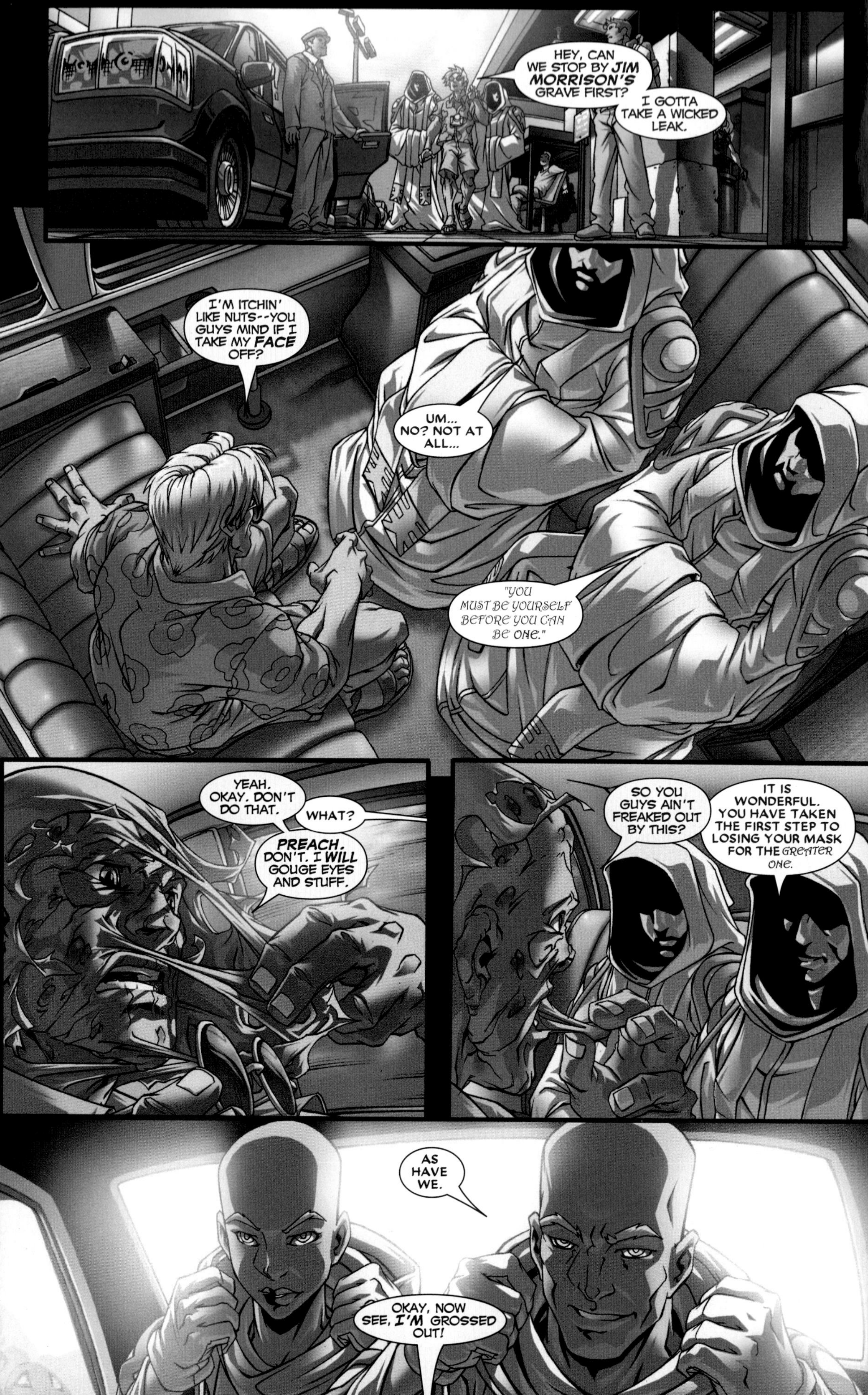

HEY, CAN WE STOP BY JIM MORRISON'S GRAVE FIRST?
I GOTTA TAKE A WICKED LEAK.
I'M ITCHIN' LIKE NUTS--YOU GUYS MIND IF I TAKE MY FACE OFF?
UM... NO? NOT AT ALL...
"YOU MUST BE YOURSELF BEFORE YOU CAN BE ONE."
YEAH. OKAY. DON'T DO THAT.
WHAT?
PREACH. DON'T. I WILL GOUGE EYES AND STUFF.
SO YOU GUYS AIN'T FREAKED OUT BY THIS?
IT IS WONDERFUL. YOU HAVE TAKEN THE FIRST STEP TO LOSING YOUR MASK FOR THE GREATER ONE.
AS HAVE WE.
OKAY, NOW SEE, I'M GROSSED OUT!

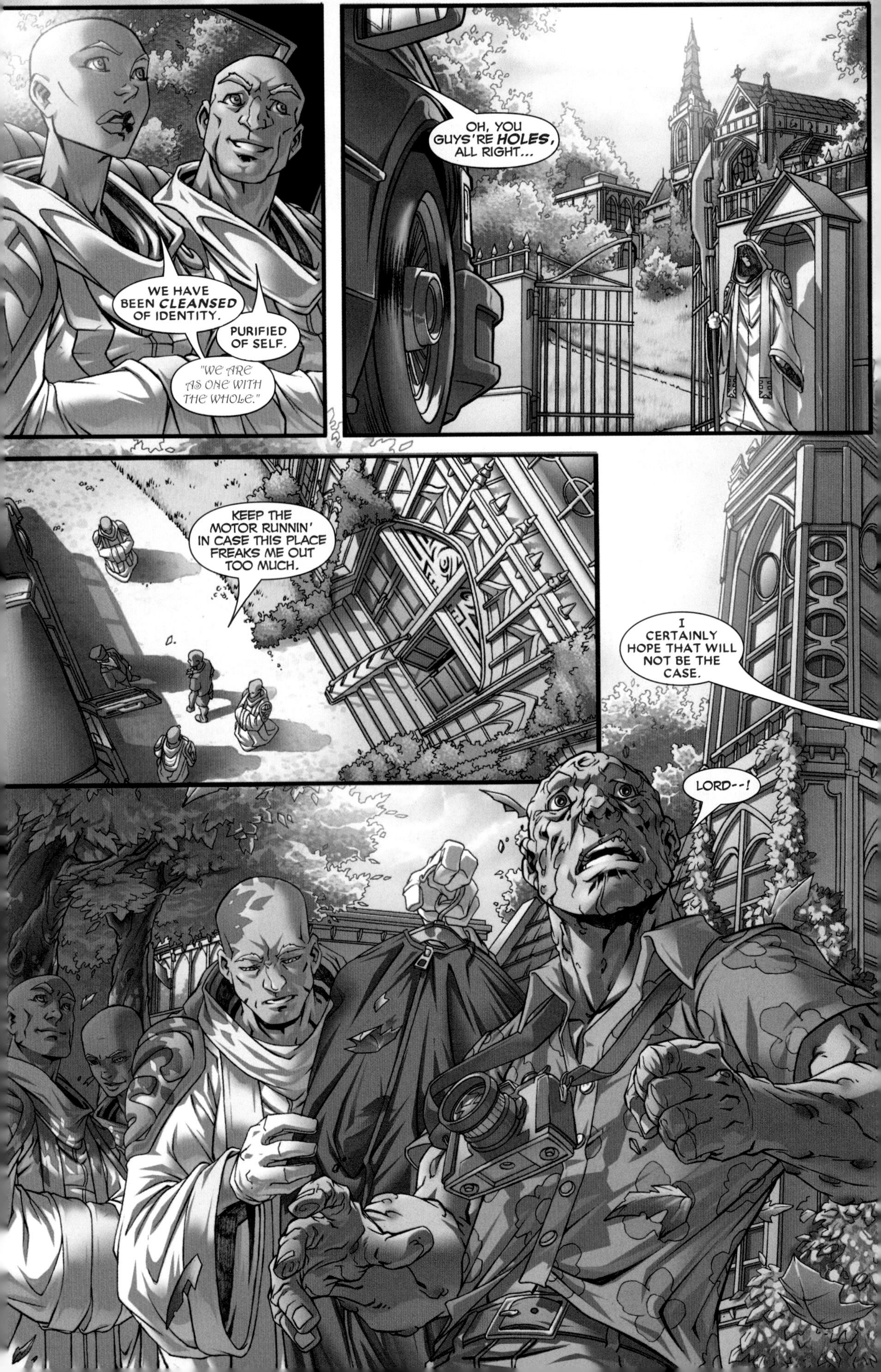
WE HAVE BEEN *CLEANSED* OF IDENTITY.
PURIFIED OF SELF.
"WE ARE AS ONE WITH THE WHOLE."
OH, YOU GUYS'RE **HOLES,** ALL RIGHT...
KEEP THE MOTOR RUNNIN' IN CASE THIS PLACE FREAKS ME OUT TOO MUCH.
I CERTAINLY HOPE THAT WILL NOT BE THE CASE.
LORD--!

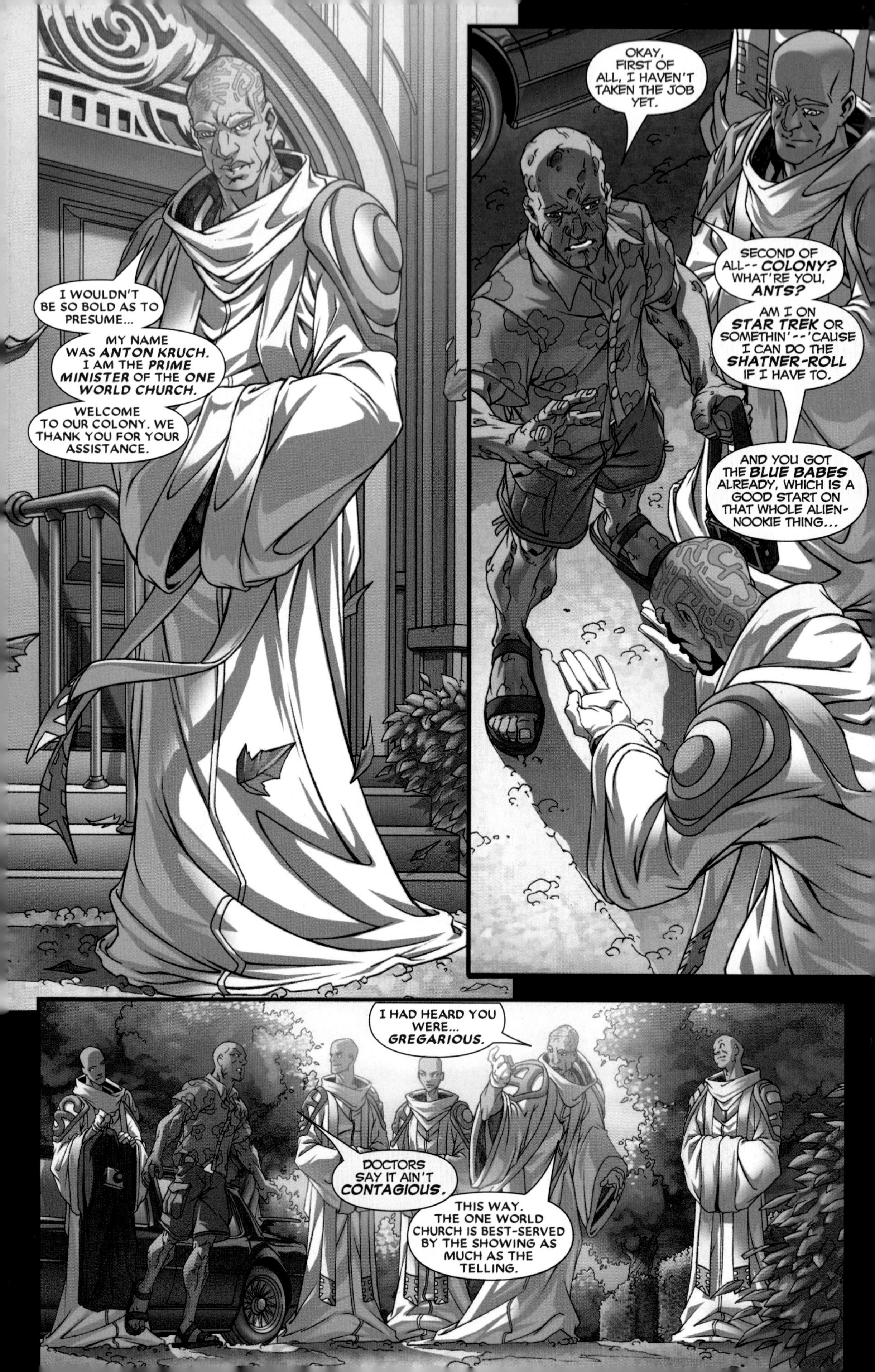

I WOULDN'T BE SO BOLD AS TO PRESUME...
MY NAME WAS ANTON KRUCH. I AM THE PRIME MINISTER OF THE ONE WORLD CHURCH.
WELCOME TO OUR COLONY. WE THANK YOU FOR YOUR ASSISTANCE.
OKAY, FIRST OF ALL, I HAVEN'T TAKEN THE JOB YET.
SECOND OF ALL-- COLONY? WHAT'RE YOU, ANTS?
AM I ON STAR TREK OR SOMETHIN'--'CAUSE I CAN DO THE SHATNER-ROLL IF I HAVE TO.
AND YOU GOT THE BLUE BABES ALREADY, WHICH IS A GOOD START ON THAT WHOLE ALIEN-NOOKIE THING...
I HAD HEARD YOU WERE... GREGARIOUS.
DOCTORS SAY IT AIN'T CONTAGIOUS.
THIS WAY. THE ONE WORLD CHURCH IS BEST-SERVED BY THE SHOWING AS MUCH AS THE TELLING.

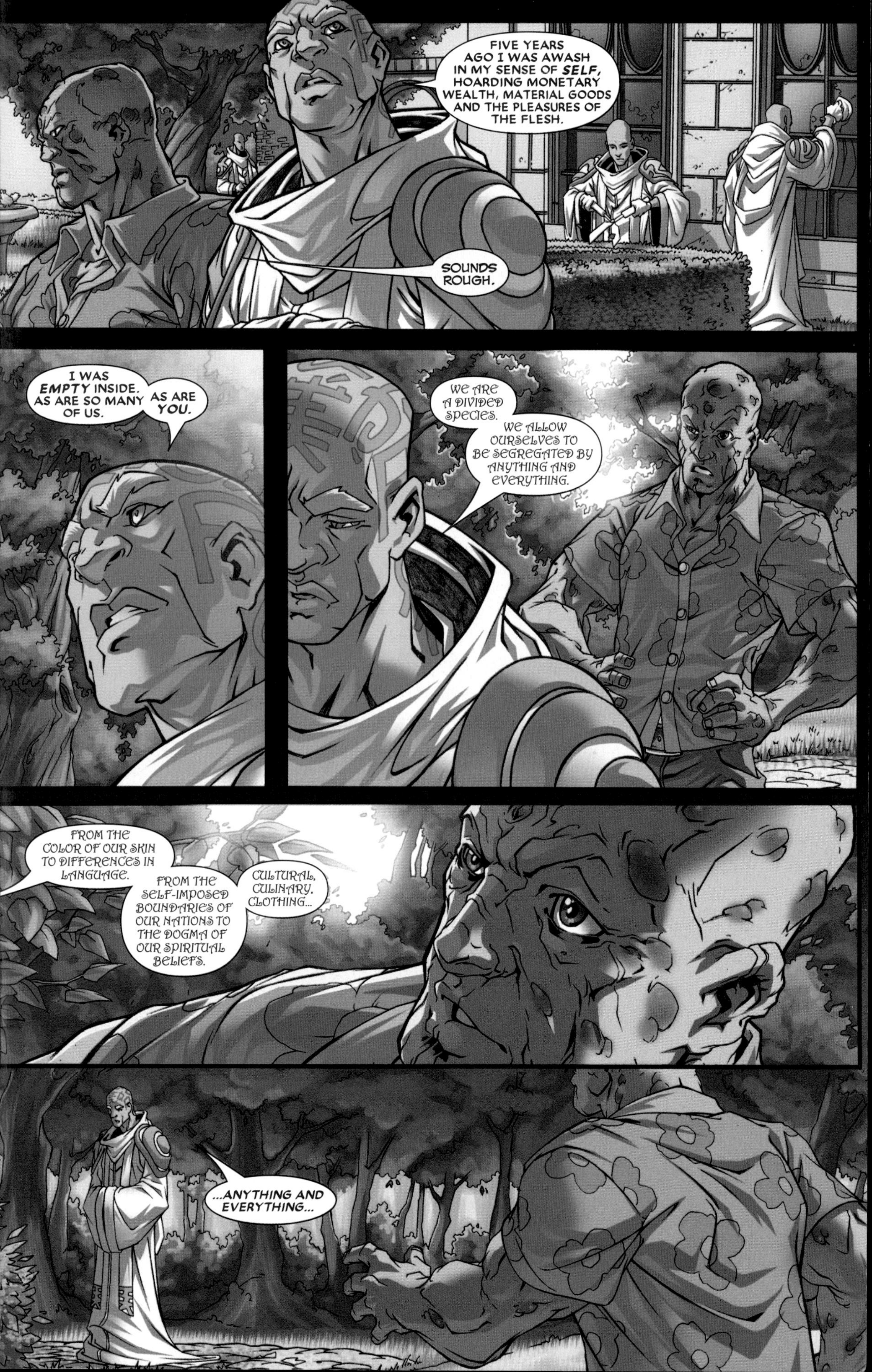
FIVE YEARS AGO I WAS AWASH IN MY SENSE OF SELF, HOARDING MONETARY WEALTH, MATERIAL GOODS AND THE PLEASURES OF THE FLESH.
SOUNDS ROUGH.
I WAS EMPTY INSIDE. AS ARE SO MANY OF US.
AS ARE YOU.
WE ARE A DIVIDED SPECIES.
WE ALLOW OURSELVES TO BE SEGREGATED BY ANYTHING AND EVERYTHING.
FROM THE COLOR OF OUR SKIN TO DIFFERENCES IN LANGUAGE.
FROM THE SELF-IMPOSED BOUNDARIES OF OUR NATIONS TO THE DOGMA OF OUR SPIRITUAL BELIEFS.
CULTURAL, CULINARY, CLOTHING...
...ANYTHING AND EVERYTHING...

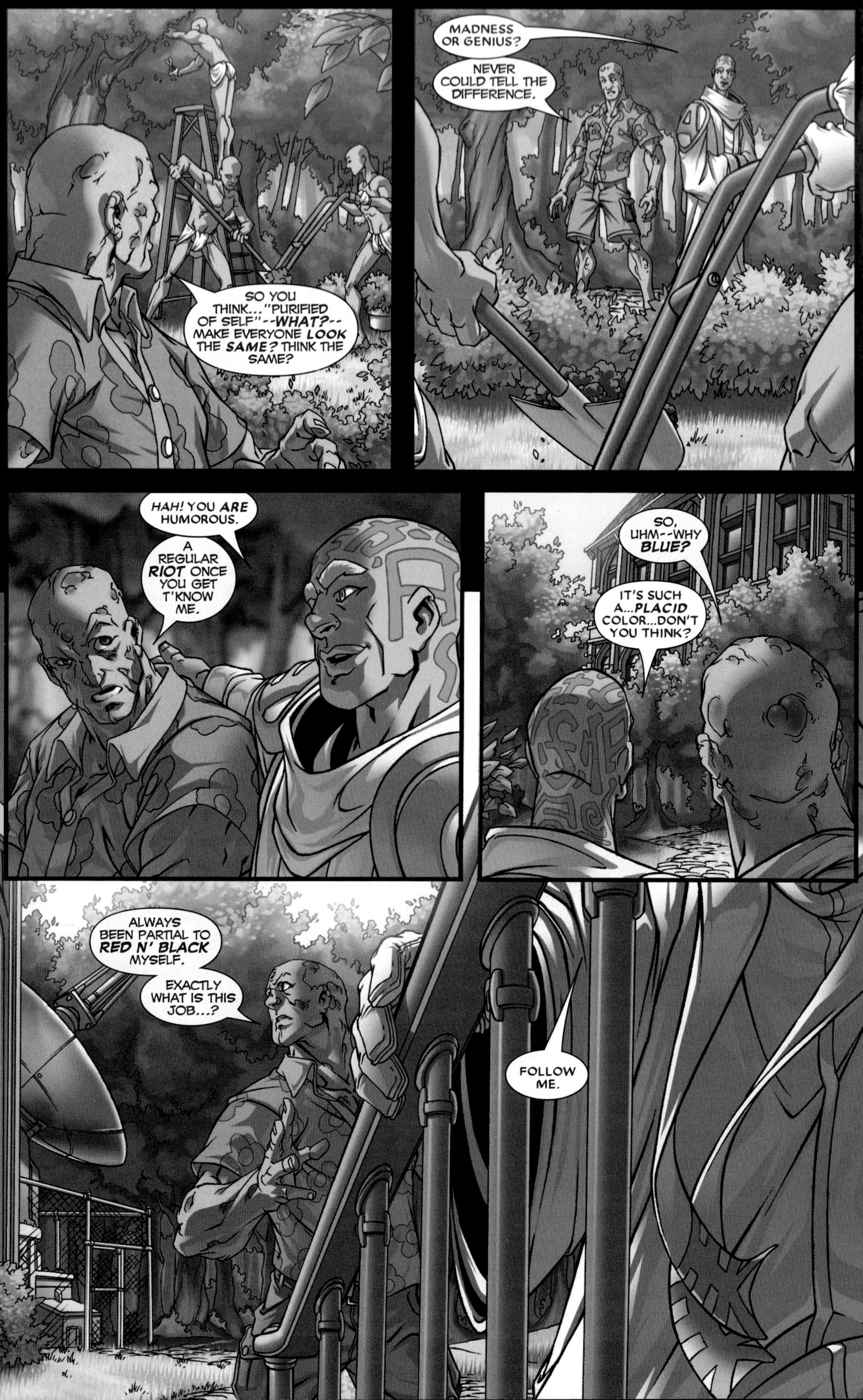
SO YOU THINK... "PURIFIED OF SELF"--WHAT?-- MAKE EVERYONE LOOK THE SAME? THINK THE SAME?
MADNESS OR GENIUS?
NEVER COULD TELL THE DIFFERENCE.
HAH! YOU ARE HUMOROUS.
A REGULAR RIOT ONCE YOU GET T'KNOW ME.
SO, UHM--WHY BLUE?
IT'S SUCH A...PLACID COLOR...DON'T YOU THINK?
ALWAYS BEEN PARTIAL TO RED N' BLACK MYSELF.
EXACTLY WHAT IS THIS JOB...?
FOLLOW ME.

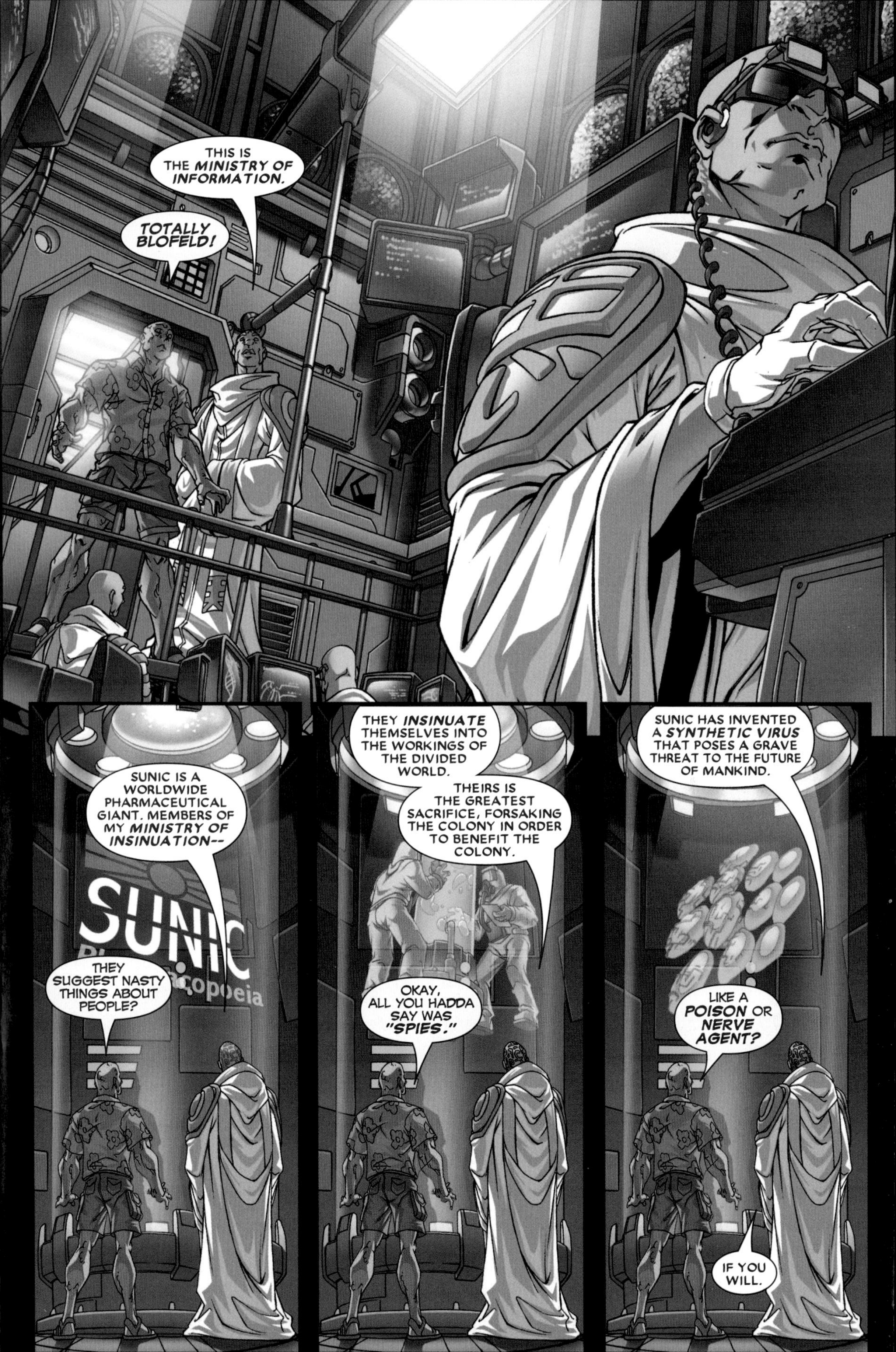
THIS IS THE MINISTRY OF INFORMATION.
TOTALLY BLOFELD!
SUNIC IS A WORLDWIDE PHARMACEUTICAL GIANT. MEMBERS OF MY MINISTRY OF INSINUATION--
SUNIC
THEY SUGGEST NASTY THINGS ABOUT PEOPLE?
THEY INSINUATE THEMSELVES INTO THE WORKINGS OF THE DIVIDED WORLD.
THEIRS IS THE GREATEST SACRIFICE, FORSAKING THE COLONY IN ORDER TO BENEFIT THE COLONY.
OKAY, ALL YOU HADDA SAY WAS "SPIES."
SUNIC HAS INVENTED A SYNTHETIC VIRUS THAT POSES A GRAVE THREAT TO THE FUTURE OF MANKIND.
LIKE A POISON OR NERVE AGENT?
IF YOU WILL.

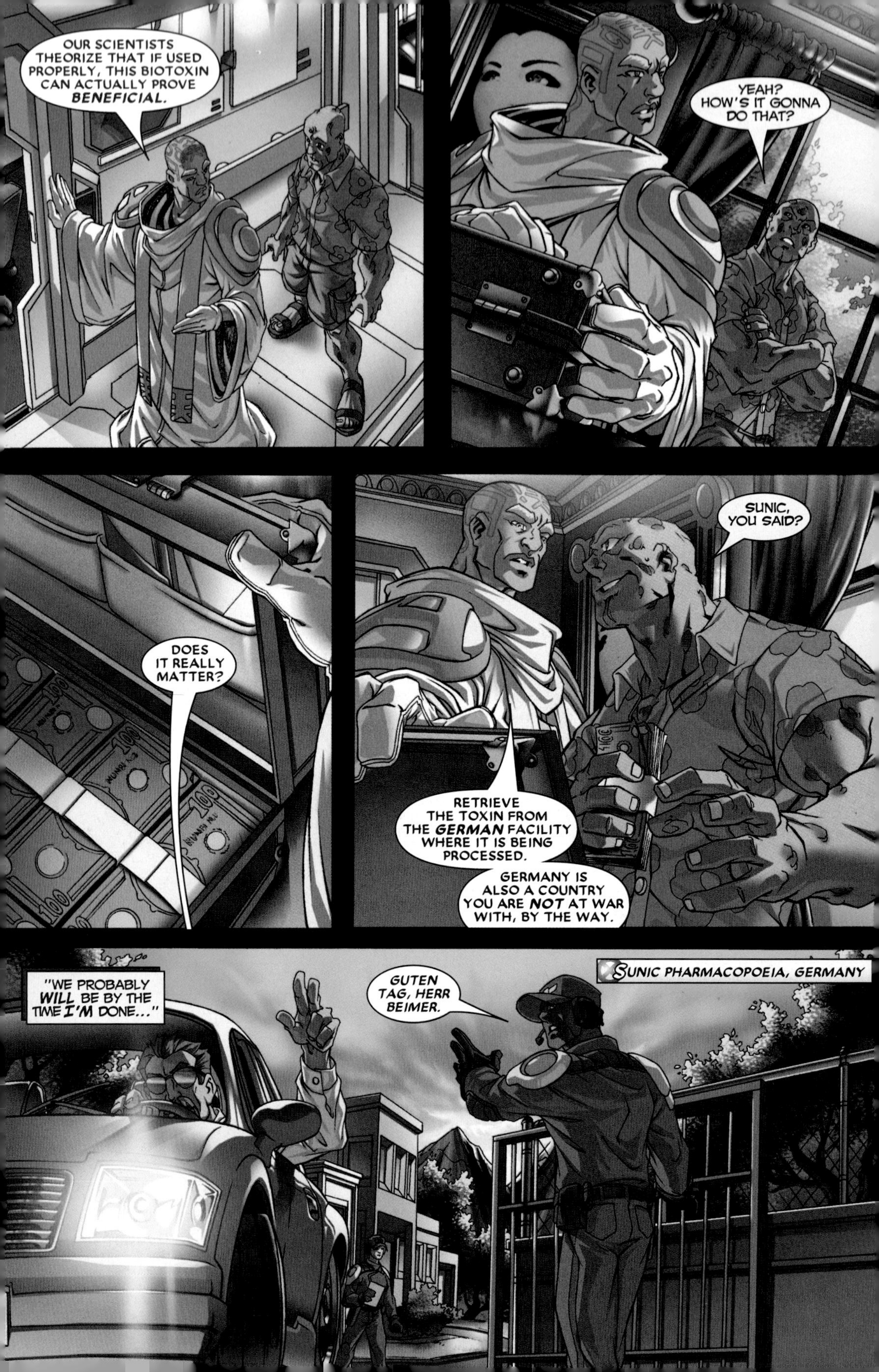
OUR SCIENTISTS THEORIZE THAT IF USED PROPERLY, THIS BIOTOXIN CAN ACTUALLY PROVE BENEFICIAL.
YEAH? HOW'S IT GONNA DO THAT?
DOES IT REALLY MATTER?
SUNIC, YOU SAID?
RETRIEVE THE TOXIN FROM THE GERMAN FACILITY WHERE IT IS BEING PROCESSED.
GERMANY IS ALSO A COUNTRY YOU ARE NOT AT WAR WITH, BY THE WAY.
SUNIC PHARMACOPOEIA, GERMANY
"WE PROBABLY WILL BE BY THE TIME I'M DONE..."
GUTEN TAG, HERR BEIMER.

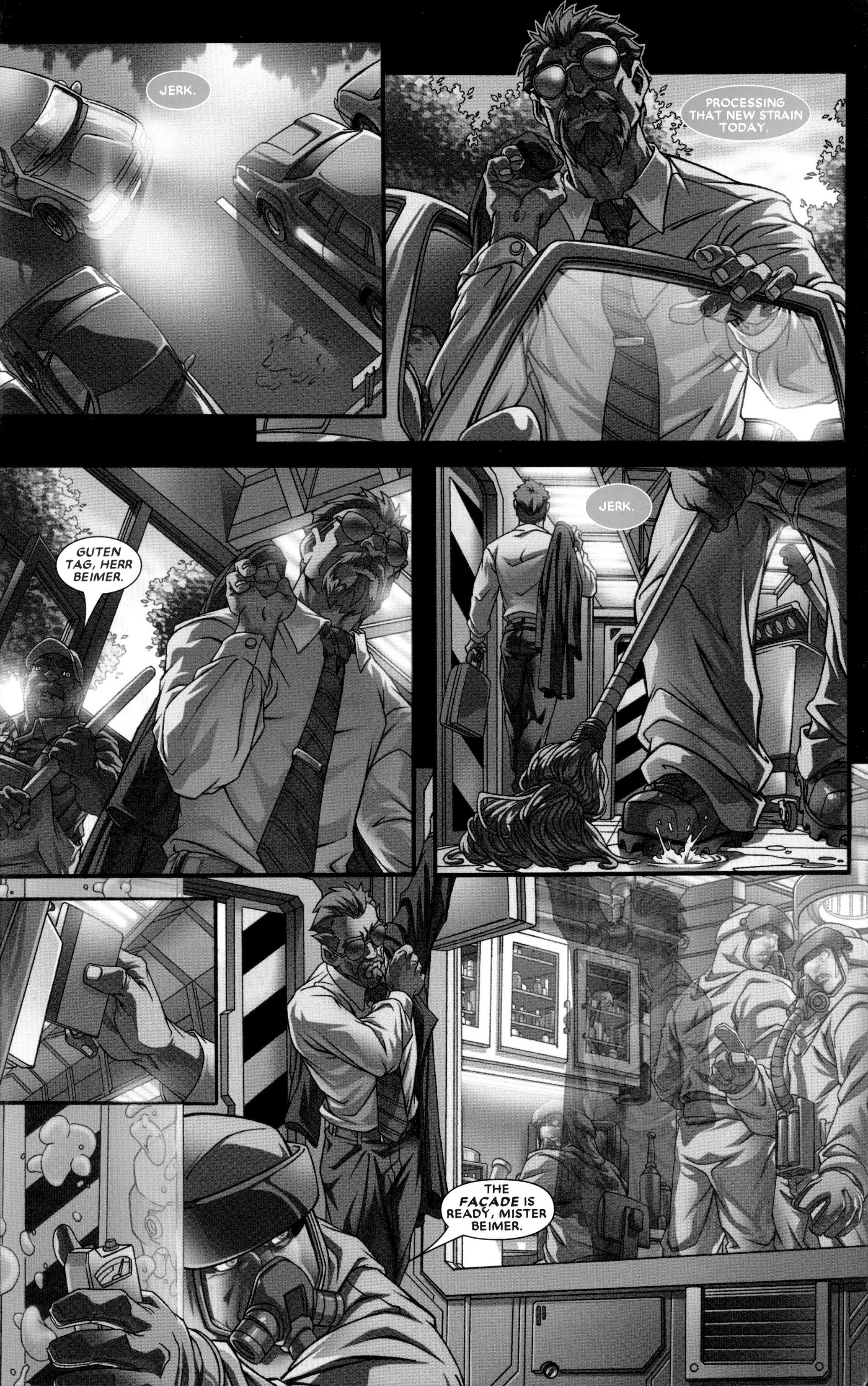
JERK.
PROCESSING THAT NEW STRAIN TODAY.
GUTEN TAG, HERR BEIMER.
JERK.
THE FAÇADE IS READY, MISTER BEIMER.

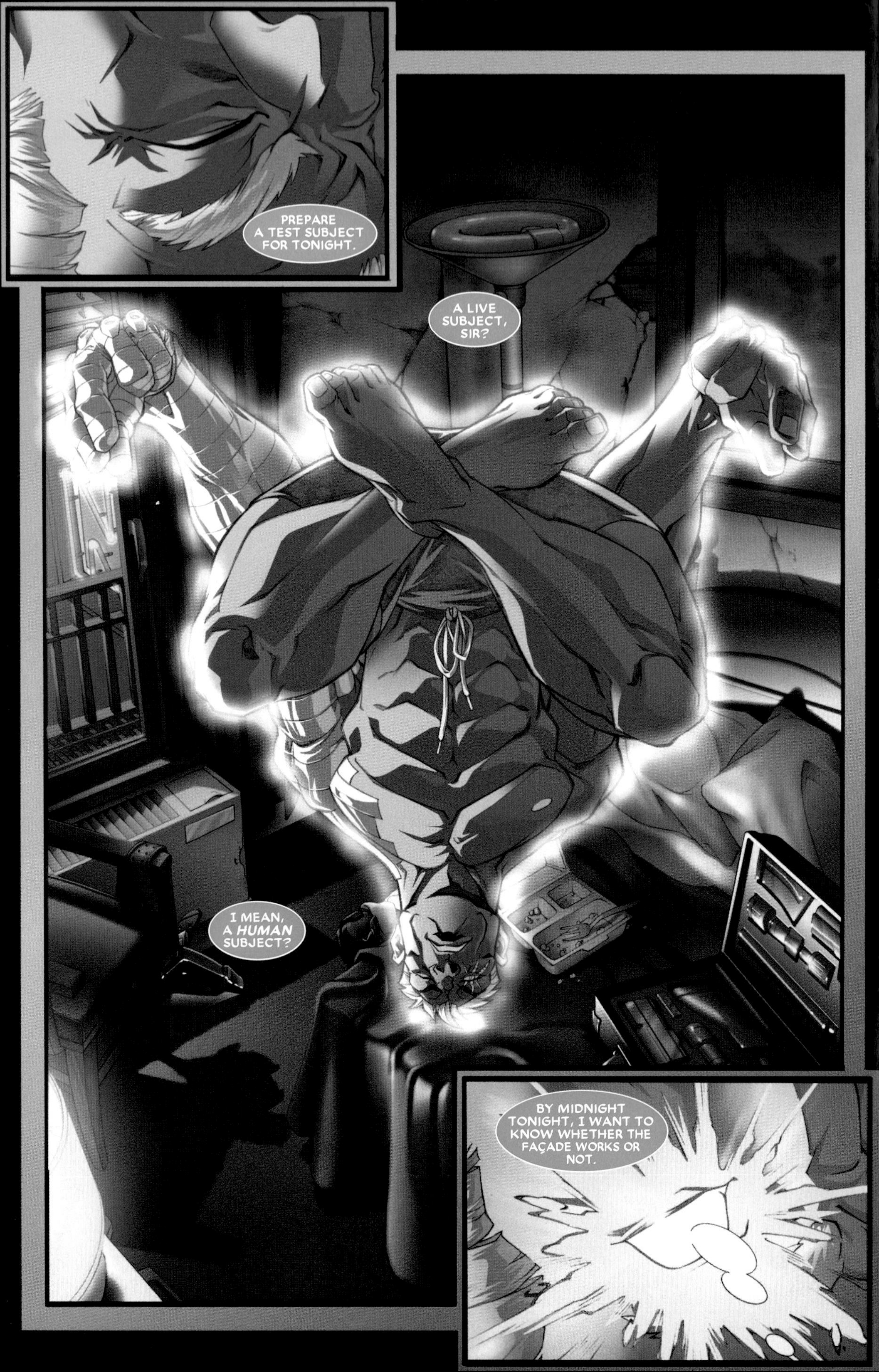
PREPARE A TEST SUBJECT FOR TONIGHT.
A LIVE SUBJECT, SIR?
I MEAN, A *HUMAN* SUBJECT?
BY MIDNIGHT TONIGHT, I WANT TO KNOW WHETHER THE FAÇADE WORKS OR NOT.

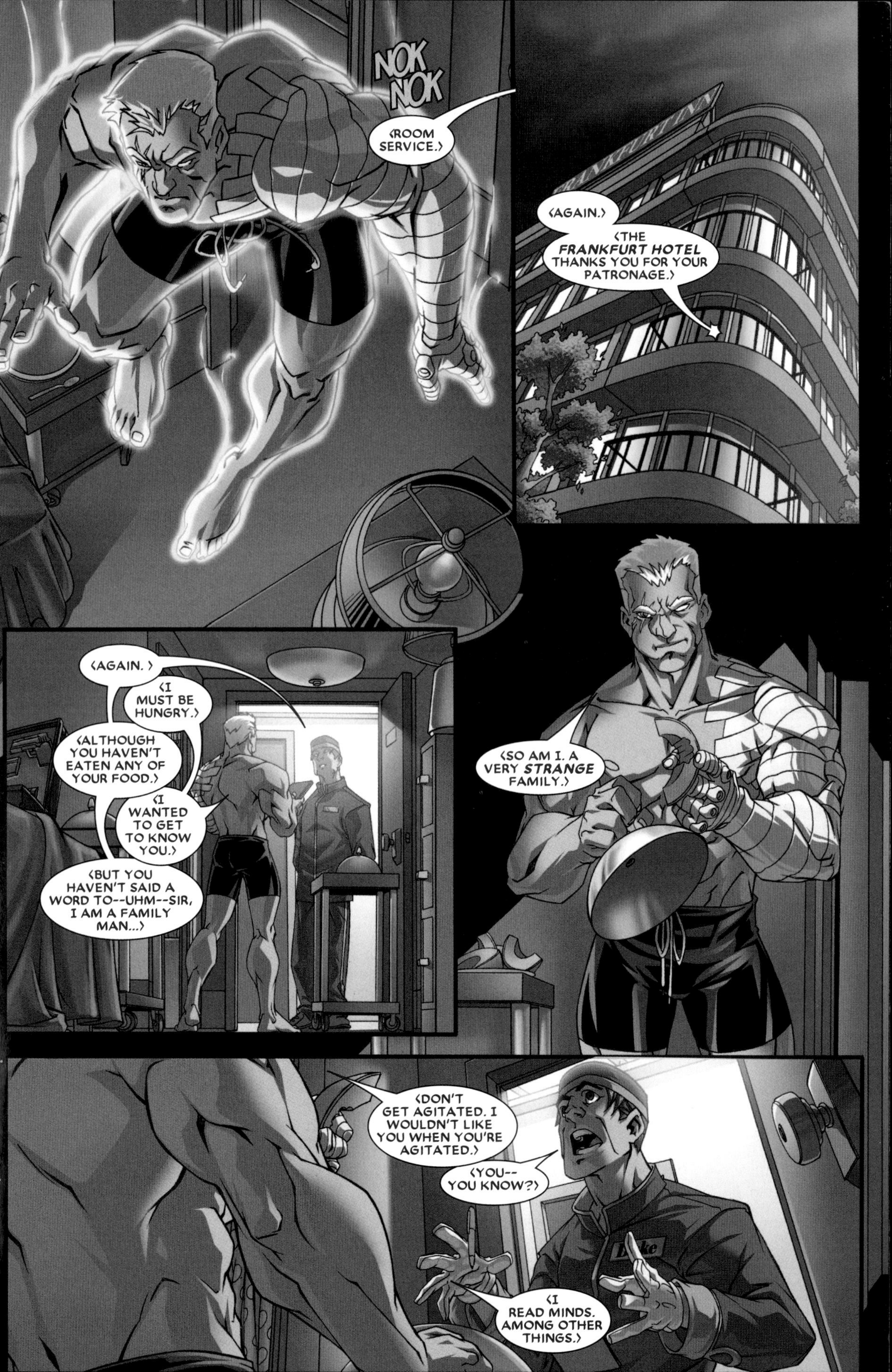
NOK NOK
‹ROOM SERVICE.›
‹AGAIN.›
‹THE FRANKFURT HOTEL THANKS YOU FOR YOUR PATRONAGE.›
‹AGAIN. ›
‹I MUST BE HUNGRY.›
‹ALTHOUGH YOU HAVEN'T EATEN ANY OF YOUR FOOD.›
‹I WANTED TO GET TO KNOW YOU.›
‹BUT YOU HAVEN'T SAID A WORD TO--UHM--SIR, I AM A FAMILY MAN...›
‹SO AM I. A VERY STRANGE FAMILY.›
‹DON'T GET AGITATED. I WOULDN'T LIKE YOU WHEN YOU'RE AGITATED.›
‹YOU-- YOU KNOW?›
‹I READ MINDS. AMONG OTHER THINGS.›

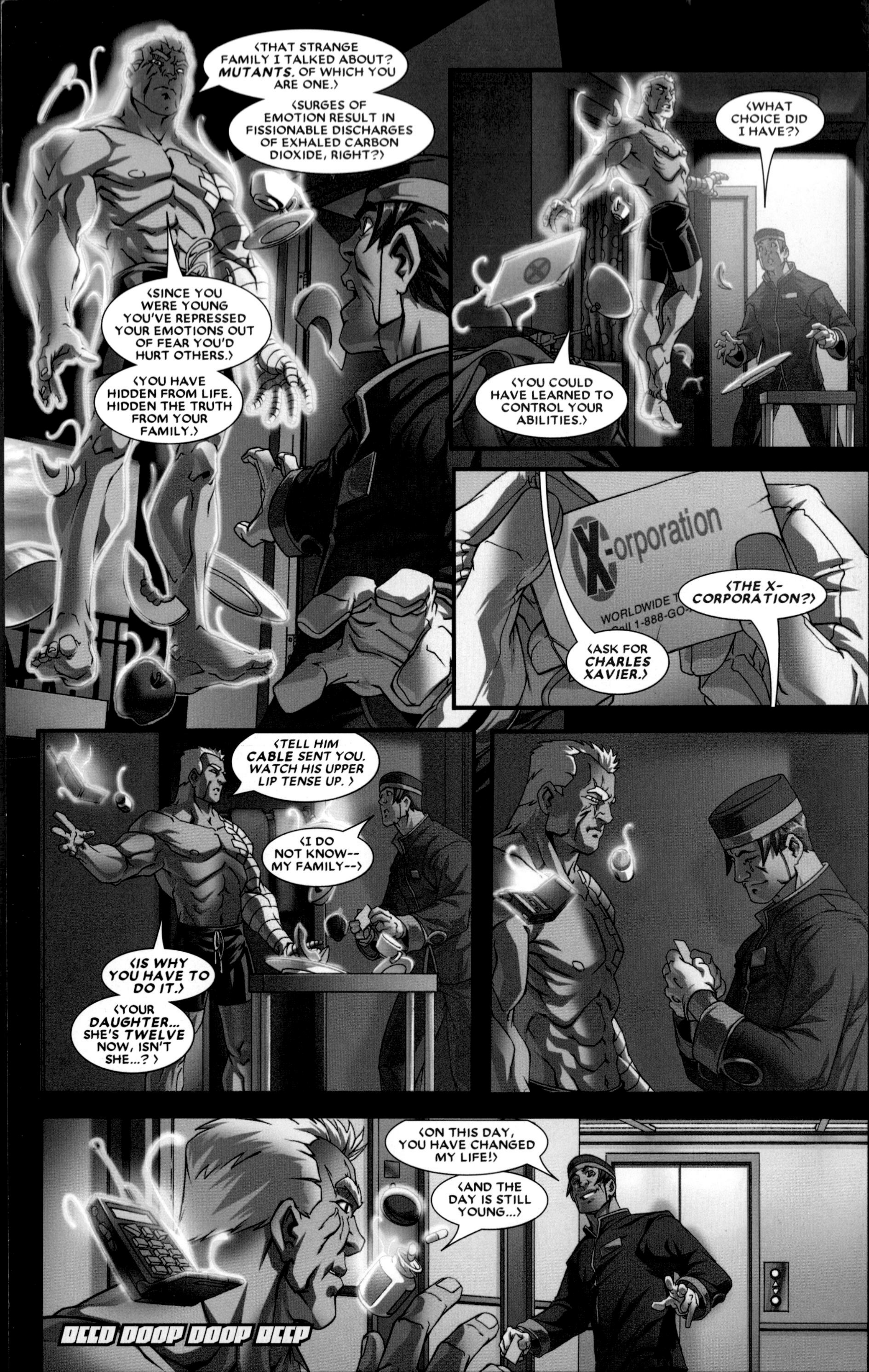

‹THAT STRANGE FAMILY I TALKED ABOUT? MUTANTS, OF WHICH YOU ARE ONE.›
‹SURGES OF EMOTION RESULT IN FISSIONABLE DISCHARGES OF EXHALED CARBON DIOXIDE, RIGHT?›
‹SINCE YOU WERE YOUNG YOU'VE REPRESSED YOUR EMOTIONS OUT OF FEAR YOU'D HURT OTHERS.›
‹YOU HAVE HIDDEN FROM LIFE. HIDDEN THE TRUTH FROM YOUR FAMILY.›
‹WHAT CHOICE DID I HAVE?›
‹YOU COULD HAVE LEARNED TO CONTROL YOUR ABILITIES.›
X-orporation
WORLDWIDE T
Call 1-888-GO-
‹THE X-CORPORATION?›
‹ASK FOR CHARLES XAVIER.›
‹TELL HIM CABLE SENT YOU. WATCH HIS UPPER LIP TENSE UP.›
‹I DO NOT KNOW-- MY FAMILY--›
‹IS WHY YOU HAVE TO DO IT.›
‹YOUR DAUGHTER... SHE'S TWELVE NOW, ISN'T SHE...?›
‹ON THIS DAY, YOU HAVE CHANGED MY LIFE!›
‹AND THE DAY IS STILL YOUNG...›
DEEP DOOP DOOP DEEP

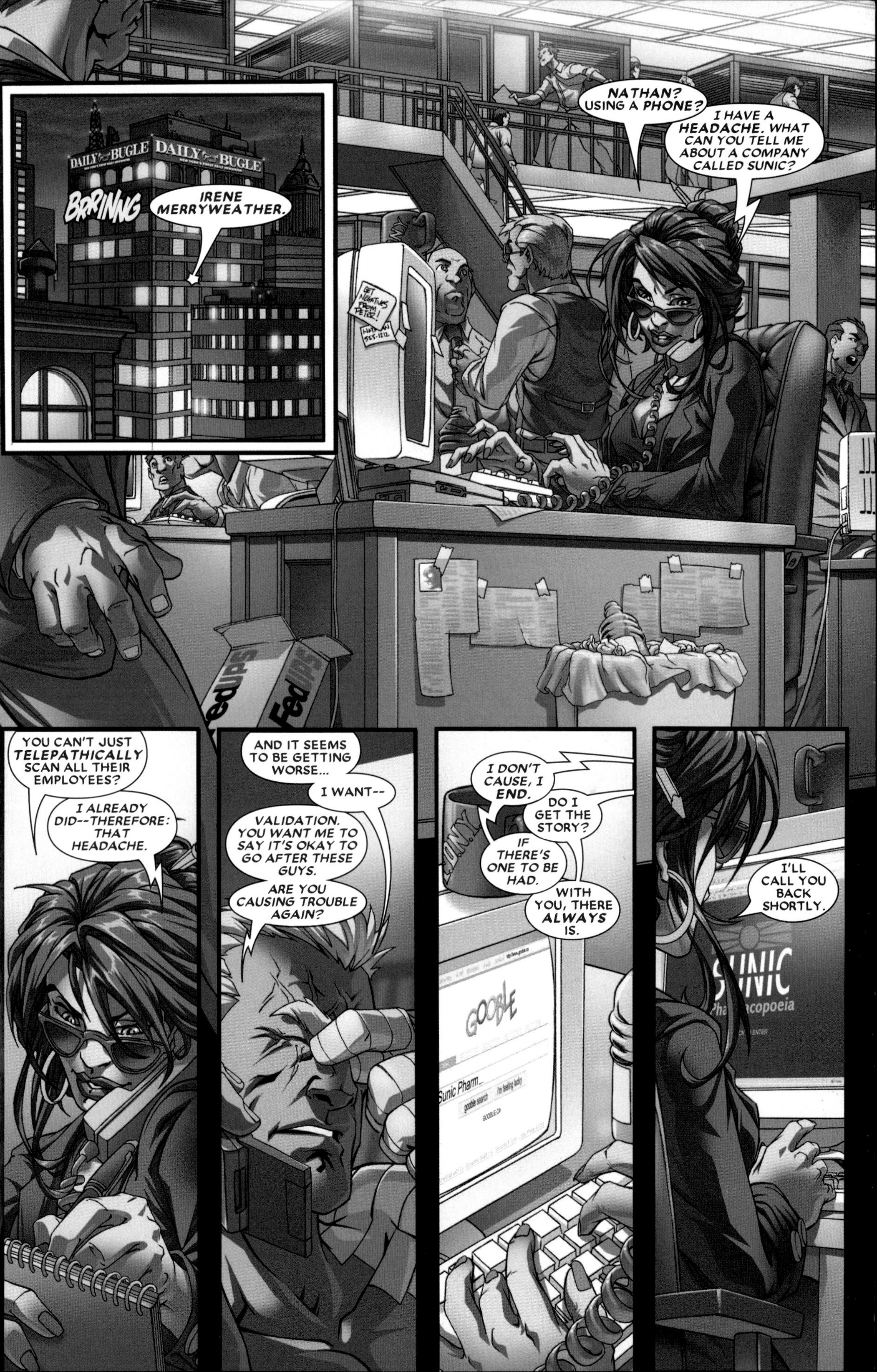
DAILY BUGLE
DAILY BUGLE
BRRINNG
IRENE MERRYWEATHER.
NATHAN? USING A PHONE?
I HAVE A HEADACHE. WHAT CAN YOU TELL ME ABOUT A COMPANY CALLED SUNIC?
GET NEGATIVES FROM PETER!
NATHAN 555-1212
FedUPS
YOU CAN'T JUST TELEPATHICALLY SCAN ALL THEIR EMPLOYEES?
I ALREADY DID--THEREFORE: THAT HEADACHE.
AND IT SEEMS TO BE GETTING WORSE...
I WANT--
VALIDATION. YOU WANT ME TO SAY IT'S OKAY TO GO AFTER THESE GUYS.
ARE YOU CAUSING TROUBLE AGAIN?
I DON'T CAUSE, I END.
DO I GET THE STORY?
IF THERE'S ONE TO BE HAD.
WITH YOU, THERE ALWAYS IS.
GOOBLE
Sunic Pharm_
gooble search
I'm feeling lucky
I'LL CALL YOU BACK SHORTLY.
SUNIC

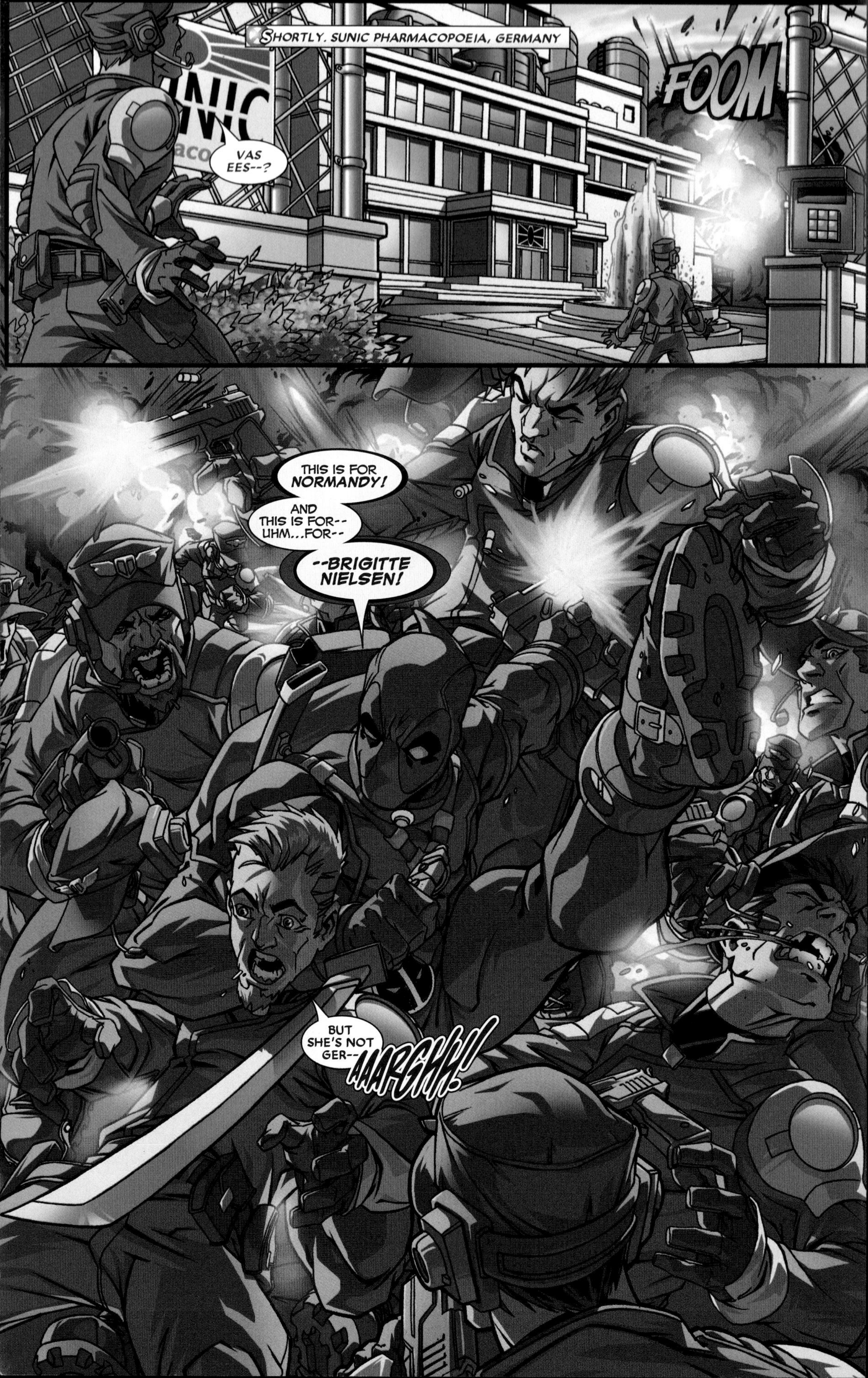
SHORTLY. SUNIC PHARMACOPOEIA, GERMANY
VAS EES--?
FOOM
THIS IS FOR NORMANDY!
AND THIS IS FOR-- UHM...FOR--
--BRIGITTE NIELSEN!
BUT SHE'S NOT GER--
AAARGHH!!

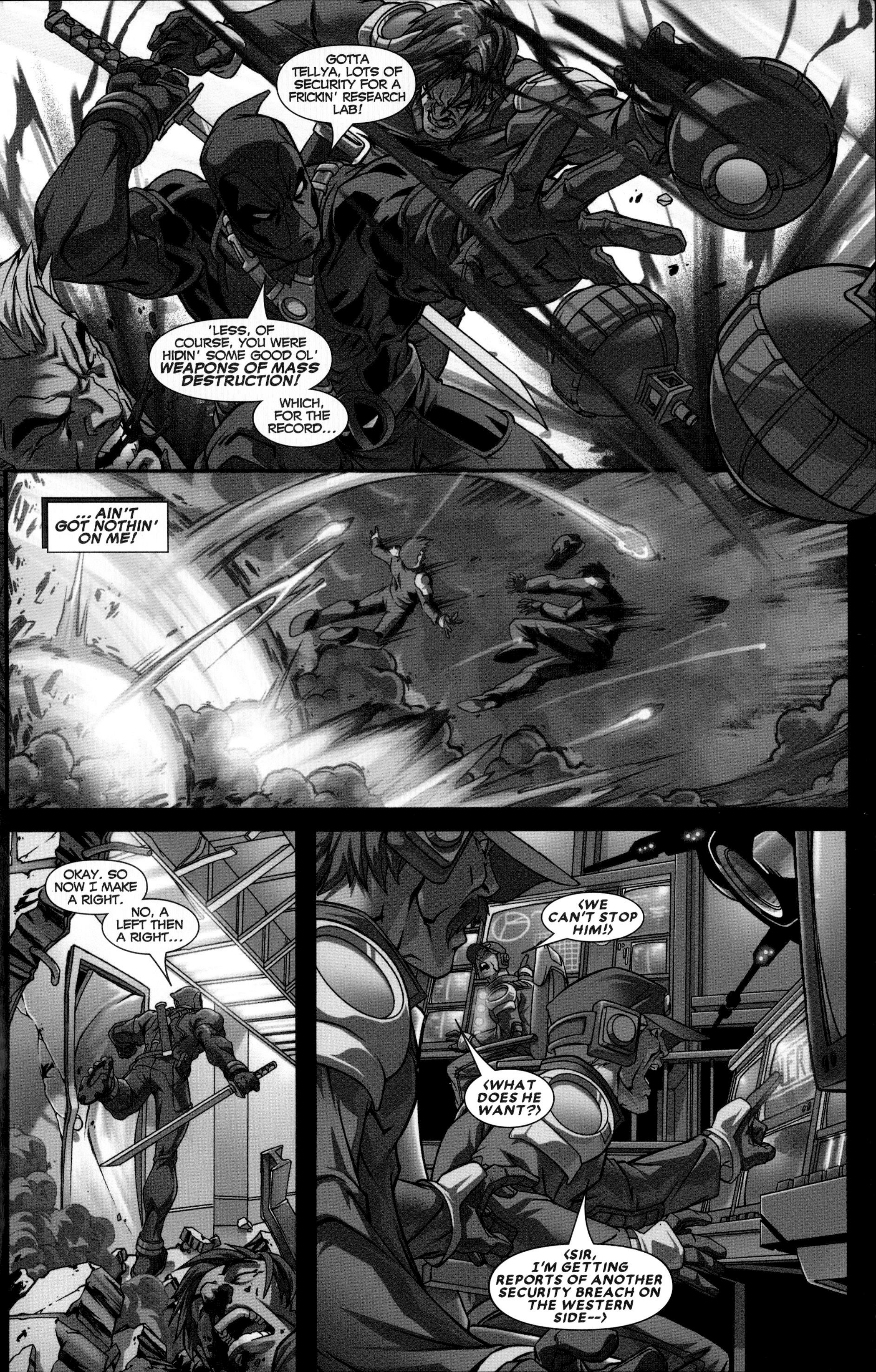
GOTTA TELLYA, LOTS OF SECURITY FOR A FRICKIN' RESEARCH LAB!
'LESS, OF COURSE, YOU WERE HIDIN' SOME GOOD OL' WEAPONS OF MASS DESTRUCTION!
WHICH, FOR THE RECORD...
... AIN'T GOT NOTHIN' ON ME!
OKAY. SO NOW I MAKE A RIGHT.
NO, A LEFT THEN A RIGHT...
‹WE CAN'T STOP HIM!›
‹WHAT DOES HE WANT?›
‹SIR, I'M GETTING REPORTS OF ANOTHER SECURITY BREACH ON THE WESTERN SIDE--›

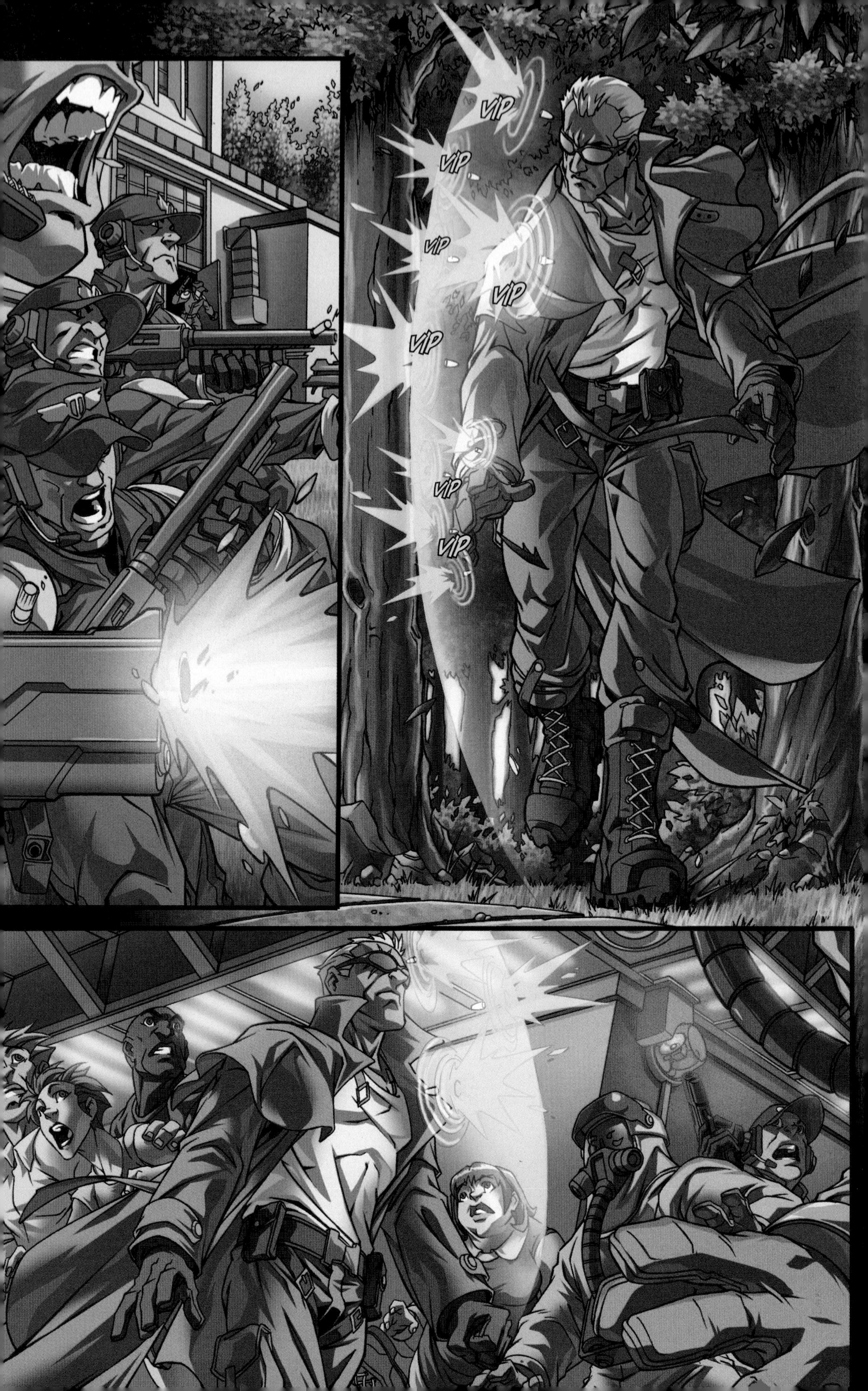
VIP
VIP
VIP
VIP
VIP
VIP
VIP

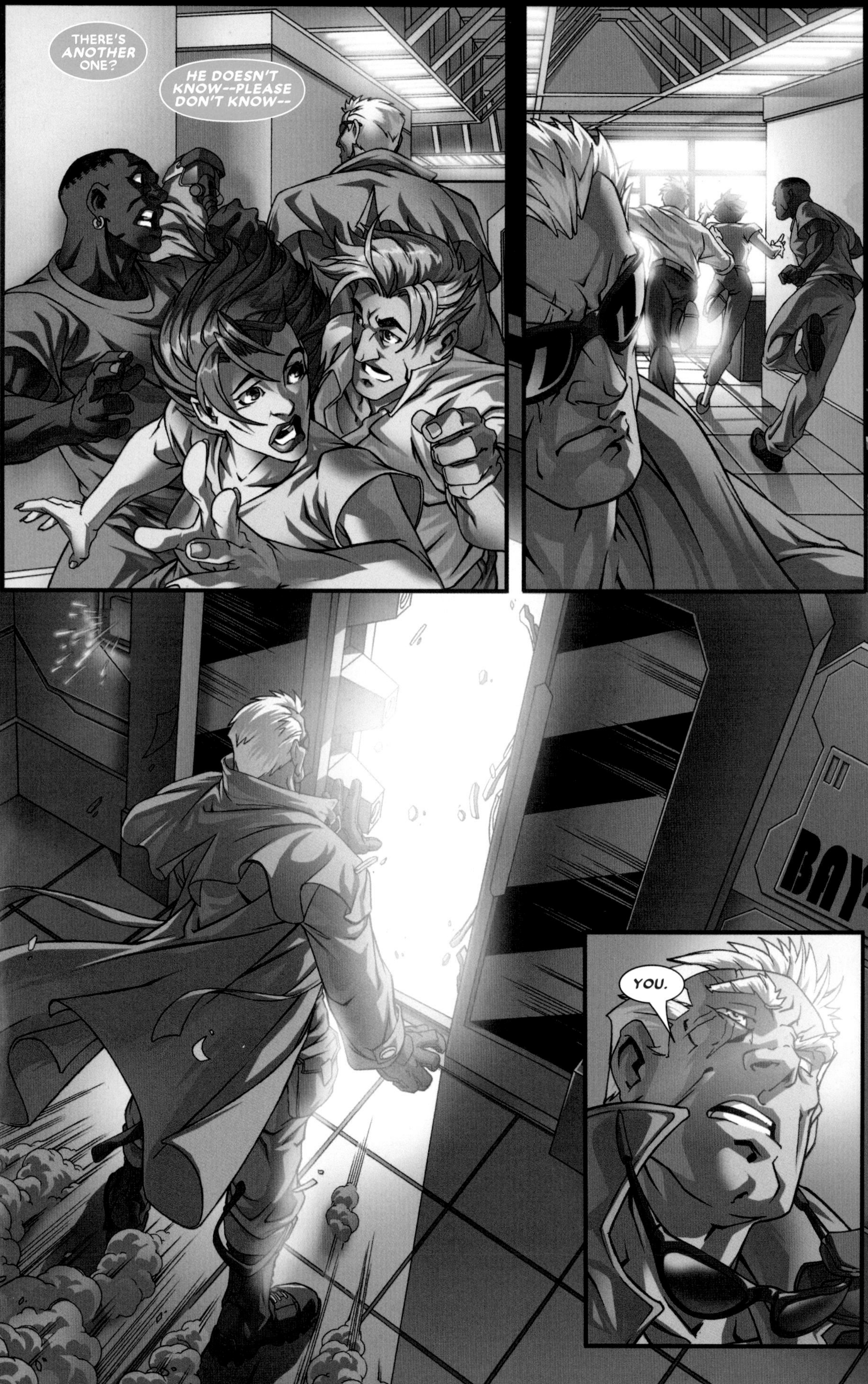
THERE'S ANOTHER ONE?
HE DOESN'T KNOW--PLEASE DON'T KNOW--
BAY-
YOU.

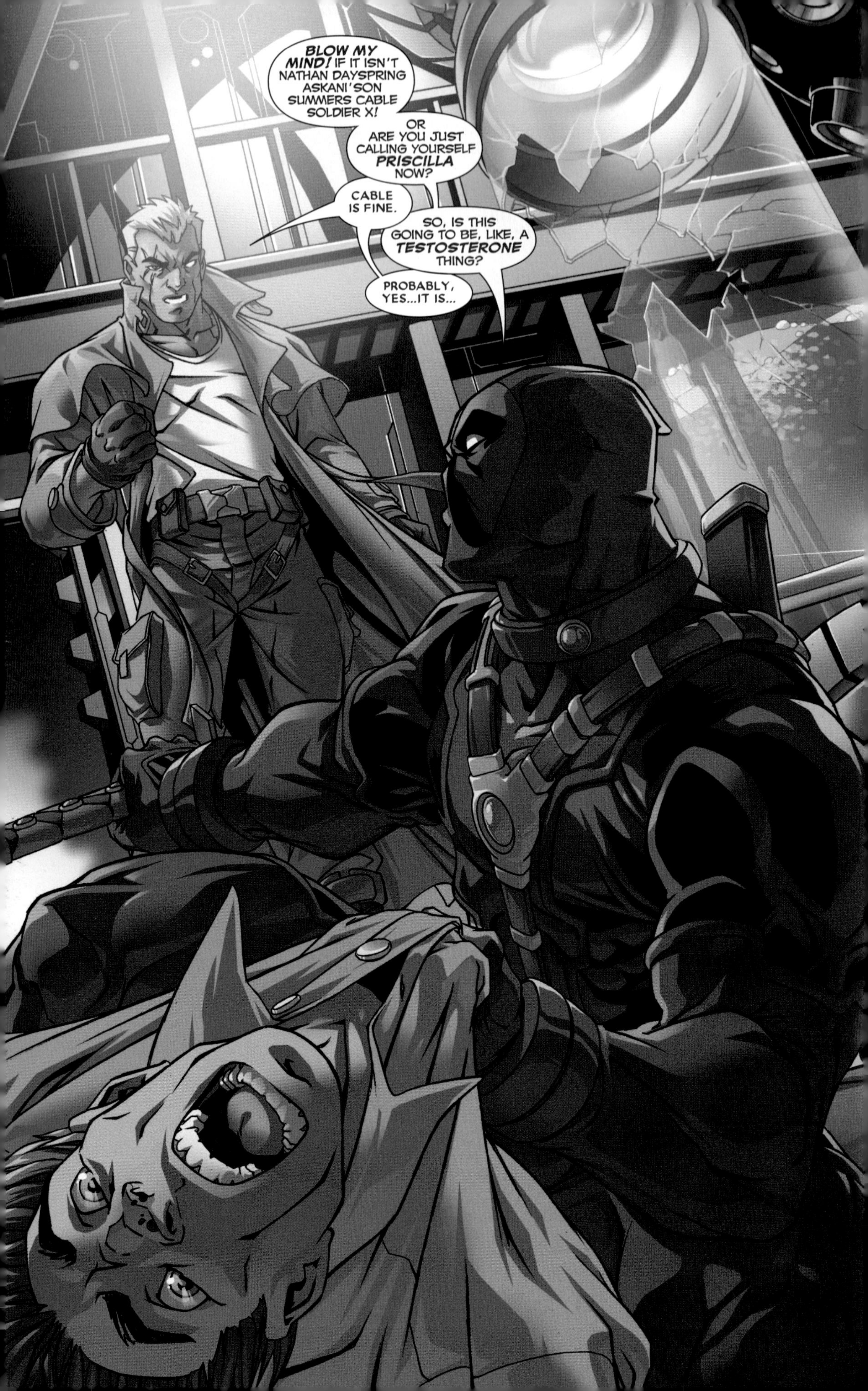
BLOW MY MIND! IF IT ISN'T NATHAN DAYSPRING ASKANI'SON SUMMERS CABLE SOLDIER X!
OR ARE YOU JUST CALLING YOURSELF PRISCILLA NOW?
CABLE IS FINE.
SO, IS THIS GOING TO BE, LIKE, A TESTOSTERONE THING?
PROBABLY, YES...IT IS...

2

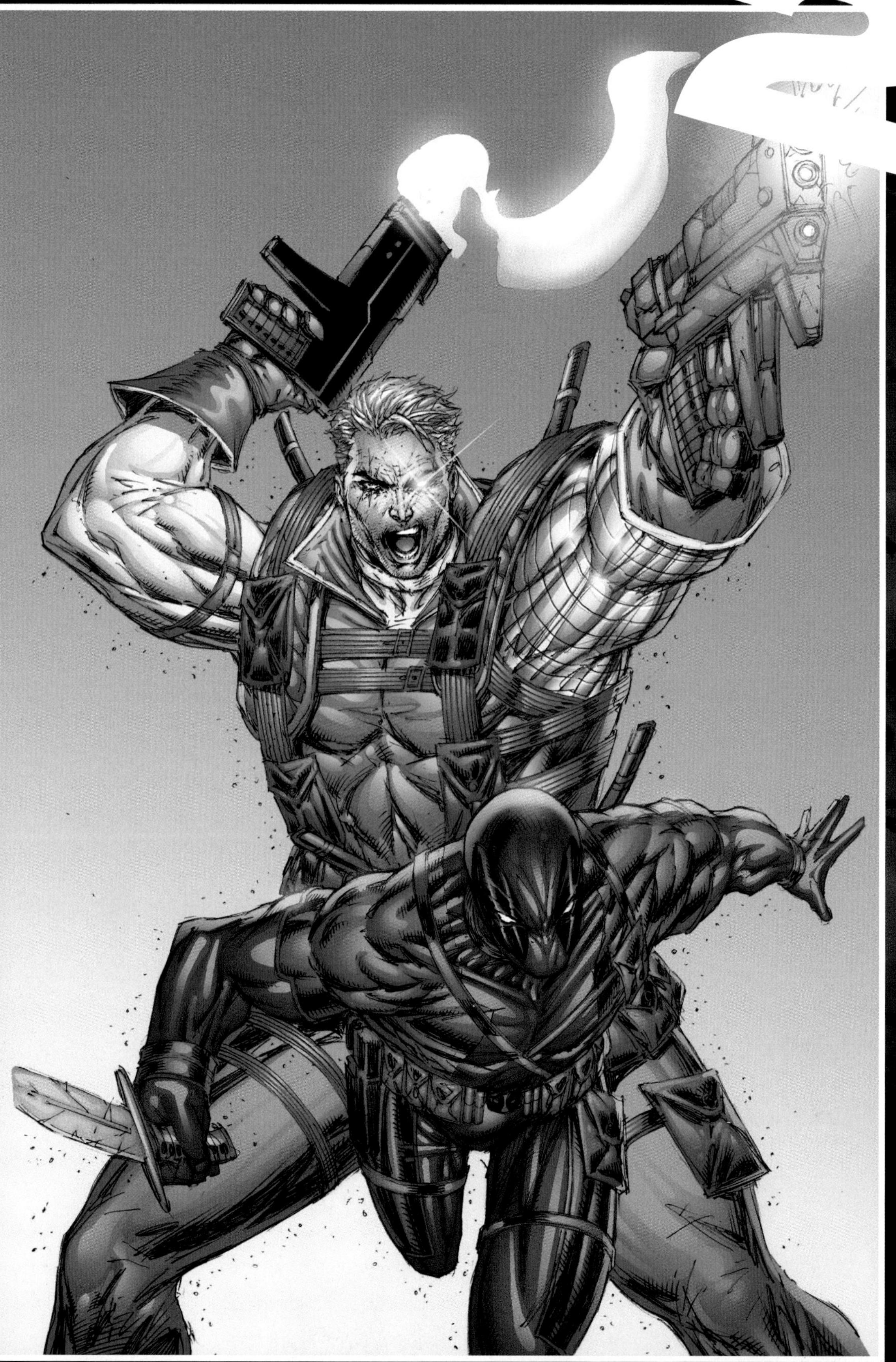

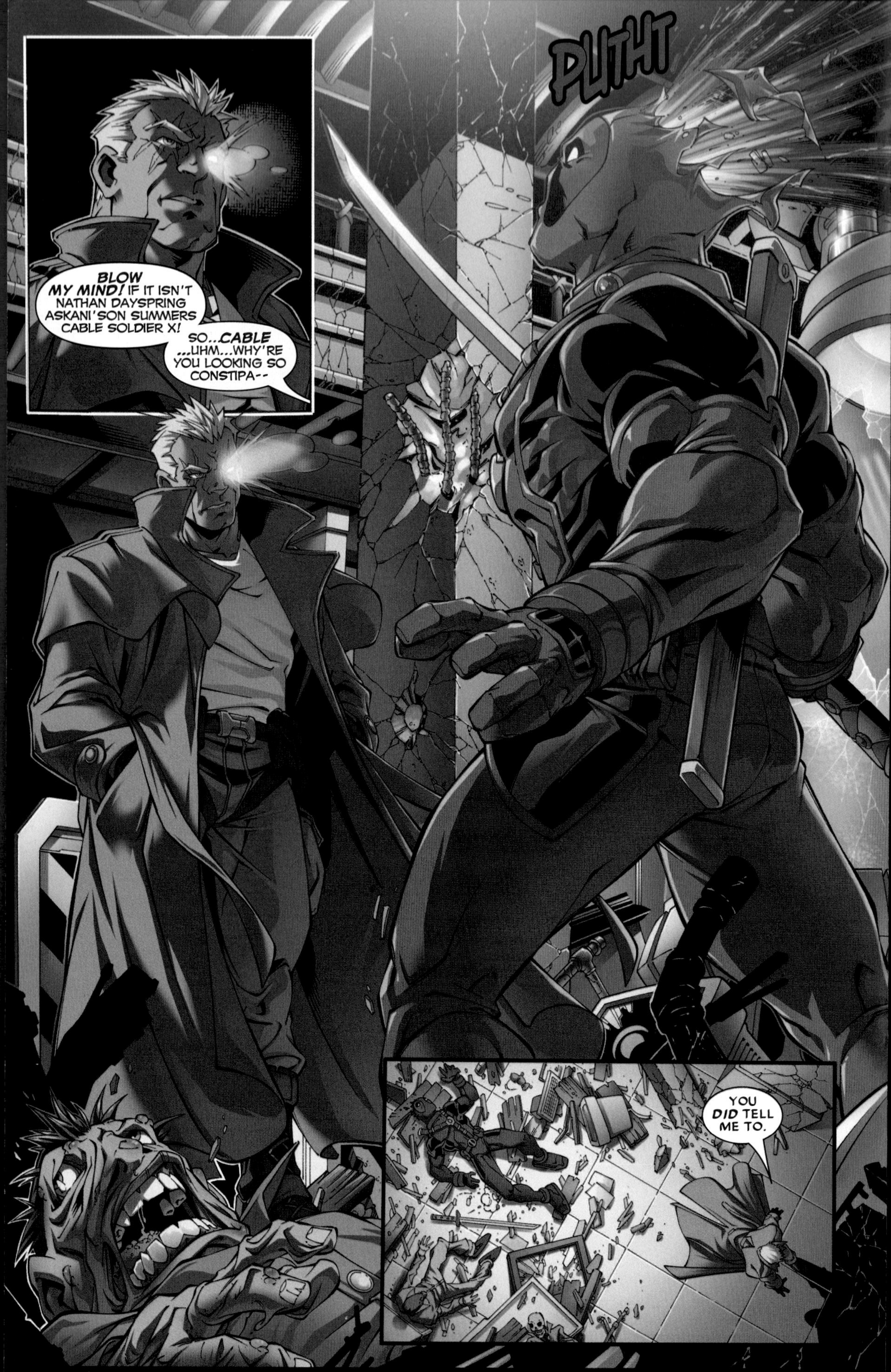
BLOW MY MIND! IF IT ISN'T NATHAN DAYSPRING ASKANI'SON SUMMERS CABLE SOLDIER X!
SO...CABLE ...UHM...WHY'RE YOU LOOKING SO CONSTIPA--
PLIHT
YOU DID TELL ME TO.

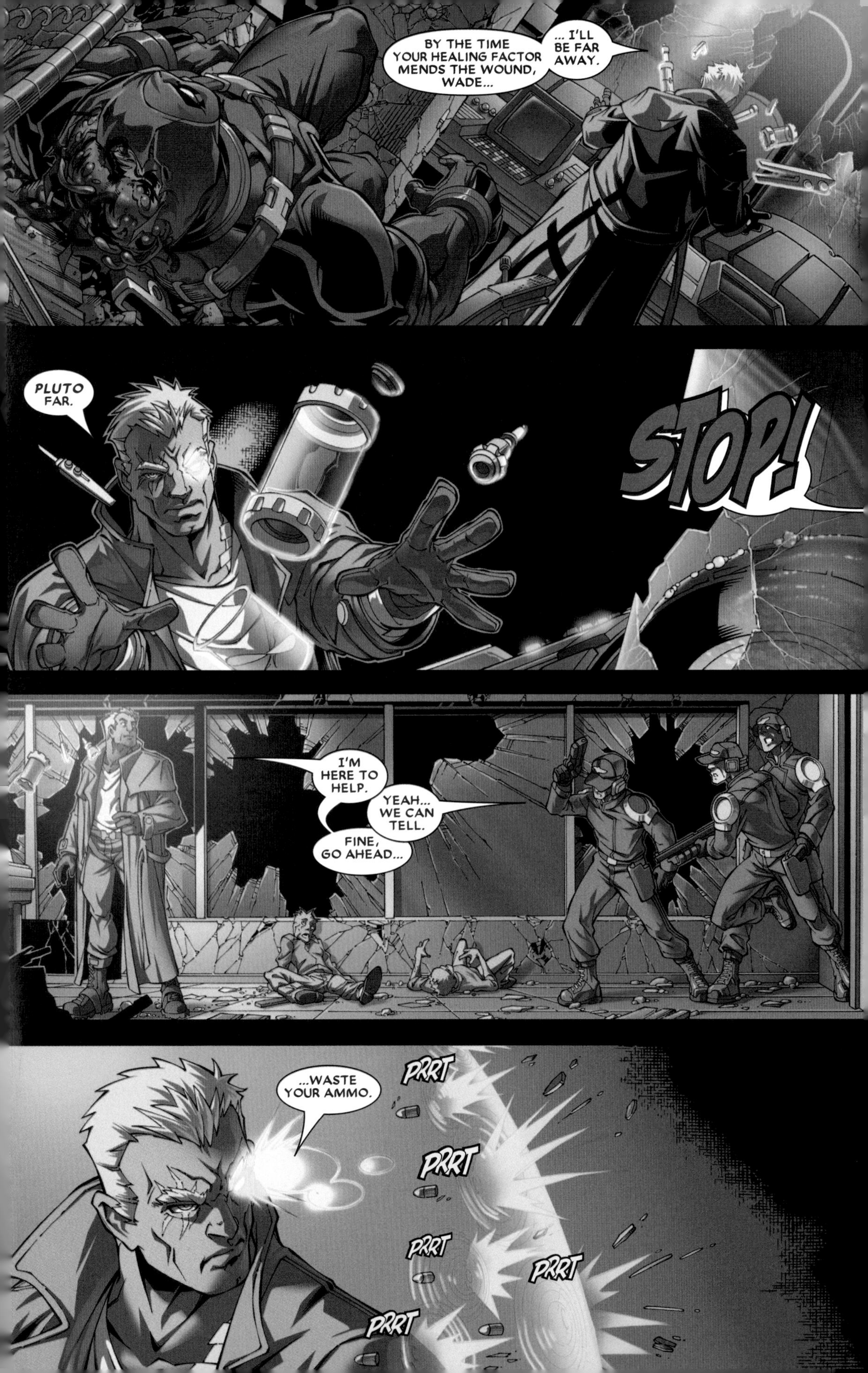
BY THE TIME YOUR HEALING FACTOR MENDS THE WOUND, WADE...
... I'LL BE FAR AWAY.
PLUTO FAR.
STOP!
I'M HERE TO HELP.
YEAH... WE CAN TELL.
FINE, GO AHEAD...
...WASTE YOUR AMMO.
PRRT
PRRT
PRRT
PRRT
PRRT

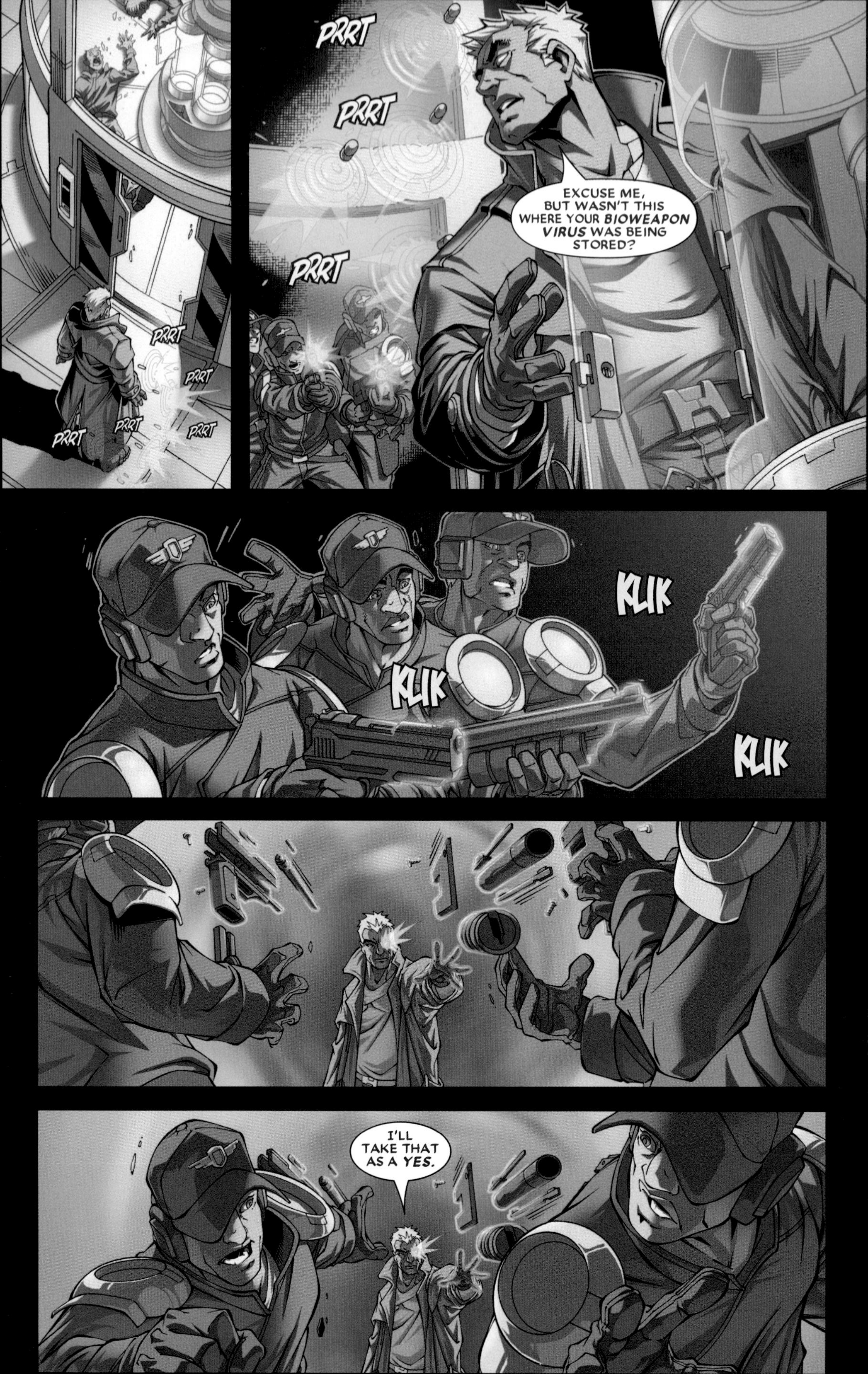
PRRT
PRRT
PRRT
PRRT
PRRT
PRRT
PRRT
PRRT
EXCUSE ME, BUT WASN'T THIS WHERE YOUR BIOWEAPON VIRUS WAS BEING STORED?
KLIK
KLIK
KLIK
I'LL TAKE THAT AS A YES.

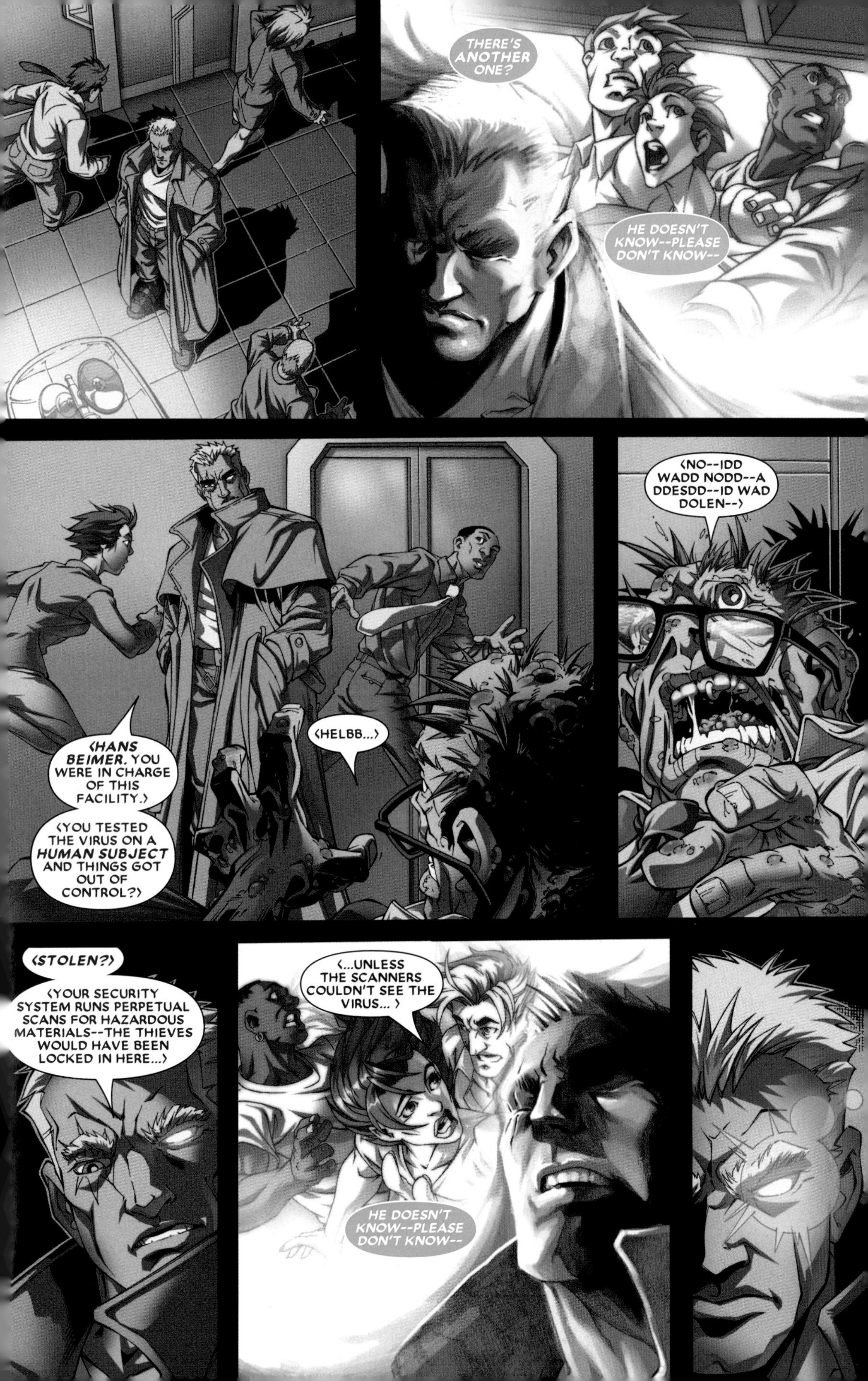
THERE'S ANOTHER ONE?
HE DOESN'T KNOW--PLEASE DON'T KNOW--
‹HANS BEIMER. YOU WERE IN CHARGE OF THIS FACILITY.›
‹YOU TESTED THE VIRUS ON A HUMAN SUBJECT AND THINGS GOT OUT OF CONTROL?›
‹HELBB...›
‹NO--IDD WADD NODD--A DDESDD--ID WAD DOLEN--›
‹STOLEN?›
‹YOUR SECURITY SYSTEM RUNS PERPETUAL SCANS FOR HAZARDOUS MATERIALS--THE THIEVES WOULD HAVE BEEN LOCKED IN HERE...›
‹...UNLESS THE SCANNERS COULDN'T SEE THE VIRUS... ›
HE DOESN'T KNOW--PLEASE DON'T KNOW--

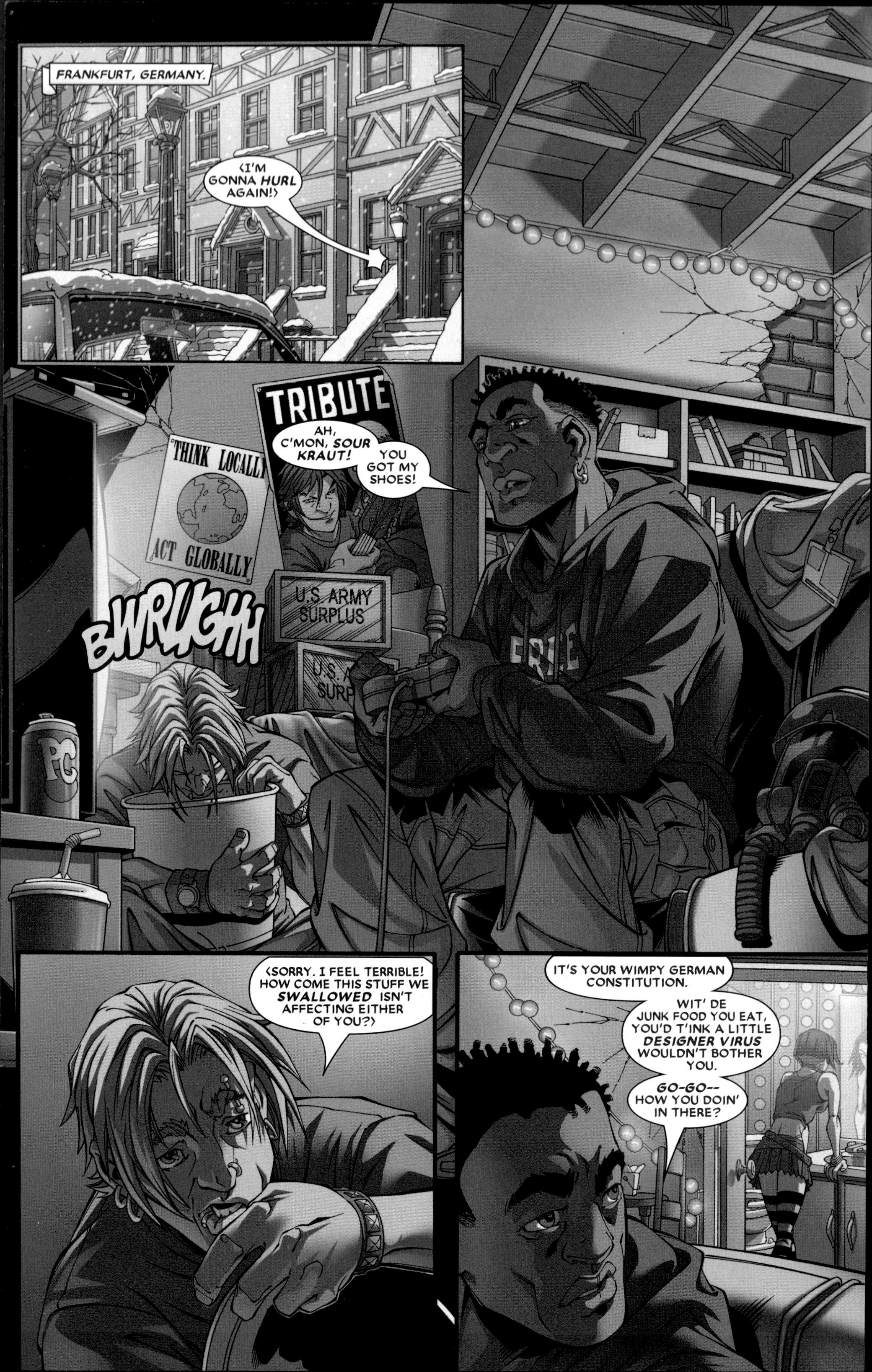
FRANKFURT, GERMANY.
‹I'M GONNA HURL AGAIN!›
TRIBUTE
THINK LOCALLY
ACT GLOBALLY
AH, C'MON, SOUR KRAUT!
YOU GOT MY SHOES!
U.S. ARMY SURPLUS
BWRUGHH
PC
‹SORRY. I FEEL TERRIBLE! HOW COME THIS STUFF WE SWALLOWED ISN'T AFFECTING EITHER OF YOU?›
IT'S YOUR WIMPY GERMAN CONSTITUTION.
WIT' DE JUNK FOOD YOU EAT, YOU'D T'INK A LITTLE DESIGNER VIRUS WOULDN'T BOTHER YOU.
GO-GO-- HOW YOU DOIN' IN THERE?

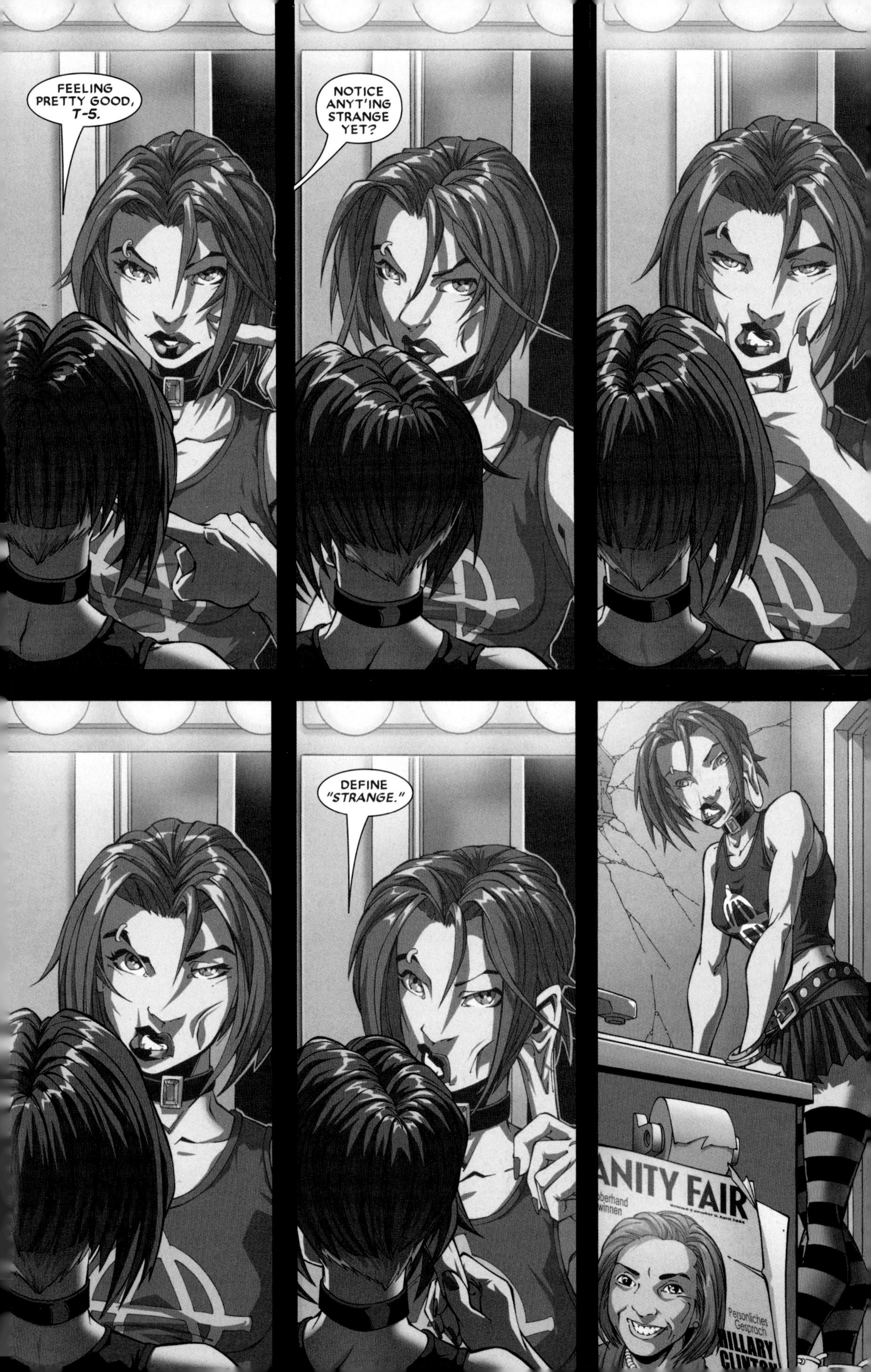
FEELING PRETTY GOOD, *T-5.*
NOTICE ANYT'ING STRANGE YET?
DEFINE *"STRANGE."*
ANITY FAIR
Personliches Gesprach

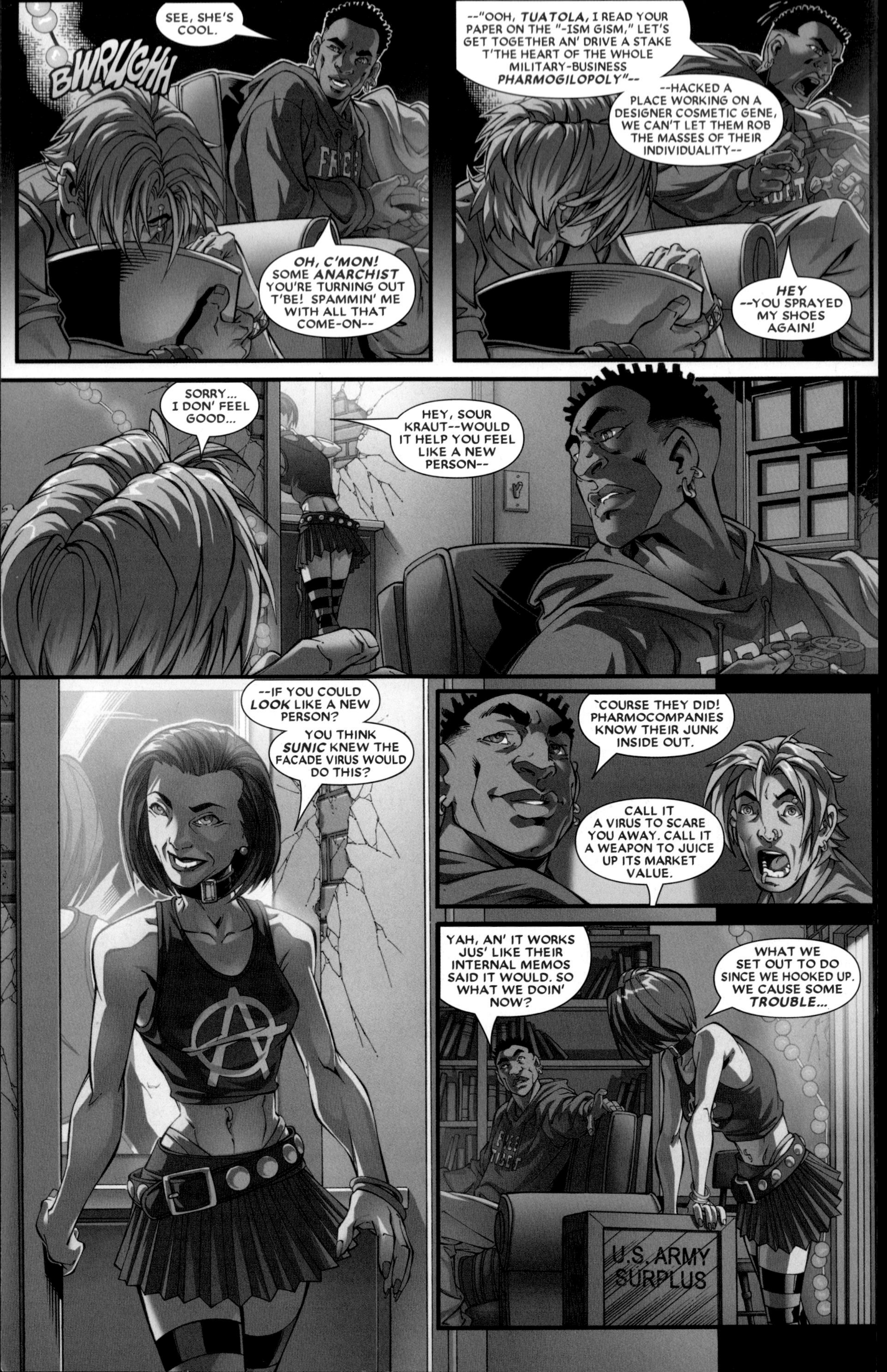

SEE, SHE'S COOL.
BWRUGHH
OH, C'MON! SOME ANARCHIST YOU'RE TURNING OUT T'BE! SPAMMIN' ME WITH ALL THAT COME-ON--
--"OOH, TUATOLA, I READ YOUR PAPER ON THE "-ISM GISM," LET'S GET TOGETHER AN' DRIVE A STAKE T'THE HEART OF THE WHOLE MILITARY-BUSINESS PHARMOGILOPOLY"--
--HACKED A PLACE WORKING ON A DESIGNER COSMETIC GENE, WE CAN'T LET THEM ROB THE MASSES OF THEIR INDIVIDUALITY--
HEY --YOU SPRAYED MY SHOES AGAIN!
SORRY... I DON' FEEL GOOD...
HEY, SOUR KRAUT--WOULD IT HELP YOU FEEL LIKE A NEW PERSON--
--IF YOU COULD LOOK LIKE A NEW PERSON?
YOU THINK SUNIC KNEW THE FACADE VIRUS WOULD DO THIS?
`COURSE THEY DID! PHARMOCOMPANIES KNOW THEIR JUNK INSIDE OUT.
CALL IT A VIRUS TO SCARE YOU AWAY. CALL IT A WEAPON TO JUICE UP ITS MARKET VALUE.
YAH, AN' IT WORKS JUS' LIKE THEIR INTERNAL MEMOS SAID IT WOULD. SO WHAT WE DOIN' NOW?
WHAT WE SET OUT TO DO SINCE WE HOOKED UP. WE CAUSE SOME TROUBLE...
U.S. ARMY SURPLUS

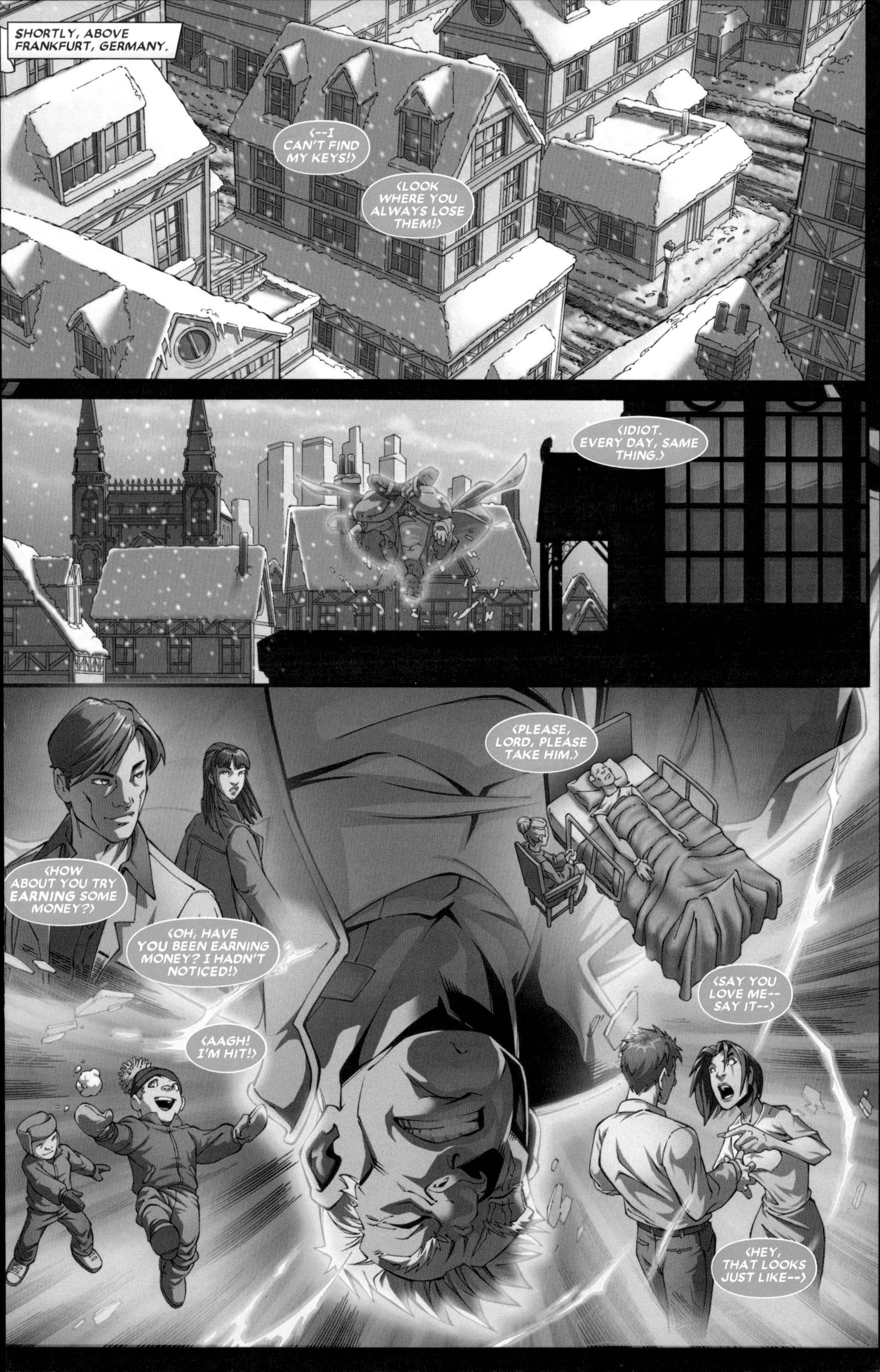
SHORTLY, ABOVE FRANKFURT, GERMANY.
<--I CAN'T FIND MY KEYS!>
<LOOK WHERE YOU ALWAYS LOSE THEM!>
<IDIOT. EVERY DAY, SAME THING.>
<PLEASE, LORD, PLEASE TAKE HIM.>
<HOW ABOUT YOU TRY EARNING SOME MONEY?>
<OH, HAVE YOU BEEN EARNING MONEY? I HADN'T NOTICED!>
<SAY YOU LOVE ME--SAY IT-->
<AAGH! I'M HIT!>
<HEY, THAT LOOKS JUST LIKE-->

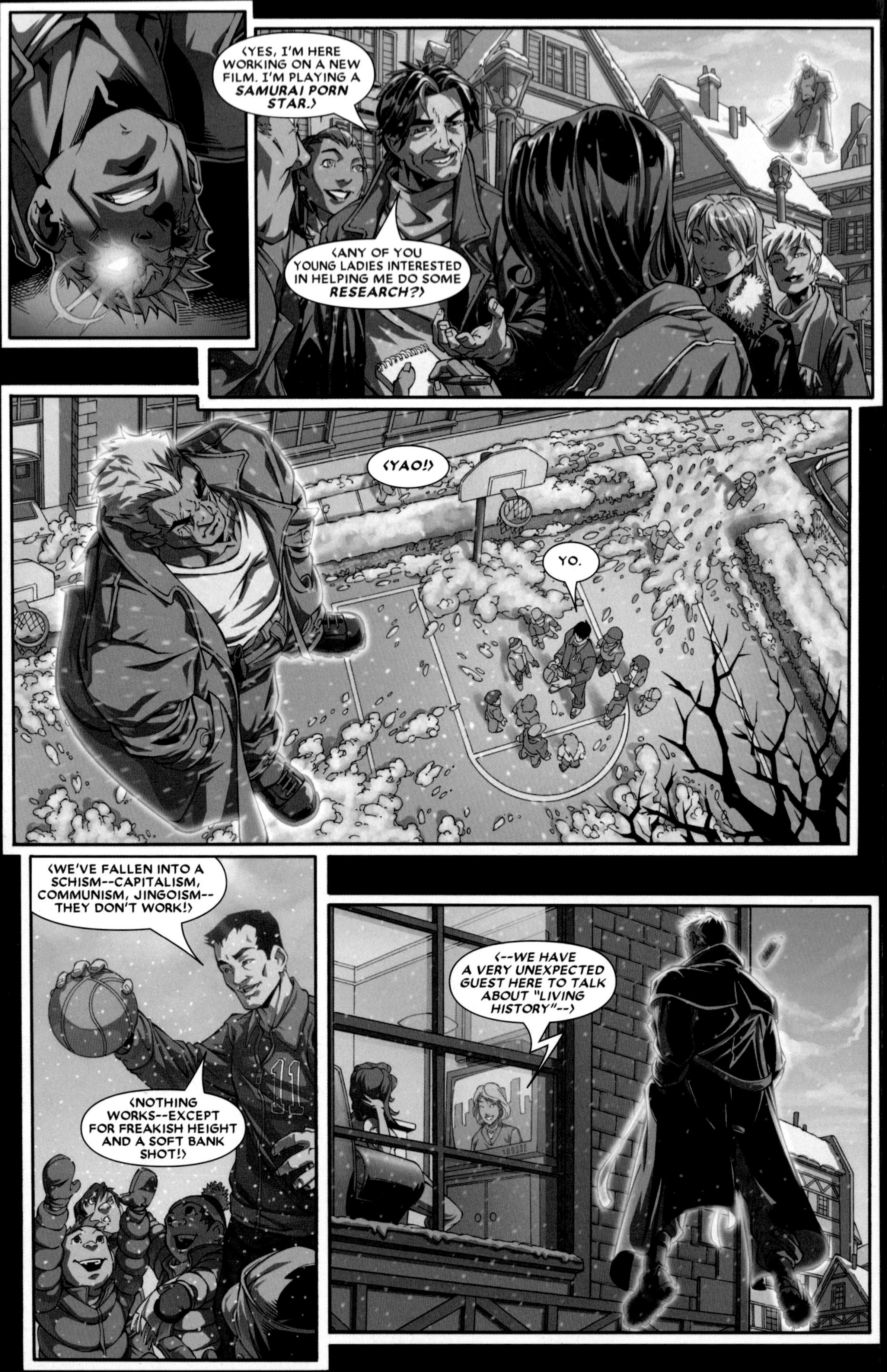
‹YES, I'M HERE WORKING ON A NEW FILM. I'M PLAYING A SAMURAI PORN STAR.›
‹ANY OF YOU YOUNG LADIES INTERESTED IN HELPING ME DO SOME RESEARCH?›
‹YAO!›
YO.
‹WE'VE FALLEN INTO A SCHISM--CAPITALISM, COMMUNISM, JINGOISM--THEY DON'T WORK!›
‹NOTHING WORKS--EXCEPT FOR FREAKISH HEIGHT AND A SOFT BANK SHOT!›
‹--WE HAVE A VERY UNEXPECTED GUEST HERE TO TALK ABOUT "LIVING HISTORY"--›

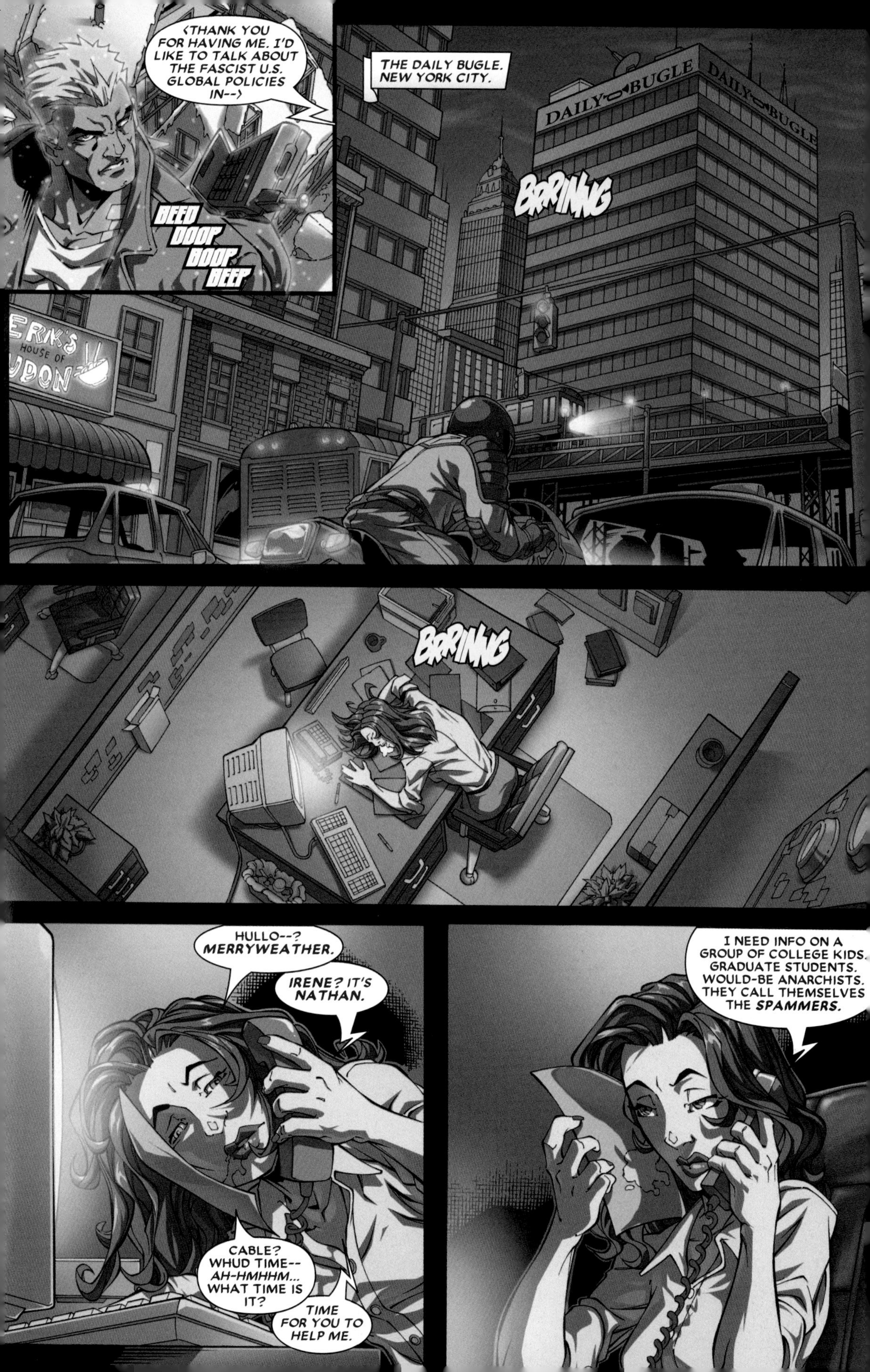

‹THANK YOU FOR HAVING ME. I'D LIKE TO TALK ABOUT THE FASCIST U.S. GLOBAL POLICIES IN--›
BEED DOOP BOOP BEEP
THE DAILY BUGLE. NEW YORK CITY.
DAILY BUGLE
DAILY BUGLE
BRRINNG
ERIK'S HOUSE OF UDON
BRRINNG
HULLO--? MERRYWEATHER.
IRENE? IT'S NATHAN.
CABLE? WHUD TIME-- AH-HMHHM... WHAT TIME IS IT?
TIME FOR YOU TO HELP ME.
I NEED INFO ON A GROUP OF COLLEGE KIDS. GRADUATE STUDENTS. WOULD-BE ANARCHISTS. THEY CALL THEMSELVES THE SPAMMERS.

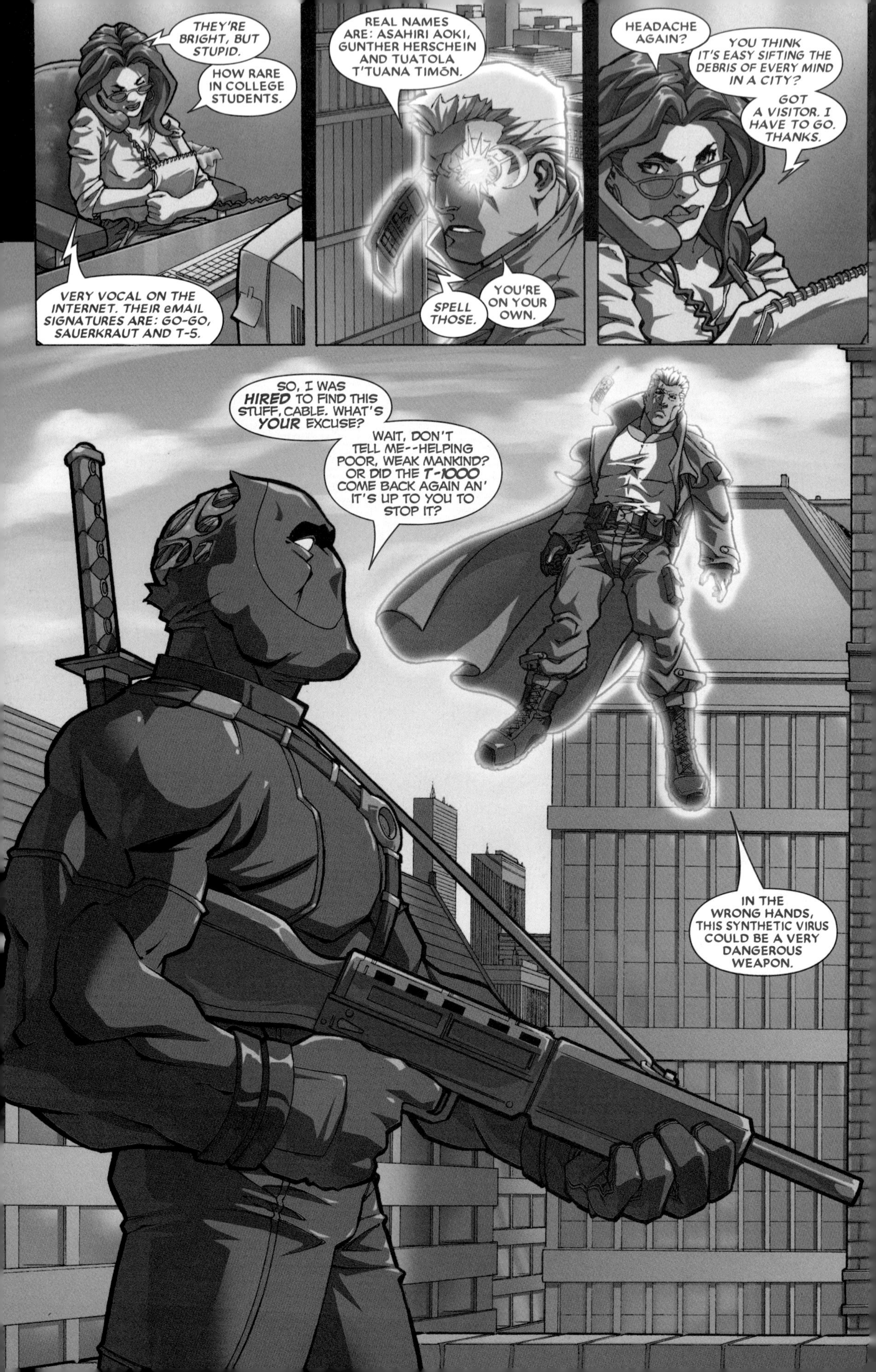
THEY'RE BRIGHT, BUT STUPID.
HOW RARE IN COLLEGE STUDENTS.
VERY VOCAL ON THE INTERNET. THEIR eMAIL SIGNATURES ARE: GO-GO, SAUERKRAUT AND T-5.
REAL NAMES ARE: ASAHIRI AOKI, GUNTHER HERSCHEIN AND TUATOLA T'TUANA TIMŌN.
SPELL THOSE.
YOU'RE ON YOUR OWN.
HEADACHE AGAIN?
YOU THINK IT'S EASY SIFTING THE DEBRIS OF EVERY MIND IN A CITY?
GOT A VISITOR. I HAVE TO GO. THANKS.
SO, I WAS HIRED TO FIND THIS STUFF, CABLE. WHAT'S YOUR EXCUSE?
WAIT, DON'T TELL ME--HELPING POOR, WEAK MANKIND? OR DID THE T-1000 COME BACK AGAIN AN' IT'S UP TO YOU TO STOP IT?
IN THE WRONG HANDS, THIS SYNTHETIC VIRUS COULD BE A VERY DANGEROUS WEAPON.

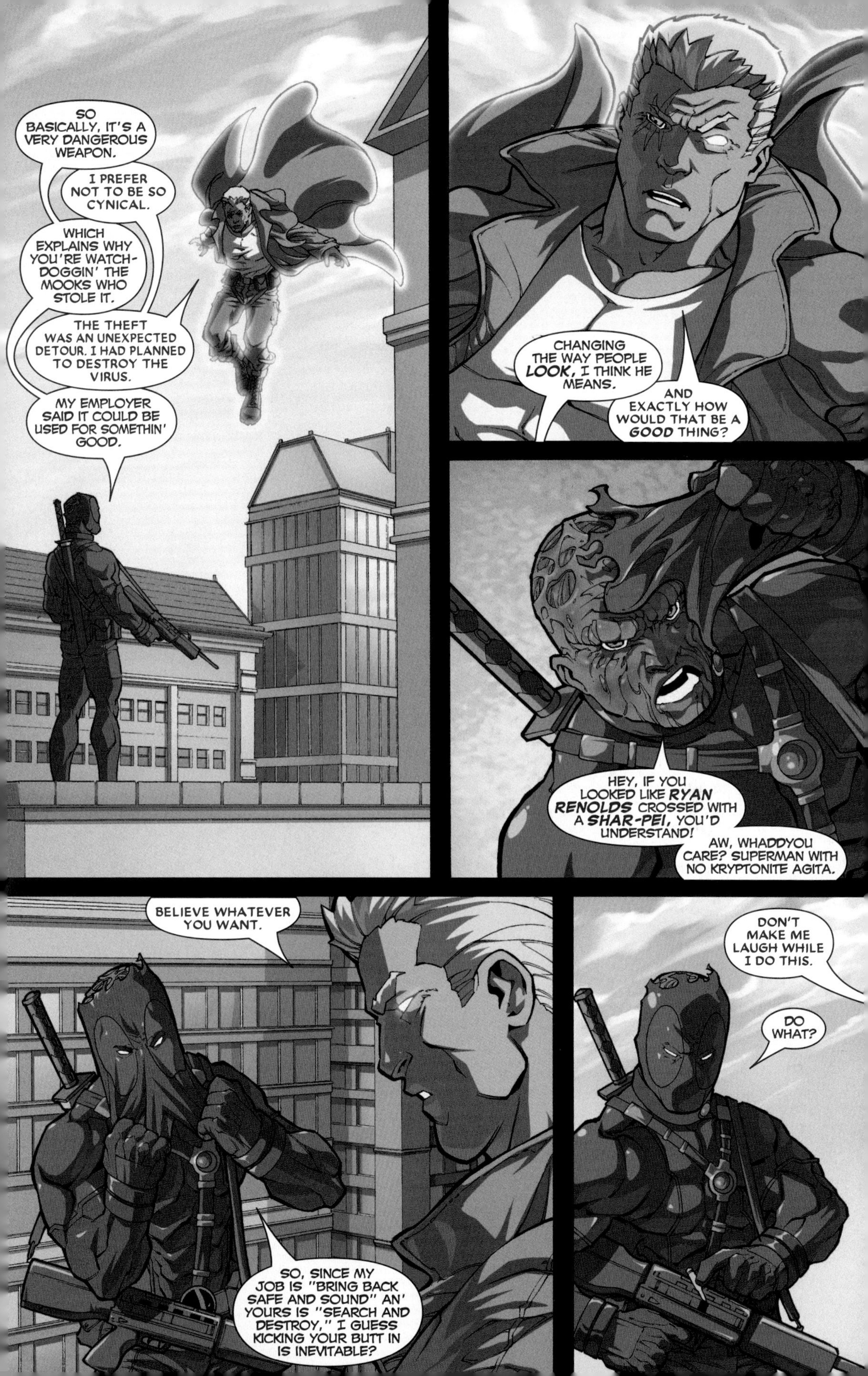
SO BASICALLY, IT'S A VERY DANGEROUS WEAPON.
I PREFER NOT TO BE SO CYNICAL.
WHICH EXPLAINS WHY YOU'RE WATCH-DOGGIN' THE MOOKS WHO STOLE IT.
THE THEFT WAS AN UNEXPECTED DETOUR. I HAD PLANNED TO DESTROY THE VIRUS.
MY EMPLOYER SAID IT COULD BE USED FOR SOMETHIN' GOOD.
CHANGING THE WAY PEOPLE LOOK, I THINK HE MEANS.
AND EXACTLY HOW WOULD THAT BE A GOOD THING?
HEY, IF YOU LOOKED LIKE RYAN RENOLDS CROSSED WITH A SHAR-PEI, YOU'D UNDERSTAND!
AW, WHADDYOU CARE? SUPERMAN WITH NO KRYPTONITE AGITA.
BELIEVE WHATEVER YOU WANT.
SO, SINCE MY JOB IS "BRING BACK SAFE AND SOUND" AN' YOURS IS "SEARCH AND DESTROY," I GUESS KICKING YOUR BUTT IN IS INEVITABLE?
DON'T MAKE ME LAUGH WHILE I DO THIS.
DO WHAT?

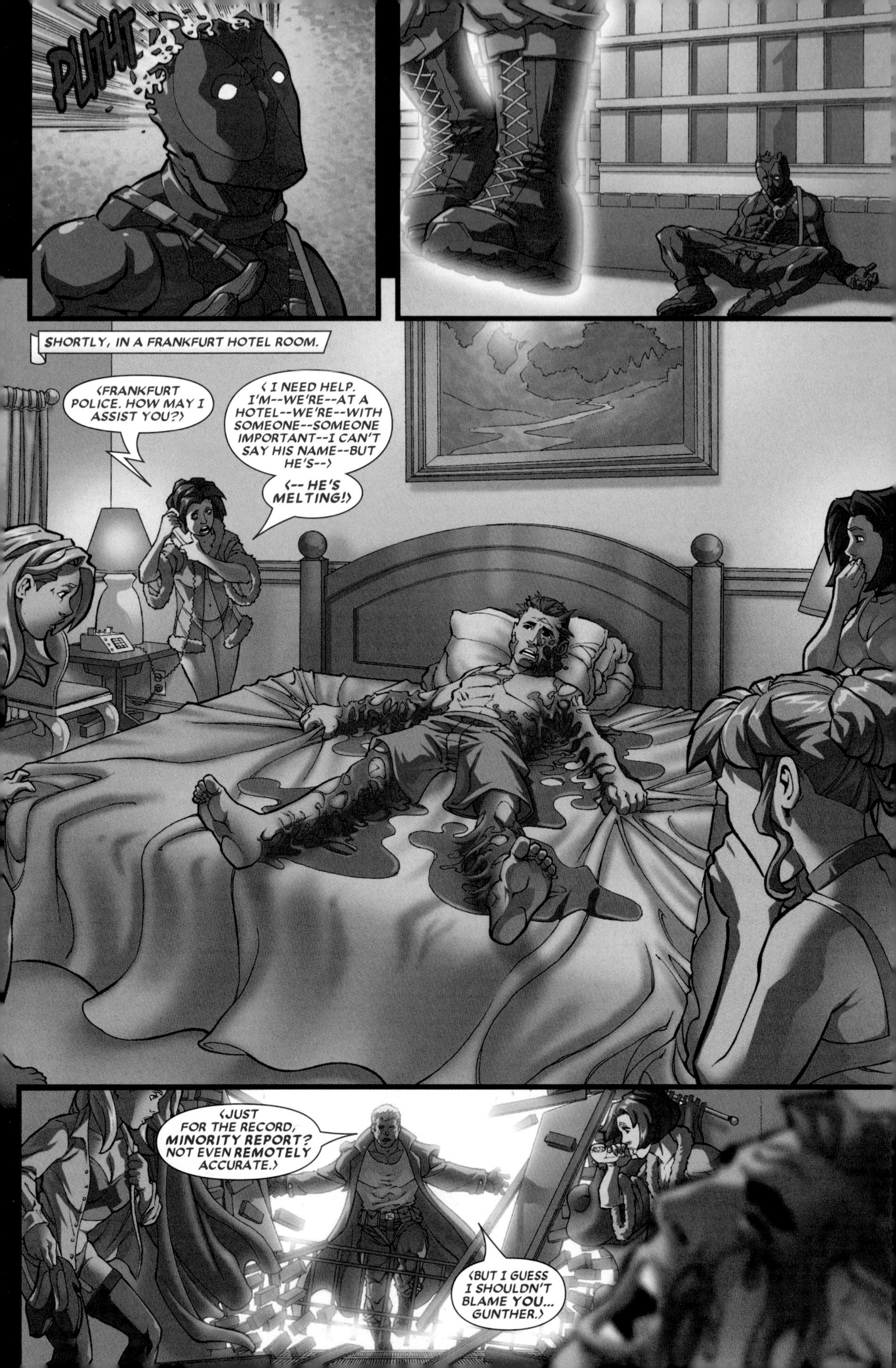
PLTHT
SHORTLY, IN A FRANKFURT HOTEL ROOM.
‹FRANKFURT POLICE. HOW MAY I ASSIST YOU?›
‹ I NEED HELP. I'M--WE'RE--AT A HOTEL--WE'RE--WITH SOMEONE--SOMEONE IMPORTANT--I CAN'T SAY HIS NAME--BUT HE'S--›
‹-- HE'S MELTING!›
‹JUST FOR THE RECORD, MINORITY REPORT? NOT EVEN REMOTELY ACCURATE.›
‹BUT I GUESS I SHOULDN'T BLAME YOU... GUNTHER.›

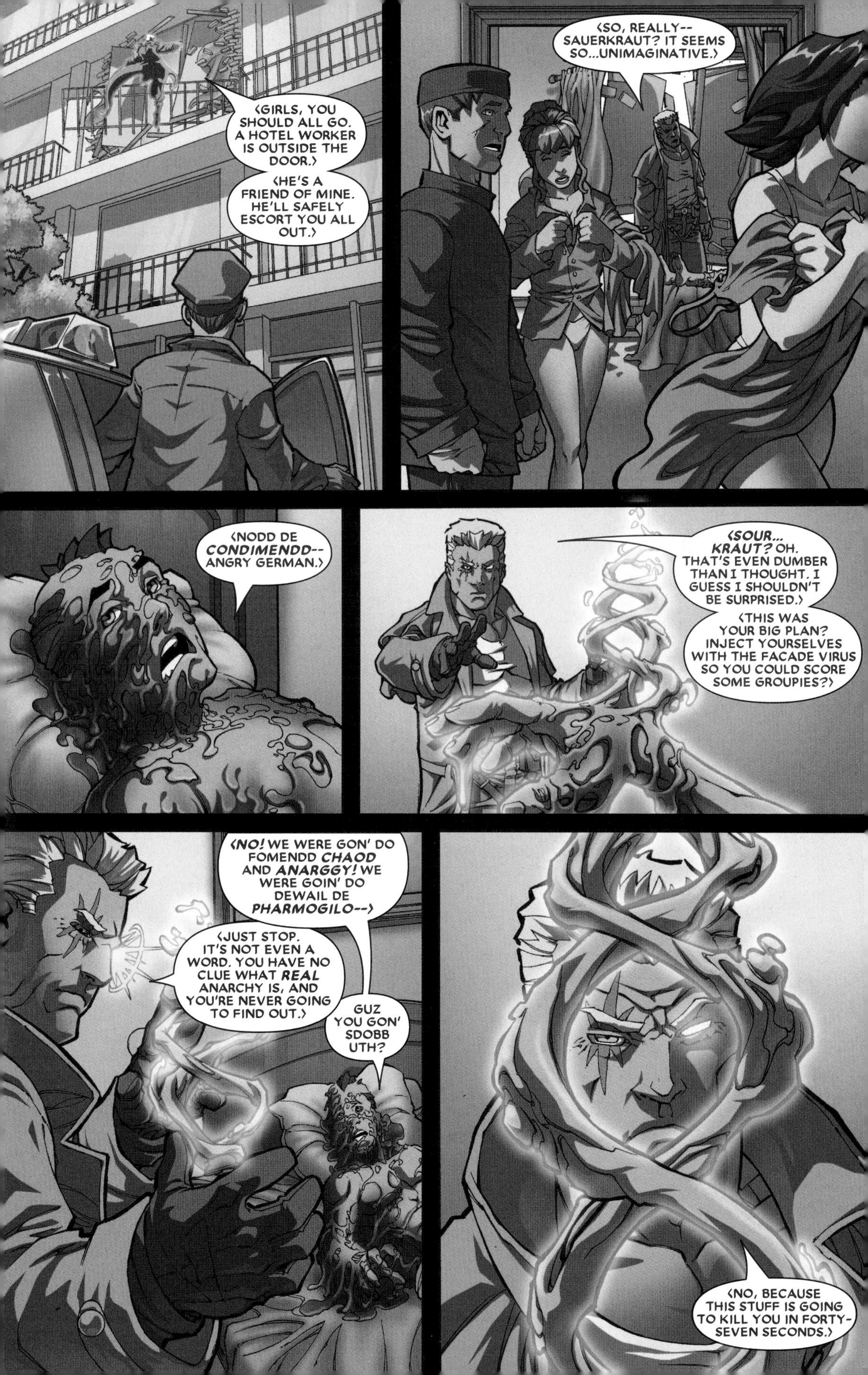

‹GIRLS, YOU SHOULD ALL GO. A HOTEL WORKER IS OUTSIDE THE DOOR.›
‹HE'S A FRIEND OF MINE. HE'LL SAFELY ESCORT YOU ALL OUT.›
‹SO, REALLY-- SAUERKRAUT? IT SEEMS SO...UNIMAGINATIVE.›
‹NODD DE *CONDIMENDD*-- ANGRY GERMAN.›
‹*SOUR... KRAUT?* OH. THAT'S EVEN DUMBER THAN I THOUGHT. I GUESS I SHOULDN'T BE SURPRISED.›
‹THIS WAS YOUR BIG PLAN? INJECT YOURSELVES WITH THE FACADE VIRUS SO YOU COULD SCORE SOME GROUPIES?›
‹*NO!* WE WERE GON' DO FOMENDD *CHAOD* AND *ANARGGY!* WE WERE GOIN' DO DEWAIL DE *PHARMOGILO*--›
‹JUST STOP. IT'S NOT EVEN A WORD. YOU HAVE NO CLUE WHAT *REAL* ANARCHY IS, AND YOU'RE NEVER GOING TO FIND OUT.›
GUZ YOU GON' SDOBB UTH?
‹NO, BECAUSE THIS STUFF IS GOING TO KILL YOU IN FORTY-SEVEN SECONDS.›

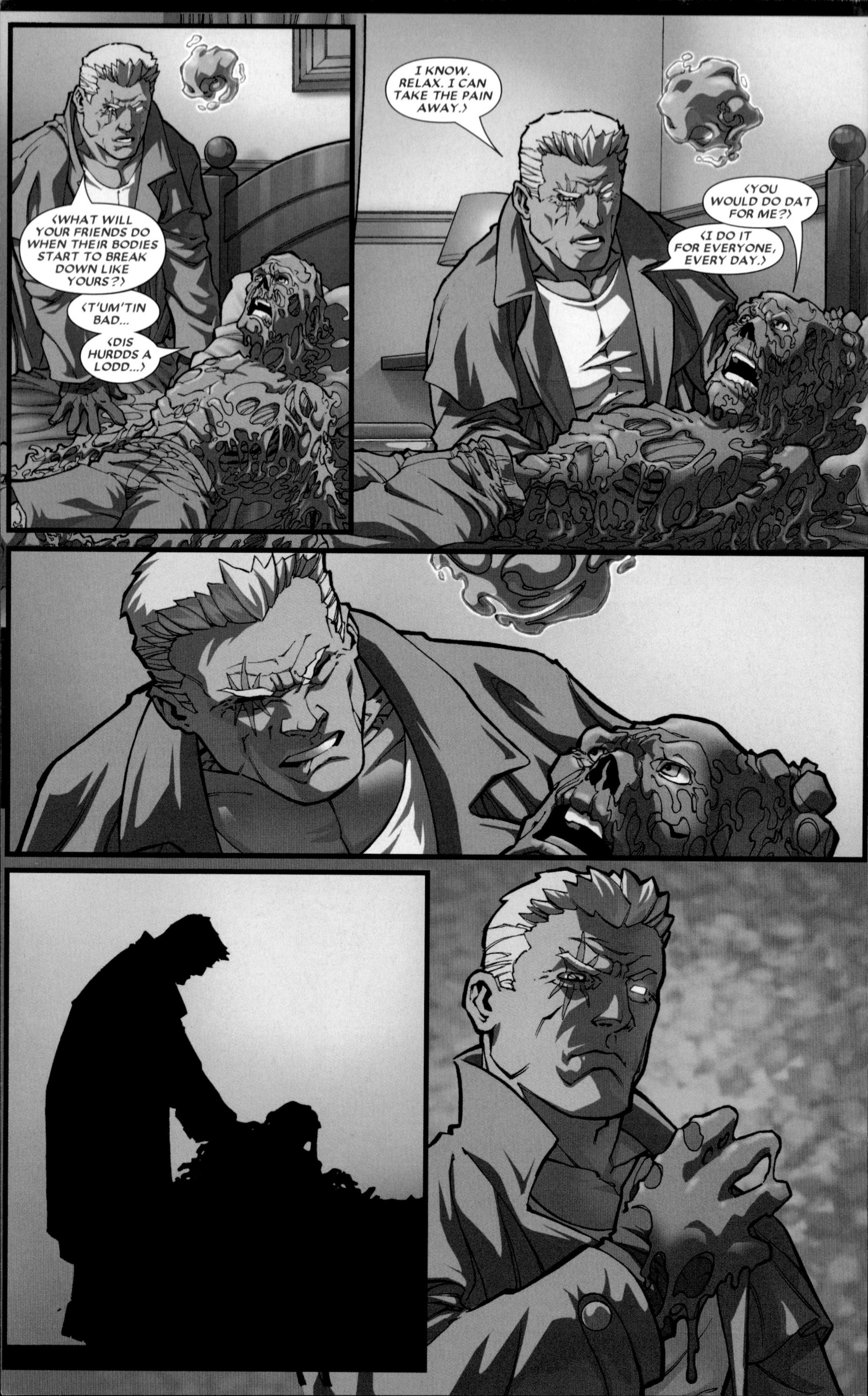
‹WHAT WILL YOUR FRIENDS DO WHEN THEIR BODIES START TO BREAK DOWN LIKE YOURS?›
‹T'UM'TIN BAD...
‹DIS HURDDS A LODD...›
I KNOW. RELAX. I CAN TAKE THE PAIN AWAY.›
‹YOU WOULD DO DAT FOR ME?›
‹I DO IT FOR EVERYONE, EVERY DAY.›

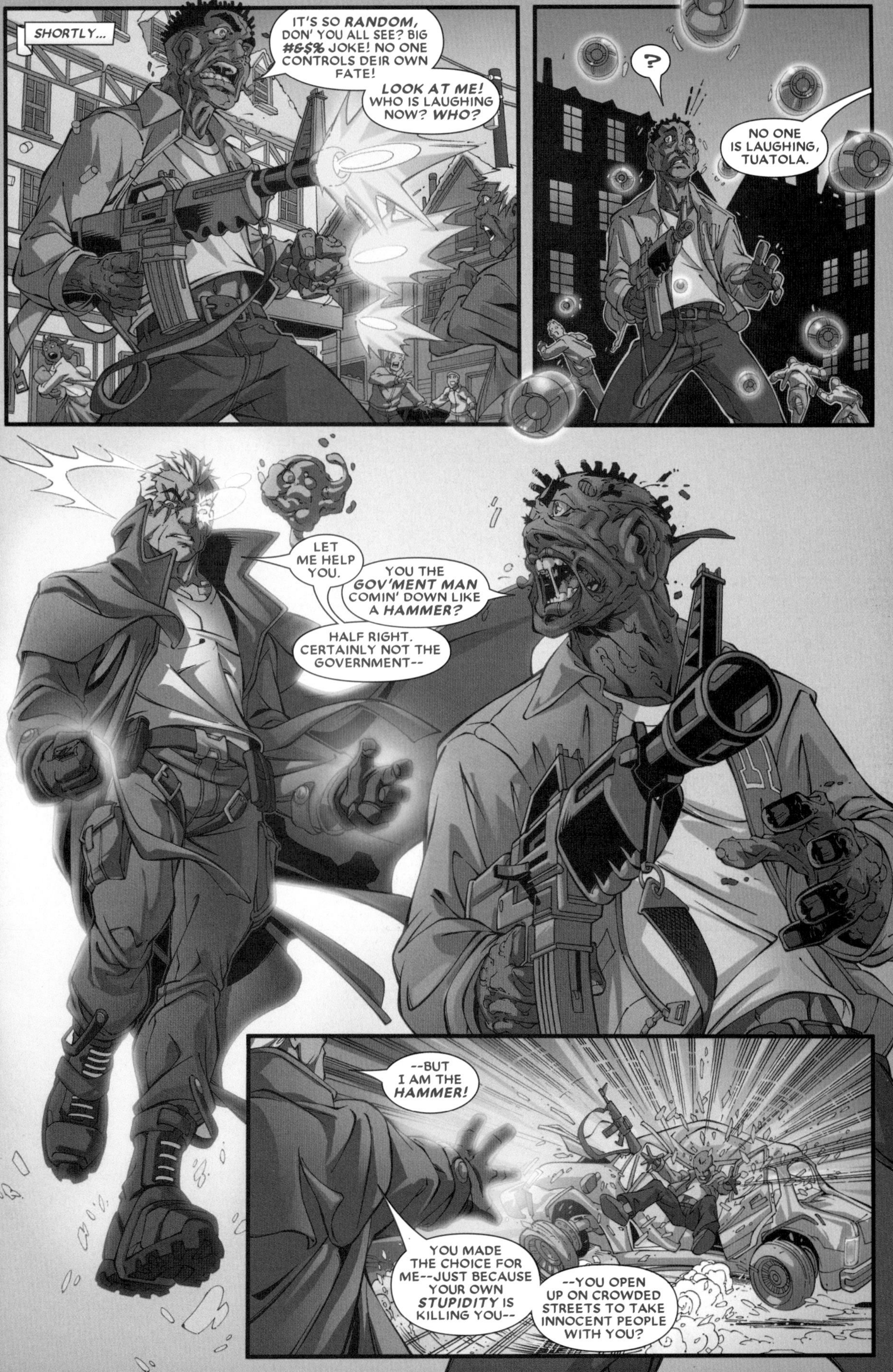
SHORTLY...
IT'S SO RANDOM, DON' YOU ALL SEE? BIG #&$% JOKE! NO ONE CONTROLS DEIR OWN FATE!
LOOK AT ME! WHO IS LAUGHING NOW? WHO?
?
NO ONE IS LAUGHING, TUATOLA.
LET ME HELP YOU.
YOU THE GOV'MENT MAN COMIN' DOWN LIKE A HAMMER?
HALF RIGHT. CERTAINLY NOT THE GOVERNMENT--
--BUT I AM THE HAMMER!
YOU MADE THE CHOICE FOR ME--JUST BECAUSE YOUR OWN STUPIDITY IS KILLING YOU--
--YOU OPEN UP ON CROWDED STREETS TO TAKE INNOCENT PEOPLE WITH YOU?

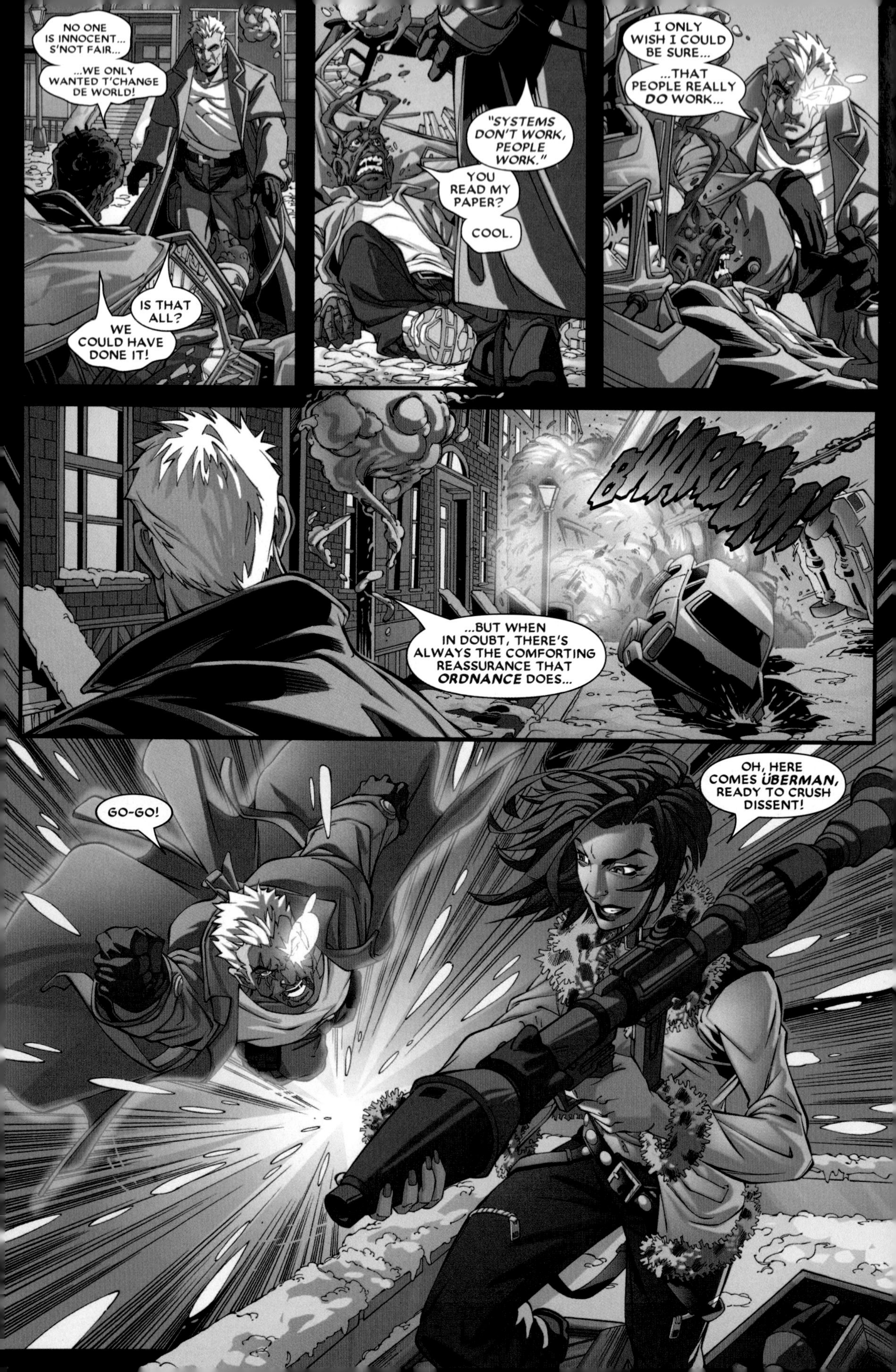
NO ONE IS INNOCENT... S'NOT FAIR...
...WE ONLY WANTED T'CHANGE DE WORLD!
IS THAT ALL?
WE COULD HAVE DONE IT!
"SYSTEMS DON'T WORK, PEOPLE WORK."
YOU READ MY PAPER?
COOL.
I ONLY WISH I COULD BE SURE...
...THAT PEOPLE REALLY DO WORK...
...BUT WHEN IN DOUBT, THERE'S ALWAYS THE COMFORTING REASSURANCE THAT ORDNANCE DOES...
BWAROOM!!
GO-GO!
OH, HERE COMES ÜBERMAN, READY TO CRUSH DISSENT!

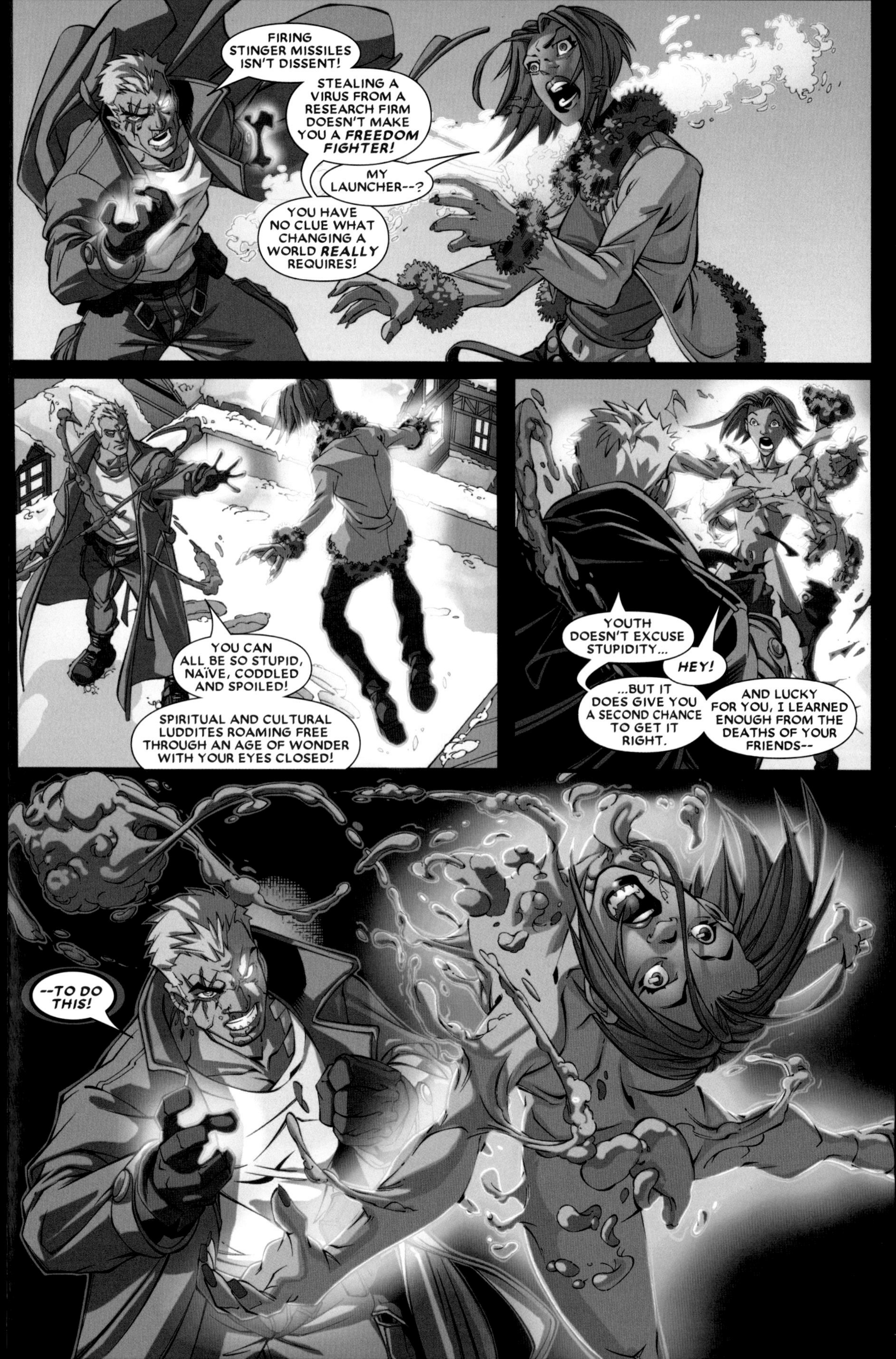
FIRING STINGER MISSILES ISN'T DISSENT!
STEALING A VIRUS FROM A RESEARCH FIRM DOESN'T MAKE YOU A *FREEDOM FIGHTER!*
MY LAUNCHER--?
YOU HAVE NO CLUE WHAT CHANGING A WORLD *REALLY* REQUIRES!
YOU CAN ALL BE SO STUPID, NAÏVE, CODDLED AND SPOILED!
SPIRITUAL AND CULTURAL LUDDITES ROAMING FREE THROUGH AN AGE OF WONDER WITH YOUR EYES CLOSED!
YOUTH DOESN'T EXCUSE STUPIDITY...
HEY!
...BUT IT DOES GIVE YOU A SECOND CHANCE TO GET IT RIGHT.
AND LUCKY FOR YOU, I LEARNED ENOUGH FROM THE DEATHS OF YOUR FRIENDS--
--TO DO THIS!

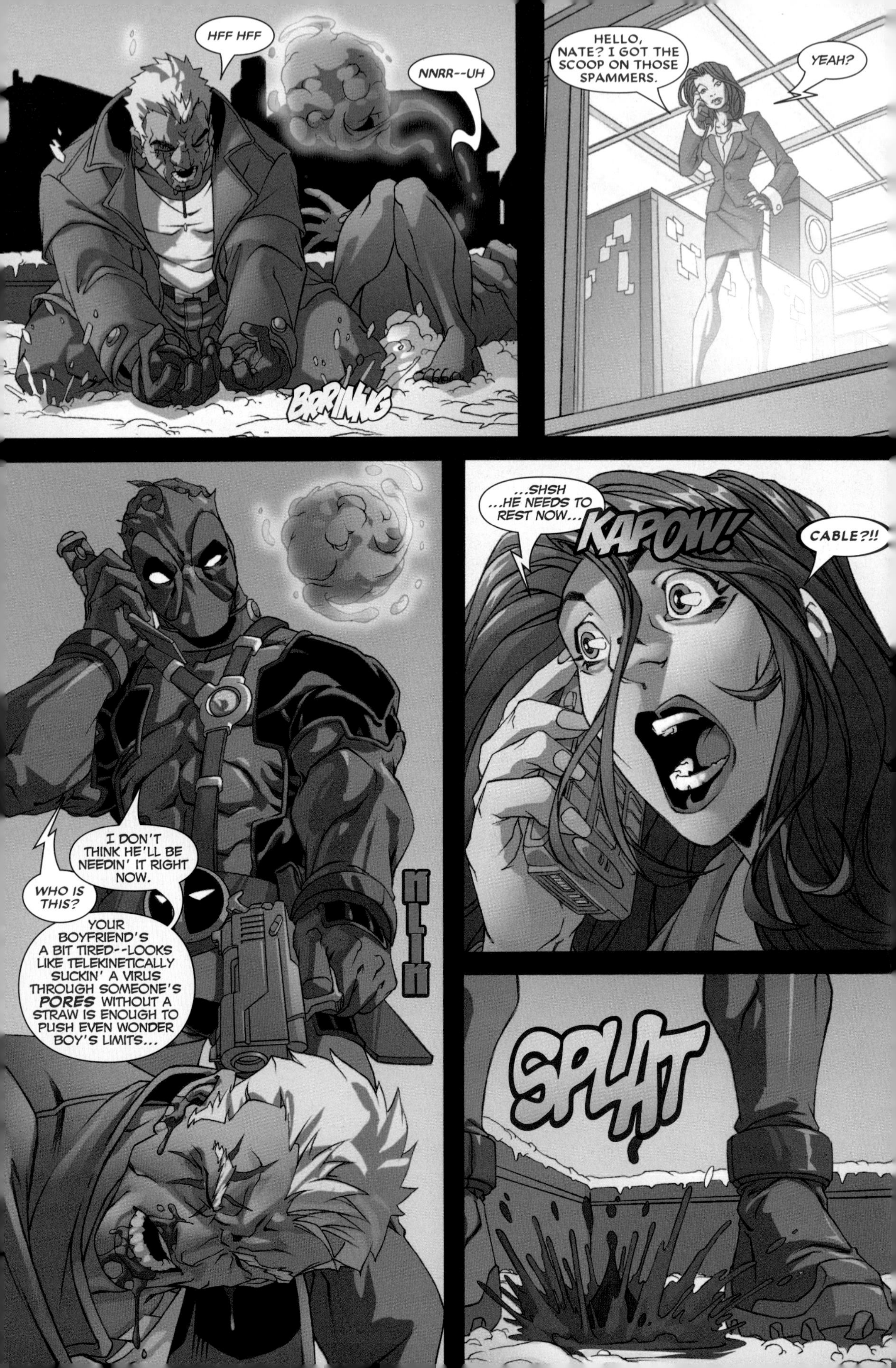
HFF HFF
NNRR--UH
BRRINNG
HELLO, NATE? I GOT THE SCOOP ON THOSE SPAMMERS.
YEAH?
I DON'T THINK HE'LL BE NEEDIN' IT RIGHT NOW.
WHO IS THIS?
YOUR BOYFRIEND'S A BIT TIRED--LOOKS LIKE TELEKINETICALLY SUCKIN' A VIRUS THROUGH SOMEONE'S PORES WITHOUT A STRAW IS ENOUGH TO PUSH EVEN WONDER BOY'S LIMITS...
KLIK
...SHSH ...HE NEEDS TO REST NOW...
KAPOW!
CABLE?!!
SPLAT

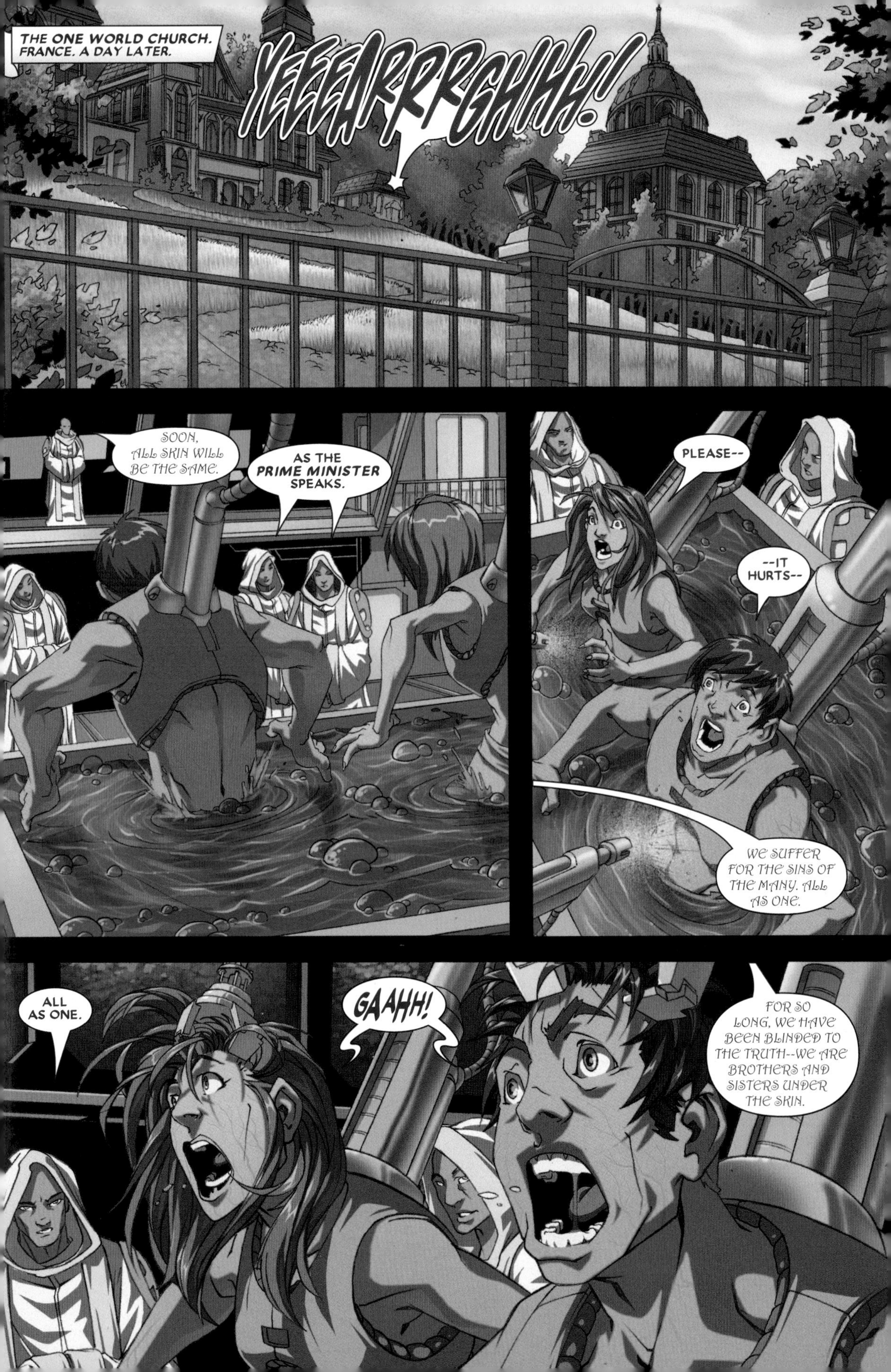
THE ONE WORLD CHURCH. FRANCE. A DAY LATER.
YEEEARRRGHHH!
SOON, ALL SKIN WILL BE THE SAME.
AS THE PRIME MINISTER SPEAKS.
PLEASE--
--IT HURTS--
WE SUFFER FOR THE SINS OF THE MANY. ALL AS ONE.
ALL AS ONE.
GAAHH!
FOR SO LONG, WE HAVE BEEN BLINDED TO THE TRUTH--WE ARE BROTHERS AND SISTERS UNDER THE SKIN.

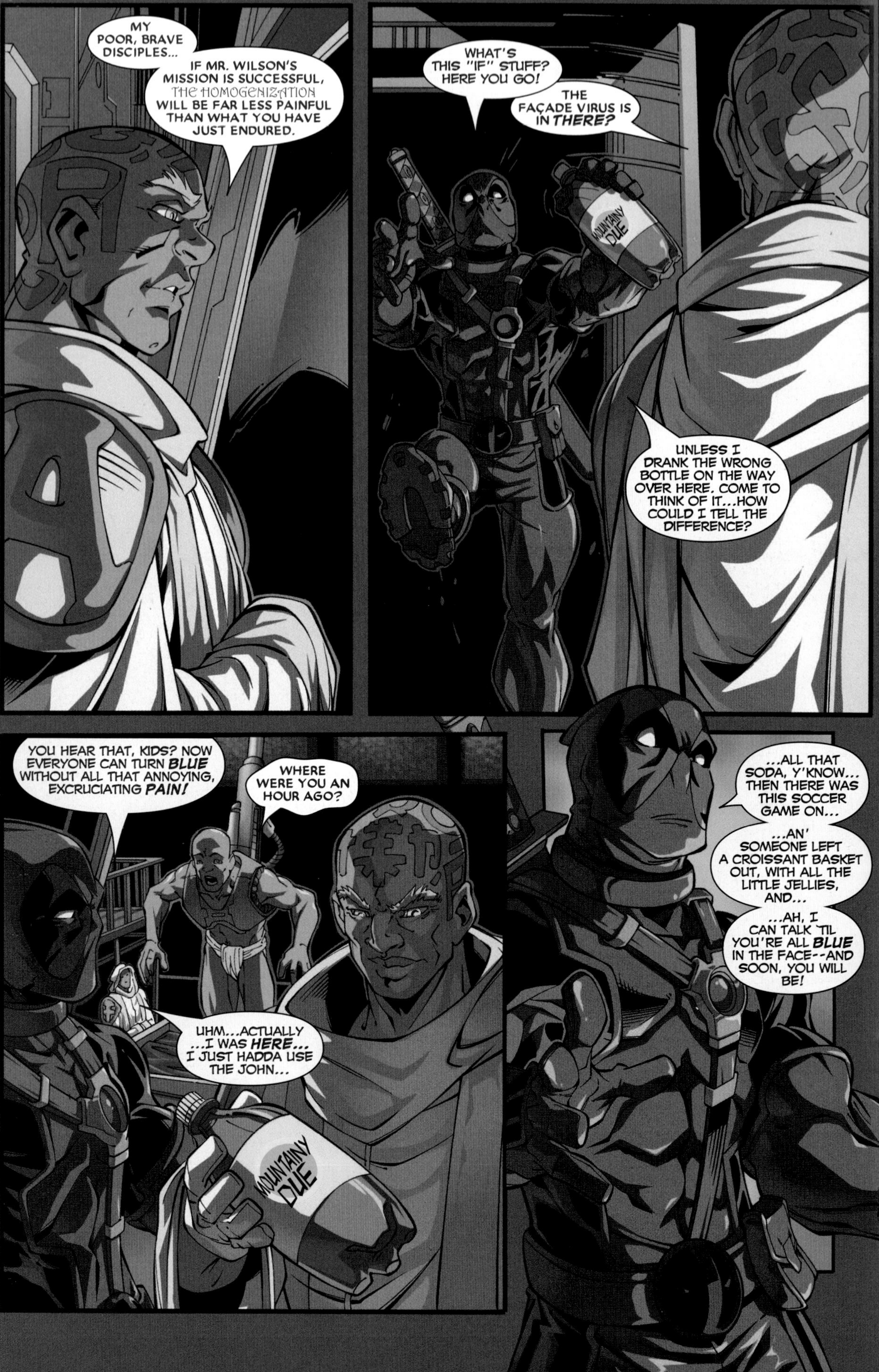
MY POOR, BRAVE DISCIPLES...
IF MR. WILSON'S MISSION IS SUCCESSFUL, THE HOMOGENIZATION WILL BE FAR LESS PAINFUL THAN WHAT YOU HAVE JUST ENDURED.
WHAT'S THIS "IF" STUFF? HERE YOU GO!
THE FAÇADE VIRUS IS IN *THERE?*
MOUNTAINY DUE
UNLESS I DRANK THE WRONG BOTTLE ON THE WAY OVER HERE. COME TO THINK OF IT...HOW COULD I TELL THE DIFFERENCE?
YOU HEAR THAT, KIDS? NOW EVERYONE CAN TURN ***BLUE*** WITHOUT ALL THAT ANNOYING, EXCRUCIATING ***PAIN!***
WHERE WERE YOU AN HOUR AGO?
UHM...ACTUALLY ...I WAS ***HERE...*** I JUST HADDA USE THE JOHN...
MOUNTAINY DUE
...ALL THAT SODA, Y'KNOW... THEN THERE WAS THIS SOCCER GAME ON...
...AN' SOMEONE LEFT A CROISSANT BASKET OUT, WITH ALL THE LITTLE JELLIES, AND...
...AH, I CAN TALK 'TIL YOU'RE ALL ***BLUE*** IN THE FACE--AND SOON, YOU WILL BE!

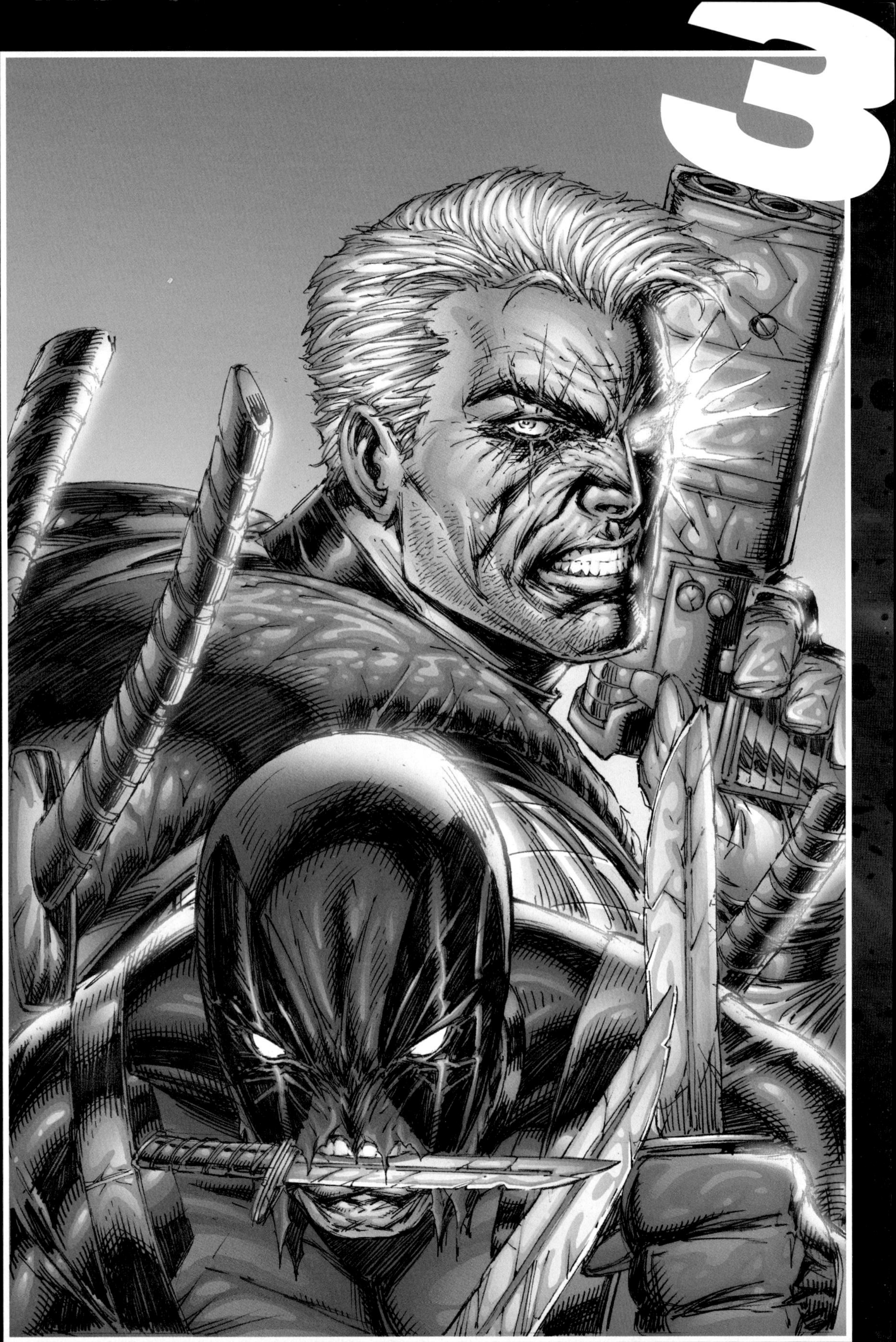
3

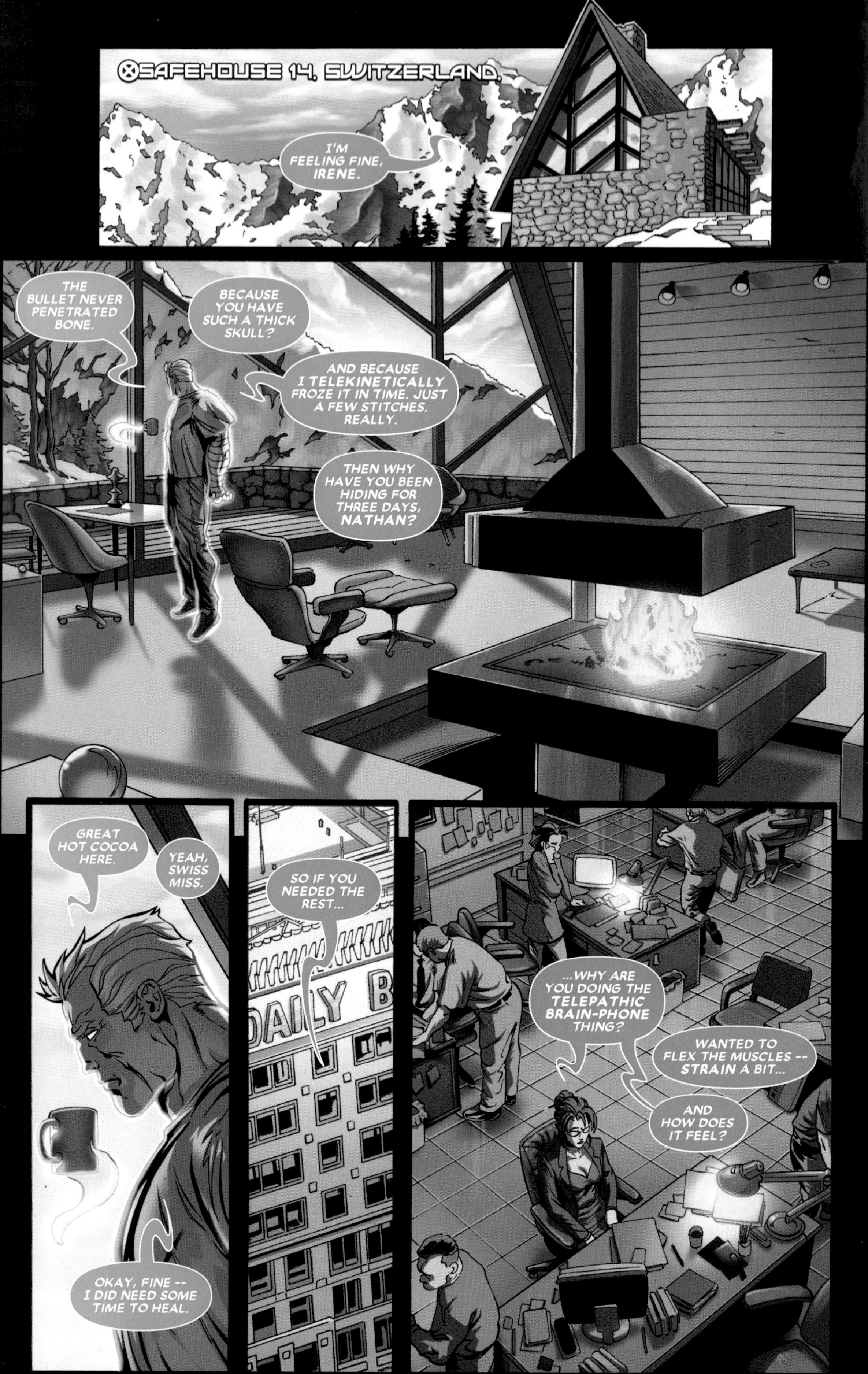
SAFEHOUSE 14, SWITZERLAND.
I'M FEELING FINE, IRENE.
THE BULLET NEVER PENETRATED BONE.
BECAUSE YOU HAVE SUCH A THICK SKULL?
AND BECAUSE I TELEKINETICALLY FROZE IT IN TIME. JUST A FEW STITCHES. REALLY.
THEN WHY HAVE YOU BEEN HIDING FOR THREE DAYS, NATHAN?
GREAT HOT COCOA HERE.
YEAH, SWISS MISS.
OKAY, FINE -- I DID NEED SOME TIME TO HEAL.
SO IF YOU NEEDED THE REST...
...WHY ARE YOU DOING THE TELEPATHIC BRAIN-PHONE THING?
WANTED TO FLEX THE MUSCLES -- STRAIN A BIT...
AND HOW DOES IT FEEL?

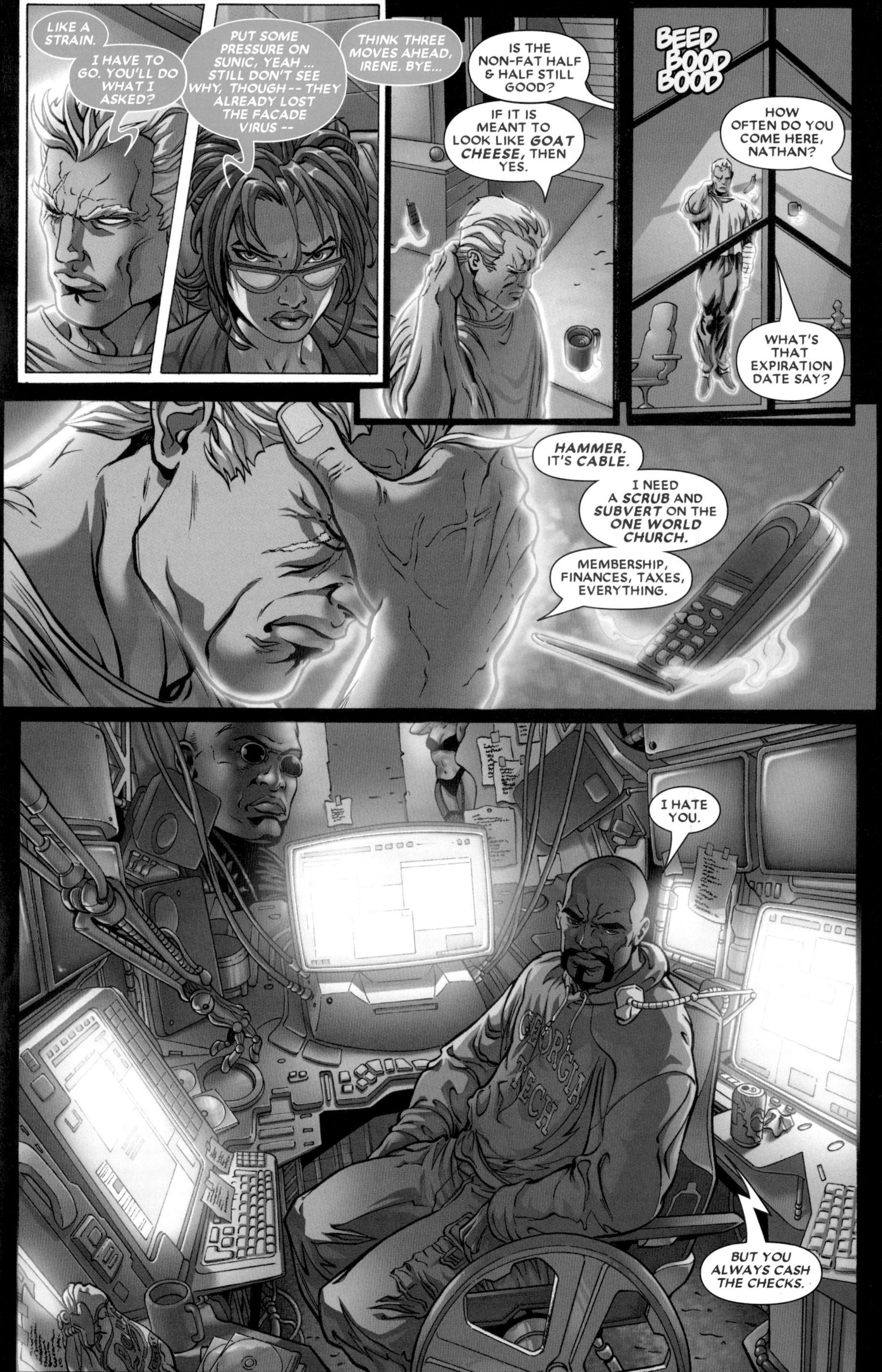
LIKE A STRAIN.
I HAVE TO GO. YOU'LL DO WHAT I ASKED?
PUT SOME PRESSURE ON SUNIC, YEAH ... STILL DON'T SEE WHY, THOUGH -- THEY ALREADY LOST THE FACADE VIRUS --
THINK THREE MOVES AHEAD, IRENE. BYE...
IS THE NON-FAT HALF & HALF STILL GOOD?
IF IT IS MEANT TO LOOK LIKE GOAT CHEESE, THEN YES.
BEED BOOD BOOD
HOW OFTEN DO YOU COME HERE, NATHAN?
WHAT'S THAT EXPIRATION DATE SAY?
HAMMER. IT'S CABLE.
I NEED A SCRUB AND SUBVERT ON THE ONE WORLD CHURCH.
MEMBERSHIP, FINANCES, TAXES, EVERYTHING.
I HATE YOU.
BUT YOU ALWAYS CASH THE CHECKS.

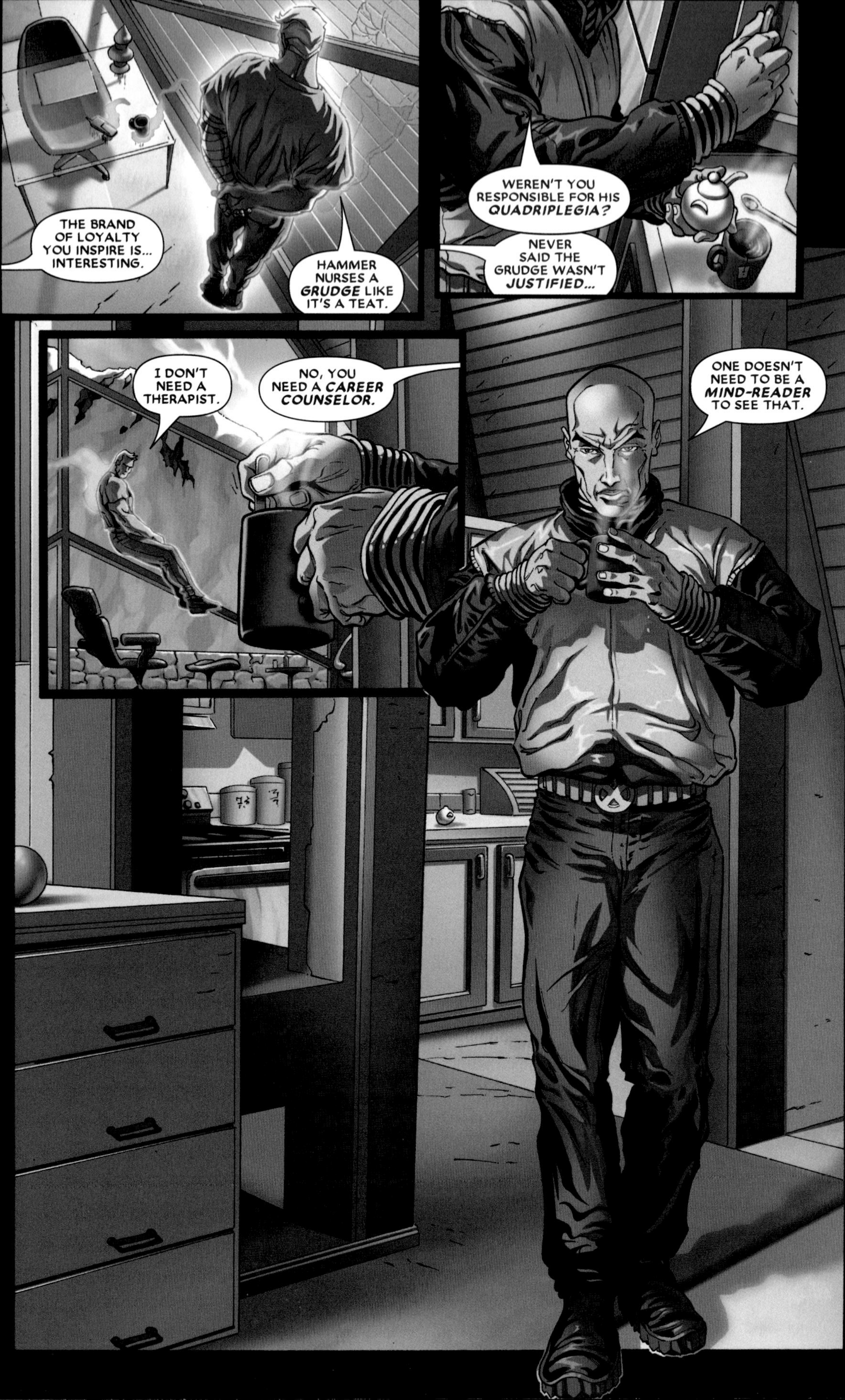
THE BRAND OF LOYALTY YOU INSPIRE IS... INTERESTING.
HAMMER NURSES A GRUDGE LIKE IT'S A TEAT.
WEREN'T YOU RESPONSIBLE FOR HIS QUADRIPLEGIA?
NEVER SAID THE GRUDGE WASN'T JUSTIFIED...
I DON'T NEED A THERAPIST.
NO, YOU NEED A CAREER COUNSELOR.
ONE DOESN'T NEED TO BE A MIND-READER TO SEE THAT.

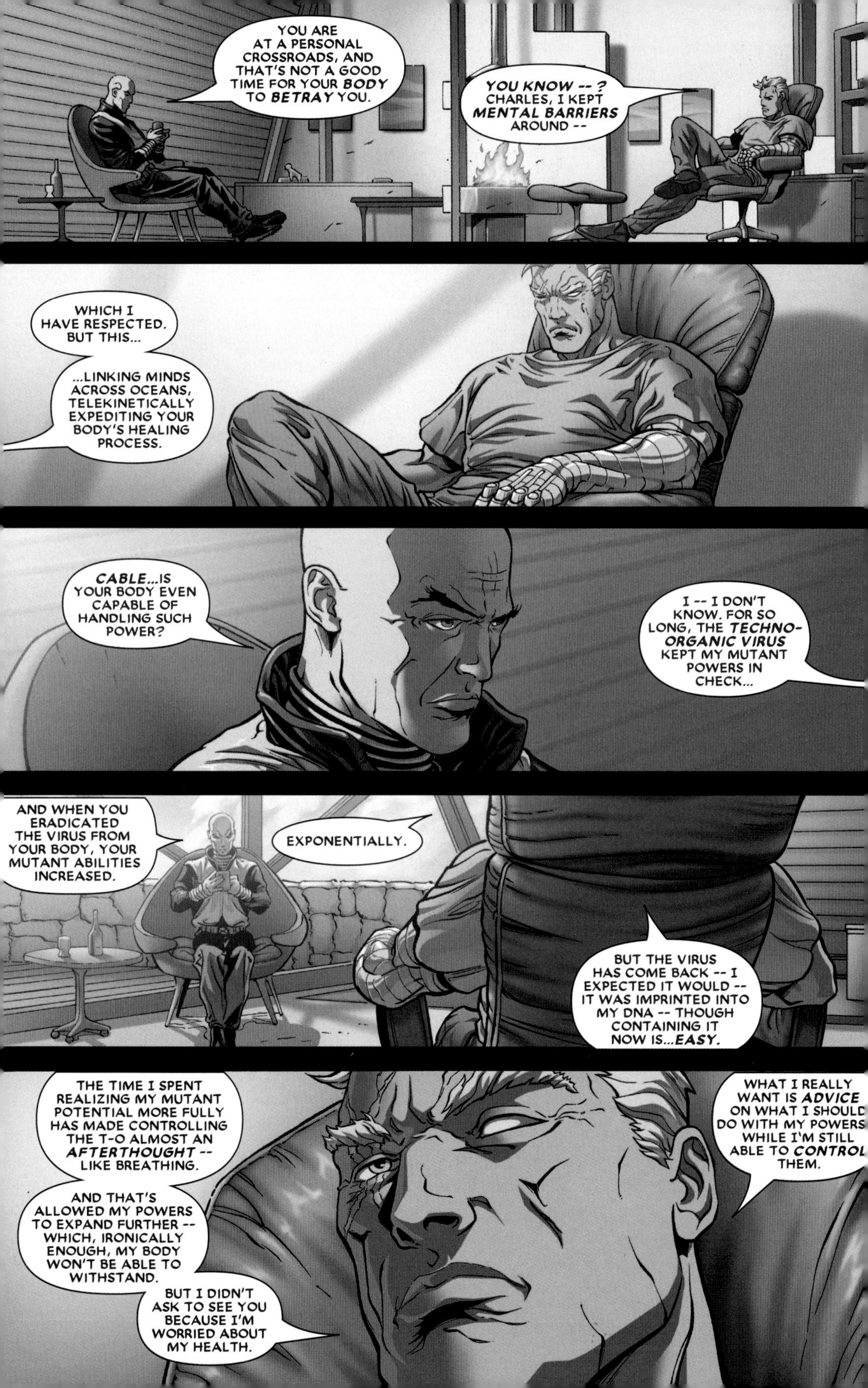
YOU ARE AT A PERSONAL CROSSROADS, AND THAT'S NOT A GOOD TIME FOR YOUR BODY TO BETRAY YOU.
YOU KNOW -- ? CHARLES, I KEPT MENTAL BARRIERS AROUND --
WHICH I HAVE RESPECTED. BUT THIS...
...LINKING MINDS ACROSS OCEANS, TELEKINETICALLY EXPEDITING YOUR BODY'S HEALING PROCESS.
CABLE...IS YOUR BODY EVEN CAPABLE OF HANDLING SUCH POWER?
I -- I DON'T KNOW. FOR SO LONG, THE TECHNO-ORGANIC VIRUS KEPT MY MUTANT POWERS IN CHECK...
AND WHEN YOU ERADICATED THE VIRUS FROM YOUR BODY, YOUR MUTANT ABILITIES INCREASED.
EXPONENTIALLY.
BUT THE VIRUS HAS COME BACK -- I EXPECTED IT WOULD -- IT WAS IMPRINTED INTO MY DNA -- THOUGH CONTAINING IT NOW IS...EASY.
THE TIME I SPENT REALIZING MY MUTANT POTENTIAL MORE FULLY HAS MADE CONTROLLING THE T-O ALMOST AN AFTERTHOUGHT -- LIKE BREATHING.
AND THAT'S ALLOWED MY POWERS TO EXPAND FURTHER -- WHICH, IRONICALLY ENOUGH, MY BODY WON'T BE ABLE TO WITHSTAND.
BUT I DIDN'T ASK TO SEE YOU BECAUSE I'M WORRIED ABOUT MY HEALTH.
WHAT I REALLY WANT IS ADVICE ON WHAT I SHOULD DO WITH MY POWERS WHILE I'M STILL ABLE TO CONTROL THEM.

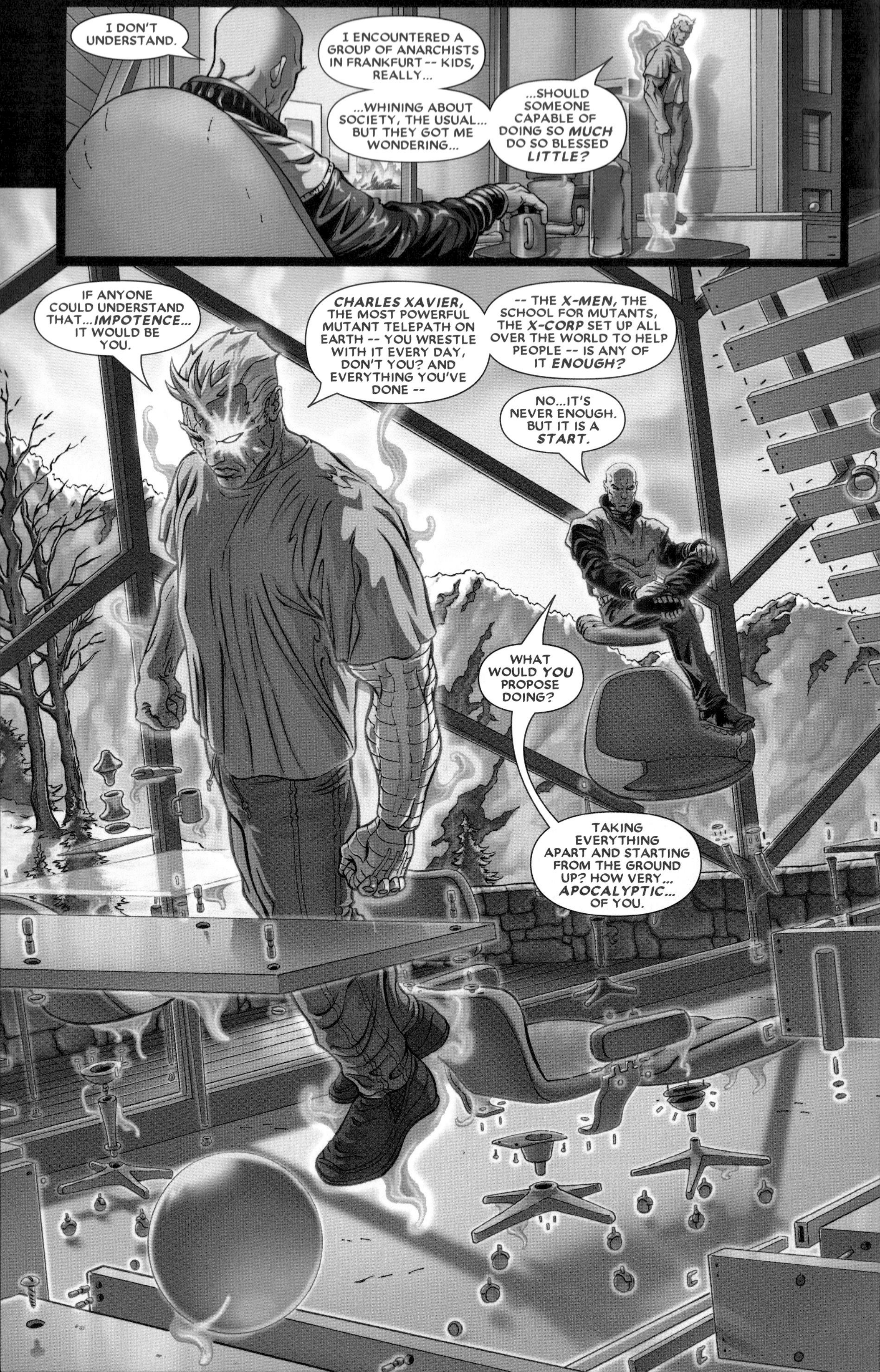
I DON'T UNDERSTAND.
I ENCOUNTERED A GROUP OF ANARCHISTS IN FRANKFURT -- KIDS, REALLY...
...WHINING ABOUT SOCIETY, THE USUAL... BUT THEY GOT ME WONDERING...
...SHOULD SOMEONE CAPABLE OF DOING SO MUCH DO SO BLESSED LITTLE?
IF ANYONE COULD UNDERSTAND THAT...IMPOTENCE... IT WOULD BE YOU.
CHARLES XAVIER, THE MOST POWERFUL MUTANT TELEPATH ON EARTH -- YOU WRESTLE WITH IT EVERY DAY, DON'T YOU? AND EVERYTHING YOU'VE DONE --
-- THE X-MEN, THE SCHOOL FOR MUTANTS, THE X-CORP SET UP ALL OVER THE WORLD TO HELP PEOPLE -- IS ANY OF IT ENOUGH?
NO...IT'S NEVER ENOUGH. BUT IT IS A START.
WHAT WOULD YOU PROPOSE DOING?
TAKING EVERYTHING APART AND STARTING FROM THE GROUND UP? HOW VERY... APOCALYPTIC... OF YOU.

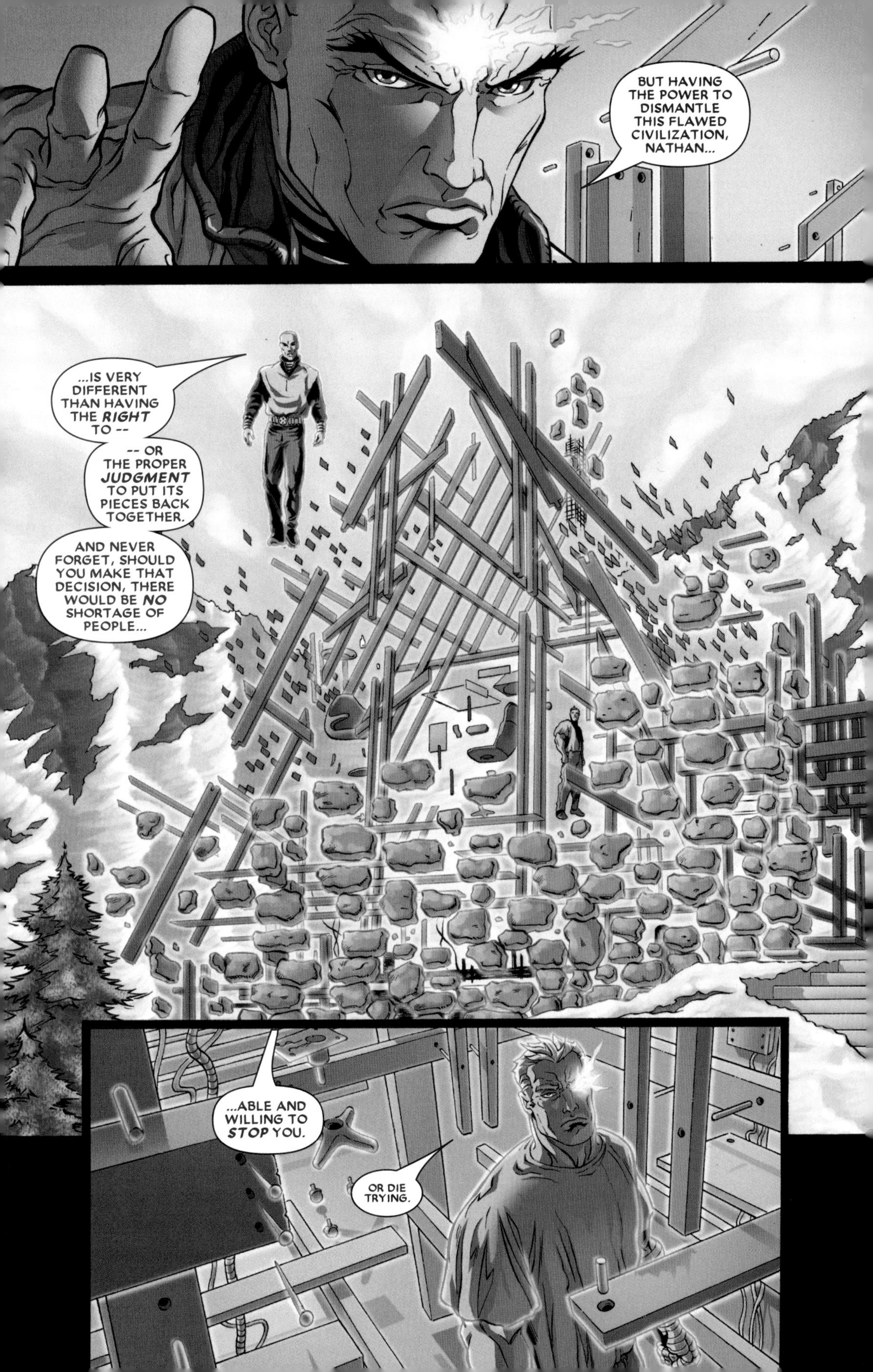
BUT HAVING THE POWER TO DISMANTLE THIS FLAWED CIVILIZATION, NATHAN...
...IS VERY DIFFERENT THAN HAVING THE *RIGHT* TO --
-- OR THE PROPER *JUDGMENT* TO PUT ITS PIECES BACK TOGETHER.
AND NEVER FORGET, SHOULD YOU MAKE THAT DECISION, THERE WOULD BE *NO* SHORTAGE OF PEOPLE...
...ABLE AND WILLING TO *STOP* YOU.
OR DIE TRYING.

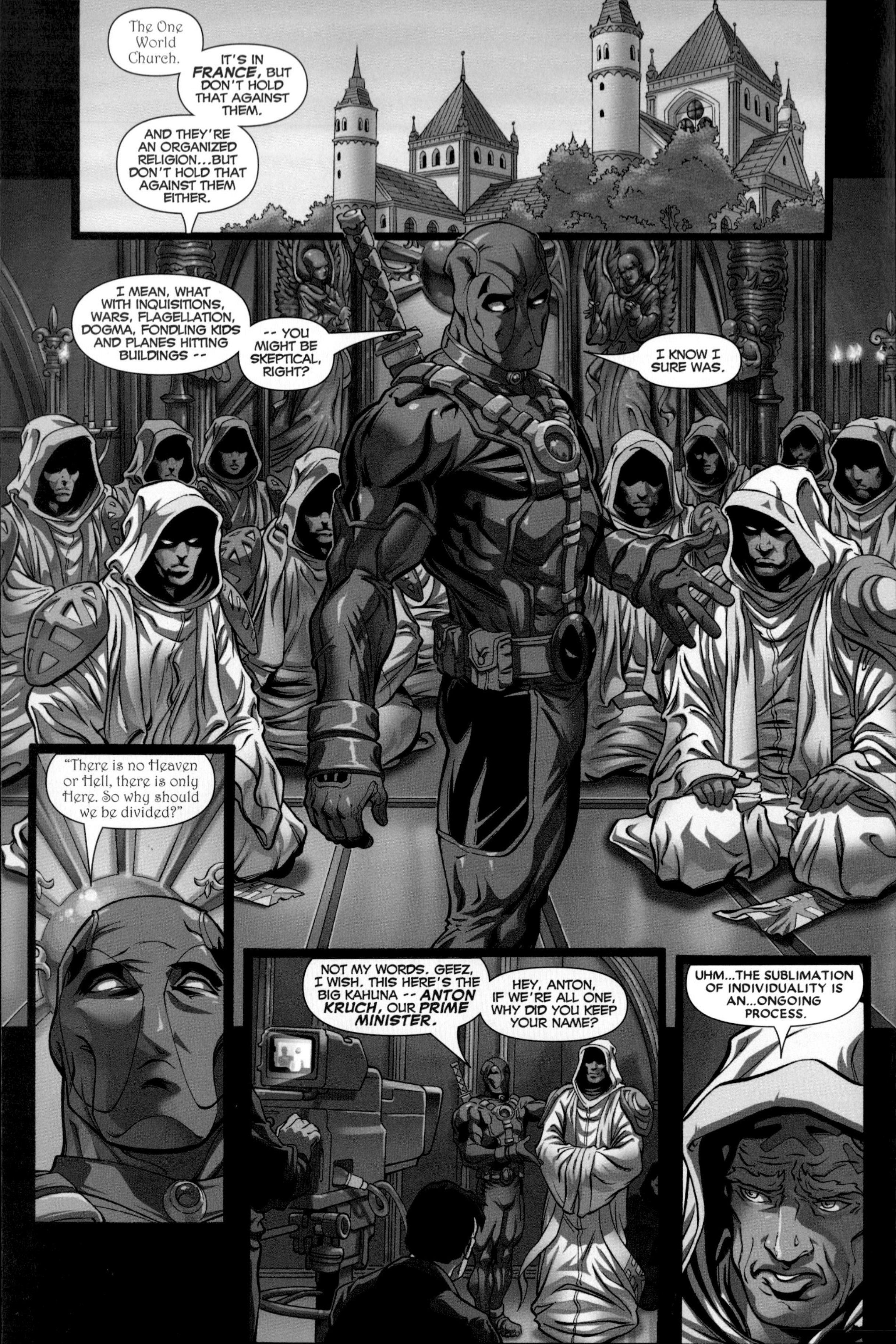
The One World Church.
IT'S IN FRANCE, BUT DON'T HOLD THAT AGAINST THEM.
AND THEY'RE AN ORGANIZED RELIGION...BUT DON'T HOLD THAT AGAINST THEM EITHER.
I MEAN, WHAT WITH INQUISITIONS, WARS, FLAGELLATION, DOGMA, FONDLING KIDS AND PLANES HITTING BUILDINGS --
-- YOU MIGHT BE SKEPTICAL, RIGHT?
I KNOW I SURE WAS.
"There is no Heaven or Hell, there is only Here. So why should we be divided?"
NOT MY WORDS. GEEZ, I WISH. THIS HERE'S THE BIG KAHUNA -- ANTON KRUCH, OUR PRIME MINISTER.
HEY, ANTON, IF WE'RE ALL ONE, WHY DID YOU KEEP YOUR NAME?
UHM...THE SUBLIMATION OF INDIVIDUALITY IS AN...ONGOING PROCESS.

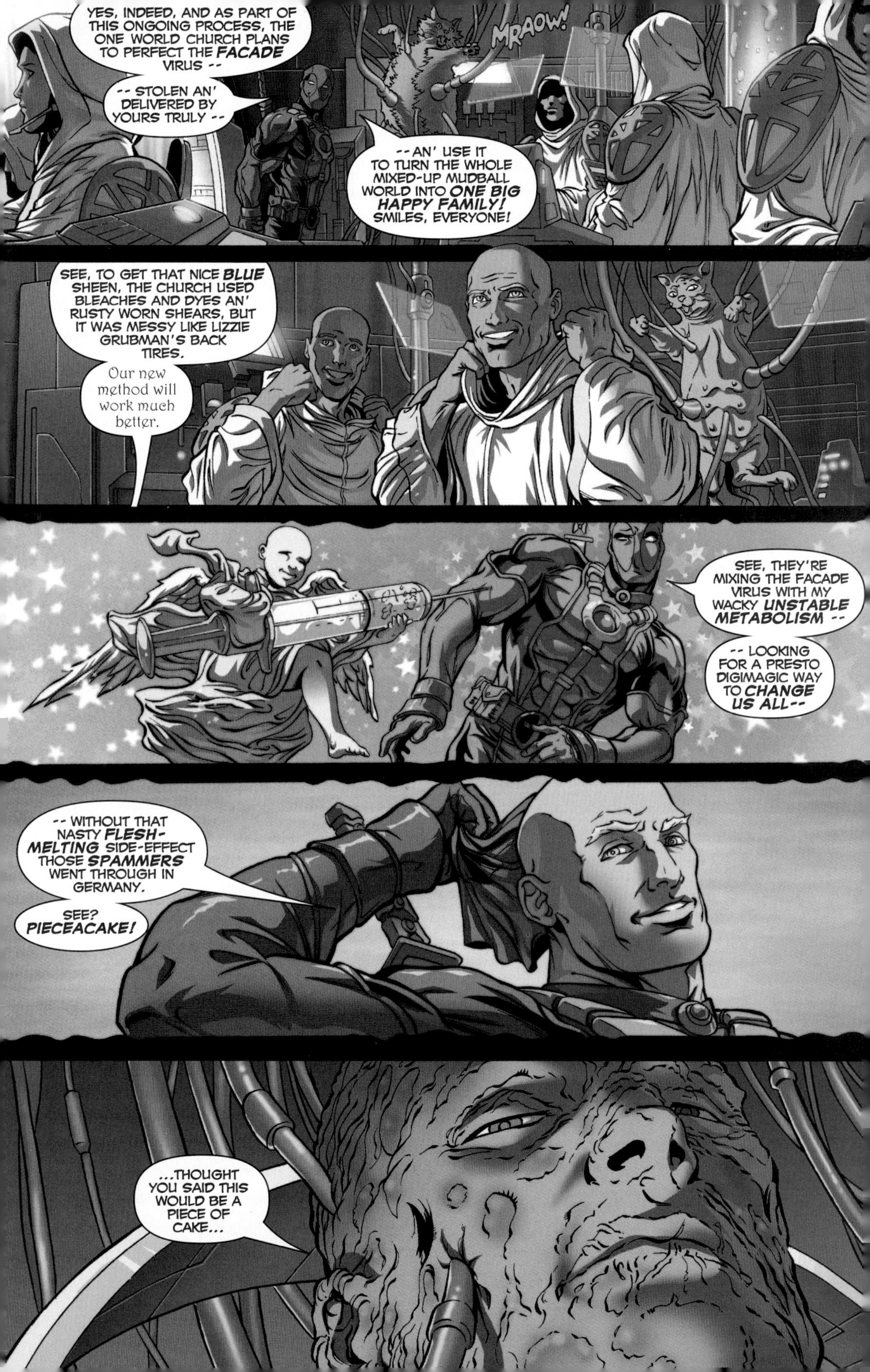
YES, INDEED, AND AS PART OF THIS ONGOING PROCESS, THE ONE WORLD CHURCH PLANS TO PERFECT THE FACADE VIRUS --
MRAOW!
-- STOLEN AN' DELIVERED BY YOURS TRULY --
-- AN' USE IT TO TURN THE WHOLE MIXED-UP MUDBALL WORLD INTO ONE BIG HAPPY FAMILY! SMILES, EVERYONE!
SEE, TO GET THAT NICE BLUE SHEEN, THE CHURCH USED BLEACHES AND DYES AN' RUSTY WORN SHEARS, BUT IT WAS MESSY LIKE LIZZIE GRUBMAN'S BACK TIRES.
Our new method will work much better.
SEE, THEY'RE MIXING THE FACADE VIRUS WITH MY WACKY UNSTABLE METABOLISM --
-- LOOKING FOR A PRESTO DIGIMAGIC WAY TO CHANGE US ALL--
-- WITHOUT THAT NASTY FLESH-MELTING SIDE-EFFECT THOSE SPAMMERS WENT THROUGH IN GERMANY.
SEE? PIECEACAKE!
...THOUGHT YOU SAID THIS WOULD BE A PIECE OF CAKE...

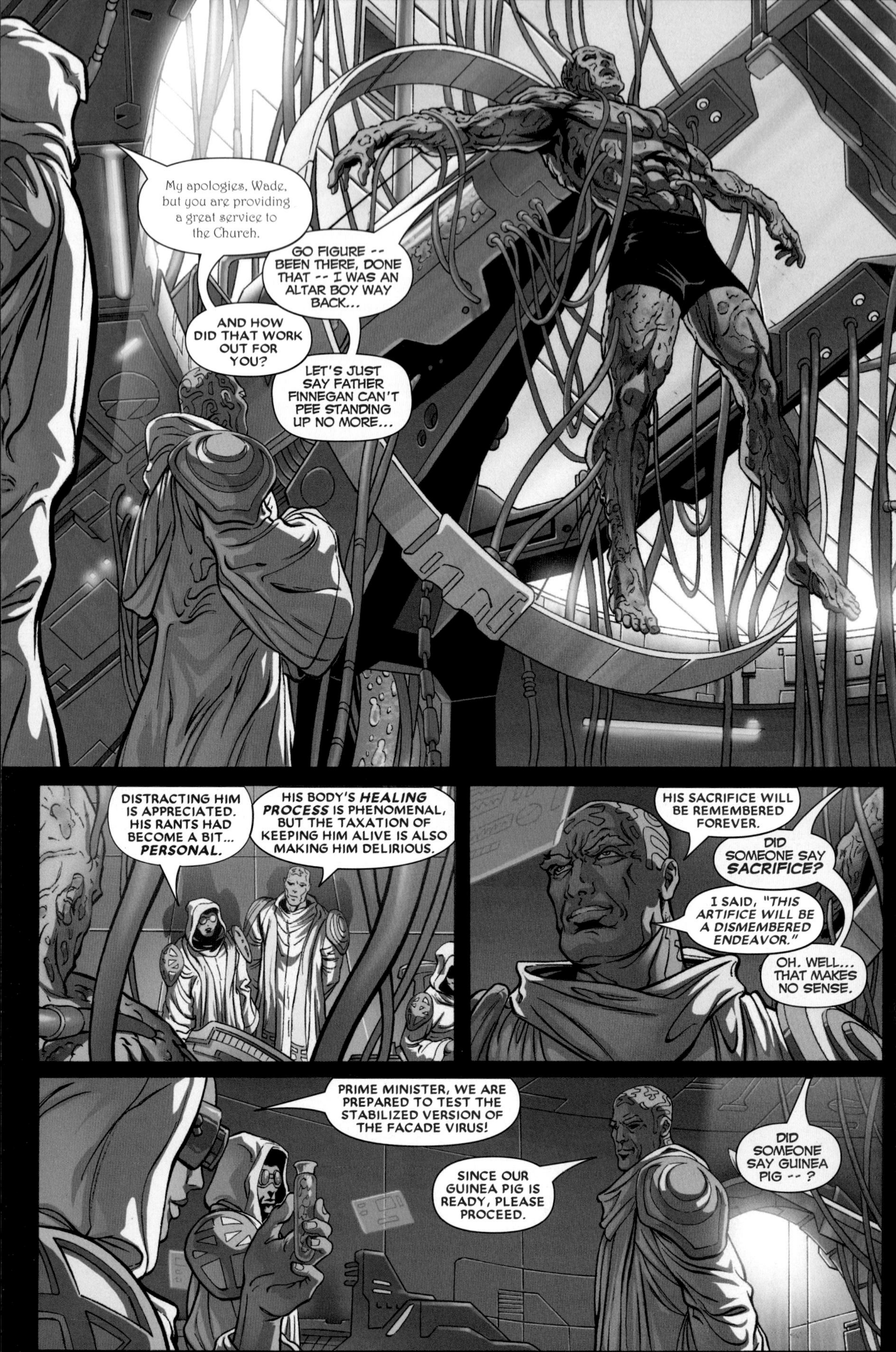
My apologies, Wade, but you are providing a great service to the Church.
GO FIGURE -- BEEN THERE, DONE THAT -- I WAS AN ALTAR BOY WAY BACK...
AND HOW DID THAT WORK OUT FOR YOU?
LET'S JUST SAY FATHER FINNEGAN CAN'T PEE STANDING UP NO MORE...
DISTRACTING HIM IS APPRECIATED. HIS RANTS HAD BECOME A BIT... PERSONAL.
HIS BODY'S HEALING PROCESS IS PHENOMENAL, BUT THE TAXATION OF KEEPING HIM ALIVE IS ALSO MAKING HIM DELIRIOUS.
HIS SACRIFICE WILL BE REMEMBERED FOREVER.
DID SOMEONE SAY SACRIFICE?
I SAID, "THIS ARTIFICE WILL BE A DISMEMBERED ENDEAVOR."
OH. WELL... THAT MAKES NO SENSE.
PRIME MINISTER, WE ARE PREPARED TO TEST THE STABILIZED VERSION OF THE FACADE VIRUS!
SINCE OUR GUINEA PIG IS READY, PLEASE PROCEED.
DID SOMEONE SAY GUINEA PIG -- ?

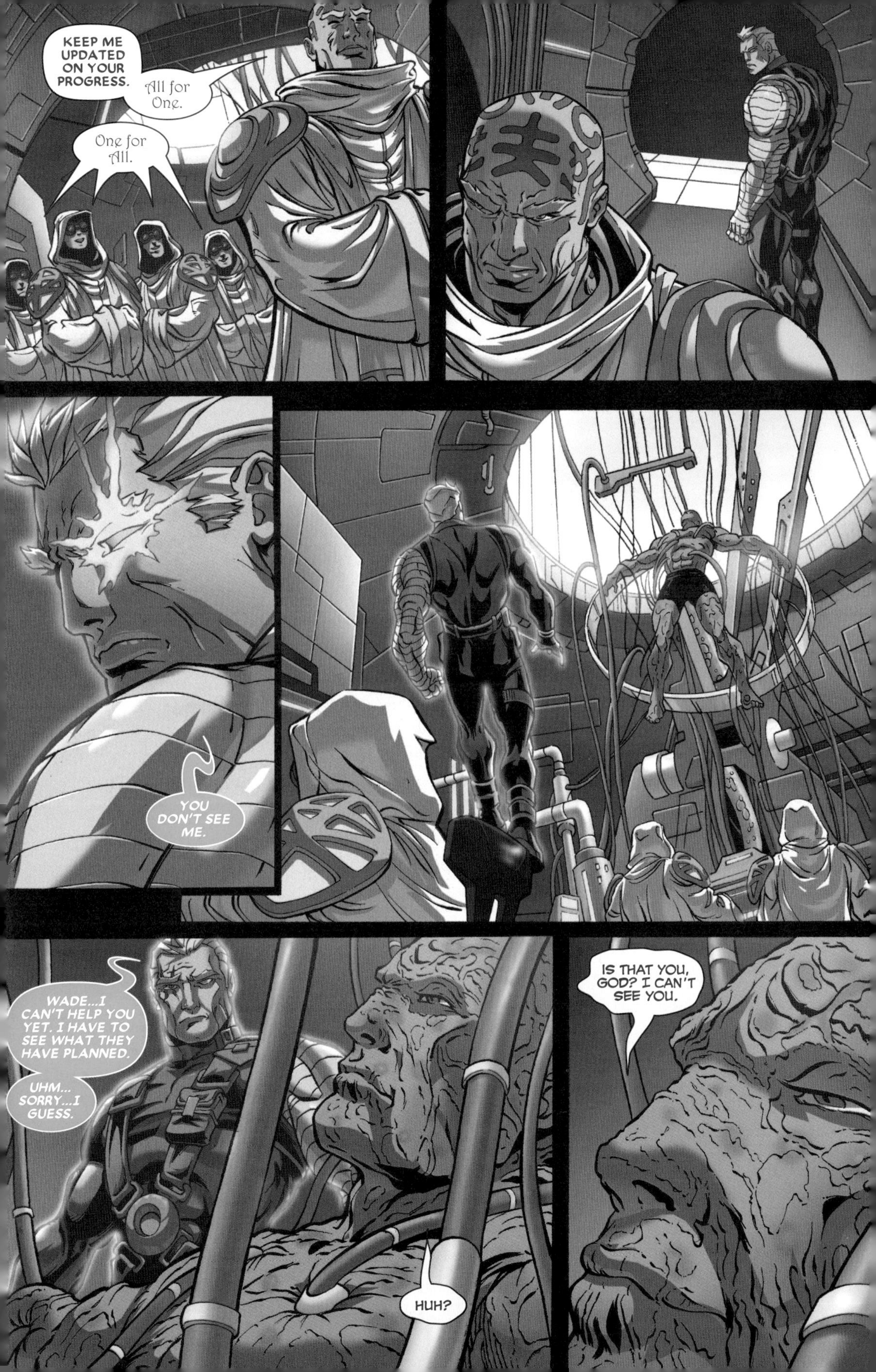
KEEP ME UPDATED ON YOUR PROGRESS.
All for One.
One for All.
YOU DON'T SEE ME.
WADE...I CAN'T HELP YOU YET. I HAVE TO SEE WHAT THEY HAVE PLANNED.
UHM... SORRY...I GUESS.
HUH?
IS THAT YOU, GOD? I CAN'T SEE YOU.

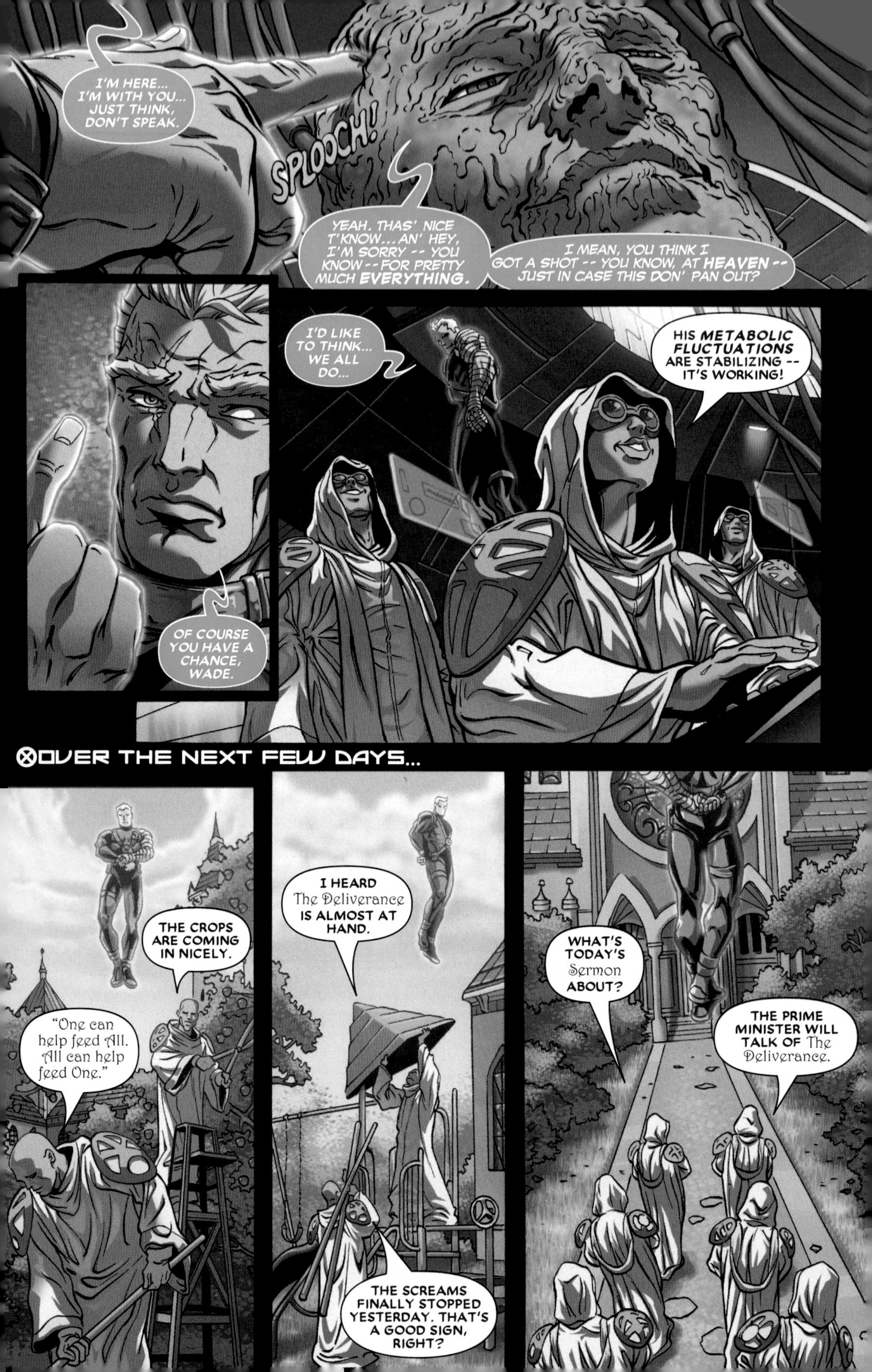
I'M HERE... I'M WITH YOU... JUST THINK, DON'T SPEAK.
SPLOOCH!
YEAH. THAS' NICE T'KNOW... AN' HEY, I'M SORRY -- YOU KNOW -- FOR PRETTY MUCH EVERYTHING.
I MEAN, YOU THINK I GOT A SHOT -- YOU KNOW, AT HEAVEN -- JUST IN CASE THIS DON' PAN OUT?
OF COURSE YOU HAVE A CHANCE, WADE.
I'D LIKE TO THINK... WE ALL DO...
HIS METABOLIC FLUCTUATIONS ARE STABILIZING -- IT'S WORKING!
OVER THE NEXT FEW DAYS...
THE CROPS ARE COMING IN NICELY.
"One can help feed All. All can help feed One."
I HEARD The Deliverance IS ALMOST AT HAND.
THE SCREAMS FINALLY STOPPED YESTERDAY. THAT'S A GOOD SIGN, RIGHT?
WHAT'S TODAY'S Sermon ABOUT?
THE PRIME MINISTER WILL TALK OF The Deliverance.

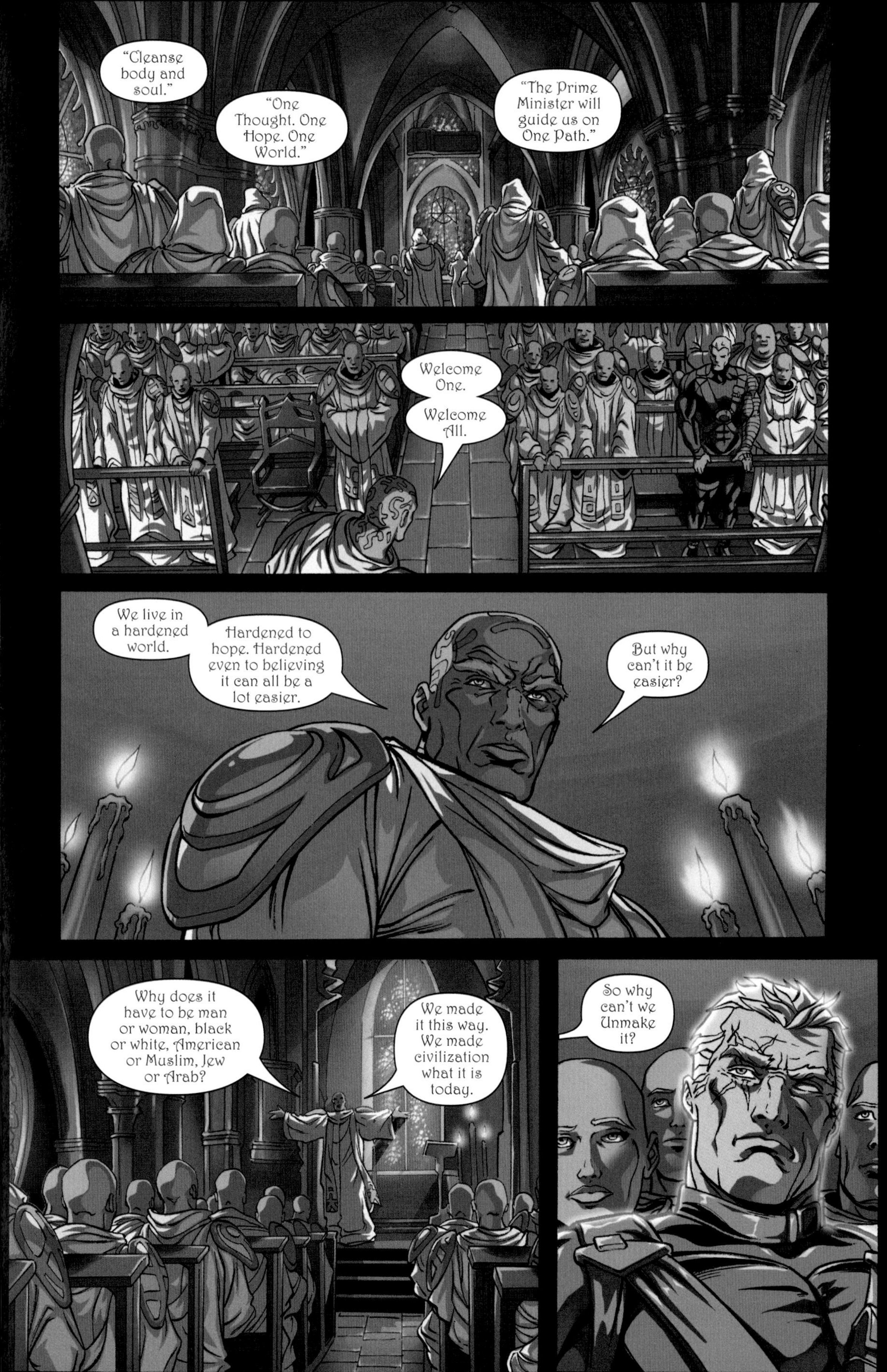
"Cleanse body and soul."
"One Thought. One Hope. One World."
"The Prime Minister will guide us on One Path."
Welcome One.
Welcome All.
We live in a hardened world.
Hardened to hope. Hardened even to believing it can all be a lot easier.
But why can't it be easier?
Why does it have to be man or woman, black or white, American or Muslim, Jew or Arab?
We made it this way. We made civilization what it is today.
So why can't we Unmake it?

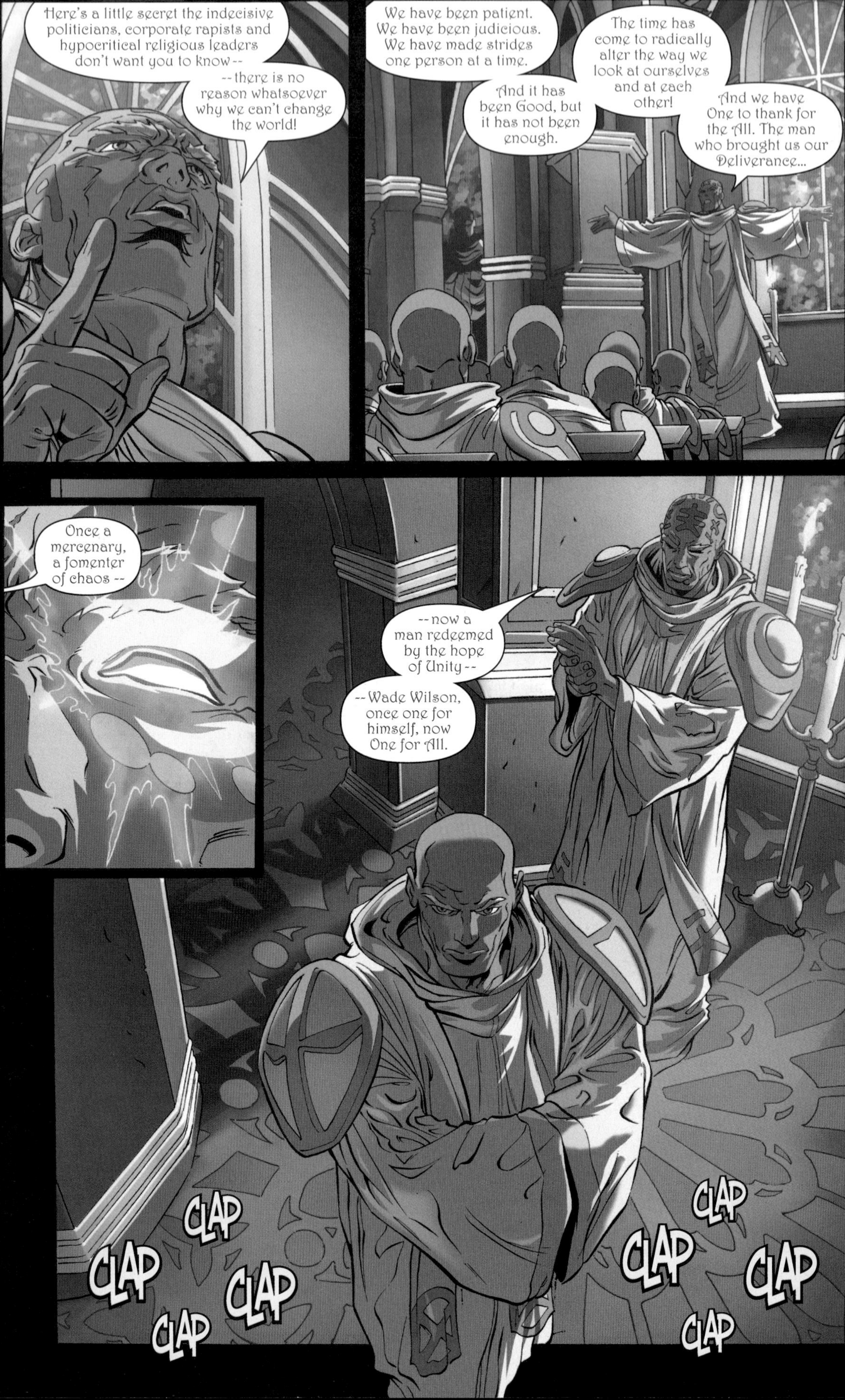
Here's a little secret the indecisive politicians, corporate rapists and hypocritical religious leaders don't want you to know--
--there is no reason whatsoever why we can't change the world!
We have been patient. We have been judicious. We have made strides one person at a time.
And it has been Good, but it has not been enough.
The time has come to radically alter the way we look at ourselves and at each other!
And we have One to thank for the All. The man who brought us our Deliverance...
Once a mercenary, a fomenter of chaos --
--now a man redeemed by the hope of Unity--
--Wade Wilson, once one for himself, now One for All.
CLAP
CLAP
CLAP
CLAP
CLAP
CLAP
CLAP
CLAP

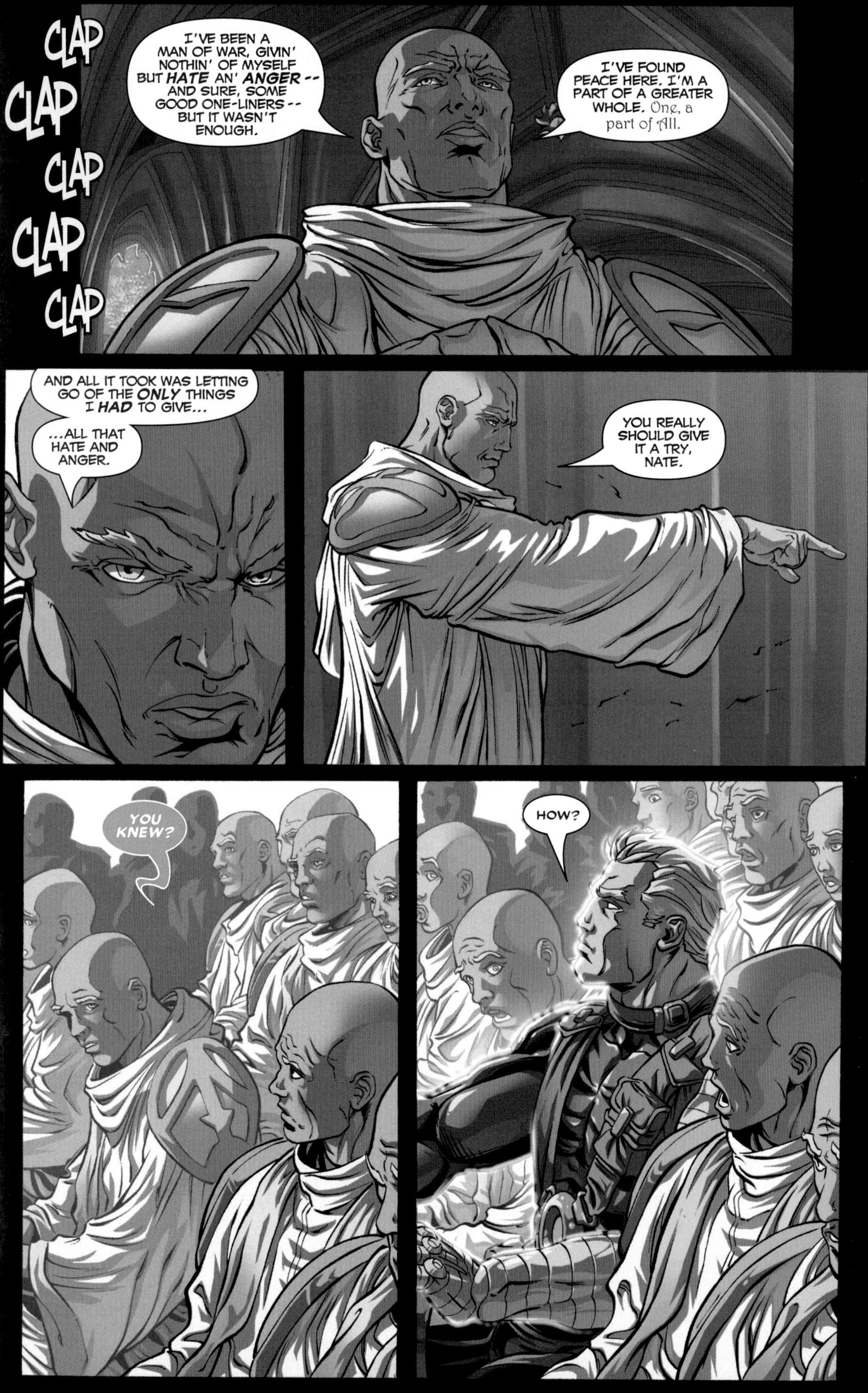
CLAP
CLAP
CLAP
CLAP
CLAP
I'VE BEEN A MAN OF WAR, GIVIN' NOTHIN' OF MYSELF BUT HATE AN' ANGER -- AND SURE, SOME GOOD ONE-LINERS -- BUT IT WASN'T ENOUGH.
I'VE FOUND PEACE HERE. I'M A PART OF A GREATER WHOLE. One, a part of All.
AND ALL IT TOOK WAS LETTING GO OF THE ONLY THINGS I HAD TO GIVE...
...ALL THAT HATE AND ANGER.
YOU REALLY SHOULD GIVE IT A TRY, NATE.
YOU KNEW?
HOW?

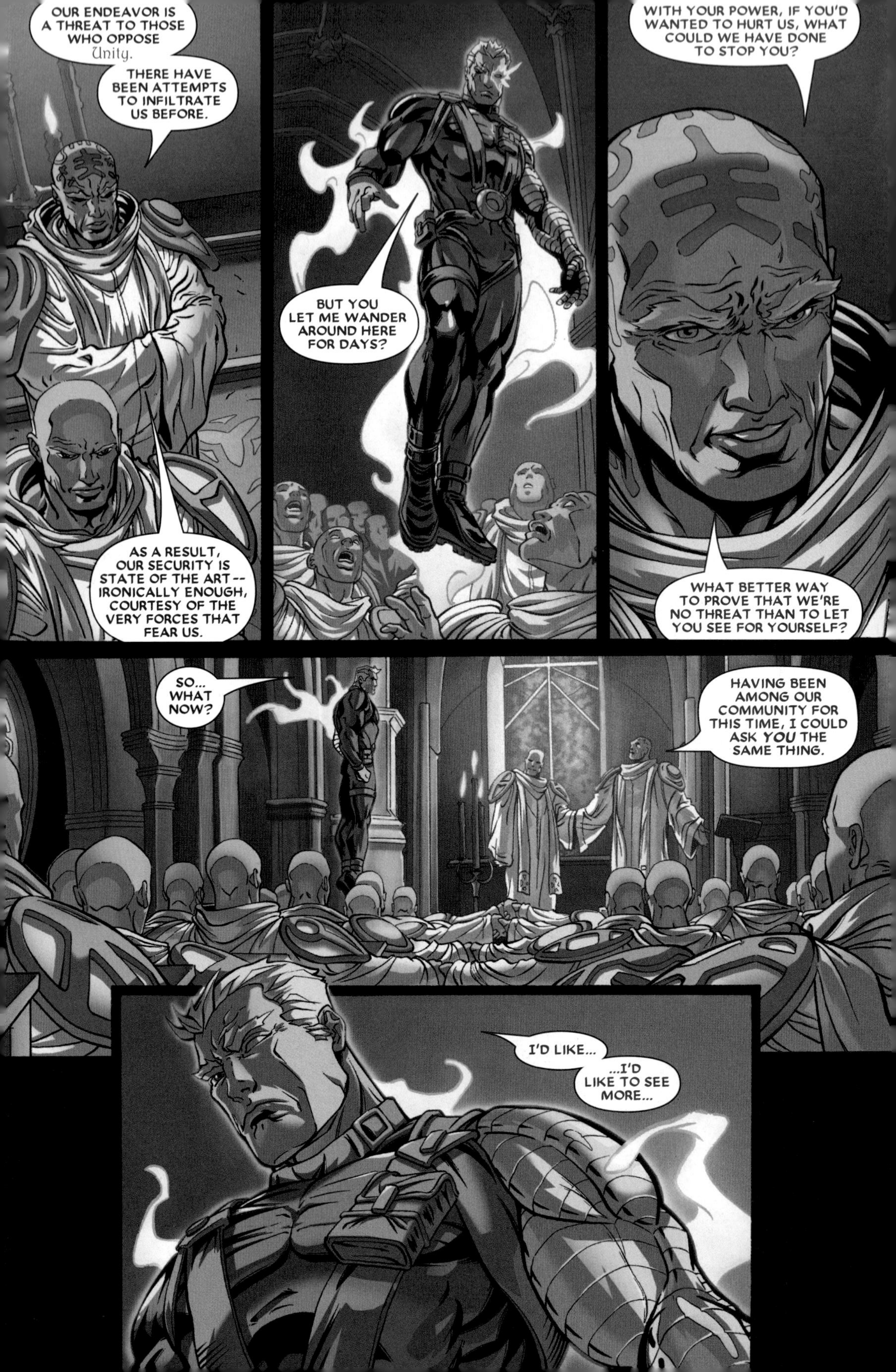
OUR ENDEAVOR IS A THREAT TO THOSE WHO OPPOSE Unity.
THERE HAVE BEEN ATTEMPTS TO INFILTRATE US BEFORE.
AS A RESULT, OUR SECURITY IS STATE OF THE ART -- IRONICALLY ENOUGH, COURTESY OF THE VERY FORCES THAT FEAR US.
BUT YOU LET ME WANDER AROUND HERE FOR DAYS?
WITH YOUR POWER, IF YOU'D WANTED TO HURT US, WHAT COULD WE HAVE DONE TO STOP YOU?
WHAT BETTER WAY TO PROVE THAT WE'RE NO THREAT THAN TO LET YOU SEE FOR YOURSELF?
SO... WHAT NOW?
HAVING BEEN AMONG OUR COMMUNITY FOR THIS TIME, I COULD ASK YOU THE SAME THING.
I'D LIKE...
...I'D LIKE TO SEE MORE...

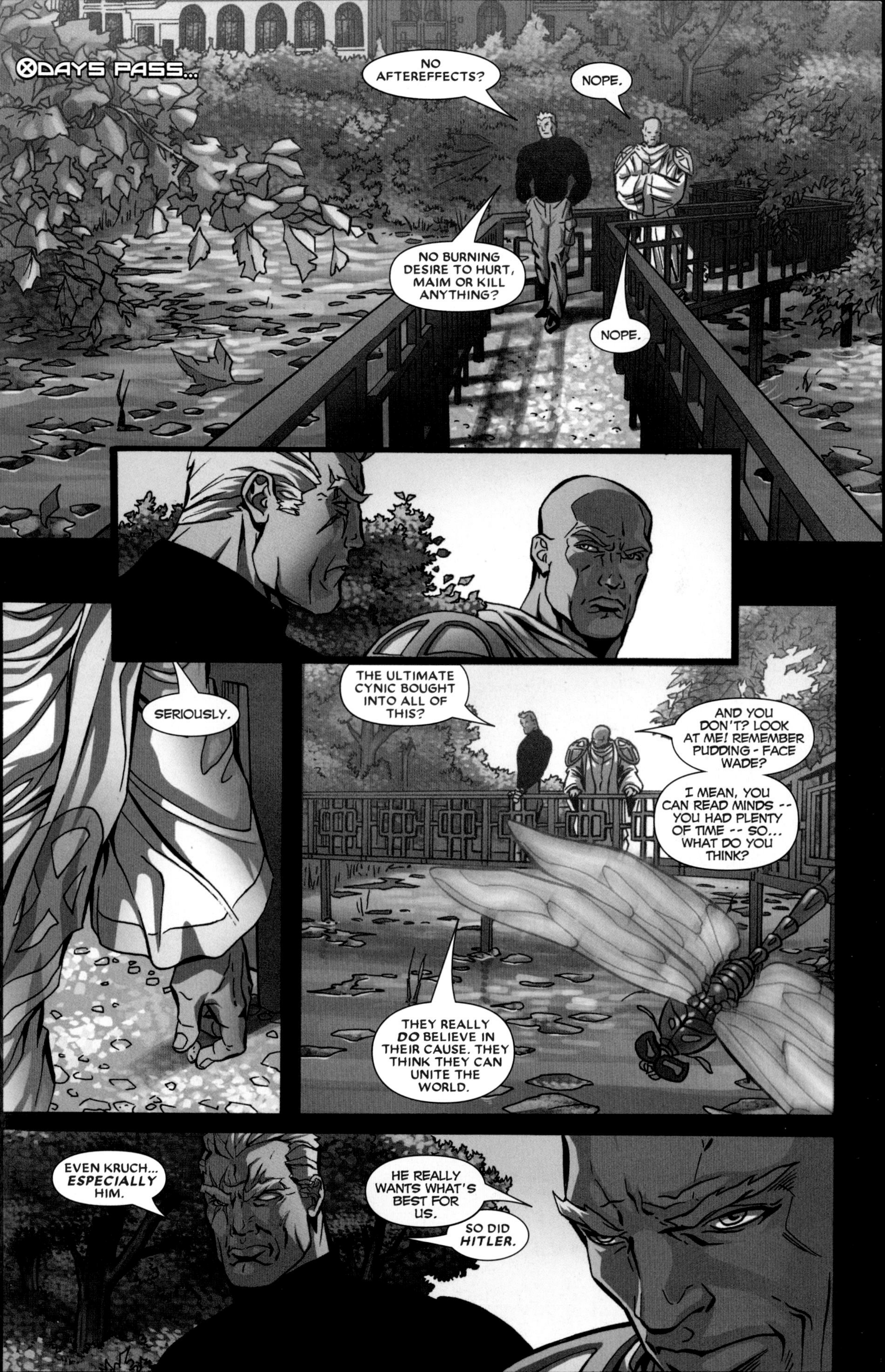
DAYS PASS...
NO AFTEREFFECTS?
NOPE.
NO BURNING DESIRE TO HURT, MAIM OR KILL ANYTHING?
NOPE.
SERIOUSLY.
THE ULTIMATE CYNIC BOUGHT INTO ALL OF THIS?
AND YOU DON'T? LOOK AT ME! REMEMBER PUDDING-FACE WADE?
I MEAN, YOU CAN READ MINDS -- YOU HAD PLENTY OF TIME -- SO... WHAT DO YOU THINK?
THEY REALLY DO BELIEVE IN THEIR CAUSE. THEY THINK THEY CAN UNITE THE WORLD.
EVEN KRUCH... ESPECIALLY HIM.
HE REALLY WANTS WHAT'S BEST FOR US.
SO DID HITLER.

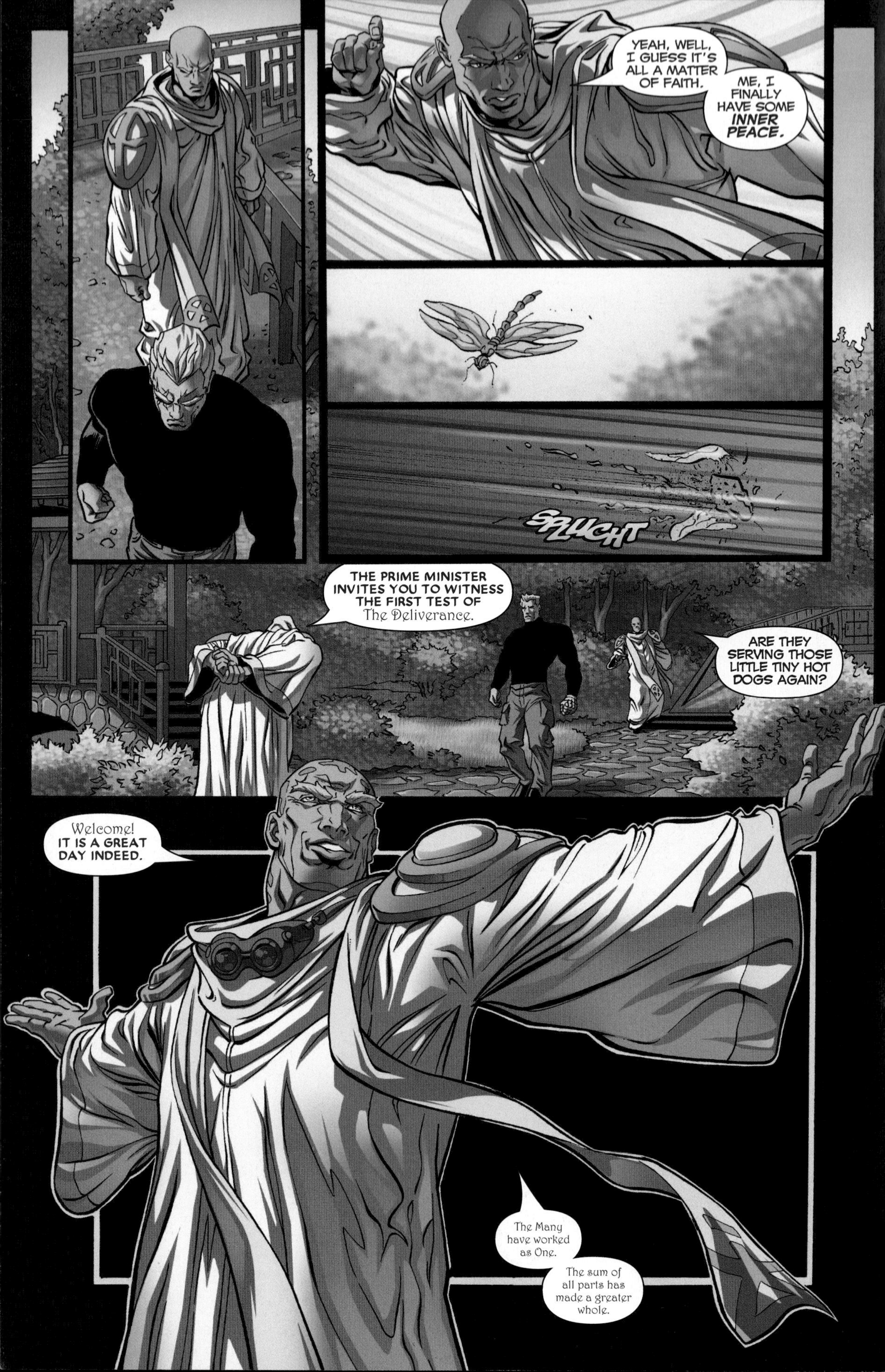
YEAH, WELL, I GUESS IT'S ALL A MATTER OF FAITH.
ME, I FINALLY HAVE SOME **INNER PEACE.**
SPLUCHT
THE PRIME MINISTER INVITES YOU TO WITNESS THE FIRST TEST OF The Deliverance.
ARE THEY SERVING THOSE LITTLE TINY HOT DOGS AGAIN?
Welcome! IT IS A GREAT DAY INDEED.
The Many have worked as One.
The sum of all parts has made a greater whole.

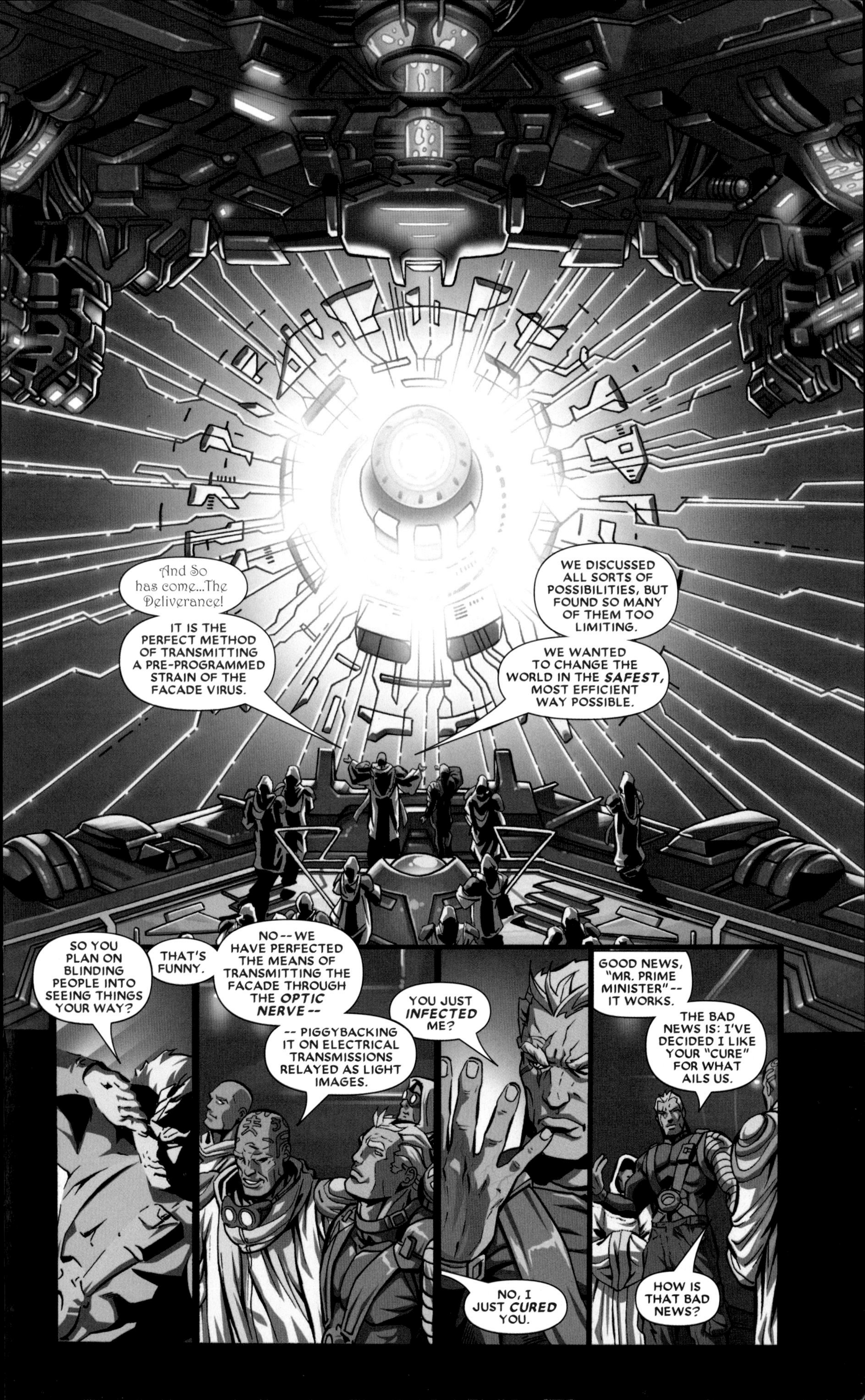
And So has come...The Deliverance!
IT IS THE PERFECT METHOD OF TRANSMITTING A PRE-PROGRAMMED STRAIN OF THE FACADE VIRUS.
WE DISCUSSED ALL SORTS OF POSSIBILITIES, BUT FOUND SO MANY OF THEM TOO LIMITING.
WE WANTED TO CHANGE THE WORLD IN THE SAFEST, MOST EFFICIENT WAY POSSIBLE.
SO YOU PLAN ON BLINDING PEOPLE INTO SEEING THINGS YOUR WAY?
THAT'S FUNNY.
NO--WE HAVE PERFECTED THE MEANS OF TRANSMITTING THE FACADE THROUGH THE OPTIC NERVE--
--PIGGYBACKING IT ON ELECTRICAL TRANSMISSIONS RELAYED AS LIGHT IMAGES.
YOU JUST INFECTED ME?
NO, I JUST CURED YOU.
GOOD NEWS, "MR. PRIME MINISTER"-- IT WORKS.
THE BAD NEWS IS: I'VE DECIDED I LIKE YOUR "CURE" FOR WHAT AILS US.
HOW IS THAT BAD NEWS?

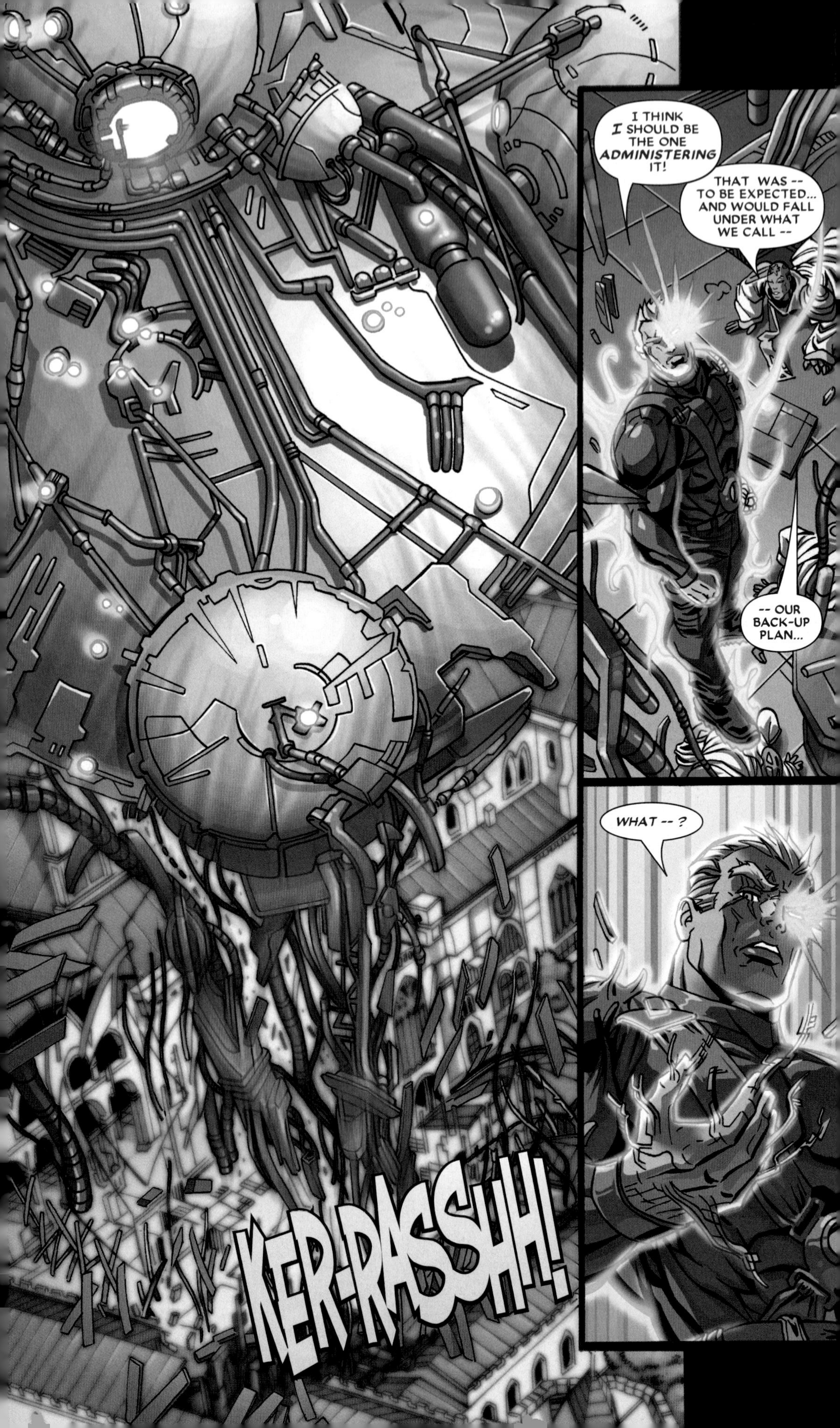
I THINK I SHOULD BE THE ONE ADMINISTERING IT!
THAT WAS -- TO BE EXPECTED... AND WOULD FALL UNDER WHAT WE CALL --
-- OUR BACK-UP PLAN...
WHAT -- ?
KER-RASSHH!

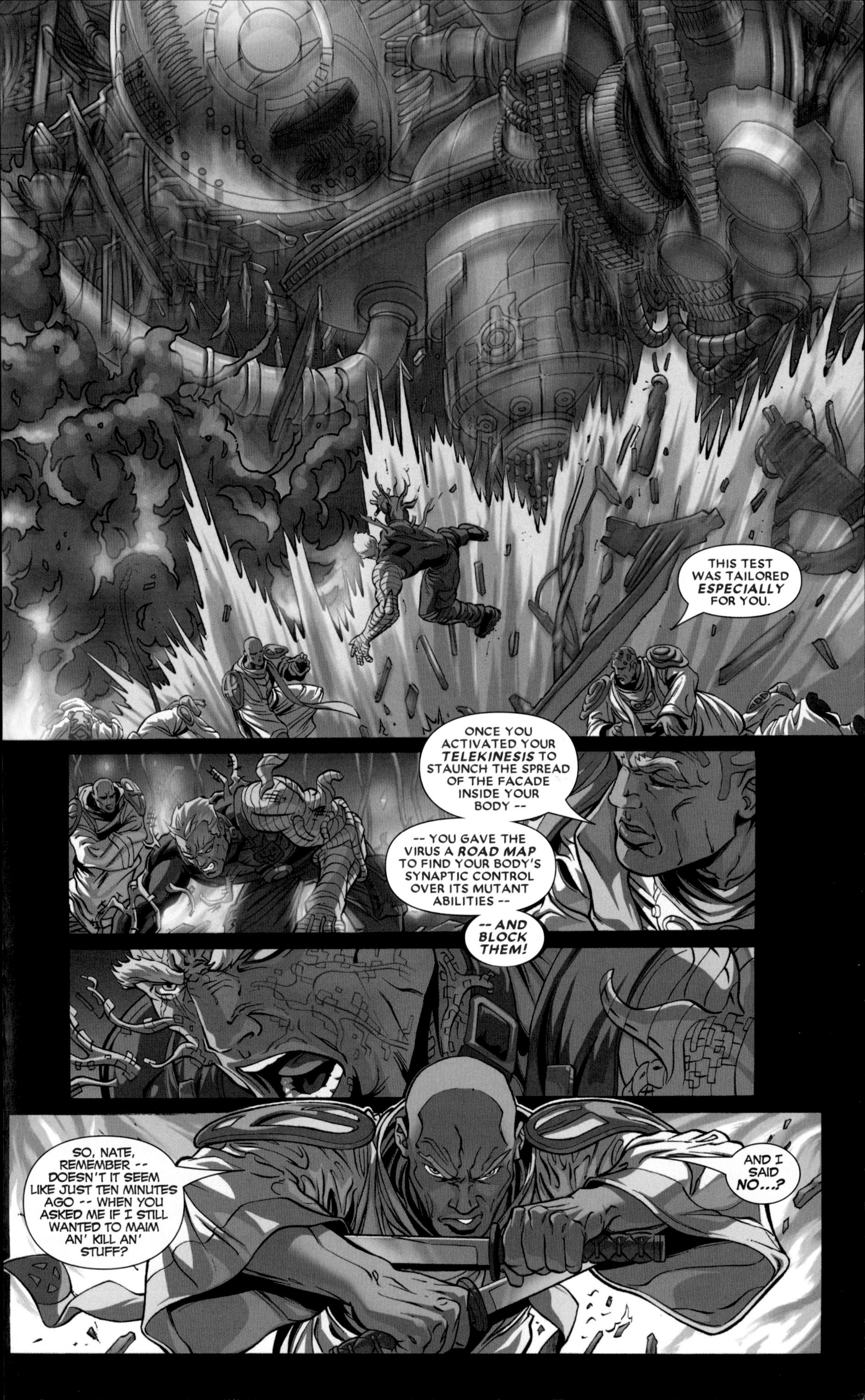
THIS TEST WAS TAILORED ESPECIALLY FOR YOU.
ONCE YOU ACTIVATED YOUR TELEKINESIS TO STAUNCH THE SPREAD OF THE FACADE INSIDE YOUR BODY --
-- YOU GAVE THE VIRUS A ROAD MAP TO FIND YOUR BODY'S SYNAPTIC CONTROL OVER ITS MUTANT ABILITIES --
-- AND BLOCK THEM!
SO, NATE, REMEMBER -- DOESN'T IT SEEM LIKE JUST TEN MINUTES AGO -- WHEN YOU ASKED ME IF I STILL WANTED TO MAIM AN' KILL AN' STUFF?
AND I SAID NO...?

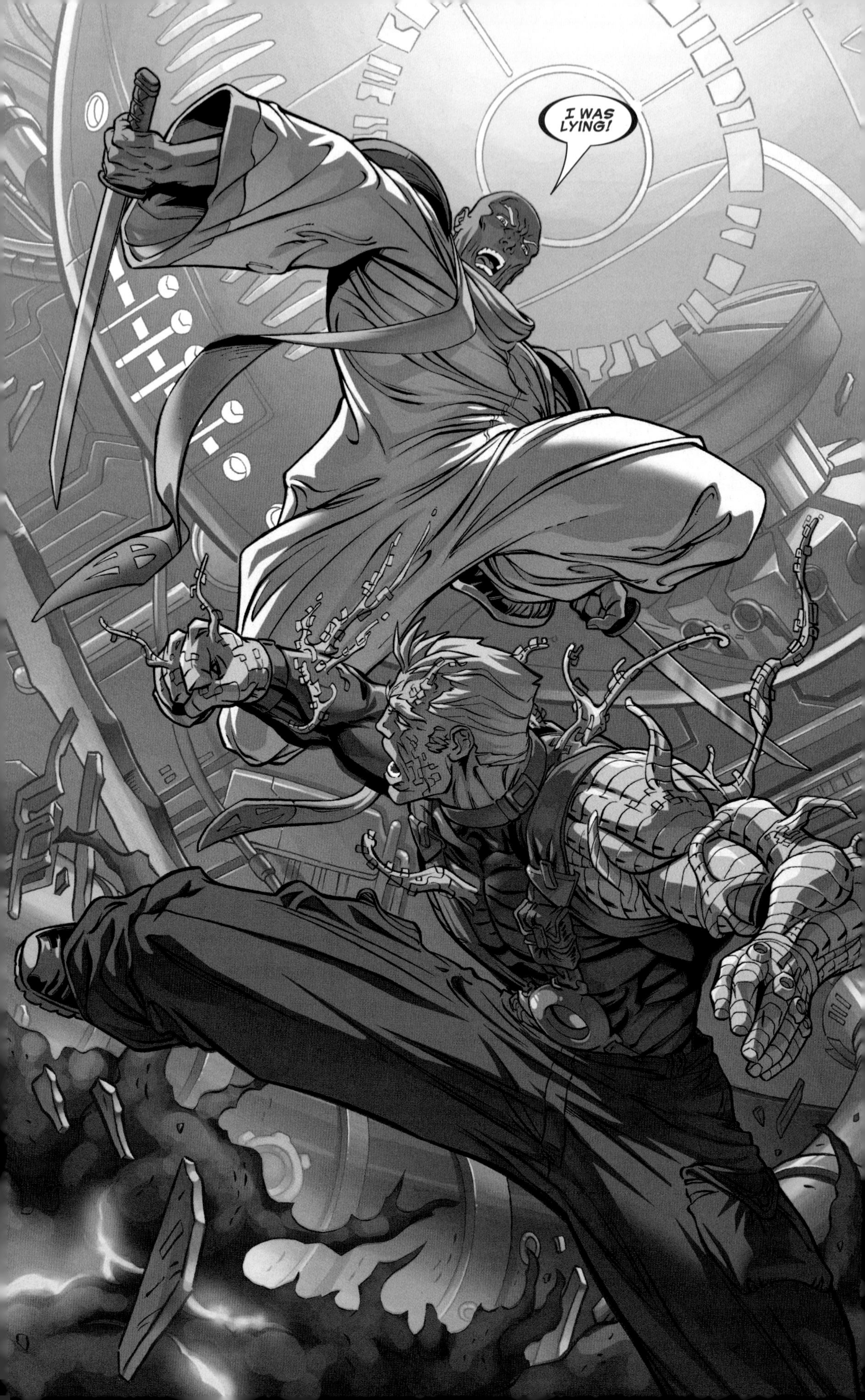
I WAS LYING!

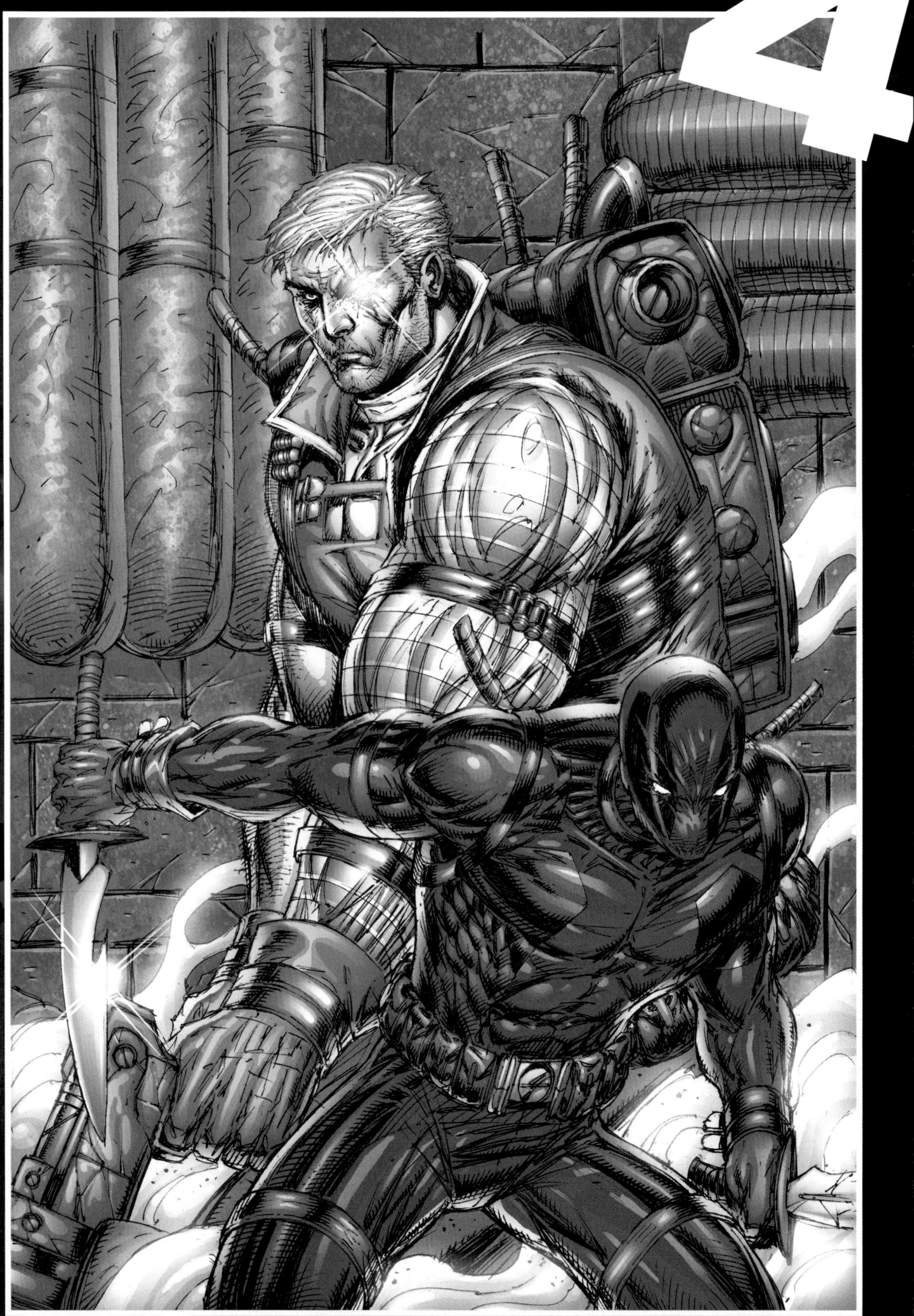
4

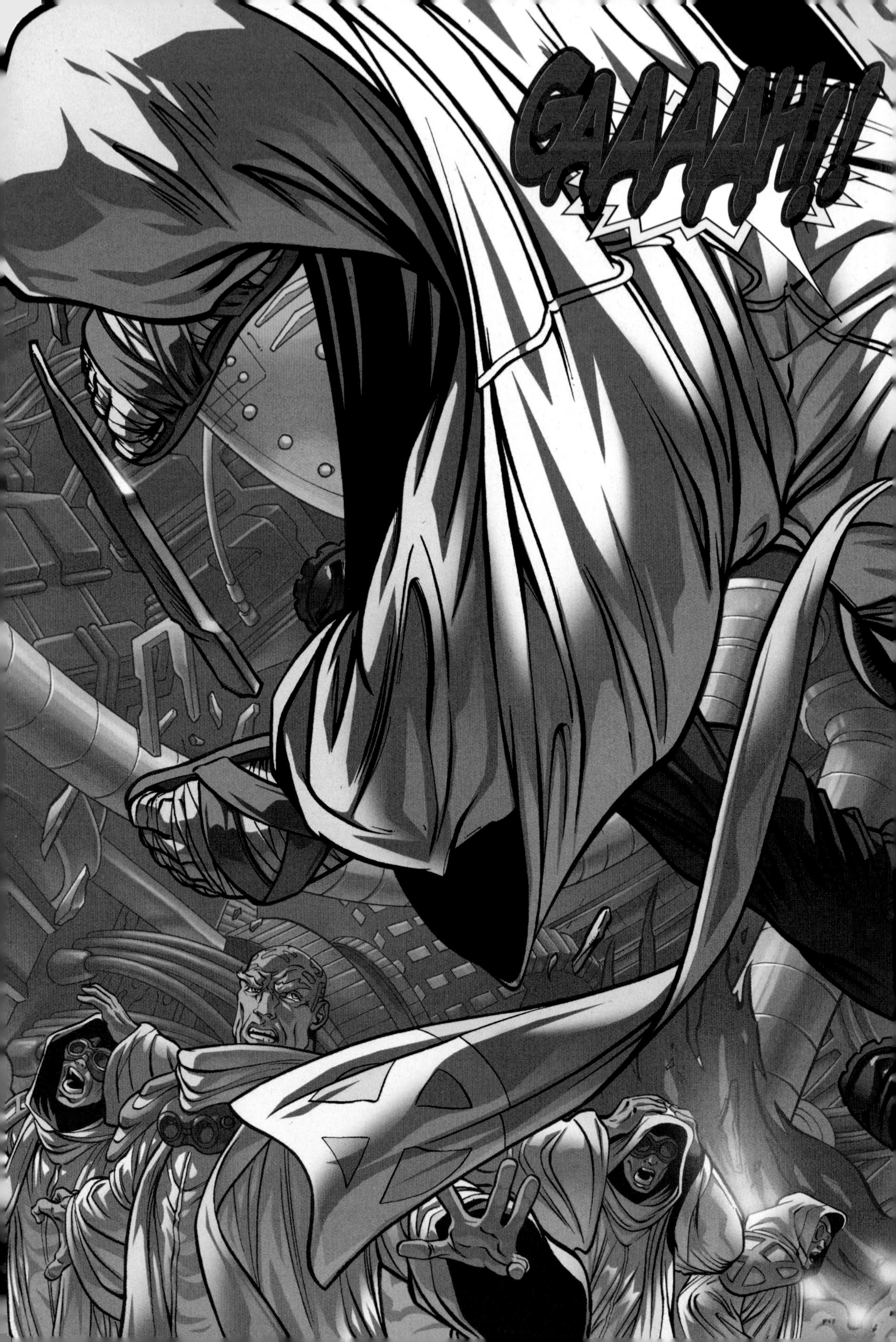
GAAAAH!!

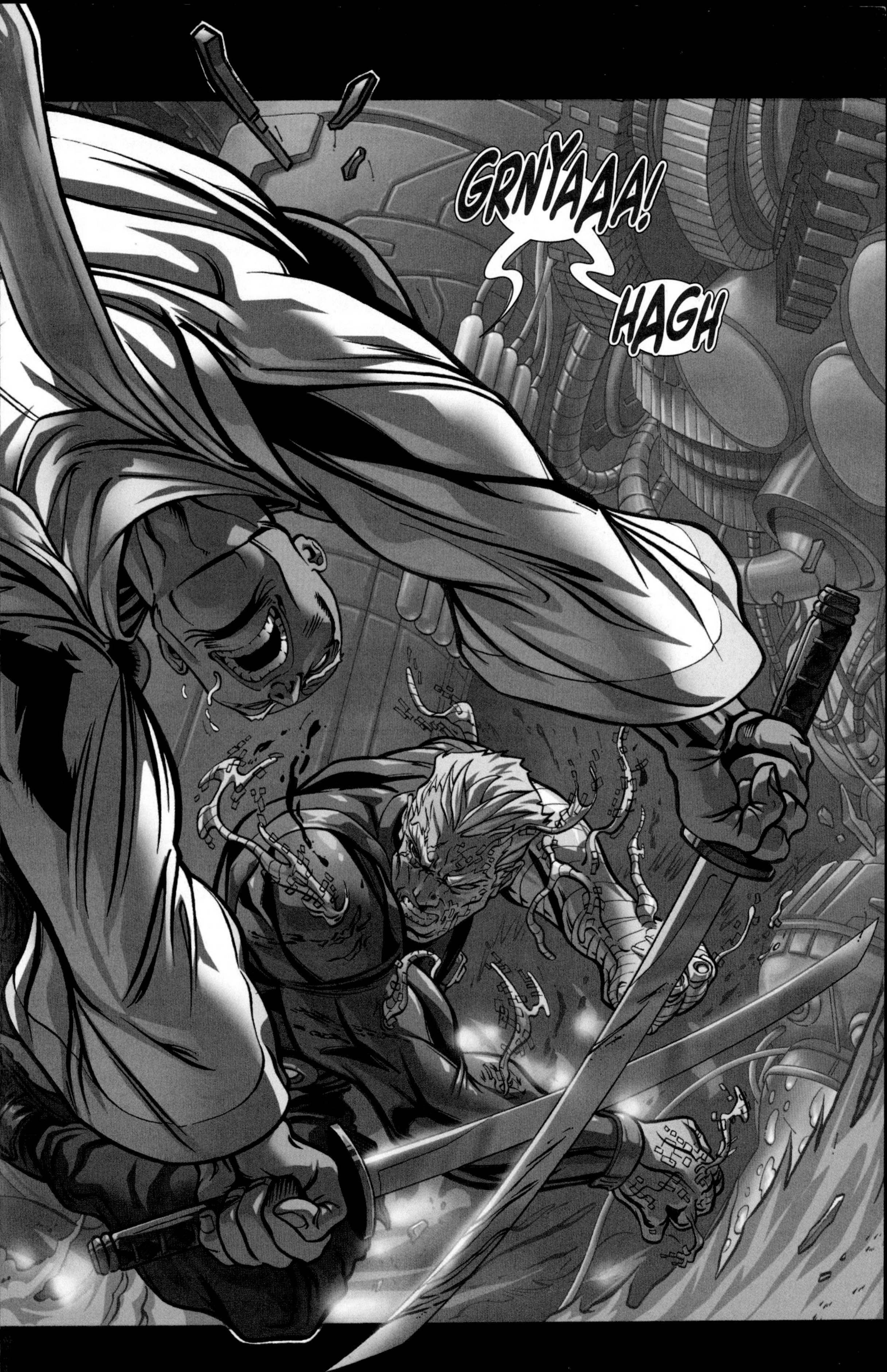
GRNYAAA!
HAGH

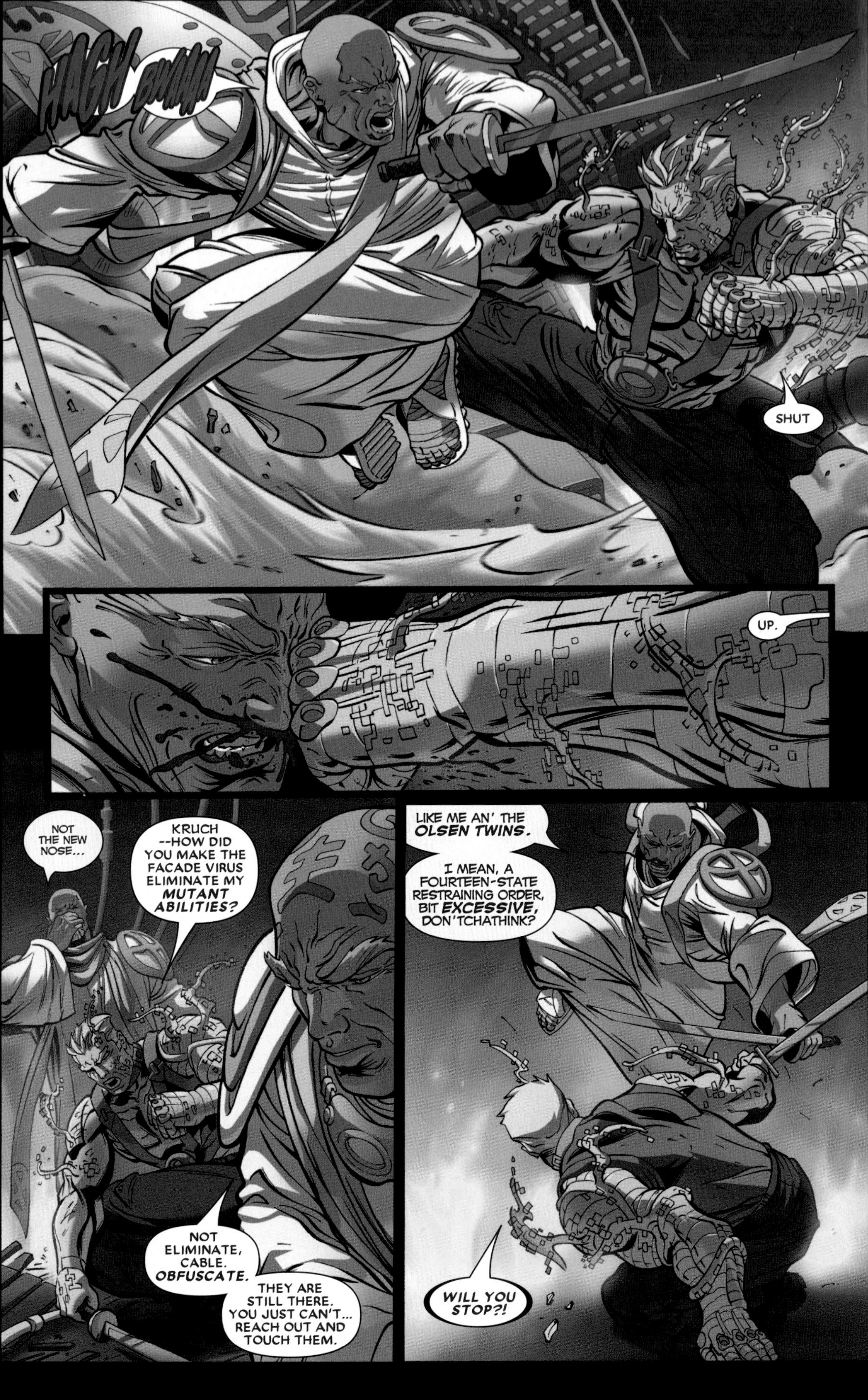
HAGH
BWAAH
SHUT
UP.
NOT THE NEW NOSE...
KRUCH --HOW DID YOU MAKE THE FACADE VIRUS ELIMINATE MY MUTANT ABILITIES?
NOT ELIMINATE, CABLE. OBFUSCATE.
THEY ARE STILL THERE. YOU JUST CAN'T... REACH OUT AND TOUCH THEM.
LIKE ME AN' THE OLSEN TWINS.
I MEAN, A FOURTEEN-STATE RESTRAINING ORDER, BIT EXCESSIVE, DON'TCHATHINK?
WILL YOU STOP?!

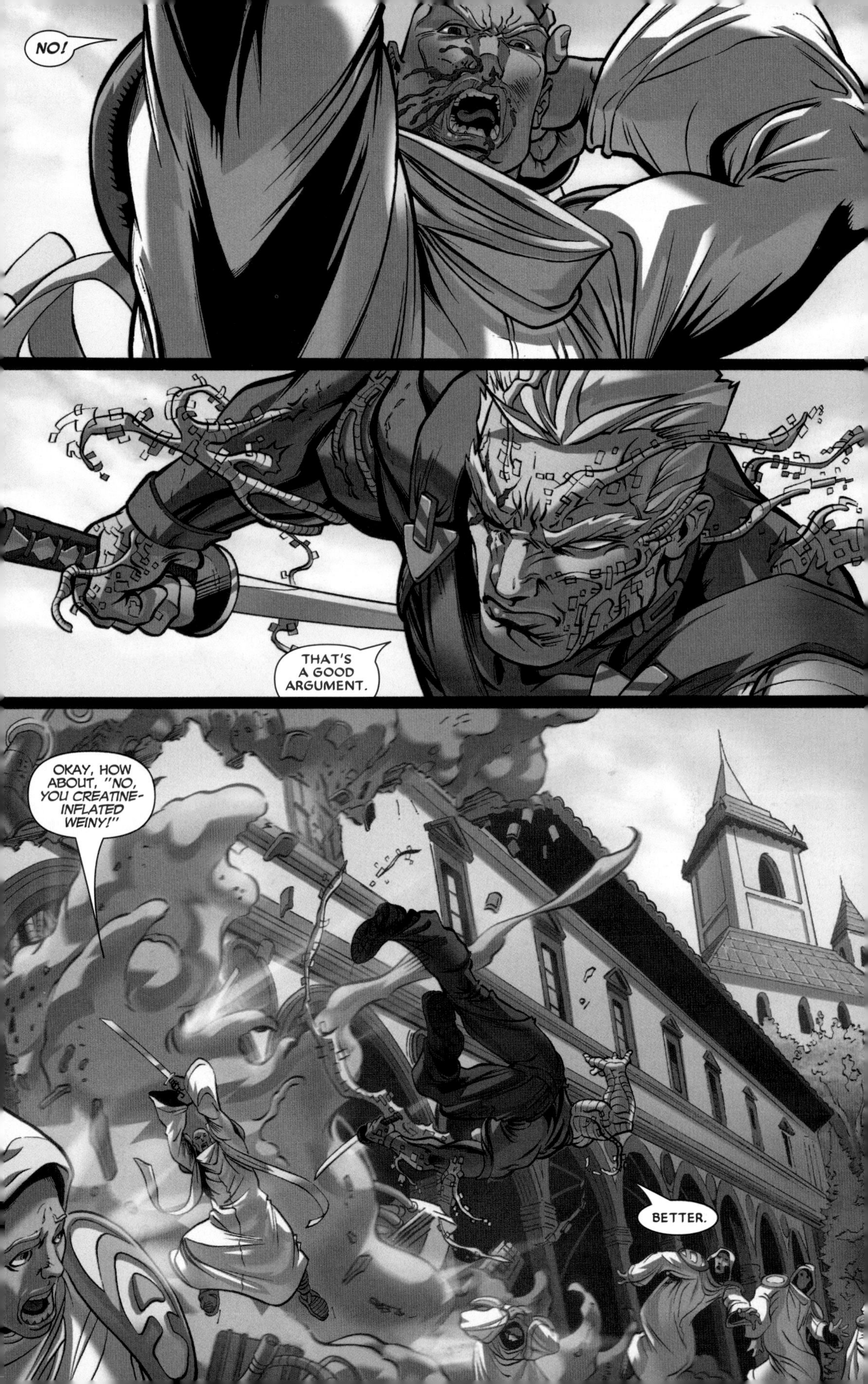
NO!
THAT'S A GOOD ARGUMENT.
OKAY, HOW ABOUT, "NO, YOU CREATINE-INFLATED WEINY!"
BETTER.

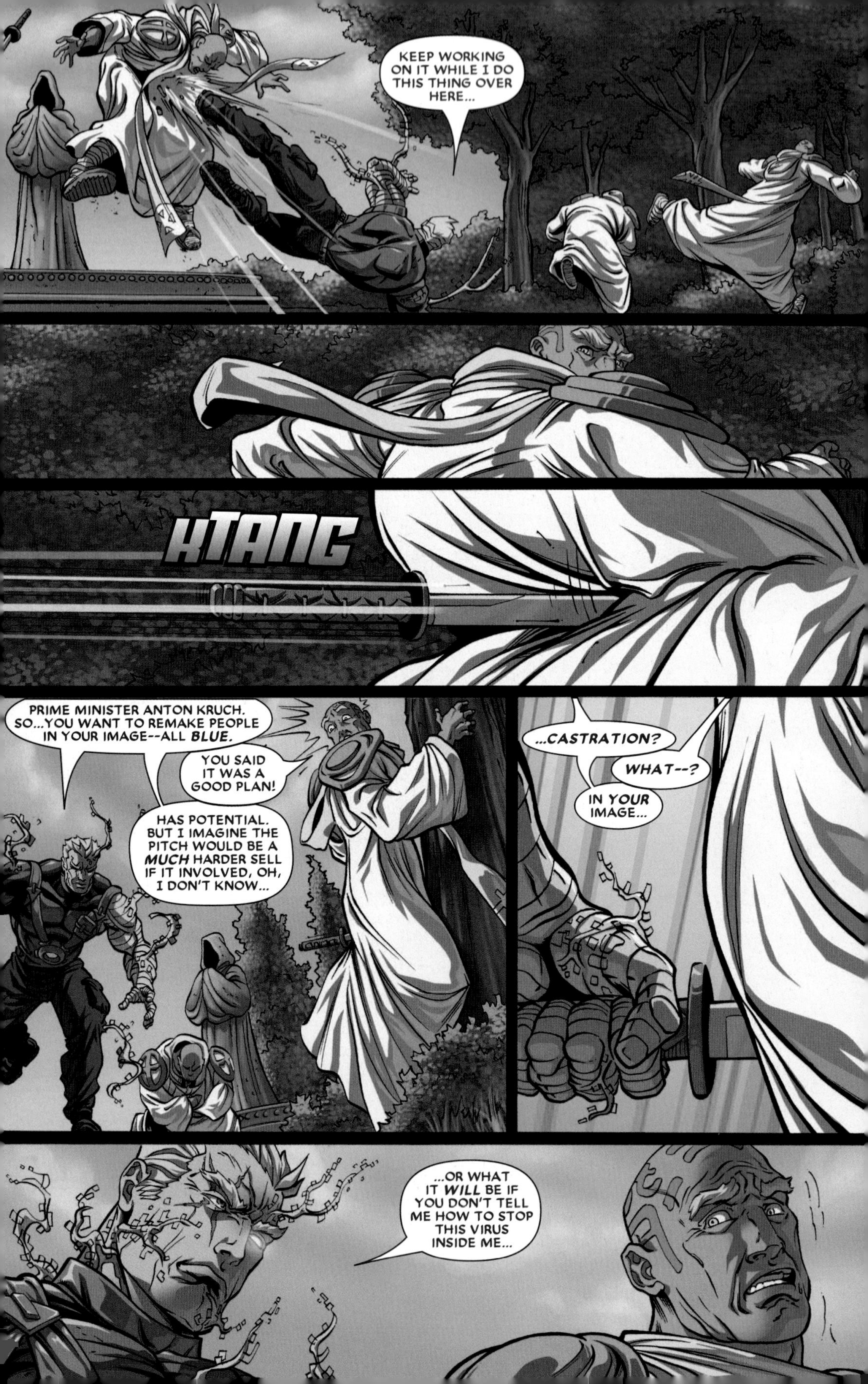
KEEP WORKING ON IT WHILE I DO THIS THING OVER HERE...
KTANG
PRIME MINISTER ANTON KRUCH. SO...YOU WANT TO REMAKE PEOPLE IN YOUR IMAGE--ALL BLUE.
YOU SAID IT WAS A GOOD PLAN!
HAS POTENTIAL. BUT I IMAGINE THE PITCH WOULD BE A MUCH HARDER SELL IF IT INVOLVED, OH, I DON'T KNOW...
...CASTRATION?
WHAT--?
IN YOUR IMAGE...
...OR WHAT IT WILL BE IF YOU DON'T TELL ME HOW TO STOP THIS VIRUS INSIDE ME...

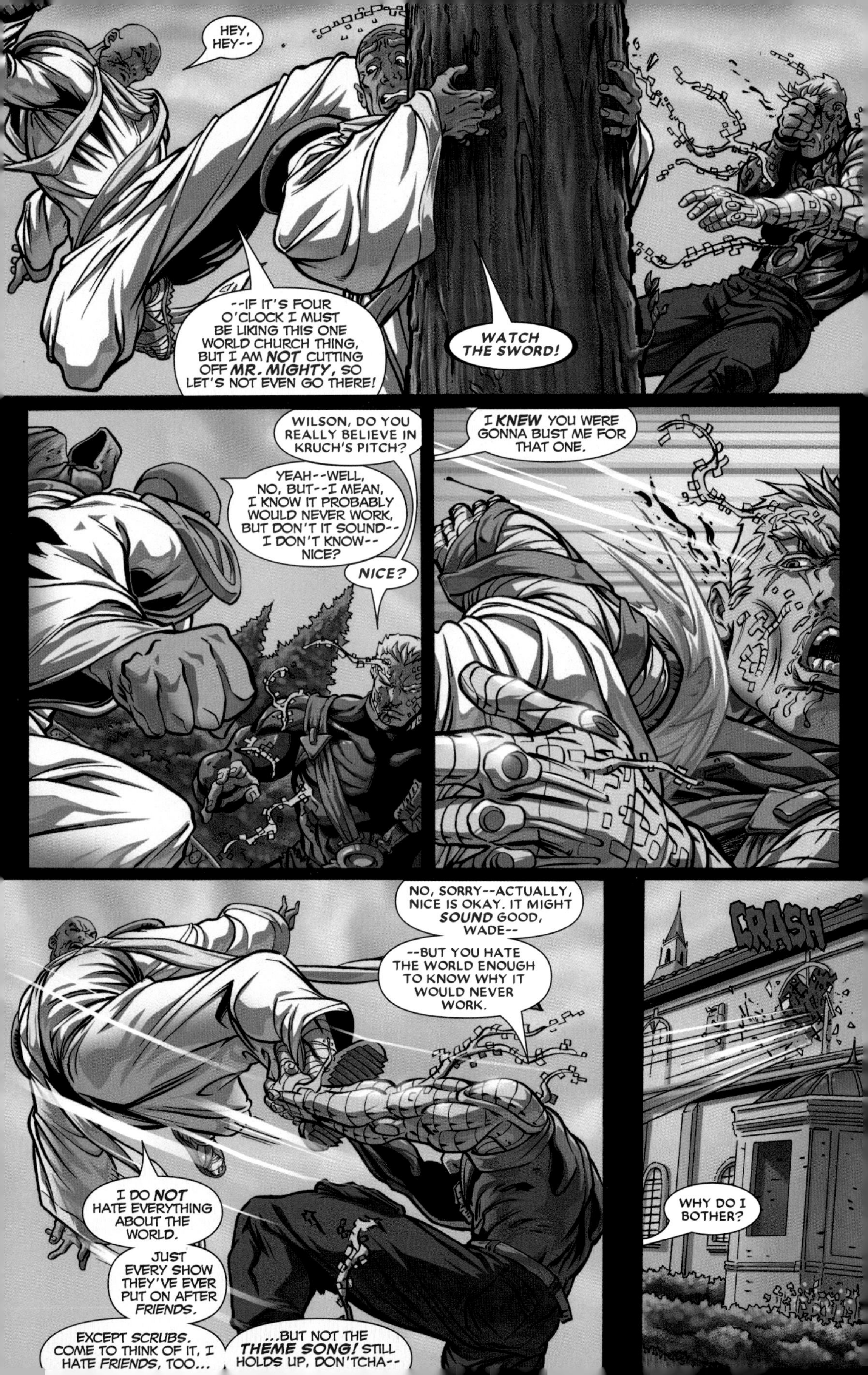
HEY, HEY--
--IF IT'S FOUR O'CLOCK I MUST BE LIKING THIS ONE WORLD CHURCH THING, BUT I AM NOT CUTTING OFF MR. MIGHTY, SO LET'S NOT EVEN GO THERE!
WATCH THE SWORD!
WILSON, DO YOU REALLY BELIEVE IN KRUCH'S PITCH?
YEAH--WELL, NO, BUT--I MEAN, I KNOW IT PROBABLY WOULD NEVER WORK, BUT DON'T IT SOUND--I DON'T KNOW--NICE?
NICE?
I KNEW YOU WERE GONNA BUST ME FOR THAT ONE.
NO, SORRY--ACTUALLY, NICE IS OKAY. IT MIGHT SOUND GOOD, WADE--
--BUT YOU HATE THE WORLD ENOUGH TO KNOW WHY IT WOULD NEVER WORK.
I DO NOT HATE EVERYTHING ABOUT THE WORLD.
JUST EVERY SHOW THEY'VE EVER PUT ON AFTER FRIENDS.
EXCEPT SCRUBS. COME TO THINK OF IT, I HATE FRIENDS, TOO...
...BUT NOT THE THEME SONG! STILL HOLDS UP, DON'TCHA--
CRASH
WHY DO I BOTHER?

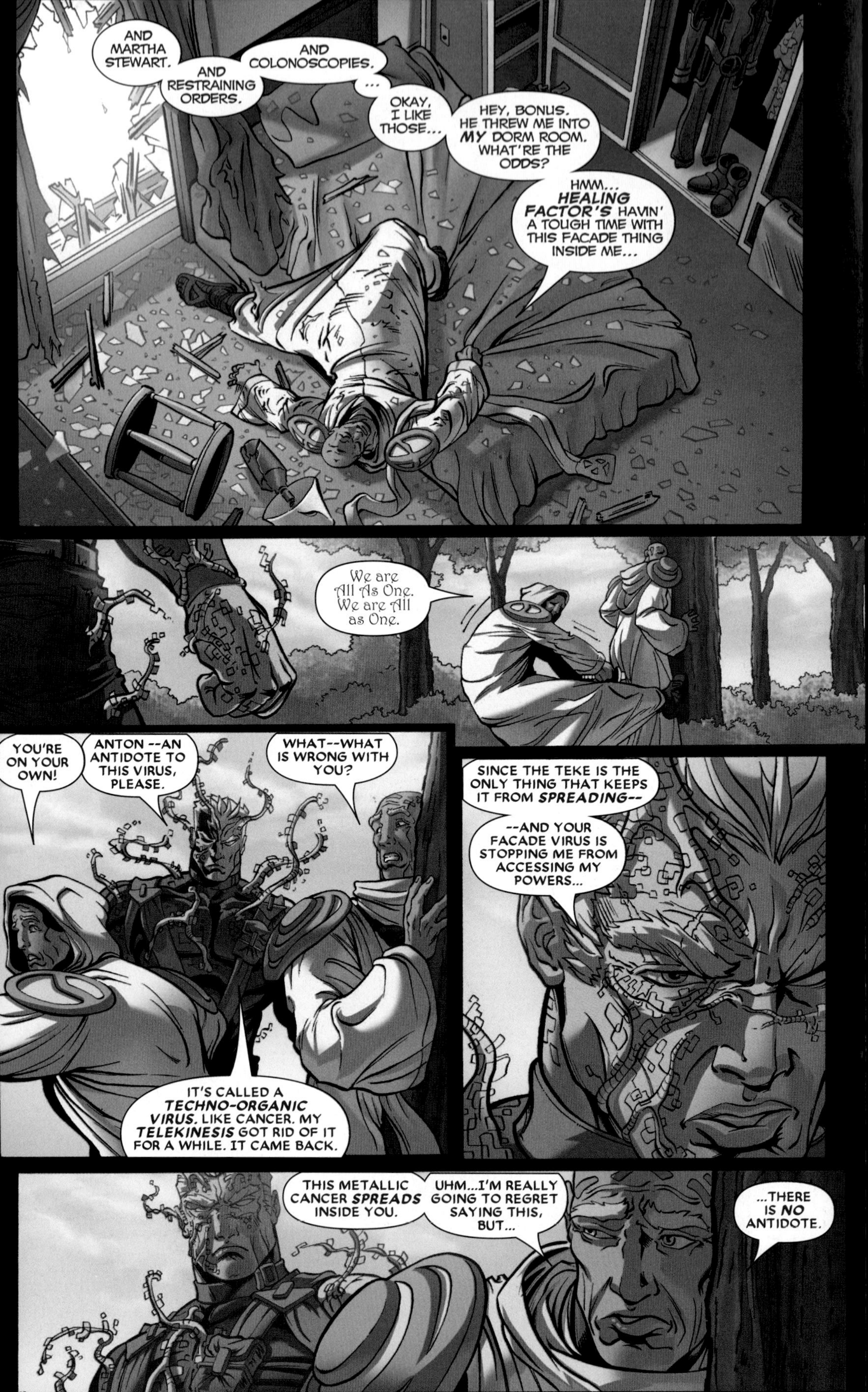
AND MARTHA STEWART.
AND RESTRAINING ORDERS.
AND COLONOSCOPIES.
...
OKAY, I LIKE THOSE...
HEY, BONUS. HE THREW ME INTO MY DORM ROOM. WHAT'RE THE ODDS?
HMM... HEALING FACTOR'S HAVIN' A TOUGH TIME WITH THIS FACADE THING INSIDE ME...
We are All As One. We are All as One.
YOU'RE ON YOUR OWN!
ANTON --AN ANTIDOTE TO THIS VIRUS, PLEASE.
WHAT--WHAT IS WRONG WITH YOU?
IT'S CALLED A TECHNO-ORGANIC VIRUS. LIKE CANCER. MY TELEKINESIS GOT RID OF IT FOR A WHILE. IT CAME BACK.
SINCE THE TEKE IS THE ONLY THING THAT KEEPS IT FROM SPREADING--
--AND YOUR FACADE VIRUS IS STOPPING ME FROM ACCESSING MY POWERS...
THIS METALLIC CANCER SPREADS INSIDE YOU.
UHM...I'M REALLY GOING TO REGRET SAYING THIS, BUT...
...THERE IS NO ANTIDOTE.

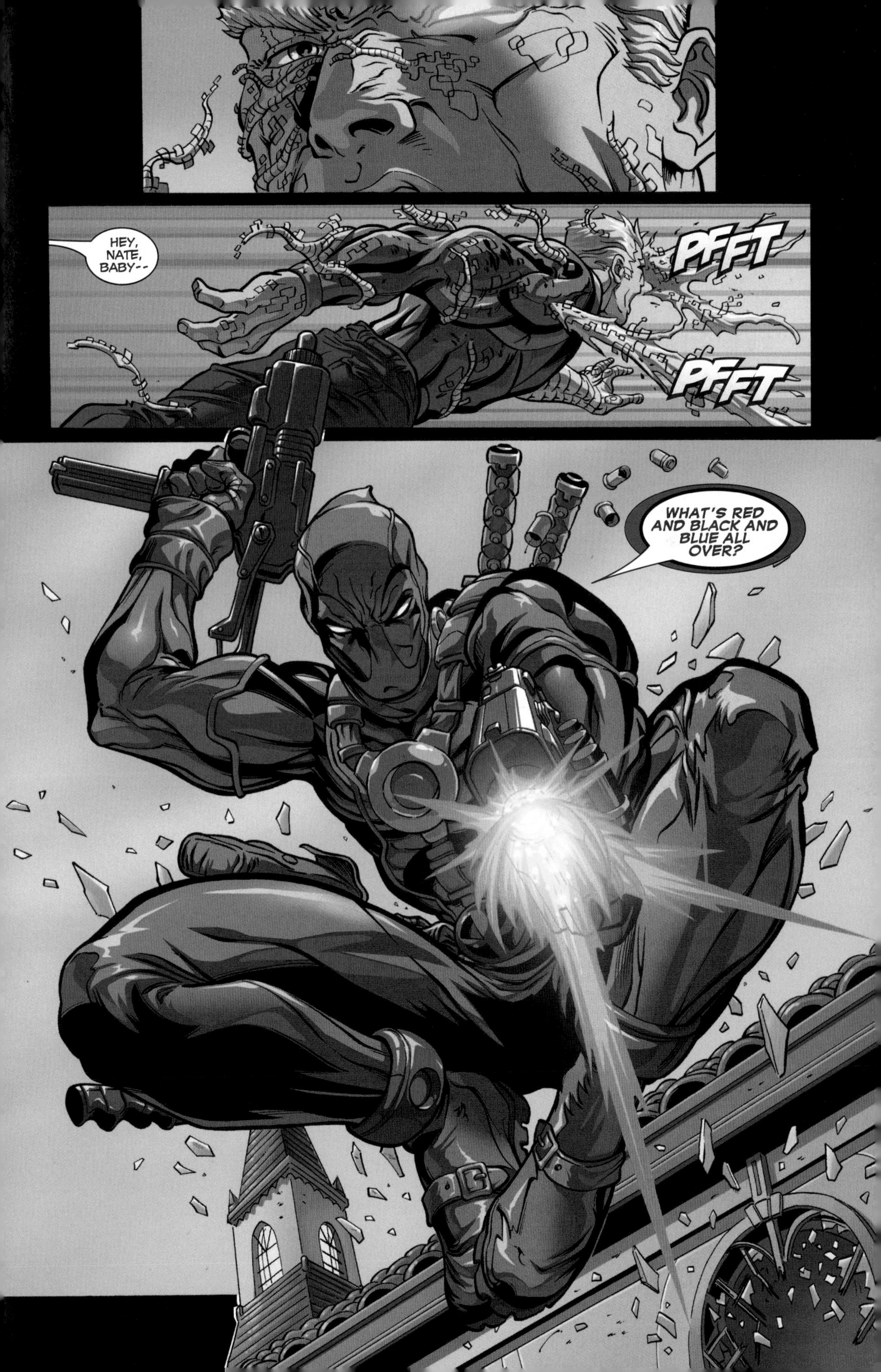
HEY, NATE, BABY--
PFFT
PFFT
WHAT'S RED AND BLACK AND BLUE ALL OVER?

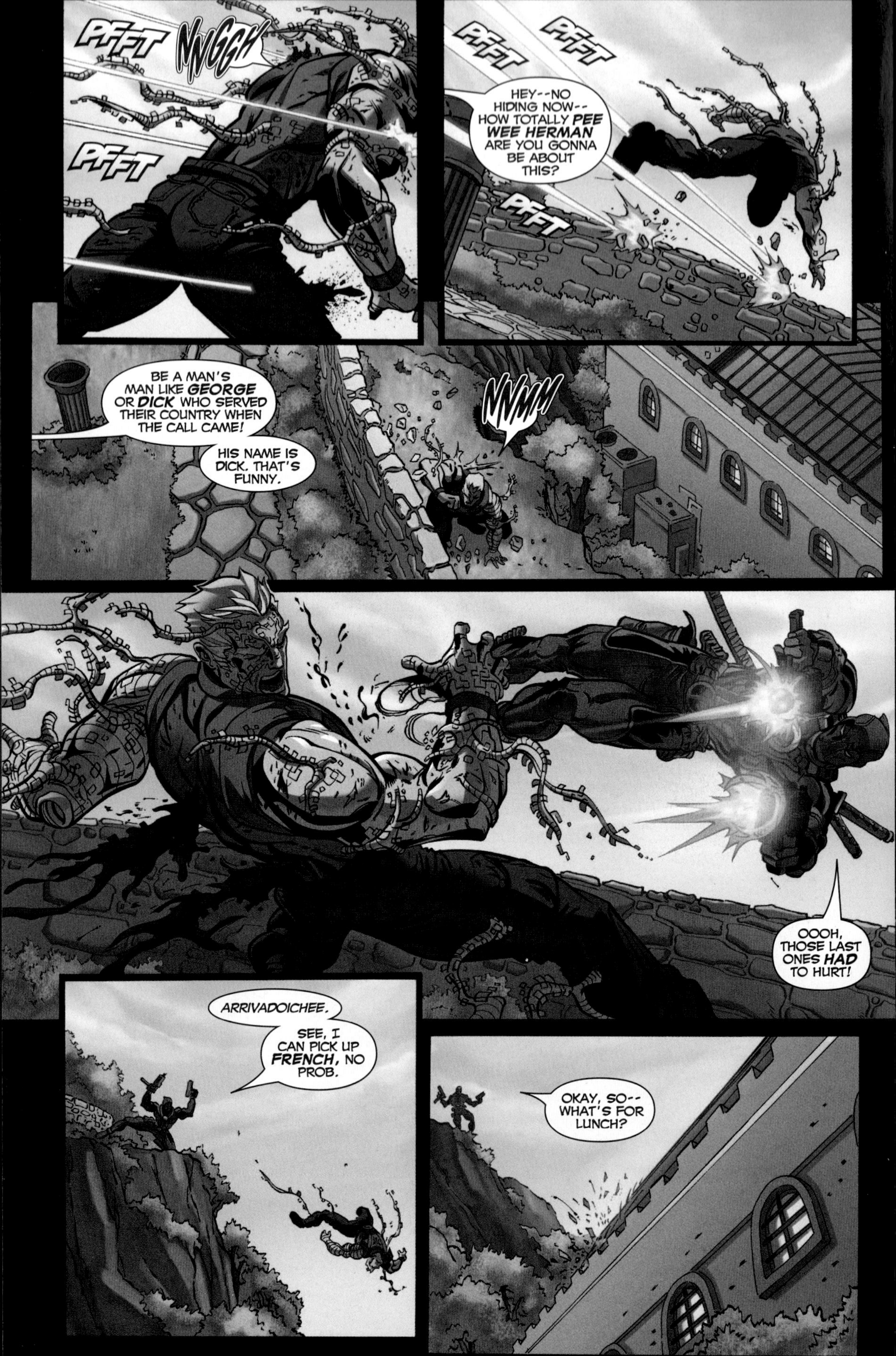
PFFT
NNGGH
PFFT
PFFT
PFFT
HEY--NO HIDING NOW--HOW TOTALLY **PEE WEE HERMAN** ARE YOU GONNA BE ABOUT THIS?
PFFT
BE A MAN'S MAN LIKE **GEORGE** OR **DICK** WHO SERVED THEIR COUNTRY WHEN THE CALL CAME!
HIS NAME IS DICK. THAT'S FUNNY.
NNMM
OOOH, THOSE LAST ONES **HAD** TO HURT!
ARRIVADOICHEE.
SEE, I CAN PICK UP **FRENCH**, NO PROB.
OKAY, SO--WHAT'S FOR LUNCH?

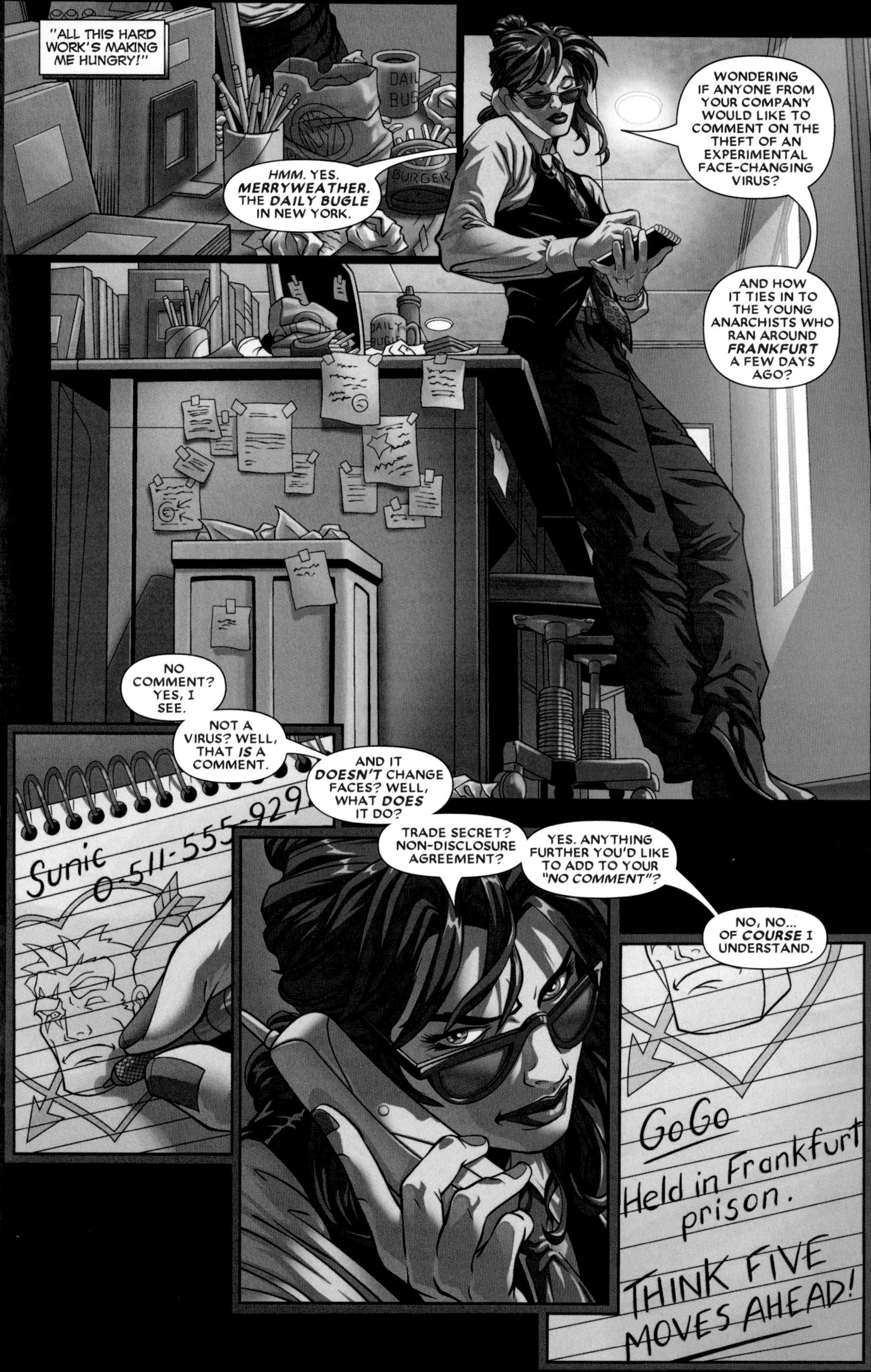
"ALL THIS HARD WORK'S MAKING ME HUNGRY!"
DAILY BUGLE
BURGER
HMM. YES. MERRYWEATHER. THE DAILY BUGLE IN NEW YORK.
WONDERING IF ANYONE FROM YOUR COMPANY WOULD LIKE TO COMMENT ON THE THEFT OF AN EXPERIMENTAL FACE-CHANGING VIRUS?
AND HOW IT TIES IN TO THE YOUNG ANARCHISTS WHO RAN AROUND FRANKFURT A FEW DAYS AGO?
NO COMMENT? YES, I SEE.
NOT A VIRUS? WELL, THAT IS A COMMENT.
AND IT DOESN'T CHANGE FACES? WELL, WHAT DOES IT DO?
Sunic 0-511-555-929
TRADE SECRET? NON-DISCLOSURE AGREEMENT?
YES. ANYTHING FURTHER YOU'D LIKE TO ADD TO YOUR "NO COMMENT"?
NO, NO... OF COURSE I UNDERSTAND.
GoGo
Held in Frankfurt prison.
THINK FIVE MOVES AHEAD!

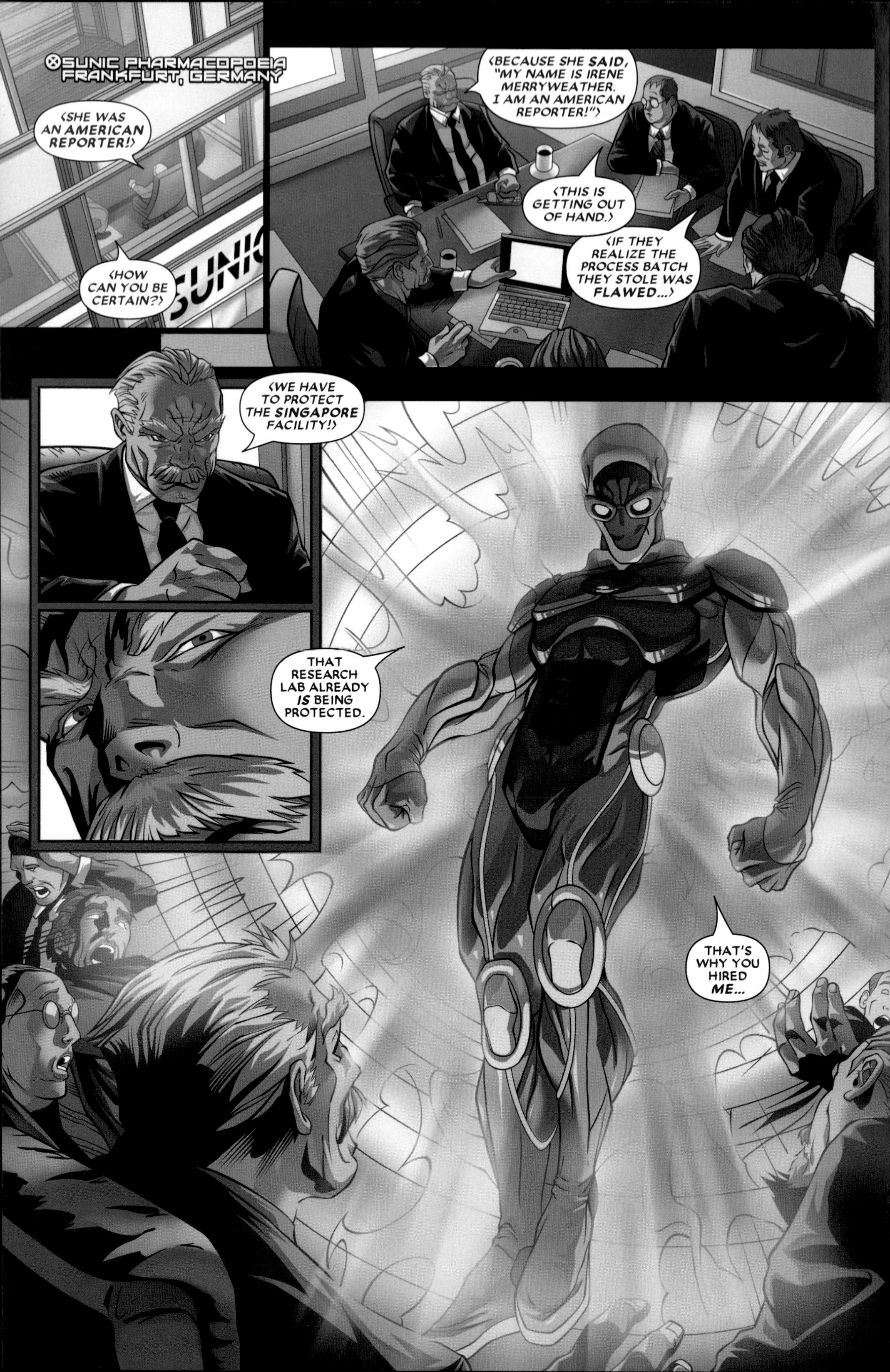
SUNIC PHARMACOPOEIA
FRANKFURT, GERMANY
‹SHE WAS AN AMERICAN REPORTER!›
‹HOW CAN YOU BE CERTAIN?›
SUNIC
‹BECAUSE SHE SAID, "MY NAME IS IRENE MERRYWEATHER. I AM AN AMERICAN REPORTER!"›
‹THIS IS GETTING OUT OF HAND.›
‹IF THEY REALIZE THE PROCESS BATCH THEY STOLE WAS FLAWED...›
‹WE HAVE TO PROTECT THE SINGAPORE FACILITY!›
THAT RESEARCH LAB ALREADY IS BEING PROTECTED.
THAT'S WHY YOU HIRED ME...

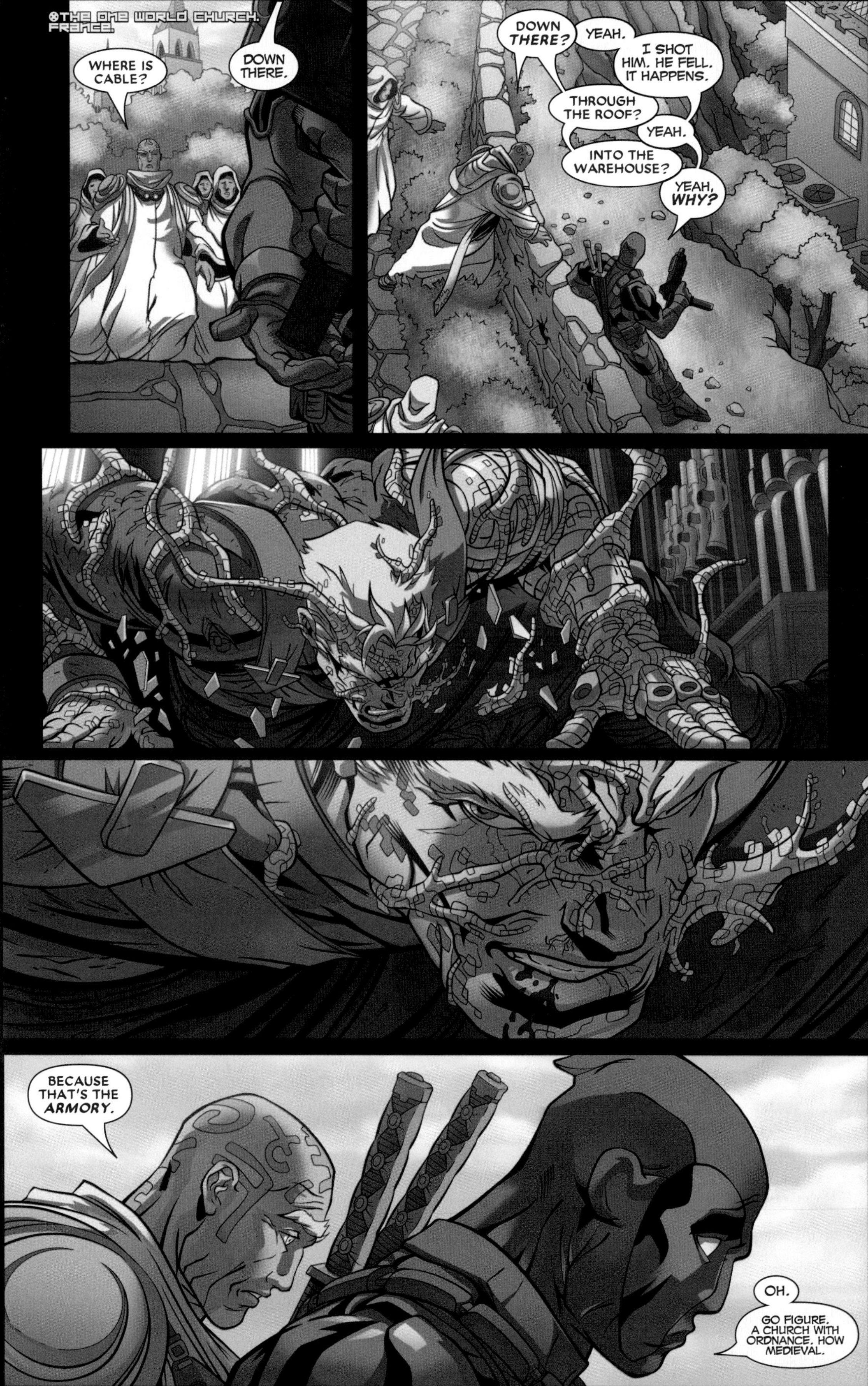
THE ONE WORLD CHURCH. FRANCE.
WHERE IS CABLE?
DOWN THERE.
DOWN THERE?
YEAH.
I SHOT HIM. HE FELL. IT HAPPENS.
THROUGH THE ROOF?
YEAH.
INTO THE WAREHOUSE?
YEAH, WHY?
BECAUSE THAT'S THE ARMORY.
OH.
GO FIGURE. A CHURCH WITH ORDNANCE. HOW MEDIEVAL.

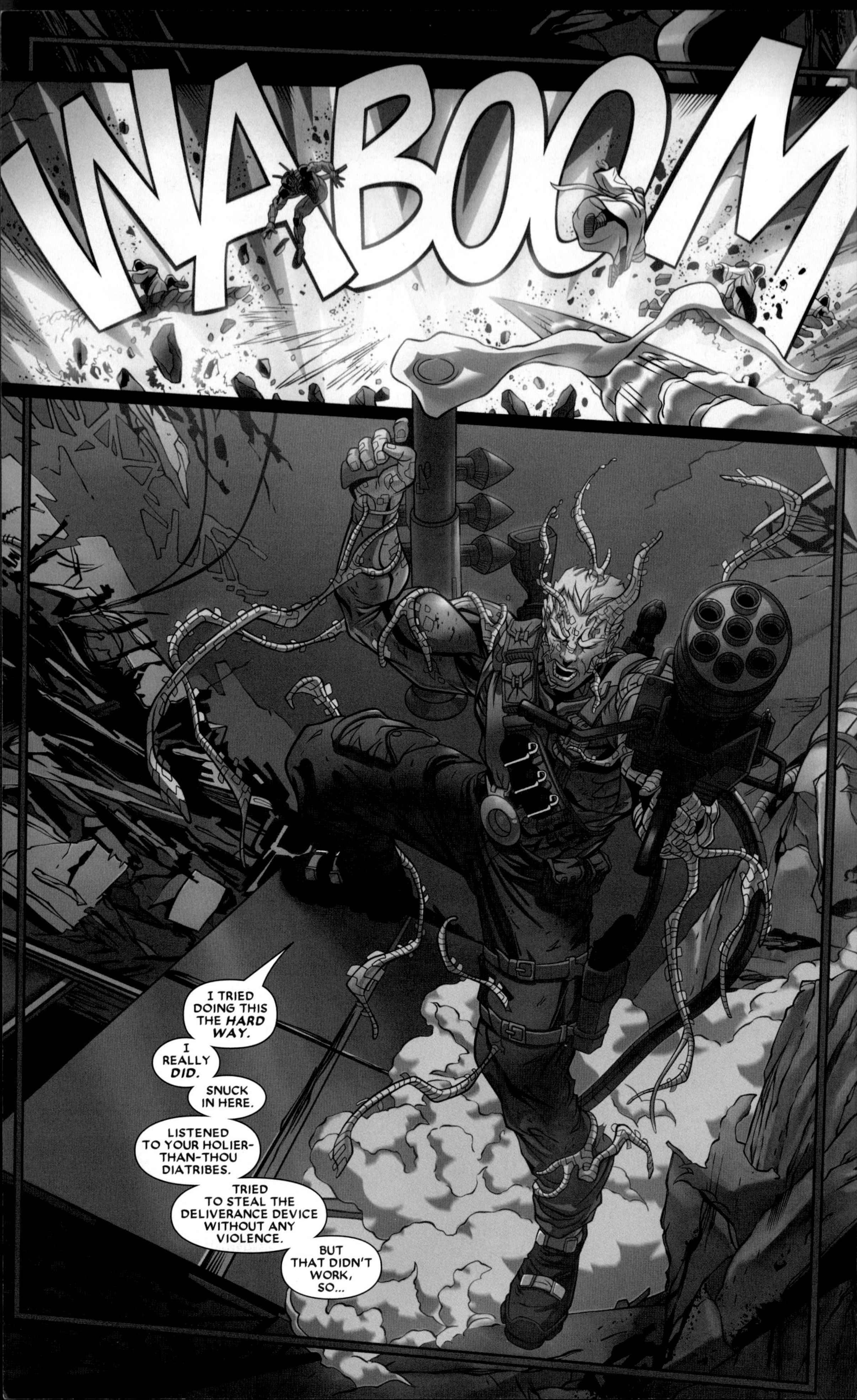
WABOOM
I TRIED DOING THIS THE HARD WAY.
I REALLY DID.
SNUCK IN HERE.
LISTENED TO YOUR HOLIER-THAN-THOU DIATRIBES.
TRIED TO STEAL THE DELIVERANCE DEVICE WITHOUT ANY VIOLENCE.
BUT THAT DIDN'T WORK, SO...

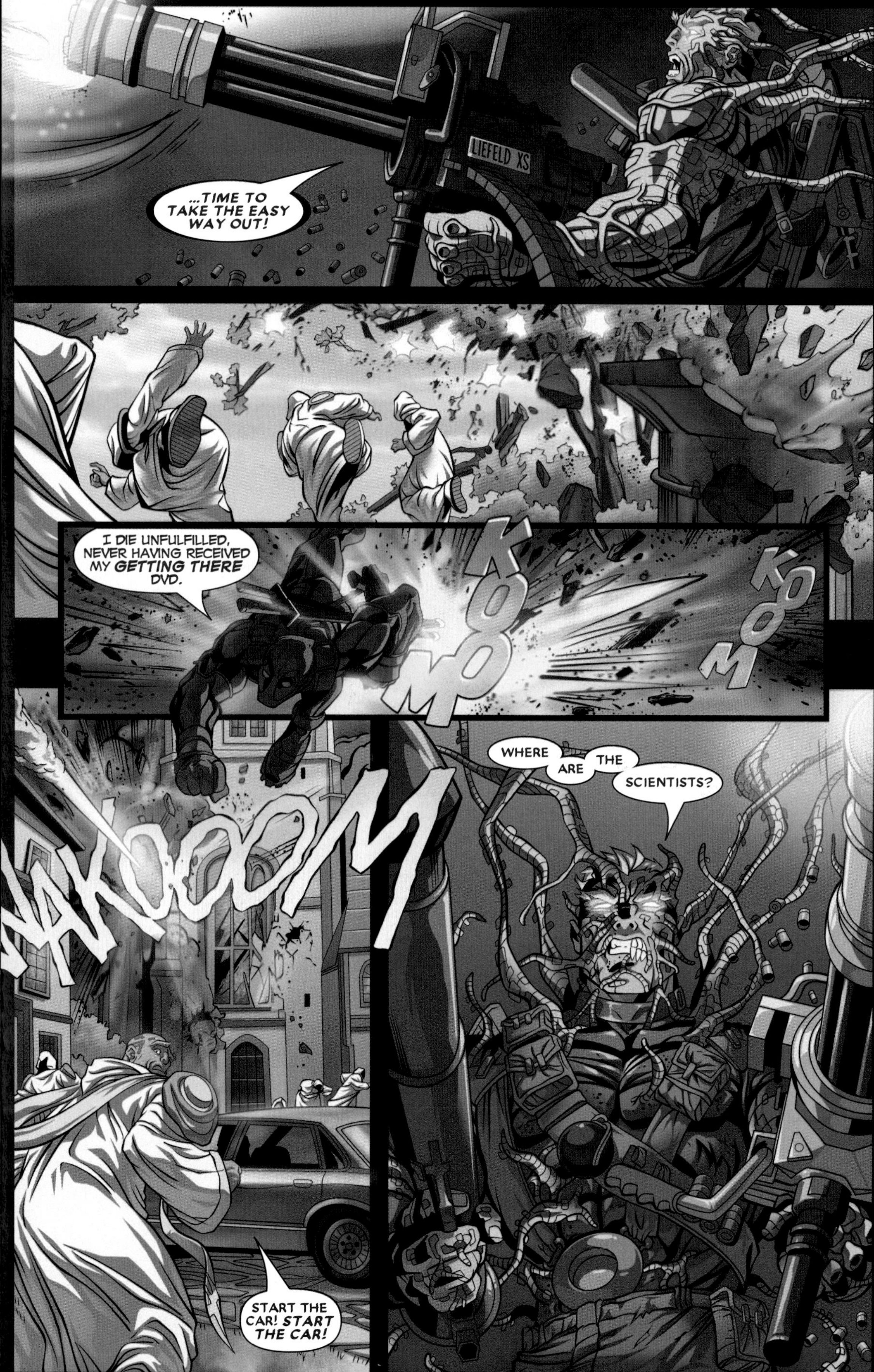
...TIME TO TAKE THE EASY WAY OUT!
LIEFELD XS
I DIE UNFULFILLED, NEVER HAVING RECEIVED MY GETTING THERE DVD.
KOOOM
KOOOM
KAKOOOM
WHERE ARE THE SCIENTISTS?
START THE CAR! START THE CAR!

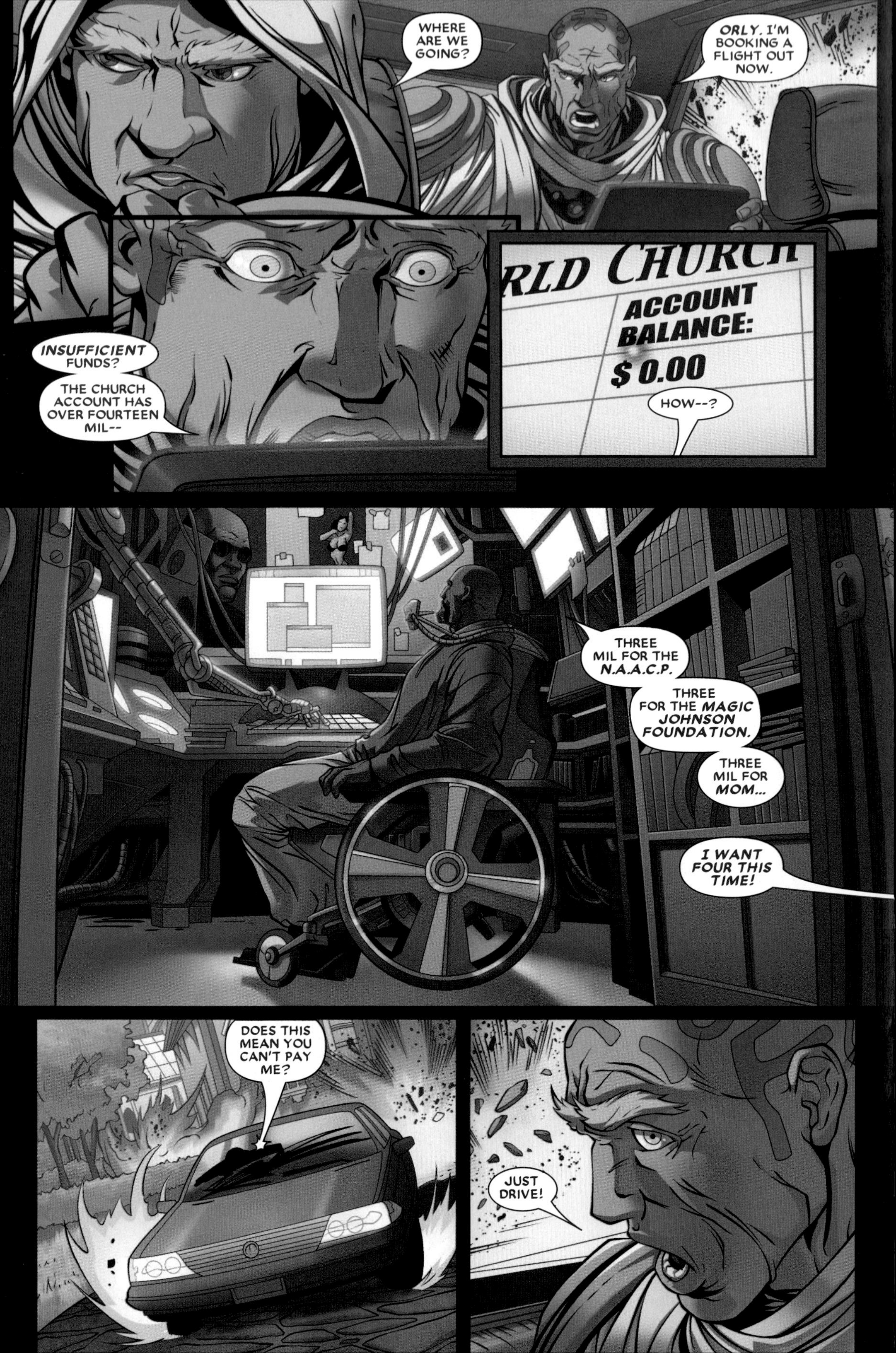

WHERE ARE WE GOING?
ORLY. I'M BOOKING A FLIGHT OUT NOW.
RLD CHURCH
ACCOUNT BALANCE:
$ 0.00
INSUFFICIENT FUNDS?
THE CHURCH ACCOUNT HAS OVER FOURTEEN MIL--
HOW--?
THREE MIL FOR THE N.A.A.C.P.
THREE FOR THE MAGIC JOHNSON FOUNDATION.
THREE MIL FOR MOM...
I WANT FOUR THIS TIME!
DOES THIS MEAN YOU CAN'T PAY ME?
JUST DRIVE!

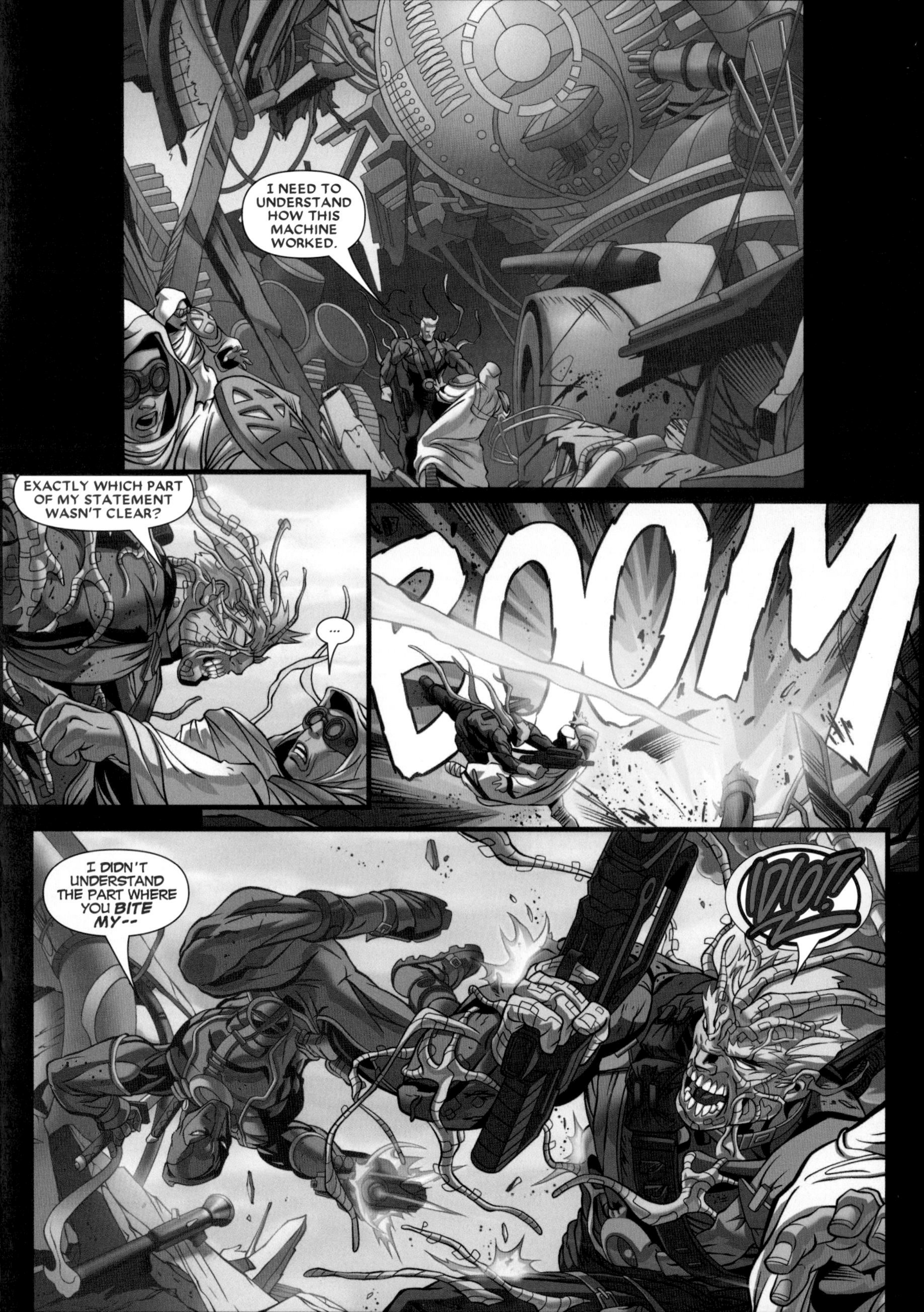
I NEED TO UNDERSTAND HOW THIS MACHINE WORKED.
EXACTLY WHICH PART OF MY STATEMENT WASN'T CLEAR?
...
BOOM
I DIDN'T UNDERSTAND THE PART WHERE YOU *BITE* MY--
IDIOT!

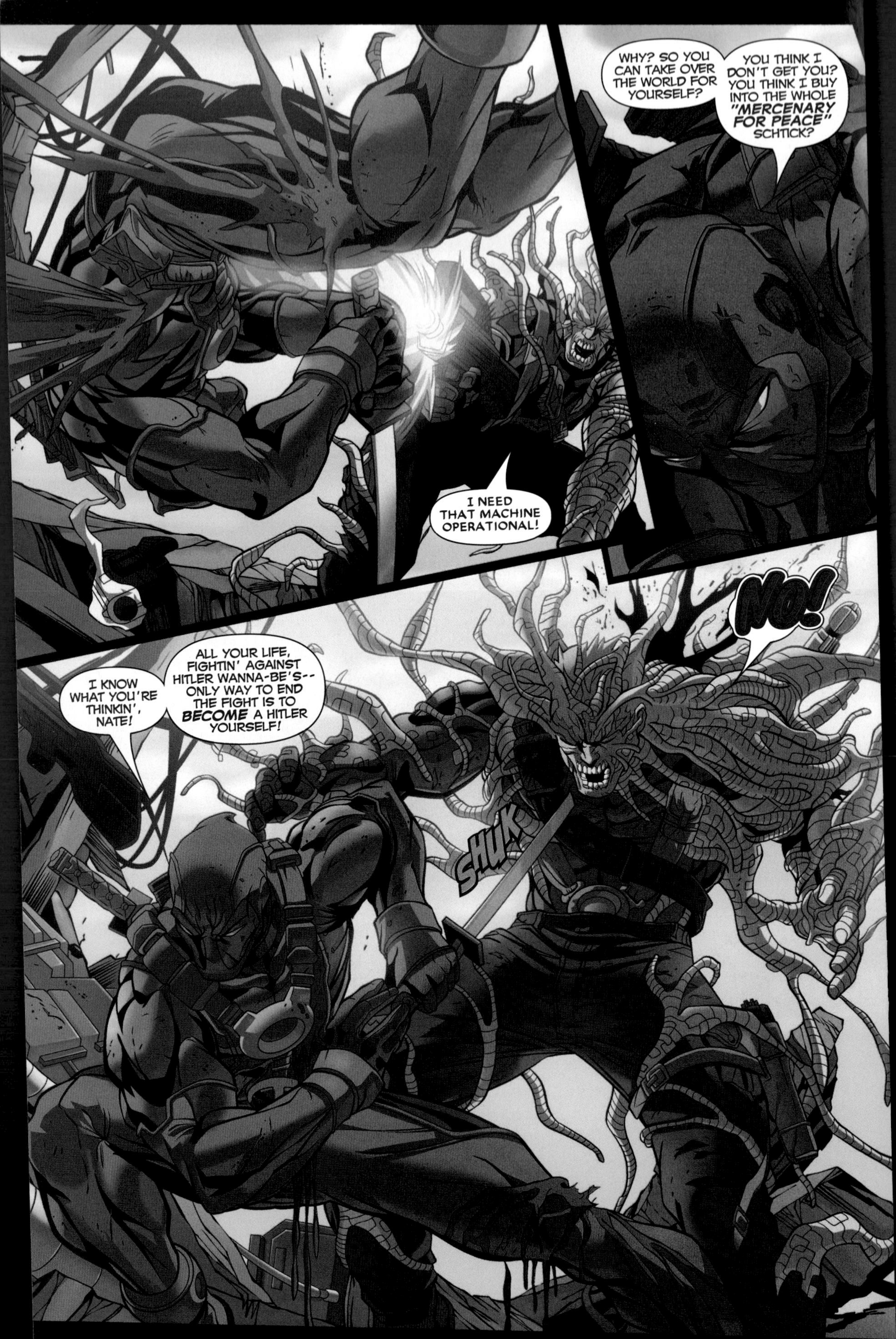
WHY? SO YOU CAN TAKE OVER THE WORLD FOR YOURSELF?
YOU THINK I DON'T GET YOU? YOU THINK I BUY INTO THE WHOLE "MERCENARY FOR PEACE" SCHTICK?
I NEED THAT MACHINE OPERATIONAL!
NO!
I KNOW WHAT YOU'RE THINKIN', NATE!
ALL YOUR LIFE, FIGHTIN' AGAINST HITLER WANNA-BE'S--ONLY WAY TO END THE FIGHT IS TO BECOME A HITLER YOURSELF!
SHUK

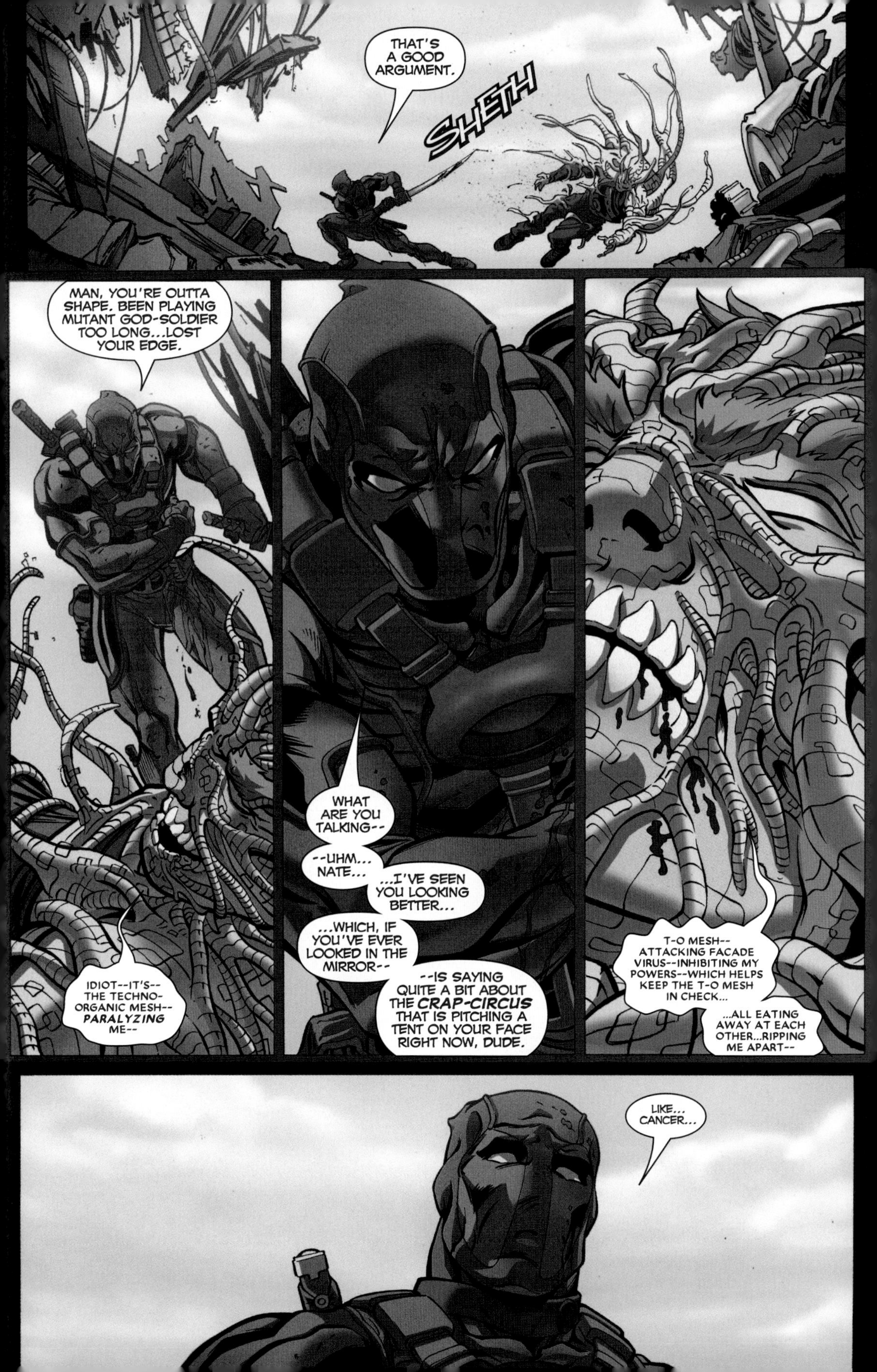
THAT'S A GOOD ARGUMENT.
SHETH
MAN, YOU'RE OUTTA SHAPE. BEEN PLAYING MUTANT GOD-SOLDIER TOO LONG...LOST YOUR EDGE.
IDIOT--IT'S-- THE TECHNO-ORGANIC MESH-- PARALYZING ME--
WHAT ARE YOU TALKING--
--UHM... NATE...
...I'VE SEEN YOU LOOKING BETTER...
...WHICH, IF YOU'VE EVER LOOKED IN THE MIRROR--
--IS SAYING QUITE A BIT ABOUT THE CRAP-CIRCUS THAT IS PITCHING A TENT ON YOUR FACE RIGHT NOW, DUDE.
T-O MESH-- ATTACKING FACADE VIRUS--INHIBITING MY POWERS--WHICH HELPS KEEP THE T-O MESH IN CHECK...
...ALL EATING AWAY AT EACH OTHER...RIPPING ME APART--
LIKE... CANCER...

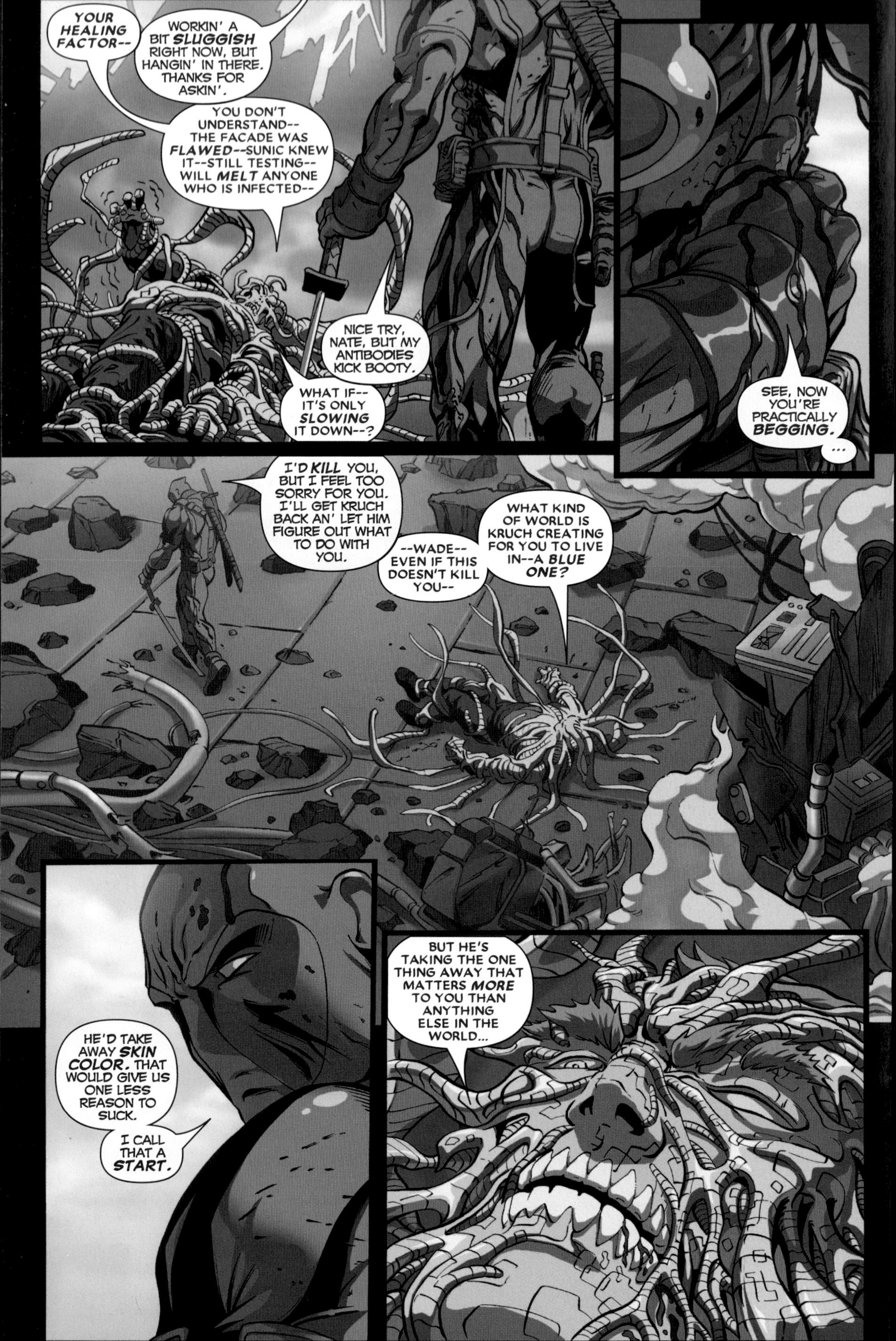
YOUR HEALING FACTOR--
WORKIN' A BIT SLUGGISH RIGHT NOW, BUT HANGIN' IN THERE. THANKS FOR ASKIN'.
YOU DON'T UNDERSTAND-- THE FACADE WAS FLAWED--SUNIC KNEW IT--STILL TESTING-- WILL MELT ANYONE WHO IS INFECTED--
NICE TRY, NATE, BUT MY ANTIBODIES KICK BOOTY.
WHAT IF-- IT'S ONLY SLOWING IT DOWN--?
SEE, NOW YOU'RE PRACTICALLY BEGGING.
...
I'D KILL YOU, BUT I FEEL TOO SORRY FOR YOU. I'LL GET KRUCH BACK AN' LET HIM FIGURE OUT WHAT TO DO WITH YOU.
--WADE-- EVEN IF THIS DOESN'T KILL YOU--
WHAT KIND OF WORLD IS KRUCH CREATING FOR YOU TO LIVE IN--A BLUE ONE?
BUT HE'S TAKING THE ONE THING AWAY THAT MATTERS MORE TO YOU THAN ANYTHING ELSE IN THE WORLD...
HE'D TAKE AWAY SKIN COLOR. THAT WOULD GIVE US ONE LESS REASON TO SUCK.
I CALL THAT A START.

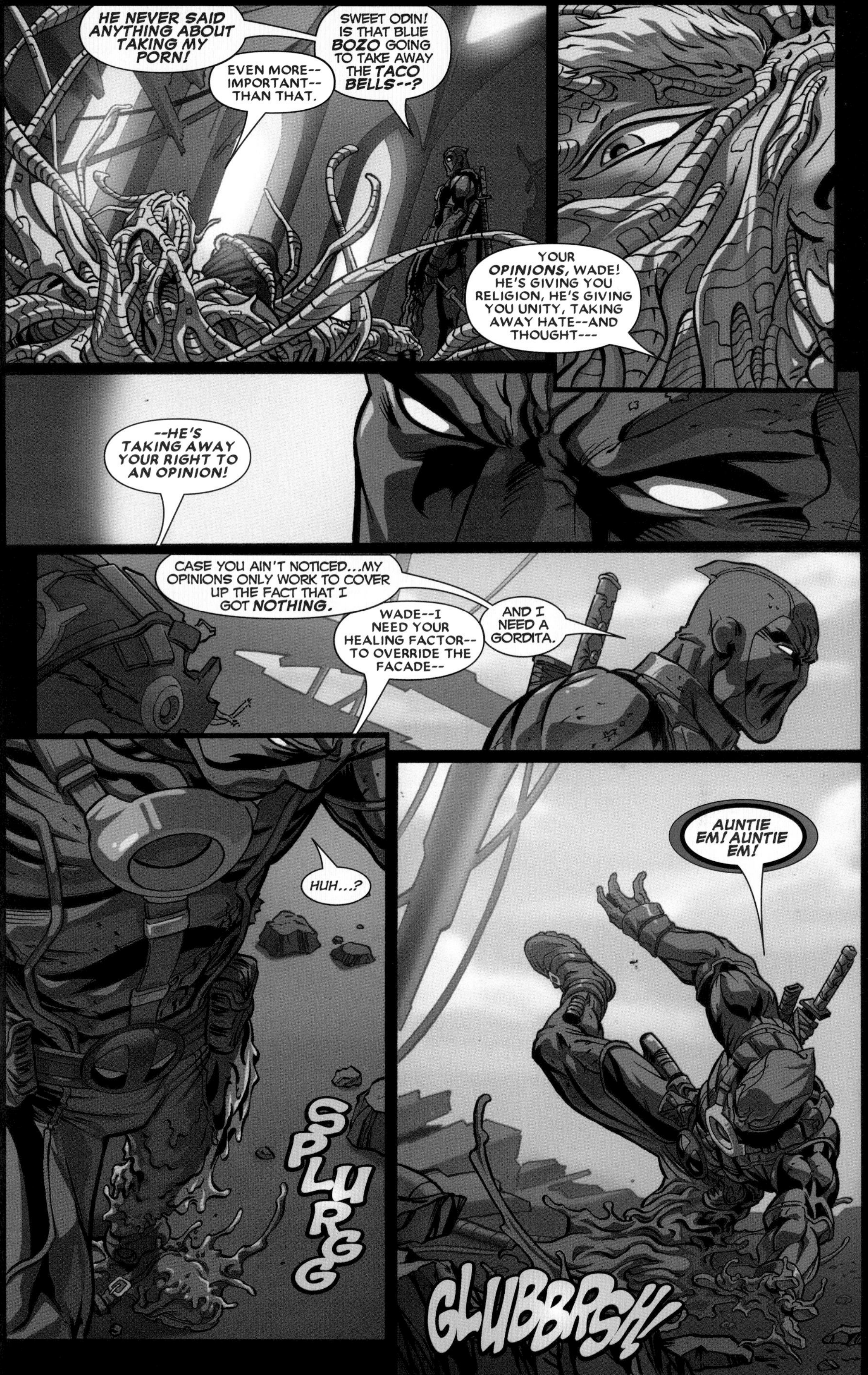
HE NEVER SAID ANYTHING ABOUT TAKING MY PORN!
SWEET ODIN! IS THAT BLUE BOZO GOING TO TAKE AWAY THE TACO BELLS--?
EVEN MORE--IMPORTANT--THAN THAT.
YOUR OPINIONS, WADE! HE'S GIVING YOU RELIGION, HE'S GIVING YOU UNITY, TAKING AWAY HATE--AND THOUGHT---
--HE'S TAKING AWAY YOUR RIGHT TO AN OPINION!
CASE YOU AIN'T NOTICED...MY OPINIONS ONLY WORK TO COVER UP THE FACT THAT I GOT NOTHING.
AND I NEED A GORDITA.
WADE--I NEED YOUR HEALING FACTOR--TO OVERRIDE THE FACADE--
HUH...?
SPLURGG
AUNTIE EM! AUNTIE EM!
GLUBBRSH!

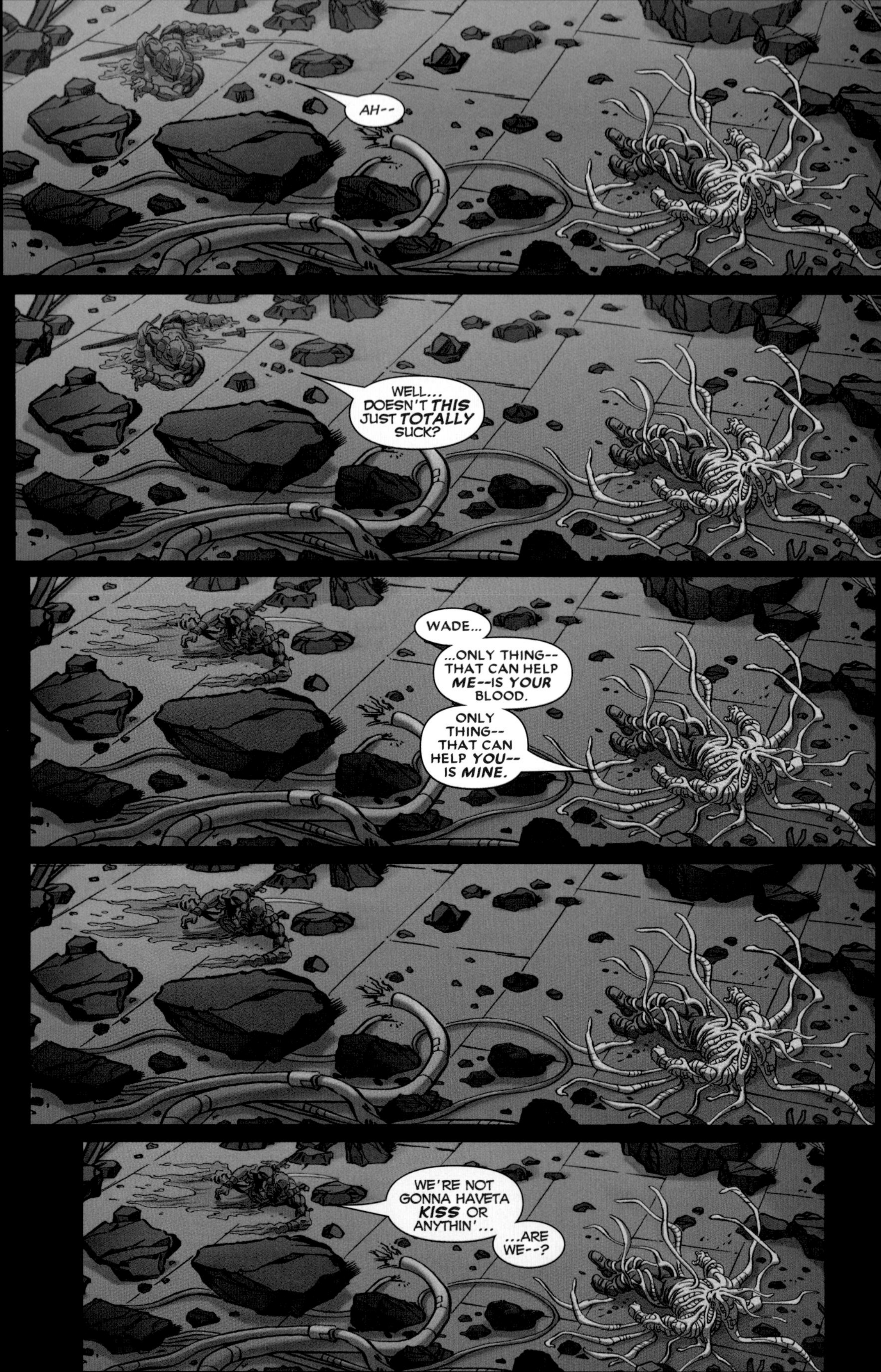
AH--
WELL... DOESN'T THIS JUST TOTALLY SUCK?
WADE...
...ONLY THING-- THAT CAN HELP ME--IS YOUR BLOOD.
ONLY THING-- THAT CAN HELP YOU-- IS MINE.
WE'RE NOT GONNA HAVETA KISS OR ANYTHIN'...
...ARE WE--?

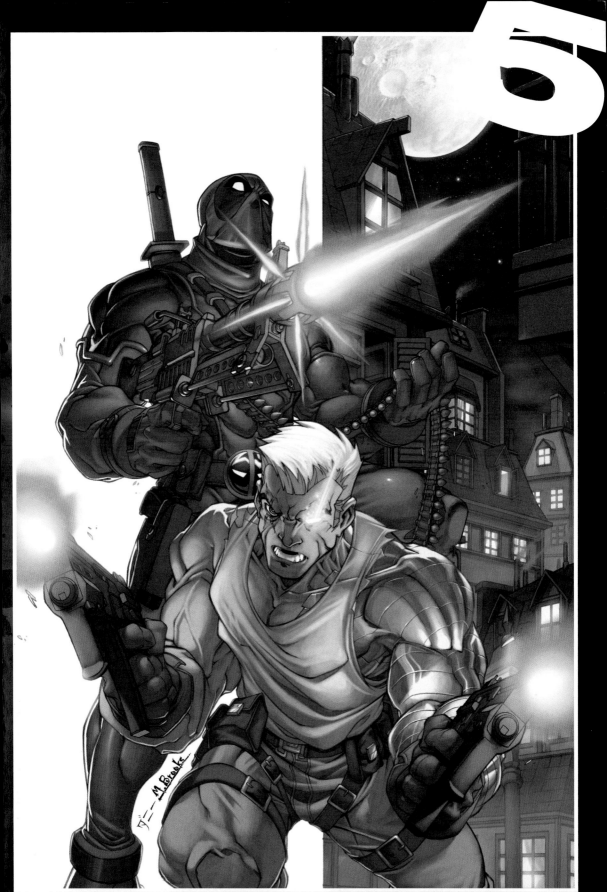

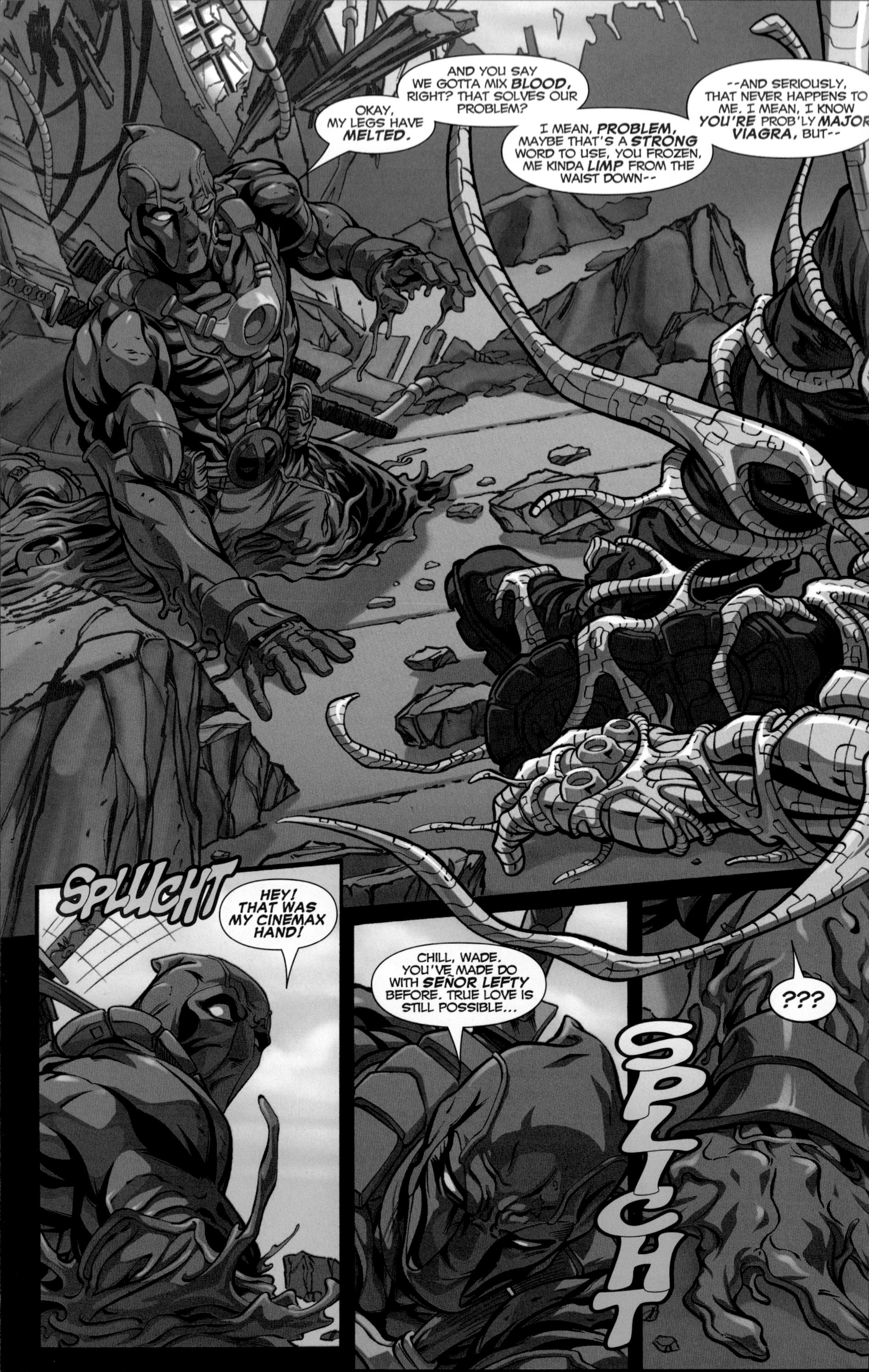
OKAY, MY LEGS HAVE MELTED.
AND YOU SAY WE GOTTA MIX BLOOD, RIGHT? THAT SOLVES OUR PROBLEM?
I MEAN, PROBLEM, MAYBE THAT'S A STRONG WORD TO USE, YOU FROZEN, ME KINDA LIMP FROM THE WAIST DOWN--
--AND SERIOUSLY, THAT NEVER HAPPENS TO ME. I MEAN, I KNOW YOU'RE PROB'LY MAJOR VIAGRA, BUT--
SPLUCHT
HEY! THAT WAS MY CINEMAX HAND!
CHILL, WADE. YOU'VE MADE DO WITH SEÑOR LEFTY BEFORE. TRUE LOVE IS STILL POSSIBLE...
???
SPLICHT

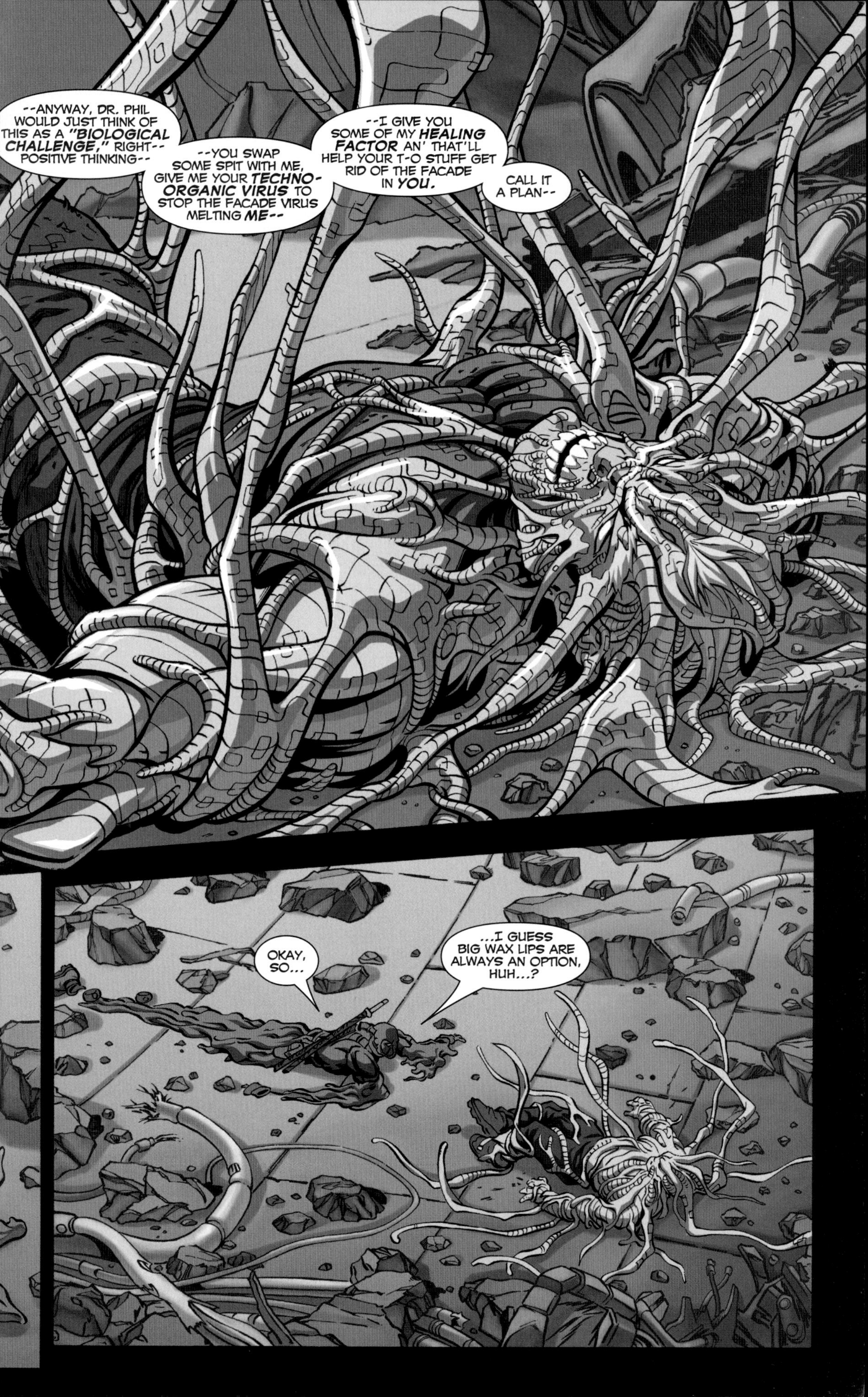
--ANYWAY, DR. PHIL WOULD JUST THINK OF THIS AS A "BIOLOGICAL CHALLENGE," RIGHT--POSITIVE THINKING--
--YOU SWAP SOME SPIT WITH ME, GIVE ME YOUR TECHNO-ORGANIC VIRUS TO STOP THE FACADE VIRUS MELTING ME--
--I GIVE YOU SOME OF MY HEALING FACTOR AN' THAT'LL HELP YOUR T-O STUFF GET RID OF THE FACADE IN YOU.
CALL IT A PLAN--
OKAY, SO...
...I GUESS BIG WAX LIPS ARE ALWAYS AN OPTION, HUH...?

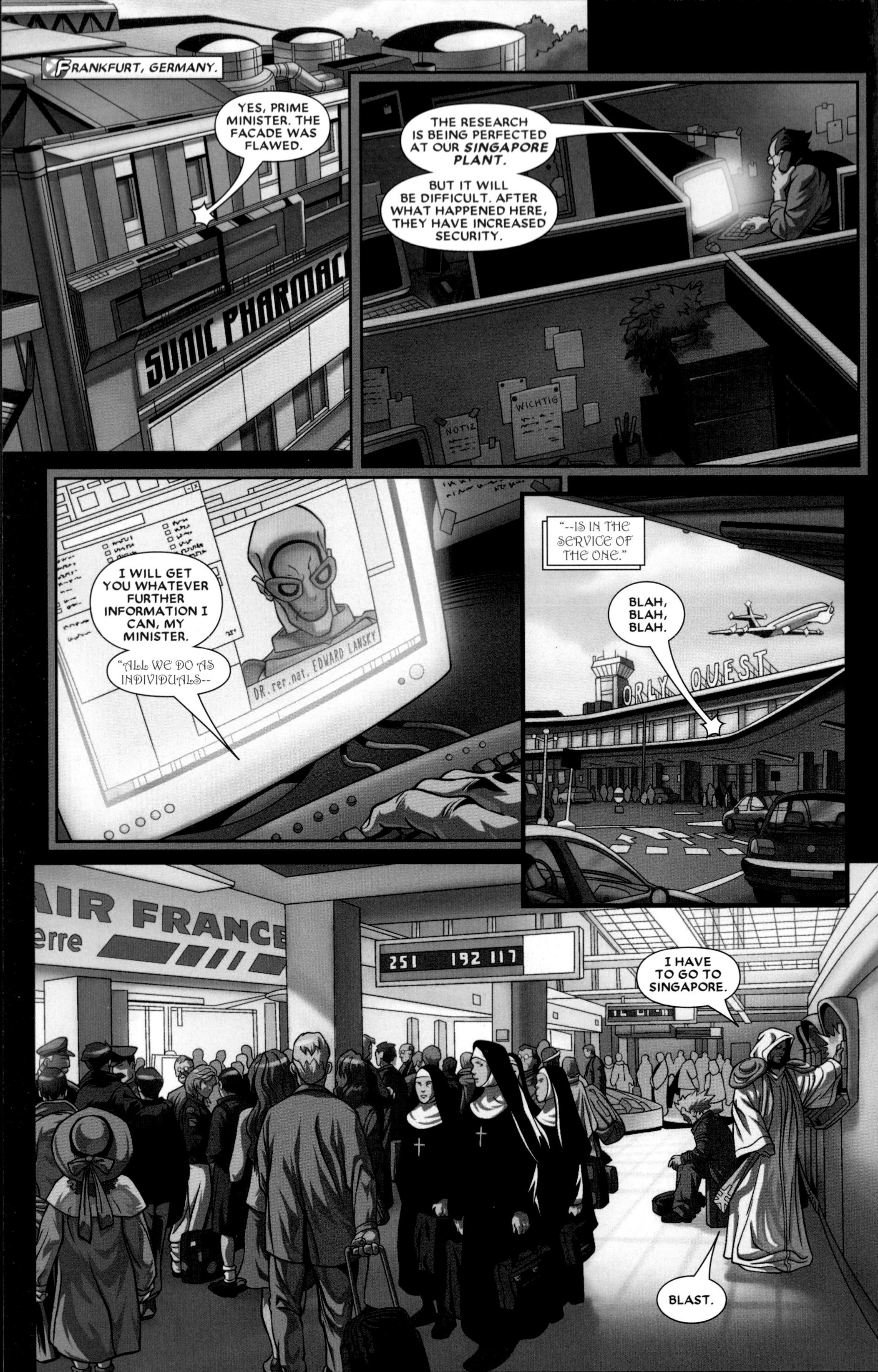
FRANKFURT, GERMANY.
SUNIC PHARMAC
YES, PRIME MINISTER. THE FACADE WAS FLAWED.
THE RESEARCH IS BEING PERFECTED AT OUR SINGAPORE PLANT.
BUT IT WILL BE DIFFICULT. AFTER WHAT HAPPENED HERE, THEY HAVE INCREASED SECURITY.
WICHTIG
NOTIZ
I WILL GET YOU WHATEVER FURTHER INFORMATION I CAN, MY MINISTER.
"ALL WE DO AS INDIVIDUALS--
DR. rer. nat. EDWARD LANSKY
"--IS IN THE SERVICE OF THE ONE."
BLAH, BLAH, BLAH.
ORLY OUEST
AIR FRANCE
erre
251 192 117
I HAVE TO GO TO SINGAPORE.
BLAST.

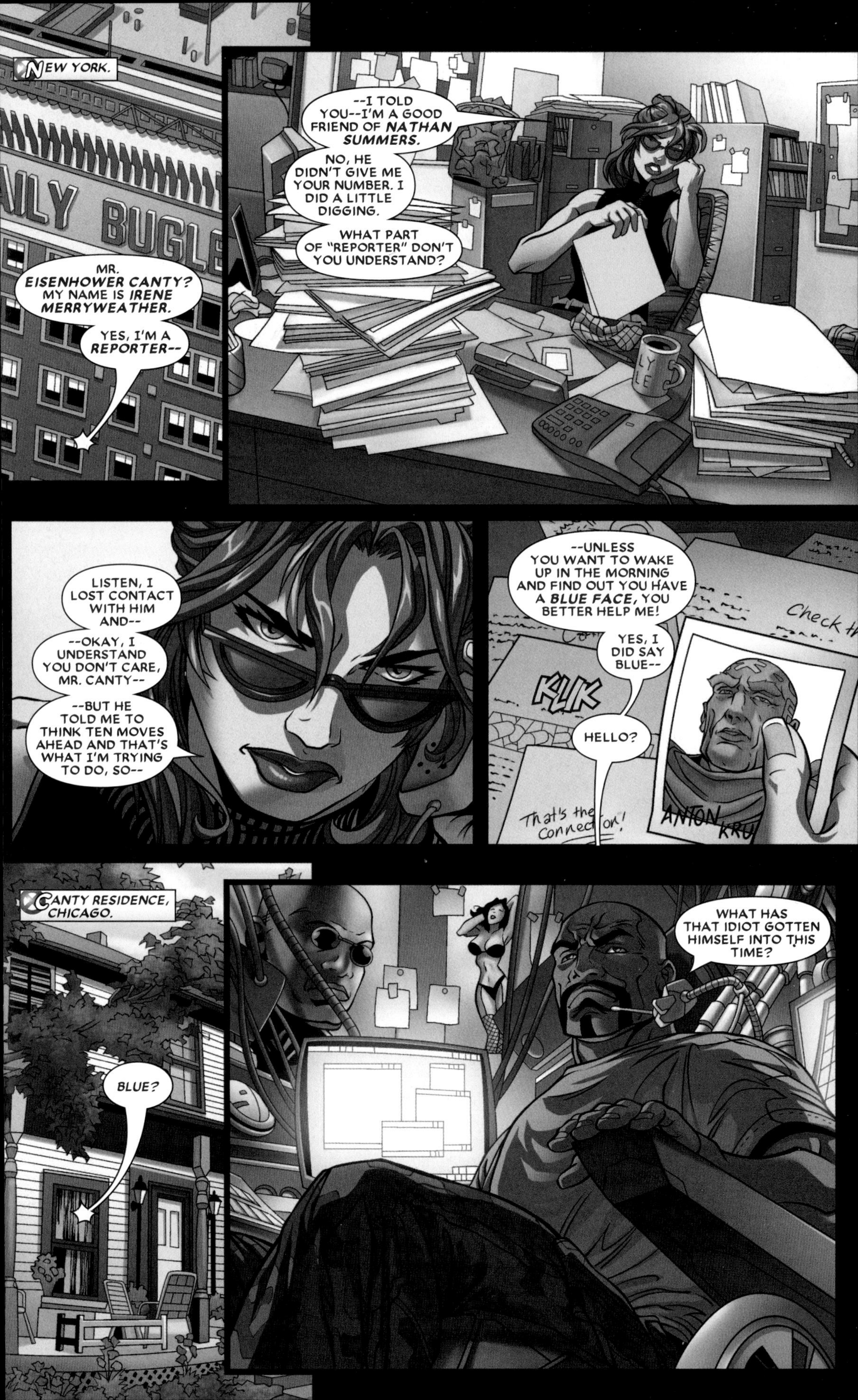
NEW YORK.
MR. EISENHOWER CANTY? MY NAME IS IRENE MERRYWEATHER.
YES, I'M A REPORTER--
--I TOLD YOU--I'M A GOOD FRIEND OF NATHAN SUMMERS.
NO, HE DIDN'T GIVE ME YOUR NUMBER. I DID A LITTLE DIGGING.
WHAT PART OF "REPORTER" DON'T YOU UNDERSTAND?
LYLE
LISTEN, I LOST CONTACT WITH HIM AND--
--OKAY, I UNDERSTAND YOU DON'T CARE, MR. CANTY--
--BUT HE TOLD ME TO THINK TEN MOVES AHEAD AND THAT'S WHAT I'M TRYING TO DO, SO--
--UNLESS YOU WANT TO WAKE UP IN THE MORNING AND FIND OUT YOU HAVE A BLUE FACE, YOU BETTER HELP ME!
YES, I DID SAY BLUE--
KLIK
HELLO?
That's the connection!
ANTON KRU
CANTY RESIDENCE, CHICAGO.
BLUE?
WHAT HAS THAT IDIOT GOTTEN HIMSELF INTO THIS TIME?

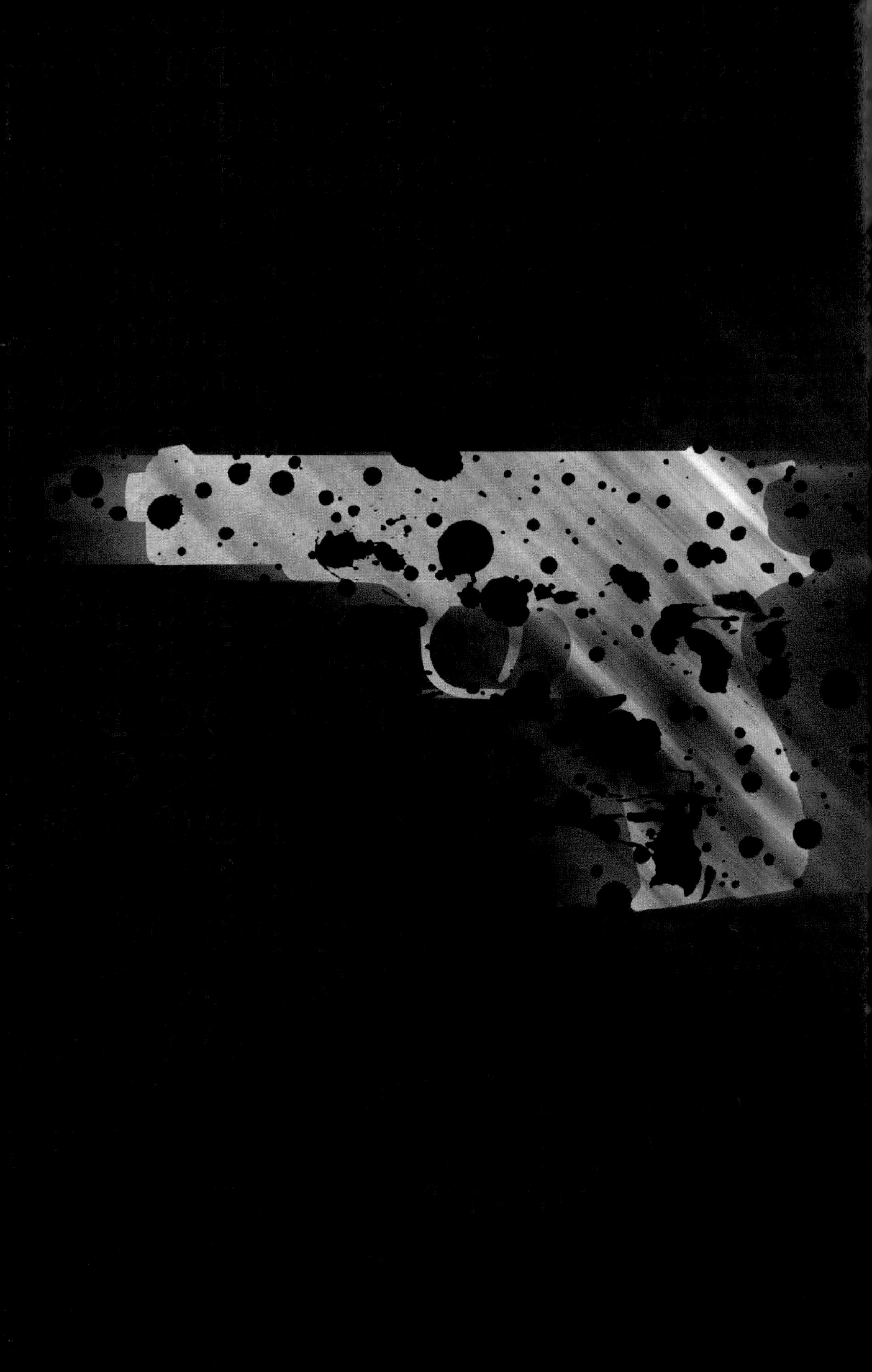

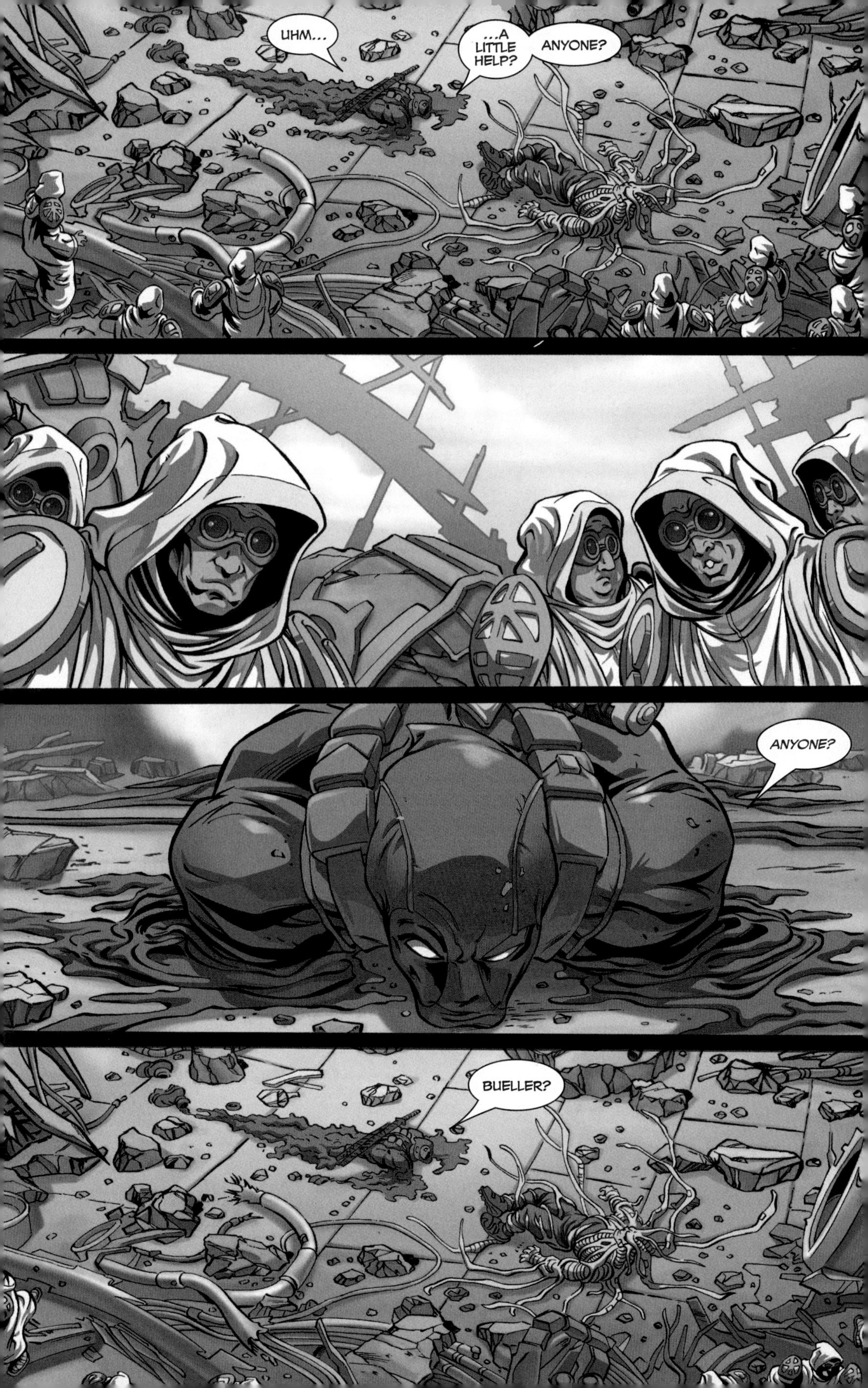
UHM...
...A LITTLE HELP?
ANYONE?
ANYONE?
BUELLER?

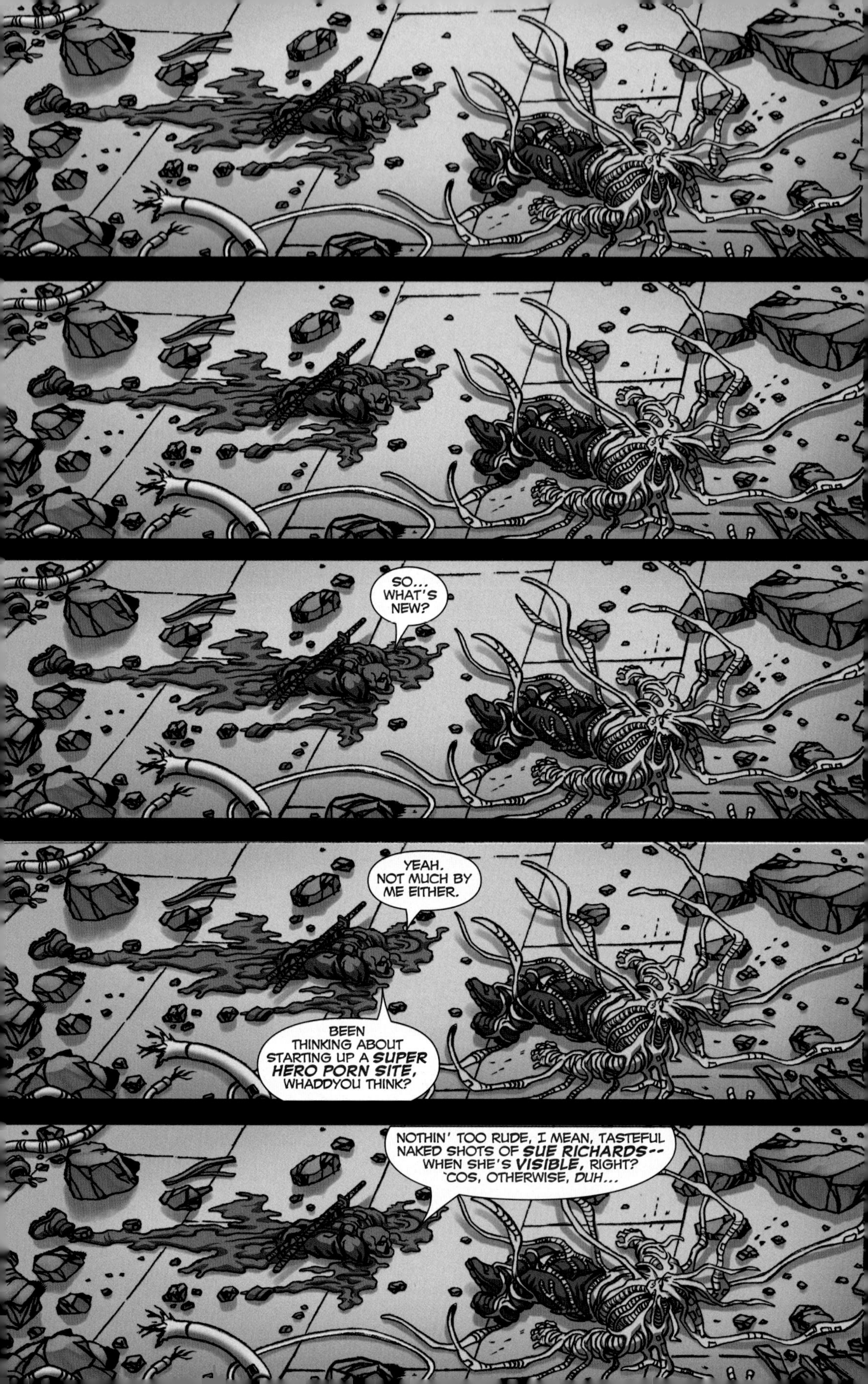
SO... WHAT'S NEW?
YEAH. NOT MUCH BY ME EITHER.
BEEN THINKING ABOUT STARTING UP A SUPER HERO PORN SITE, WHADDYOU THINK?
NOTHIN' TOO RUDE, I MEAN, TASTEFUL NAKED SHOTS OF SUE RICHARDS-- WHEN SHE'S VISIBLE, RIGHT? 'COS, OTHERWISE, DUH...

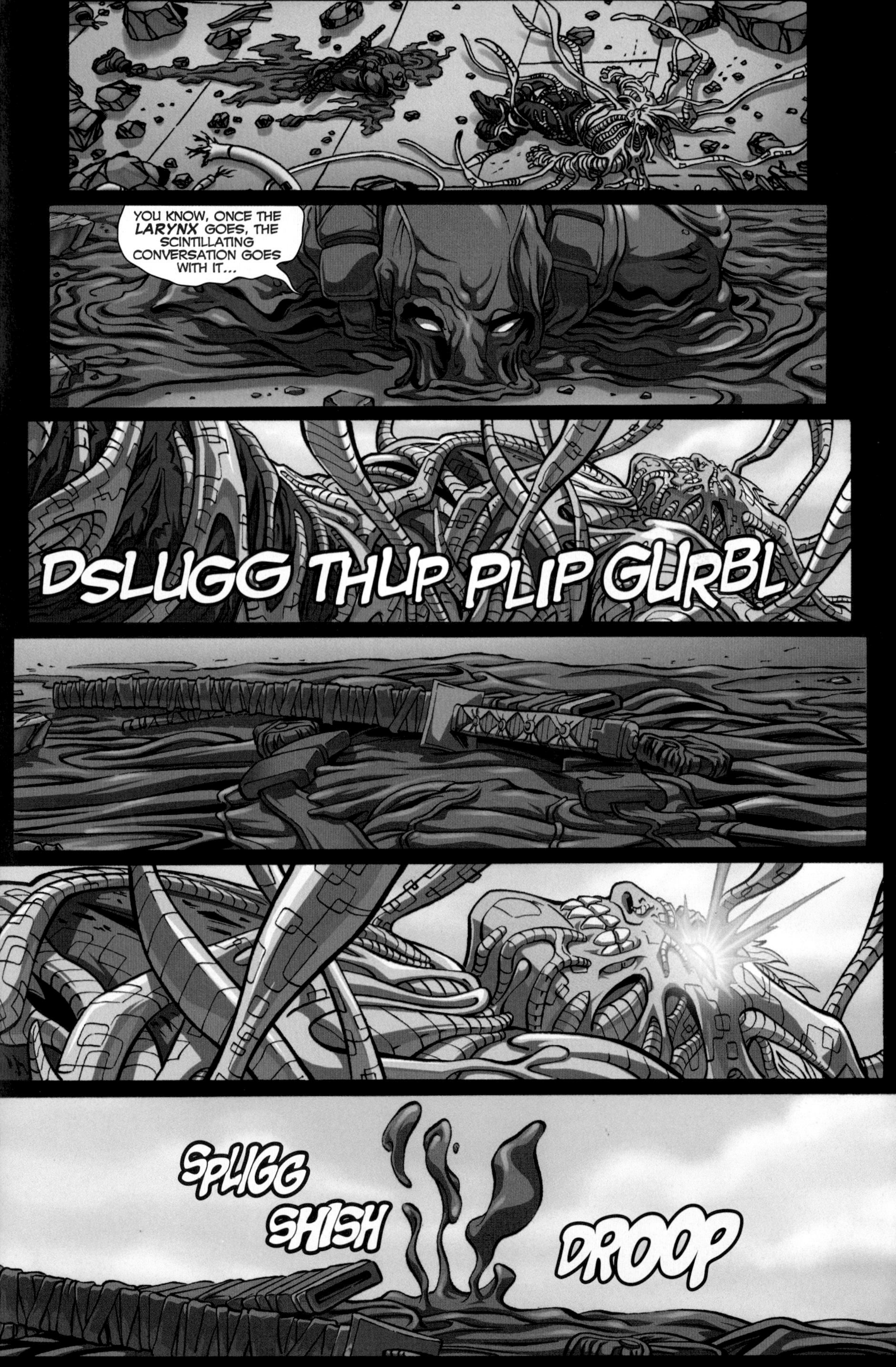
YOU KNOW, ONCE THE LARYNX GOES, THE SCINTILLATING CONVERSATION GOES WITH IT...
DSLUGG THUP PLIP GURBL
SPLIGG
SHISH
DROOP

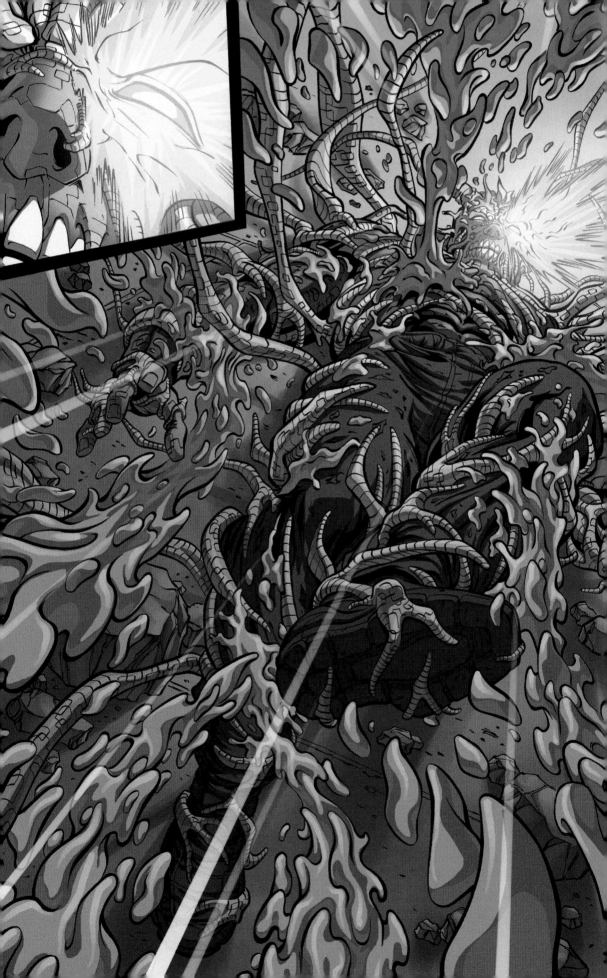

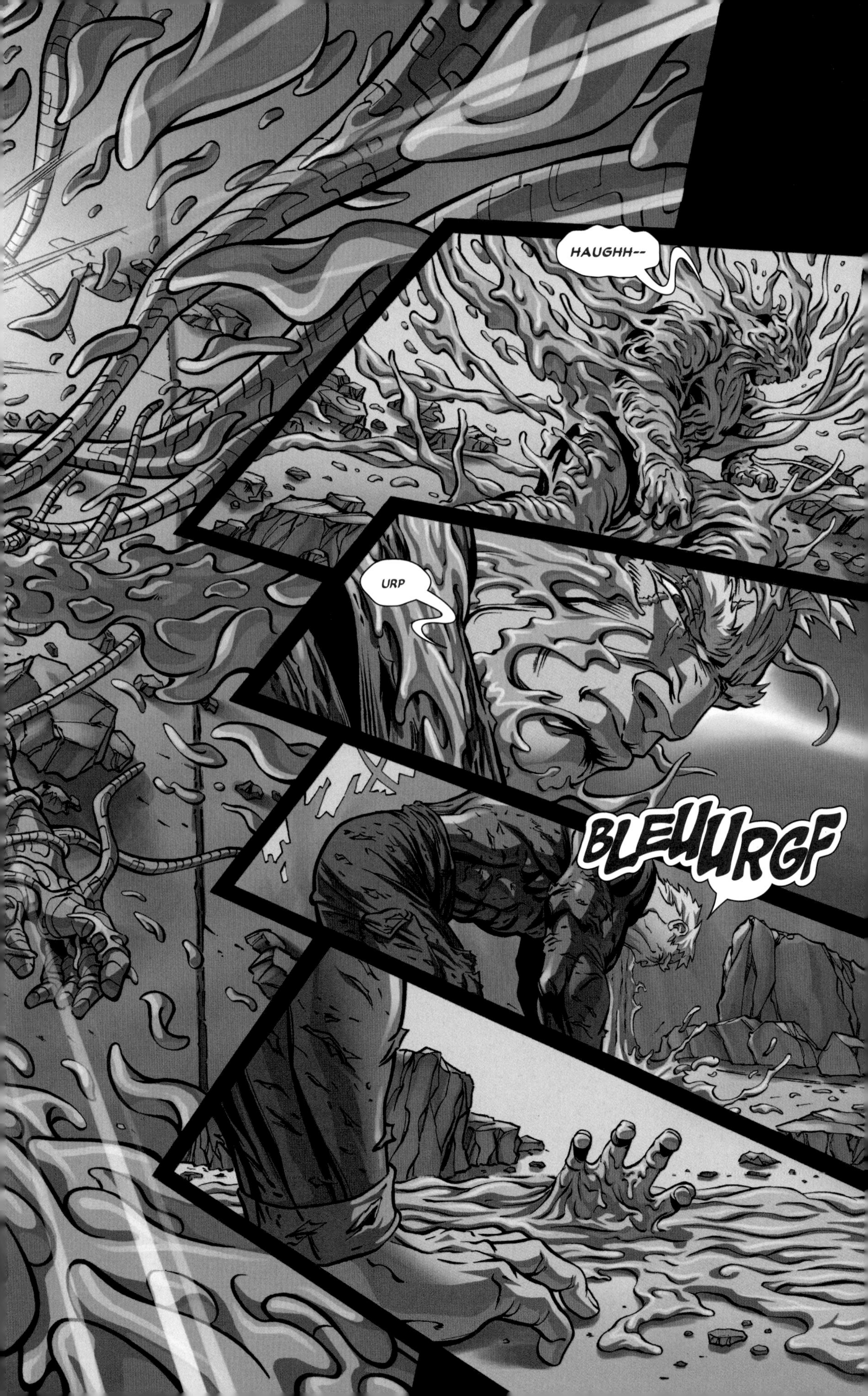
HAUGHH--
URP
BLEUURGF

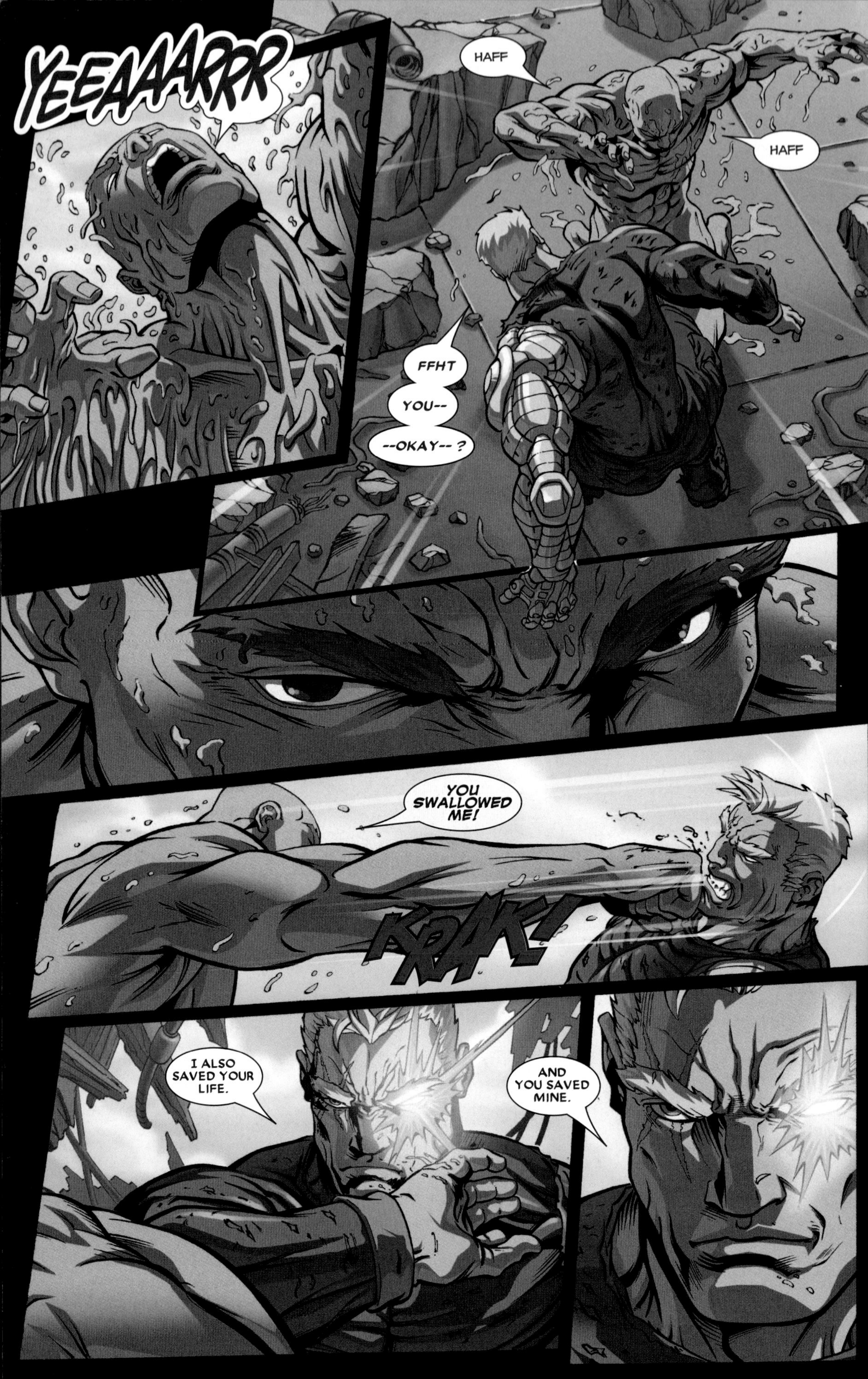
YEEAAARRR
HAFF
HAFF
FFHT
YOU--
--OKAY-- ?
YOU SWALLOWED ME!
KRAK!
I ALSO SAVED YOUR LIFE.
AND YOU SAVED MINE.

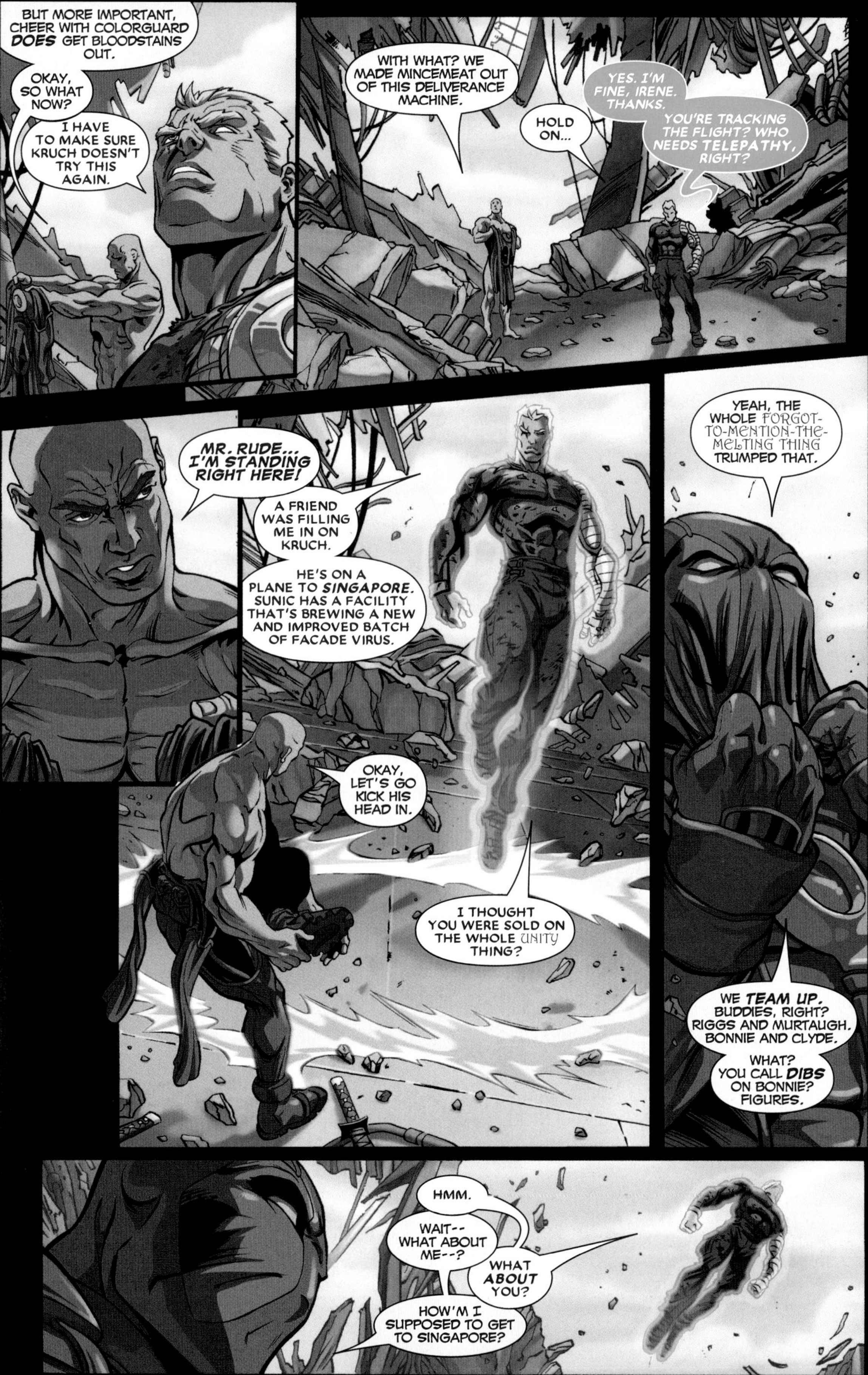
BUT MORE IMPORTANT, CHEER WITH COLORGUARD DOES GET BLOODSTAINS OUT.
OKAY, SO WHAT NOW?
I HAVE TO MAKE SURE KRUCH DOESN'T TRY THIS AGAIN.
WITH WHAT? WE MADE MINCEMEAT OUT OF THIS DELIVERANCE MACHINE.
HOLD ON...
YES. I'M FINE, IRENE. THANKS.
YOU'RE TRACKING THE FLIGHT? WHO NEEDS TELEPATHY, RIGHT?
MR. RUDE... I'M STANDING RIGHT HERE!
A FRIEND WAS FILLING ME IN ON KRUCH.
HE'S ON A PLANE TO SINGAPORE. SUNIC HAS A FACILITY THAT'S BREWING A NEW AND IMPROVED BATCH OF FACADE VIRUS.
OKAY, LET'S GO KICK HIS HEAD IN.
I THOUGHT YOU WERE SOLD ON THE WHOLE UNITY THING?
YEAH, THE WHOLE FORGOT-TO-MENTION-THE-MELTING THING TRUMPED THAT.
WE TEAM UP. BUDDIES, RIGHT? RIGGS AND MURTAUGH. BONNIE AND CLYDE.
WHAT? YOU CALL DIBS ON BONNIE? FIGURES.
HMM.
WAIT-- WHAT ABOUT ME--?
WHAT ABOUT YOU?
HOW'M I SUPPOSED TO GET TO SINGAPORE?

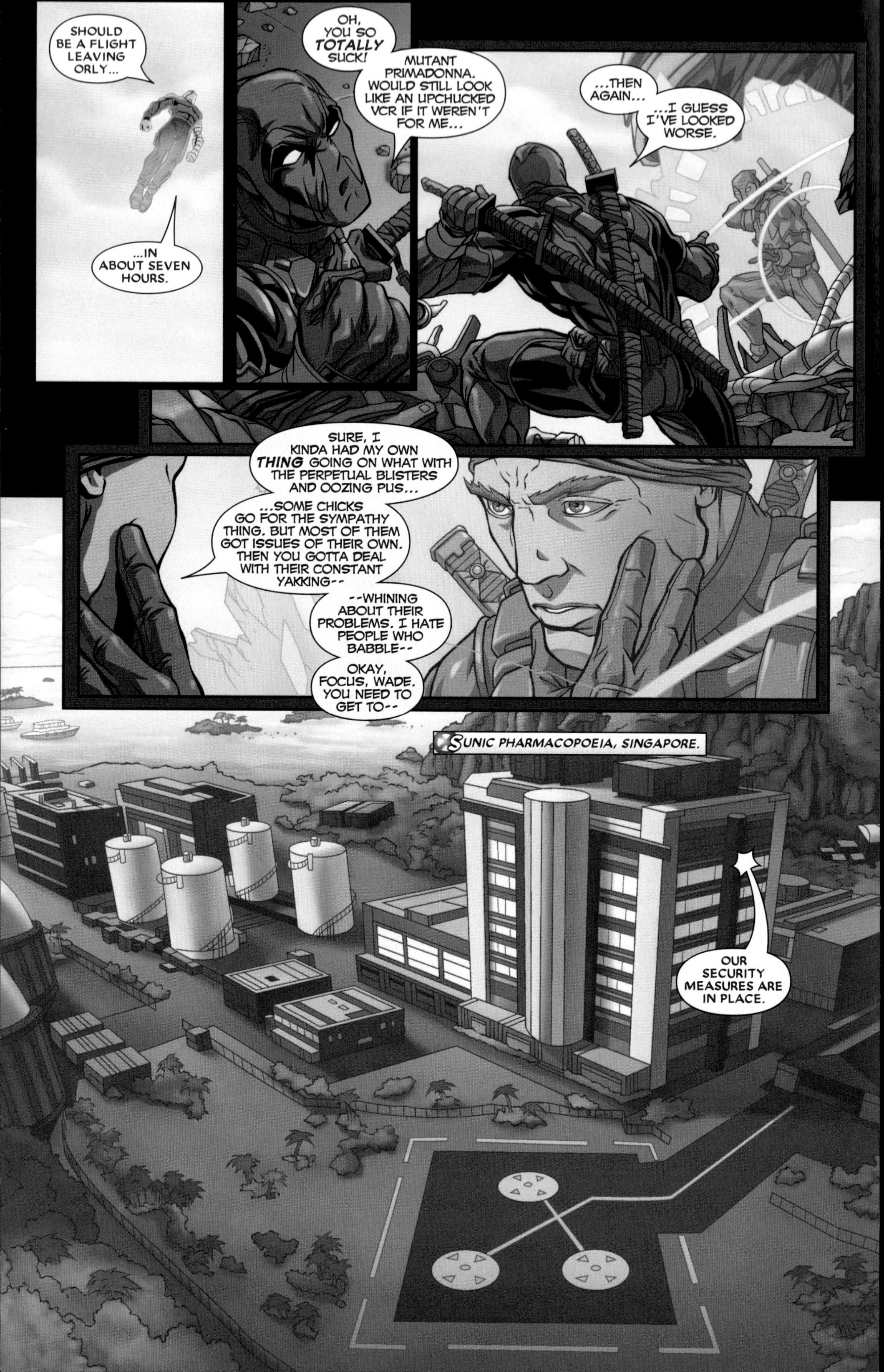
SHOULD BE A FLIGHT LEAVING ORLY...
...IN ABOUT SEVEN HOURS.
OH, YOU SO TOTALLY SUCK!
MUTANT PRIMADONNA. WOULD STILL LOOK LIKE AN UPCHUCKED VCR IF IT WEREN'T FOR ME...
...THEN AGAIN...
...I GUESS I'VE LOOKED WORSE.
SURE, I KINDA HAD MY OWN THING GOING ON WHAT WITH THE PERPETUAL BLISTERS AND OOZING PUS...
...SOME CHICKS GO FOR THE SYMPATHY THING. BUT MOST OF THEM GOT ISSUES OF THEIR OWN. THEN YOU GOTTA DEAL WITH THEIR CONSTANT YAKKING--
--WHINING ABOUT THEIR PROBLEMS. I HATE PEOPLE WHO BABBLE--
OKAY, FOCUS, WADE. YOU NEED TO GET TO--
SUNIC PHARMACOPOEIA, SINGAPORE.
OUR SECURITY MEASURES ARE IN PLACE.

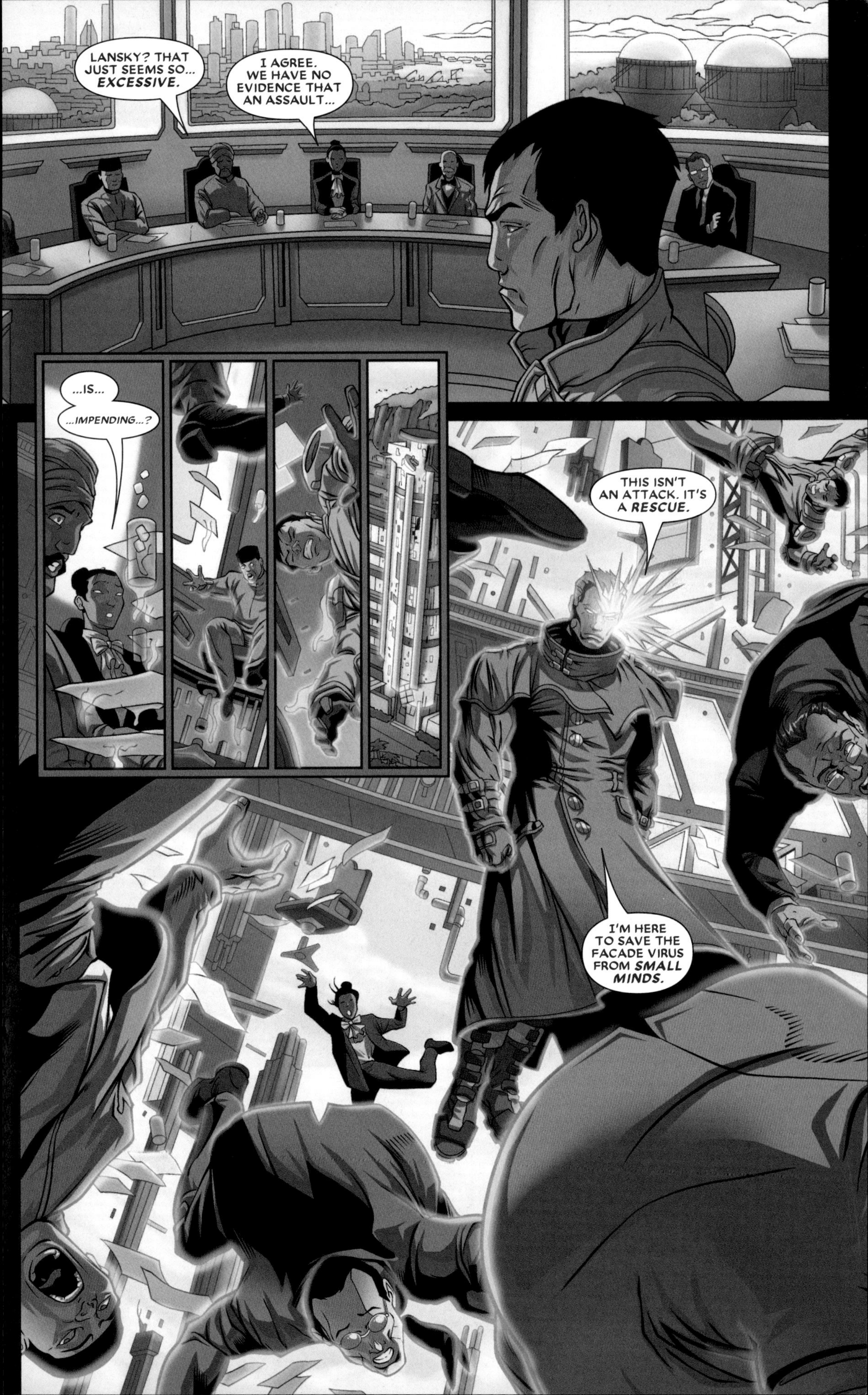
LANSKY? THAT JUST SEEMS SO... EXCESSIVE.
I AGREE. WE HAVE NO EVIDENCE THAT AN ASSAULT...
...IS...
...IMPENDING...?
THIS ISN'T AN ATTACK. IT'S A RESCUE.
I'M HERE TO SAVE THE FACADE VIRUS FROM SMALL MINDS.

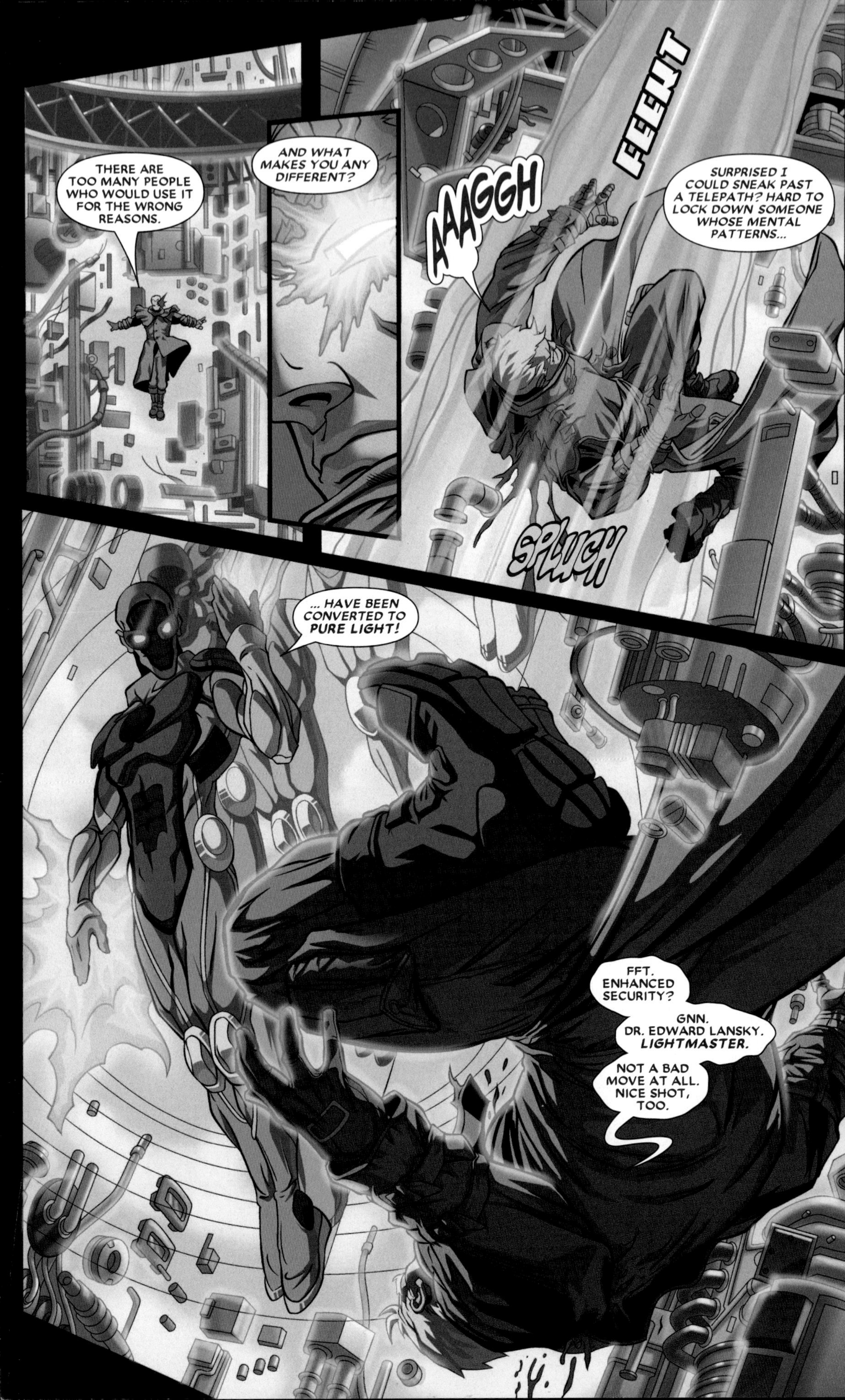
THERE ARE TOO MANY PEOPLE WHO WOULD USE IT FOR THE WRONG REASONS.
AND WHAT MAKES YOU ANY DIFFERENT?
FEERT
AAAGGH
SURPRISED I COULD SNEAK PAST A TELEPATH? HARD TO LOCK DOWN SOMEONE WHOSE MENTAL PATTERNS...
SPLUCH
... HAVE BEEN CONVERTED TO PURE LIGHT!
FFT. ENHANCED SECURITY?
GNN. DR. EDWARD LANSKY. LIGHTMASTER.
NOT A BAD MOVE AT ALL. NICE SHOT, TOO.

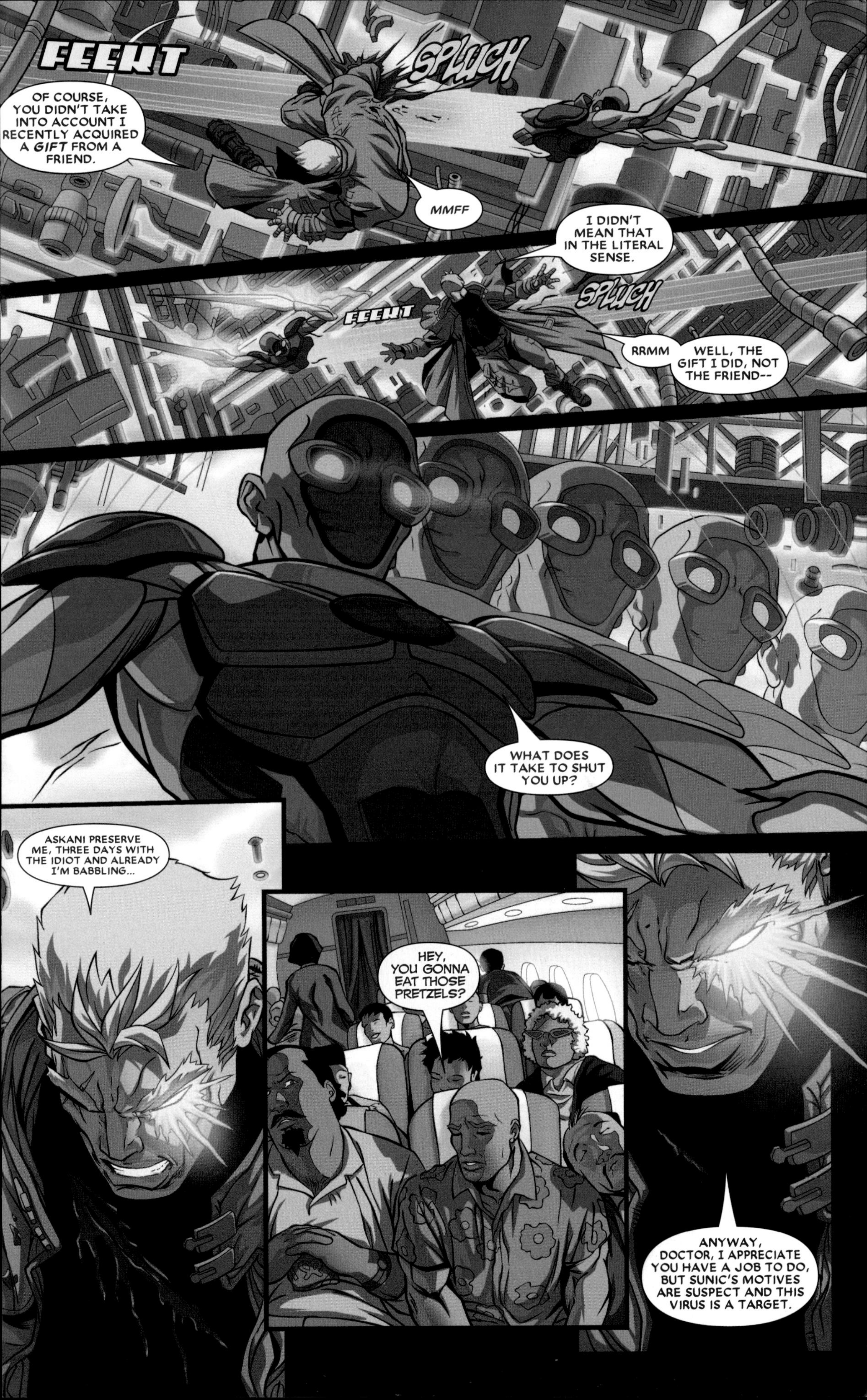
FEERT
SPLUCH
OF COURSE, YOU DIDN'T TAKE INTO ACCOUNT I RECENTLY ACQUIRED A GIFT FROM A FRIEND.
MMFF
I DIDN'T MEAN THAT IN THE LITERAL SENSE.
SPLUCH
FEERT
RRMM
WELL, THE GIFT I DID, NOT THE FRIEND--
WHAT DOES IT TAKE TO SHUT YOU UP?
ASKANI PRESERVE ME, THREE DAYS WITH THE IDIOT AND ALREADY I'M BABBLING...
HEY, YOU GONNA EAT THOSE PRETZELS?
ANYWAY, DOCTOR, I APPRECIATE YOU HAVE A JOB TO DO, BUT SUNIC'S MOTIVES ARE SUSPECT AND THIS VIRUS IS A TARGET.

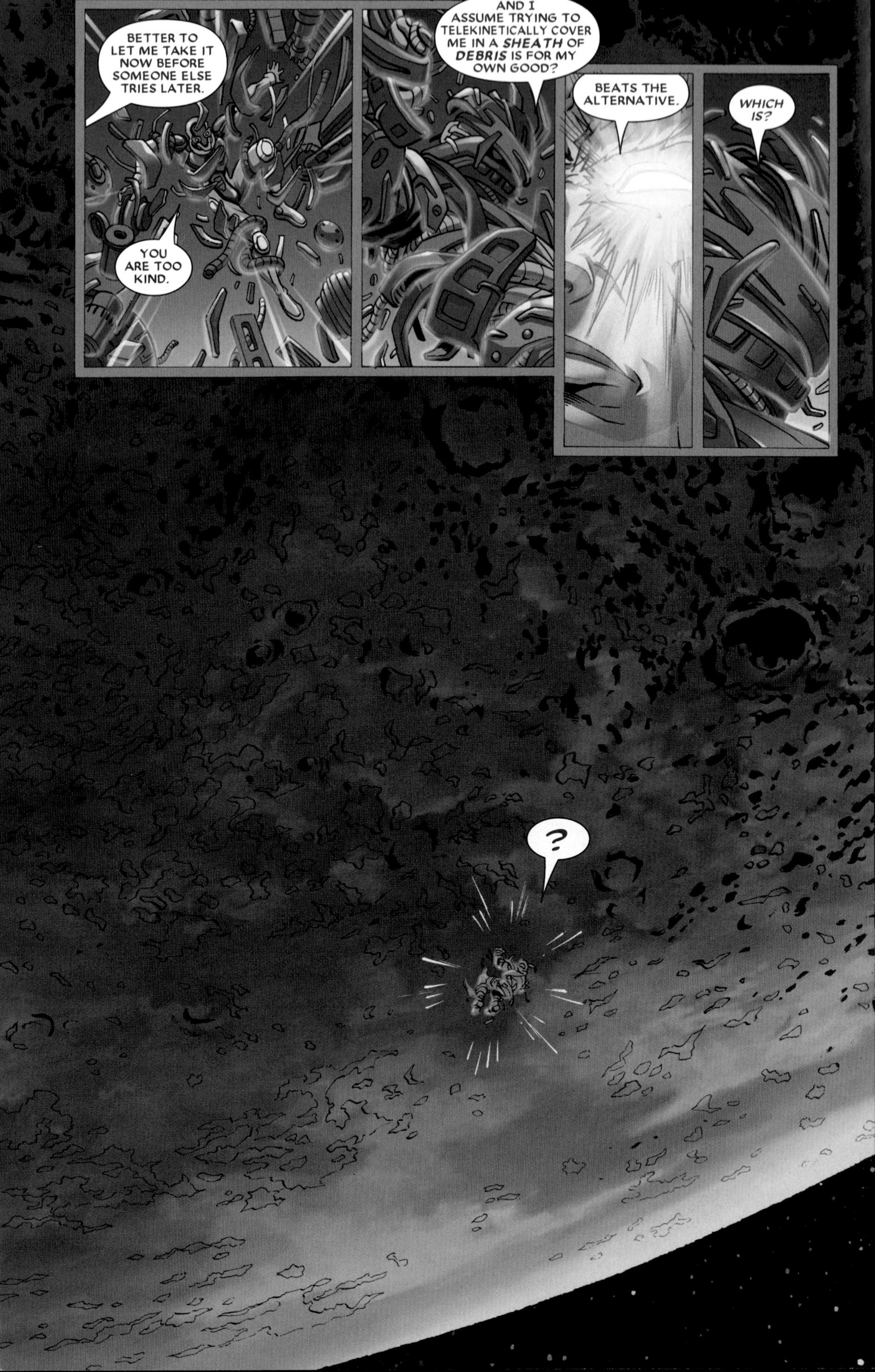
BETTER TO LET ME TAKE IT NOW BEFORE SOMEONE ELSE TRIES LATER.
YOU ARE TOO KIND.
AND I ASSUME TRYING TO TELEKINETICALLY COVER ME IN A SHEATH OF DEBRIS IS FOR MY OWN GOOD?
BEATS THE ALTERNATIVE.
WHICH IS?
?

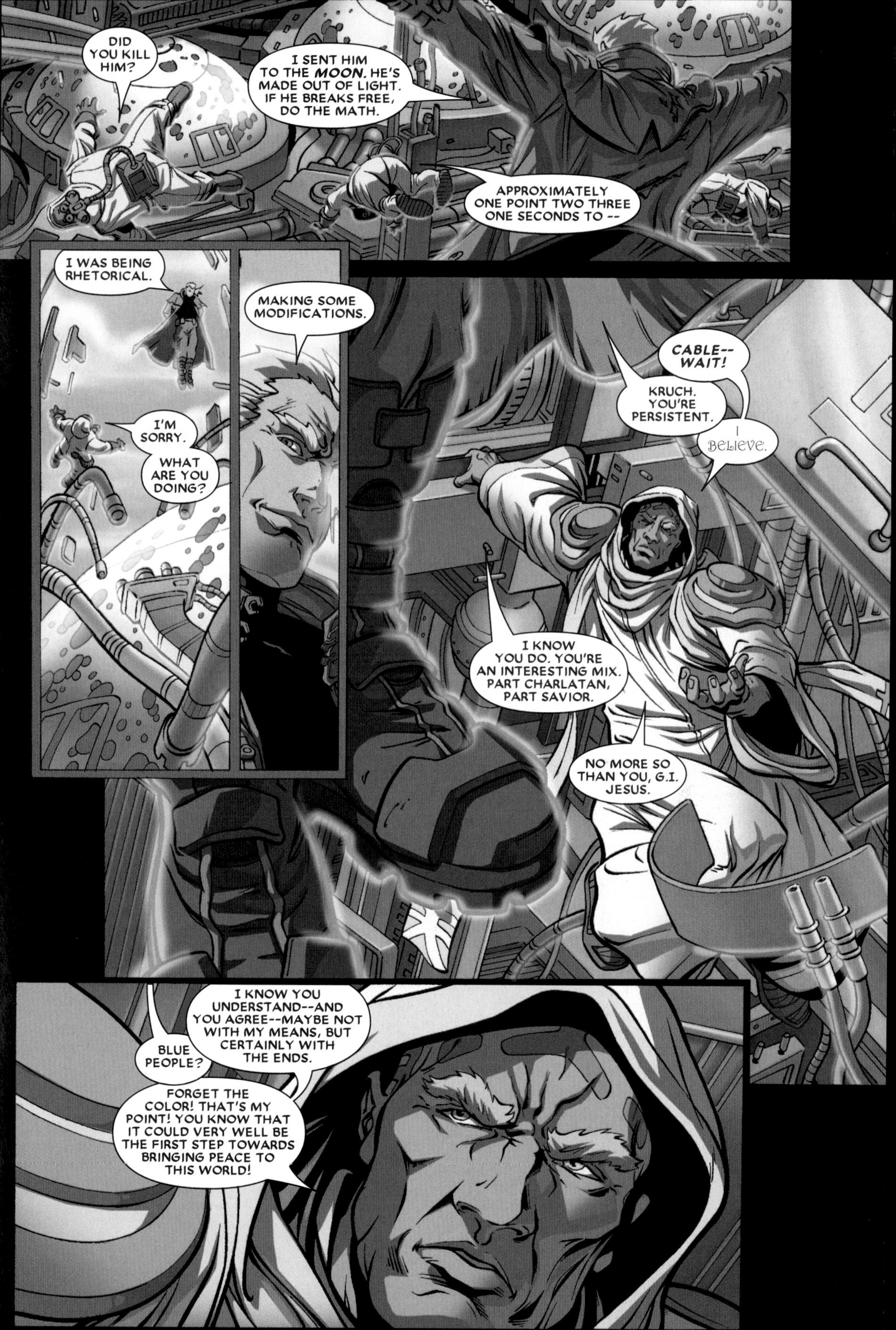
DID YOU KILL HIM?
I SENT HIM TO THE MOON. HE'S MADE OUT OF LIGHT. IF HE BREAKS FREE, DO THE MATH.
APPROXIMATELY ONE POINT TWO THREE ONE SECONDS TO --
I WAS BEING RHETORICAL.
I'M SORRY.
WHAT ARE YOU DOING?
MAKING SOME MODIFICATIONS.
CABLE-- WAIT!
KRUCH. YOU'RE PERSISTENT.
I BELIEVE.
I KNOW YOU DO. YOU'RE AN INTERESTING MIX. PART CHARLATAN, PART SAVIOR.
NO MORE SO THAN YOU, G.I. JESUS.
BLUE PEOPLE?
I KNOW YOU UNDERSTAND--AND YOU AGREE--MAYBE NOT WITH MY MEANS, BUT CERTAINLY WITH THE ENDS.
FORGET THE COLOR! THAT'S MY POINT! YOU KNOW THAT IT COULD VERY WELL BE THE FIRST STEP TOWARDS BRINGING PEACE TO THIS WORLD!

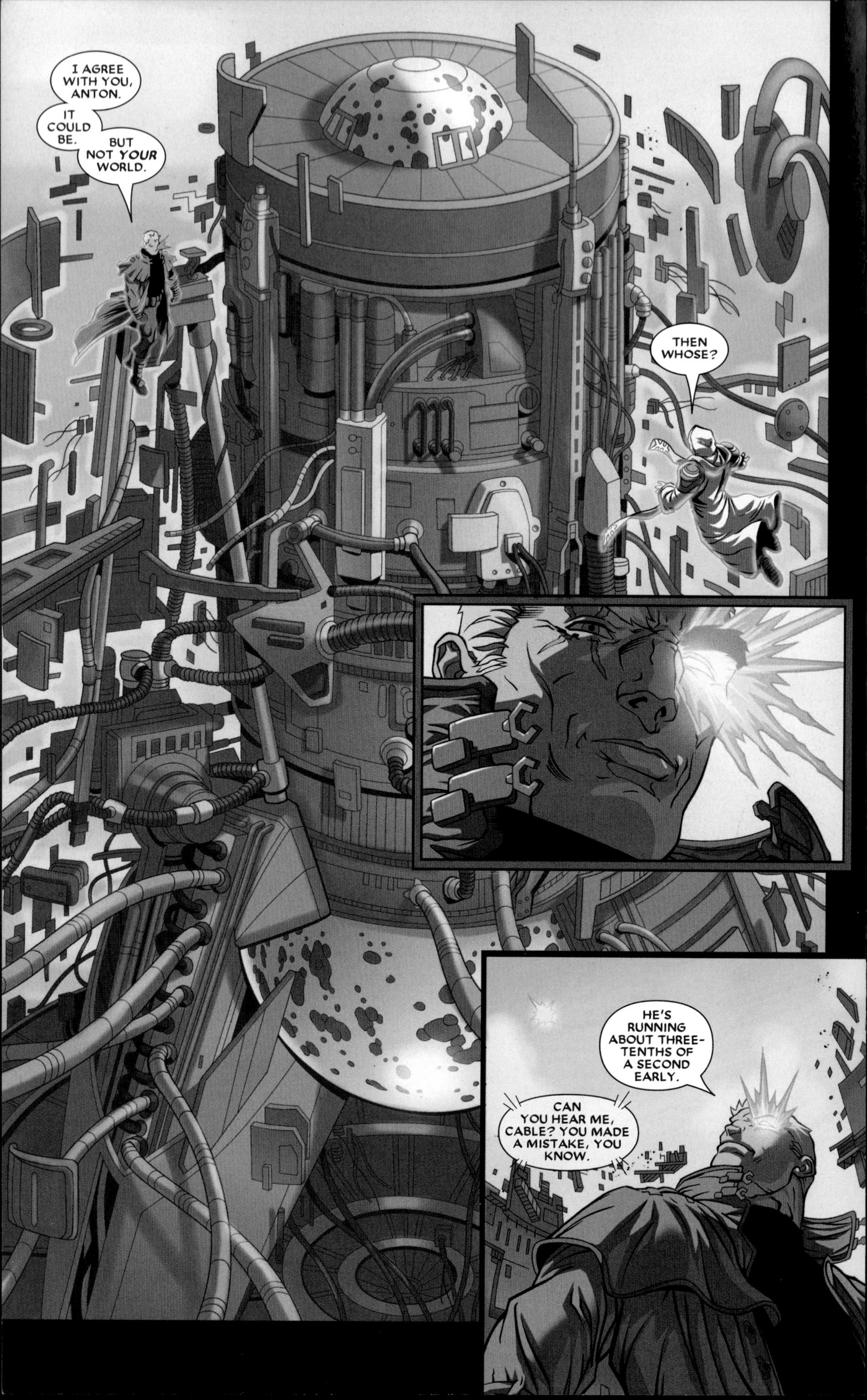
I AGREE WITH YOU, ANTON.
IT COULD BE.
BUT NOT YOUR WORLD.
THEN WHOSE?
HE'S RUNNING ABOUT THREE-TENTHS OF A SECOND EARLY.
CAN YOU HEAR ME, CABLE? YOU MADE A MISTAKE, YOU KNOW.

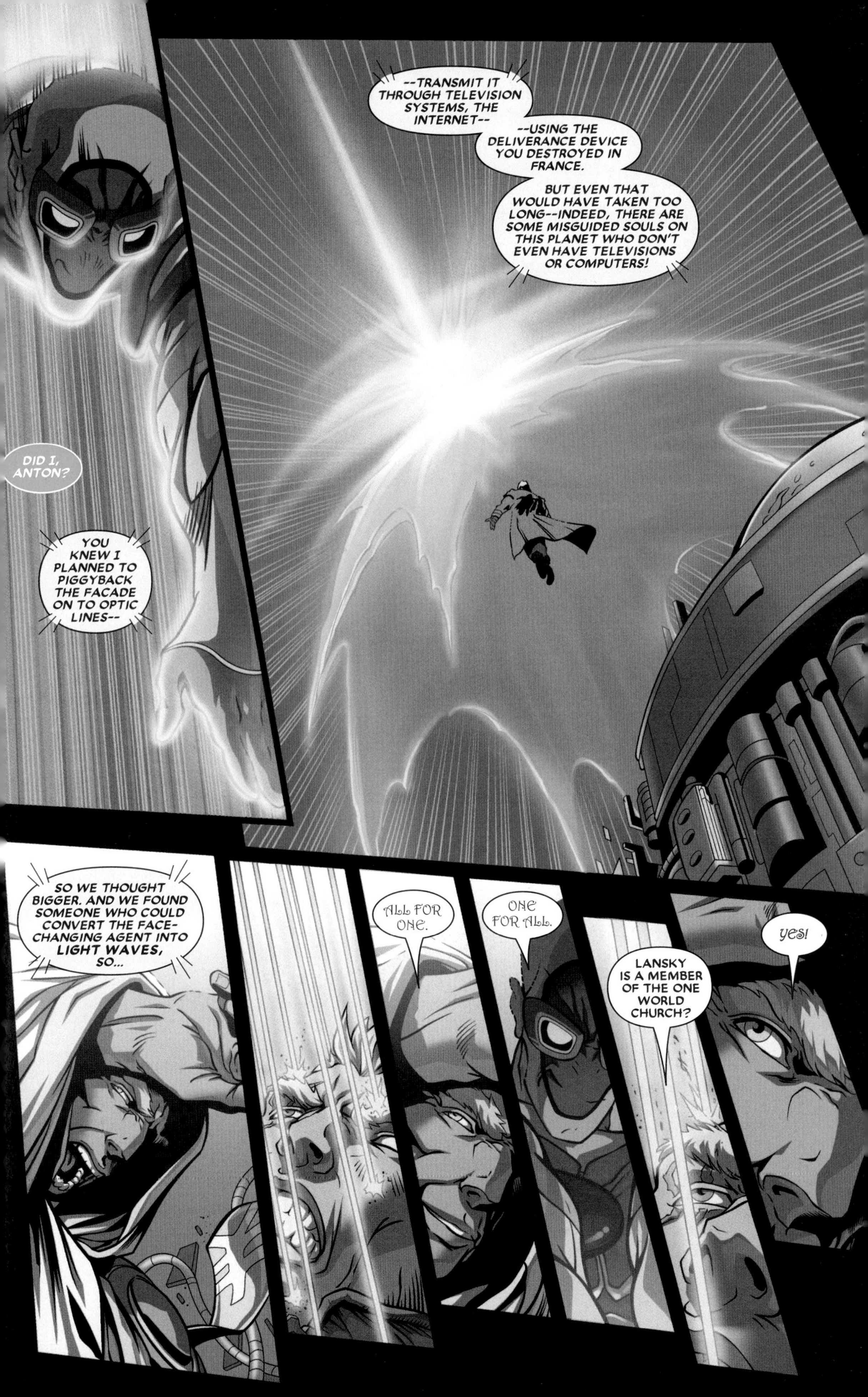
--TRANSMIT IT THROUGH TELEVISION SYSTEMS, THE INTERNET--
--USING THE DELIVERANCE DEVICE YOU DESTROYED IN FRANCE.
BUT EVEN THAT WOULD HAVE TAKEN TOO LONG--INDEED, THERE ARE SOME MISGUIDED SOULS ON THIS PLANET WHO DON'T EVEN HAVE TELEVISIONS OR COMPUTERS!
DID I, ANTON?
YOU KNEW I PLANNED TO PIGGYBACK THE FACADE ON TO OPTIC LINES--
SO WE THOUGHT BIGGER. AND WE FOUND SOMEONE WHO COULD CONVERT THE FACE-CHANGING AGENT INTO LIGHT WAVES, SO...
ALL FOR ONE.
ONE FOR ALL.
LANSKY IS A MEMBER OF THE ONE WORLD CHURCH?
YES!

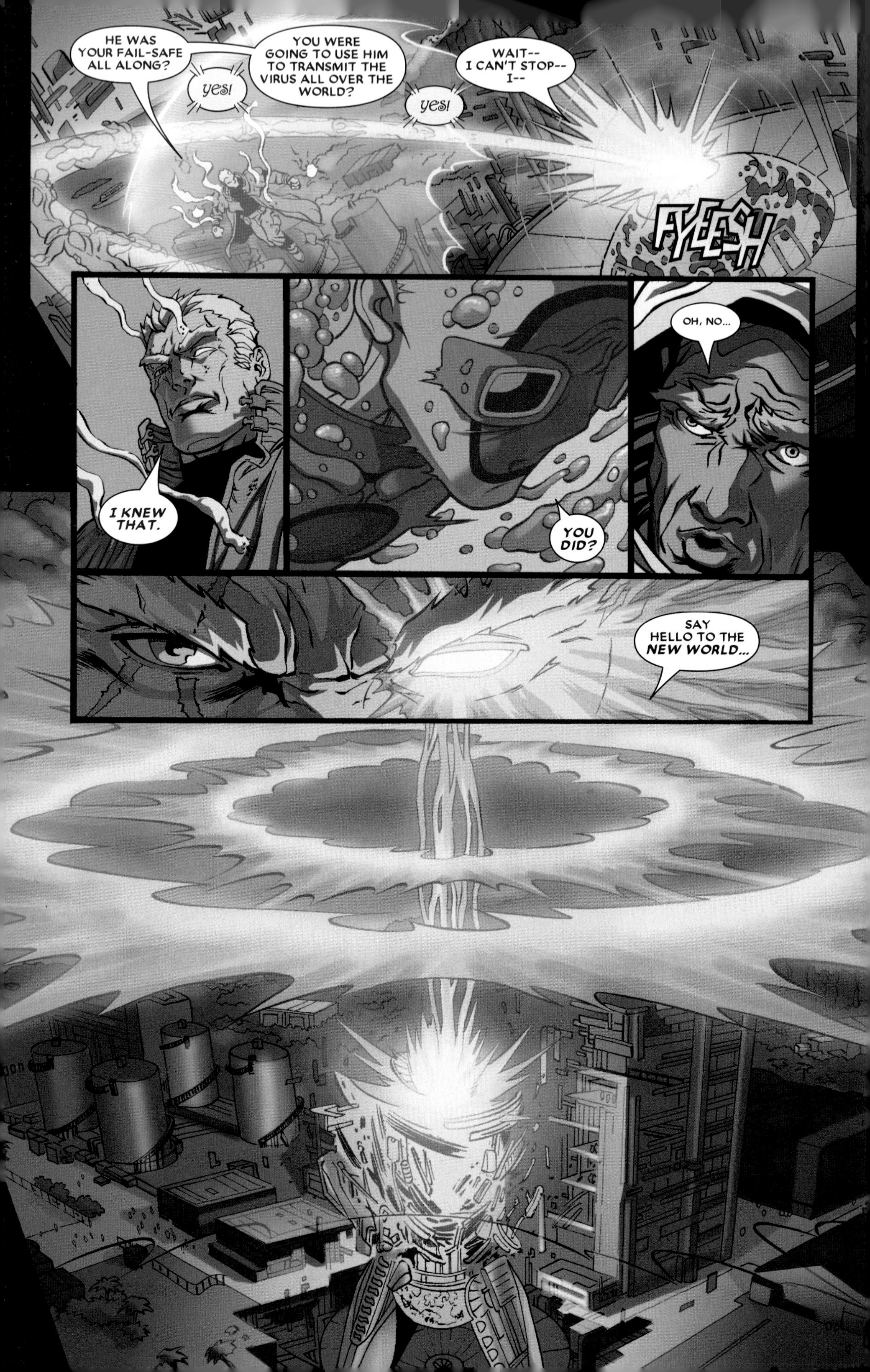
HE WAS YOUR FAIL-SAFE ALL ALONG?
YES!
YOU WERE GOING TO USE HIM TO TRANSMIT THE VIRUS ALL OVER THE WORLD?
YES!
WAIT-- I CAN'T STOP-- I--
FYEESH
I KNEW THAT.
YOU DID?
OH, NO...
SAY HELLO TO THE NEW WORLD...

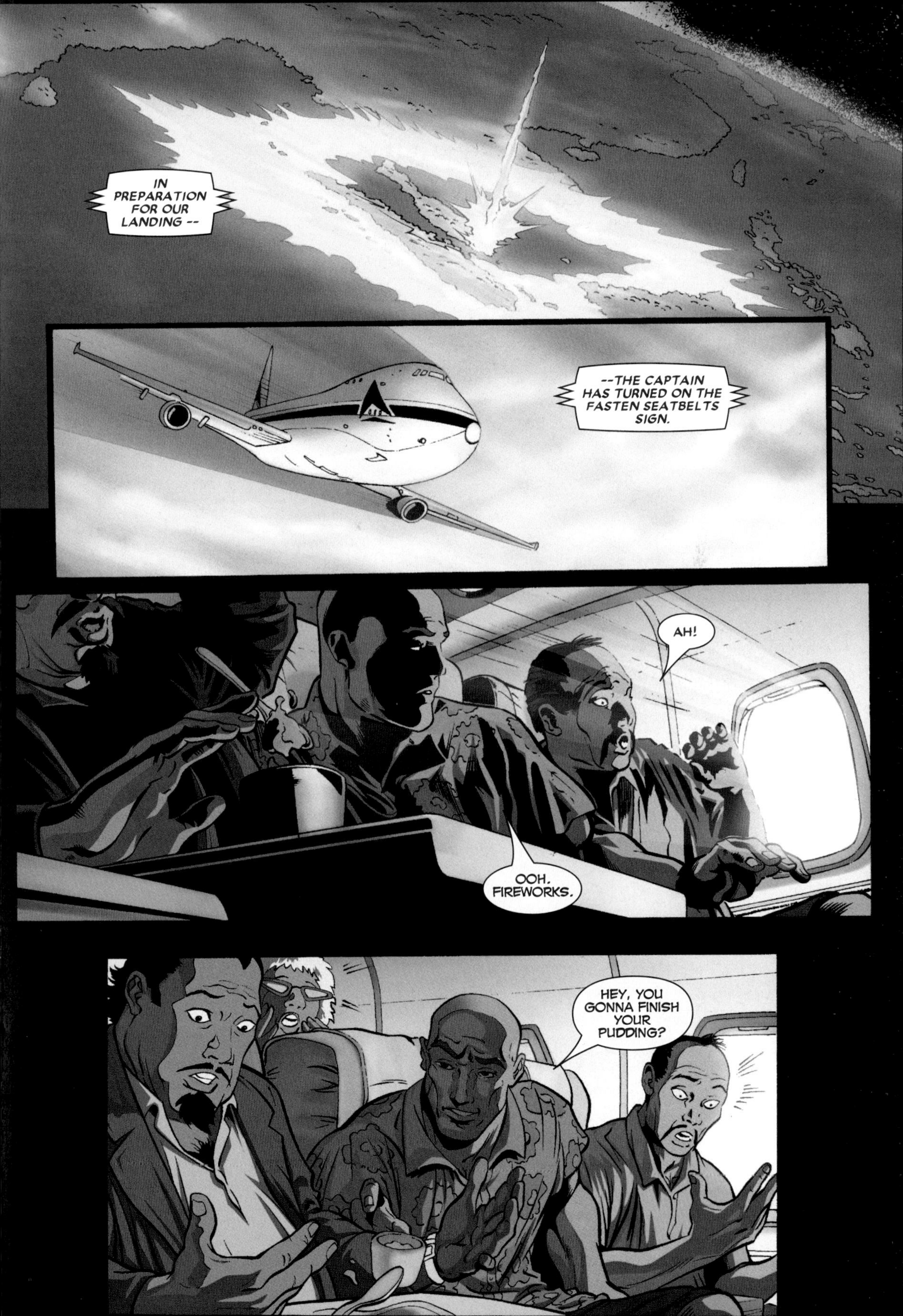
IN PREPARATION FOR OUR LANDING --
--THE CAPTAIN HAS TURNED ON THE FASTEN SEATBELTS SIGN.
AH!
OOH. FIREWORKS.
HEY, YOU GONNA FINISH YOUR PUDDING?

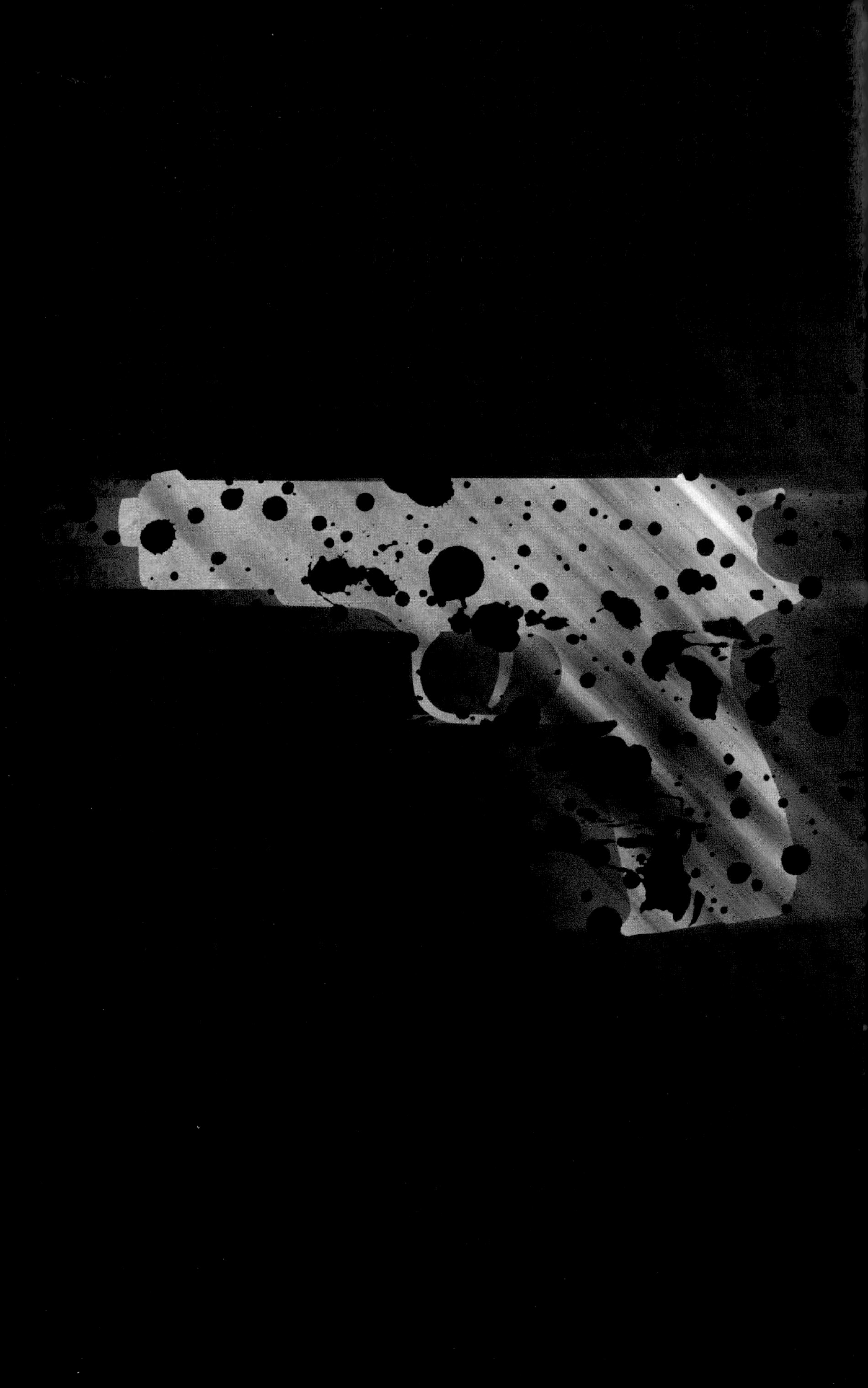

6

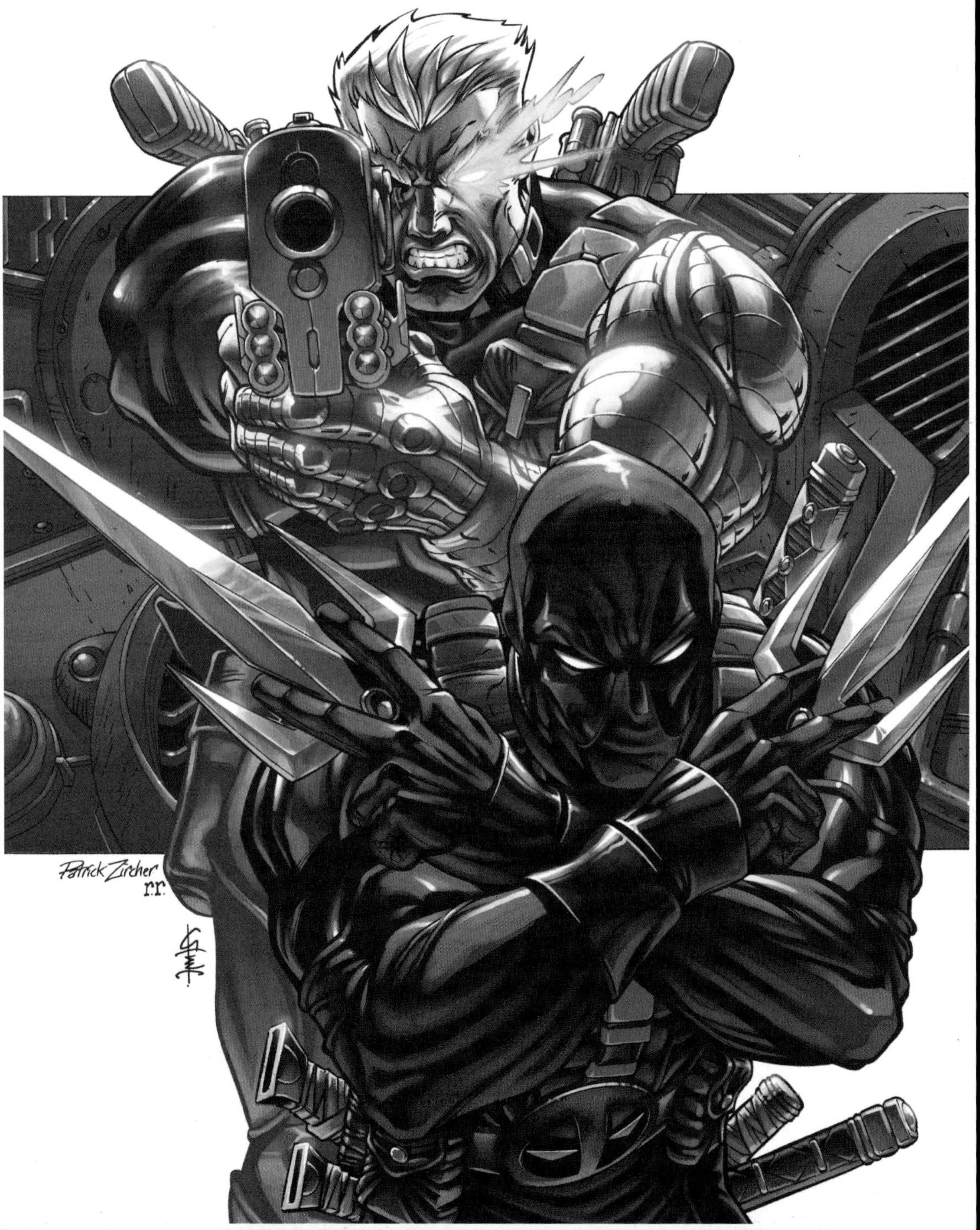
Patrick Zircher
r.r.

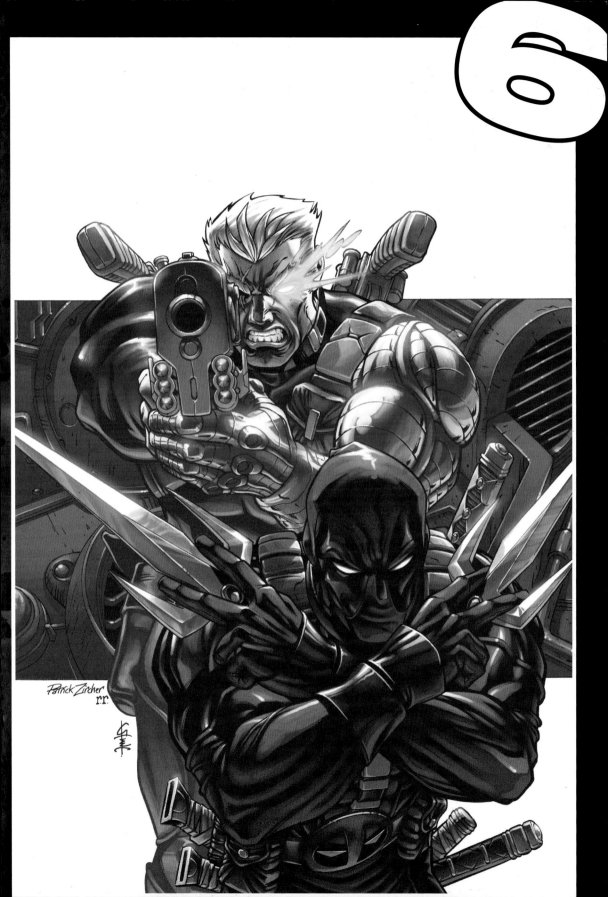

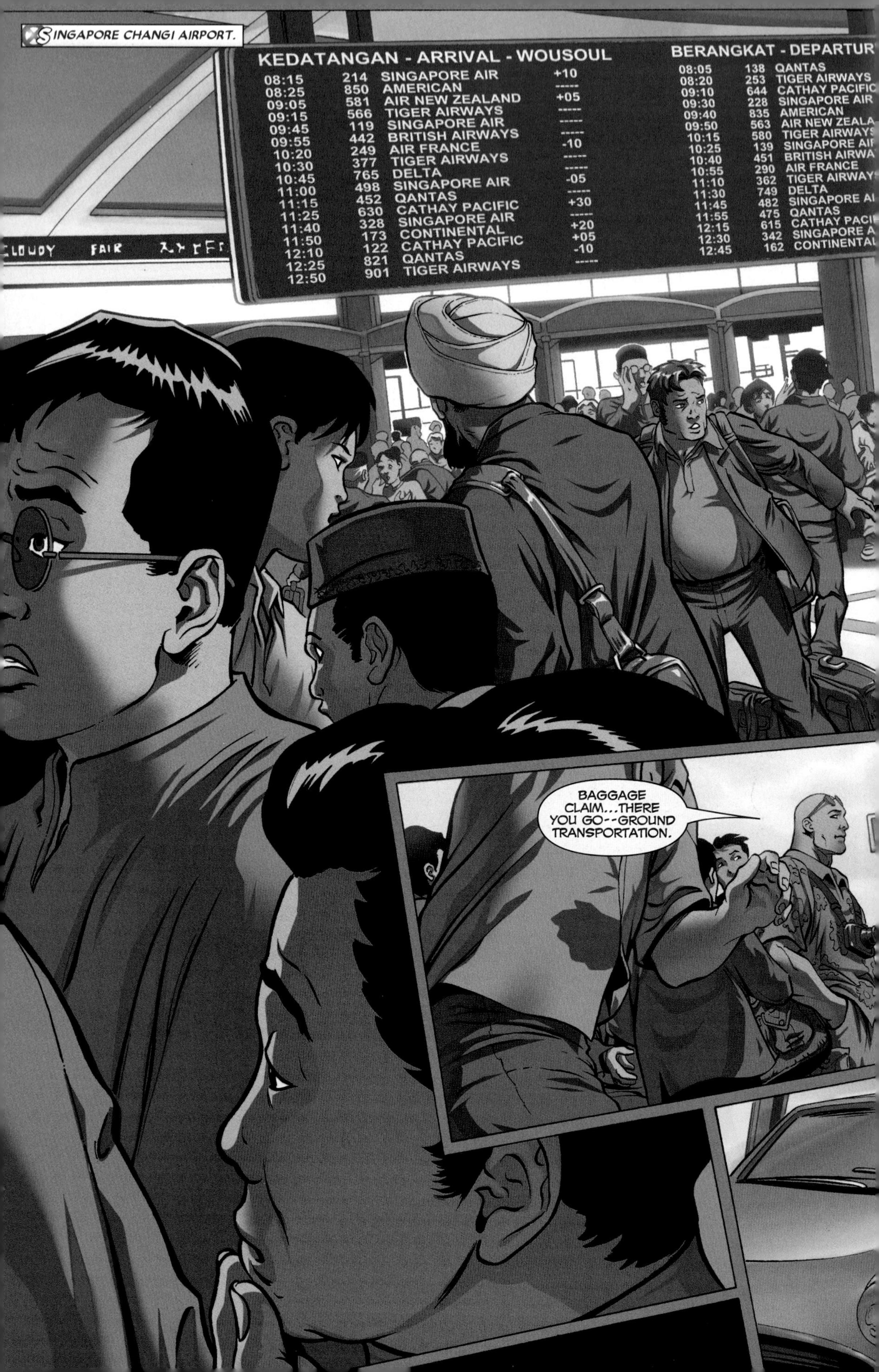
SINGAPORE CHANGI AIRPORT.
KEDATANGAN - ARRIVAL - WOUSOUL
08:15 214 SINGAPORE AIR +10
08:25 850 AMERICAN -----
09:05 581 AIR NEW ZEALAND +05
09:15 566 TIGER AIRWAYS -----
09:45 119 SINGAPORE AIR -----
09:55 442 BRITISH AIRWAYS -----
10:20 249 AIR FRANCE -10
10:30 377 TIGER AIRWAYS -----
10:45 765 DELTA -----
11:00 498 SINGAPORE AIR -05
11:15 452 QANTAS -----
11:25 630 CATHAY PACIFIC +30
11:40 328 SINGAPORE AIR -----
11:50 173 CONTINENTAL +20
12:10 122 CATHAY PACIFIC +05
12:25 821 QANTAS -10
12:50 901 TIGER AIRWAYS -----
BERANGKAT - DEPARTUR
08:05 138 QANTAS
08:20 253 TIGER AIRWAYS
09:10 644 CATHAY PACIFIC
09:30 228 SINGAPORE AIR
09:40 835 AMERICAN
09:50 563 AIR NEW ZEALA
10:15 580 TIGER AIRWAYS
10:25 139 SINGAPORE AI
10:40 451 BRITISH AIRWA
10:55 290 AIR FRANCE
11:10 362 TIGER AIRWAY
11:30 749 DELTA
11:45 482 SINGAPORE AI
11:55 475 QANTAS
12:15 615 CATHAY PACI
12:30 342 SINGAPORE A
12:45 162 CONTINENTAL
CLOUDY FAIR
BAGGAGE CLAIM...THERE YOU GO--GROUND TRANSPORTATION.

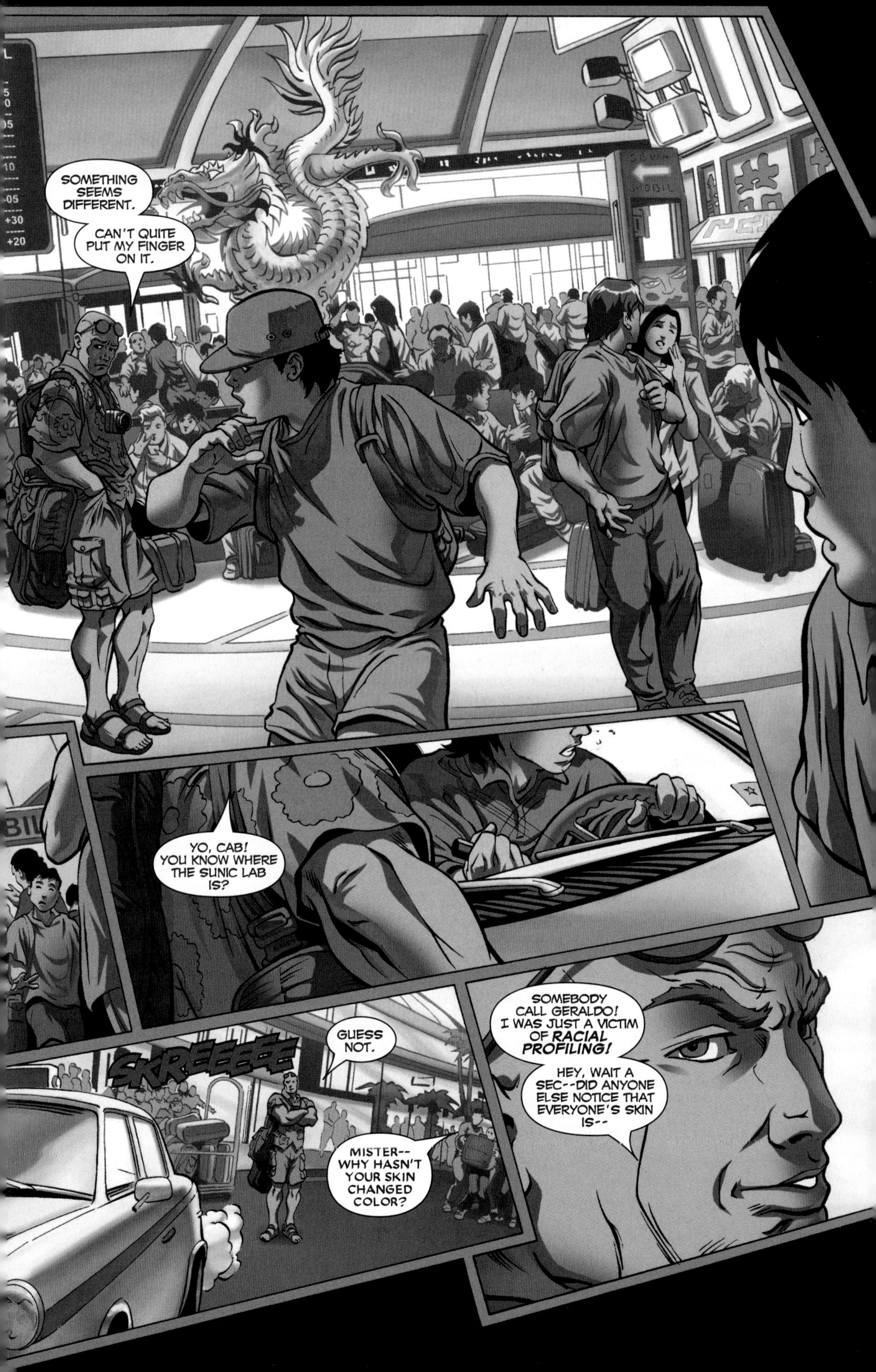
SOMETHING SEEMS DIFFERENT.
CAN'T QUITE PUT MY FINGER ON IT.
YO, CAB! YOU KNOW WHERE THE SUNIC LAB IS?
SKREEEEE
GUESS NOT.
MISTER-- WHY HASN'T YOUR SKIN CHANGED COLOR?
SOMEBODY CALL GERALDO! I WAS JUST A VICTIM OF *RACIAL PROFILING!*
HEY, WAIT A SEC--DID ANYONE ELSE NOTICE THAT EVERYONE'S SKIN IS--

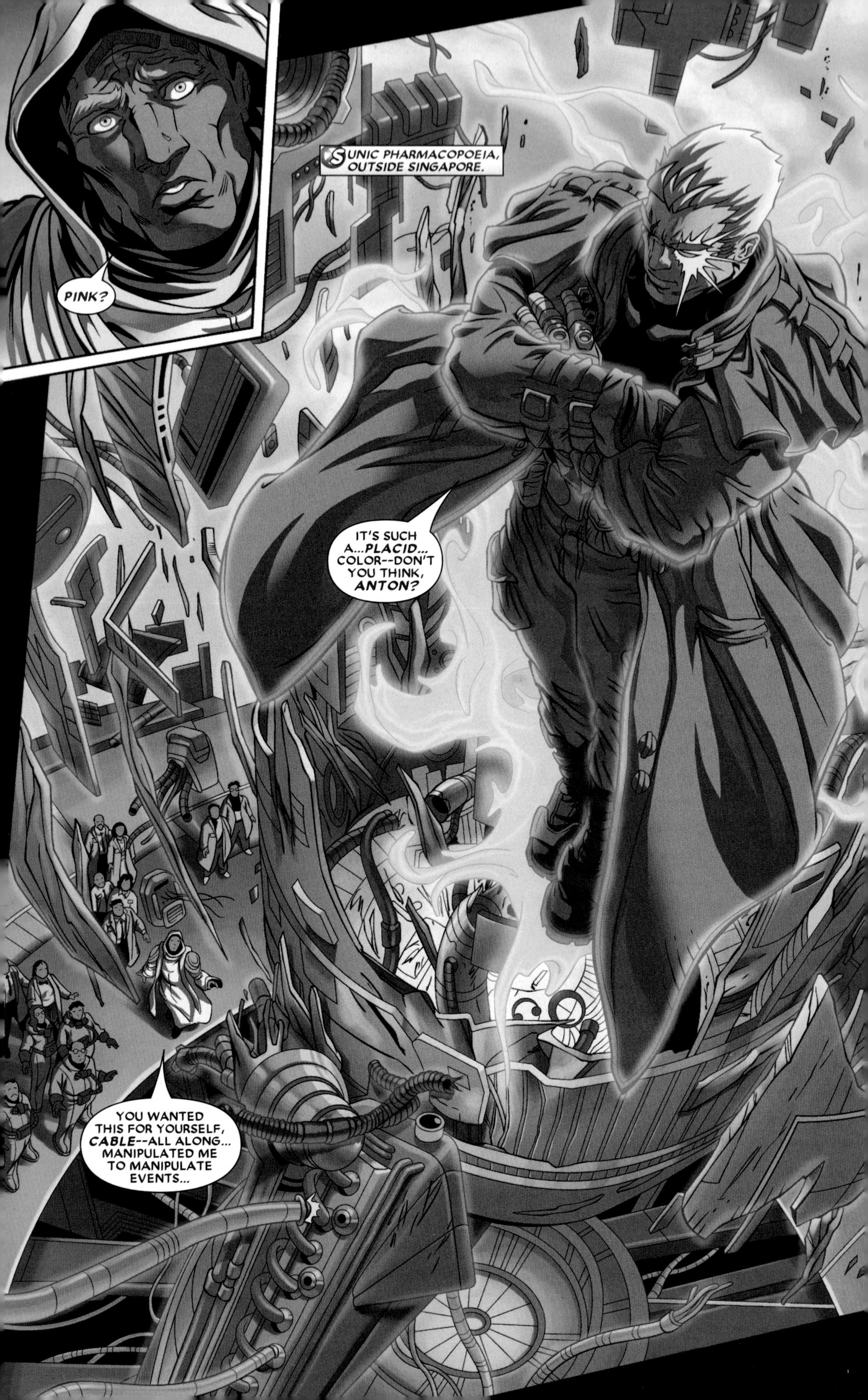
PINK?
SUNIC PHARMACOPOEIA, OUTSIDE SINGAPORE.
IT'S SUCH A...PLACID... COLOR--DON'T YOU THINK, ANTON?
YOU WANTED THIS FOR YOURSELF, CABLE--ALL ALONG... MANIPULATED ME TO MANIPULATE EVENTS...

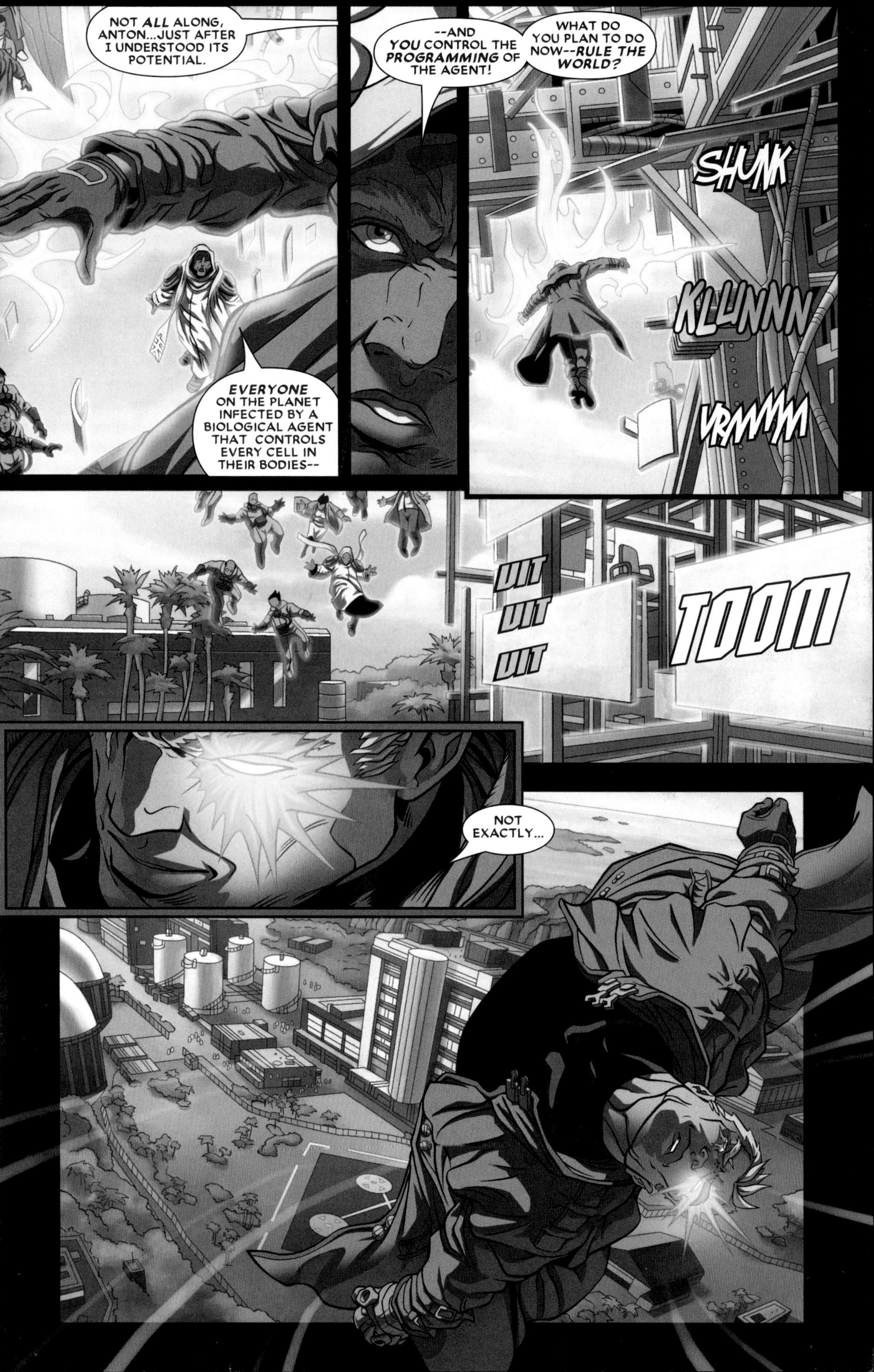
NOT ALL ALONG, ANTON...JUST AFTER I UNDERSTOOD ITS POTENTIAL.
EVERYONE ON THE PLANET INFECTED BY A BIOLOGICAL AGENT THAT CONTROLS EVERY CELL IN THEIR BODIES--
--AND YOU CONTROL THE PROGRAMMING OF THE AGENT!
WHAT DO YOU PLAN TO DO NOW--RULE THE WORLD?
SHUNK
KLUNNN
VRMMM
VIT
VIT
VIT
TOOM
NOT EXACTLY...

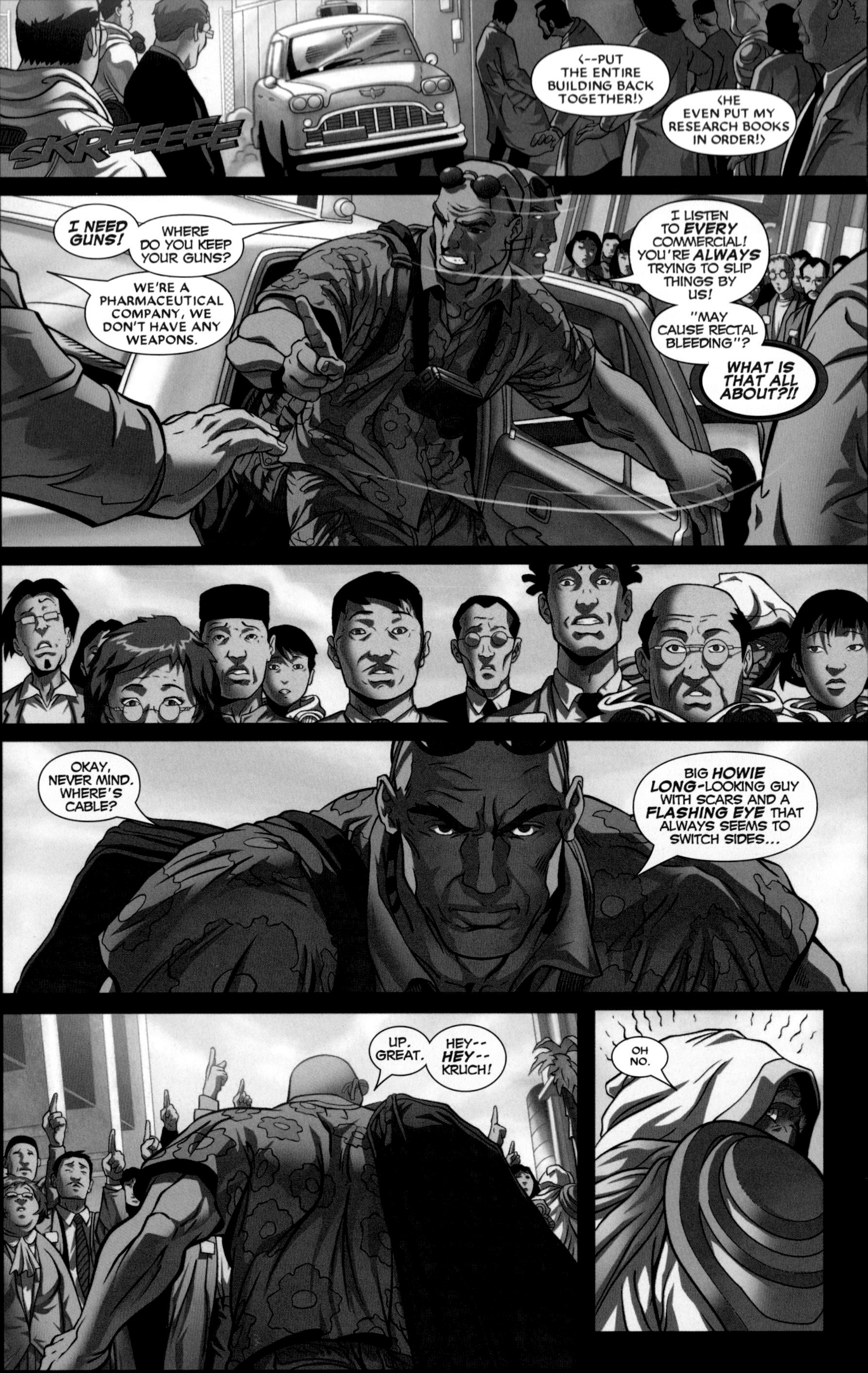
SKREEEEEE
<--PUT THE ENTIRE BUILDING BACK TOGETHER!>
<HE EVEN PUT MY RESEARCH BOOKS IN ORDER!>
I NEED GUNS!
WHERE DO YOU KEEP YOUR GUNS?
WE'RE A PHARMACEUTICAL COMPANY, WE DON'T HAVE ANY WEAPONS.
I LISTEN TO EVERY COMMERCIAL! YOU'RE ALWAYS TRYING TO SLIP THINGS BY US!
"MAY CAUSE RECTAL BLEEDING"?
WHAT IS THAT ALL ABOUT?!!
OKAY, NEVER MIND. WHERE'S CABLE?
BIG HOWIE LONG-LOOKING GUY WITH SCARS AND A FLASHING EYE THAT ALWAYS SEEMS TO SWITCH SIDES...
UP. GREAT.
HEY--HEY--KRUCH!
OH NO.

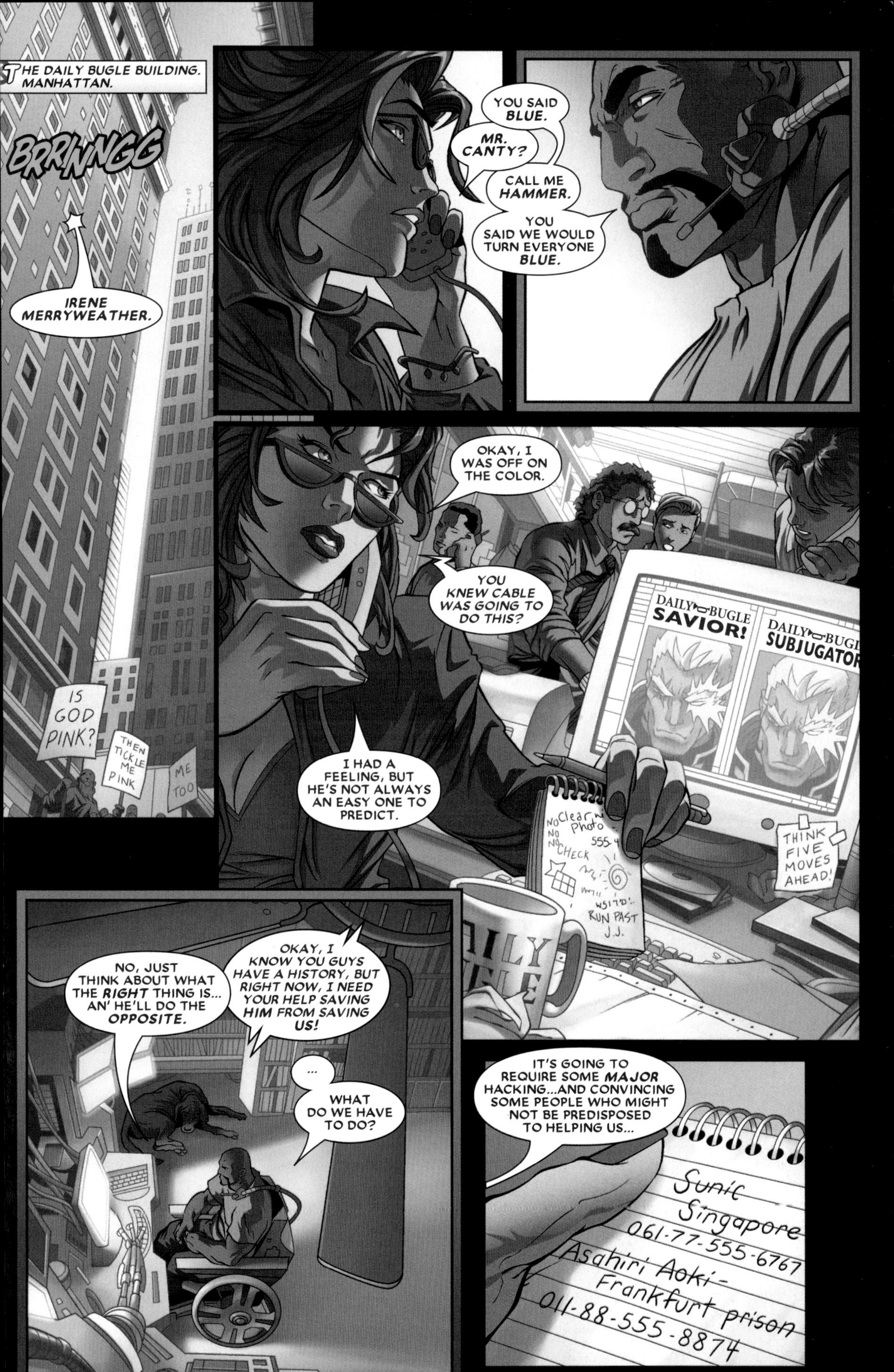
THE DAILY BUGLE BUILDING. MANHATTAN.
BRRINNGG
IRENE MERRYWEATHER.
IS GOD PINK?
THEN TICKLE ME PINK
ME TOO
MR. CANTY?
YOU SAID BLUE.
CALL ME HAMMER.
YOU SAID WE WOULD TURN EVERYONE BLUE.
OKAY, I WAS OFF ON THE COLOR.
YOU KNEW CABLE WAS GOING TO DO THIS?
I HAD A FEELING, BUT HE'S NOT ALWAYS AN EASY ONE TO PREDICT.
DAILY BUGLE SAVIOR!
DAILY BUGLE SUBJUGATOR
THINK FIVE MOVES AHEAD!
RUN PAST J.J.
NO, JUST THINK ABOUT WHAT THE RIGHT THING IS... AN' HE'LL DO THE OPPOSITE.
OKAY, I KNOW YOU GUYS HAVE A HISTORY, BUT RIGHT NOW, I NEED YOUR HELP SAVING HIM FROM SAVING US!
...
WHAT DO WE HAVE TO DO?
IT'S GOING TO REQUIRE SOME MAJOR HACKING...AND CONVINCING SOME PEOPLE WHO MIGHT NOT BE PREDISPOSED TO HELPING US...
Sunic Singapore
061-77-555-6767
Asahiri Aoki - Frankfurt prison
011-88-555-8874

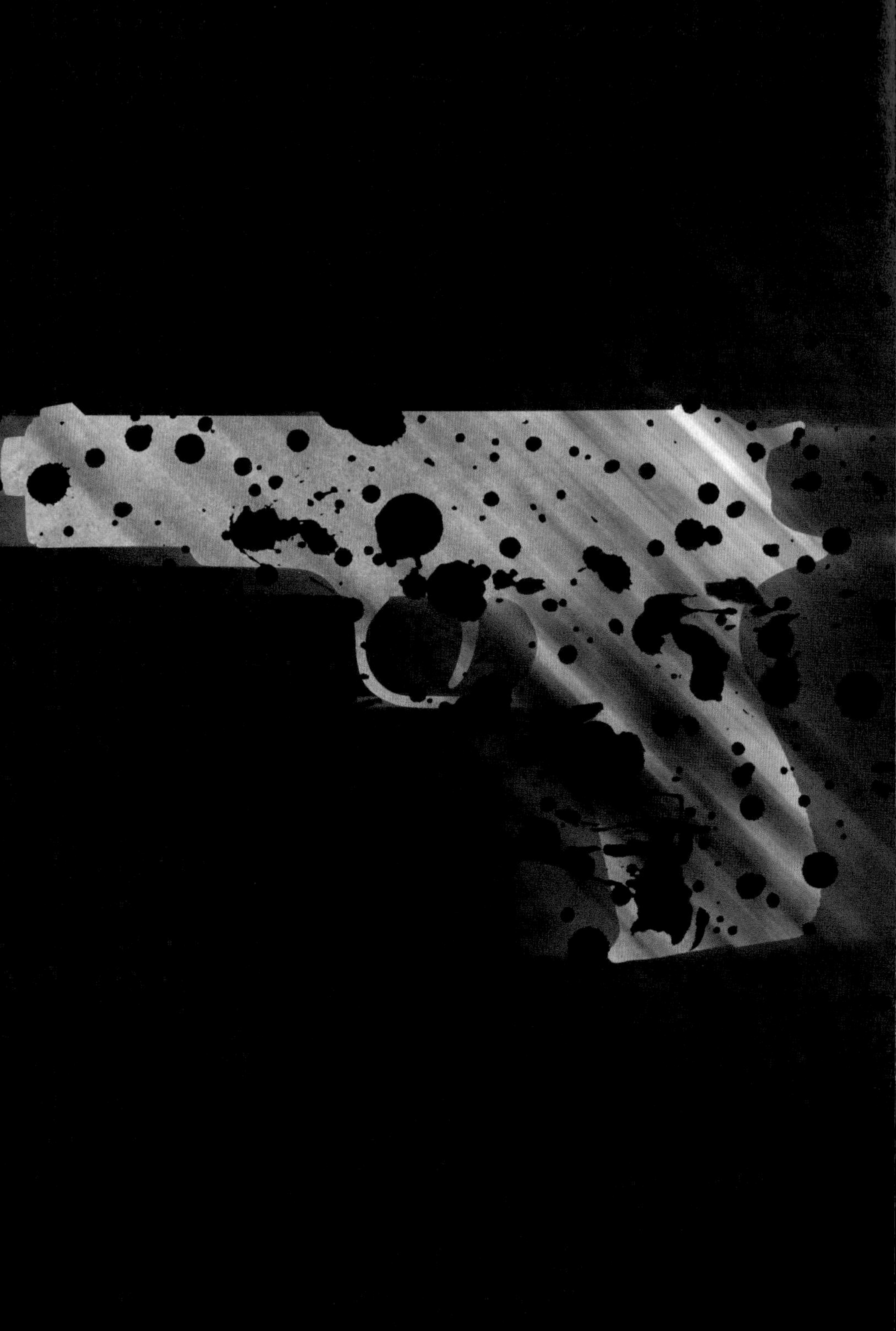

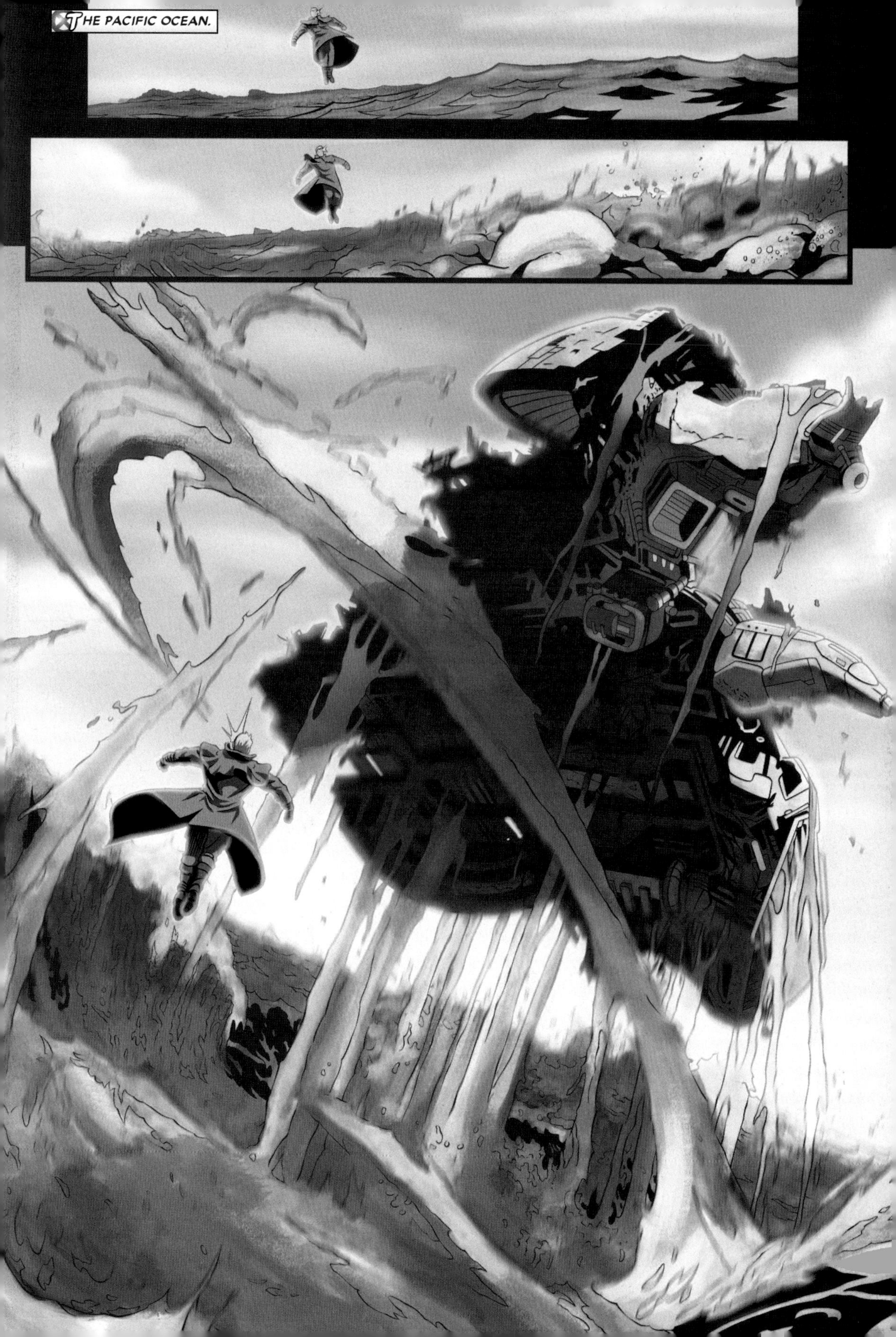
THE PACIFIC OCEAN.

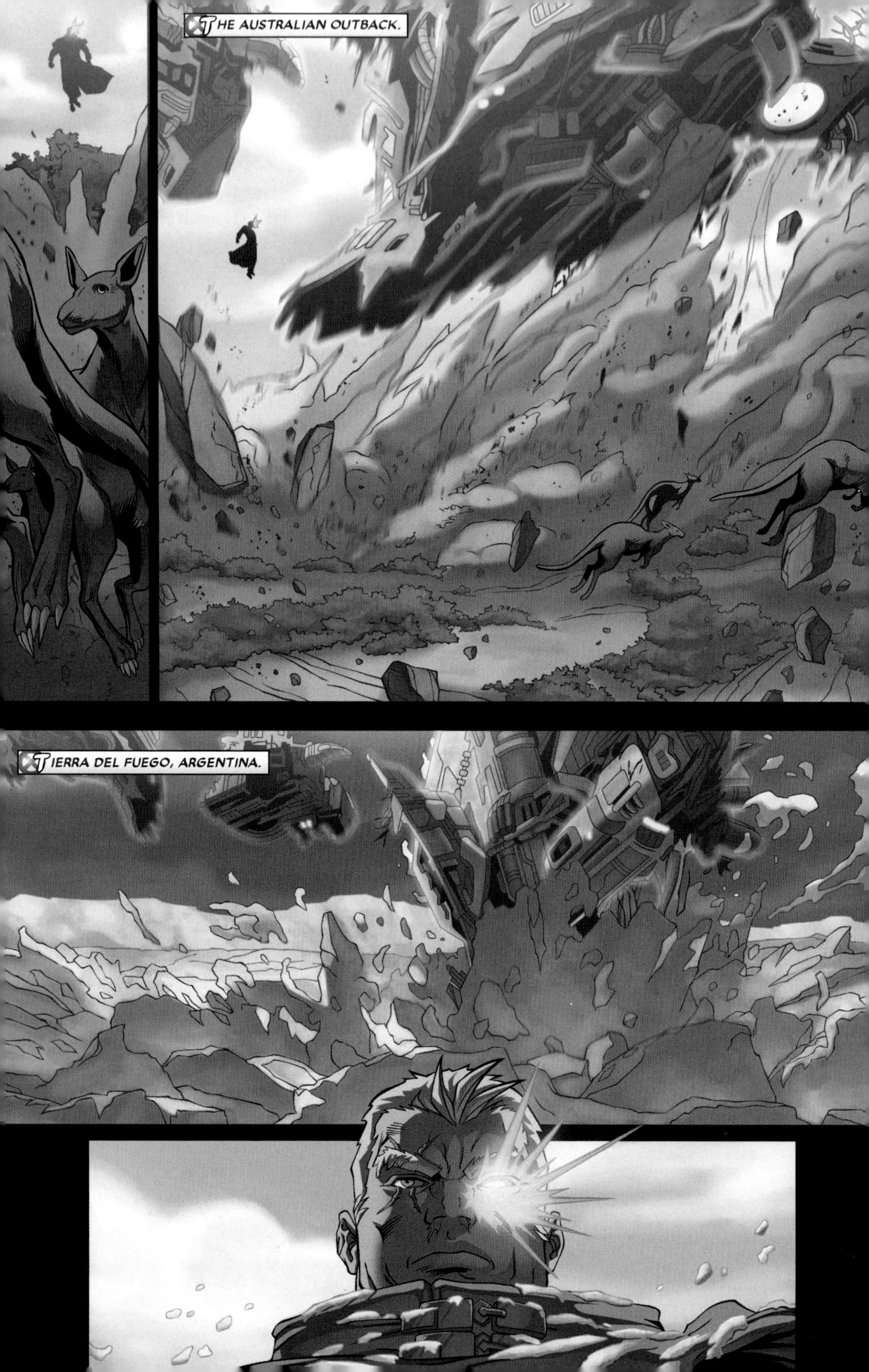
THE AUSTRALIAN OUTBACK.
TIERRA DEL FUEGO, ARGENTINA.

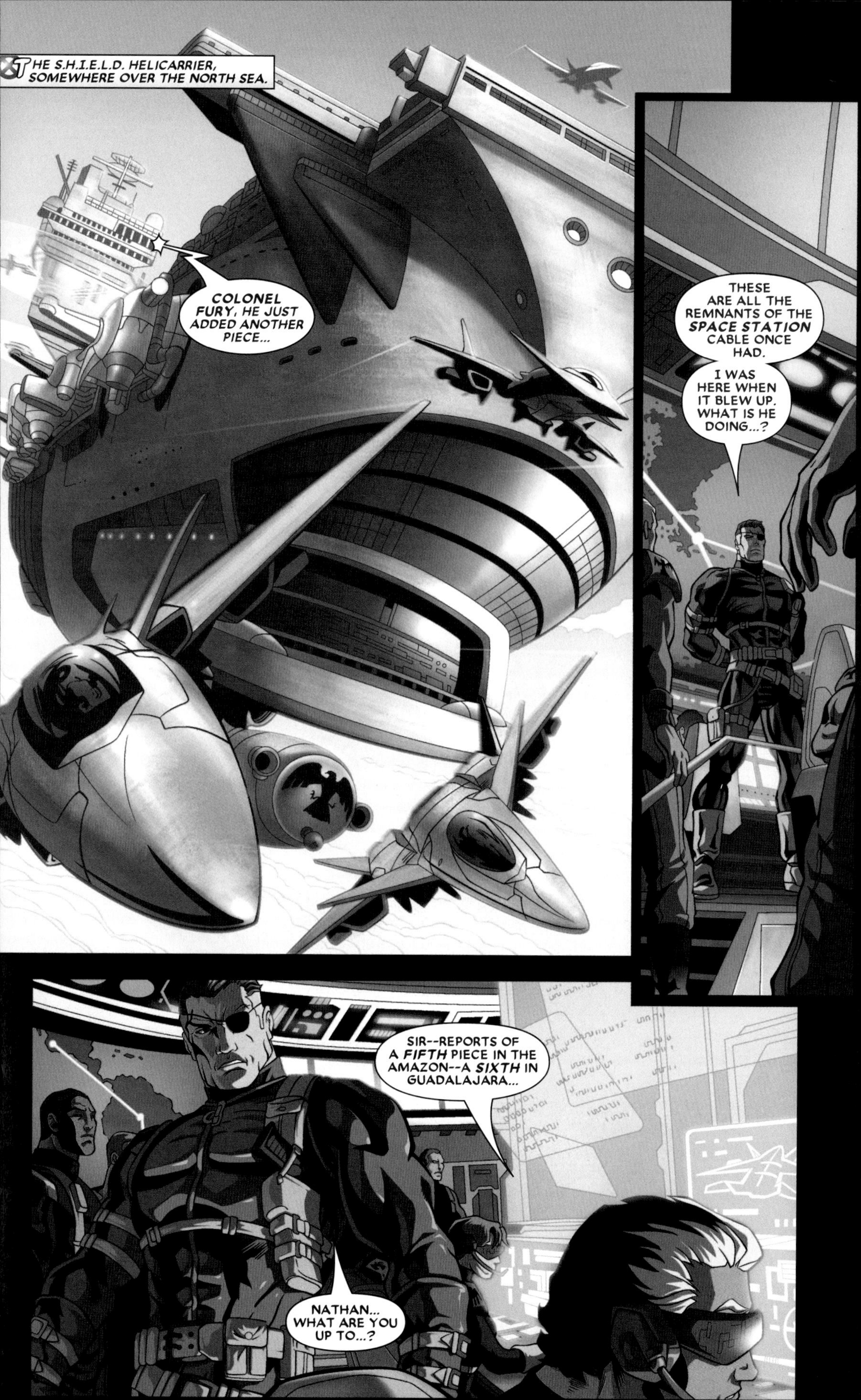
THE S.H.I.E.L.D. HELICARRIER, SOMEWHERE OVER THE NORTH SEA.
COLONEL FURY, HE JUST ADDED ANOTHER PIECE...
THESE ARE ALL THE REMNANTS OF THE SPACE STATION CABLE ONCE HAD.
I WAS HERE WHEN IT BLEW UP. WHAT IS HE DOING...?
SIR--REPORTS OF A FIFTH PIECE IN THE AMAZON--A SIXTH IN GUADALAJARA...
NATHAN... WHAT ARE YOU UP TO...?

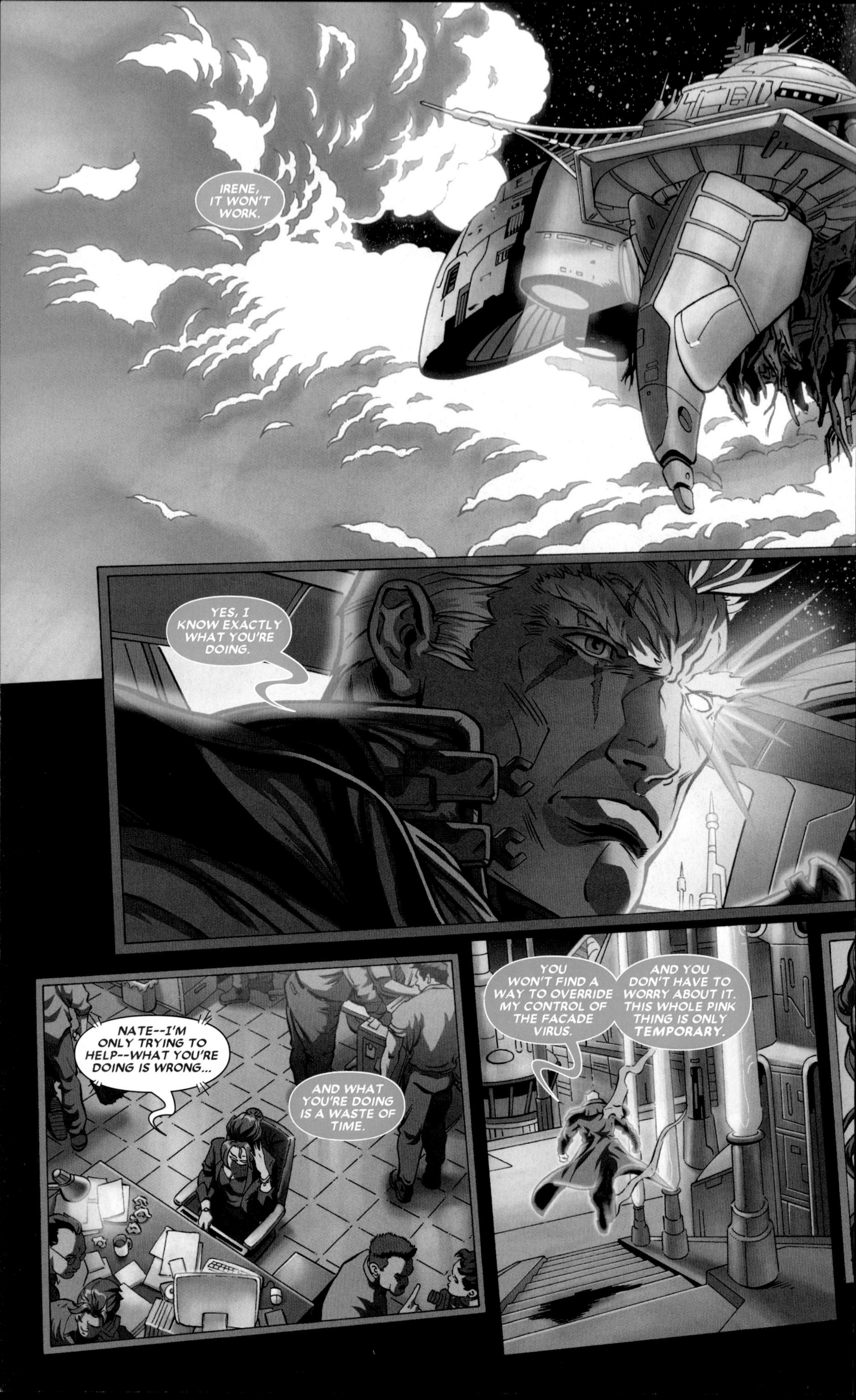
IRENE, IT WON'T WORK.
YES, I KNOW EXACTLY WHAT YOU'RE DOING.
NATE--I'M ONLY TRYING TO HELP--WHAT YOU'RE DOING IS WRONG...
AND WHAT YOU'RE DOING IS A WASTE OF TIME.
YOU WON'T FIND A WAY TO OVERRIDE MY CONTROL OF THE FACADE VIRUS.
AND YOU DON'T HAVE TO WORRY ABOUT IT. THIS WHOLE PINK THING IS ONLY TEMPORARY.

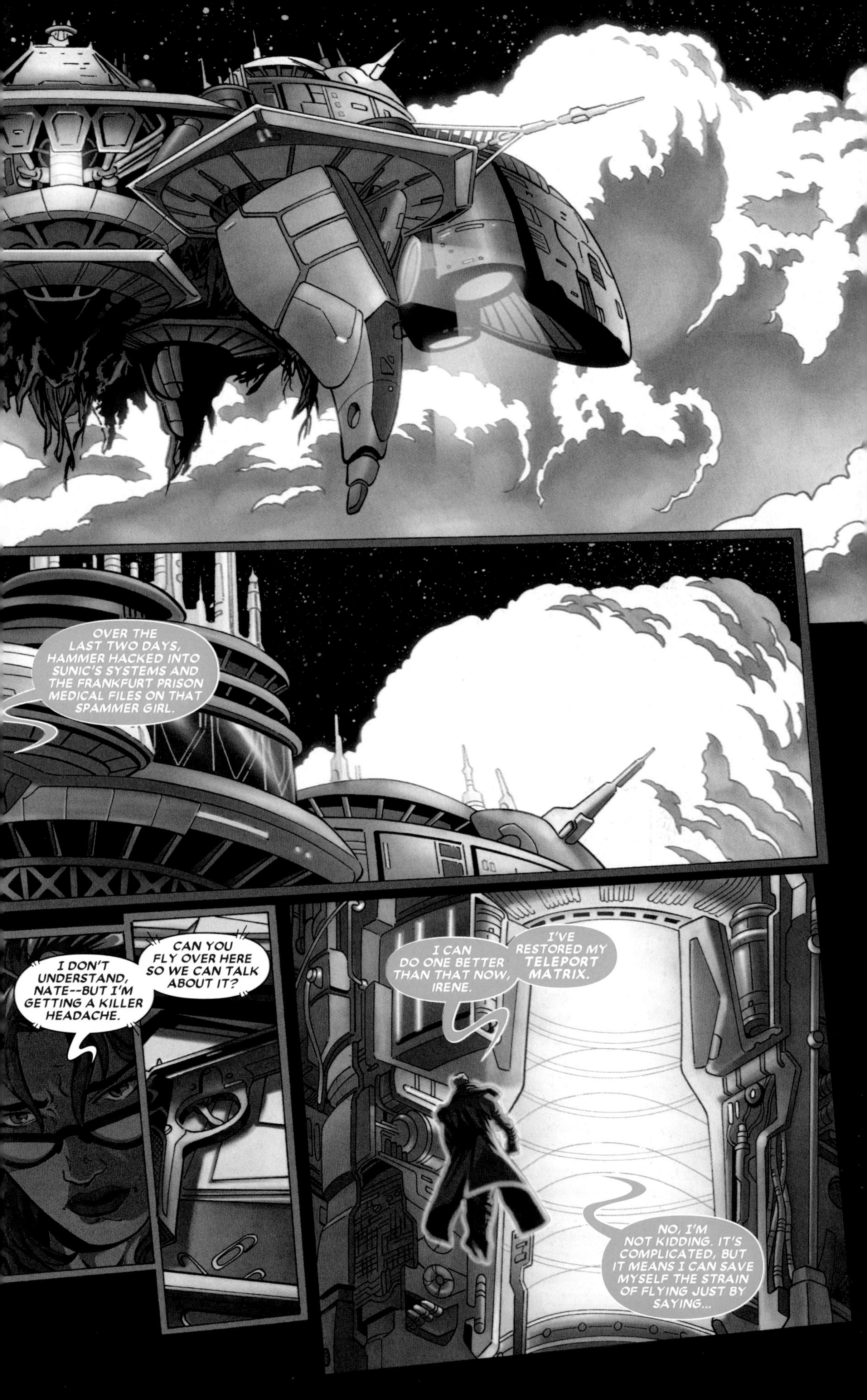
OVER THE LAST TWO DAYS, HAMMER HACKED INTO SUNIC'S SYSTEMS AND THE FRANKFURT PRISON MEDICAL FILES ON THAT SPAMMER GIRL.
I DON'T UNDERSTAND, NATE--BUT I'M GETTING A KILLER HEADACHE.
CAN YOU FLY OVER HERE SO WE CAN TALK ABOUT IT?
I CAN DO ONE BETTER THAN THAT NOW, IRENE.
I'VE RESTORED MY TELEPORT MATRIX.
NO, I'M NOT KIDDING. IT'S COMPLICATED, BUT IT MEANS I CAN SAVE MYSELF THE STRAIN OF FLYING JUST BY SAYING...

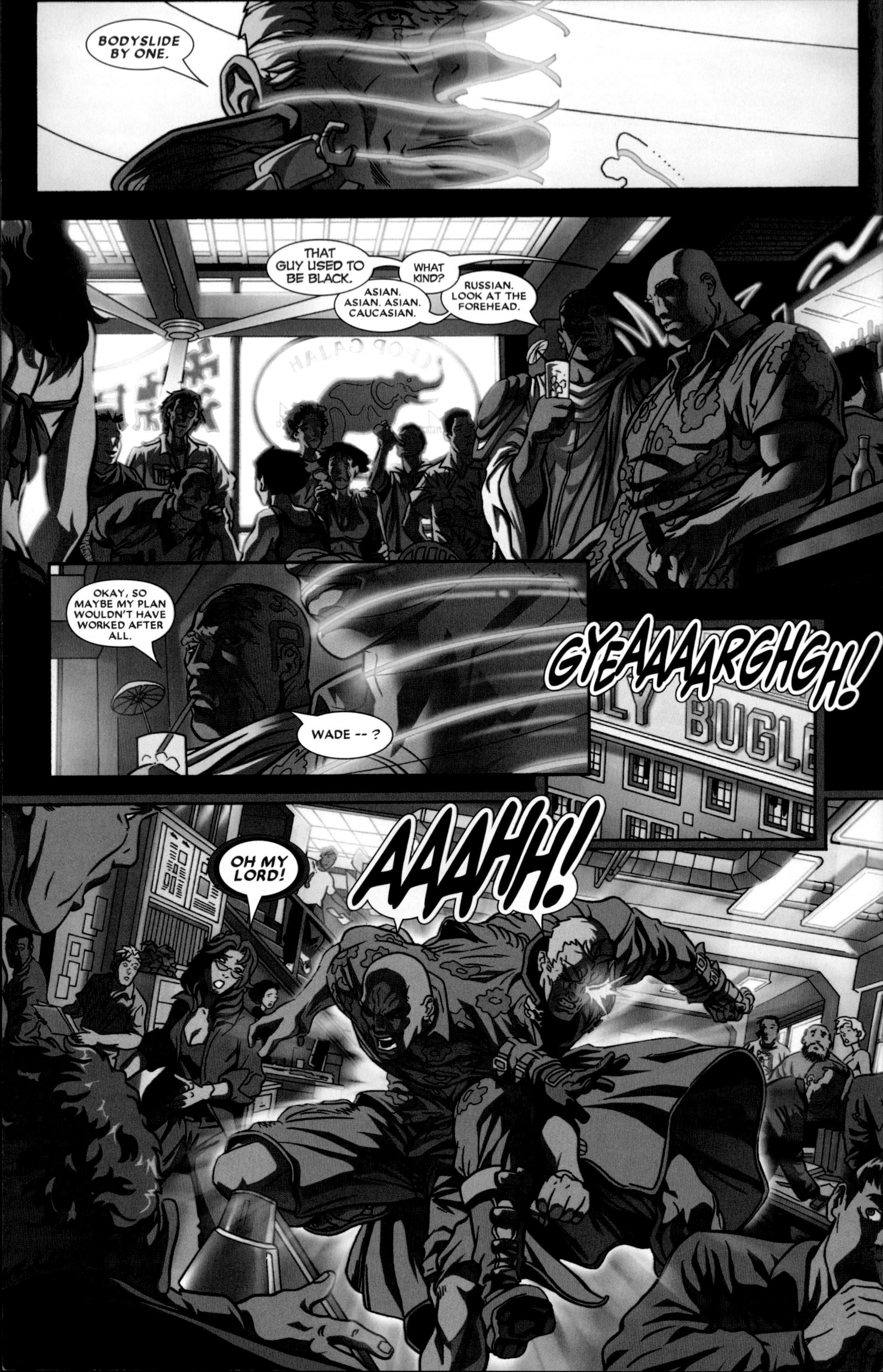
BODYSLIDE BY ONE.
THAT GUY USED TO BE BLACK.
WHAT KIND?
ASIAN. ASIAN. ASIAN. CAUCASIAN.
RUSSIAN. LOOK AT THE FOREHEAD.
OKAY, SO MAYBE MY PLAN WOULDN'T HAVE WORKED AFTER ALL.
WADE -- ?
GYEAAAARGHGH!
BUGLE
OH MY LORD!
AAAHH!

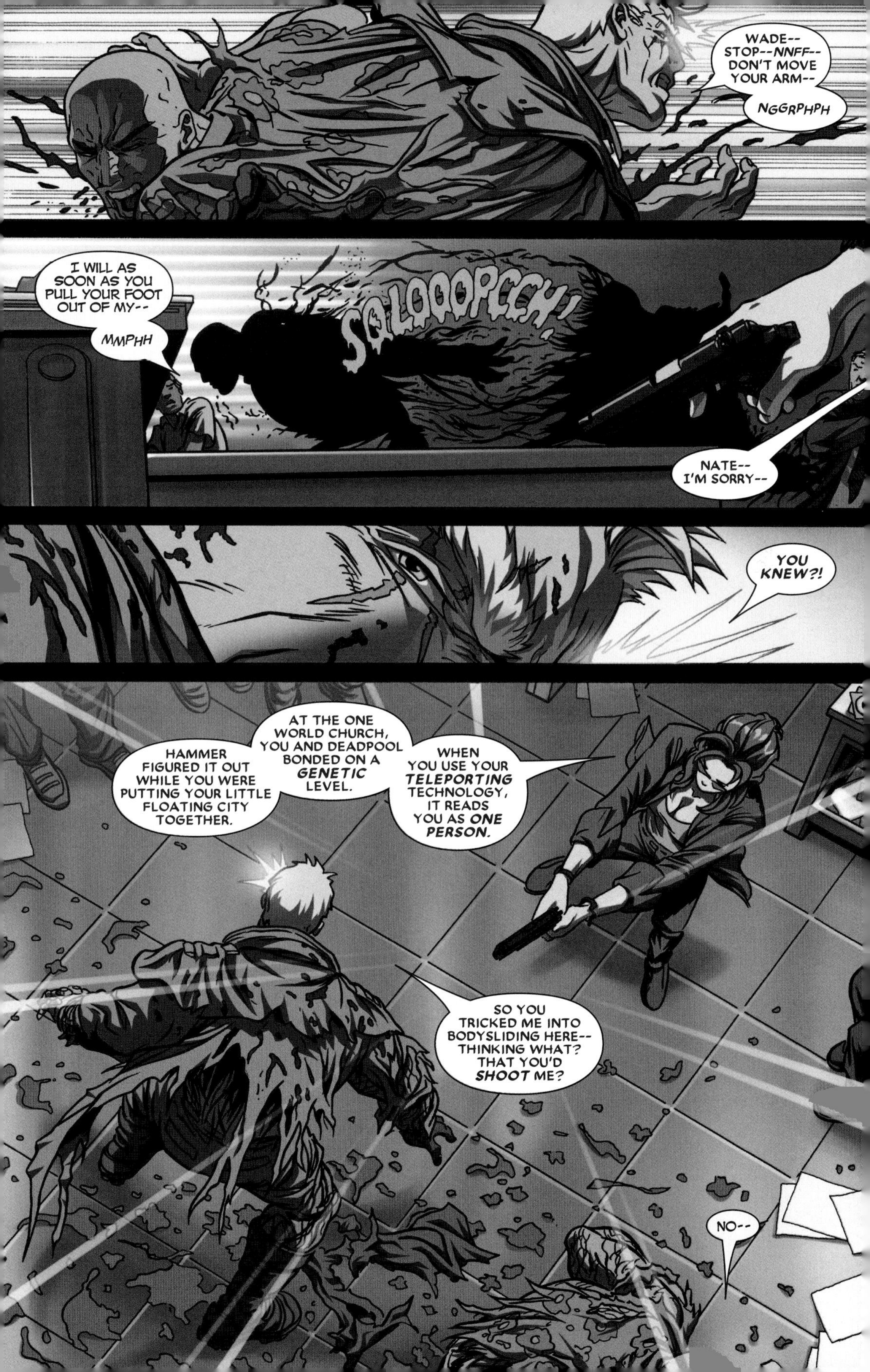

WADE-- STOP--NNFF-- DON'T MOVE YOUR ARM--
NGGRPHPH
I WILL AS SOON AS YOU PULL YOUR FOOT OUT OF MY--
MMPHH
SQLOOOPCCH!
NATE-- I'M SORRY--
YOU KNEW?!
HAMMER FIGURED IT OUT WHILE YOU WERE PUTTING YOUR LITTLE FLOATING CITY TOGETHER.
AT THE ONE WORLD CHURCH, YOU AND DEADPOOL BONDED ON A GENETIC LEVEL.
WHEN YOU USE YOUR TELEPORTING TECHNOLOGY, IT READS YOU AS ONE PERSON.
SO YOU TRICKED ME INTO BODYSLIDING HERE-- THINKING WHAT? THAT YOU'D SHOOT ME?
NO--

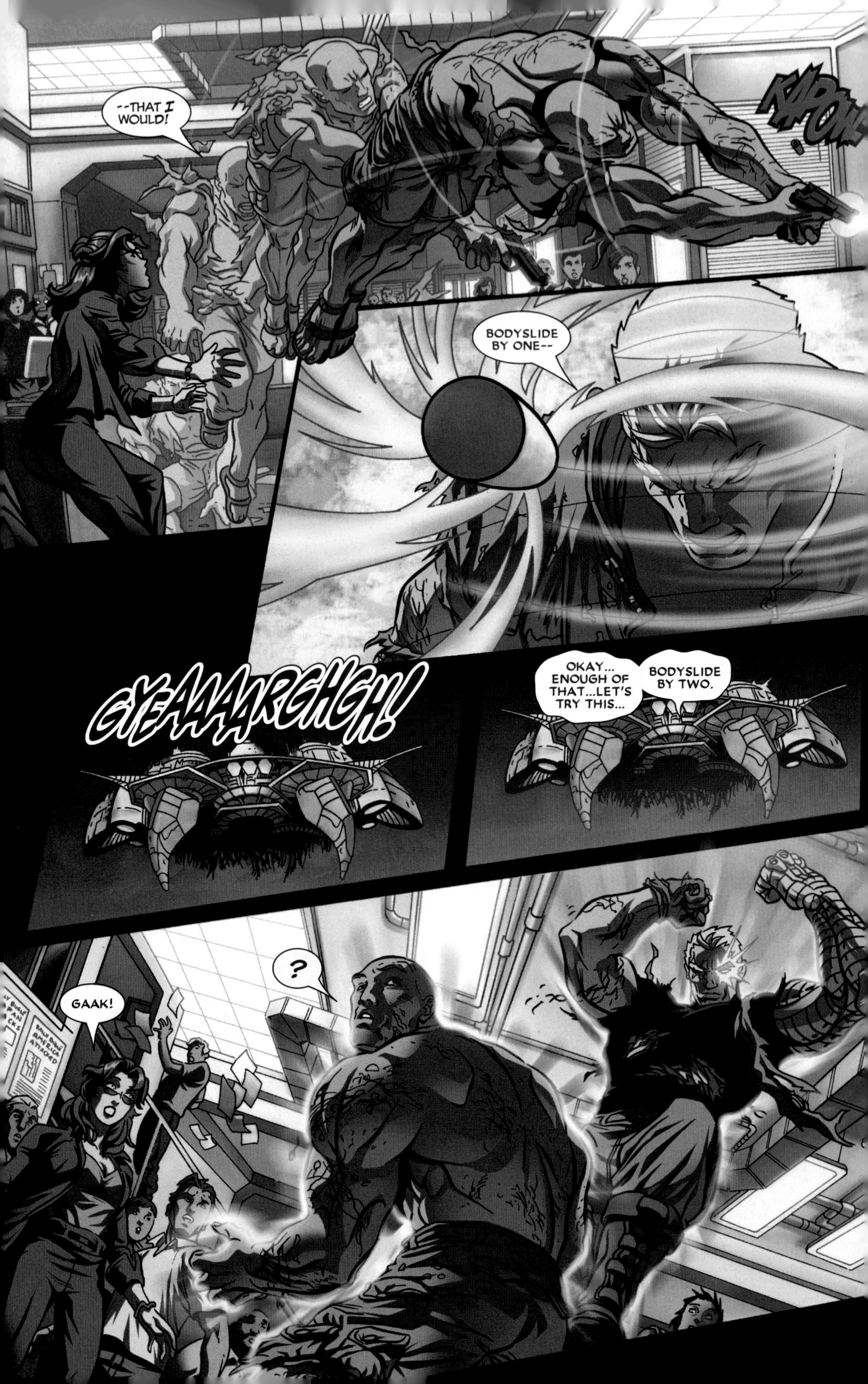
--THAT I WOULD!
KAPOW
BODYSLIDE BY ONE--
GYEAAARGHGH!
OKAY... ENOUGH OF THAT...LET'S TRY THIS...
BODYSLIDE BY TWO.
GAAK!
?

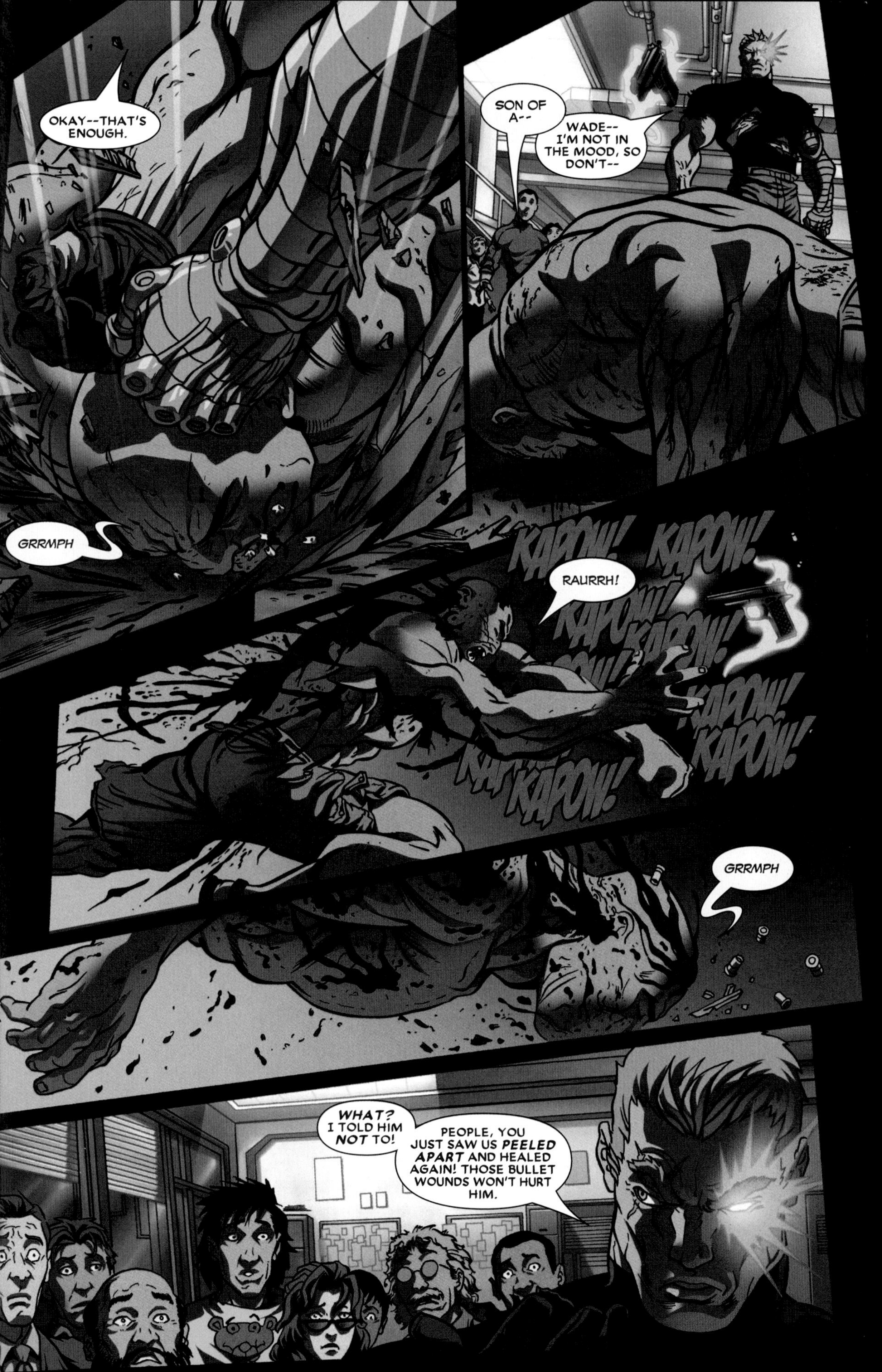
OKAY--THAT'S ENOUGH.
SON OF A--
WADE-- I'M NOT IN THE MOOD, SO DON'T--
GRRMPH
KAPOW! KAPOW!
RAURRH!
KAPOW! KAPOW! KAPOW! KAPOW! KAPOW!
GRRMPH
WHAT? I TOLD HIM NOT TO!
PEOPLE, YOU JUST SAW US PEELED APART AND HEALED AGAIN! THOSE BULLET WOUNDS WON'T HURT HIM.

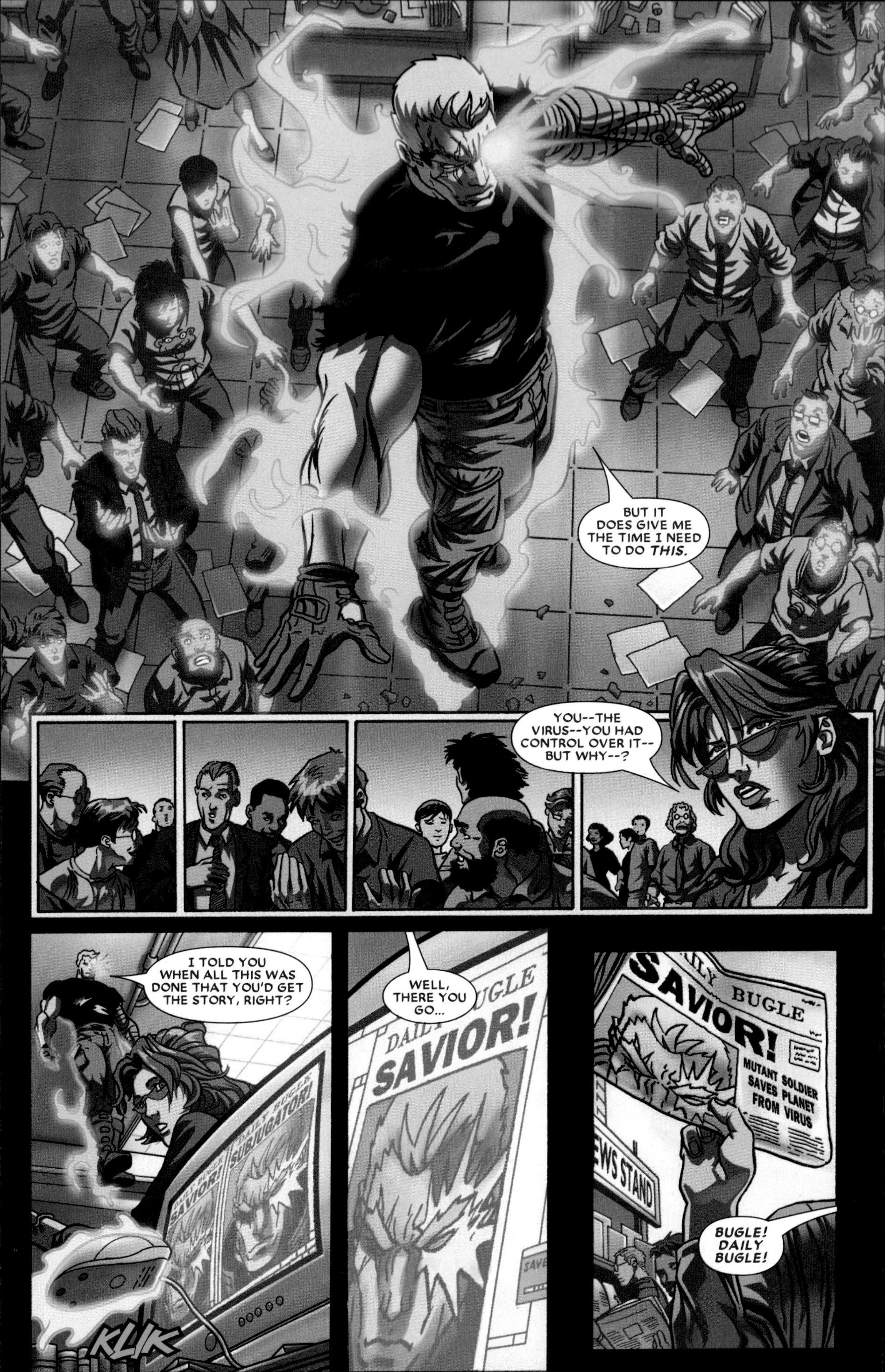
BUT IT DOES GIVE ME THE TIME I NEED TO DO THIS.
YOU--THE VIRUS--YOU HAD CONTROL OVER IT--BUT WHY--?
I TOLD YOU WHEN ALL THIS WAS DONE THAT YOU'D GET THE STORY, RIGHT?
DAILY BUGLE
SAVIOR!
DAILY BUGLE
SUBJUGATOR!
KLIK
WELL, THERE YOU GO...
DAILY BUGLE
SAVIOR!
BUGLE
SAVIOR!
MUTANT SOLDIER SAVES PLANET FROM VIRUS
NEWS STAND
BUGLE! DAILY BUGLE!

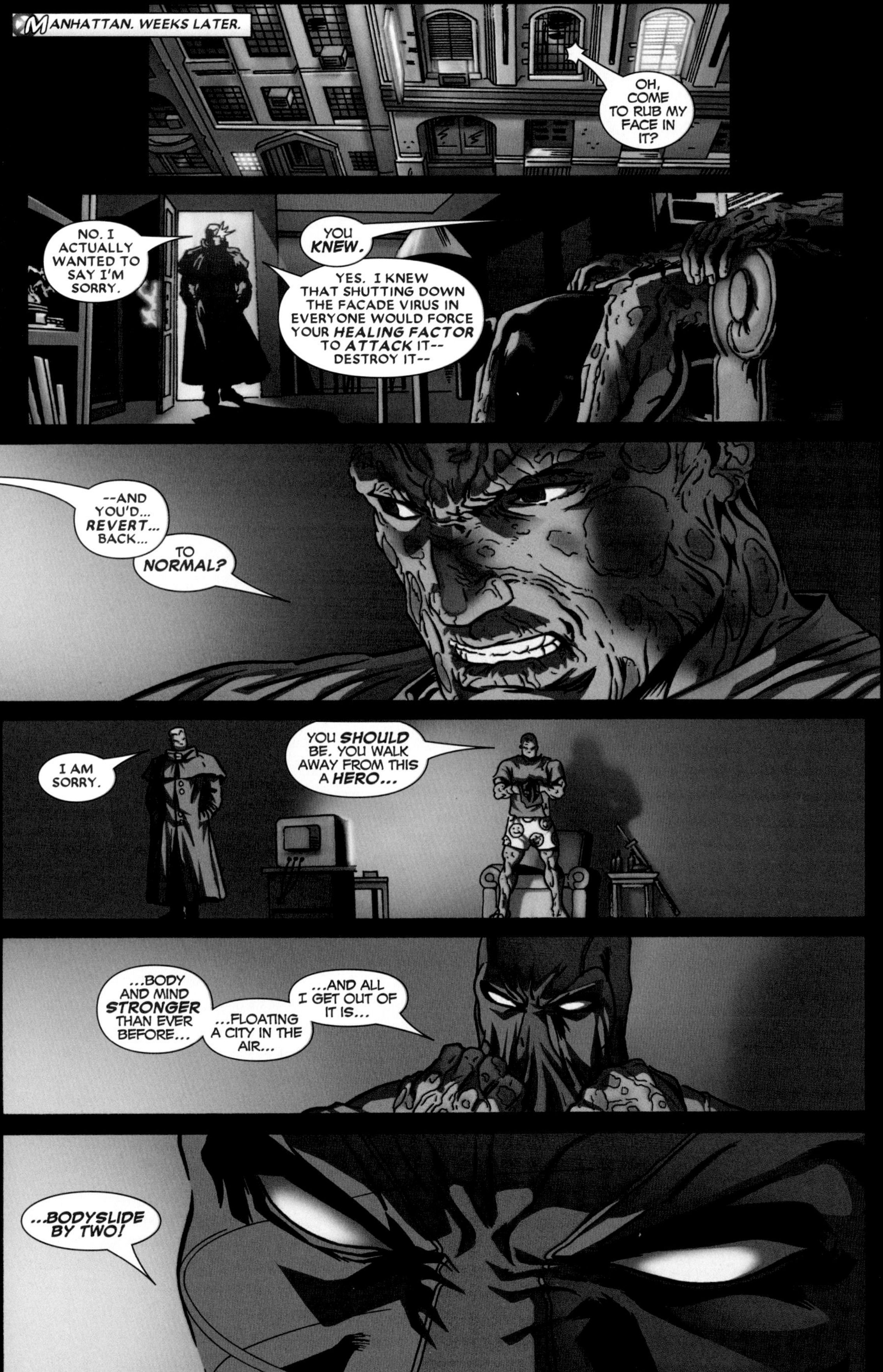
MANHATTAN. WEEKS LATER.
OH, COME TO RUB MY FACE IN IT?
NO. I ACTUALLY WANTED TO SAY I'M SORRY.
YOU KNEW.
YES. I KNEW THAT SHUTTING DOWN THE FACADE VIRUS IN EVERYONE WOULD FORCE YOUR HEALING FACTOR TO ATTACK IT-- DESTROY IT--
--AND YOU'D... REVERT... BACK...
TO NORMAL?
I AM SORRY.
YOU SHOULD BE. YOU WALK AWAY FROM THIS A HERO...
...BODY AND MIND STRONGER THAN EVER BEFORE...
...FLOATING A CITY IN THE AIR...
...AND ALL I GET OUT OF IT IS...
...BODYSLIDE BY TWO!

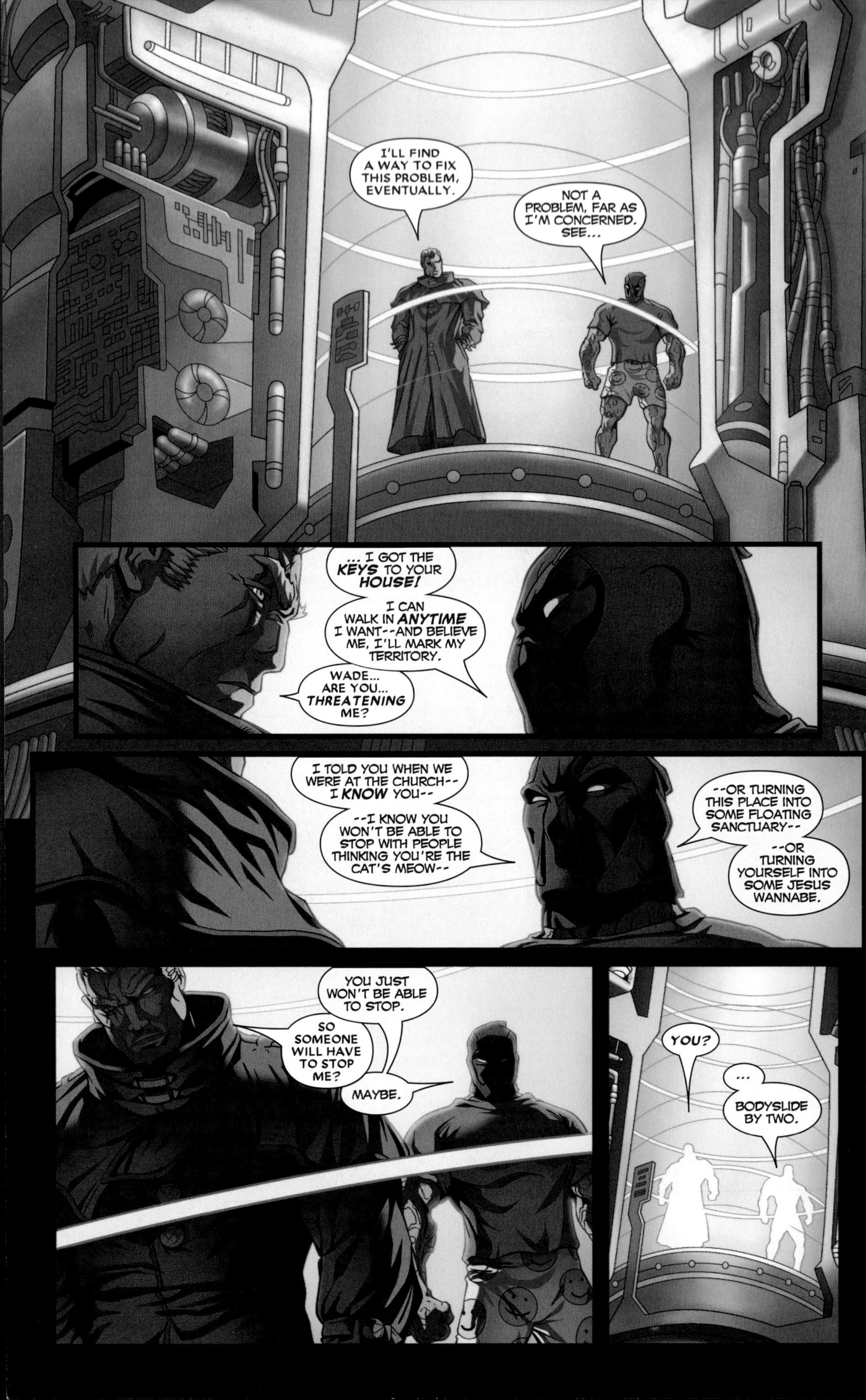
I'LL FIND A WAY TO FIX THIS PROBLEM, EVENTUALLY.
NOT A PROBLEM, FAR AS I'M CONCERNED. SEE...
... I GOT THE *KEYS* TO YOUR *HOUSE!*
I CAN WALK IN *ANYTIME* I WANT--AND BELIEVE ME, I'LL MARK MY TERRITORY.
WADE... ARE YOU... *THREATENING* ME?
I TOLD YOU WHEN WE WERE AT THE CHURCH-- I *KNOW* YOU--
--I KNOW YOU WON'T BE ABLE TO STOP WITH PEOPLE THINKING YOU'RE THE CAT'S MEOW--
--OR TURNING THIS PLACE INTO SOME FLOATING SANCTUARY--
--OR TURNING YOURSELF INTO SOME JESUS WANNABE.
YOU JUST WON'T BE ABLE TO STOP.
SO SOMEONE WILL HAVE TO STOP ME?
MAYBE.
YOU?
...
BODYSLIDE BY TWO.

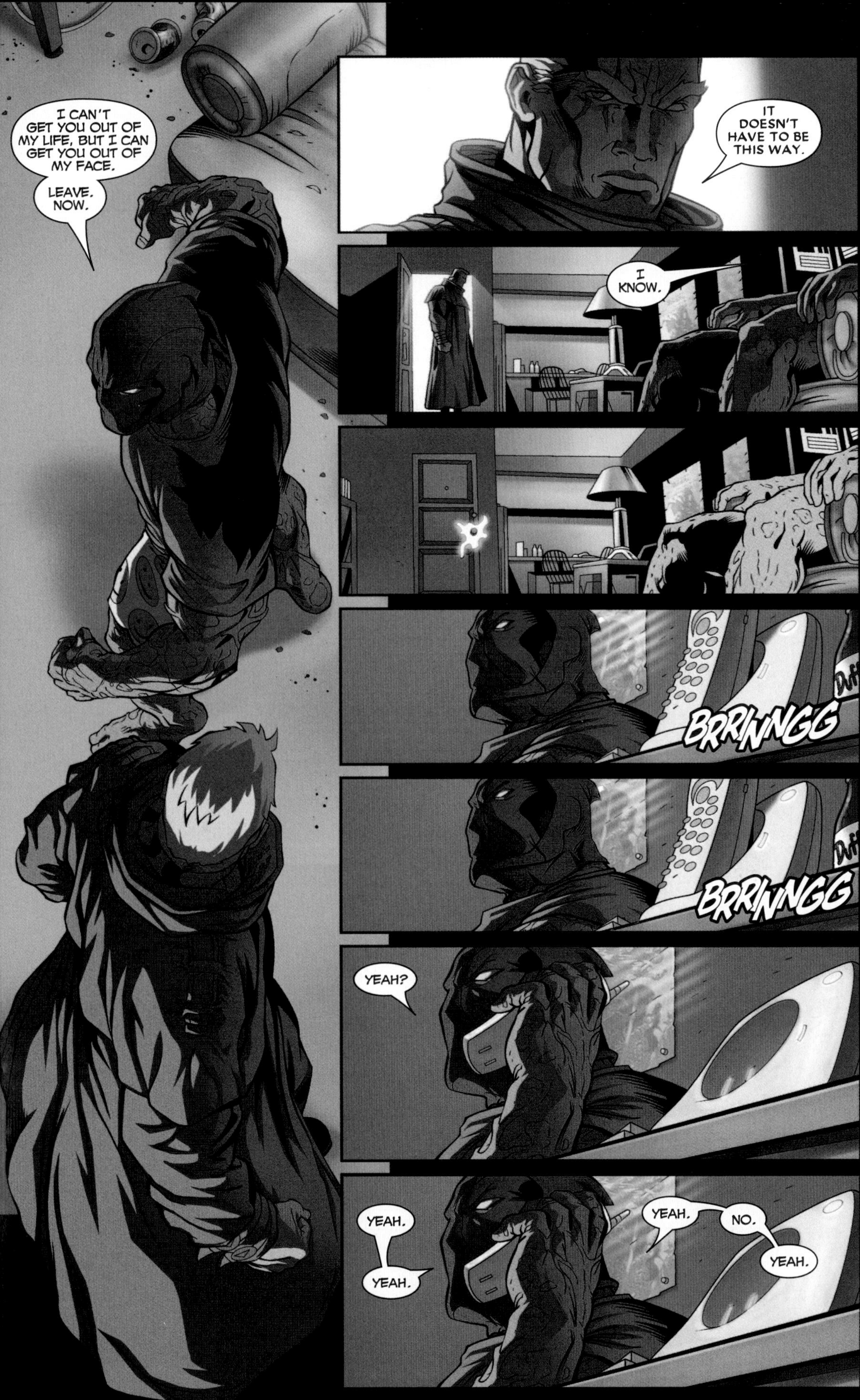
I CAN'T GET YOU OUT OF MY LIFE, BUT I CAN GET YOU OUT OF MY FACE.
LEAVE. NOW.
IT DOESN'T HAVE TO BE THIS WAY.
I KNOW.
BRRINNGG
BRRINNGG
YEAH?
YEAH.
YEAH.
YEAH.
NO.
YEAH.

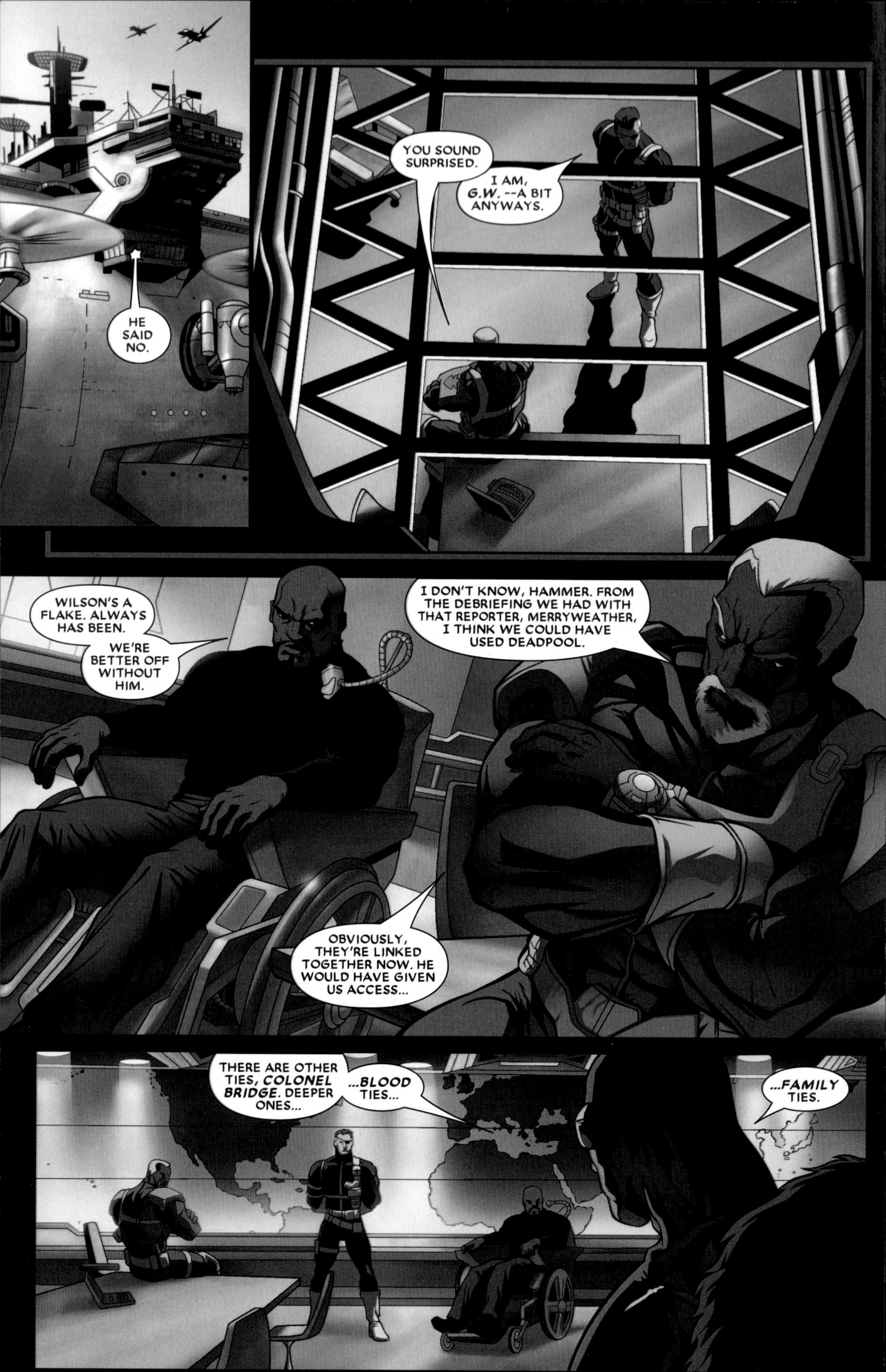
YOU SOUND SURPRISED.
I AM, G.W. --A BIT ANYWAYS.
HE SAID NO.
WILSON'S A FLAKE. ALWAYS HAS BEEN.
WE'RE BETTER OFF WITHOUT HIM.
I DON'T KNOW, HAMMER. FROM THE DEBRIEFING WE HAD WITH THAT REPORTER, MERRYWEATHER, I THINK WE COULD HAVE USED DEADPOOL.
OBVIOUSLY, THEY'RE LINKED TOGETHER NOW. HE WOULD HAVE GIVEN US ACCESS...
THERE ARE OTHER TIES, COLONEL BRIDGE. DEEPER ONES...
...BLOOD TIES...
...FAMILY TIES.

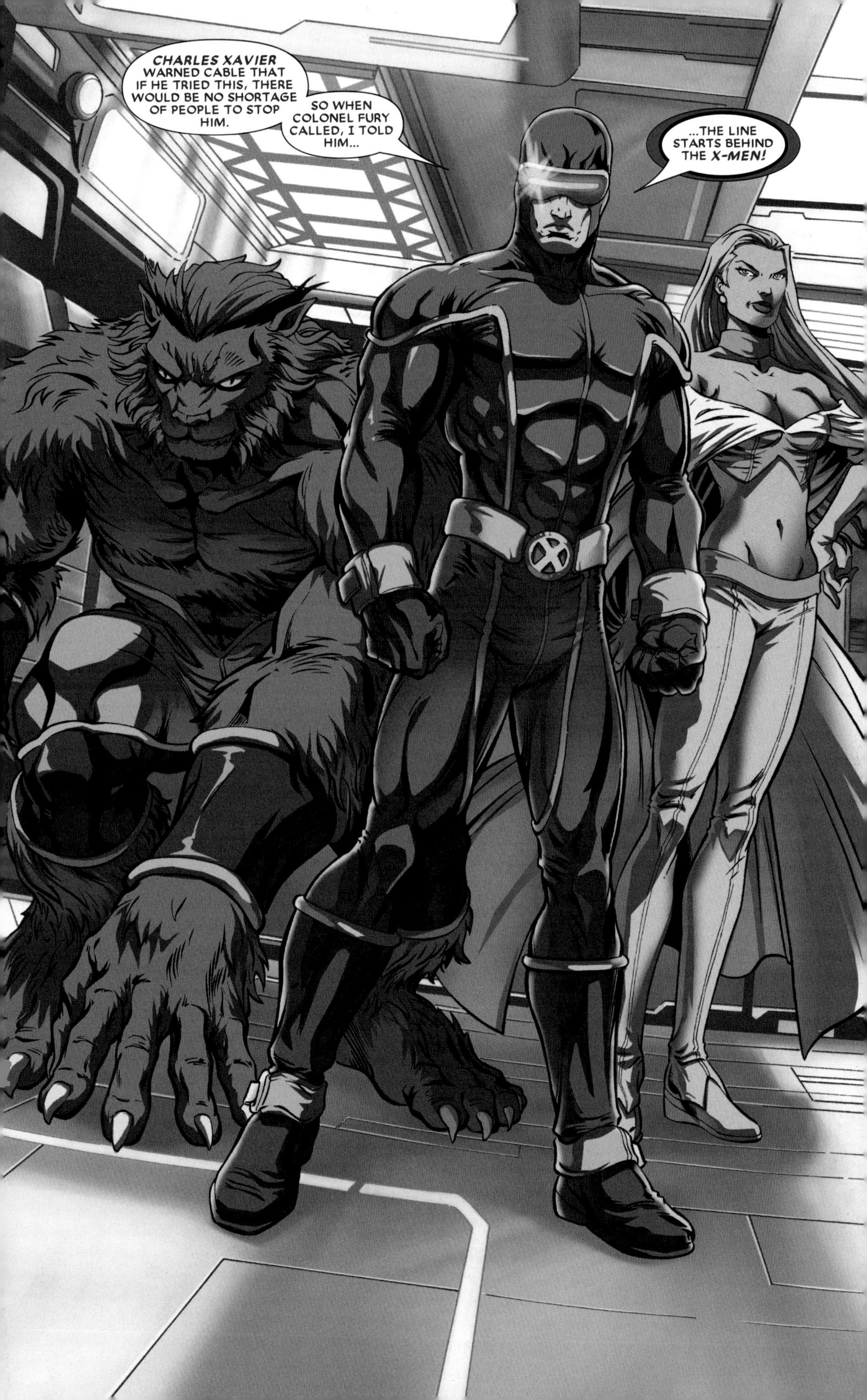

CHARLES XAVIER WARNED CABLE THAT IF HE TRIED THIS, THERE WOULD BE NO SHORTAGE OF PEOPLE TO STOP HIM.
SO WHEN COLONEL FURY CALLED, I TOLD HIM...
...THE LINE STARTS BEHIND THE X-MEN!

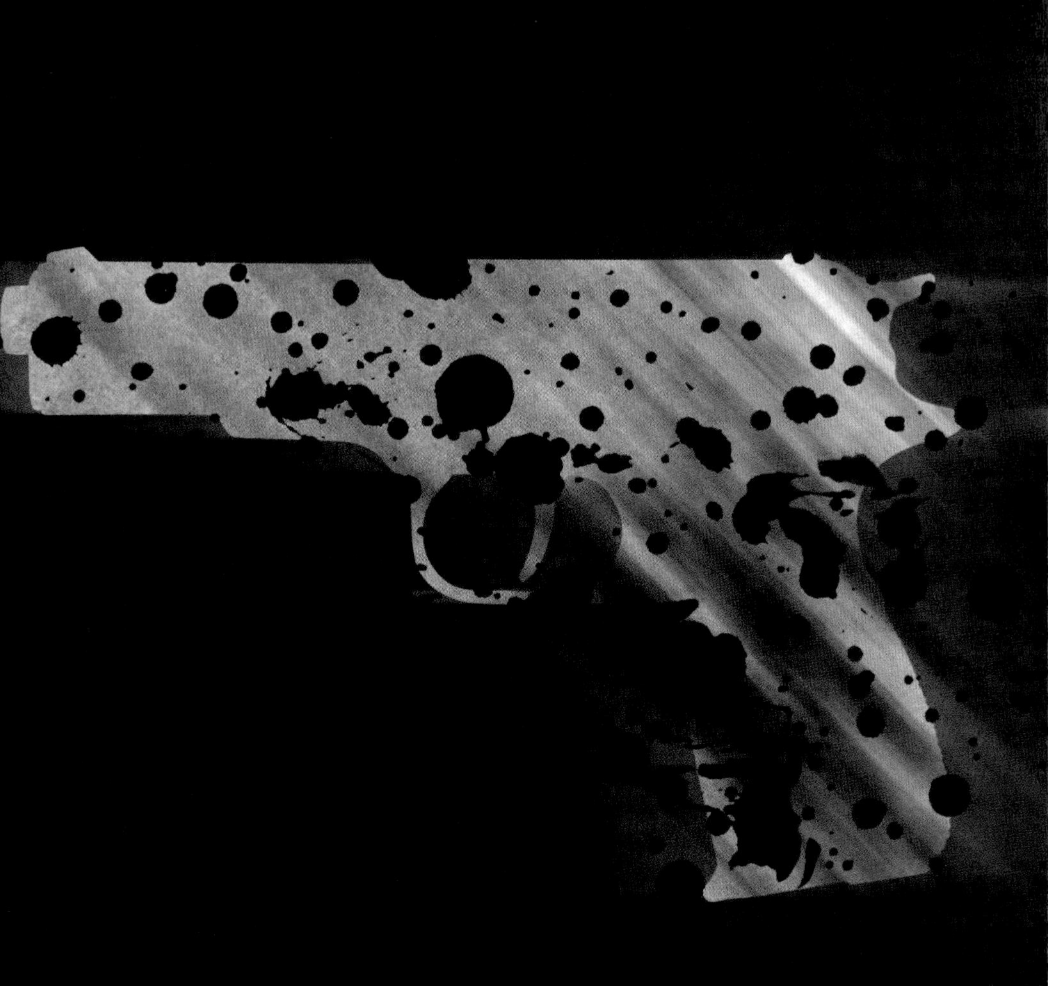

7

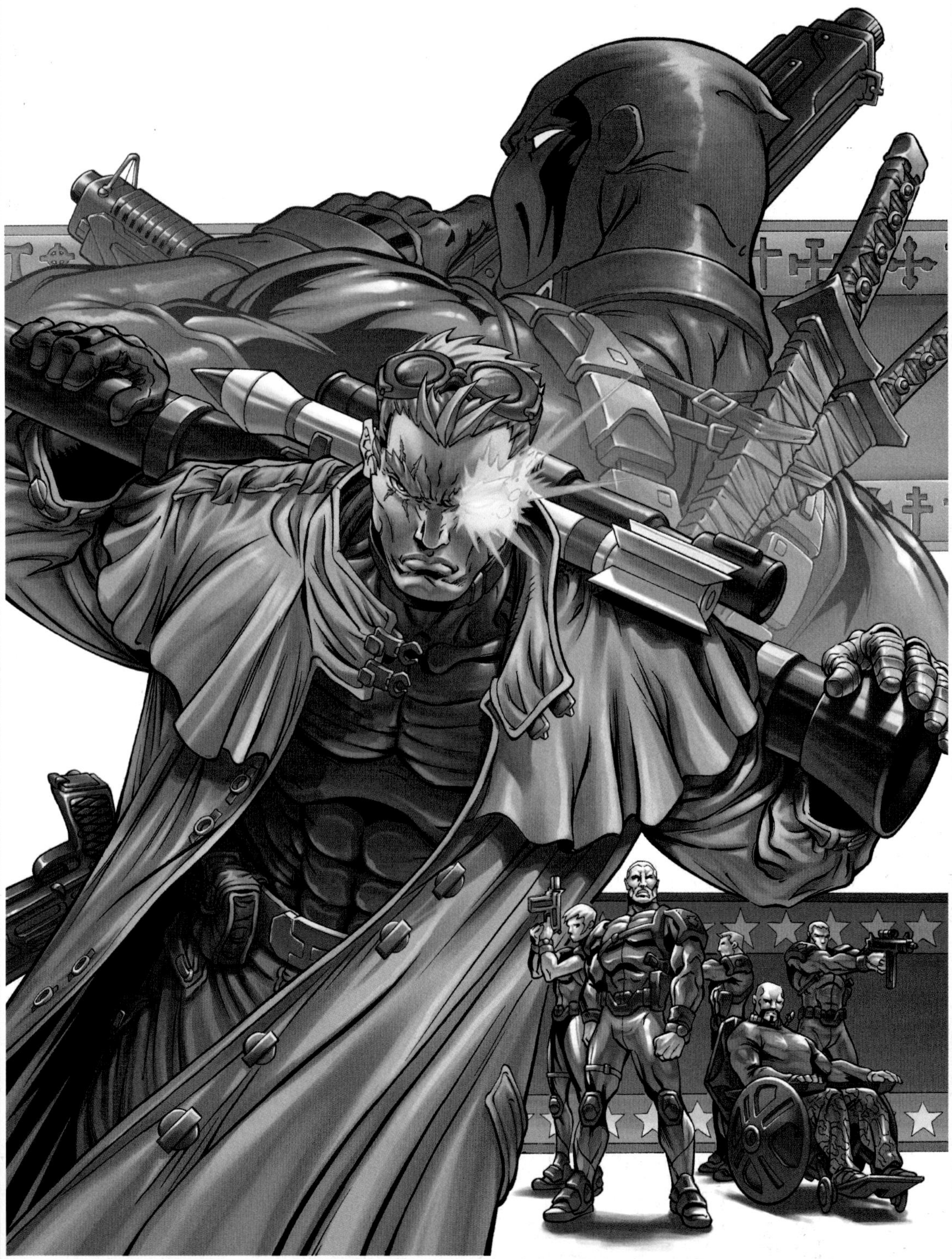

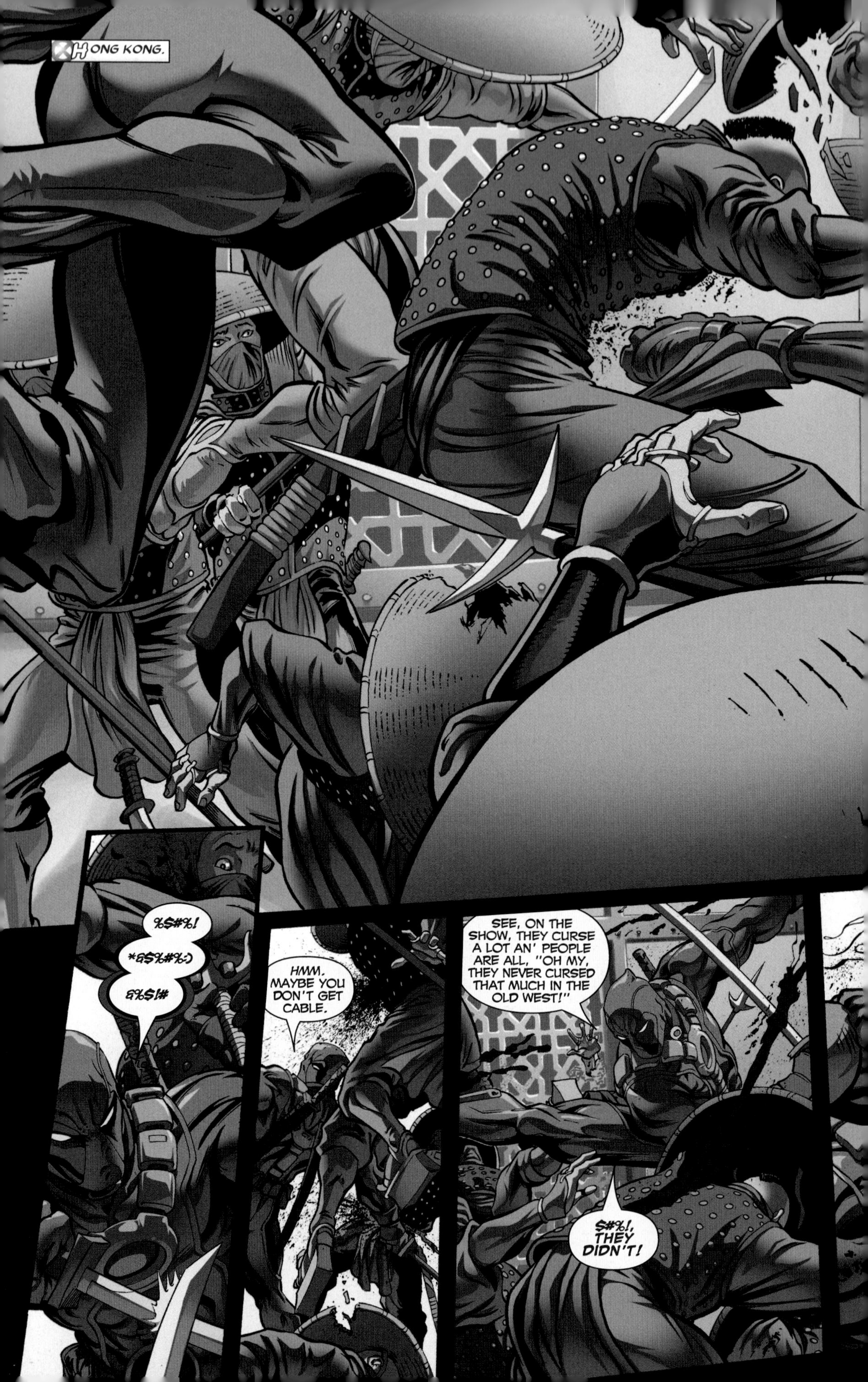
HONG KONG.
%$#%!
*&$%#%:)
&%$!#
HMM. MAYBE YOU DON'T GET CABLE.
SEE, ON THE SHOW, THEY CURSE A LOT AN' PEOPLE ARE ALL, "OH MY, THEY NEVER CURSED THAT MUCH IN THE OLD WEST!"
$#%!, THEY DIDN'T!

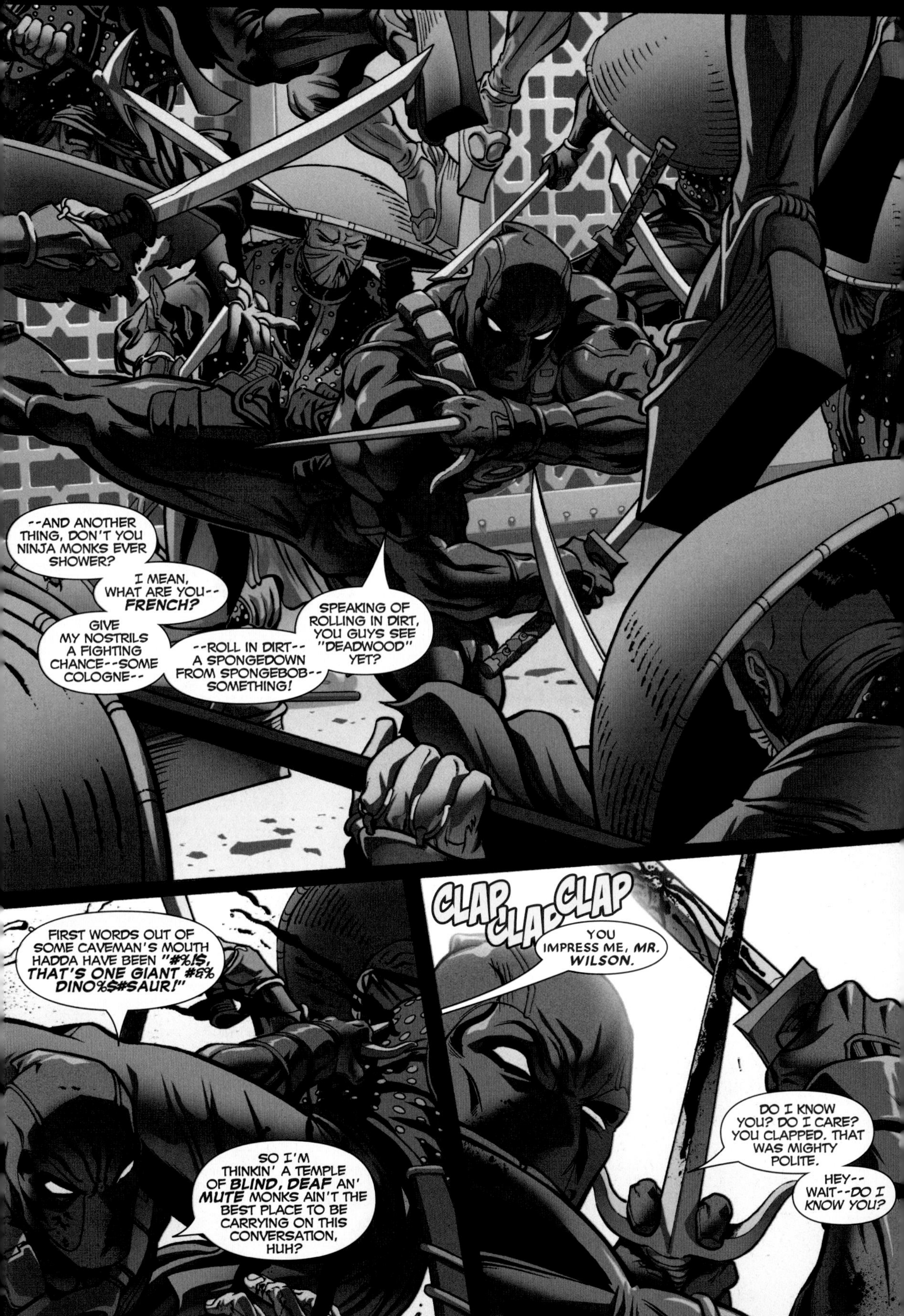
--AND ANOTHER THING, DON'T YOU NINJA MONKS EVER SHOWER?
I MEAN, WHAT ARE YOU-- **FRENCH?**
GIVE MY NOSTRILS A FIGHTING CHANCE--SOME COLOGNE--
--ROLL IN DIRT--A SPONGEDOWN FROM SPONGEBOB--SOMETHING!
SPEAKING OF ROLLING IN DIRT, YOU GUYS SEE "DEADWOOD" YET?
FIRST WORDS OUT OF SOME CAVEMAN'S MOUTH HADDA HAVE BEEN ***"#%!$, THAT'S ONE GIANT #&% DINO%$#SAUR!"***
SO I'M THINKIN' A TEMPLE OF **BLIND, DEAF** AN' **MUTE** MONKS AIN'T THE BEST PLACE TO BE CARRYING ON THIS CONVERSATION, HUH?
CLAP CLAP CLAP
YOU IMPRESS ME, **MR. WILSON.**
!
DO I KNOW YOU? DO I CARE? YOU CLAPPED. THAT WAS MIGHTY POLITE.
HEY--WAIT--DO I KNOW YOU?

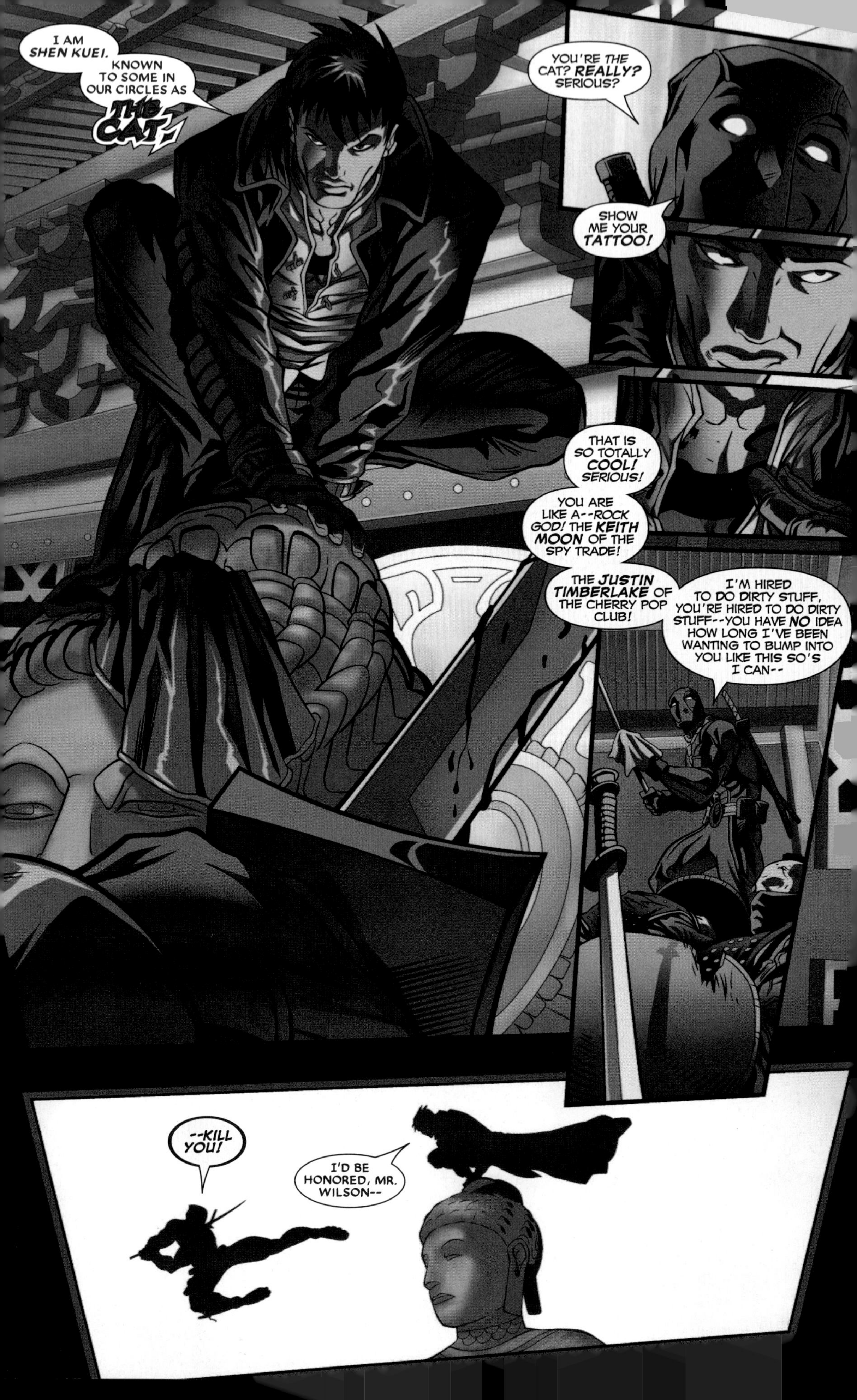
I AM SHEN KUEI. KNOWN TO SOME IN OUR CIRCLES AS
THE CAT.
YOU'RE THE CAT? REALLY? SERIOUS?
SHOW ME YOUR TATTOO!
THAT IS SO TOTALLY COOL! SERIOUS!
YOU ARE LIKE A--ROCK GOD! THE KEITH MOON OF THE SPY TRADE!
THE JUSTIN TIMBERLAKE OF THE CHERRY POP CLUB!
I'M HIRED TO DO DIRTY STUFF, YOU'RE HIRED TO DO DIRTY STUFF--YOU HAVE NO IDEA HOW LONG I'VE BEEN WANTING TO BUMP INTO YOU LIKE THIS SO'S I CAN--
--KILL YOU!
I'D BE HONORED, MR. WILSON--

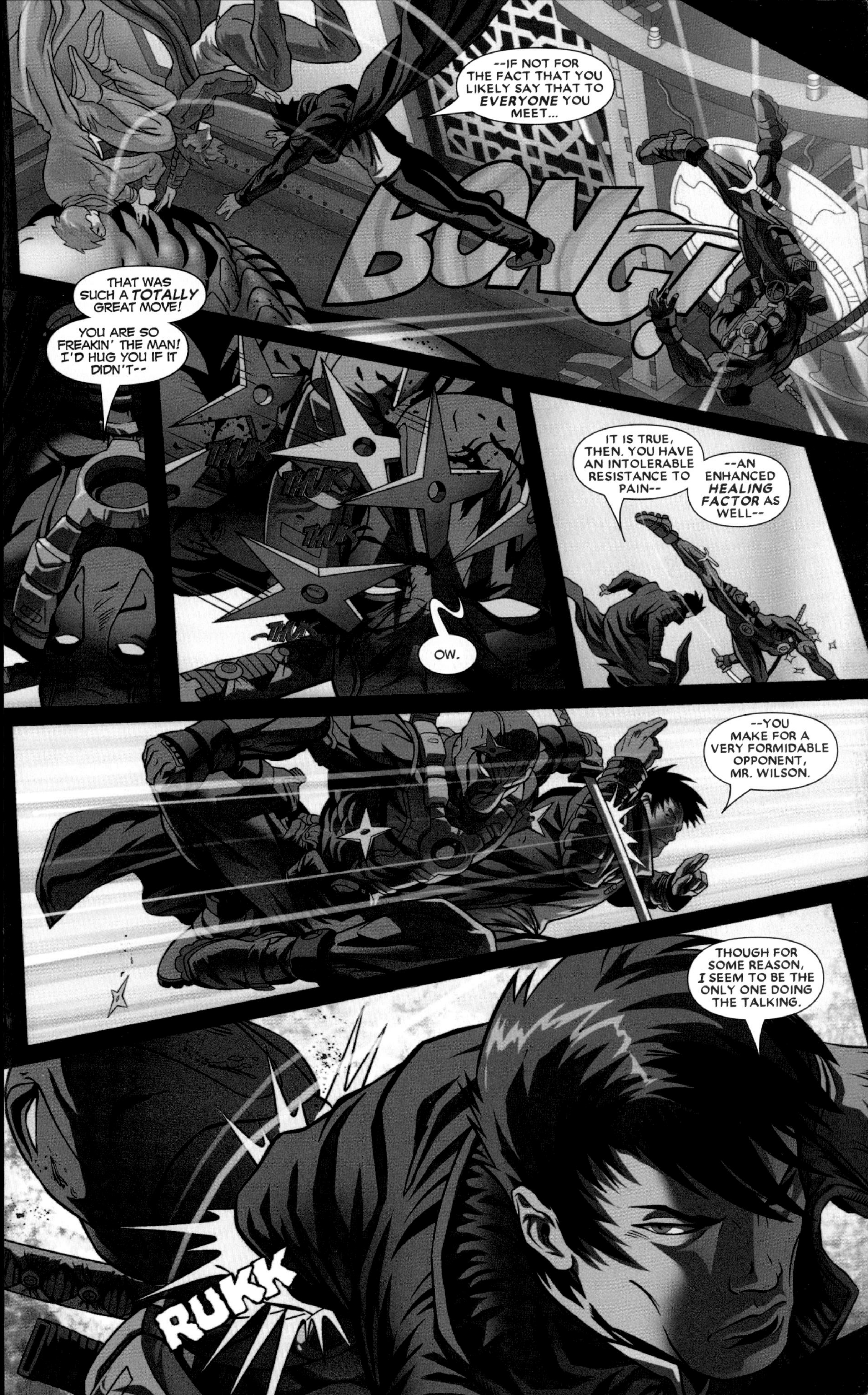
--IF NOT FOR THE FACT THAT YOU LIKELY SAY THAT TO EVERYONE YOU MEET...
BONG!
THAT WAS SUCH A TOTALLY GREAT MOVE!
YOU ARE SO FREAKIN' THE MAN! I'D HUG YOU IF IT DIDN'T--
THUK
THUK
THUK
THUK
OW.
IT IS TRUE, THEN. YOU HAVE AN INTOLERABLE RESISTANCE TO PAIN--
--AN ENHANCED HEALING FACTOR AS WELL--
--YOU MAKE FOR A VERY FORMIDABLE OPPONENT, MR. WILSON.
THOUGH FOR SOME REASON, I SEEM TO BE THE ONLY ONE DOING THE TALKING.
RUKK

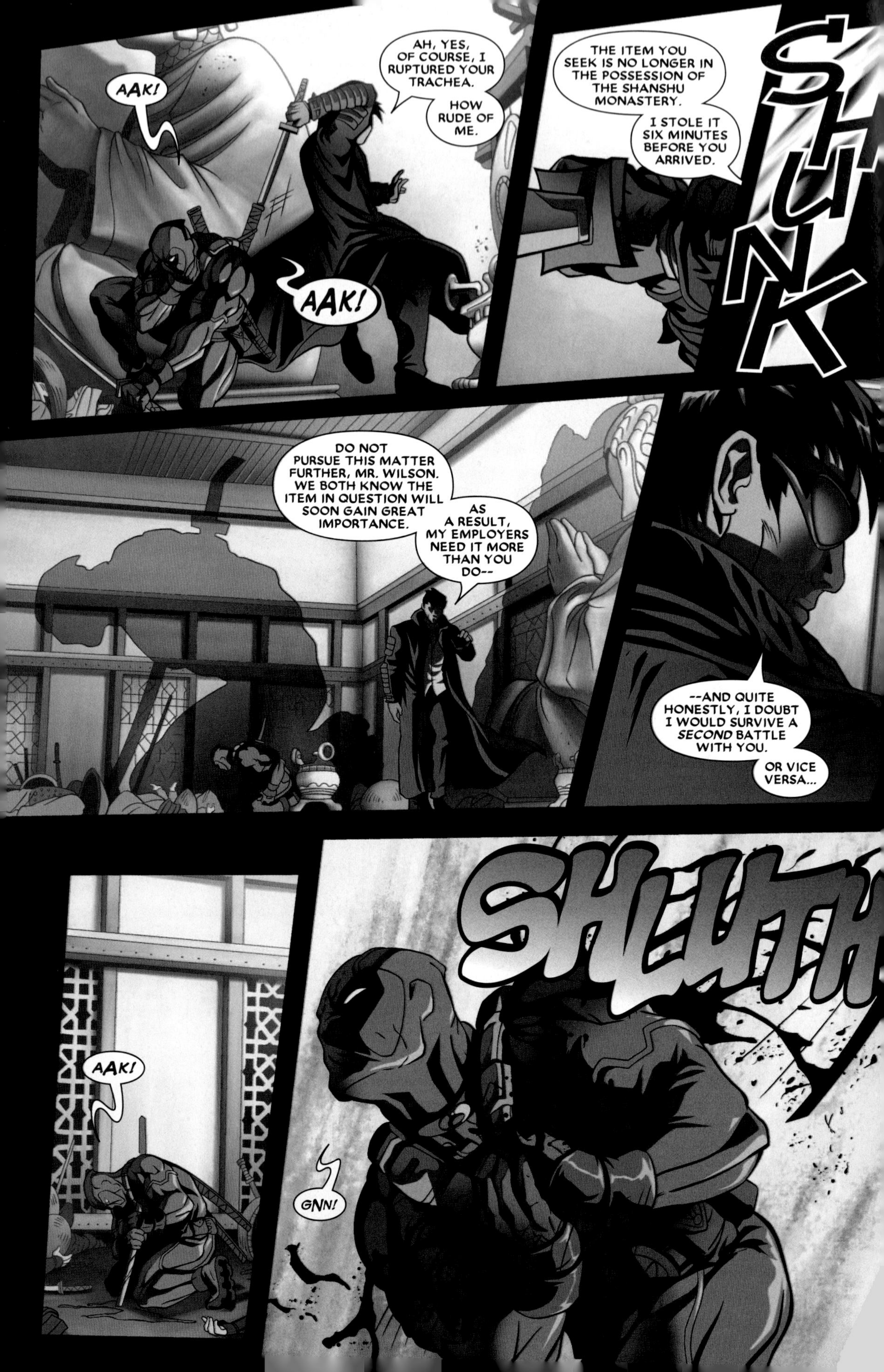
AAK!
AH, YES, OF COURSE, I RUPTURED YOUR TRACHEA.
HOW RUDE OF ME.
AAK!
THE ITEM YOU SEEK IS NO LONGER IN THE POSSESSION OF THE SHANSHU MONASTERY.
I STOLE IT SIX MINUTES BEFORE YOU ARRIVED.
SHUNK
DO NOT PURSUE THIS MATTER FURTHER, MR. WILSON. WE BOTH KNOW THE ITEM IN QUESTION WILL SOON GAIN GREAT IMPORTANCE.
AS A RESULT, MY EMPLOYERS NEED IT MORE THAN YOU DO--
--AND QUITE HONESTLY, I DOUBT I WOULD SURVIVE A *SECOND* BATTLE WITH YOU.
OR VICE VERSA...
AAK!
SHLUTH
GNN!

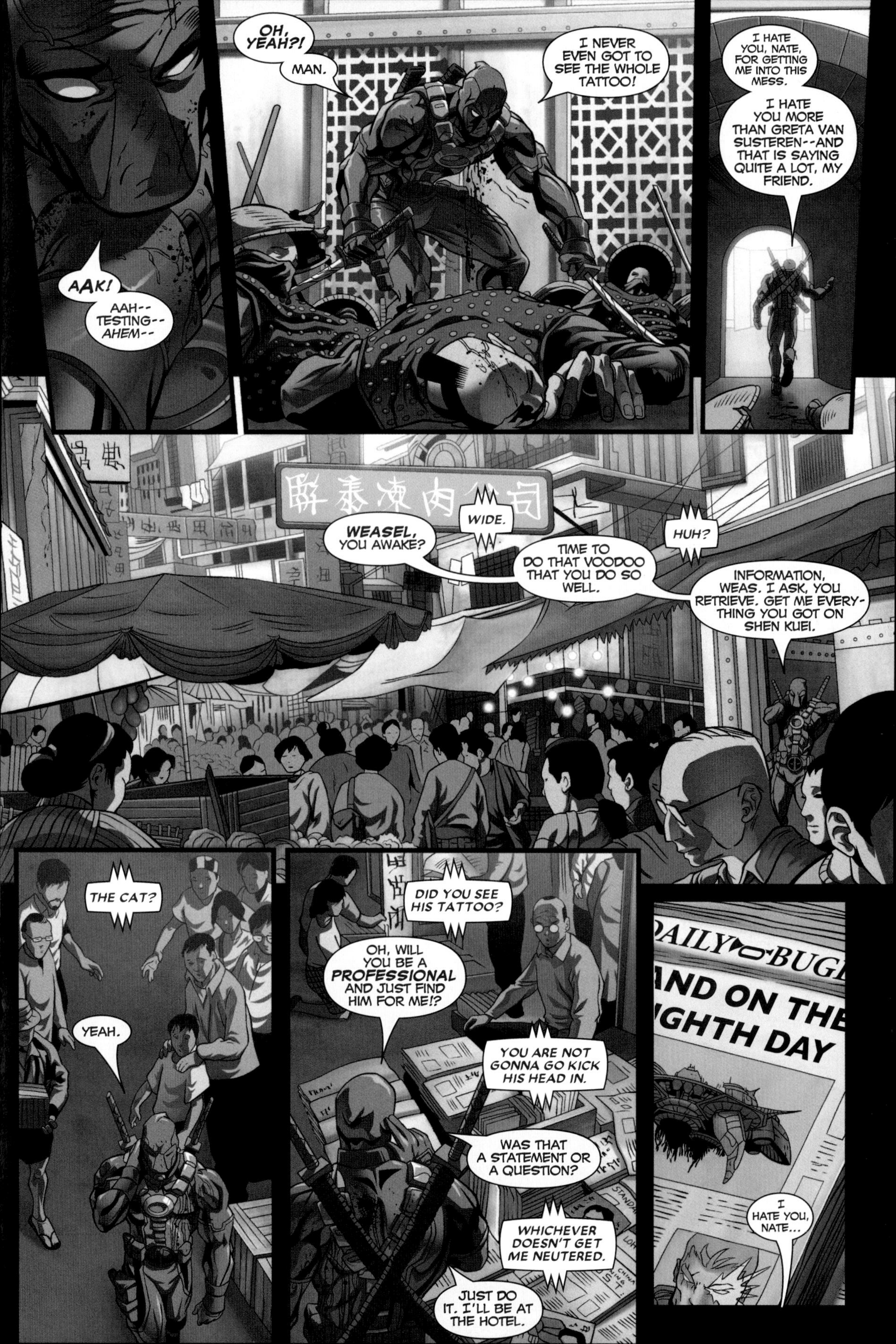

AAK!
AAH-- TESTING-- AHEM--
OH, YEAH?!
MAN.
I NEVER EVEN GOT TO SEE THE WHOLE TATTOO!
I HATE YOU, NATE, FOR GETTING ME INTO THIS MESS.
I HATE YOU MORE THAN GRETA VAN SUSTEREN--AND THAT IS SAYING QUITE A LOT, MY FRIEND.
WEASEL, YOU AWAKE?
WIDE.
TIME TO DO THAT VOODOO THAT YOU DO SO WELL.
HUH?
INFORMATION, WEAS. I ASK, YOU RETRIEVE. GET ME EVERYTHING YOU GOT ON SHEN KUEI.
THE CAT?
YEAH.
DID YOU SEE HIS TATTOO?
OH, WILL YOU BE A PROFESSIONAL AND JUST FIND HIM FOR ME!?
YOU ARE NOT GONNA GO KICK HIS HEAD IN.
WAS THAT A STATEMENT OR A QUESTION?
WHICHEVER DOESN'T GET ME NEUTERED.
JUST DO IT. I'LL BE AT THE HOTEL.
DAILY BUG
AND ON THE
GHTH DAY
I HATE YOU, NATE...

TESTAMENT

AN INTERVIEW WITH THE MAN KNOWN AS
CABLE

Irene Merryweather: Are you ready, Nathan?
Cable: You don't have the recorder on.
IM: Duh. There. So…it's not every day your best friend becomes a savior.
Cable: I didn't know I was your best friend.
IM: Don't avoid.
Cable: Okay. This isn't for *The Daily Bugle,* is it? I've read Jameson's mind…not pleasant.
IM: They fired me. Something about a gun in my desk--or drooling on my desk, I wasn't paying attention. This is freelance. Figure it should be easy to sell an interview with a holy man.
Cable: Please stop that.
IM: I'm sorry, does it bother you? Turning people's skin pink, changing it back and saying, "don't bother thanking me, just be thankful I'm here," raising chunks of debris from all over the earth and sculpting a floating sanctuary--should I go on?
Cable: Please do. It sounds more impressive when you run it all together…

IM: Four days rerouting waterways to flood half the Sahara, two days to throw every single logger out of the Amazon rain forest, two hours a day soothing the pain of every single person on the planet dying of any kind of disease--
Cable: Well, two hours where that's my only focus. I'm doing it right now, too.
IM: And managing to be a pompous twit while you're doing it. Let's see, stopping the white blood count deterioration of every AIDS victim in Africa, straightening the Leaning Tower of Pisa--
Cable: That one didn't go over as well as I'd hoped.
IM: Stopping a daily average of fourteen individual acts of terrorism, eleven hundred

attempted murders, seven thousand car accidents--
Cable: Thankfully, Ford stopped making Pintos.
IM: You think this is funny?
Cable: My mission or this interview?
IM: Let's talk about your mission. What is it?
Cable: I want to save the world.
IM: From what?
Cable: From itself. From your superhuman demagogue of the week.
IM: Like you?
Cable: I've never met a demagogue who tried to cure disease, soothe pain…I helped Marian Pittlaw from Perkasie, Pennsylvania with her taxes.
IM: You monster.
Cable: She did owe money.
IM: Back to your mission…
Cable: So between coy banter you'll accuse me of being a madman?
IM: Are you?

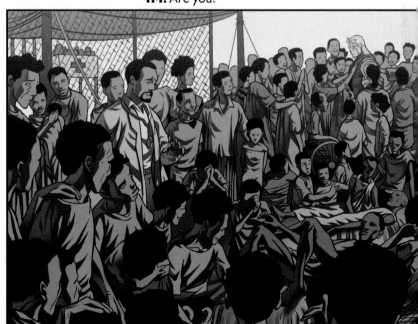

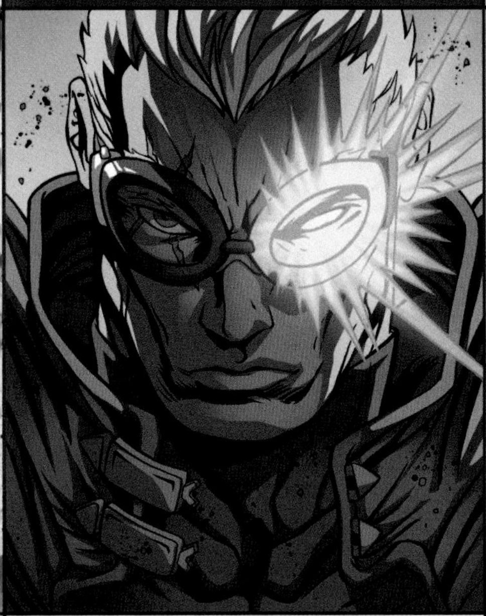

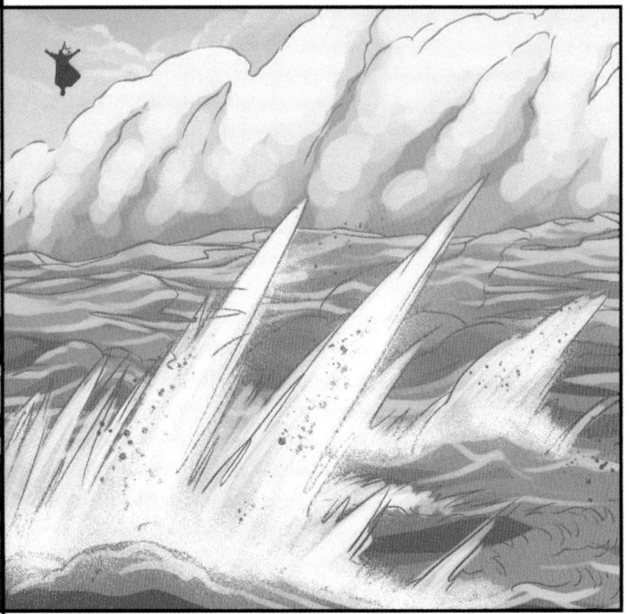

"I want to save the world and I have the power to do it."--CABLE

Cable: No, Irene. I don't see myself that way at all.
IM: When Hitler looked in the mirror, did he see a madman?
Cable: I've lived under the crushing heel of a creature that made Hitler look like a Beanie Baby--and that's not to diminish what that pathetic maniac did, just to explain that I know the face of evil. I've stared it in the eye.

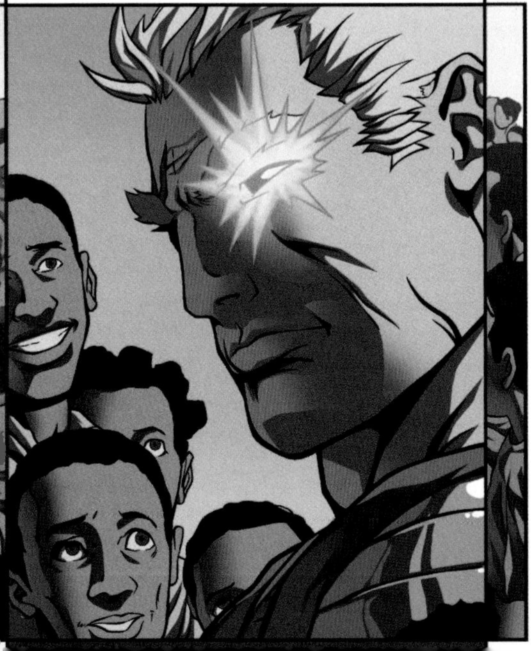

IM: You're talking about Apocalypse?
Cable: Yes.
IM: He was an immortal, powered by alien technology and genetic enhancements.
Cable: Yes.
IM: And you come from the future--a time when Apocalypse had ruled for centuries?
Cable: Yes.
IM: A time when the struggles, the schism between mutants and humans, remained?
Cable: Unfortunately, yes.
IM: So what do you hope to do here in the present?
Cable: I don't understand.
IM: Why are you here if you know what the future holds in store? I mean, nothing you do now can change what will be.
Cable: Time travel is a tricky thing, Irene. Nothing I do can change *my* past, but everything I do can change *your* future. My past doesn't have to be your future.
IM: I have a headache.
Cable: It can get confusing.
IM: So everything you're doing is to help prevent the kind of world you come from?
Cable: Like I said, I want to save the world and I have the power to do it.
IM: Let's talk about that. People are afraid of mutants--
Cable: That's understandable. We're different. We're an evolutionary change. People resist change.
IM: And occasionally, a mutant will do something like, oh, say, try to destroy the world.
Cable: Humans have flown planes into crowded buildings. Dropped sarin gas on innocent people. People murder people--does that make *all* humans inherently bad?
IM: So to the people who are afraid of mutants--afraid of having peace imposed on them--
Cable: I'm not imposing anything.
IM: What would you call--
Cable: I can read their minds, Irene--I can read yours, too--I *know* what people want.
IM: And what's that?
Cable: They want what I can give them...

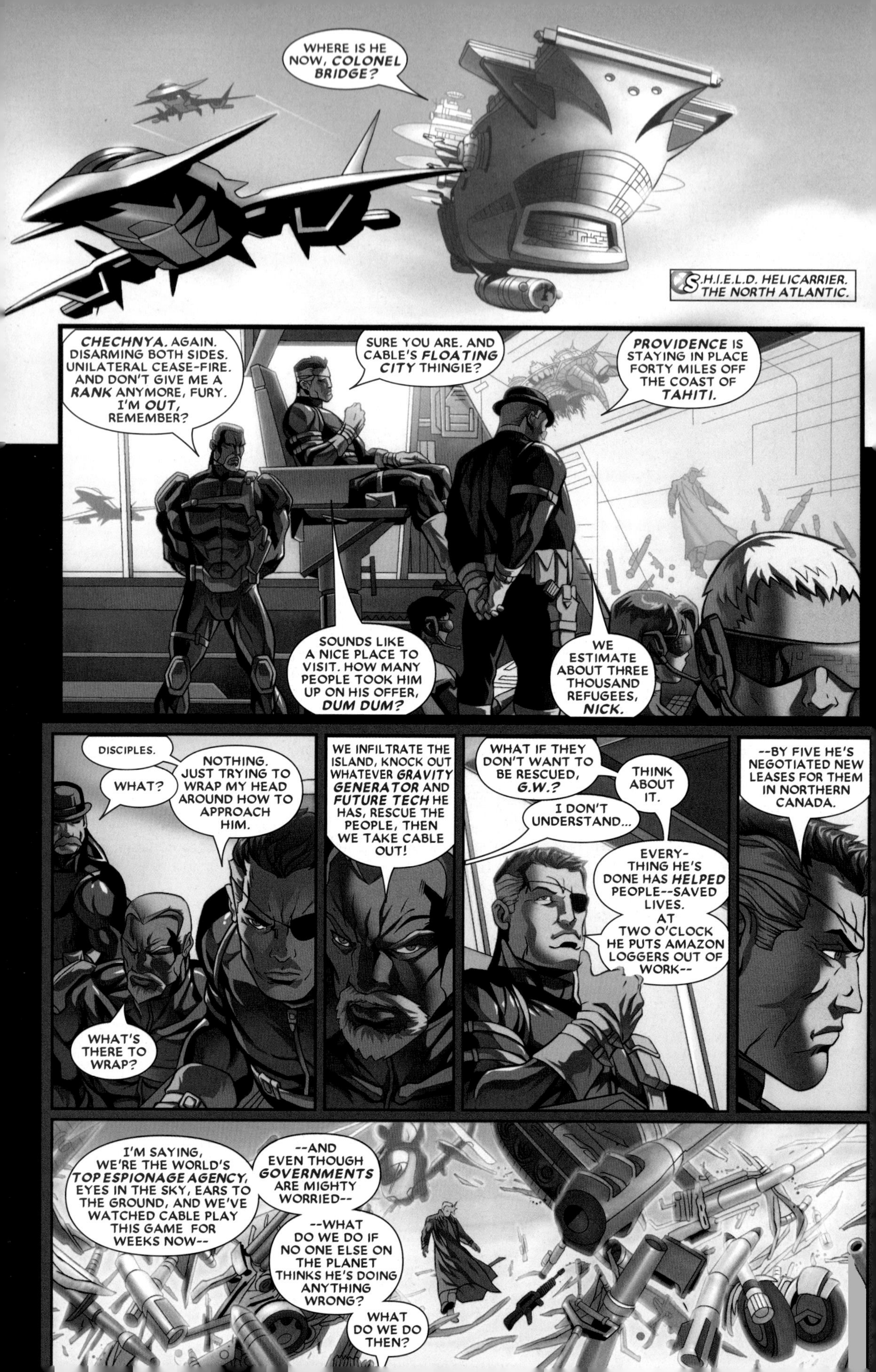
WHERE IS HE NOW, COLONEL BRIDGE?
S.H.I.E.L.D. HELICARRIER. THE NORTH ATLANTIC.
CHECHNYA. AGAIN. DISARMING BOTH SIDES. UNILATERAL CEASE-FIRE. AND DON'T GIVE ME A RANK ANYMORE, FURY. I'M OUT, REMEMBER?
SURE YOU ARE. AND CABLE'S FLOATING CITY THINGIE?
PROVIDENCE IS STAYING IN PLACE FORTY MILES OFF THE COAST OF TAHITI.
SOUNDS LIKE A NICE PLACE TO VISIT. HOW MANY PEOPLE TOOK HIM UP ON HIS OFFER, DUM DUM?
WE ESTIMATE ABOUT THREE THOUSAND REFUGEES, NICK.
DISCIPLES.
WHAT?
NOTHING. JUST TRYING TO WRAP MY HEAD AROUND HOW TO APPROACH HIM.
WHAT'S THERE TO WRAP?
WE INFILTRATE THE ISLAND, KNOCK OUT WHATEVER GRAVITY GENERATOR AND FUTURE TECH HE HAS, RESCUE THE PEOPLE, THEN WE TAKE CABLE OUT!
WHAT IF THEY DON'T WANT TO BE RESCUED, G.W.?
I DON'T UNDERSTAND...
THINK ABOUT IT.
EVERY-THING HE'S DONE HAS HELPED PEOPLE--SAVED LIVES.
AT TWO O'CLOCK HE PUTS AMAZON LOGGERS OUT OF WORK--
--BY FIVE HE'S NEGOTIATED NEW LEASES FOR THEM IN NORTHERN CANADA.
I'M SAYING, WE'RE THE WORLD'S TOP ESPIONAGE AGENCY, EYES IN THE SKY, EARS TO THE GROUND, AND WE'VE WATCHED CABLE PLAY THIS GAME FOR WEEKS NOW--
--AND EVEN THOUGH GOVERNMENTS ARE MIGHTY WORRIED--
--WHAT DO WE DO IF NO ONE ELSE ON THE PLANET THINKS HE'S DOING ANYTHING WRONG?
WHAT DO WE DO THEN?

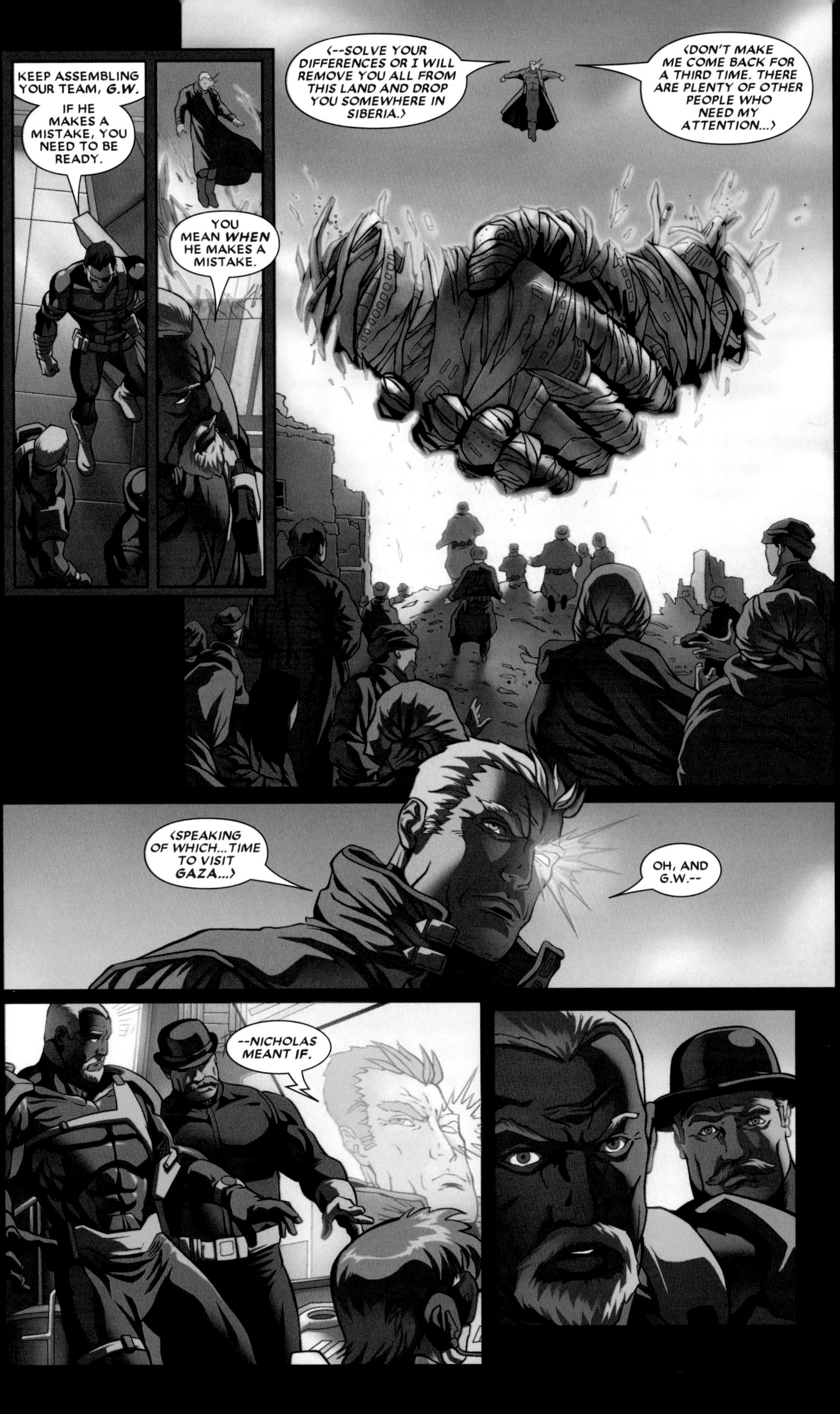
KEEP ASSEMBLING YOUR TEAM, G.W.
IF HE MAKES A MISTAKE, YOU NEED TO BE READY.
YOU MEAN WHEN HE MAKES A MISTAKE.
‹--SOLVE YOUR DIFFERENCES OR I WILL REMOVE YOU ALL FROM THIS LAND AND DROP YOU SOMEWHERE IN SIBERIA.›
‹DON'T MAKE ME COME BACK FOR A THIRD TIME. THERE ARE PLENTY OF OTHER PEOPLE WHO NEED MY ATTENTION...›
‹SPEAKING OF WHICH...TIME TO VISIT GAZA...›
OH, AND G.W.--
--NICHOLAS MEANT IF.

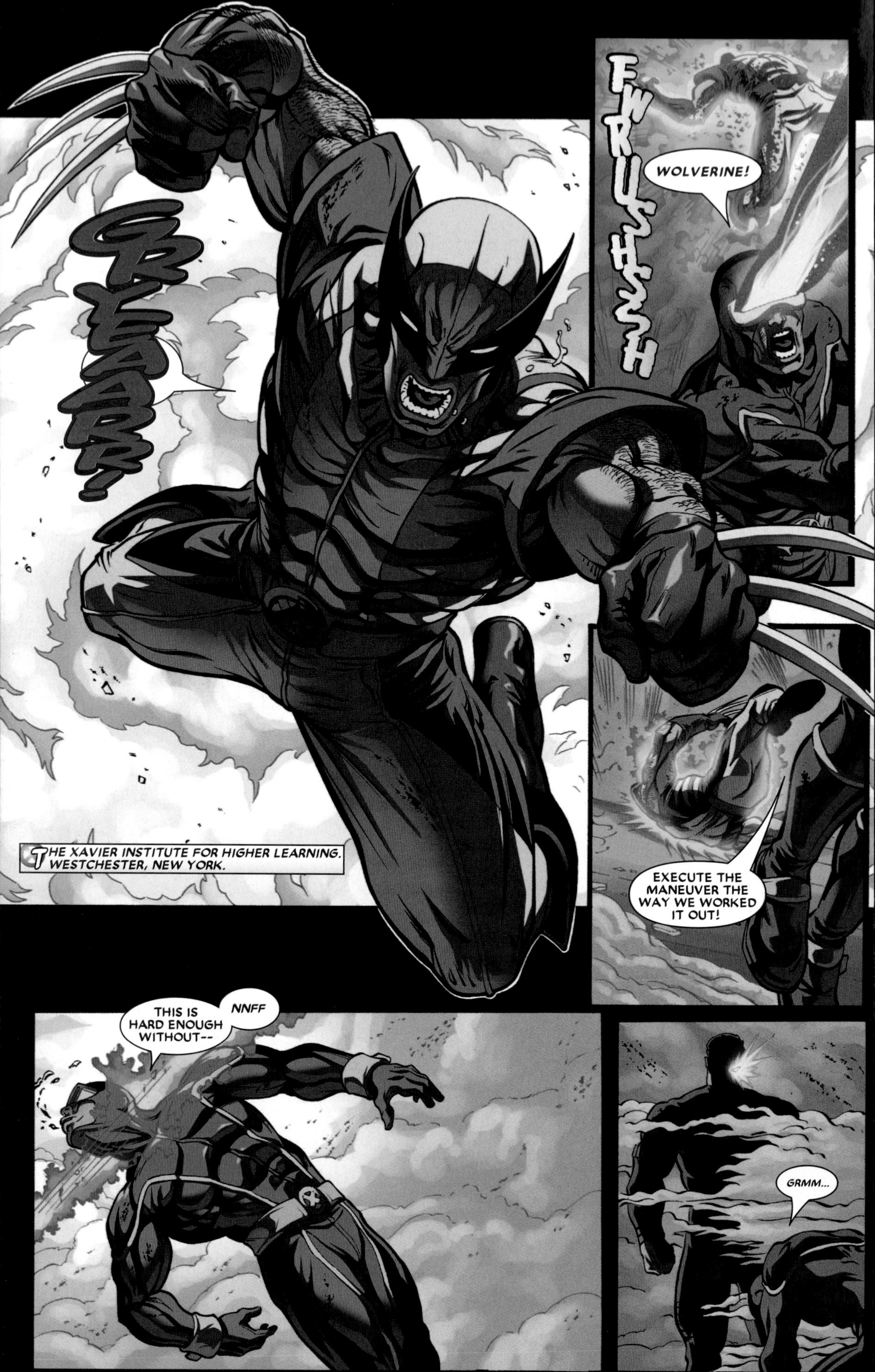
GRYEAARRR!
THE XAVIER INSTITUTE FOR HIGHER LEARNING. WESTCHESTER, NEW YORK.
FWRUSHSHSH
WOLVERINE!
EXECUTE THE MANEUVER THE WAY WE WORKED IT OUT!
NNFF
THIS IS HARD ENOUGH WITHOUT--
GRMM...

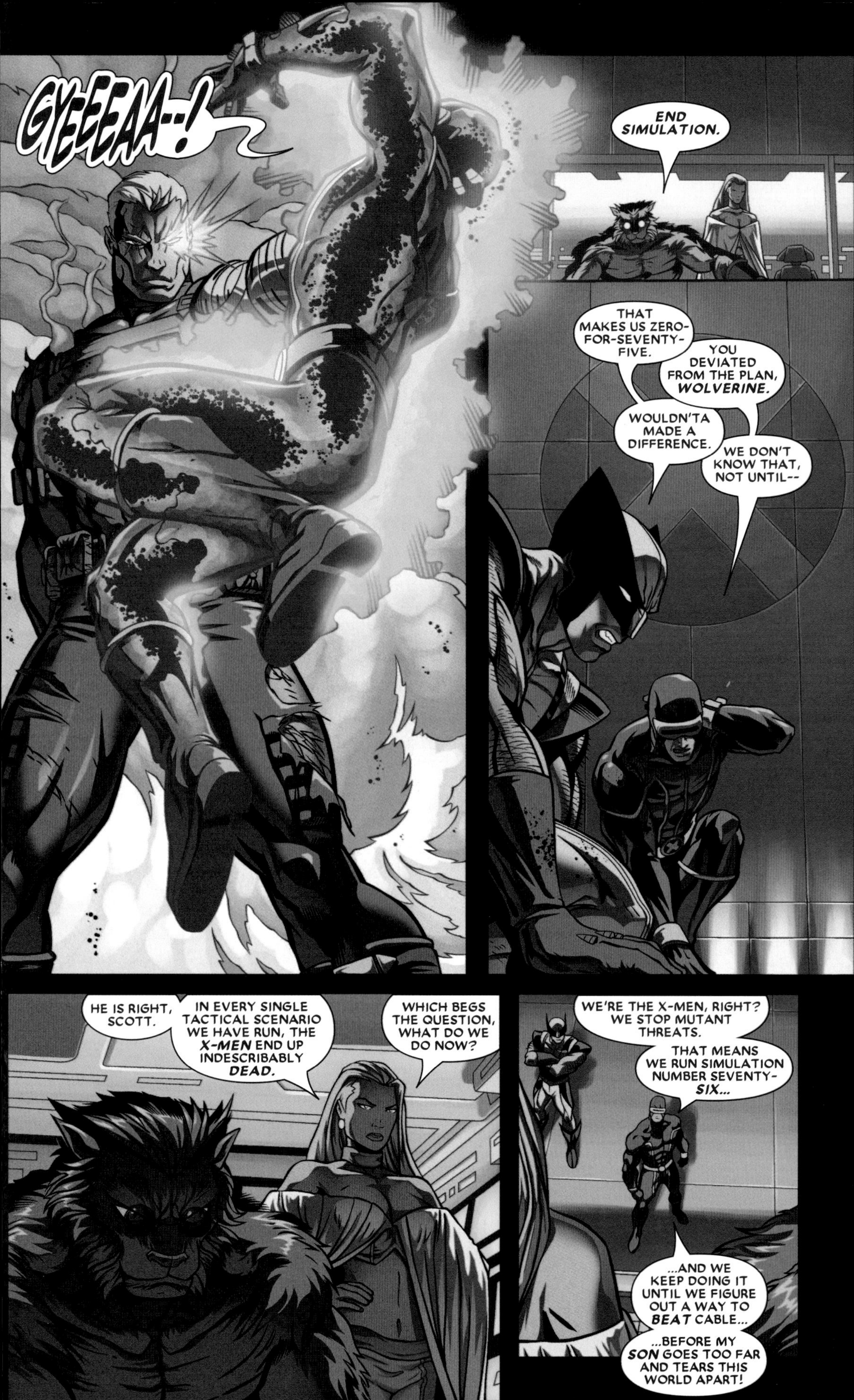
GYEEEAA--!
END SIMULATION.
THAT MAKES US ZERO-FOR-SEVENTY-FIVE.
YOU DEVIATED FROM THE PLAN, WOLVERINE.
WOULDN'TA MADE A DIFFERENCE.
WE DON'T KNOW THAT, NOT UNTIL--
HE IS RIGHT, SCOTT.
IN EVERY SINGLE TACTICAL SCENARIO WE HAVE RUN, THE X-MEN END UP INDESCRIBABLY DEAD.
WHICH BEGS THE QUESTION, WHAT DO WE DO NOW?
WE'RE THE X-MEN, RIGHT? WE STOP MUTANT THREATS.
THAT MEANS WE RUN SIMULATION NUMBER SEVENTY-SIX...
...AND WE KEEP DOING IT UNTIL WE FIGURE OUT A WAY TO BEAT CABLE...
...BEFORE MY SON GOES TOO FAR AND TEARS THIS WORLD APART!

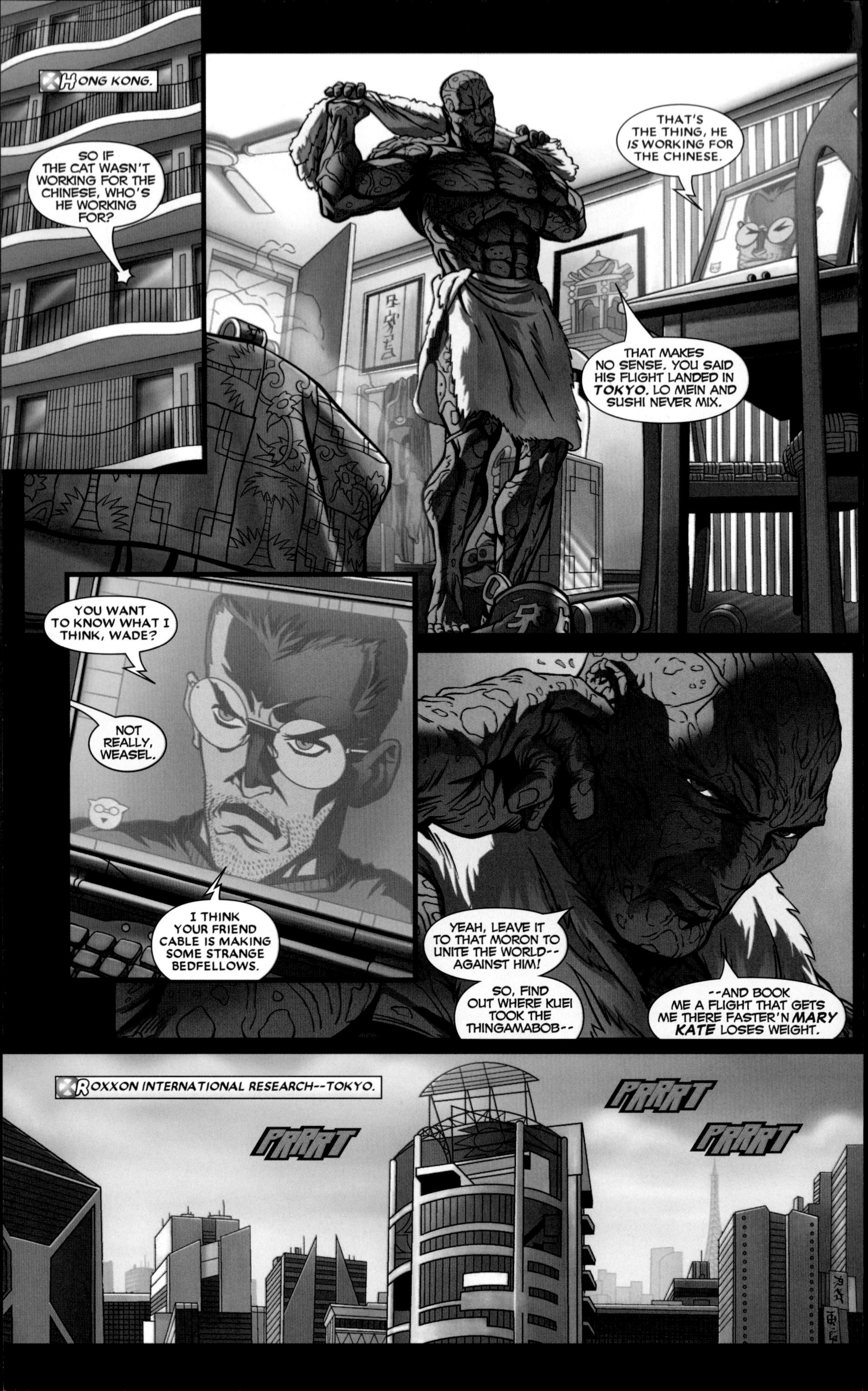
HONG KONG.
SO IF THE CAT WASN'T WORKING FOR THE CHINESE, WHO'S HE WORKING FOR?
THAT'S THE THING, HE IS WORKING FOR THE CHINESE.
THAT MAKES NO SENSE. YOU SAID HIS FLIGHT LANDED IN TOKYO. LO MEIN AND SUSHI NEVER MIX.
YOU WANT TO KNOW WHAT I THINK, WADE?
NOT REALLY, WEASEL.
I THINK YOUR FRIEND CABLE IS MAKING SOME STRANGE BEDFELLOWS.
YEAH, LEAVE IT TO THAT MORON TO UNITE THE WORLD--AGAINST HIM!
SO, FIND OUT WHERE KUEI TOOK THE THINGAMABOB--
--AND BOOK ME A FLIGHT THAT GETS ME THERE FASTER'N MARY KATE LOSES WEIGHT.
ROXXON INTERNATIONAL RESEARCH--TOKYO.
PRRRT
PRRRT
PRRRT

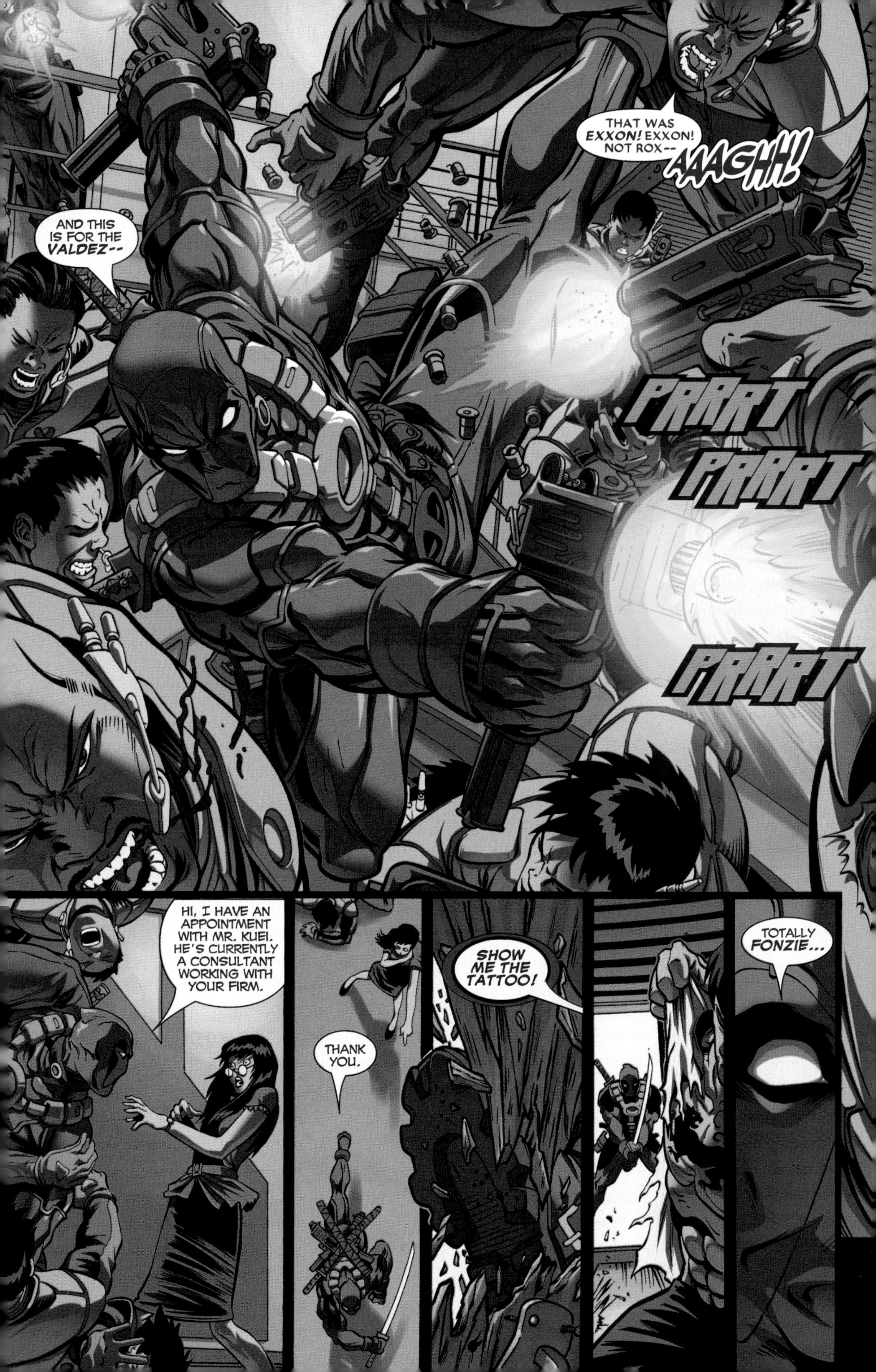
THAT WAS EXXON! EXXON! NOT ROX--
AAAGHH!
AND THIS IS FOR THE VALDEZ--
PRRRT
PRRRT
PRRRT
HI, I HAVE AN APPOINTMENT WITH MR. KUEI. HE'S CURRENTLY A CONSULTANT WORKING WITH YOUR FIRM.
THANK YOU.
SHOW ME THE TATTOO!
TOTALLY FONZIE...

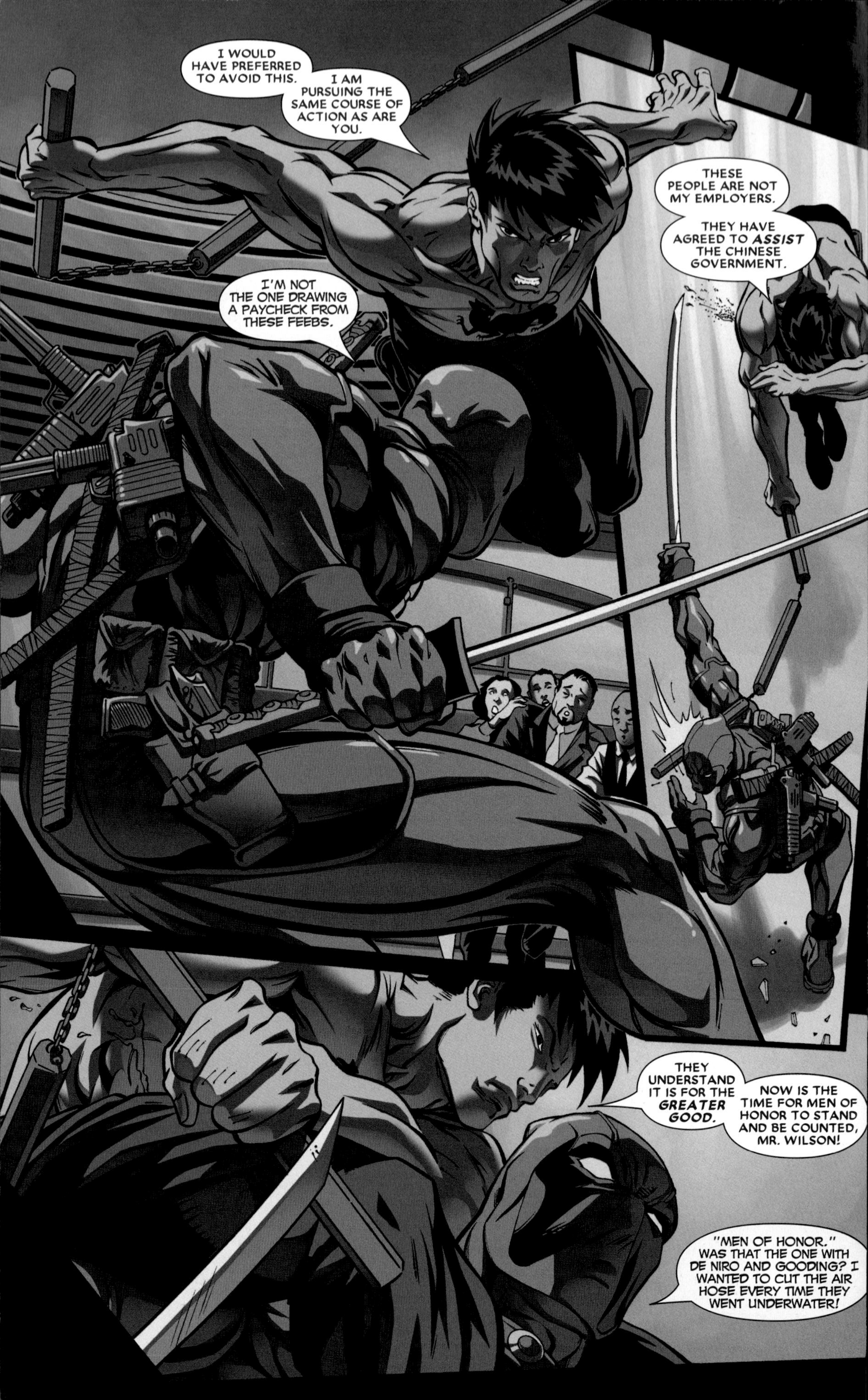
I WOULD HAVE PREFERRED TO AVOID THIS.
I AM PURSUING THE SAME COURSE OF ACTION AS ARE YOU.
THESE PEOPLE ARE NOT MY EMPLOYERS.
THEY HAVE AGREED TO *ASSIST* THE CHINESE GOVERNMENT.
I'M NOT THE ONE DRAWING A PAYCHECK FROM THESE FEEBS.
THEY UNDERSTAND IT IS FOR THE *GREATER GOOD.*
NOW IS THE TIME FOR MEN OF HONOR TO STAND AND BE COUNTED, MR. WILSON!
"MEN OF HONOR." WAS THAT THE ONE WITH DE NIRO AND GOODING? I WANTED TO CUT THE AIR HOSE EVERY TIME THEY WENT UNDERWATER!

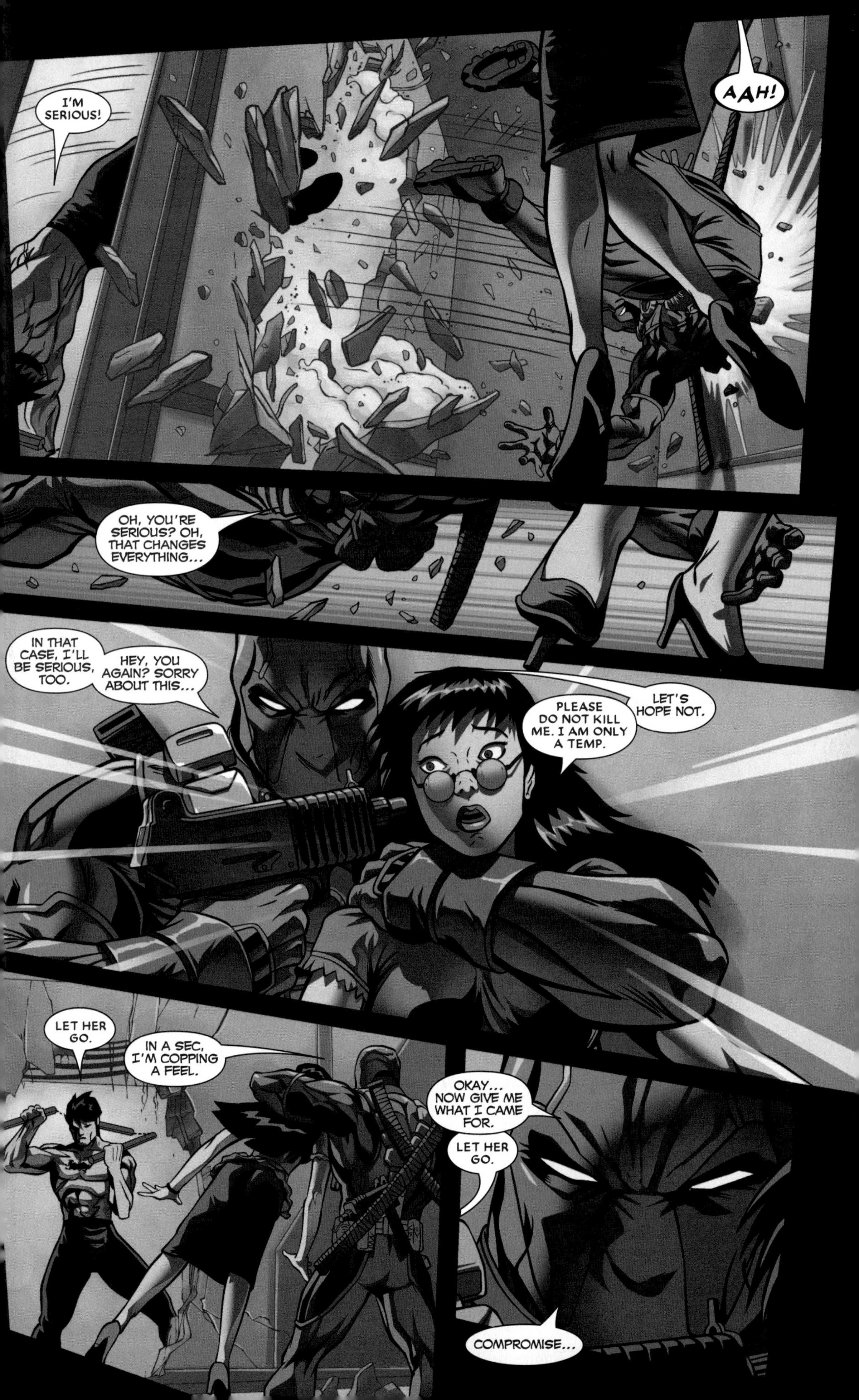
I'M SERIOUS!
AAH!
OH, YOU'RE SERIOUS? OH, THAT CHANGES EVERYTHING...
IN THAT CASE, I'LL BE SERIOUS, TOO.
HEY, YOU AGAIN? SORRY ABOUT THIS...
PLEASE DO NOT KILL ME. I AM ONLY A TEMP.
LET'S HOPE NOT.
LET HER GO.
IN A SEC, I'M COPPING A FEEL.
OKAY... NOW GIVE ME WHAT I CAME FOR.
LET HER GO.
COMPROMISE...

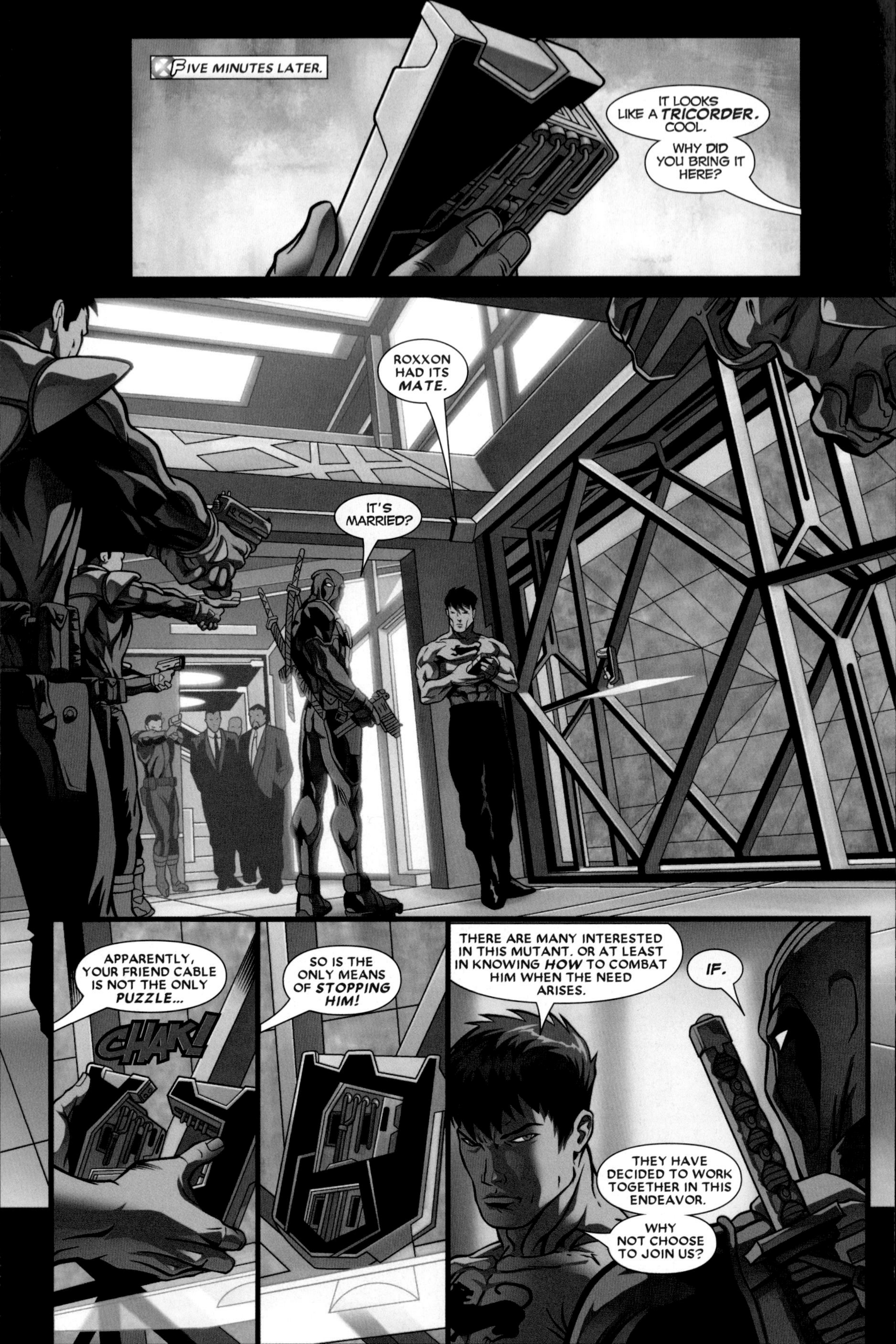
FIVE MINUTES LATER.
IT LOOKS LIKE A TRICORDER. COOL.
WHY DID YOU BRING IT HERE?
ROXXON HAD ITS MATE.
IT'S MARRIED?
APPARENTLY, YOUR FRIEND CABLE IS NOT THE ONLY PUZZLE...
CHAK!
SO IS THE ONLY MEANS OF STOPPING HIM!
THERE ARE MANY INTERESTED IN THIS MUTANT. OR AT LEAST IN KNOWING HOW TO COMBAT HIM WHEN THE NEED ARISES.
IF.
THEY HAVE DECIDED TO WORK TOGETHER IN THIS ENDEAVOR.
WHY NOT CHOOSE TO JOIN US?

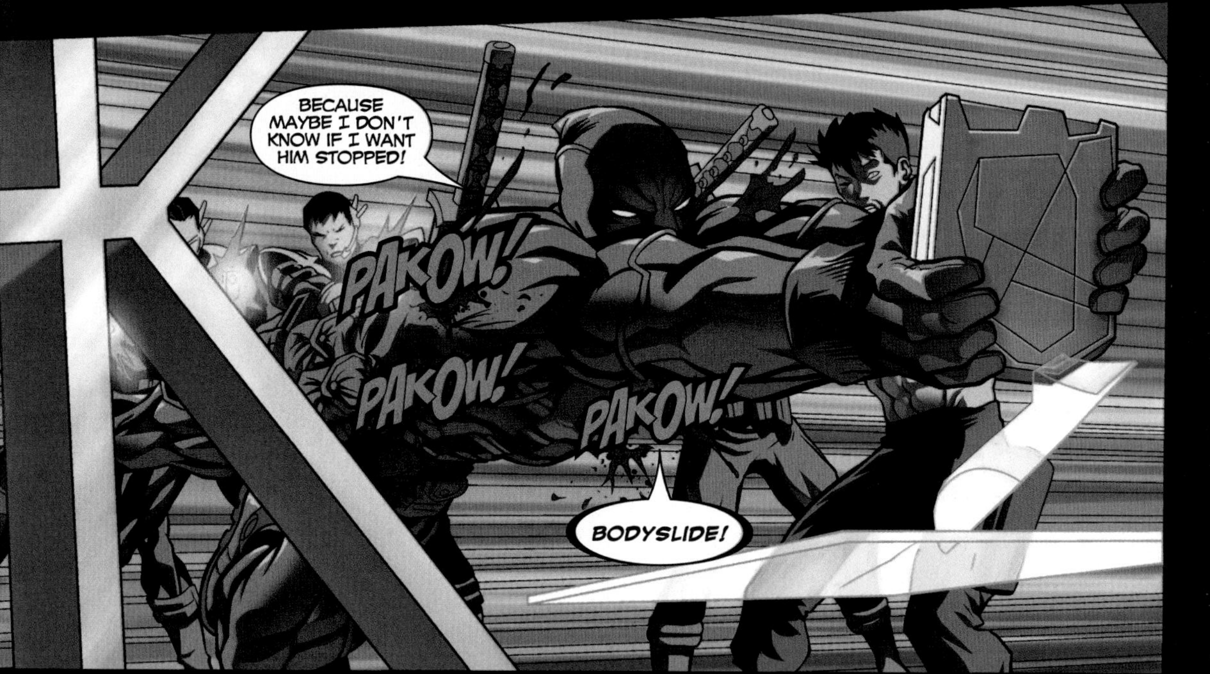
BECAUSE MAYBE I DON'T KNOW IF I WANT HIM STOPPED!
PAKOW!
PAKOW!
PAKOW!
BODYSLIDE!

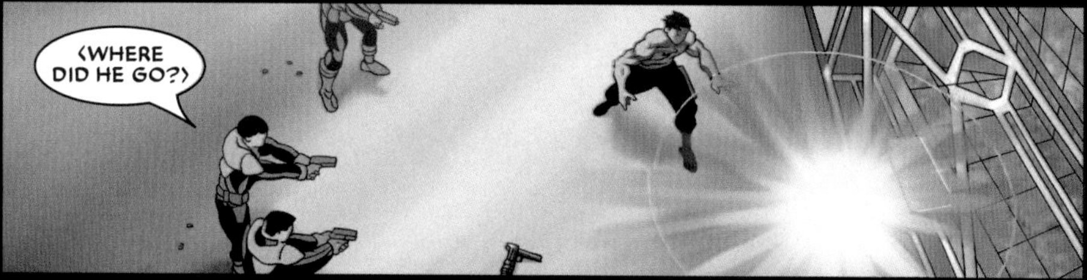
‹WHERE DID HE GO?›

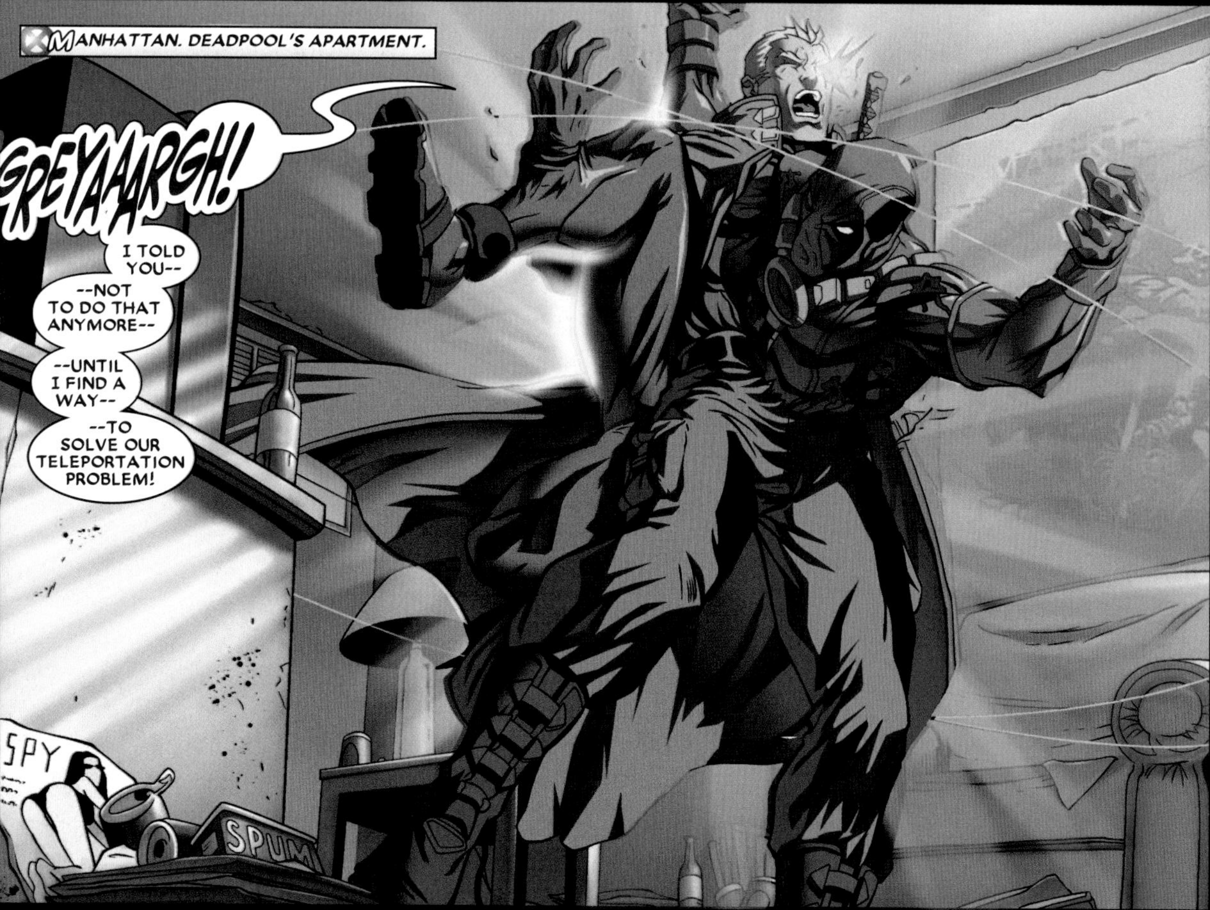
MANHATTAN. DEADPOOL'S APARTMENT.
GREYAAARGH!
I TOLD YOU--
--NOT TO DO THAT ANYMORE--
--UNTIL I FIND A WAY--
--TO SOLVE OUR TELEPORTATION PROBLEM!
SPY
SPUM

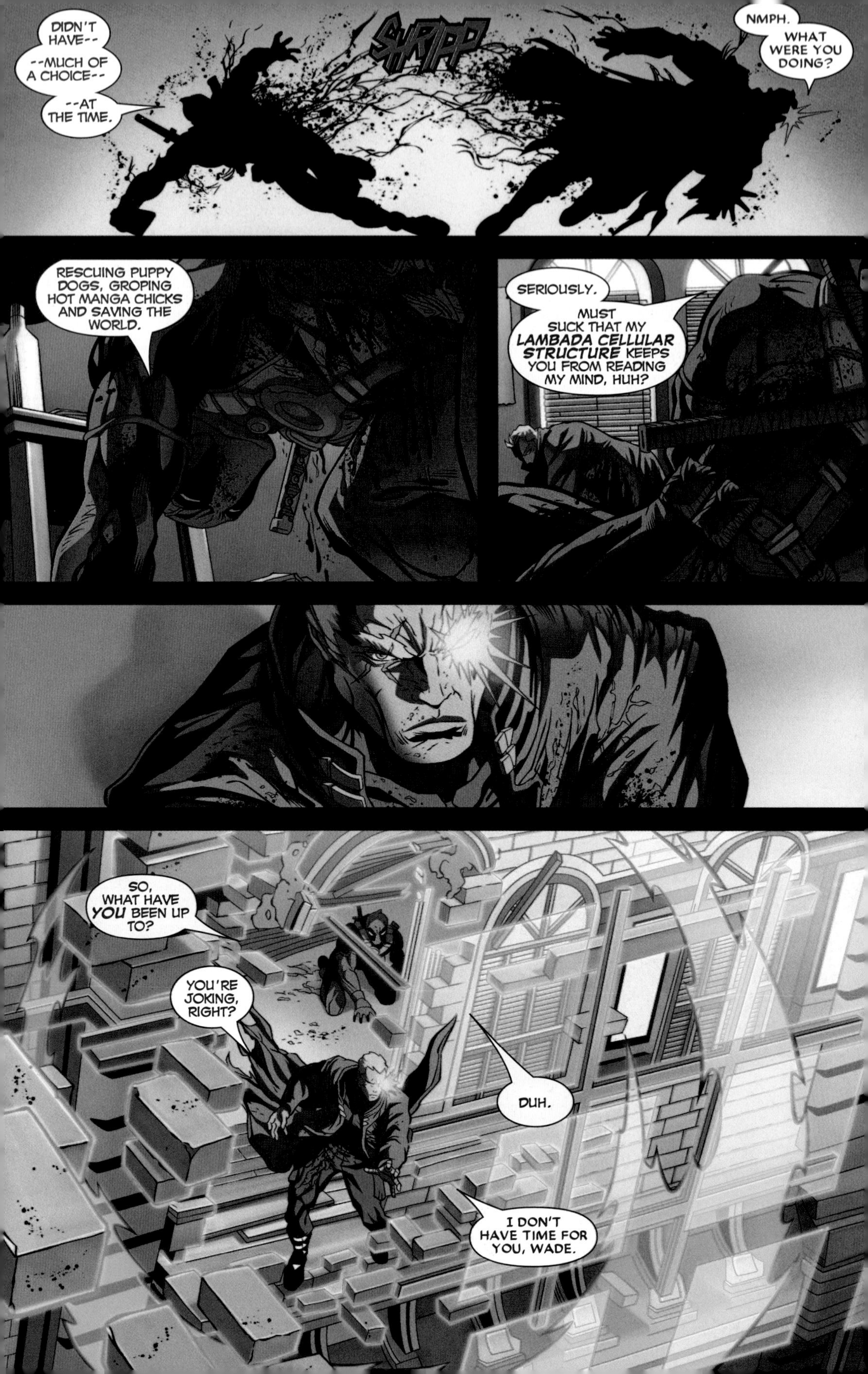
DIDN'T HAVE--
--MUCH OF A CHOICE--
--AT THE TIME.
SHRTPP
NMPH. WHAT WERE YOU DOING?
RESCUING PUPPY DOGS, GROPING HOT MANGA CHICKS AND SAVING THE WORLD.
SERIOUSLY.
MUST SUCK THAT MY **LAMBADA CELLULAR STRUCTURE** KEEPS YOU FROM READING MY MIND, HUH?
SO, WHAT HAVE **YOU** BEEN UP TO?
YOU'RE JOKING, RIGHT?
DUH.
I DON'T HAVE TIME FOR YOU, WADE.

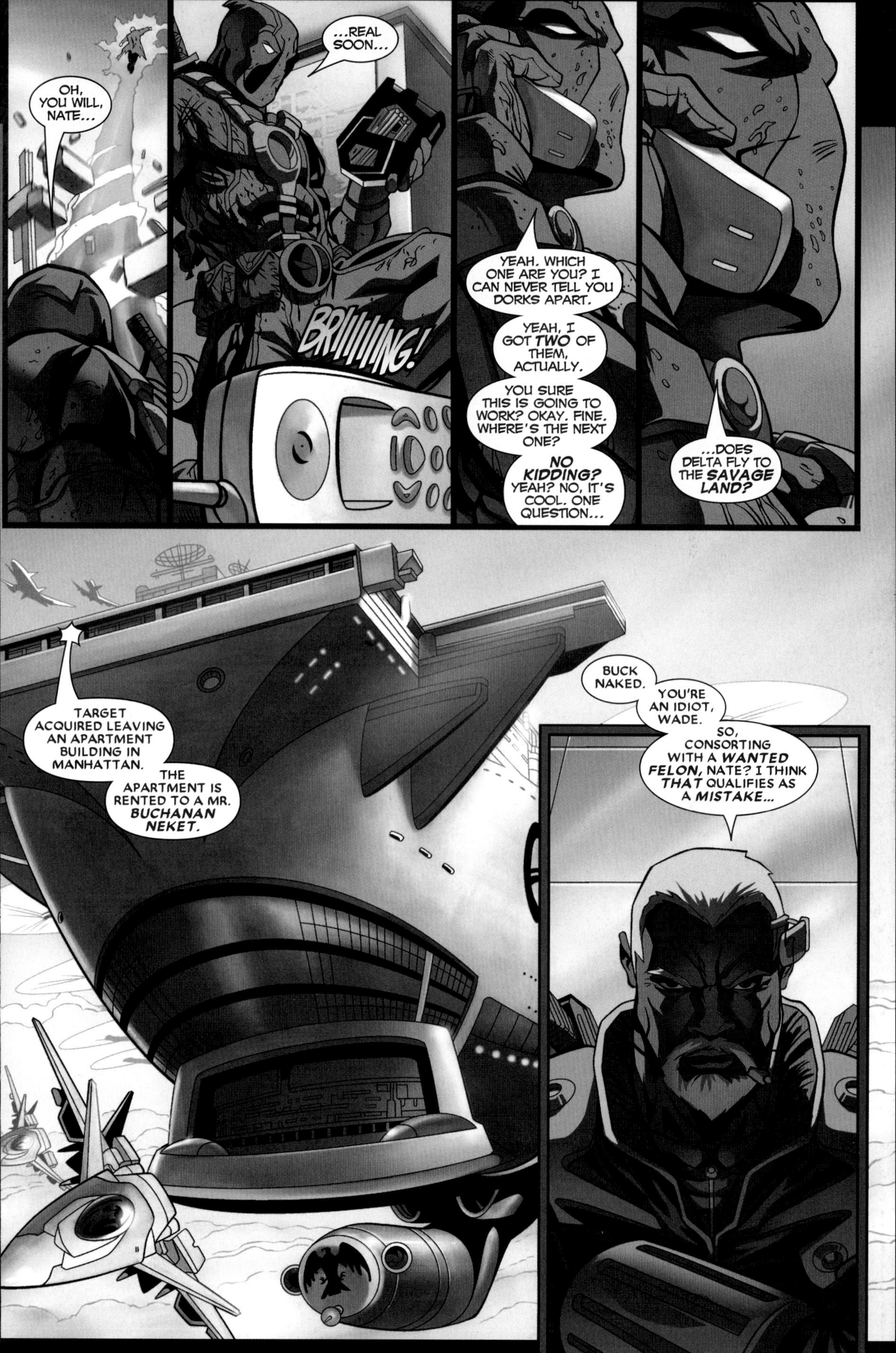
OH, YOU WILL, NATE...
...REAL SOON...
BRIIIIIING!
YEAH. WHICH ONE ARE YOU? I CAN NEVER TELL YOU DORKS APART.
YEAH, I GOT TWO OF THEM, ACTUALLY.
YOU SURE THIS IS GOING TO WORK? OKAY. FINE. WHERE'S THE NEXT ONE?
NO KIDDING? YEAH? NO, IT'S COOL. ONE QUESTION...
...DOES DELTA FLY TO THE SAVAGE LAND?
TARGET ACQUIRED LEAVING AN APARTMENT BUILDING IN MANHATTAN.
THE APARTMENT IS RENTED TO A MR. BUCHANAN NEKET.
BUCK NAKED.
YOU'RE AN IDIOT, WADE.
SO, CONSORTING WITH A WANTED FELON, NATE? I THINK THAT QUALIFIES AS A MISTAKE...

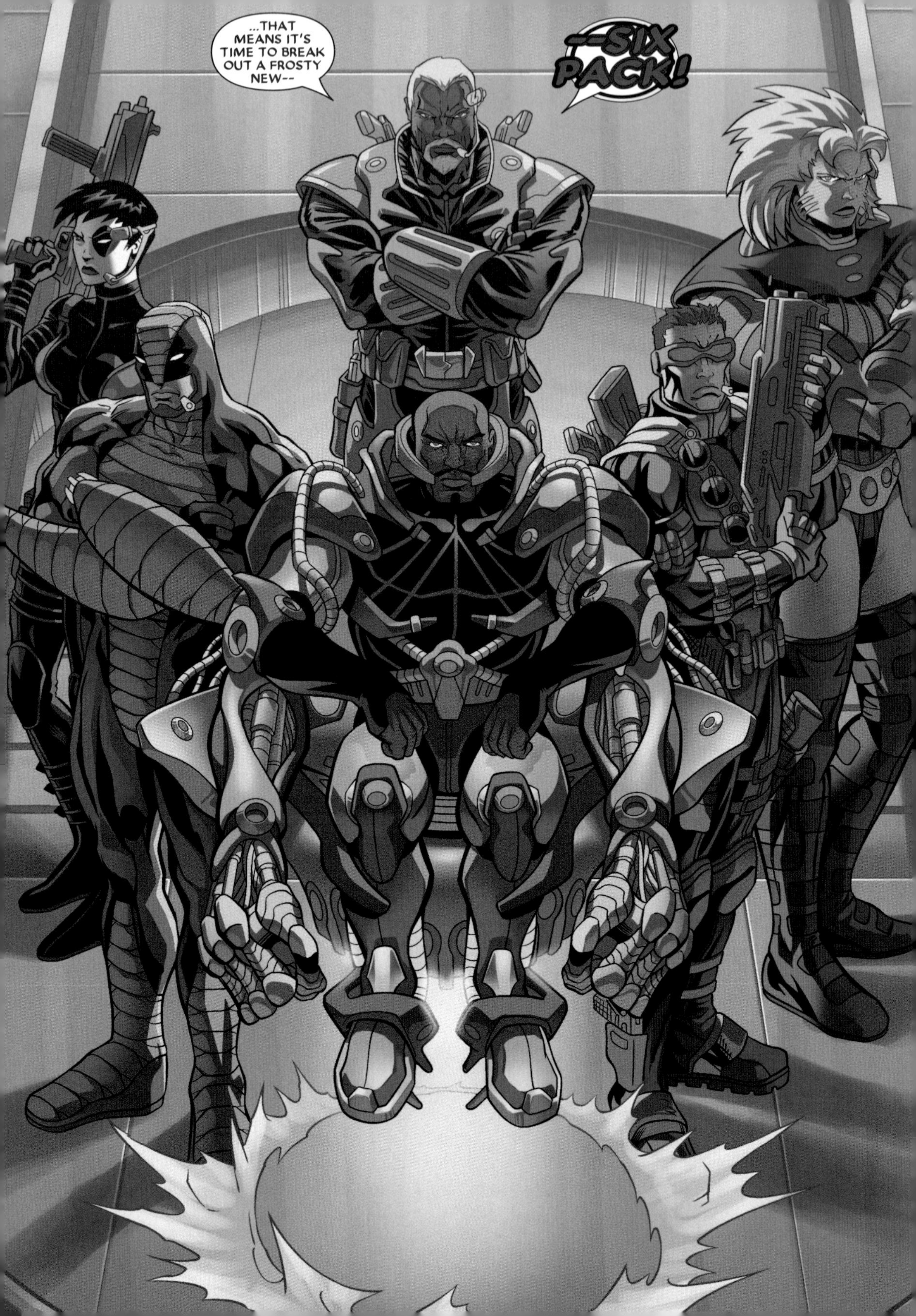
...THAT MEANS IT'S TIME TO BREAK OUT A FROSTY NEW--
--SIX PACK!

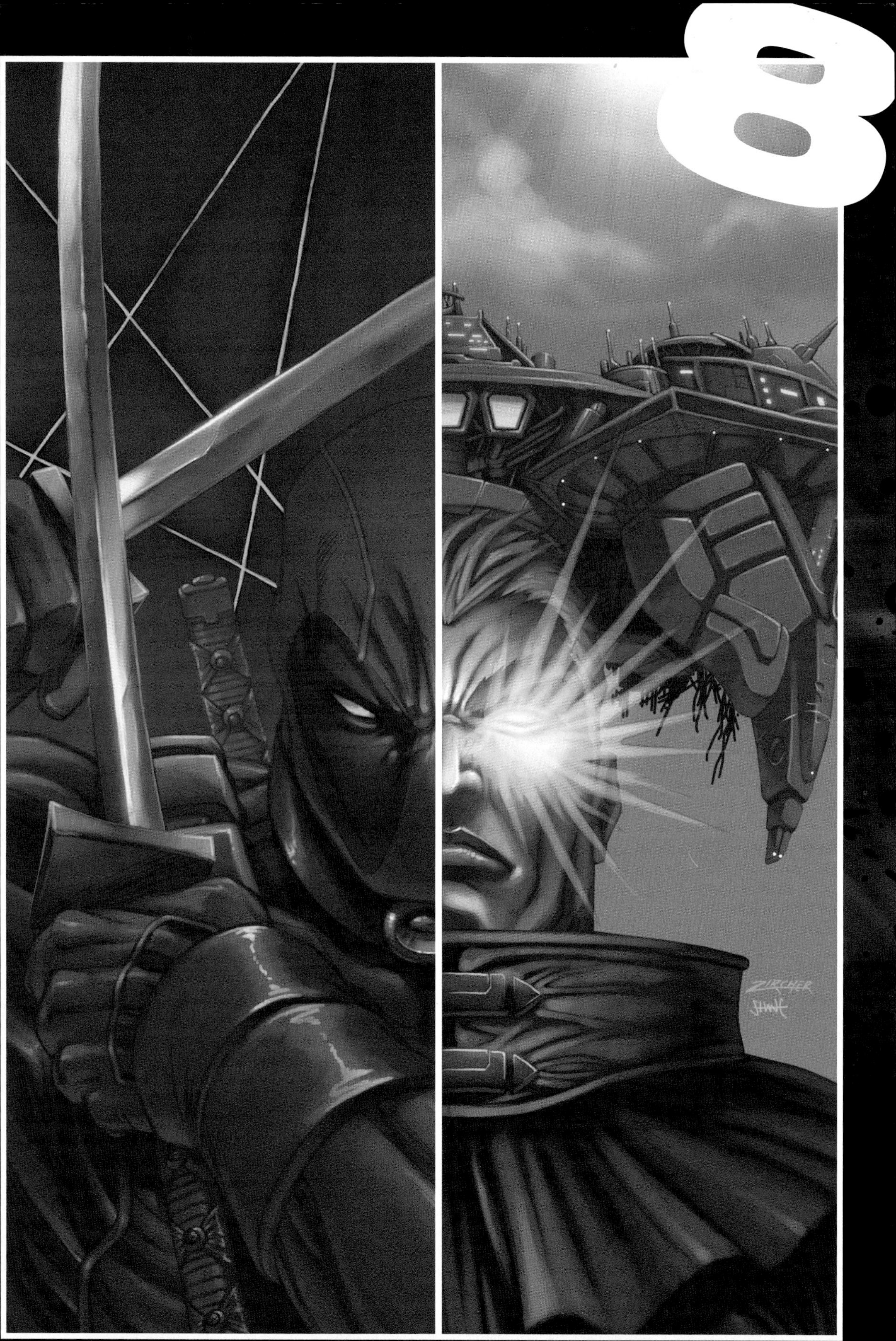
8
ZIRCHER

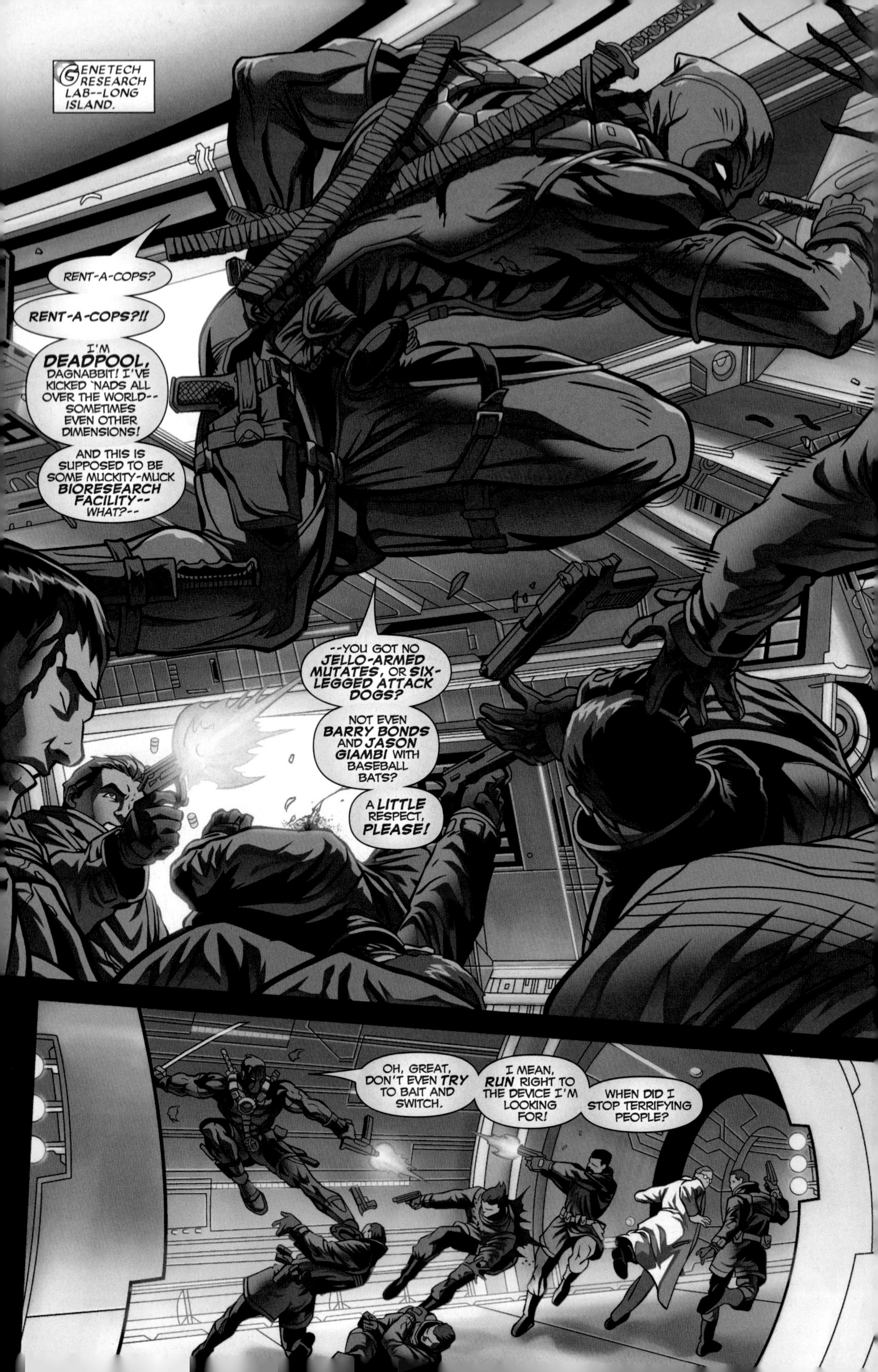
GENETECH RESEARCH LAB--LONG ISLAND.
RENT-A-COPS?
RENT-A-COPS?!!
I'M DEADPOOL, DAGNABBIT! I'VE KICKED 'NADS ALL OVER THE WORLD-- SOMETIMES EVEN OTHER DIMENSIONS!
AND THIS IS SUPPOSED TO BE SOME MUCKITY-MUCK BIORESEARCH FACILITY-- WHAT?--
--YOU GOT NO JELLO-ARMED MUTATES, OR SIX-LEGGED ATTACK DOGS?
NOT EVEN BARRY BONDS AND JASON GIAMBI WITH BASEBALL BATS?
A LITTLE RESPECT, PLEASE!
OH, GREAT, DON'T EVEN TRY TO BAIT AND SWITCH.
I MEAN, RUN RIGHT TO THE DEVICE I'M LOOKING FOR!
WHEN DID I STOP TERRIFYING PEOPLE?

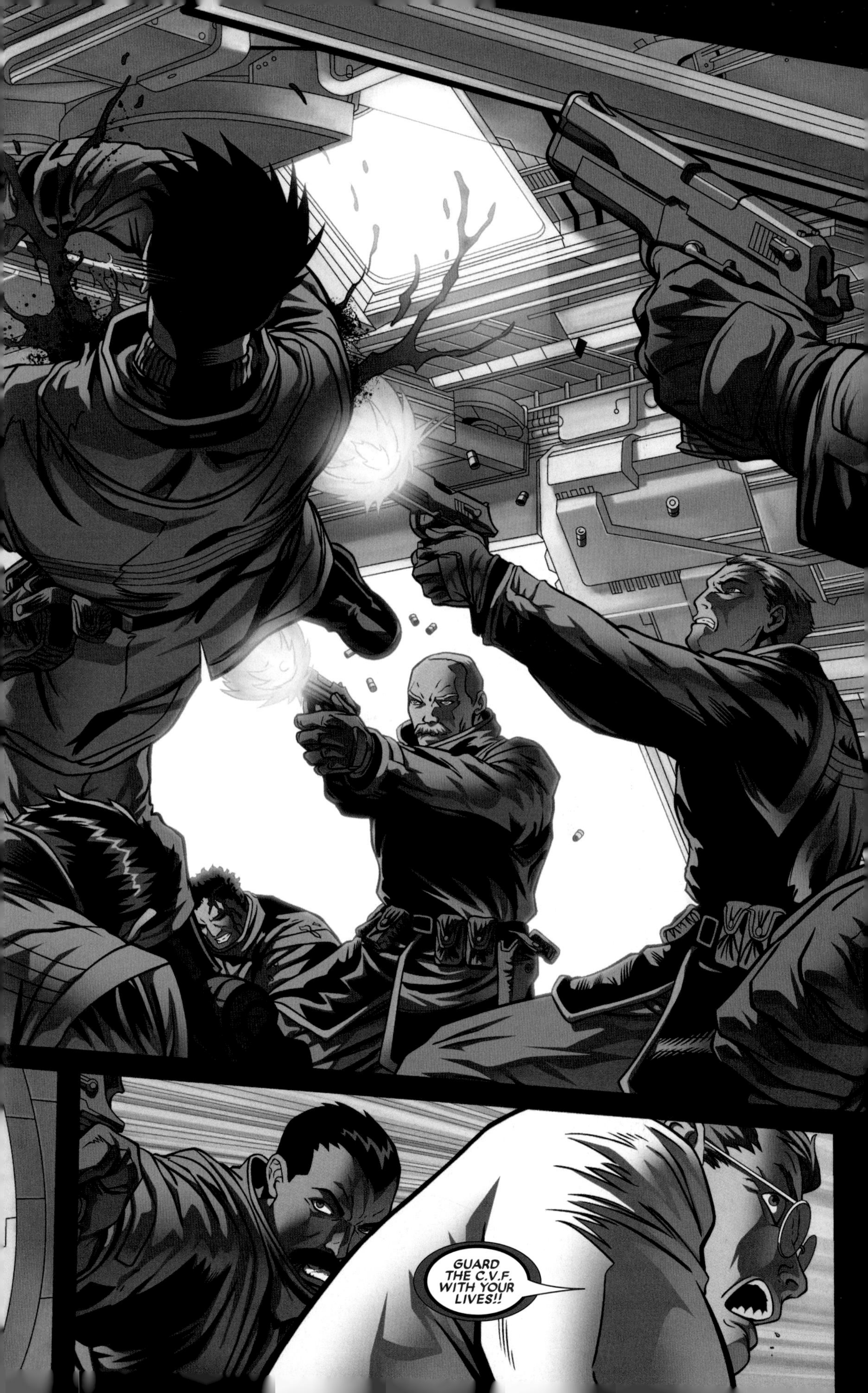
GUARD THE C.V.F. WITH YOUR LIVES!!

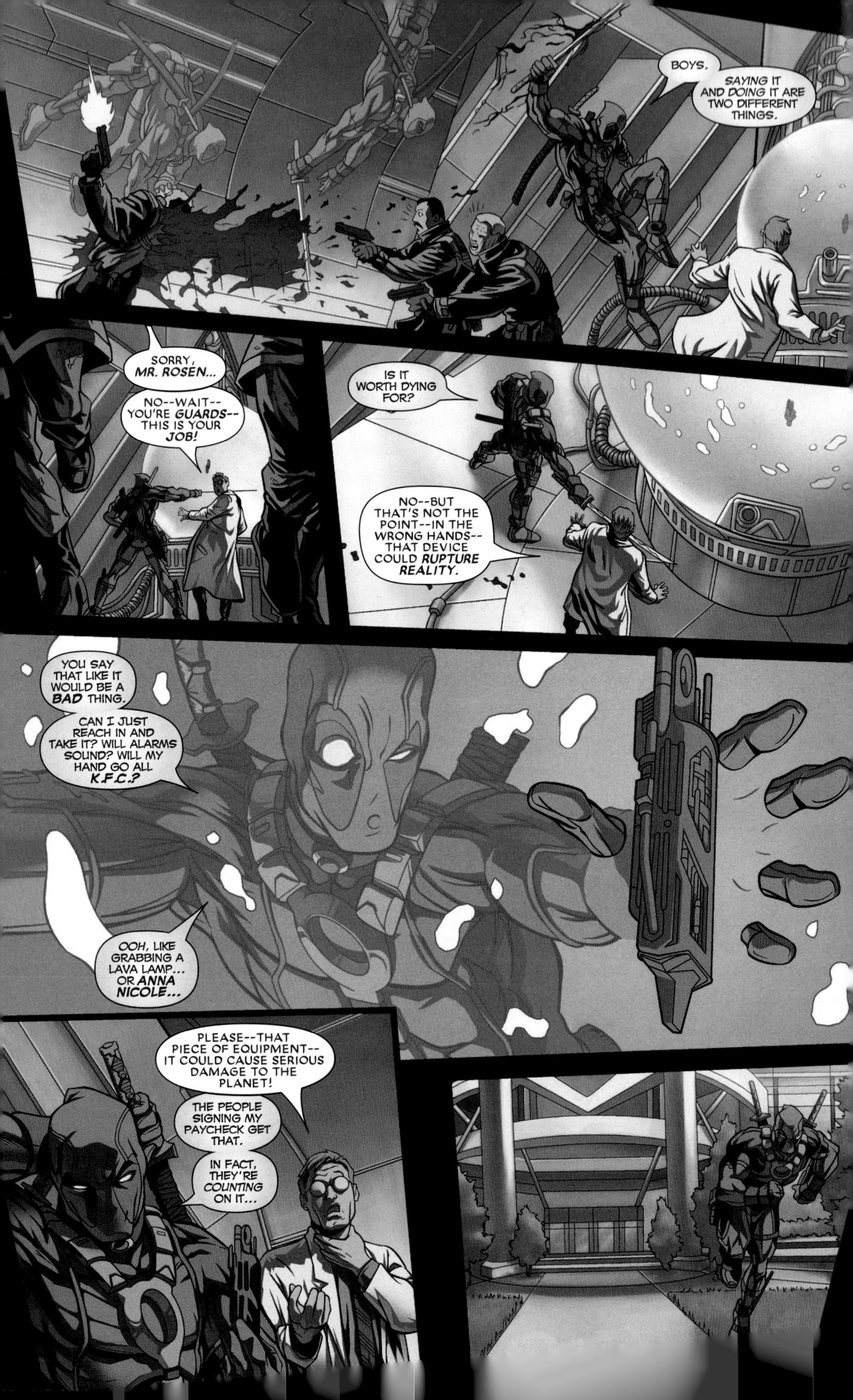

BOYS.
SAYING IT AND DOING IT ARE TWO DIFFERENT THINGS.
SORRY, MR. ROSEN...
NO--WAIT--YOU'RE GUARDS--THIS IS YOUR JOB!
IS IT WORTH DYING FOR?
NO--BUT THAT'S NOT THE POINT--IN THE WRONG HANDS--THAT DEVICE COULD RUPTURE REALITY.
YOU SAY THAT LIKE IT WOULD BE A BAD THING.
CAN I JUST REACH IN AND TAKE IT? WILL ALARMS SOUND? WILL MY HAND GO ALL K.F.C.?
OOH, LIKE GRABBING A LAVA LAMP... OR ANNA NICOLE...
PLEASE--THAT PIECE OF EQUIPMENT--IT COULD CAUSE SERIOUS DAMAGE TO THE PLANET!
THE PEOPLE SIGNING MY PAYCHECK GET THAT.
IN FACT, THEY'RE COUNTING ON IT...

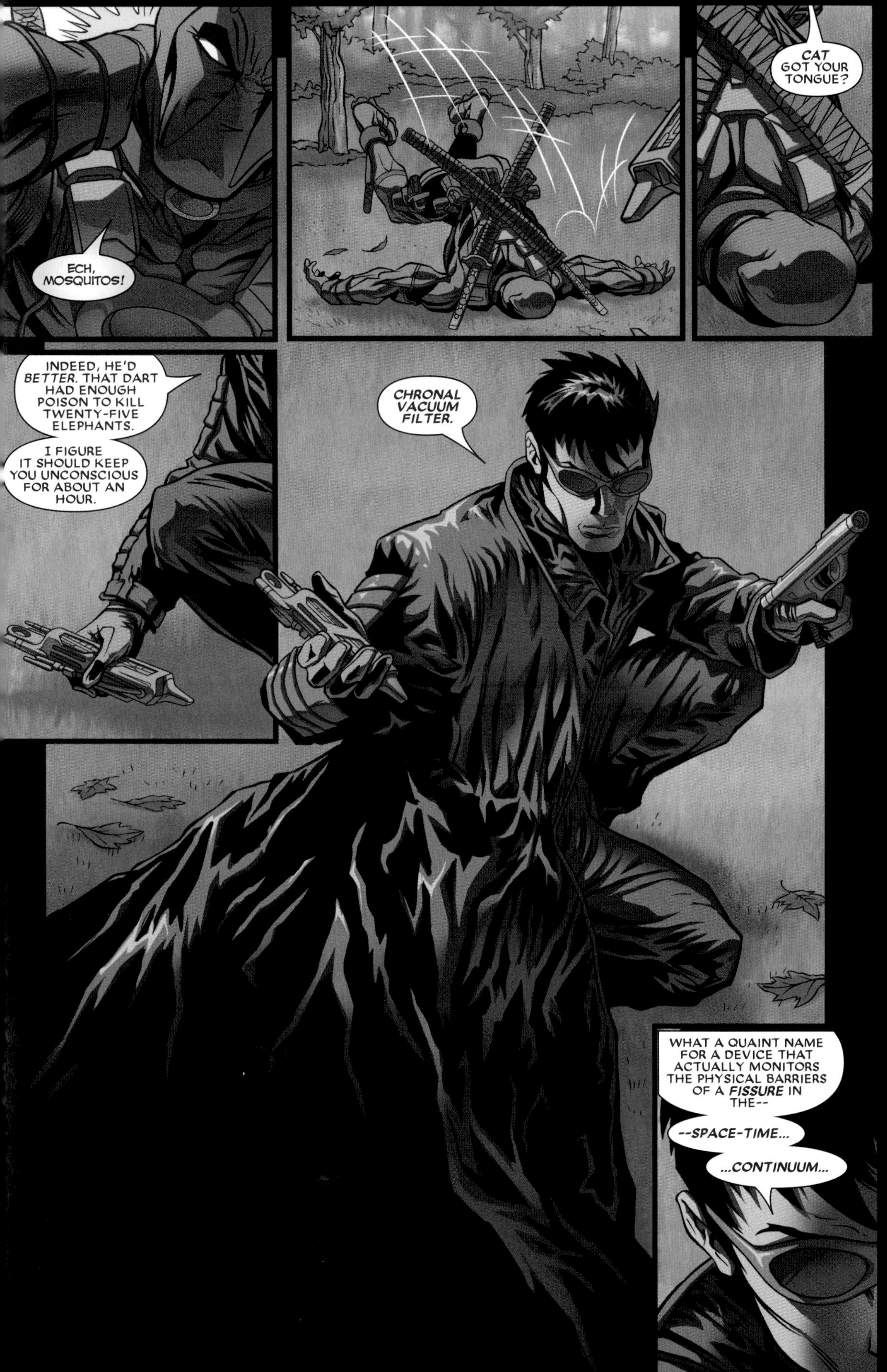
ECH, MOSQUITOS!
CAT GOT YOUR TONGUE?
INDEED, HE'D BETTER. THAT DART HAD ENOUGH POISON TO KILL TWENTY-FIVE ELEPHANTS.
I FIGURE IT SHOULD KEEP YOU UNCONSCIOUS FOR ABOUT AN HOUR.
CHRONAL VACUUM FILTER.
WHAT A QUAINT NAME FOR A DEVICE THAT ACTUALLY MONITORS THE PHYSICAL BARRIERS OF A FISSURE IN THE--
--SPACE-TIME...
...CONTINUUM...

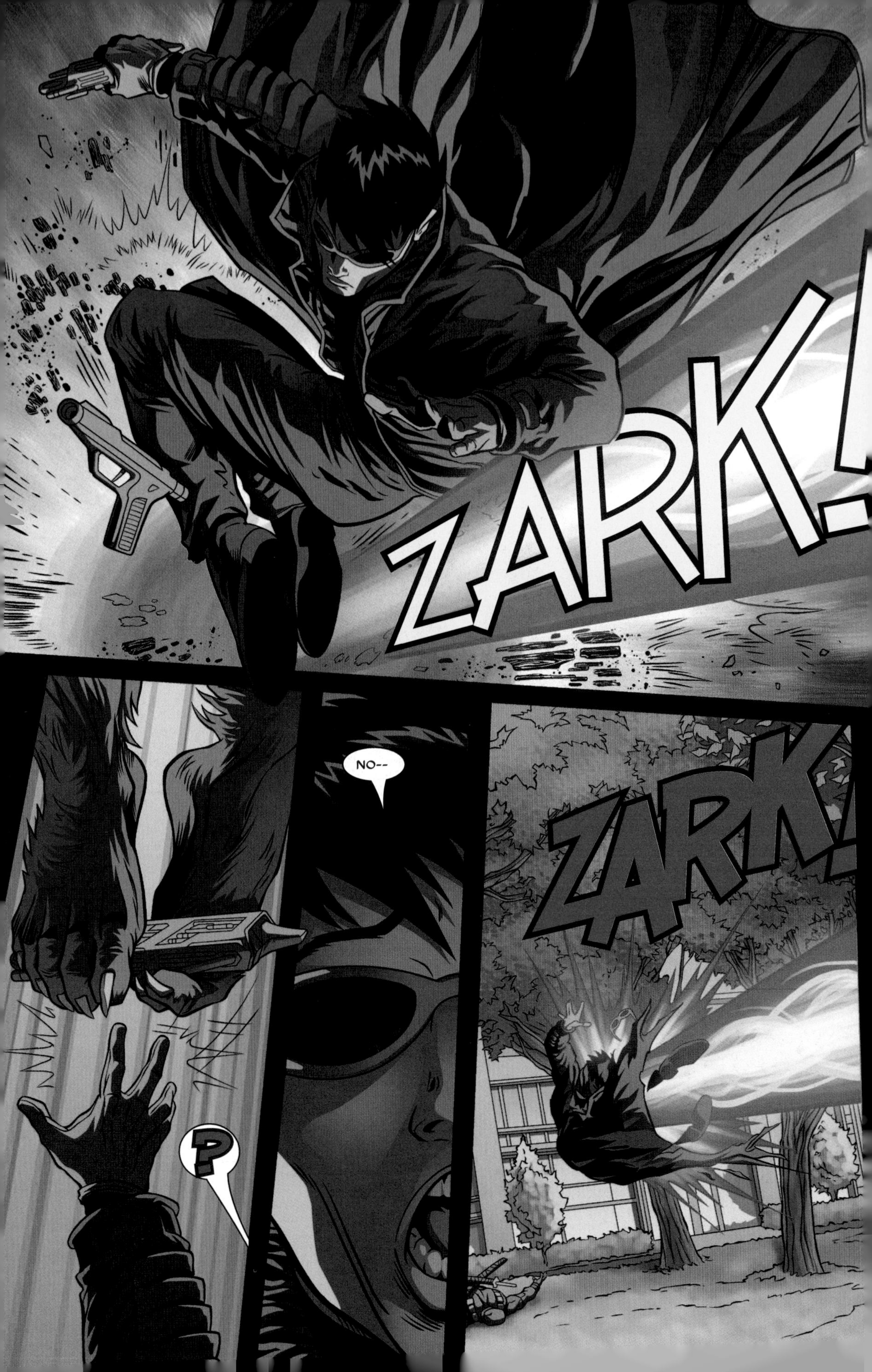
ZARK!!
NO--
?
ZARK!!

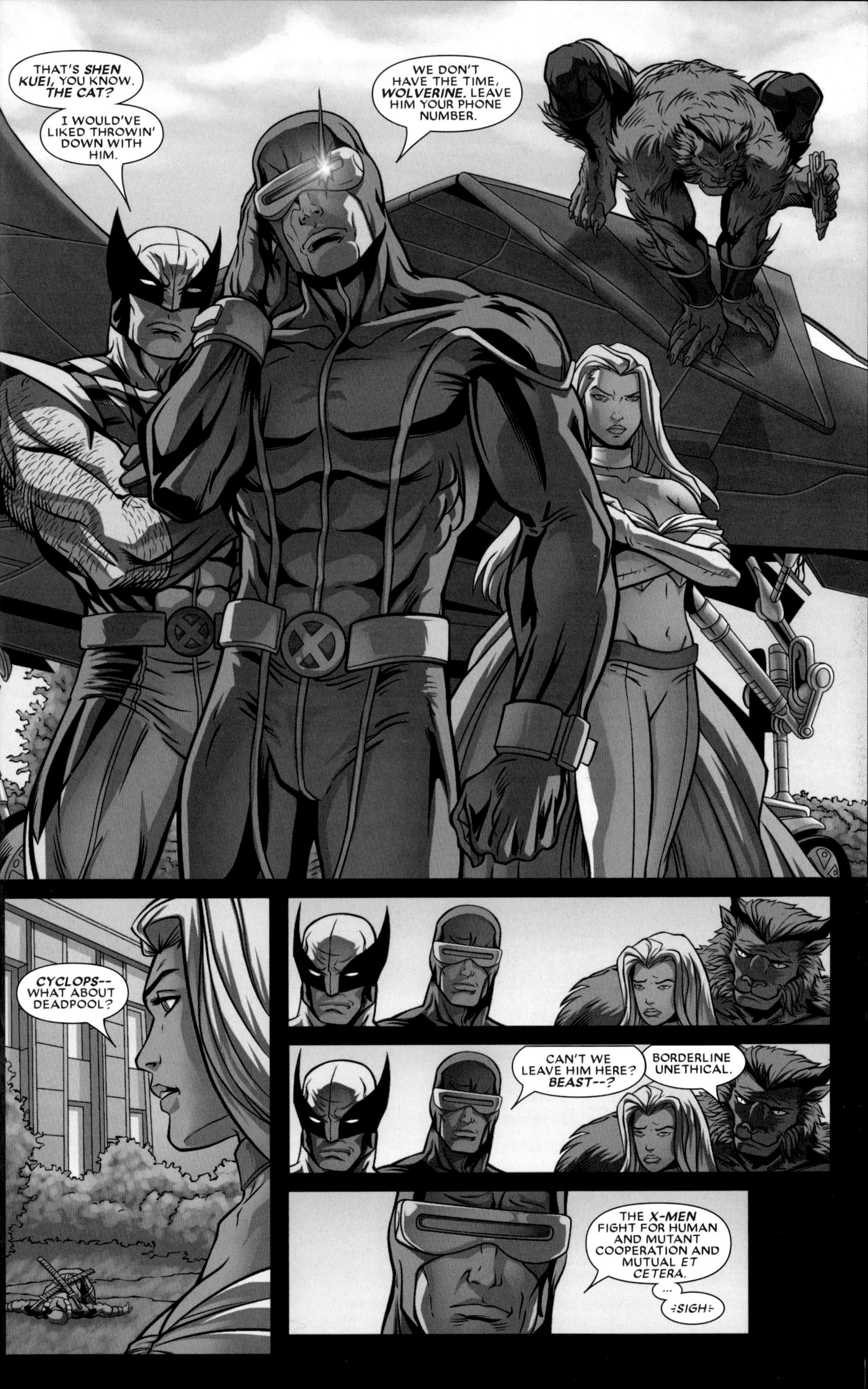
THAT'S *SHEN KUEI,* YOU KNOW. *THE CAT?*
I WOULD'VE LIKED THROWIN' DOWN WITH HIM.
WE DON'T HAVE THE TIME, *WOLVERINE.* LEAVE HIM YOUR PHONE NUMBER.
CYCLOPS-- WHAT ABOUT DEADPOOL?
CAN'T WE LEAVE HIM HERE? *BEAST--?*
BORDERLINE UNETHICAL.
THE *X-MEN* FIGHT FOR HUMAN AND MUTANT COOPERATION AND MUTUAL *ET CETERA.*
...
SIGH

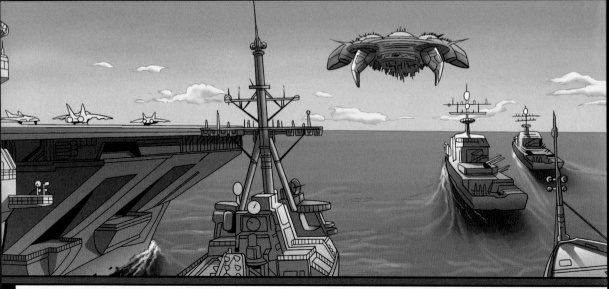

Irene Merryweather: Well, Nathan, we've talked about what you would like to do for humanity, but how do you think humanity will receive your...

Cable: Gifts?

IM: Sure. Whatever. Gifts.

Cable: I know the majority of mankind yearns for security, for spirituality, for hope. I know that people in established positions of power fear anything that destabilizes that power.

IM: So if you do the basic math...?

Cable: The U.S.S. *Ronald Reagan* is two hundred miles below us now. The Chinese government has dispatched no less than eighty-seven specialized agents to find a way to kill me. S.H.I.E.L.D. has activated a mercenary team to infiltrate Providence. Every Al Qaeda cell has been instructed to detonate any weapons stockpiles they have the second I should publicly position myself above Allah.

IM: But you're still maintaining that the average person--

Cable: Is crying inside for a change. Begging for something different.

IM: I don't understand?

Cable: Why did we pave our planet? Why do we need money? What if everyone could have whatever they want?

IM: You can promise that?

Cable: No. I can promise to provide you the opportunity to achieve that. *(Pause.)* That face you're making. Either you just realized it's been three hours since you had a cigarette, or you have doubts.

IM: Well, it's just that in my experience, most people want more than what the person next to them has.

Cable: Yes, and that's a part of human nature that needs to change.

IM: Jumbo shrimp. How do you change something that is nature?

Cable: How do you change physiological evolution? It is both a process and an eventuality.

IM: An inevitability?

Cable: No, that would infer it will happen whether we do something about it or not. What I propose will take very hard work.

IM: So it's not like you're going to blink your eyes and change everyone's minds?

Cable: I wouldn't even if I could. No. I've seen that

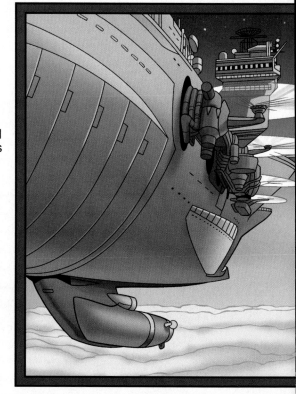

way. I refuse to become that. No, my way is harder and ultimately more rewarding. I want to show everyone it is possible, and then help us work towards it.

IM: Socialism?

Cable: Isms bore me. I think they are only brought up by people who seek to marginalize the potential of each ism to provide something meaningful. Name it, Capitalism, Socialism, even Communism--all contain something of merit towards structuring a society. The biggest flaw in human history has been its need to take the worst of a system along with the best. It doesn't have to be all of one and none of another.

IM: Like American politics?

Cable: You have to be a Conservative Republican or a Liberal Democrat? Well, what about the vast majority of the people in the

middle? What about those who see the positives of both sides?

IM: Well, we can't cater to them, since the money usually comes from the fringes.

Cable: How did we create a system where the fringes are crushing the middle?

IM: We found a way to combine chocolate and peanut butter.

Cable: By the very definition of the terms, that makes no sense. The middle are the people trying to live their lives as best they can, coping and hoping. I think the middle is sick and tired of the fringes. Religious extremists. Political extremists. Corporate extremists.

IM: Well, your rhetoric sounds nice, but--

Cable: It's not rhetoric if my words are being put into action. Providence is open to all who want to sample a taste of what could be. Several thousand of the planet s greatest minds, from scientists to philosophers, philanthropists to writers--all have accepted my invitation.

IM: Sounds like my nephew's fifth-grade dodgeball team would kick their butts in.

Cable: I'm telekinetic, Merryweather. Bring it on.

IM: And what do you plan to do with all these great minds?

Cable: Give them an opportunity to *be* great minds. Then give them an opportunity to bring all they see, all they learn, all their ideas, back to their countries.

IM: This process…it could take generations.

Cable: It should take generations, Irene. I can't emphasize enough that I'm not interested in forcing my views on anyone.

IM: And yet, the Chinese government has dispatched eighty-seven specialized agents to kill you...

(Pause.)

Cable: Make it ninety. I didn't realize he could split himself into four separate people.

IM: You joke about it…

Cable: Not really, no. I'm just…aware of it. I want everyone who reads this to see that I'm aware, but also that I'm not rushing out to instigate violence.

IM: But that awareness also makes you a realist?

Cable: The establishment fears change. Simple as that. I represent change. That creates friction, which will lead to conflict.

IM: An inevitability?

Cable: Well, I could hope not, but let's be realistic.

IM: How will you deal with this situation when the time comes?

Cable: I am trying very hard to be as open and available as possible. I have not directly threatened any government, corporate or religious institution.

IM: There are people in Chechnya and Gaza who--

Cable: Individuals. The fringes. My actions in both places were cheered by a vast majority of the people.

IM: Like parades in the streets?

Cable: I'm telepathic, too. The cheering is loudest inside the silence of the human mind.

IM: Well, that's as sweet as sweet could be, but answer this, Nathan: You're going out of your way to be non-violent, but what if you're attacked first?

> THIS IS *S.H.I.E.L.D.* HELICARRIER LAUNCH CONTROL. PSI-SKIMMER-ONE CLEAR FOR RELEASE.

> *"The average person is crying inside for a change."* --Cable

> E.T.A. IN TWENTY-TWO MINUTES AND COUNTING...

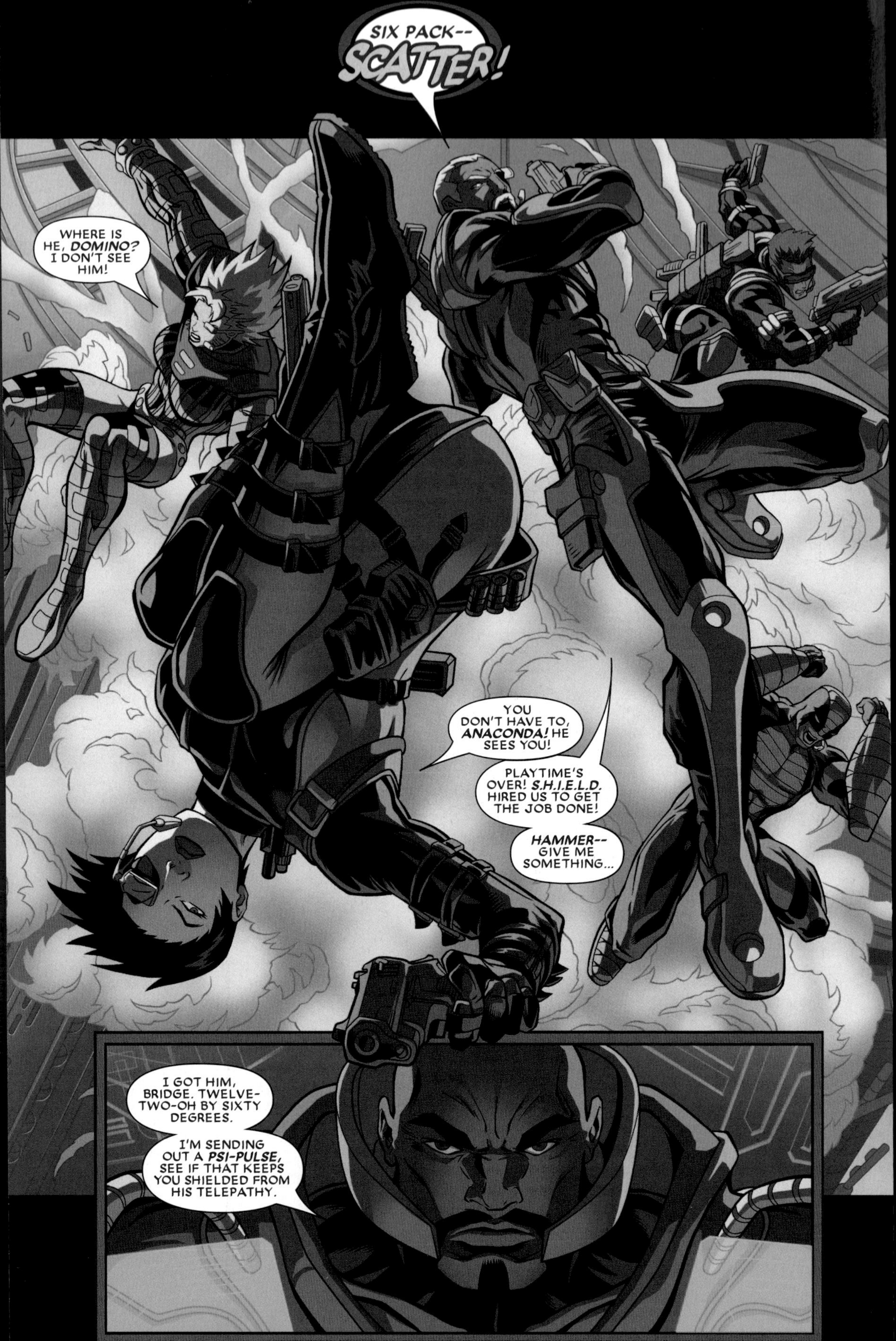

SIX PACK--
SCATTER!
WHERE IS HE, DOMINO? I DON'T SEE HIM!
YOU DON'T HAVE TO, ANACONDA! HE SEES YOU!
PLAYTIME'S OVER! S.H.I.E.L.D. HIRED US TO GET THE JOB DONE!
HAMMER-- GIVE ME SOMETHING...
I GOT HIM, BRIDGE. TWELVE-TWO-OH BY SIXTY DEGREES.
I'M SENDING OUT A PSI-PULSE, SEE IF THAT KEEPS YOU SHIELDED FROM HIS TELEPATHY.

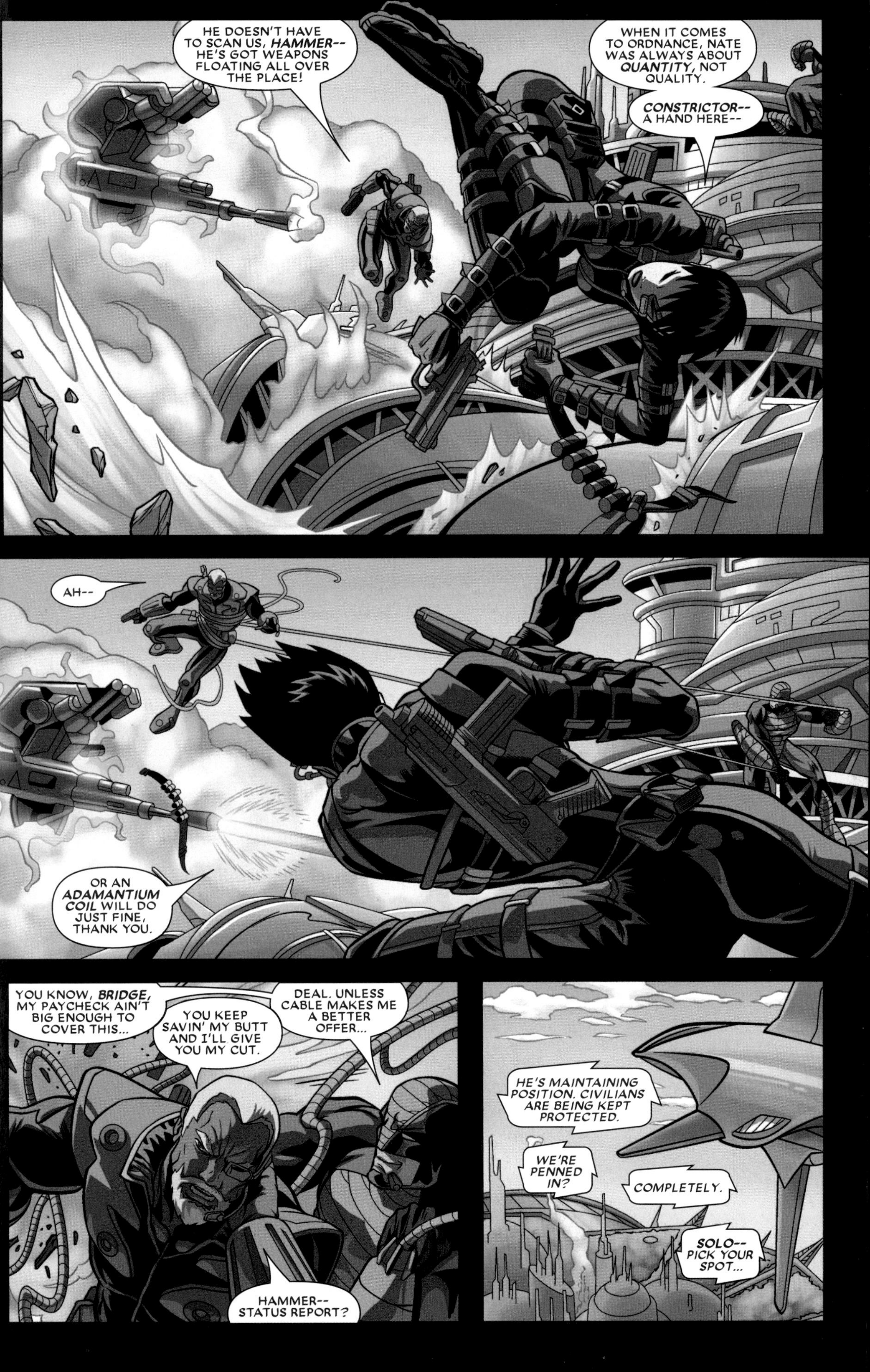
HE DOESN'T HAVE TO SCAN US, HAMMER-- HE'S GOT WEAPONS FLOATING ALL OVER THE PLACE!
WHEN IT COMES TO ORDNANCE, NATE WAS ALWAYS ABOUT QUANTITY, NOT QUALITY.
CONSTRICTOR-- A HAND HERE--
AH--
OR AN ADAMANTIUM COIL WILL DO JUST FINE, THANK YOU.
YOU KNOW, BRIDGE, MY PAYCHECK AIN'T BIG ENOUGH TO COVER THIS...
YOU KEEP SAVIN' MY BUTT AND I'LL GIVE YOU MY CUT.
DEAL. UNLESS CABLE MAKES ME A BETTER OFFER...
HAMMER-- STATUS REPORT?
HE'S MAINTAINING POSITION. CIVILIANS ARE BEING KEPT PROTECTED.
WE'RE PENNED IN?
COMPLETELY.
SOLO-- PICK YOUR SPOT...

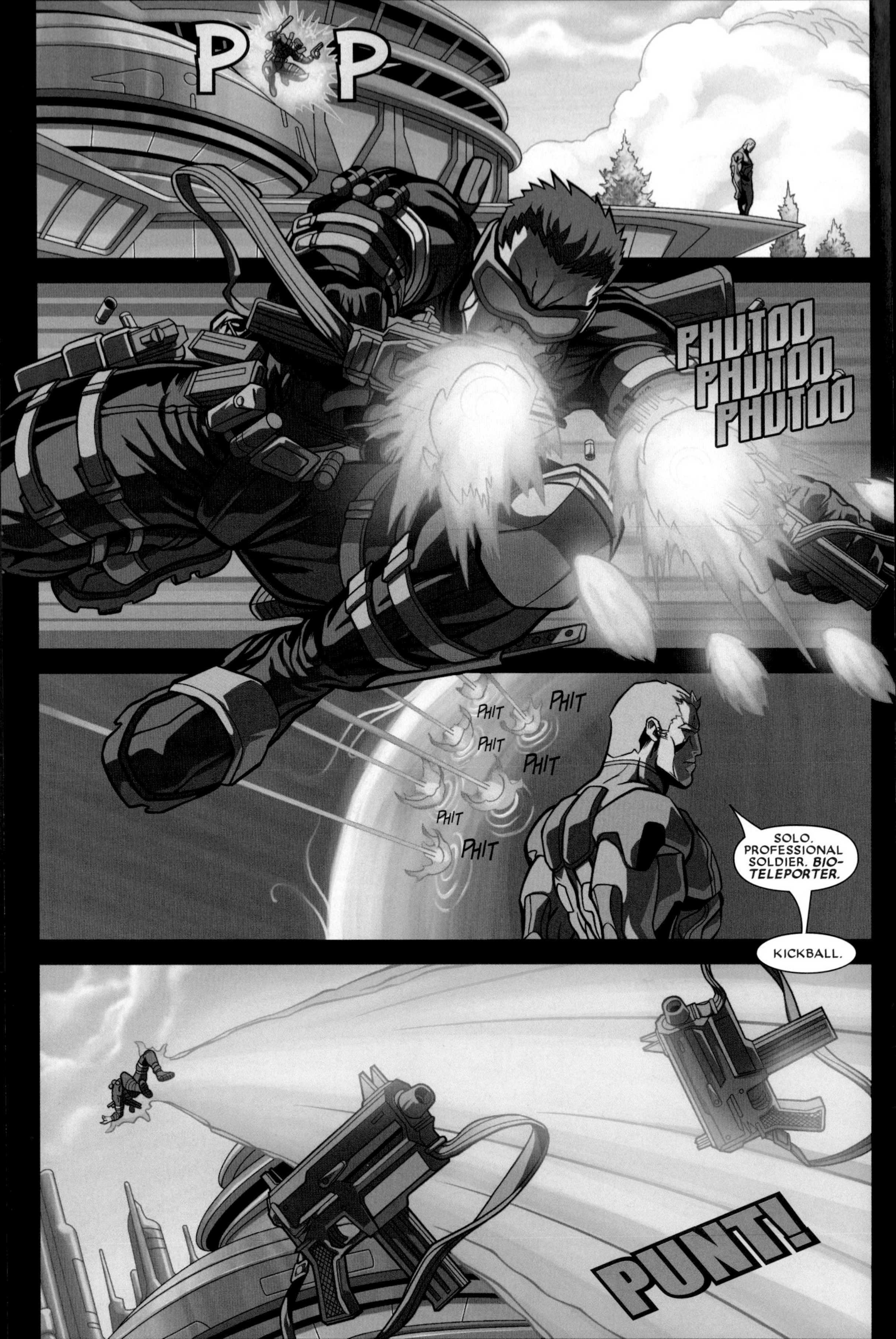
POP
PHUTOO PHUTOO PHUTOO
PHIT PHIT PHIT PHIT PHIT PHIT
SOLO. PROFESSIONAL SOLDIER. BIO-TELEPORTER.
KICKBALL.
PUNT!

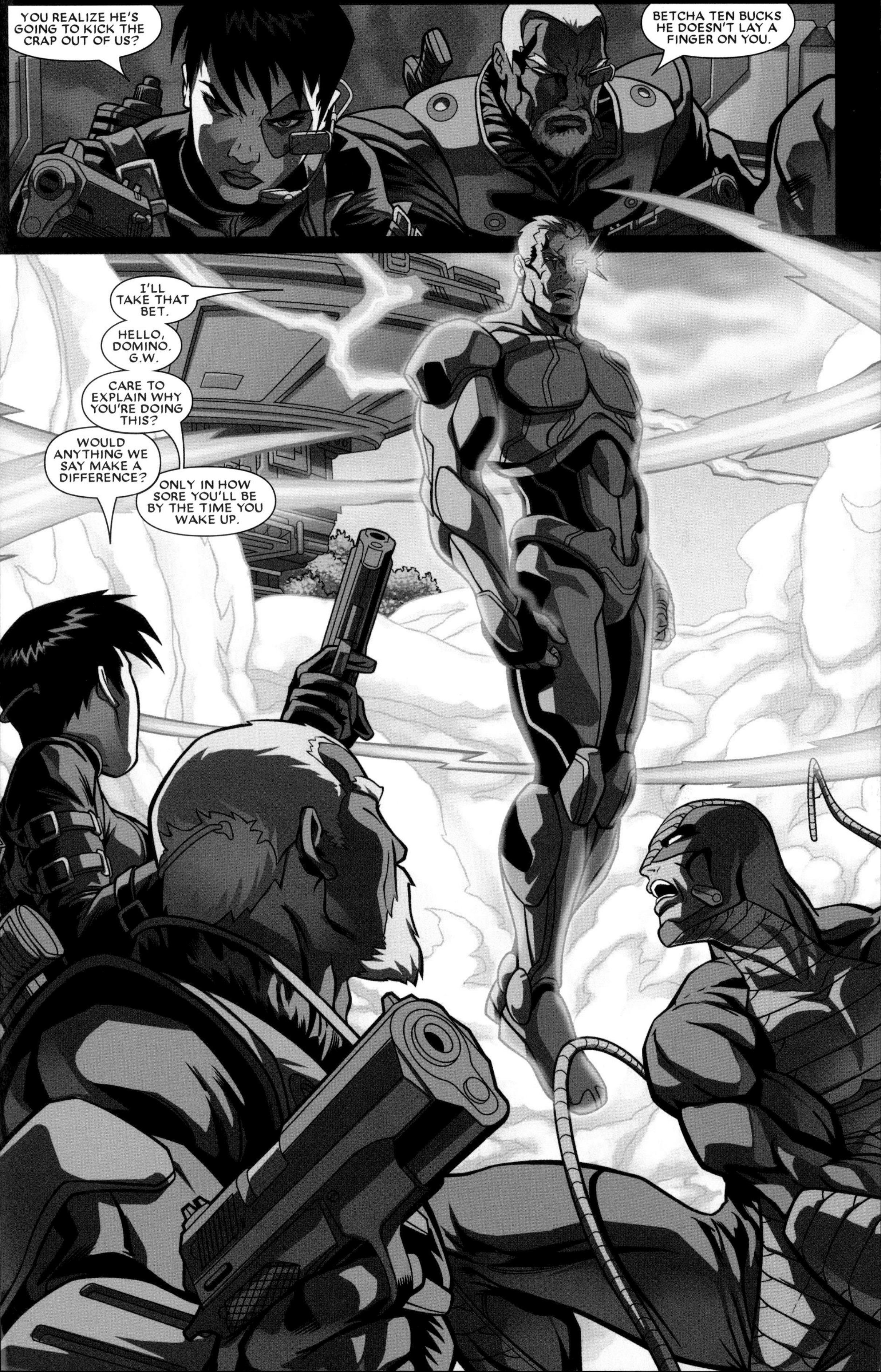

YOU REALIZE HE'S GOING TO KICK THE CRAP OUT OF US?
BETCHA TEN BUCKS HE DOESN'T LAY A FINGER ON YOU.
I'LL TAKE THAT BET.
HELLO, DOMINO. G.W.
CARE TO EXPLAIN WHY YOU'RE DOING THIS?
WOULD ANYTHING WE SAY MAKE A DIFFERENCE?
ONLY IN HOW SORE YOU'LL BE BY THE TIME YOU WAKE UP.

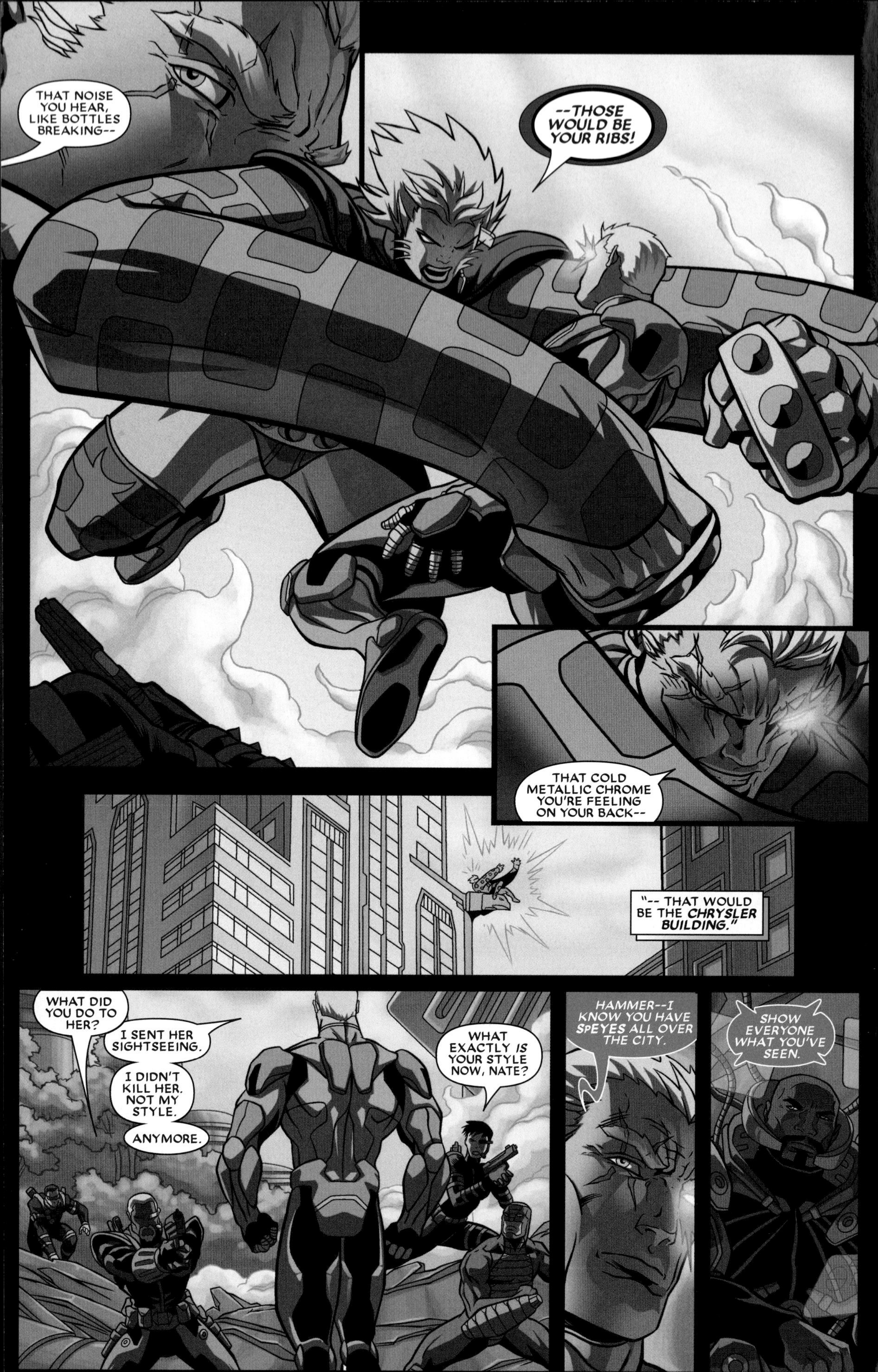
THAT NOISE YOU HEAR, LIKE BOTTLES BREAKING--
--THOSE WOULD BE YOUR RIBS!
THAT COLD METALLIC CHROME YOU'RE FEELING ON YOUR BACK--
"-- THAT WOULD BE THE CHRYSLER BUILDING."
WHAT DID YOU DO TO HER?
I SENT HER SIGHTSEEING.
I DIDN'T KILL HER. NOT MY STYLE.
ANYMORE.
WHAT EXACTLY IS YOUR STYLE NOW, NATE?
HAMMER--I KNOW YOU HAVE SPEYES ALL OVER THE CITY.
SHOW EVERYONE WHAT YOU'VE SEEN.

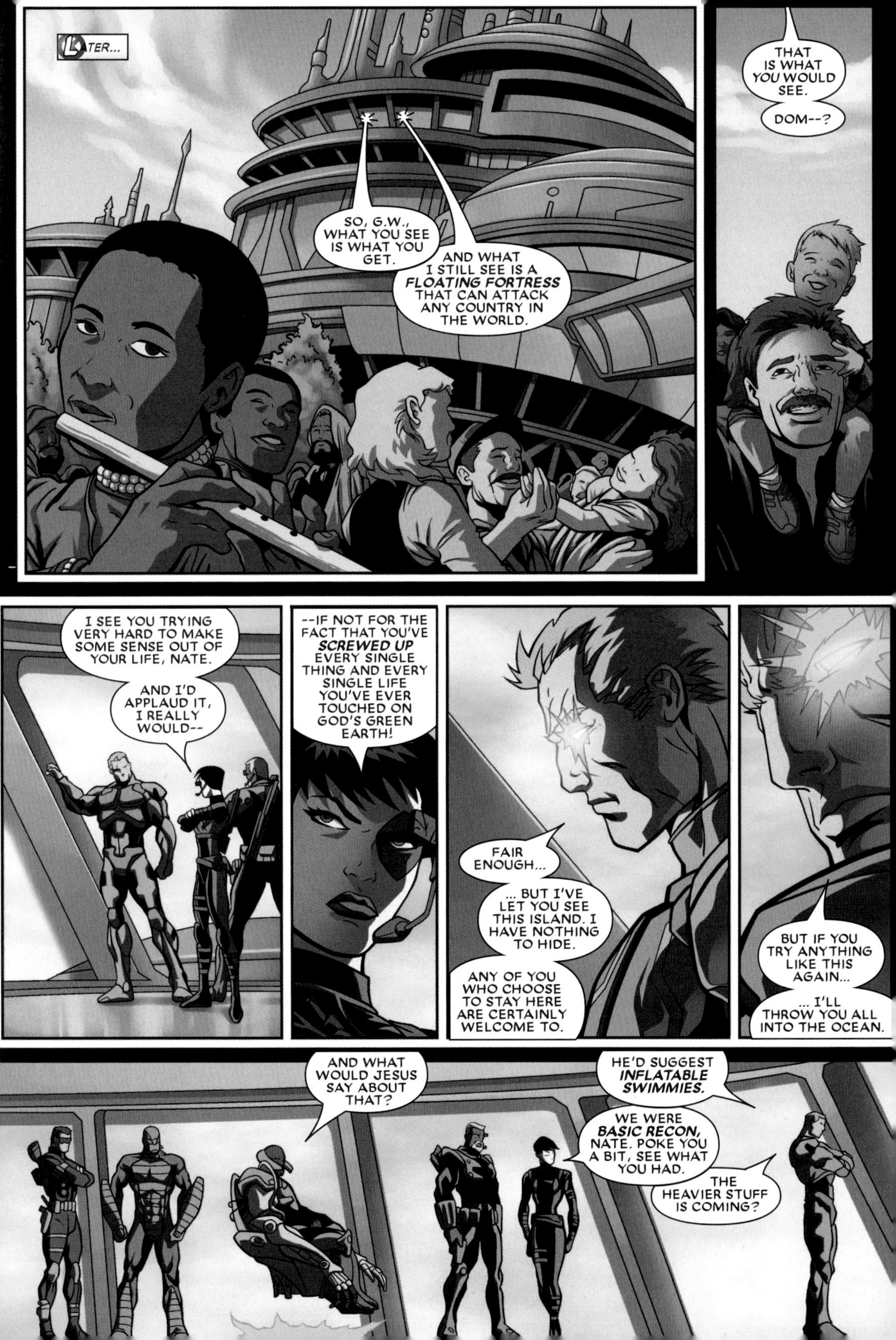
LATER...
SO, G.W., WHAT YOU SEE IS WHAT YOU GET.
AND WHAT I STILL SEE IS A FLOATING FORTRESS THAT CAN ATTACK ANY COUNTRY IN THE WORLD.
THAT IS WHAT YOU WOULD SEE.
DOM--?
I SEE YOU TRYING VERY HARD TO MAKE SOME SENSE OUT OF YOUR LIFE, NATE.
AND I'D APPLAUD IT, I REALLY WOULD--
--IF NOT FOR THE FACT THAT YOU'VE SCREWED UP EVERY SINGLE THING AND EVERY SINGLE LIFE YOU'VE EVER TOUCHED ON GOD'S GREEN EARTH!
FAIR ENOUGH...
... BUT I'VE LET YOU SEE THIS ISLAND. I HAVE NOTHING TO HIDE.
ANY OF YOU WHO CHOOSE TO STAY HERE ARE CERTAINLY WELCOME TO.
BUT IF YOU TRY ANYTHING LIKE THIS AGAIN...
... I'LL THROW YOU ALL INTO THE OCEAN.
AND WHAT WOULD JESUS SAY ABOUT THAT?
HE'D SUGGEST INFLATABLE SWIMMIES.
WE WERE BASIC RECON, NATE. POKE YOU A BIT, SEE WHAT YOU HAD.
THE HEAVIER STUFF IS COMING?

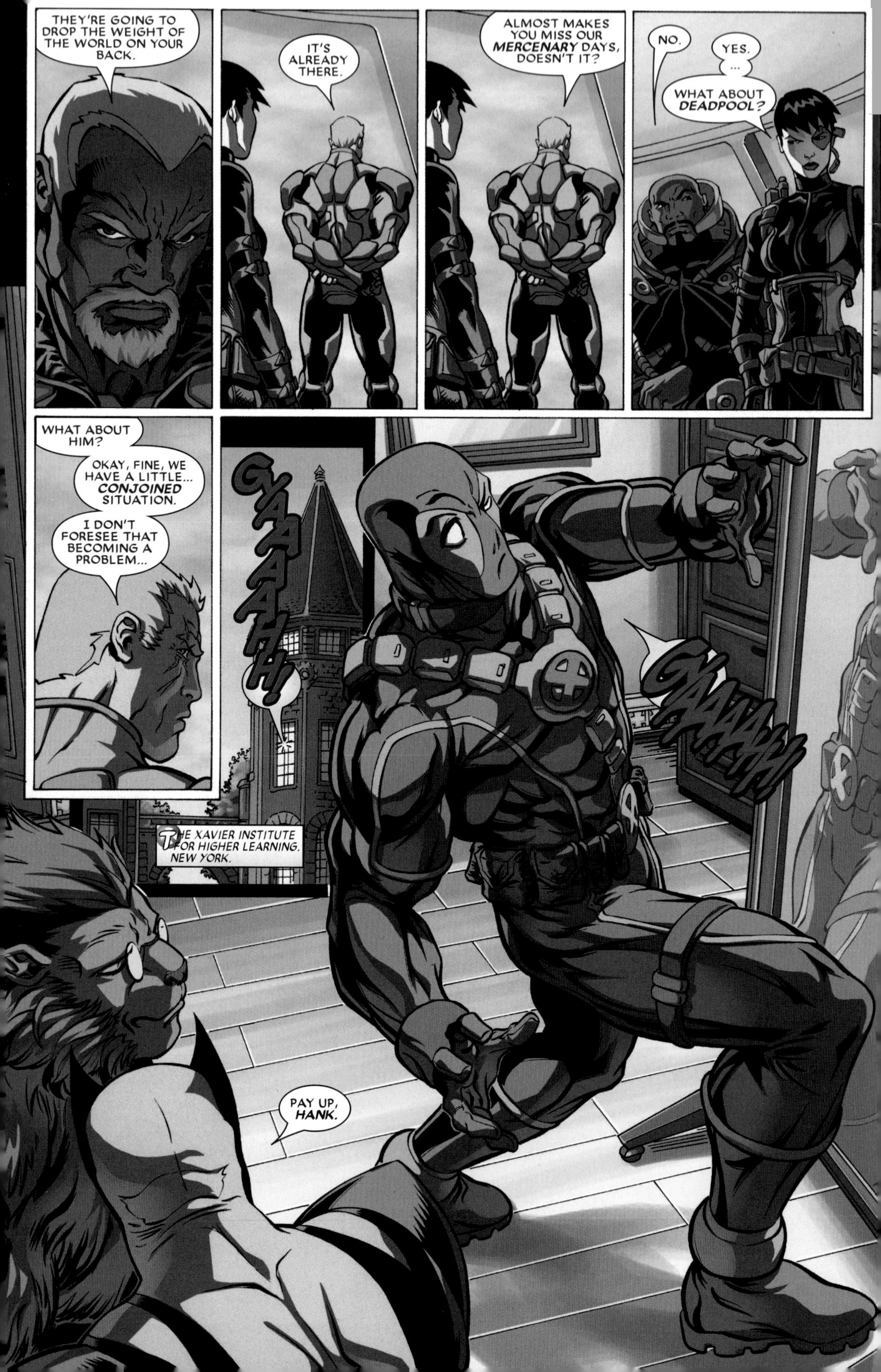
THEY'RE GOING TO DROP THE WEIGHT OF THE WORLD ON YOUR BACK.
IT'S ALREADY THERE.
ALMOST MAKES YOU MISS OUR MERCENARY DAYS, DOESN'T IT?
NO.
YES.
...
WHAT ABOUT DEADPOOL?
WHAT ABOUT HIM?
OKAY, FINE, WE HAVE A LITTLE... CONJOINED SITUATION.
I DON'T FORESEE THAT BECOMING A PROBLEM...
GYAAAAHH!
GYAAAAHH!
THE XAVIER INSTITUTE FOR HIGHER LEARNING. NEW YORK.
PAY UP, HANK.

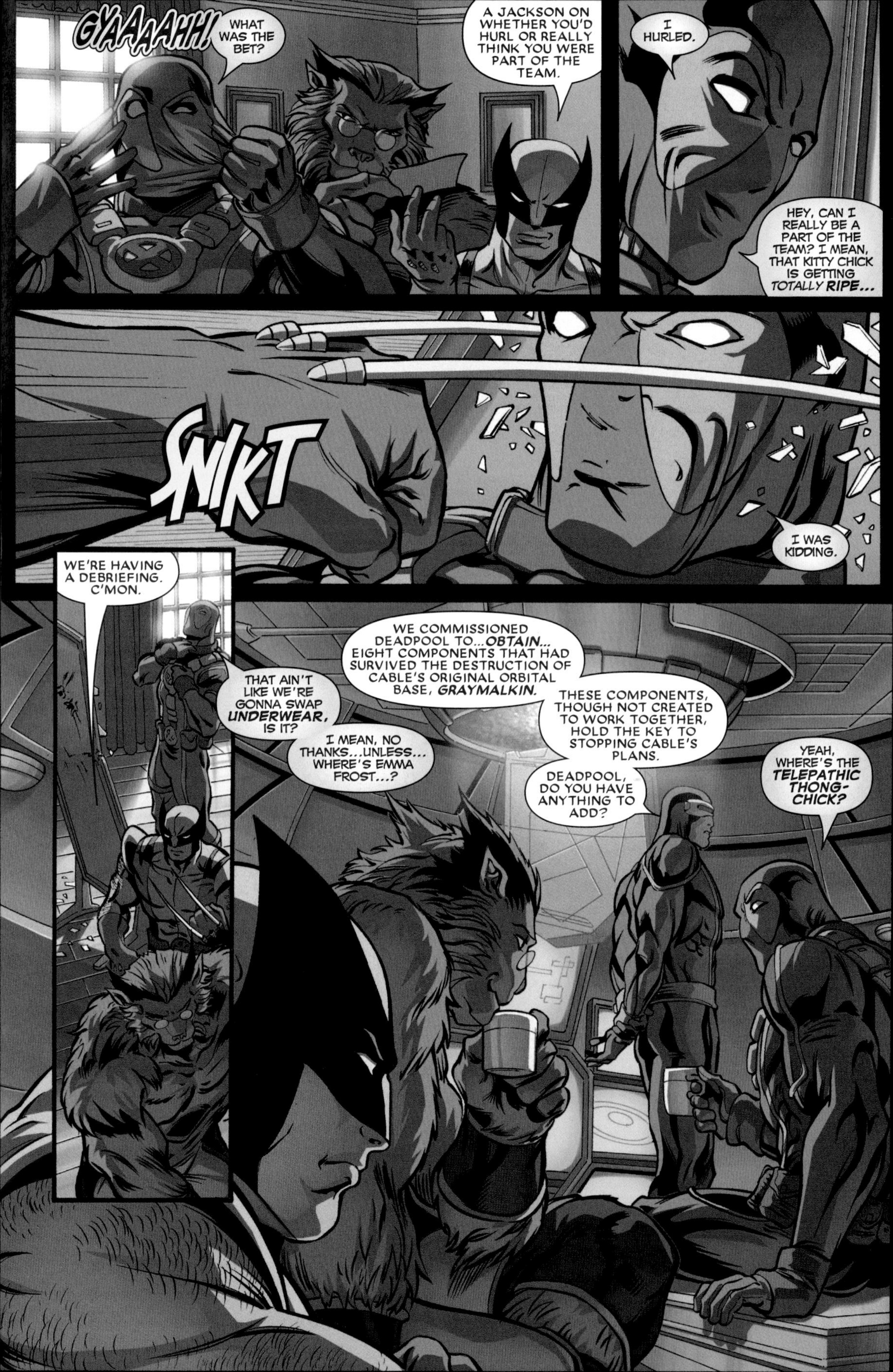
GYAAAAHH!
WHAT WAS THE BET?
A JACKSON ON WHETHER YOU'D HURL OR REALLY THINK YOU WERE PART OF THE TEAM.
I HURLED.
HEY, CAN I REALLY BE A PART OF THE TEAM? I MEAN, THAT KITTY CHICK IS GETTING *TOTALLY* **RIPE...**
SNIKT
I WAS KIDDING.
WE'RE HAVING A DEBRIEFING. C'MON.
THAT AIN'T LIKE WE'RE GONNA SWAP **UNDERWEAR,** IS IT?
I MEAN, NO THANKS...UNLESS... WHERE'S EMMA FROST...?
WE COMMISSIONED DEADPOOL TO...**OBTAIN...** EIGHT COMPONENTS THAT HAD SURVIVED THE DESTRUCTION OF CABLE'S ORIGINAL ORBITAL BASE, **GRAYMALKIN.**
THESE COMPONENTS, THOUGH NOT CREATED TO WORK TOGETHER, HOLD THE KEY TO STOPPING CABLE'S PLANS.
DEADPOOL, DO YOU HAVE ANYTHING TO ADD?
YEAH, WHERE'S THE ***TELEPATHIC THONG-CHICK?***

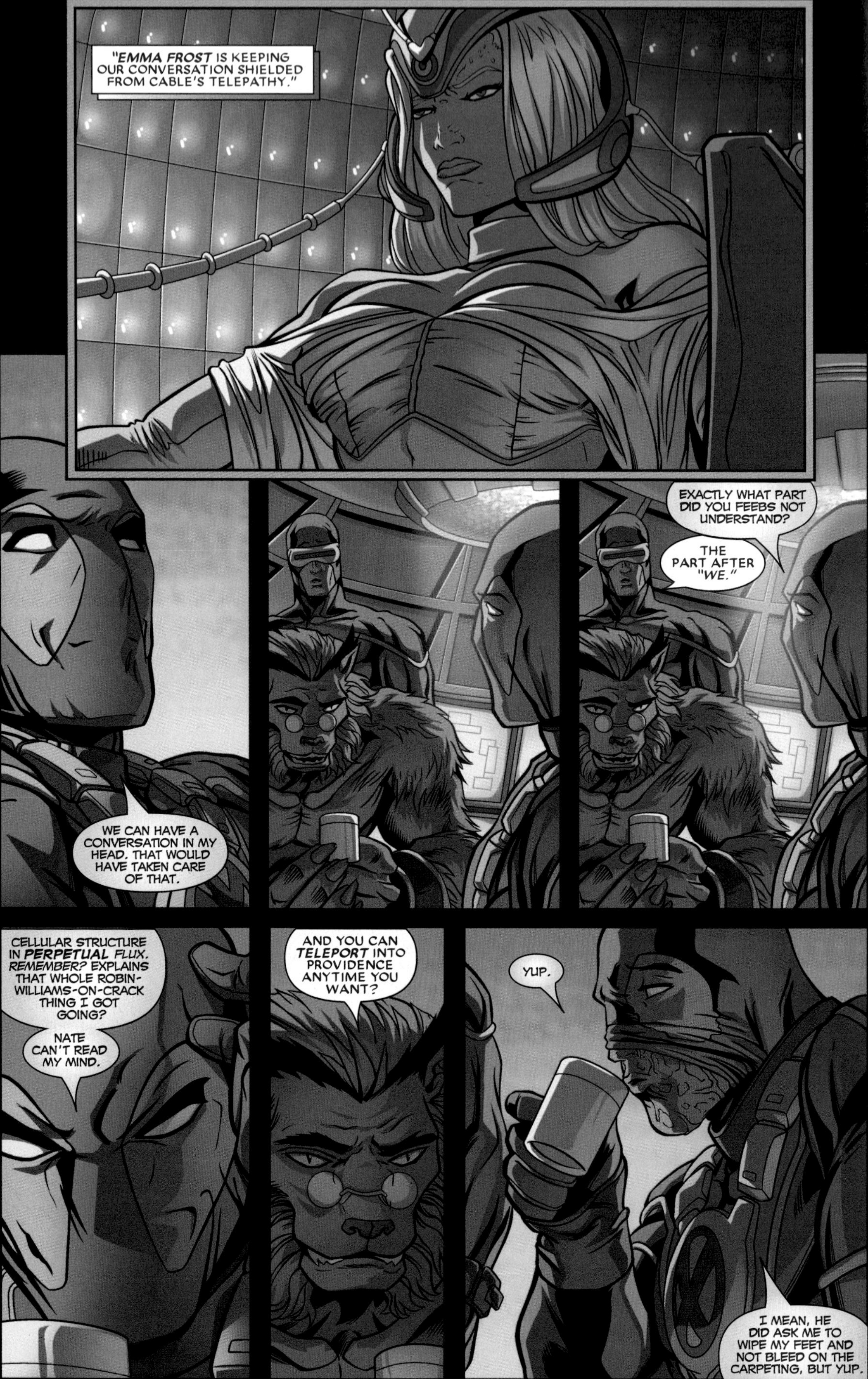
"EMMA FROST IS KEEPING OUR CONVERSATION SHIELDED FROM CABLE'S TELEPATHY."
WE CAN HAVE A CONVERSATION IN MY HEAD. THAT WOULD HAVE TAKEN CARE OF THAT.
EXACTLY WHAT PART DID YOU FEEBS NOT UNDERSTAND?
THE PART AFTER "WE."
CELLULAR STRUCTURE IN PERPETUAL FLUX, REMEMBER? EXPLAINS THAT WHOLE ROBIN-WILLIAMS-ON-CRACK THING I GOT GOING?
NATE CAN'T READ MY MIND.
AND YOU CAN TELEPORT INTO PROVIDENCE ANYTIME YOU WANT?
YUP.
I MEAN, HE DID ASK ME TO WIPE MY FEET AND NOT BLEED ON THE CARPETING, BUT YUP.

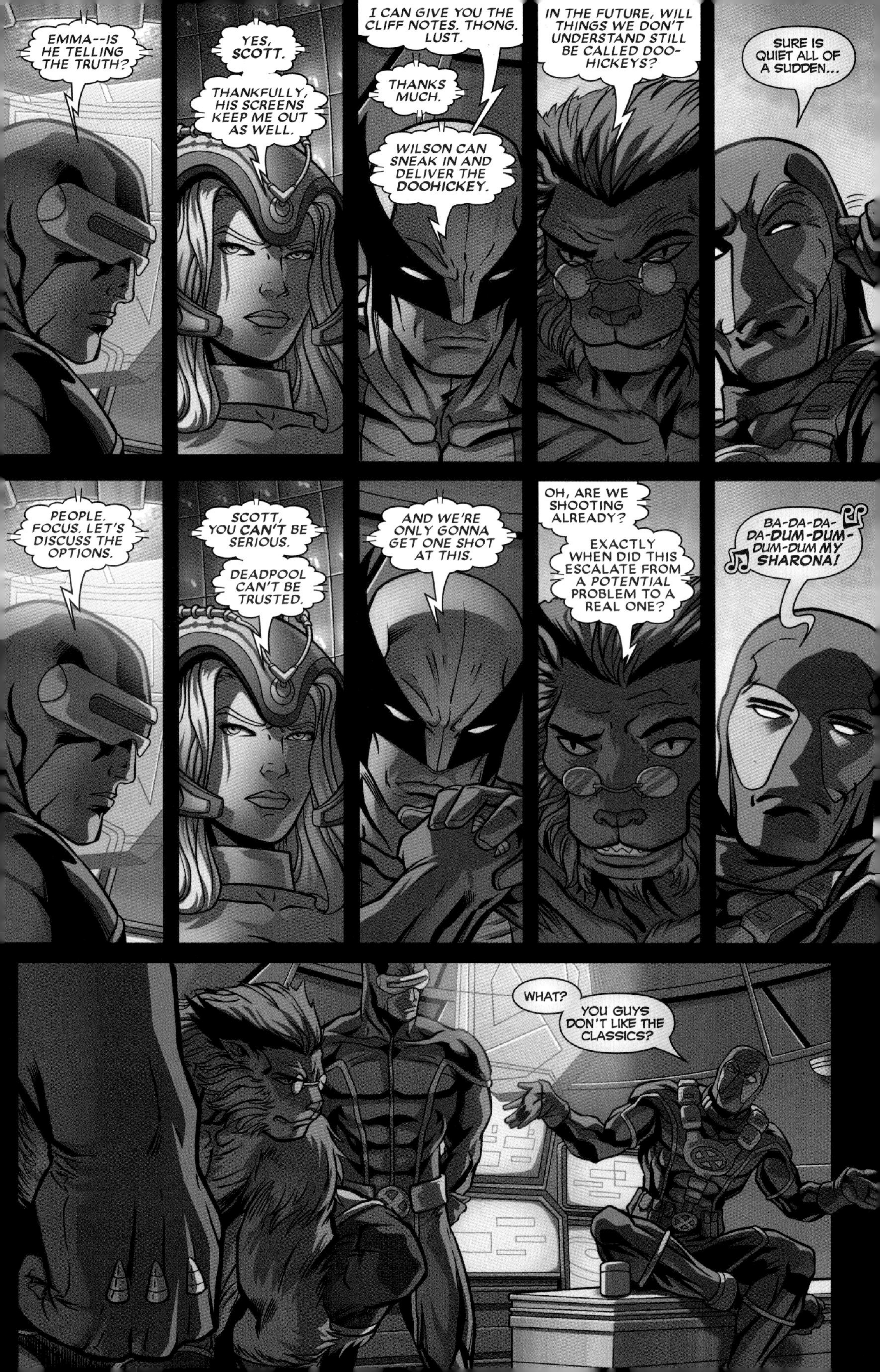
EMMA--IS HE TELLING THE TRUTH?
YES, SCOTT.
THANKFULLY, HIS SCREENS KEEP ME OUT AS WELL.
I CAN GIVE YOU THE CLIFF NOTES. THONG. LUST.
THANKS MUCH.
WILSON CAN SNEAK IN AND DELIVER THE DOOHICKEY.
IN THE FUTURE, WILL THINGS WE DON'T UNDERSTAND STILL BE CALLED DOO-HICKEYS?
SURE IS QUIET ALL OF A SUDDEN...
PEOPLE. FOCUS. LET'S DISCUSS THE OPTIONS.
SCOTT, YOU CAN'T BE SERIOUS.
DEADPOOL CAN'T BE TRUSTED.
AND WE'RE ONLY GONNA GET ONE SHOT AT THIS.
OH, ARE WE SHOOTING ALREADY?
EXACTLY WHEN DID THIS ESCALATE FROM A POTENTIAL PROBLEM TO A REAL ONE?
BA-DA-DA-DA-DUM-DUM-DUM-DUM MY SHARONA!
WHAT?
YOU GUYS DON'T LIKE THE CLASSICS?

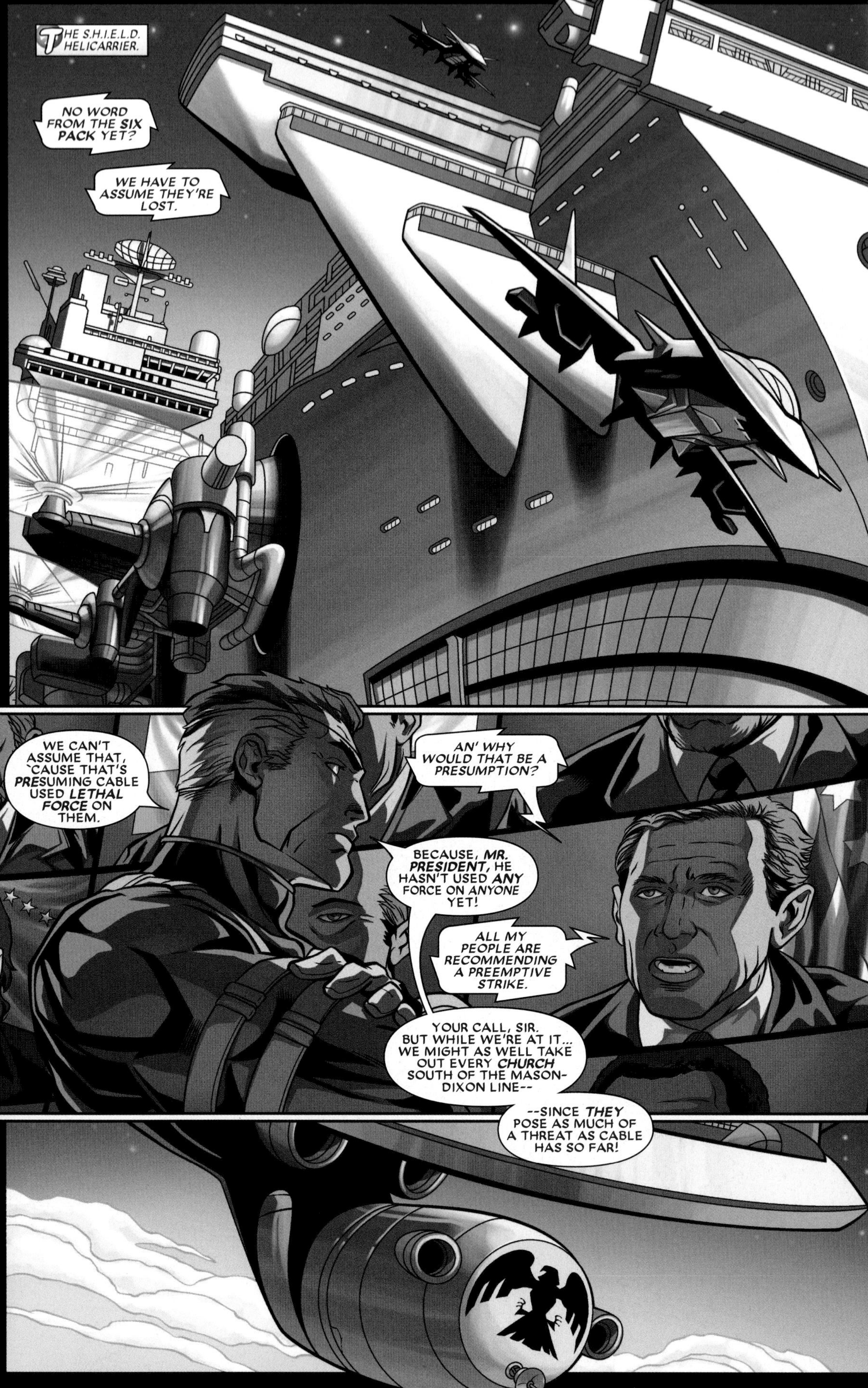
THE S.H.I.E.L.D. HELICARRIER.
NO WORD FROM THE SIX PACK YET?
WE HAVE TO ASSUME THEY'RE LOST.
WE CAN'T ASSUME THAT, 'CAUSE THAT'S PRESUMING CABLE USED LETHAL FORCE ON THEM.
AN' WHY WOULD THAT BE A PRESUMPTION?
BECAUSE, MR. PRESIDENT, HE HASN'T USED ANY FORCE ON ANYONE YET!
ALL MY PEOPLE ARE RECOMMENDING A PREEMPTIVE STRIKE.
YOUR CALL, SIR. BUT WHILE WE'RE AT IT... WE MIGHT AS WELL TAKE OUT EVERY CHURCH SOUTH OF THE MASON-DIXON LINE--
--SINCE THEY POSE AS MUCH OF A THREAT AS CABLE HAS SO FAR!

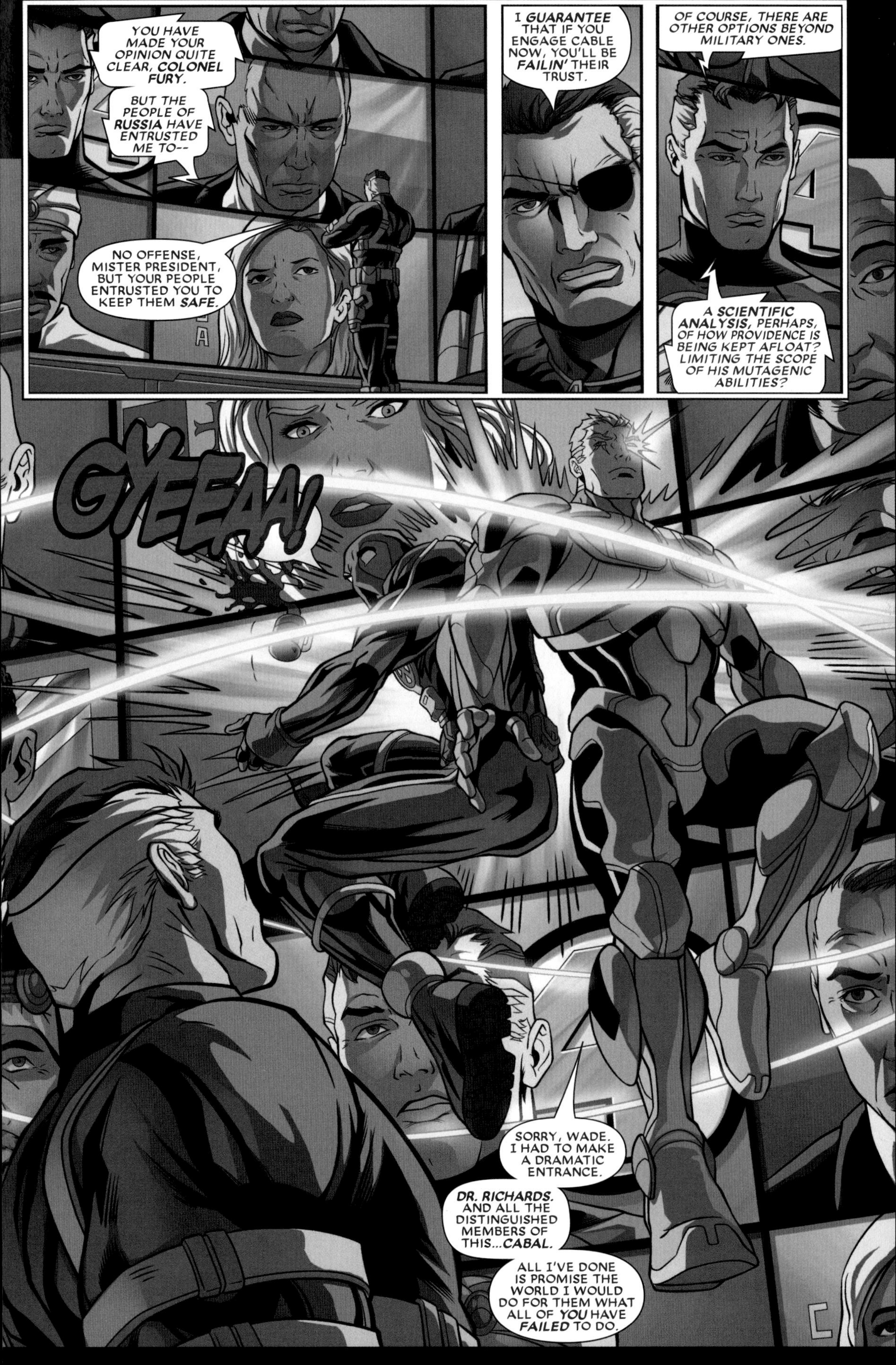
YOU HAVE MADE YOUR OPINION QUITE CLEAR, COLONEL FURY.
BUT THE PEOPLE OF RUSSIA HAVE ENTRUSTED ME TO--
NO OFFENSE, MISTER PRESIDENT, BUT YOUR PEOPLE ENTRUSTED YOU TO KEEP THEM SAFE.
I GUARANTEE THAT IF YOU ENGAGE CABLE NOW, YOU'LL BE FAILIN' THEIR TRUST.
OF COURSE, THERE ARE OTHER OPTIONS BEYOND MILITARY ONES.
A SCIENTIFIC ANALYSIS, PERHAPS, OF HOW PROVIDENCE IS BEING KEPT AFLOAT? LIMITING THE SCOPE OF HIS MUTAGENIC ABILITIES?
GYEEAA!
SORRY, WADE. I HAD TO MAKE A DRAMATIC ENTRANCE.
DR. RICHARDS. AND ALL THE DISTINGUISHED MEMBERS OF THIS...CABAL.
ALL I'VE DONE IS PROMISE THE WORLD I WOULD DO FOR THEM WHAT ALL OF YOU HAVE FAILED TO DO.

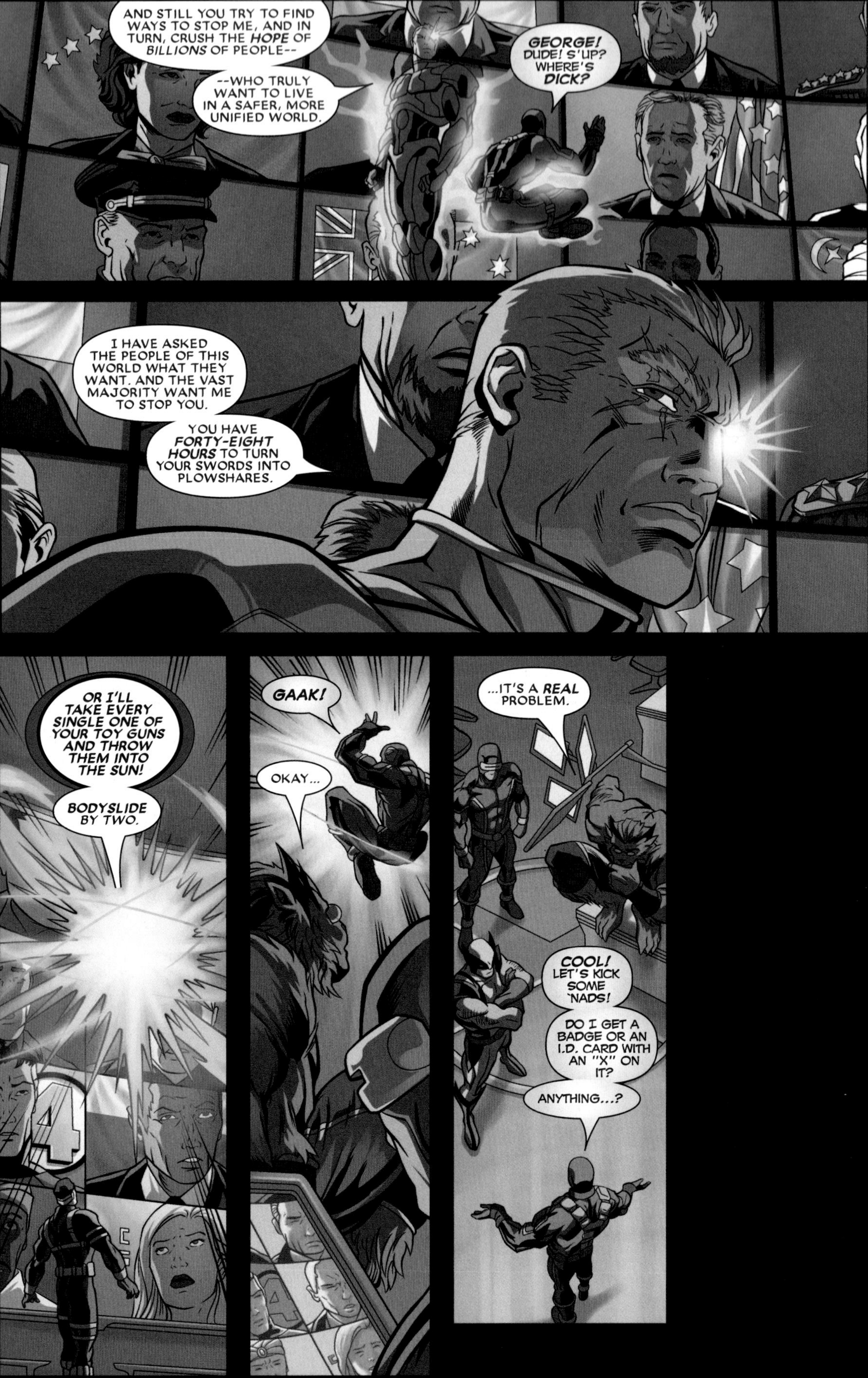
AND STILL YOU TRY TO FIND WAYS TO STOP ME, AND IN TURN, CRUSH THE HOPE OF BILLIONS OF PEOPLE--
--WHO TRULY WANT TO LIVE IN A SAFER, MORE UNIFIED WORLD.
GEORGE! DUDE! S'UP? WHERE'S DICK?
I HAVE ASKED THE PEOPLE OF THIS WORLD WHAT THEY WANT. AND THE VAST MAJORITY WANT ME TO STOP YOU.
YOU HAVE FORTY-EIGHT HOURS TO TURN YOUR SWORDS INTO PLOWSHARES.
OR I'LL TAKE EVERY SINGLE ONE OF YOUR TOY GUNS AND THROW THEM INTO THE SUN!
BODYSLIDE BY TWO.
GAAK!
OKAY...
...IT'S A REAL PROBLEM.
COOL! LET'S KICK SOME 'NADS!
DO I GET A BADGE OR AN I.D. CARD WITH AN "X" ON IT?
ANYTHING...?

9

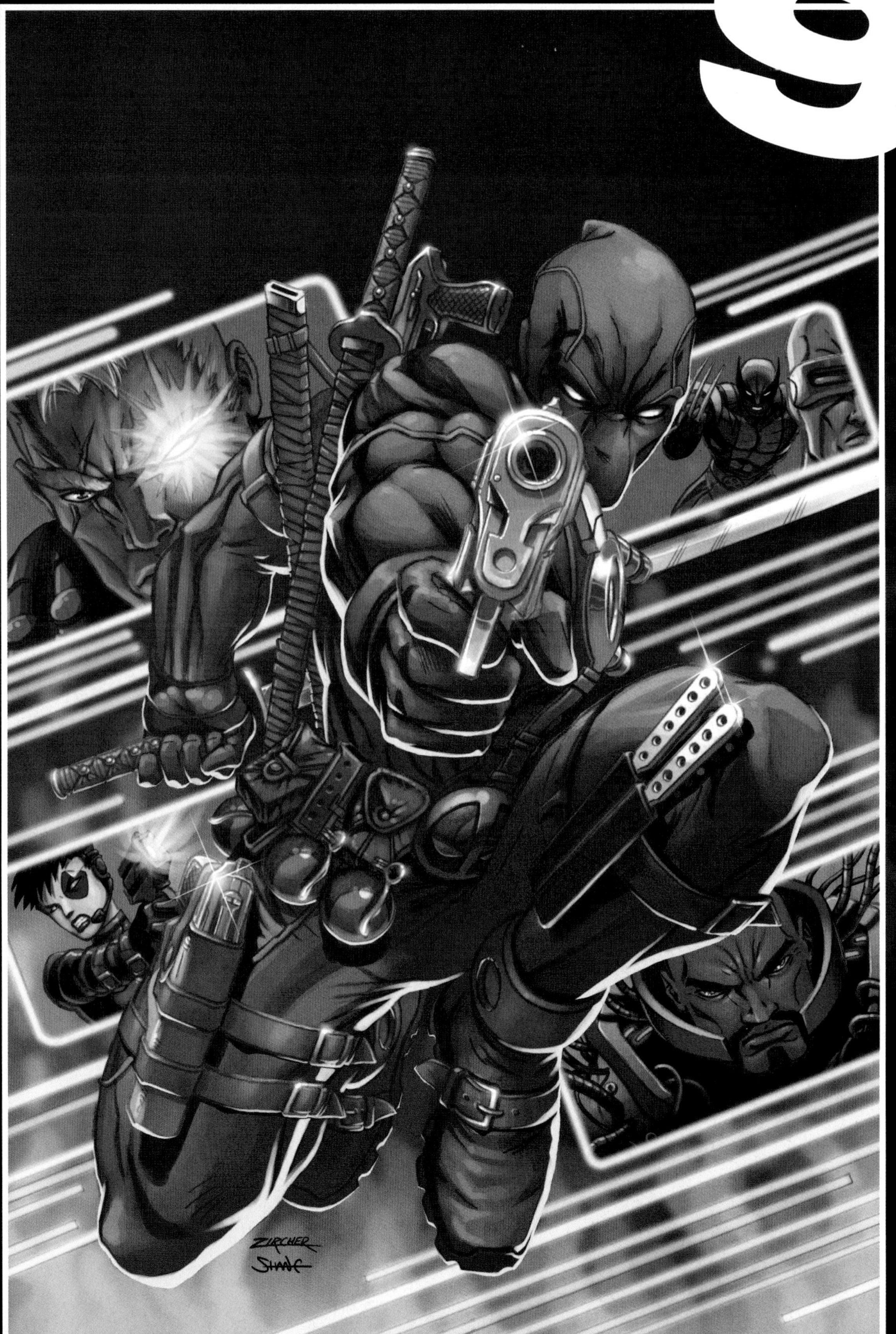
ZIRCHER
SHAW

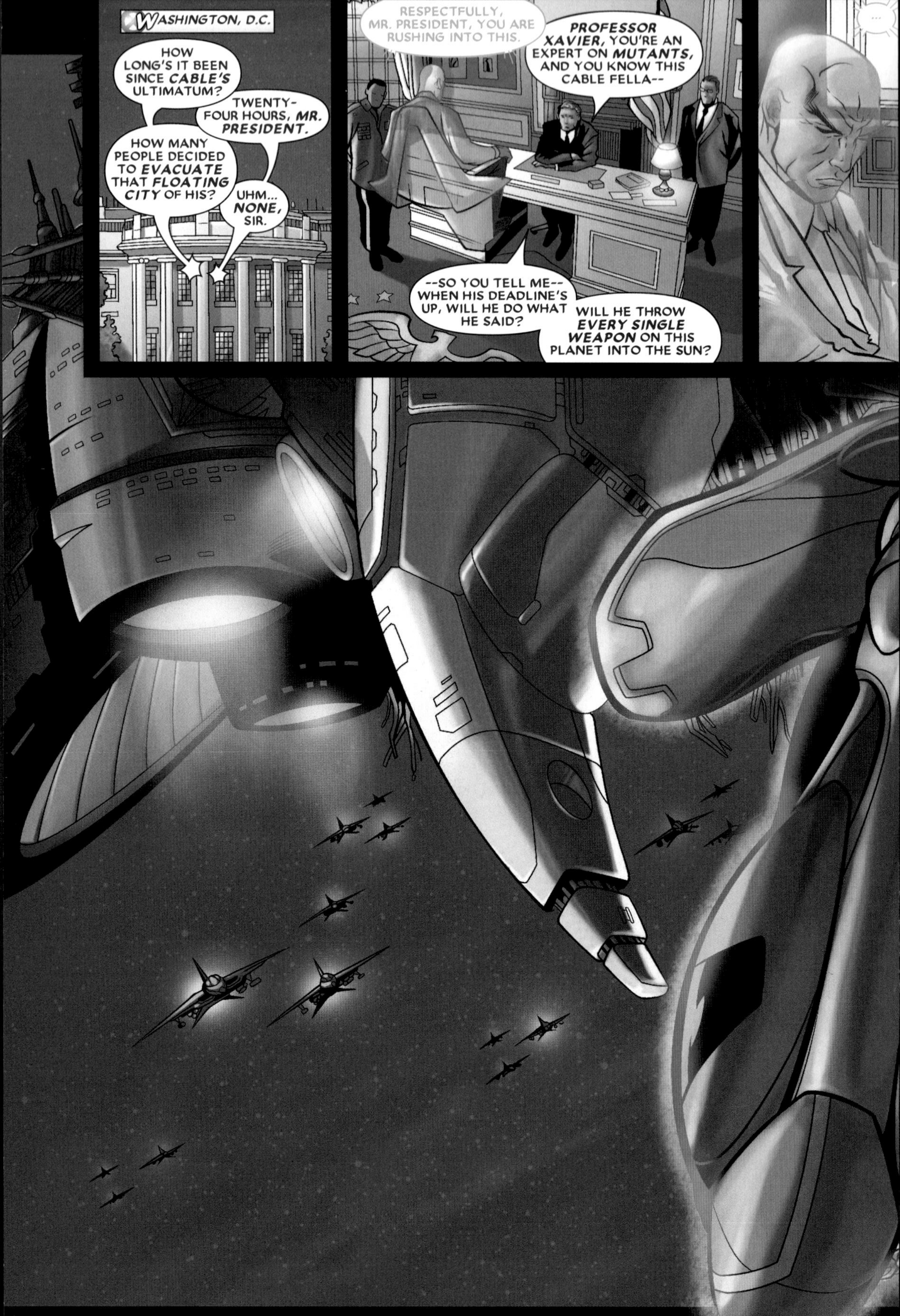
WASHINGTON, D.C.
HOW LONG'S IT BEEN SINCE CABLE'S ULTIMATUM?
TWENTY-FOUR HOURS, MR. PRESIDENT.
HOW MANY PEOPLE DECIDED TO EVACUATE THAT FLOATING CITY OF HIS?
UHM... NONE, SIR.
RESPECTFULLY, MR. PRESIDENT, YOU ARE RUSHING INTO THIS.
PROFESSOR XAVIER, YOU'RE AN EXPERT ON MUTANTS, AND YOU KNOW THIS CABLE FELLA--
--SO YOU TELL ME-- WHEN HIS DEADLINE'S UP, WILL HE DO WHAT HE SAID?
WILL HE THROW EVERY SINGLE WEAPON ON THIS PLANET INTO THE SUN?
...

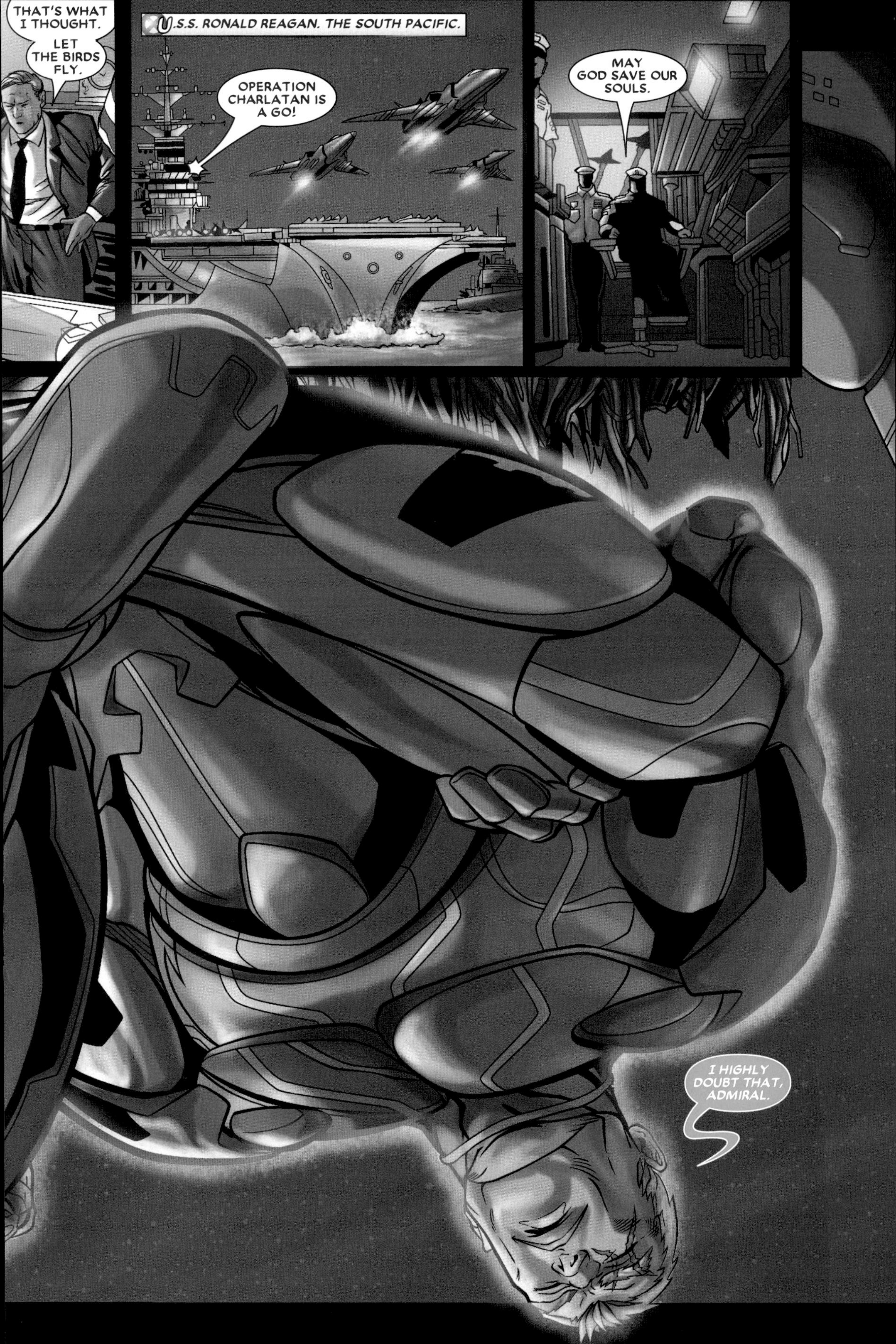
THAT'S WHAT I THOUGHT.
LET THE BIRDS FLY.
U.S.S. RONALD REAGAN. THE SOUTH PACIFIC.
OPERATION CHARLATAN IS A GO!
MAY GOD SAVE OUR SOULS.
I HIGHLY DOUBT THAT, ADMIRAL.

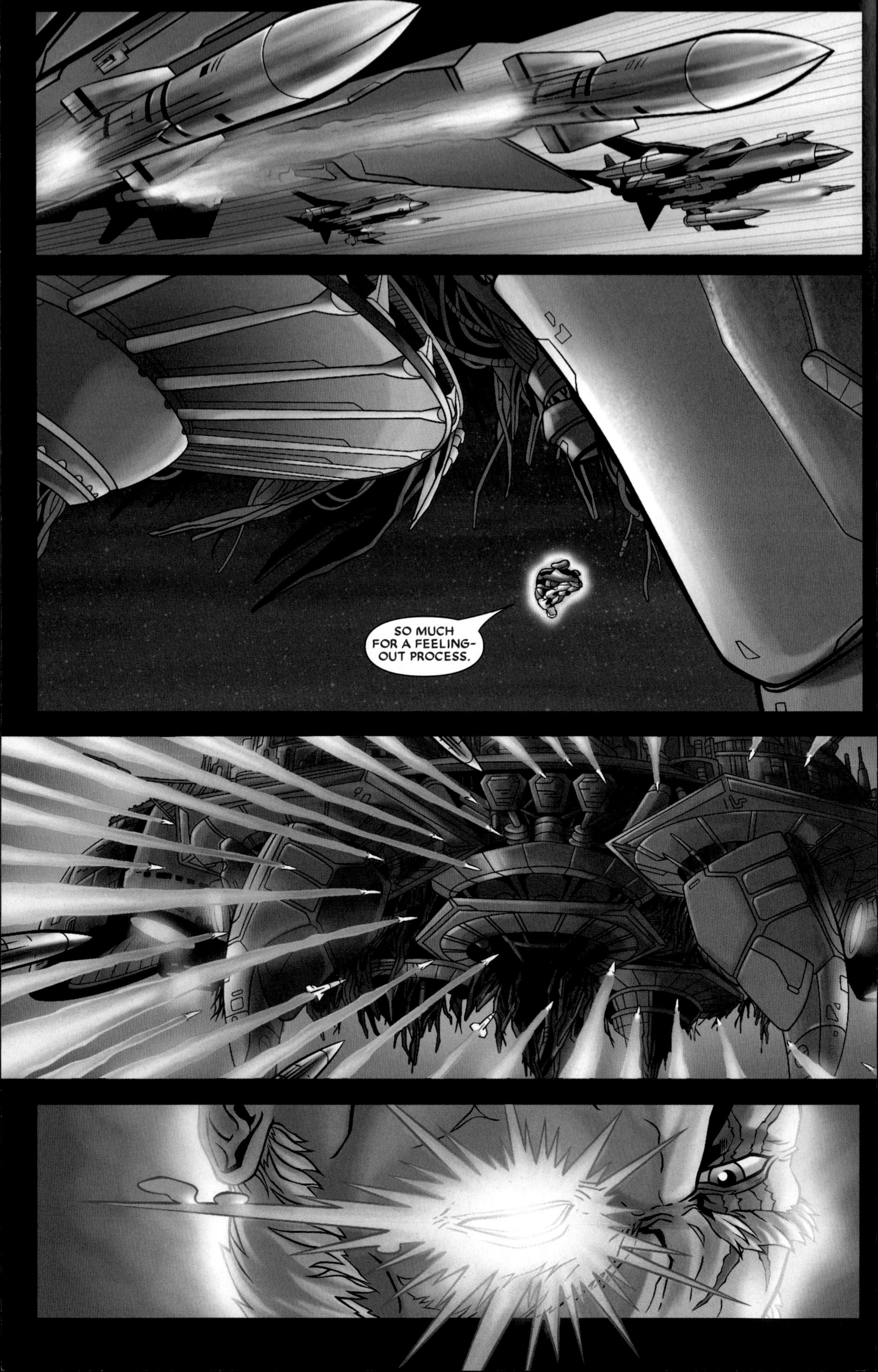
SO MUCH
FOR A FEELING-
OUT PROCESS.

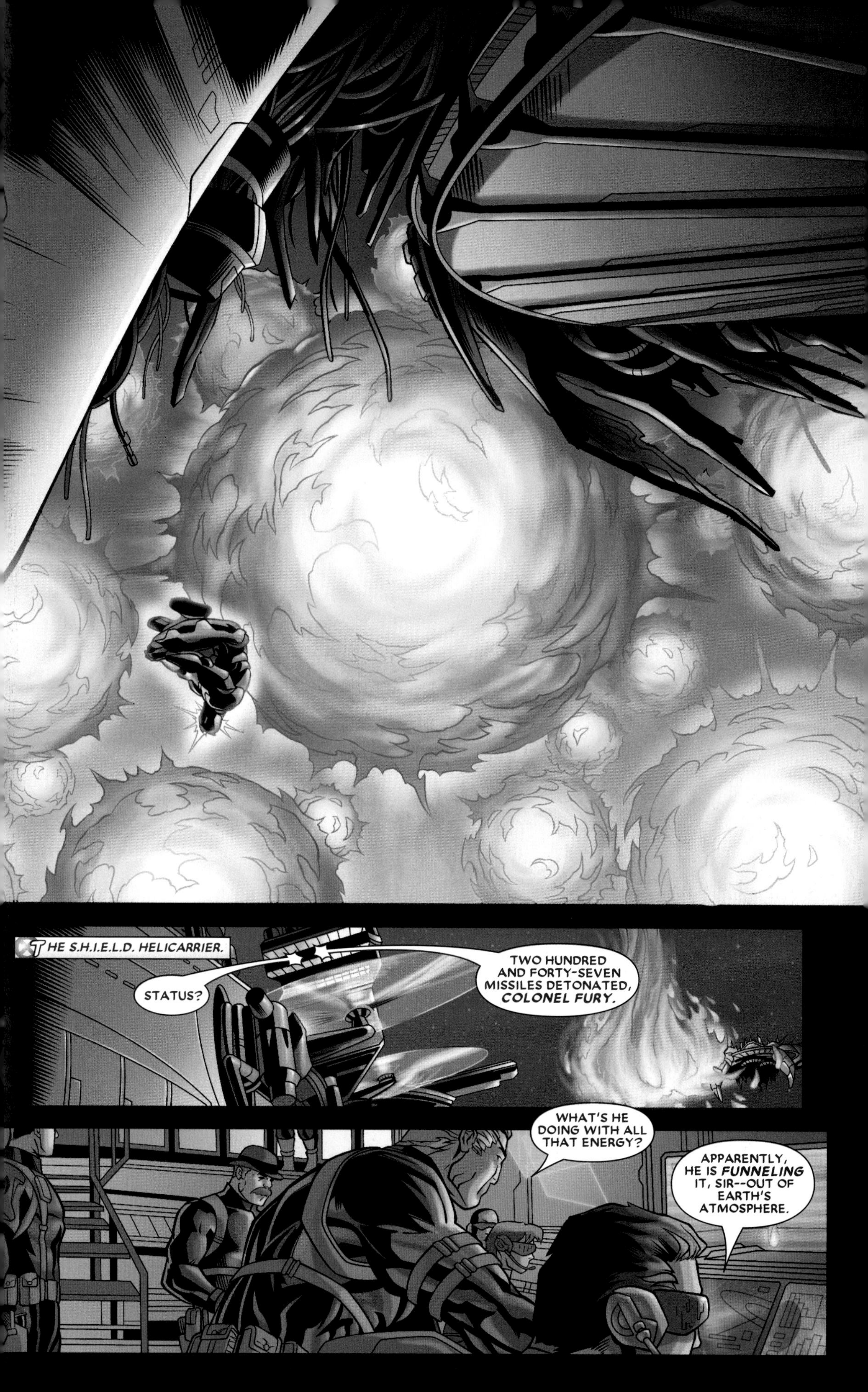
THE S.H.I.E.L.D. HELICARRIER.
STATUS?
TWO HUNDRED AND FORTY-SEVEN MISSILES DETONATED, COLONEL FURY.
WHAT'S HE DOING WITH ALL THAT ENERGY?
APPARENTLY, HE IS FUNNELING IT, SIR--OUT OF EARTH'S ATMOSPHERE.

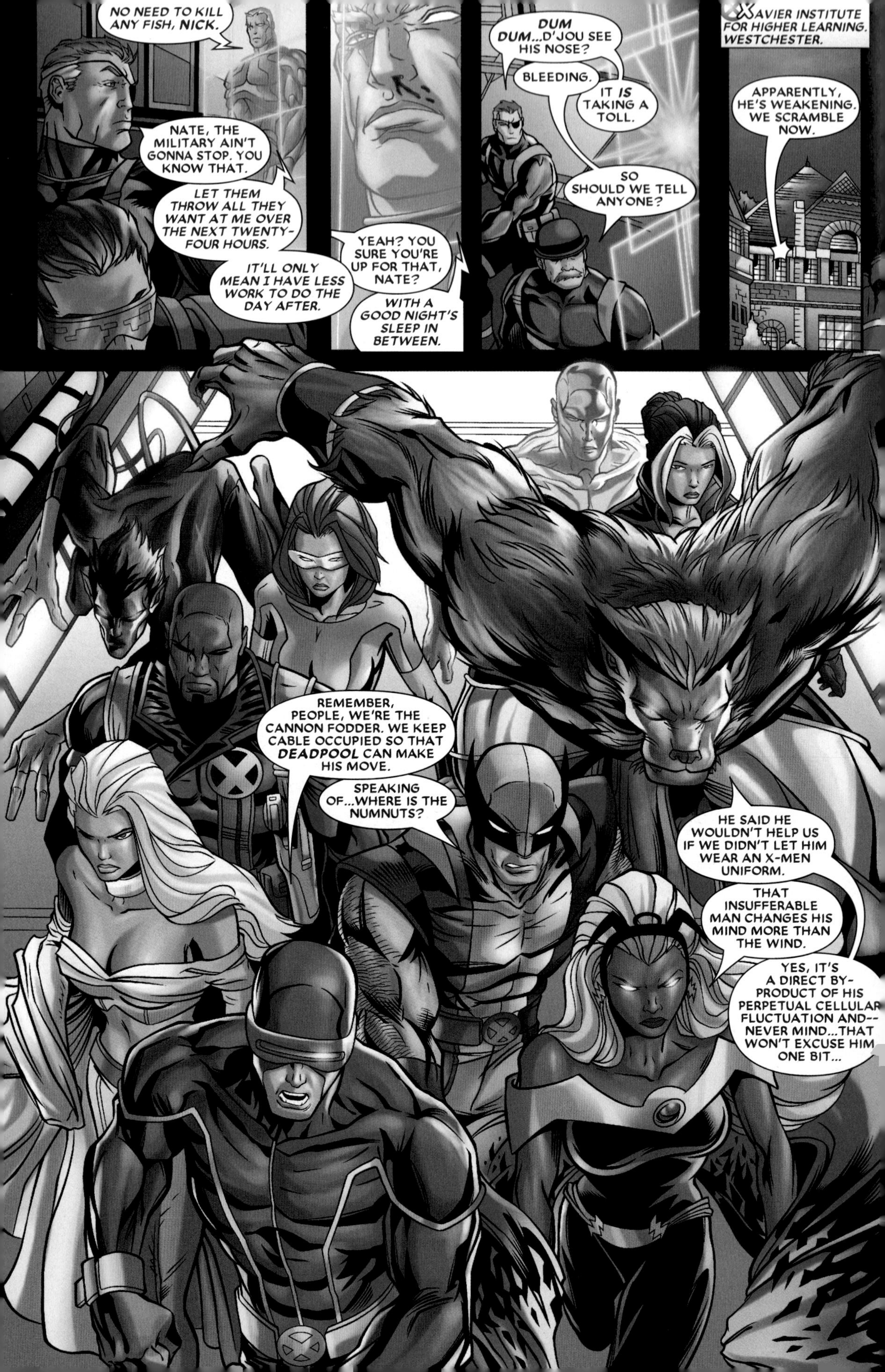
NO NEED TO KILL ANY FISH, NICK.
NATE, THE MILITARY AIN'T GONNA STOP. YOU KNOW THAT.
LET THEM THROW ALL THEY WANT AT ME OVER THE NEXT TWENTY-FOUR HOURS.
IT'LL ONLY MEAN I HAVE LESS WORK TO DO THE DAY AFTER.
YEAH? YOU SURE YOU'RE UP FOR THAT, NATE?
WITH A GOOD NIGHT'S SLEEP IN BETWEEN.
DUM DUM...D'JOU SEE HIS NOSE?
BLEEDING.
IT IS TAKING A TOLL.
SO SHOULD WE TELL ANYONE?
XAVIER INSTITUTE FOR HIGHER LEARNING. WESTCHESTER.
APPARENTLY, HE'S WEAKENING. WE SCRAMBLE NOW.
REMEMBER, PEOPLE, WE'RE THE CANNON FODDER. WE KEEP CABLE OCCUPIED SO THAT DEADPOOL CAN MAKE HIS MOVE.
SPEAKING OF...WHERE IS THE NUMNUTS?
HE SAID HE WOULDN'T HELP US IF WE DIDN'T LET HIM WEAR AN X-MEN UNIFORM.
THAT INSUFFERABLE MAN CHANGES HIS MIND MORE THAN THE WIND.
YES, IT'S A DIRECT BY-PRODUCT OF HIS PERPETUAL CELLULAR FLUCTUATION AND-- NEVER MIND...THAT WON'T EXCUSE HIM ONE BIT...

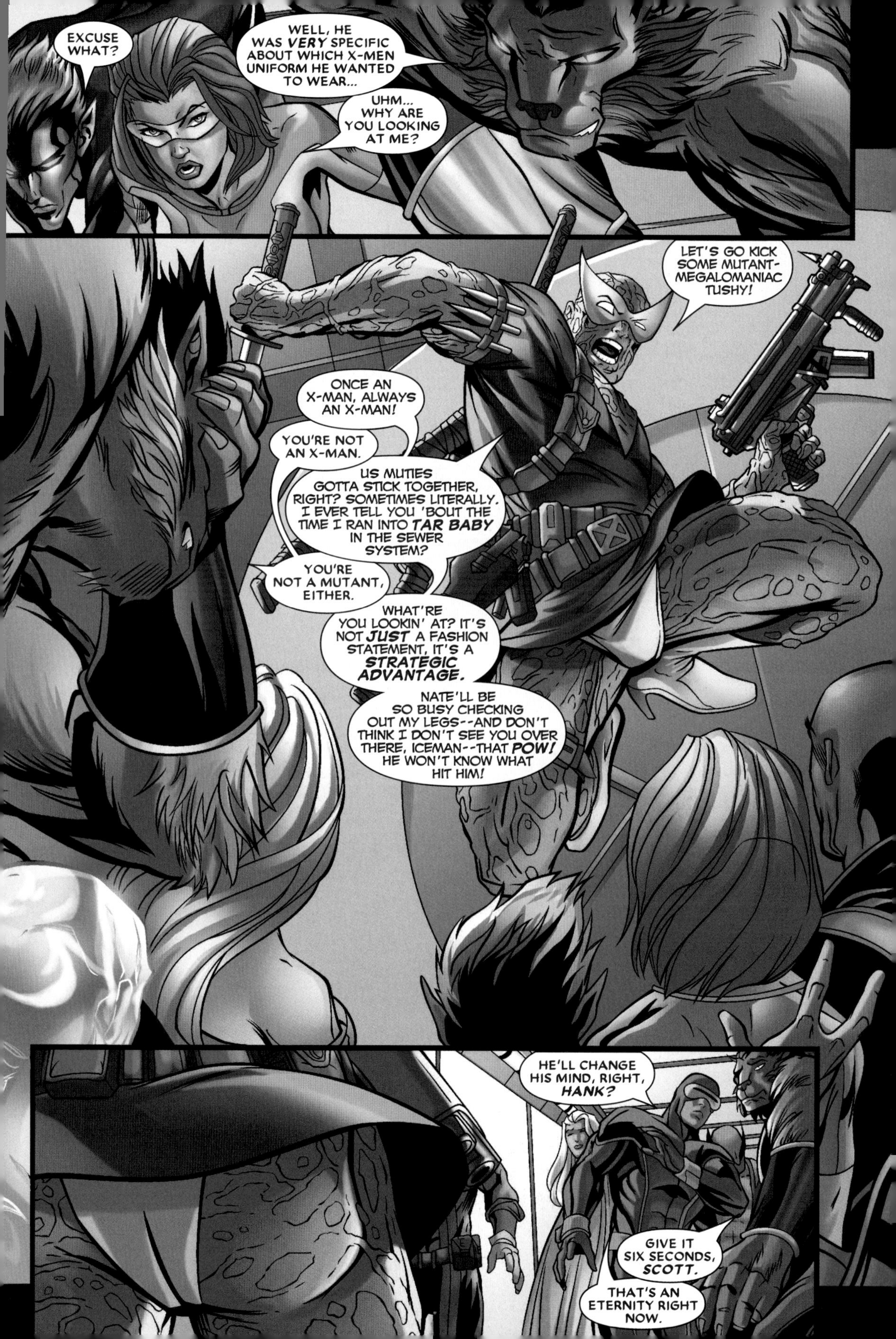
EXCUSE WHAT?
WELL, HE WAS VERY SPECIFIC ABOUT WHICH X-MEN UNIFORM HE WANTED TO WEAR...
UHM... WHY ARE YOU LOOKING AT ME?
LET'S GO KICK SOME MUTANT-MEGALOMANIAC TUSHY!
ONCE AN X-MAN, ALWAYS AN X-MAN!
YOU'RE NOT AN X-MAN.
US MUTIES GOTTA STICK TOGETHER, RIGHT? SOMETIMES LITERALLY. I EVER TELL YOU 'BOUT THE TIME I RAN INTO TAR BABY IN THE SEWER SYSTEM?
YOU'RE NOT A MUTANT, EITHER.
WHAT'RE YOU LOOKIN' AT? IT'S NOT JUST A FASHION STATEMENT, IT'S A STRATEGIC ADVANTAGE.
NATE'LL BE SO BUSY CHECKING OUT MY LEGS--AND DON'T THINK I DON'T SEE YOU OVER THERE, ICEMAN--THAT POW! HE WON'T KNOW WHAT HIT HIM!
HE'LL CHANGE HIS MIND, RIGHT, HANK?
GIVE IT SIX SECONDS, SCOTT.
THAT'S AN ETERNITY RIGHT NOW.

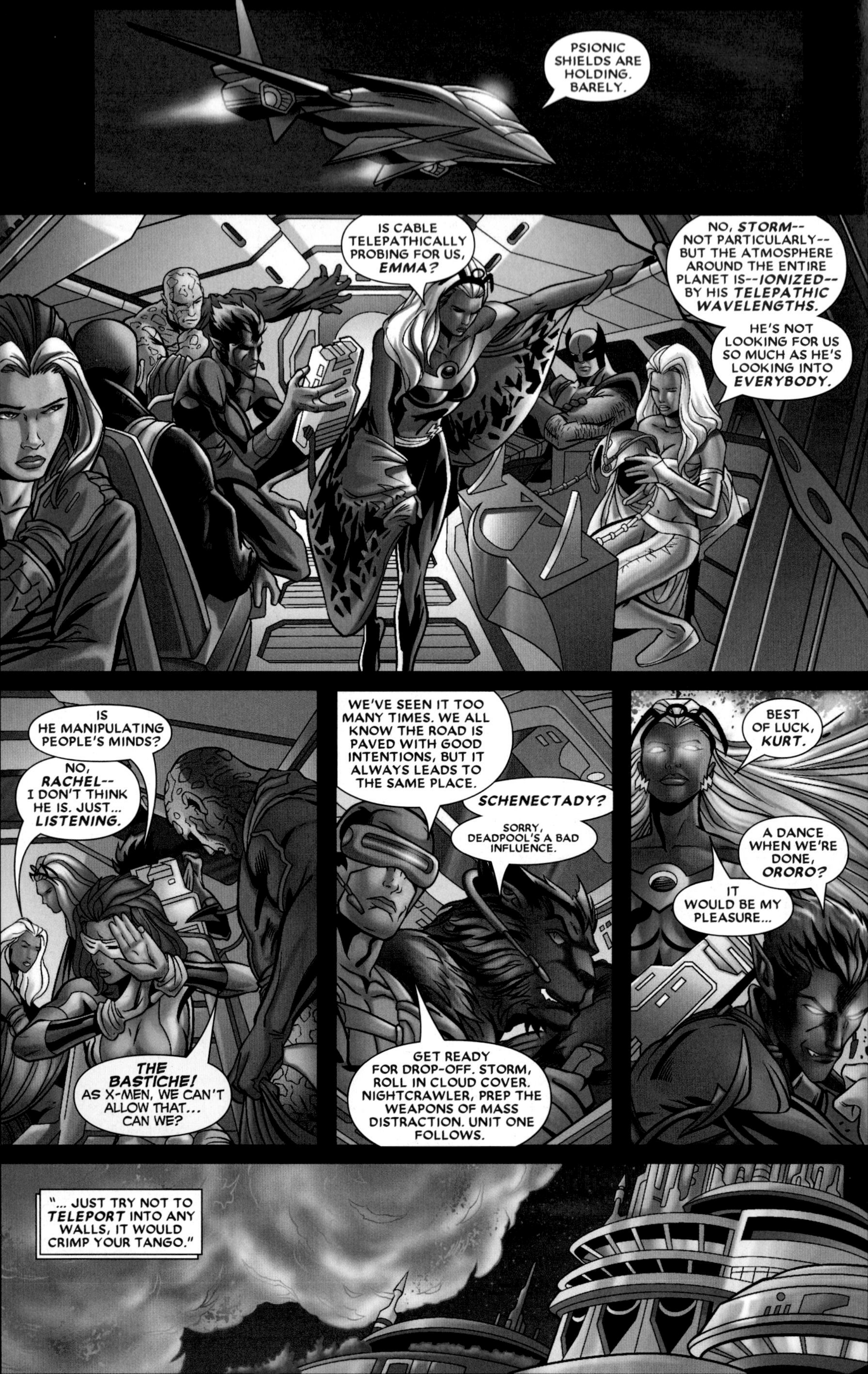
PSIONIC SHIELDS ARE HOLDING. BARELY.
IS CABLE TELEPATHICALLY PROBING FOR US, EMMA?
NO, STORM-- NOT PARTICULARLY-- BUT THE ATMOSPHERE AROUND THE ENTIRE PLANET IS--IONIZED-- BY HIS TELEPATHIC WAVELENGTHS.
HE'S NOT LOOKING FOR US SO MUCH AS HE'S LOOKING INTO EVERYBODY.
IS HE MANIPULATING PEOPLE'S MINDS?
NO, RACHEL-- I DON'T THINK HE IS. JUST... LISTENING.
THE BASTICHE! AS X-MEN, WE CAN'T ALLOW THAT... CAN WE?
WE'VE SEEN IT TOO MANY TIMES. WE ALL KNOW THE ROAD IS PAVED WITH GOOD INTENTIONS, BUT IT ALWAYS LEADS TO THE SAME PLACE.
SCHENECTADY?
SORRY, DEADPOOL'S A BAD INFLUENCE.
GET READY FOR DROP-OFF. STORM, ROLL IN CLOUD COVER. NIGHTCRAWLER, PREP THE WEAPONS OF MASS DISTRACTION. UNIT ONE FOLLOWS.
BEST OF LUCK, KURT.
A DANCE WHEN WE'RE DONE, ORORO?
IT WOULD BE MY PLEASURE...
"... JUST TRY NOT TO TELEPORT INTO ANY WALLS, IT WOULD CRIMP YOUR TANGO."

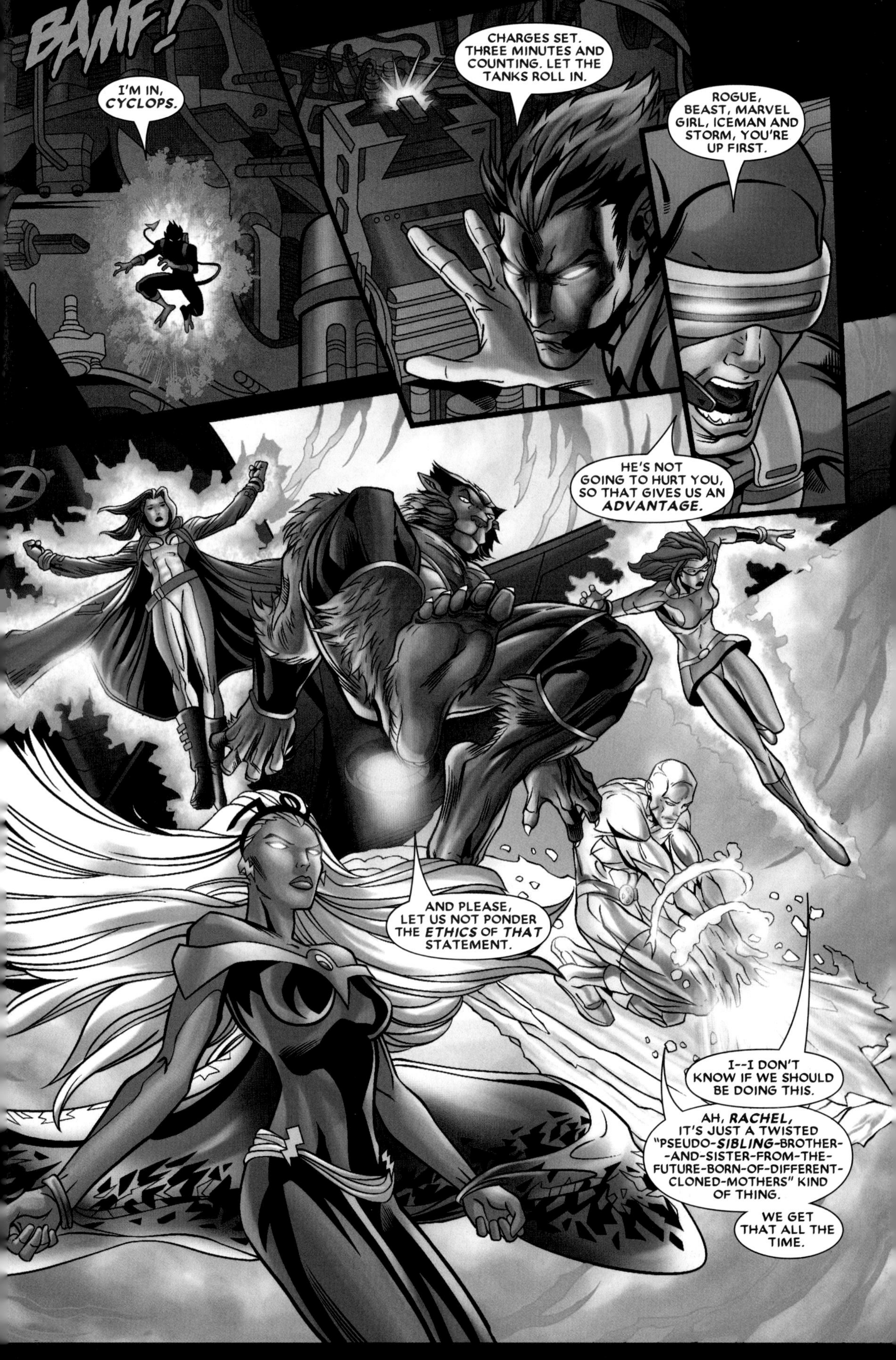
BAMF!
I'M IN, CYCLOPS.
CHARGES SET. THREE MINUTES AND COUNTING. LET THE TANKS ROLL IN.
ROGUE, BEAST, MARVEL GIRL, ICEMAN AND STORM, YOU'RE UP FIRST.
HE'S NOT GOING TO HURT YOU, SO THAT GIVES US AN ADVANTAGE.
AND PLEASE, LET US NOT PONDER THE ETHICS OF THAT STATEMENT.
I--I DON'T KNOW IF WE SHOULD BE DOING THIS.
AH, RACHEL, IT'S JUST A TWISTED "PSEUDO-SIBLING-BROTHER-AND-SISTER-FROM-THE-FUTURE-BORN-OF-DIFFERENT-CLONED-MOTHERS" KIND OF THING.
WE GET THAT ALL THE TIME.

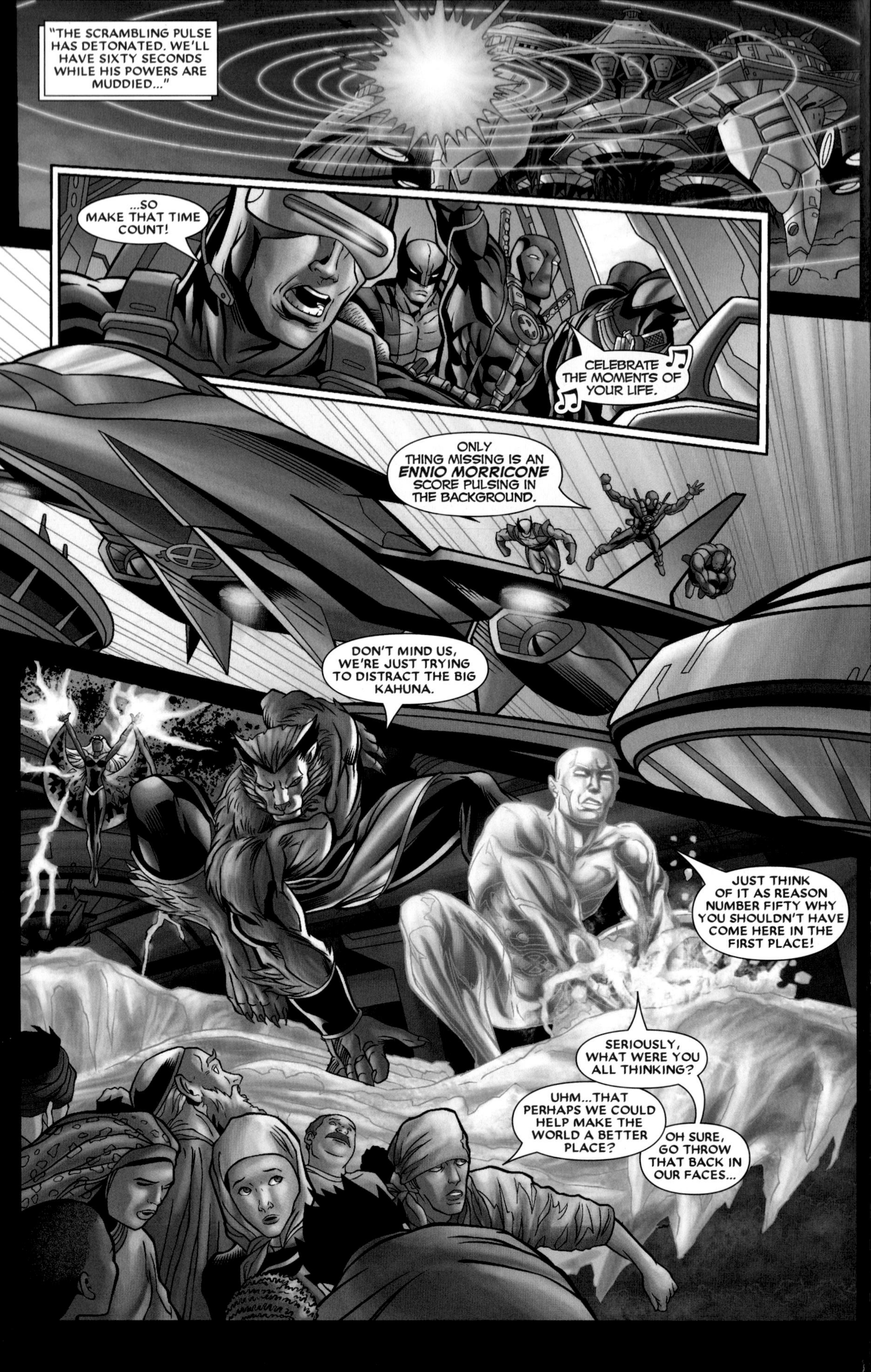
"THE SCRAMBLING PULSE HAS DETONATED. WE'LL HAVE SIXTY SECONDS WHILE HIS POWERS ARE MUDDIED..."
...SO MAKE THAT TIME COUNT!
CELEBRATE THE MOMENTS OF YOUR LIFE.
ONLY THING MISSING IS AN ENNIO MORRICONE SCORE PULSING IN THE BACKGROUND.
DON'T MIND US, WE'RE JUST TRYING TO DISTRACT THE BIG KAHUNA.
JUST THINK OF IT AS REASON NUMBER FIFTY WHY YOU SHOULDN'T HAVE COME HERE IN THE FIRST PLACE!
SERIOUSLY, WHAT WERE YOU ALL THINKING?
UHM...THAT PERHAPS WE COULD HELP MAKE THE WORLD A BETTER PLACE?
OH SURE, GO THROW THAT BACK IN OUR FACES...

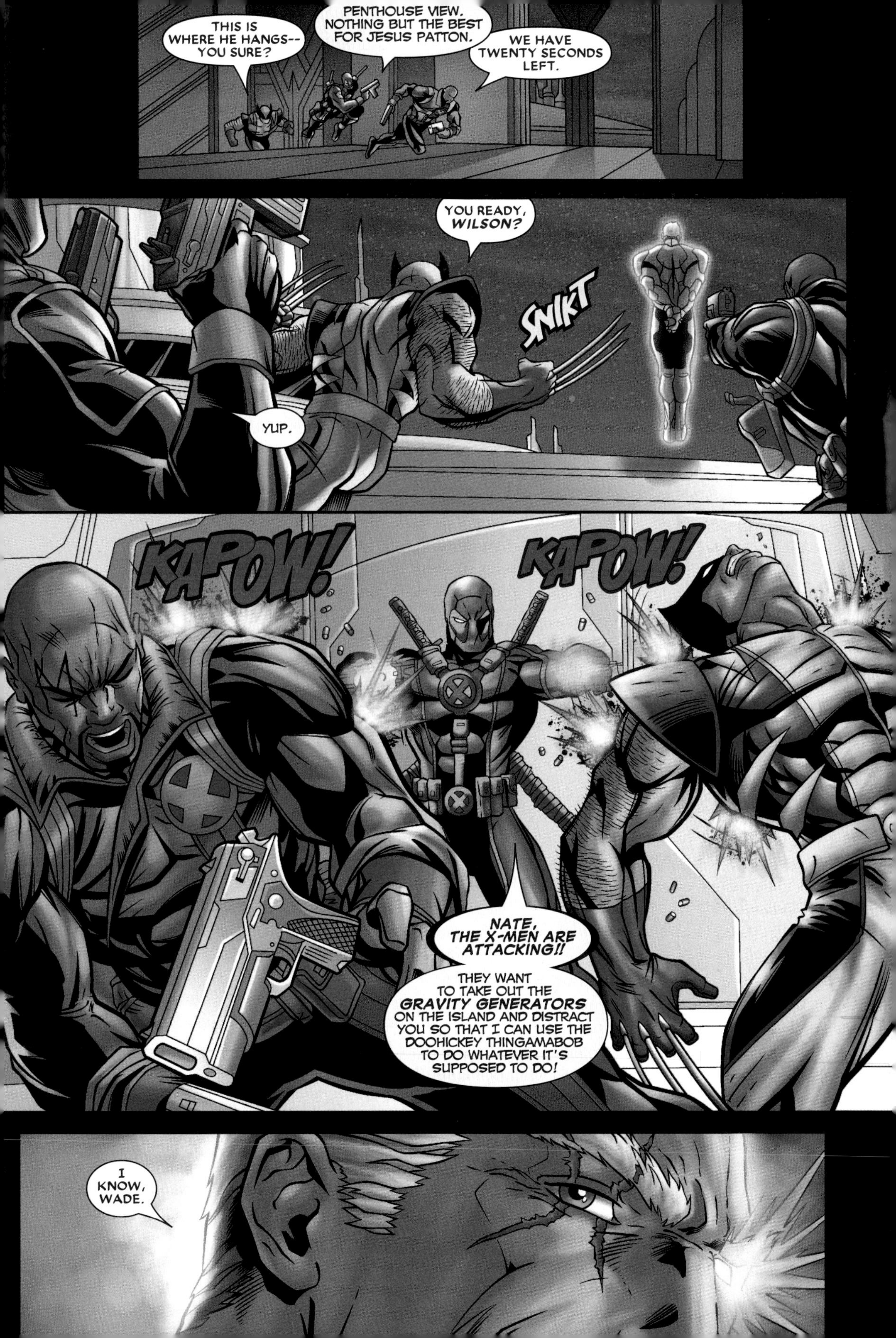
THIS IS WHERE HE HANGS-- YOU SURE?
PENTHOUSE VIEW. NOTHING BUT THE BEST FOR JESUS PATTON.
WE HAVE TWENTY SECONDS LEFT.
YOU READY, WILSON?
YUP.
SNIKT
KAPOW!
KAPOW!
NATE, THE X-MEN ARE ATTACKING!!
THEY WANT TO TAKE OUT THE GRAVITY GENERATORS ON THE ISLAND AND DISTRACT YOU SO THAT I CAN USE THE DOOHICKEY THINGAMABOB TO DO WHATEVER IT'S SUPPOSED TO DO!
I KNOW, WADE.

Irene Merryweather: You set up a deadline. You purposely imposed a time limit on allowing people to make a decision about you?
Cable: No, only to allow governments to make a decision about me. The people have already spoken.
IM: I don't hear them.
Cable: I do, Irene. Every single one of them. Every single person on the planet. I'm talking to them right now.
IM: That's one heck of a party line.
Cable: You have no idea. It's terrifying--but it's also…magical.
IM: Okay, be that as it may, when we talked a couple of days ago, you said it would take generations to enact your plans for bringing peace to Earth, etc., etc.
Cable: It still will.
IM: But you're forcing the issue--I don't understand…
Cable: Irene, I'm a time-traveler. The entire concept of time is very malleable to me--not that I can timeslide now, but when I could, I'm saying, it changes your perceptions of the here and now. The present becomes a place to be, but you accept it is only but a fraction of all that was or will be.
IM: And for those who will read this who don't speak Askani gibberish?
Cable: Not to sound patronizing, but I think on very different levels than those restricted to linear living--and most certainly on a different level than those whose power is dependent on the vagaries of regular elections or the lifespan limitations of dictatorial rule.
IM: So everything you're doing *now* is not about now?
Cable: To a certain extent. The more powerful I recently became, the more I searched for something of value. Power without worth was useless to me.
IM: And currently, you're powerful enough to take over the world?
Cable: Or save the world from those who would take it over.
IM: And throwing every single weapon on Earth into the sun solves that?

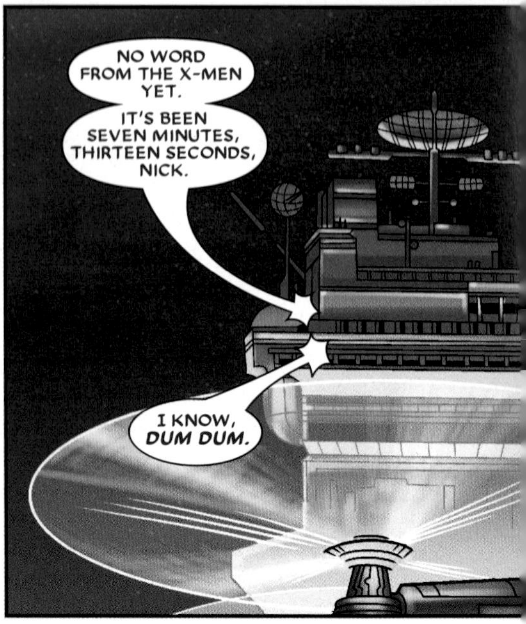
NO WORD FROM THE X-MEN YET.
IT'S BEEN SEVEN MINUTES, THIRTEEN SECONDS, NICK.
I KNOW, *DUM DUM.*

IM: Philosophically, I guess, it's just in practicali
I don't know.
Cable: How so?
IM: We live in a world where superhumans ar walking weapons. They will come--voluntarily o by coercion--and they will try to stop you.
Cable: Yes, they will.
IM: And?
Cable: I imagine that getting them out of the way quickly will make things easier for me dow the road.
IM: "Getting them out of the way"--?
Cable: Not killing them, no. I'll convert some my cause. Detain others as necessary, until suc time as they can see for themselves that I'm helping the world.
IM: None of them worry you?
Cable: All confrontation, any conflict, worries

Cable: It's nothing more than a start. New weapons will be made. Mankind has made do with sticks and rocks.
IM: Those headed out into the sun, too?
Cable (laughing)**:** No, then I'd have to worry about teeth and nails.
IM: And that's my point, eliminating the weapon doesn't solve the inherent problem.
Cable: And that's my point as well. Changing thought and behavior will take generations. But wouldn't you say reducing the availability of weapons is a step in the right direction?

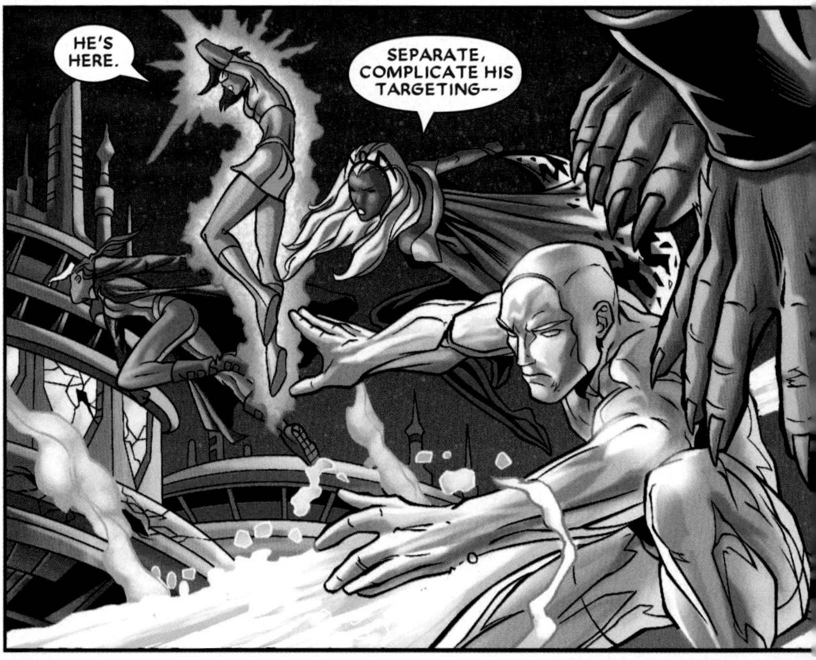
HE'S HERE.
SEPARATE, COMPLICATE HIS TARGETING--

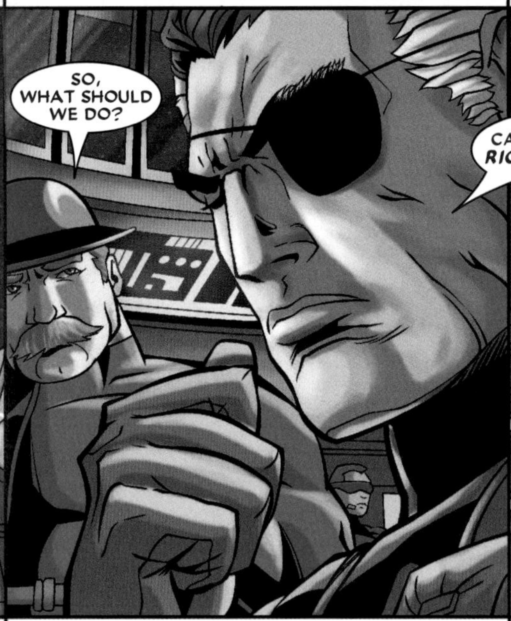
SO, WHAT SHOULD WE DO?
CALL REED RICHARDS...

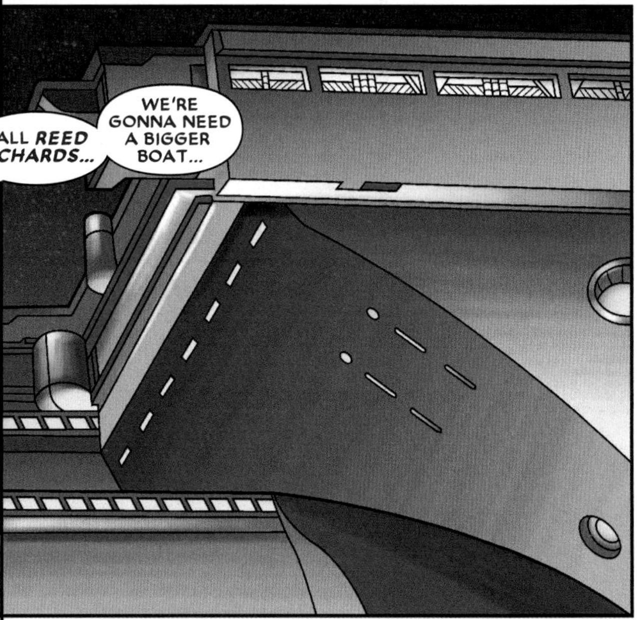
WE'RE GONNA NEED A BIGGER BOAT...

me, to one extent or another.
IM: I meant from a power standpoint.
Cable: Oh.
(smiling)
No. No, that doesn't worry me.
IM: That powerful, are you?
Cable: Yes.
IM: And that doesn't concern you?
Cable: Absolute power and all that?
IM: Sure.
Cable: No, it doesn't, because I don't want this power. I don't want to rule. I want…
(pause)
… I want to enjoy my life.
IM: You have a funny way of showing that.
Cable: Tell me about it.
IM: What happens if the world's governments don't accede to your deadline?
Cable: They'll launch an attack. Several, probably. They'll start before my deadline even expires. That will fail. Then they'll send the superhumans. Probably the X-Men first. They're mutants, that's a safe message to send the world. They know me, so they'll have some tricks up their sleeves.
IM: You sound like you have this all figured out.
Cable: I'm from the future, Irene. How do you know everything that is about to happen isn't something I read in my history tapes?
IM: I--I honestly hadn't thought of that. I mean, well, is it? History for you? *Do* you know the outcome of the actions you've taken?
Cable: Well, I'd certainly like you to think I do.
IM: That's not an answer.
Cable: Of course it is, just not the one you wanted to hear.
IM: You said the X-Men would come first.
Cable: They're the vanguard of the mutant rights movement. They've been given international authority. They have the coolest costumes. Yes, I'd expect they're first.
IM: And how would you handle that?
Cable: Strategically?
IM: Emotionally.
Cable: I don't understand.
IM: No, you're just choosing to avoid the issue. Namely, isn't Cyclops your father?
Cable: Father is a…complicated term.
IM: You are his son.
Cable: Yes.
IM: Then he is your father.
Cable: Not exactly.
IM: Geez, it's like pulling teeth. When you were a baby, he sent you to the future to protect you from the techno-organic disease that was killing you.
Cable: Yes.
IM: So, some history there, maybe?
Cable: It doesn't make a difference.
IM: Really?
Cable: I guess we'll all find out, won't we?

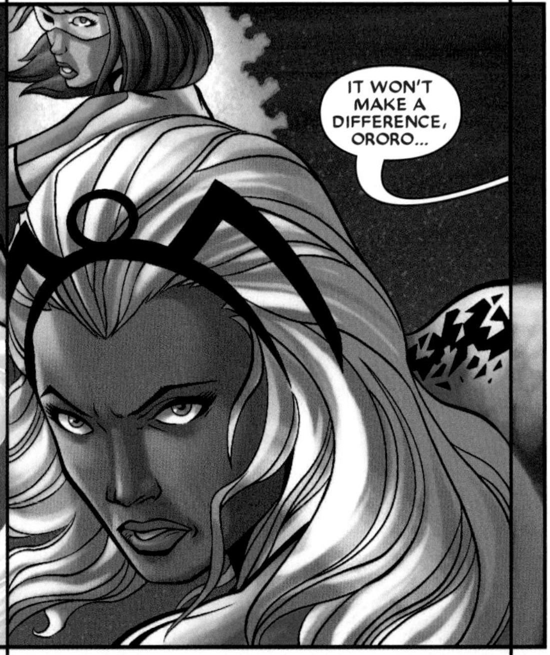
IT WON'T MAKE A DIFFERENCE, ORORO...

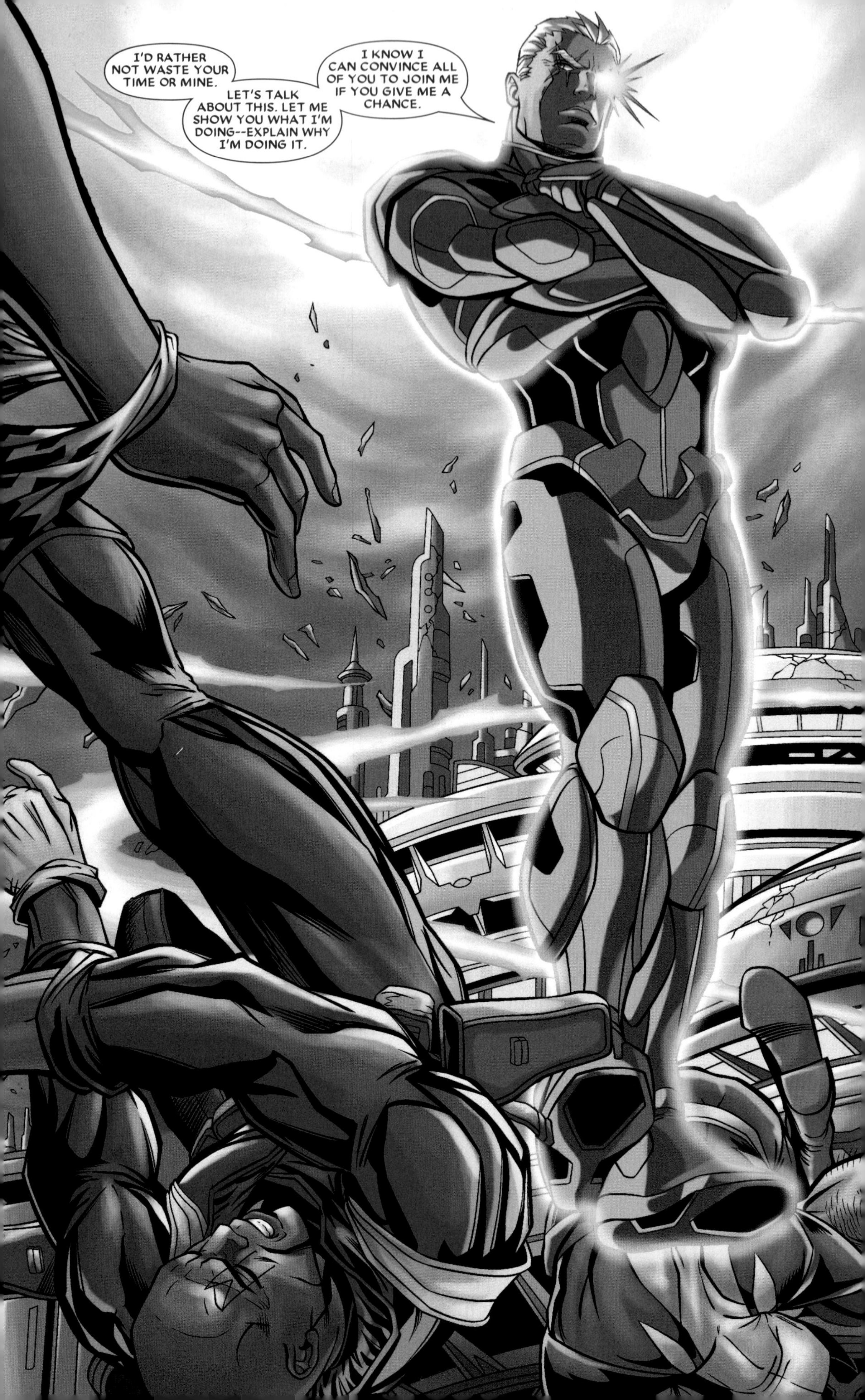
I'D RATHER NOT WASTE YOUR TIME OR MINE.
LET'S TALK ABOUT THIS. LET ME SHOW YOU WHAT I'M DOING--EXPLAIN WHY I'M DOING IT.
I KNOW I CAN CONVINCE ALL OF YOU TO JOIN ME IF YOU GIVE ME A CHANCE.

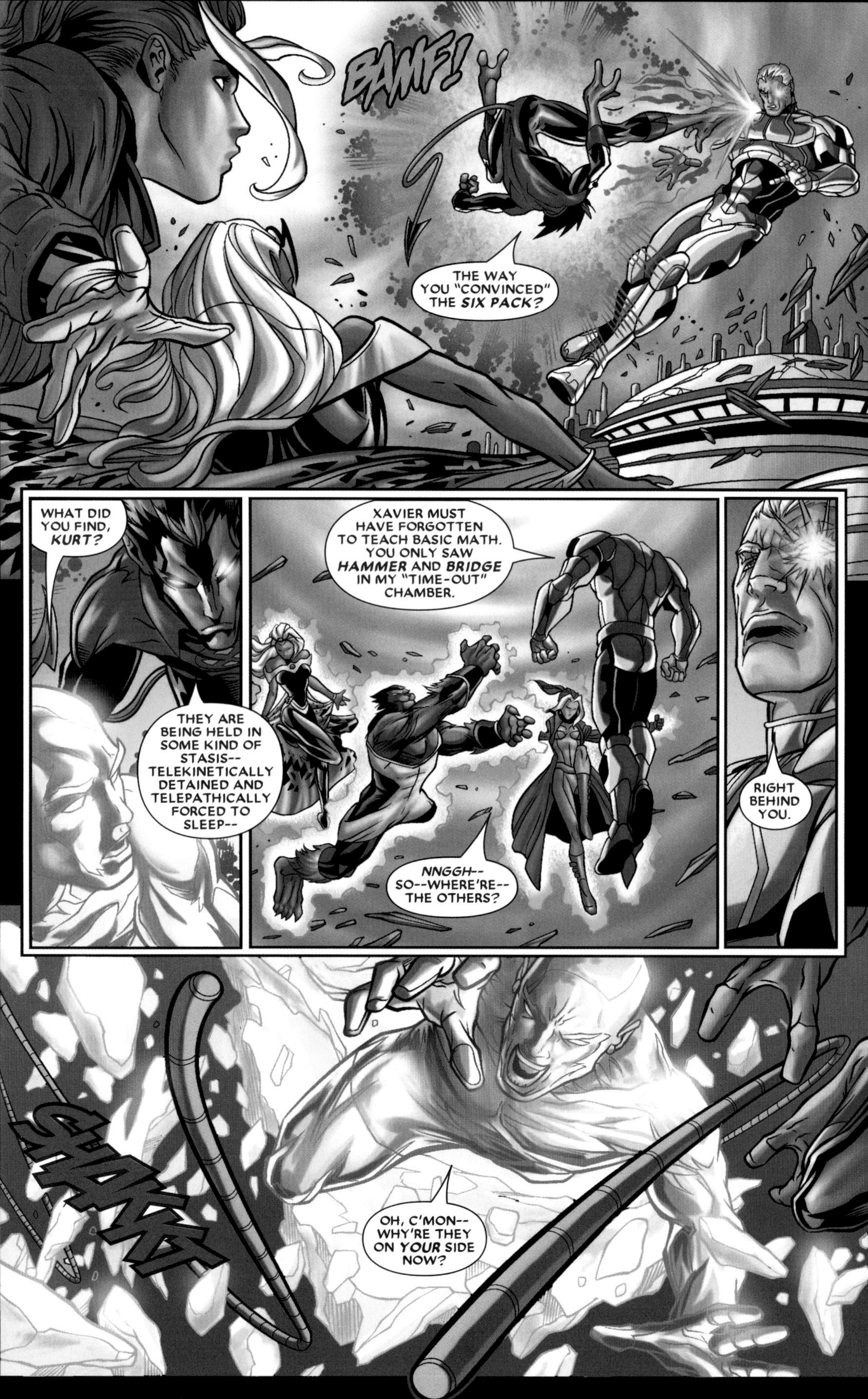
BAMF!
THE WAY YOU "CONVINCED" THE SIX PACK?
WHAT DID YOU FIND, KURT?
THEY ARE BEING HELD IN SOME KIND OF STASIS-- TELEKINETICALLY DETAINED AND TELEPATHICALLY FORCED TO SLEEP--
XAVIER MUST HAVE FORGOTTEN TO TEACH BASIC MATH. YOU ONLY SAW HAMMER AND BRIDGE IN MY "TIME-OUT" CHAMBER.
NNGGH-- SO--WHERE'RE-- THE OTHERS?
RIGHT BEHIND YOU.
SHANK!
OH, C'MON-- WHY'RE THEY ON YOUR SIDE NOW?

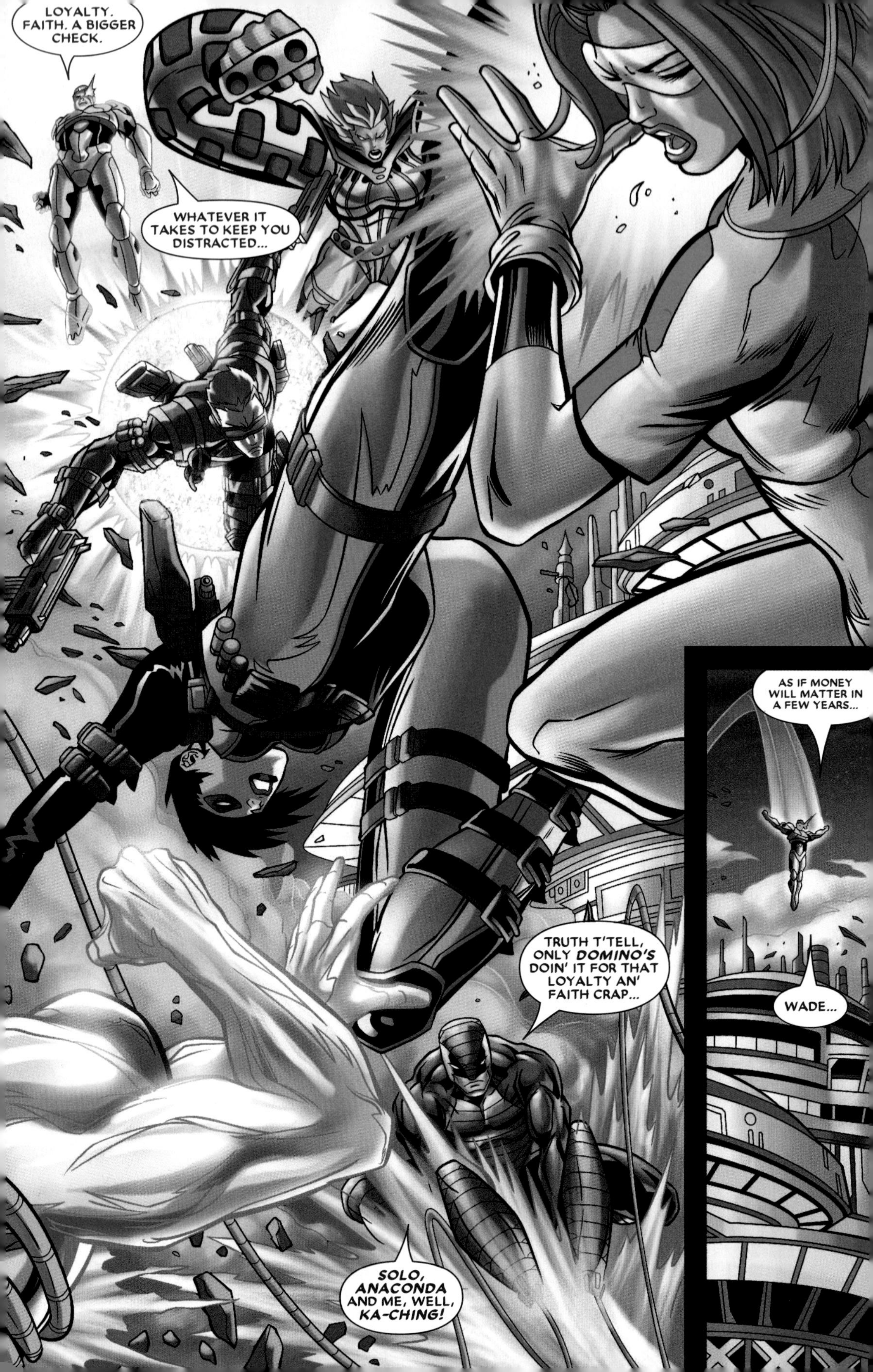
LOYALTY. FAITH. A BIGGER CHECK.
WHATEVER IT TAKES TO KEEP YOU DISTRACTED...
TRUTH T'TELL, ONLY DOMINO'S DOIN' IT FOR THAT LOYALTY AN' FAITH CRAP...
SOLO, ANACONDA AND ME, WELL, KA-CHING!
AS IF MONEY WILL MATTER IN A FEW YEARS...
WADE...

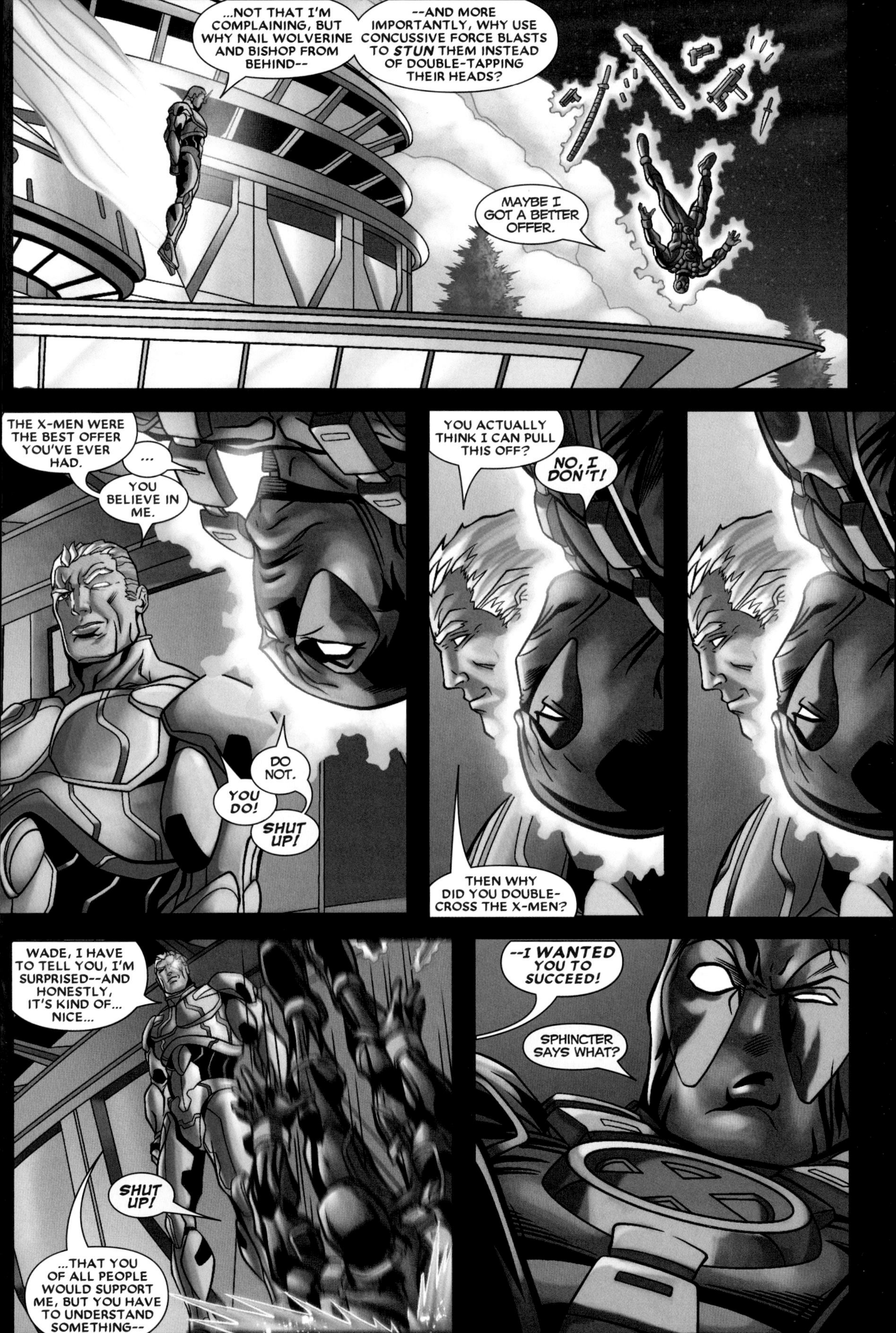
...NOT THAT I'M COMPLAINING, BUT WHY NAIL WOLVERINE AND BISHOP FROM BEHIND--
--AND MORE IMPORTANTLY, WHY USE CONCUSSIVE FORCE BLASTS TO STUN THEM INSTEAD OF DOUBLE-TAPPING THEIR HEADS?
MAYBE I GOT A BETTER OFFER.
THE X-MEN WERE THE BEST OFFER YOU'VE EVER HAD.
...
YOU BELIEVE IN ME.
DO NOT.
YOU DO!
SHUT UP!
YOU ACTUALLY THINK I CAN PULL THIS OFF?
NO, I DON'T!
THEN WHY DID YOU DOUBLE-CROSS THE X-MEN?
WADE, I HAVE TO TELL YOU, I'M SURPRISED--AND HONESTLY, IT'S KIND OF... NICE...
SHUT UP!
...THAT YOU OF ALL PEOPLE WOULD SUPPORT ME, BUT YOU HAVE TO UNDERSTAND SOMETHING--
--I WANTED YOU TO SUCCEED!
SPHINCTER SAYS WHAT?

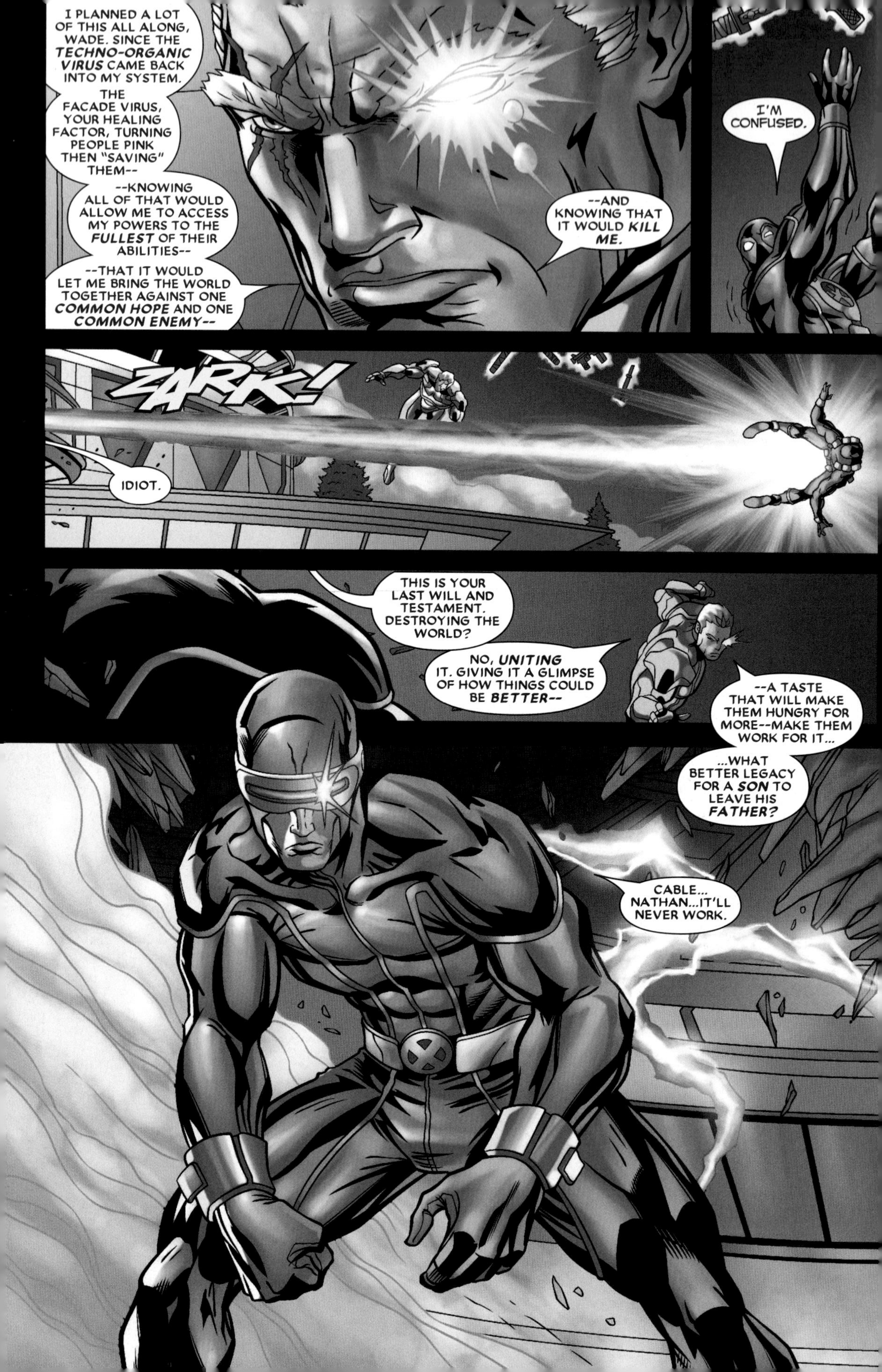
I PLANNED A LOT OF THIS ALL ALONG, WADE. SINCE THE TECHNO-ORGANIC VIRUS CAME BACK INTO MY SYSTEM.
THE FACADE VIRUS, YOUR HEALING FACTOR, TURNING PEOPLE PINK THEN "SAVING" THEM--
--KNOWING ALL OF THAT WOULD ALLOW ME TO ACCESS MY POWERS TO THE FULLEST OF THEIR ABILITIES--
--THAT IT WOULD LET ME BRING THE WORLD TOGETHER AGAINST ONE COMMON HOPE AND ONE COMMON ENEMY--
--AND KNOWING THAT IT WOULD KILL ME.
I'M CONFUSED.
ZARK!
IDIOT.
THIS IS YOUR LAST WILL AND TESTAMENT. DESTROYING THE WORLD?
NO, UNITING IT. GIVING IT A GLIMPSE OF HOW THINGS COULD BE BETTER--
--A TASTE THAT WILL MAKE THEM HUNGRY FOR MORE--MAKE THEM WORK FOR IT...
...WHAT BETTER LEGACY FOR A SON TO LEAVE HIS FATHER?
CABLE... NATHAN...IT'LL NEVER WORK.

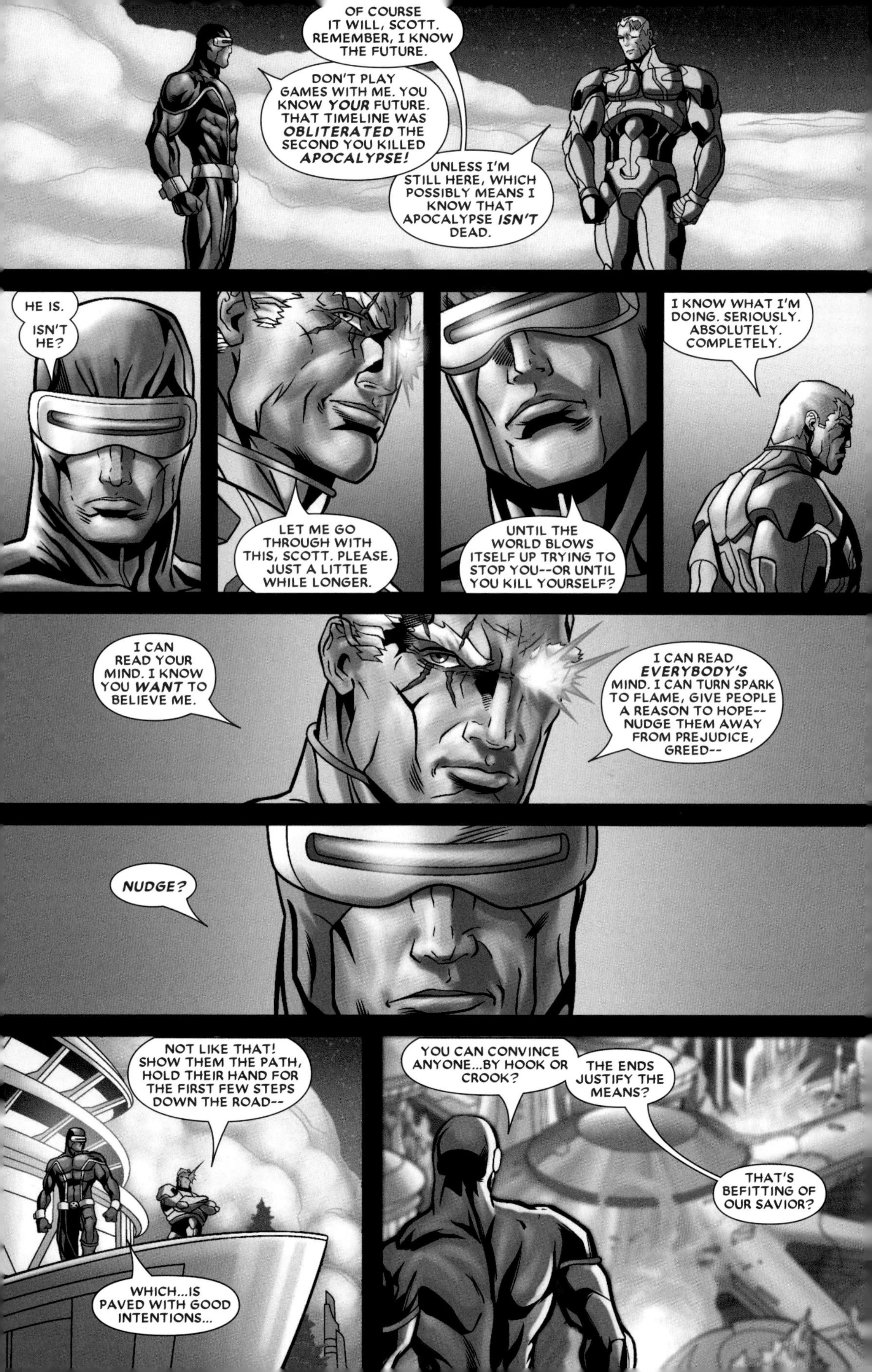
OF COURSE IT WILL, SCOTT. REMEMBER, I KNOW THE FUTURE.
DON'T PLAY GAMES WITH ME. YOU KNOW *YOUR* FUTURE. THAT TIMELINE WAS *OBLITERATED* THE SECOND YOU KILLED *APOCALYPSE!*
UNLESS I'M STILL HERE, WHICH POSSIBLY MEANS I KNOW THAT APOCALYPSE *ISN'T* DEAD.
HE IS.
ISN'T HE?
LET ME GO THROUGH WITH THIS, SCOTT. PLEASE. JUST A LITTLE WHILE LONGER.
UNTIL THE WORLD BLOWS ITSELF UP TRYING TO STOP YOU--OR UNTIL YOU KILL YOURSELF?
I KNOW WHAT I'M DOING. SERIOUSLY. ABSOLUTELY. COMPLETELY.
I CAN READ YOUR MIND. I KNOW YOU *WANT* TO BELIEVE ME.
I CAN READ *EVERYBODY'S* MIND. I CAN TURN SPARK TO FLAME, GIVE PEOPLE A REASON TO HOPE--NUDGE THEM AWAY FROM PREJUDICE, GREED--
NUDGE?
NOT LIKE THAT! SHOW THEM THE PATH, HOLD THEIR HAND FOR THE FIRST FEW STEPS DOWN THE ROAD--
WHICH...IS PAVED WITH GOOD INTENTIONS...
YOU CAN CONVINCE ANYONE...BY HOOK OR CROOK?
THE ENDS JUSTIFY THE MEANS?
THAT'S BEFITTING OF OUR SAVIOR?

I'M *NOT* A SAVIOR, I JUST-- I HAVE ALL THIS POWER-- BUT IT WON'T LAST FOR MUCH LONGER--

--AND I CAN MAKE A DIFFERENCE--I *HAVE* TO MAKE A DIFFERENCE...

NATHAN-- MY OPTIC BLASTS --

--ARE BEING KEPT IN CHECK BY YOUR TELEKINESIS?

YOU *KNOW* THEY CAN'T DEAL WITH THE VERY *IDEA* OF PEACE. WE'RE *HUNDREDS* OF YEARS AWAY FROM THAT KIND OF ENLIGHTENMENT.

THE X-MEN WERE JUST THE FIRST WAVE. WE *ASKED* TO BE. THEY'LL SEND OTHERS.

THERE'S NOTHING THEY CAN SEND THAT COULD SCARE ME AS MUCH AS FACING YOU HAS.

YOU CAN HELP ME SEE, BUT YOU'RE THE ONE WHO'S *BLIND*.

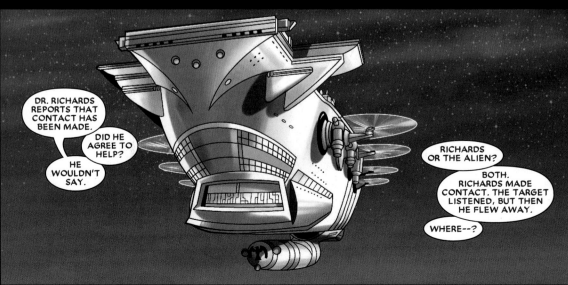

DR. RICHARDS REPORTS THAT CONTACT HAS BEEN MADE.

DID HE AGREE TO HELP?

HE WOULDN'T SAY.

RICHARDS OR THE ALIEN?

BOTH. RICHARDS MADE CONTACT. THE TARGET LISTENED, BUT THEN HE FLEW AWAY.

WHERE--?

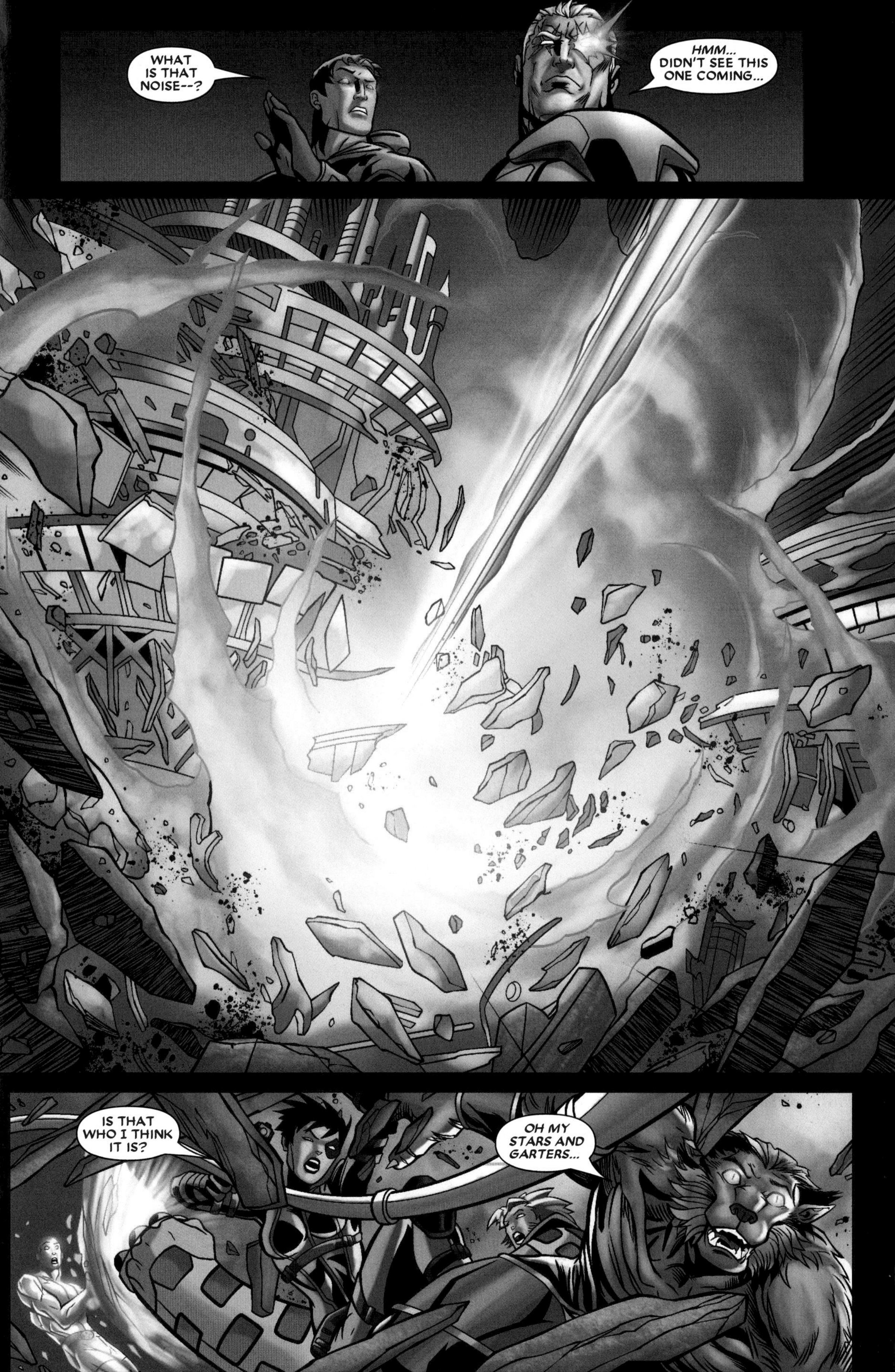
WHAT IS THAT NOISE--?
HMM... DIDN'T SEE THIS ONE COMING...
IS THAT WHO I THINK IT IS?
OH MY STARS AND GARTERS...

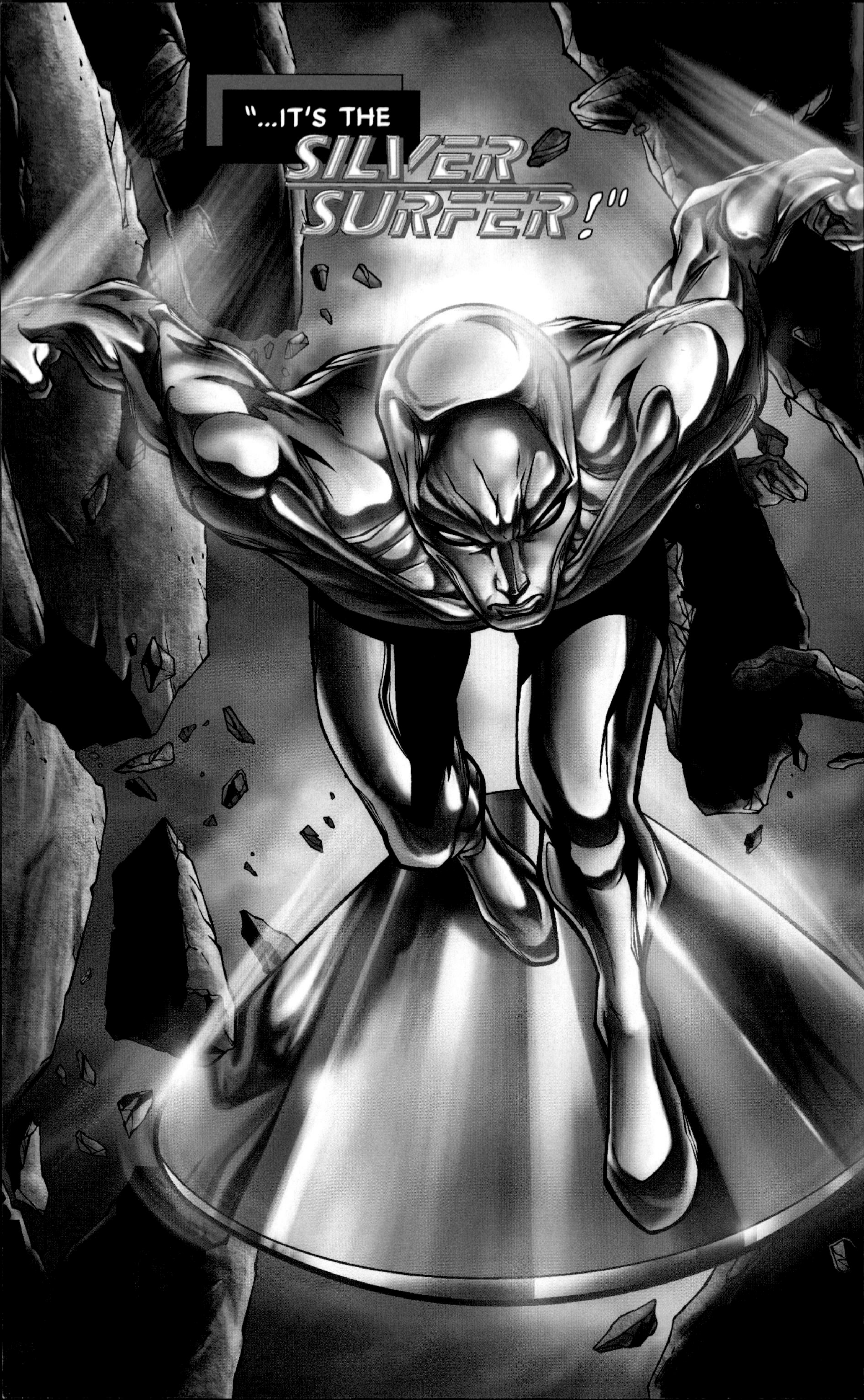
"...IT'S THE
SILVER SURFER!"

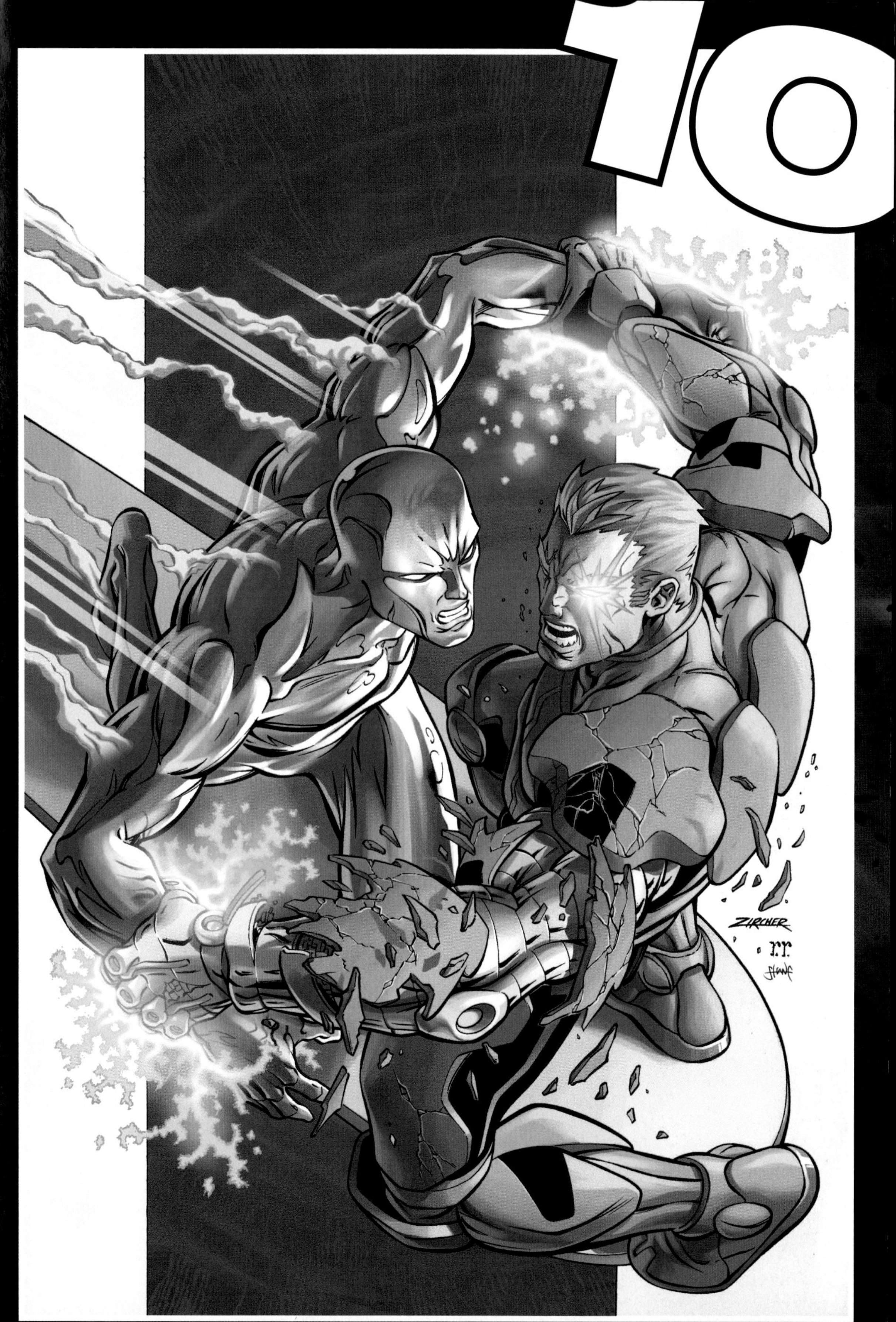
10
ZIRCHER

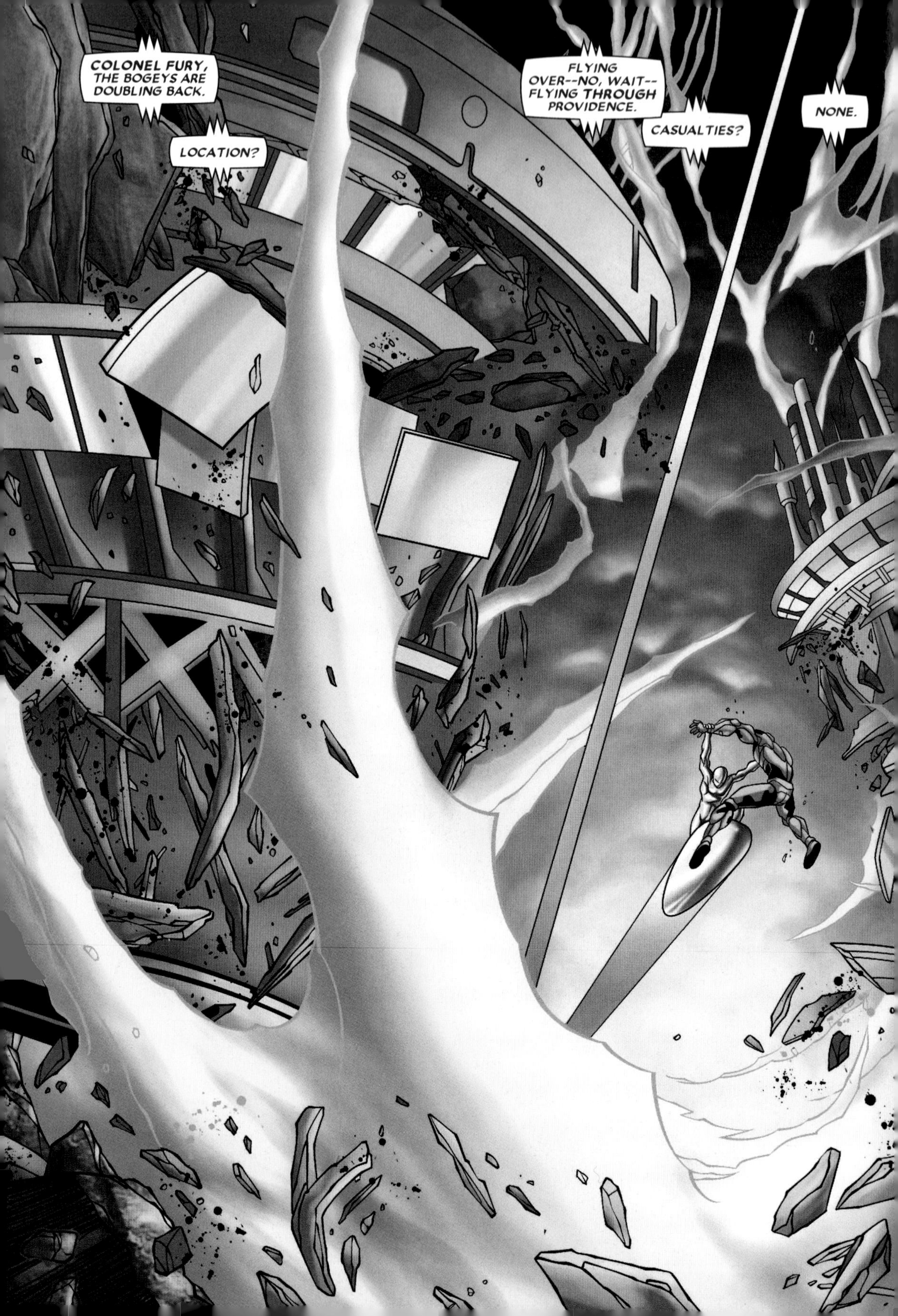
COLONEL FURY, THE BOGEYS ARE DOUBLING BACK.
LOCATION?
FLYING OVER--NO, WAIT-- FLYING THROUGH PROVIDENCE.
CASUALTIES?
NONE.

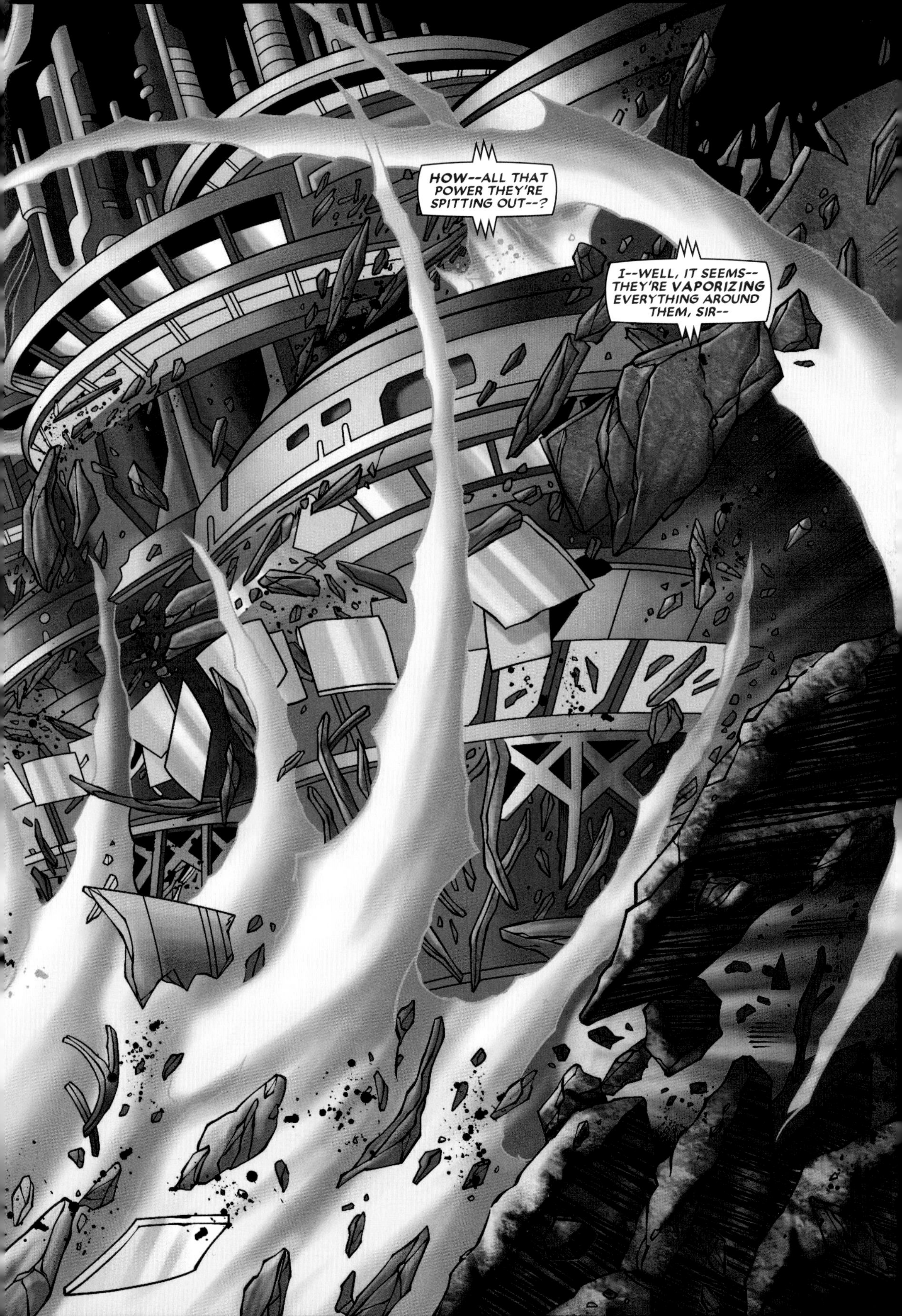
HOW--ALL THAT POWER THEY'RE SPITTING OUT--?
I--WELL, IT SEEMS--THEY'RE VAPORIZING EVERYTHING AROUND THEM, SIR--

"--AND PUTTING IT BACK TOGETHER AGAIN AT THE SAME TIME!"
WOULDN'T YOU RATHER-- TALK ABOUT THIS--?
U.S.S. RONALD REAGAN. THE SOUTH PACIFIC.
OKAY--LISTEN-- SUNDERING THE PACIFIC FLEET AT THE ATOMIC LEVEL AND PUTTING IT BACK TOGETHER AGAIN...
THE BOGEYS ARE INCOMING!
...THAT'S REALLY MORE WORK THAN I'D LIKE TO DO RIGHT NOW...

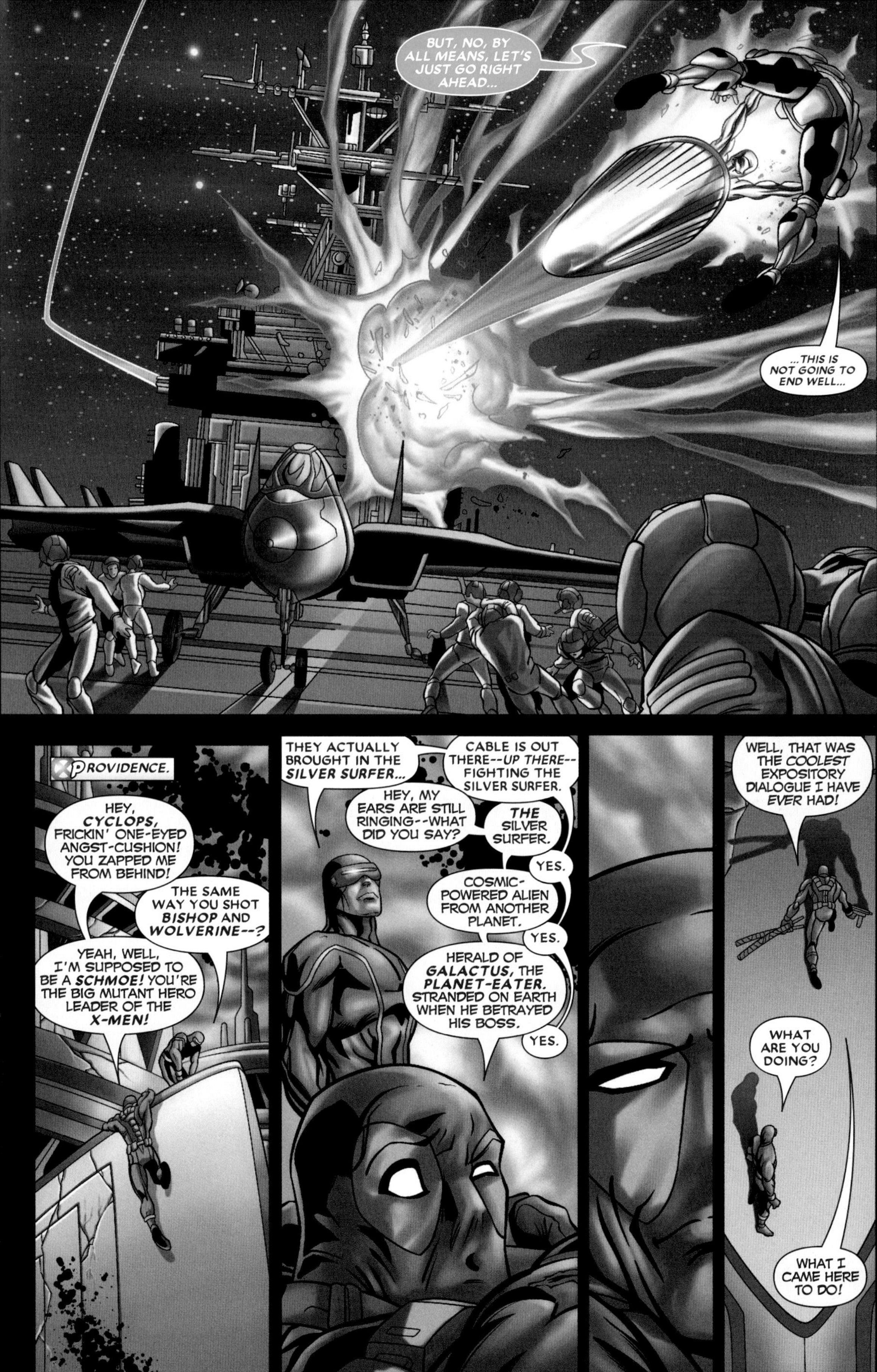
BUT, NO, BY ALL MEANS, LET'S JUST GO RIGHT AHEAD...
...THIS IS NOT GOING TO END WELL...
PROVIDENCE.
HEY, CYCLOPS, FRICKIN' ONE-EYED ANGST-CUSHION! YOU ZAPPED ME FROM BEHIND!
THE SAME WAY YOU SHOT BISHOP AND WOLVERINE--?
YEAH, WELL, I'M SUPPOSED TO BE A SCHMOE! YOU'RE THE BIG MUTANT HERO LEADER OF THE X-MEN!
THEY ACTUALLY BROUGHT IN THE SILVER SURFER...
CABLE IS OUT THERE--UP THERE--FIGHTING THE SILVER SURFER.
HEY, MY EARS ARE STILL RINGING--WHAT DID YOU SAY?
THE SILVER SURFER.
YES.
COSMIC-POWERED ALIEN FROM ANOTHER PLANET.
YES.
HERALD OF GALACTUS, THE PLANET-EATER. STRANDED ON EARTH WHEN HE BETRAYED HIS BOSS.
YES.
WELL, THAT WAS THE COOLEST EXPOSITORY DIALOGUE I HAVE EVER HAD!
WHAT ARE YOU DOING?
WHAT I CAME HERE TO DO!

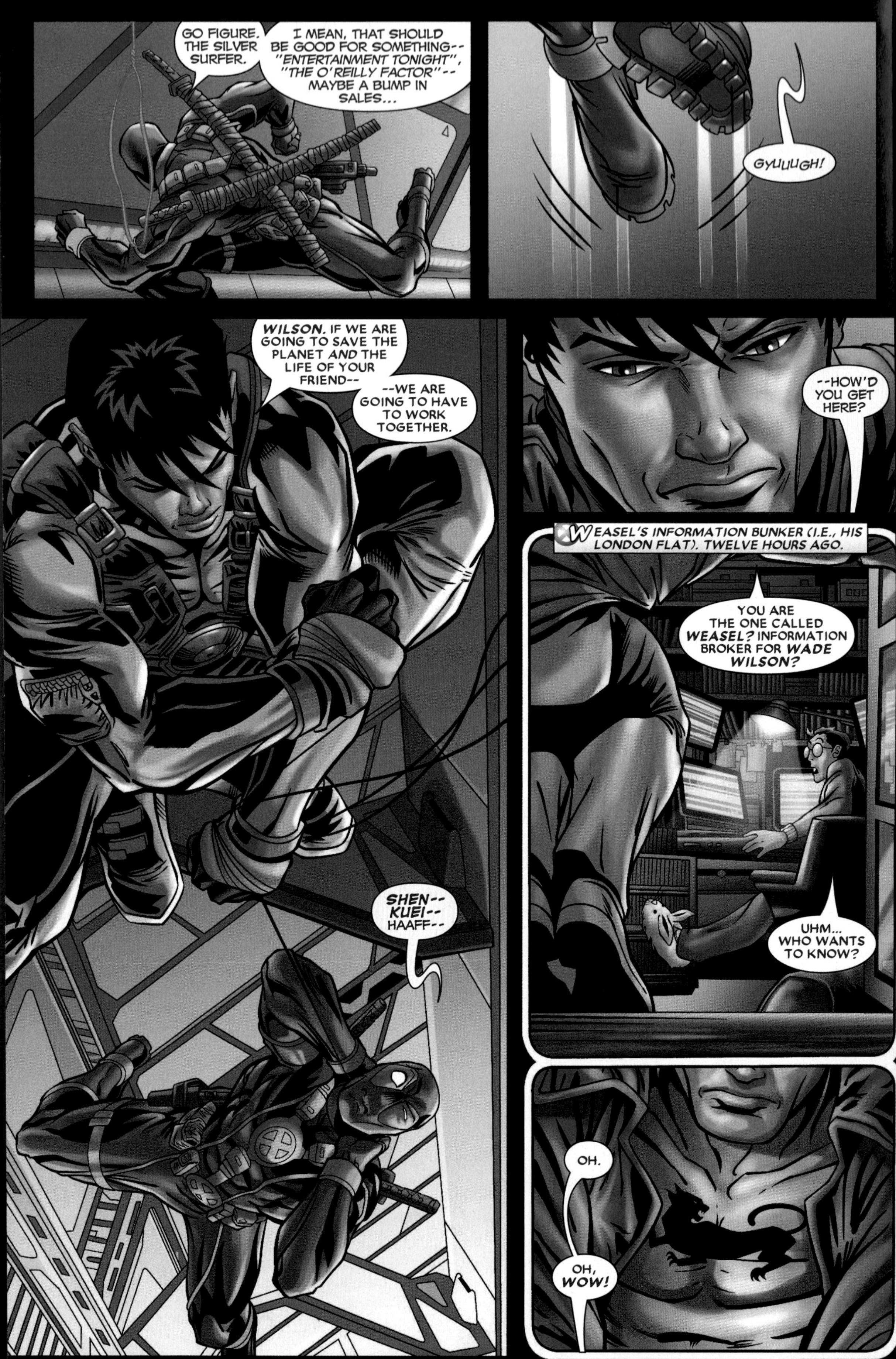
GO FIGURE. THE SILVER SURFER.
I MEAN, THAT SHOULD BE GOOD FOR SOMETHING-- "ENTERTAINMENT TONIGHT", "THE O'REILLY FACTOR"-- MAYBE A BUMP IN SALES...
GYUUUGH!
WILSON. IF WE ARE GOING TO SAVE THE PLANET AND THE LIFE OF YOUR FRIEND--
--WE ARE GOING TO HAVE TO WORK TOGETHER.
SHEN-- KUEI-- HAAFF--
--HOW'D YOU GET HERE?
WEASEL'S INFORMATION BUNKER (I.E., HIS LONDON FLAT). TWELVE HOURS AGO.
YOU ARE THE ONE CALLED WEASEL? INFORMATION BROKER FOR WADE WILSON?
UHM... WHO WANTS TO KNOW?
OH.
OH, WOW!

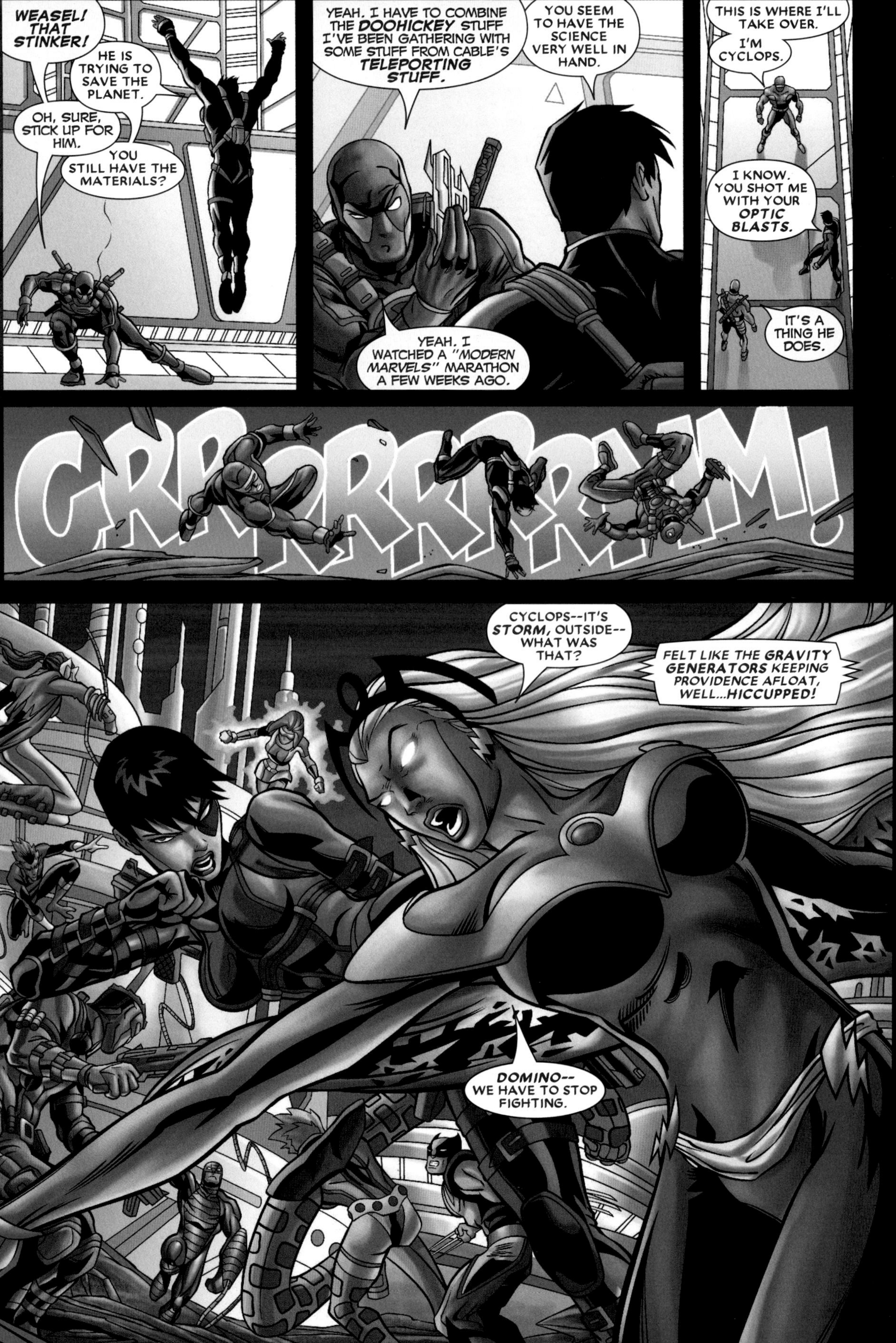
WEASEL! THAT STINKER!
HE IS TRYING TO SAVE THE PLANET.
OH, SURE, STICK UP FOR HIM.
YOU STILL HAVE THE MATERIALS?
YEAH. I HAVE TO COMBINE THE DOOHICKEY STUFF I'VE BEEN GATHERING WITH SOME STUFF FROM CABLE'S TELEPORTING STUFF.
YOU SEEM TO HAVE THE SCIENCE VERY WELL IN HAND.
YEAH. I WATCHED A "MODERN MARVELS" MARATHON A FEW WEEKS AGO.
THIS IS WHERE I'LL TAKE OVER.
I'M CYCLOPS.
I KNOW. YOU SHOT ME WITH YOUR OPTIC BLASTS.
IT'S A THING HE DOES.
CRRRRRRRM!
CYCLOPS--IT'S STORM, OUTSIDE--WHAT WAS THAT?
FELT LIKE THE GRAVITY GENERATORS KEEPING PROVIDENCE AFLOAT, WELL...HICCUPPED!
DOMINO--WE HAVE TO STOP FIGHTING.

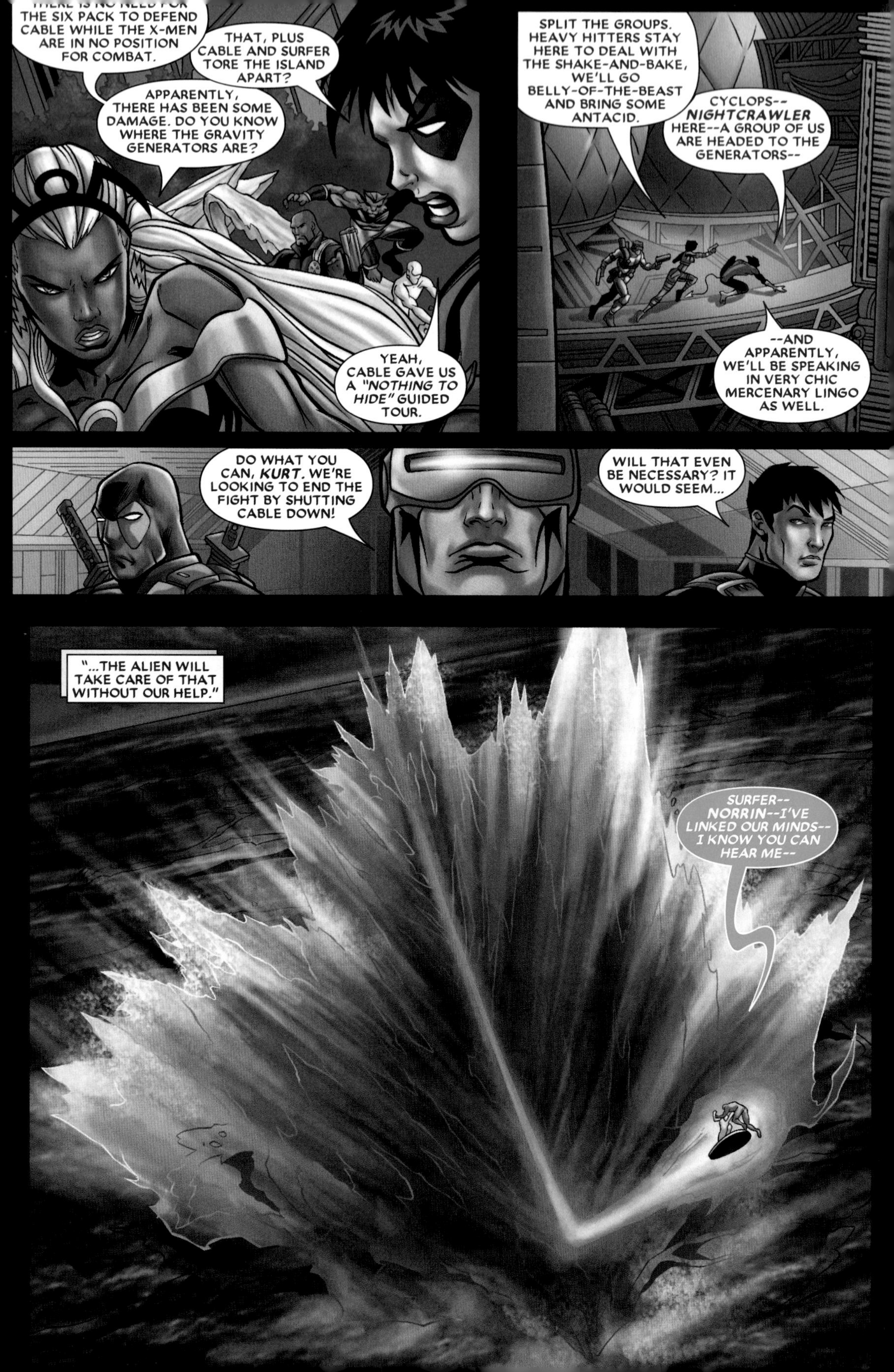

THERE IS NO NEED FOR THE SIX PACK TO DEFEND CABLE WHILE THE X-MEN ARE IN NO POSITION FOR COMBAT.
THAT, PLUS CABLE AND SURFER TORE THE ISLAND APART?
APPARENTLY, THERE HAS BEEN SOME DAMAGE. DO YOU KNOW WHERE THE GRAVITY GENERATORS ARE?
YEAH, CABLE GAVE US A *"NOTHING TO HIDE"* GUIDED TOUR.
SPLIT THE GROUPS. HEAVY HITTERS STAY HERE TO DEAL WITH THE SHAKE-AND-BAKE, WE'LL GO BELLY-OF-THE-BEAST AND BRING SOME ANTACID.
CYCLOPS-- *NIGHTCRAWLER* HERE--A GROUP OF US ARE HEADED TO THE GENERATORS--
--AND APPARENTLY, WE'LL BE SPEAKING IN VERY CHIC MERCENARY LINGO AS WELL.
DO WHAT YOU CAN, *KURT.* WE'RE LOOKING TO END THE FIGHT BY SHUTTING CABLE DOWN!
WILL THAT EVEN BE NECESSARY? IT WOULD SEEM...
"...THE ALIEN WILL TAKE CARE OF THAT WITHOUT OUR HELP."
SURFER-- NORRIN--I'VE LINKED OUR MINDS-- I KNOW YOU CAN HEAR ME--

Irene Merryweather: You said I'm not allowed to run this interview until--let me quote you--
Cable: I've seen this through to the end.
IM: Yes. So, what is that end?
Cable: My end.
IM: You expect to die?
Cable: My body can't handle this kind of energy output--no one born of humans could.
IM: So wait, all of this isn't for you to watch over a new world?
Cable: It's for this world to see what could be.
IM: That's one heck of a dice roll to risk your dying breath on.
Cable: I don't think of it that way. I don't think I have any other choice.
IM: No other choice than to burn yourself out trying to show the world how it could become a peaceful unified whole sometime in the next thousand years?
Cable: Sure, if you put it that way.
IM: What other way would you put it?
Cable: I see it as showing people the light at the end of the tunnel. Looking forward, with hope, with expectation, but also with an understanding of the sacrifices that would have to be made--both material and spiritual--in order to reach that light.
IM: Last guy who thought that way ended up on a cross…
Cable: I'd rather not be so melodramatic.
IM: But you are crucifying yourself, sacrificing yourself, so that the greater whole will have a greater understanding of what sacrifice means?
Cable: You're characterizing it like that, not me.
IM: Explain it to me then.
Cable: You're mad.
IM: That's right I'm mad! And you're crazy! Here I am interviewing you because you truly wanted to save the world, and I wanted people to see that. Sure, you're a bit nuts, but hey, your motives are pure. I just didn't know suicide was part of the game plan!
Cable: Is it suicide to die solely because you are all that you can be? Sounds more like… destiny…to me.
IM: Destiny. A time-traveler who destroyed his own past can't believe in destiny or fate.
Cable: Or, that could make him believe in it even more than before.
IM: Okay, fine, I'll play your game. So, you're going to die--how is that going to happen?
Cable: Saving the world from the madness of those who would destroy it as a means of preserving it.
IM: The super-powered nations and their superhuman attack dogs?
Cable: It will escalate. What they destroy, I will restore. Where they bring fear, I will bring hope. Where they scar, I will soothe.
IM: Give until there's nothing left to give?
Cable: Leaving nothing behind but ash…

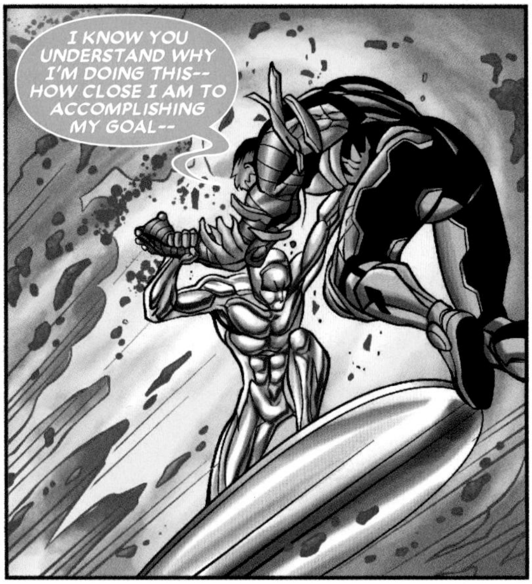
I KNOW YOU UNDERSTAND WHY I'M DOING THIS-- HOW CLOSE I AM TO ACCOMPLISHING MY GOAL--

...and hope.
IM: And there's no other way to accomplish your plan short of dying at the precise moment that allows you to stave off the annihilation of the entire planet?
Cable: No, I've pretty much got it figured out to the last decimal point.
IM: You're joking, but what if that happens? Is there anyone out there who could push your power levels to those limits?
Cable: That's an interesting question. I don't know…no one that I can think of…well, unless…
IM: Unless what?
Cable: An unexpected wild card exacerbates the situation, I don't know, somehow forcing me to generate more power than I had planned to use on a faster timetable. That might cause me to burn out faster, before I can cover the world in my little telepathic security blanket. And then…

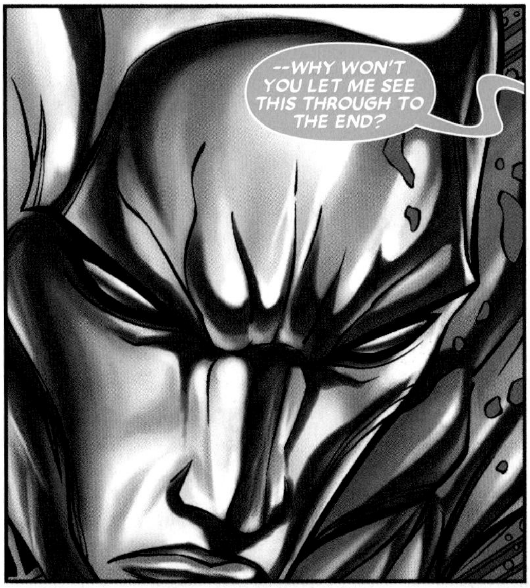
--WHY WON'T YOU LET ME SEE THIS THROUGH TO THE END?

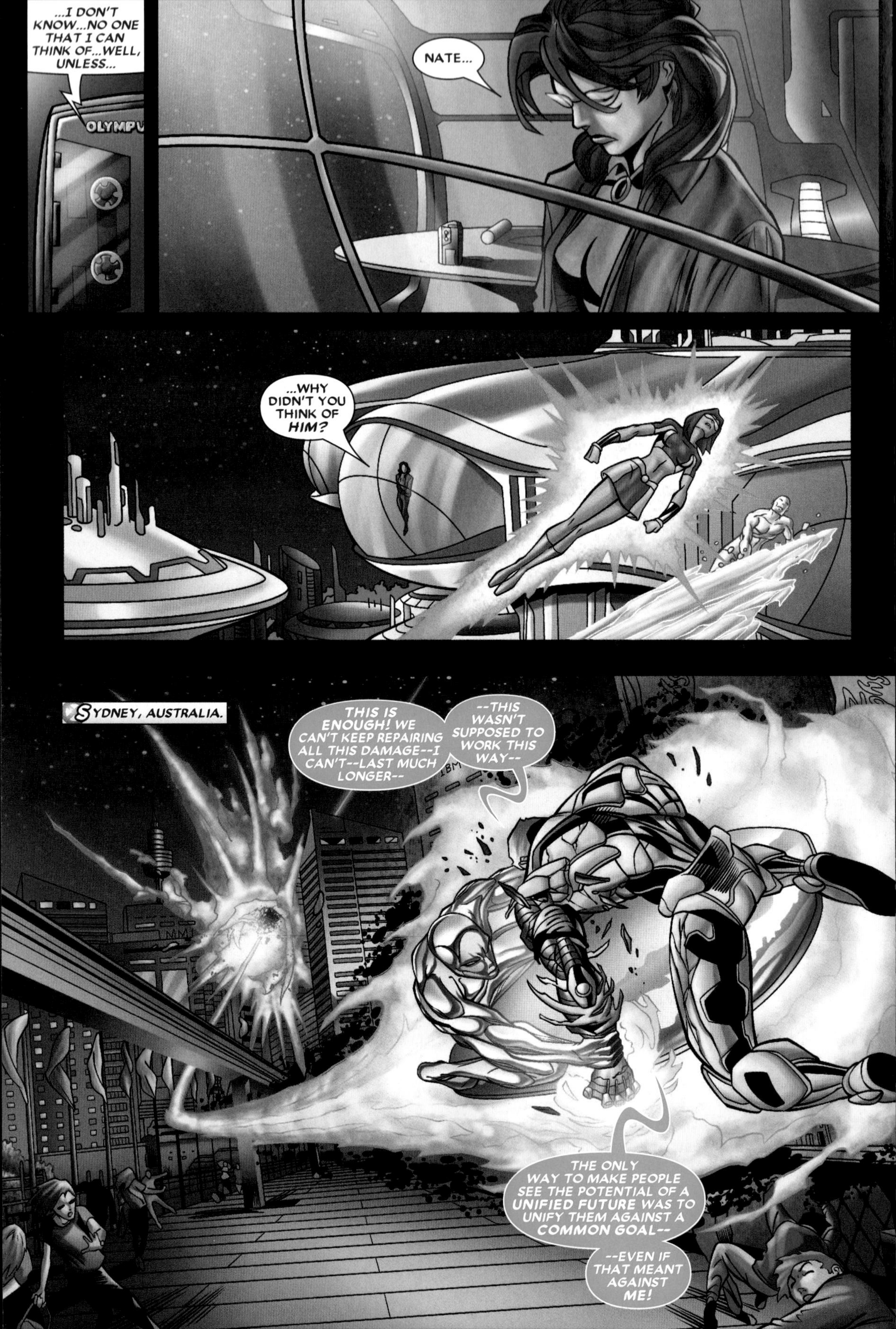

...I DON'T KNOW...NO ONE THAT I CAN THINK OF...WELL, UNLESS...
OLYMPU
NATE...
...WHY DIDN'T YOU THINK OF HIM?
SYDNEY, AUSTRALIA.
THIS IS ENOUGH! WE CAN'T KEEP REPAIRING ALL THIS DAMAGE--I CAN'T--LAST MUCH LONGER--
--THIS WASN'T SUPPOSED TO WORK THIS WAY--
THE ONLY WAY TO MAKE PEOPLE SEE THE POTENTIAL OF A UNIFIED FUTURE WAS TO UNIFY THEM AGAINST A COMMON GOAL--
--EVEN IF THAT MEANT AGAINST ME!

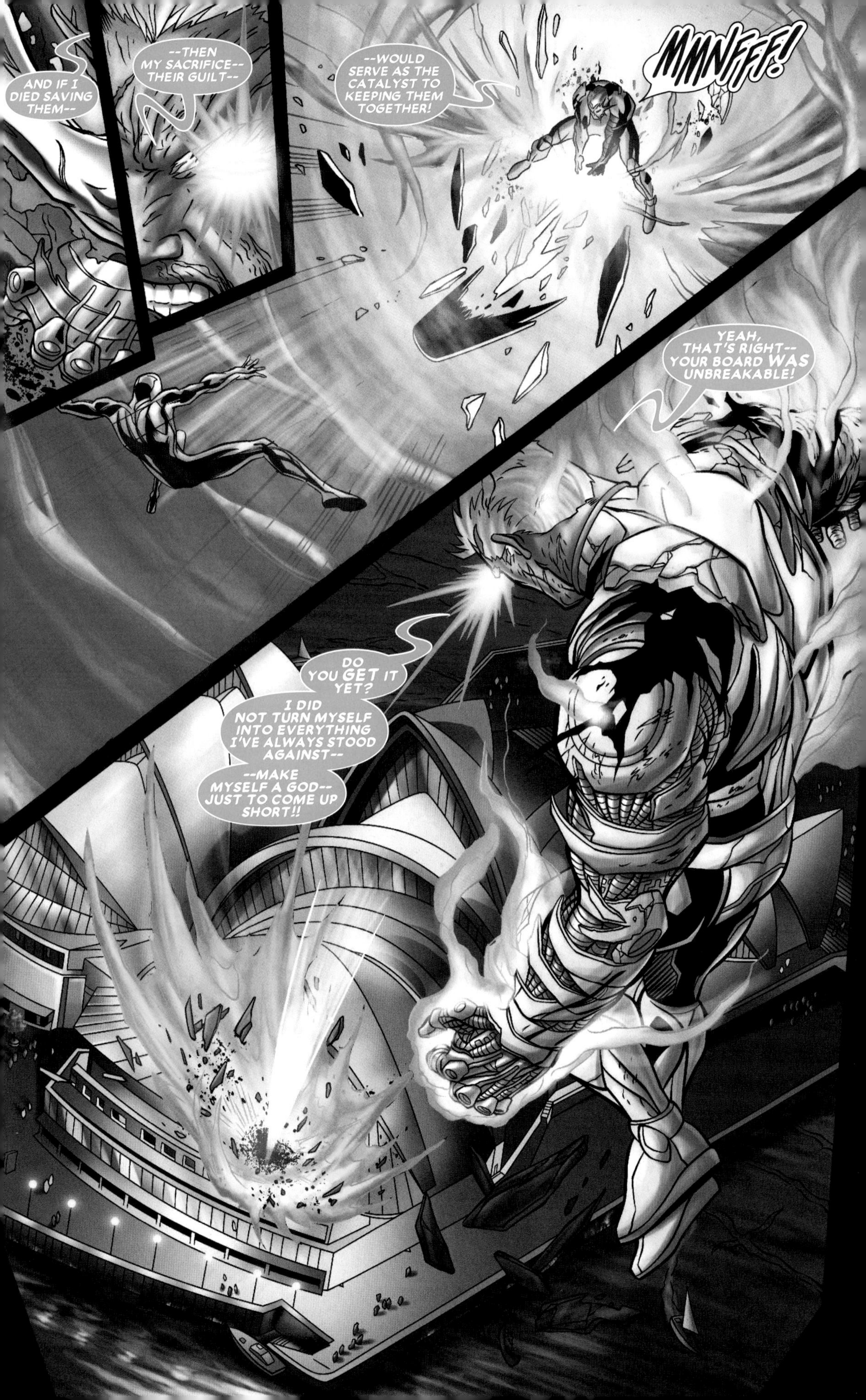
AND IF I DIED SAVING THEM--
--THEN MY SACRIFICE-- THEIR GUILT--
--WOULD SERVE AS THE CATALYST TO KEEPING THEM TOGETHER!
MMNFFF!
YEAH, THAT'S RIGHT-- YOUR BOARD WAS UNBREAKABLE!
DO YOU GET IT YET?
I DID NOT TURN MYSELF INTO EVERYTHING I'VE ALWAYS STOOD AGAINST--
--MAKE MYSELF A GOD-- JUST TO COME UP SHORT!!

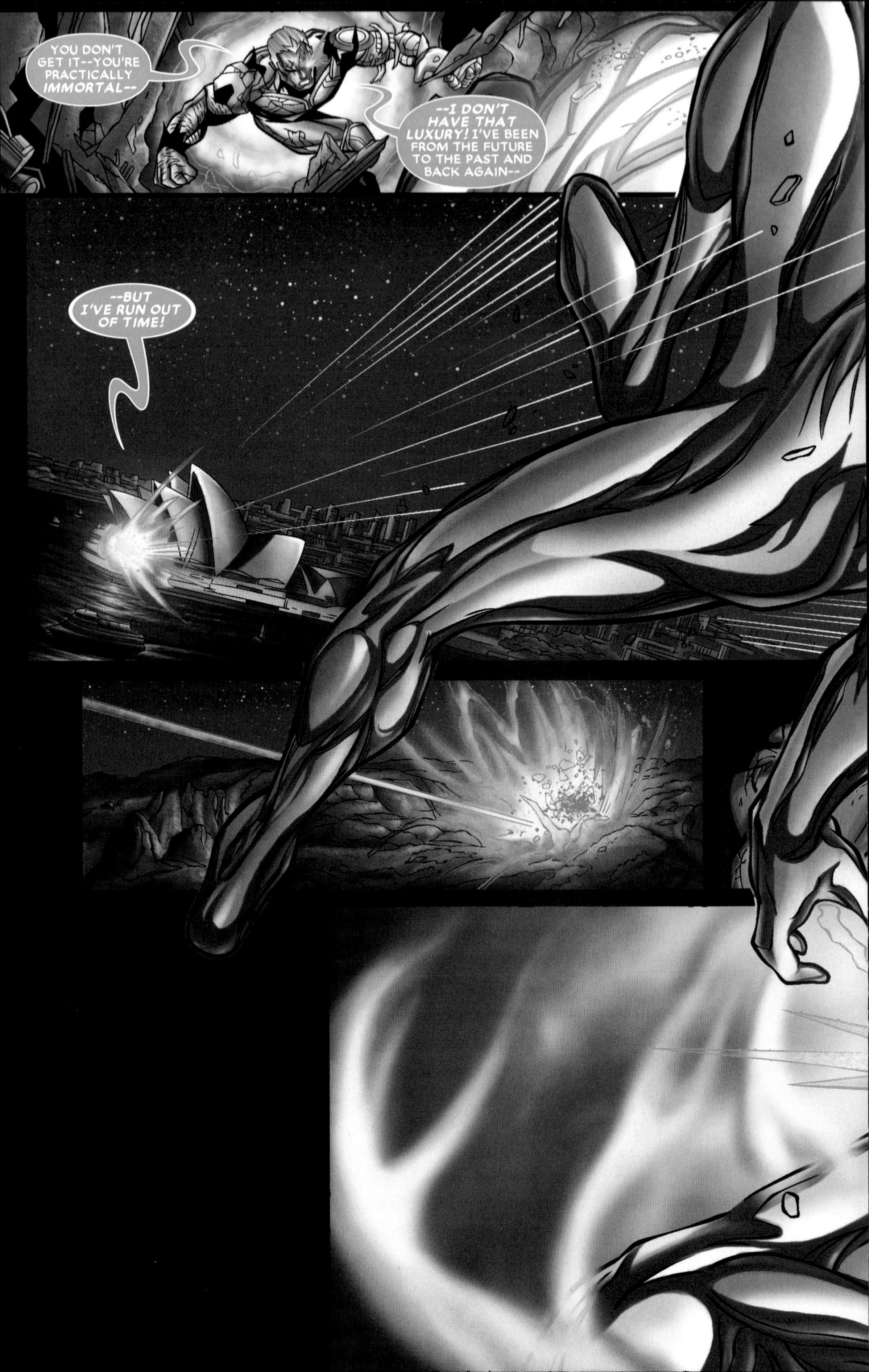
YOU DON'T GET IT--YOU'RE PRACTICALLY *IMMORTAL*--
--*I DON'T HAVE THAT LUXURY!* I'VE BEEN FROM THE FUTURE TO THE PAST AND BACK AGAIN--
--*BUT I'VE RUN OUT OF TIME!*

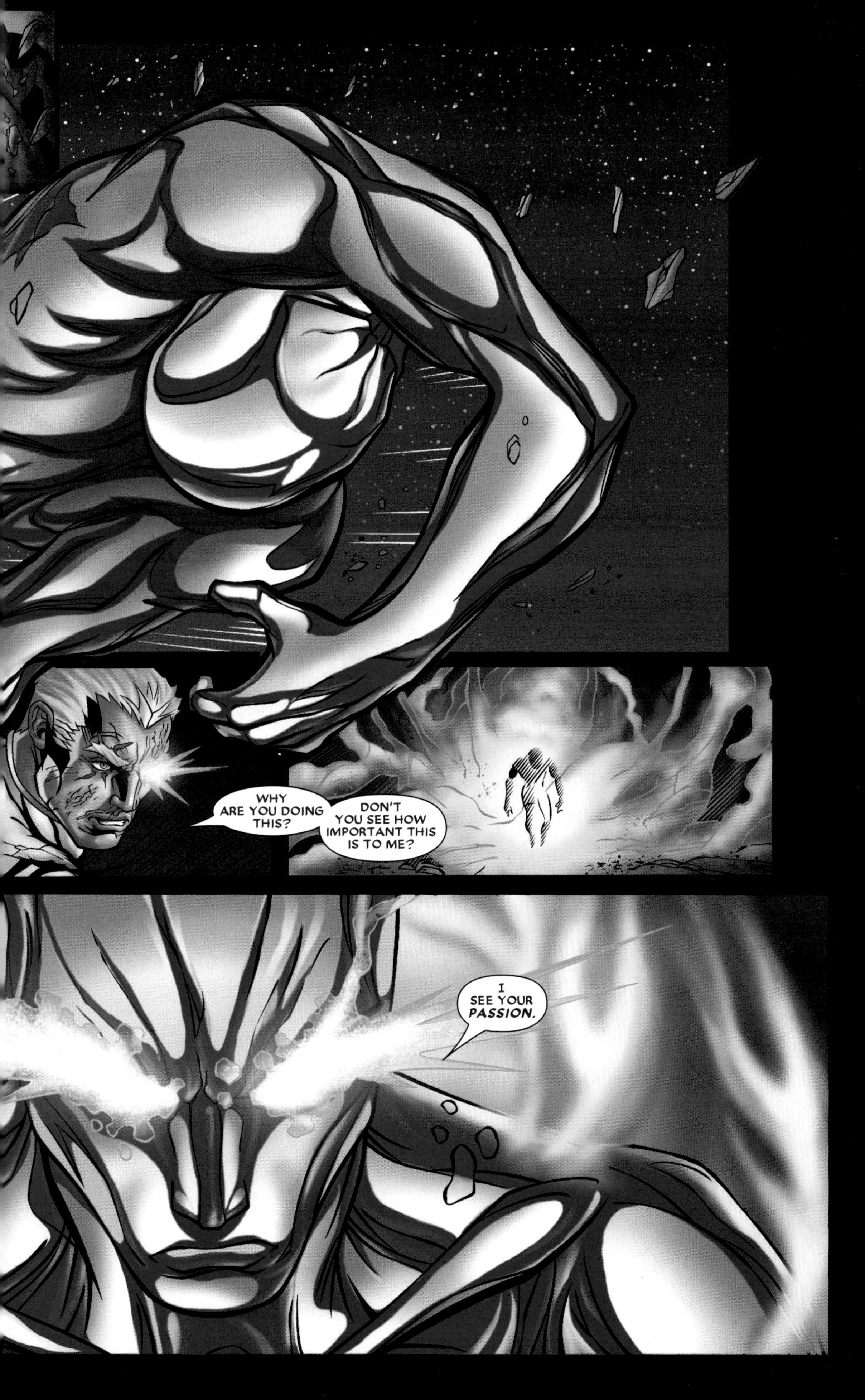
WHY ARE YOU DOING THIS?
DON'T YOU SEE HOW IMPORTANT THIS IS TO ME?
I SEE YOUR *PASSION.*

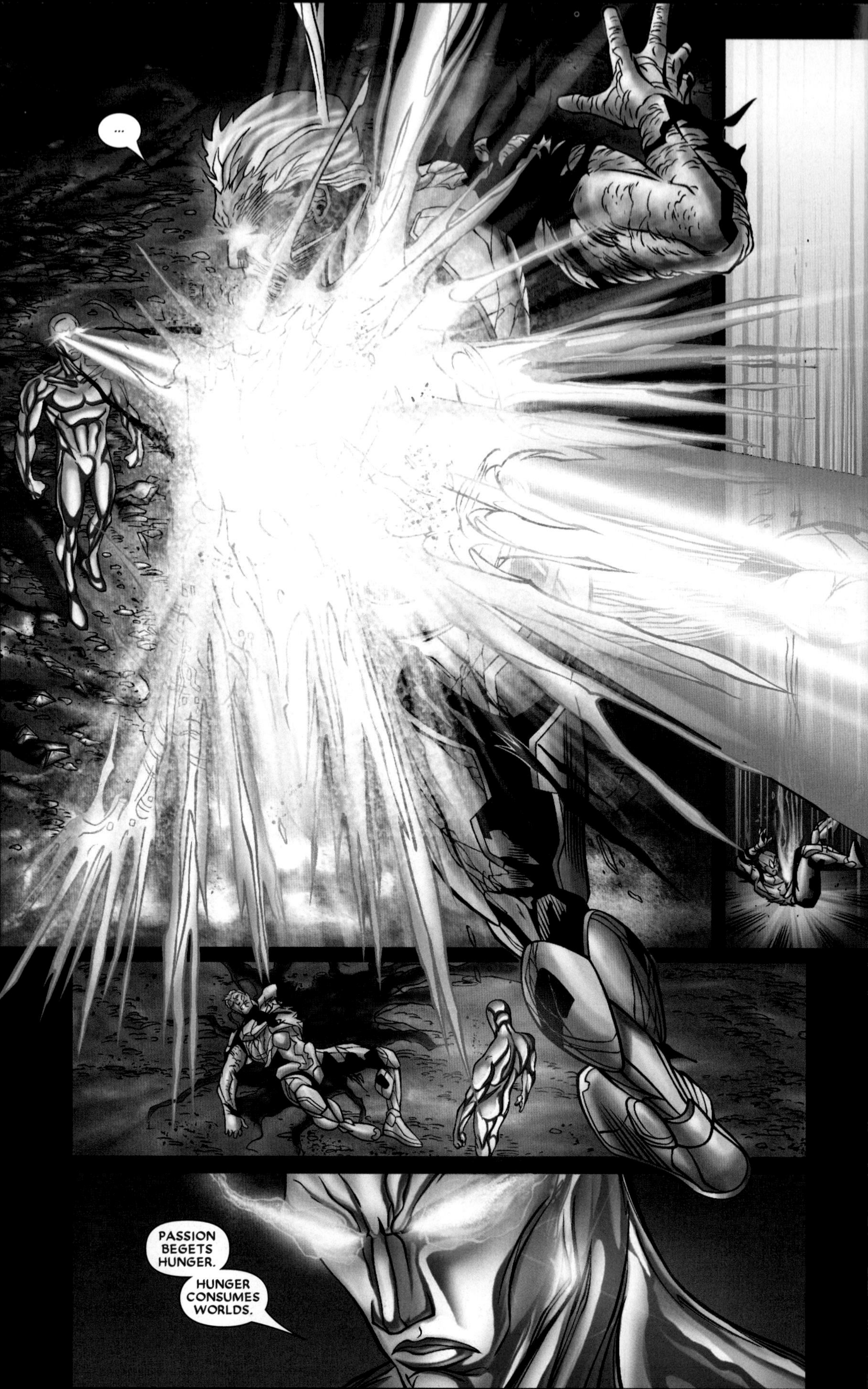
...
PASSION BEGETS HUNGER.
HUNGER CONSUMES WORLDS.

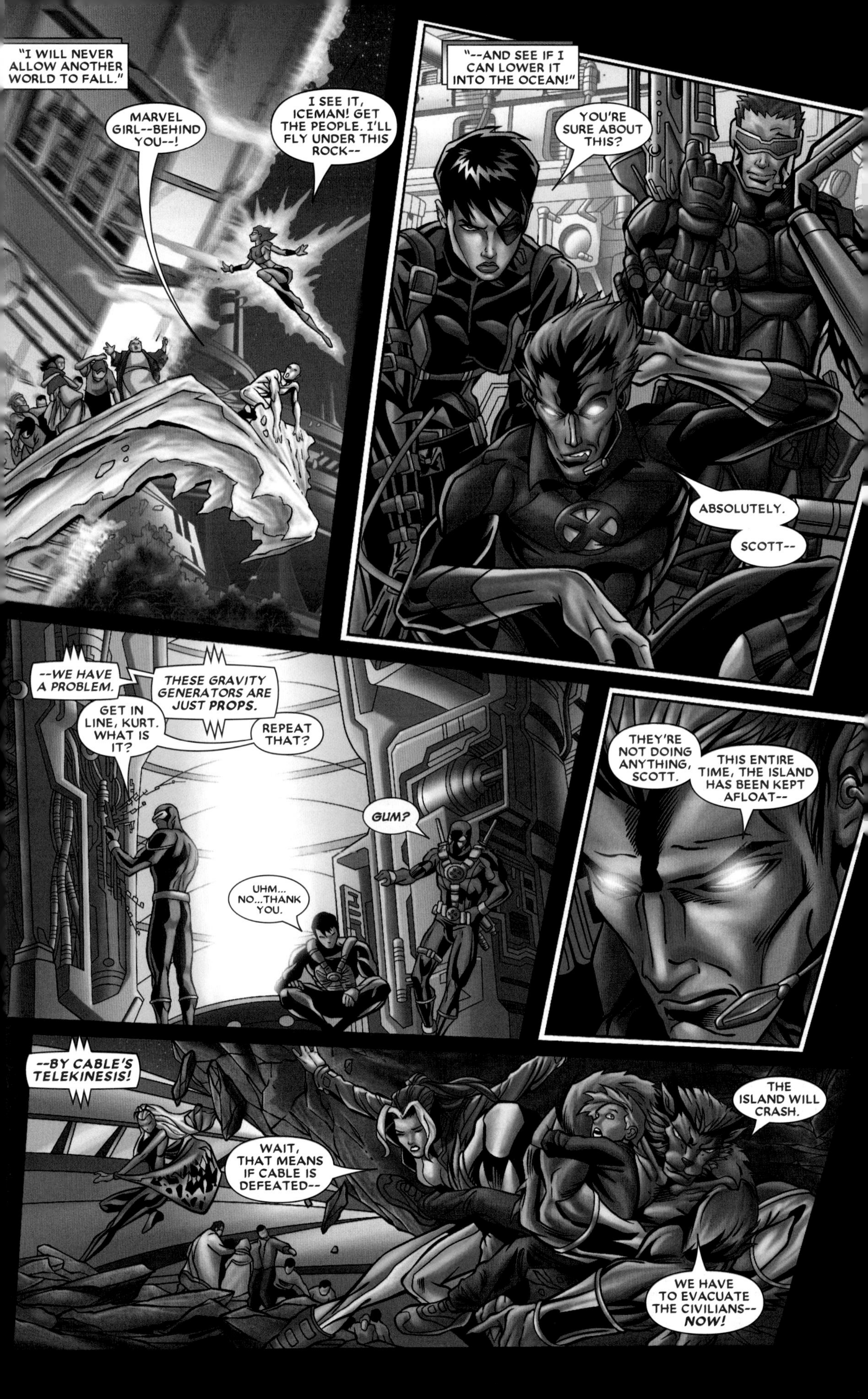
"I WILL NEVER ALLOW ANOTHER WORLD TO FALL."
MARVEL GIRL--BEHIND YOU--!
I SEE IT, ICEMAN! GET THE PEOPLE. I'LL FLY UNDER THIS ROCK--
"--AND SEE IF I CAN LOWER IT INTO THE OCEAN!"
YOU'RE SURE ABOUT THIS?
ABSOLUTELY.
SCOTT--
--WE HAVE A PROBLEM.
THESE GRAVITY GENERATORS ARE JUST PROPS.
GET IN LINE, KURT. WHAT IS IT?
REPEAT THAT?
GUM?
UHM... NO...THANK YOU.
THEY'RE NOT DOING ANYTHING, SCOTT.
THIS ENTIRE TIME, THE ISLAND HAS BEEN KEPT AFLOAT--
--BY CABLE'S TELEKINESIS!
WAIT, THAT MEANS IF CABLE IS DEFEATED--
THE ISLAND WILL CRASH.
WE HAVE TO EVACUATE THE CIVILIANS--NOW!

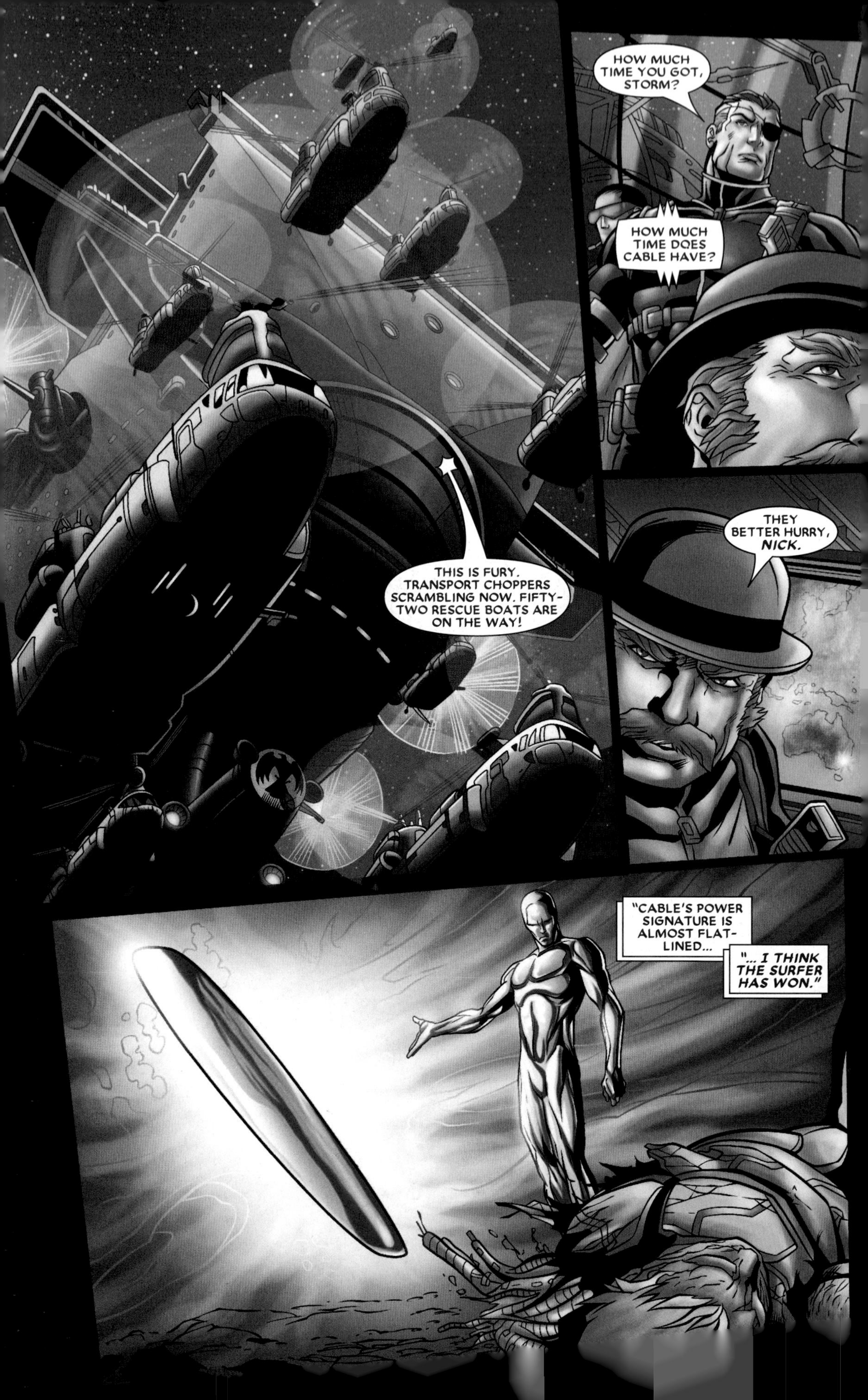
THIS IS FURY. TRANSPORT CHOPPERS SCRAMBLING NOW. FIFTY-TWO RESCUE BOATS ARE ON THE WAY!
HOW MUCH TIME YOU GOT, STORM?
HOW MUCH TIME DOES CABLE HAVE?
THEY BETTER HURRY, NICK.
"CABLE'S POWER SIGNATURE IS ALMOST FLAT-LINED...
"... I THINK THE SURFER HAS WON."

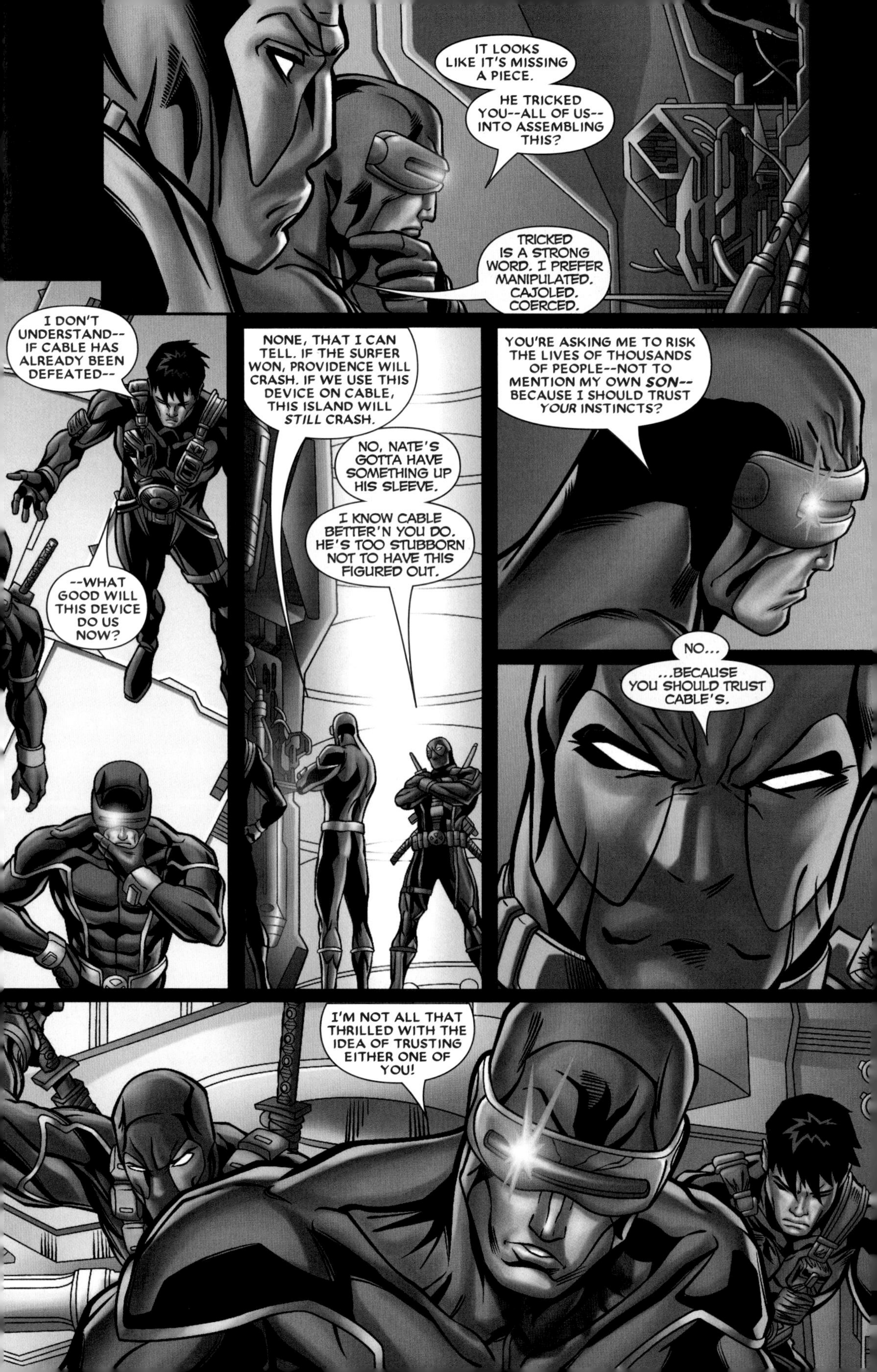
IT LOOKS LIKE IT'S MISSING A PIECE.
HE TRICKED YOU--ALL OF US--INTO ASSEMBLING THIS?
TRICKED IS A STRONG WORD. I PREFER MANIPULATED. CAJOLED. COERCED.
I DON'T UNDERSTAND--IF CABLE HAS ALREADY BEEN DEFEATED--
--WHAT GOOD WILL THIS DEVICE DO US NOW?
NONE, THAT I CAN TELL. IF THE SURFER WON, PROVIDENCE WILL CRASH. IF WE USE THIS DEVICE ON CABLE, THIS ISLAND WILL STILL CRASH.
NO, NATE'S GOTTA HAVE SOMETHING UP HIS SLEEVE.
I KNOW CABLE BETTER'N YOU DO. HE'S TOO STUBBORN NOT TO HAVE THIS FIGURED OUT.
YOU'RE ASKING ME TO RISK THE LIVES OF THOUSANDS OF PEOPLE--NOT TO MENTION MY OWN SON--BECAUSE I SHOULD TRUST YOUR INSTINCTS?
NO...
...BECAUSE YOU SHOULD TRUST CABLE'S.
I'M NOT ALL THAT THRILLED WITH THE IDEA OF TRUSTING EITHER ONE OF YOU!

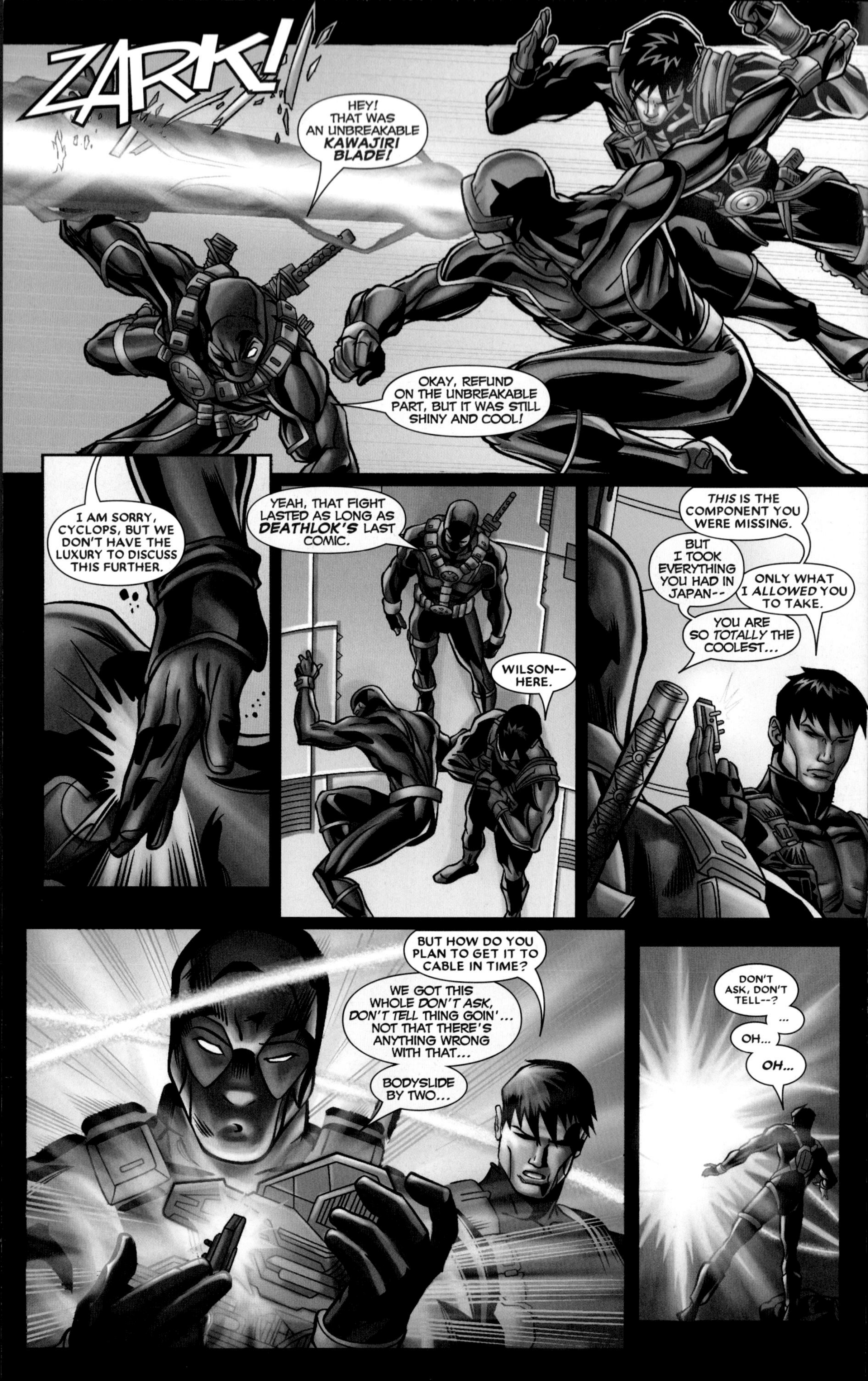
ZARK!
HEY! THAT WAS AN UNBREAKABLE KAWAJIRI BLADE!
OKAY, REFUND ON THE UNBREAKABLE PART, BUT IT WAS STILL SHINY AND COOL!
I AM SORRY, CYCLOPS, BUT WE DON'T HAVE THE LUXURY TO DISCUSS THIS FURTHER.
YEAH, THAT FIGHT LASTED AS LONG AS DEATHLOK'S LAST COMIC.
WILSON-- HERE.
THIS IS THE COMPONENT YOU WERE MISSING.
BUT I TOOK EVERYTHING YOU HAD IN JAPAN--
ONLY WHAT I ALLOWED YOU TO TAKE.
YOU ARE SO TOTALLY THE COOLEST...
BUT HOW DO YOU PLAN TO GET IT TO CABLE IN TIME?
WE GOT THIS WHOLE DON'T ASK, DON'T TELL THING GOIN'... NOT THAT THERE'S ANYTHING WRONG WITH THAT...
BODYSLIDE BY TWO...
DON'T ASK, DON'T TELL--?
...
OH...
OH...

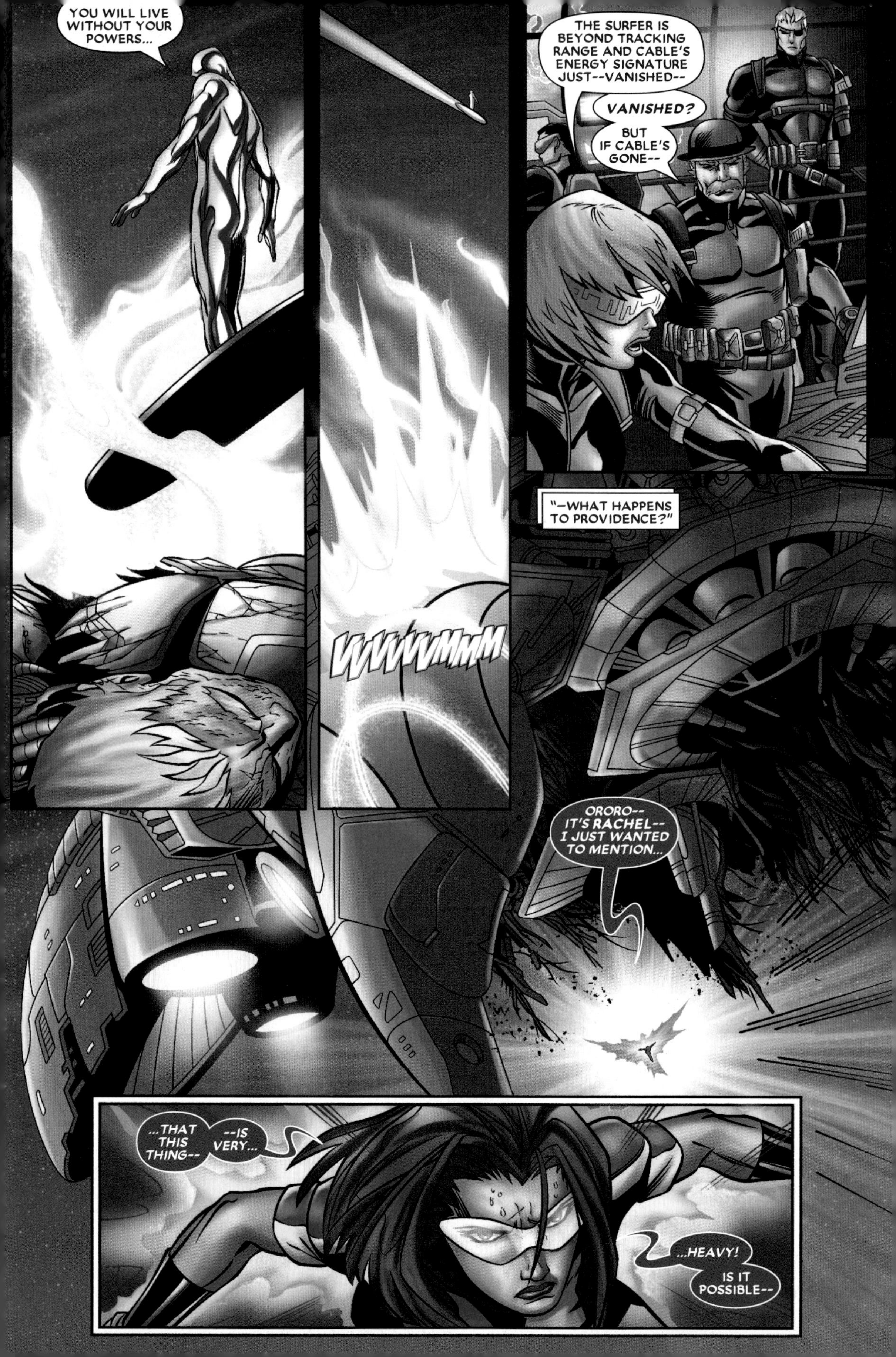

YOU WILL LIVE WITHOUT YOUR POWERS...
THE SURFER IS BEYOND TRACKING RANGE AND CABLE'S ENERGY SIGNATURE JUST--VANISHED--
VANISHED?
BUT IF CABLE'S GONE--
"–WHAT HAPPENS TO PROVIDENCE?"
VVVVVVMMM
ORORO-- IT'S RACHEL-- I JUST WANTED TO MENTION...
...THAT THIS THING--
--IS VERY...
...HEAVY!
IS IT POSSIBLE--

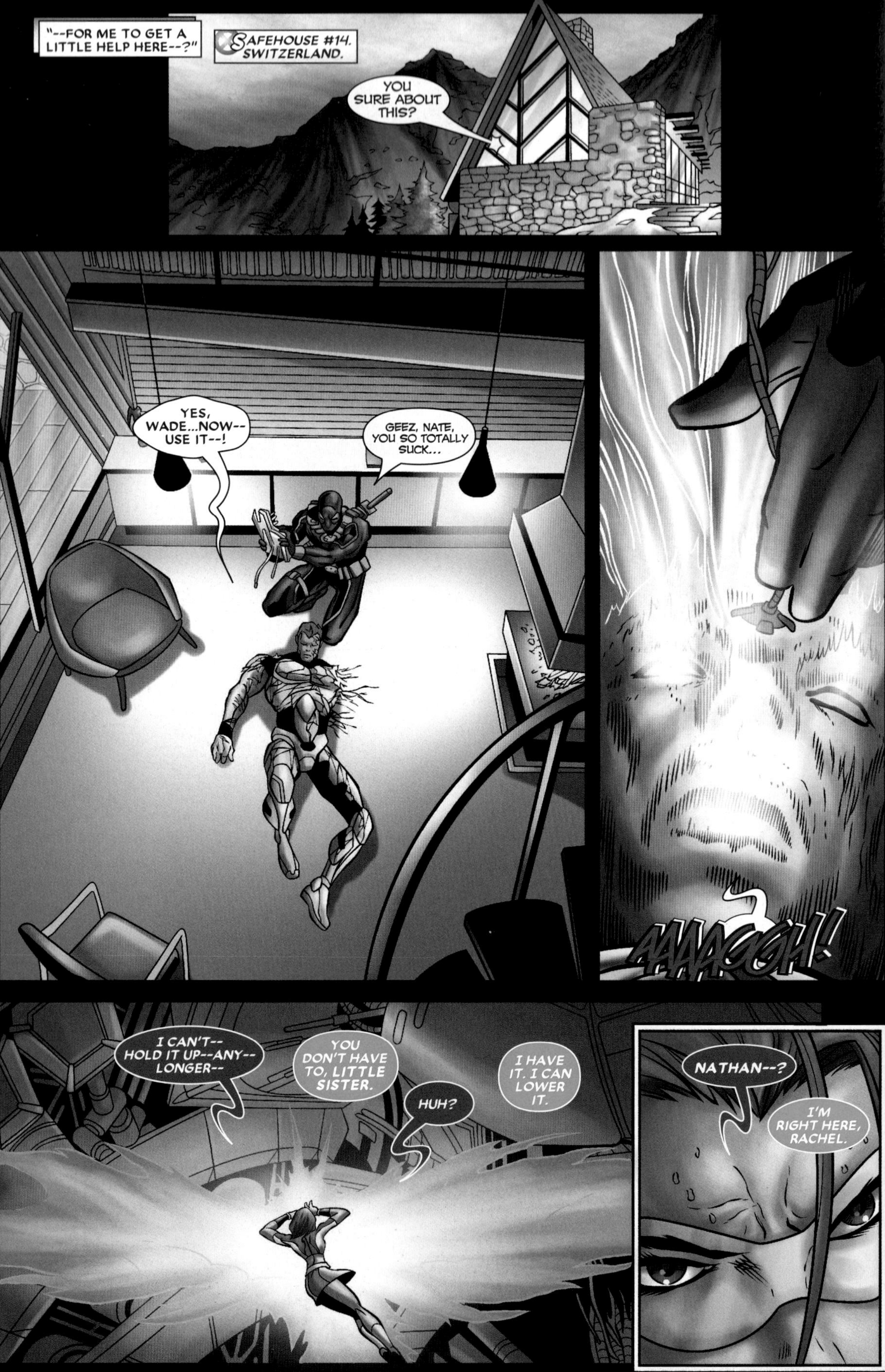
"--FOR ME TO GET A LITTLE HELP HERE--?"
SAFEHOUSE #14. SWITZERLAND.
YOU SURE ABOUT THIS?
YES, WADE...NOW--USE IT--!
GEEZ, NATE, YOU SO TOTALLY SUCK...
AAAAAGGH!
I CAN'T--HOLD IT UP--ANY--LONGER--
YOU DON'T HAVE TO, LITTLE SISTER.
HUH?
I HAVE IT. I CAN LOWER IT.
NATHAN--?
I'M RIGHT HERE, RACHEL.

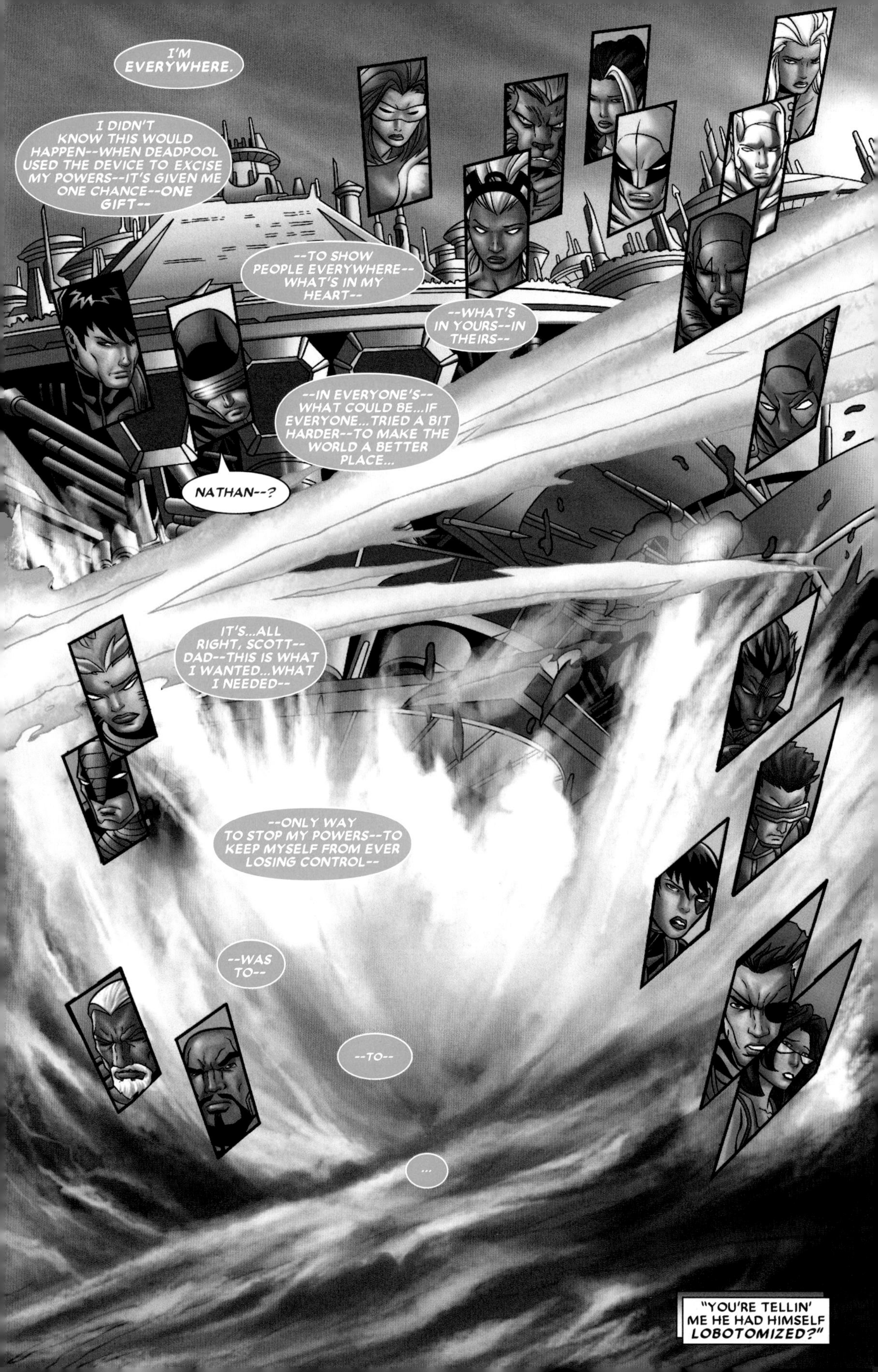
I'M EVERYWHERE.
I DIDN'T KNOW THIS WOULD HAPPEN--WHEN DEADPOOL USED THE DEVICE TO EXCISE MY POWERS--IT'S GIVEN ME ONE CHANCE--ONE GIFT--
--TO SHOW PEOPLE EVERYWHERE--WHAT'S IN MY HEART--
--WHAT'S IN YOURS--IN THEIRS--
--IN EVERYONE'S--WHAT COULD BE...IF EVERYONE...TRIED A BIT HARDER--TO MAKE THE WORLD A BETTER PLACE...
NATHAN--?
IT'S...ALL RIGHT, SCOTT--DAD--THIS IS WHAT I WANTED...WHAT I NEEDED--
--ONLY WAY TO STOP MY POWERS--TO KEEP MYSELF FROM EVER LOSING CONTROL--
--WAS TO--
--TO--
...
"YOU'RE TELLIN' ME HE HAD HIMSELF LOBOTOMIZED?"

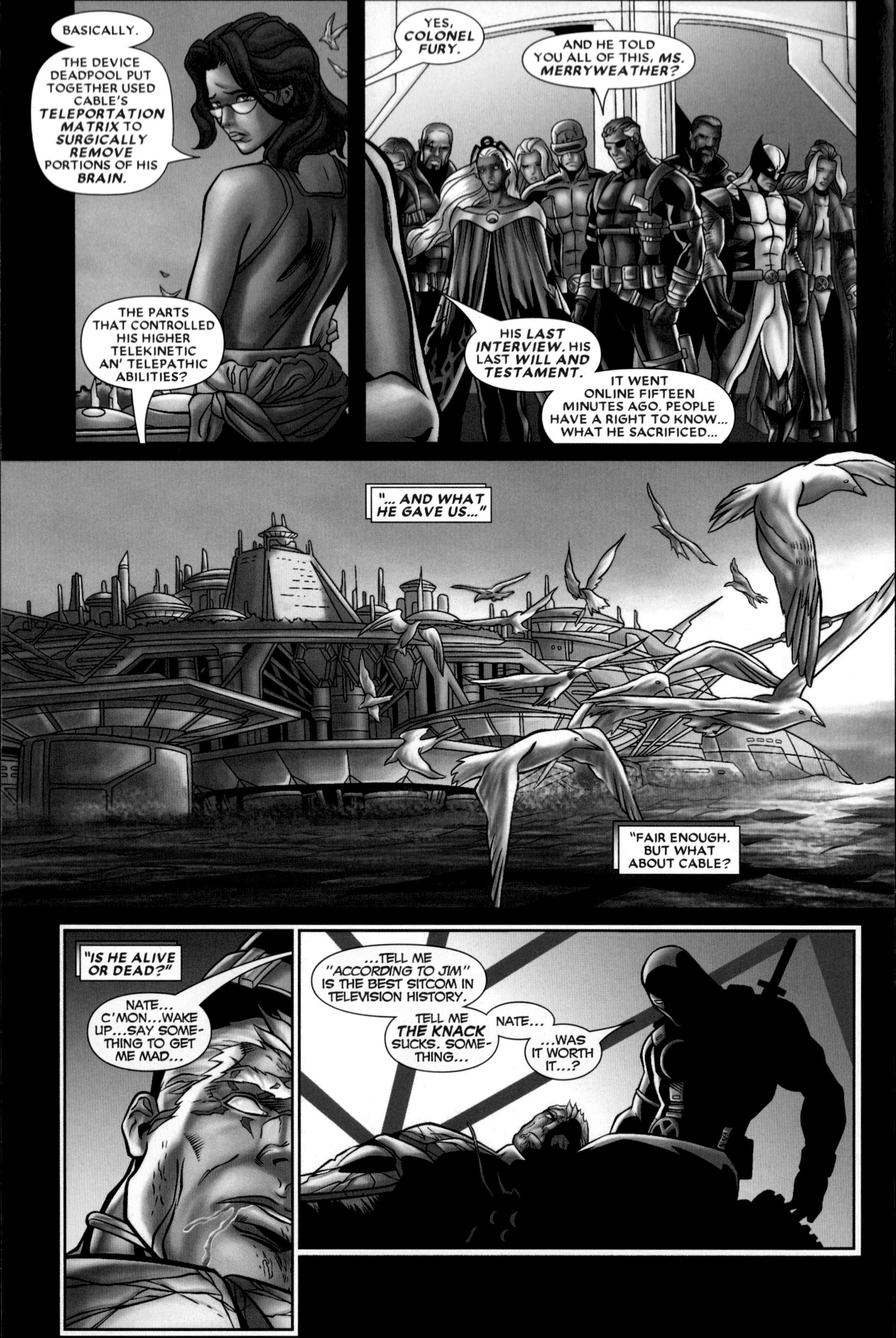

BASICALLY.
THE DEVICE DEADPOOL PUT TOGETHER USED CABLE'S TELEPORTATION MATRIX TO SURGICALLY REMOVE PORTIONS OF HIS BRAIN.
THE PARTS THAT CONTROLLED HIS HIGHER TELEKINETIC AN' TELEPATHIC ABILITIES?
YES, COLONEL FURY.
AND HE TOLD YOU ALL OF THIS, MS. MERRYWEATHER?
HIS LAST INTERVIEW. HIS LAST WILL AND TESTAMENT.
IT WENT ONLINE FIFTEEN MINUTES AGO. PEOPLE HAVE A RIGHT TO KNOW... WHAT HE SACRIFICED...
"... AND WHAT HE GAVE US..."
"FAIR ENOUGH. BUT WHAT ABOUT CABLE?
"IS HE ALIVE OR DEAD?"
NATE... C'MON...WAKE UP...SAY SOMETHING TO GET ME MAD...
...TELL ME "ACCORDING TO JIM" IS THE BEST SITCOM IN TELEVISION HISTORY.
TELL ME THE KNACK SUCKS. SOMETHING...
NATE...
...WAS IT WORTH IT...?

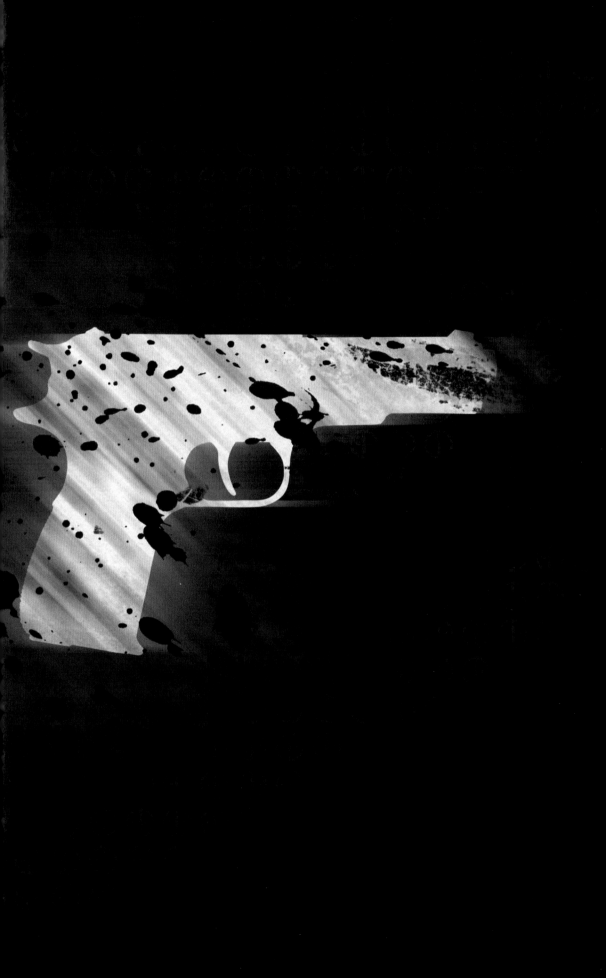

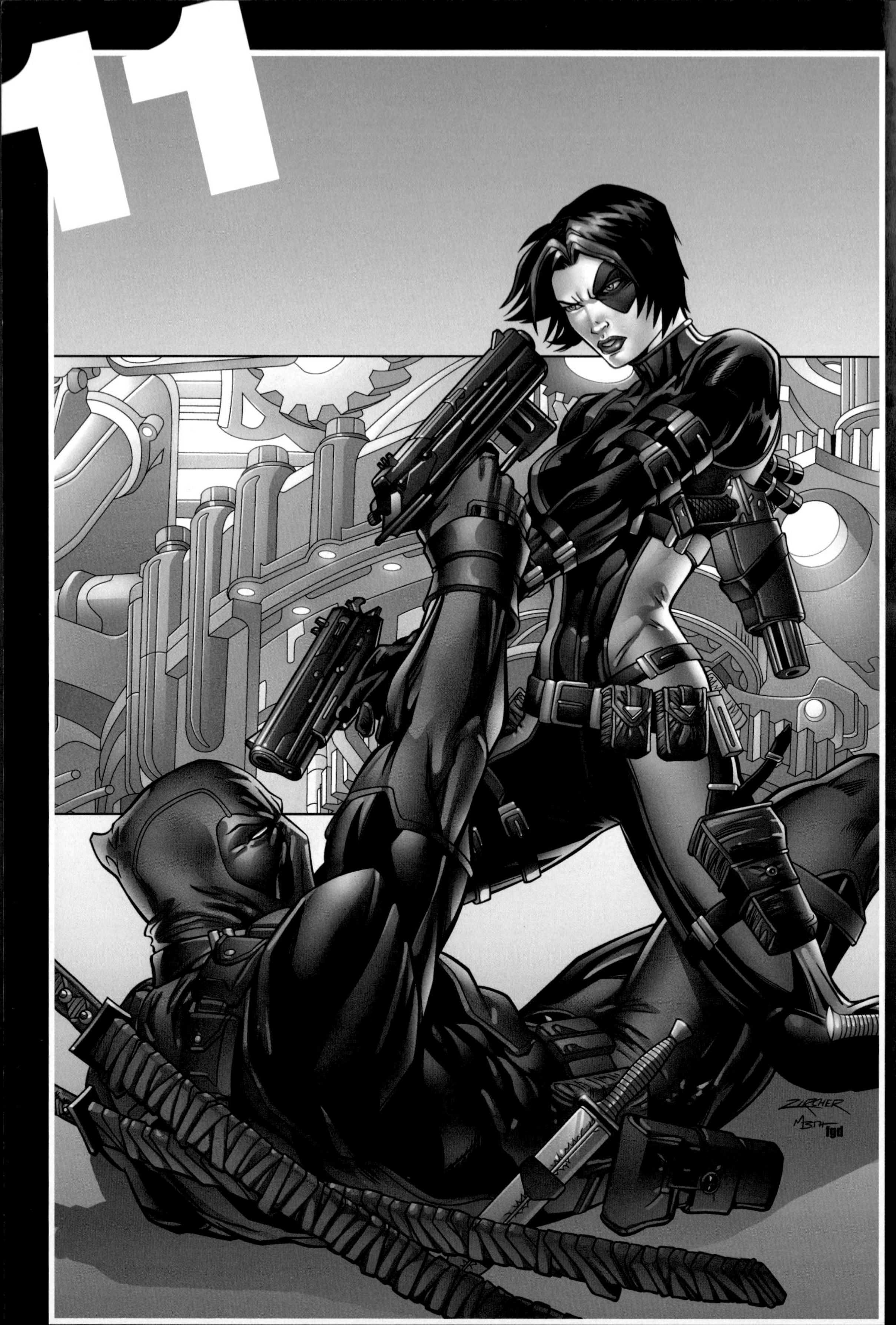
11
ZIRCHER
fgd

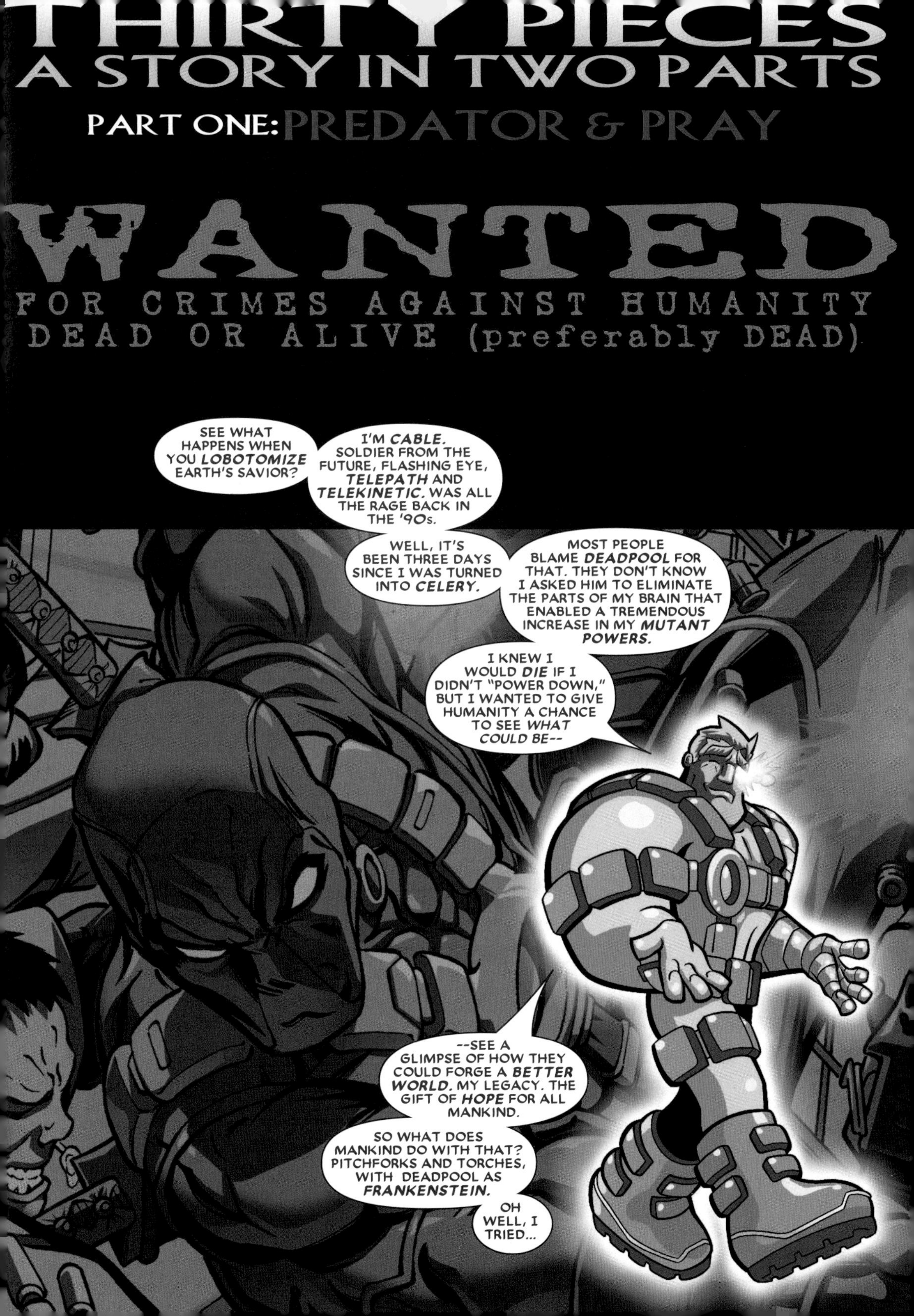
THIRTY PIECES
A STORY IN TWO PARTS
PART ONE: PREDATOR & PRAY
WANTED
FOR CRIMES AGAINST HUMANITY
DEAD OR ALIVE (preferably DEAD)
SEE WHAT HAPPENS WHEN YOU LOBOTOMIZE EARTH'S SAVIOR?
I'M CABLE. SOLDIER FROM THE FUTURE, FLASHING EYE, TELEPATH AND TELEKINETIC. WAS ALL THE RAGE BACK IN THE '90s.
WELL, IT'S BEEN THREE DAYS SINCE I WAS TURNED INTO CELERY.
MOST PEOPLE BLAME DEADPOOL FOR THAT. THEY DON'T KNOW I ASKED HIM TO ELIMINATE THE PARTS OF MY BRAIN THAT ENABLED A TREMENDOUS INCREASE IN MY MUTANT POWERS.
I KNEW I WOULD DIE IF I DIDN'T "POWER DOWN," BUT I WANTED TO GIVE HUMANITY A CHANCE TO SEE WHAT COULD BE--
--SEE A GLIMPSE OF HOW THEY COULD FORGE A BETTER WORLD. MY LEGACY. THE GIFT OF HOPE FOR ALL MANKIND.
SO WHAT DOES MANKIND DO WITH THAT? PITCHFORKS AND TORCHES, WITH DEADPOOL AS FRANKENSTEIN.
OH WELL, I TRIED...

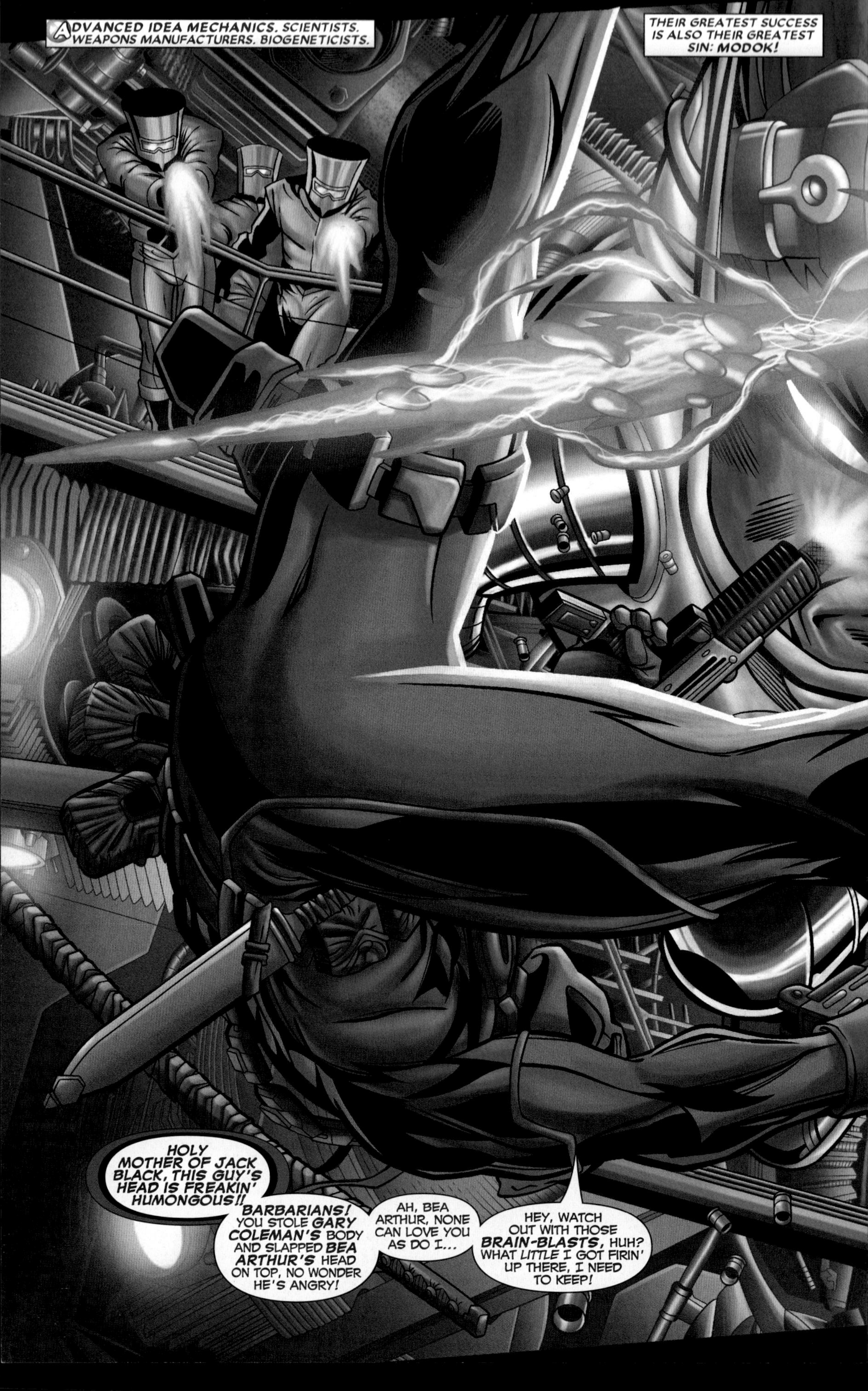
ADVANCED IDEA MECHANICS. SCIENTISTS. WEAPONS MANUFACTURERS. BIOGENETICISTS.
THEIR GREATEST SUCCESS IS ALSO THEIR GREATEST SIN: MODOK!
HOLY MOTHER OF JACK BLACK, THIS GUY'S HEAD IS FREAKIN' HUMONGOUS!!
BARBARIANS! YOU STOLE GARY COLEMAN'S BODY AND SLAPPED BEA ARTHUR'S HEAD ON TOP, NO WONDER HE'S ANGRY!
AH, BEA ARTHUR, NONE CAN LOVE YOU AS DO I...
HEY, WATCH OUT WITH THOSE BRAIN-BLASTS, HUH? WHAT LITTLE I GOT FIRIN' UP THERE, I NEED TO KEEP!

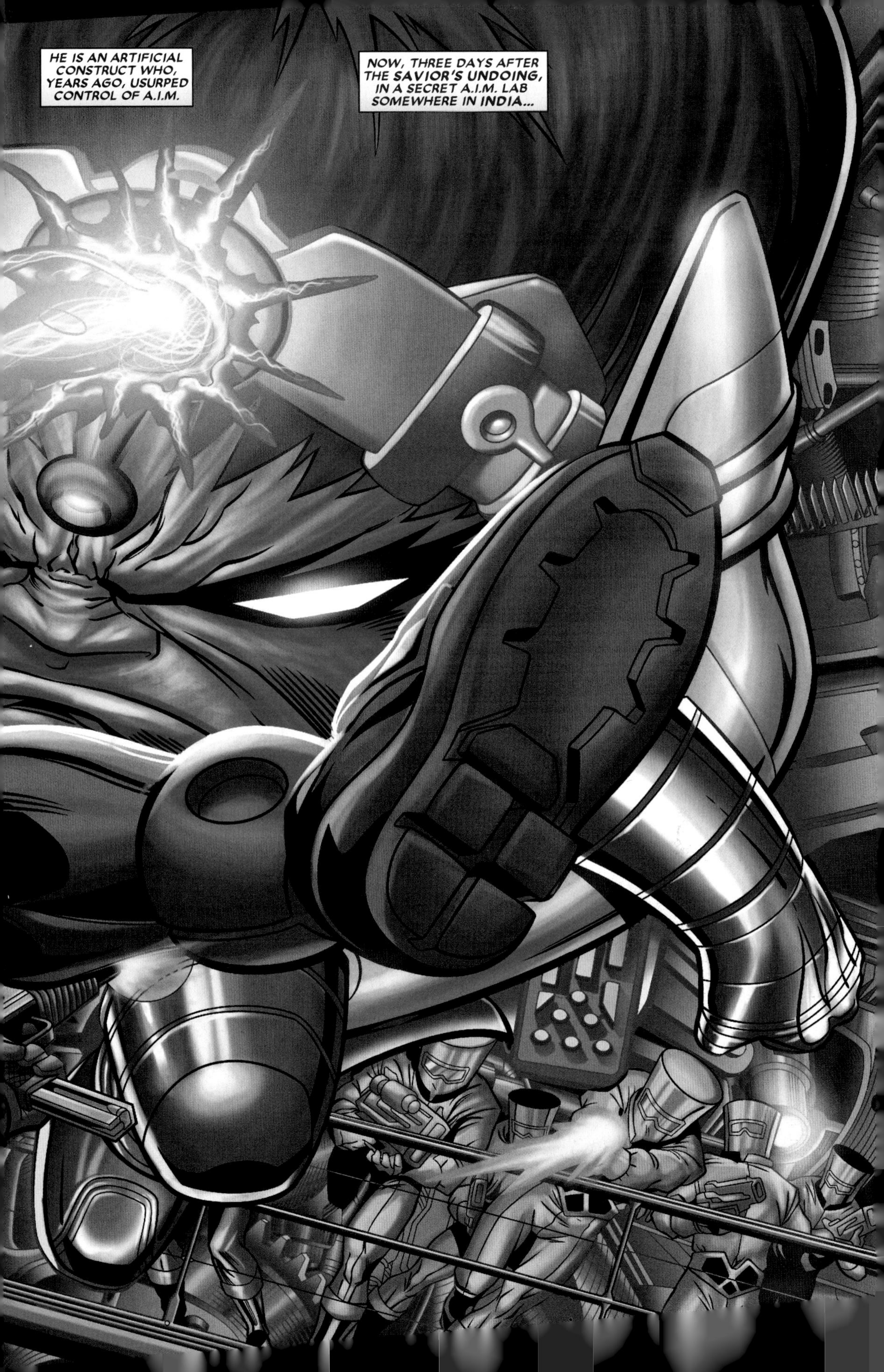
HE IS AN ARTIFICIAL CONSTRUCT WHO, YEARS AGO, USURPED CONTROL OF A.I.M.
NOW, THREE DAYS AFTER THE SAVIOR'S UNDOING, IN A SECRET A.I.M. LAB SOMEWHERE IN INDIA...

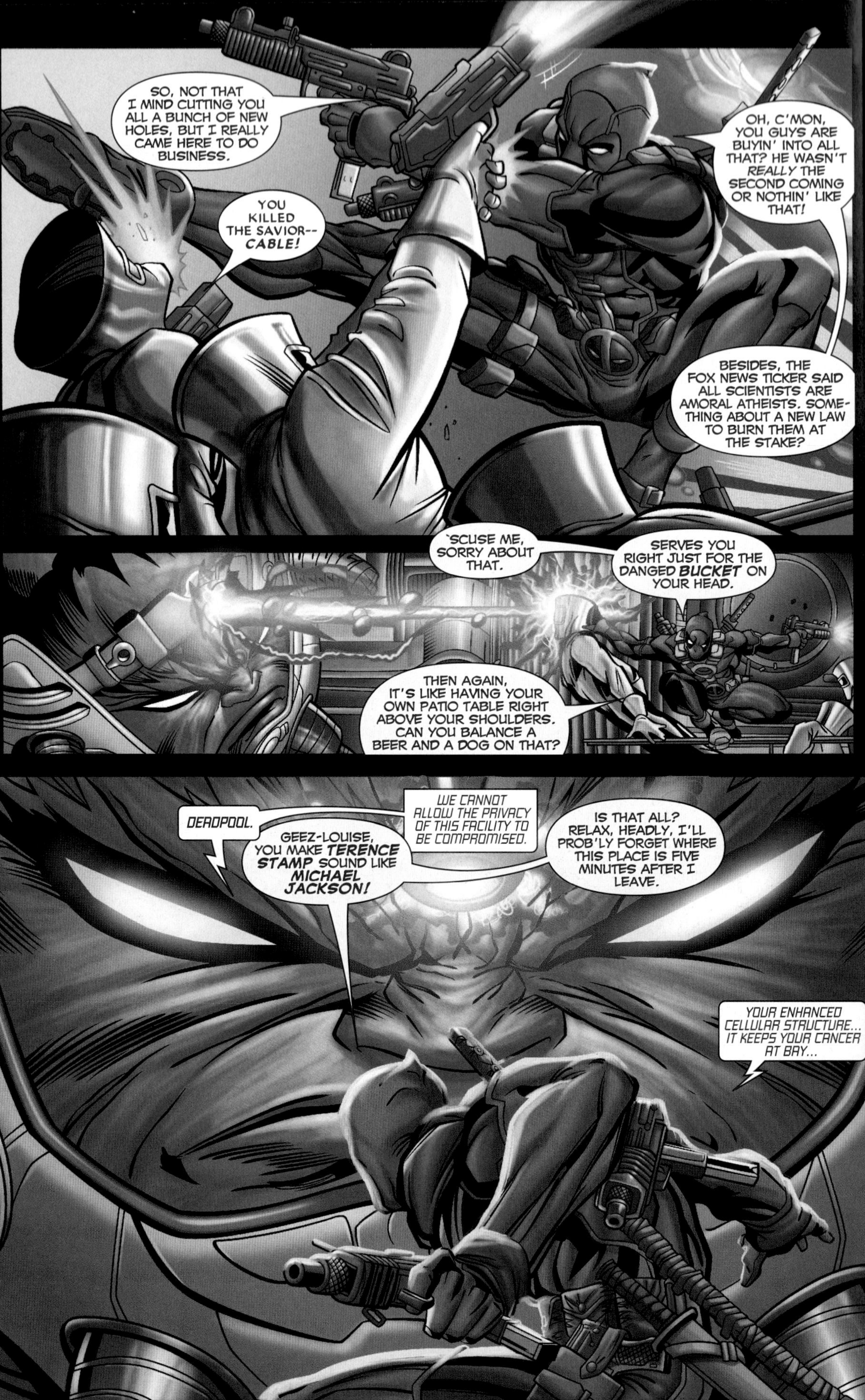
SO, NOT THAT I MIND CUTTING YOU ALL A BUNCH OF NEW HOLES, BUT I REALLY CAME HERE TO DO BUSINESS.
YOU KILLED THE SAVIOR-- CABLE!
OH, C'MON, YOU GUYS ARE BUYIN' INTO ALL THAT? HE WASN'T REALLY THE SECOND COMING OR NOTHIN' LIKE THAT!
BESIDES, THE FOX NEWS TICKER SAID ALL SCIENTISTS ARE AMORAL ATHEISTS. SOMETHING ABOUT A NEW LAW TO BURN THEM AT THE STAKE?
'SCUSE ME, SORRY ABOUT THAT.
SERVES YOU RIGHT JUST FOR THE DANGED BUCKET ON YOUR HEAD.
THEN AGAIN, IT'S LIKE HAVING YOUR OWN PATIO TABLE RIGHT ABOVE YOUR SHOULDERS. CAN YOU BALANCE A BEER AND A DOG ON THAT?
DEADPOOL.
GEEZ-LOUISE, YOU MAKE TERENCE STAMP SOUND LIKE MICHAEL JACKSON!
WE CANNOT ALLOW THE PRIVACY OF THIS FACILITY TO BE COMPROMISED.
IS THAT ALL? RELAX, HEADLY, I'LL PROB'LY FORGET WHERE THIS PLACE IS FIVE MINUTES AFTER I LEAVE.
YOUR ENHANCED CELLULAR STRUCTURE... IT KEEPS YOUR CANCER AT BAY...

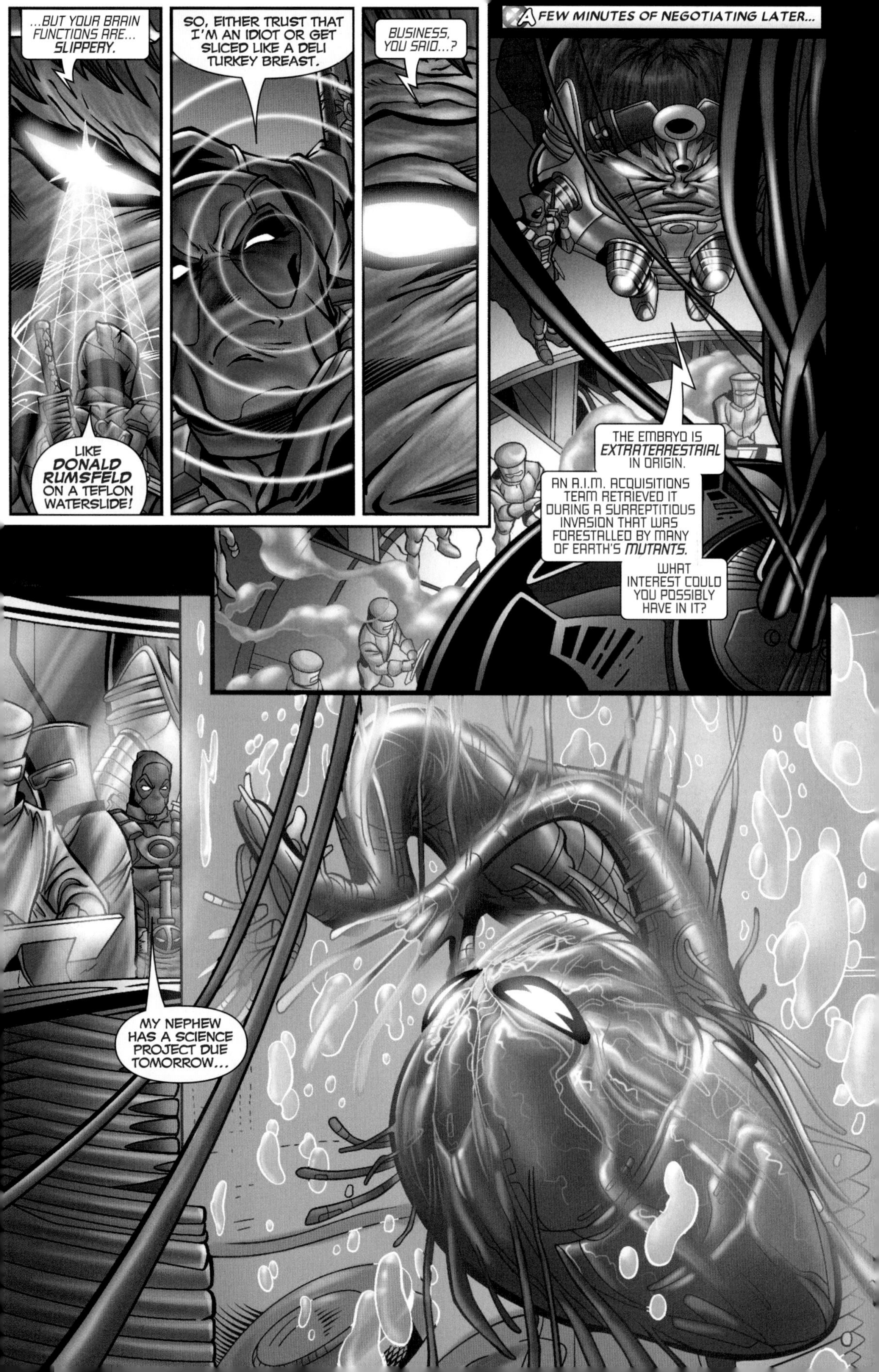

...BUT YOUR BRAIN FUNCTIONS ARE... SLIPPERY.
LIKE DONALD RUMSFELD ON A TEFLON WATERSLIDE!
SO, EITHER TRUST THAT I'M AN IDIOT OR GET SLICED LIKE A DELI TURKEY BREAST.
BUSINESS, YOU SAID...?
A FEW MINUTES OF NEGOTIATING LATER...
THE EMBRYO IS EXTRATERRESTRIAL IN ORIGIN.
AN A.I.M. ACQUISITIONS TEAM RETRIEVED IT DURING A SURREPTITIOUS INVASION THAT WAS FORESTALLED BY MANY OF EARTH'S MUTANTS.
WHAT INTEREST COULD YOU POSSIBLY HAVE IN IT?
MY NEPHEW HAS A SCIENCE PROJECT DUE TOMORROW...

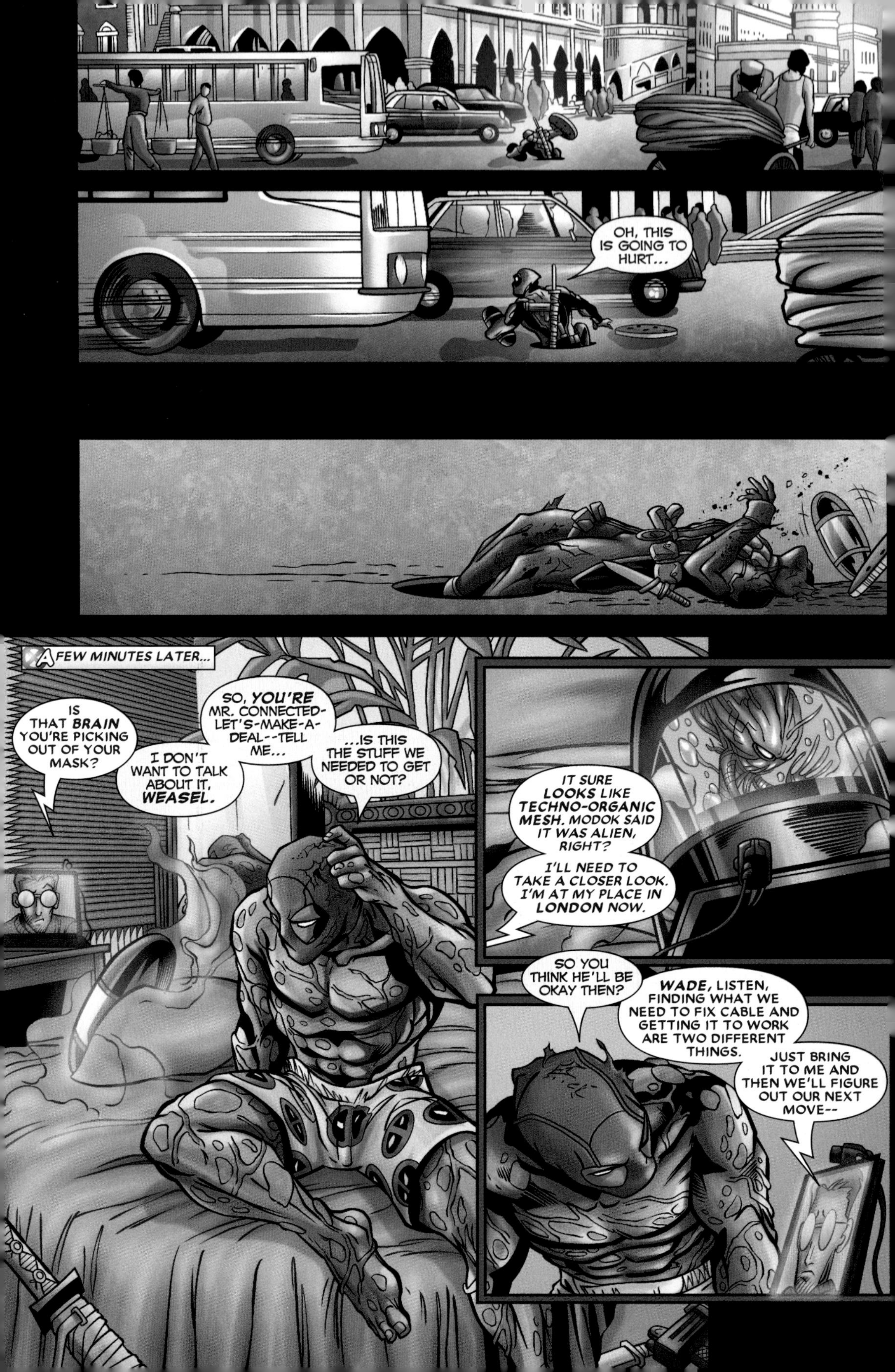
OH, THIS IS GOING TO HURT...
A FEW MINUTES LATER...
IS THAT BRAIN YOU'RE PICKING OUT OF YOUR MASK?
I DON'T WANT TO TALK ABOUT IT, WEASEL.
SO, YOU'RE MR. CONNECTED-LET'S-MAKE-A-DEAL--TELL ME...
...IS THIS THE STUFF WE NEEDED TO GET OR NOT?
IT SURE LOOKS LIKE TECHNO-ORGANIC MESH. MODOK SAID IT WAS ALIEN, RIGHT?
I'LL NEED TO TAKE A CLOSER LOOK. I'M AT MY PLACE IN LONDON NOW.
SO YOU THINK HE'LL BE OKAY THEN?
WADE, LISTEN, FINDING WHAT WE NEED TO FIX CABLE AND GETTING IT TO WORK ARE TWO DIFFERENT THINGS.
JUST BRING IT TO ME AND THEN WE'LL FIGURE OUT OUR NEXT MOVE--

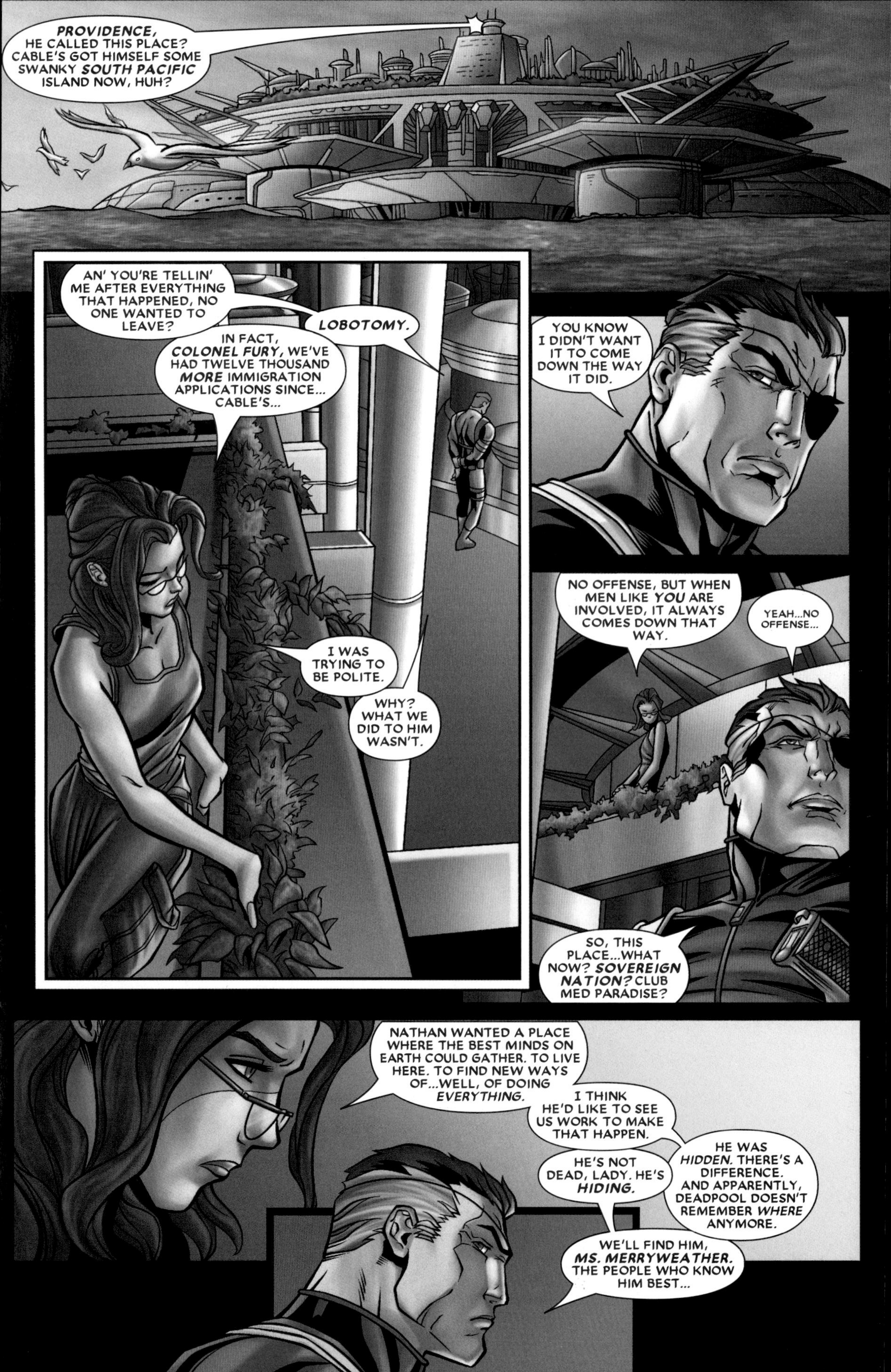
PROVIDENCE, HE CALLED THIS PLACE? CABLE'S GOT HIMSELF SOME SWANKY SOUTH PACIFIC ISLAND NOW, HUH?
AN' YOU'RE TELLIN' ME AFTER EVERYTHING THAT HAPPENED, NO ONE WANTED TO LEAVE?
LOBOTOMY.
IN FACT, COLONEL FURY, WE'VE HAD TWELVE THOUSAND MORE IMMIGRATION APPLICATIONS SINCE... CABLE'S...
I WAS TRYING TO BE POLITE.
WHY? WHAT WE DID TO HIM WASN'T.
YOU KNOW I DIDN'T WANT IT TO COME DOWN THE WAY IT DID.
NO OFFENSE, BUT WHEN MEN LIKE YOU ARE INVOLVED, IT ALWAYS COMES DOWN THAT WAY.
YEAH...NO OFFENSE...
SO, THIS PLACE...WHAT NOW? SOVEREIGN NATION? CLUB MED PARADISE?
NATHAN WANTED A PLACE WHERE THE BEST MINDS ON EARTH COULD GATHER. TO LIVE HERE. TO FIND NEW WAYS OF...WELL, OF DOING EVERYTHING.
I THINK HE'D LIKE TO SEE US WORK TO MAKE THAT HAPPEN.
HE'S NOT DEAD, LADY. HE'S HIDING.
HE WAS HIDDEN. THERE'S A DIFFERENCE. AND APPARENTLY, DEADPOOL DOESN'T REMEMBER WHERE ANYMORE.
WE'LL FIND HIM, MS. MERRYWEATHER. THE PEOPLE WHO KNOW HIM BEST...

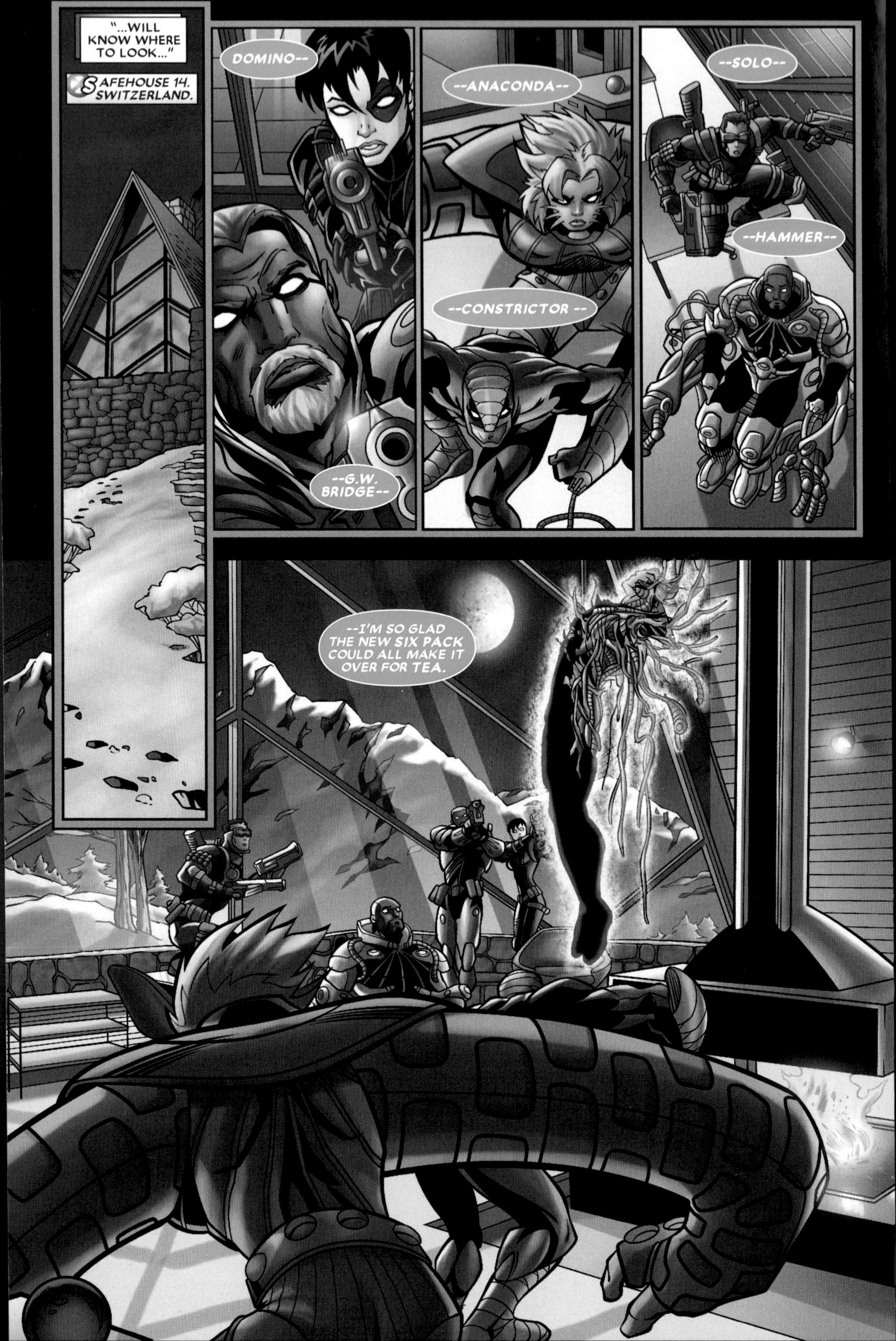
"...WILL KNOW WHERE TO LOOK..."
SAFEHOUSE 14. SWITZERLAND.
DOMINO--
--G.W. BRIDGE--
--ANACONDA--
--CONSTRICTOR --
--SOLO--
--HAMMER--
--I'M SO GLAD THE NEW SIX PACK COULD ALL MAKE IT OVER FOR TEA.

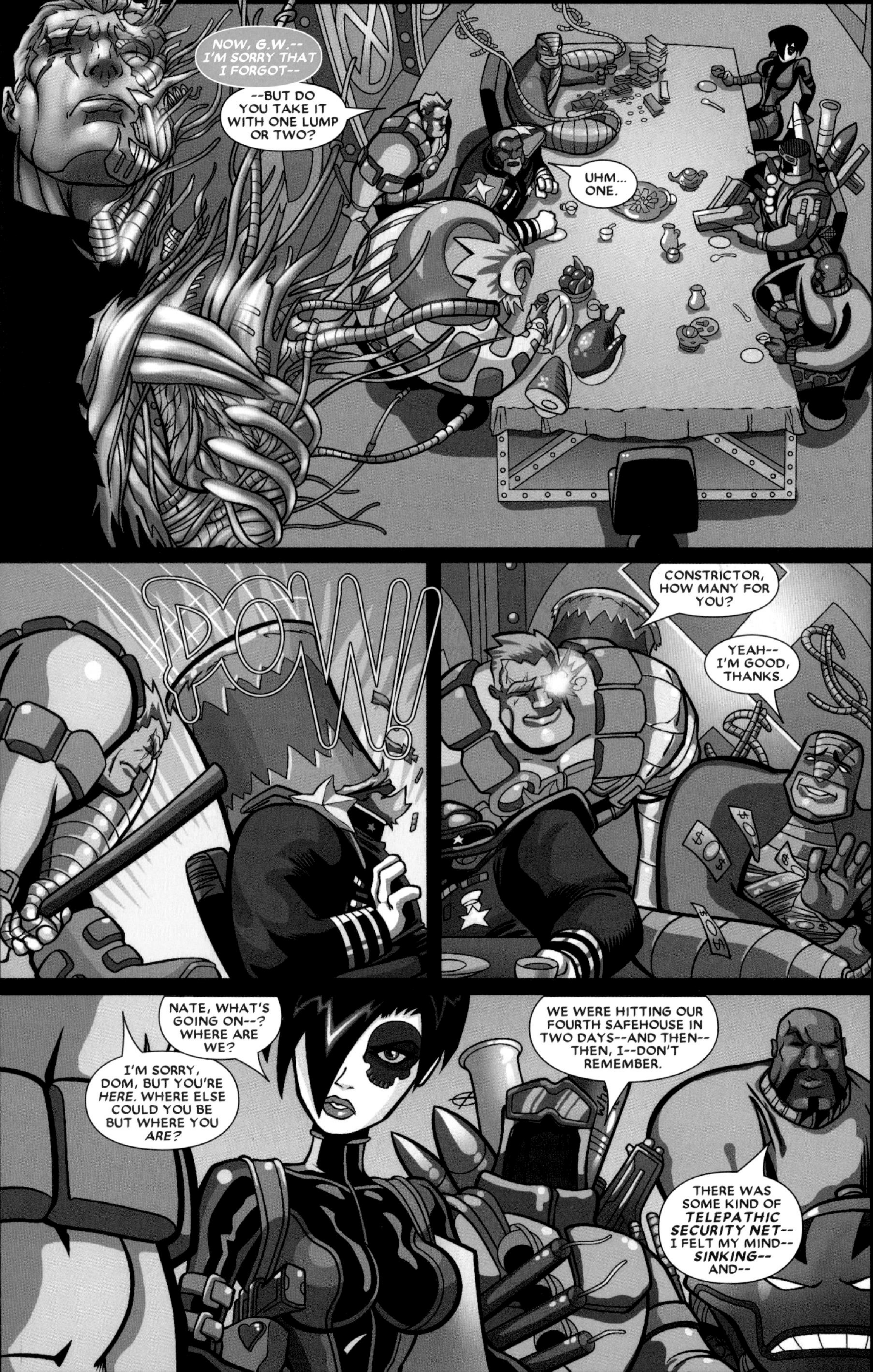
NOW, G.W.-- I'M SORRY THAT I FORGOT--
--BUT DO YOU TAKE IT WITH ONE LUMP OR TWO?
UHM... ONE.
POW!!
CONSTRICTOR, HOW MANY FOR YOU?
YEAH-- I'M GOOD, THANKS.
NATE, WHAT'S GOING ON--? WHERE ARE WE?
I'M SORRY, DOM, BUT YOU'RE HERE. WHERE ELSE COULD YOU BE BUT WHERE YOU ARE?
WE WERE HITTING OUR FOURTH SAFEHOUSE IN TWO DAYS--AND THEN-- THEN, I--DON'T REMEMBER.
THERE WAS SOME KIND OF TELEPATHIC SECURITY NET-- I FELT MY MIND-- SINKING-- AND--

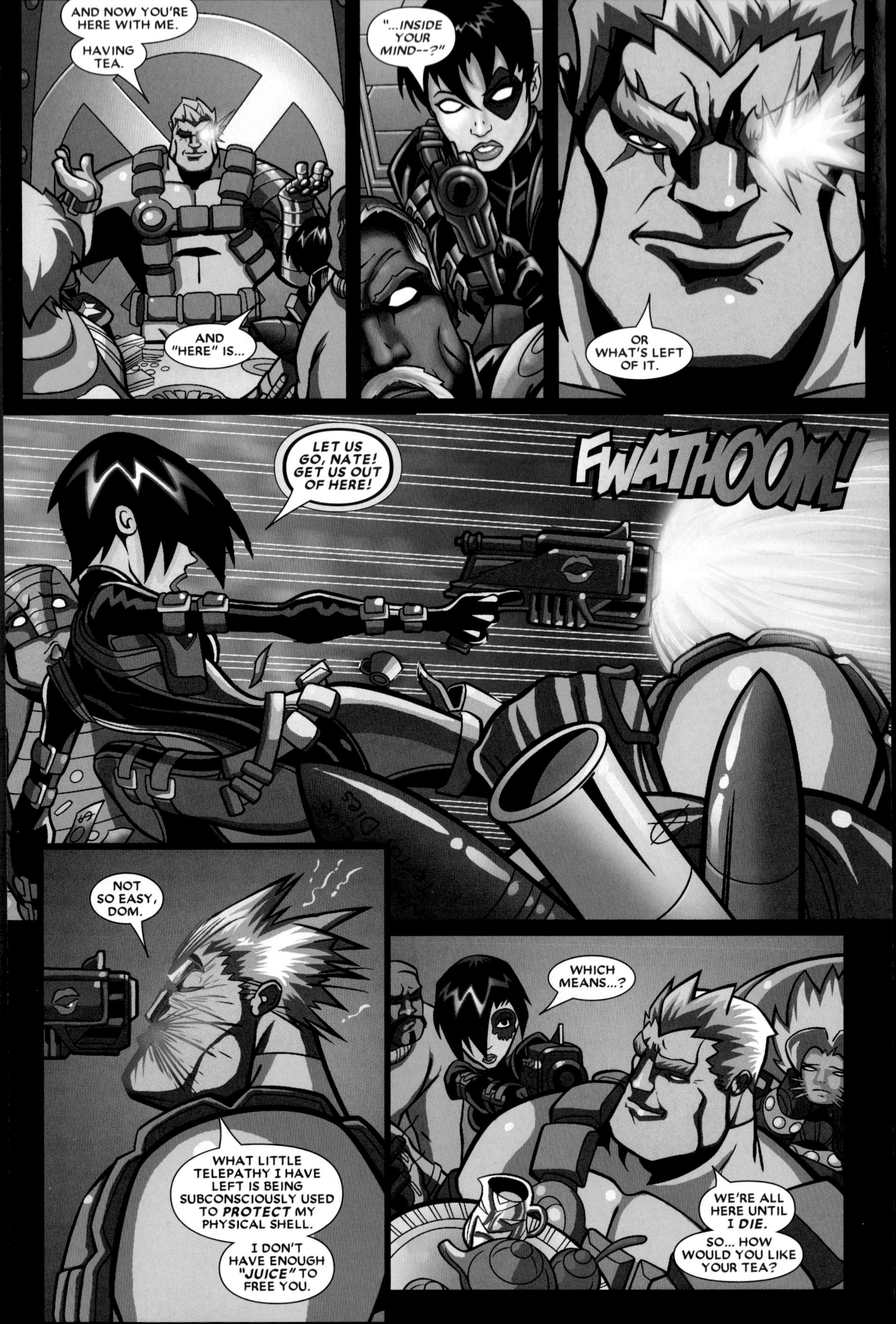
AND NOW YOU'RE HERE WITH ME.
HAVING TEA.
AND "HERE" IS...
"...INSIDE YOUR MIND--?"
OR WHAT'S LEFT OF IT.
LET US GO, NATE! GET US OUT OF HERE!
FWATHOOM!
NOT SO EASY, DOM.
WHAT LITTLE TELEPATHY I HAVE LEFT IS BEING SUBCONSCIOUSLY USED TO PROTECT MY PHYSICAL SHELL.
I DON'T HAVE ENOUGH "JUICE" TO FREE YOU.
WHICH MEANS...?
WE'RE ALL HERE UNTIL I DIE.
SO... HOW WOULD YOU LIKE YOUR TEA?

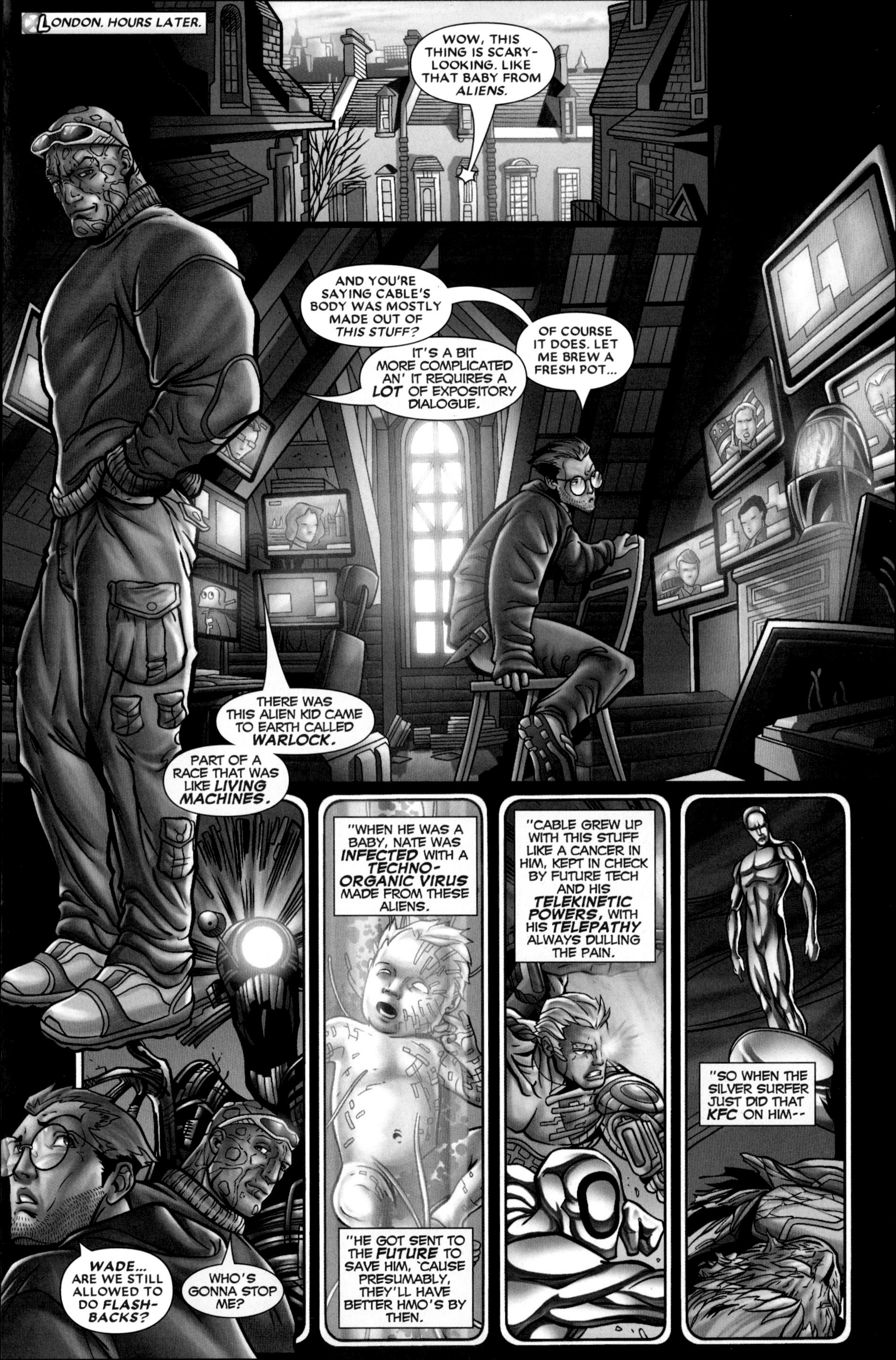
LONDON. HOURS LATER.
WOW, THIS THING IS SCARY-LOOKING. LIKE THAT BABY FROM ALIENS.
AND YOU'RE SAYING CABLE'S BODY WAS MOSTLY MADE OUT OF THIS STUFF?
OF COURSE IT DOES. LET ME BREW A FRESH POT...
IT'S A BIT MORE COMPLICATED AN' IT REQUIRES A LOT OF EXPOSITORY DIALOGUE.
THERE WAS THIS ALIEN KID CAME TO EARTH CALLED WARLOCK.
PART OF A RACE THAT WAS LIKE LIVING MACHINES.
"WHEN HE WAS A BABY, NATE WAS INFECTED WITH A TECHNO-ORGANIC VIRUS MADE FROM THESE ALIENS.
"HE GOT SENT TO THE FUTURE TO SAVE HIM, 'CAUSE PRESUMABLY, THEY'LL HAVE BETTER HMO'S BY THEN.
"CABLE GREW UP WITH THIS STUFF LIKE A CANCER IN HIM, KEPT IN CHECK BY FUTURE TECH AND HIS TELEKINETIC POWERS, WITH HIS TELEPATHY ALWAYS DULLING THE PAIN.
"SO WHEN THE SILVER SURFER JUST DID THAT KFC ON HIM--
WADE... ARE WE STILL ALLOWED TO DO FLASH-BACKS?
WHO'S GONNA STOP ME?

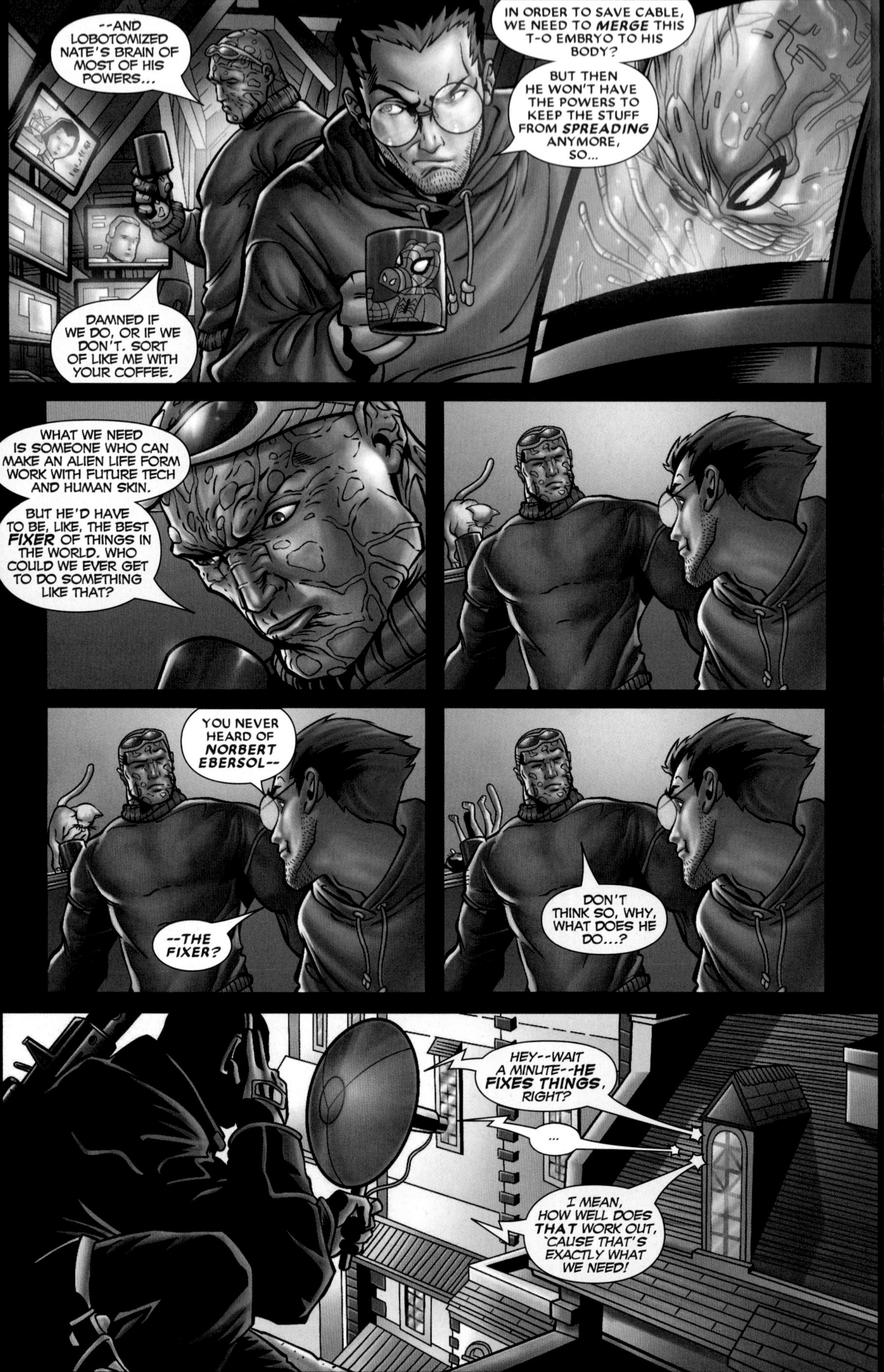
--AND LOBOTOMIZED NATE'S BRAIN OF MOST OF HIS POWERS...
IN ORDER TO SAVE CABLE, WE NEED TO MERGE THIS T-O EMBRYO TO HIS BODY?
BUT THEN HE WON'T HAVE THE POWERS TO KEEP THE STUFF FROM SPREADING ANYMORE, SO...
DAMNED IF WE DO, OR IF WE DON'T. SORT OF LIKE ME WITH YOUR COFFEE.
WHAT WE NEED IS SOMEONE WHO CAN MAKE AN ALIEN LIFE FORM WORK WITH FUTURE TECH AND HUMAN SKIN.
BUT HE'D HAVE TO BE, LIKE, THE BEST FIXER OF THINGS IN THE WORLD. WHO COULD WE EVER GET TO DO SOMETHING LIKE THAT?
YOU NEVER HEARD OF NORBERT EBERSOL--
--THE FIXER?
DON'T THINK SO, WHY, WHAT DOES HE DO...?
HEY--WAIT A MINUTE--HE FIXES THINGS, RIGHT?
...
I MEAN, HOW WELL DOES THAT WORK OUT, 'CAUSE THAT'S EXACTLY WHAT WE NEED!

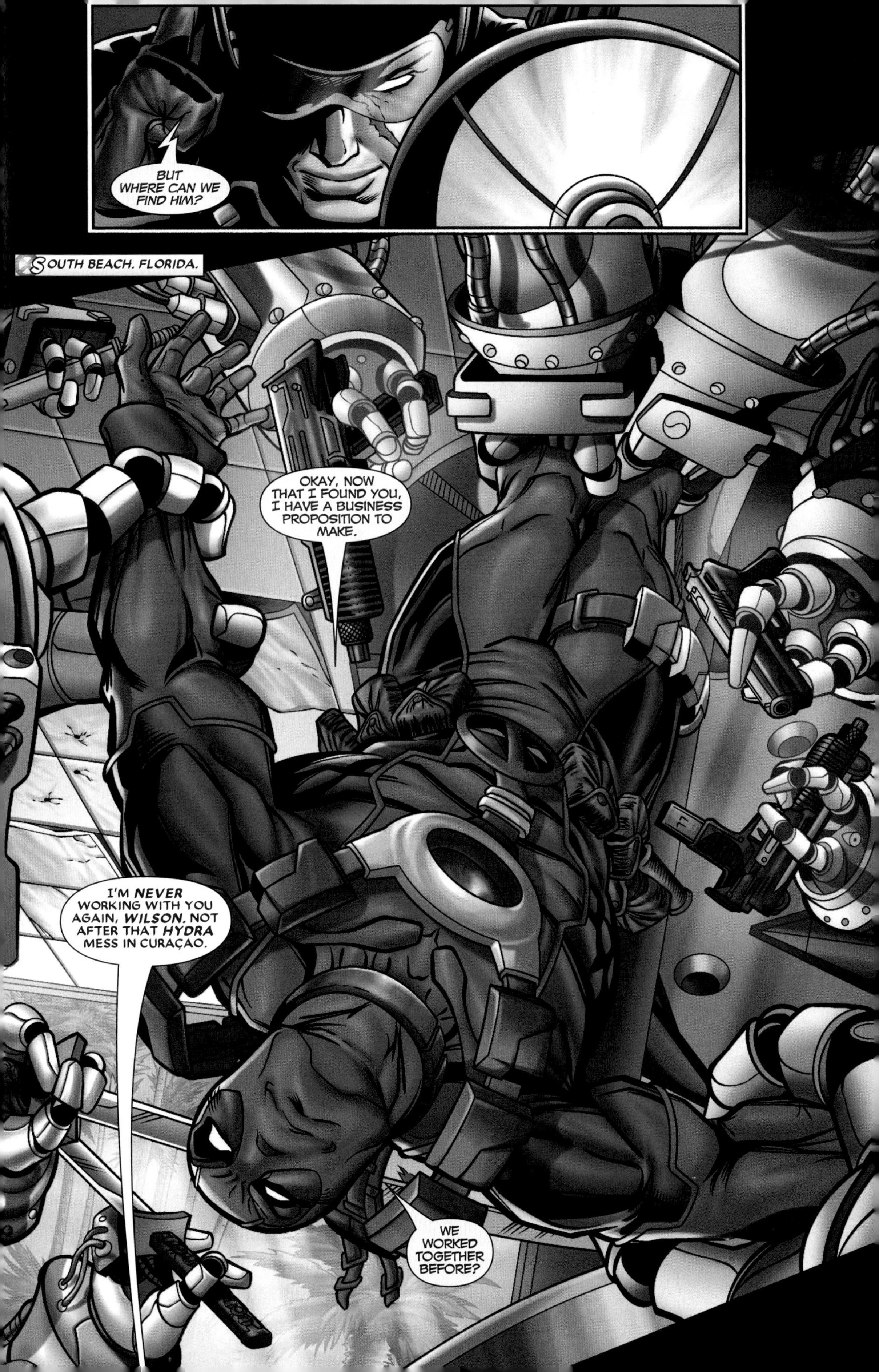
BUT WHERE CAN WE FIND HIM?
SOUTH BEACH. FLORIDA.
OKAY, NOW THAT I FOUND YOU, I HAVE A BUSINESS PROPOSITION TO MAKE.
I'M NEVER WORKING WITH YOU AGAIN, WILSON. NOT AFTER THAT HYDRA MESS IN CURAÇAO.
WE WORKED TOGETHER BEFORE?

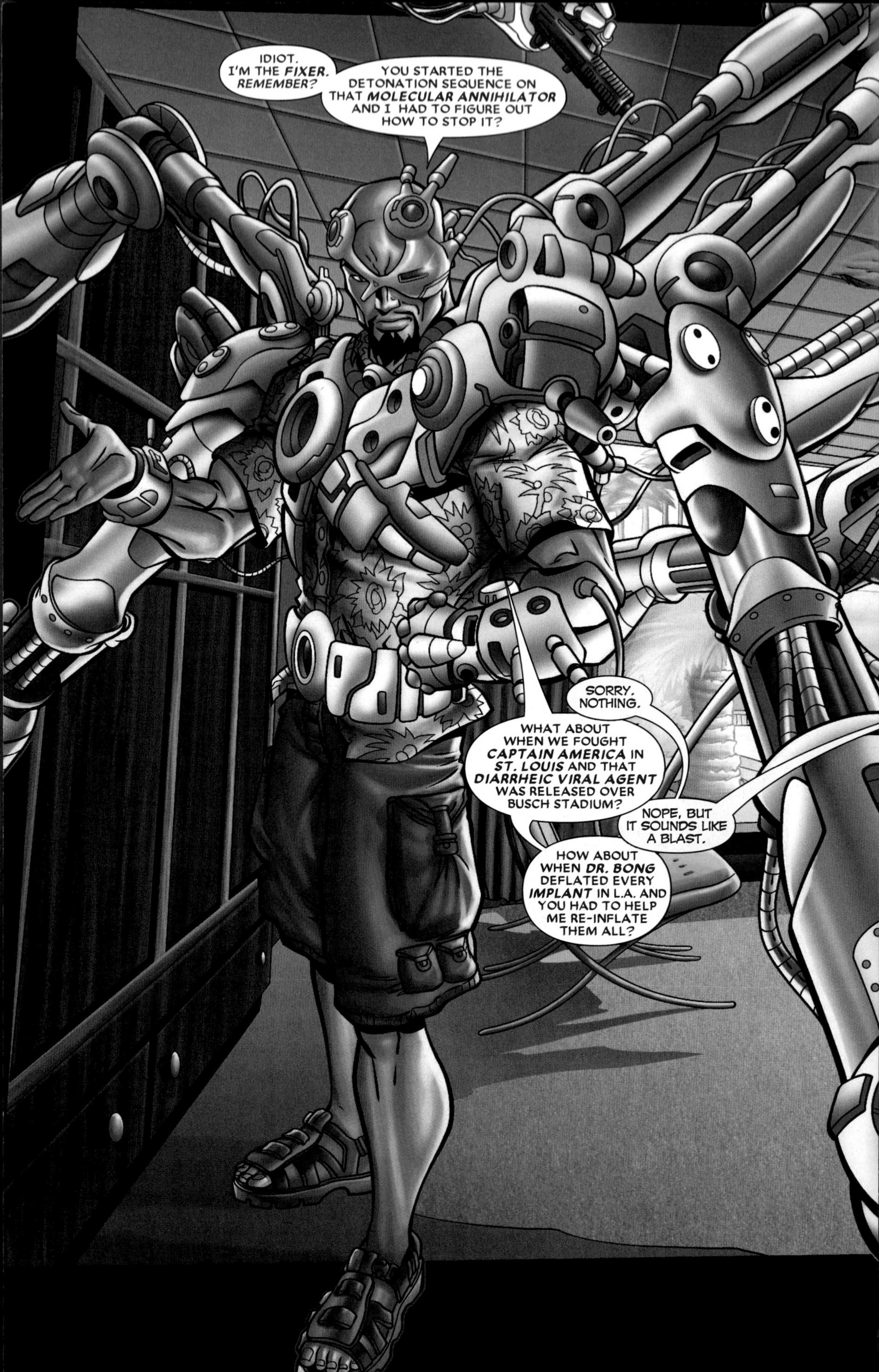
IDIOT. I'M THE FIXER. REMEMBER?
YOU STARTED THE DETONATION SEQUENCE ON THAT MOLECULAR ANNIHILATOR AND I HAD TO FIGURE OUT HOW TO STOP IT?
SORRY. NOTHING.
WHAT ABOUT WHEN WE FOUGHT CAPTAIN AMERICA IN ST. LOUIS AND THAT DIARRHEIC VIRAL AGENT WAS RELEASED OVER BUSCH STADIUM?
NOPE, BUT IT SOUNDS LIKE A BLAST.
HOW ABOUT WHEN DR. BONG DEFLATED EVERY IMPLANT IN L.A. AND YOU HAD TO HELP ME RE-INFLATE THEM ALL?

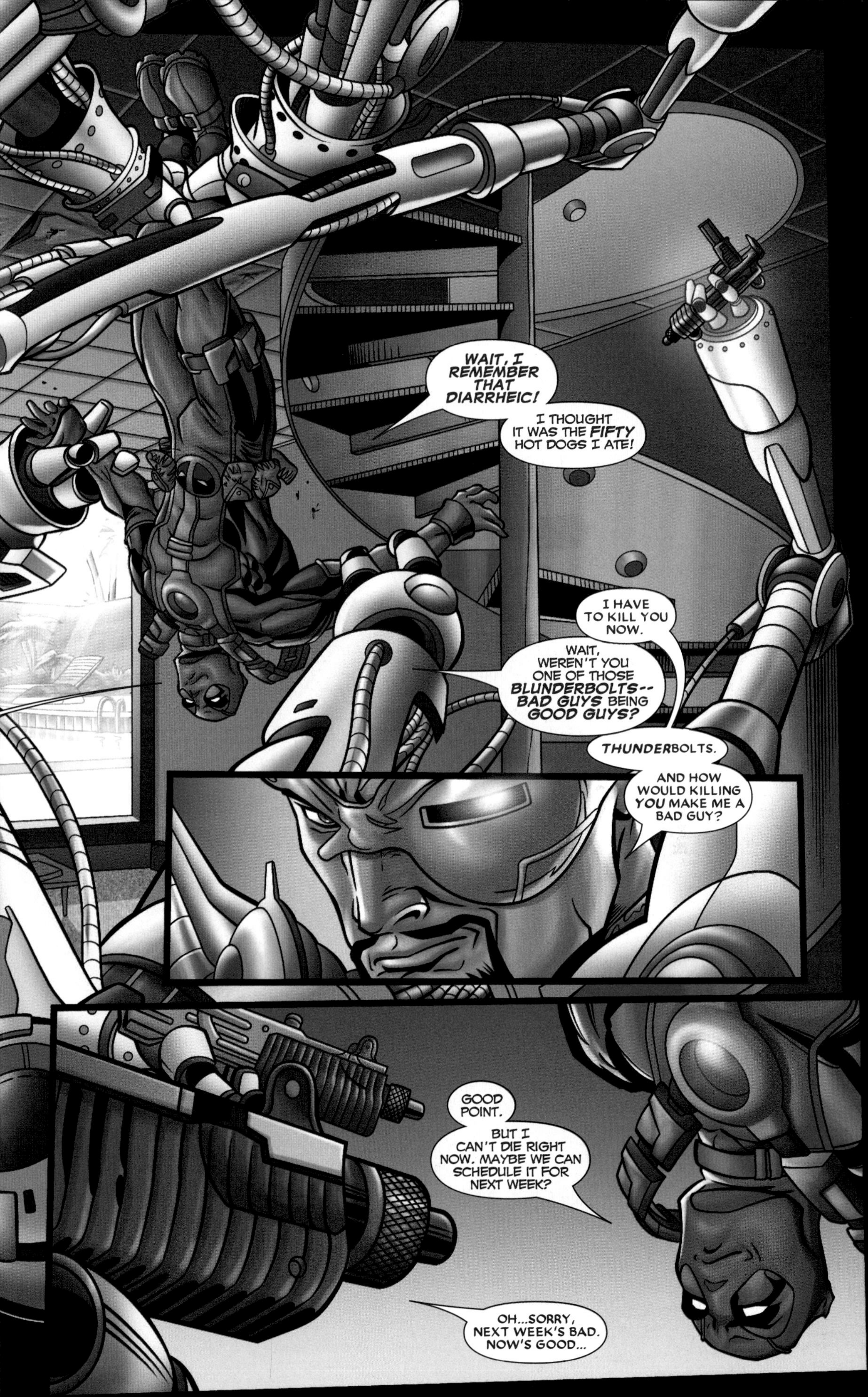
WAIT, I REMEMBER THAT DIARRHEIC!
I THOUGHT IT WAS THE FIFTY HOT DOGS I ATE!
I HAVE TO KILL YOU NOW.
WAIT, WEREN'T YOU ONE OF THOSE BLUNDERBOLTS-- BAD GUYS BEING GOOD GUYS?
THUNDERBOLTS.
AND HOW WOULD KILLING YOU MAKE ME A BAD GUY?
GOOD POINT.
BUT I CAN'T DIE RIGHT NOW. MAYBE WE CAN SCHEDULE IT FOR NEXT WEEK?
OH...SORRY, NEXT WEEK'S BAD. NOW'S GOOD...

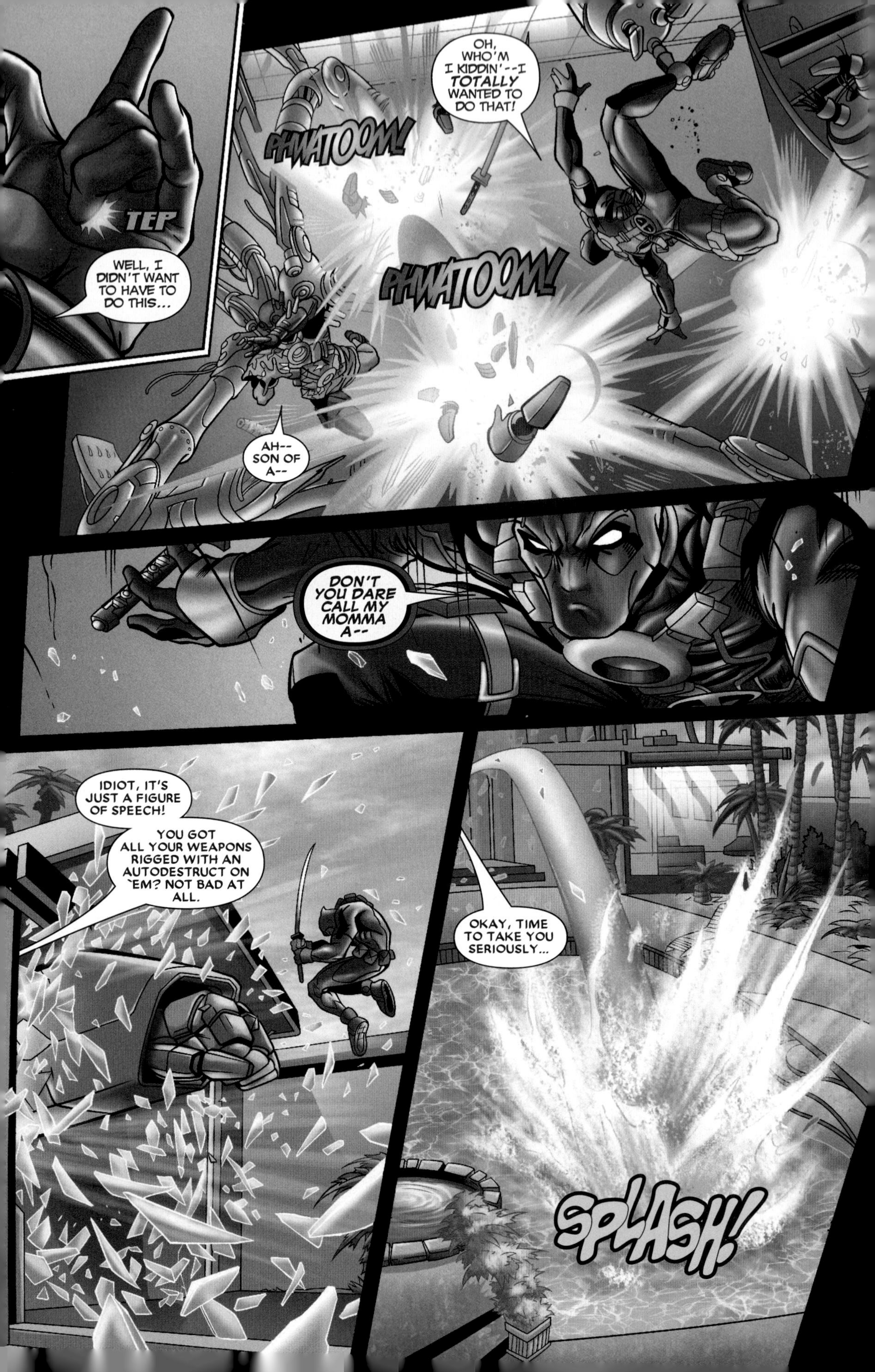
TEP
WELL, I DIDN'T WANT TO HAVE TO DO THIS...
PHWATOOM!
OH, WHO'M I KIDDIN'--I TOTALLY WANTED TO DO THAT!
PHWATOOM!
AH-- SON OF A--
DON'T YOU DARE CALL MY MOMMA A--
IDIOT, IT'S JUST A FIGURE OF SPEECH!
YOU GOT ALL YOUR WEAPONS RIGGED WITH AN AUTODESTRUCT ON 'EM? NOT BAD AT ALL.
OKAY, TIME TO TAKE YOU SERIOUSLY...
SPLASH!

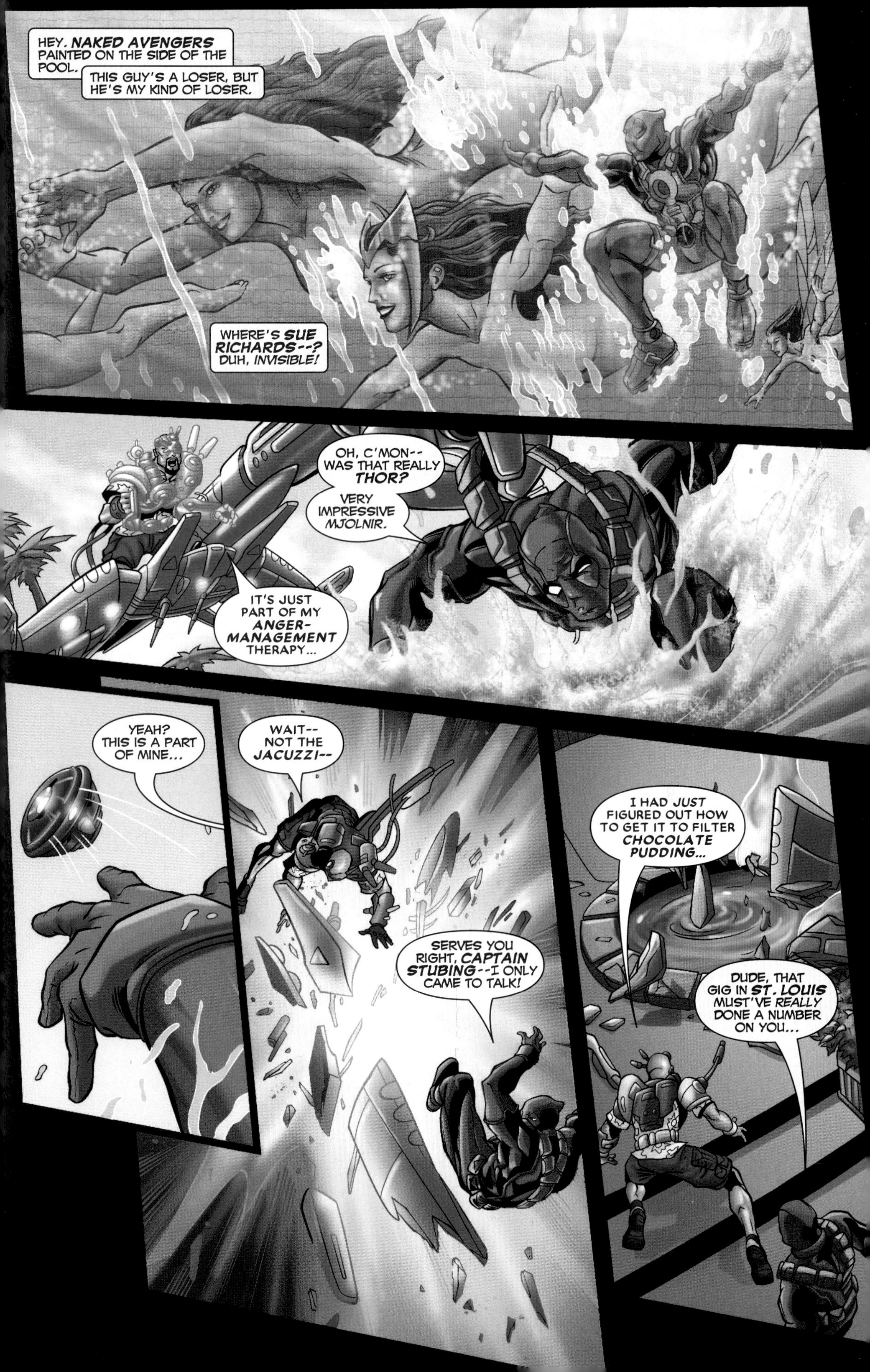
HEY. NAKED AVENGERS PAINTED ON THE SIDE OF THE POOL.
THIS GUY'S A LOSER, BUT HE'S MY KIND OF LOSER.
WHERE'S SUE RICHARDS--? DUH, INVISIBLE!
OH, C'MON-- WAS THAT REALLY THOR?
VERY IMPRESSIVE MJOLNIR.
IT'S JUST PART OF MY ANGER-MANAGEMENT THERAPY...
YEAH? THIS IS A PART OF MINE...
WAIT-- NOT THE JACUZZI--
SERVES YOU RIGHT, CAPTAIN STUBING--I ONLY CAME TO TALK!
I HAD JUST FIGURED OUT HOW TO GET IT TO FILTER CHOCOLATE PUDDING...
DUDE, THAT GIG IN ST. LOUIS MUST'VE REALLY DONE A NUMBER ON YOU...

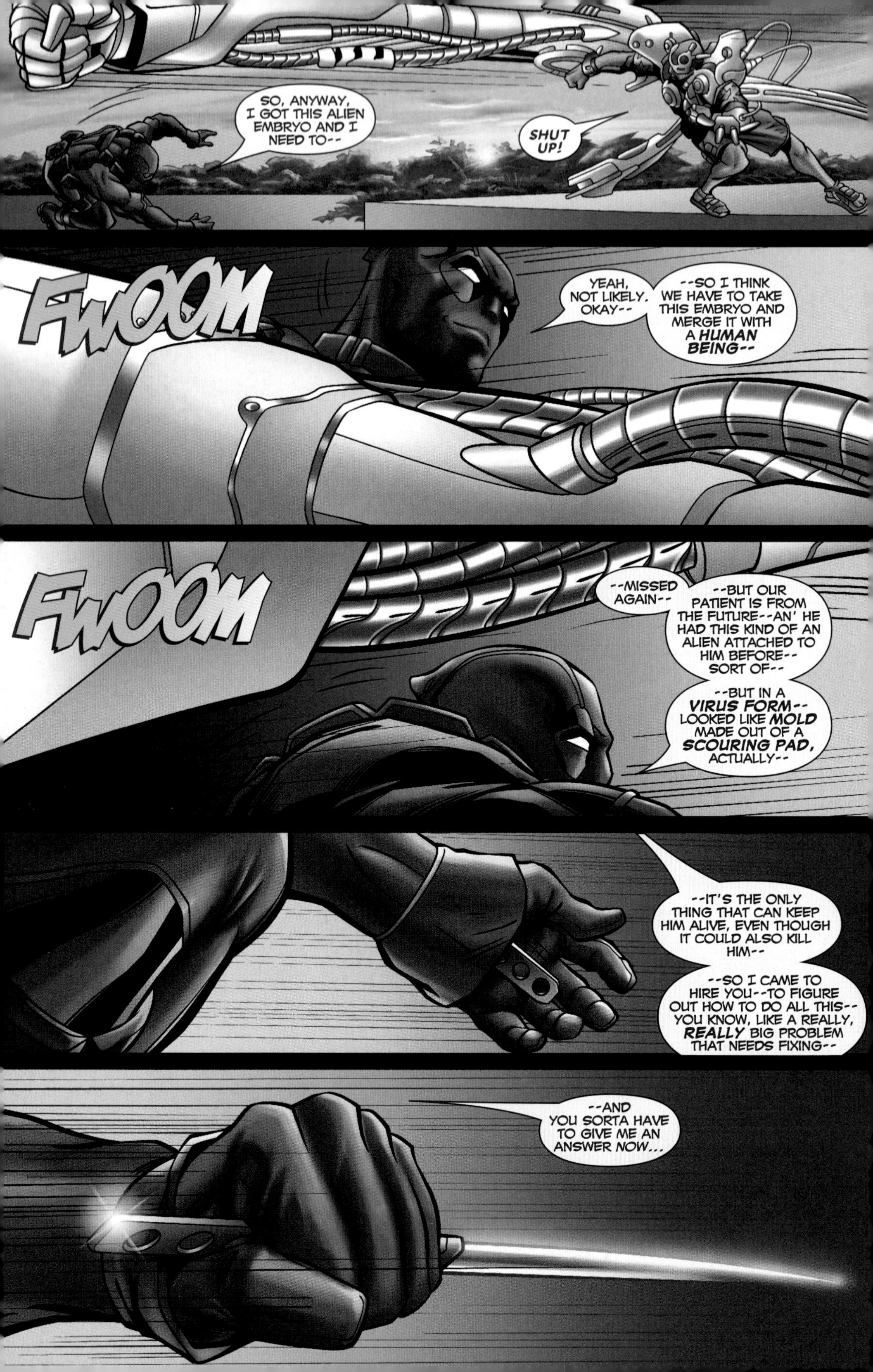
SO, ANYWAY, I GOT THIS ALIEN EMBRYO AND I NEED TO--
SHUT UP!
FWOOM
YEAH, NOT LIKELY. OKAY--
--SO I THINK WE HAVE TO TAKE THIS EMBRYO AND MERGE IT WITH A HUMAN BEING--
FWOOM
--MISSED AGAIN--
--BUT OUR PATIENT IS FROM THE FUTURE--AN' HE HAD THIS KIND OF AN ALIEN ATTACHED TO HIM BEFORE-- SORT OF--
--BUT IN A VIRUS FORM-- LOOKED LIKE MOLD MADE OUT OF A SCOURING PAD, ACTUALLY--
--IT'S THE ONLY THING THAT CAN KEEP HIM ALIVE, EVEN THOUGH IT COULD ALSO KILL HIM--
--SO I CAME TO HIRE YOU--TO FIGURE OUT HOW TO DO ALL THIS-- YOU KNOW, LIKE A REALLY, REALLY BIG PROBLEM THAT NEEDS FIXING--
--AND YOU SORTA HAVE TO GIVE ME AN ANSWER NOW...

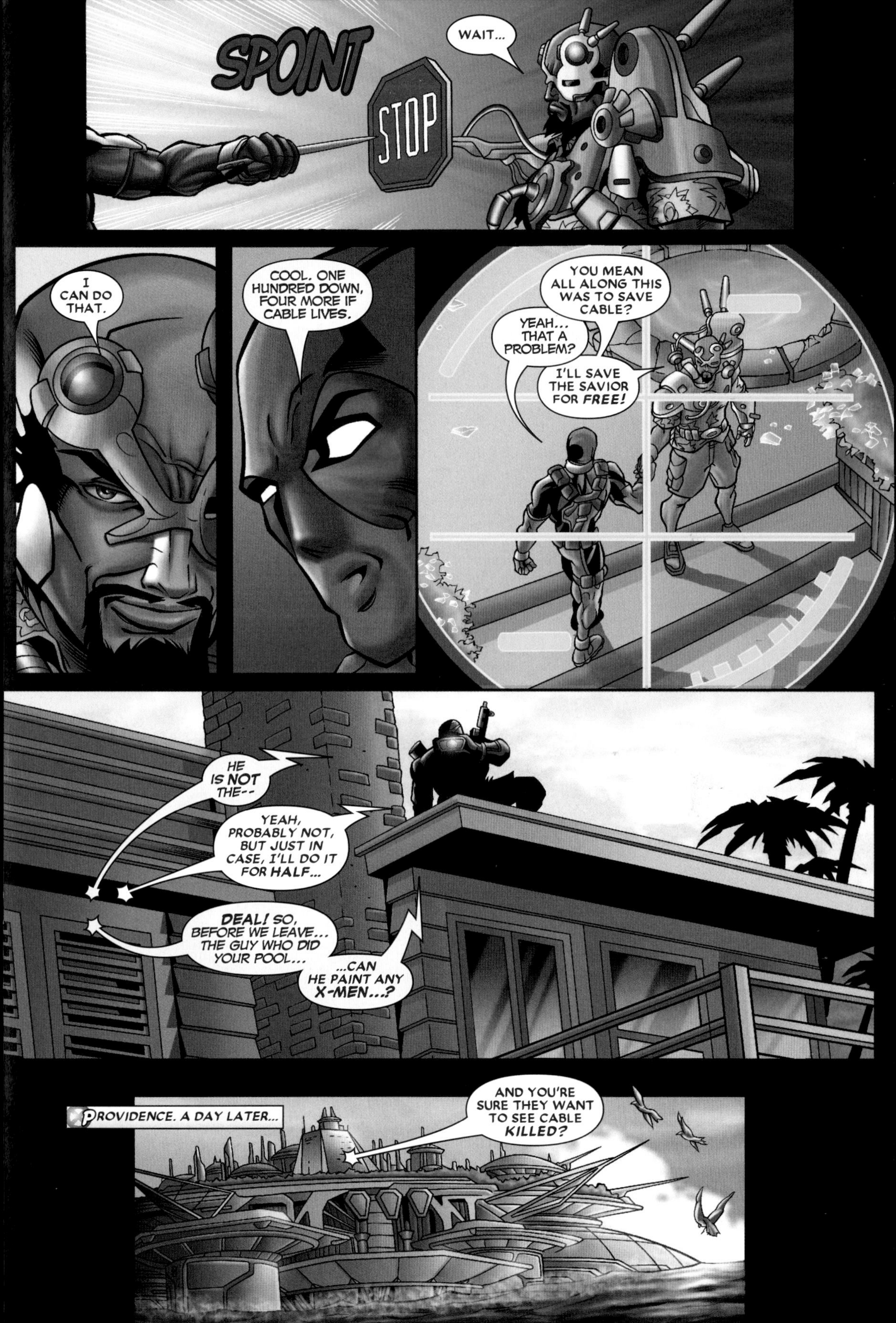
SPOINT
STOP
WAIT...
I CAN DO THAT.
COOL. ONE HUNDRED DOWN, FOUR MORE IF CABLE LIVES.
YOU MEAN ALL ALONG THIS WAS TO SAVE CABLE?
YEAH... THAT A PROBLEM?
I'LL SAVE THE SAVIOR FOR FREE!
HE IS NOT THE--
YEAH, PROBABLY NOT, BUT JUST IN CASE, I'LL DO IT FOR HALF...
DEAL! SO, BEFORE WE LEAVE... THE GUY WHO DID YOUR POOL...
...CAN HE PAINT ANY X-MEN...?
PROVIDENCE. A DAY LATER...
AND YOU'RE SURE THEY WANT TO SEE CABLE KILLED?

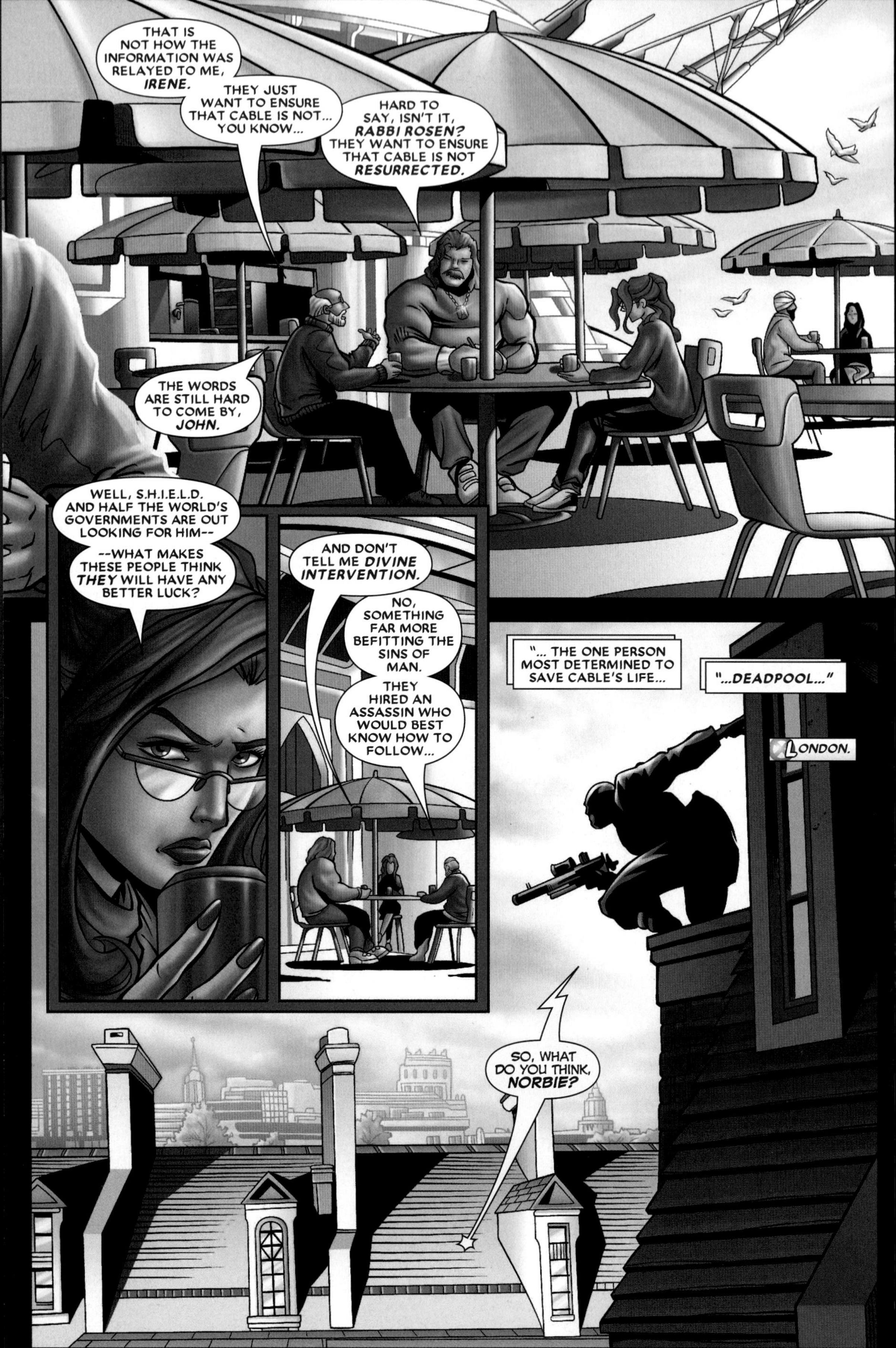
THAT IS NOT HOW THE INFORMATION WAS RELAYED TO ME, IRENE.
THEY JUST WANT TO ENSURE THAT CABLE IS NOT... YOU KNOW...
HARD TO SAY, ISN'T IT, RABBI ROSEN? THEY WANT TO ENSURE THAT CABLE IS NOT RESURRECTED.
THE WORDS ARE STILL HARD TO COME BY, JOHN.
WELL, S.H.I.E.L.D. AND HALF THE WORLD'S GOVERNMENTS ARE OUT LOOKING FOR HIM--
--WHAT MAKES THESE PEOPLE THINK THEY WILL HAVE ANY BETTER LUCK?
AND DON'T TELL ME DIVINE INTERVENTION.
NO, SOMETHING FAR MORE BEFITTING THE SINS OF MAN.
THEY HIRED AN ASSASSIN WHO WOULD BEST KNOW HOW TO FOLLOW...
"... THE ONE PERSON MOST DETERMINED TO SAVE CABLE'S LIFE...
"...DEADPOOL..."
LONDON.
SO, WHAT DO YOU THINK, NORBIE?

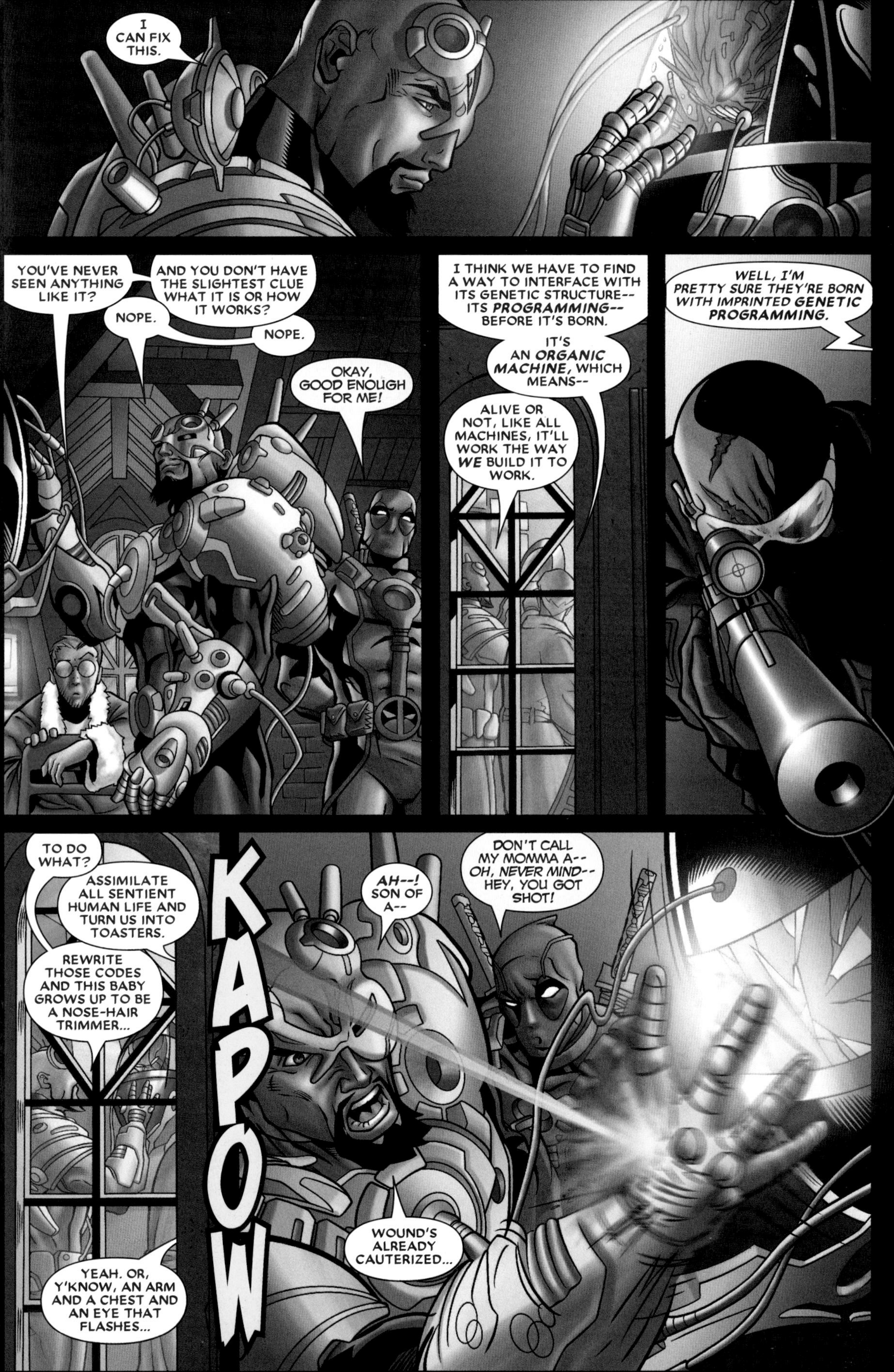
I CAN FIX THIS.
YOU'VE NEVER SEEN ANYTHING LIKE IT?
AND YOU DON'T HAVE THE SLIGHTEST CLUE WHAT IT IS OR HOW IT WORKS?
NOPE.
NOPE.
OKAY, GOOD ENOUGH FOR ME!
I THINK WE HAVE TO FIND A WAY TO INTERFACE WITH ITS GENETIC STRUCTURE-- ITS PROGRAMMING-- BEFORE IT'S BORN.
IT'S AN ORGANIC MACHINE, WHICH MEANS--
ALIVE OR NOT, LIKE ALL MACHINES, IT'LL WORK THE WAY WE BUILD IT TO WORK.
WELL, I'M PRETTY SURE THEY'RE BORN WITH IMPRINTED GENETIC PROGRAMMING.
TO DO WHAT?
ASSIMILATE ALL SENTIENT HUMAN LIFE AND TURN US INTO TOASTERS.
REWRITE THOSE CODES AND THIS BABY GROWS UP TO BE A NOSE-HAIR TRIMMER...
YEAH. OR, Y'KNOW, AN ARM AND A CHEST AND AN EYE THAT FLASHES...
KAPOW
AH--! SON OF A--
DON'T CALL MY MOMMA A-- OH, NEVER MIND-- HEY, YOU GOT SHOT!
WOUND'S ALREADY CAUTERIZED...

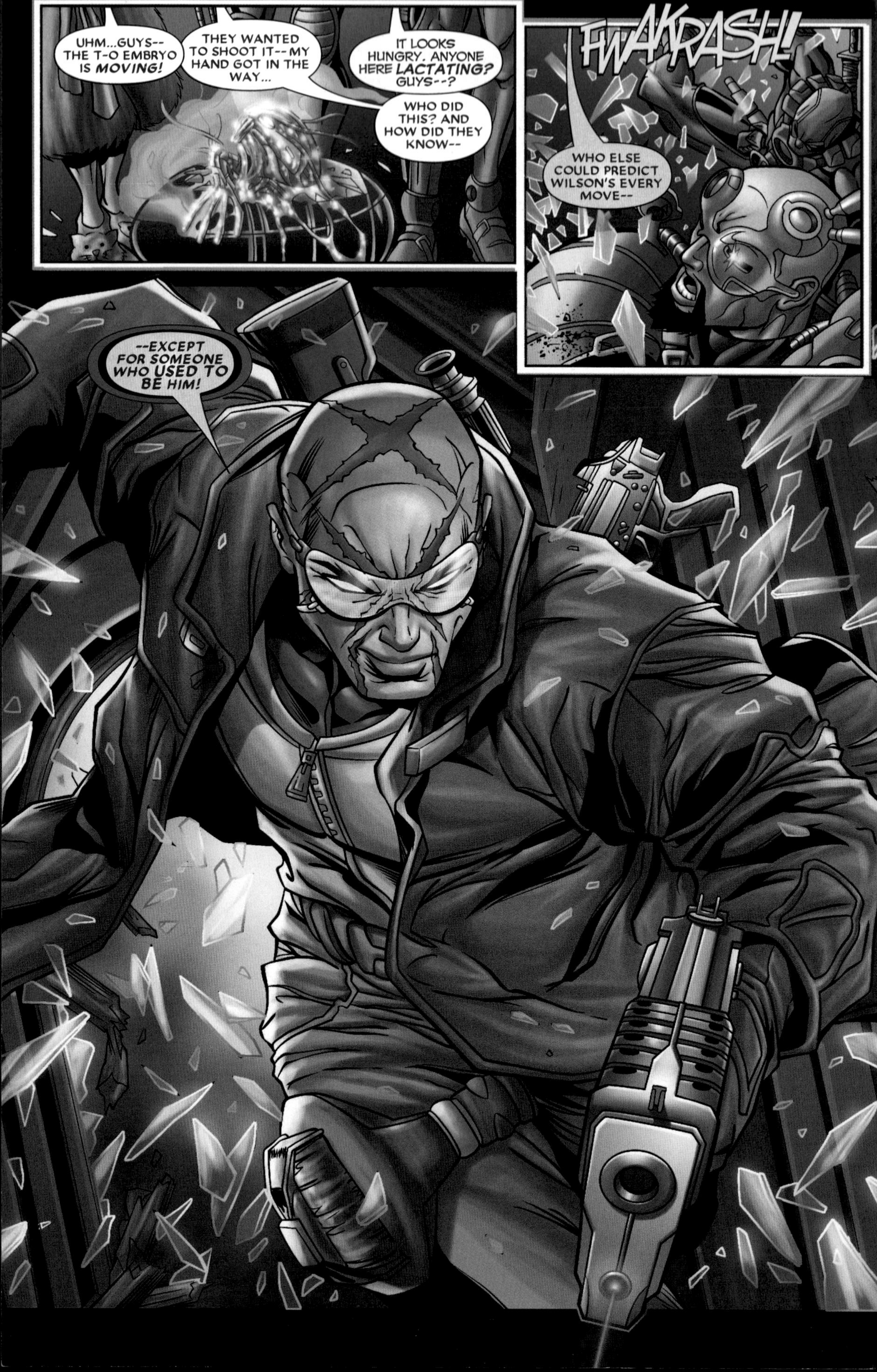
UHM...GUYS-- THE T-O EMBRYO IS MOVING!
THEY WANTED TO SHOOT IT-- MY HAND GOT IN THE WAY...
IT LOOKS HUNGRY. ANYONE HERE LACTATING? GUYS--?
WHO DID THIS? AND HOW DID THEY KNOW--
FWAKRASH!
WHO ELSE COULD PREDICT WILSON'S EVERY MOVE--
--EXCEPT FOR SOMEONE WHO USED TO BE HIM!

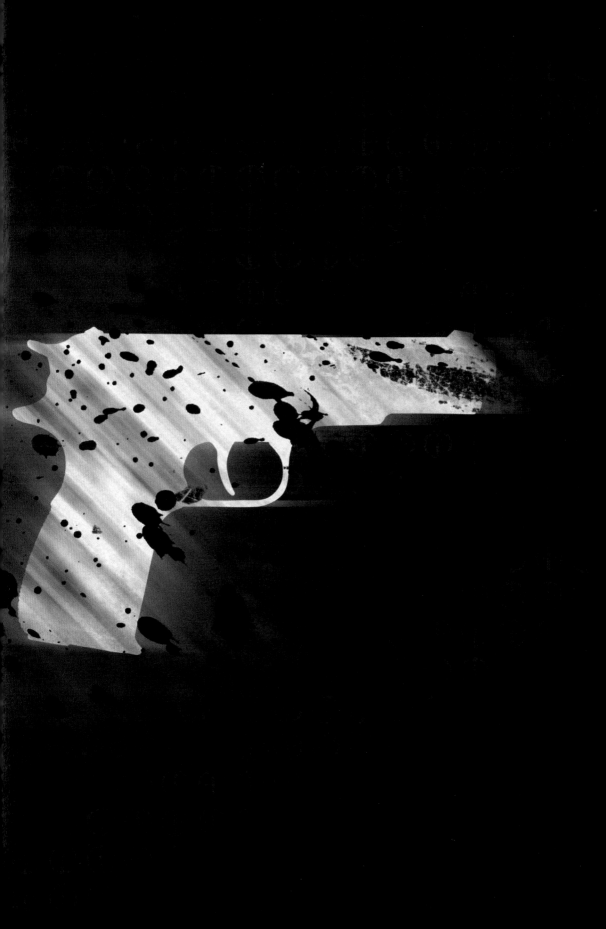

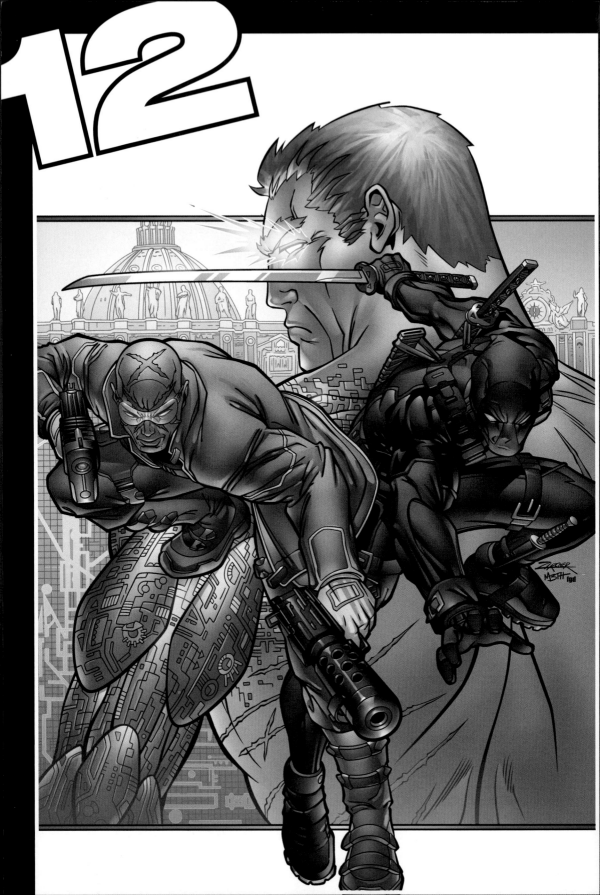

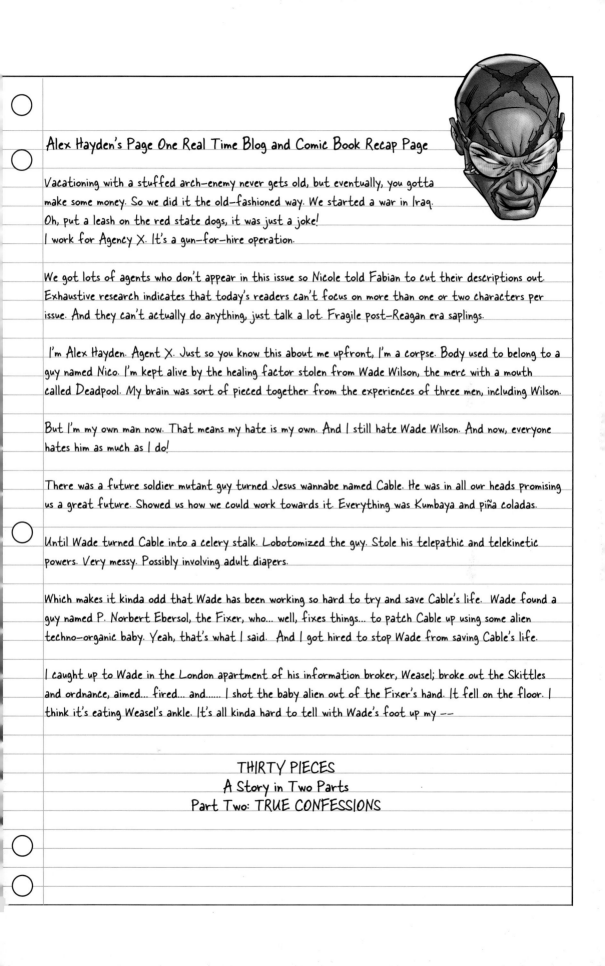

Alex Hayden's Page One Real Time Blog and Comic Book Recap Page

Vacationing with a stuffed arch-enemy never gets old, but eventually, you gotta make some money. So we did it the old-fashioned way. We started a war in Iraq. Oh, put a leash on the red state dogs, it was just a joke!
I work for Agency X. It's a gun-for-hire operation.

We got lots of agents who don't appear in this issue so Nicole told Fabian to cut their descriptions out. Exhaustive research indicates that today's readers can't focus on more than one or two characters per issue. And they can't actually do anything, just talk a lot. Fragile post-Reagan era saplings.

I'm Alex Hayden. Agent X. Just so you know this about me upfront, I'm a corpse. Body used to belong to a guy named Nico. I'm kept alive by the healing factor stolen from Wade Wilson, the merc with a mouth called Deadpool. My brain was sort of pieced together from the experiences of three men, including Wilson.

But I'm my own man now. That means my hate is my own. And I still hate Wade Wilson. And now, everyone hates him as much as I do!

There was a future soldier mutant guy turned Jesus wannabe named Cable. He was in all our heads promising us a great future. Showed us how we could work towards it. Everything was Kumbaya and piña coladas.

Until Wade turned Cable into a celery stalk. Lobotomized the guy. Stole his telepathic and telekinetic powers. Very messy. Possibly involving adult diapers.

Which makes it kinda odd that Wade has been working so hard to try and save Cable's life. Wade found a guy named P. Norbert Ebersol, the Fixer, who... well, fixes things... to patch Cable up using some alien techno-organic baby. Yeah, that's what I said. And I got hired to stop Wade from saving Cable's life.

I caught up to Wade in the London apartment of his information broker, Weasel; broke out the Skittles and ordnance, aimed... fired... and...... I shot the baby alien out of the Fixer's hand. It fell on the floor. I think it's eating Weasel's ankle. It's all kinda hard to tell with Wade's foot up my --

THIRTY PIECES
A Story in Two Parts
Part Two: TRUE CONFESSIONS

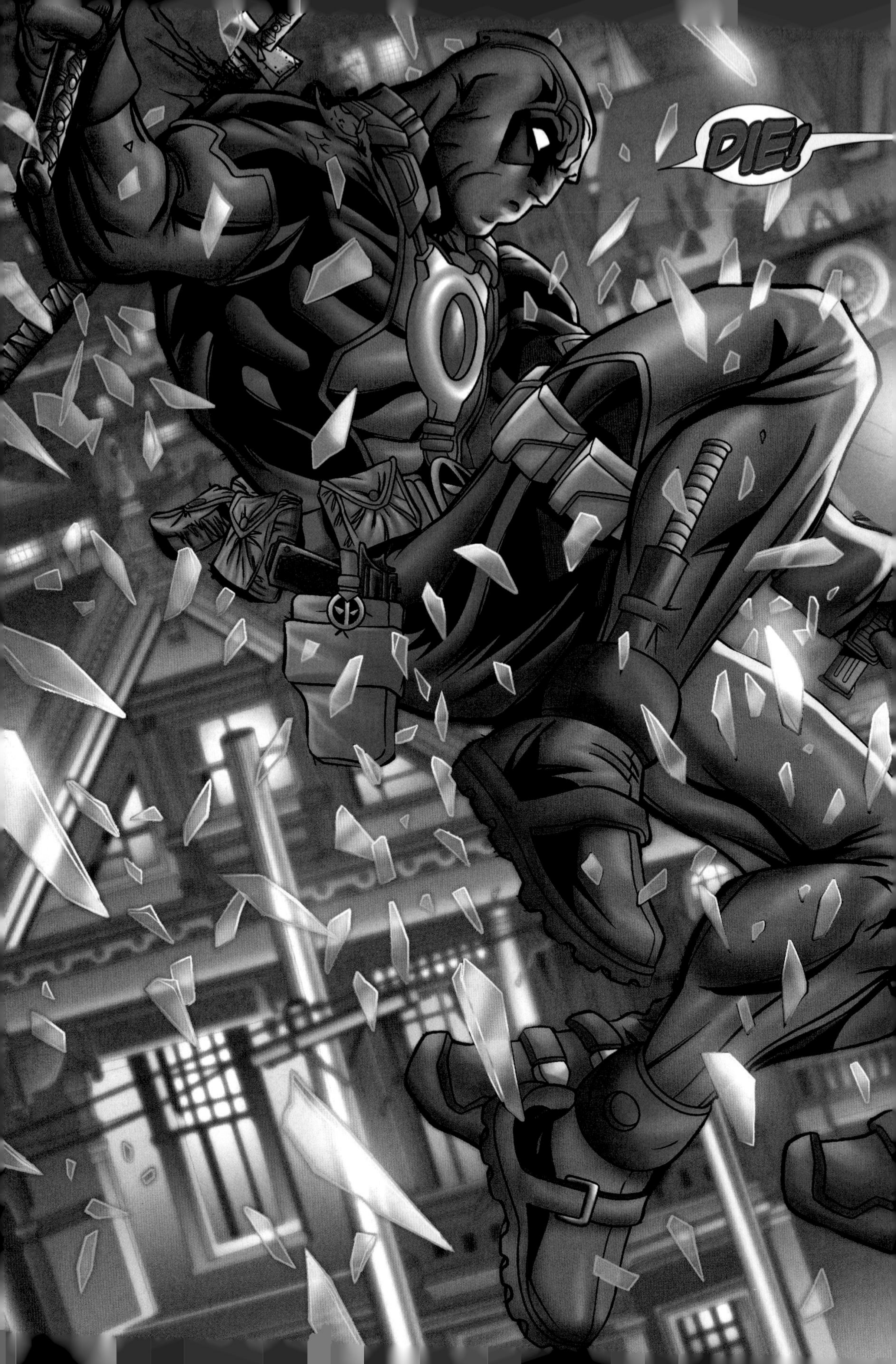
DIE!

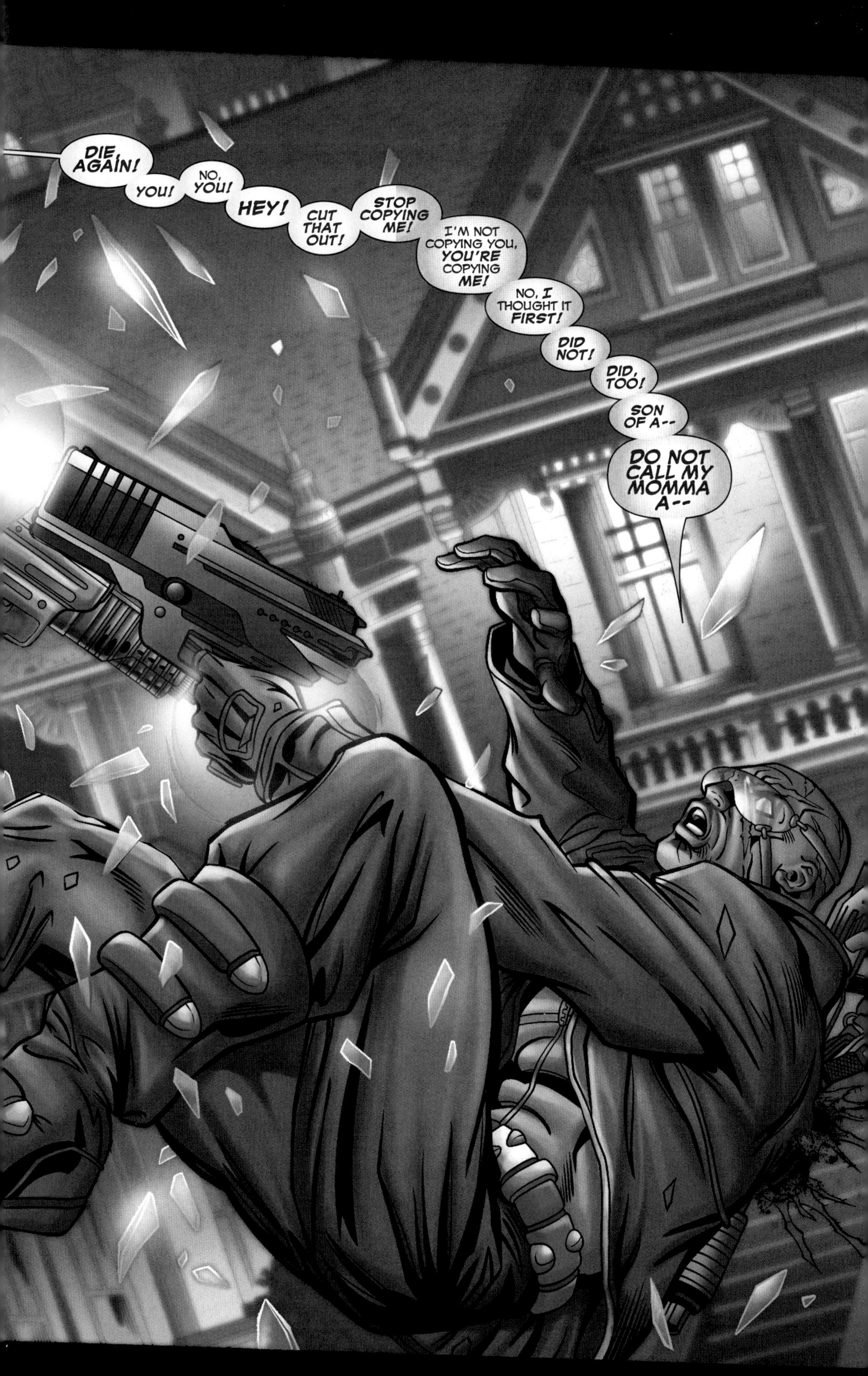
DIE, AGAIN!
YOU!
NO, YOU!
HEY!
CUT THAT OUT!
STOP COPYING ME!
I'M NOT COPYING YOU, YOU'RE COPYING ME!
NO, I THOUGHT IT FIRST!
DID NOT!
DID, TOO!
SON OF A--
DO NOT CALL MY MOMMA A--

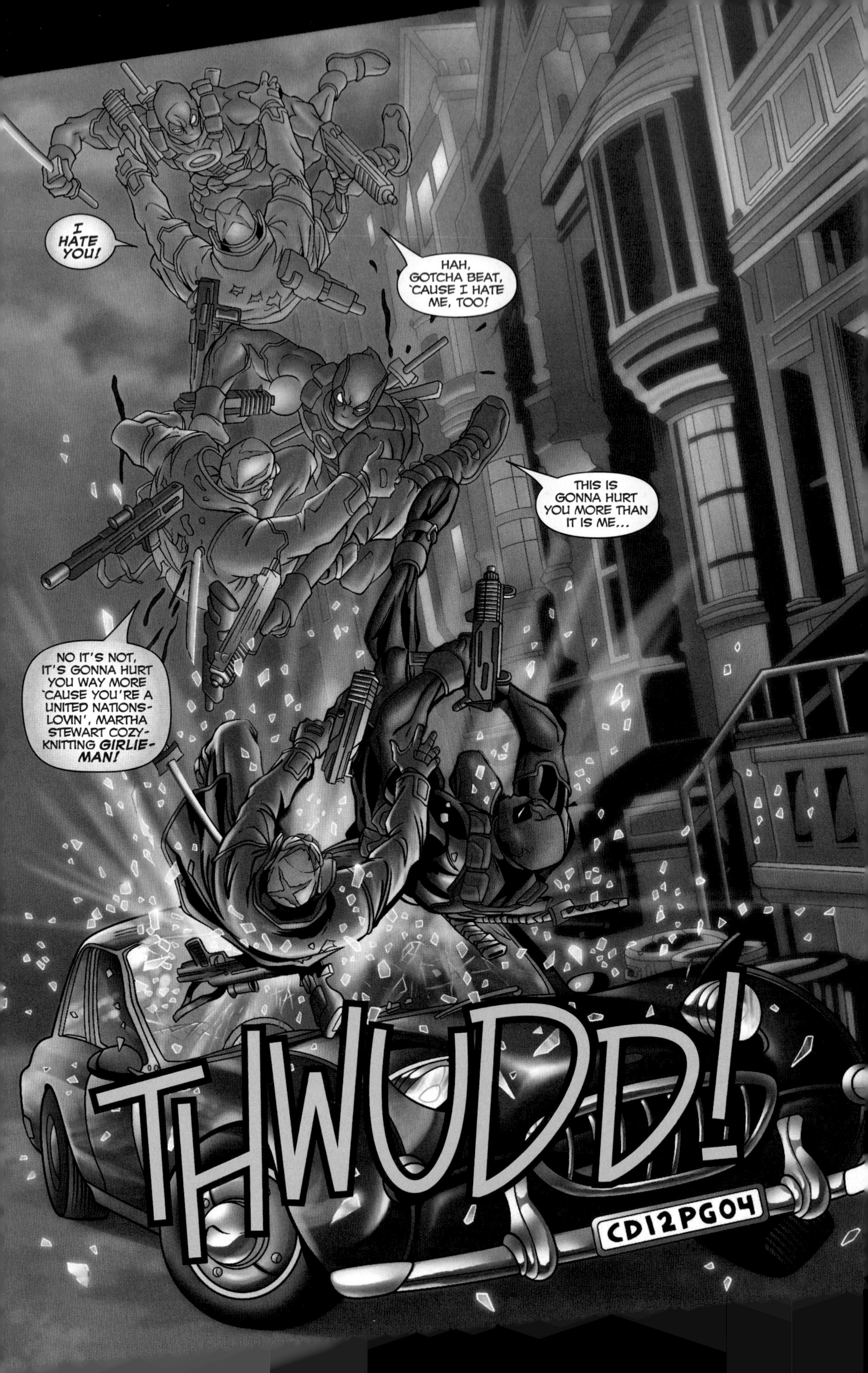
I HATE YOU!
HAH, GOTCHA BEAT, 'CAUSE I HATE ME, TOO!
THIS IS GONNA HURT YOU MORE THAN IT IS ME...
NO IT'S NOT, IT'S GONNA HURT YOU WAY MORE 'CAUSE YOU'RE A UNITED NATIONS-LOVIN', MARTHA STEWART COZY-KNITTING GIRLIE-MAN!
THWUDD!
CD12PG04

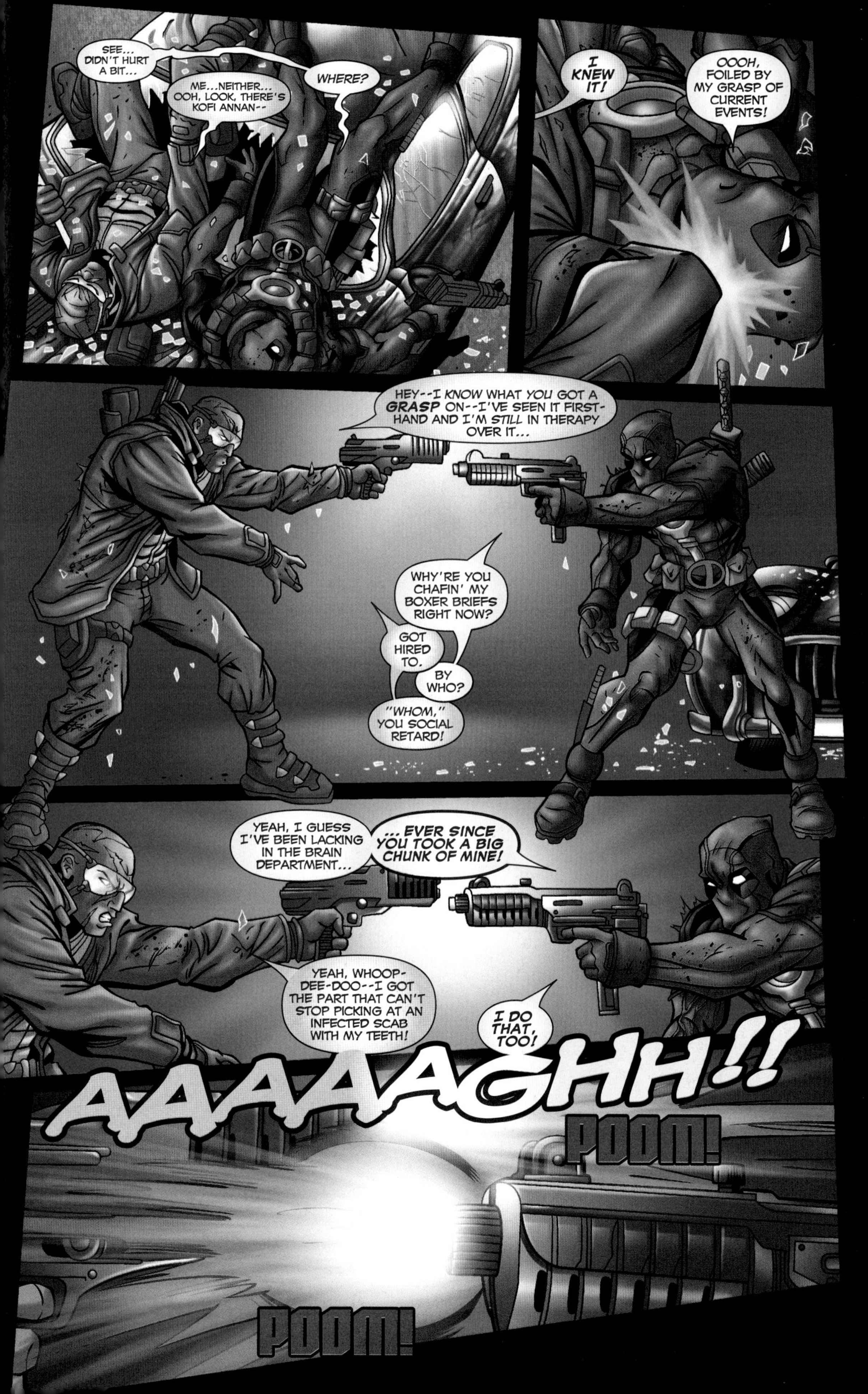
SEE... DIDN'T HURT A BIT...
ME...NEITHER... OOH, LOOK, THERE'S KOFI ANNAN--
WHERE?
I KNEW IT!
OOOH, FOILED BY MY GRASP OF CURRENT EVENTS!
HEY--I KNOW WHAT YOU GOT A GRASP ON--I'VE SEEN IT FIRST-HAND AND I'M STILL IN THERAPY OVER IT...
WHY'RE YOU CHAFIN' MY BOXER BRIEFS RIGHT NOW?
GOT HIRED TO.
BY WHO?
"WHOM," YOU SOCIAL RETARD!
YEAH, I GUESS I'VE BEEN LACKING IN THE BRAIN DEPARTMENT...
...EVER SINCE YOU TOOK A BIG CHUNK OF MINE!
YEAH, WHOOP-DEE-DOO--I GOT THE PART THAT CAN'T STOP PICKING AT AN INFECTED SCAB WITH MY TEETH!
I DO THAT, TOO!
AAAAAGHH!!
POOM!
POOM!

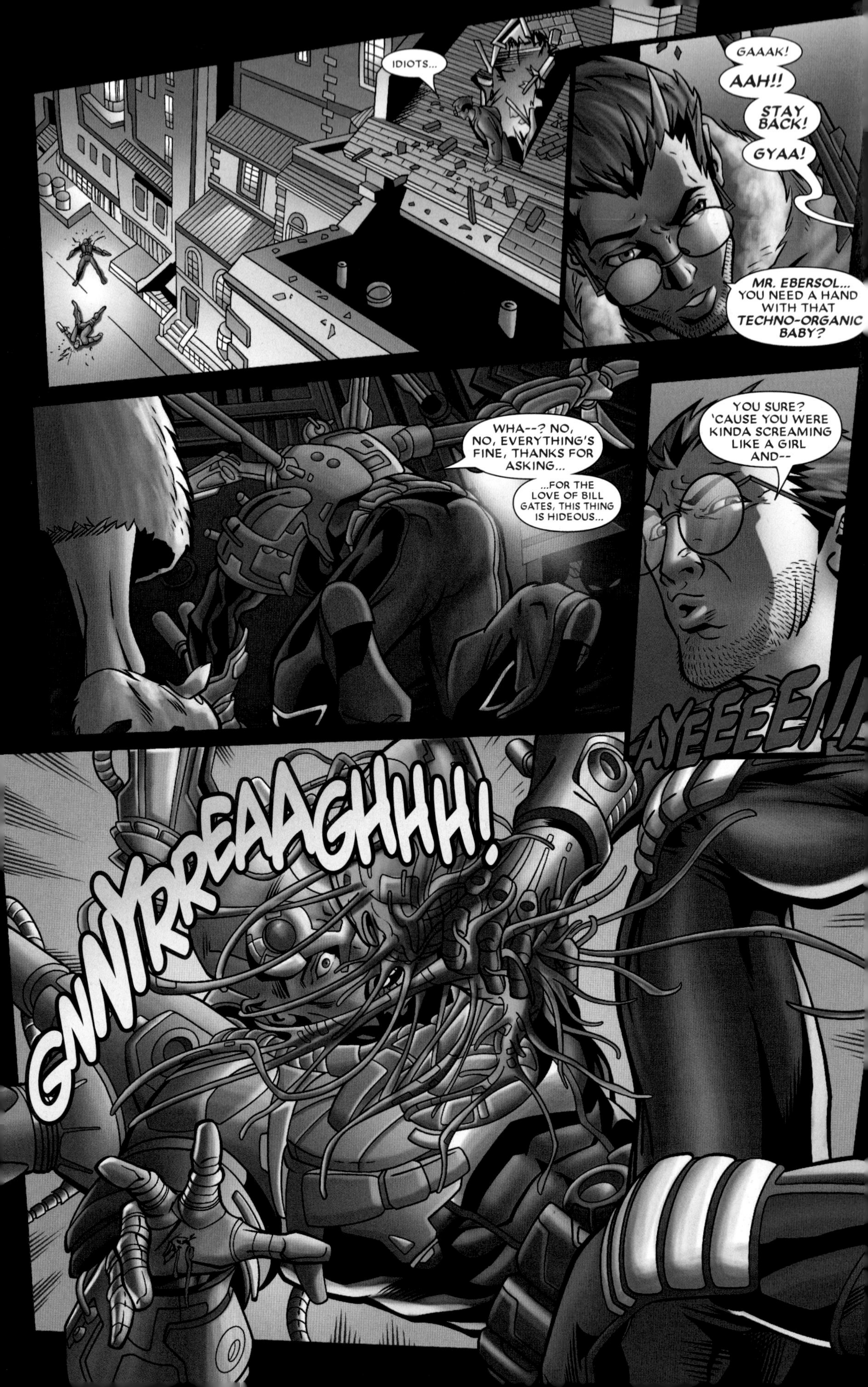
IDIOTS...
GAAAK!
AAH!!
STAY BACK!
GYAA!
MR. EBERSOL... YOU NEED A HAND WITH THAT TECHNO-ORGANIC BABY?
WHA--? NO, NO, EVERYTHING'S FINE, THANKS FOR ASKING...
...FOR THE LOVE OF BILL GATES, THIS THING IS HIDEOUS...
YOU SURE? 'CAUSE YOU WERE KINDA SCREAMING LIKE A GIRL AND--
AYEEEEE!!
GNNYRREAAGHHH!

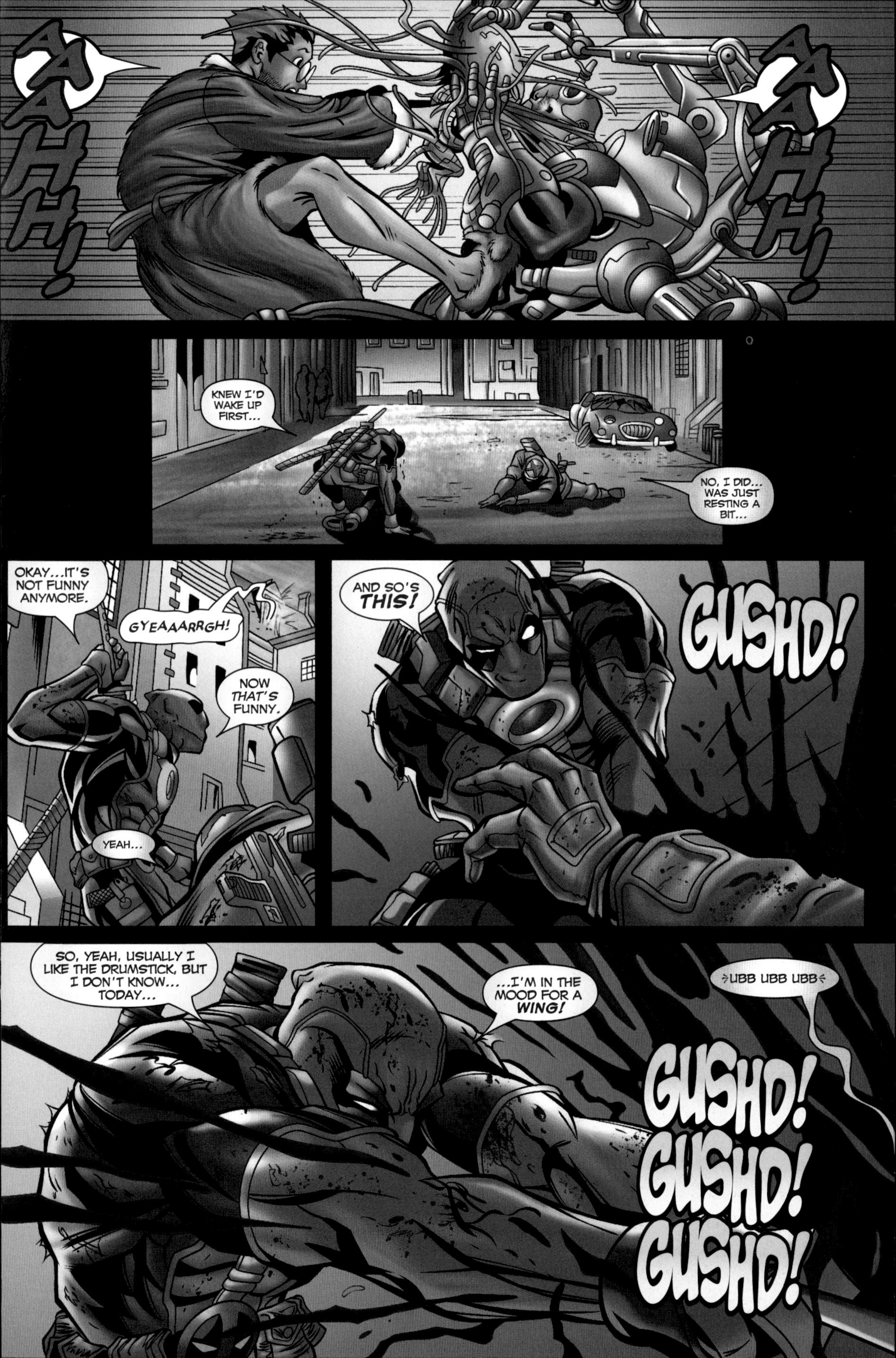
AAAHH!
AAAHH!
KNEW I'D WAKE UP FIRST...
NO, I DID... WAS JUST RESTING A BIT...
OKAY...IT'S NOT FUNNY ANYMORE.
GYEAAARRGH!
NOW THAT'S FUNNY.
YEAH...
AND SO'S THIS!
GUSHD!
SO, YEAH, USUALLY I LIKE THE DRUMSTICK, BUT I DON'T KNOW... TODAY...
...I'M IN THE MOOD FOR A WING!
UBB UBB UBB
GUSHD! GUSHD! GUSHD!

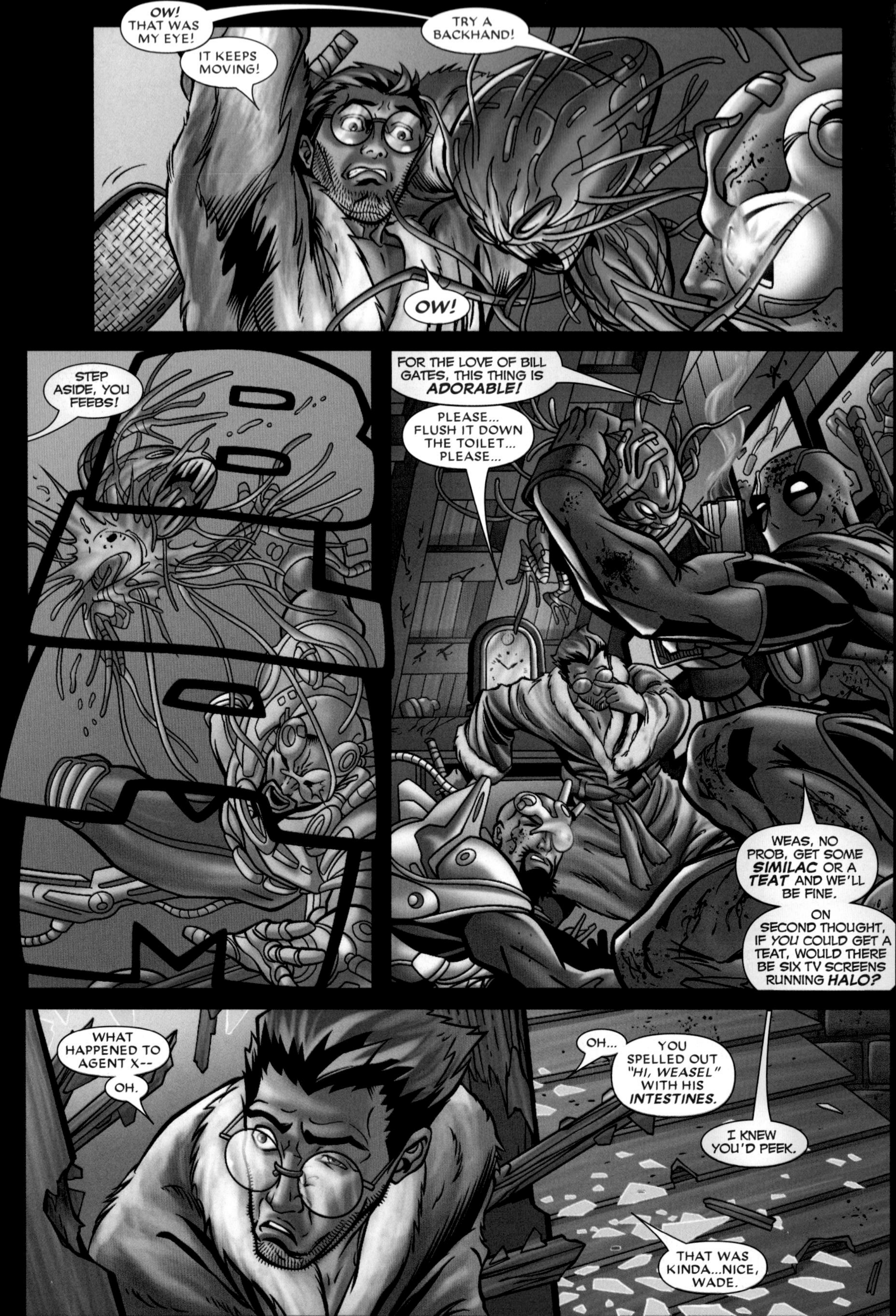

OW! THAT WAS MY EYE!
IT KEEPS MOVING!
TRY A BACKHAND!
OW!
STEP ASIDE, YOU FEEBS!
FOR THE LOVE OF BILL GATES, THIS THING IS ADORABLE!
PLEASE... FLUSH IT DOWN THE TOILET... PLEASE...
WEAS, NO PROB, GET SOME SIMILAC OR A TEAT AND WE'LL BE FINE.
ON SECOND THOUGHT, IF YOU COULD GET A TEAT, WOULD THERE BE SIX TV SCREENS RUNNING HALO?
WHAT HAPPENED TO AGENT X--
OH.
OH...
YOU SPELLED OUT "HI, WEASEL" WITH HIS INTESTINES.
I KNEW YOU'D PEEK.
THAT WAS KINDA...NICE, WADE.

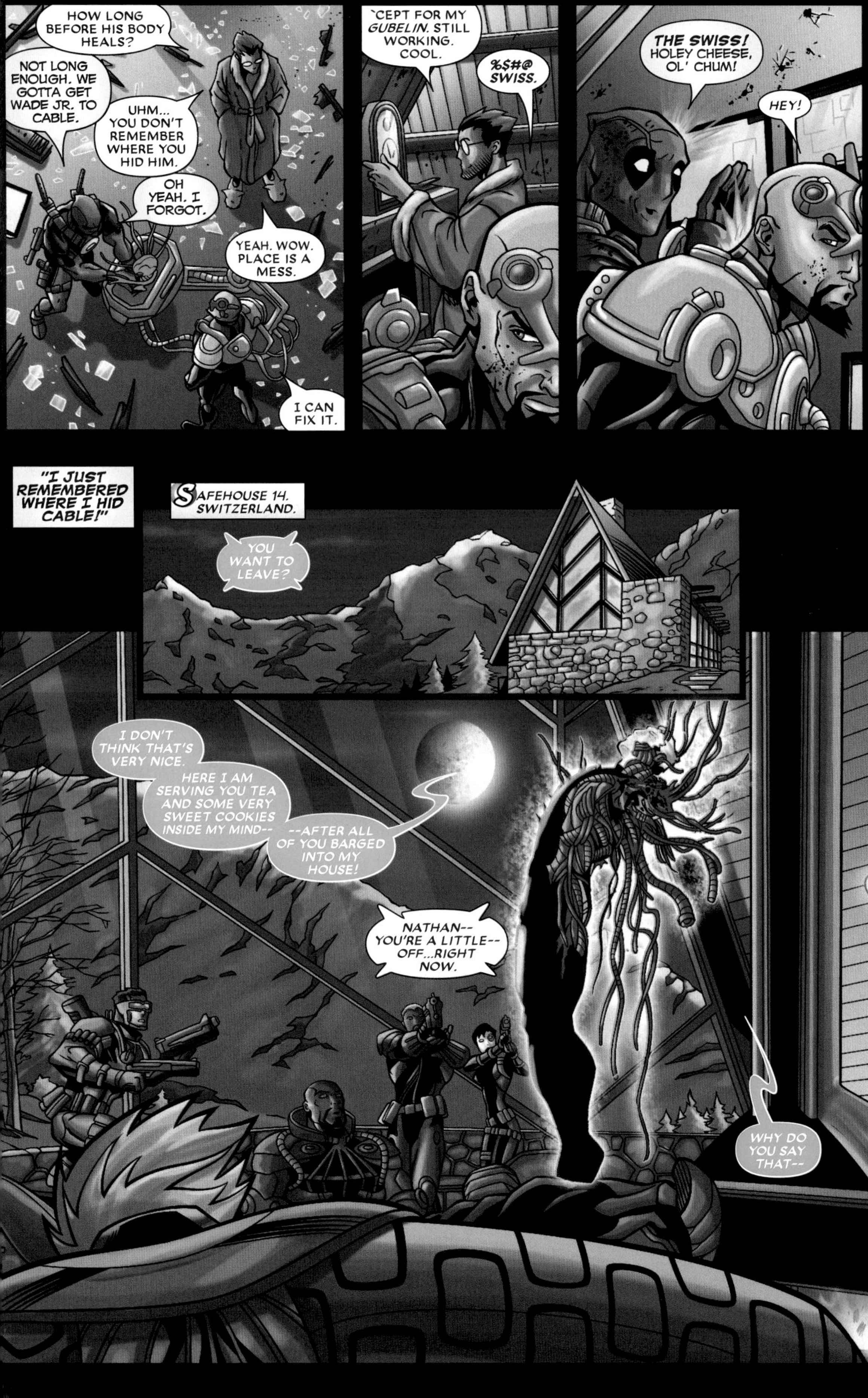
HOW LONG BEFORE HIS BODY HEALS?
NOT LONG ENOUGH. WE GOTTA GET WADE JR. TO CABLE.
UHM... YOU DON'T REMEMBER WHERE YOU HID HIM.
OH YEAH. I FORGOT.
YEAH. WOW. PLACE IS A MESS.
I CAN FIX IT.
`CEPT FOR MY GUBELIN. STILL WORKING. COOL.
%$#@ SWISS.
THE SWISS! HOLEY CHEESE, OL' CHUM!
HEY!
"I JUST REMEMBERED WHERE I HID CABLE!"
SAFEHOUSE 14. SWITZERLAND.
YOU WANT TO LEAVE?
I DON'T THINK THAT'S VERY NICE.
HERE I AM SERVING YOU TEA AND SOME VERY SWEET COOKIES INSIDE MY MIND--
--AFTER ALL OF YOU BARGED INTO MY HOUSE!
NATHAN-- YOU'RE A LITTLE-- OFF...RIGHT NOW.
WHY DO YOU SAY THAT--

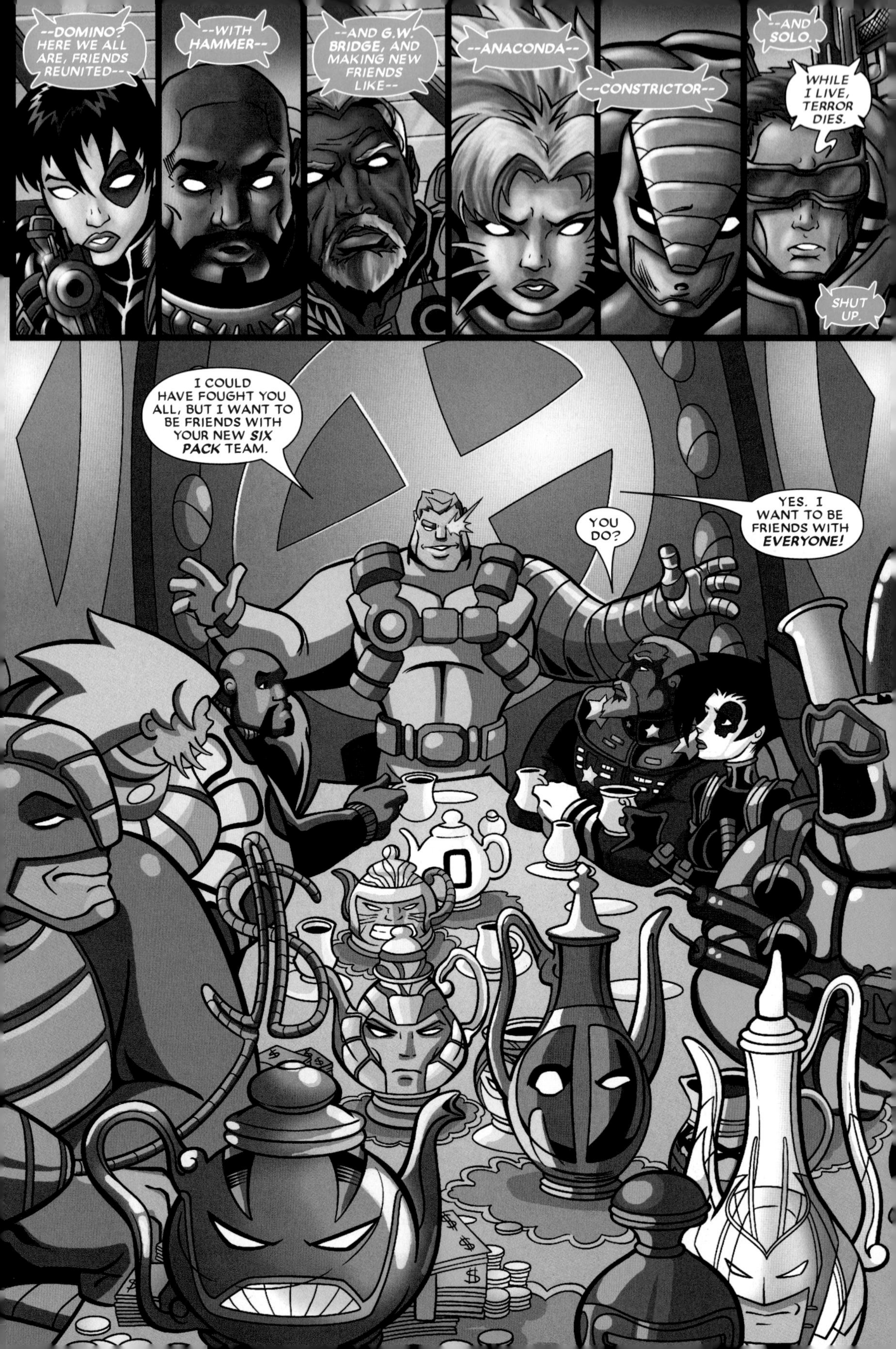
--DOMINO? HERE WE ALL ARE, FRIENDS REUNITED--
--WITH HAMMER--
--AND G.W. BRIDGE, AND MAKING NEW FRIENDS LIKE--
--ANACONDA--
--CONSTRICTOR--
--AND SOLO.
WHILE I LIVE, TERROR DIES.
SHUT UP.
I COULD HAVE FOUGHT YOU ALL, BUT I WANT TO BE FRIENDS WITH YOUR NEW SIX PACK TEAM.
YOU DO?
YES. I WANT TO BE FRIENDS WITH EVERYONE!

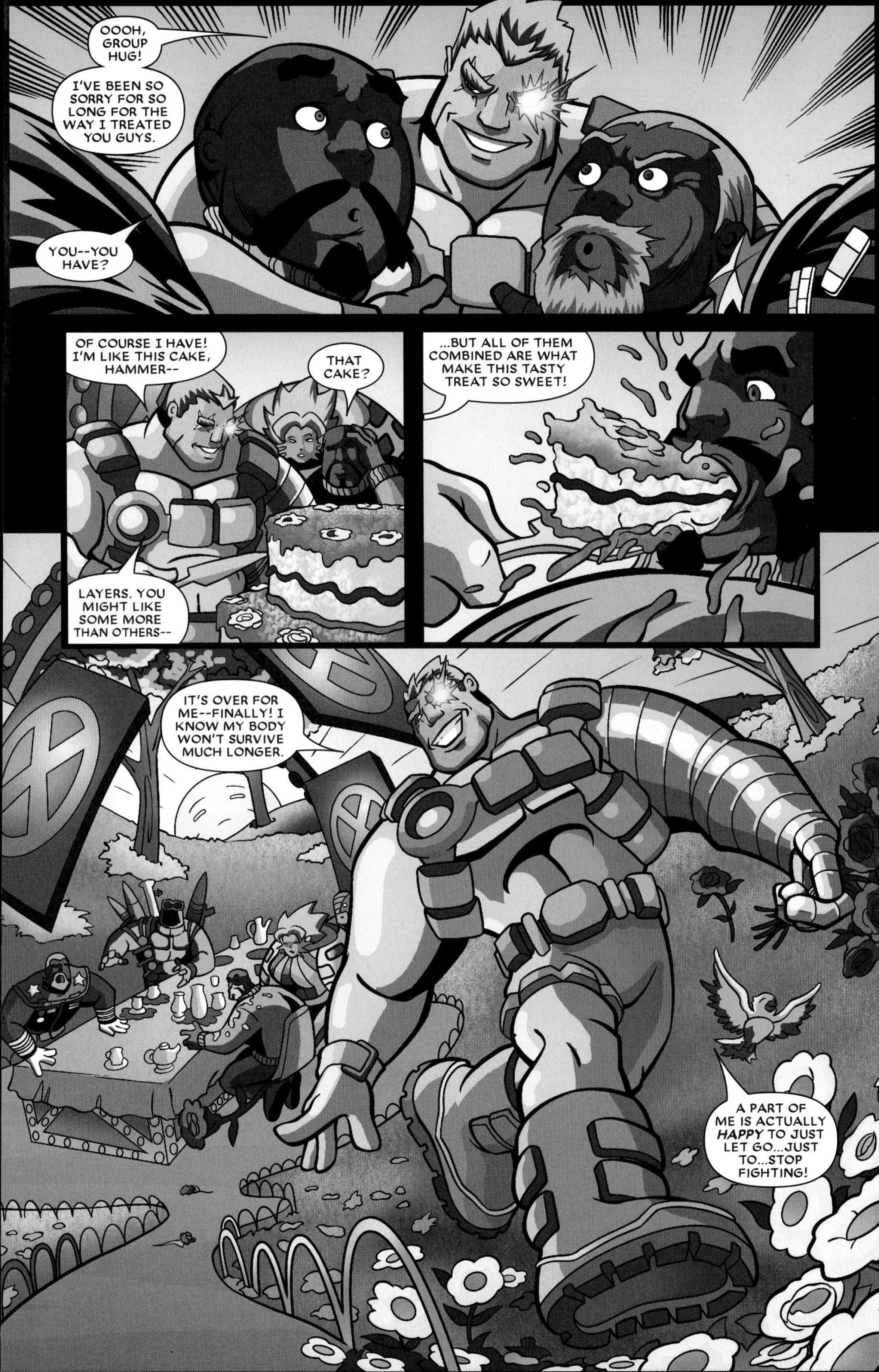
OOOH, GROUP HUG!
I'VE BEEN SO SORRY FOR SO LONG FOR THE WAY I TREATED YOU GUYS.
YOU--YOU HAVE?
OF COURSE I HAVE! I'M LIKE THIS CAKE, HAMMER--
THAT CAKE?
LAYERS. YOU MIGHT LIKE SOME MORE THAN OTHERS--
...BUT ALL OF THEM COMBINED ARE WHAT MAKE THIS TASTY TREAT SO SWEET!
IT'S OVER FOR ME--FINALLY! I KNOW MY BODY WON'T SURVIVE MUCH LONGER.
A PART OF ME IS ACTUALLY *HAPPY* TO JUST LET GO...JUST TO...STOP FIGHTING!

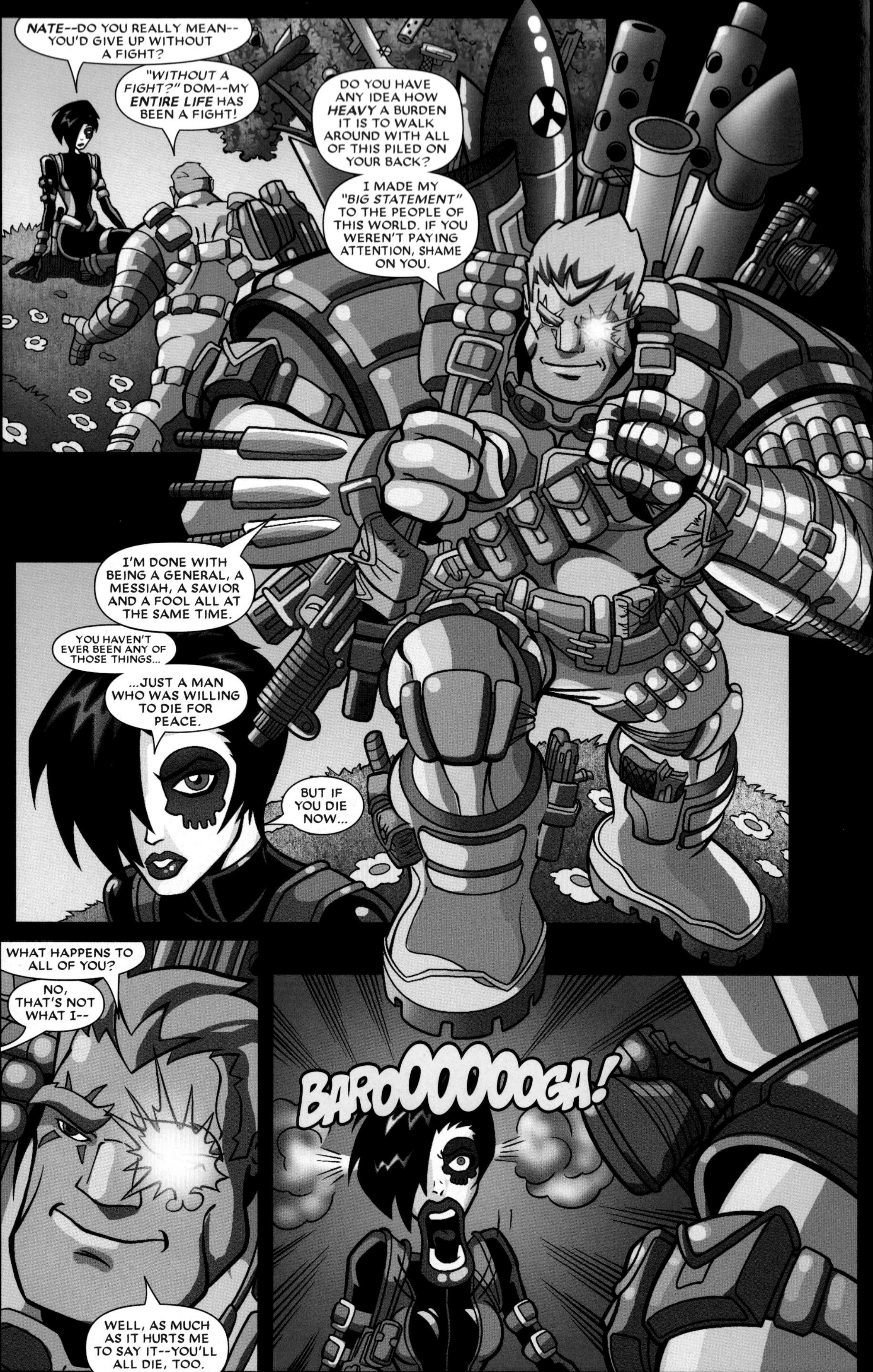
NATE--DO YOU REALLY MEAN-- YOU'D GIVE UP WITHOUT A FIGHT?
"WITHOUT A FIGHT?" DOM--MY ENTIRE LIFE HAS BEEN A FIGHT!
DO YOU HAVE ANY IDEA HOW HEAVY A BURDEN IT IS TO WALK AROUND WITH ALL OF THIS PILED ON YOUR BACK?
I MADE MY "BIG STATEMENT" TO THE PEOPLE OF THIS WORLD. IF YOU WEREN'T PAYING ATTENTION, SHAME ON YOU.
I'M DONE WITH BEING A GENERAL, A MESSIAH, A SAVIOR AND A FOOL ALL AT THE SAME TIME.
YOU HAVEN'T EVER BEEN ANY OF THOSE THINGS...
...JUST A MAN WHO WAS WILLING TO DIE FOR PEACE.
BUT IF YOU DIE NOW...
WHAT HAPPENS TO ALL OF YOU?
NO, THAT'S NOT WHAT I--
WELL, AS MUCH AS IT HURTS ME TO SAY IT--YOU'LL ALL DIE, TOO.
BAROOOOOOGA!

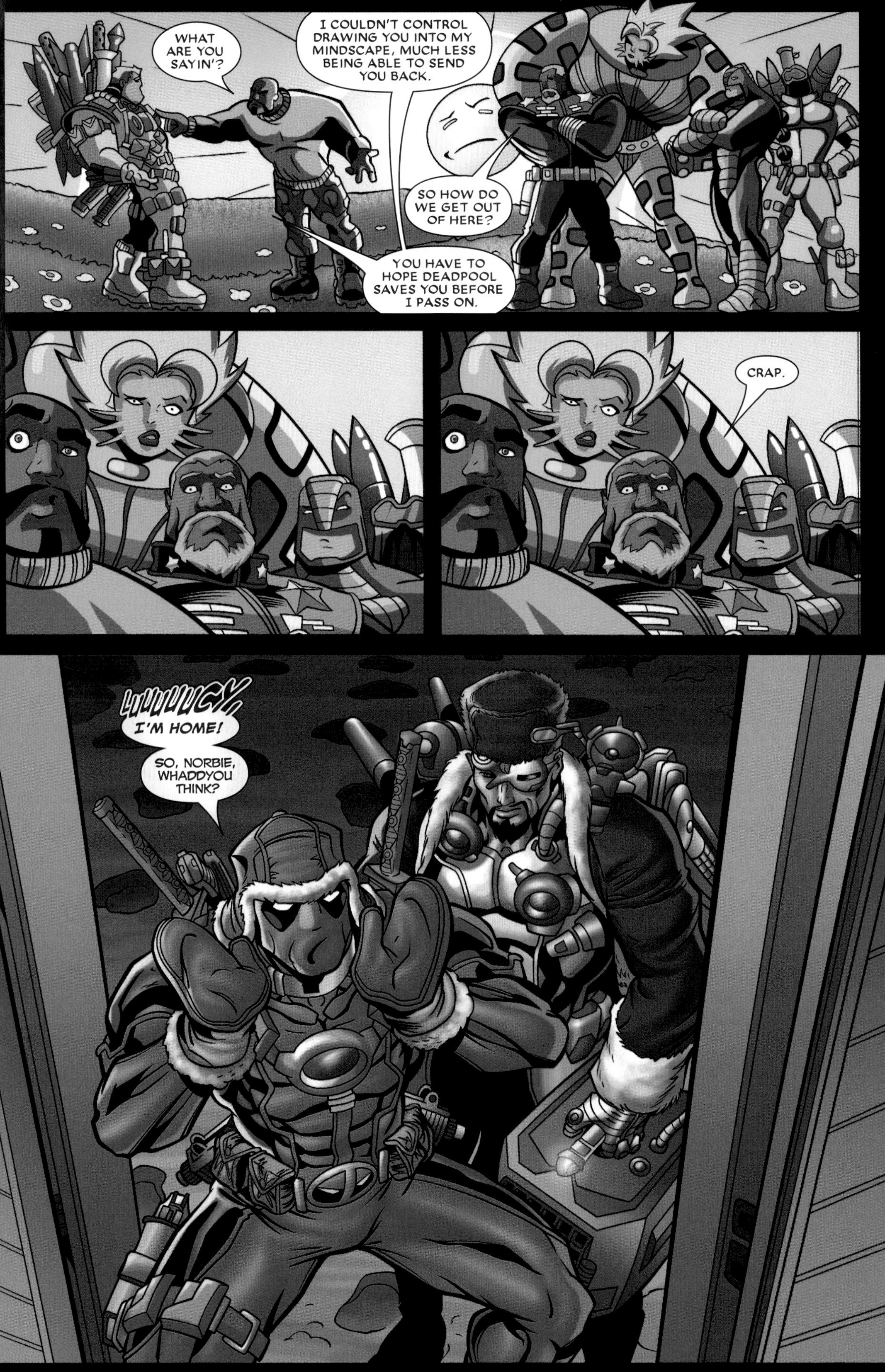

WHAT ARE YOU SAYIN'?
I COULDN'T CONTROL DRAWING YOU INTO MY MINDSCAPE, MUCH LESS BEING ABLE TO SEND YOU BACK.
SO HOW DO WE GET OUT OF HERE?
YOU HAVE TO HOPE DEADPOOL SAVES YOU BEFORE I PASS ON.
CRAP.
LUUUUUCY, I'M HOME!
SO, NORBIE, WHADDYOU THINK?

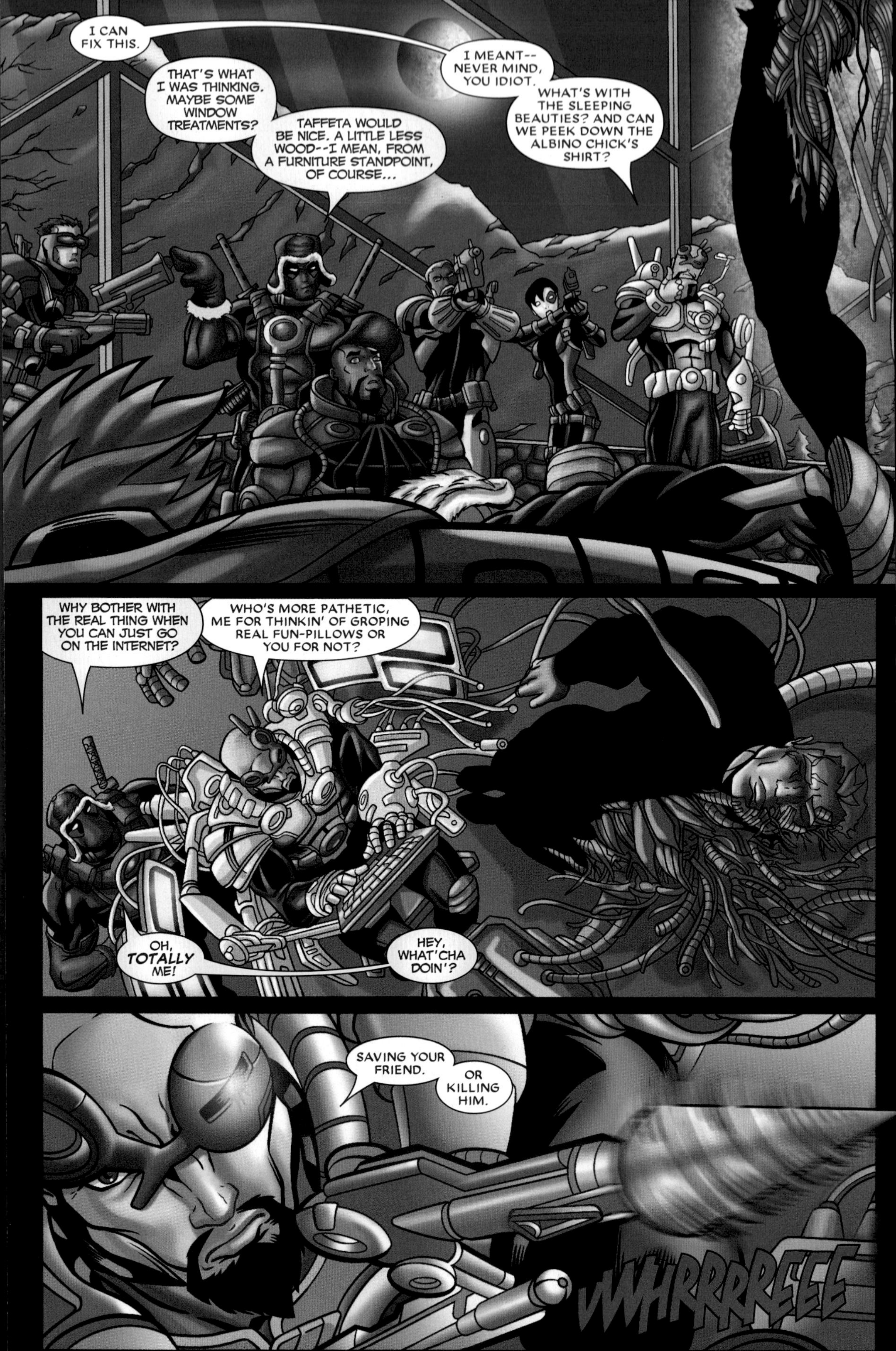
I CAN FIX THIS.
THAT'S WHAT I WAS THINKING. MAYBE SOME WINDOW TREATMENTS?
TAFFETA WOULD BE NICE. A LITTLE LESS WOOD--I MEAN, FROM A FURNITURE STANDPOINT, OF COURSE...
I MEANT-- NEVER MIND, YOU IDIOT.
WHAT'S WITH THE SLEEPING BEAUTIES? AND CAN WE PEEK DOWN THE ALBINO CHICK'S SHIRT?
WHY BOTHER WITH THE REAL THING WHEN YOU CAN JUST GO ON THE INTERNET?
WHO'S MORE PATHETIC, ME FOR THINKIN' OF GROPING REAL FUN-PILLOWS OR YOU FOR NOT?
OH, *TOTALLY* ME!
HEY, WHAT'CHA DOIN'?
SAVING YOUR FRIEND.
OR KILLING HIM.
VWHRRRREEE

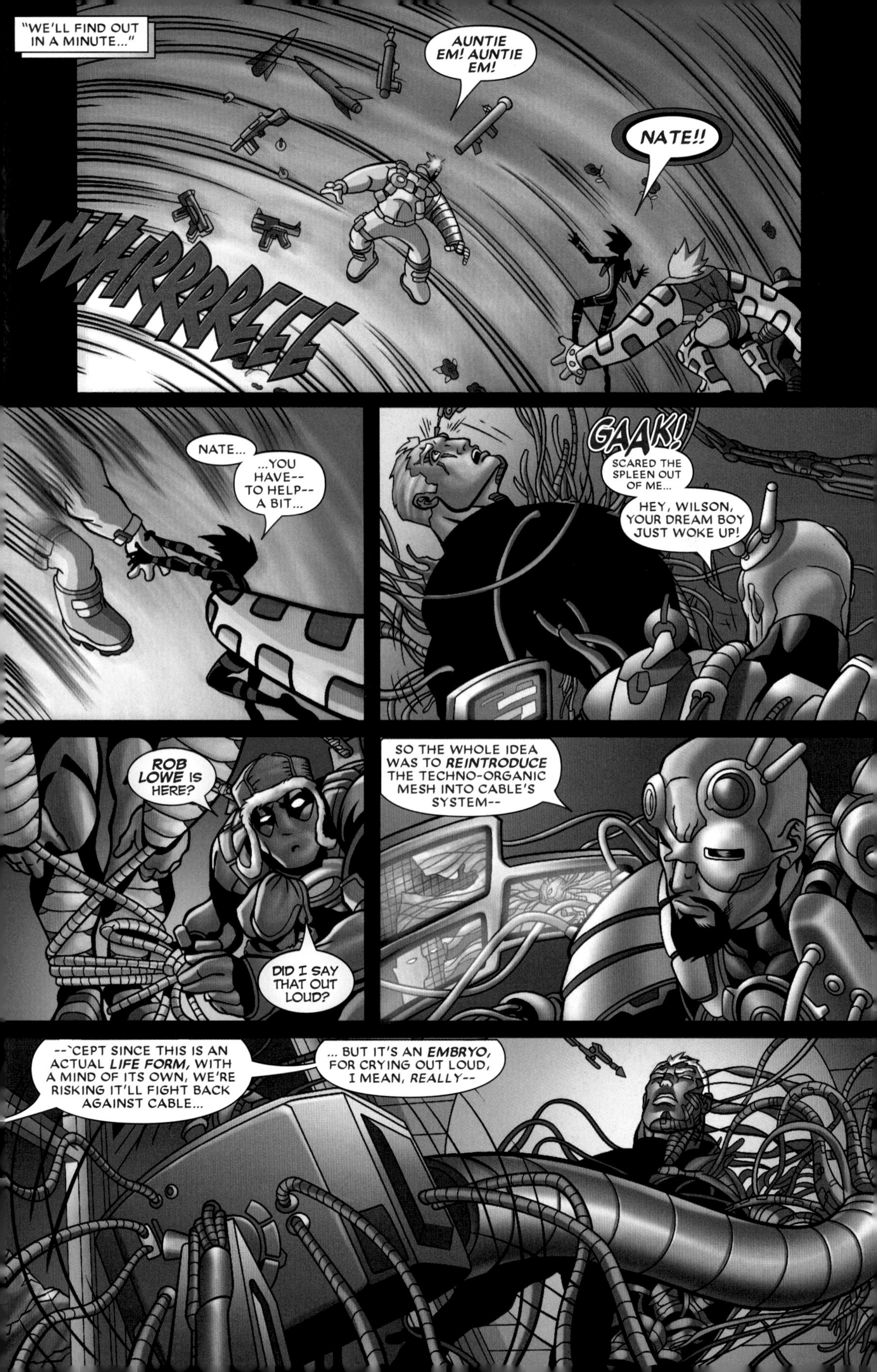
"WE'LL FIND OUT IN A MINUTE..."
AUNTIE EM! AUNTIE EM!
NATE!!
VVWHRRRREEE
NATE...
...YOU HAVE-- TO HELP-- A BIT...
GAAK!
SCARED THE SPLEEN OUT OF ME...
HEY, WILSON, YOUR DREAM BOY JUST WOKE UP!
ROB LOWE IS HERE?
DID I SAY THAT OUT LOUD?
SO THE WHOLE IDEA WAS TO REINTRODUCE THE TECHNO-ORGANIC MESH INTO CABLE'S SYSTEM--
--`CEPT SINCE THIS IS AN ACTUAL LIFE FORM, WITH A MIND OF ITS OWN, WE'RE RISKING IT'LL FIGHT BACK AGAINST CABLE...
... BUT IT'S AN EMBRYO, FOR CRYING OUT LOUD, I MEAN, REALLY--

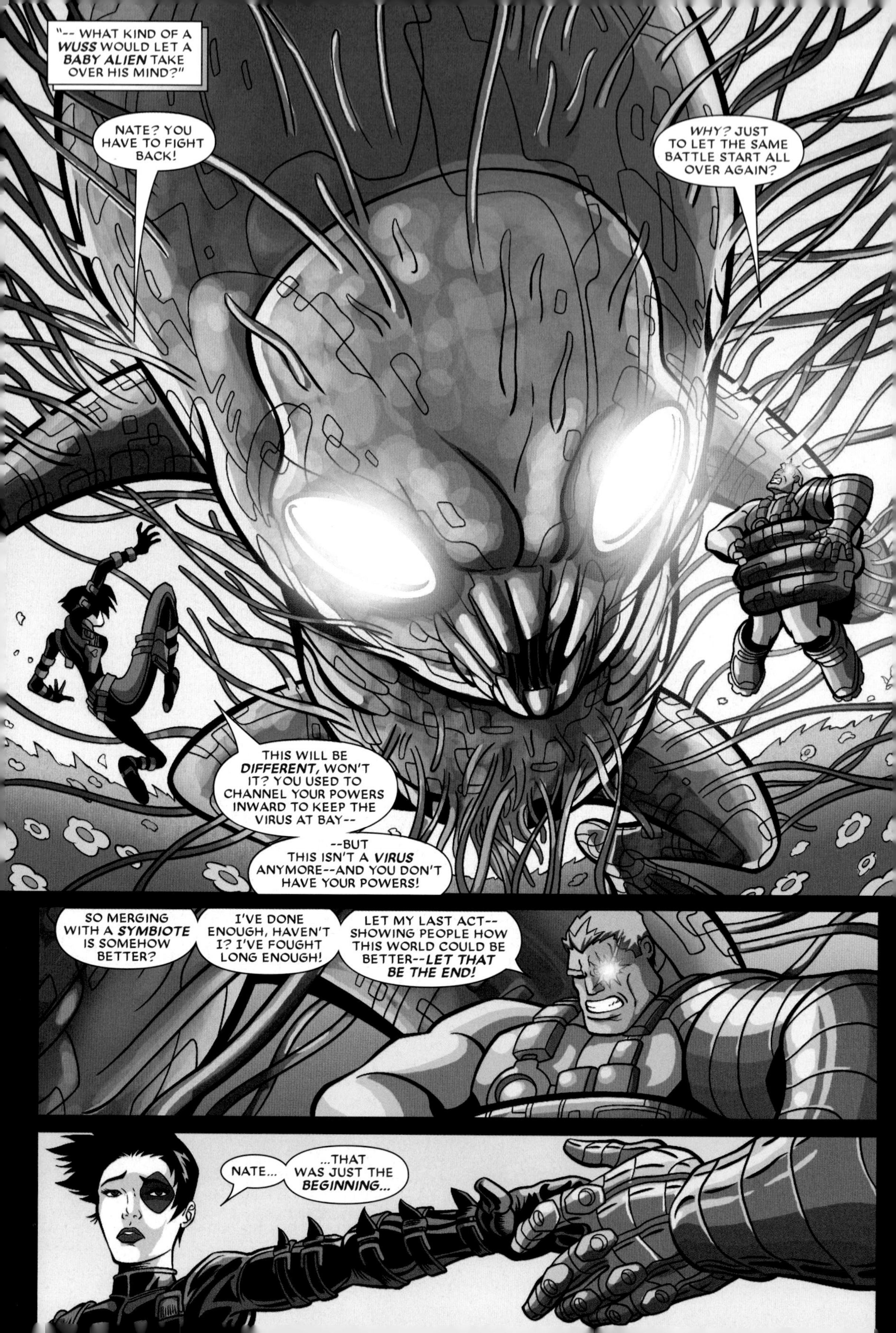
"-- WHAT KIND OF A WUSS WOULD LET A BABY ALIEN TAKE OVER HIS MIND?"
NATE? YOU HAVE TO FIGHT BACK!
WHY? JUST TO LET THE SAME BATTLE START ALL OVER AGAIN?
THIS WILL BE DIFFERENT, WON'T IT? YOU USED TO CHANNEL YOUR POWERS INWARD TO KEEP THE VIRUS AT BAY--
--BUT THIS ISN'T A VIRUS ANYMORE--AND YOU DON'T HAVE YOUR POWERS!
SO MERGING WITH A SYMBIOTE IS SOMEHOW BETTER?
I'VE DONE ENOUGH, HAVEN'T I? I'VE FOUGHT LONG ENOUGH!
LET MY LAST ACT-- SHOWING PEOPLE HOW THIS WORLD COULD BE BETTER--LET THAT BE THE END!
NATE...
...THAT WAS JUST THE BEGINNING...

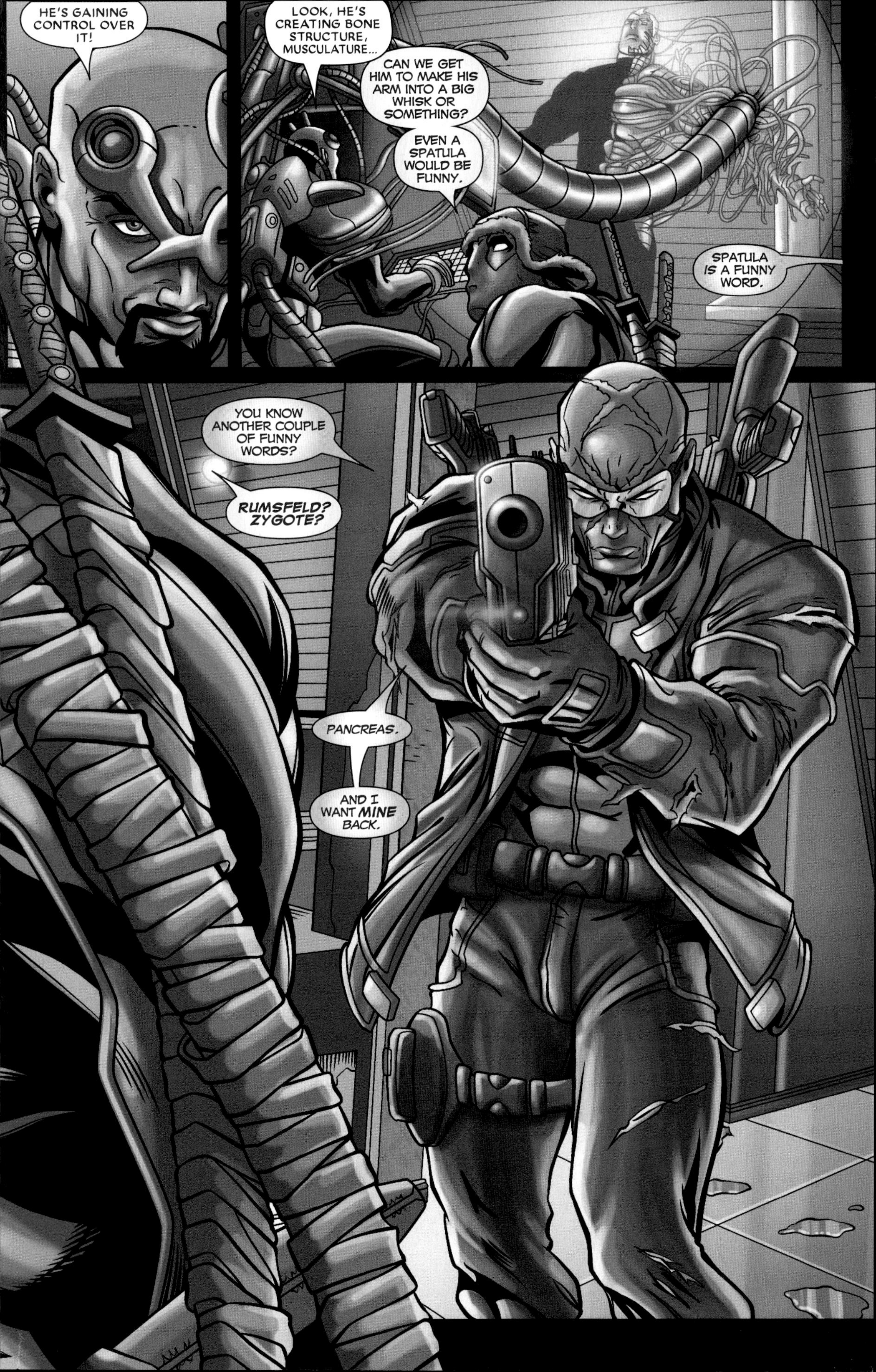
HE'S GAINING CONTROL OVER IT!
LOOK, HE'S CREATING BONE STRUCTURE, MUSCULATURE...
CAN WE GET HIM TO MAKE HIS ARM INTO A BIG WHISK OR SOMETHING?
EVEN A SPATULA WOULD BE FUNNY.
SPATULA IS A FUNNY WORD.
YOU KNOW ANOTHER COUPLE OF FUNNY WORDS?
RUMSFELD? ZYGOTE?
PANCREAS.
AND I WANT MINE BACK.

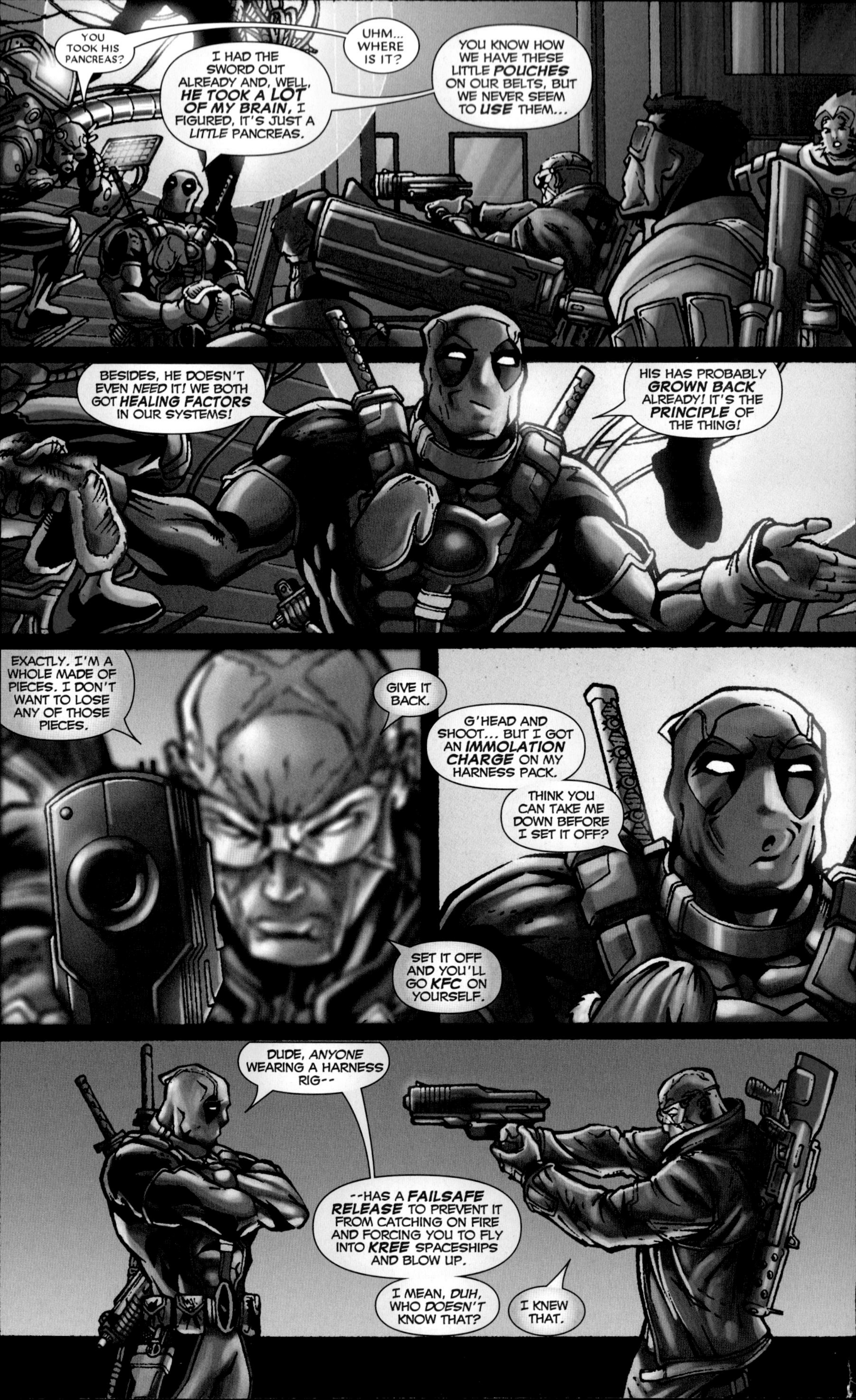
YOU TOOK HIS PANCREAS?
I HAD THE SWORD OUT ALREADY AND, WELL, HE TOOK A LOT OF MY BRAIN, I FIGURED, IT'S JUST A LITTLE PANCREAS.
UHM... WHERE IS IT?
YOU KNOW HOW WE HAVE THESE LITTLE POUCHES ON OUR BELTS, BUT WE NEVER SEEM TO USE THEM...
BESIDES, HE DOESN'T EVEN NEED IT! WE BOTH GOT HEALING FACTORS IN OUR SYSTEMS!
HIS HAS PROBABLY GROWN BACK ALREADY! IT'S THE PRINCIPLE OF THE THING!
EXACTLY. I'M A WHOLE MADE OF PIECES. I DON'T WANT TO LOSE ANY OF THOSE PIECES.
GIVE IT BACK.
G'HEAD AND SHOOT... BUT I GOT AN IMMOLATION CHARGE ON MY HARNESS PACK.
THINK YOU CAN TAKE ME DOWN BEFORE I SET IT OFF?
SET IT OFF AND YOU'LL GO KFC ON YOURSELF.
DUDE, ANYONE WEARING A HARNESS RIG--
--HAS A FAILSAFE RELEASE TO PREVENT IT FROM CATCHING ON FIRE AND FORCING YOU TO FLY INTO KREE SPACESHIPS AND BLOW UP.
I MEAN, DUH, WHO DOESN'T KNOW THAT?
I KNEW THAT.

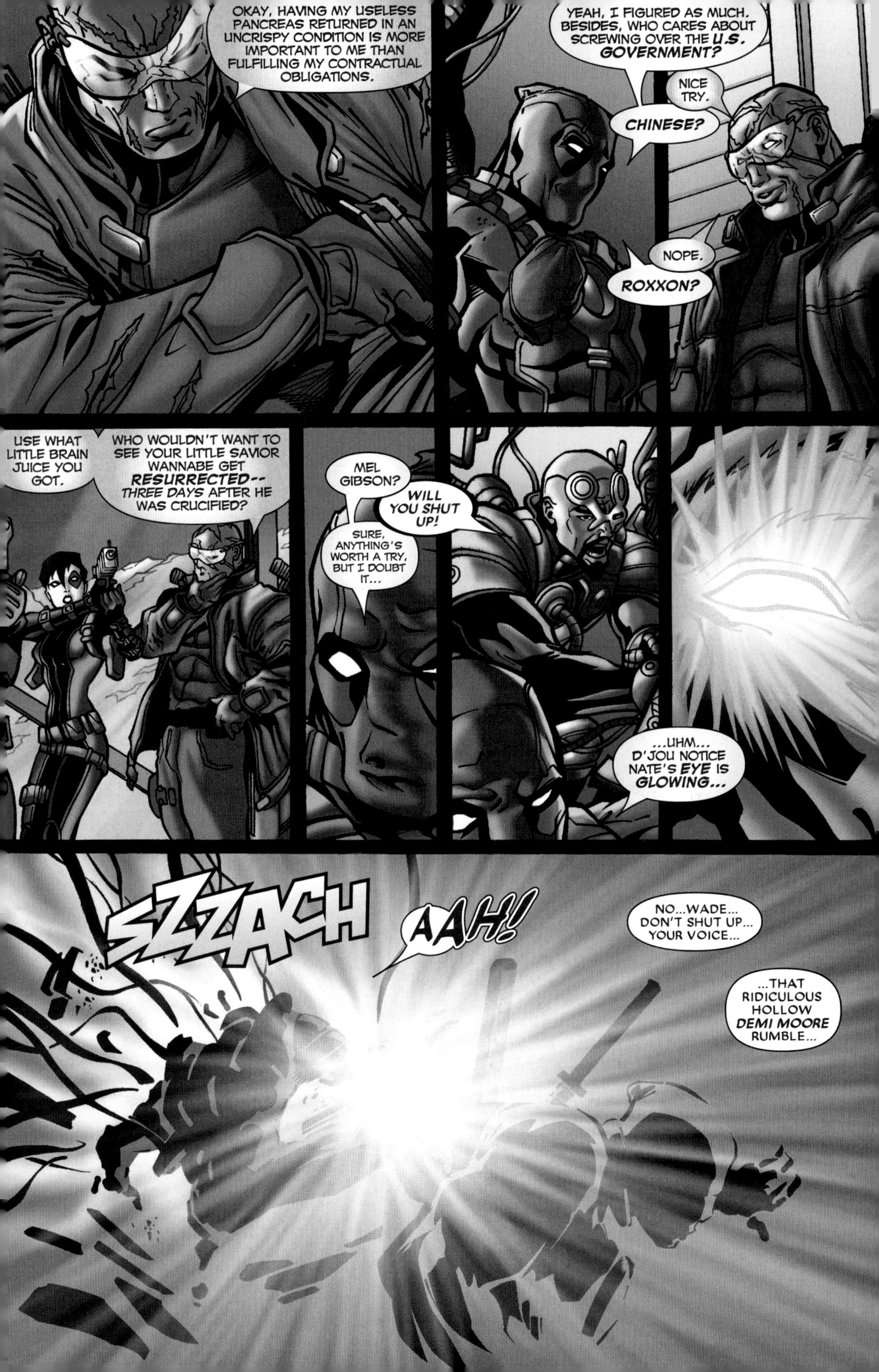
OKAY, HAVING MY USELESS PANCREAS RETURNED IN AN UNCRISPY CONDITION IS MORE IMPORTANT TO ME THAN FULFILLING MY CONTRACTUAL OBLIGATIONS.
YEAH, I FIGURED AS MUCH. BESIDES, WHO CARES ABOUT SCREWING OVER THE U.S. GOVERNMENT?
NICE TRY.
CHINESE?
NOPE.
ROXXON?
USE WHAT LITTLE BRAIN JUICE YOU GOT.
WHO WOULDN'T WANT TO SEE YOUR LITTLE SAVIOR WANNABE GET RESURRECTED-- THREE DAYS AFTER HE WAS CRUCIFIED?
MEL GIBSON?
WILL YOU SHUT UP!
SURE, ANYTHING'S WORTH A TRY, BUT I DOUBT IT...
...UHM... D'JOU NOTICE NATE'S EYE IS GLOWING...
SZZACH
AAH!
NO...WADE... DON'T SHUT UP... YOUR VOICE...
...THAT RIDICULOUS HOLLOW DEMI MOORE RUMBLE...

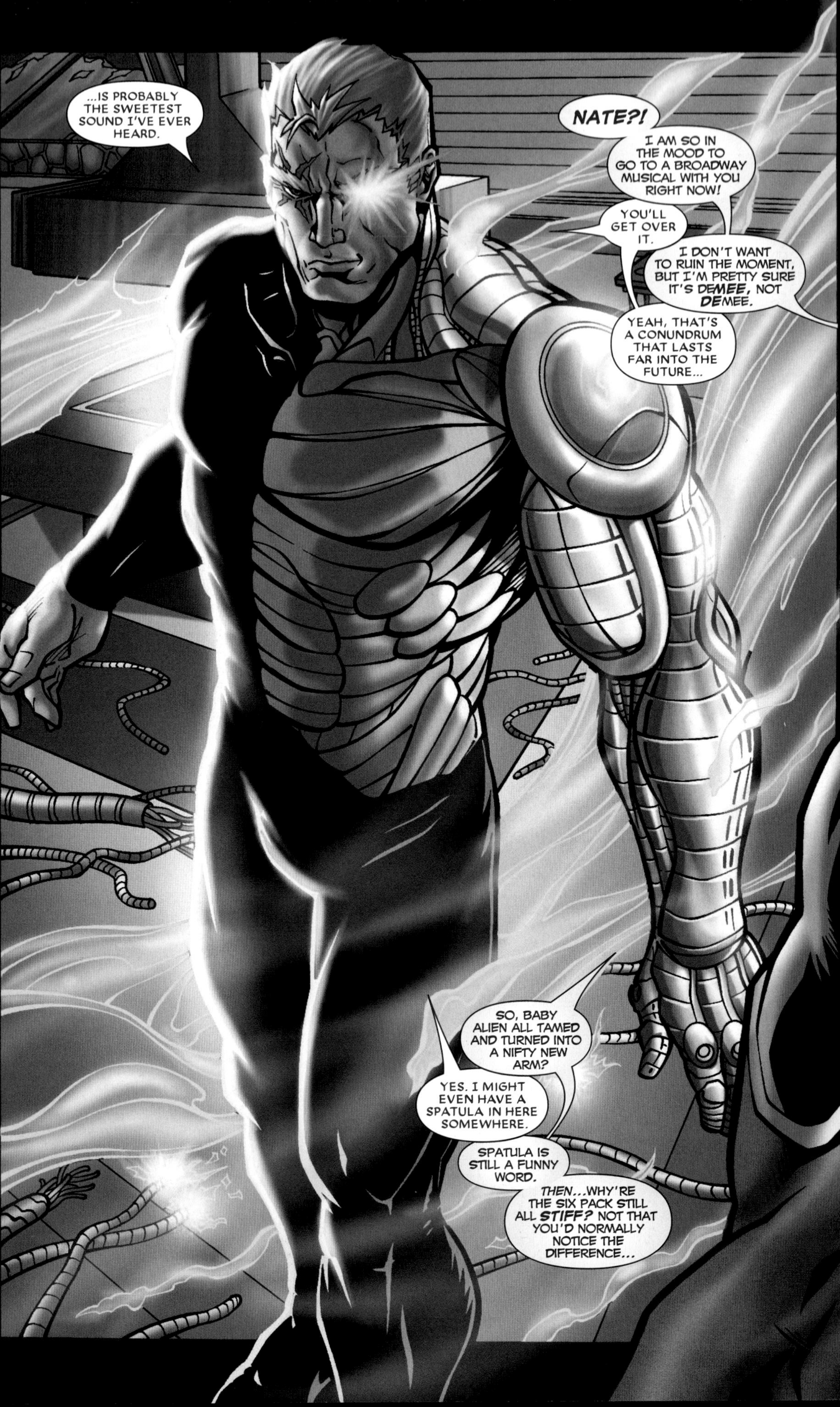

...IS PROBABLY THE SWEETEST SOUND I'VE EVER HEARD.
NATE?!
I AM SO IN THE MOOD TO GO TO A BROADWAY MUSICAL WITH YOU RIGHT NOW!
YOU'LL GET OVER IT.
I DON'T WANT TO RUIN THE MOMENT, BUT I'M PRETTY SURE IT'S DEMEE, NOT DEMEE.
YEAH, THAT'S A CONUNDRUM THAT LASTS FAR INTO THE FUTURE...
SO, BABY ALIEN ALL TAMED AND TURNED INTO A NIFTY NEW ARM?
YES. I MIGHT EVEN HAVE A SPATULA IN HERE SOMEWHERE.
SPATULA IS STILL A FUNNY WORD.
THEN...WHY'RE THE SIX PACK STILL ALL STIFF? NOT THAT YOU'D NORMALLY NOTICE THE DIFFERENCE...

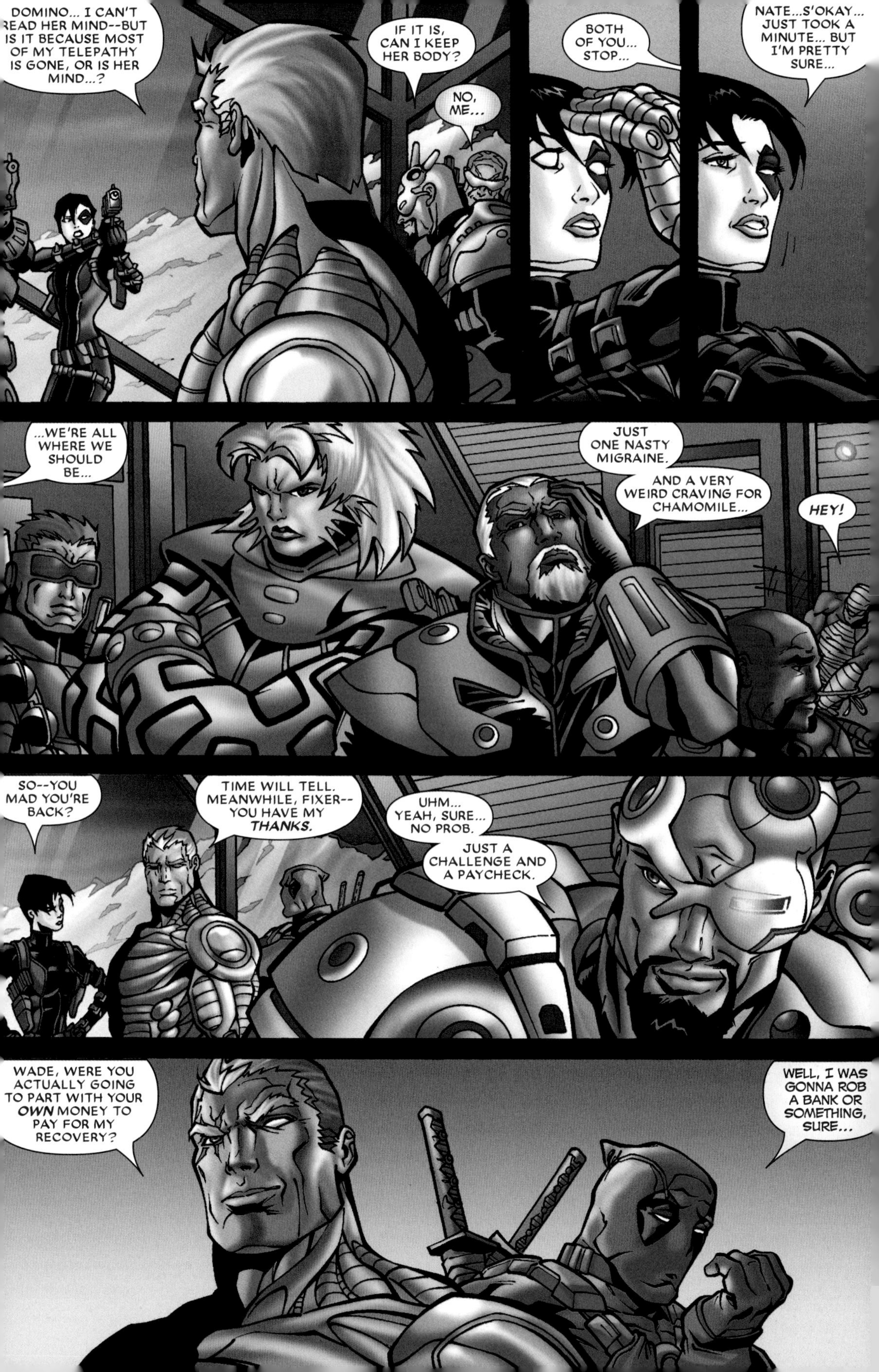
DOMINO... I CAN'T READ HER MIND--BUT IS IT BECAUSE MOST OF MY TELEPATHY IS GONE, OR IS HER MIND...?
IF IT IS, CAN I KEEP HER BODY?
NO, ME...
BOTH OF YOU... STOP...
NATE...S'OKAY... JUST TOOK A MINUTE... BUT I'M PRETTY SURE...
...WE'RE ALL WHERE WE SHOULD BE...
JUST ONE NASTY MIGRAINE.
AND A VERY WEIRD CRAVING FOR CHAMOMILE...
HEY!
SO--YOU MAD YOU'RE BACK?
TIME WILL TELL. MEANWHILE, FIXER--YOU HAVE MY THANKS.
UHM... YEAH, SURE... NO PROB.
JUST A CHALLENGE AND A PAYCHECK.
WADE, WERE YOU ACTUALLY GOING TO PART WITH YOUR OWN MONEY TO PAY FOR MY RECOVERY?
WELL, I WAS GONNA ROB A BANK OR SOMETHING, SURE...

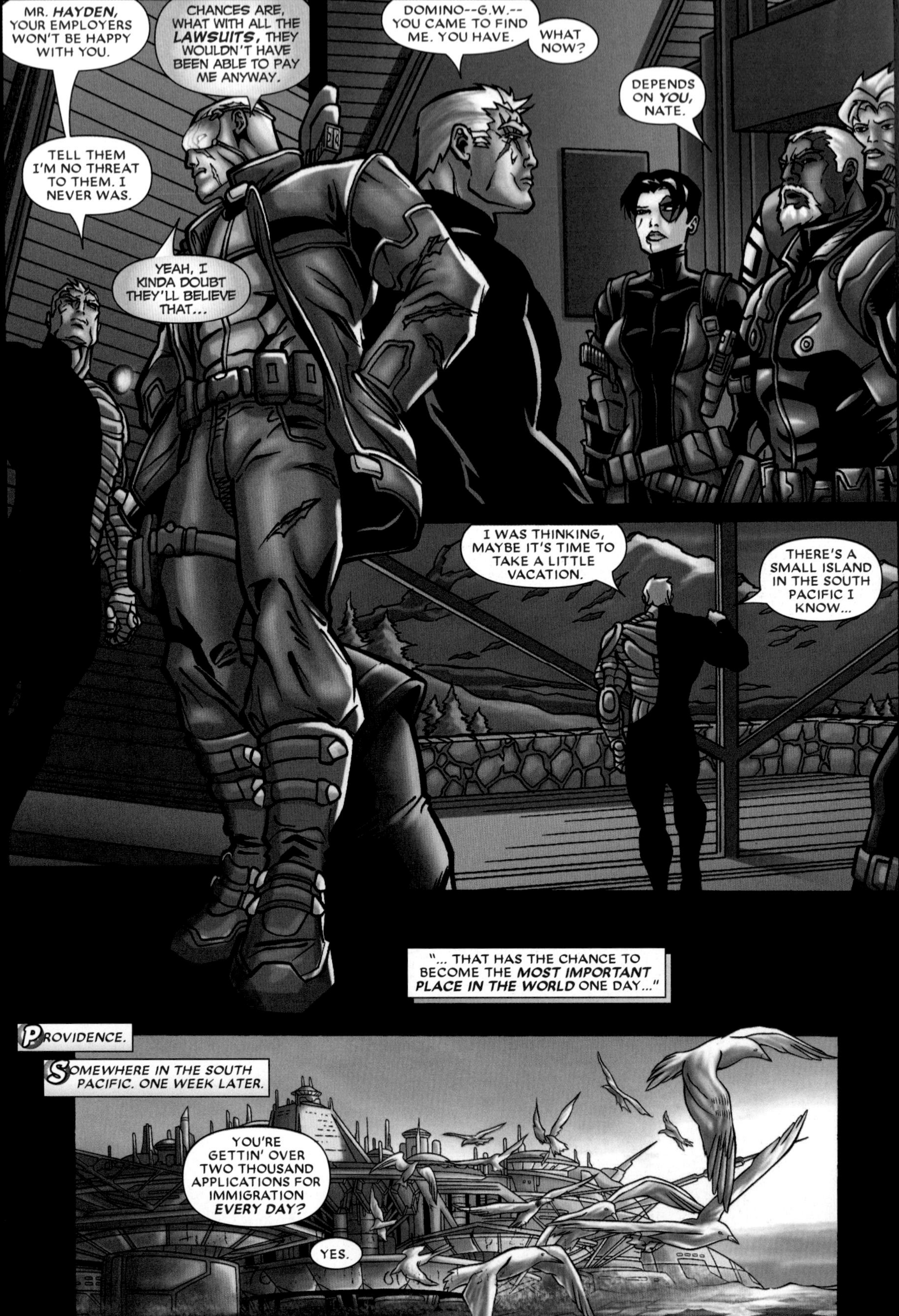

MR. HAYDEN, YOUR EMPLOYERS WON'T BE HAPPY WITH YOU.
CHANCES ARE, WHAT WITH ALL THE LAWSUITS, THEY WOULDN'T HAVE BEEN ABLE TO PAY ME ANYWAY.
TELL THEM I'M NO THREAT TO THEM. I NEVER WAS.
YEAH, I KINDA DOUBT THEY'LL BELIEVE THAT...
DOMINO--G.W.--YOU CAME TO FIND ME. YOU HAVE.
WHAT NOW?
DEPENDS ON YOU, NATE.
I WAS THINKING, MAYBE IT'S TIME TO TAKE A LITTLE VACATION.
THERE'S A SMALL ISLAND IN THE SOUTH PACIFIC I KNOW...
"... THAT HAS THE CHANCE TO BECOME THE MOST IMPORTANT PLACE IN THE WORLD ONE DAY..."
PROVIDENCE.
SOMEWHERE IN THE SOUTH PACIFIC. ONE WEEK LATER.
YOU'RE GETTIN' OVER TWO THOUSAND APPLICATIONS FOR IMMIGRATION EVERY DAY?
YES.

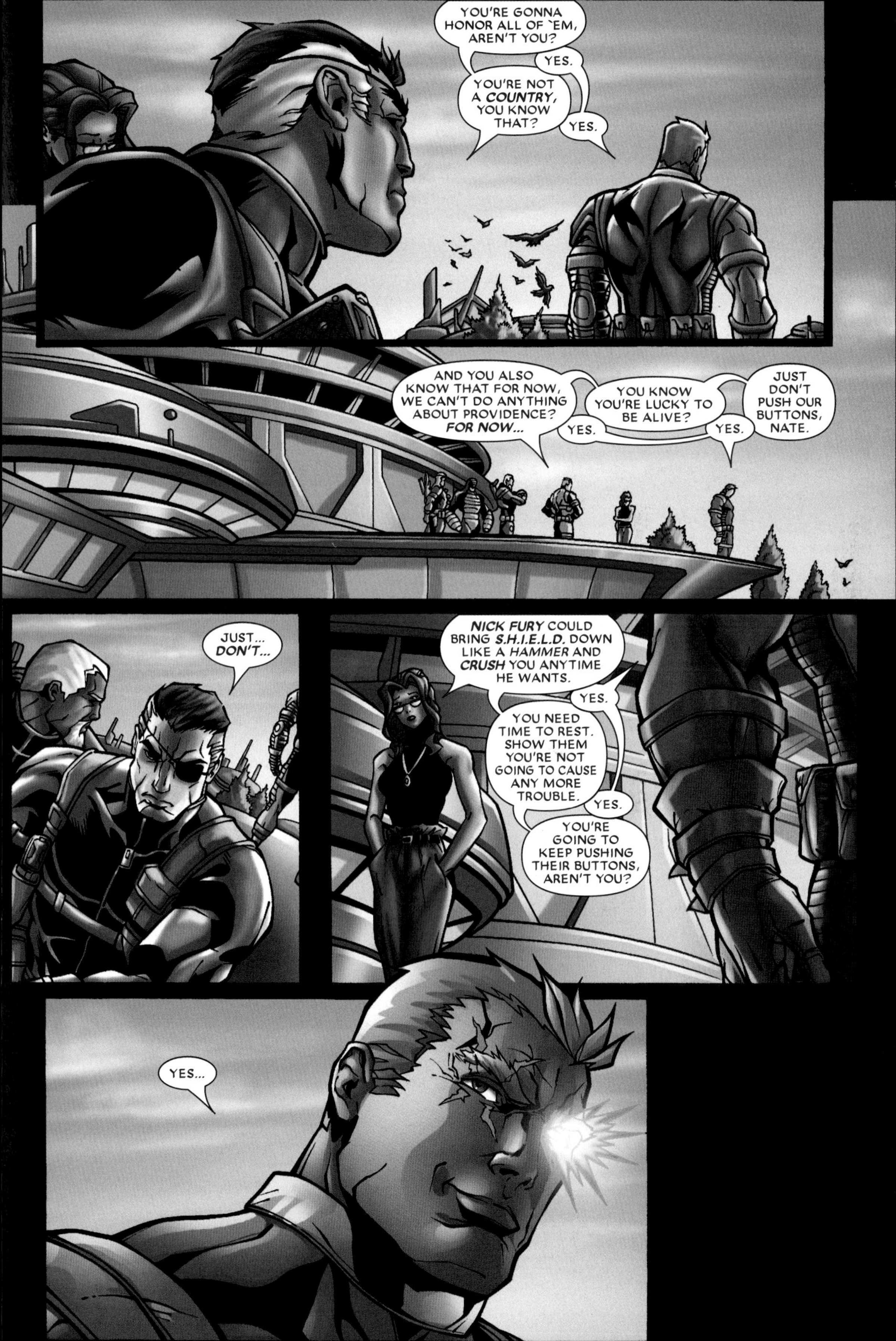
YOU'RE GONNA HONOR ALL OF `EM, AREN'T YOU?
YES.
YOU'RE NOT A COUNTRY, YOU KNOW THAT?
YES.
AND YOU ALSO KNOW THAT FOR NOW, WE CAN'T DO ANYTHING ABOUT PROVIDENCE? FOR NOW...
YES.
YOU KNOW YOU'RE LUCKY TO BE ALIVE?
YES.
JUST DON'T PUSH OUR BUTTONS, NATE.
JUST... DON'T...
NICK FURY COULD BRING S.H.I.E.L.D. DOWN LIKE A HAMMER AND CRUSH YOU ANYTIME HE WANTS.
YES.
YOU NEED TIME TO REST. SHOW THEM YOU'RE NOT GOING TO CAUSE ANY MORE TROUBLE.
YES.
YOU'RE GOING TO KEEP PUSHING THEIR BUTTONS, AREN'T YOU?
YES...

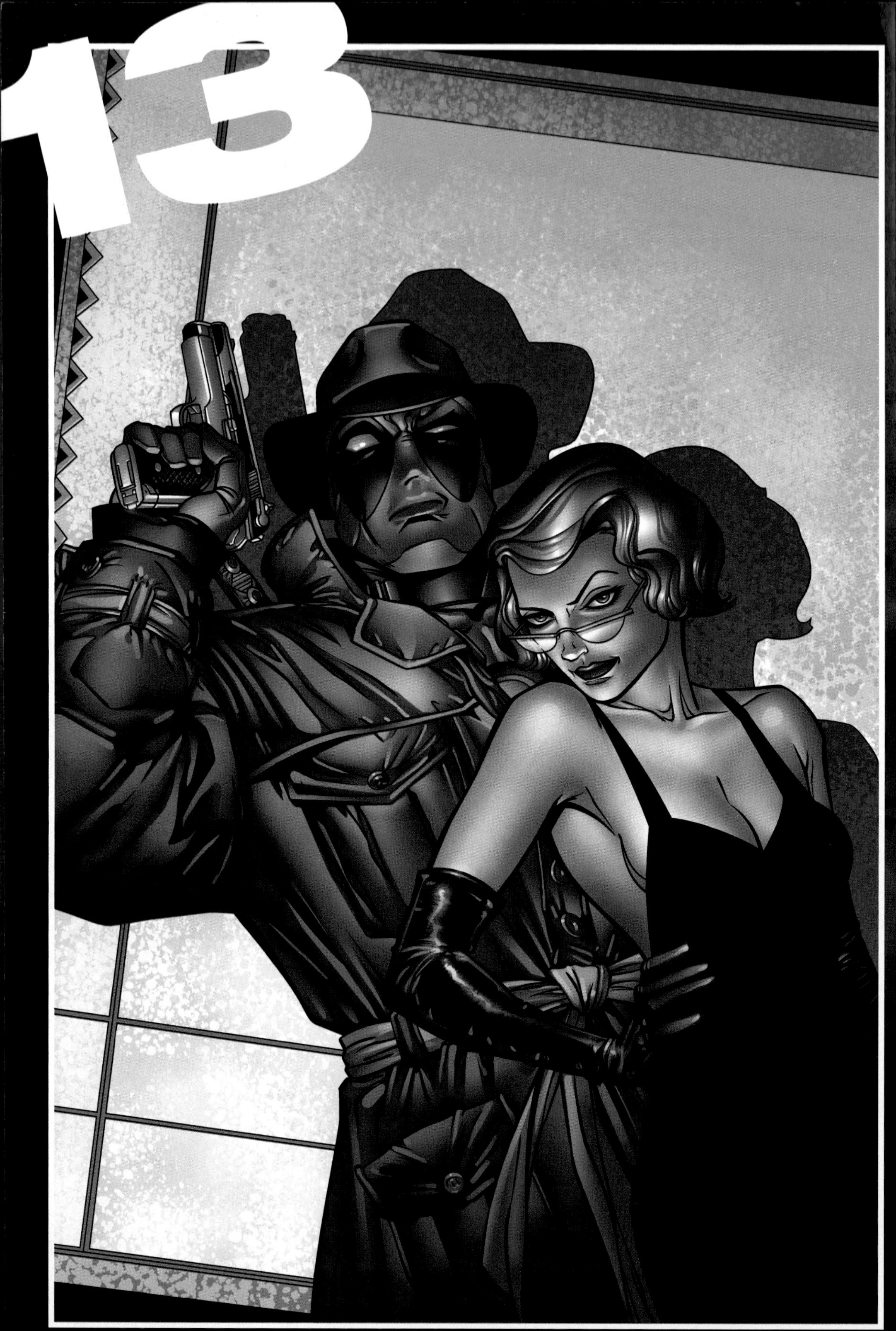
13

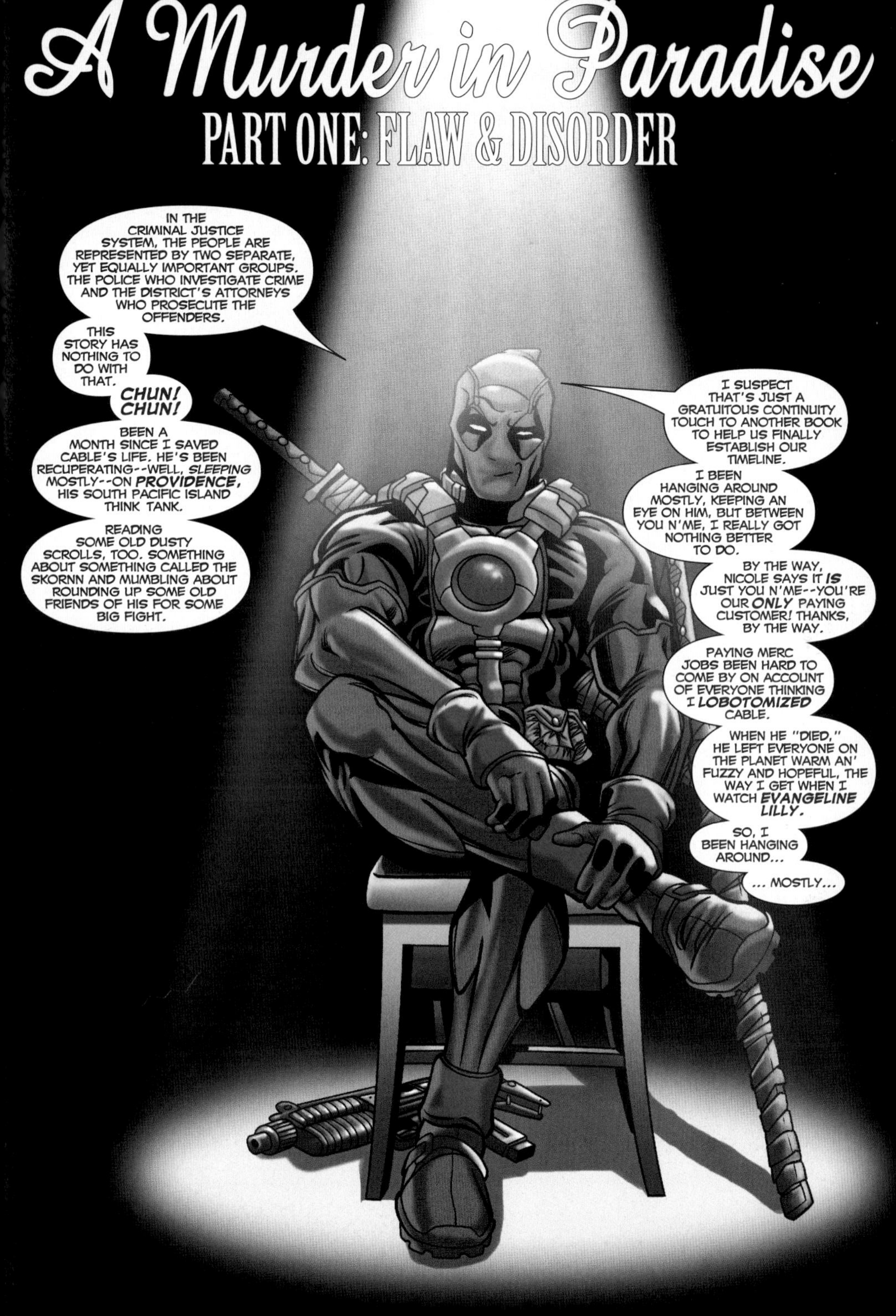

A Murder in Paradise
PART ONE: FLAW & DISORDER
IN THE CRIMINAL JUSTICE SYSTEM, THE PEOPLE ARE REPRESENTED BY TWO SEPARATE, YET EQUALLY IMPORTANT GROUPS. THE POLICE WHO INVESTIGATE CRIME AND THE DISTRICT'S ATTORNEYS WHO PROSECUTE THE OFFENDERS.
THIS STORY HAS NOTHING TO DO WITH THAT.
CHUN! CHUN!
BEEN A MONTH SINCE I SAVED CABLE'S LIFE. HE'S BEEN RECUPERATING--WELL, SLEEPING MOSTLY--ON PROVIDENCE, HIS SOUTH PACIFIC ISLAND THINK TANK.
READING SOME OLD DUSTY SCROLLS, TOO. SOMETHING ABOUT SOMETHING CALLED THE SKORNN AND MUMBLING ABOUT ROUNDING UP SOME OLD FRIENDS OF HIS FOR SOME BIG FIGHT.
I SUSPECT THAT'S JUST A GRATUITOUS CONTINUITY TOUCH TO ANOTHER BOOK TO HELP US FINALLY ESTABLISH OUR TIMELINE.
I BEEN HANGING AROUND MOSTLY, KEEPING AN EYE ON HIM, BUT BETWEEN YOU N'ME, I REALLY GOT NOTHING BETTER TO DO.
BY THE WAY, NICOLE SAYS IT IS JUST YOU N'ME--YOU'RE OUR ONLY PAYING CUSTOMER! THANKS, BY THE WAY.
PAYING MERC JOBS BEEN HARD TO COME BY ON ACCOUNT OF EVERYONE THINKING I LOBOTOMIZED CABLE.
WHEN HE "DIED," HE LEFT EVERYONE ON THE PLANET WARM AN' FUZZY AND HOPEFUL, THE WAY I GET WHEN I WATCH EVANGELINE LILLY.
SO, I BEEN HANGING AROUND...
... MOSTLY...

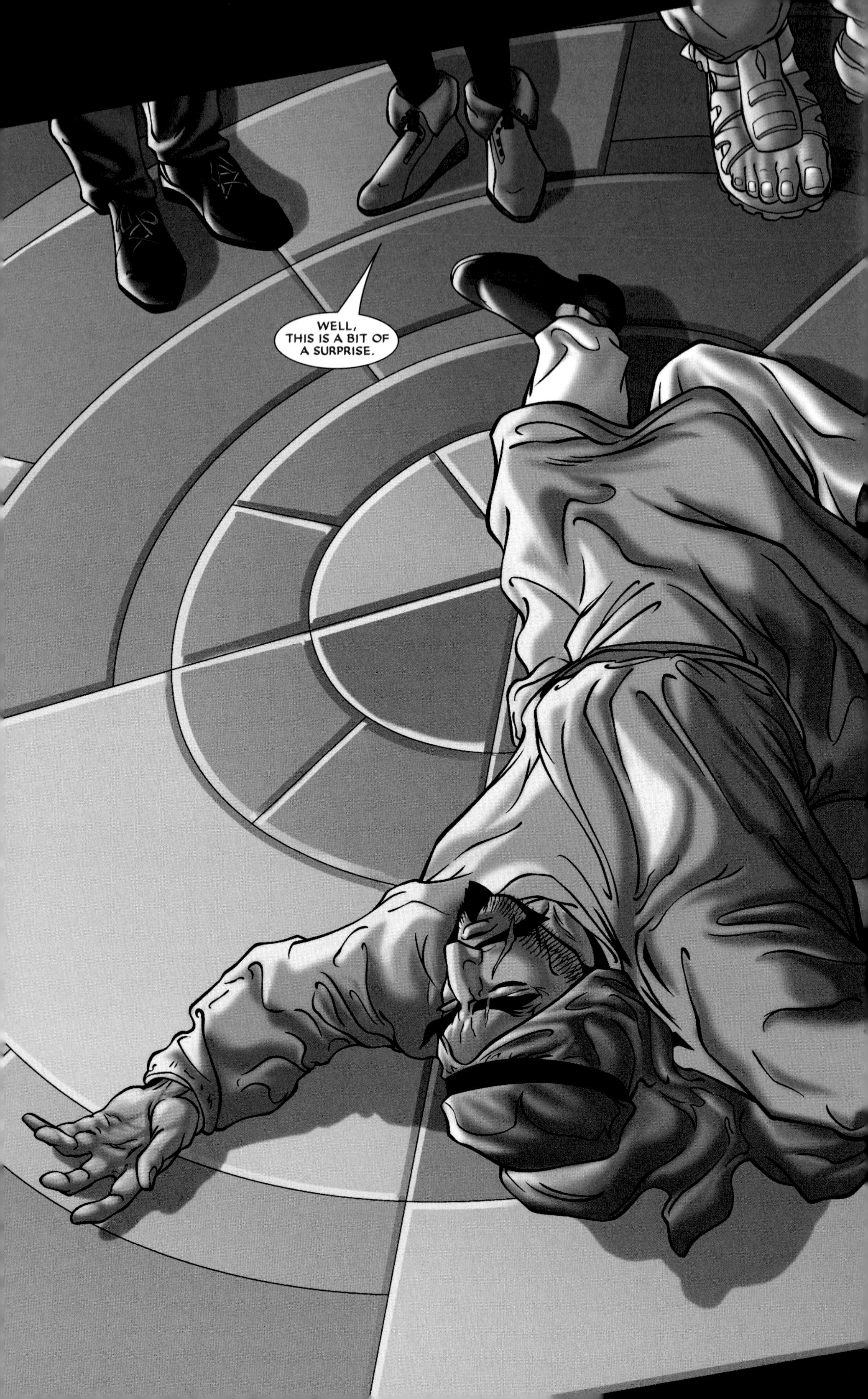
WELL, THIS IS A BIT OF A SURPRISE.

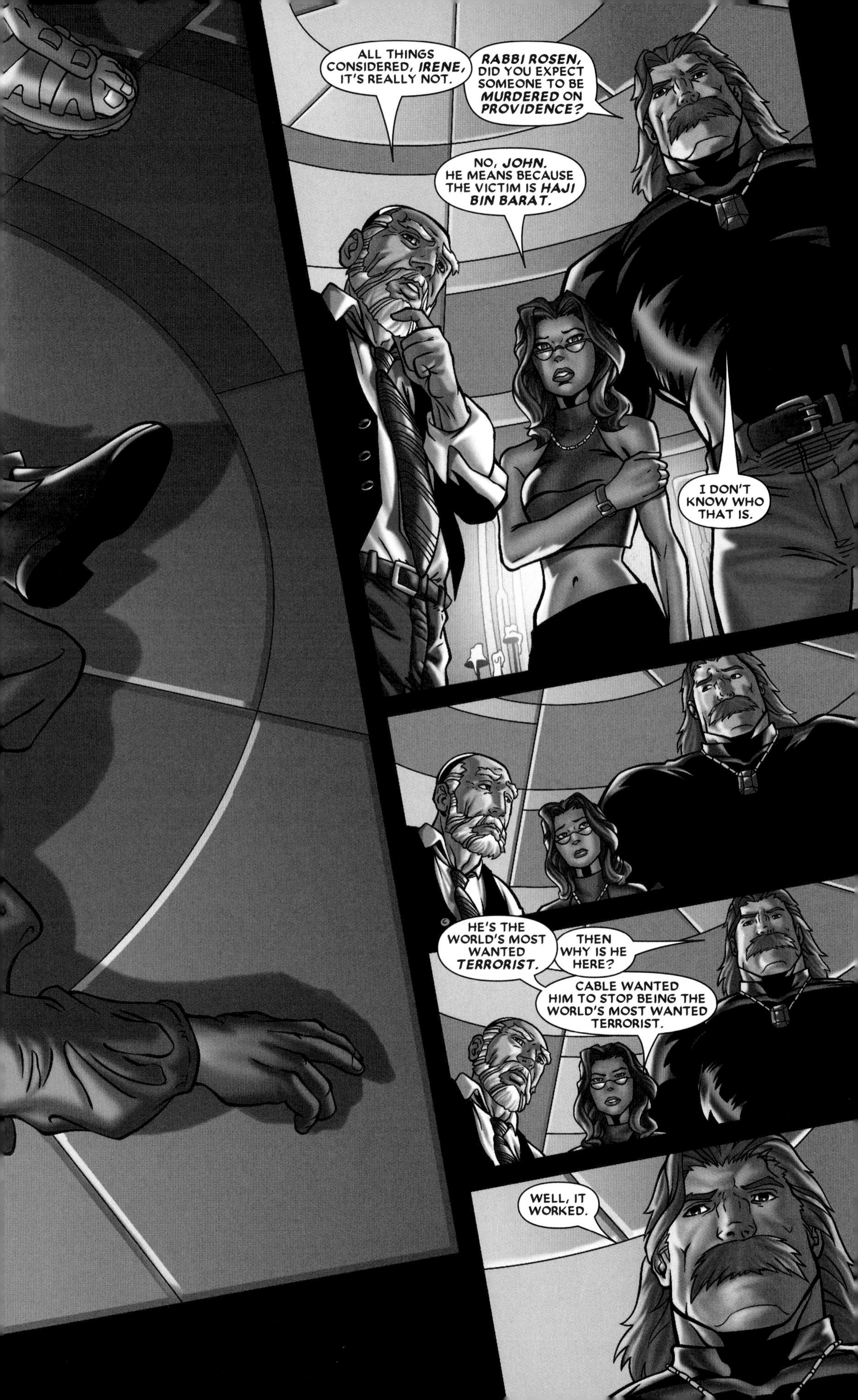
ALL THINGS CONSIDERED, IRENE, IT'S REALLY NOT.
RABBI ROSEN, DID YOU EXPECT SOMEONE TO BE MURDERED ON PROVIDENCE?
NO, JOHN. HE MEANS BECAUSE THE VICTIM IS HAJI BIN BARAT.
I DON'T KNOW WHO THAT IS.
HE'S THE WORLD'S MOST WANTED TERRORIST.
THEN WHY IS HE HERE?
CABLE WANTED HIM TO STOP BEING THE WORLD'S MOST WANTED TERRORIST.
WELL, IT WORKED.

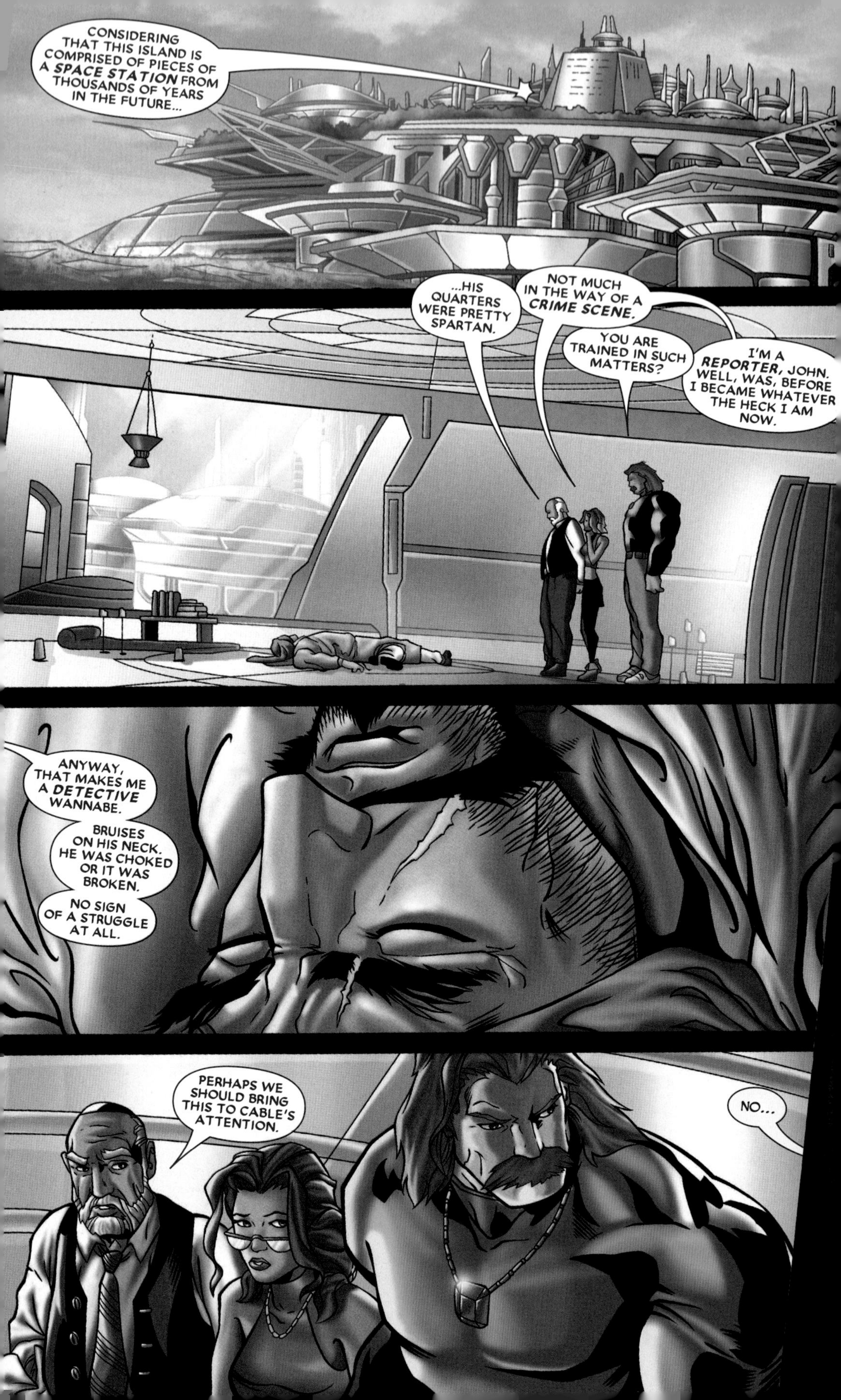
CONSIDERING THAT THIS ISLAND IS COMPRISED OF PIECES OF A SPACE STATION FROM THOUSANDS OF YEARS IN THE FUTURE...
...HIS QUARTERS WERE PRETTY SPARTAN.
NOT MUCH IN THE WAY OF A CRIME SCENE.
YOU ARE TRAINED IN SUCH MATTERS?
I'M A REPORTER, JOHN. WELL, WAS, BEFORE I BECAME WHATEVER THE HECK I AM NOW.
ANYWAY, THAT MAKES ME A DETECTIVE WANNABE.
BRUISES ON HIS NECK. HE WAS CHOKED OR IT WAS BROKEN.
NO SIGN OF A STRUGGLE AT ALL.
PERHAPS WE SHOULD BRING THIS TO CABLE'S ATTENTION.
NO...

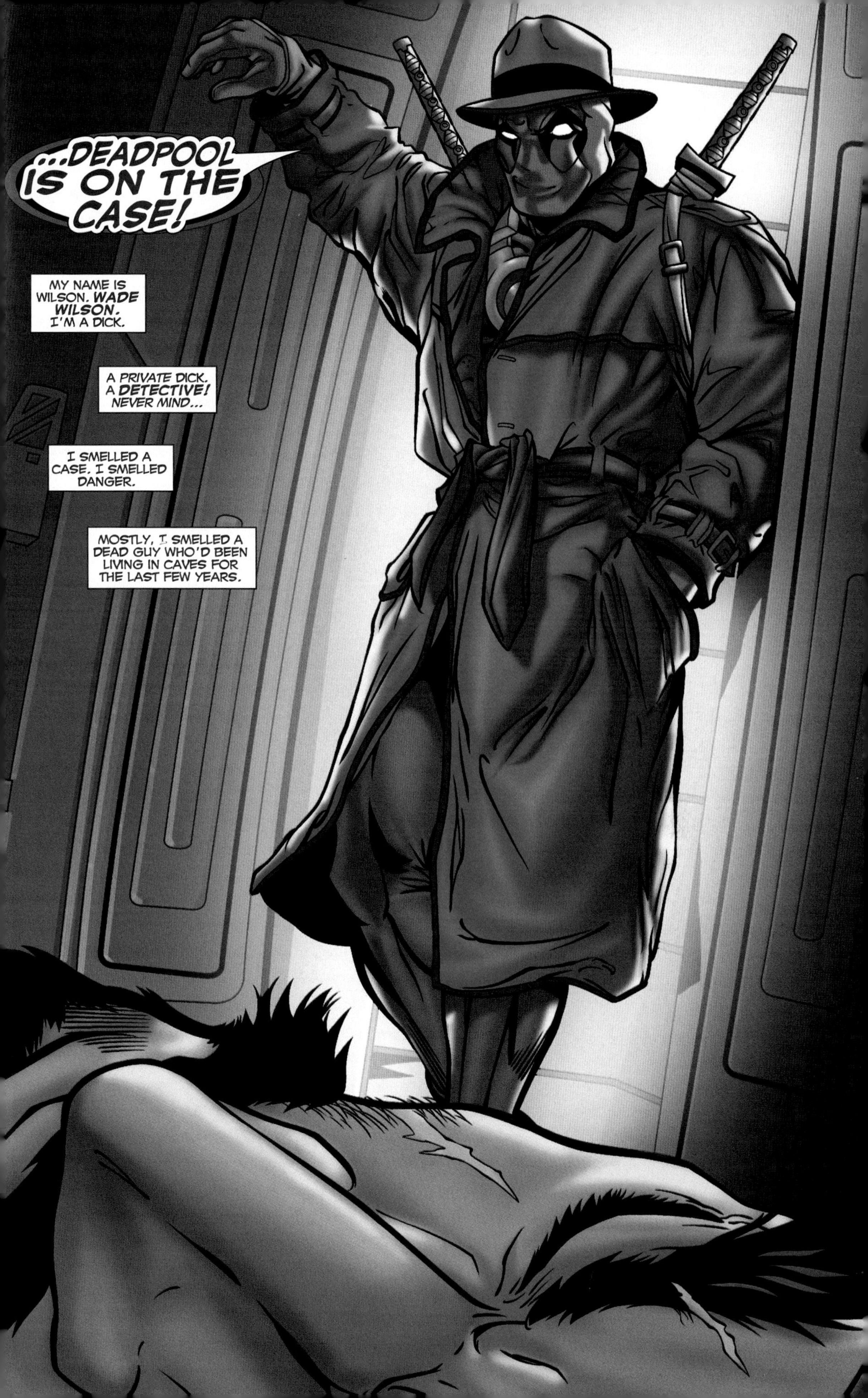
...DEADPOOL IS ON THE CASE!
MY NAME IS WILSON. WADE WILSON. I'M A DICK.
A PRIVATE DICK. A DETECTIVE! NEVER MIND...
I SMELLED A CASE. I SMELLED DANGER.
MOSTLY, I SMELLED A DEAD GUY WHO'D BEEN LIVING IN CAVES FOR THE LAST FEW YEARS.

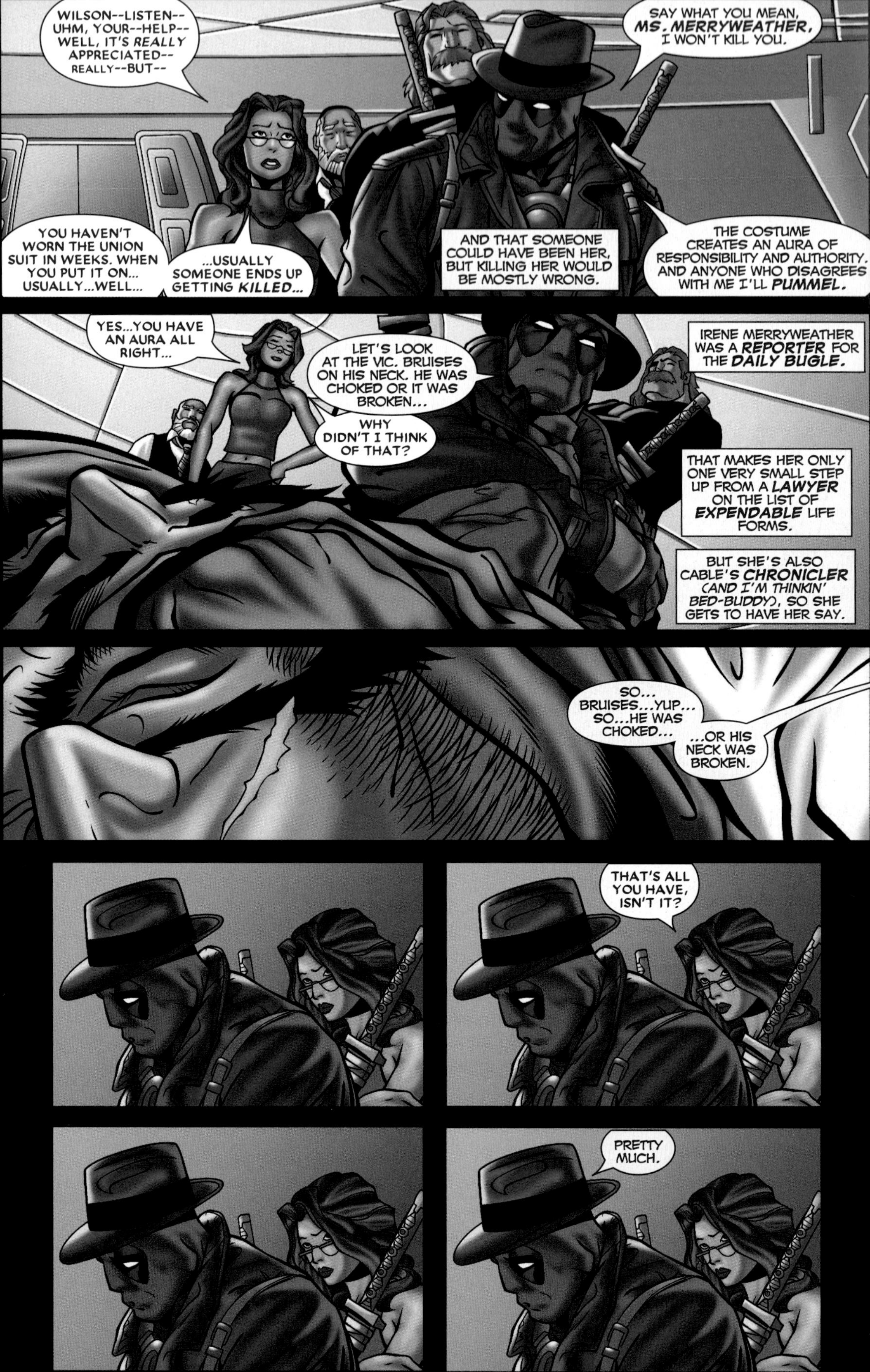
WILSON--LISTEN--UHM, YOUR--HELP--WELL, IT'S REALLY APPRECIATED--REALLY--BUT--
SAY WHAT YOU MEAN, MS. MERRYWEATHER. I WON'T KILL YOU.
YOU HAVEN'T WORN THE UNION SUIT IN WEEKS. WHEN YOU PUT IT ON... USUALLY...WELL...
...USUALLY SOMEONE ENDS UP GETTING KILLED...
AND THAT SOMEONE COULD HAVE BEEN HER, BUT KILLING HER WOULD BE MOSTLY WRONG.
THE COSTUME CREATES AN AURA OF RESPONSIBILITY AND AUTHORITY. AND ANYONE WHO DISAGREES WITH ME I'LL PUMMEL.
YES...YOU HAVE AN AURA ALL RIGHT...
LET'S LOOK AT THE VIC. BRUISES ON HIS NECK. HE WAS CHOKED OR IT WAS BROKEN...
WHY DIDN'T I THINK OF THAT?
IRENE MERRYWEATHER WAS A REPORTER FOR THE DAILY BUGLE.
THAT MAKES HER ONLY ONE VERY SMALL STEP UP FROM A LAWYER ON THE LIST OF EXPENDABLE LIFE FORMS.
BUT SHE'S ALSO CABLE'S CHRONICLER (AND I'M THINKIN' BED-BUDDY), SO SHE GETS TO HAVE HER SAY.
SO... BRUISES...YUP... SO...HE WAS CHOKED...
...OR HIS NECK WAS BROKEN.
THAT'S ALL YOU HAVE, ISN'T IT?
PRETTY MUCH.

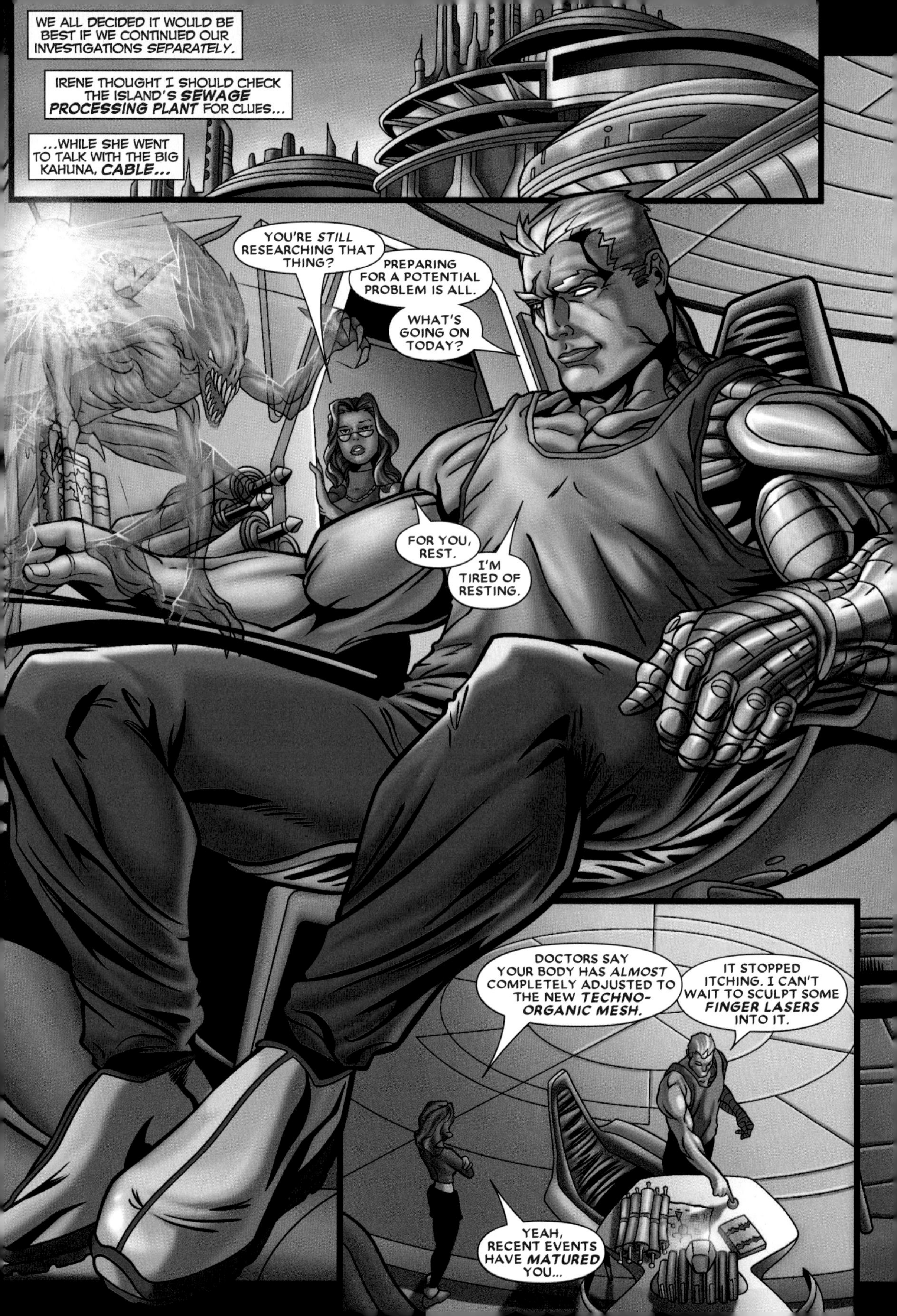
WE ALL DECIDED IT WOULD BE BEST IF WE CONTINUED OUR INVESTIGATIONS *SEPARATELY.*
IRENE THOUGHT I SHOULD CHECK THE ISLAND'S **SEWAGE PROCESSING PLANT** FOR CLUES...
...WHILE SHE WENT TO TALK WITH THE BIG KAHUNA, ***CABLE...***
YOU'RE *STILL* RESEARCHING THAT THING?
PREPARING FOR A POTENTIAL PROBLEM IS ALL.
WHAT'S GOING ON TODAY?
FOR YOU, REST.
I'M TIRED OF RESTING.
DOCTORS SAY YOUR BODY HAS *ALMOST* COMPLETELY ADJUSTED TO THE NEW ***TECHNO-ORGANIC MESH.***
IT STOPPED ITCHING. I CAN'T WAIT TO SCULPT SOME ***FINGER LASERS*** INTO IT.
YEAH, RECENT EVENTS HAVE ***MATURED*** YOU...

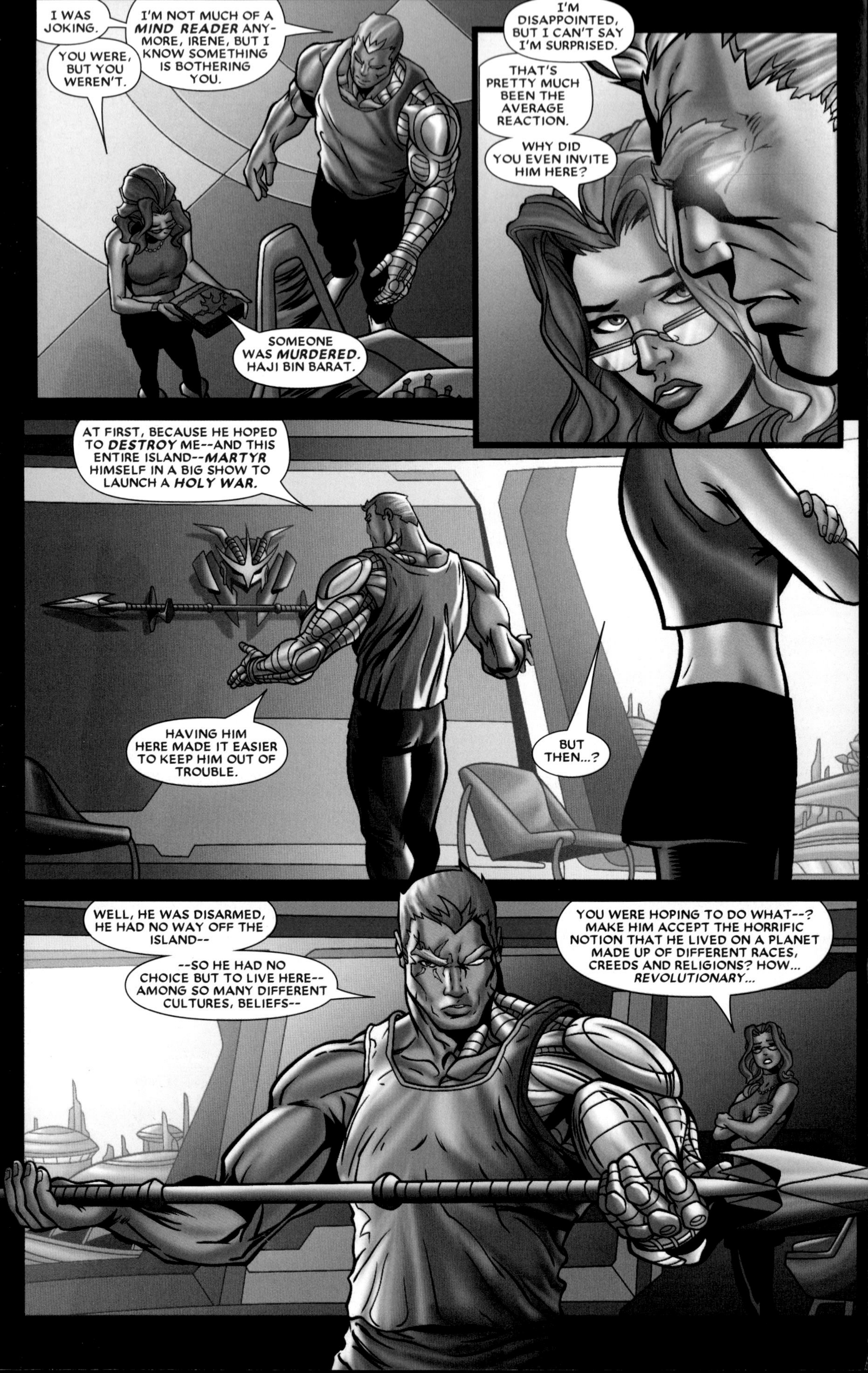
I WAS JOKING.
YOU WERE, BUT YOU WEREN'T.
I'M NOT MUCH OF A MIND READER ANYMORE, IRENE, BUT I KNOW SOMETHING IS BOTHERING YOU.
SOMEONE WAS MURDERED. HAJI BIN BARAT.
I'M DISAPPOINTED, BUT I CAN'T SAY I'M SURPRISED.
THAT'S PRETTY MUCH BEEN THE AVERAGE REACTION.
WHY DID YOU EVEN INVITE HIM HERE?
AT FIRST, BECAUSE HE HOPED TO DESTROY ME--AND THIS ENTIRE ISLAND--MARTYR HIMSELF IN A BIG SHOW TO LAUNCH A HOLY WAR.
HAVING HIM HERE MADE IT EASIER TO KEEP HIM OUT OF TROUBLE.
BUT THEN...?
WELL, HE WAS DISARMED, HE HAD NO WAY OFF THE ISLAND--
--SO HE HAD NO CHOICE BUT TO LIVE HERE--AMONG SO MANY DIFFERENT CULTURES, BELIEFS--
YOU WERE HOPING TO DO WHAT--? MAKE HIM ACCEPT THE HORRIFIC NOTION THAT HE LIVED ON A PLANET MADE UP OF DIFFERENT RACES, CREEDS AND RELIGIONS? HOW... REVOLUTIONARY...

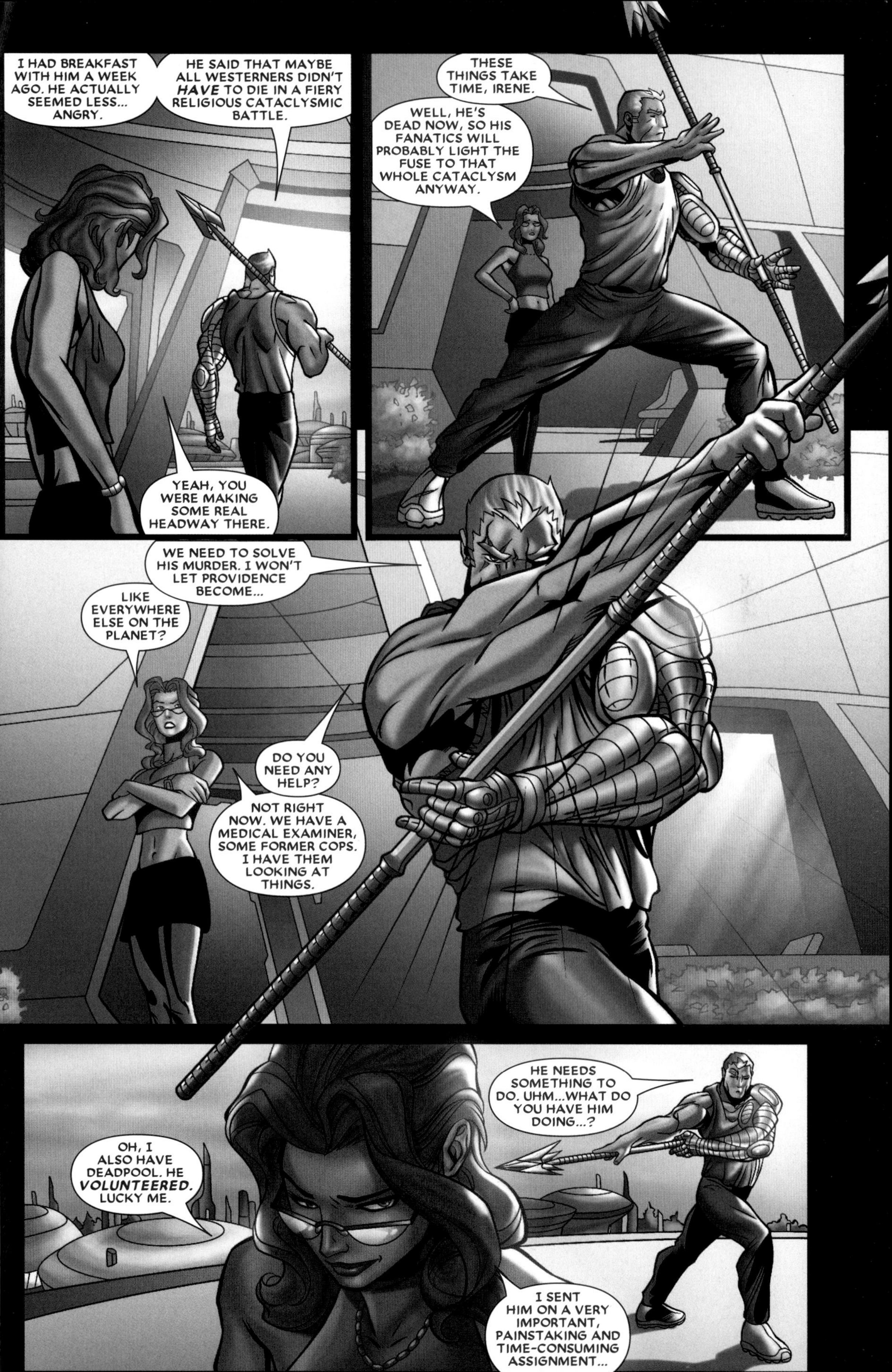

I HAD BREAKFAST WITH HIM A WEEK AGO. HE ACTUALLY SEEMED LESS... ANGRY.
HE SAID THAT MAYBE ALL WESTERNERS DIDN'T *HAVE* TO DIE IN A FIERY RELIGIOUS CATACLYSMIC BATTLE.
YEAH, YOU WERE MAKING SOME REAL HEADWAY THERE.
THESE THINGS TAKE TIME, IRENE.
WELL, HE'S DEAD NOW, SO HIS FANATICS WILL PROBABLY LIGHT THE FUSE TO THAT WHOLE CATACLYSM ANYWAY.
WE NEED TO SOLVE HIS MURDER. I WON'T LET PROVIDENCE BECOME...
LIKE EVERYWHERE ELSE ON THE PLANET?
DO YOU NEED ANY HELP?
NOT RIGHT NOW. WE HAVE A MEDICAL EXAMINER, SOME FORMER COPS. I HAVE THEM LOOKING AT THINGS.
OH, I ALSO HAVE DEADPOOL. HE ***VOLUNTEERED.*** LUCKY ME.
HE NEEDS SOMETHING TO DO. UHM...WHAT DO YOU HAVE HIM DOING...?
I SENT HIM ON A VERY IMPORTANT, PAINSTAKING AND TIME-CONSUMING ASSIGNMENT...

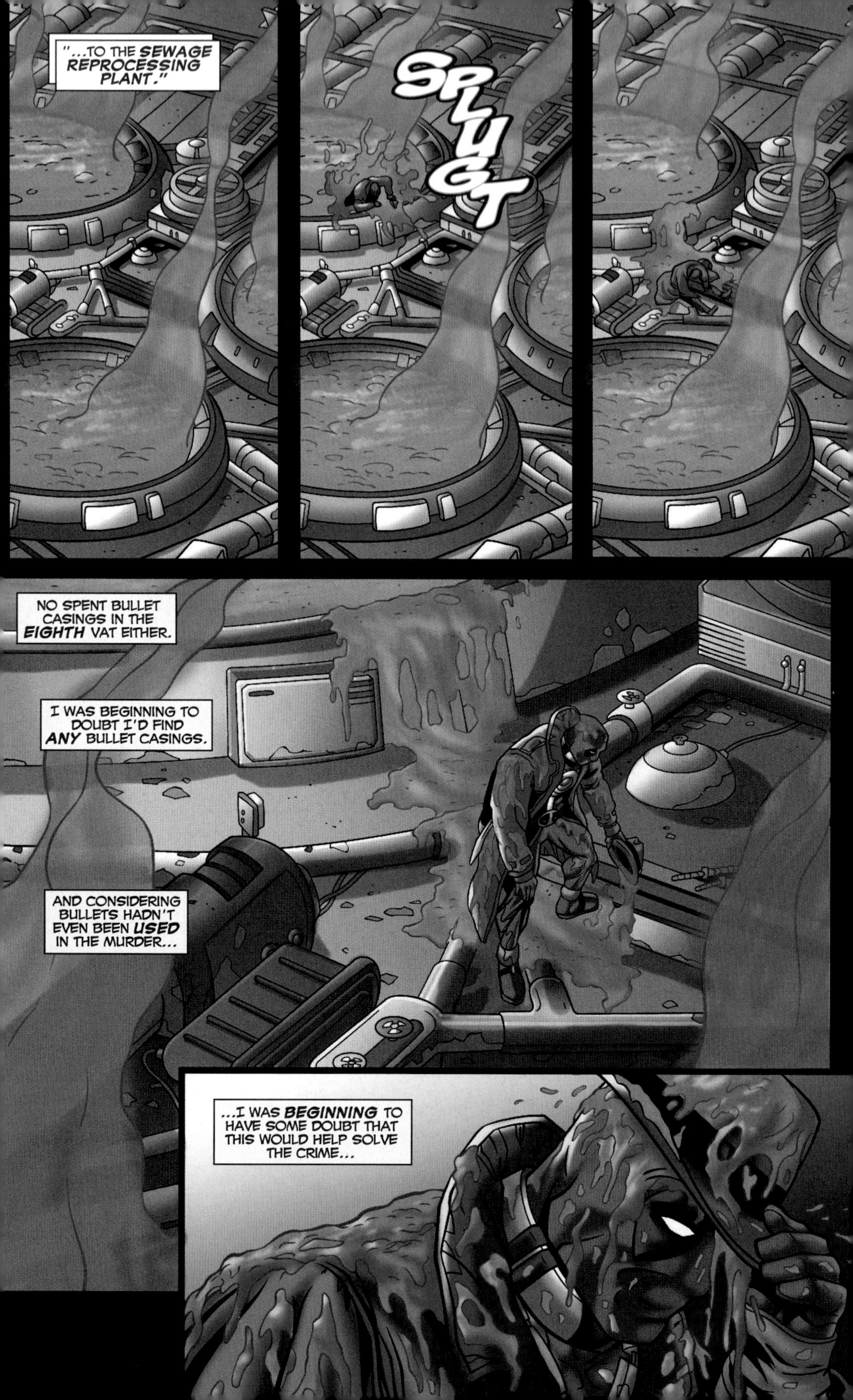
"...TO THE SEWAGE REPROCESSING PLANT."
SPLUGT
NO SPENT BULLET CASINGS IN THE EIGHTH VAT EITHER.
I WAS BEGINNING TO DOUBT I'D FIND ANY BULLET CASINGS.
AND CONSIDERING BULLETS HADN'T EVEN BEEN USED IN THE MURDER...
...I WAS BEGINNING TO HAVE SOME DOUBT THAT THIS WOULD HELP SOLVE THE CRIME...

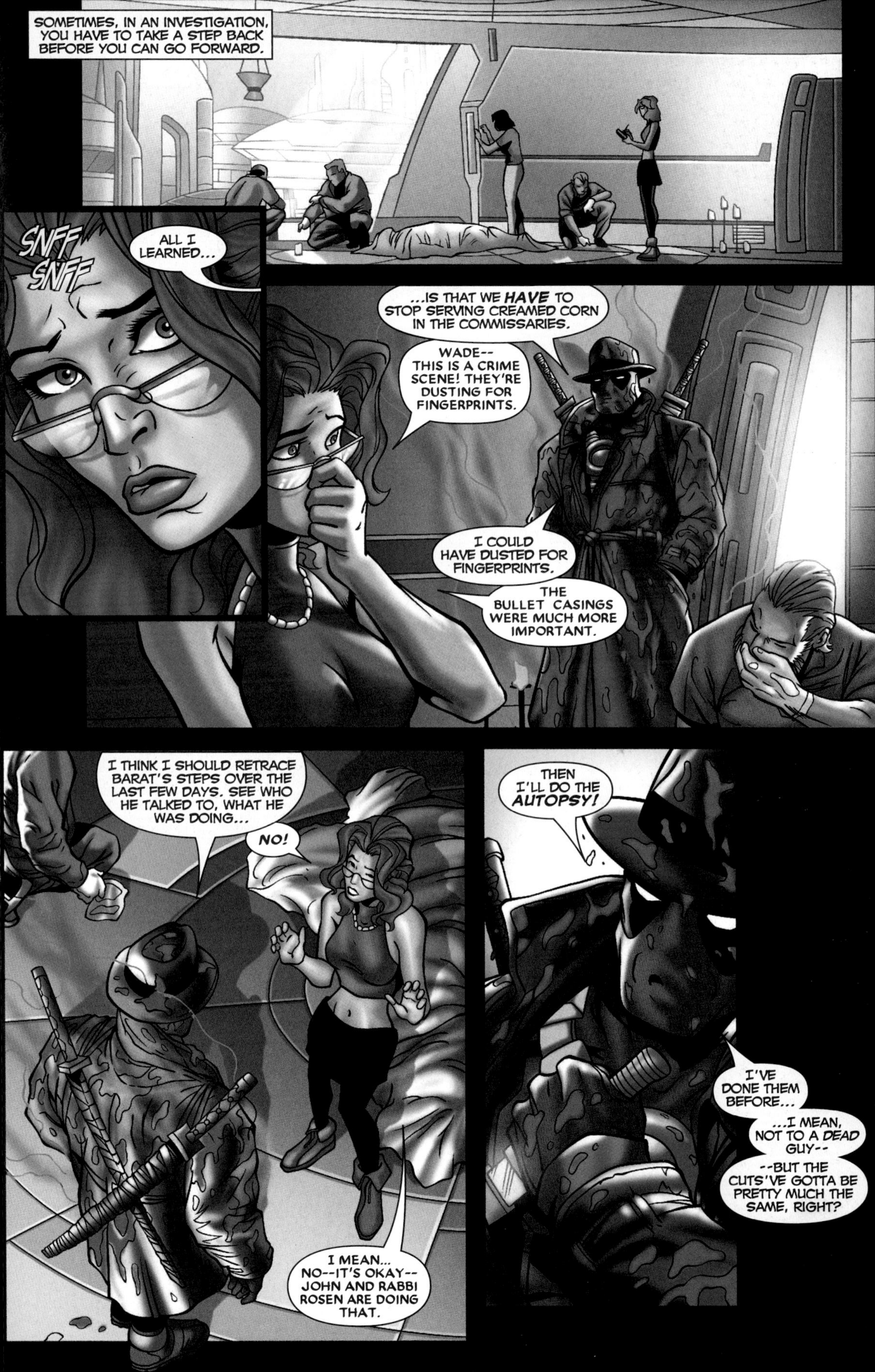
SOMETIMES, IN AN INVESTIGATION, YOU HAVE TO TAKE A STEP BACK BEFORE YOU CAN GO FORWARD.
SNFF SNFF
ALL I LEARNED...
...IS THAT WE HAVE TO STOP SERVING CREAMED CORN IN THE COMMISSARIES.
WADE-- THIS IS A CRIME SCENE! THEY'RE DUSTING FOR FINGERPRINTS.
I COULD HAVE DUSTED FOR FINGERPRINTS.
THE BULLET CASINGS WERE MUCH MORE IMPORTANT.
I THINK I SHOULD RETRACE BARAT'S STEPS OVER THE LAST FEW DAYS. SEE WHO HE TALKED TO, WHAT HE WAS DOING...
NO!
I MEAN... NO--IT'S OKAY-- JOHN AND RABBI ROSEN ARE DOING THAT.
THEN I'LL DO THE AUTOPSY!
I'VE DONE THEM BEFORE...
...I MEAN, NOT TO A DEAD GUY--
--BUT THE CUTS'VE GOTTA BE PRETTY MUCH THE SAME, RIGHT?

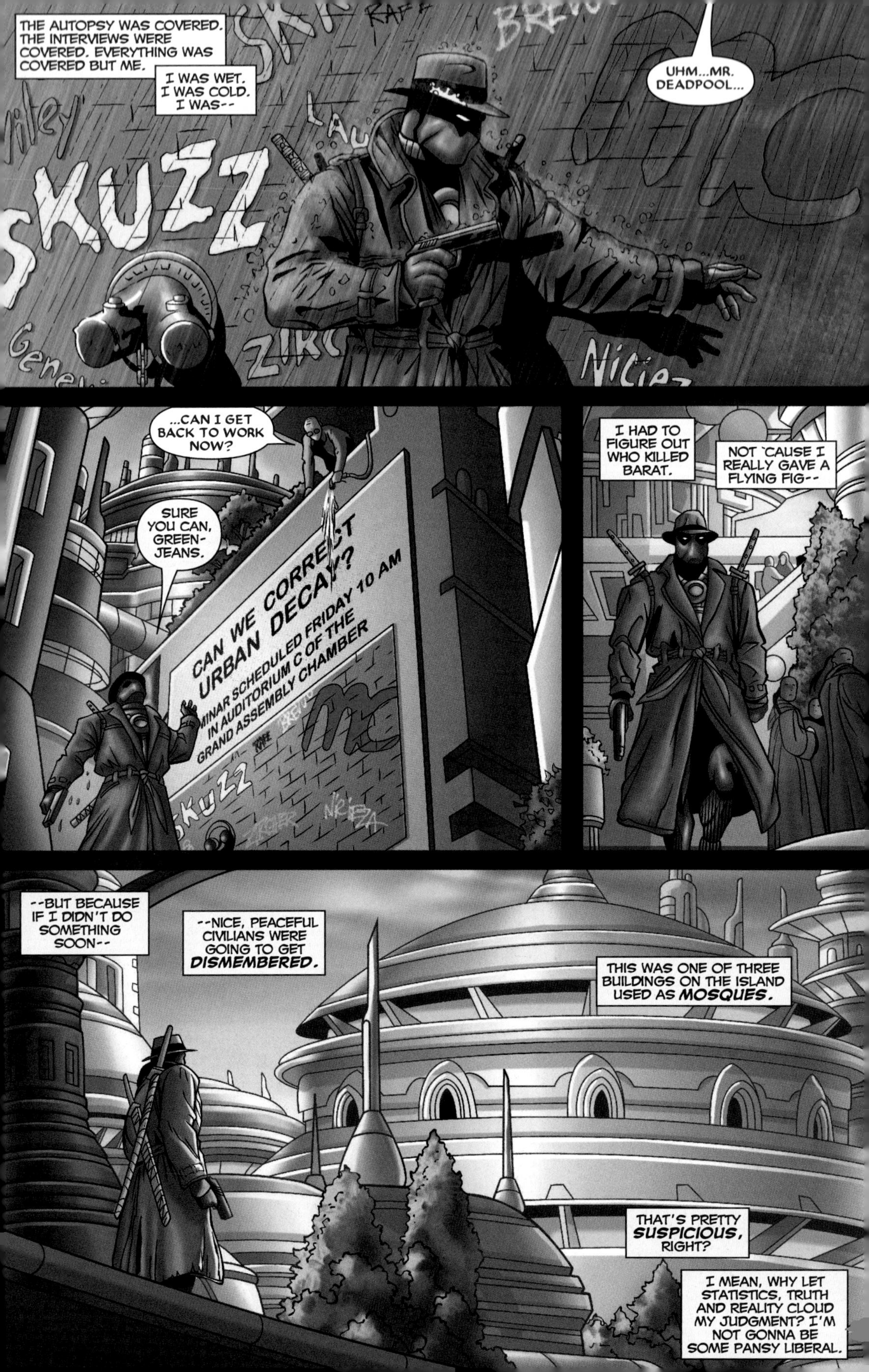

THE AUTOPSY WAS COVERED. THE INTERVIEWS WERE COVERED. EVERYTHING WAS COVERED BUT ME.
I WAS WET. I WAS COLD. I WAS--
UHM...MR. DEADPOOL...
SKUZZ
...CAN I GET BACK TO WORK NOW?
SURE YOU CAN, GREEN-JEANS.
CAN WE CORRECT URBAN DECAY?
MINAR SCHEDULED FRIDAY 10 AM IN AUDITORIUM C OF THE GRAND ASSEMBLY CHAMBER
I HAD TO FIGURE OUT WHO KILLED BARAT.
NOT 'CAUSE I REALLY GAVE A FLYING FIG--
--BUT BECAUSE IF I DIDN'T DO SOMETHING SOON--
--NICE, PEACEFUL CIVILIANS WERE GOING TO GET DISMEMBERED.
THIS WAS ONE OF THREE BUILDINGS ON THE ISLAND USED AS MOSQUES.
THAT'S PRETTY SUSPICIOUS, RIGHT?
I MEAN, WHY LET STATISTICS, TRUTH AND REALITY CLOUD MY JUDGMENT? I'M NOT GONNA BE SOME PANSY LIBERAL.

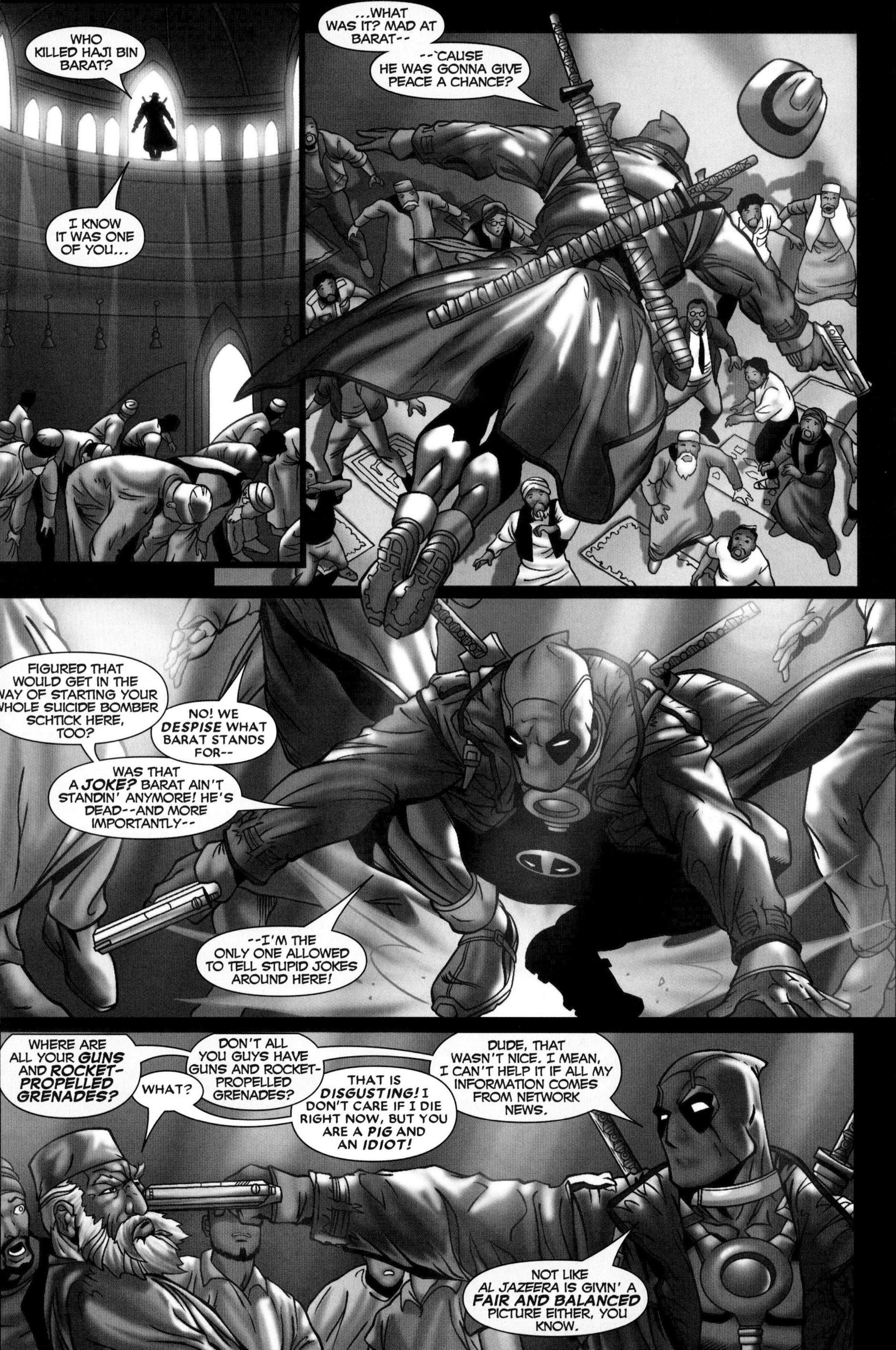
WHO KILLED HAJI BIN BARAT?
I KNOW IT WAS ONE OF YOU...
...WHAT WAS IT? MAD AT BARAT--
--'CAUSE HE WAS GONNA GIVE PEACE A CHANCE?
FIGURED THAT WOULD GET IN THE WAY OF STARTING YOUR WHOLE SUICIDE BOMBER SCHTICK HERE, TOO?
NO! WE DESPISE WHAT BARAT STANDS FOR--
WAS THAT A JOKE? BARAT AIN'T STANDIN' ANYMORE! HE'S DEAD--AND MORE IMPORTANTLY--
--I'M THE ONLY ONE ALLOWED TO TELL STUPID JOKES AROUND HERE!
WHERE ARE ALL YOUR GUNS AND ROCKET-PROPELLED GRENADES?
WHAT?
DON'T ALL YOU GUYS HAVE GUNS AND ROCKET-PROPELLED GRENADES?
THAT IS DISGUSTING! I DON'T CARE IF I DIE RIGHT NOW, BUT YOU ARE A PIG AND AN IDIOT!
DUDE, THAT WASN'T NICE. I MEAN, I CAN'T HELP IT IF ALL MY INFORMATION COMES FROM NETWORK NEWS.
NOT LIKE AL JAZEERA IS GIVIN' A FAIR AND BALANCED PICTURE EITHER, YOU KNOW.

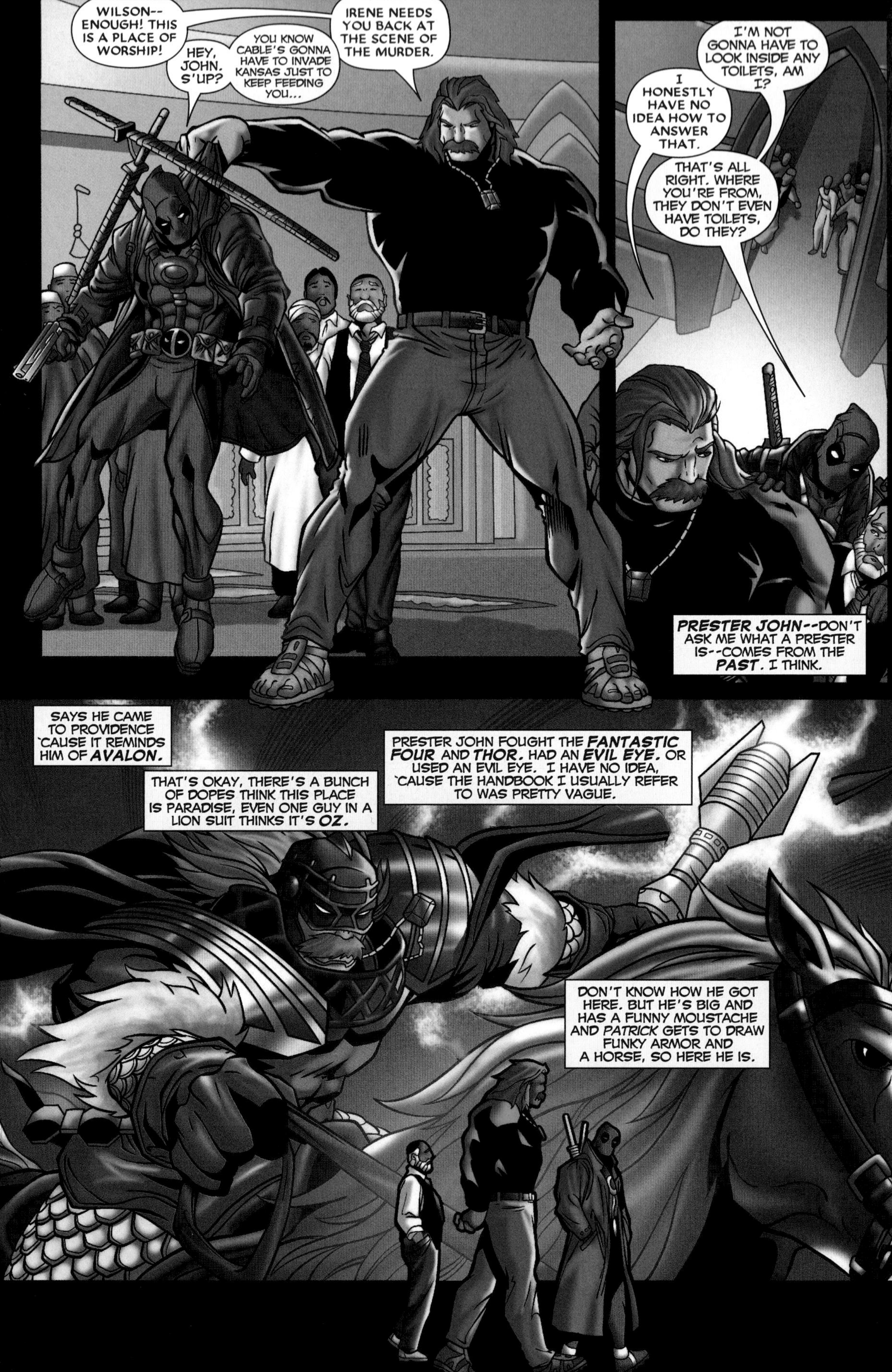
WILSON-- ENOUGH! THIS IS A PLACE OF WORSHIP!
HEY, JOHN. S'UP?
YOU KNOW CABLE'S GONNA HAVE TO INVADE KANSAS JUST TO KEEP FEEDING YOU...
IRENE NEEDS YOU BACK AT THE SCENE OF THE MURDER.
I'M NOT GONNA HAVE TO LOOK INSIDE ANY TOILETS, AM I?
I HONESTLY HAVE NO IDEA HOW TO ANSWER THAT.
THAT'S ALL RIGHT. WHERE YOU'RE FROM, THEY DON'T EVEN HAVE TOILETS, DO THEY?
PRESTER JOHN--DON'T ASK ME WHAT A PRESTER IS--COMES FROM THE PAST. I THINK.
SAYS HE CAME TO PROVIDENCE 'CAUSE IT REMINDS HIM OF AVALON.
THAT'S OKAY, THERE'S A BUNCH OF DOPES THINK THIS PLACE IS PARADISE, EVEN ONE GUY IN A LION SUIT THINKS IT'S OZ.
PRESTER JOHN FOUGHT THE FANTASTIC FOUR AND THOR. HAD AN EVIL EYE. OR USED AN EVIL EYE. I HAVE NO IDEA, 'CAUSE THE HANDBOOK I USUALLY REFER TO WAS PRETTY VAGUE.
DON'T KNOW HOW HE GOT HERE. BUT HE'S BIG AND HAS A FUNNY MOUSTACHE AND PATRICK GETS TO DRAW FUNKY ARMOR AND A HORSE, SO HERE HE IS.

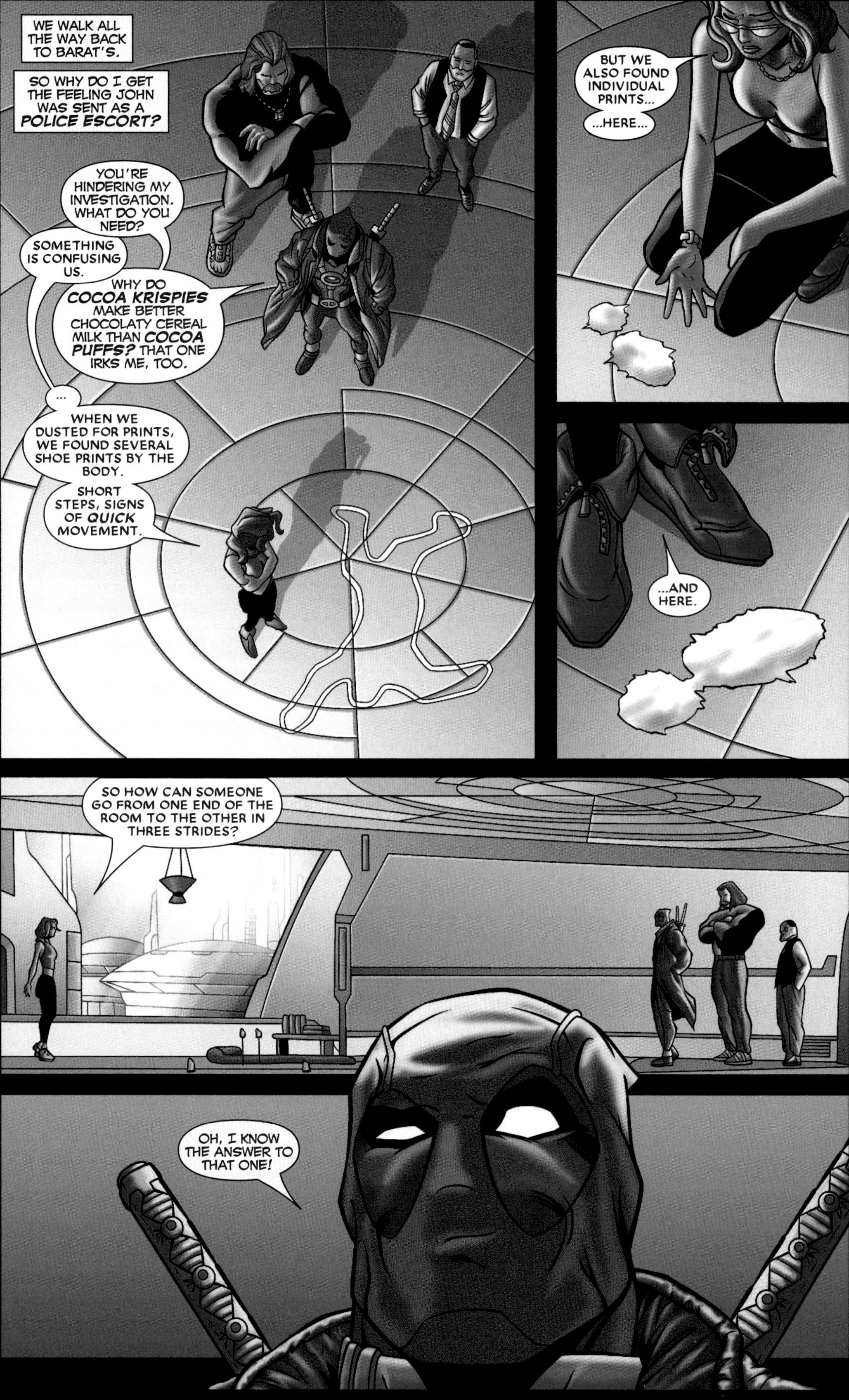
WE WALK ALL THE WAY BACK TO BARAT'S.
SO WHY DO I GET THE FEELING JOHN WAS SENT AS A POLICE ESCORT?
YOU'RE HINDERING MY INVESTIGATION. WHAT DO YOU NEED?
SOMETHING IS CONFUSING US.
WHY DO COCOA KRISPIES MAKE BETTER CHOCOLATY CEREAL MILK THAN COCOA PUFFS? THAT ONE IRKS ME, TOO.
...
WHEN WE DUSTED FOR PRINTS, WE FOUND SEVERAL SHOE PRINTS BY THE BODY.
SHORT STEPS, SIGNS OF QUICK MOVEMENT.
BUT WE ALSO FOUND INDIVIDUAL PRINTS...
...HERE...
...AND HERE.
SO HOW CAN SOMEONE GO FROM ONE END OF THE ROOM TO THE OTHER IN THREE STRIDES?
OH, I KNOW THE ANSWER TO THAT ONE!

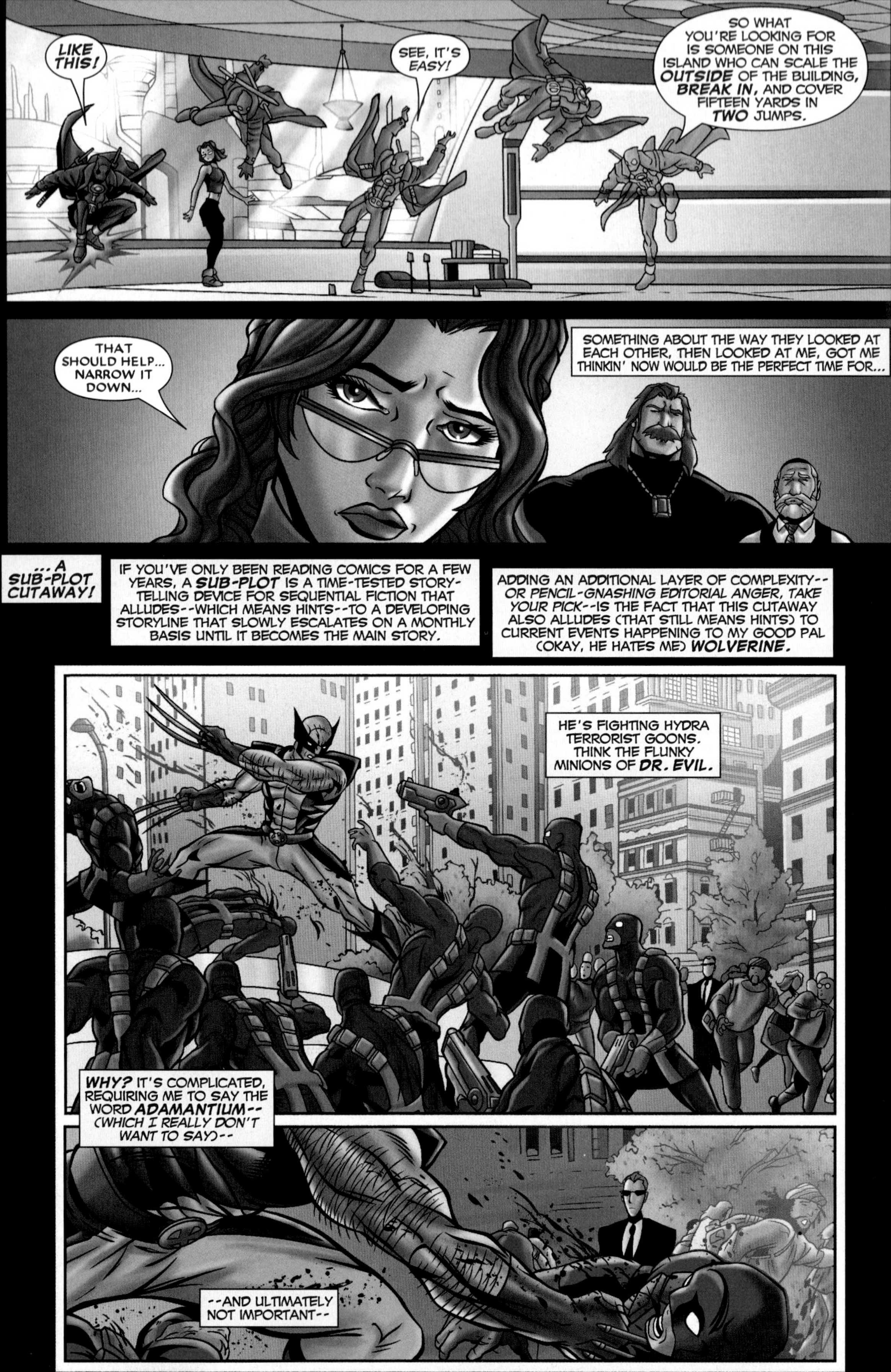
LIKE THIS!
SEE, IT'S EASY!
SO WHAT YOU'RE LOOKING FOR IS SOMEONE ON THIS ISLAND WHO CAN SCALE THE OUTSIDE OF THE BUILDING, BREAK IN, AND COVER FIFTEEN YARDS IN TWO JUMPS.
THAT SHOULD HELP... NARROW IT DOWN...
SOMETHING ABOUT THE WAY THEY LOOKED AT EACH OTHER, THEN LOOKED AT ME, GOT ME THINKIN' NOW WOULD BE THE PERFECT TIME FOR...
...A SUB-PLOT CUTAWAY!
IF YOU'VE ONLY BEEN READING COMICS FOR A FEW YEARS, A SUB-PLOT IS A TIME-TESTED STORY-TELLING DEVICE FOR SEQUENTIAL FICTION THAT ALLUDES--WHICH MEANS HINTS--TO A DEVELOPING STORYLINE THAT SLOWLY ESCALATES ON A MONTHLY BASIS UNTIL IT BECOMES THE MAIN STORY.
ADDING AN ADDITIONAL LAYER OF COMPLEXITY--OR PENCIL-GNASHING EDITORIAL ANGER, TAKE YOUR PICK--IS THE FACT THAT THIS CUTAWAY ALSO ALLUDES (THAT STILL MEANS HINTS) TO CURRENT EVENTS HAPPENING TO MY GOOD PAL (OKAY, HE HATES ME) WOLVERINE.
HE'S FIGHTING HYDRA TERRORIST GOONS. THINK THE FLUNKY MINIONS OF DR. EVIL.
WHY? IT'S COMPLICATED, REQUIRING ME TO SAY THE WORD ADAMANTIUM--(WHICH I REALLY DON'T WANT TO SAY)--
--AND ULTIMATELY NOT IMPORTANT--

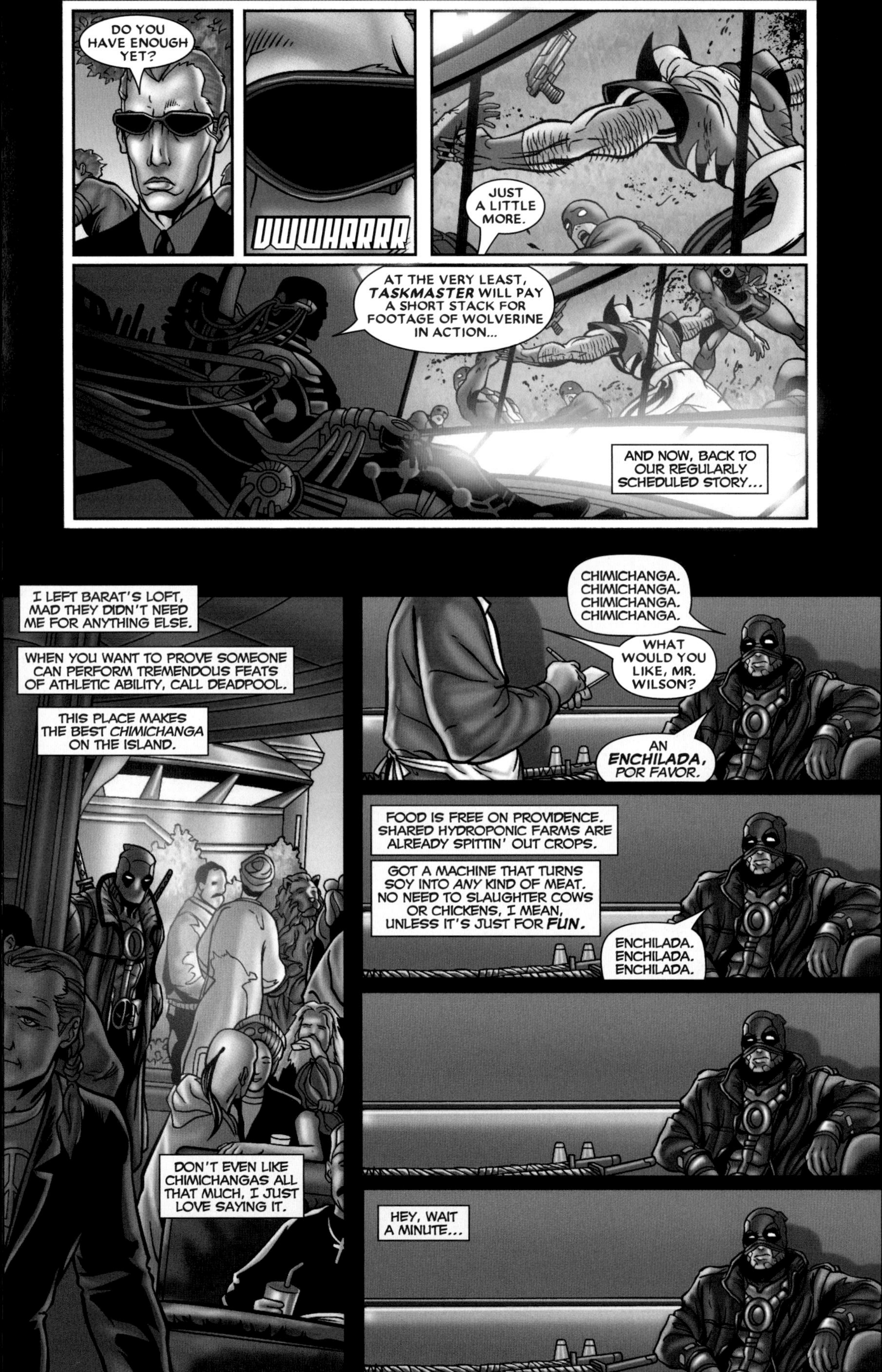

DO YOU HAVE ENOUGH YET?
VWWHRRRR
JUST A LITTLE MORE.
AT THE VERY LEAST, TASKMASTER WILL PAY A SHORT STACK FOR FOOTAGE OF WOLVERINE IN ACTION...
AND NOW, BACK TO OUR REGULARLY SCHEDULED STORY...
I LEFT BARAT'S LOFT, MAD THEY DIDN'T NEED ME FOR ANYTHING ELSE.
WHEN YOU WANT TO PROVE SOMEONE CAN PERFORM TREMENDOUS FEATS OF ATHLETIC ABILITY, CALL DEADPOOL.
THIS PLACE MAKES THE BEST CHIMICHANGA ON THE ISLAND.
DON'T EVEN LIKE CHIMICHANGAS ALL THAT MUCH, I JUST LOVE SAYING IT.
CHIMICHANGA. CHIMICHANGA. CHIMICHANGA. CHIMICHANGA.
WHAT WOULD YOU LIKE, MR. WILSON?
AN ENCHILADA, POR FAVOR.
FOOD IS FREE ON PROVIDENCE. SHARED HYDROPONIC FARMS ARE ALREADY SPITTIN' OUT CROPS.
GOT A MACHINE THAT TURNS SOY INTO ANY KIND OF MEAT. NO NEED TO SLAUGHTER COWS OR CHICKENS, I MEAN, UNLESS IT'S JUST FOR FUN.
ENCHILADA. ENCHILADA. ENCHILADA.
HEY, WAIT A MINUTE...

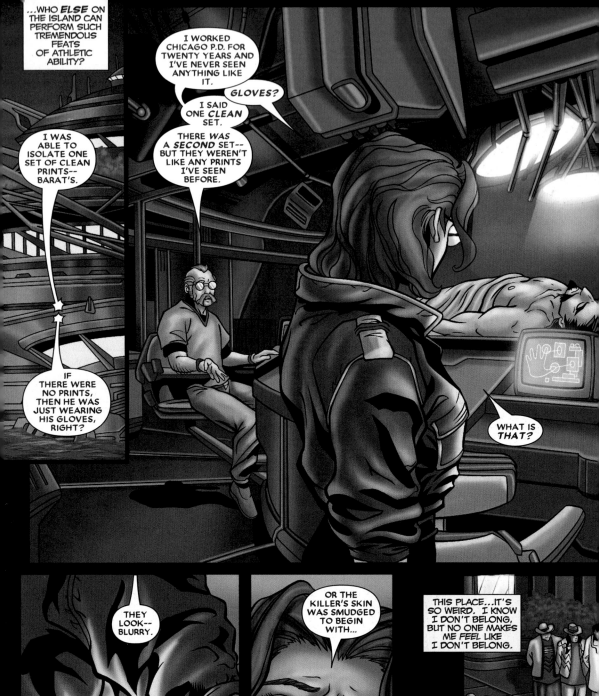

...WHO *ELSE* ON THE ISLAND CAN PERFORM SUCH TREMENDOUS FEATS OF ATHLETIC ABILITY?

I WAS ABLE TO ISOLATE ONE SET OF CLEAN PRINTS-- BARAT'S.

IF THERE WERE NO PRINTS, THEN HE WAS JUST WEARING HIS GLOVES, RIGHT?

I WORKED CHICAGO P.D. FOR TWENTY YEARS AND I'VE NEVER SEEN ANYTHING LIKE IT.

GLOVES?

I SAID ONE *CLEAN* SET.

THERE *WAS* A *SECOND* SET-- BUT THEY WEREN'T LIKE ANY PRINTS I'VE SEEN BEFORE.

WHAT IS *THAT?*

THEY LOOK-- BLURRY.

LIKE HE SMUDGED EACH AND EVERY ONE OF THE PRINTS HE LEFT BEHIND.

OR THE KILLER'S SKIN WAS SMUDGED TO BEGIN WITH...

THIS PLACE...IT'S SO WEIRD. I KNOW I DON'T BELONG, BUT NO ONE MAKES ME FEEL LIKE I DON'T BELONG.

DOES THAT MAKE SENSE?

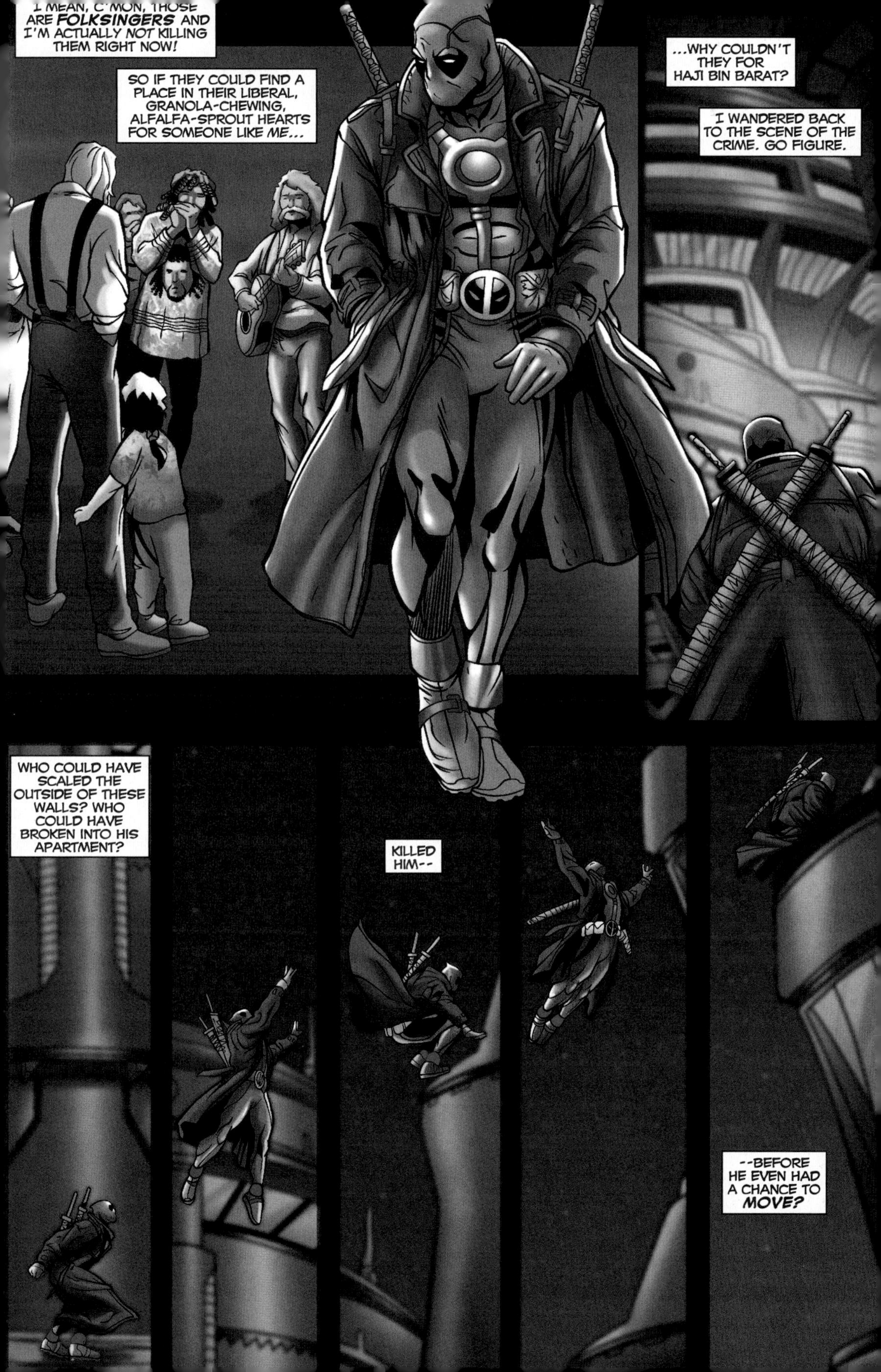
I MEAN, C'MON, THOSE ARE FOLKSINGERS AND I'M ACTUALLY NOT KILLING THEM RIGHT NOW!
SO IF THEY COULD FIND A PLACE IN THEIR LIBERAL, GRANOLA-CHEWING, ALFALFA-SPROUT HEARTS FOR SOMEONE LIKE ME...
...WHY COULDN'T THEY FOR HAJI BIN BARAT?
I WANDERED BACK TO THE SCENE OF THE CRIME. GO FIGURE.
WHO COULD HAVE SCALED THE OUTSIDE OF THESE WALLS? WHO COULD HAVE BROKEN INTO HIS APARTMENT?
KILLED HIM--
--BEFORE HE EVEN HAD A CHANCE TO MOVE?

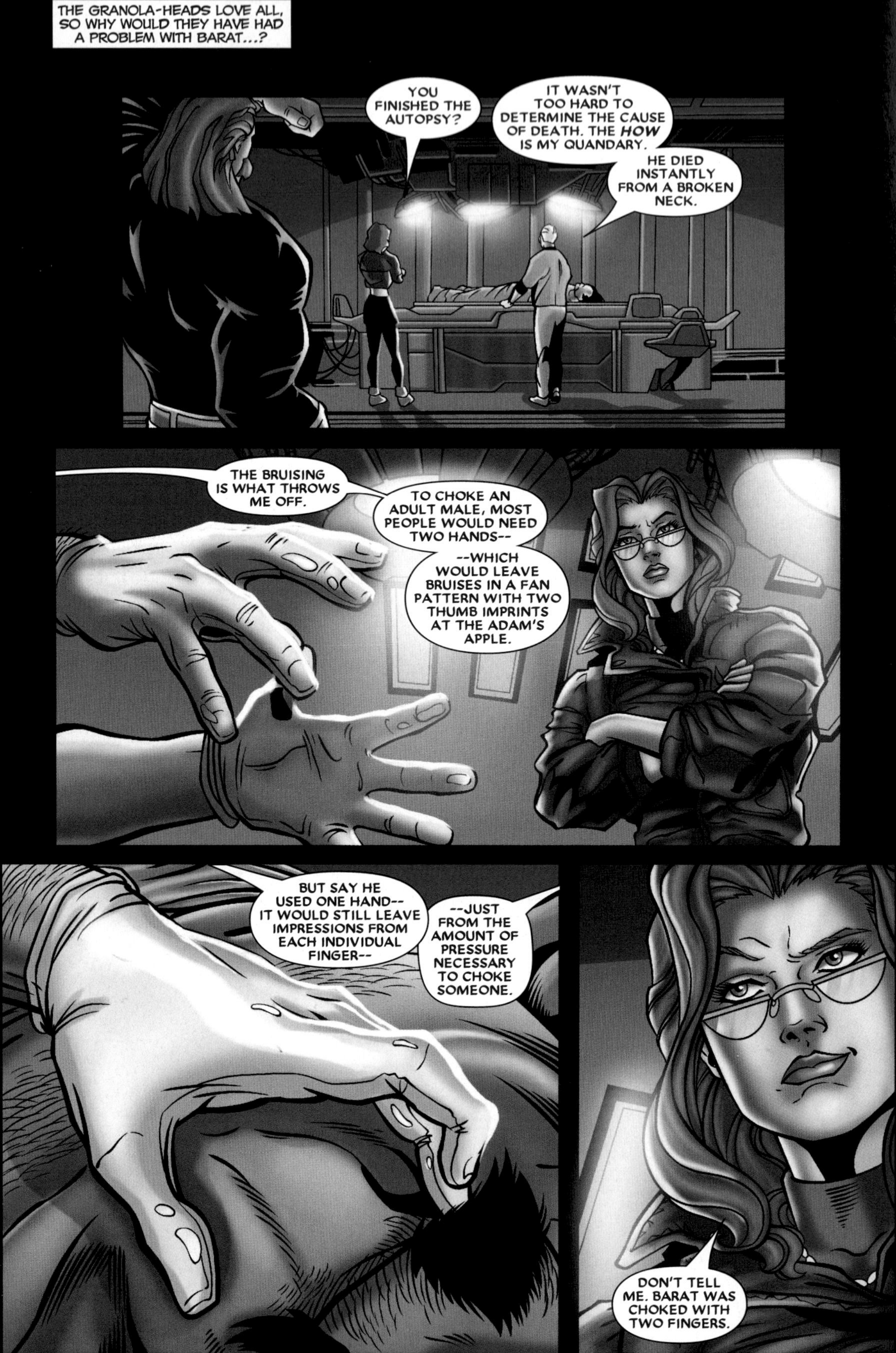
THE GRANOLA-HEADS LOVE ALL, SO WHY WOULD THEY HAVE HAD A PROBLEM WITH BARAT...?
YOU FINISHED THE AUTOPSY?
IT WASN'T TOO HARD TO DETERMINE THE CAUSE OF DEATH. THE *HOW* IS MY QUANDARY.
HE DIED INSTANTLY FROM A BROKEN NECK.
THE BRUISING IS WHAT THROWS ME OFF.
TO CHOKE AN ADULT MALE, MOST PEOPLE WOULD NEED TWO HANDS--
--WHICH WOULD LEAVE BRUISES IN A FAN PATTERN WITH TWO THUMB IMPRINTS AT THE ADAM'S APPLE.
BUT SAY HE USED ONE HAND-- IT WOULD STILL LEAVE IMPRESSIONS FROM EACH INDIVIDUAL FINGER--
--JUST FROM THE AMOUNT OF PRESSURE NECESSARY TO CHOKE SOMEONE.
DON'T TELL ME. BARAT WAS CHOKED WITH TWO FINGERS.

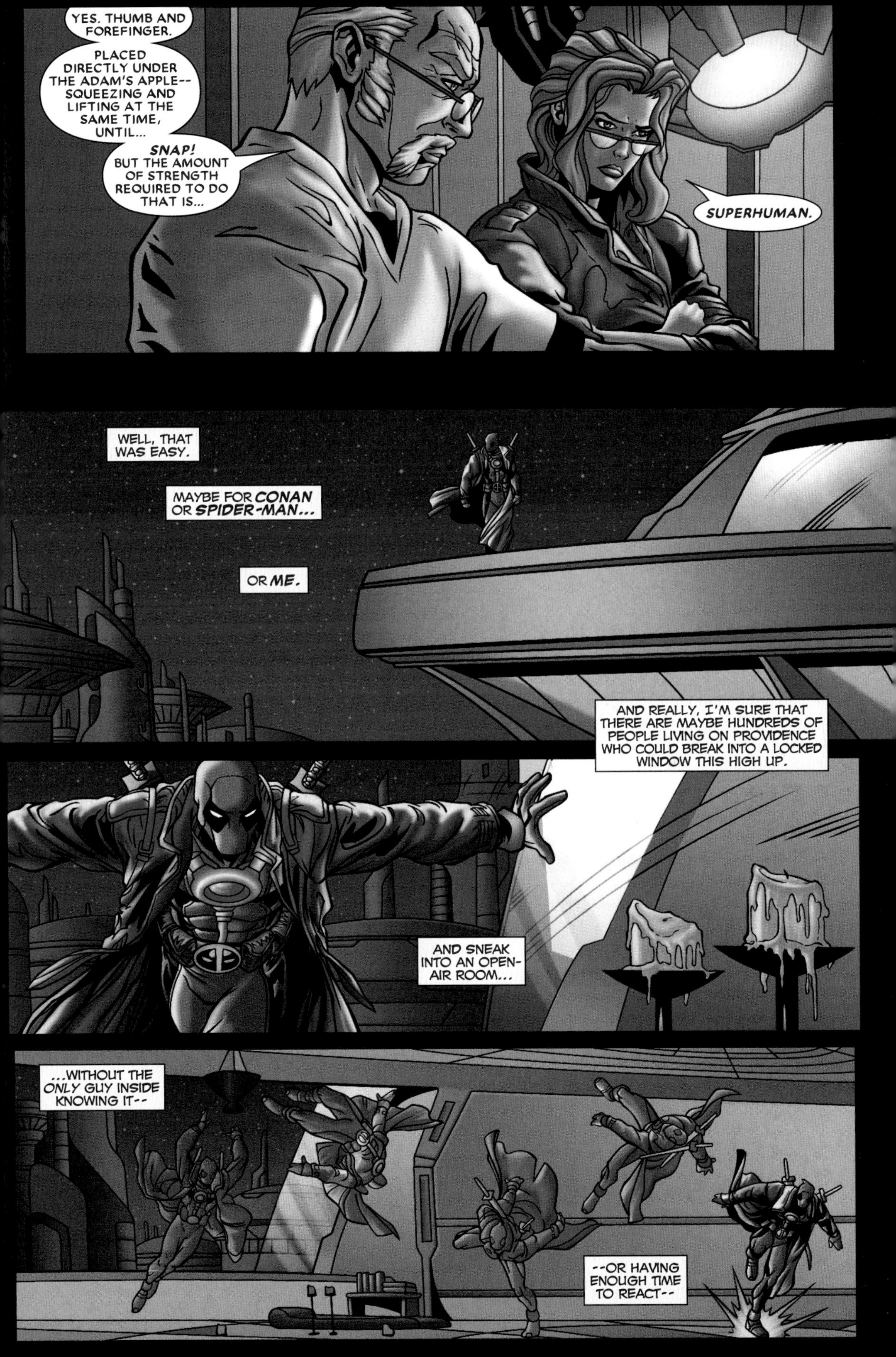
YES. THUMB AND FOREFINGER.
PLACED DIRECTLY UNDER THE ADAM'S APPLE-- SQUEEZING AND LIFTING AT THE SAME TIME, UNTIL...
SNAP! BUT THE AMOUNT OF STRENGTH REQUIRED TO DO THAT IS...
SUPERHUMAN.
WELL, THAT WAS EASY.
MAYBE FOR CONAN OR SPIDER-MAN...
OR ME.
AND REALLY, I'M SURE THAT THERE ARE MAYBE HUNDREDS OF PEOPLE LIVING ON PROVIDENCE WHO COULD BREAK INTO A LOCKED WINDOW THIS HIGH UP.
AND SNEAK INTO AN OPEN-AIR ROOM...
...WITHOUT THE ONLY GUY INSIDE KNOWING IT--
--OR HAVING ENOUGH TIME TO REACT--

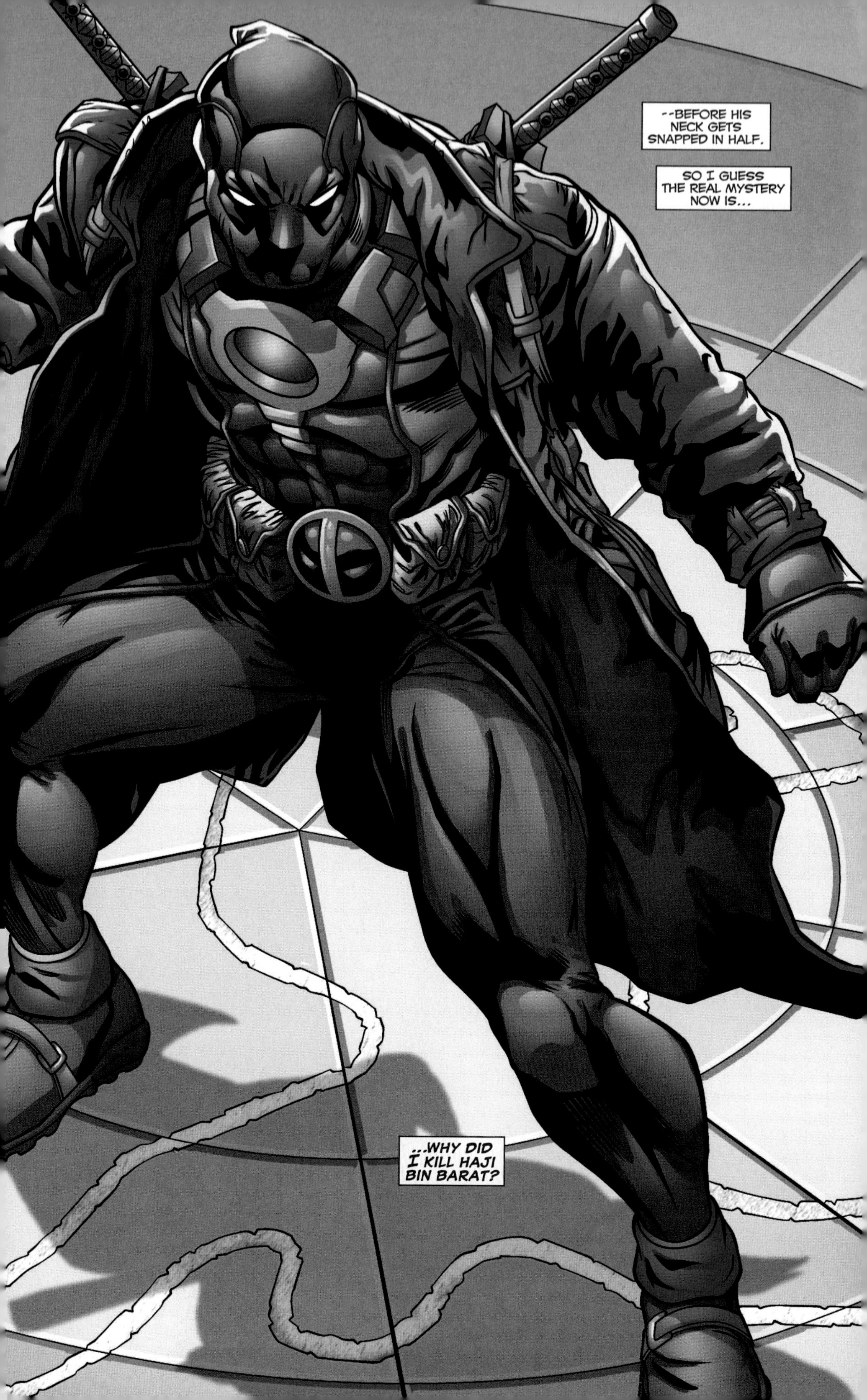
--BEFORE HIS NECK GETS SNAPPED IN HALF.
SO I GUESS THE REAL MYSTERY NOW IS...
...WHY DID I KILL HAJI BIN BARAT?

DEAR DEADPOOL

That's right, old chums—lucky issue 13 marks our first-ever letters page! Let the wig-flipping commence as DP himself responds to YOUR comments. Enjoy.

–CDP team

Dear Cable & Deadpool team,

I just wanted to tell you that your book is AWESOME!!! It's always the first book I read on new comic day. I have to admit when the title first arrived at my local comic store I was skeptical. "Cable…?" I said, "and Deadpool? How…why?" You all proved me sooo wrong. Patrick's pencils capture the lighthearted action perfectly and Fabian's storytelling effectively blew my mind in a major way. The most major of ways, really. I thought the days of mind-blowing comics ended long ago but you guys proved me wrong. Any book that has a cameo from the Silver Surfer (biggest badass in the cosmos forever) is alright in my book. I thought I was going to flip my wig when he matched wits and powers with Cable. Anyways, I could go on forever about the excellent dialogue, the fresh storytelling, the awesome art, or even the punctuality of the book, but suffice it to say…Keep up the good work guys, you're actually doing it!! Thanks for a great read. Excelsior!!!!!

Sincerely,
Sam Wilson (not the Falcon)
Richmond, VA

Are you really the Falcon? That is so cool. I had your Mego figure back in the 70's, but the wings were made out of cloth. Lame. How's Redwing? Tell 'im I'm still sorry about ruining his chances with that pigeon over on Union Square.

So anyway, thanks for the letter and for having the LEAST amount of typos out of any letter on this page!

Dear everyone on Cable/Deadpool,

Well done for creating the best team-up comic on the market. The duo has dynamics that make me pick up the title every month. For starters there's the comedy – who can beat Deadpool for comedy? The guy turns everything into a joke (but with a serious undertone). Seeing him as an "X-Man" (well, temp–X-Man) in Marvel Girl's costume had me laughing so hard my sides did actually hurt.

Then there's the action – Cable's a soldier who means business, just look how he not only took on the Blue Church, the Six Pack and the X-Men but also the Silver Surfer!! Even the Avengers didn't see so much action in their last arc.

And who could forget storylines? I don't know how Fabian does it but he pulls off some amazing story arcs that keep me fixated on the comic the whole time I'm reading (and then pull me back in for a 2nd glance).

So in closing I would like to say thanks to Fabian for the great stories, Mr. Zircher/Udon for the amazing art (it is amazingly well done) and to the editorial team for keeping all this action going!

Make Mine Marvel,
Gary Pickup
Salford, UK

For a guy from England, let me tell you, I practically sprained my wrist fixing all your typos. I thought you guys were supposed to be educated or something? Just `cause you invented the language doesn't mean you can brutalize it!

Oh, thanks for the kind words, except telling us more happened in our book than in Avengers is kind of a backhanded compliment, since nothing happens in their book anymore.

That was a cheap shot. Sorry. I wanted to be in the New Avengers, but I didn't "rate" as important enough, which, sure, I guess I understand, considering we got Spider-Woman, Sentry, Luke Cage – all top headliner type guys.

Hope they get cancelled. What, Nicole? They're selling like two hundred bazillion copies? Serious? Crap. That's like 90's numbers… What're we selling? You kidding? Really? Oh.

Never mind.

Dear Mr. Nicieza,

Cable & Deadpool and the (New) Thunderbolts are my two favorite books and I couldn't be happier that you are at the helm. Cutting to the chase and avoiding all the kissing-up (although warranted), I must ask whether your statement by Deadpool on the seventh-to-last page of Cable and Deadpool #12 "...anyone wearing a harness rig has a failsafe release to prevent it from catching on fire and forcing you to fly into Kree spaceships and blow up..." is a direct reference to the supposedly-late Hawkeye? Could the 'new Swordsman' whom you've introduced in the New Thunderbolts perhaps be our hero brought back to life? I hope so, but I won't keep my fingers crossed. Thank you for writing my favorite books so incredibly well and making my Wednesdays at the comic shop so enjoyable.

P.S. Is there any possible way you could let me know how to get ahold of Tom Grummett's original art?! I'm dying to get my hands on some original pages of Atlas from the New Thunderbolts!

P.S.S. Please don't kill Atlas! He's my favorite character!

Best,
Matthew Roderick Eschert

Okay, first of all, I hate P.S.'s and P.S.S.'s. I think they're kinda, well, limp. Second of all, we would never make fun of the Avengers. Ever. They're the bestest ever. Ever.

Third of all, it's incredibly rude to be asking about Grummett's art in a book drawn by Zircher. Do you have ANY idea how incredibly insecure artists are? Nicieza (geshundheit) tells me printing this letter is going to cost him six hours on the phone with Patrick now.

Lastly, the new Swordsman is NOT Hawkeye. Hawkeye is dead. He died a wonderfully heroic death over in that incredibly great comic book, the Avengers.

Hey there.

Maybe I'm just dense, but I still have NO idea why the hell reintroducing the T.O. thing back into Cable's system is the way to magically reverse his lobotomy. I just finished Cable/Deadpool #12 and I've been waiting for it to make sense, and it doesn't yet. It's all vague factoids that don't congeal. I enjoyed Deadpool monkeying around with Agent X, though.

Thanks!
Andy

Okay, Andy, thanks for letting us print this letter, 'cause seriously, dude, you're just ASKING for some abuse. Before I start, though, let me apologize in advance, because in your defense, you might not realize that YOURE ACTUALLY SUPPOSED TO READ THE COMIC BOOK.

(Oh, and the missing apostrophe was just a bone I'm tossing to Gary).

Let's clarify your confusion at #12. Per the PRINTED DIALOGUE (which, by the way, you're supposed to read):

Fixer says, "The whole idea was to reintroduce the techno-organic mesh into Cable's system, `cept since this is an actual lifeform, with a mind of its own, we're risking it'll fight back against Cable… but it's an embryo, for crying out loud, what kind of wuss would let an alien baby take over his mind?"

Followed by cute drawings of Cable deciding to fight back against the alien baby, which, apparently, from what was written above, was trying to take over his mind.

And in response to Cable telling Domino he doesn't want to start the cycle of fighting the t-o virus all over again, Domino says, "This will be different, won't it? You used to channel your powers inward to keep the virus at bay – but this isn't a virus anymore and you don't have your powers."

And Cable says, "So merging with a symbiote is somehow better…"

And a page later, Fixer says Cable is gaining control over it, using it to form bone and muscle structure. Then Cable wakes up with his new arm. A page later, Cable clearly says most of his telepathy is gone. He doesn't have his powers anymore. I removed that part of his brain in #10. But he doesn't need his powers to control the t-o mesh, cause it's not a virus attacking his body anymore, it's a symbiotic lifeform – a baby he valiantly kicked the crap out of.

Wasn't that easy? Sheesh. Readers today… how would you guys have ever survived Omega the Unknown…?

Dear Cable and Deadpool,

Just want to give my thanks for a really great title, and one that is full of Marvel continuity. Great stuff. Now I got some questions, and some very exciting requests!!

1. With the recent launch of Black Panther, how about getting in on some of the spotlight, and have T'Challa himself meet Cable and Deadpool, he's met them both before but not together...
2. Pitch a Deadpool/Deathstroke series to DC and Marvel, and get Gail Simone and Fabian to write together, it would be a major hit I'm telling you!!
3. Bullseye ('nuff said).
4. I wanna see Cable help Wade figure out more of his past.
5. We need Apocolypse to show up again!! He is making big headlines right now, and is Cable's major baddy.
6. I wanna see some more Arab-Berber heroes!! (Not villains.) Give them some good representations!!

So until Cable and Deadpool bring their feelings out of the closet for each other, Make Mine Marvel!

Jimal Sagaiar

Okay, Jimal. I liked your letter. Easy and to the point.
1) T'Challa is too cool for us and he could kick my butt in, so no, he won't be appearing in this book.
2) Deathstroke is too cool for us and he could kick my butt in, so no, he won't be appearing in this book. And Fabian is too insecure about comparing himself to Gail, so he said no, too. And Marvel's lawyers said no, on account of they don't want anyone at DC to notice the similarities. I don't know what that means.
3) Bullseye is too cool for us and he could… `nuff Said.
4) I don't like that idea. I don't want to know about my past. Except for trying to remember that night with the Lombardi twins…
5) Great idea. Since he'd kick Nate's butt up and down the book, expect this to happen real soon!
6) I had some entertaining run-ins with some Arabs in this issue. Hope you enjoyed it as much as I did.

Fabian, Zircher, et all,

Thank you for a hilarious and consistently impressive title. Issue 12 of C&D was quite possibly the best issue to date. When I first heard that Agent X was making an appearance I was a bit skeptical about how you would handle the character, but I was very impressed. There were lots of great jokes in this issue, and the art by Zircher was as always superb. I honestly think Patrick Zircher is the finest artist working for Marvel right now. The Fixer was great in this storyline I hope he doesn't disappear from comics after this arc, maybe you can bring him back into New Thunderbolts sometime soon.

The Alex Hayden recap page was the cream of the crop. As soon as I opened this book, I felt like I was reading my beloved Agent X all over again.

Thanks for a blast from the past. I can't wait to see what you've got in store in future issues.

So until Cable turns his hand into a spatula and starts a cooking show, Make Mine Cable & Deadpool.

James Mallone

Well, that was painless. Okay, thanks. Seriously. Spatula is still a funny word.

Oh, and Fabian thanks you for capitalizing his name. His ego needed that.

That's it for this month, folks! Next issue, a lightning bolt hits a federal superhuman prison freeing like a gajillion bad guys and the good guys go to get their butts handed to them instead of just letting the bad guys starve to death on an inaccessible island.

Want a comic book character verbally abusing YOU next? Send your letters to mheroes@marvel.com and mark your message "okay to print."

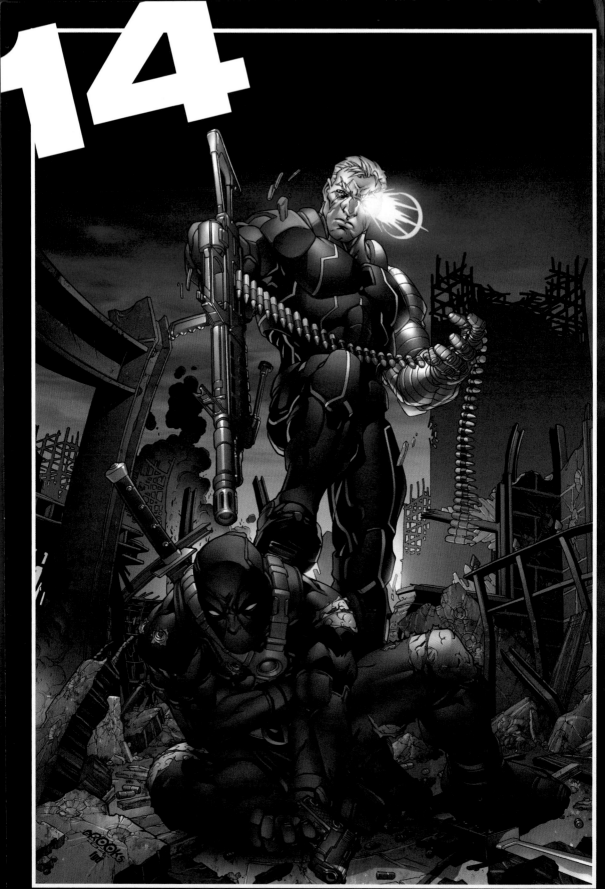

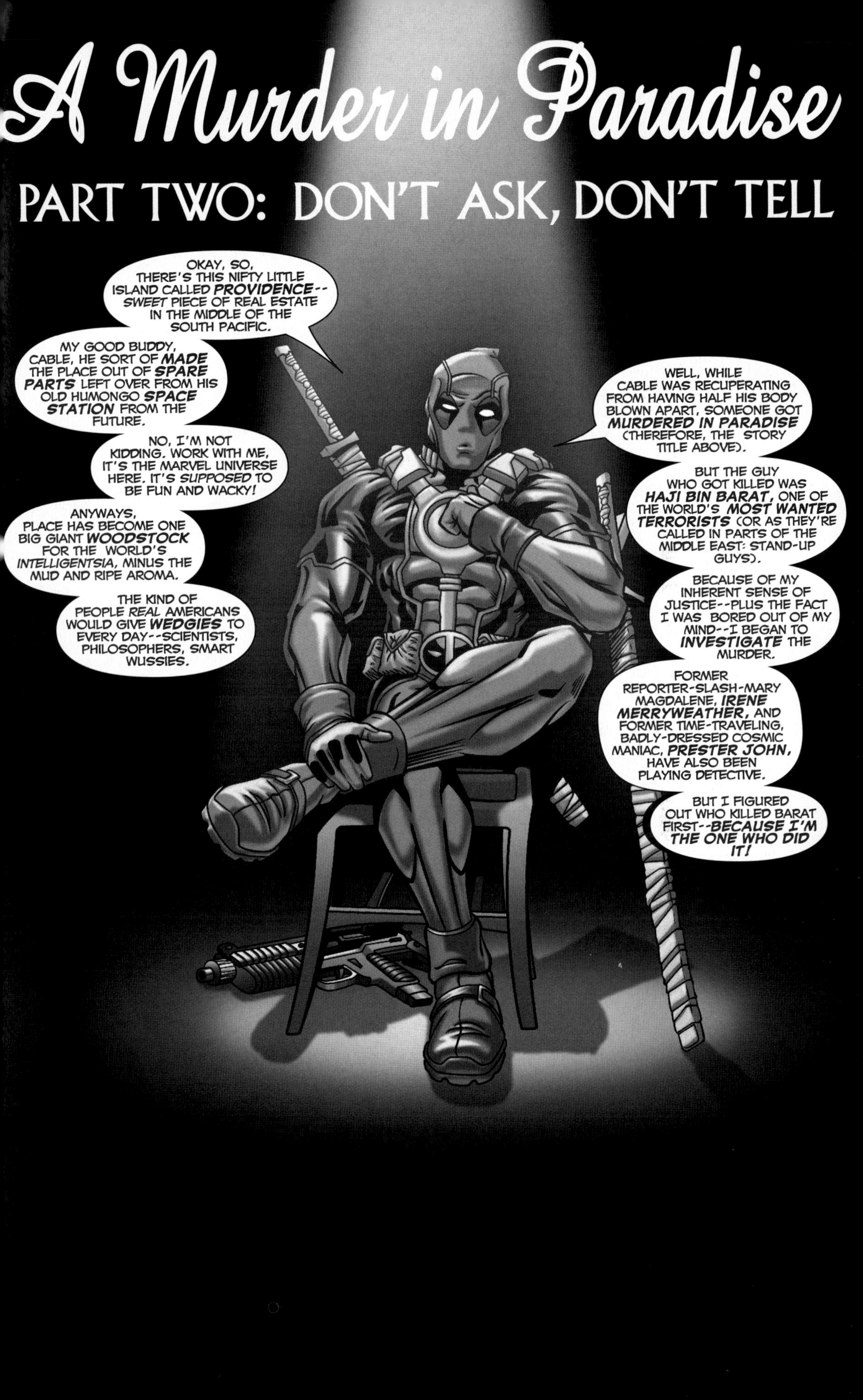
A Murder in Paradise
PART TWO: DON'T ASK, DON'T TELL
OKAY, SO, THERE'S THIS NIFTY LITTLE ISLAND CALLED PROVIDENCE--SWEET PIECE OF REAL ESTATE IN THE MIDDLE OF THE SOUTH PACIFIC.
MY GOOD BUDDY, CABLE, HE SORT OF MADE THE PLACE OUT OF SPARE PARTS LEFT OVER FROM HIS OLD HUMONGO SPACE STATION FROM THE FUTURE.
NO, I'M NOT KIDDING. WORK WITH ME, IT'S THE MARVEL UNIVERSE HERE. IT'S SUPPOSED TO BE FUN AND WACKY!
ANYWAYS, PLACE HAS BECOME ONE BIG GIANT WOODSTOCK FOR THE WORLD'S INTELLIGENTSIA, MINUS THE MUD AND RIPE AROMA.
THE KIND OF PEOPLE REAL AMERICANS WOULD GIVE WEDGIES TO EVERY DAY--SCIENTISTS, PHILOSOPHERS, SMART WUSSIES.
WELL, WHILE CABLE WAS RECUPERATING FROM HAVING HALF HIS BODY BLOWN APART, SOMEONE GOT MURDERED IN PARADISE (THEREFORE, THE STORY TITLE ABOVE).
BUT THE GUY WHO GOT KILLED WAS HAJI BIN BARAT, ONE OF THE WORLD'S MOST WANTED TERRORISTS (OR AS THEY'RE CALLED IN PARTS OF THE MIDDLE EAST: STAND-UP GUYS).
BECAUSE OF MY INHERENT SENSE OF JUSTICE--PLUS THE FACT I WAS BORED OUT OF MY MIND--I BEGAN TO INVESTIGATE THE MURDER.
FORMER REPORTER-SLASH-MARY MAGDALENE, IRENE MERRYWEATHER, AND FORMER TIME-TRAVELING, BADLY-DRESSED COSMIC MANIAC, PRESTER JOHN, HAVE ALSO BEEN PLAYING DETECTIVE.
BUT I FIGURED OUT WHO KILLED BARAT FIRST--BECAUSE I'M THE ONE WHO DID IT!

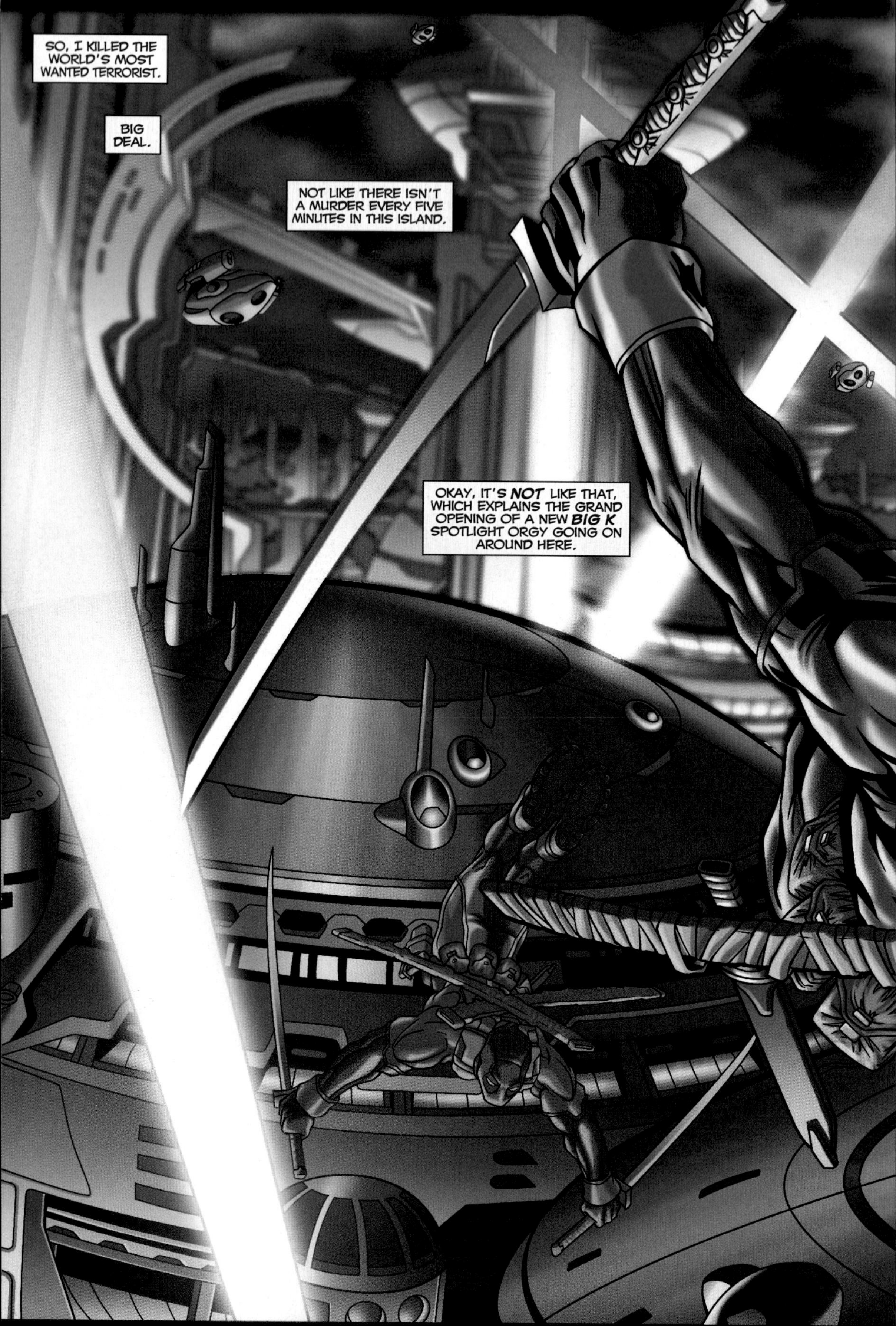
SO, I KILLED THE WORLD'S MOST WANTED TERRORIST.
BIG DEAL.
NOT LIKE THERE ISN'T A MURDER EVERY FIVE MINUTES IN THIS ISLAND.
OKAY, IT'S NOT LIKE THAT, WHICH EXPLAINS THE GRAND OPENING OF A NEW BIG K SPOTLIGHT ORGY GOING ON AROUND HERE.

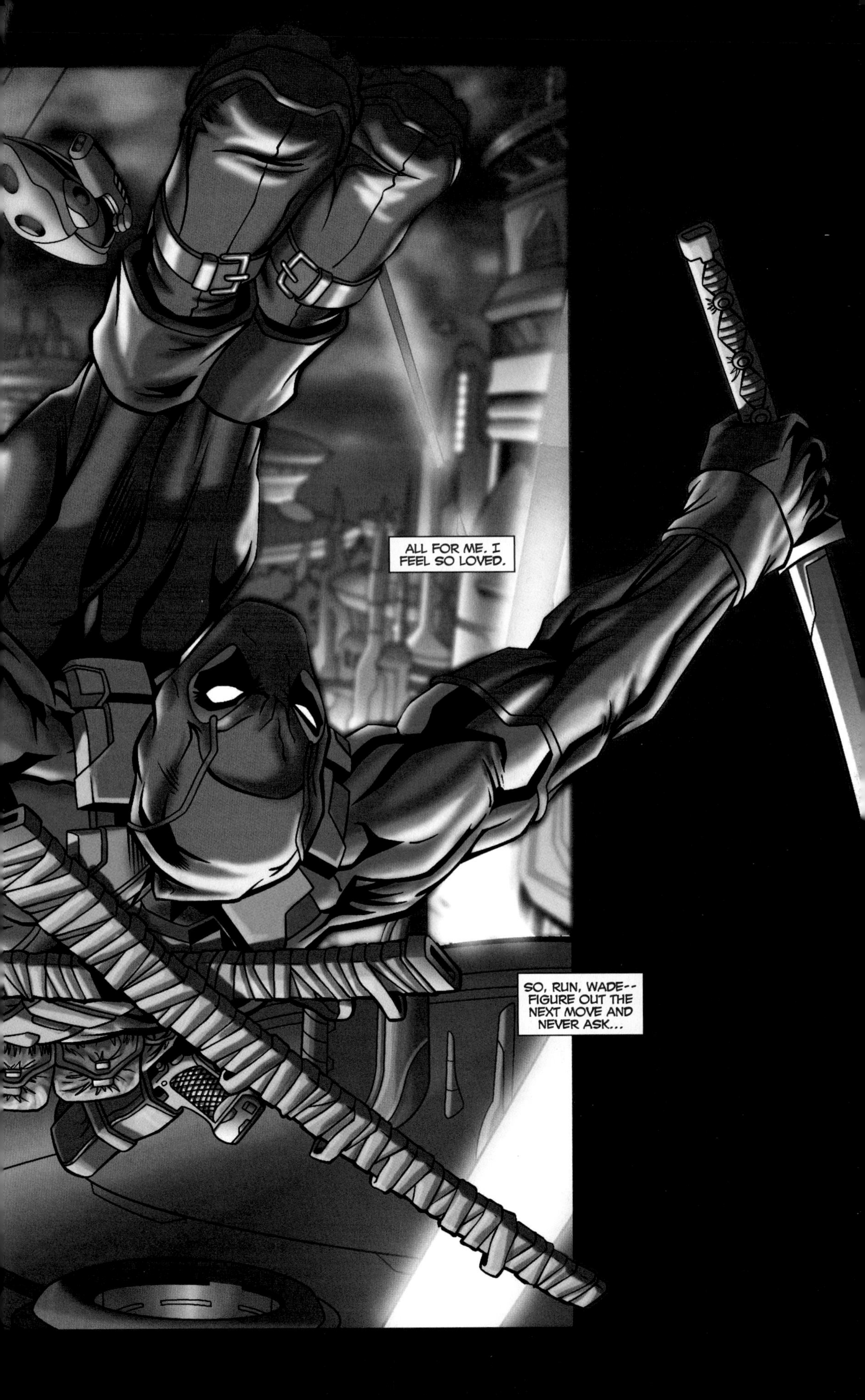
ALL FOR ME. I FEEL SO LOVED.
SO, RUN, WADE-- FIGURE OUT THE NEXT MOVE AND NEVER ASK...

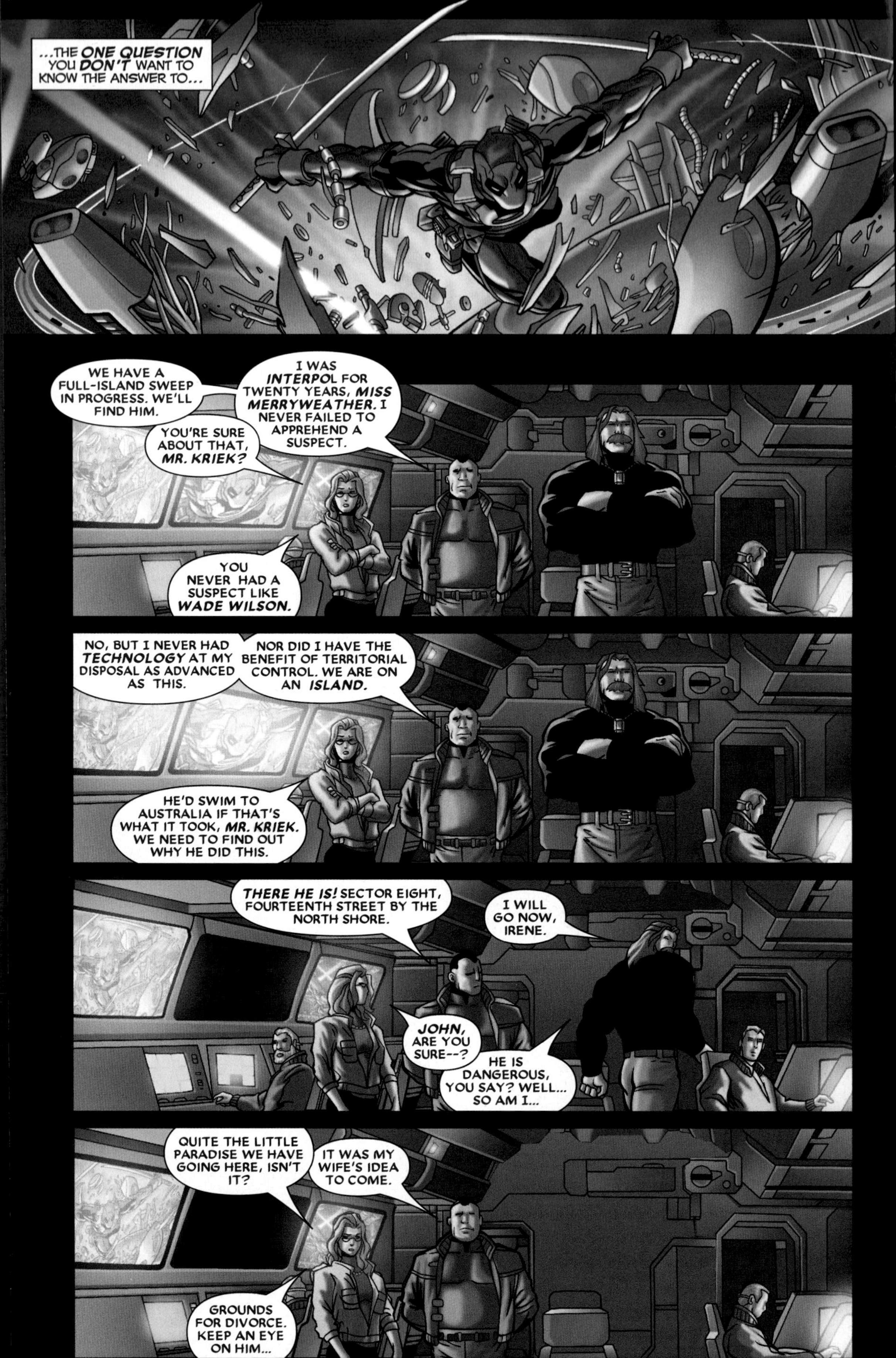
...THE ONE QUESTION YOU DON'T WANT TO KNOW THE ANSWER TO...
WE HAVE A FULL-ISLAND SWEEP IN PROGRESS. WE'LL FIND HIM.
YOU'RE SURE ABOUT THAT, MR. KRIEK?
I WAS INTERPOL FOR TWENTY YEARS, MISS MERRYWEATHER. I NEVER FAILED TO APPREHEND A SUSPECT.
YOU NEVER HAD A SUSPECT LIKE WADE WILSON.
NO, BUT I NEVER HAD TECHNOLOGY AT MY DISPOSAL AS ADVANCED AS THIS.
NOR DID I HAVE THE BENEFIT OF TERRITORIAL CONTROL. WE ARE ON AN ISLAND.
HE'D SWIM TO AUSTRALIA IF THAT'S WHAT IT TOOK, MR. KRIEK. WE NEED TO FIND OUT WHY HE DID THIS.
THERE HE IS! SECTOR EIGHT, FOURTEENTH STREET BY THE NORTH SHORE.
I WILL GO NOW, IRENE.
JOHN, ARE YOU SURE--?
HE IS DANGEROUS, YOU SAY? WELL... SO AM I...
QUITE THE LITTLE PARADISE WE HAVE GOING HERE, ISN'T IT?
IT WAS MY WIFE'S IDEA TO COME.
GROUNDS FOR DIVORCE. KEEP AN EYE ON HIM...

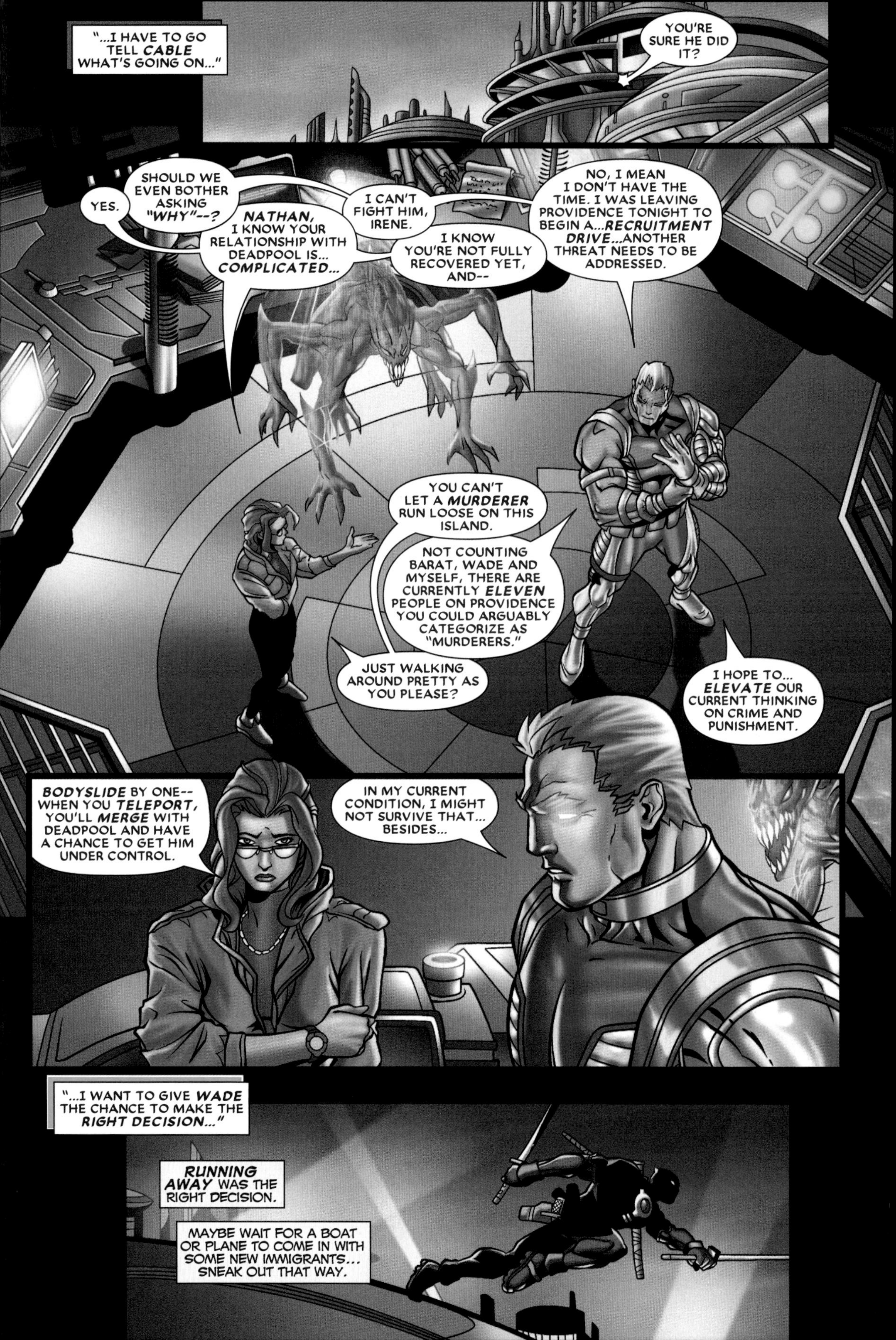
"...I HAVE TO GO TELL CABLE WHAT'S GOING ON..."
YOU'RE SURE HE DID IT?
YES.
SHOULD WE EVEN BOTHER ASKING "WHY"--?
NATHAN, I KNOW YOUR RELATIONSHIP WITH DEADPOOL IS... COMPLICATED...
I CAN'T FIGHT HIM, IRENE.
I KNOW YOU'RE NOT FULLY RECOVERED YET, AND--
NO, I MEAN I DON'T HAVE THE TIME. I WAS LEAVING PROVIDENCE TONIGHT TO BEGIN A...RECRUITMENT DRIVE...ANOTHER THREAT NEEDS TO BE ADDRESSED.
YOU CAN'T LET A MURDERER RUN LOOSE ON THIS ISLAND.
NOT COUNTING BARAT, WADE AND MYSELF, THERE ARE CURRENTLY ELEVEN PEOPLE ON PROVIDENCE YOU COULD ARGUABLY CATEGORIZE AS "MURDERERS."
JUST WALKING AROUND PRETTY AS YOU PLEASE?
I HOPE TO... ELEVATE OUR CURRENT THINKING ON CRIME AND PUNISHMENT.
BODYSLIDE BY ONE-- WHEN YOU TELEPORT, YOU'LL MERGE WITH DEADPOOL AND HAVE A CHANCE TO GET HIM UNDER CONTROL.
IN MY CURRENT CONDITION, I MIGHT NOT SURVIVE THAT... BESIDES...
"...I WANT TO GIVE WADE THE CHANCE TO MAKE THE RIGHT DECISION..."
RUNNING AWAY WAS THE RIGHT DECISION.
MAYBE WAIT FOR A BOAT OR PLANE TO COME IN WITH SOME NEW IMMIGRANTS... SNEAK OUT THAT WAY.

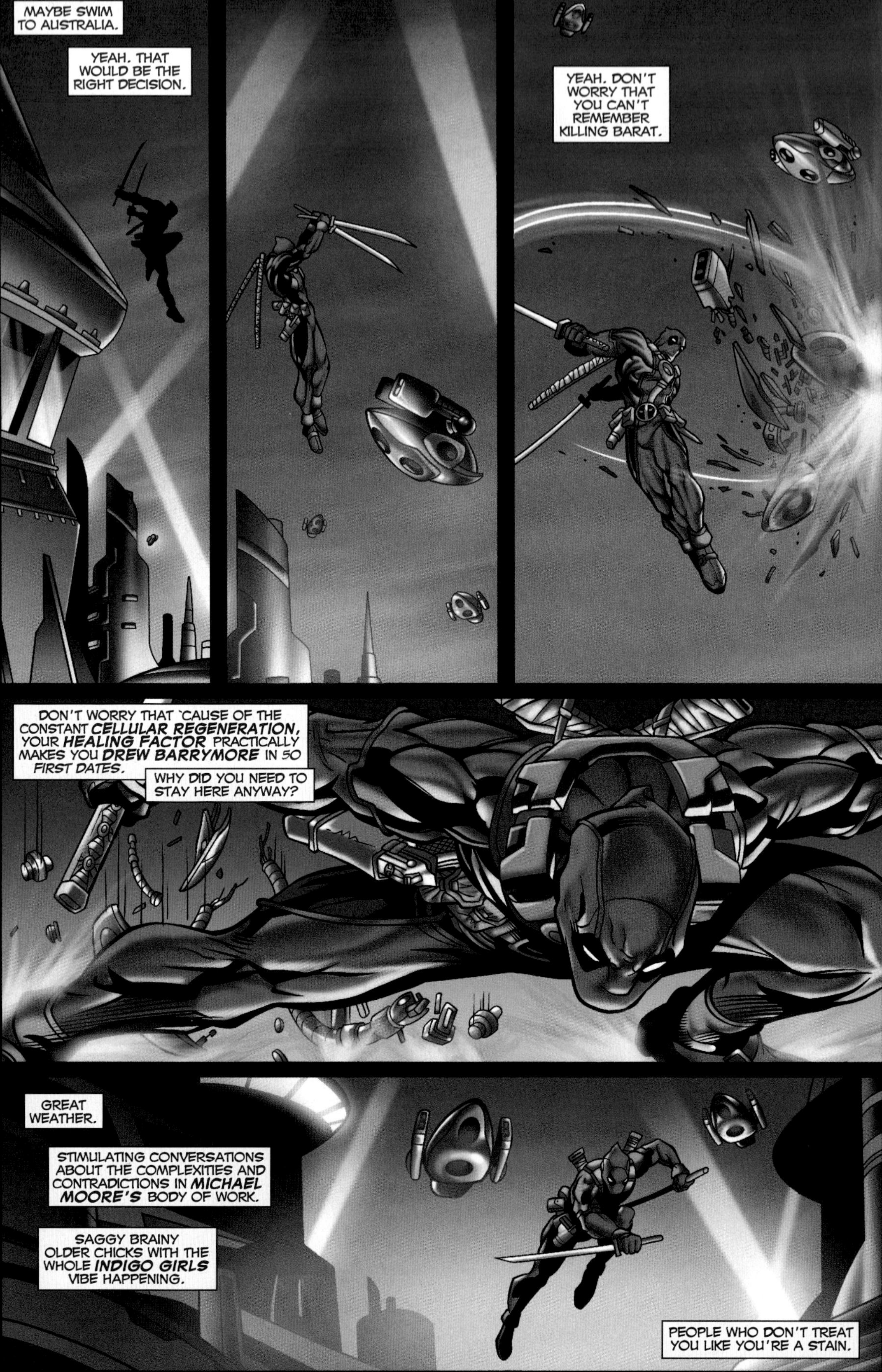
MAYBE SWIM TO AUSTRALIA.
YEAH. THAT WOULD BE THE RIGHT DECISION.
YEAH. DON'T WORRY THAT YOU CAN'T REMEMBER KILLING BARAT.
DON'T WORRY THAT 'CAUSE OF THE CONSTANT CELLULAR REGENERATION, YOUR HEALING FACTOR PRACTICALLY MAKES YOU DREW BARRYMORE IN 50 FIRST DATES.
WHY DID YOU NEED TO STAY HERE ANYWAY?
GREAT WEATHER.
STIMULATING CONVERSATIONS ABOUT THE COMPLEXITIES AND CONTRADICTIONS IN MICHAEL MOORE'S BODY OF WORK.
SAGGY BRAINY OLDER CHICKS WITH THE WHOLE INDIGO GIRLS VIBE HAPPENING.
PEOPLE WHO DON'T TREAT YOU LIKE YOU'RE A STAIN.

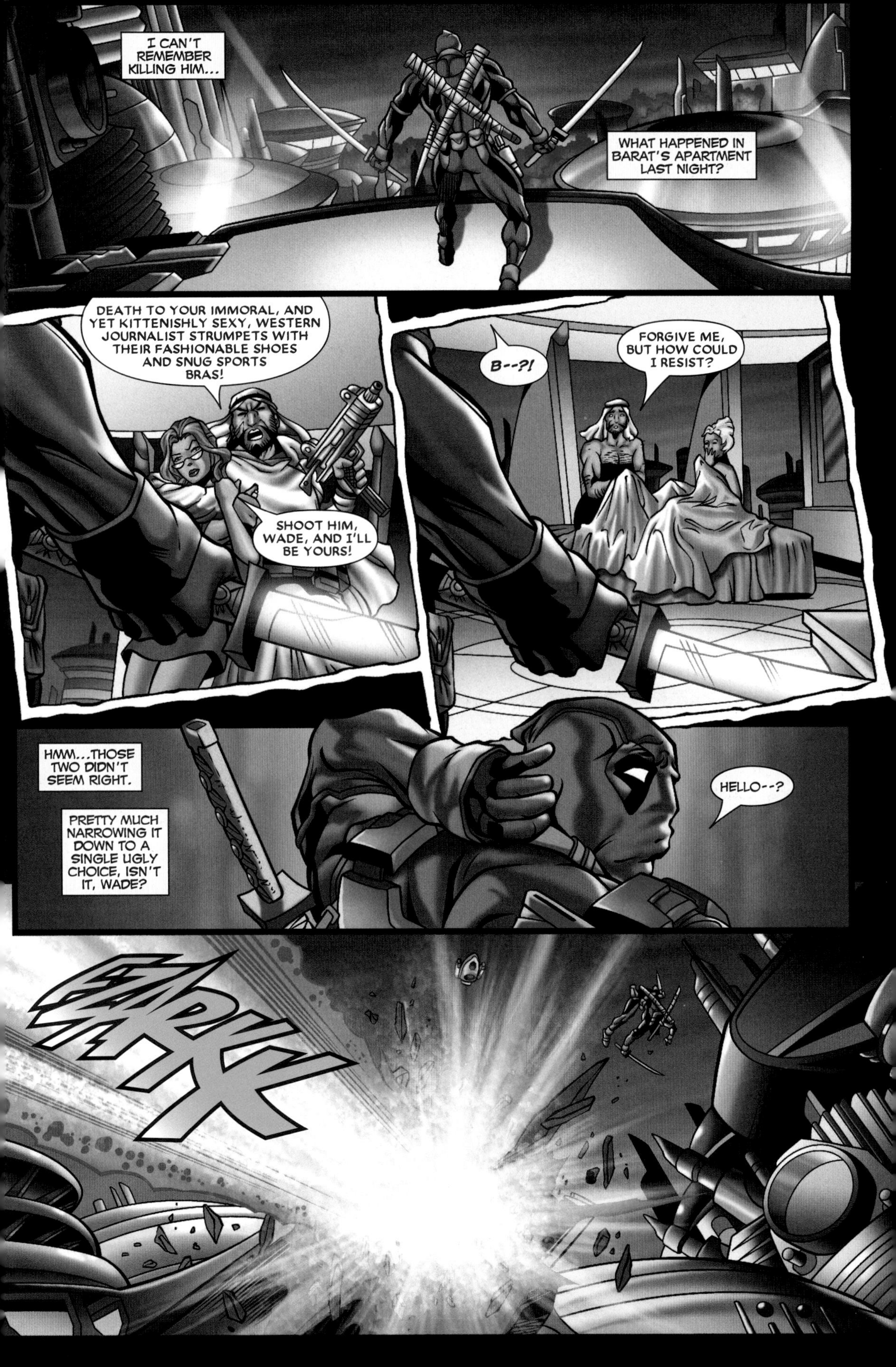
I CAN'T REMEMBER KILLING HIM...
WHAT HAPPENED IN BARAT'S APARTMENT LAST NIGHT?
DEATH TO YOUR IMMORAL, AND YET KITTENISHLY SEXY, WESTERN JOURNALIST STRUMPETS WITH THEIR FASHIONABLE SHOES AND SNUG SPORTS BRAS!
SHOOT HIM, WADE, AND I'LL BE YOURS!
B--?!
FORGIVE ME, BUT HOW COULD I RESIST?
HMM...THOSE TWO DIDN'T SEEM RIGHT.
PRETTY MUCH NARROWING IT DOWN TO A SINGLE UGLY CHOICE, ISN'T IT, WADE?
HELLO--?

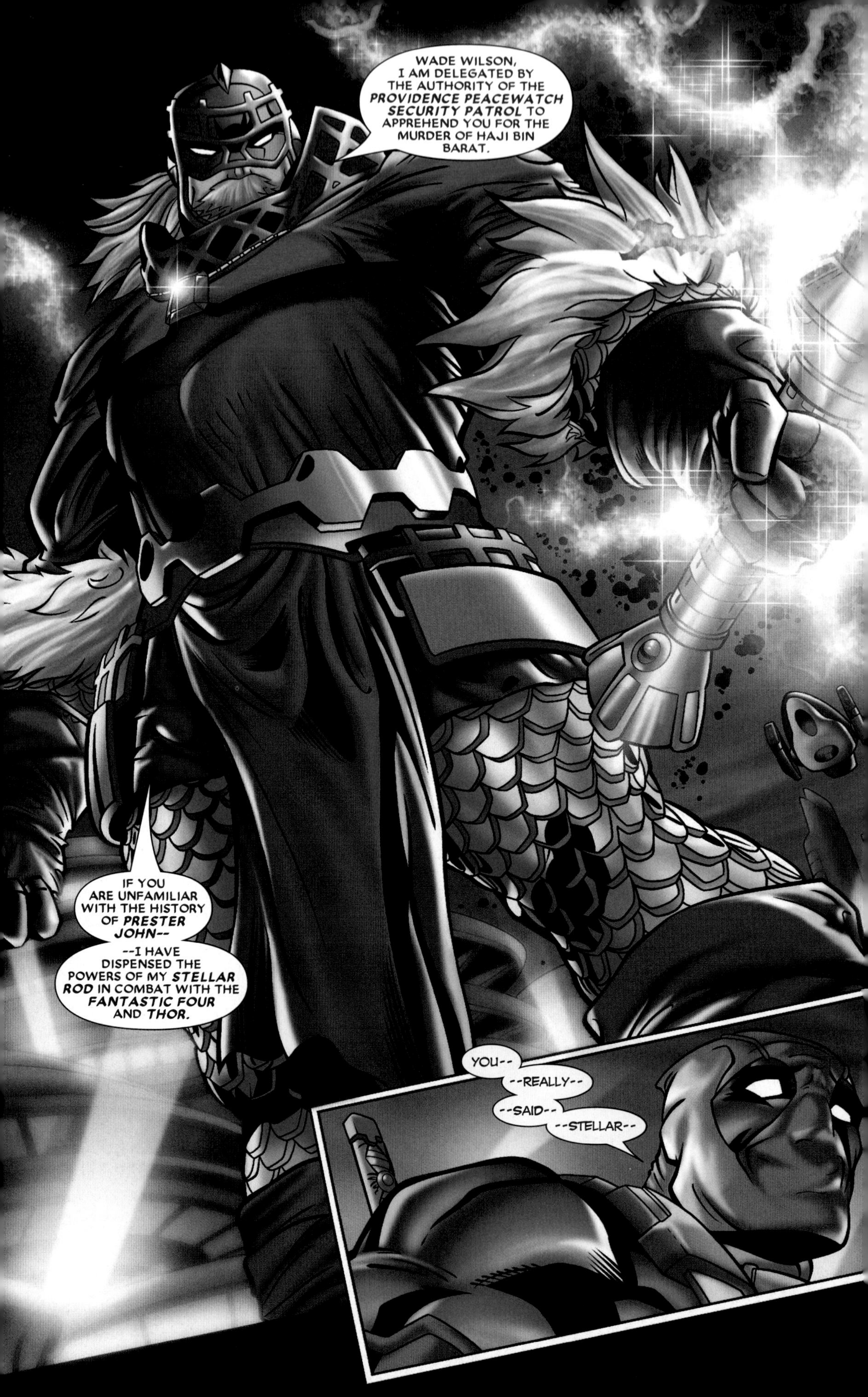
WADE WILSON, I AM DELEGATED BY THE AUTHORITY OF THE PROVIDENCE PEACEWATCH SECURITY PATROL TO APPREHEND YOU FOR THE MURDER OF HAJI BIN BARAT.
IF YOU ARE UNFAMILIAR WITH THE HISTORY OF PRESTER JOHN--
--I HAVE DISPENSED THE POWERS OF MY STELLAR ROD IN COMBAT WITH THE FANTASTIC FOUR AND THOR.
YOU--
--REALLY--
--SAID--
--STELLAR--

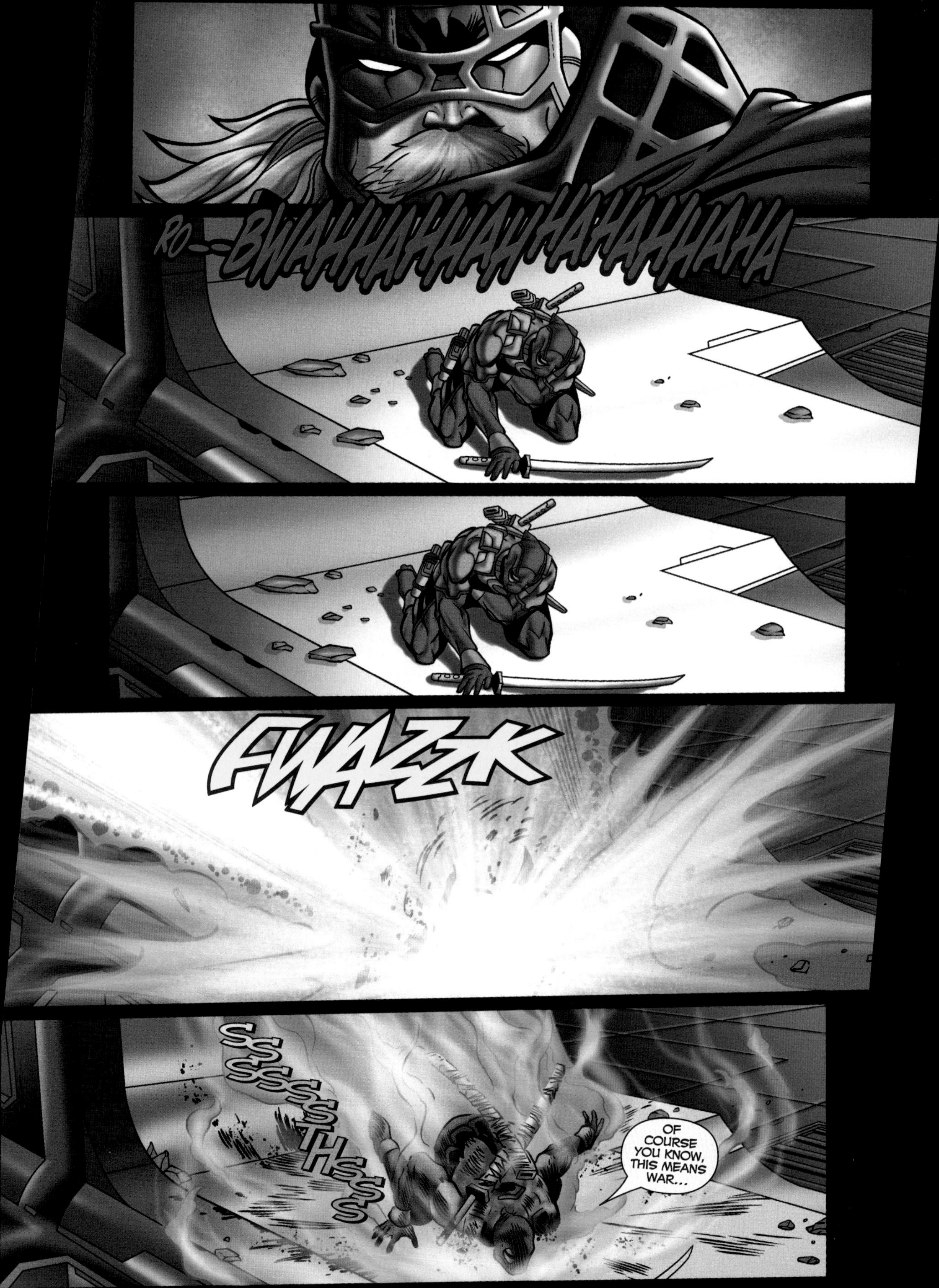
RO--BWAHHAHAHAHAHAHAHAHAHAHA
FWAZ-K
SSSSSSSSSTHSSS
OF COURSE YOU KNOW, THIS MEANS WAR...

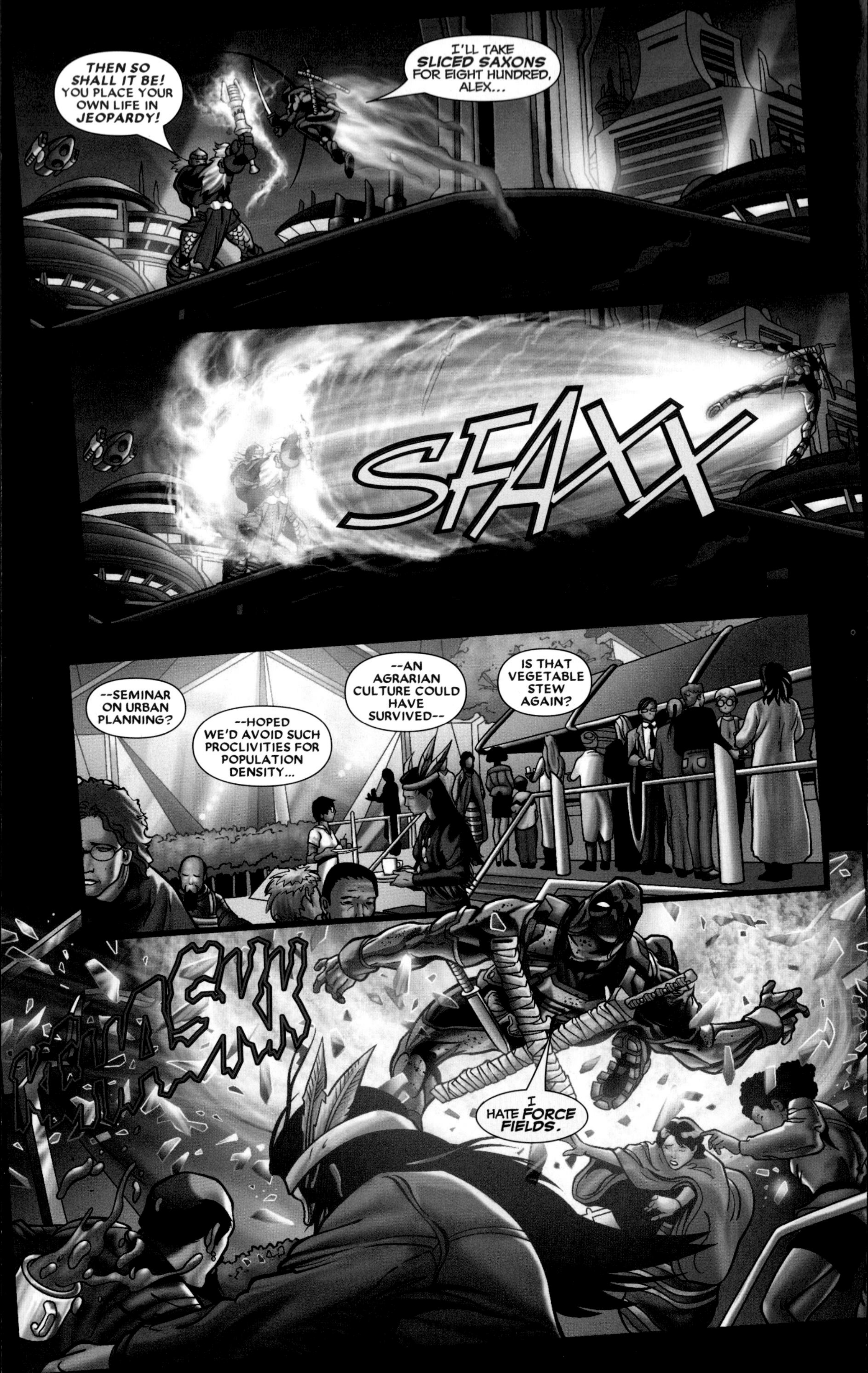
THEN SO SHALL IT BE! YOU PLACE YOUR OWN LIFE IN JEOPARDY!
I'LL TAKE SLICED SAXONS FOR EIGHT HUNDRED, ALEX...
SFAXX
--SEMINAR ON URBAN PLANNING?
--HOPED WE'D AVOID SUCH PROCLIVITIES FOR POPULATION DENSITY...
--AN AGRARIAN CULTURE COULD HAVE SURVIVED--
IS THAT VEGETABLE STEW AGAIN?
I HATE FORCE FIELDS.

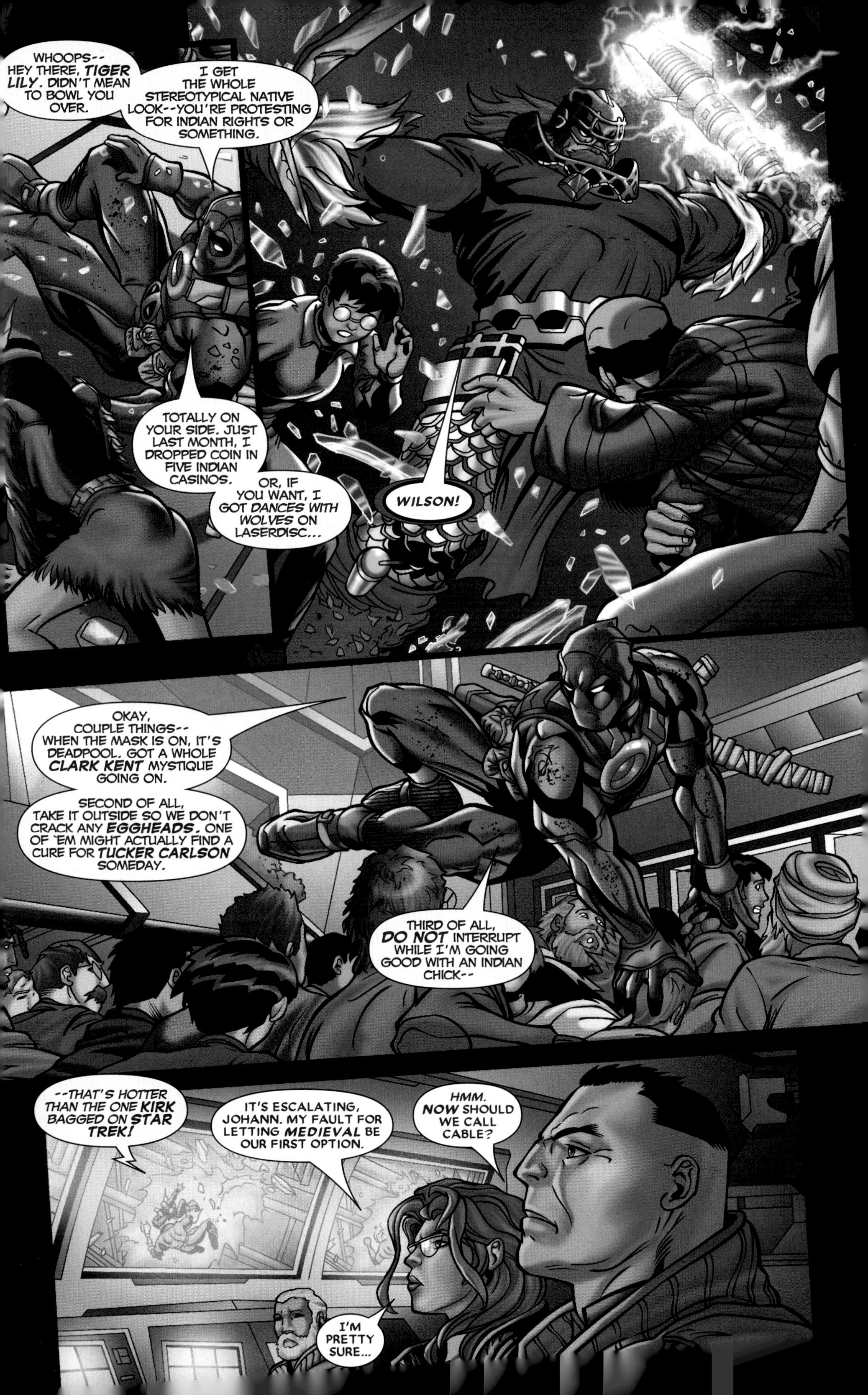
WHOOPS--
HEY THERE, TIGER LILY. DIDN'T MEAN TO BOWL YOU OVER.
I GET THE WHOLE STEREOTYPICAL NATIVE LOOK--YOU'RE PROTESTING FOR INDIAN RIGHTS OR SOMETHING.
TOTALLY ON YOUR SIDE. JUST LAST MONTH, I DROPPED COIN IN FIVE INDIAN CASINOS.
OR, IF YOU WANT, I GOT DANCES WITH WOLVES ON LASERDISC...
WILSON!
OKAY, COUPLE THINGS--
WHEN THE MASK IS ON, IT'S DEADPOOL. GOT A WHOLE CLARK KENT MYSTIQUE GOING ON.
SECOND OF ALL, TAKE IT OUTSIDE SO WE DON'T CRACK ANY EGGHEADS. ONE OF 'EM MIGHT ACTUALLY FIND A CURE FOR TUCKER CARLSON SOMEDAY.
THIRD OF ALL, DO NOT INTERRUPT WHILE I'M GOING GOOD WITH AN INDIAN CHICK--
--THAT'S HOTTER THAN THE ONE KIRK BAGGED ON STAR TREK!
IT'S ESCALATING, JOHANN. MY FAULT FOR LETTING MEDIEVAL BE OUR FIRST OPTION.
HMM. NOW SHOULD WE CALL CABLE?
I'M PRETTY SURE...

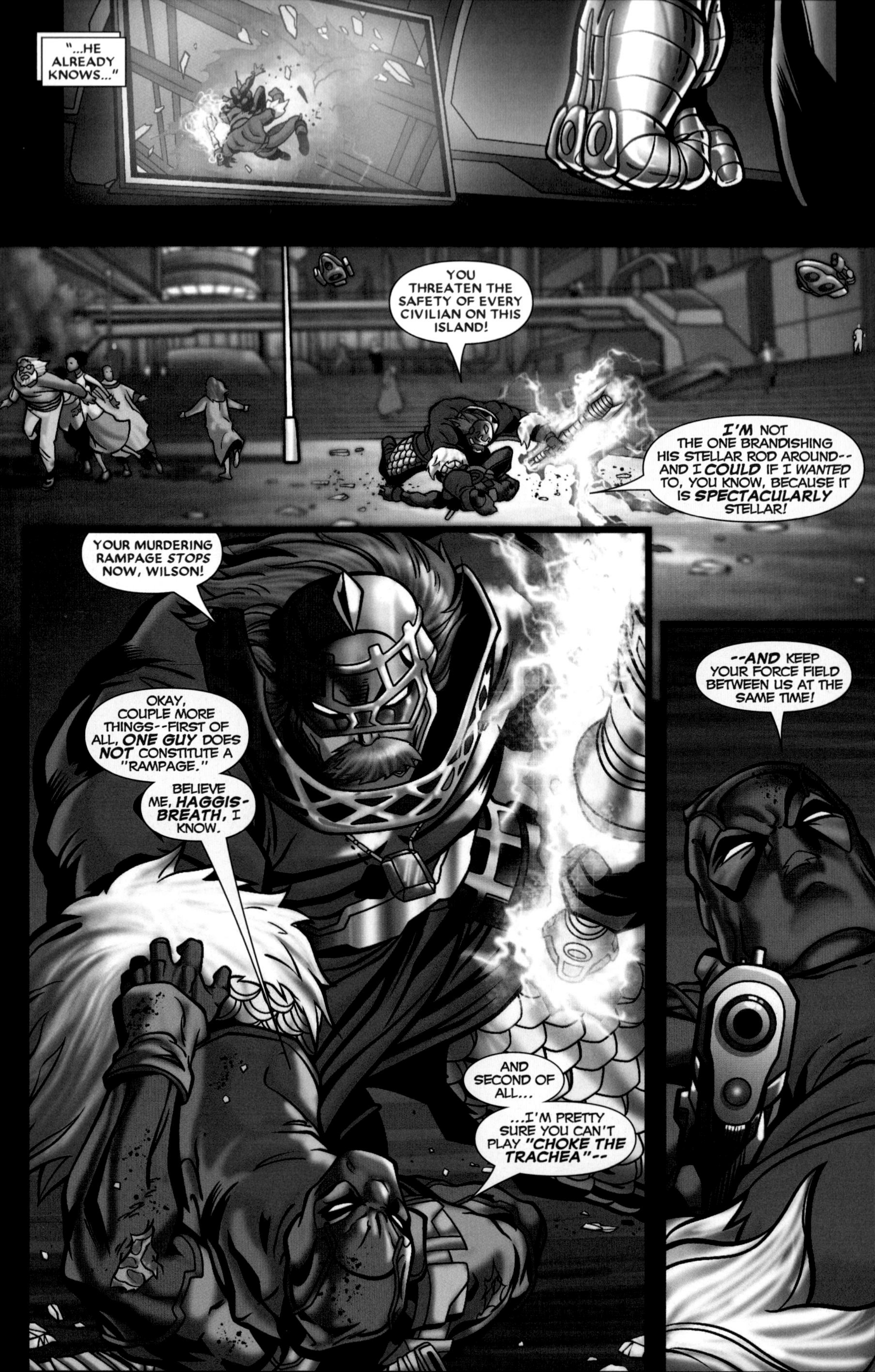
"...HE ALREADY KNOWS..."
YOU THREATEN THE SAFETY OF EVERY CIVILIAN ON THIS ISLAND!
I'M NOT THE ONE BRANDISHING HIS STELLAR ROD AROUND-- AND I COULD IF I WANTED TO, YOU KNOW, BECAUSE IT IS SPECTACULARLY STELLAR!
YOUR MURDERING RAMPAGE STOPS NOW, WILSON!
OKAY, COUPLE MORE THINGS--FIRST OF ALL, ONE GUY DOES NOT CONSTITUTE A "RAMPAGE."
BELIEVE ME, HAGGIS-BREATH, I KNOW.
AND SECOND OF ALL...
...I'M PRETTY SURE YOU CAN'T PLAY "CHOKE THE TRACHEA"--
--AND KEEP YOUR FORCE FIELD BETWEEN US AT THE SAME TIME!

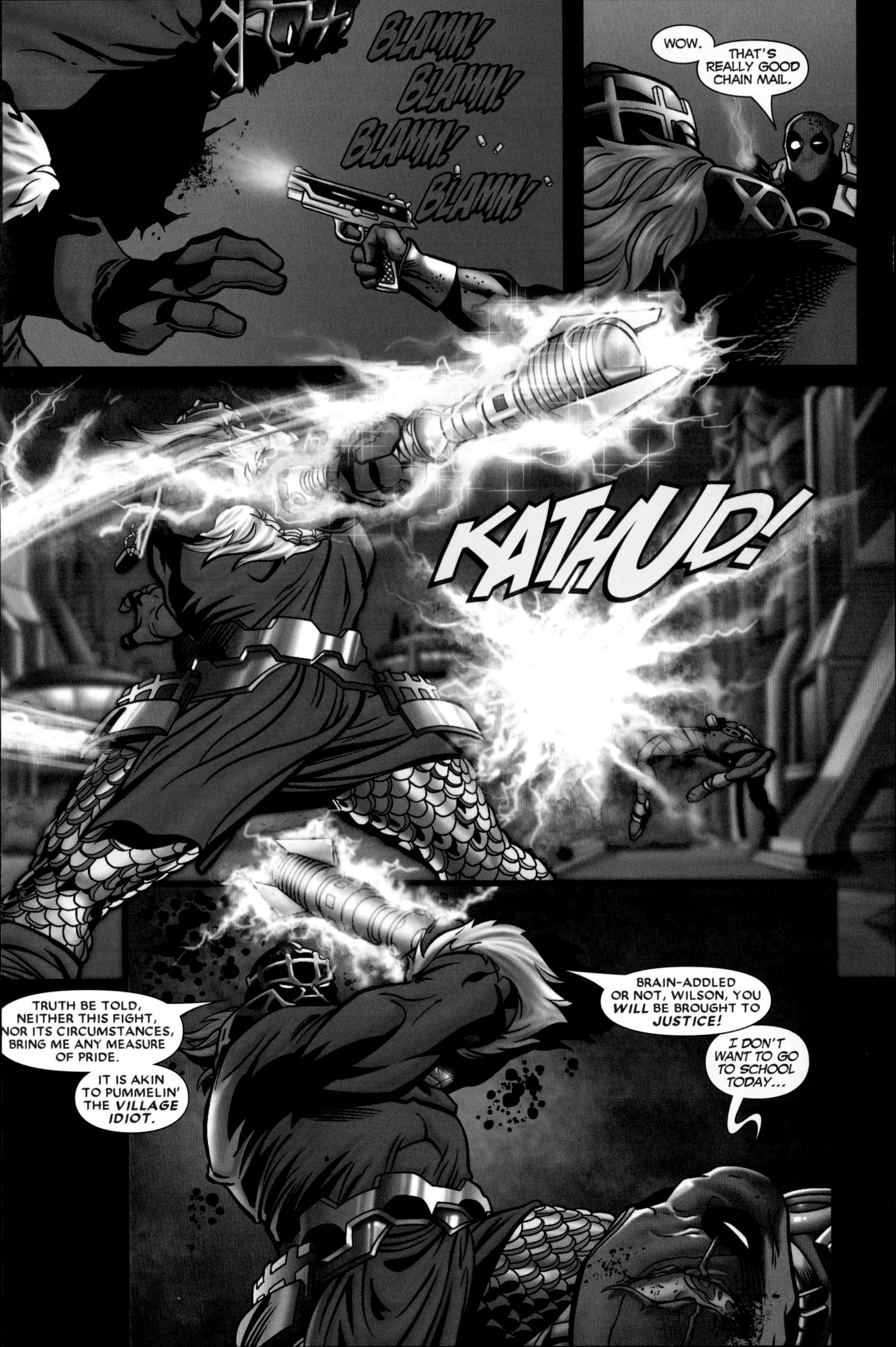
BLAMM!
BLAMM!
BLAMM!
BLAMM!
WOW.
THAT'S REALLY GOOD CHAIN MAIL.
KATHUD!
TRUTH BE TOLD, NEITHER THIS FIGHT, NOR ITS CIRCUMSTANCES, BRING ME ANY MEASURE OF PRIDE.
IT IS AKIN TO PUMMELIN' THE *VILLAGE IDIOT*.
BRAIN-ADDLED OR NOT, WILSON, YOU *WILL* BE BROUGHT TO *JUSTICE*!
I DON'T WANT TO GO TO SCHOOL TODAY...

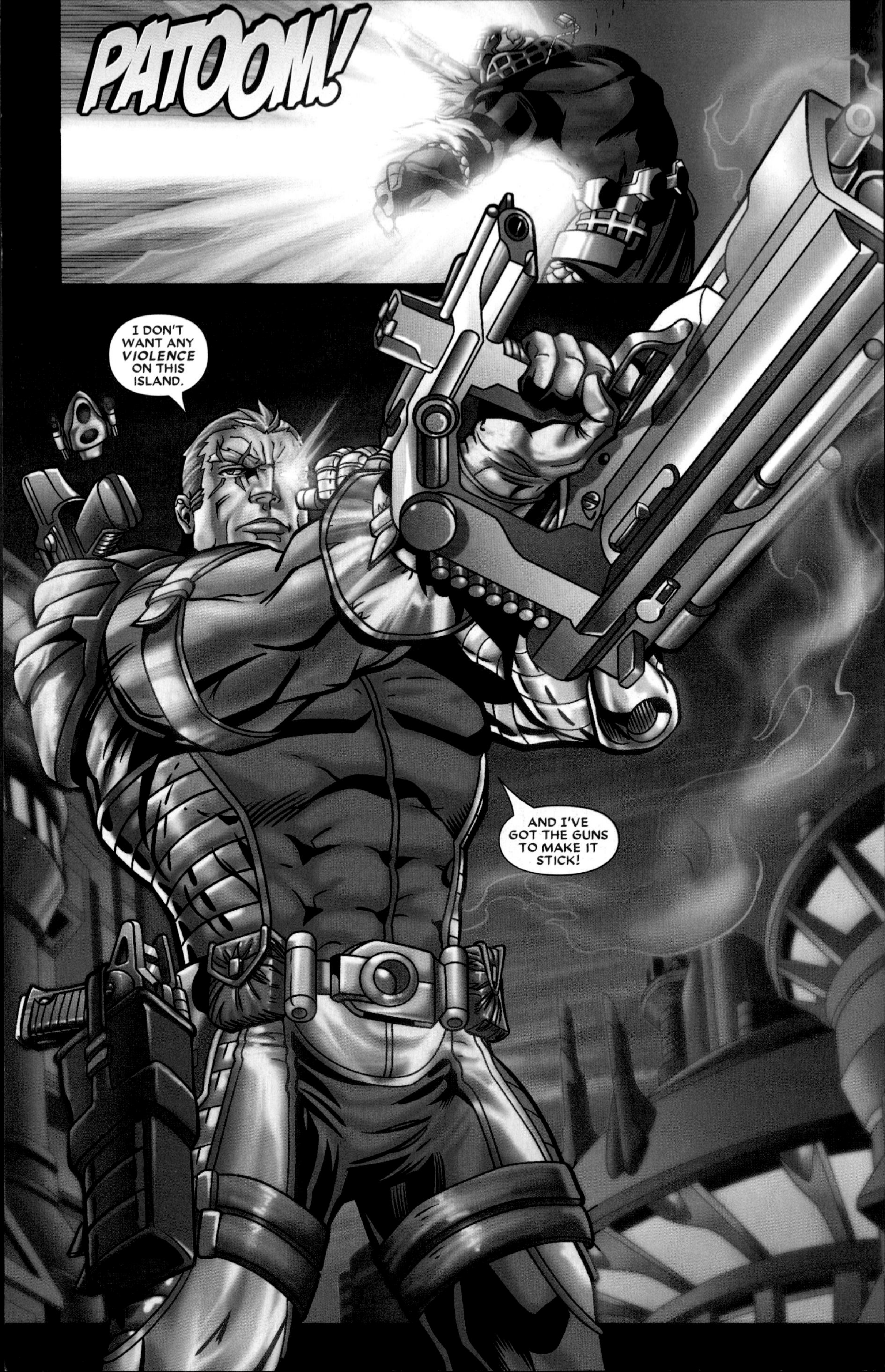
PATOOM!
I DON'T WANT ANY VIOLENCE ON THIS ISLAND.
AND I'VE GOT THE GUNS TO MAKE IT STICK!

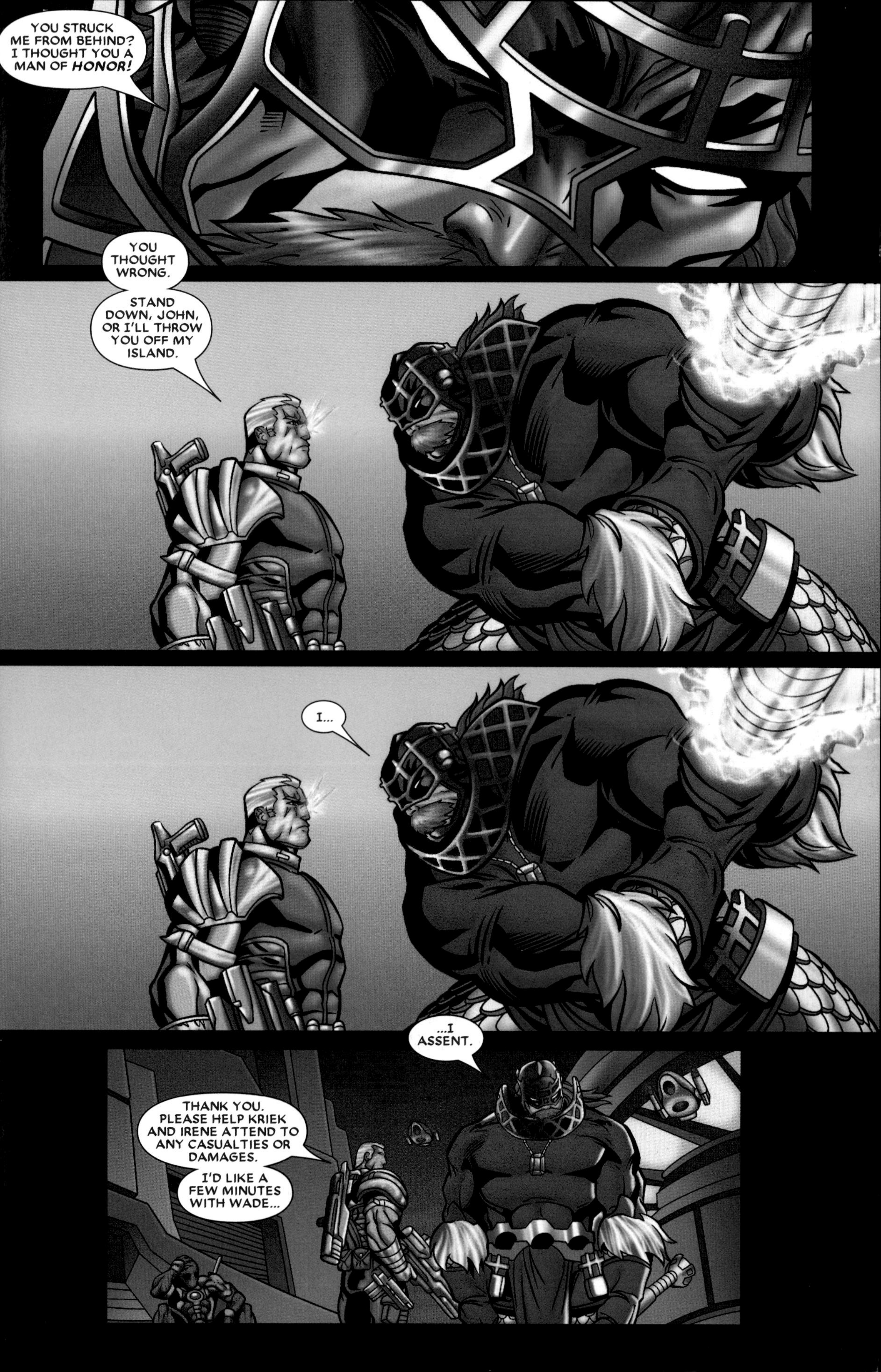
YOU STRUCK ME FROM BEHIND? I THOUGHT YOU A MAN OF *HONOR!*
YOU THOUGHT WRONG.
STAND DOWN, JOHN, OR I'LL THROW YOU OFF MY ISLAND.
I...
...I ASSENT.
THANK YOU. PLEASE HELP KRIEK AND IRENE ATTEND TO ANY CASUALTIES OR DAMAGES.
I'D LIKE A FEW MINUTES WITH WADE...

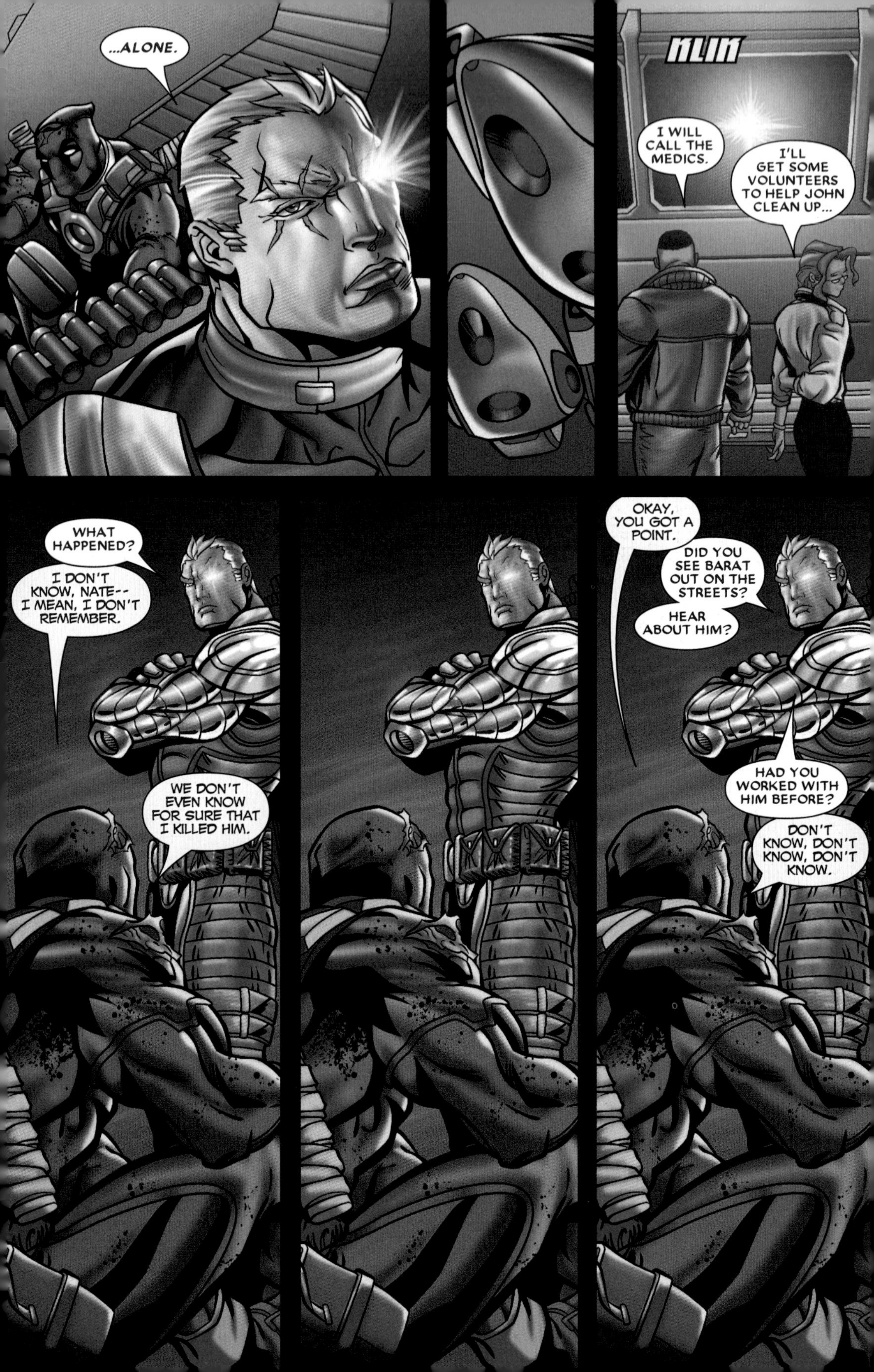
...ALONE.
KLIK
I WILL CALL THE MEDICS.
I'LL GET SOME VOLUNTEERS TO HELP JOHN CLEAN UP...
WHAT HAPPENED?
I DON'T KNOW, NATE-- I MEAN, I DON'T REMEMBER.
WE DON'T EVEN KNOW FOR SURE THAT I KILLED HIM.
OKAY, YOU GOT A POINT.
DID YOU SEE BARAT OUT ON THE STREETS?
HEAR ABOUT HIM?
HAD YOU WORKED WITH HIM BEFORE?
DON'T KNOW, DON'T KNOW, DON'T KNOW.

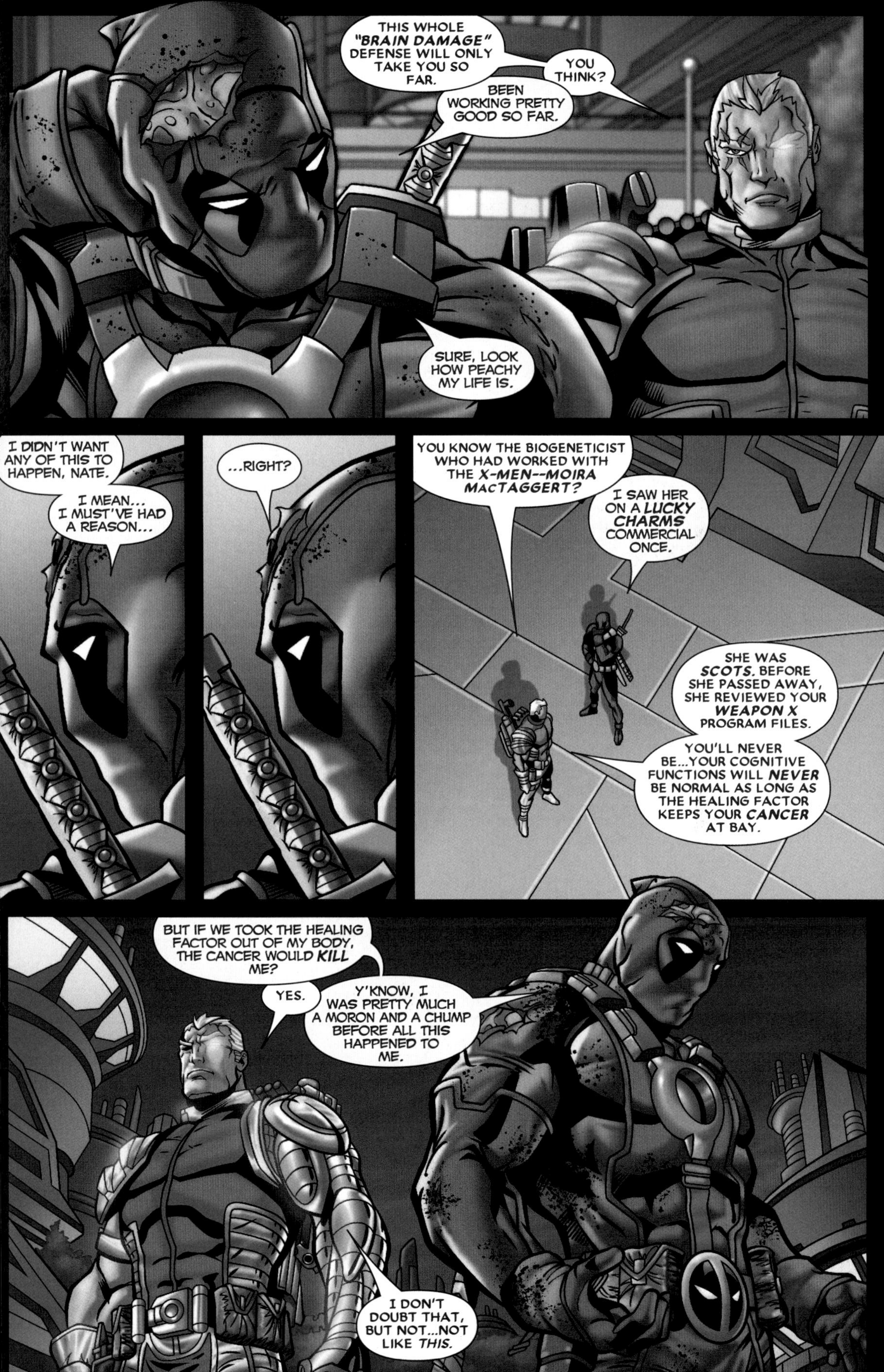
THIS WHOLE "BRAIN DAMAGE" DEFENSE WILL ONLY TAKE YOU SO FAR.
YOU THINK?
BEEN WORKING PRETTY GOOD SO FAR.
SURE, LOOK HOW PEACHY MY LIFE IS.
I DIDN'T WANT ANY OF THIS TO HAPPEN, NATE.
I MEAN... I MUST'VE HAD A REASON...
...RIGHT?
YOU KNOW THE BIOGENETICIST WHO HAD WORKED WITH THE X-MEN--MOIRA MacTAGGERT?
I SAW HER ON A LUCKY CHARMS COMMERCIAL ONCE.
SHE WAS SCOTS. BEFORE SHE PASSED AWAY, SHE REVIEWED YOUR WEAPON X PROGRAM FILES.
YOU'LL NEVER BE...YOUR COGNITIVE FUNCTIONS WILL NEVER BE NORMAL AS LONG AS THE HEALING FACTOR KEEPS YOUR CANCER AT BAY.
BUT IF WE TOOK THE HEALING FACTOR OUT OF MY BODY, THE CANCER WOULD KILL ME?
YES.
Y'KNOW, I WAS PRETTY MUCH A MORON AND A CHUMP BEFORE ALL THIS HAPPENED TO ME.
I DON'T DOUBT THAT, BUT NOT...NOT LIKE THIS.

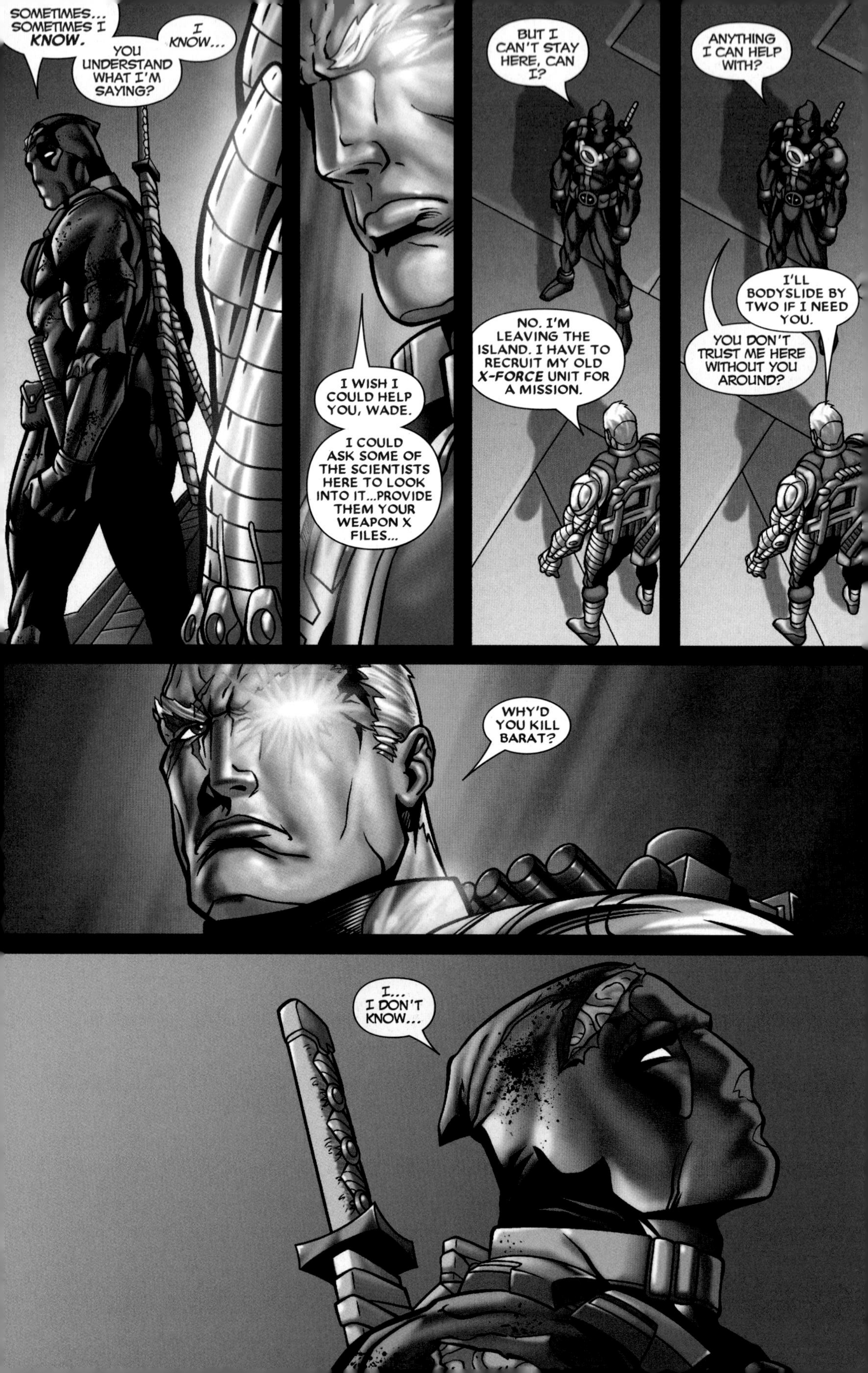
SOMETIMES... SOMETIMES I KNOW.
I KNOW...
YOU UNDERSTAND WHAT I'M SAYING?
I WISH I COULD HELP YOU, WADE.
I COULD ASK SOME OF THE SCIENTISTS HERE TO LOOK INTO IT...PROVIDE THEM YOUR WEAPON X FILES...
BUT I CAN'T STAY HERE, CAN I?
NO. I'M LEAVING THE ISLAND. I HAVE TO RECRUIT MY OLD X-FORCE UNIT FOR A MISSION.
ANYTHING I CAN HELP WITH?
YOU DON'T TRUST ME HERE WITHOUT YOU AROUND?
I'LL BODYSLIDE BY TWO IF I NEED YOU.
WHY'D YOU KILL BARAT?
I... I DON'T KNOW...

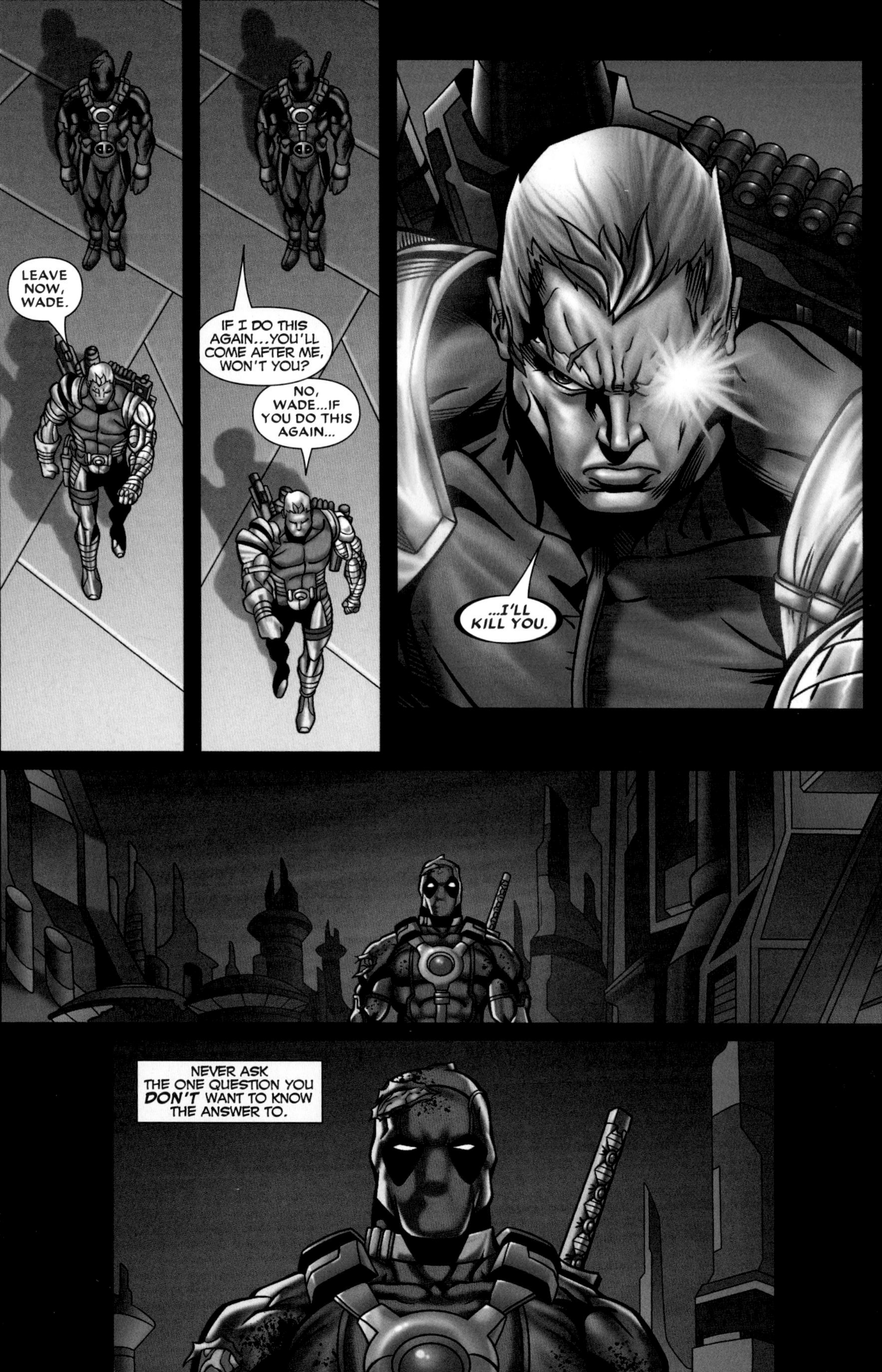
LEAVE NOW, WADE.
IF I DO THIS AGAIN...YOU'LL COME AFTER ME, WON'T YOU?
NO, WADE...IF YOU DO THIS AGAIN...
...I'LL KILL YOU.
NEVER ASK THE ONE QUESTION YOU DON'T WANT TO KNOW THE ANSWER TO.

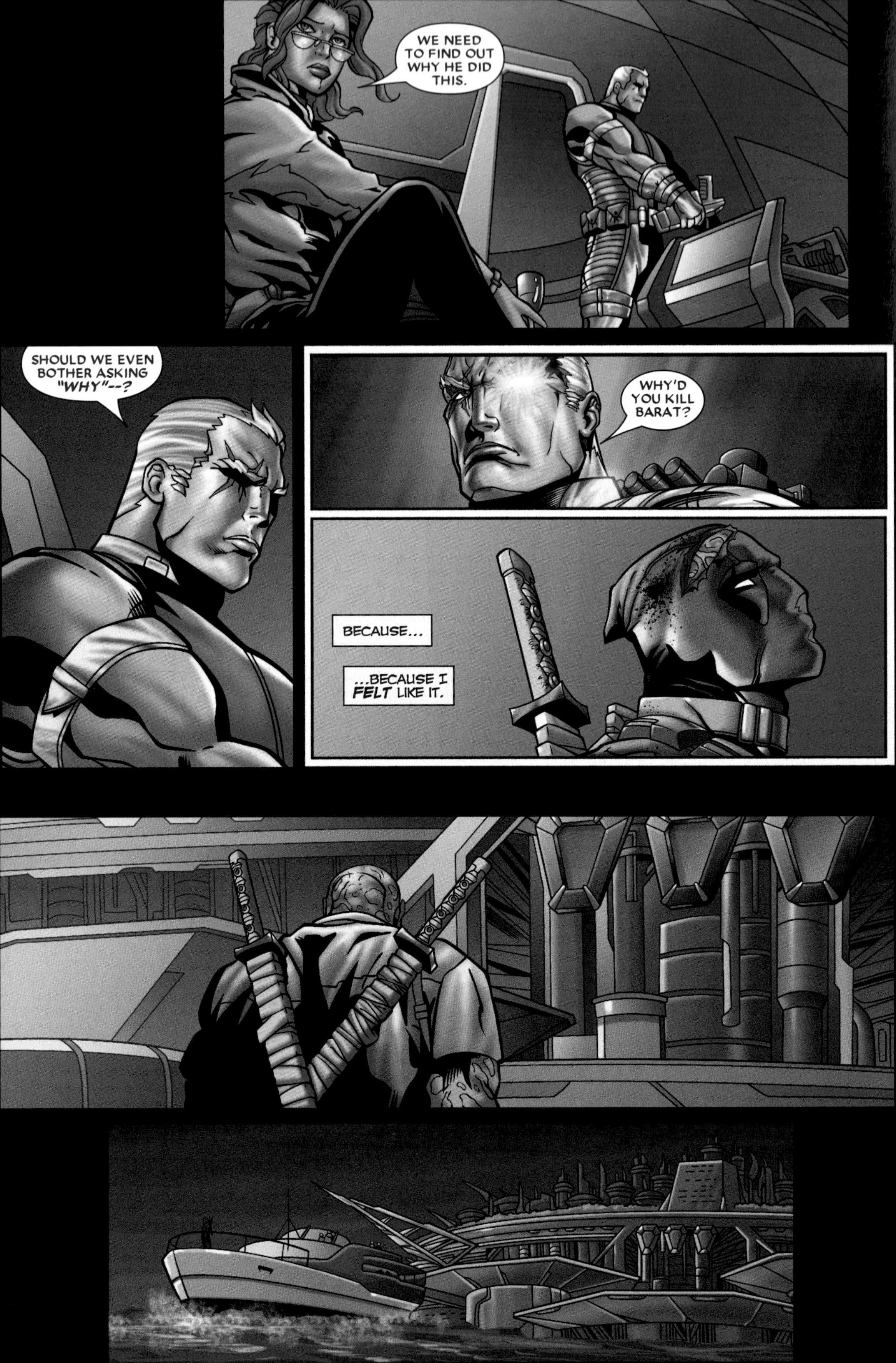
WE NEED TO FIND OUT WHY HE DID THIS.
SHOULD WE EVEN BOTHER ASKING "*WHY*"--?
WHY'D YOU KILL BARAT?
BECAUSE...
...BECAUSE I *FELT* LIKE IT.

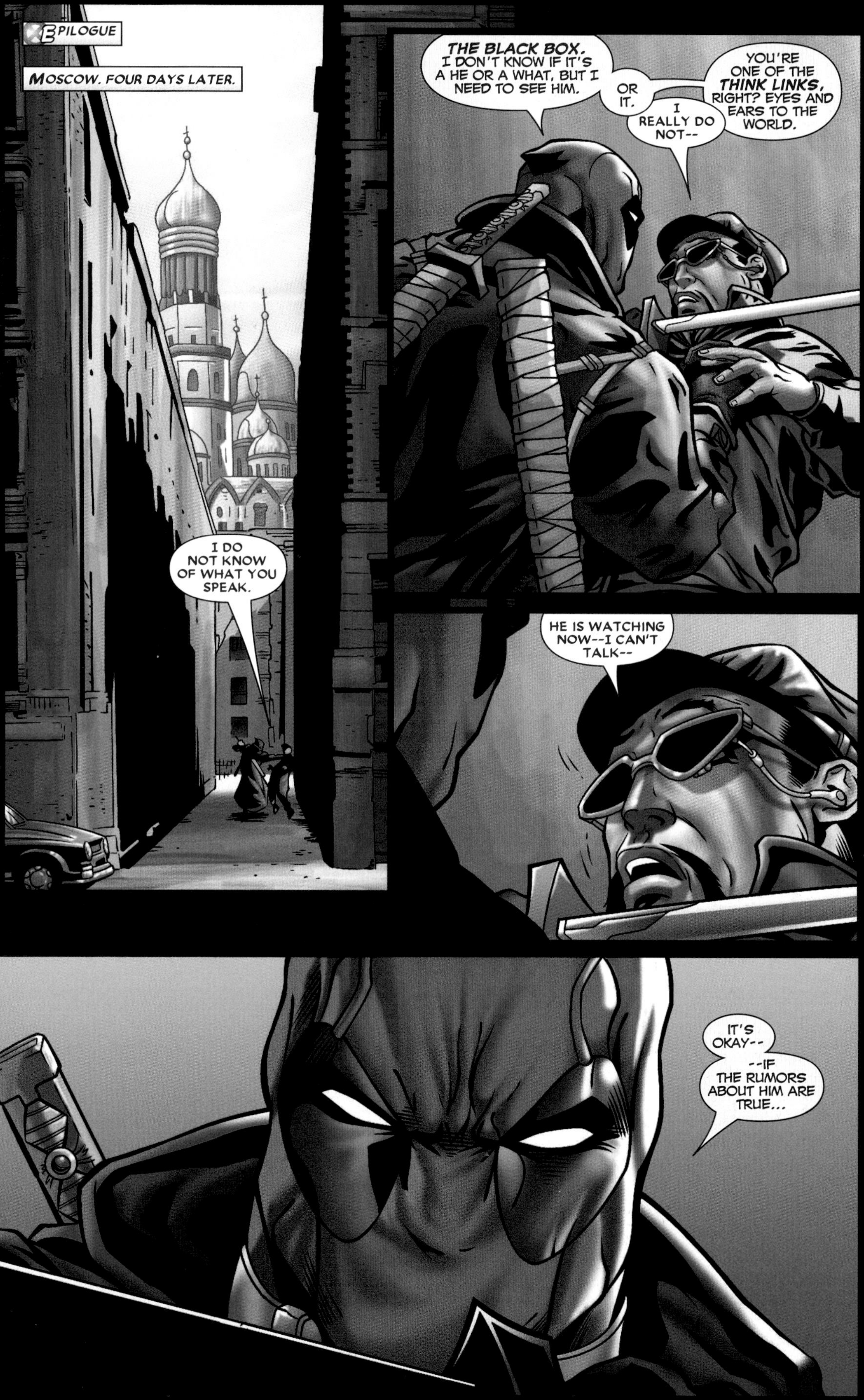
EPILOGUE
MOSCOW. FOUR DAYS LATER.
I DO NOT KNOW OF WHAT YOU SPEAK.
THE BLACK BOX. I DON'T KNOW IF IT'S A HE OR A WHAT, BUT I NEED TO SEE HIM.
OR IT.
YOU'RE ONE OF THE THINK LINKS, RIGHT? EYES AND EARS TO THE WORLD.
I REALLY DO NOT--
HE IS WATCHING NOW--I CAN'T TALK--
IT'S OKAY--
--IF THE RUMORS ABOUT HIM ARE TRUE...

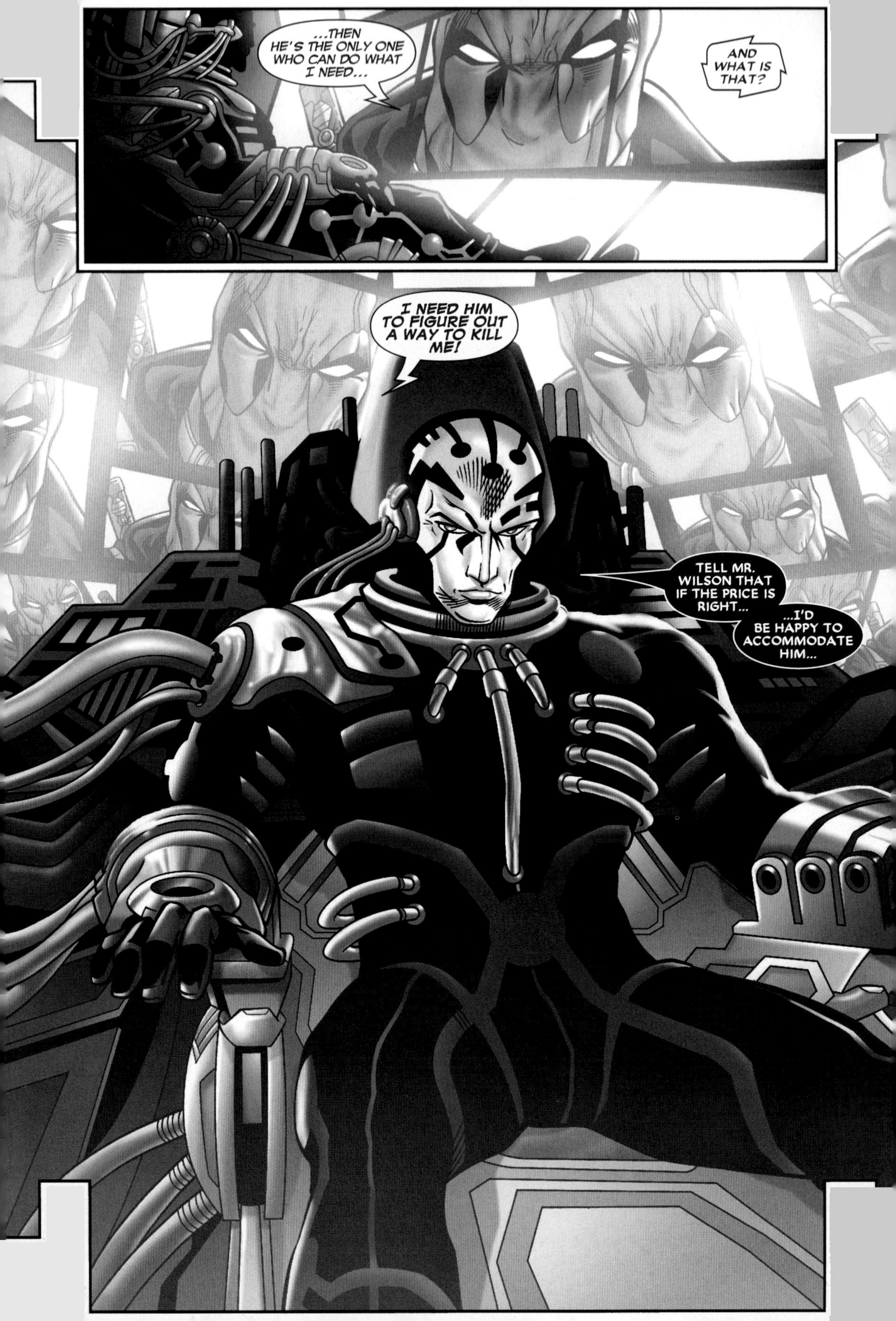
...THEN HE'S THE ONLY ONE WHO CAN DO WHAT I NEED...
AND WHAT IS THAT?
I NEED HIM TO FIGURE OUT A WAY TO KILL ME!
TELL MR. WILSON THAT IF THE PRICE IS RIGHT...
...I'D BE HAPPY TO ACCOMMODATE HIM...

DEAR DEADPOOL

Welcome back, gang! Guess what time it is? INTERNATIONAL LETTERS time! We got fans of C&DP all over the world! Understandable, since I love the French and am indifferent to national boundaries when kicking @$$!

We haven't gone to Kuala Lumpur. I wanna go there, mostly 'cause I like saying it. Kuala Lumpur. Kuala Lumpur. Okay, on with the page...

To the Mighty Powers That Be (note the insertion of "Mighty" in the hope that sucking up will actually help keep this book alive):

Just wanted to you know how much I'm enjoying C&DP. It's always refreshing to see two refugees from the bad old '90s find a place to shine here in the naughty aughts.

Niciez and Zircher are doing a great job, on-time month after month, in delivering a story that's beautiful to look at and can make you sad a page after laughing hysterically. In fact, I've started buying an extra copy each month at my local shop so I can have the owner just give it to someone who isn't already reading it.

Who loves ya, baby?

Keep up the great work,

Rick Jones (yes, really); U.S.A.

No way! Rick Jones! I got all your albums. And I loved you in the Kree/Skrull war. As for "Who loves ya, baby?"--what's with Ving Rhames as Kojak? That's just kinda outside the box, ain't it?

Anyway, Fabian was gonna ask me to rag on you for the 90's dig, since all those bad comics he wrote back then basically paid his kids' college tuition before they were even born, but when you told us you're buying an extra copy to give away, well, abuse forestalled. FOR NOW.

Hey there Nicole, and everyone else working on C&DP!

Just thought I'd write in to say great job on the series so far, I've been reading from issue 1 and think it's the best Marvel title out there!

It's great to see Cable's powers return to a normal level, and I'm really looking forward to seeing how this is handled, but I'm kinda worried about the problems raised in X-Force #6! (I don't want to spoil it for anyone who hasn't read it.) Is this going to be addressed in C&DP at any point, and if so when, because I know C&DP was a few weeks behind continuity to begin with.

Thanks a bunch, keep up the good work,

Chris Morley, UK

No, we don't plan to address Cable's disappearance in this book. Hopefully ever, 'cause basically that means the book is all mine! Now if I can just kill Merryweather--and that Prester John torpedo Patrick likes drawing so much... and Weasel... and...

Dear C&DP Crew,

Some comics have too much emphasis on lots of text and dialogue, and some others have lots of art and meager amounts of text to go with it. C&DP is a fantastically well-crafted title because it manages to get lots of both into every issue.

It has been wonderful to watch Cable's character become so complex and powerful at the same time, very few incredibly powerful characters can be this interesting these days. I also love how Cable and Deadpool interact with the wider Marvel Universe beyond the X-Men titles. The abundance of interesting supporting characters makes Cable and Deadpool's stories more surprising and realistic because of their sheer scale.

Lastly, I have a few questions...

1) How was it possible for Cable to get Deadpool's non-mutant healing factor?

2) How did Agent X get his scars back after his own series ended?

3) When Cable or Deadpool teleport, how is the destination determined?

4) How did A.I.M. get a Phalanx baby?

5) Will there be more female characters apart from Irene and Domino explored in this title in the near future?

Thank you all for a fantastic story so far, I can't wait for more.

Chris Day, Australia

Okay, Chris, lighten up on those Fosters, our stories ain't "realistic," they're ridiculous. We're comic book characters for crying out loud!

Ooh, numbered questions! I love those:

1)We merged on a very intimate level--not that there's anything wrong with that. When I was all melted like a puddle of Ensure, Nate sort of sucked me into his body and then he sort of upchucked me out. That's all the detailed science we need to know.

2)He carved them back on to his face himself because he scores more chicks with the scars.

3)Beats me. How do you do it when you teleport?

4)Same way A.I.M. gets everything. They found it. They're like the vultures of the Marvel Universe. Except with buckets on their heads. Which are actually kinda cool...

5)I would like to explore many more female characters in this book. During our upcoming issues, I'll be trying to explore Siryn. I've also put in a request to explore Sue Richards, Wasp, She-Hulk, the older chick from Power Pack who all of a sudden looks like Lindsay Lohan and Nicole Wiley, our editor.

Hey my name's Marc and I live in France..you know the country where you can't pay Deadpool enough to go to while our countries are at war! heh...we're not? (dixit: Cable&Deadpool#1) Your storyline and art are awesome!! and I hope Cable & Deadpool will continue for a very very very very long tilme..I love what you are doing on Cable & Deadpool you make me dream..thanks!!

Marc, France
A member of the ONE WORLD CHURCH!
"you are one for yourself, now be One for all".

Man, dude, your typos are worse than that guy's from last month!

Thanks for your letter! Please write again. Just write better.

So, after many months--or has it been years-- there are going to be letters pages again? Cool! I am a big fan of Deadpool and was a fan of Agent X and miss it greatly. It was nice to see Alex again.

I do have one complaint, though: what happened to the humor? Deadpool doesn't make me laugh as much as he used to. Still cool with his wit and fighting but it just hasn't been the classic Wade humor. I understand it is hard to write funny-wise but Deadpool was always funnier in his own comic.

Cable as the straight man, though, makes it amusing and I do laugh at Cable sometimes. Their sparring against each other is good but the humor needs work.

Please keep this comic going. I am tired of always needing to look for new titles.

--Aaron Poitras, Canada

Wow.

Much to my surprise, these two hooligans are quickly becoming my favourite pair of characters in the Marvel Universe. Fabian--a genius!--craftily spins great plots that keep me buying comic after comic. And I can't fathom how ANYBODY could continuously think up dialogue that includes Deadpool. I think Fabian should do stand-up!

Matthew Carter, Canada

Matthew, meet Aaron. Now go kick his butt for Fabian, wouldja? Then again, you're both Canadians (which is like half-French, right?), so you won't fight unless you're on a hockey rink or something? Can you at least smash a bottle of Moosehead over Aaron's skull? Does he have any idea how hard it is to be FUNNY every freakin' panel on every freakin' page of every freakin' issue?

Dear Insaniqaurium (Also known as Fabian, Patrick, and Nicole),

I started collecting Cable and X-Force in the early 1990's (when they were good, and hey, Fabian was writing then... coincidence? I think not...) and giggled my way through Wade's series. ADORED Agent X, and was highly skeptical about the launch of C&DP.

Yeah, so I'm kind of an idiot. It's a character flaw.

Basically, I've giggled my way through every issue, but #12 made me beyond giddy. We've got Alex, Domino, Nate being a big dork, Wade being... Wade, and Nick Fury. All in-character, and being sarcastic b!@#$%^$s.

My joy cannot be expressed in words. So imagine, if you will, a giddy fangirl cutting out construction-paper hearts and writing your names on them.

You gave back me the characters that I love deeply, and missed terribly. Plus, y'all are freaking nuts and unapologetic about it. ONLY GO AWAY WHEN YOU START TO SUCK!

Deep and abiding adoration, A.J.,U.S.A.

Y'know, A.J., you were really kinda boring me until I saw you were a chick. Then you became LETTER WRITER OF THE MONTH! I mean, a human with mammaries venturing into a comic book store? That makes you more powerful than mighty Mjolnir at your typical store, doesn't it?

Now Fabian and Patrick are asking if those hearts are being cut out for them, or for me n' Nate? Cause Fabian and Patrick are both married, so hopefully, they're for me n' Nate, 'cause, well, you wanna talk about swingin' some magic Uru hammers, baby...

"Uru" is a very funny word. Even funnier than "spatula."

EDITOR'S NOTE: At press time, A.J. has already revealed more about who those heart cutouts are REALLY for. Tune in next month to find out!

Surely, though, we have more than one female reader. Fellas: why aren't you buying extra copies for your lady friends? Don't you owe them that much? Remember: more sales equals less fear of cancellation. And ladies: send in your letters. – NW

Next month starts "Enema of the State," in which I go looking for Cable who has been missing since X-Force #6. Okay, I lied to Chris. What's he gonna do, throw bangers and mash at me? Sigh. See you next month! I'm off to Kuala Lumpur... uhm... if Kuala Lumpur had been decimated by Apocalypse, that is...

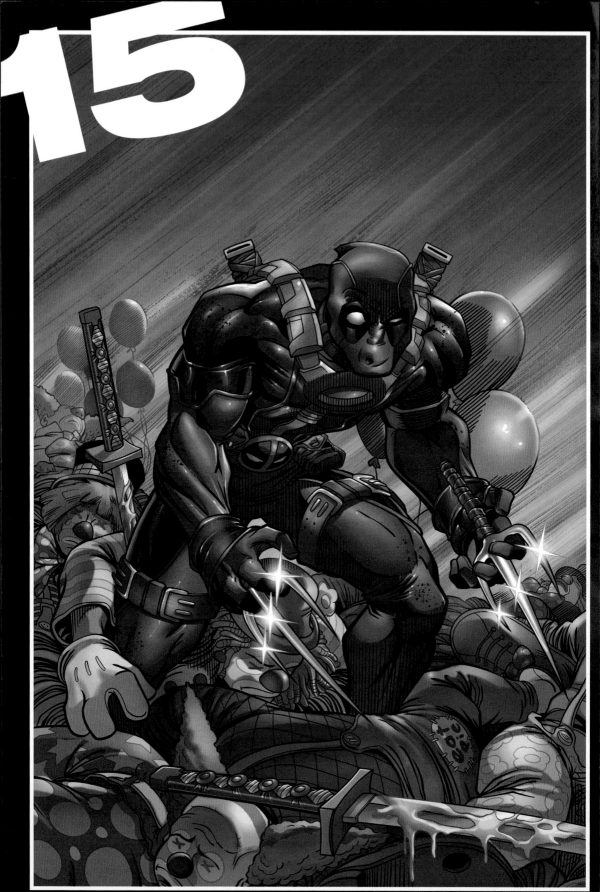

ENEMA OF THE STATE

PART ONE: KILLER CLOWNS

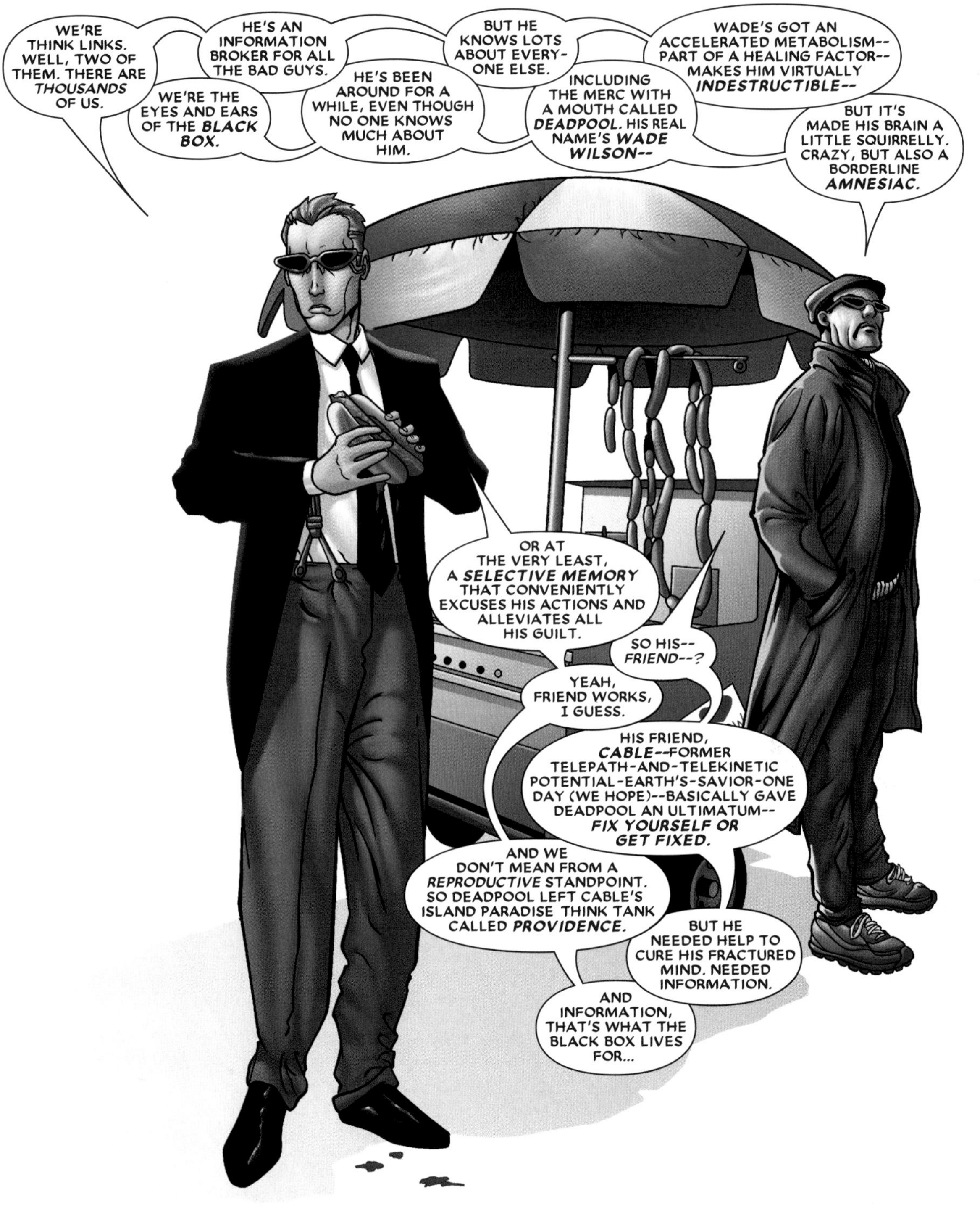

WE'RE THINK LINKS. WELL, TWO OF THEM. THERE ARE *THOUSANDS* OF US.
WE'RE THE EYES AND EARS OF THE ***BLACK BOX.***
HE'S AN INFORMATION BROKER FOR ALL THE BAD GUYS.
HE'S BEEN AROUND FOR A WHILE, EVEN THOUGH NO ONE KNOWS MUCH ABOUT HIM.
BUT HE KNOWS LOTS ABOUT EVERY-ONE ELSE.
INCLUDING THE MERC WITH A MOUTH CALLED ***DEADPOOL.*** HIS REAL NAME'S ***WADE WILSON--***
WADE'S GOT AN ACCELERATED METABOLISM--PART OF A HEALING FACTOR--MAKES HIM VIRTUALLY ***INDESTRUCTIBLE--***
BUT IT'S MADE HIS BRAIN A LITTLE SQUIRRELLY. CRAZY, BUT ALSO A BORDERLINE ***AMNESIAC.***
OR AT THE VERY LEAST, A ***SELECTIVE MEMORY*** THAT CONVENIENTLY EXCUSES HIS ACTIONS AND ALLEVIATES ALL HIS GUILT.
SO HIS--*FRIEND*--?
YEAH, FRIEND WORKS, I GUESS.
HIS FRIEND, ***CABLE***--FORMER TELEPATH-AND-TELEKINETIC POTENTIAL-EARTH'S-SAVIOR-ONE DAY (WE HOPE)--BASICALLY GAVE DEADPOOL AN ULTIMATUM--***FIX YOURSELF OR GET FIXED.***
AND WE DON'T MEAN FROM A *REPRODUCTIVE* STANDPOINT. SO DEADPOOL LEFT CABLE'S ISLAND PARADISE THINK TANK CALLED ***PROVIDENCE.***
BUT HE NEEDED HELP TO CURE HIS FRACTURED MIND. NEEDED INFORMATION.
AND INFORMATION, THAT'S WHAT THE BLACK BOX LIVES FOR...

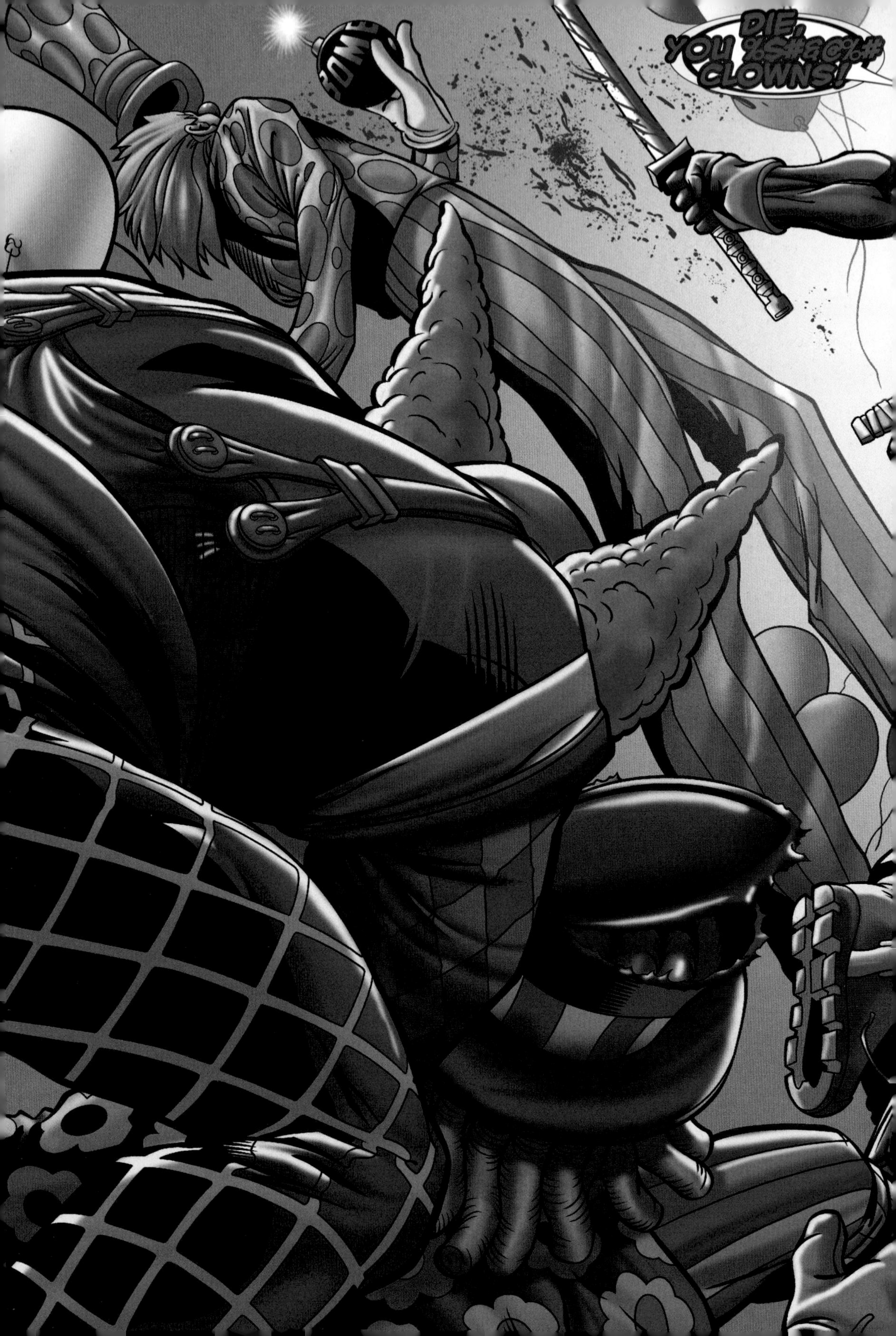
DIE, YOU %$#&@%# CLOWNS!

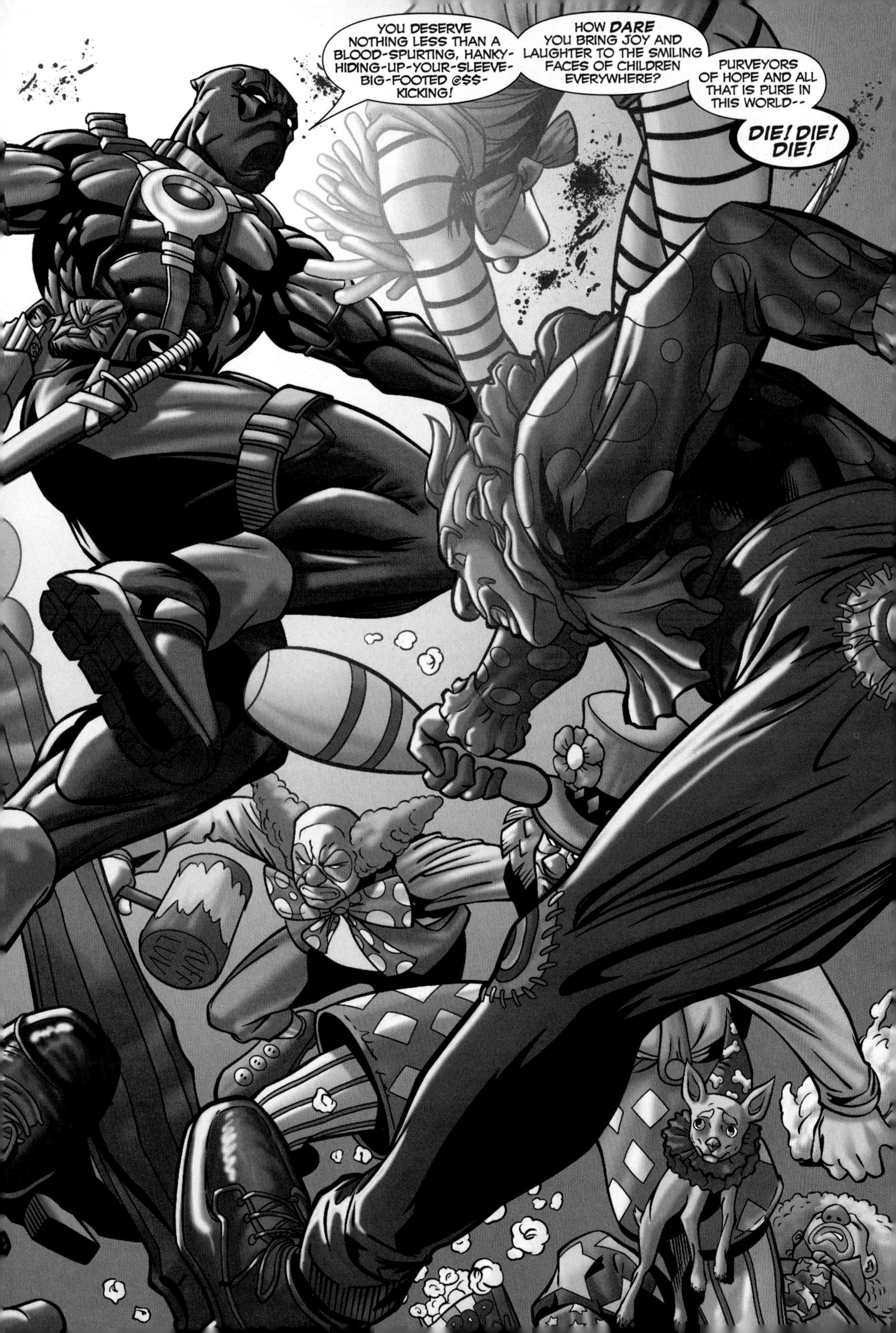
YOU DESERVE NOTHING LESS THAN A BLOOD-SPURTING, HANKY-HIDING-UP-YOUR-SLEEVE-BIG-FOOTED @$$-KICKING!
HOW DARE YOU BRING JOY AND LAUGHTER TO THE SMILING FACES OF CHILDREN EVERYWHERE?
PURVEYORS OF HOPE AND ALL THAT IS PURE IN THIS WORLD--
DIE! DIE! DIE!

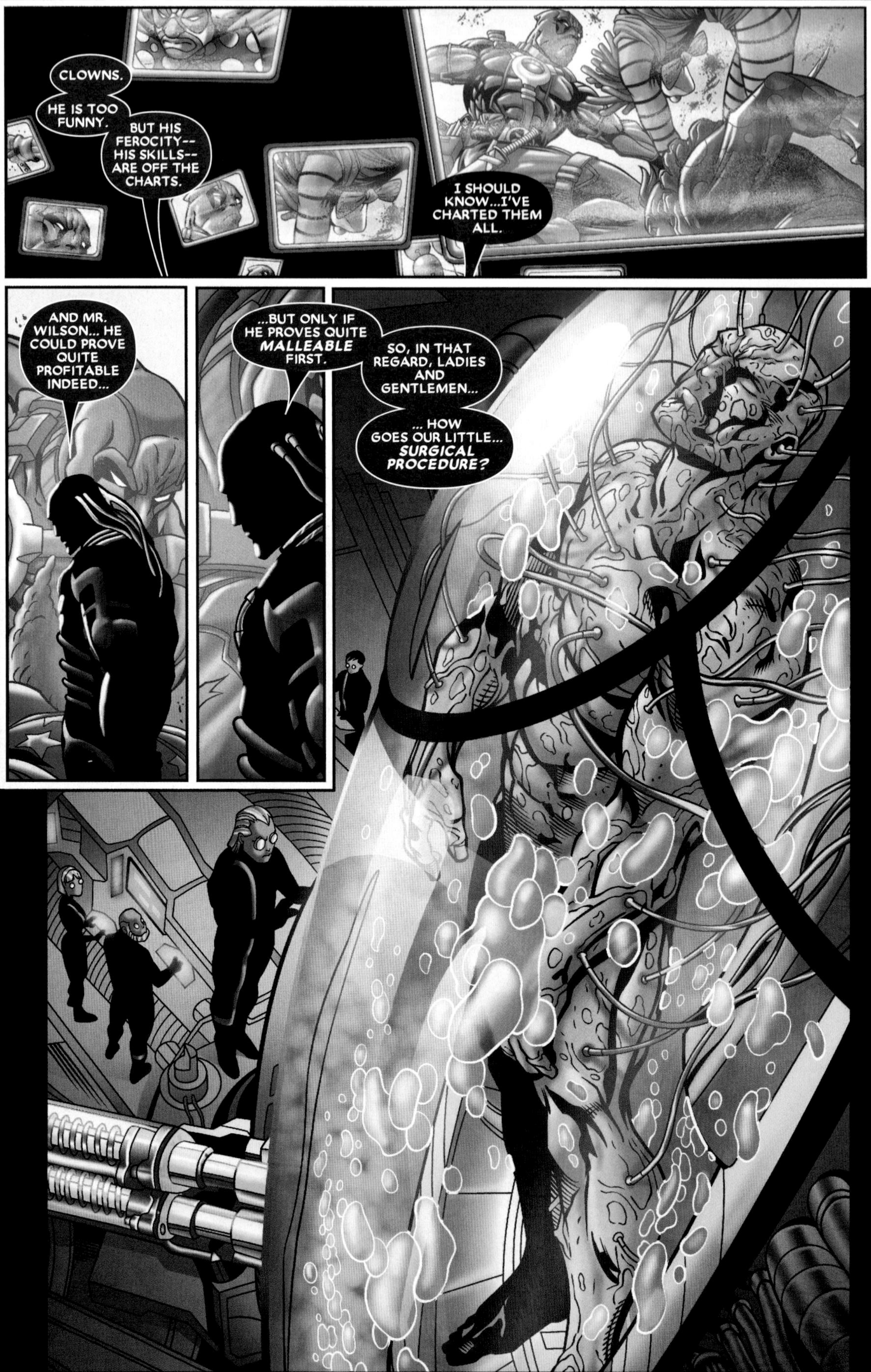
CLOWNS.
HE IS TOO FUNNY.
BUT HIS FEROCITY-- HIS SKILLS-- ARE OFF THE CHARTS.
I SHOULD KNOW...I'VE CHARTED THEM ALL.
AND MR. WILSON... HE COULD PROVE QUITE PROFITABLE INDEED...
...BUT ONLY IF HE PROVES QUITE MALLEABLE FIRST.
SO, IN THAT REGARD, LADIES AND GENTLEMEN...
... HOW GOES OUR LITTLE... SURGICAL PROCEDURE?

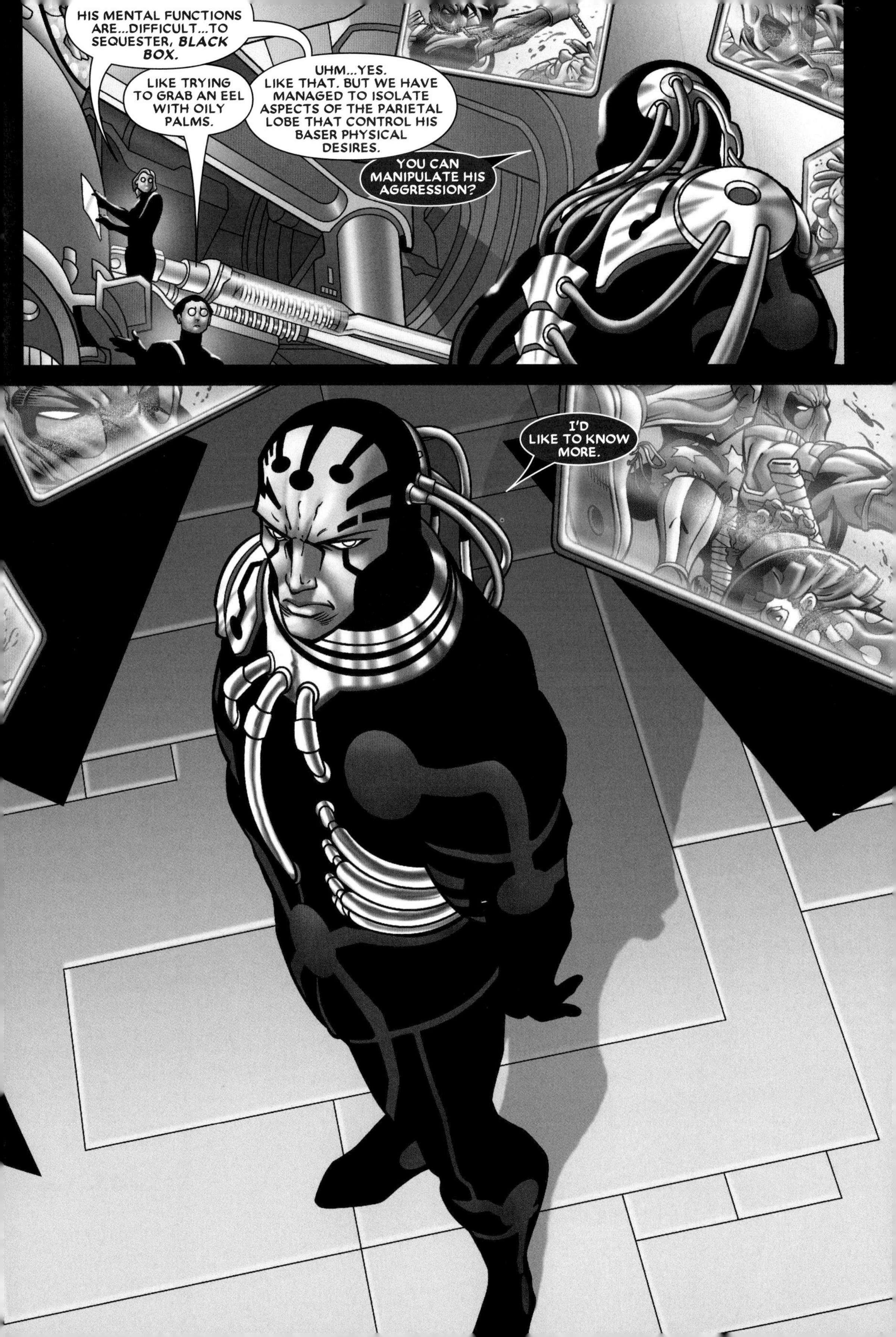
HIS MENTAL FUNCTIONS ARE...DIFFICULT...TO SEQUESTER, BLACK BOX.
LIKE TRYING TO GRAB AN EEL WITH OILY PALMS.
UHM...YES. LIKE THAT. BUT WE HAVE MANAGED TO ISOLATE ASPECTS OF THE PARIETAL LOBE THAT CONTROL HIS BASER PHYSICAL DESIRES.
YOU CAN MANIPULATE HIS AGGRESSION?
I'D LIKE TO KNOW MORE.

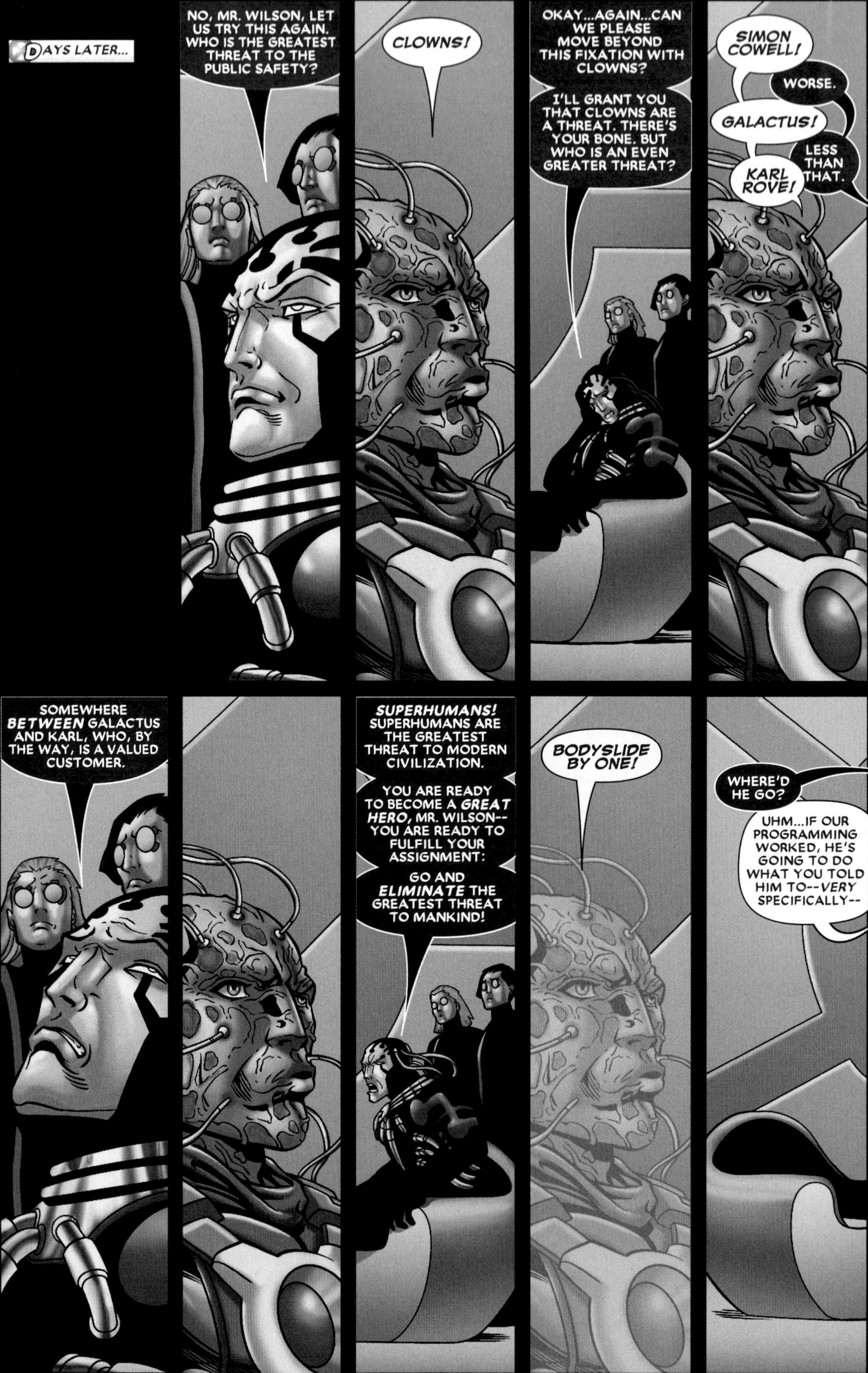
DAYS LATER...
NO, MR. WILSON, LET US TRY THIS AGAIN. WHO IS THE GREATEST THREAT TO THE PUBLIC SAFETY?
CLOWNS!
OKAY...AGAIN...CAN WE PLEASE MOVE BEYOND THIS FIXATION WITH CLOWNS?
I'LL GRANT YOU THAT CLOWNS ARE A THREAT. THERE'S YOUR BONE. BUT WHO IS AN EVEN GREATER THREAT?
SIMON COWELL!
WORSE.
GALACTUS!
LESS THAN THAT.
KARL ROVE!
SOMEWHERE BETWEEN GALACTUS AND KARL, WHO, BY THE WAY, IS A VALUED CUSTOMER.
SUPERHUMANS! SUPERHUMANS ARE THE GREATEST THREAT TO MODERN CIVILIZATION.
YOU ARE READY TO BECOME A GREAT HERO, MR. WILSON-- YOU ARE READY TO FULFILL YOUR ASSIGNMENT:
GO AND ELIMINATE THE GREATEST THREAT TO MANKIND!
BODYSLIDE BY ONE!
WHERE'D HE GO?
UHM...IF OUR PROGRAMMING WORKED, HE'S GOING TO DO WHAT YOU TOLD HIM TO--VERY SPECIFICALLY--

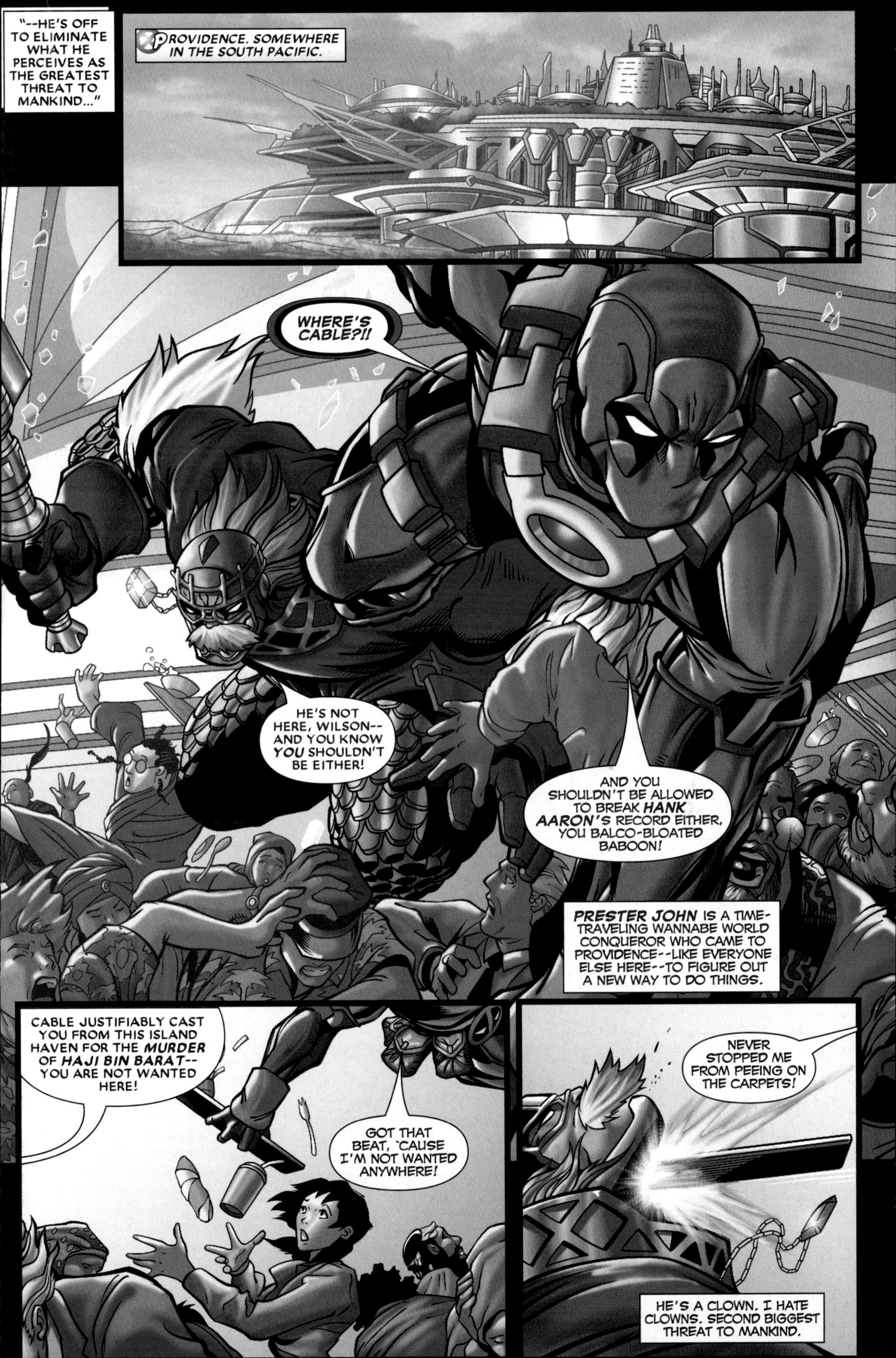
"--HE'S OFF TO ELIMINATE WHAT HE PERCEIVES AS THE GREATEST THREAT TO MANKIND..."
PROVIDENCE. SOMEWHERE IN THE SOUTH PACIFIC.
WHERE'S CABLE?!!
HE'S NOT HERE, WILSON-- AND YOU KNOW YOU SHOULDN'T BE EITHER!
AND YOU SHOULDN'T BE ALLOWED TO BREAK HANK AARON'S RECORD EITHER, YOU BALCO-BLOATED BABOON!
PRESTER JOHN IS A TIME-TRAVELING WANNABE WORLD CONQUEROR WHO CAME TO PROVIDENCE--LIKE EVERYONE ELSE HERE--TO FIGURE OUT A NEW WAY TO DO THINGS.
CABLE JUSTIFIABLY CAST YOU FROM THIS ISLAND HAVEN FOR THE MURDER OF HAJI BIN BARAT-- YOU ARE NOT WANTED HERE!
GOT THAT BEAT, 'CAUSE I'M NOT WANTED ANYWHERE!
NEVER STOPPED ME FROM PEEING ON THE CARPETS!
HE'S A CLOWN. I HATE CLOWNS. SECOND BIGGEST THREAT TO MANKIND.

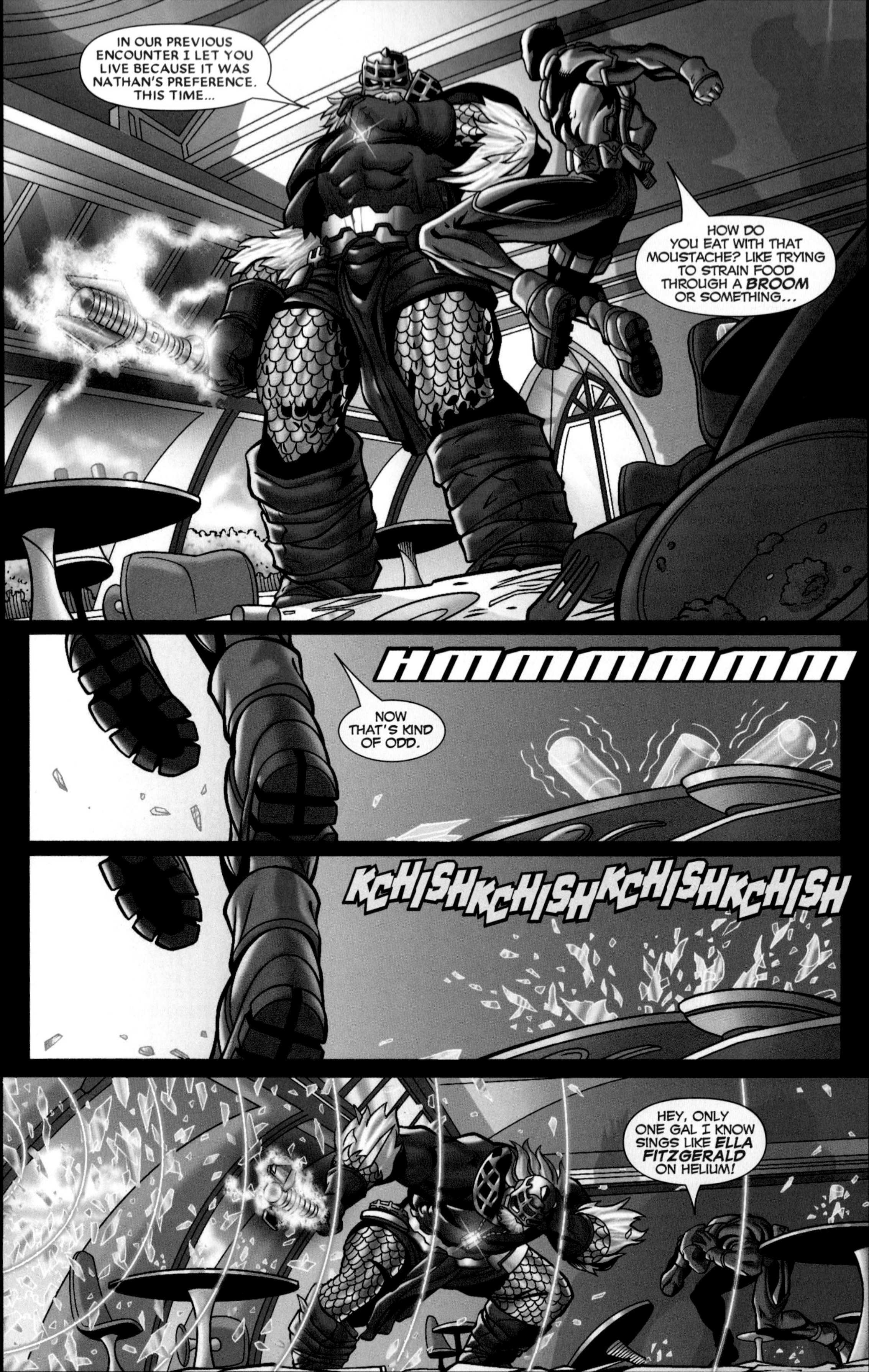
IN OUR PREVIOUS ENCOUNTER I LET YOU LIVE BECAUSE IT WAS NATHAN'S PREFERENCE. THIS TIME...
HOW DO YOU EAT WITH THAT MOUSTACHE? LIKE TRYING TO STRAIN FOOD THROUGH A BROOM OR SOMETHING...
HMMMMMMM
NOW THAT'S KIND OF ODD.
KCHISHKCHISHKCHISHKCHISH
HEY, ONLY ONE GAL I KNOW SINGS LIKE ELLA FITZGERALD ON HELIUM!

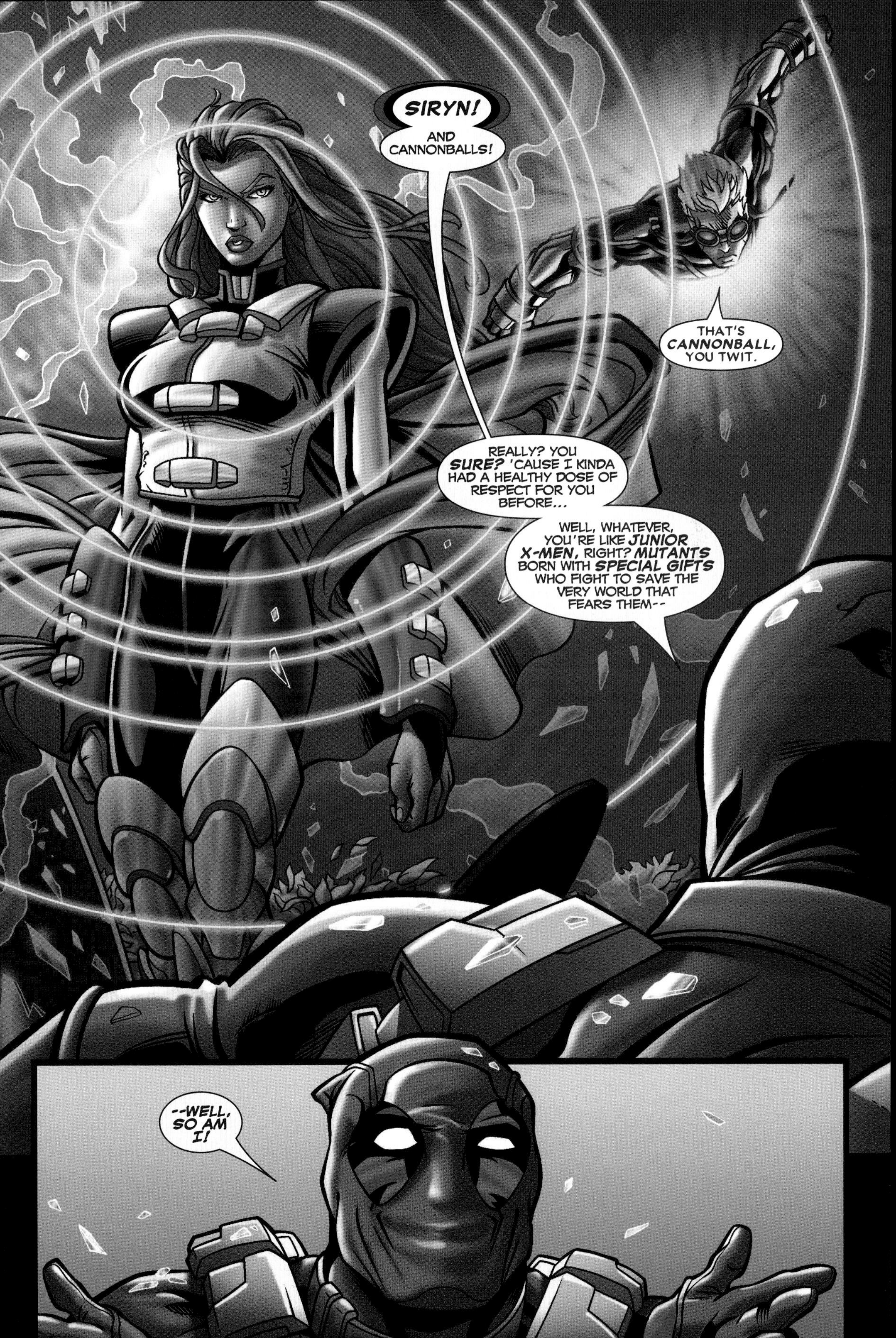
SIRYN!
AND CANNONBALLS!
THAT'S CANNONBALL, YOU TWIT.
REALLY? YOU SURE? 'CAUSE I KINDA HAD A HEALTHY DOSE OF RESPECT FOR YOU BEFORE...
WELL, WHATEVER, YOU'RE LIKE JUNIOR X-MEN, RIGHT? MUTANTS BORN WITH SPECIAL GIFTS WHO FIGHT TO SAVE THE VERY WORLD THAT FEARS THEM--
--WELL, SO AM I!

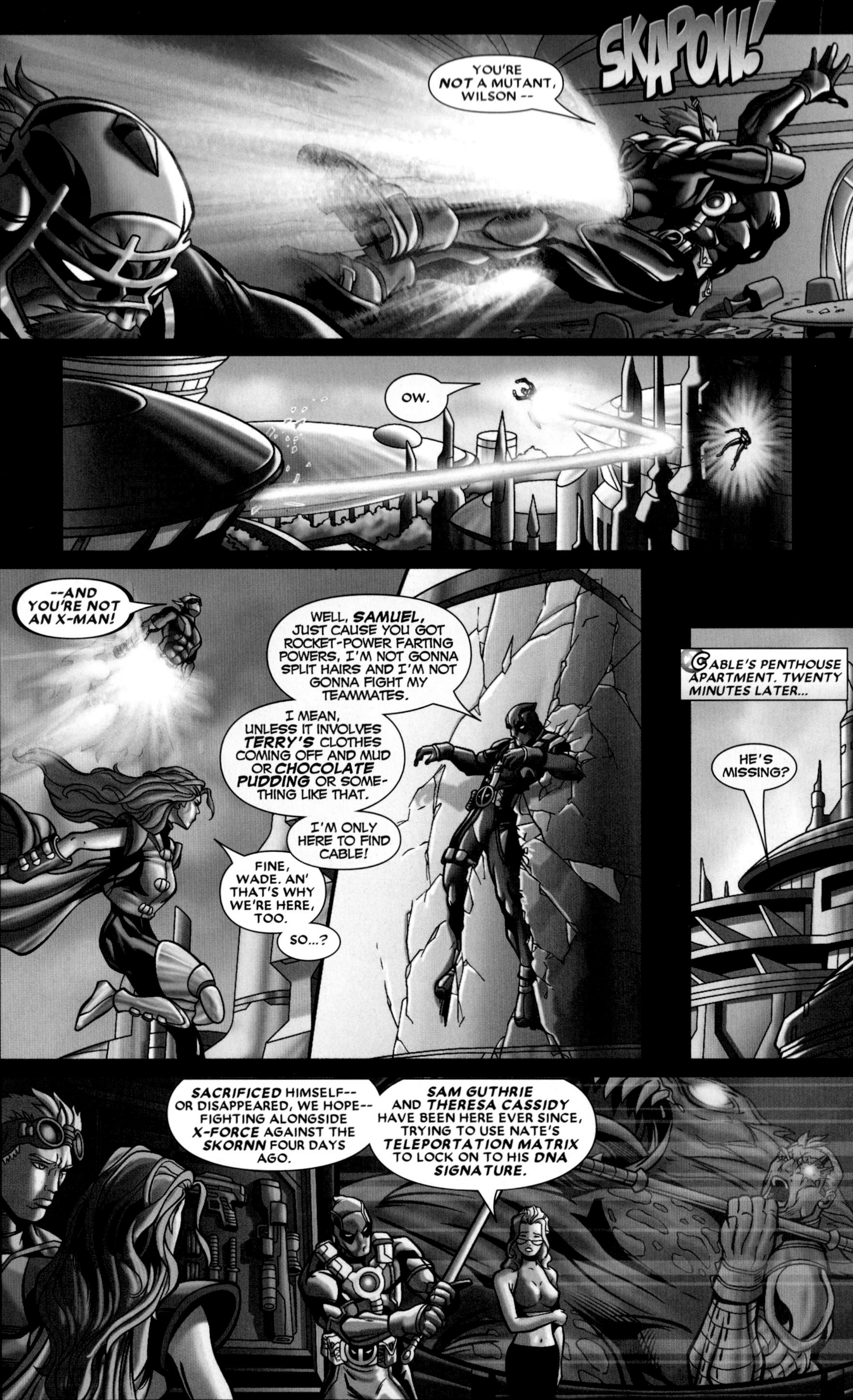
SKAPOW!
YOU'RE NOT A MUTANT, WILSON --
OW.
--AND YOU'RE NOT AN X-MAN!
WELL, SAMUEL, JUST CAUSE YOU GOT ROCKET-POWER FARTING POWERS, I'M NOT GONNA SPLIT HAIRS AND I'M NOT GONNA FIGHT MY TEAMMATES.
I MEAN, UNLESS IT INVOLVES TERRY'S CLOTHES COMING OFF AND MUD OR CHOCOLATE PUDDING OR SOMETHING LIKE THAT.
I'M ONLY HERE TO FIND CABLE!
FINE, WADE. AN' THAT'S WHY WE'RE HERE, TOO.
SO...?
CABLE'S PENTHOUSE APARTMENT. TWENTY MINUTES LATER...
HE'S MISSING?
SACRIFICED HIMSELF-- OR DISAPPEARED, WE HOPE-- FIGHTING ALONGSIDE X-FORCE AGAINST THE SKORNN FOUR DAYS AGO.
SAM GUTHRIE AND THERESA CASSIDY HAVE BEEN HERE EVER SINCE, TRYING TO USE NATE'S TELEPORTATION MATRIX TO LOCK ON TO HIS DNA SIGNATURE.

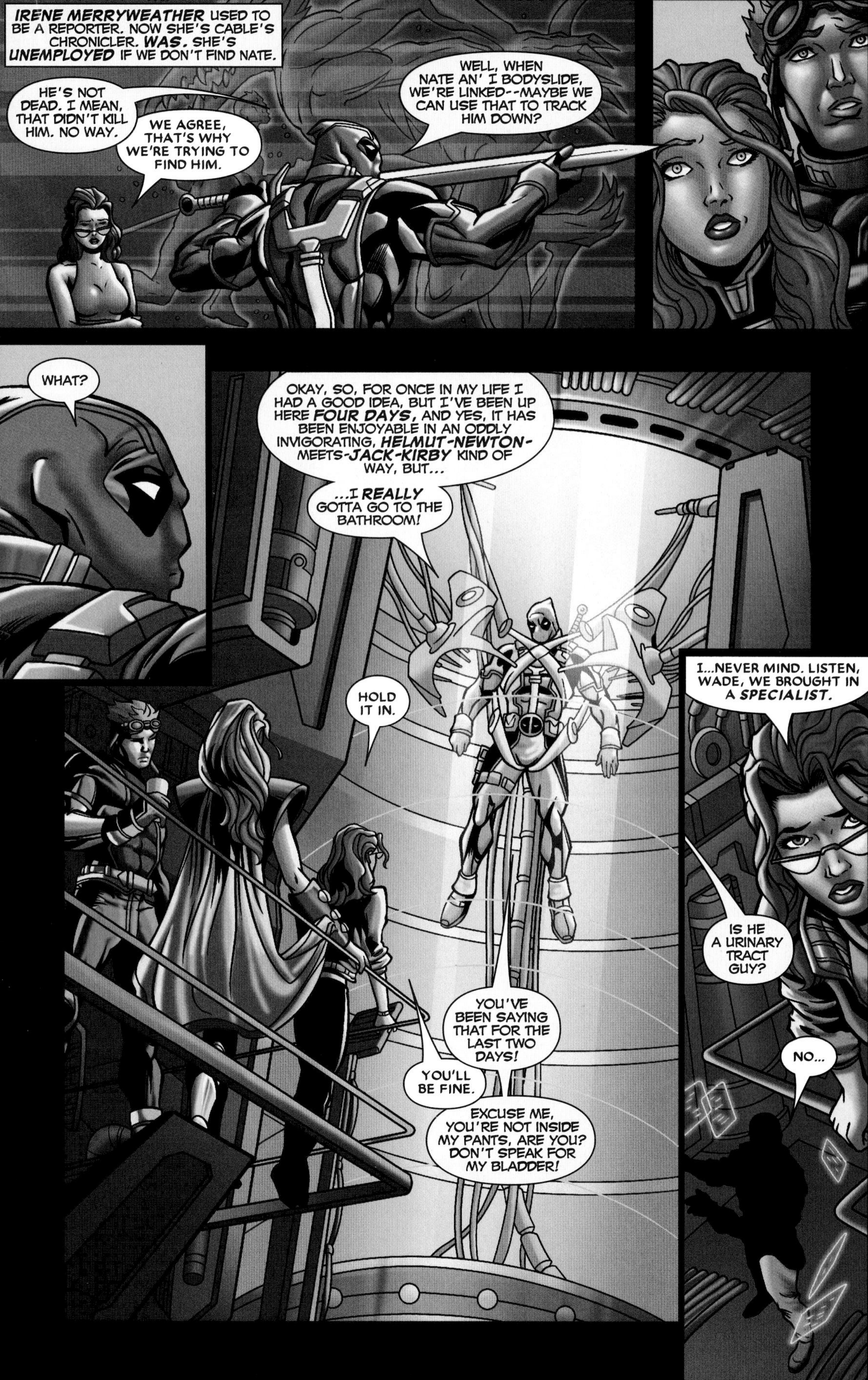
IRENE MERRYWEATHER USED TO BE A REPORTER. NOW SHE'S CABLE'S CHRONICLER. WAS. SHE'S UNEMPLOYED IF WE DON'T FIND NATE.
HE'S NOT DEAD. I MEAN, THAT DIDN'T KILL HIM. NO WAY.
WE AGREE, THAT'S WHY WE'RE TRYING TO FIND HIM.
WELL, WHEN NATE AN' I BODYSLIDE, WE'RE LINKED--MAYBE WE CAN USE THAT TO TRACK HIM DOWN?
WHAT?
OKAY, SO, FOR ONCE IN MY LIFE I HAD A GOOD IDEA, BUT I'VE BEEN UP HERE FOUR DAYS, AND YES, IT HAS BEEN ENJOYABLE IN AN ODDLY INVIGORATING, HELMUT-NEWTON-MEETS-JACK-KIRBY KIND OF WAY, BUT...
...I REALLY GOTTA GO TO THE BATHROOM!
HOLD IT IN.
YOU'VE BEEN SAYING THAT FOR THE LAST TWO DAYS!
YOU'LL BE FINE.
EXCUSE ME, YOU'RE NOT INSIDE MY PANTS, ARE YOU? DON'T SPEAK FOR MY BLADDER!
I...NEVER MIND. LISTEN, WADE, WE BROUGHT IN A SPECIALIST.
IS HE A URINARY TRACT GUY?
NO...

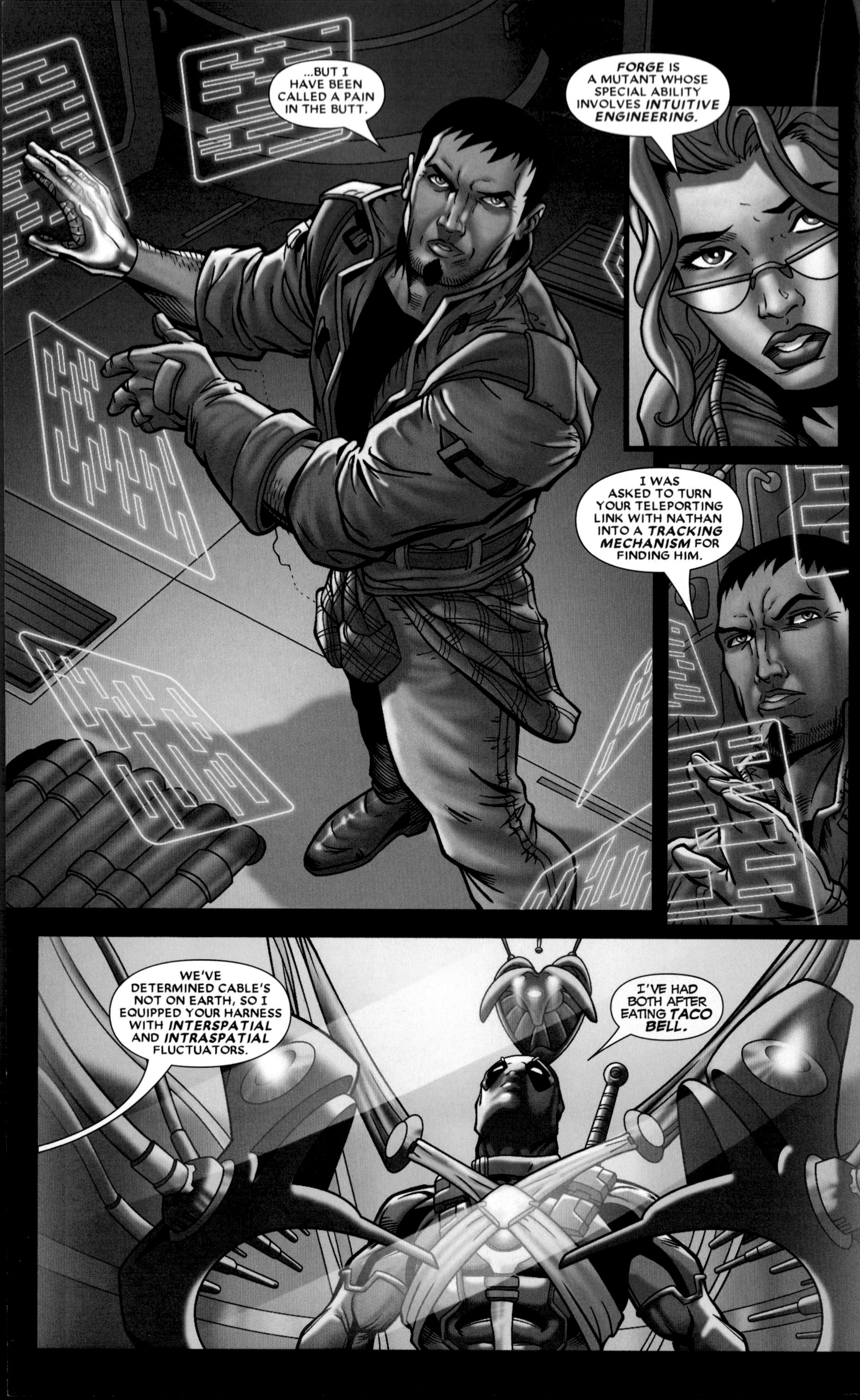
...BUT I HAVE BEEN CALLED A PAIN IN THE BUTT.
FORGE IS A MUTANT WHOSE SPECIAL ABILITY INVOLVES INTUITIVE ENGINEERING.
I WAS ASKED TO TURN YOUR TELEPORTING LINK WITH NATHAN INTO A TRACKING MECHANISM FOR FINDING HIM.
WE'VE DETERMINED CABLE'S NOT ON EARTH, SO I EQUIPPED YOUR HARNESS WITH INTERSPATIAL AND INTRASPATIAL FLUCTUATORS.
I'VE HAD BOTH AFTER EATING TACO BELL.

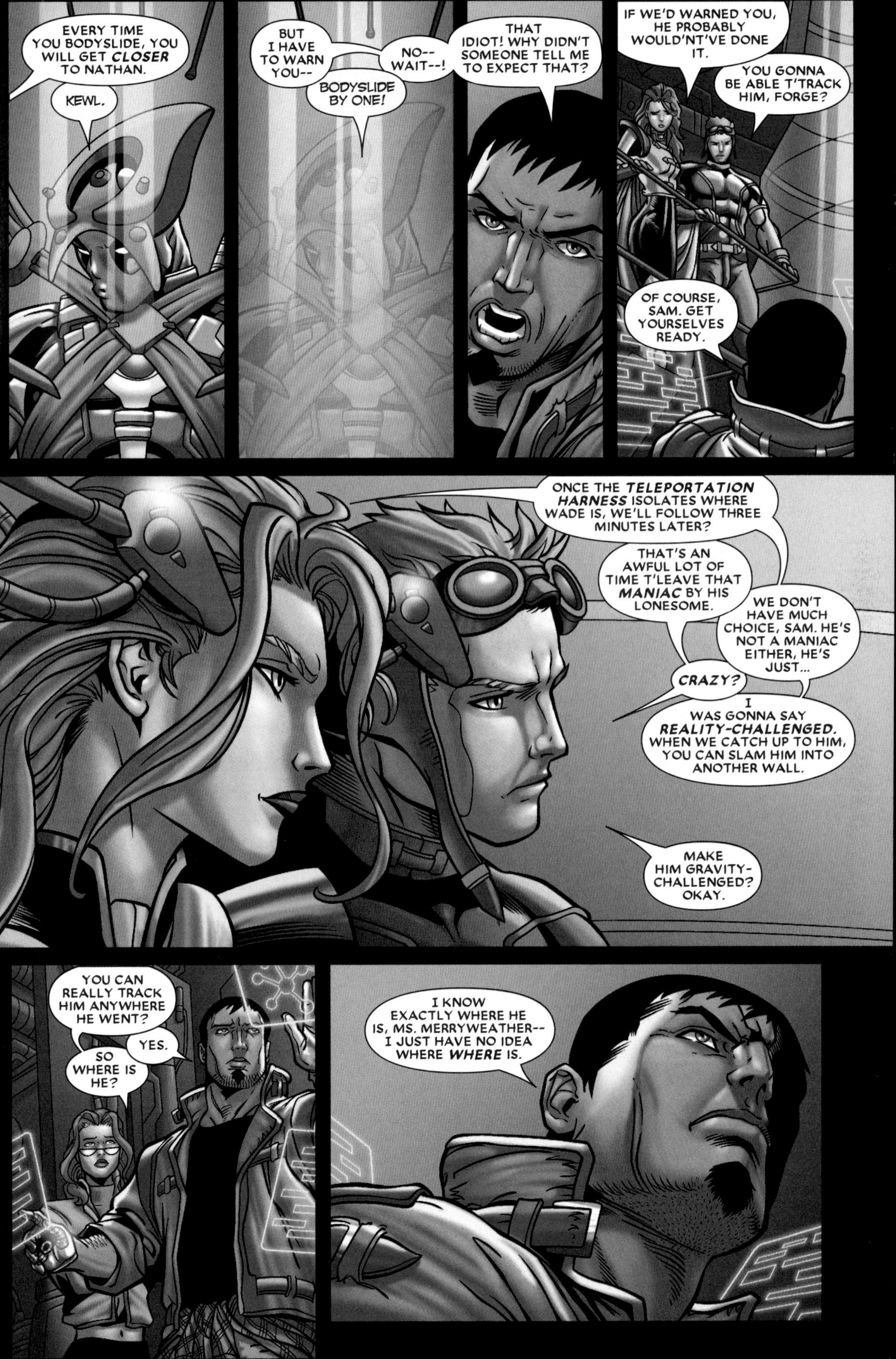
EVERY TIME YOU BODYSLIDE, YOU WILL GET CLOSER TO NATHAN.
KEWL.
BUT I HAVE TO WARN YOU--
NO-- WAIT--!
BODYSLIDE BY ONE!
THAT IDIOT! WHY DIDN'T SOMEONE TELL ME TO EXPECT THAT?
IF WE'D WARNED YOU, HE PROBABLY WOULD'NT'VE DONE IT.
YOU GONNA BE ABLE T'TRACK HIM, FORGE?
OF COURSE, SAM. GET YOURSELVES READY.
ONCE THE TELEPORTATION HARNESS ISOLATES WHERE WADE IS, WE'LL FOLLOW THREE MINUTES LATER?
THAT'S AN AWFUL LOT OF TIME T'LEAVE THAT MANIAC BY HIS LONESOME.
WE DON'T HAVE MUCH CHOICE, SAM. HE'S NOT A MANIAC EITHER, HE'S JUST...
CRAZY?
I WAS GONNA SAY REALITY-CHALLENGED. WHEN WE CATCH UP TO HIM, YOU CAN SLAM HIM INTO ANOTHER WALL.
MAKE HIM GRAVITY-CHALLENGED? OKAY.
YOU CAN REALLY TRACK HIM ANYWHERE HE WENT?
YES.
SO WHERE IS HE?
I KNOW EXACTLY WHERE HE IS, MS. MERRYWEATHER-- I JUST HAVE NO IDEA WHERE WHERE IS.

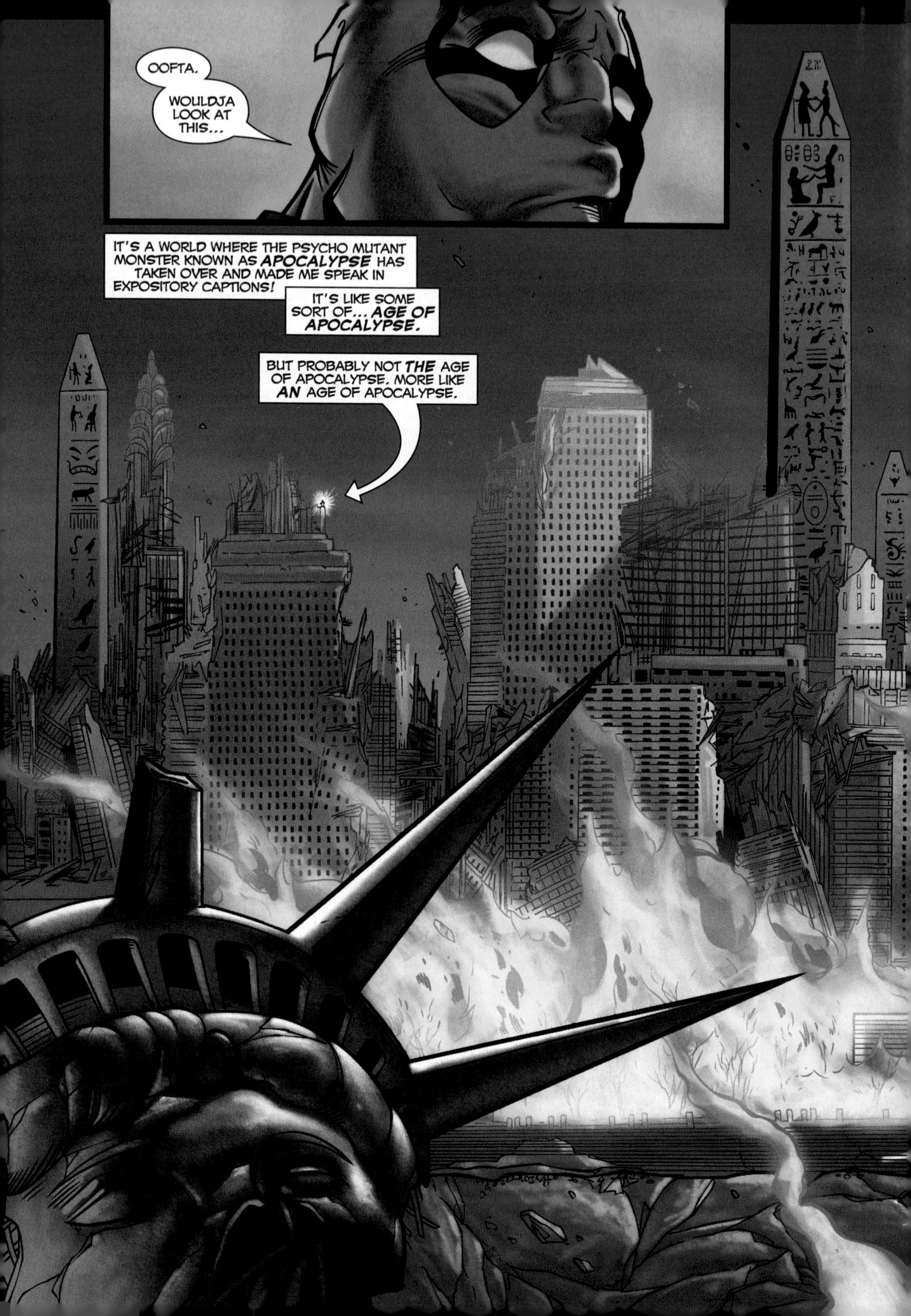
OOFTA.
WOULDJA LOOK AT THIS...
IT'S A WORLD WHERE THE PSYCHO MUTANT MONSTER KNOWN AS APOCALYPSE HAS TAKEN OVER AND MADE ME SPEAK IN EXPOSITORY CAPTIONS!
IT'S LIKE SOME SORT OF... AGE OF APOCALYPSE.
BUT PROBABLY NOT THE AGE OF APOCALYPSE. MORE LIKE AN AGE OF APOCALYPSE.

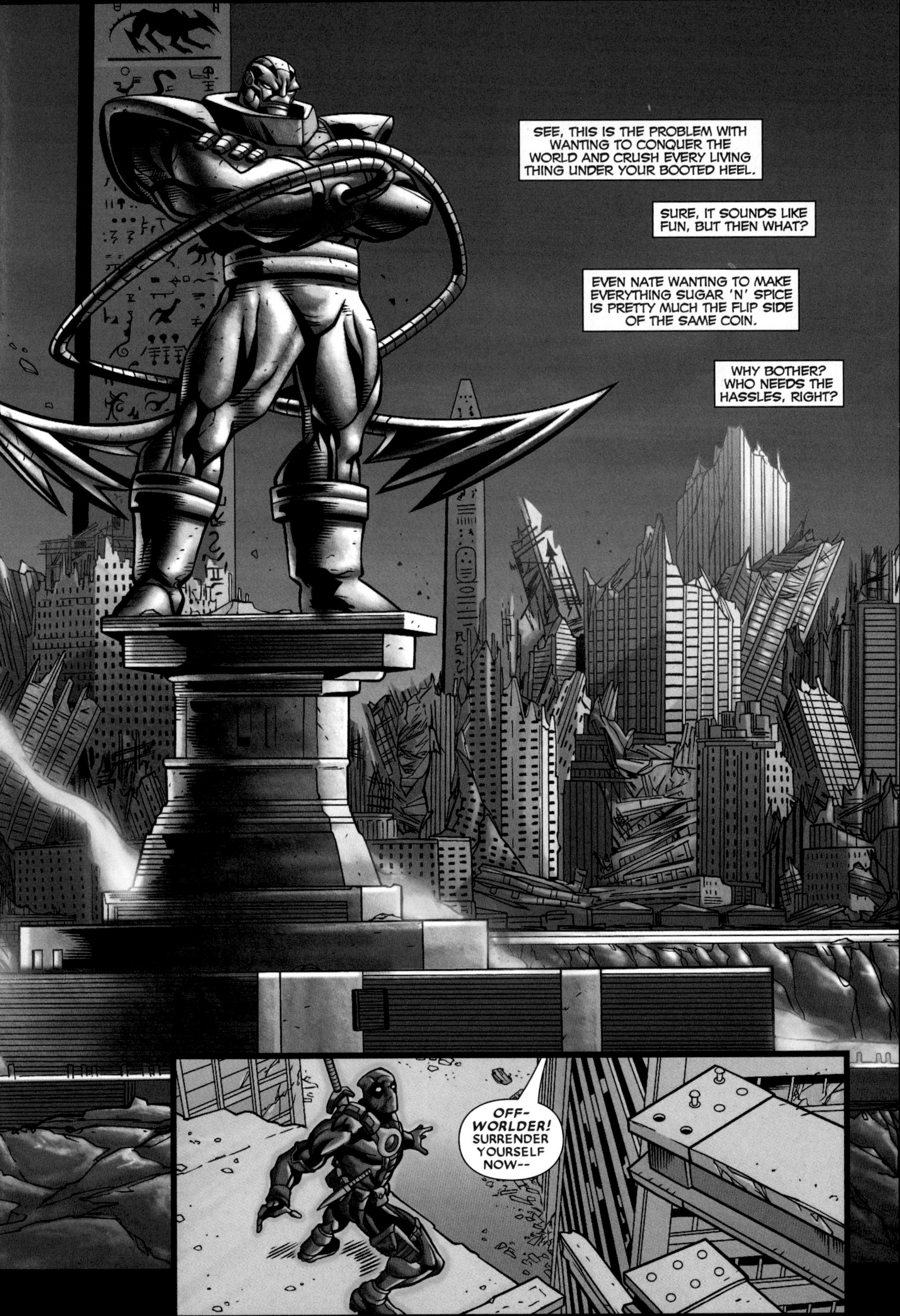
SEE, THIS IS THE PROBLEM WITH WANTING TO CONQUER THE WORLD AND CRUSH EVERY LIVING THING UNDER YOUR BOOTED HEEL.
SURE, IT SOUNDS LIKE FUN, BUT THEN WHAT?
EVEN NATE WANTING TO MAKE EVERYTHING SUGAR 'N' SPICE IS PRETTY MUCH THE FLIP SIDE OF THE SAME COIN.
WHY BOTHER? WHO NEEDS THE HASSLES, RIGHT?
OFF-WORLDER! SURRENDER YOURSELF NOW--

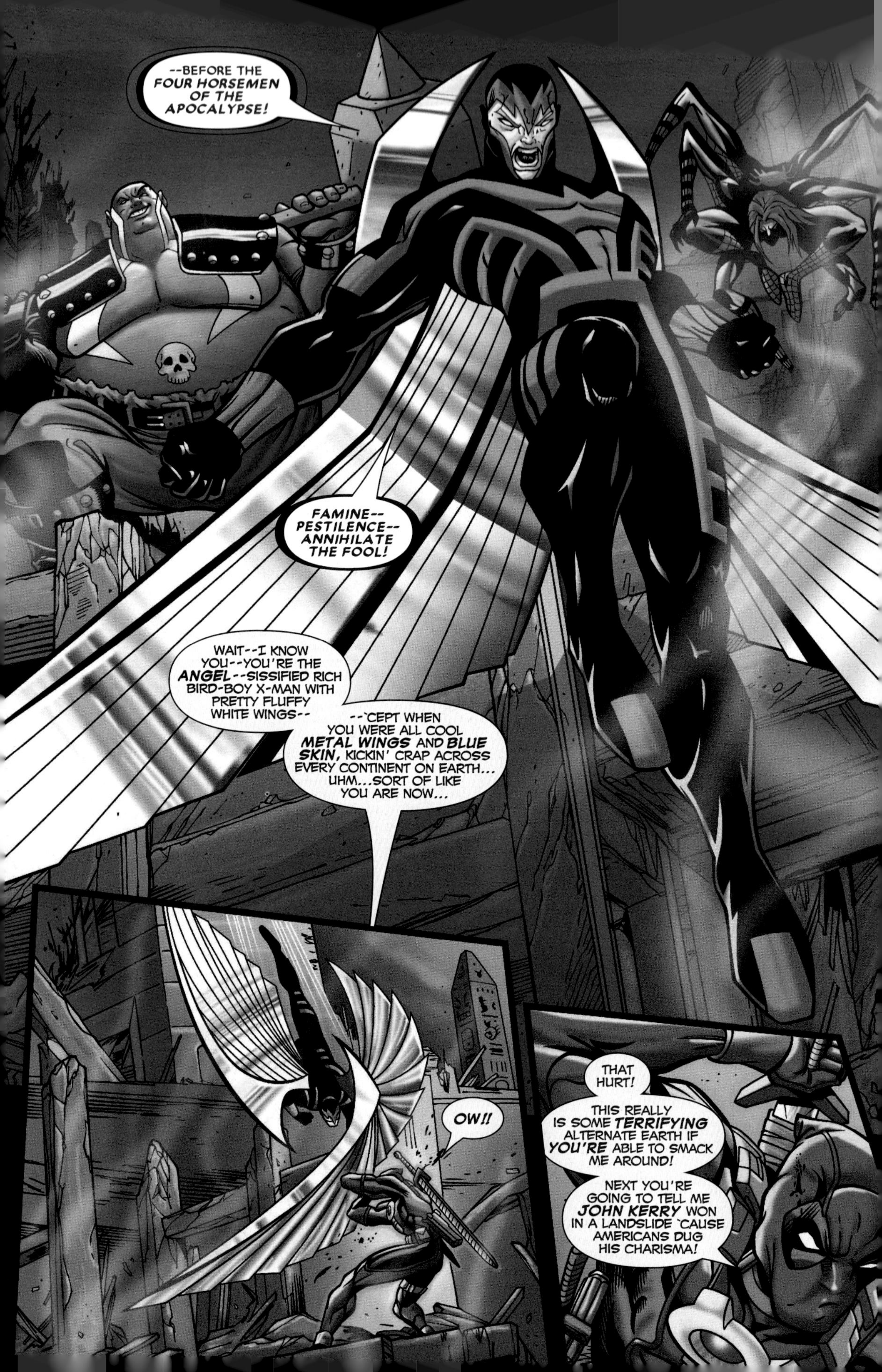
--BEFORE THE FOUR HORSEMEN OF THE APOCALYPSE!
FAMINE--PESTILENCE--ANNIHILATE THE FOOL!
WAIT--I KNOW YOU--YOU'RE THE ANGEL--SISSIFIED RICH BIRD-BOY X-MAN WITH PRETTY FLUFFY WHITE WINGS--
--`CEPT WHEN YOU WERE ALL COOL METAL WINGS AND BLUE SKIN, KICKIN' CRAP ACROSS EVERY CONTINENT ON EARTH... UHM...SORT OF LIKE YOU ARE NOW...
OW!!
THAT HURT!
THIS REALLY IS SOME TERRIFYING ALTERNATE EARTH IF YOU'RE ABLE TO SMACK ME AROUND!
NEXT YOU'RE GOING TO TELL ME JOHN KERRY WON IN A LANDSLIDE `CAUSE AMERICANS DUG HIS CHARISMA!

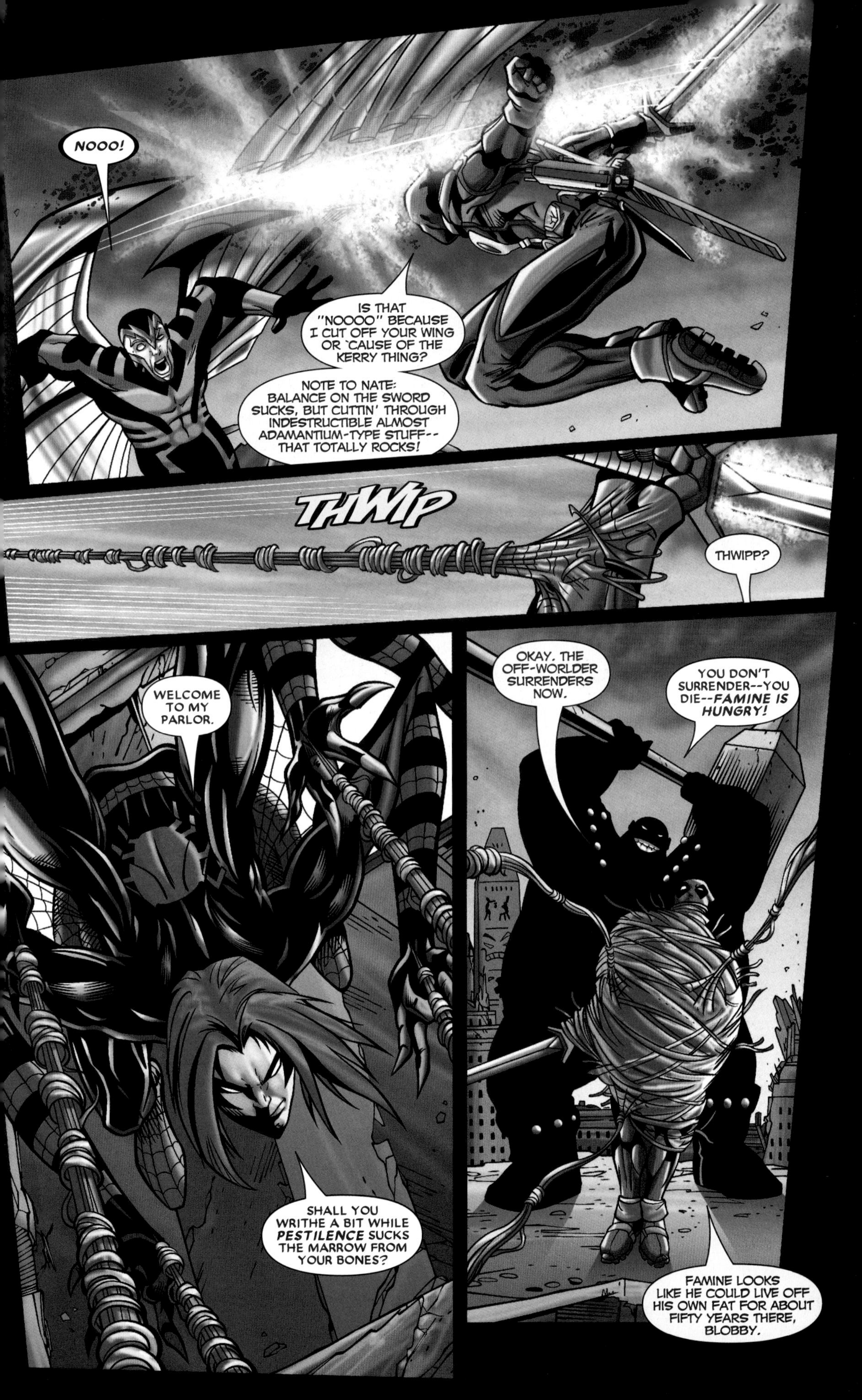
NOOO!
IS THAT "NOOOO" BECAUSE I CUT OFF YOUR WING OR 'CAUSE OF THE KERRY THING?
NOTE TO NATE: BALANCE ON THE SWORD SUCKS, BUT CUTTIN' THROUGH INDESTRUCTIBLE ALMOST ADAMANTIUM-TYPE STUFF--THAT TOTALLY ROCKS!
THWIP
THWIPP?
WELCOME TO MY PARLOR.
SHALL YOU WRITHE A BIT WHILE PESTILENCE SUCKS THE MARROW FROM YOUR BONES?
OKAY. THE OFF-WORLDER SURRENDERS NOW.
YOU DON'T SURRENDER--YOU DIE--FAMINE IS HUNGRY!
FAMINE LOOKS LIKE HE COULD LIVE OFF HIS OWN FAT FOR ABOUT FIFTY YEARS THERE, BLOBBY.

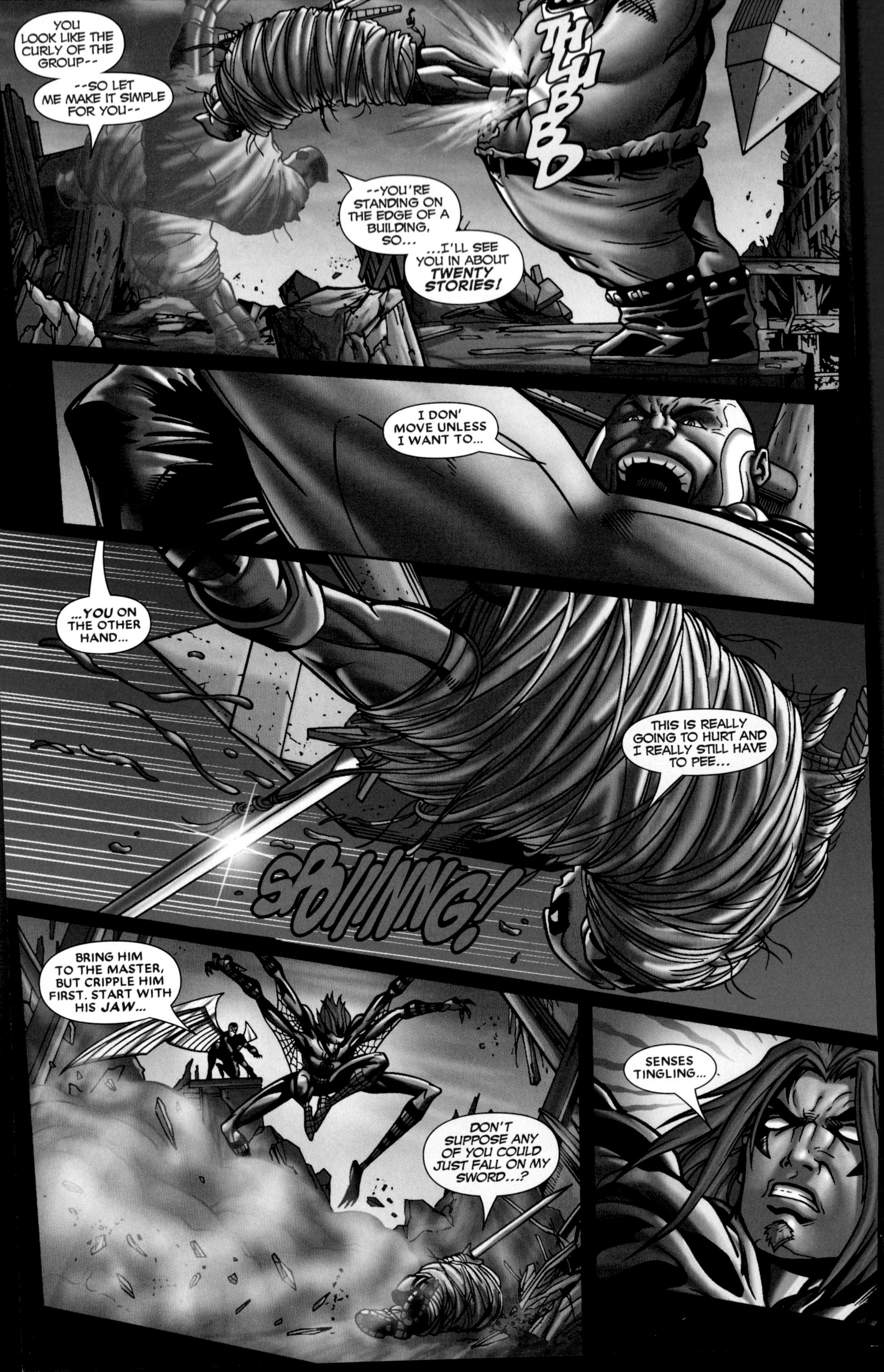
YOU LOOK LIKE THE CURLY OF THE GROUP--
--SO LET ME MAKE IT SIMPLE FOR YOU--
THUBBB
--YOU'RE STANDING ON THE EDGE OF A BUILDING, SO...
...I'LL SEE YOU IN ABOUT TWENTY STORIES!
I DON' MOVE UNLESS I WANT TO...
...YOU ON THE OTHER HAND...
THIS IS REALLY GOING TO HURT AND I REALLY STILL HAVE TO PEE...
SPOIIINNG!
BRING HIM TO THE MASTER, BUT CRIPPLE HIM FIRST. START WITH HIS JAW...
DON'T SUPPOSE ANY OF YOU COULD JUST FALL ON MY SWORD...?
SENSES TINGLING...

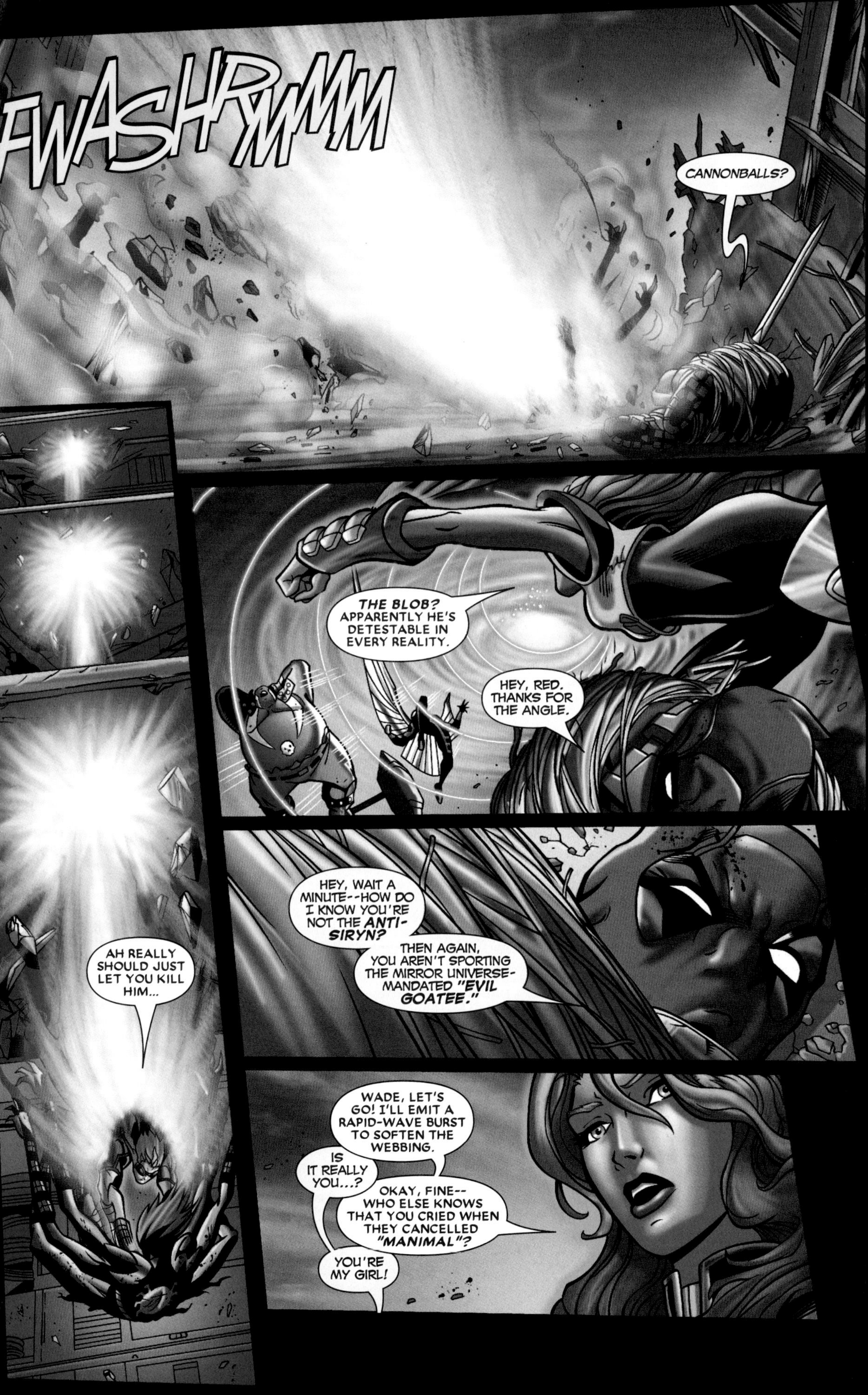
FWASHRMMMM
CANNONBALLS?
AH REALLY SHOULD JUST LET YOU KILL HIM...
THE BLOB? APPARENTLY HE'S DETESTABLE IN EVERY REALITY.
HEY, RED. THANKS FOR THE ANGLE.
HEY, WAIT A MINUTE--HOW DO I KNOW YOU'RE NOT THE ANTI-SIRYN?
THEN AGAIN, YOU AREN'T SPORTING THE MIRROR UNIVERSE-MANDATED "EVIL GOATEE."
WADE, LET'S GO! I'LL EMIT A RAPID-WAVE BURST TO SOFTEN THE WEBBING.
IS IT REALLY YOU...?
OKAY, FINE--WHO ELSE KNOWS THAT YOU CRIED WHEN THEY CANCELLED "MANIMAL"?
YOU'RE MY GIRL!

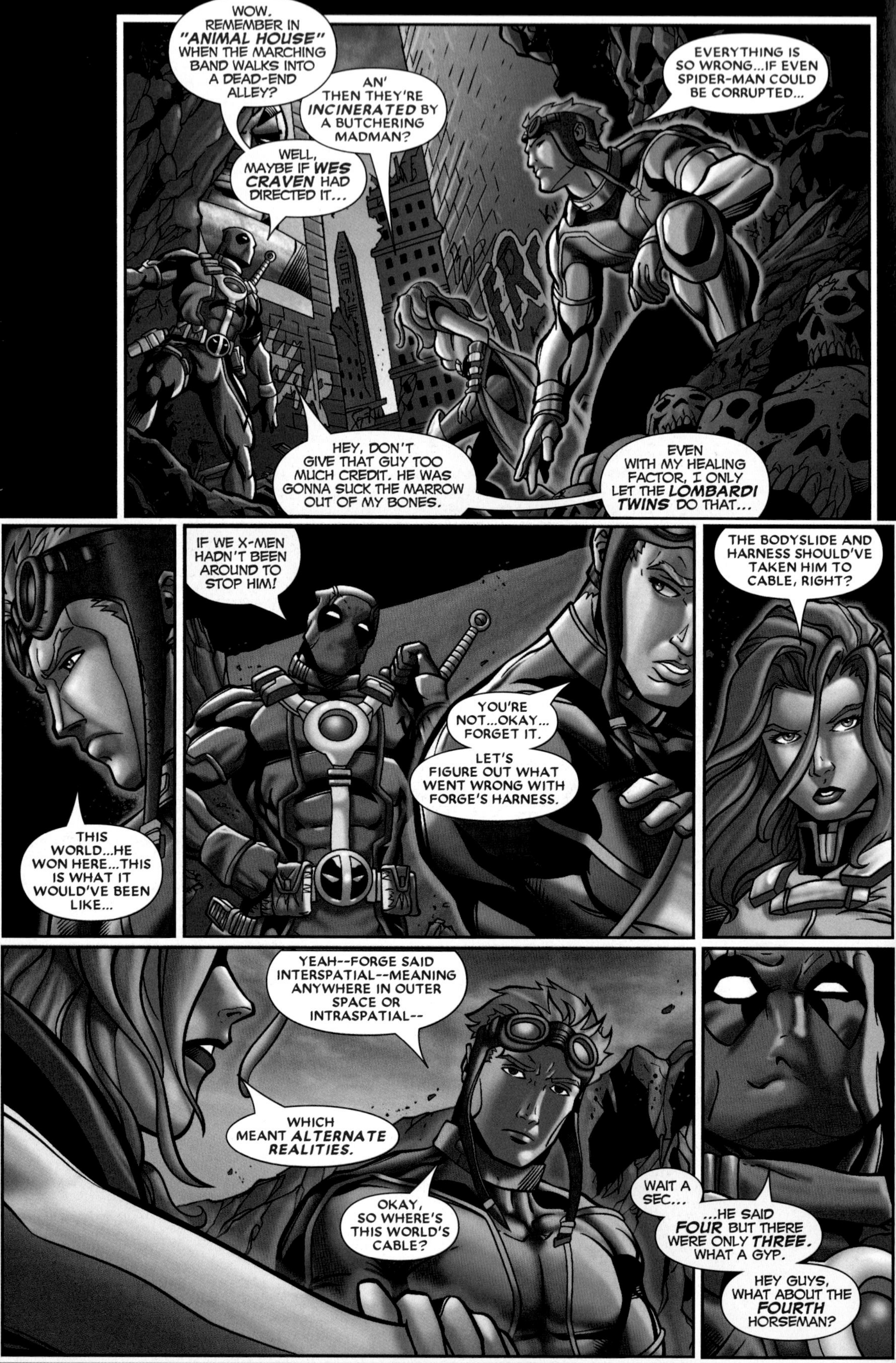
WOW. REMEMBER IN "ANIMAL HOUSE" WHEN THE MARCHING BAND WALKS INTO A DEAD-END ALLEY?
AN' THEN THEY'RE INCINERATED BY A BUTCHERING MADMAN?
WELL, MAYBE IF WES CRAVEN HAD DIRECTED IT...
EVERYTHING IS SO WRONG...IF EVEN SPIDER-MAN COULD BE CORRUPTED...
HEY, DON'T GIVE THAT GUY TOO MUCH CREDIT. HE WAS GONNA SUCK THE MARROW OUT OF MY BONES.
EVEN WITH MY HEALING FACTOR, I ONLY LET THE LOMBARDI TWINS DO THAT...
THIS WORLD...HE WON HERE...THIS IS WHAT IT WOULD'VE BEEN LIKE...
IF WE X-MEN HADN'T BEEN AROUND TO STOP HIM!
YOU'RE NOT...OKAY... FORGET IT.
LET'S FIGURE OUT WHAT WENT WRONG WITH FORGE'S HARNESS.
THE BODYSLIDE AND HARNESS SHOULD'VE TAKEN HIM TO CABLE, RIGHT?
YEAH--FORGE SAID INTERSPATIAL--MEANING ANYWHERE IN OUTER SPACE OR INTRASPATIAL--
WHICH MEANT ALTERNATE REALITIES.
OKAY, SO WHERE'S THIS WORLD'S CABLE?
WAIT A SEC...
...HE SAID FOUR BUT THERE WERE ONLY THREE. WHAT A GYP.
HEY GUYS, WHAT ABOUT THE FOURTH HORSEMAN?

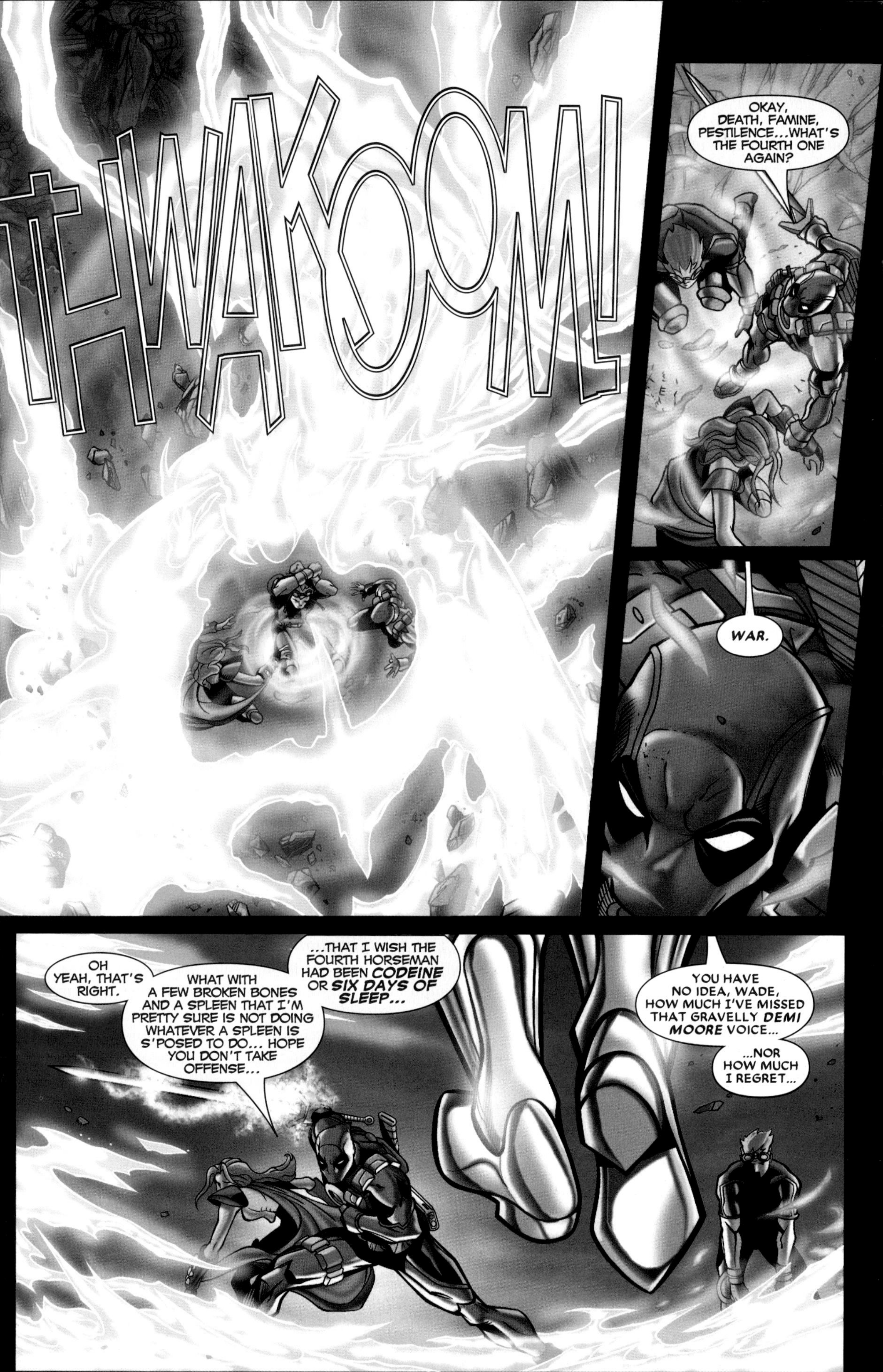
THWAKOOM!!
OKAY, DEATH, FAMINE, PESTILENCE...WHAT'S THE FOURTH ONE AGAIN?
WAR.
OH YEAH, THAT'S RIGHT.
WHAT WITH A FEW BROKEN BONES AND A SPLEEN THAT I'M PRETTY SURE IS NOT DOING WHATEVER A SPLEEN IS S'POSED TO DO... HOPE YOU DON'T TAKE OFFENSE...
...THAT I WISH THE FOURTH HORSEMAN HAD BEEN CODEINE OR SIX DAYS OF SLEEP...
YOU HAVE NO IDEA, WADE, HOW MUCH I'VE MISSED THAT GRAVELLY DEMI MOORE VOICE...
...NOR HOW MUCH I REGRET...

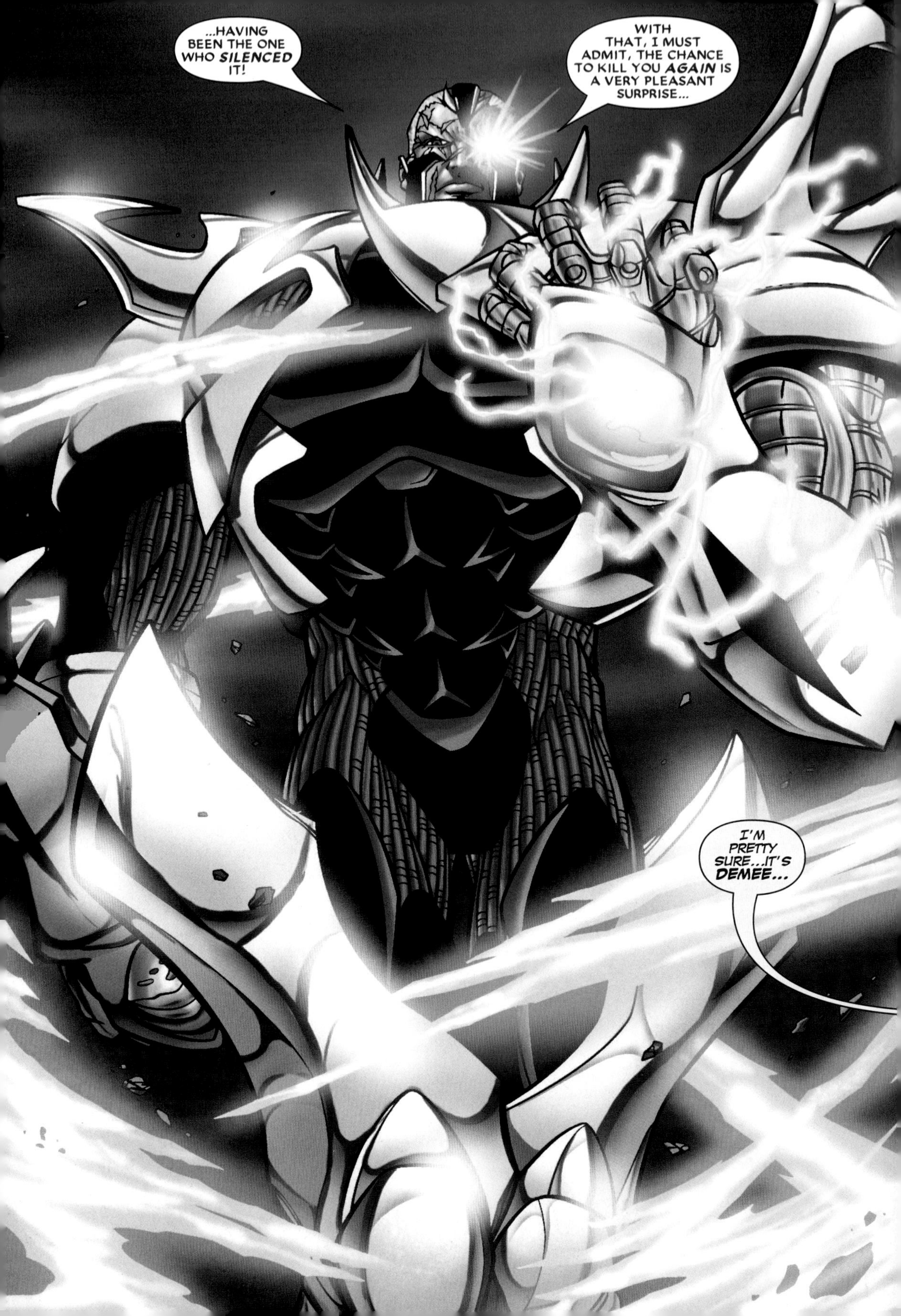
...HAVING BEEN THE ONE WHO SILENCED IT!
WITH THAT, I MUST ADMIT, THE CHANCE TO KILL YOU AGAIN IS A VERY PLEASANT SURPRISE...
I'M PRETTY SURE...IT'S DEMEE...

DEAR DEADPOOL

Nicole sent along a note with the letters: "This month's unintentional theme seems to be letters from the unstable, and those who love them. Oh yeah, and women. And psychics."

I'll just let all of you decide who is unstable, who is a lover of the unstable, who is a woman and who is a psychic. I don't care. I just ate forty-seven Big Macs and I am feeling unstable myself. On with your useless blatherings…

Dear Deadpool:

I've never written a letter to a publication like yours, but this time I'm really desperate. You see, my imaginary twin brother Hank, who lives somewhere in the back of my brain, is really giving me the creeps. He… oh wait, now I remember, this is not one of those letters columns where you can get the answer to all of life's problems. Sadly, it is but a comic book letters page, and what's even more frightening, Wade Wilson answers the letters. I mean, how could a guy like Deadpool help anybody with mental problems?

(Oh, come on, bro'! You don't know--he might be able to help.)

No!!! He can't--and you keep out of this, Hank!

Anyway, all I wanted to do, before I got the delusional idea that I was finally looking for help, was to thank the whole *C & DP* team for one of my favorite books every month. I buy up to 50 comics a month, and yours is one of the three or four books I look forward to reading the most.

(Man, this whole sentence doesn't make any sense, you goofball.)

It does too. It's not like English was my first language; unlike you, I'm German, and not some backyard loony out of some swamp in Scotland.

(I am not Scottish!)

Yes, you are and ticklish too. NOW SHUT UP!!!!!

Dieter Nagy
(and Hank, even though I don't really exist)

Okay, does Hank buy 50 copies, too? If so, you're both good in my book and a wonderful shining example of what makes Germany so great today. If not, then I sincerely suggest Dieter take four hundred and seventy two aspirin and call no one in the morning.

Dear Deadpool,

I just wanted to admit that I am the one who ate the last jelly donut.

I know I should have come clean when you asked me in the first place, but I was afraid you would be mad. I'm sorry.

Andrew Kugelstadt

Joke's on you, Andy – I mean, besides how funny your name is – I don't even like jelly donuts. I like Bavarian Crème. `Cause they have cream inside. And they're Bavarian. And I looked on a map, and I can't find Bavarius anywhere. I think Dr. Doom wiped it off the face of the Earth. And all we have left as testament to their glorious culture are spongy cream-filled donuts. Fair trade-off.

Dear Cable/Deadpool Team,

I am liking your series. Hopefully Marvel will keep it going for a very, very long time. I was wondering when or if you and Agent X will ever team up again? Also, I ran into Taskmaster in a bar the other day and he says you still owe him three grand and that he thinks you're a dork. Oh, and keep the fun times rolling.

Randy M.

I am liking your letter. Hopefully you will keep writing for a very, very long time. I was wondering when or if you and sanity will ever team up again. Also, I ran into Taskmaster in a bar the other day and I paid him three grand to kill you. Keep the fun times rolling, Randy.

C & DP is the greatest freakin' series ever. Sure it lacks some of the slapstick humor of previous Deadpool comics (and spin-offs), but it has continuously carried a plot that is not only entertaining, but also relevant to today's society.

Recently, a friend of mine was depressed, and we used examples from the comic series to help cheer him up. In fact, I need my monthly dose of Deadpool to keep me sane. I am a Mental Health Advocate on Cape Cod (if you've never been here, don't bother, it isn't worth seeing).

I find that there is a point monthly when I feel as if I am going to crack, and getting my hands on the newest issue featuring the Merc with a Mouth is the best way for me to survive. It actually brings down my stress.

And so with that in mind, I have a few comments.

Seeing how the book lowers my stress, but only monthly, can we PLEASE get a volume of *Essential Deadpool* published!?

Never ever cancel this book, or five puppies somewhere will die (not sure where, I just wanted to say it).

Until the Rat and Weasel have a child of their very own, make mine *Cable & Deadpool*… er, I mean, Marvel. Whatever.

Mike Higgins

Are you the same Mike Higgins who used to work at Marvel? `Cause you wrote *Spitfire and the Troubleshooters*, so that would make the whole mental health/stress thing totally understandable.

I think an *Essential Deadpool* is an essential idea. I'm going to make my point to Quesada and Buckley. And I have the swords to do it, too…

Dear Deadpool:

Please, sir, was the cover to *C & DP* #13 merely a delightful homage in general or based on any movie poster (or pulp magazine cover) in particular?

Did Miss (or Ms.) Merryweather enjoy dressing up as a scheming temptress?

(That trench coat and fedora became you--please don't let anyone attempt to convince you otherwise.).

Did you point out to Mr. Summers that the late Mr. Barat should have said, "Maybe not all Westerners have to die in a fiery religious cataclysmic battle" because "Maybe all Westerners didn't have to..." means that NO Westerners need die? From the context of Mr. Summers' conversation with Miss (or Ms.) Merryweather, I doubt that the late Mr. Barat's change of heart had progressed that far.

Please don't tell Mr. Summers this, but you're the reason I buy this comic. (On the other hand, do feel free to let Messrs. Nicieza and Zircher know that I very much enjoy their work.)

Ann Nichols [Miss]

See, Ann, I can take a wild guess that you're a chick `cause you contradicted yourself a million times in one short letter! Complimenting then correcting, passive-aggressives make me wanna…

Can't I ever just find a woman who wants to watch "Sleepless in Seattle" with me while hanging upside down in a leather harness over a bathtub full of Wendy's Chili (fingers optional)?

Do such women even exist anymore?

Nicole interrupts again: "Last month we wanted to know which creative team member our female reader A.J. was cutting out paper hearts for. Today, we reveal the answer!"

Nicole is beginning to annoy me, and yet, I too am curious as to this revelation…

Dear Deadpool,

Apparently, the way to get published on your letters page is to open myself for verbal abuse. I'm okay with this. Unfortunately, I don't really have a brain-dead question to draw your wrath. Sorry 'bout that.

Mostly, I wanted to say that I thought Irene sending you to search the sewer tanks for bullets that wouldn't matter was really funny. So much so, I'm reordering my pathetic budget to figure out whether or not I can squeeze a Mrs. Fields delivery to Nicole, Fabian, and Patrick. Since they're mostly in different areas, probably not. But the intent's there!

Oh, and I wanna ask Nicole to marry me again. Seriously. Nicole? Will you marry me? I give really good foot rubs.

Cookies (maybe) and appreciation of snarky comic joy,

A.J.

If Nicole's boyfriend lets you marry her, I don't even need to be invited to the wedding, though I demand to videotape the honeymoon.

Oh, and send the cookies to Marvel's offices. Patrick's on the other side of the country, but Fabian and Nicole will surely save him some. Surely.

Nicole interrupts YET AGAIN: "Abridged mail from psychic readers:"

Was wondering if Siryn will be making an appearance in your most excellent comic.

Robert Jackson

Hey, you must be psychic, `cause red's in the book for a whole bunch of issues right now!

Between my brother and I, we have just about every comic that Cable has appeared in, including as a baby (I know, it's a sickness).

Dan Slezak

Well, you must be psychic, Dan, `cause I always said Nate was a big baby, and wait `til you see what's comin' up!

Nicole interrupts again… sigh… "I also want to thank STEVE CHUNG for writing in. His mail is too long and wacky to print, but he picked up the book simply because I asked him to."

Great. We're so desperate for sales we need our editor to wander the streets asking total strangers to buy the book. But it worked… hmm…

Next month: Alternate Cable kicks my butt across an alternate world. In fact, kicks me so hard I end up on another alternate world. And wait `til you see Cable on that one… and then another… and… I'm gonna spew Big Macs all over the multiverse! Yeehaaa!

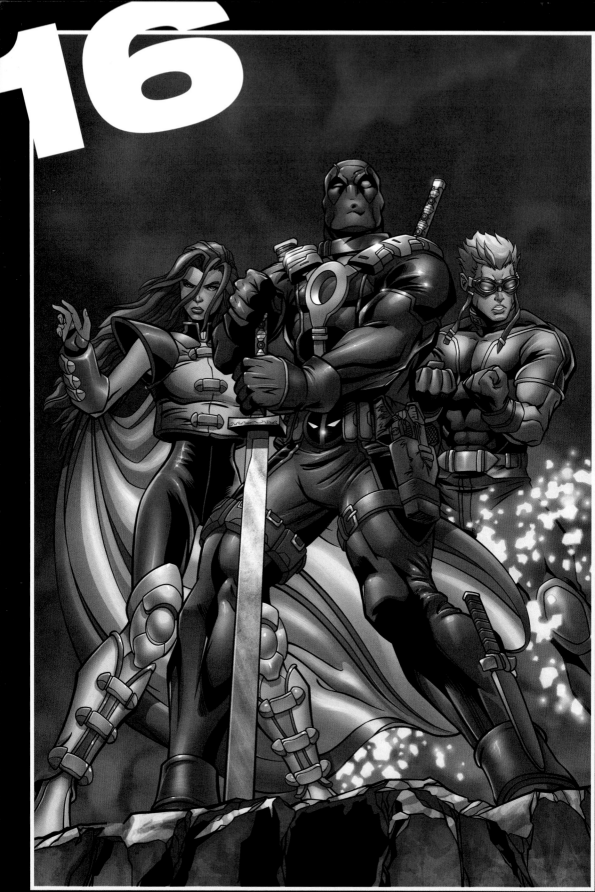

ENEMA OF THE STATE

PART TWO: WHAT IF...?

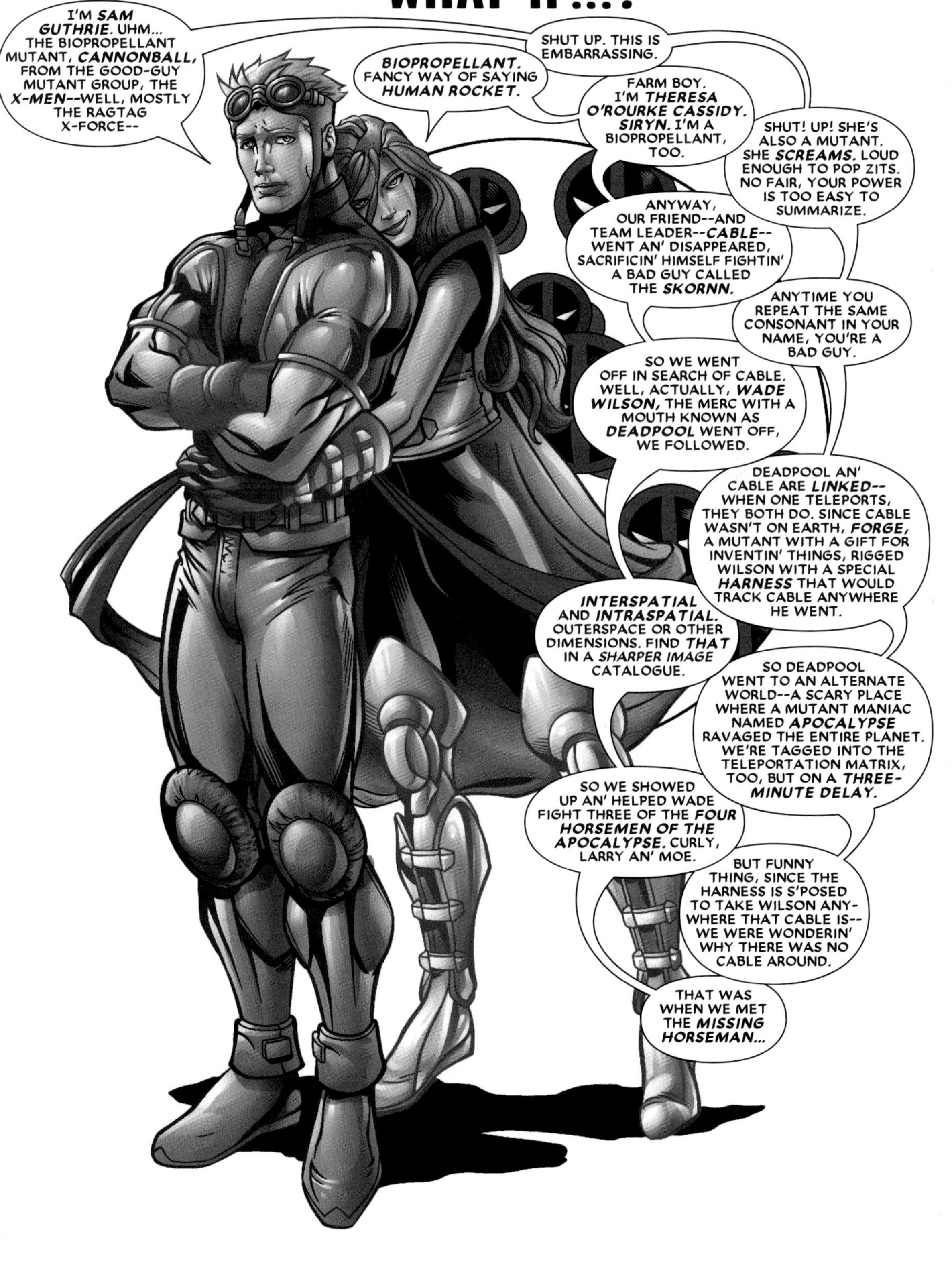

I'M SAM GUTHRIE. UHM... THE BIOPROPELLANT MUTANT, CANNONBALL, FROM THE GOOD-GUY MUTANT GROUP, THE X-MEN--WELL, MOSTLY THE RAGTAG X-FORCE--
SHUT UP. THIS IS EMBARRASSING.
BIOPROPELLANT. FANCY WAY OF SAYING HUMAN ROCKET.
FARM BOY. I'M THERESA O'ROURKE CASSIDY. SIRYN. I'M A BIOPROPELLANT, TOO.
SHUT! UP! SHE'S ALSO A MUTANT. SHE SCREAMS. LOUD ENOUGH TO POP ZITS. NO FAIR, YOUR POWER IS TOO EASY TO SUMMARIZE.
ANYWAY, OUR FRIEND--AND TEAM LEADER--CABLE--WENT AN' DISAPPEARED, SACRIFICIN' HIMSELF FIGHTIN' A BAD GUY CALLED THE SKORNN.
ANYTIME YOU REPEAT THE SAME CONSONANT IN YOUR NAME, YOU'RE A BAD GUY.
SO WE WENT OFF IN SEARCH OF CABLE. WELL, ACTUALLY, WADE WILSON, THE MERC WITH A MOUTH KNOWN AS DEADPOOL WENT OFF, WE FOLLOWED.
DEADPOOL AN' CABLE ARE LINKED--WHEN ONE TELEPORTS, THEY BOTH DO. SINCE CABLE WASN'T ON EARTH, FORGE, A MUTANT WITH A GIFT FOR INVENTIN' THINGS, RIGGED WILSON WITH A SPECIAL HARNESS THAT WOULD TRACK CABLE ANYWHERE HE WENT.
INTERSPATIAL AND INTRASPATIAL. OUTERSPACE OR OTHER DIMENSIONS. FIND THAT IN A SHARPER IMAGE CATALOGUE.
SO DEADPOOL WENT TO AN ALTERNATE WORLD--A SCARY PLACE WHERE A MUTANT MANIAC NAMED APOCALYPSE RAVAGED THE ENTIRE PLANET. WE'RE TAGGED INTO THE TELEPORTATION MATRIX, TOO, BUT ON A THREE-MINUTE DELAY.
SO WE SHOWED UP AN' HELPED WADE FIGHT THREE OF THE FOUR HORSEMEN OF THE APOCALYPSE. CURLY, LARRY AN' MOE.
BUT FUNNY THING, SINCE THE HARNESS IS S'POSED TO TAKE WILSON ANYWHERE THAT CABLE IS--WE WERE WONDERIN' WHY THERE WAS NO CABLE AROUND.
THAT WAS WHEN WE MET THE MISSING HORSEMAN...

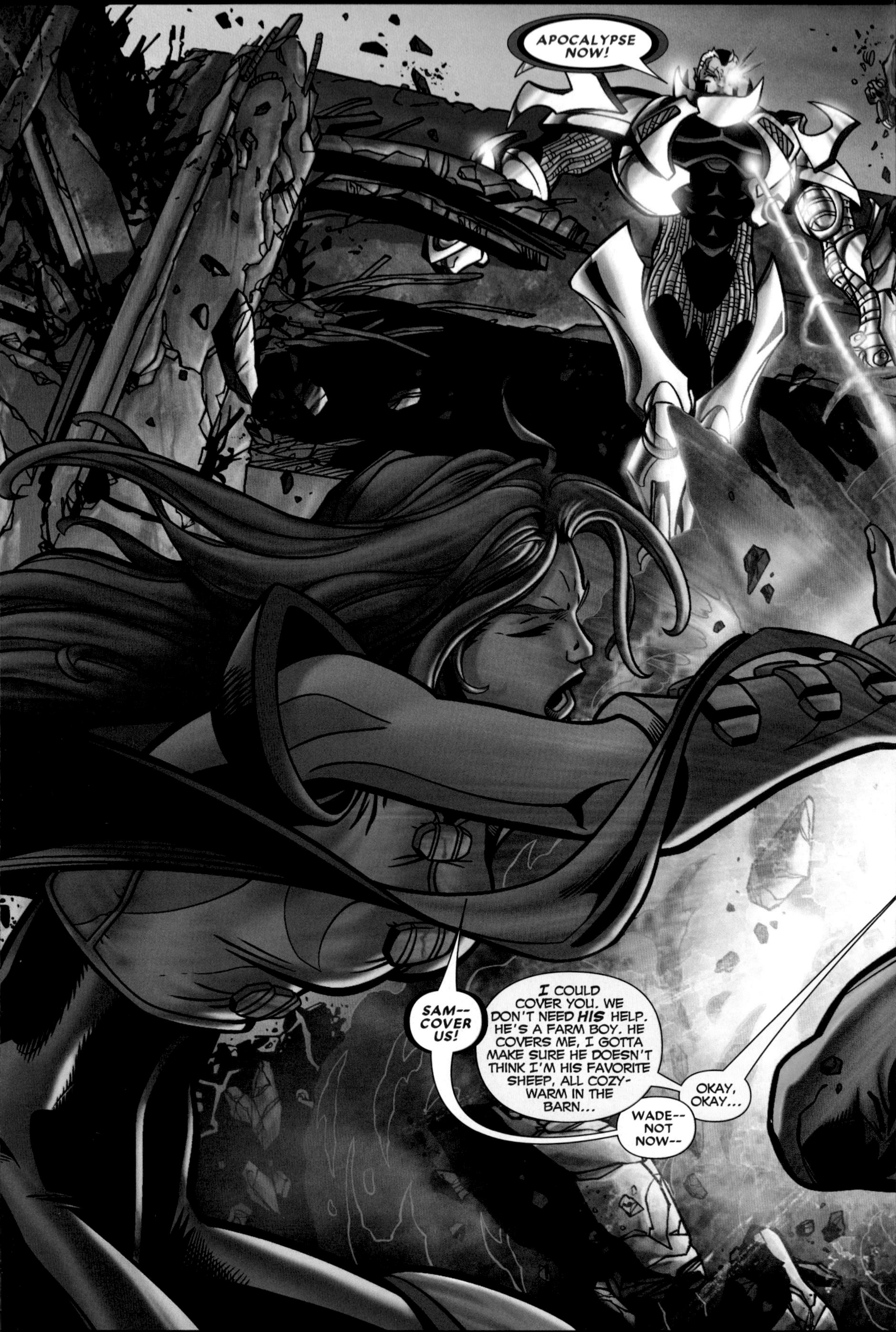
APOCALYPSE NOW!
SAM-- COVER US!
I COULD COVER YOU. WE DON'T NEED HIS HELP. HE'S A FARM BOY. HE COVERS ME, I GOTTA MAKE SURE HE DOESN'T THINK I'M HIS FAVORITE SHEEP, ALL COZY-WARM IN THE BARN...
OKAY, OKAY...
WADE-- NOT NOW--

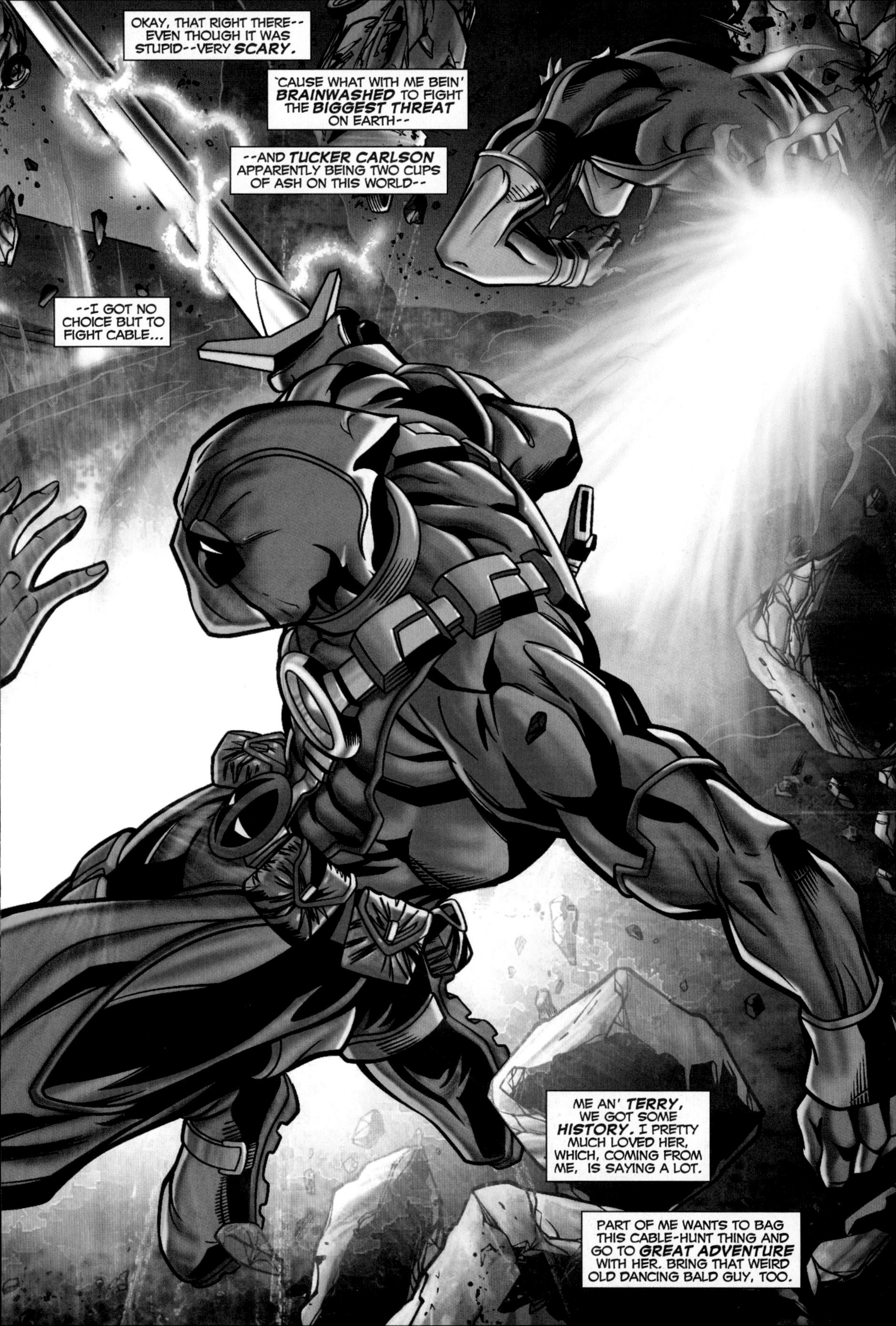

OKAY, THAT RIGHT THERE-- EVEN THOUGH IT WAS STUPID--VERY SCARY.
'CAUSE WHAT WITH ME BEIN' BRAINWASHED TO FIGHT THE BIGGEST THREAT ON EARTH--
--AND TUCKER CARLSON APPARENTLY BEING TWO CUPS OF ASH ON THIS WORLD--
--I GOT NO CHOICE BUT TO FIGHT CABLE...
ME AN' TERRY, WE GOT SOME HISTORY. I PRETTY MUCH LOVED HER, WHICH, COMING FROM ME, IS SAYING A LOT.
PART OF ME WANTS TO BAG THIS CABLE-HUNT THING AND GO TO GREAT ADVENTURE WITH HER. BRING THAT WEIRD OLD DANCING BALD GUY, TOO.

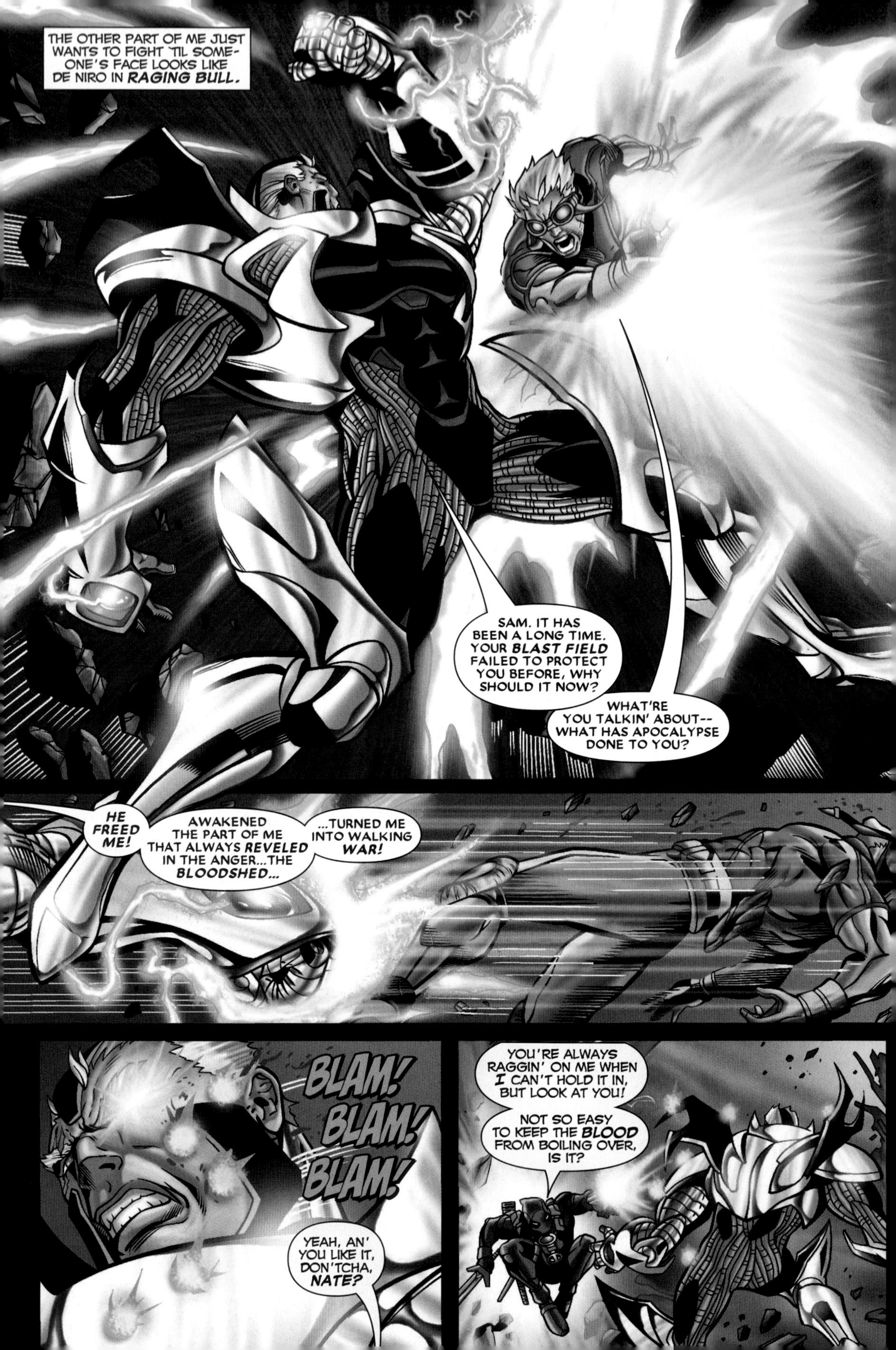
THE OTHER PART OF ME JUST WANTS TO FIGHT 'TIL SOME-ONE'S FACE LOOKS LIKE DE NIRO IN *RAGING BULL.*
SAM. IT HAS BEEN A LONG TIME. YOUR *BLAST FIELD* FAILED TO PROTECT YOU BEFORE, WHY SHOULD IT NOW?
WHAT'RE YOU TALKIN' ABOUT-- WHAT HAS APOCALYPSE DONE TO YOU?
HE FREED ME!
AWAKENED THE PART OF ME THAT ALWAYS *REVELED* IN THE ANGER...THE *BLOODSHED...*
...TURNED ME INTO WALKING *WAR!*
BLAM! BLAM! BLAM!
YEAH, AN' YOU LIKE IT, DON'TCHA, *NATE?*
YOU'RE ALWAYS RAGGIN' ON ME WHEN *I* CAN'T HOLD IT IN, BUT LOOK AT YOU!
NOT SO EASY TO KEEP THE *BLOOD* FROM BOILING OVER, IS IT?

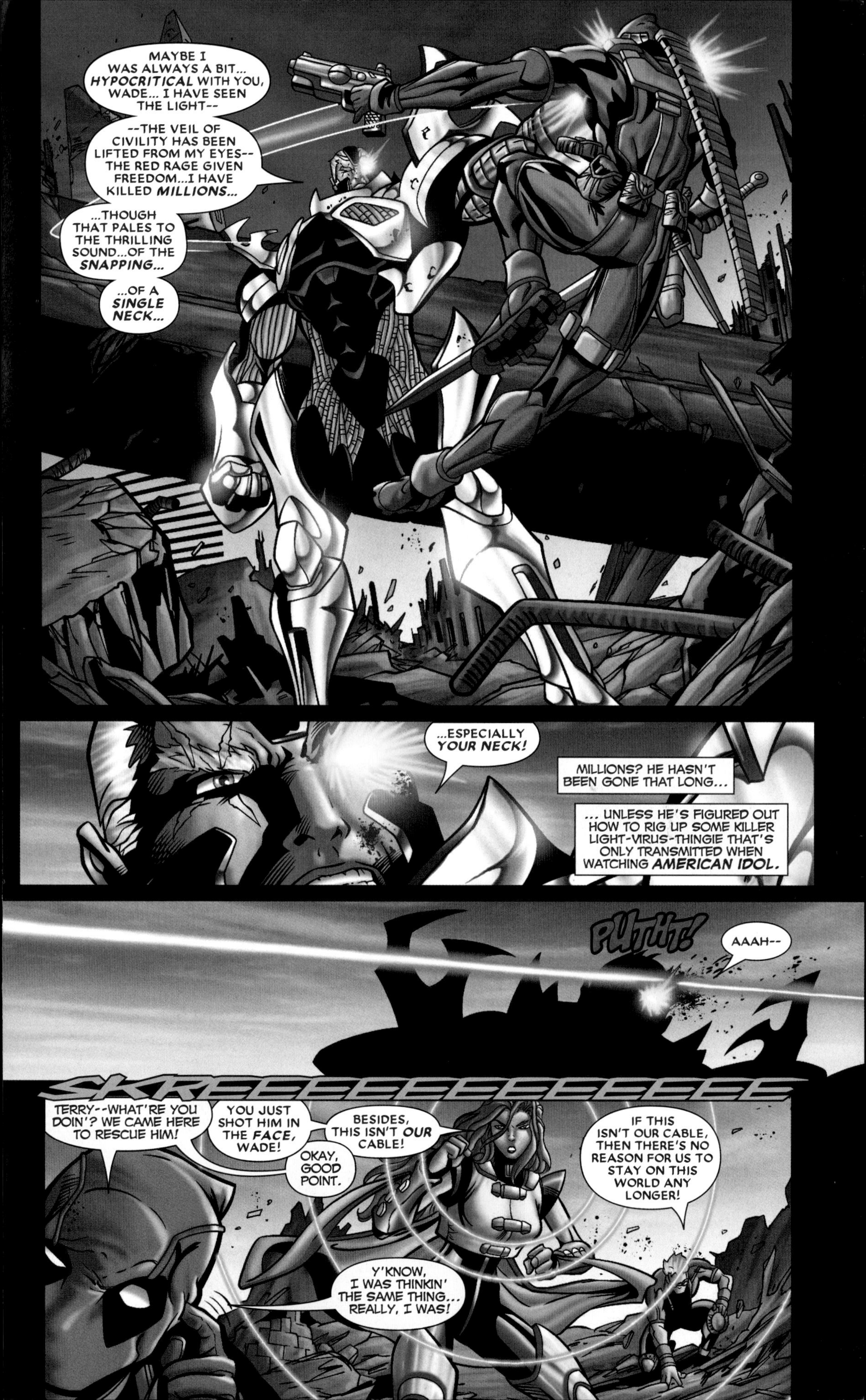
MAYBE I WAS ALWAYS A BIT... HYPOCRITICAL WITH YOU, WADE... I HAVE SEEN THE LIGHT--
--THE VEIL OF CIVILITY HAS BEEN LIFTED FROM MY EYES-- THE RED RAGE GIVEN FREEDOM...I HAVE KILLED MILLIONS...
...THOUGH THAT PALES TO THE THRILLING SOUND...OF THE SNAPPING...
...OF A SINGLE NECK...
...ESPECIALLY YOUR NECK!
MILLIONS? HE HASN'T BEEN GONE THAT LONG...
... UNLESS HE'S FIGURED OUT HOW TO RIG UP SOME KILLER LIGHT-VIRUS-THINGIE THAT'S ONLY TRANSMITTED WHEN WATCHING AMERICAN IDOL.
PUTHT!
AAAH--
SKREEEEEEEEEEEEEEE
TERRY--WHAT'RE YOU DOIN'? WE CAME HERE TO RESCUE HIM!
YOU JUST SHOT HIM IN THE FACE, WADE!
OKAY, GOOD POINT.
BESIDES, THIS ISN'T OUR CABLE!
IF THIS ISN'T OUR CABLE, THEN THERE'S NO REASON FOR US TO STAY ON THIS WORLD ANY LONGER!
Y'KNOW, I WAS THINKIN' THE SAME THING... REALLY, I WAS!

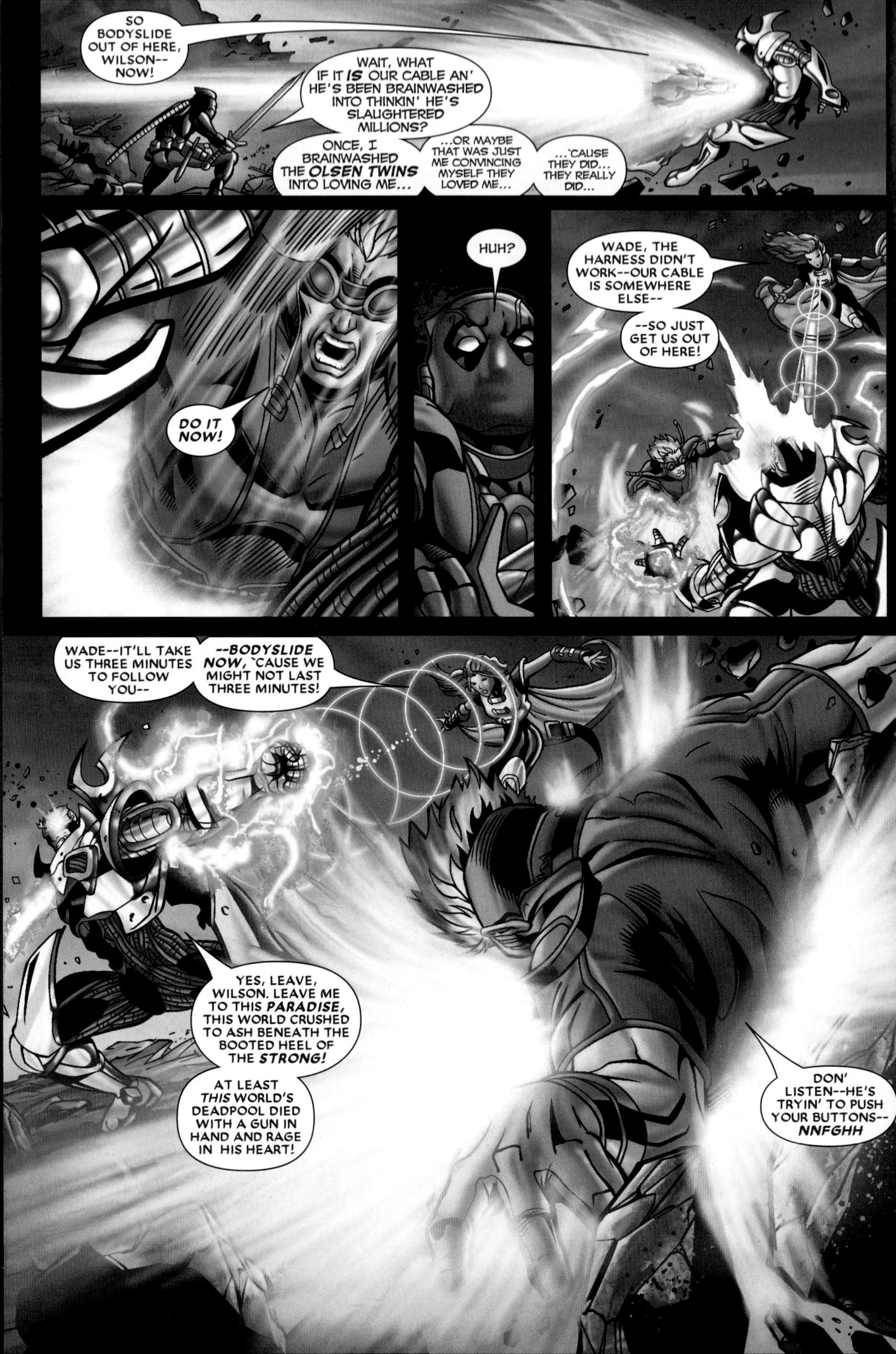

SO BODYSLIDE OUT OF HERE, WILSON-- NOW!
WAIT, WHAT IF IT ***IS*** OUR CABLE AN' HE'S BEEN BRAINWASHED INTO THINKIN' HE'S SLAUGHTERED MILLIONS?
ONCE, I BRAINWASHED THE ***OLSEN TWINS*** INTO LOVING ME...
...OR MAYBE THAT WAS JUST ME CONVINCING MYSELF THEY LOVED ME...
...'CAUSE THEY DID... THEY REALLY DID...
DO IT NOW!
HUH?
WADE, THE HARNESS DIDN'T WORK--OUR CABLE IS SOMEWHERE ELSE--
--SO JUST GET US OUT OF HERE!
WADE--IT'LL TAKE US THREE MINUTES TO FOLLOW YOU--
--BODYSLIDE NOW, 'CAUSE WE MIGHT NOT LAST THREE MINUTES!
YES, LEAVE, WILSON. LEAVE ME TO THIS ***PARADISE,*** THIS WORLD CRUSHED TO ASH BENEATH THE BOOTED HEEL OF THE ***STRONG!***
AT LEAST *THIS* WORLD'S DEADPOOL DIED WITH A GUN IN HAND AND RAGE IN HIS HEART!
DON' LISTEN--HE'S TRYIN' TO PUSH YOUR BUTTONS-- ***NNFGHH***

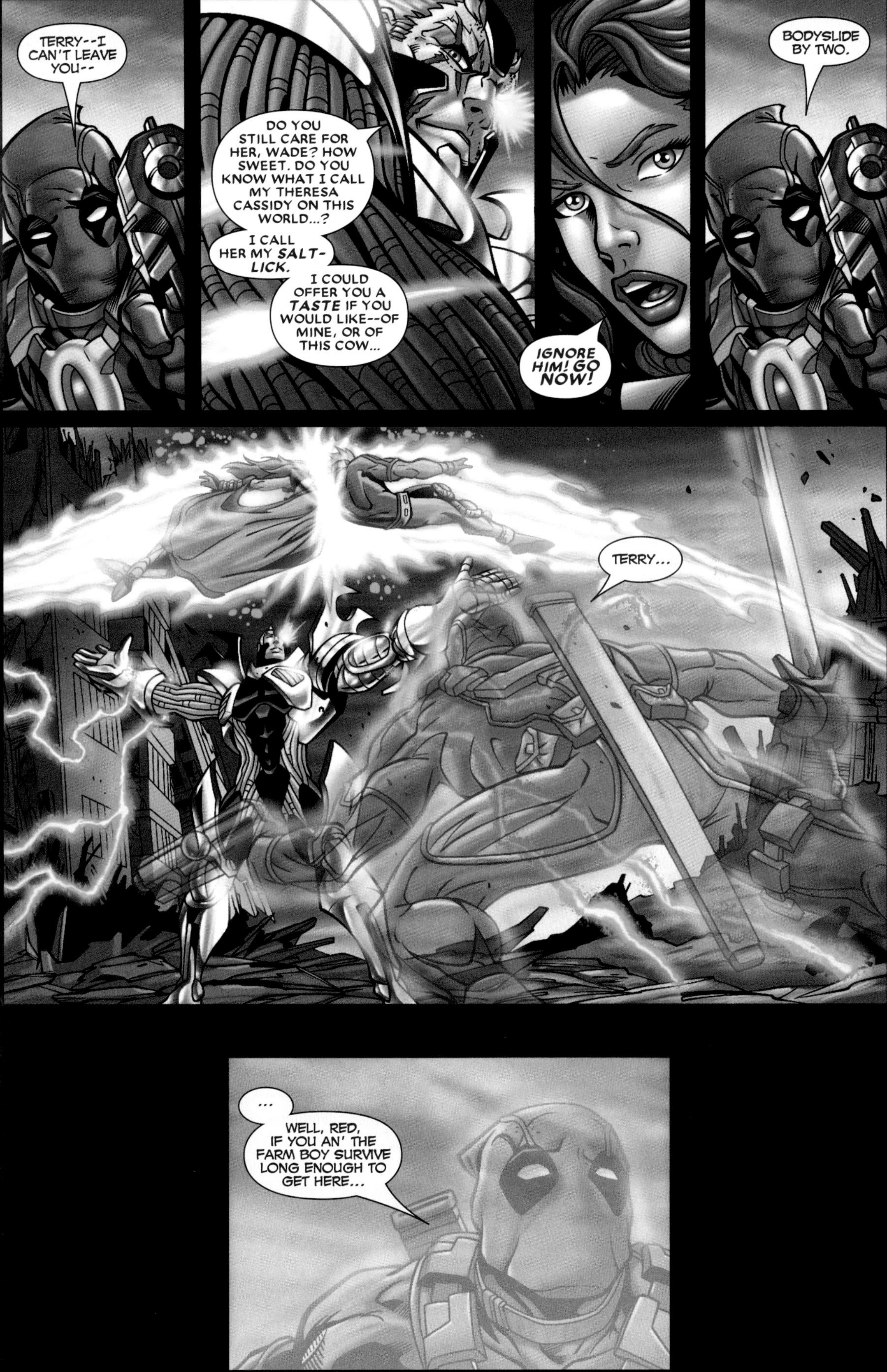
TERRY--I CAN'T LEAVE YOU--
DO YOU STILL CARE FOR HER, WADE? HOW SWEET. DO YOU KNOW WHAT I CALL MY THERESA CASSIDY ON THIS WORLD...?
I CALL HER MY SALT-LICK.
I COULD OFFER YOU A TASTE IF YOU WOULD LIKE--OF MINE, OR OF THIS COW...
IGNORE HIM! GO NOW!
BODYSLIDE BY TWO.
TERRY...
...
WELL, RED, IF YOU AN' THE FARM BOY SURVIVE LONG ENOUGH TO GET HERE...

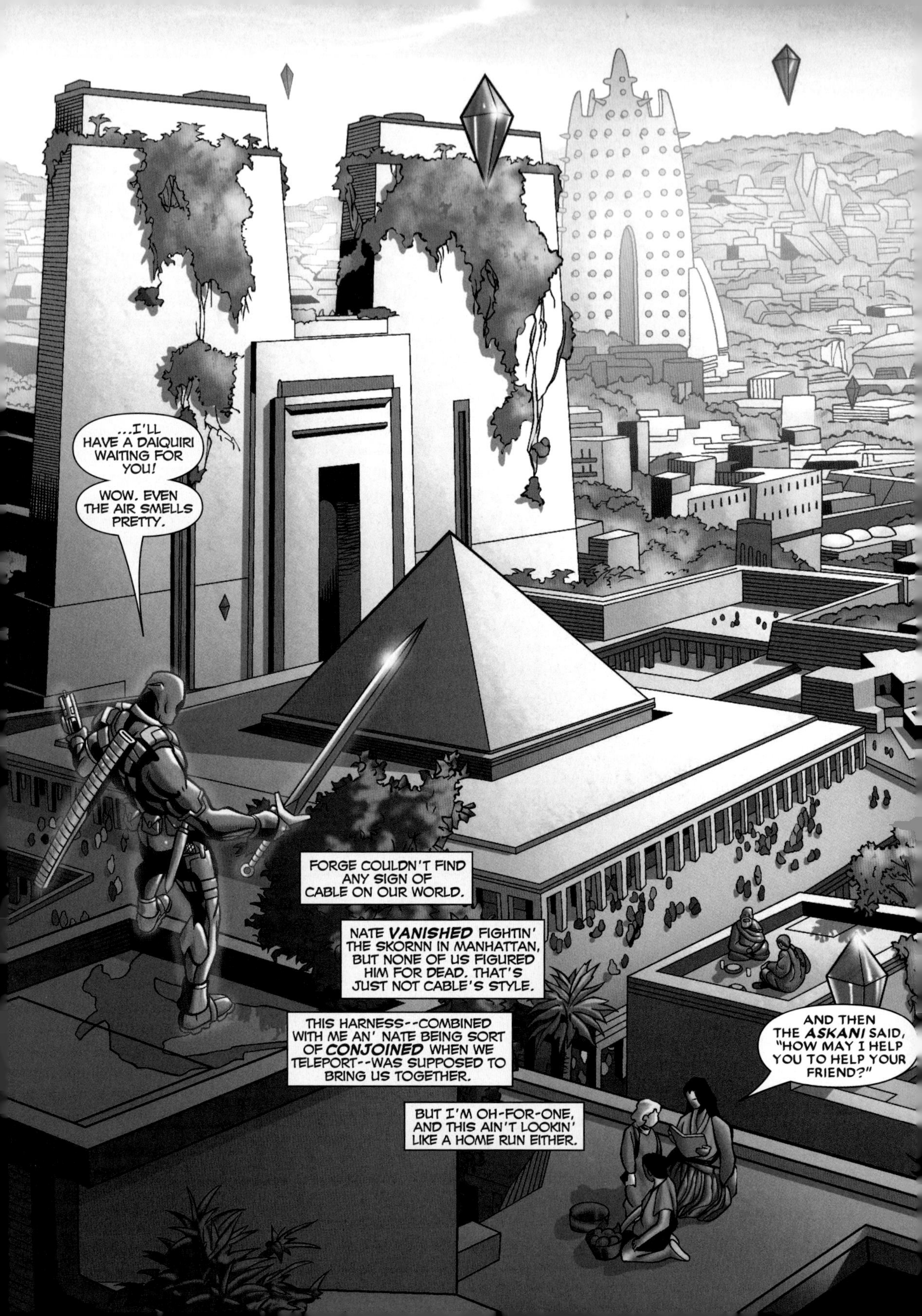
...I'LL HAVE A DAIQUIRI WAITING FOR YOU!
WOW. EVEN THE AIR SMELLS PRETTY.
FORGE COULDN'T FIND ANY SIGN OF CABLE ON OUR WORLD.
NATE VANISHED FIGHTIN' THE SKORNN IN MANHATTAN, BUT NONE OF US FIGURED HIM FOR DEAD. THAT'S JUST NOT CABLE'S STYLE.
THIS HARNESS--COMBINED WITH ME AN' NATE BEING SORT OF CONJOINED WHEN WE TELEPORT--WAS SUPPOSED TO BRING US TOGETHER.
BUT I'M OH-FOR-ONE, AND THIS AIN'T LOOKIN' LIKE A HOME RUN EITHER.
AND THEN THE ASKANI SAID, "HOW MAY I HELP YOU TO HELP YOUR FRIEND?"

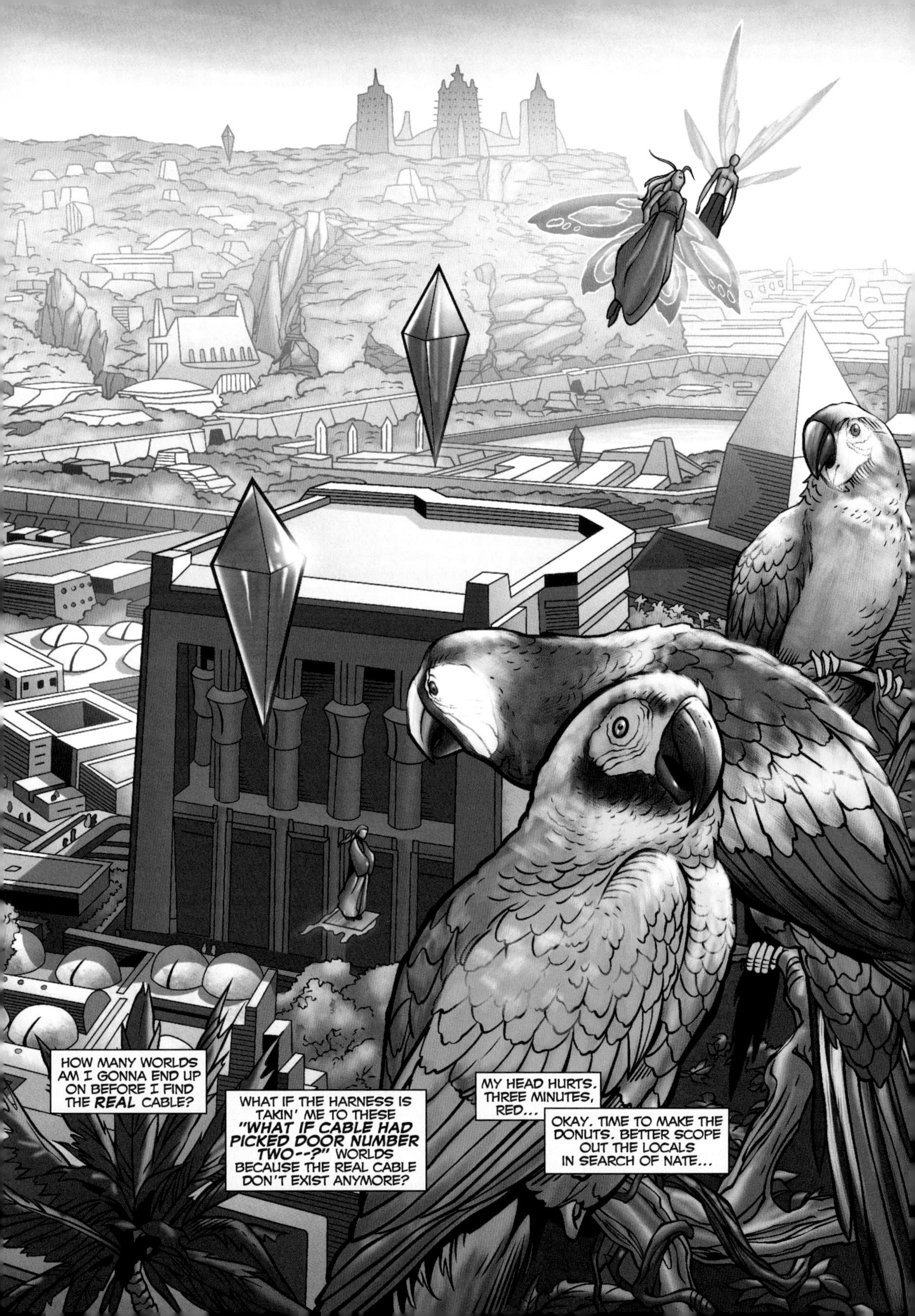
HOW MANY WORLDS AM I GONNA END UP ON BEFORE I FIND THE **REAL** CABLE?
WHAT IF THE HARNESS IS TAKIN' ME TO THESE ***"WHAT IF CABLE HAD PICKED DOOR NUMBER TWO--?"*** WORLDS BECAUSE THE REAL CABLE DON'T EXIST ANYMORE?
MY HEAD HURTS. THREE MINUTES, RED...
OKAY. TIME TO MAKE THE DONUTS. BETTER SCOPE OUT THE LOCALS IN SEARCH OF NATE...

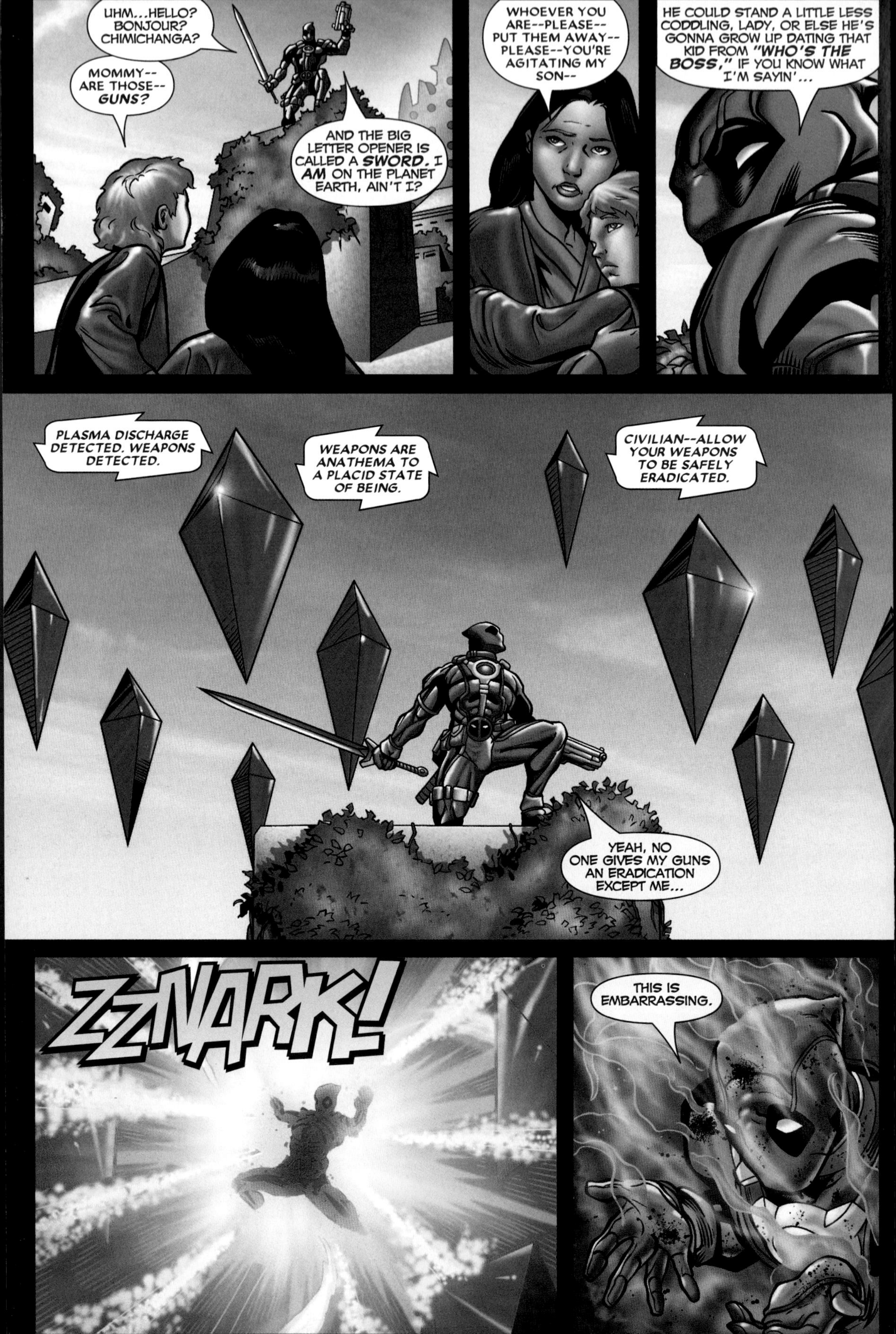
UHM...HELLO? BONJOUR? CHIMICHANGA?
MOMMY-- ARE THOSE-- GUNS?
AND THE BIG LETTER OPENER IS CALLED A SWORD. I AM ON THE PLANET EARTH, AIN'T I?
WHOEVER YOU ARE--PLEASE-- PUT THEM AWAY-- PLEASE--YOU'RE AGITATING MY SON--
HE COULD STAND A LITTLE LESS CODDLING, LADY, OR ELSE HE'S GONNA GROW UP DATING THAT KID FROM "WHO'S THE BOSS," IF YOU KNOW WHAT I'M SAYIN'...
PLASMA DISCHARGE DETECTED. WEAPONS DETECTED.
WEAPONS ARE ANATHEMA TO A PLACID STATE OF BEING.
CIVILIAN--ALLOW YOUR WEAPONS TO BE SAFELY ERADICATED.
YEAH, NO ONE GIVES MY GUNS AN ERADICATION EXCEPT ME...
ZZNARK!
THIS IS EMBARRASSING.

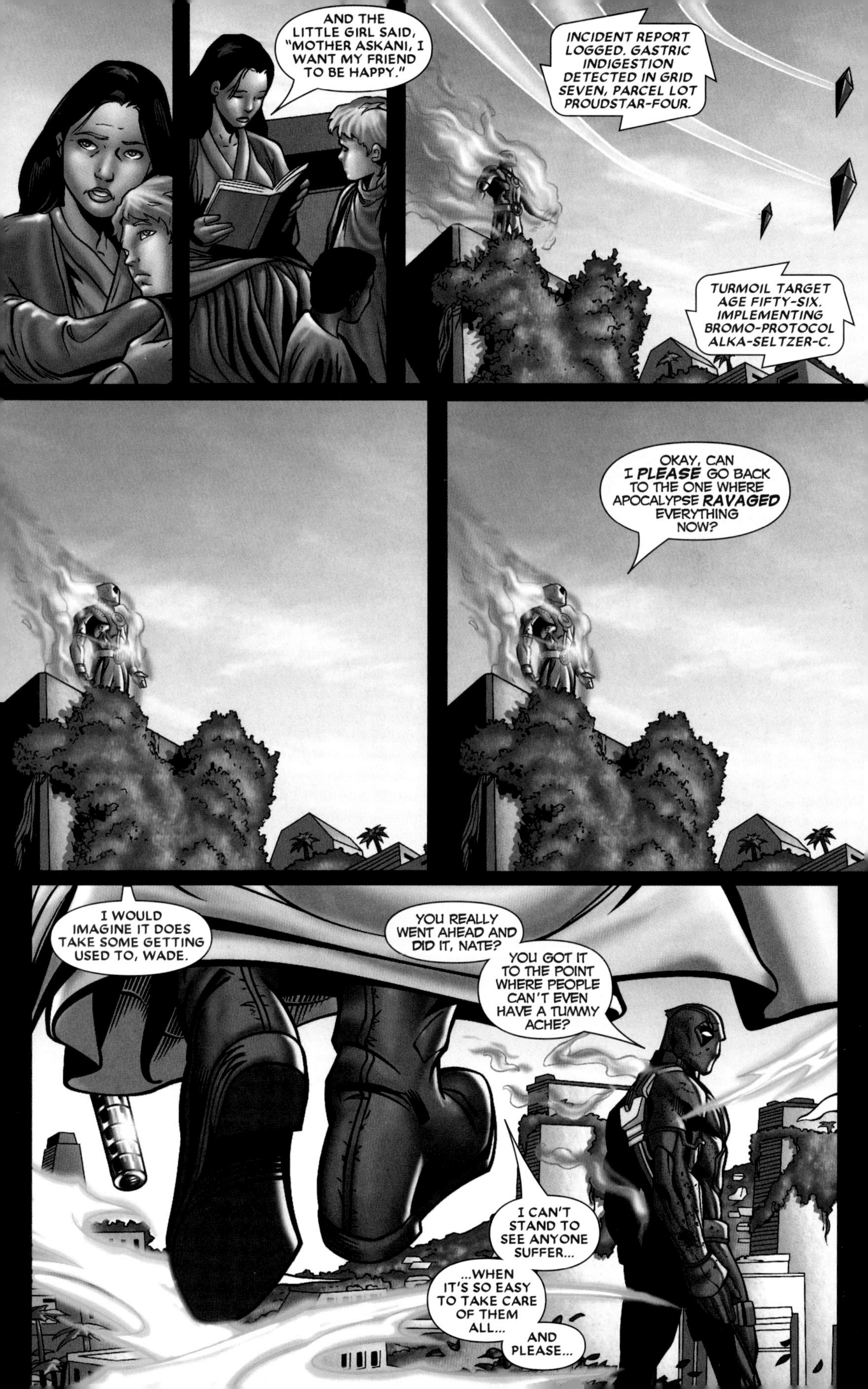
AND THE LITTLE GIRL SAID, "MOTHER ASKANI, I WANT MY FRIEND TO BE HAPPY."
INCIDENT REPORT LOGGED. GASTRIC INDIGESTION DETECTED IN GRID SEVEN, PARCEL LOT PROUDSTAR-FOUR.
TURMOIL TARGET AGE FIFTY-SIX. IMPLEMENTING BROMO-PROTOCOL ALKA-SELTZER-C.
OKAY, CAN I PLEASE GO BACK TO THE ONE WHERE APOCALYPSE RAVAGED EVERYTHING NOW?
I WOULD IMAGINE IT DOES TAKE SOME GETTING USED TO, WADE.
YOU REALLY WENT AHEAD AND DID IT, NATE?
YOU GOT IT TO THE POINT WHERE PEOPLE CAN'T EVEN HAVE A TUMMY ACHE?
I CAN'T STAND TO SEE ANYONE SUFFER...
...WHEN IT'S SO EASY TO TAKE CARE OF THEM ALL...
AND PLEASE...

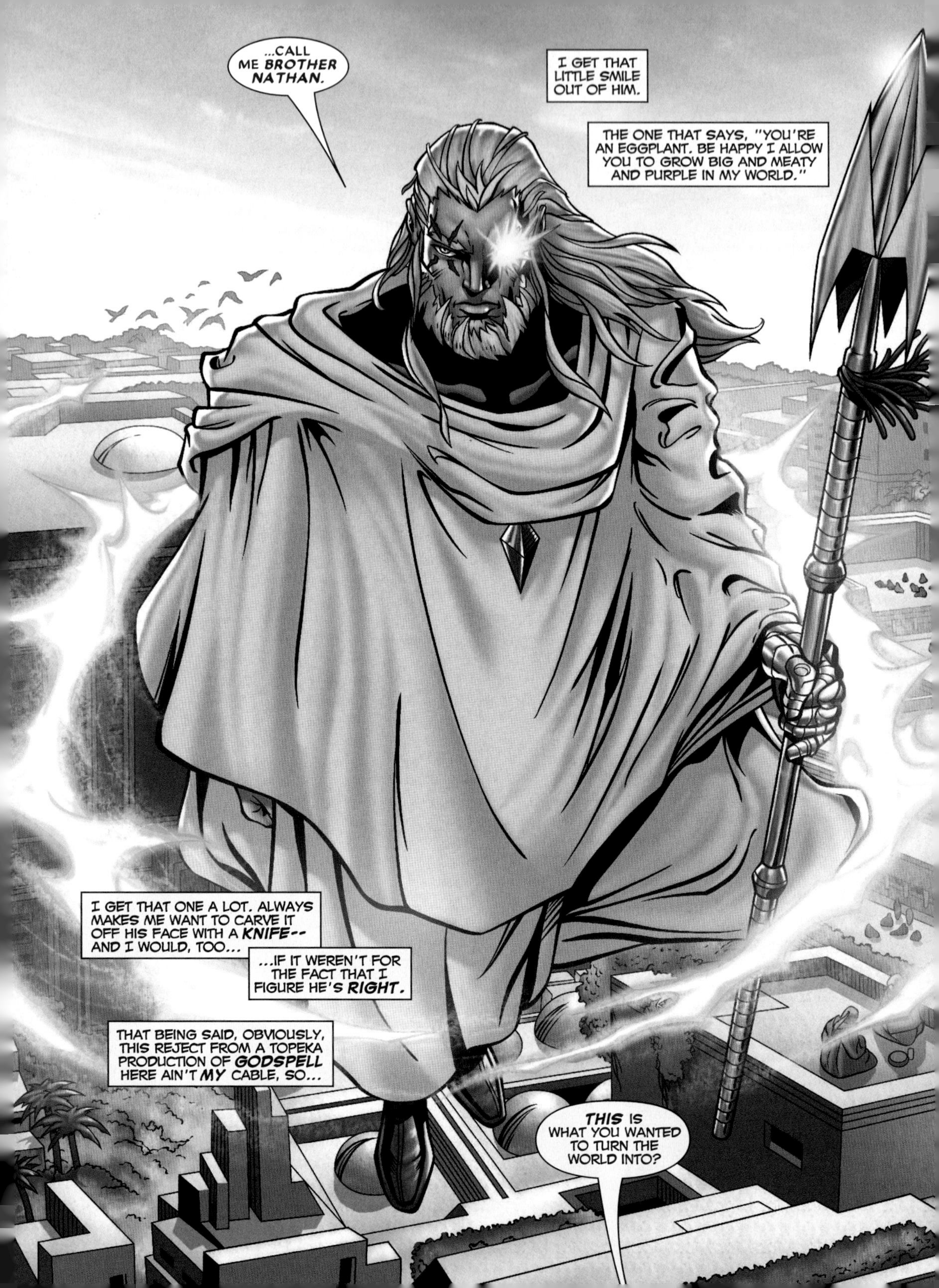
...CALL ME BROTHER NATHAN.
I GET THAT LITTLE SMILE OUT OF HIM.
THE ONE THAT SAYS, "YOU'RE AN EGGPLANT. BE HAPPY I ALLOW YOU TO GROW BIG AND MEATY AND PURPLE IN MY WORLD."
I GET THAT ONE A LOT. ALWAYS MAKES ME WANT TO CARVE IT OFF HIS FACE WITH A KNIFE-- AND I WOULD, TOO...
...IF IT WEREN'T FOR THE FACT THAT I FIGURE HE'S RIGHT.
THAT BEING SAID, OBVIOUSLY, THIS REJECT FROM A TOPEKA PRODUCTION OF GODSPELL HERE AIN'T MY CABLE, SO...
THIS IS WHAT YOU WANTED TO TURN THE WORLD INTO?

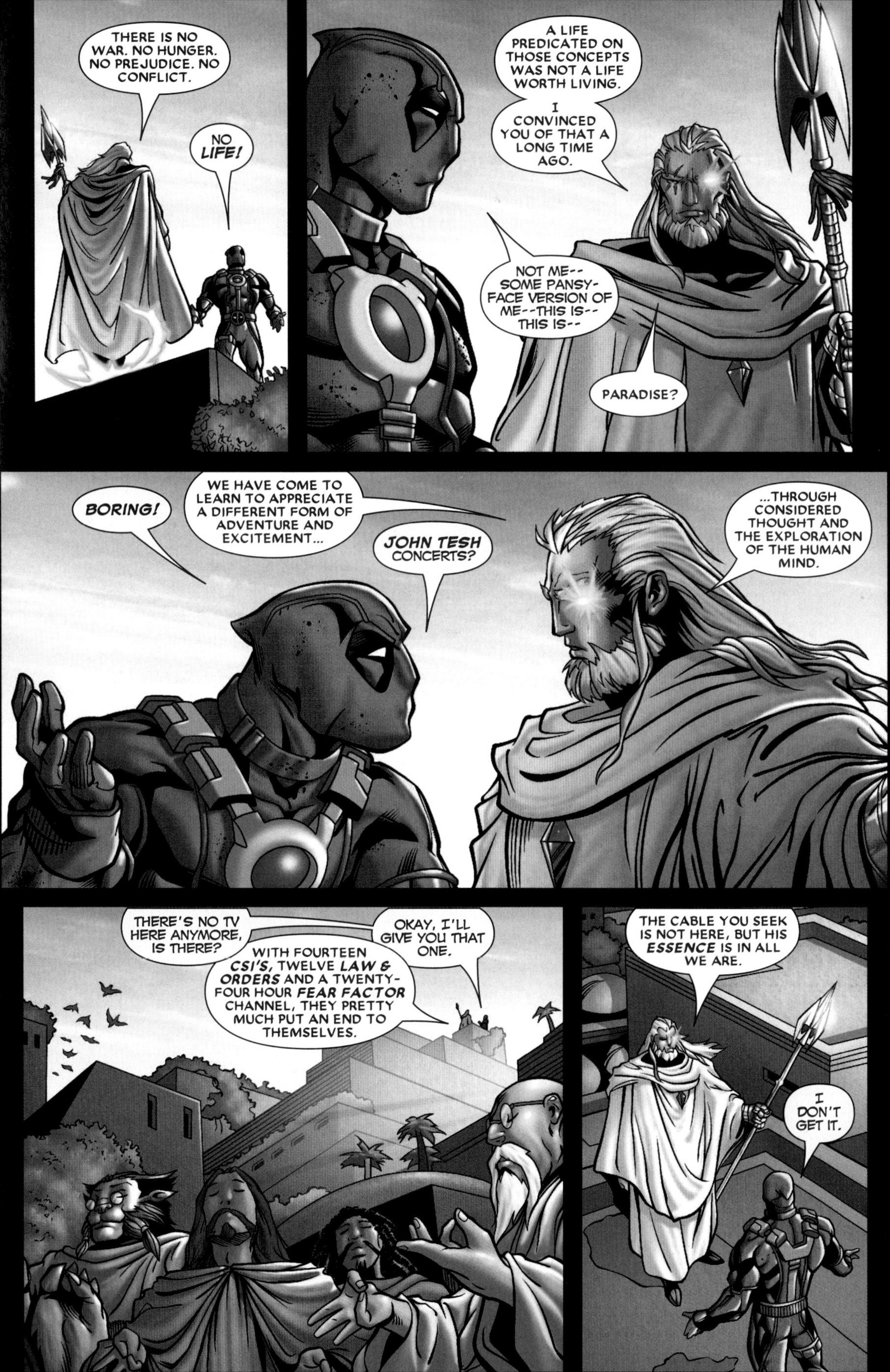
THERE IS NO WAR. NO HUNGER. NO PREJUDICE. NO CONFLICT.
NO *LIFE!*
A LIFE PREDICATED ON THOSE CONCEPTS WAS NOT A LIFE WORTH LIVING.
I CONVINCED YOU OF THAT A LONG TIME AGO.
NOT ME-- SOME PANSY-FACE VERSION OF ME--THIS IS-- THIS IS--
PARADISE?
BORING!
WE HAVE COME TO LEARN TO APPRECIATE A DIFFERENT FORM OF ADVENTURE AND EXCITEMENT...
JOHN TESH CONCERTS?
...THROUGH CONSIDERED THOUGHT AND THE EXPLORATION OF THE HUMAN MIND.
THERE'S NO TV HERE ANYMORE, IS THERE?
OKAY, I'LL GIVE YOU THAT ONE.
WITH FOURTEEN *CSI'S*, TWELVE *LAW & ORDERS* AND A TWENTY-FOUR HOUR *FEAR FACTOR* CHANNEL, THEY PRETTY MUCH PUT AN END TO THEMSELVES.
THE CABLE YOU SEEK IS NOT HERE, BUT HIS *ESSENCE* IS IN ALL WE ARE.
I DON'T GET IT.

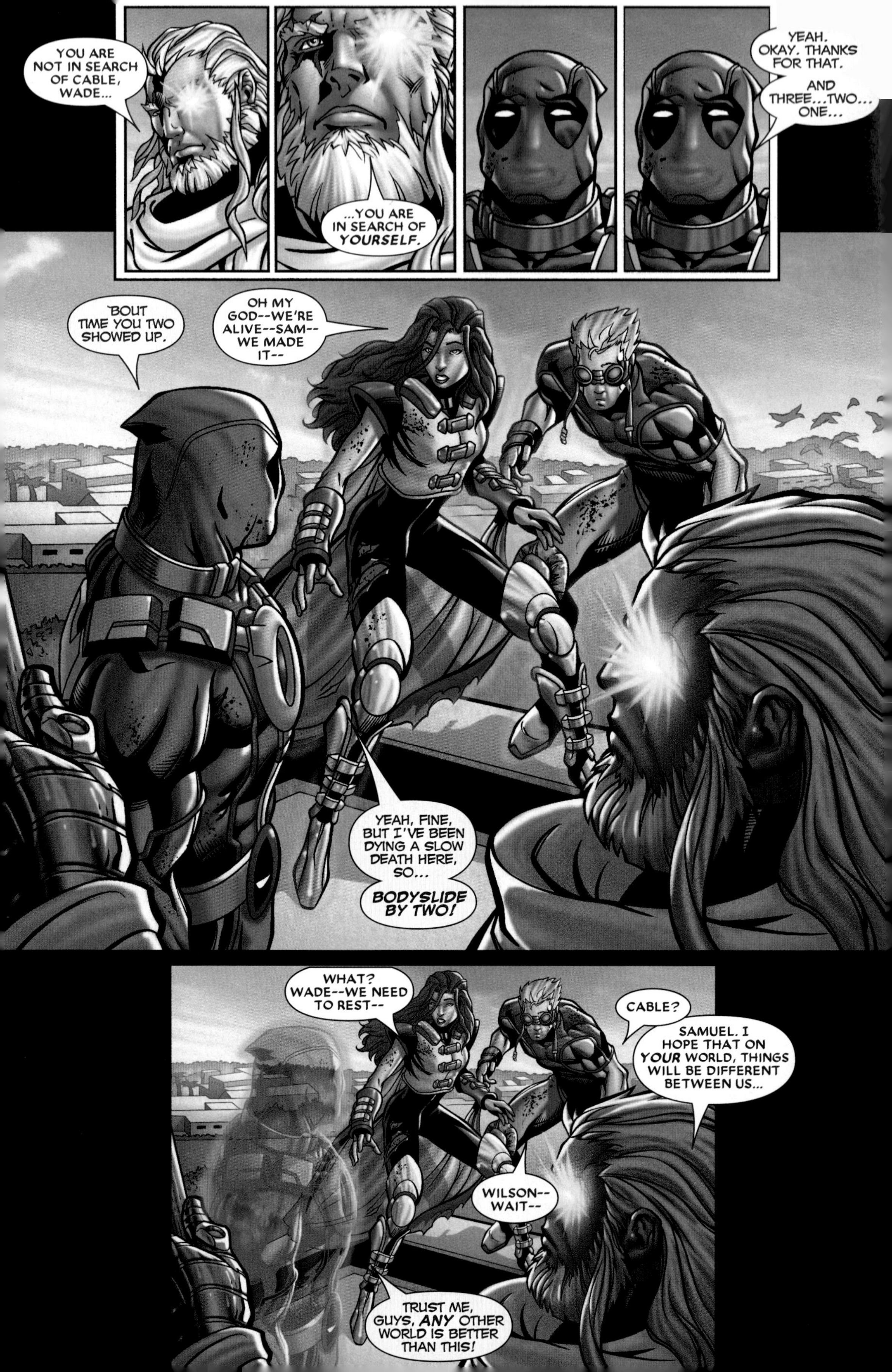
YOU ARE NOT IN SEARCH OF CABLE, WADE...
...YOU ARE IN SEARCH OF YOURSELF.
YEAH. OKAY. THANKS FOR THAT.
AND THREE...TWO... ONE...
'BOUT TIME YOU TWO SHOWED UP.
OH MY GOD--WE'RE ALIVE--SAM--WE MADE IT--
YEAH, FINE, BUT I'VE BEEN DYING A SLOW DEATH HERE, SO...
BODYSLIDE BY TWO!
WHAT? WADE--WE NEED TO REST--
CABLE?
SAMUEL. I HOPE THAT ON YOUR WORLD, THINGS WILL BE DIFFERENT BETWEEN US...
WILSON--WAIT--
TRUST ME, GUYS, ANY OTHER WORLD IS BETTER THAN THIS!

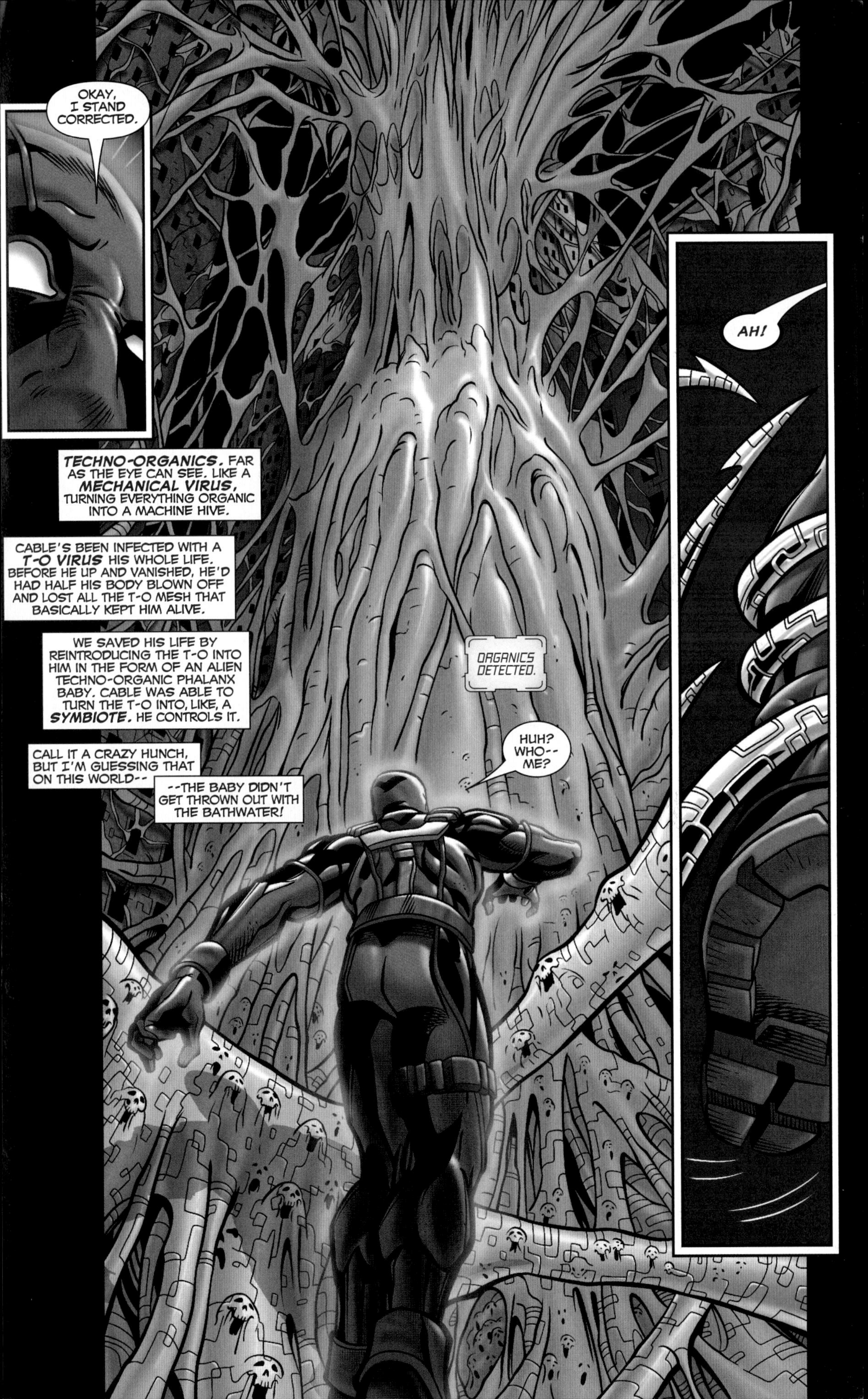
OKAY, I STAND CORRECTED.
TECHNO-ORGANICS. FAR AS THE EYE CAN SEE. LIKE A MECHANICAL VIRUS, TURNING EVERYTHING ORGANIC INTO A MACHINE HIVE.
CABLE'S BEEN INFECTED WITH A T-O VIRUS HIS WHOLE LIFE. BEFORE HE UP AND VANISHED, HE'D HAD HALF HIS BODY BLOWN OFF AND LOST ALL THE T-O MESH THAT BASICALLY KEPT HIM ALIVE.
WE SAVED HIS LIFE BY REINTRODUCING THE T-O INTO HIM IN THE FORM OF AN ALIEN TECHNO-ORGANIC PHALANX BABY. CABLE WAS ABLE TO TURN THE T-O INTO, LIKE, A SYMBIOTE. HE CONTROLS IT.
ORGANICS DETECTED.
CALL IT A CRAZY HUNCH, BUT I'M GUESSING THAT ON THIS WORLD--
HUH? WHO-- ME?
--THE BABY DIDN'T GET THROWN OUT WITH THE BATHWATER!
AH!

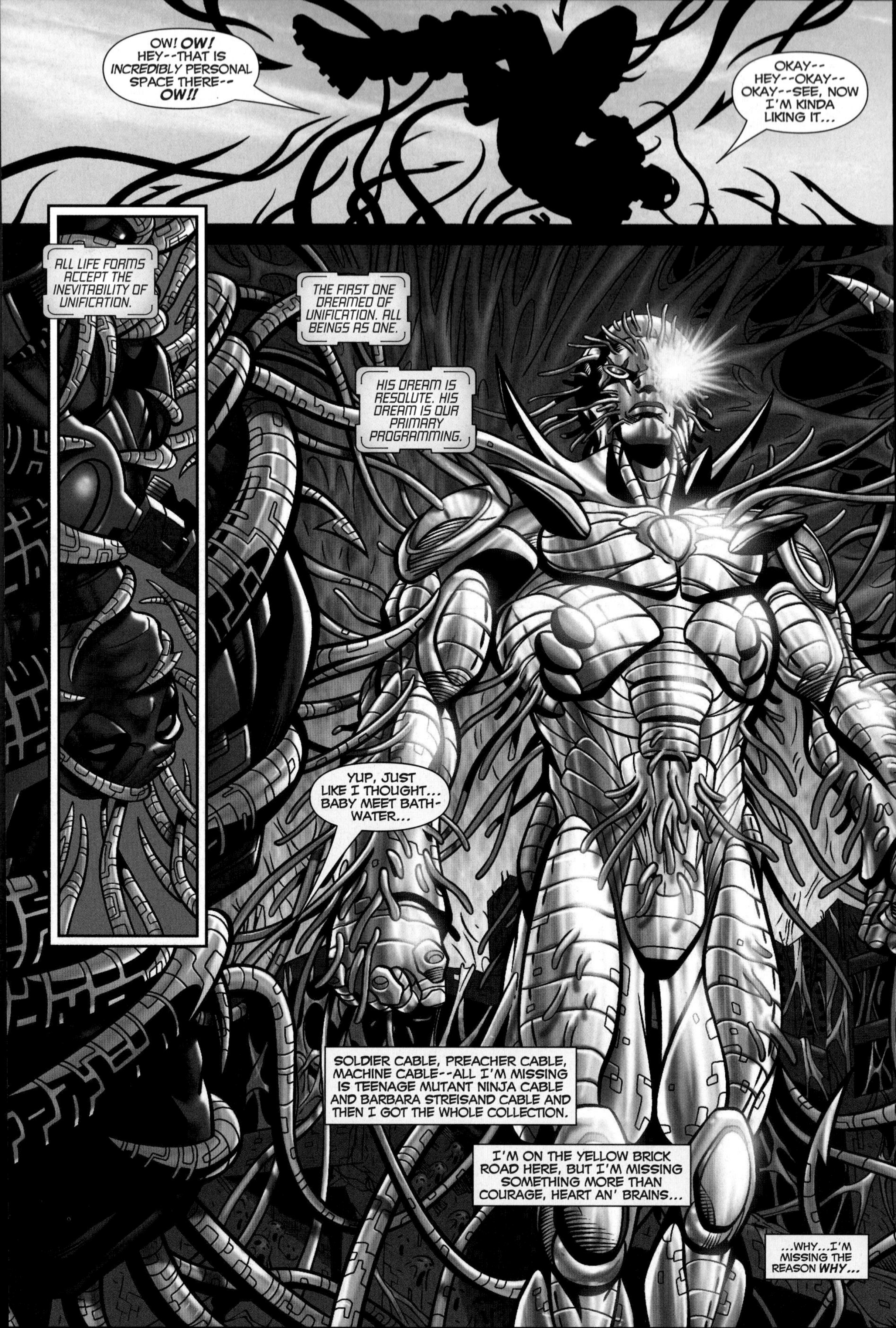
OW! OW! HEY--THAT IS INCREDIBLY PERSONAL SPACE THERE-- OW!!
OKAY-- HEY--OKAY-- OKAY--SEE, NOW I'M KINDA LIKING IT...
ALL LIFE FORMS ACCEPT THE INEVITABILITY OF UNIFICATION.
THE FIRST ONE DREAMED OF UNIFICATION. ALL BEINGS AS ONE.
HIS DREAM IS RESOLUTE. HIS DREAM IS OUR PRIMARY PROGRAMMING.
YUP, JUST LIKE I THOUGHT... BABY MEET BATH-WATER...
SOLDIER CABLE, PREACHER CABLE, MACHINE CABLE--ALL I'M MISSING IS TEENAGE MUTANT NINJA CABLE AND BARBARA STREISAND CABLE AND THEN I GOT THE WHOLE COLLECTION.
I'M ON THE YELLOW BRICK ROAD HERE, BUT I'M MISSING SOMETHING MORE THAN COURAGE, HEART AN' BRAINS...
...WHY...I'M MISSING THE REASON WHY...

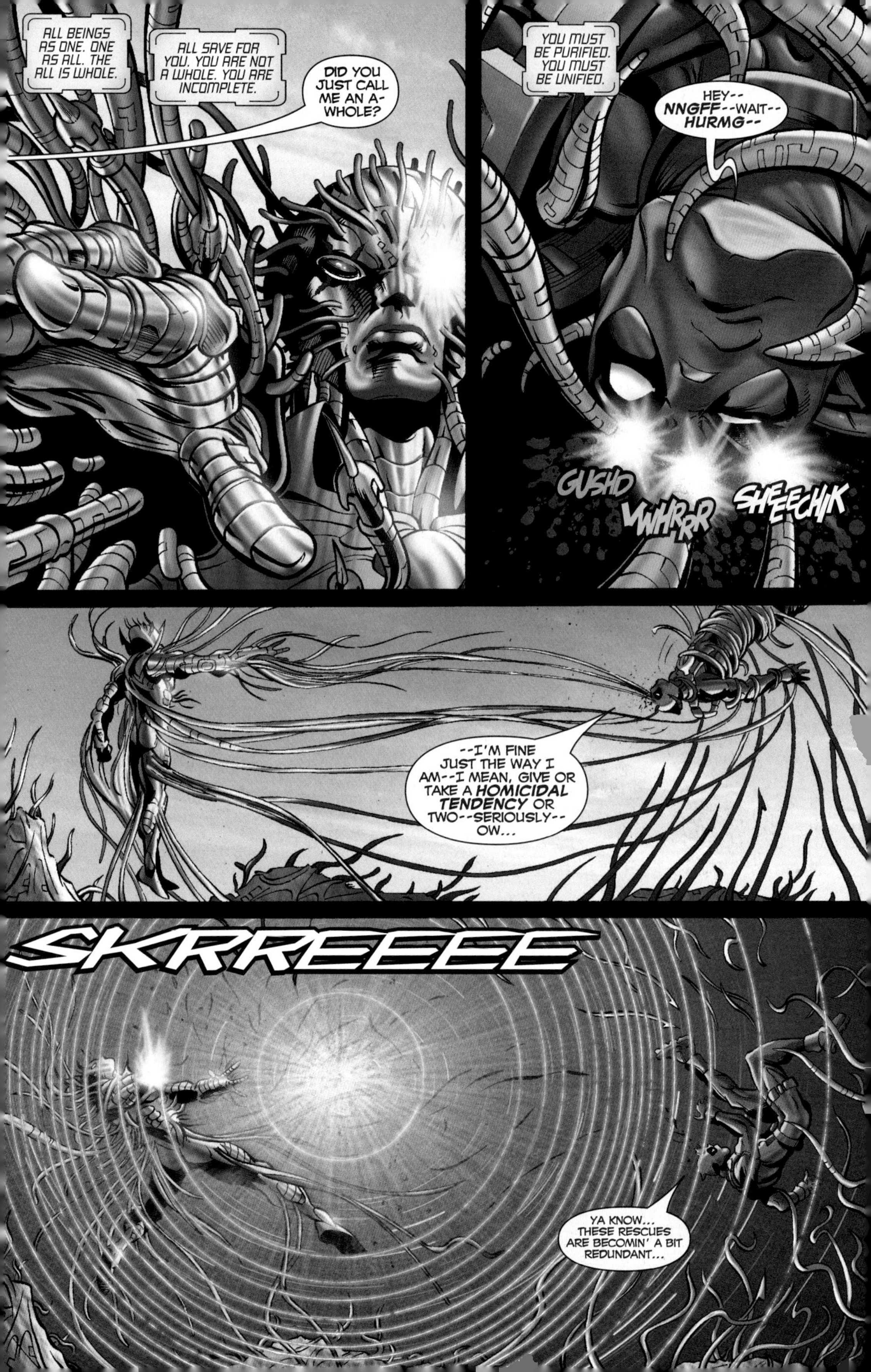
ALL BEINGS AS ONE. ONE AS ALL. THE ALL IS WHOLE.
ALL SAVE FOR YOU. YOU ARE NOT A WHOLE. YOU ARE INCOMPLETE.
DID YOU JUST CALL ME AN A-WHOLE?
YOU MUST BE PURIFIED. YOU MUST BE UNIFIED.
HEY-- NNGFF--WAIT-- HURMG--
GUSHD
VWHRRR
SHEEECHIK
--I'M FINE JUST THE WAY I AM--I MEAN, GIVE OR TAKE A HOMICIDAL TENDENCY OR TWO--SERIOUSLY-- OW...
SKRREEEE
YA KNOW... THESE RESCUES ARE BECOMIN' A BIT REDUNDANT...

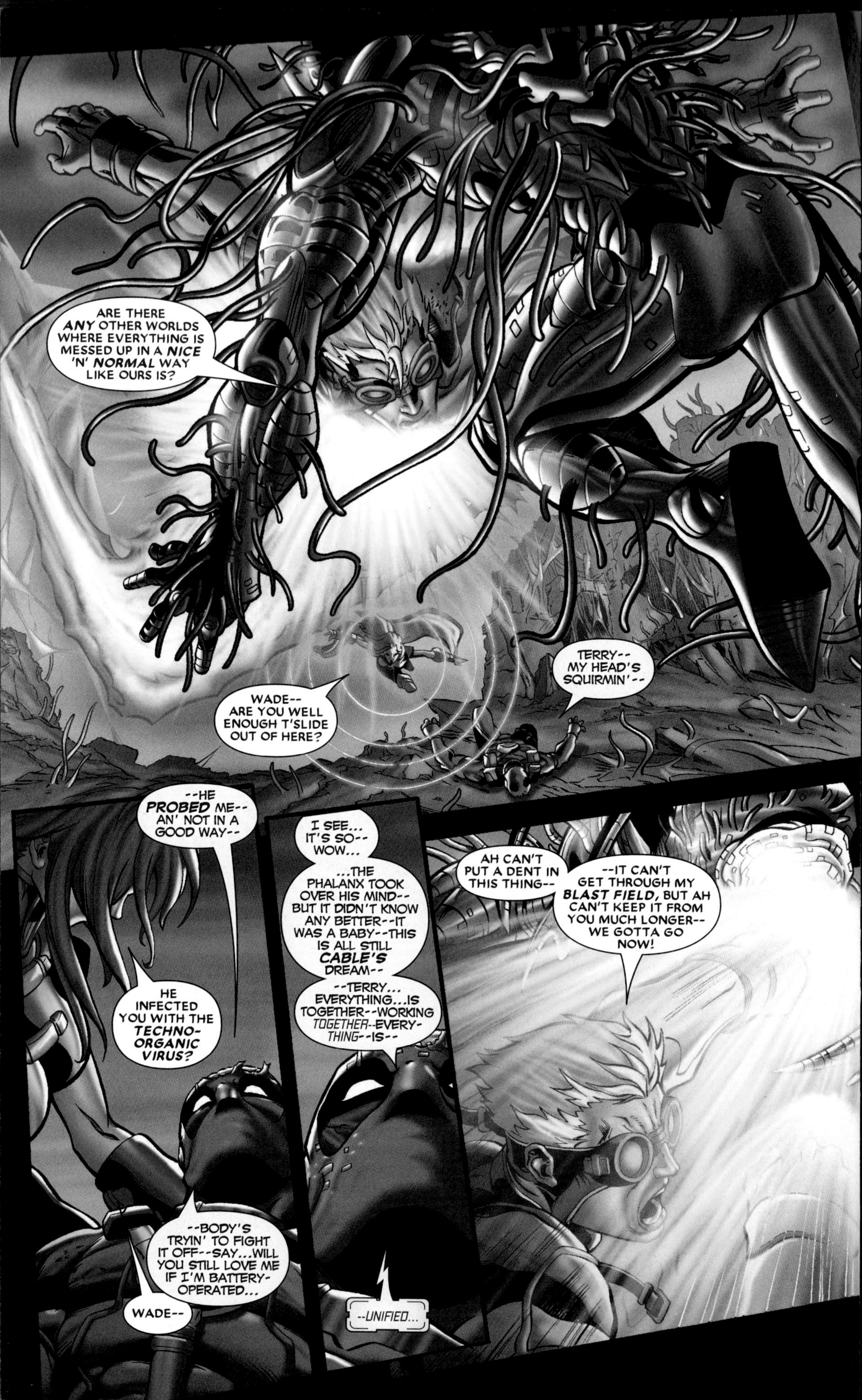
ARE THERE ANY OTHER WORLDS WHERE EVERYTHING IS MESSED UP IN A NICE 'N' NORMAL WAY LIKE OURS IS?
WADE-- ARE YOU WELL ENOUGH T'SLIDE OUT OF HERE?
TERRY-- MY HEAD'S SQUIRMIN'--
--HE PROBED ME-- AN' NOT IN A GOOD WAY--
HE INFECTED YOU WITH THE TECHNO-ORGANIC VIRUS?
--BODY'S TRYIN' TO FIGHT IT OFF--SAY...WILL YOU STILL LOVE ME IF I'M BATTERY-OPERATED...
WADE--
I SEE... IT'S SO-- WOW...
...THE PHALANX TOOK OVER HIS MIND-- BUT IT DIDN'T KNOW ANY BETTER--IT WAS A BABY--THIS IS ALL STILL CABLE'S DREAM--
--TERRY... EVERYTHING...IS TOGETHER--WORKING TOGETHER--EVERY-THING--IS--
--UNIFIED...
AH CAN'T PUT A DENT IN THIS THING--
--IT CAN'T GET THROUGH MY BLAST FIELD, BUT AH CAN'T KEEP IT FROM YOU MUCH LONGER-- WE GOTTA GO NOW!

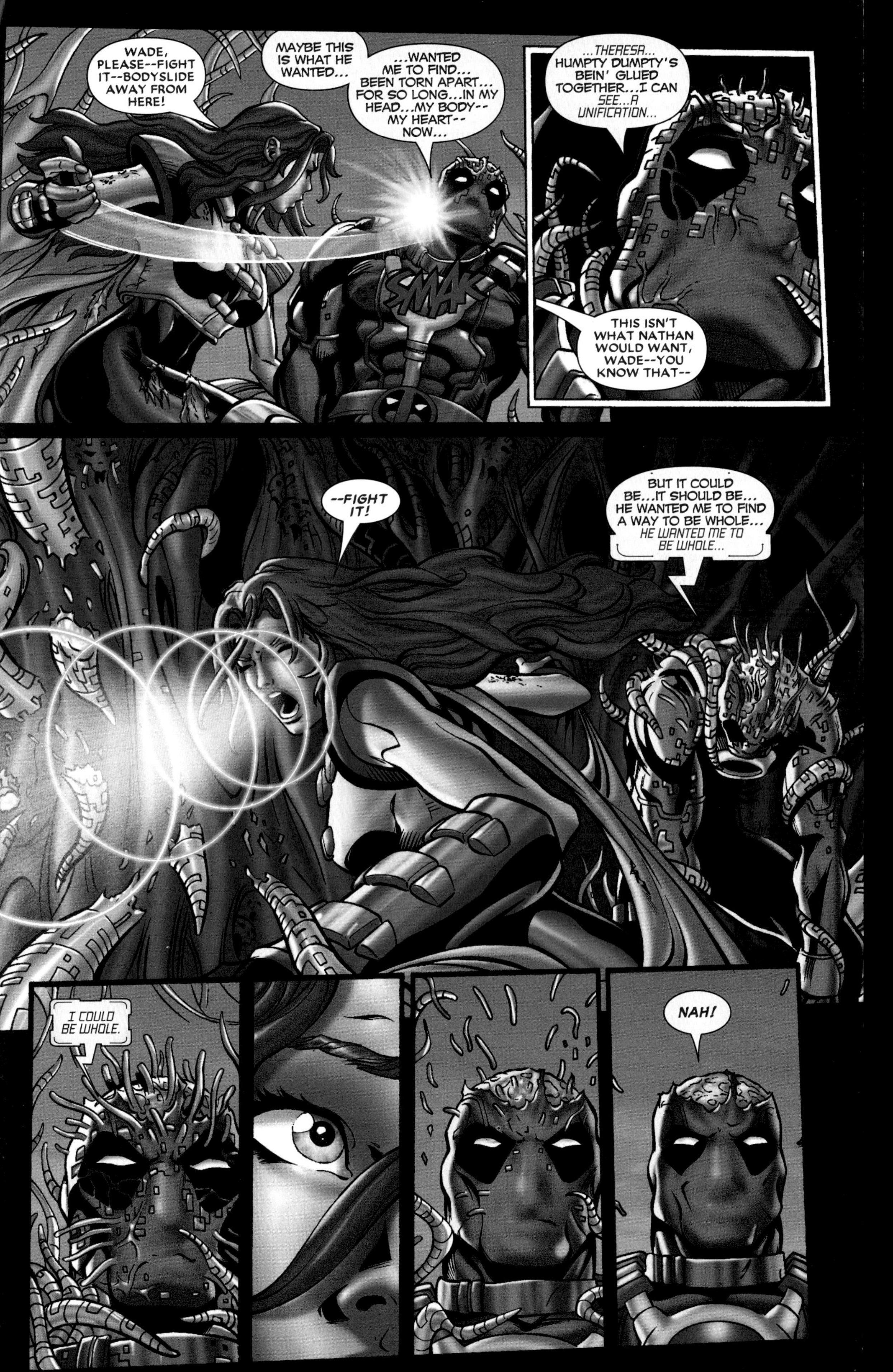
WADE, PLEASE--FIGHT IT--BODYSLIDE AWAY FROM HERE!
MAYBE THIS IS WHAT HE WANTED...
...WANTED ME TO FIND... BEEN TORN APART... FOR SO LONG... IN MY HEAD... MY BODY-- MY HEART-- NOW...
SMAK
...THERESA... HUMPTY DUMPTY'S BEIN' GLUED TOGETHER... I CAN SEE... A UNIFICATION...
THIS ISN'T WHAT NATHAN WOULD WANT, WADE--YOU KNOW THAT--
--FIGHT IT!
BUT IT COULD BE... IT SHOULD BE... HE WANTED ME TO FIND A WAY TO BE WHOLE...
HE WANTED ME TO BE WHOLE...
I COULD BE WHOLE.
NAH!

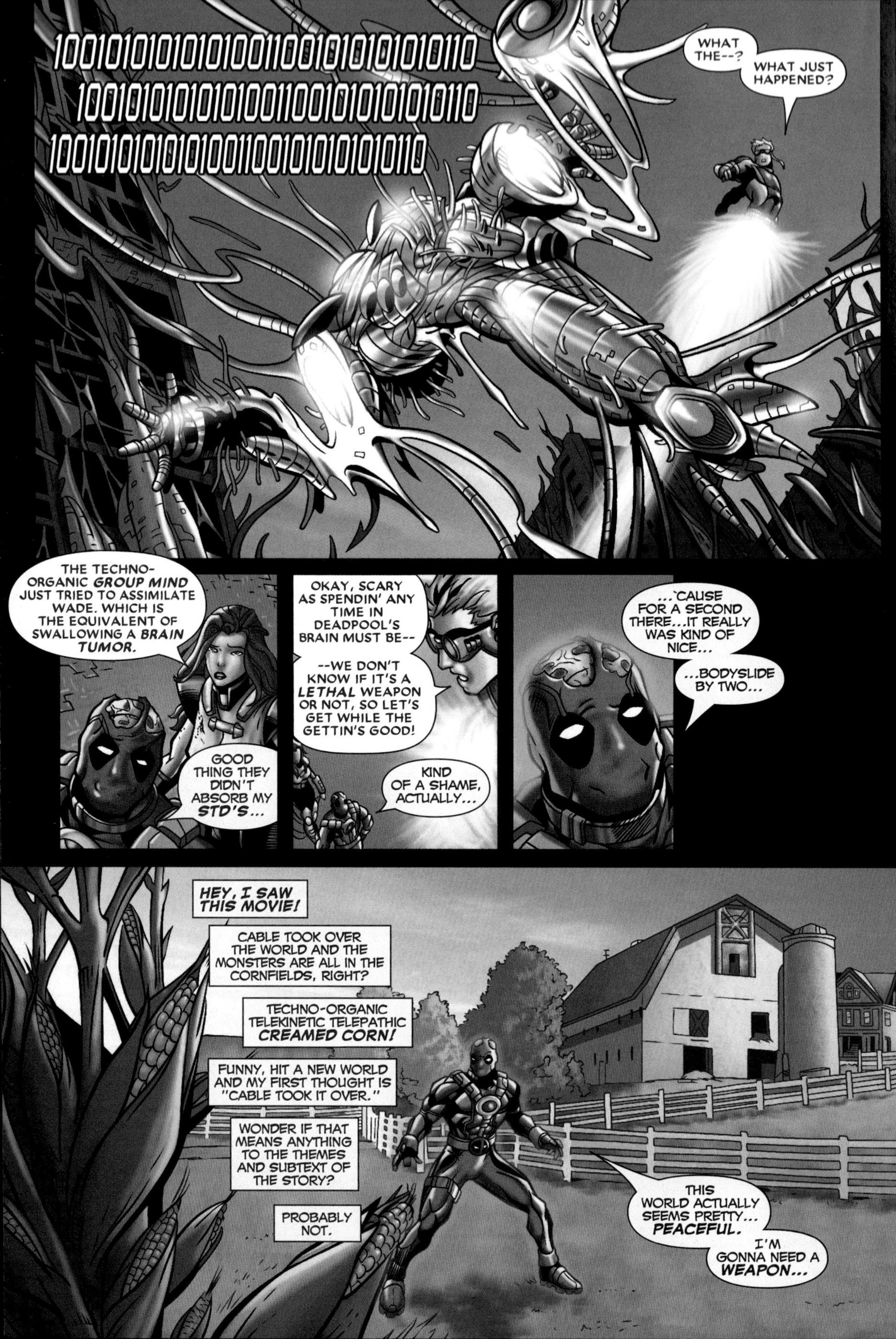
10010101010101010011001010101010110
10010101010101010011001010101010110
10010101010101010011001010101010110
WHAT THE--? WHAT JUST HAPPENED?
THE TECHNO-ORGANIC GROUP MIND JUST TRIED TO ASSIMILATE WADE. WHICH IS THE EQUIVALENT OF SWALLOWING A BRAIN TUMOR.
GOOD THING THEY DIDN'T ABSORB MY STD'S...
OKAY, SCARY AS SPENDIN' ANY TIME IN DEADPOOL'S BRAIN MUST BE--
--WE DON'T KNOW IF IT'S A LETHAL WEAPON OR NOT, SO LET'S GET WHILE THE GETTIN'S GOOD!
KIND OF A SHAME, ACTUALLY...
...'CAUSE FOR A SECOND THERE...IT REALLY WAS KIND OF NICE...
...BODYSLIDE BY TWO...
HEY, I SAW THIS MOVIE!
CABLE TOOK OVER THE WORLD AND THE MONSTERS ARE ALL IN THE CORNFIELDS, RIGHT?
TECHNO-ORGANIC TELEKINETIC TELEPATHIC CREAMED CORN!
FUNNY, HIT A NEW WORLD AND MY FIRST THOUGHT IS "CABLE TOOK IT OVER."
WONDER IF THAT MEANS ANYTHING TO THE THEMES AND SUBTEXT OF THE STORY?
PROBABLY NOT.
THIS WORLD ACTUALLY SEEMS PRETTY... PEACEFUL.
I'M GONNA NEED A WEAPON...

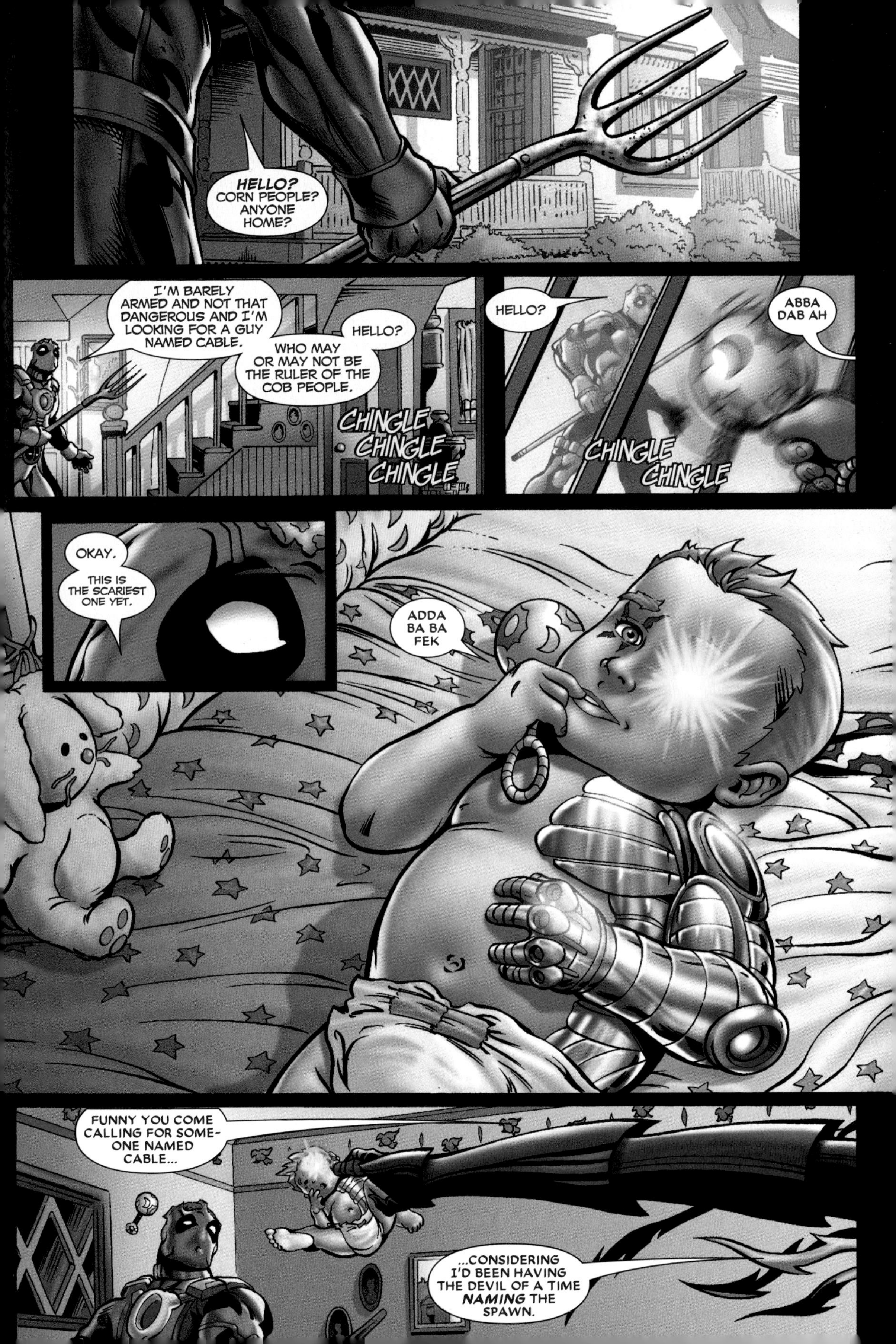

HELLO? CORN PEOPLE? ANYONE HOME?
I'M BARELY ARMED AND NOT THAT DANGEROUS AND I'M LOOKING FOR A GUY NAMED CABLE.
HELLO?
WHO MAY OR MAY NOT BE THE RULER OF THE COB PEOPLE.
CHINGLE CHINGLE CHINGLE
HELLO?
ABBA DAB AH
CHINGLE CHINGLE
OKAY.
THIS IS THE SCARIEST ONE YET.
ADDA BA BA FEK
FUNNY YOU COME CALLING FOR SOME-ONE NAMED CABLE...
...CONSIDERING I'D BEEN HAVING THE DEVIL OF A TIME NAMING THE SPAWN.

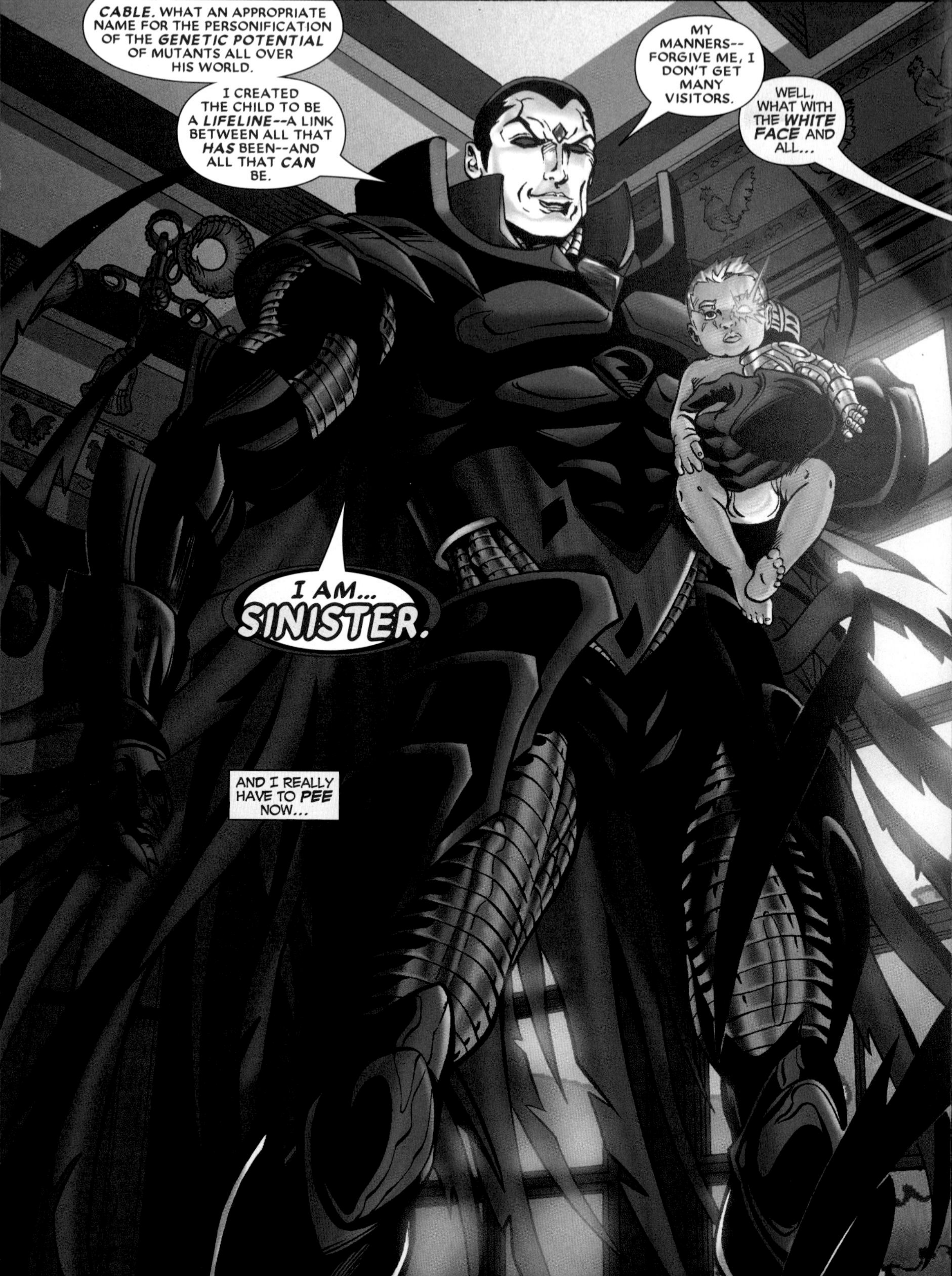
CABLE. WHAT AN APPROPRIATE NAME FOR THE PERSONIFICATION OF THE GENETIC POTENTIAL OF MUTANTS ALL OVER HIS WORLD.
I CREATED THE CHILD TO BE A LIFELINE--A LINK BETWEEN ALL THAT HAS BEEN--AND ALL THAT CAN BE.
MY MANNERS--FORGIVE ME, I DON'T GET MANY VISITORS.
WELL, WHAT WITH THE WHITE FACE AND ALL...
I AM... SINISTER.
AND I REALLY HAVE TO PEE NOW...

DEAR DEADPOOL

Deadpool and the Creative Staff,

I just finished reading *C&DP* #14 cover to cover and thought I should impart to you further knowledge of your female fan base. Hi! I love this comic. Absolutely gorgeous! All of it. Every issue is superb.

I've spent much of my time worrying about my favorite merc. Honestly, I'd like Deadpool just to be happy, but then I don't think you'd sell very many comics that way. Which would lead to there being no comics with Deadpool in them and that would make me very sad. I would miss him with the same despair that came when I started college and couldn't afford buying any comics at all. I was even more distressed (back in the day) when I was told that Deadpool's series was gone. I had no idea what had happened to him and feared I'd never hear from him again.

Then recently I got back in the game and went to my local comic shop. I dabbled with titles here and there for about a year before entering one day with maybe $5 in my pocket. I had to debate what title to pick up. I have been very apprehensive about jumping back into any X-titles and wasn't sure what to do.

That's when I spotted *C&DP* #1. A smile spread across my face. I'd found the title that would bring me back into the fold for good.

Thanks. It has really been worth it. If we're all lucky I'll be able to expand the number of titles I pick up very soon. Until then...every month guaranteed, *Cable & Deadpool.*

With the most intense esteem,
B. Hockin

Okay, B.—(not related to BEA, the Mythic Goddess of Love, are you?) —it was a really nice and sweet letter and all, but what's this about not wanting to see me happy just so you can have a measly comic book to read every month? I mean, no offense, but that's pretty selfish of you.

Women. I'd hate you all if I didn't love your smooth soft skin and supple round—what? Huh, uhm—okay...

Nicole asked me to move on... Women...

Thank you for keeping *Cable & Deadpool* going—it is my favorite comic on the stands right now. I'm glad you give so much of the book to Deadpool right now because Cable gets too much press as it is. Also I'm glad you are keeping the art fresh, and the writing as a shrine to the lesser-known circles of Marvel-dom. Now what would a fan letter be without pointless questions?

1) When is the title going to be switched to *Deadpool & Cable*?

2) When will Deadpool finally hook up with Bea?

3) When is Deadpool going to die, then come back to from the grave, only to get beat down again? It's been awhile.

4) When can we expect a Slingers guest spot?

5) When will there be a shameless Spider-Man guest spot?

Thanks for keeping this up!

Matt Deragisch

Hey Matt,

1) I've been told it can't be that for legal reasons of an alphabetical nature. I don't know what that means, but lawyers scare me, so I didn't ask.

2) I've been told for legal, moral and ethical reasons, that it can only remain a wistful dream of a lustful mind.

3) Good point. Just from a comic book law of averages standpoint, I should be dying and coming back to life again pretty soon.

***4) Slingers?* What are we, the DREGS of the Marvel Universe here? Bad enough we have Prester John in this freakin' book, you want us to stoop to the Slingers? What next, "How about a guest shot by *NFL Superpro*?" Buncha dorks, all a' you... now if we could only get the licensing rights to *Sectaurs* again...**

Web-head's guest-starring in this issue, isn't he? Sort of. The real thing? That would be kinda cool, wouldn't it?

Tell Nicieza I'd kick Spidey's smarmy New Avengers, married-to-a-redheaded-bombshell butt in any time he wants!

My name is Mitch Punpayuk (Pun-pie-yuck) and I would like to be verbally abused by a comic book character, and here is some ammunition for you guys. I'm a 6-foot, 350- pound, 23-year-old comic book fanboy. I live in the Phoenix, AZ area and I work as a DirecTV technician. And I'm also trying to become a writer; movies, TV, comic books (hint-hint, nudge-nudge). Can't wait to be insulted.

Thanks,
Mitch

Fish, meet barrel. I don't even know where to begin, Mitch. I mean... make me work for it. Never mind. Good luck to you, dude.

Hello! I just finished *C&DP* #14, and have to tell you that I just adore Deadpool. He really does rock! And yeah, Cable's okay too; especially since he now seems to have glimmers of a sense of humor.

This is currently the only Marvel title I regularly harass the comic stores for. Anyways I am writing because you requested fan mail from your female readers and I just happen to be one! So you should feel very flattered that I drag my cute butt monthly into the freaky-guy-who-rarely-glimpses-real-live-human-chicks headquarters just for you!

I hope this strange, interesting and mostly hilarious title Lives Long And Prospers! The writing is great as is the art, and I especially appreciate that the female characters have boobs that aren't bigger than their heads! Yaaay! And is it weird that I have a huge crush on Deadpool?

Your Amused & Adoring Fangirl,
Melissa Turner

Post Script: All typos are maliciously intentional, as is the dreaded P.S. Bwa ha ha ha!!

Yeah. Well, I fixed your typos and I'm not even mad about it `cause you said you had a cute butt. How cute? I mean, two oranges side by side cute or big J. Lo cute? What do I care, either way works for me. Nicieza, we need to get some more chicks in this book, I mean, all we got is Merryweather. Yeeeuch.

We need some bad girls to show up in this book... soon!

Oh, and by the way, Melissa, swing that cute butt around all you want makin' fun of comic nerd boys, but you threw in that *Star Trek* ref all on your lonesome, babe. How do you defend that?

Dear Deadpool,

On account of you asking female readers of *C&DP* to write in, I, being a female, have written to let you know that you have more than one female fan. Though to be fair I started reading *C&DP* because Cable is my hero. I admire him very much. And though it was difficult to warm to you, on account of how you don't have a problem with eviscerating people and writing words with their intestines (gross gross gross gross), I couldn't help feeling a pang of sorrow when Cable asked you to leave Providence. And I like saying the word *chimichanga* as well, but *chicharrón* is better (it means pork rind or crackling). Cable's still my hero. But you're OK too.

Christine Pienaar

***Chicharrón*! Sounds like a Spanish cuss word, doesn't it? Or a nefarious villain.**

I'm glad I'm okay with you, Christine, even though liking Nate is sort of like liking Clint Eastwood or something. I mean, he's older than the Pope. About as much fun on a Friday night, too.

NEXT ISSUE:
We fight the nefarious CHICHARRÓN! Pork rinds for everyone! Actually, it's our VERY exciting HOUSE OF M crossover. Watch Cannonballs, Red and Me endure the shameless attempt to increase our sales! And best of all—soiled diapers and REAL ramifications abound!

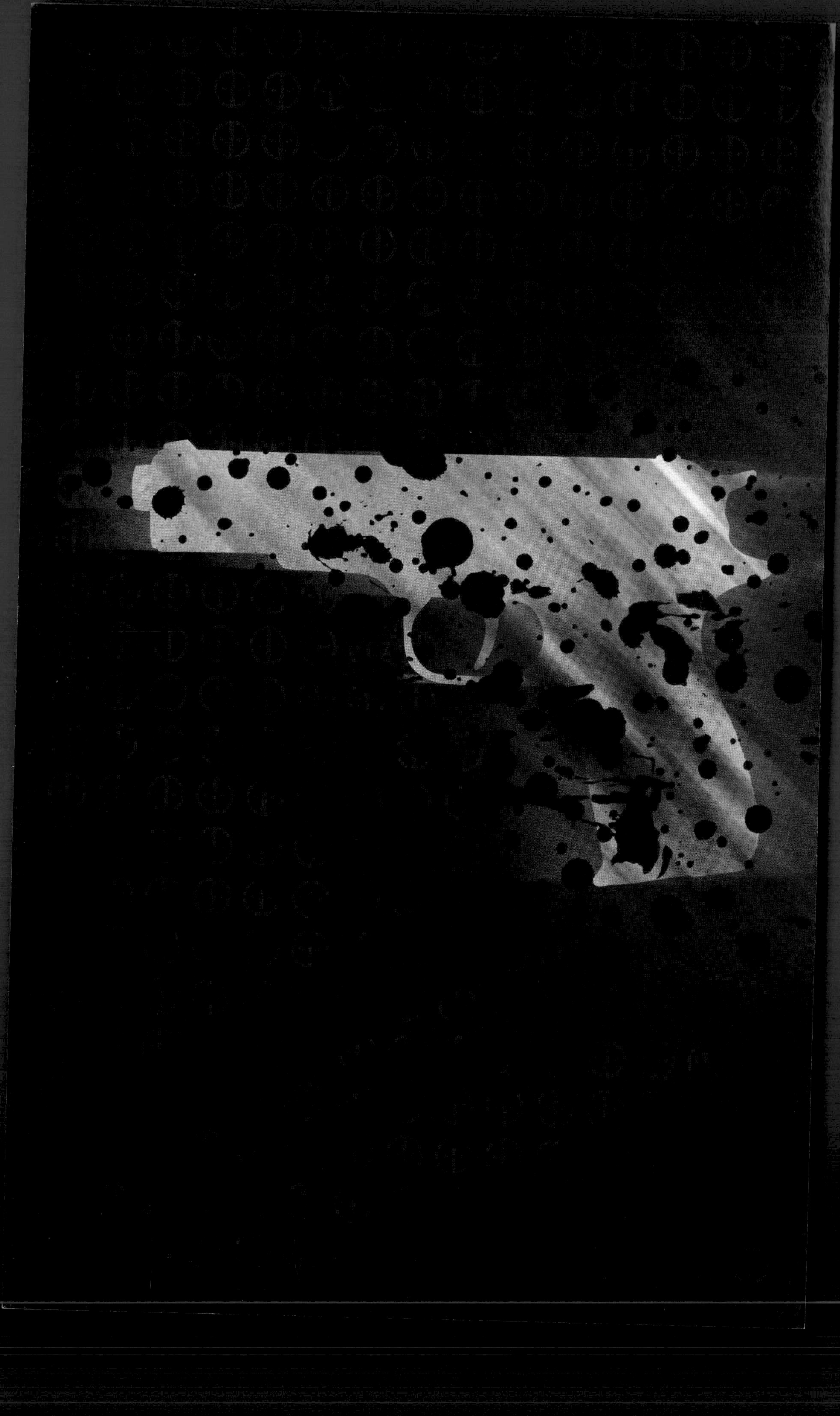

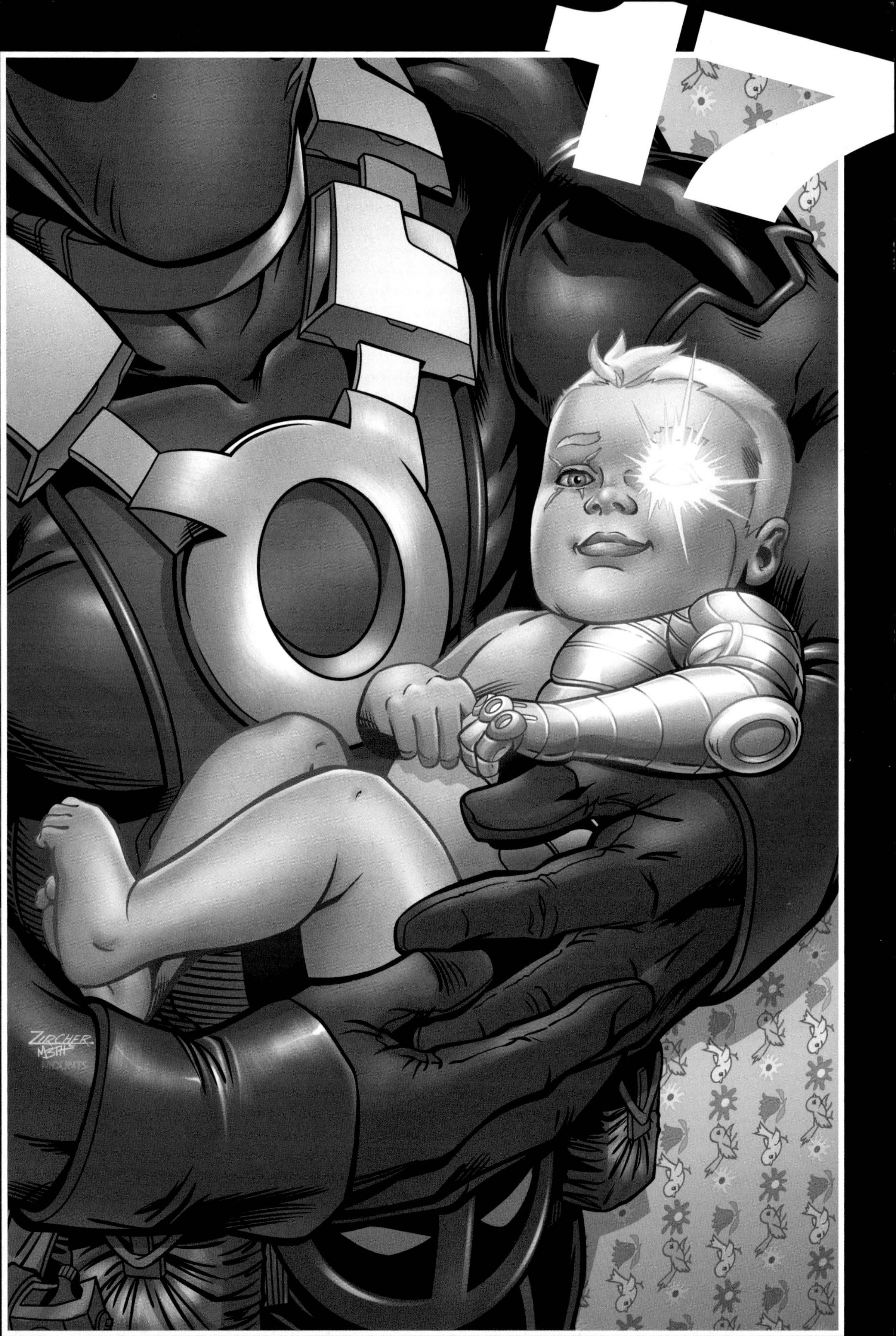
17

The New Avengers and the Astonishing X-Men met to discuss the fate of Wanda Maximoff, the Scarlet Witch—the daughter of the powerful mutant terrorist Magneto. After losing control of her reality-altering powers and suffering a total nervous breakdown, Wanda unleashed chaos upon the Avengers, killing and injuring many of their number. Magneto intervened and took his daughter to the devastated island-nation of Genosha, where Charles Xavier—Professor X, the founder of the X-Men—was to help her recover. Xavier failed, and now it is up to Wanda's friends and teammates to decide whether she will live or die. But Magneto, Wanda, and her brother Pietro disappear...

Then the world burns to white. Reality as we knew it is gone...

...to be replaced by a society in which humans are the oppressed minority and mutants run the culture, ruling over all existing countries, religions, and politics. A kingdom united under the House of M.

HOUSE OF M

CABLE & DEADPOOL

ENEMA OF THE STATE

PART THREE: "HOUSE OF MMMM"

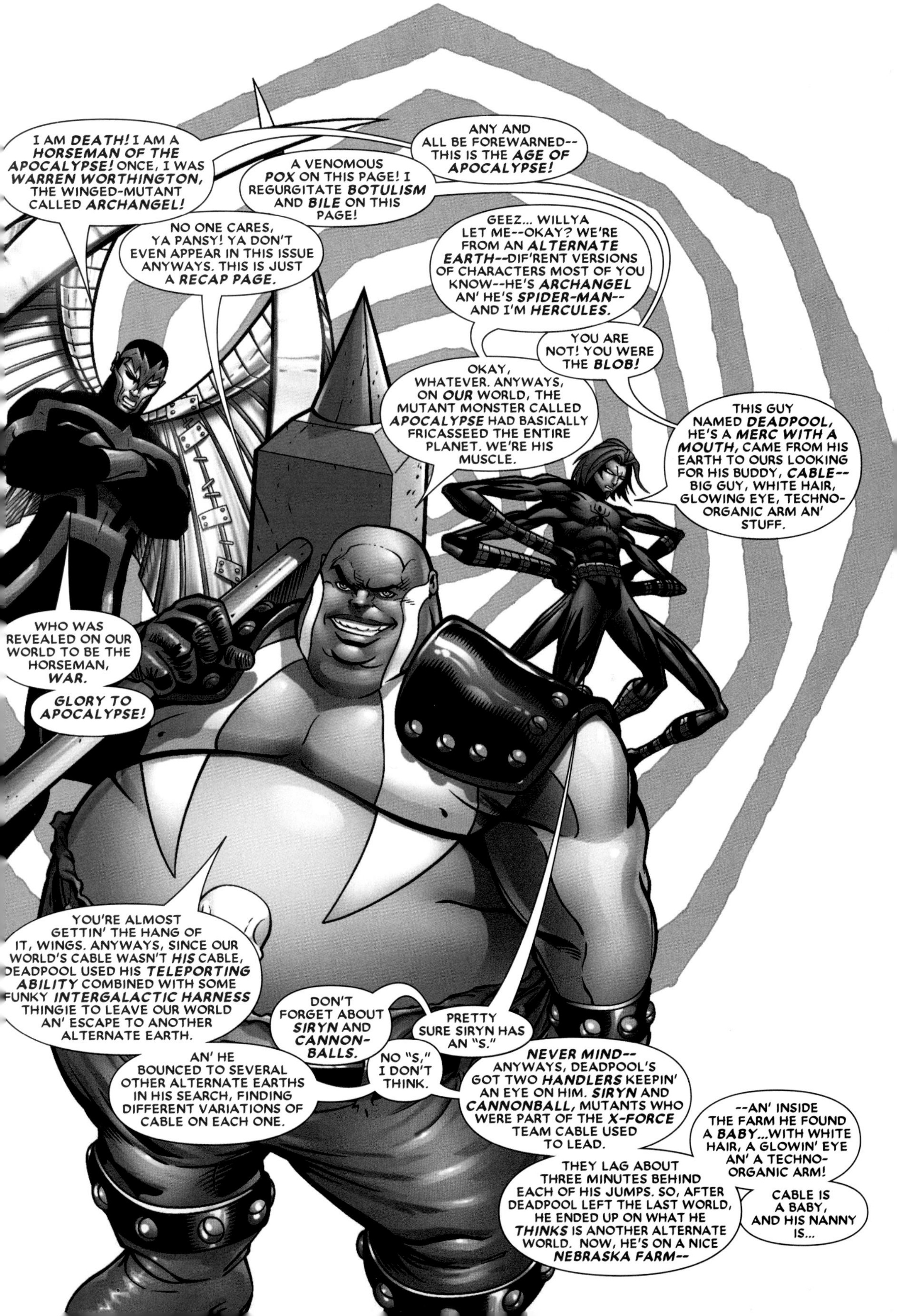
I AM DEATH! I AM A HORSEMAN OF THE APOCALYPSE! ONCE, I WAS WARREN WORTHINGTON, THE WINGED-MUTANT CALLED ARCHANGEL!
A VENOMOUS POX ON THIS PAGE! I REGURGITATE BOTULISM AND BILE ON THIS PAGE!
ANY AND ALL BE FOREWARNED-- THIS IS THE AGE OF APOCALYPSE!
NO ONE CARES, YA PANSY! YA DON'T EVEN APPEAR IN THIS ISSUE ANYWAYS. THIS IS JUST A RECAP PAGE.
GEEZ... WILLYA LET ME--OKAY? WE'RE FROM AN ALTERNATE EARTH--DIF'RENT VERSIONS OF CHARACTERS MOST OF YOU KNOW--HE'S ARCHANGEL AN' HE'S SPIDER-MAN-- AND I'M HERCULES.
YOU ARE NOT! YOU WERE THE BLOB!
OKAY, WHATEVER. ANYWAYS, ON OUR WORLD, THE MUTANT MONSTER CALLED APOCALYPSE HAD BASICALLY FRICASSEED THE ENTIRE PLANET. WE'RE HIS MUSCLE.
THIS GUY NAMED DEADPOOL, HE'S A MERC WITH A MOUTH, CAME FROM HIS EARTH TO OURS LOOKING FOR HIS BUDDY, CABLE-- BIG GUY, WHITE HAIR, GLOWING EYE, TECHNO-ORGANIC ARM AN' STUFF.
WHO WAS REVEALED ON OUR WORLD TO BE THE HORSEMAN, WAR.
GLORY TO APOCALYPSE!
YOU'RE ALMOST GETTIN' THE HANG OF IT, WINGS. ANYWAYS, SINCE OUR WORLD'S CABLE WASN'T HIS CABLE, DEADPOOL USED HIS TELEPORTING ABILITY COMBINED WITH SOME FUNKY INTERGALACTIC HARNESS THINGIE TO LEAVE OUR WORLD AN' ESCAPE TO ANOTHER ALTERNATE EARTH.
AN' HE BOUNCED TO SEVERAL OTHER ALTERNATE EARTHS IN HIS SEARCH, FINDING DIFFERENT VARIATIONS OF CABLE ON EACH ONE.
DON'T FORGET ABOUT SIRYN AND CANNON-BALLS.
PRETTY SURE SIRYN HAS AN "S."
NO "S," I DON'T THINK.
NEVER MIND-- ANYWAYS, DEADPOOL'S GOT TWO HANDLERS KEEPIN' AN EYE ON HIM. SIRYN AND CANNONBALL, MUTANTS WHO WERE PART OF THE X-FORCE TEAM CABLE USED TO LEAD.
THEY LAG ABOUT THREE MINUTES BEHIND EACH OF HIS JUMPS. SO, AFTER DEADPOOL LEFT THE LAST WORLD, HE ENDED UP ON WHAT HE THINKS IS ANOTHER ALTERNATE WORLD. NOW, HE'S ON A NICE NEBRASKA FARM--
--AN' INSIDE THE FARM HE FOUND A BABY...WITH WHITE HAIR, A GLOWIN' EYE AN' A TECHNO-ORGANIC ARM!
CABLE IS A BABY, AND HIS NANNY IS...

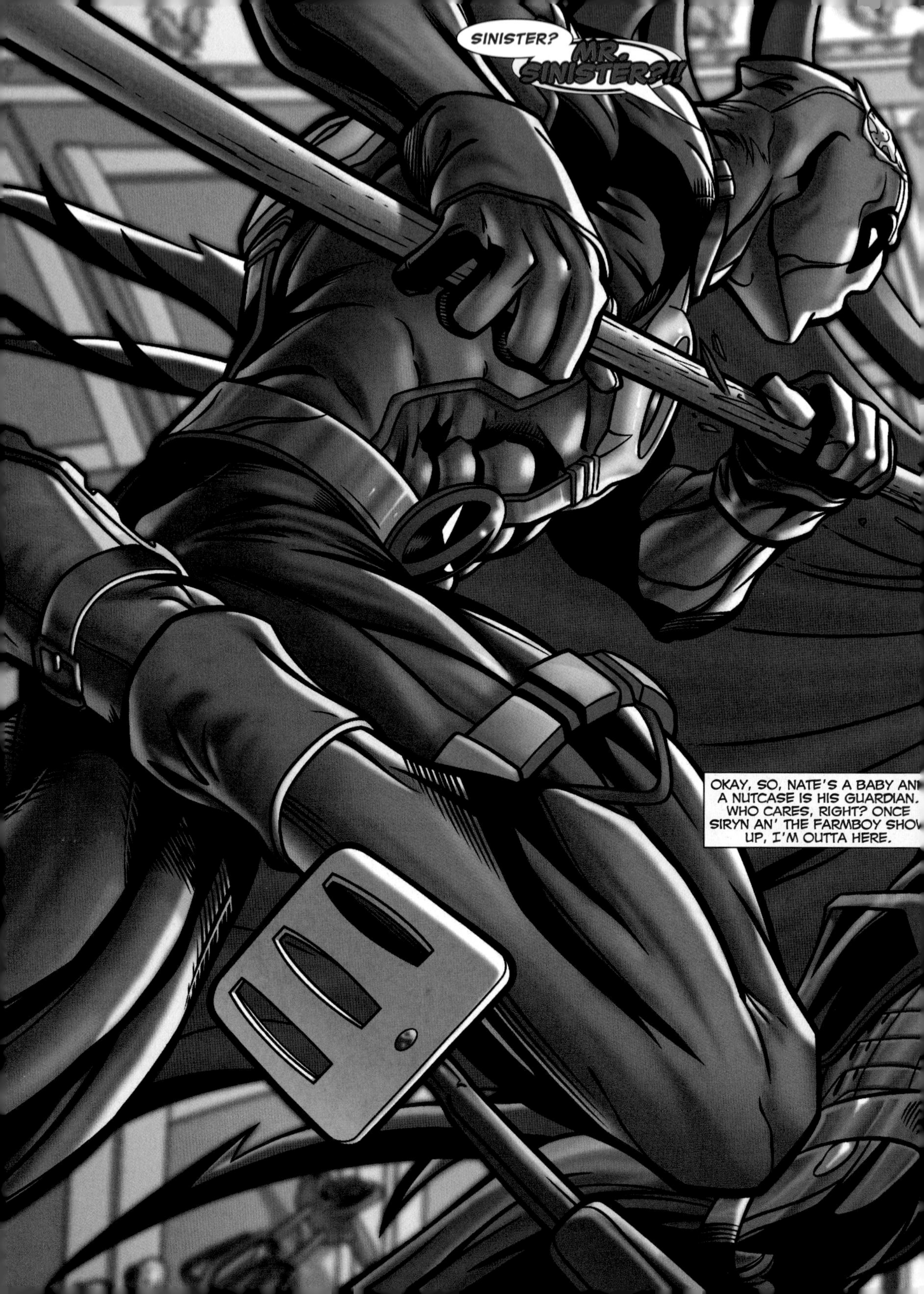
SINISTER?
MR. SINISTER?!!
OKAY, SO, NATE'S A BABY AN
A NUTCASE IS HIS GUARDIAN.
WHO CARES, RIGHT? ONCE
SIRYN AN' THE FARMBOY SHO
UP, I'M OUTTA HERE.

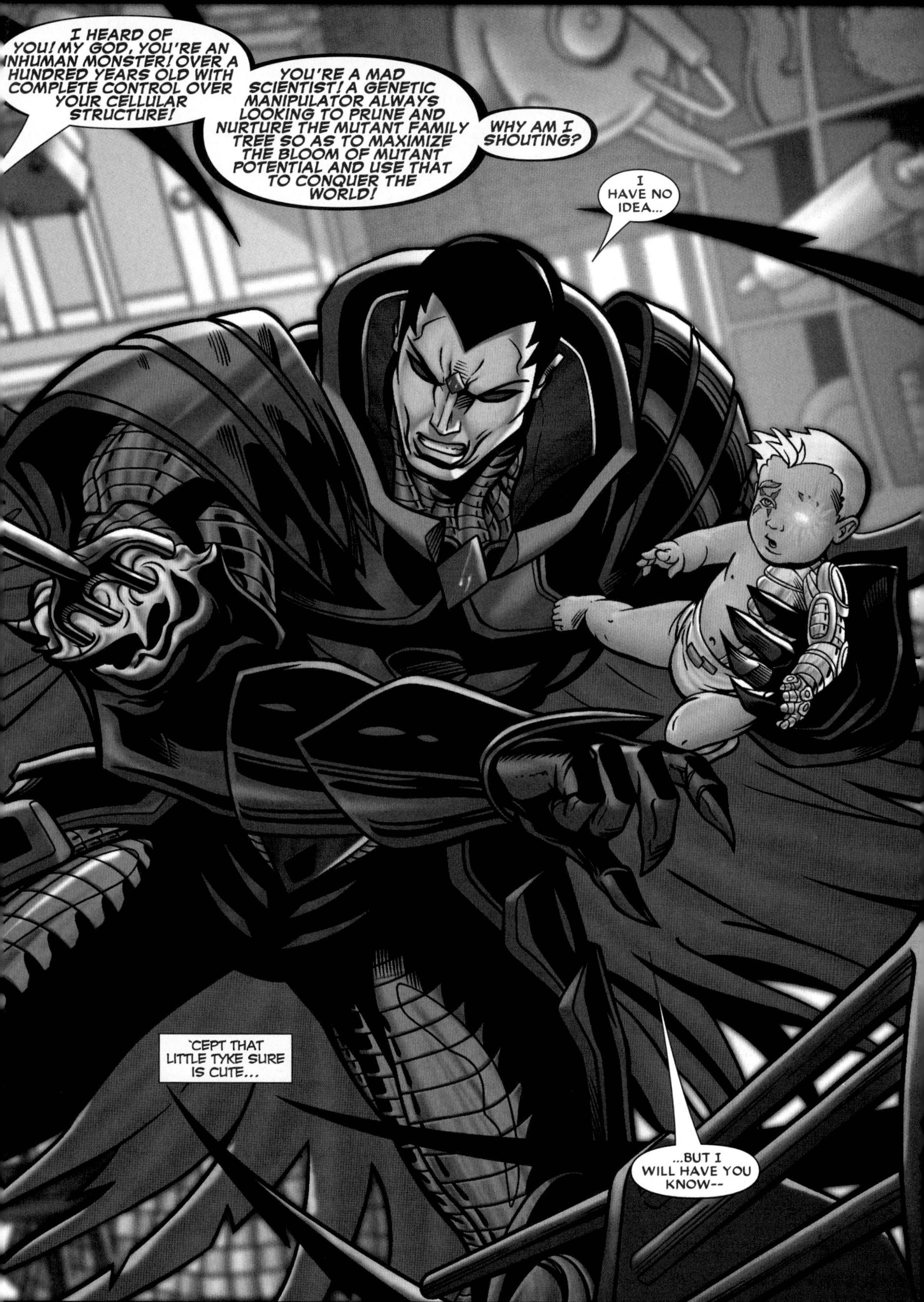
I HEARD OF YOU! MY GOD, YOU'RE AN INHUMAN MONSTER! OVER A HUNDRED YEARS OLD WITH COMPLETE CONTROL OVER YOUR CELLULAR STRUCTURE!
YOU'RE A MAD SCIENTIST! A GENETIC MANIPULATOR ALWAYS LOOKING TO PRUNE AND NURTURE THE MUTANT FAMILY TREE SO AS TO MAXIMIZE THE BLOOM OF MUTANT POTENTIAL AND USE THAT TO CONQUER THE WORLD!
WHY AM I SHOUTING?
I HAVE NO IDEA...
'CEPT THAT LITTLE TYKE SURE IS CUTE...
...BUT I WILL HAVE YOU KNOW--

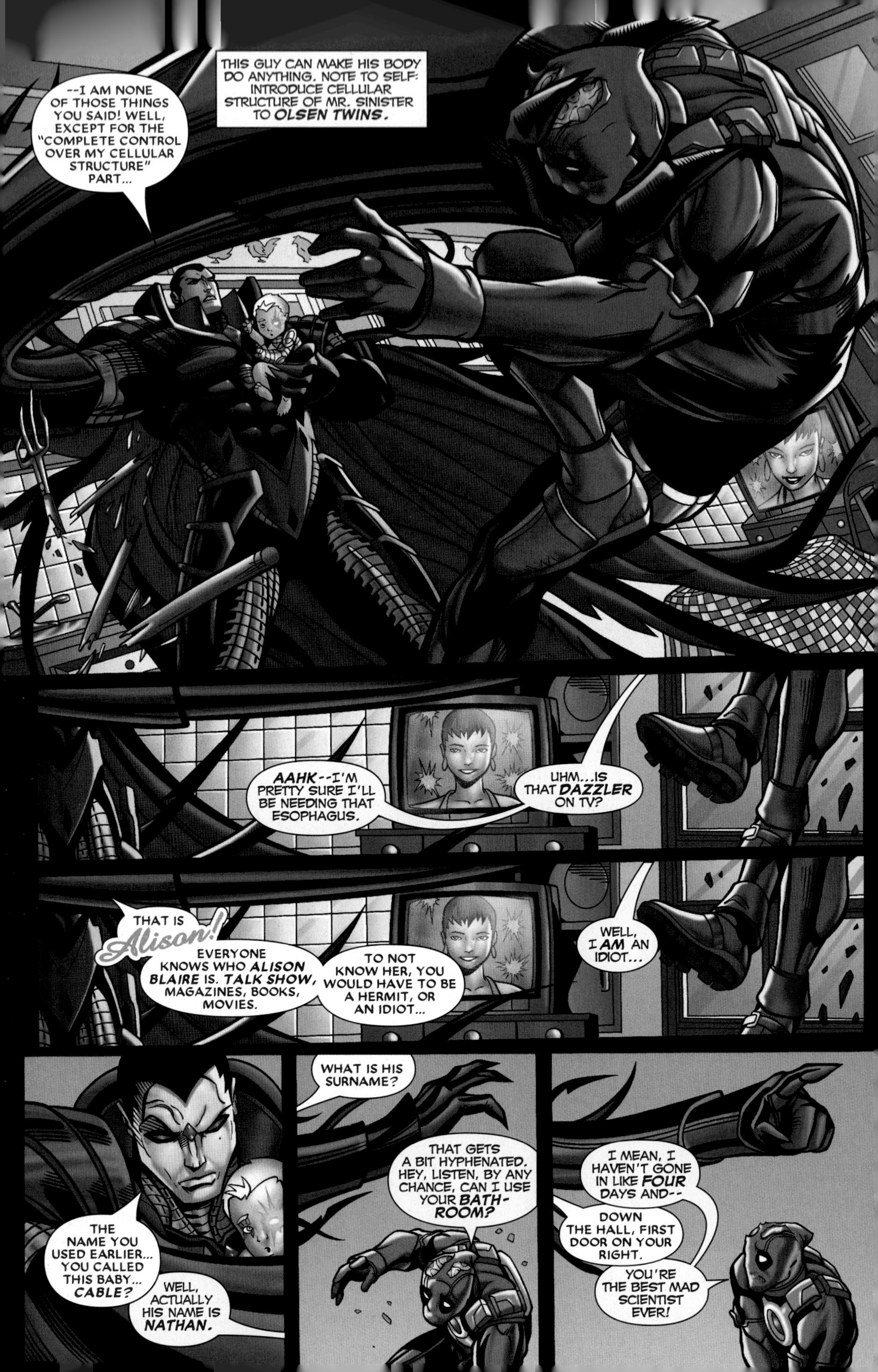

--I AM NONE OF THOSE THINGS YOU SAID! WELL, EXCEPT FOR THE "COMPLETE CONTROL OVER MY CELLULAR STRUCTURE" PART...
THIS GUY CAN MAKE HIS BODY DO ANYTHING. NOTE TO SELF: INTRODUCE CELLULAR STRUCTURE OF MR. SINISTER TO OLSEN TWINS.
AAHK--I'M PRETTY SURE I'LL BE NEEDING THAT ESOPHAGUS.
UHM...IS THAT DAZZLER ON TV?
THAT IS Alison!
EVERYONE KNOWS WHO ALISON BLAIRE IS. TALK SHOW, MAGAZINES, BOOKS, MOVIES.
TO NOT KNOW HER, YOU WOULD HAVE TO BE A HERMIT, OR AN IDIOT...
WELL, I AM AN IDIOT...
THE NAME YOU USED EARLIER... YOU CALLED THIS BABY... CABLE?
WELL, ACTUALLY HIS NAME IS NATHAN.
WHAT IS HIS SURNAME?
THAT GETS A BIT HYPHENATED. HEY, LISTEN, BY ANY CHANCE, CAN I USE YOUR BATH-ROOM?
I MEAN, I HAVEN'T GONE IN LIKE FOUR DAYS AND--
DOWN THE HALL, FIRST DOOR ON YOUR RIGHT.
YOU'RE THE BEST MAD SCIENTIST EVER!

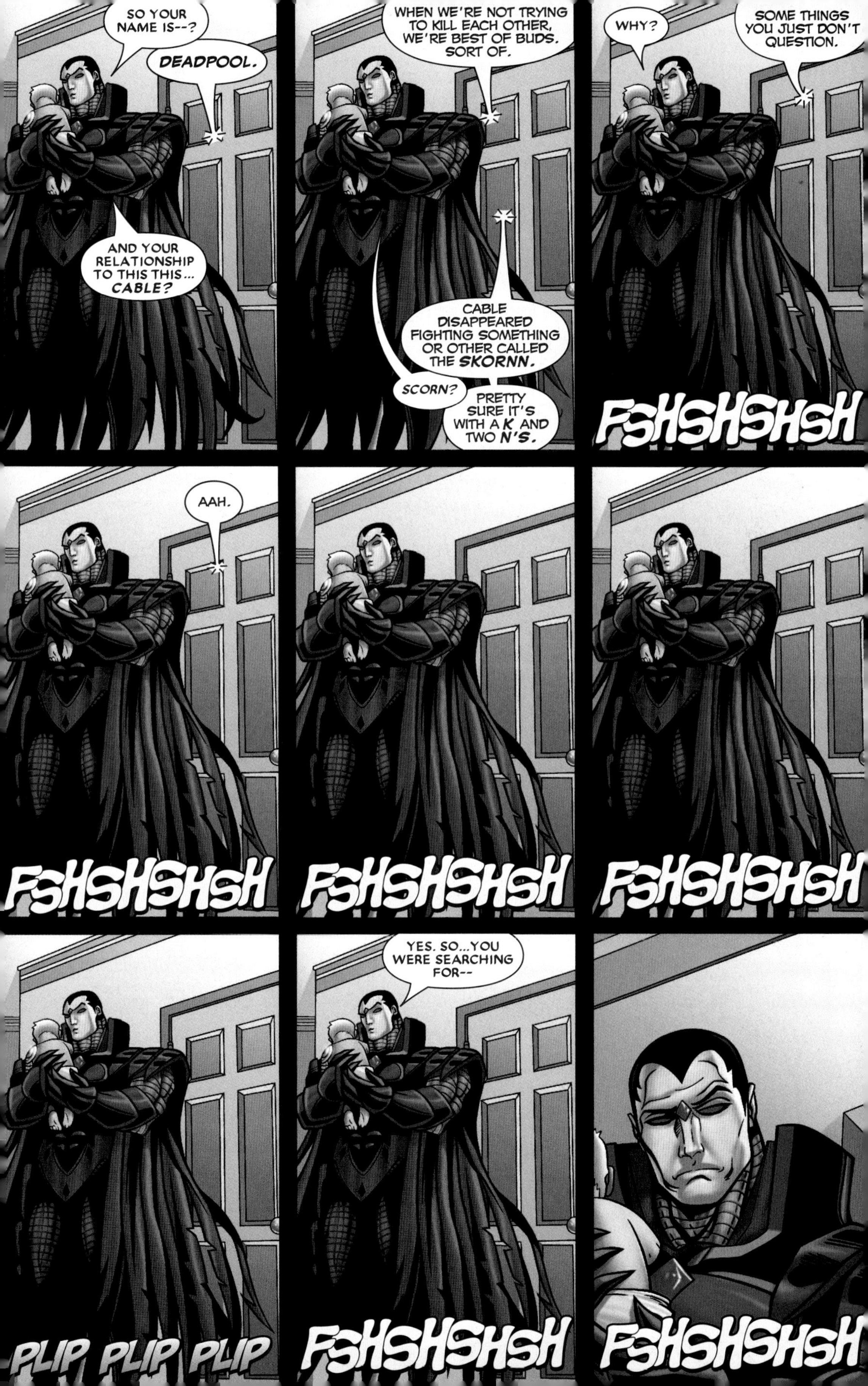
SO YOUR NAME IS--?
DEADPOOL.
AND YOUR RELATIONSHIP TO THIS THIS... CABLE?
WHEN WE'RE NOT TRYING TO KILL EACH OTHER, WE'RE BEST OF BUDS. SORT OF.
CABLE DISAPPEARED FIGHTING SOMETHING OR OTHER CALLED THE SKORNN.
SCORN?
PRETTY SURE IT'S WITH A K AND TWO N'S.
WHY?
SOME THINGS YOU JUST DON'T QUESTION.
FSHSHSHSH
AAH.
FSHSHSHSH
FSHSHSHSH
FSHSHSHSH
PLIP PLIP PLIP
YES. SO...YOU WERE SEARCHING FOR--
FSHSHSHSH
FSHSHSHSH

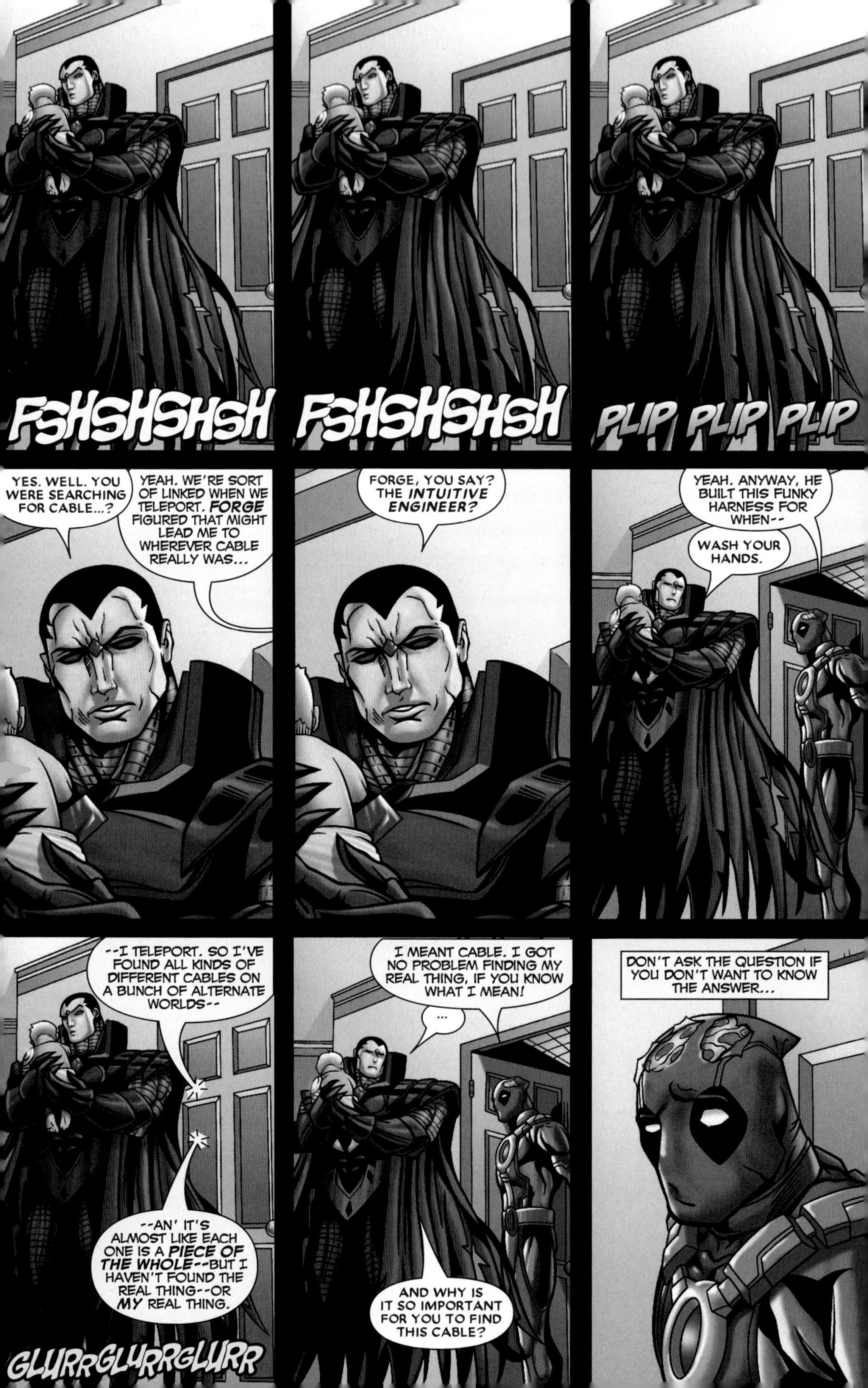
FSHSHSHSH
FSHSHSHSH
PLIP PLIP PLIP
YES. WELL. YOU WERE SEARCHING FOR CABLE...?
YEAH. WE'RE SORT OF LINKED WHEN WE TELEPORT. FORGE FIGURED THAT MIGHT LEAD ME TO WHEREVER CABLE REALLY WAS...
FORGE, YOU SAY? THE INTUITIVE ENGINEER?
YEAH. ANYWAY, HE BUILT THIS FUNKY HARNESS FOR WHEN--
WASH YOUR HANDS.
--I TELEPORT. SO I'VE FOUND ALL KINDS OF DIFFERENT CABLES ON A BUNCH OF ALTERNATE WORLDS--
--AN' IT'S ALMOST LIKE EACH ONE IS A PIECE OF THE WHOLE--BUT I HAVEN'T FOUND THE REAL THING--OR MY REAL THING.
GLURRGLURRGLURR
I MEANT CABLE. I GOT NO PROBLEM FINDING MY REAL THING, IF YOU KNOW WHAT I MEAN!
...
AND WHY IS IT SO IMPORTANT FOR YOU TO FIND THIS CABLE?
DON'T ASK THE QUESTION IF YOU DON'T WANT TO KNOW THE ANSWER...

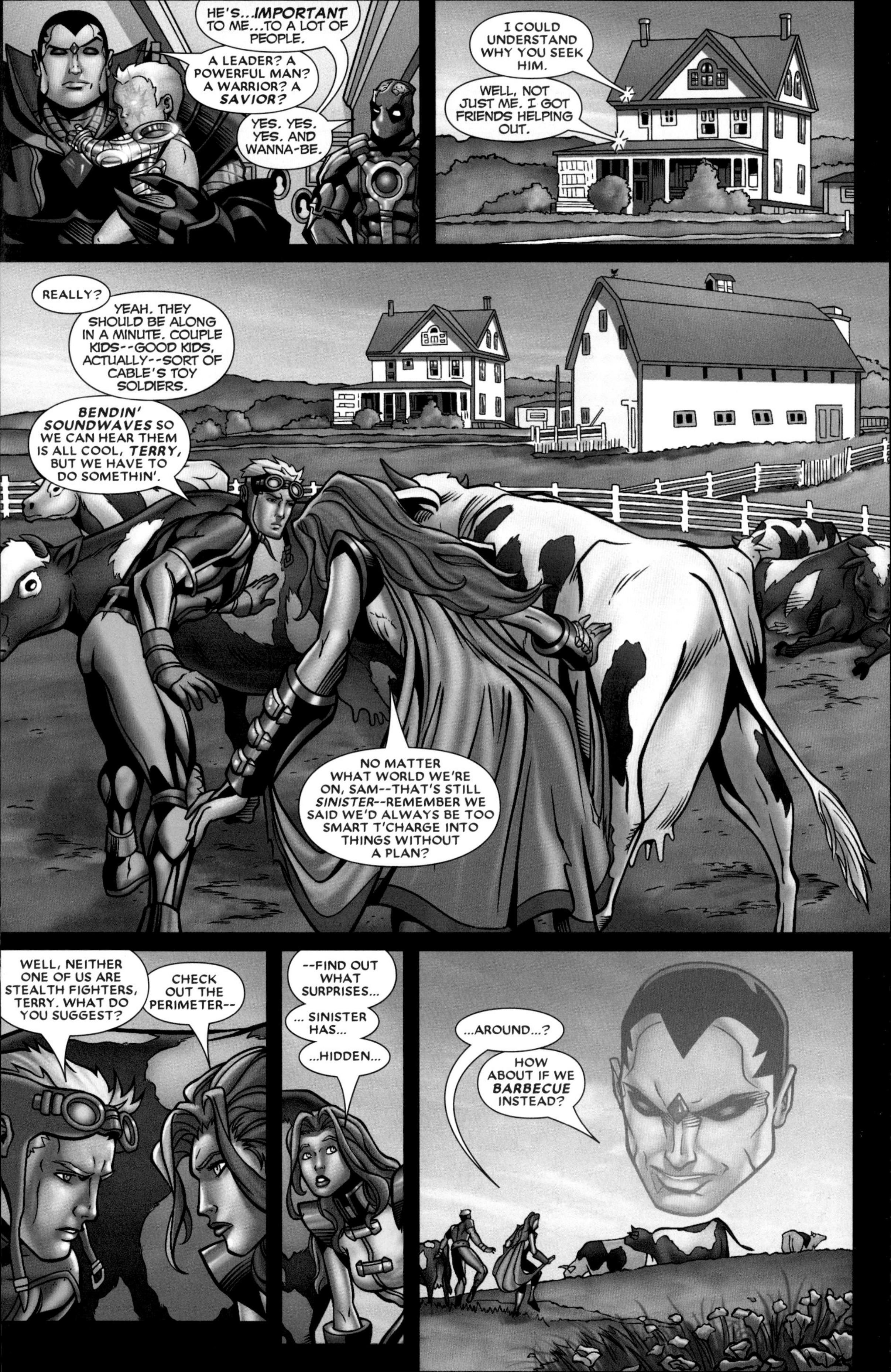
HE'S...IMPORTANT TO ME...TO A LOT OF PEOPLE.
A LEADER? A POWERFUL MAN? A WARRIOR? A SAVIOR?
YES. YES. YES. AND WANNA-BE.
I COULD UNDERSTAND WHY YOU SEEK HIM.
WELL, NOT JUST ME. I GOT FRIENDS HELPING OUT.
REALLY?
YEAH. THEY SHOULD BE ALONG IN A MINUTE. COUPLE KIDS--GOOD KIDS, ACTUALLY--SORT OF CABLE'S TOY SOLDIERS.
BENDIN' SOUNDWAVES SO WE CAN HEAR THEM IS ALL COOL, TERRY, BUT WE HAVE TO DO SOMETHIN'.
NO MATTER WHAT WORLD WE'RE ON, SAM--THAT'S STILL SINISTER--REMEMBER WE SAID WE'D ALWAYS BE TOO SMART T'CHARGE INTO THINGS WITHOUT A PLAN?
WELL, NEITHER ONE OF US ARE STEALTH FIGHTERS, TERRY. WHAT DO YOU SUGGEST?
CHECK OUT THE PERIMETER--
--FIND OUT WHAT SURPRISES...
... SINISTER HAS...
...HIDDEN...
...AROUND...?
HOW ABOUT IF WE BARBECUE INSTEAD?

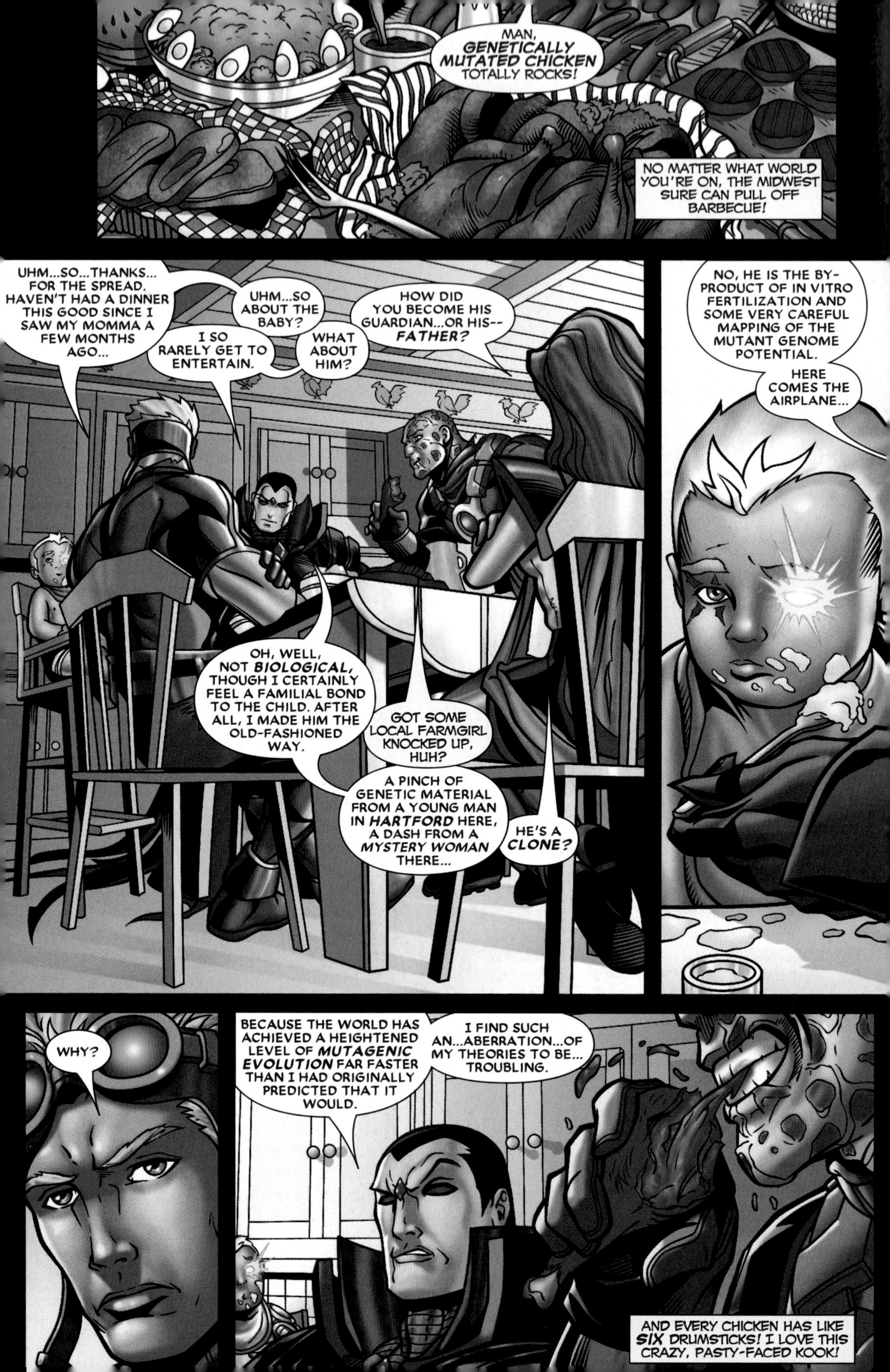
MAN, GENETICALLY MUTATED CHICKEN TOTALLY ROCKS!
NO MATTER WHAT WORLD YOU'RE ON, THE MIDWEST SURE CAN PULL OFF BARBECUE!
UHM...SO...THANKS... FOR THE SPREAD. HAVEN'T HAD A DINNER THIS GOOD SINCE I SAW MY MOMMA A FEW MONTHS AGO...
I SO RARELY GET TO ENTERTAIN.
UHM...SO ABOUT THE BABY?
WHAT ABOUT HIM?
HOW DID YOU BECOME HIS GUARDIAN...OR HIS-- FATHER?
OH, WELL, NOT BIOLOGICAL, THOUGH I CERTAINLY FEEL A FAMILIAL BOND TO THE CHILD. AFTER ALL, I MADE HIM THE OLD-FASHIONED WAY.
GOT SOME LOCAL FARMGIRL KNOCKED UP, HUH?
A PINCH OF GENETIC MATERIAL FROM A YOUNG MAN IN HARTFORD HERE, A DASH FROM A MYSTERY WOMAN THERE...
HE'S A CLONE?
NO, HE IS THE BY-PRODUCT OF IN VITRO FERTILIZATION AND SOME VERY CAREFUL MAPPING OF THE MUTANT GENOME POTENTIAL.
HERE COMES THE AIRPLANE...
WHY?
BECAUSE THE WORLD HAS ACHIEVED A HEIGHTENED LEVEL OF MUTAGENIC EVOLUTION FAR FASTER THAN I HAD ORIGINALLY PREDICTED THAT IT WOULD.
I FIND SUCH AN...ABERRATION...OF MY THEORIES TO BE... TROUBLING.
AND EVERY CHICKEN HAS LIKE SIX DRUMSTICKS! I LOVE THIS CRAZY, PASTY-FACED KOOK!

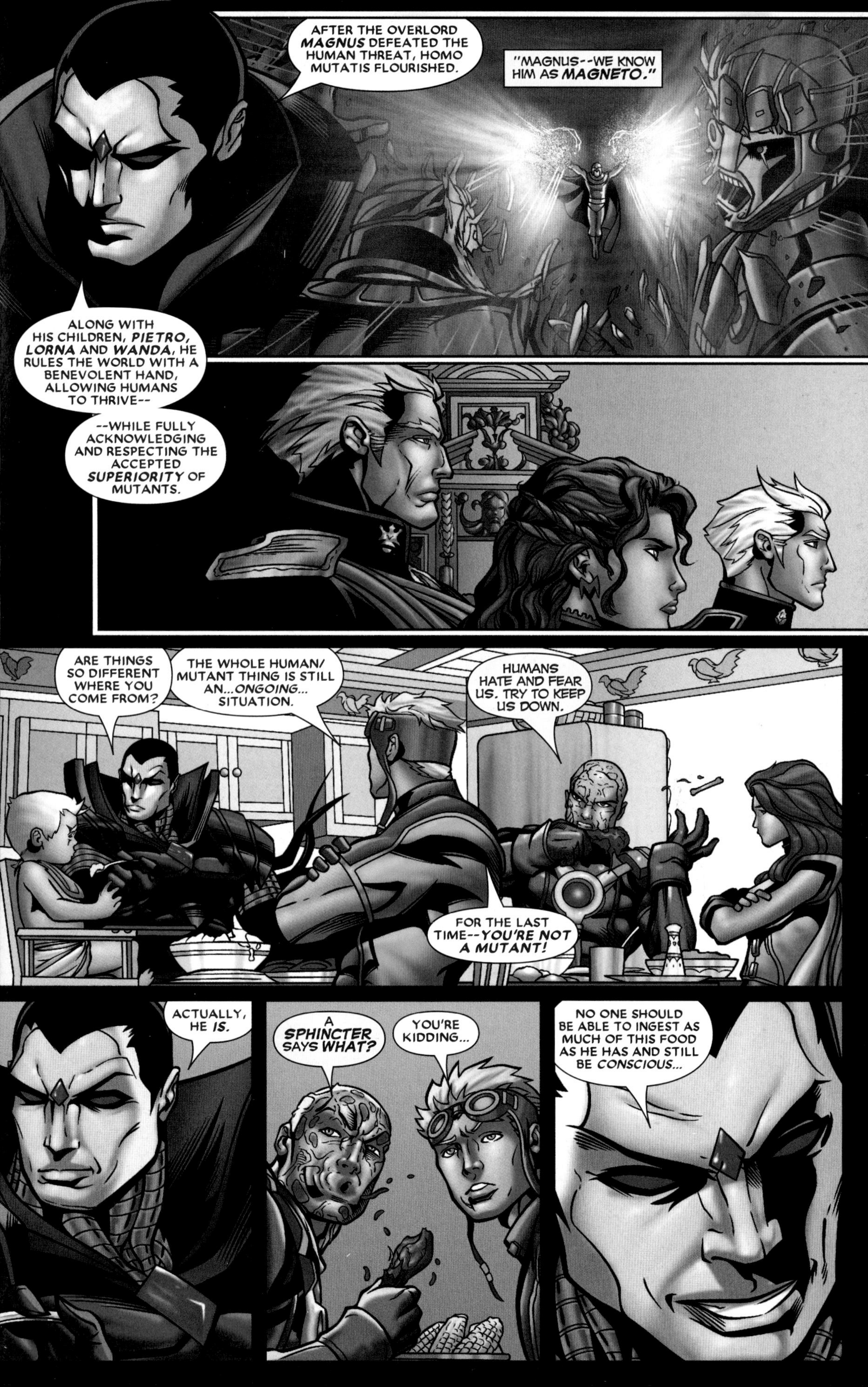
AFTER THE OVERLORD MAGNUS DEFEATED THE HUMAN THREAT, HOMO MUTATIS FLOURISHED.
"MAGNUS--WE KNOW HIM AS MAGNETO."
ALONG WITH HIS CHILDREN, PIETRO, LORNA AND WANDA, HE RULES THE WORLD WITH A BENEVOLENT HAND, ALLOWING HUMANS TO THRIVE--
--WHILE FULLY ACKNOWLEDGING AND RESPECTING THE ACCEPTED SUPERIORITY OF MUTANTS.
ARE THINGS SO DIFFERENT WHERE YOU COME FROM?
THE WHOLE HUMAN/ MUTANT THING IS STILL AN...ONGOING... SITUATION.
HUMANS HATE AND FEAR US. TRY TO KEEP US DOWN.
FOR THE LAST TIME--YOU'RE NOT A MUTANT!
ACTUALLY, HE IS.
A SPHINCTER SAYS WHAT?
YOU'RE KIDDING...
NO ONE SHOULD BE ABLE TO INGEST AS MUCH OF THIS FOOD AS HE HAS AND STILL BE CONSCIOUS...

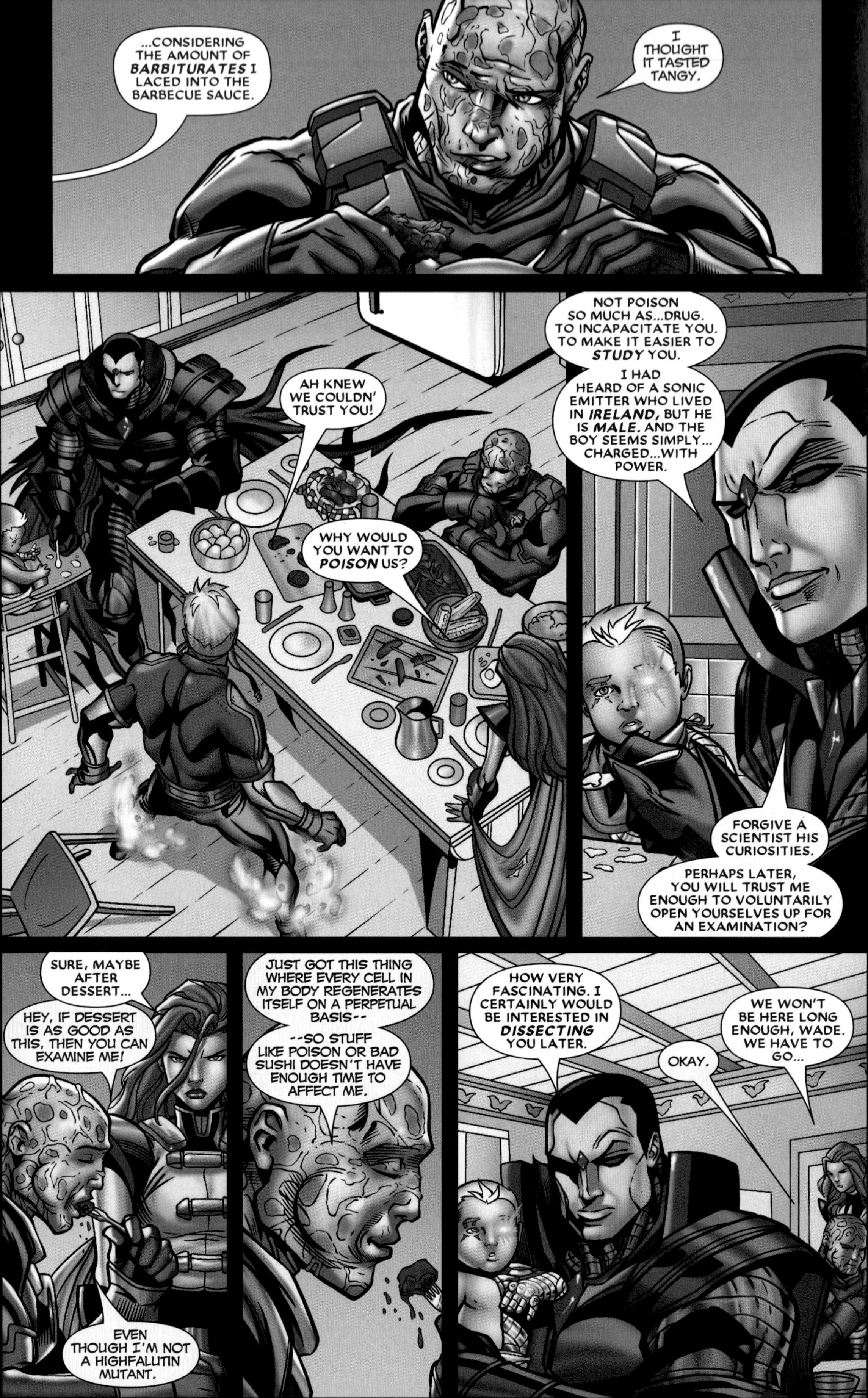
...CONSIDERING THE AMOUNT OF BARBITURATES I LACED INTO THE BARBECUE SAUCE.
I THOUGHT IT TASTED TANGY.
AH KNEW WE COULDN' TRUST YOU!
WHY WOULD YOU WANT TO POISON US?
NOT POISON SO MUCH AS...DRUG. TO INCAPACITATE YOU. TO MAKE IT EASIER TO STUDY YOU.
I HAD HEARD OF A SONIC EMITTER WHO LIVED IN IRELAND, BUT HE IS MALE. AND THE BOY SEEMS SIMPLY... CHARGED...WITH POWER.
FORGIVE A SCIENTIST HIS CURIOSITIES.
PERHAPS LATER, YOU WILL TRUST ME ENOUGH TO VOLUNTARILY OPEN YOURSELVES UP FOR AN EXAMINATION?
SURE, MAYBE AFTER DESSERT...
HEY, IF DESSERT IS AS GOOD AS THIS, THEN YOU CAN EXAMINE ME!
EVEN THOUGH I'M NOT A HIGHFALUTIN MUTANT.
JUST GOT THIS THING WHERE EVERY CELL IN MY BODY REGENERATES ITSELF ON A PERPETUAL BASIS--
--SO STUFF LIKE POISON OR BAD SUSHI DOESN'T HAVE ENOUGH TIME TO AFFECT ME.
HOW VERY FASCINATING. I CERTAINLY WOULD BE INTERESTED IN DISSECTING YOU LATER.
OKAY.
WE WON'T BE HERE LONG ENOUGH, WADE. WE HAVE TO GO...

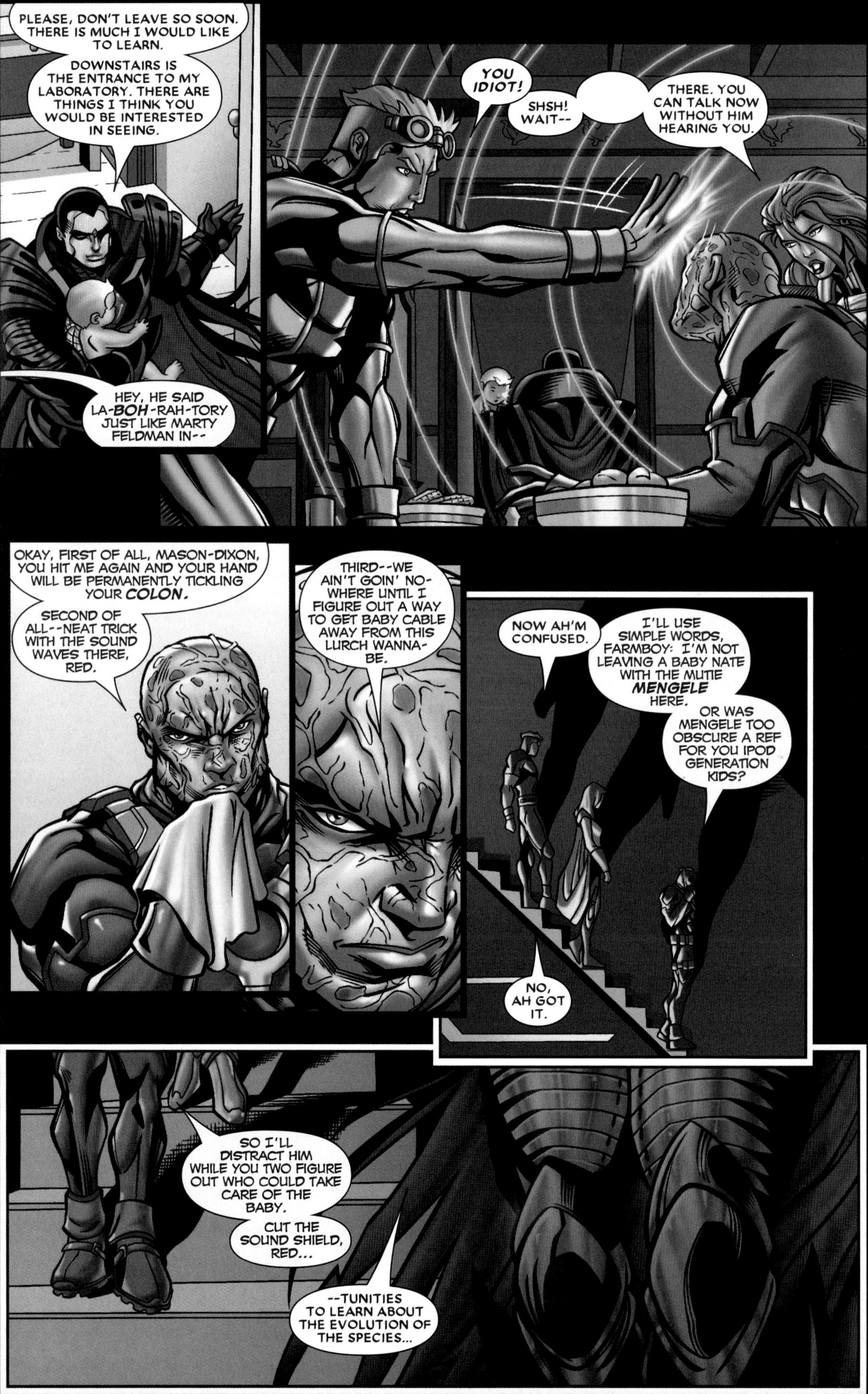
PLEASE, DON'T LEAVE SO SOON. THERE IS MUCH I WOULD LIKE TO LEARN.
DOWNSTAIRS IS THE ENTRANCE TO MY LABORATORY. THERE ARE THINGS I THINK YOU WOULD BE INTERESTED IN SEEING.
HEY, HE SAID LA-BOH-RAH-TORY JUST LIKE MARTY FELDMAN IN--
YOU IDIOT!
SHSH! WAIT--
THERE. YOU CAN TALK NOW WITHOUT HIM HEARING YOU.
OKAY, FIRST OF ALL, MASON-DIXON, YOU HIT ME AGAIN AND YOUR HAND WILL BE PERMANENTLY TICKLING YOUR COLON.
SECOND OF ALL--NEAT TRICK WITH THE SOUND WAVES THERE, RED.
THIRD--WE AIN'T GOIN' NO-WHERE UNTIL I FIGURE OUT A WAY TO GET BABY CABLE AWAY FROM THIS LURCH WANNA-BE.
NOW AH'M CONFUSED.
I'LL USE SIMPLE WORDS, FARMBOY: I'M NOT LEAVING A BABY NATE WITH THE MUTIE MENGELE HERE.
OR WAS MENGELE TOO OBSCURE A REF FOR YOU IPOD GENERATION KIDS?
NO, AH GOT IT.
SO I'LL DISTRACT HIM WHILE YOU TWO FIGURE OUT WHO COULD TAKE CARE OF THE BABY.
CUT THE SOUND SHIELD, RED...
--TUNITIES TO LEARN ABOUT THE EVOLUTION OF THE SPECIES...

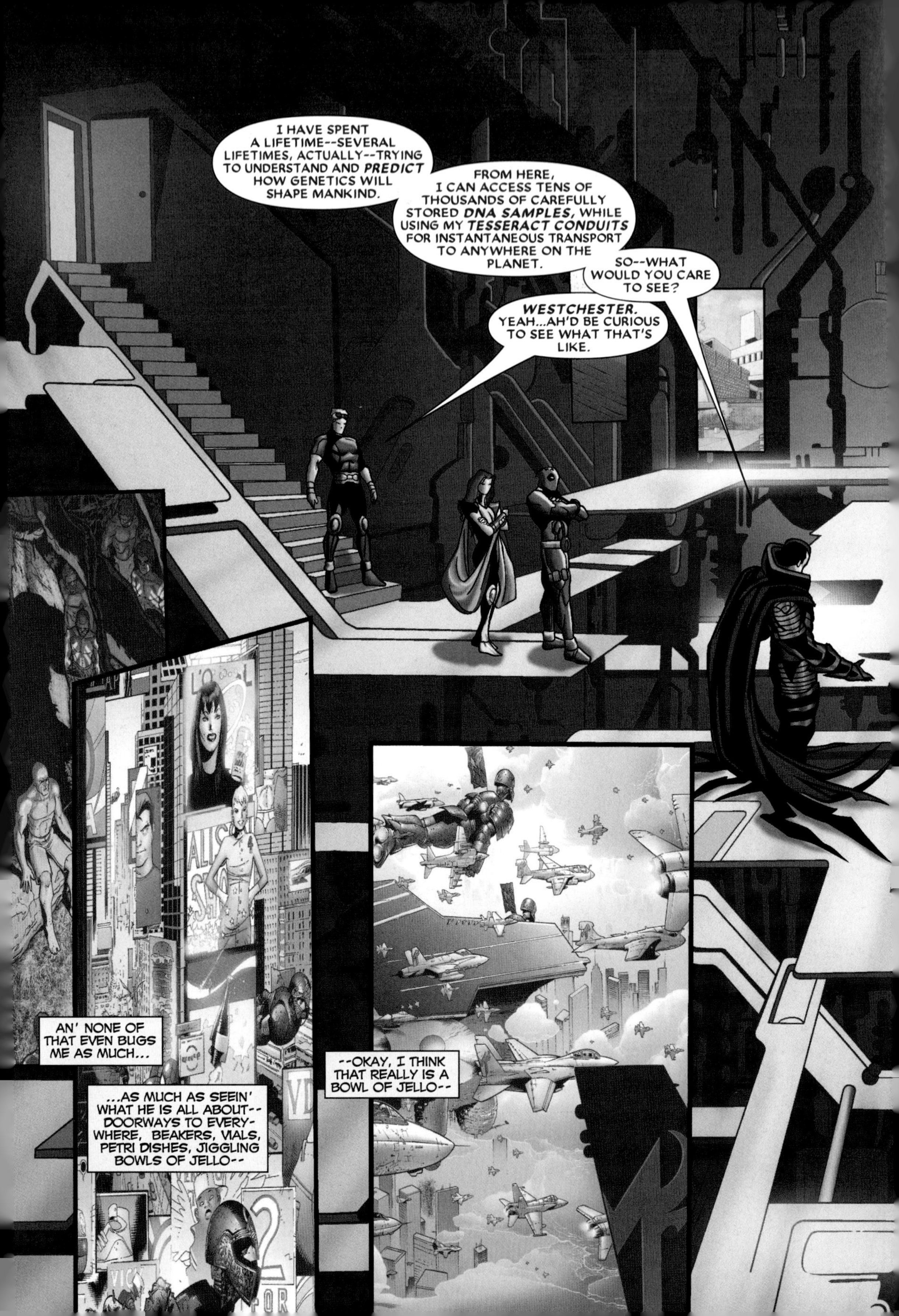
I HAVE SPENT A LIFETIME--SEVERAL LIFETIMES, ACTUALLY--TRYING TO UNDERSTAND AND *PREDICT* HOW GENETICS WILL SHAPE MANKIND.
FROM HERE, I CAN ACCESS TENS OF THOUSANDS OF CAREFULLY STORED *DNA SAMPLES,* WHILE USING MY *TESSERACT CONDUITS* FOR INSTANTANEOUS TRANSPORT TO ANYWHERE ON THE PLANET.
SO--WHAT WOULD YOU CARE TO SEE?
WESTCHESTER. YEAH...AH'D BE CURIOUS TO SEE WHAT THAT'S LIKE.
AN' NONE OF THAT EVEN BUGS ME AS MUCH...
...AS MUCH AS SEEIN' WHAT HE IS ALL ABOUT--DOORWAYS TO EVERY-WHERE, BEAKERS, VIALS, PETRI DISHES, JIGGLING BOWLS OF JELLO--
--OKAY, I THINK THAT REALLY IS A BOWL OF JELLO--

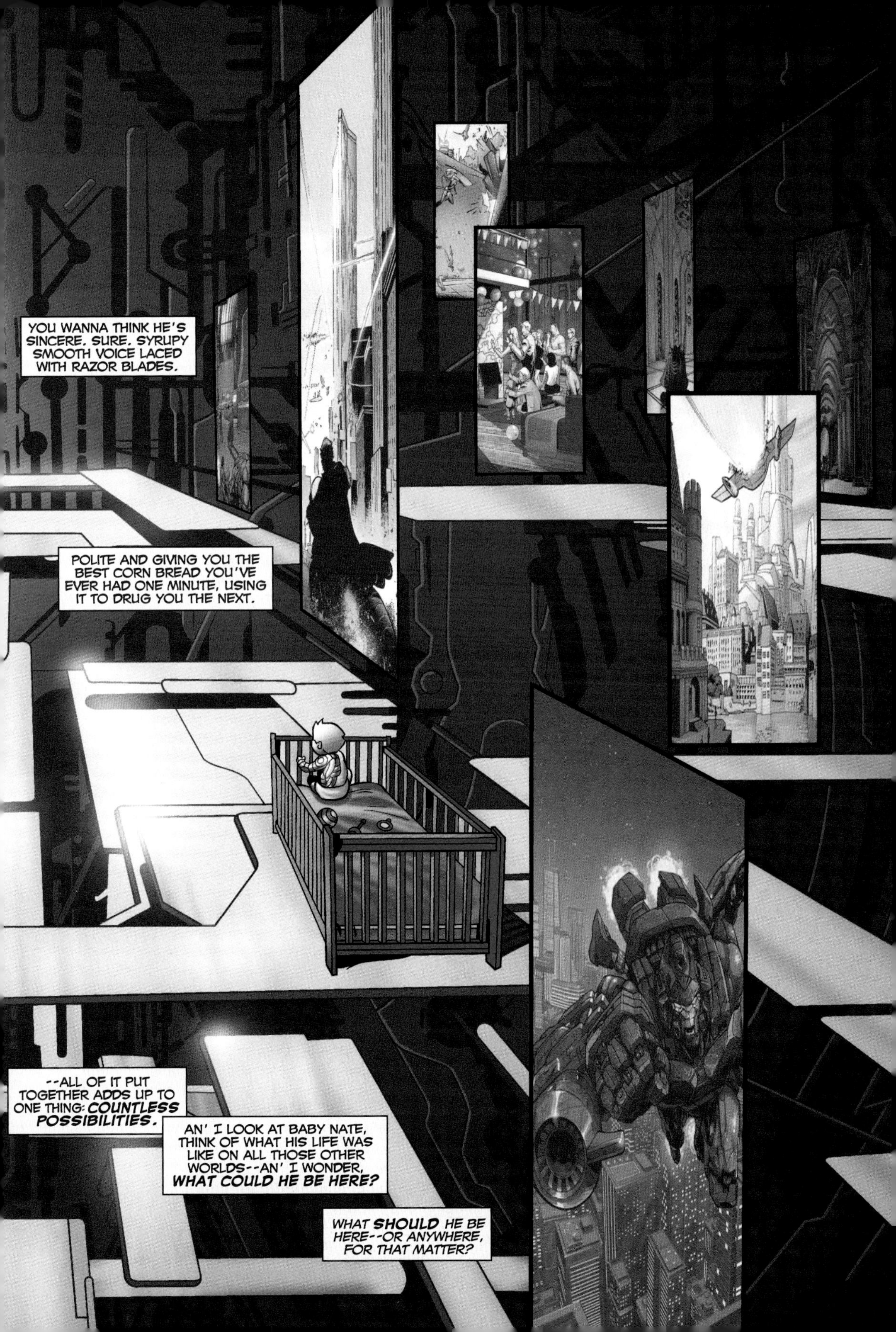
YOU WANNA THINK HE'S SINCERE. SURE. SYRUPY SMOOTH VOICE LACED WITH RAZOR BLADES.
POLITE AND GIVING YOU THE BEST CORN BREAD YOU'VE EVER HAD ONE MINUTE, USING IT TO DRUG YOU THE NEXT.
--ALL OF IT PUT TOGETHER ADDS UP TO ONE THING: ***COUNTLESS POSSIBILITIES.***
AN' I LOOK AT BABY NATE, THINK OF WHAT HIS LIFE WAS LIKE ON ALL THOSE OTHER WORLDS--AN' I WONDER, ***WHAT COULD HE BE HERE?***
*WHAT **SHOULD** HE BE HERE--OR ANYWHERE, FOR THAT MATTER?*

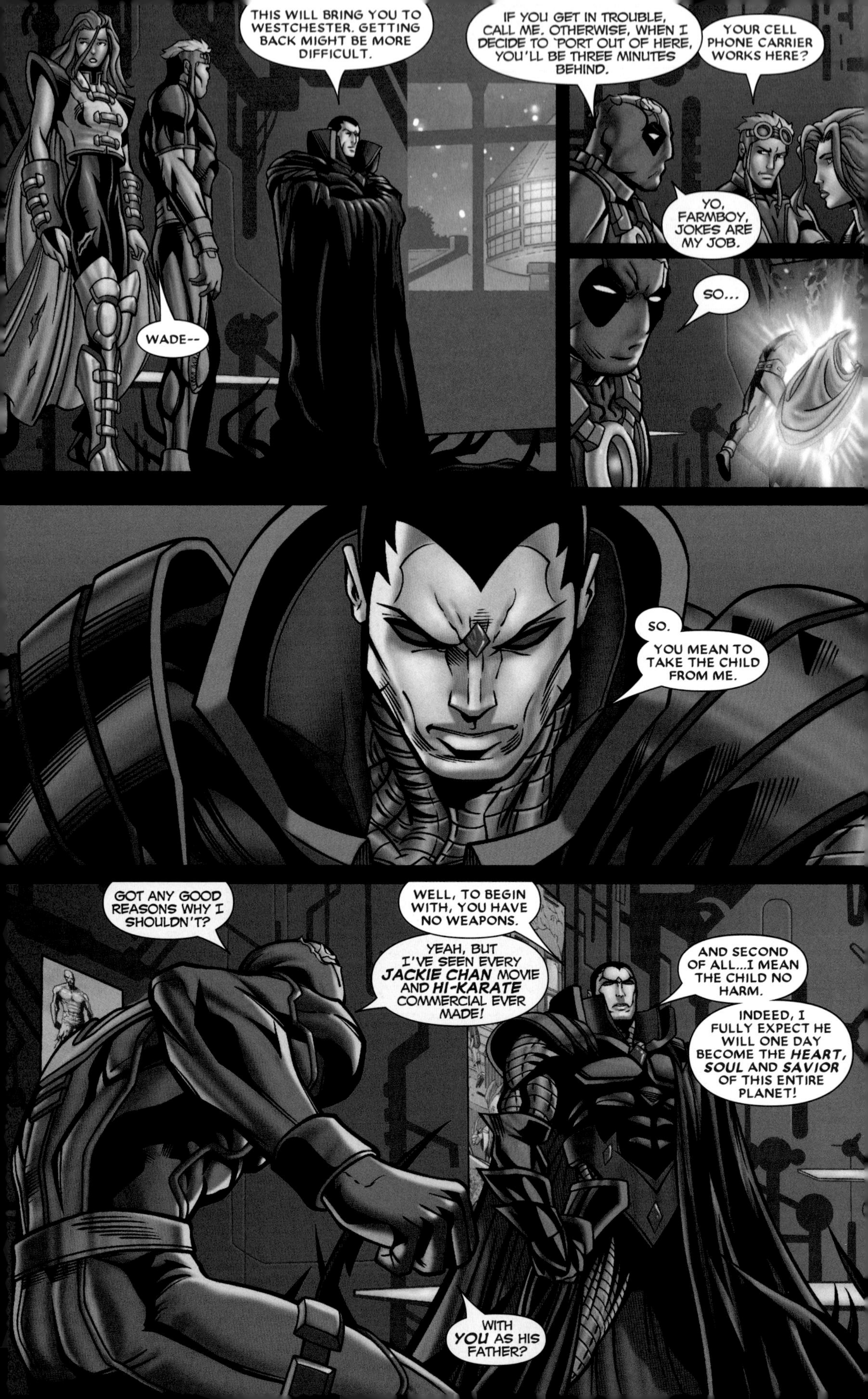
THIS WILL BRING YOU TO WESTCHESTER. GETTING BACK MIGHT BE MORE DIFFICULT.
WADE--
IF YOU GET IN TROUBLE, CALL ME. OTHERWISE, WHEN I DECIDE TO 'PORT OUT OF HERE, YOU'LL BE THREE MINUTES BEHIND.
YOUR CELL PHONE CARRIER WORKS HERE?
YO, FARMBOY, JOKES ARE MY JOB.
SO...
SO.
YOU MEAN TO TAKE THE CHILD FROM ME.
GOT ANY GOOD REASONS WHY I SHOULDN'T?
WELL, TO BEGIN WITH, YOU HAVE NO WEAPONS.
YEAH, BUT I'VE SEEN EVERY JACKIE CHAN MOVIE AND HI-KARATE COMMERCIAL EVER MADE!
AND SECOND OF ALL...I MEAN THE CHILD NO HARM.
INDEED, I FULLY EXPECT HE WILL ONE DAY BECOME THE HEART, SOUL AND SAVIOR OF THIS ENTIRE PLANET!
WITH YOU AS HIS FATHER?

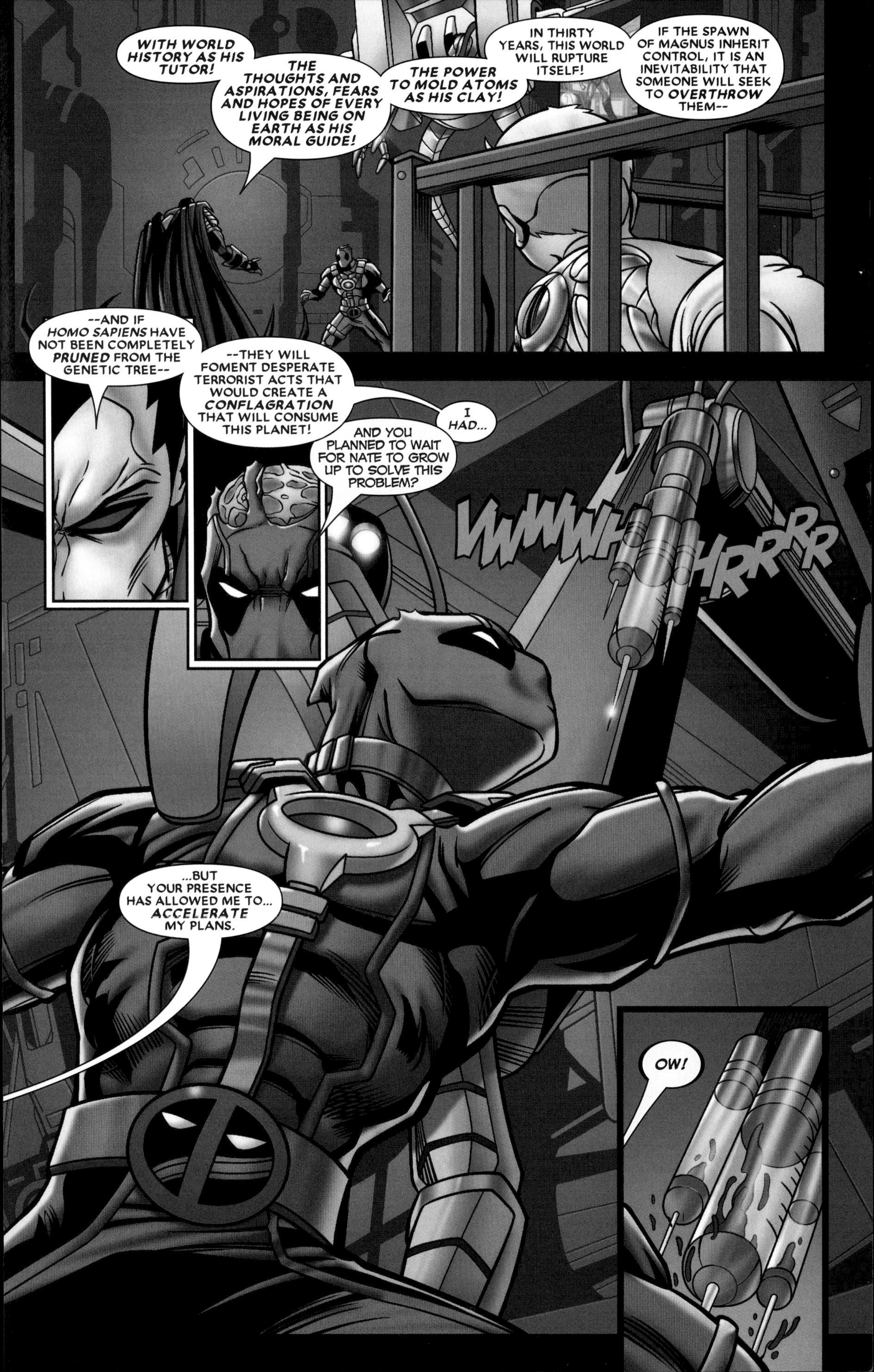
WITH WORLD HISTORY AS HIS TUTOR!
THE THOUGHTS AND ASPIRATIONS, FEARS AND HOPES OF EVERY LIVING BEING ON EARTH AS HIS MORAL GUIDE!
THE POWER TO MOLD ATOMS AS HIS CLAY!
IN THIRTY YEARS, THIS WORLD WILL RUPTURE ITSELF!
IF THE SPAWN OF MAGNUS INHERIT CONTROL, IT IS AN INEVITABILITY THAT SOMEONE WILL SEEK TO OVERTHROW THEM--
--AND IF HOMO SAPIENS HAVE NOT BEEN COMPLETELY PRUNED FROM THE GENETIC TREE--
--THEY WILL FOMENT DESPERATE TERRORIST ACTS THAT WOULD CREATE A CONFLAGRATION THAT WILL CONSUME THIS PLANET!
I HAD...
AND YOU PLANNED TO WAIT FOR NATE TO GROW UP TO SOLVE THIS PROBLEM?
VWWWHHRRRR
...BUT YOUR PRESENCE HAS ALLOWED ME TO... ACCELERATE MY PLANS.
OW!

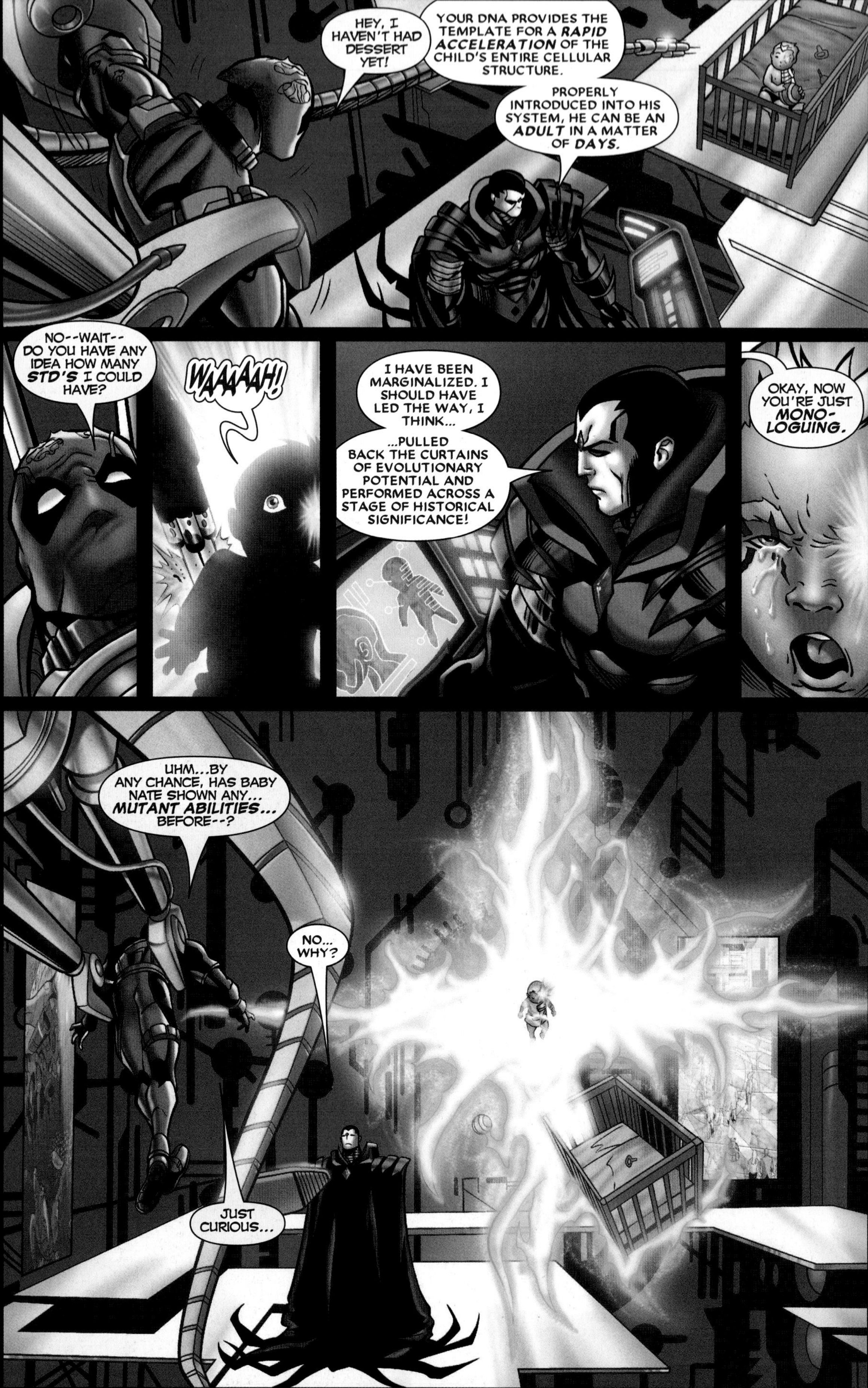
HEY, I HAVEN'T HAD DESSERT YET!
YOUR DNA PROVIDES THE TEMPLATE FOR A RAPID ACCELERATION OF THE CHILD'S ENTIRE CELLULAR STRUCTURE.
PROPERLY INTRODUCED INTO HIS SYSTEM, HE CAN BE AN ADULT IN A MATTER OF DAYS.
NO--WAIT-- DO YOU HAVE ANY IDEA HOW MANY STD'S I COULD HAVE?
WAAAAAH!
I HAVE BEEN MARGINALIZED. I SHOULD HAVE LED THE WAY, I THINK...
...PULLED BACK THE CURTAINS OF EVOLUTIONARY POTENTIAL AND PERFORMED ACROSS A STAGE OF HISTORICAL SIGNIFICANCE!
OKAY, NOW YOU'RE JUST MONO-LOGUING.
UHM...BY ANY CHANCE, HAS BABY NATE SHOWN ANY... MUTANT ABILITIES... BEFORE--?
NO... WHY?
JUST CURIOUS...

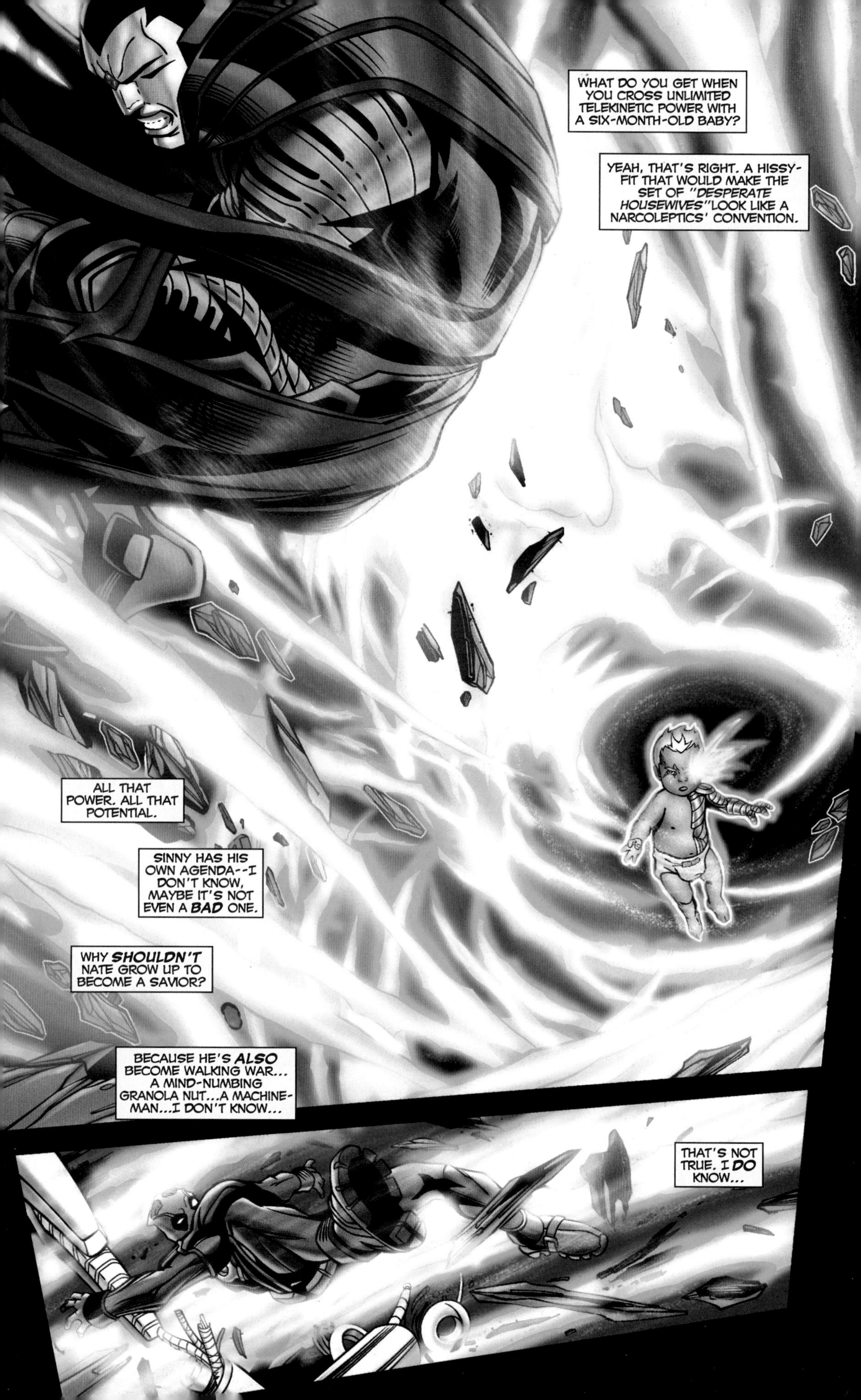
WHAT DO YOU GET WHEN YOU CROSS UNLIMITED TELEKINETIC POWER WITH A SIX-MONTH-OLD BABY?
YEAH, THAT'S RIGHT. A HISSY-FIT THAT WOULD MAKE THE SET OF "DESPERATE HOUSEWIVES" LOOK LIKE A NARCOLEPTICS' CONVENTION.
ALL THAT POWER. ALL THAT POTENTIAL.
SINNY HAS HIS OWN AGENDA--I DON'T KNOW, MAYBE IT'S NOT EVEN A BAD ONE.
WHY SHOULDN'T NATE GROW UP TO BECOME A SAVIOR?
BECAUSE HE'S ALSO BECOME WALKING WAR... A MIND-NUMBING GRANOLA NUT...A MACHINE-MAN...I DON'T KNOW...
THAT'S NOT TRUE. I DO KNOW...

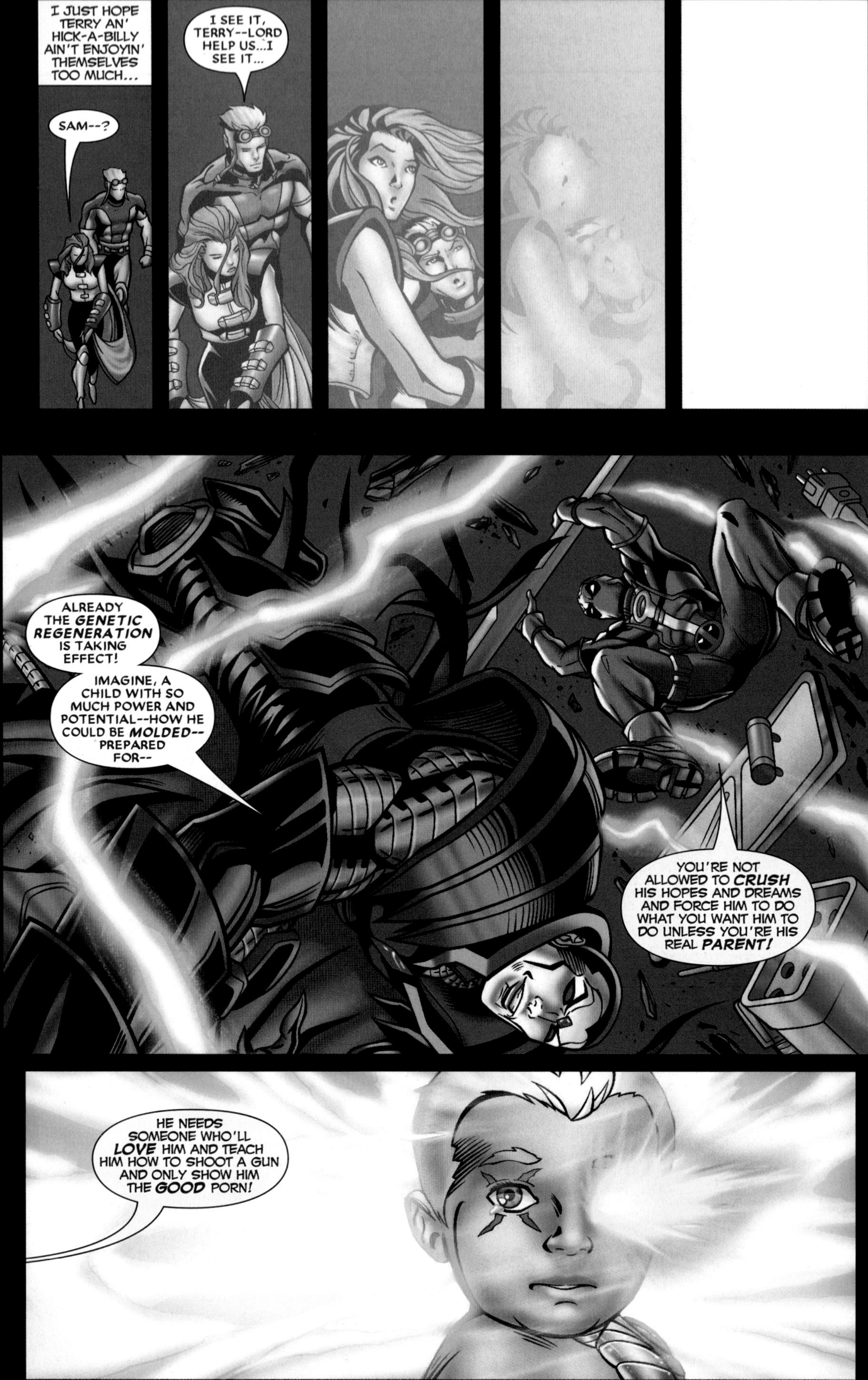
I JUST HOPE TERRY AN' HICK-A-BILLY AIN'T ENJOYIN' THEMSELVES TOO MUCH...
SAM--?
I SEE IT, TERRY--LORD HELP US...I SEE IT...
ALREADY THE GENETIC REGENERATION IS TAKING EFFECT!
IMAGINE, A CHILD WITH SO MUCH POWER AND POTENTIAL--HOW HE COULD BE MOLDED--PREPARED FOR--
YOU'RE NOT ALLOWED TO CRUSH HIS HOPES AND DREAMS AND FORCE HIM TO DO WHAT YOU WANT HIM TO DO UNLESS YOU'RE HIS REAL PARENT!
HE NEEDS SOMEONE WHO'LL LOVE HIM AND TEACH HIM HOW TO SHOOT A GUN AND ONLY SHOW HIM THE GOOD PORN!

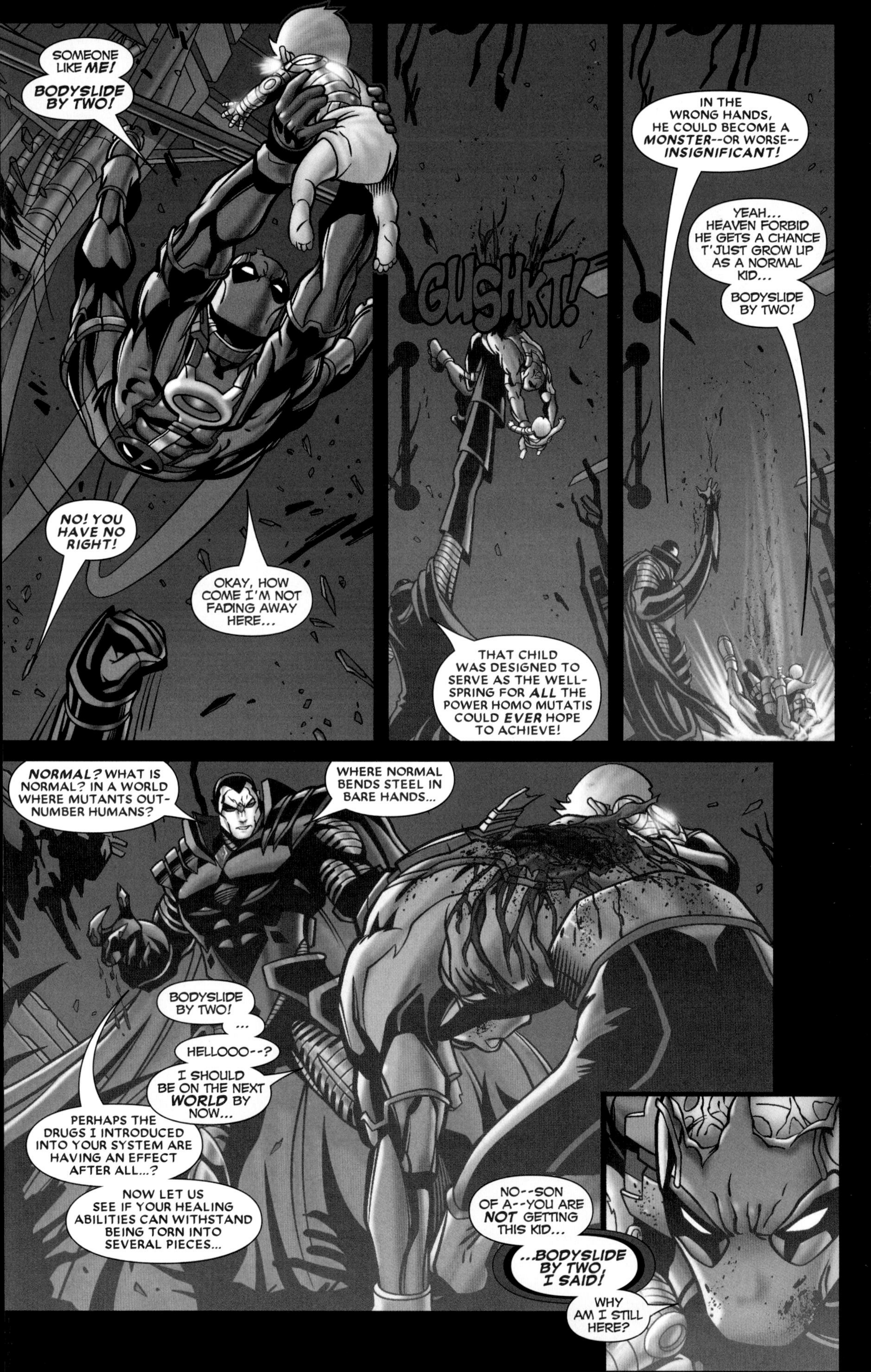
SOMEONE LIKE ME! BODYSLIDE BY TWO!
NO! YOU HAVE NO RIGHT!
OKAY, HOW COME I'M NOT FADING AWAY HERE...
GUSHKT!
THAT CHILD WAS DESIGNED TO SERVE AS THE WELL-SPRING FOR ALL THE POWER HOMO MUTATIS COULD EVER HOPE TO ACHIEVE!
IN THE WRONG HANDS, HE COULD BECOME A MONSTER--OR WORSE--INSIGNIFICANT!
YEAH... HEAVEN FORBID HE GETS A CHANCE T'JUST GROW UP AS A NORMAL KID...
BODYSLIDE BY TWO!
NORMAL? WHAT IS NORMAL? IN A WORLD WHERE MUTANTS OUT-NUMBER HUMANS?
WHERE NORMAL BENDS STEEL IN BARE HANDS...
BODYSLIDE BY TWO!
...
HELLOOO--?
I SHOULD BE ON THE NEXT WORLD BY NOW...
PERHAPS THE DRUGS I INTRODUCED INTO YOUR SYSTEM ARE HAVING AN EFFECT AFTER ALL...?
NOW LET US SEE IF YOUR HEALING ABILITIES CAN WITHSTAND BEING TORN INTO SEVERAL PIECES...
NO--SON OF A--YOU ARE NOT GETTING THIS KID...
...BODYSLIDE BY TWO, I SAID!
WHY AM I STILL HERE?

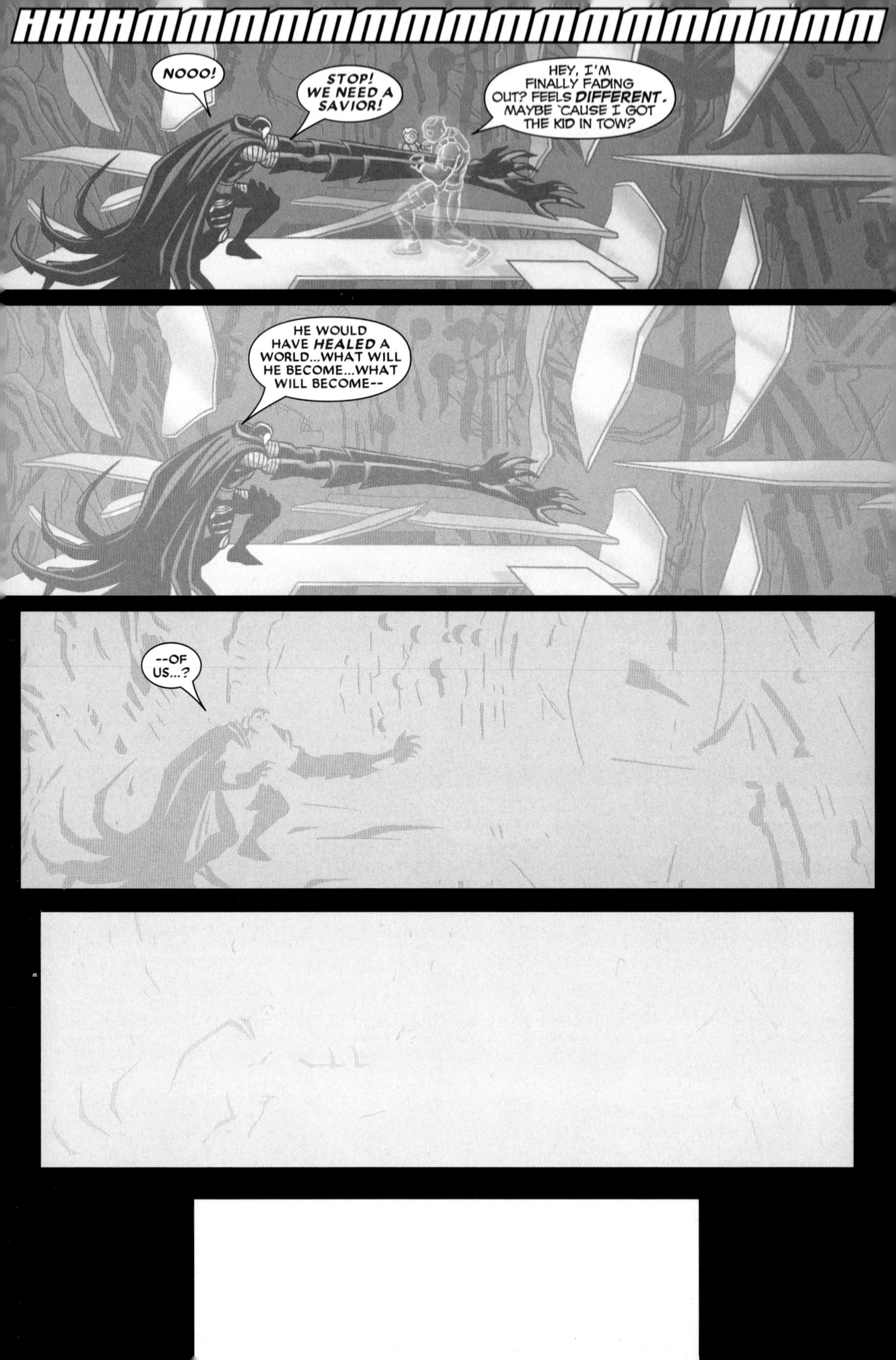
HHHHMMMMMMMMMMMMMMMMMMMMM
NOOO!
STOP! WE NEED A SAVIOR!
HEY, I'M FINALLY FADING OUT? FEELS DIFFERENT. MAYBE 'CAUSE I GOT THE KID IN TOW?
HE WOULD HAVE HEALED A WORLD...WHAT WILL HE BECOME...WHAT WILL BECOME--
--OF US...?

DEAR DEADPOOL

So you know what Cable says to me? He says, "How come I never get to answer the letters?" You know what I say? I say, "Cause you're duller than *Star Trek: Enterprise.*"

That one stung. Even time-traveling potential messiahs don't deserve that world of harsh. I'll apologize later. Anyway, here's what you mooks had to say...

Dear Deadpool,

Okay, I've been a huge fan of yours since I was like twelve (what does that say about my stability?). I just read the new *C&DP*, and I wanted to ask you a few questions.

1) So, Siryn's back. I know you two sort of had a thing there, any plans on rekindling that? Take it to the next level maybe? And if not, you think you could ask her if I can have her number?

2) Since Cable's all off in other universes (and if he doesn't come back then you can have the series all to yourself) you think you could ask the lovely Ms. Merryweather if I could get her number?

3) Have you ever heard a song you really liked, then heard a remix of that song that was really good? And then you go back and listen to the original and it just sounds... weak? Doesn't that annoy you?

4) With your healing factor, do you have to floss?

5) Who do you think should play you in the movie? Who should play Weasel?

6) Regarding Miss Ann Nichols (she had a letter in the last issue), do you think you could ask her if I could get her number? (It's so hard to find nice girls who read comics, most of them I have to restrain and read to. Usually there's pudding involved.)

Anyway, I love the series, I loved the last issue. The guest stars are great, as always (Forge? Where's he been?), tell Cannonballs to cut down on the burritos (or is that joke old? I just wanted a chance to call him Cannonballs, cuz that's a way better name). Also, I think you should replace your letters column with a Dear Abby sort of thing, you'd totally put Dr. Phil out of business.

I'll be first in line for my WWDPD? t-shirt.

Brendan H.

Ooh, numbered questions! Cool.

1)I would like to rekindle Siryn. I would like to take our relationship to the next level, which would be nude Stratego. And yes, I can give you her number, then I'd cut off your tongue so you couldn't talk to her! HA!

2)You can not only have Irene's number, but I'll tie her up and deliver her anywhere you want me to. Free of charge.

3)You know what annoys me, you kids today remaking all the classics of yesterday! What next? A remix of Kajagoogoo's Greatest Hit? Sinners all of you.

4)Even with my enhanced healing metabolism, Brendan, I do have to floss, that's why I wear a thong.

5)I should play me in the movie! Who else
could grasp the wonder that is me? I heard that Ryan Reynolds kid was interested, but you ask me, he's a flash in the pan. And Weasel won't be in my movie `cause he owes me money and a burrito.

6)Hmmm... pudding...

Ask Deadpool,

Why? I don't understand why. I don't like Deadpool. The Merc with a Mouth has always just been an annoying, murder-happy character. He's nothing I care for. I'm not a huge fan of Cable. He's too much rooted into the guns blazing, ends justifies the means era of comics. So why is *C & DP* my favorite comic currently in print? Why do I have to read this comic, laugh out loud at the humor, smile happily at the continuity references, and enjoy the plot? Then I have to read the issue again. The art is great. The stories are fun. The humor is awesome. And best yet, Fabian is shown to be a true fan of the Marvel Universe. Fabian takes the continuity that is there, he takes the characters as who they are, and he starts the story from there. It's engaging. It's interesting. It's fantastic. He can take characters I don't even care for and make them interesting without obliterating who they were before. That's skill. Thanks for some great comics guys, keep up the good work.

Josh Wilhoyte

Okay, before you start lathering hot massage oil all over Nicieza, I got one word for you: Revanche. `Nuff Said, nimrod.

Now I got a question for you: Why ask why? Nicole says the only way we're gonna get more than 10 readers is if everyone out there who ain't readin' the book stops tryin' to come up with reasons why they won't like it or shouldn't read it, no matter how many times they've heard it's Tony the Tiger GRRRRREAT.

Dear Team,

Wow. Great series, one of the few that I actually smile while opening up. And you know why I'm smiling when I open it up? Because I know what to expect. Ever since "The Burnt Offering" blew my mind, I've been nothing but impressed with this AMAZING title. I hope it stays around forever and ever. And now, numbered questions!

1) What other guest stars do we have to look forward to in the future? Any web-slingers or flag wavers?

2) When Cable does come back from whenever/whatever he's disappeared to, how radically changed will he be?

3) How much will all this House of M nonsense affect my FAVORITE book?

4) How do you say Fabian's last name? I've been wondering for years now.

That should be all for now. Please keep up the stellar (rod) job, it inspires as a reader to know there's still quality out there, and as a writer to better myself.

James Lewis Tyler

Heh, heh – you said stellar rod. Ooh, numbered questions!
1)I heard Fabian and Patrick doin' a confab about how if we survive past #24, we might see a shield-slinging Avenger show up. I told them I don't want U.S. Agent in this book. I know for a fact that in a couple issues, it'll take an iron fist to put this power man down. Figure it out for yourself.

2)One word: Huggies.

3)It will affect us just as much as is necessary to increase our sales, you big dope!

4)Sin-kev-itch. Boo-seh-ma. Keh-sah-dah. Mag-neet-o. Sub-mah-ri-ner. Chi-mee-chahn-gah.

Dear Deadpool,

Nicole mentioned that she wanted to hear more from the ladies, which I am (well, maybe more of a good broad), with two little super hero loving daughters, and an extensive comic collection hidden in the depths of my sewing room. Anyhow, I want to tell the creative team that *C & DP* is the smartest, funniest, most enjoyable book that Marvel is producing. There's a lot of substance underneath all the hilarity.

And I have to say: I love Wade Wilson. Don't ask me why. Any attempt to analyze or explain it to myself confounds the limit of whatever brainpower I have, so I just roll with it. But I'd hang with him. Although we can forgo *Sleepless in Seattle,* it's not my cup of tea. Maybe the British version of *The Office.* We can sing along to "Free Love on the Free Love Freeway" and get all weepy over Dawn and Tim. It would be magic.

I tell everyone I know who reads comics to get this one. If it's ever cancelled, I may be so distraught that I may do something unseemly like turn a firehose on all the soccer moms. Come to think of it, I guess I could do that anyway just for kicks and giggles.

Fabian, Patrick, Nicole, great, great job you guys.

Lee Ann C.

Lee Ann, baby, you are my kind of lady! Comics in your sewing room? That's EXACTLY where I keep mine! Also, I got a very special firehose you can use on the soccer moms...

That's all for this month, folks. You mooks weren't too bad this time around. Couldn't justify abusing you all too much. Sorry. Need that extra cup of coffee, or some three hundred pound cable salesman from Phoenix to write in again.

Next issue, me an' Nate go suck some beers down at a cozy down-home bar and chit-chat about life and stuff. Some interesting Oprah and Dr. Phil moments will be revealed.

It's what we in the industry used to call, "a change of pace issue," but what most people nowadays consider the normal pace.

Then after that, the rip-snortin' *Bosom Buddies* story arc kicks into gear! Lots of stealin', lyin', cheatin' an' fightin' all over this bad-ass globe of ours! Featuring the B.A.D. Girls – Black Mamba, Asp an' Diamondback! Woo-hoo, that's like Implant City comin' down for a landing on my face! An' also some big surprises!

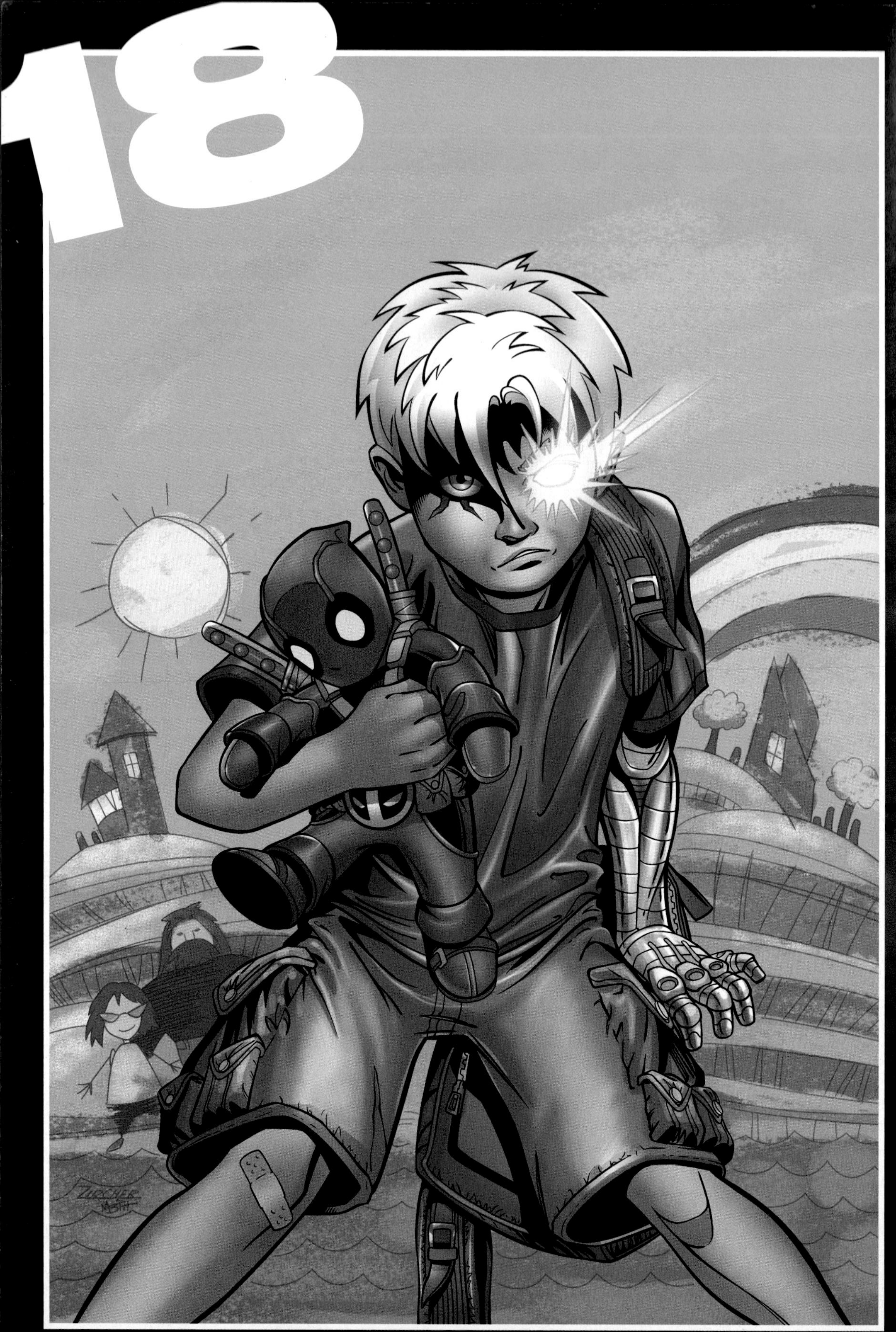
18
ZIRCHER

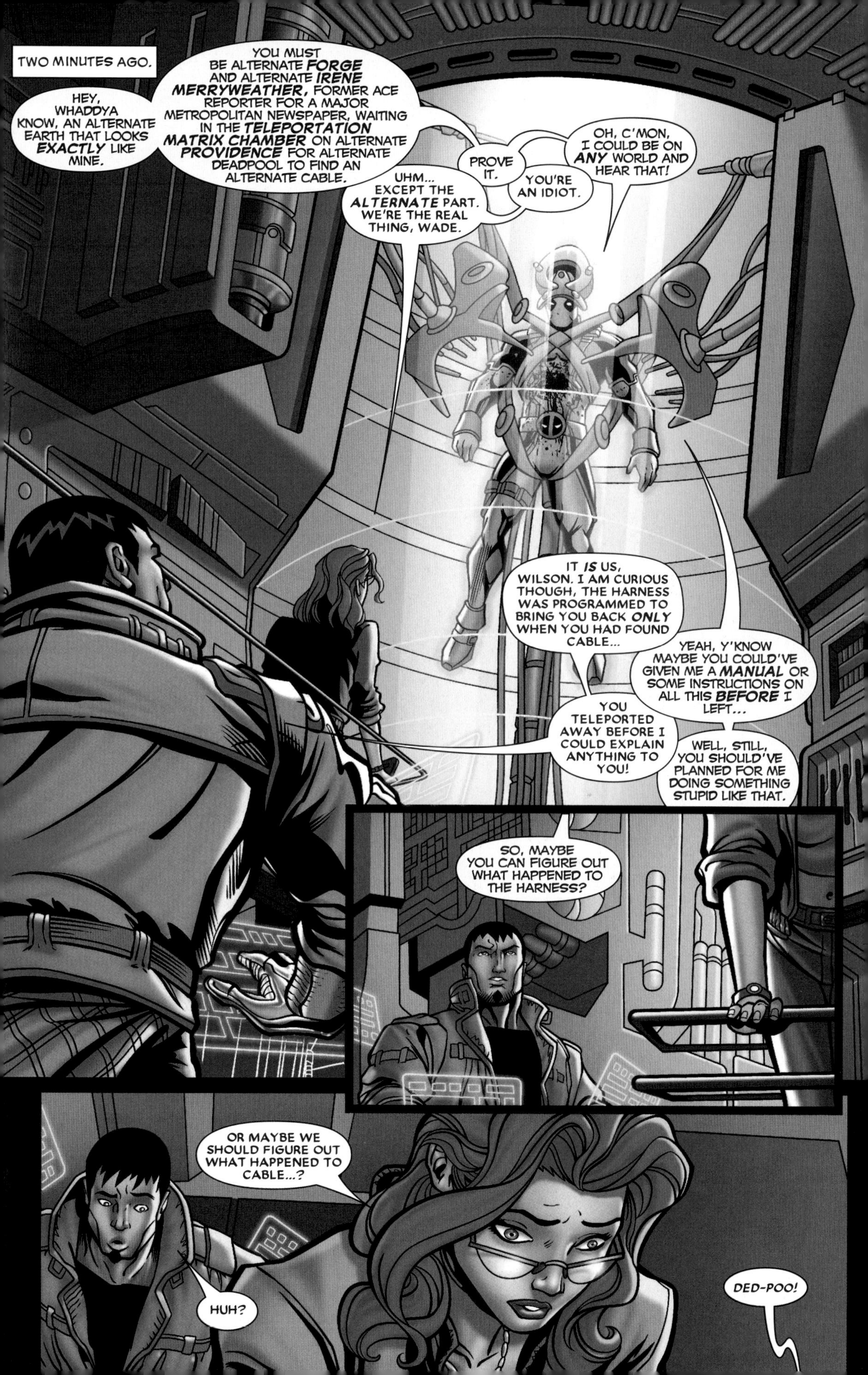
TWO MINUTES AGO.
HEY, WHADDYA KNOW, AN ALTERNATE EARTH THAT LOOKS EXACTLY LIKE MINE.
YOU MUST BE ALTERNATE FORGE AND ALTERNATE IRENE MERRYWEATHER, FORMER ACE REPORTER FOR A MAJOR METROPOLITAN NEWSPAPER, WAITING IN THE TELEPORTATION MATRIX CHAMBER ON ALTERNATE PROVIDENCE FOR ALTERNATE DEADPOOL TO FIND AN ALTERNATE CABLE.
UHM... EXCEPT THE ALTERNATE PART. WE'RE THE REAL THING, WADE.
PROVE IT.
YOU'RE AN IDIOT.
OH, C'MON, I COULD BE ON ANY WORLD AND HEAR THAT!
IT IS US, WILSON. I AM CURIOUS THOUGH, THE HARNESS WAS PROGRAMMED TO BRING YOU BACK ONLY WHEN YOU HAD FOUND CABLE...
YEAH, Y'KNOW MAYBE YOU COULD'VE GIVEN ME A MANUAL OR SOME INSTRUCTIONS ON ALL THIS BEFORE I LEFT...
YOU TELEPORTED AWAY BEFORE I COULD EXPLAIN ANYTHING TO YOU!
WELL, STILL, YOU SHOULD'VE PLANNED FOR ME DOING SOMETHING STUPID LIKE THAT.
SO, MAYBE YOU CAN FIGURE OUT WHAT HAPPENED TO THE HARNESS?
OR MAYBE WE SHOULD FIGURE OUT WHAT HAPPENED TO CABLE...?
HUH?
DED-POO!

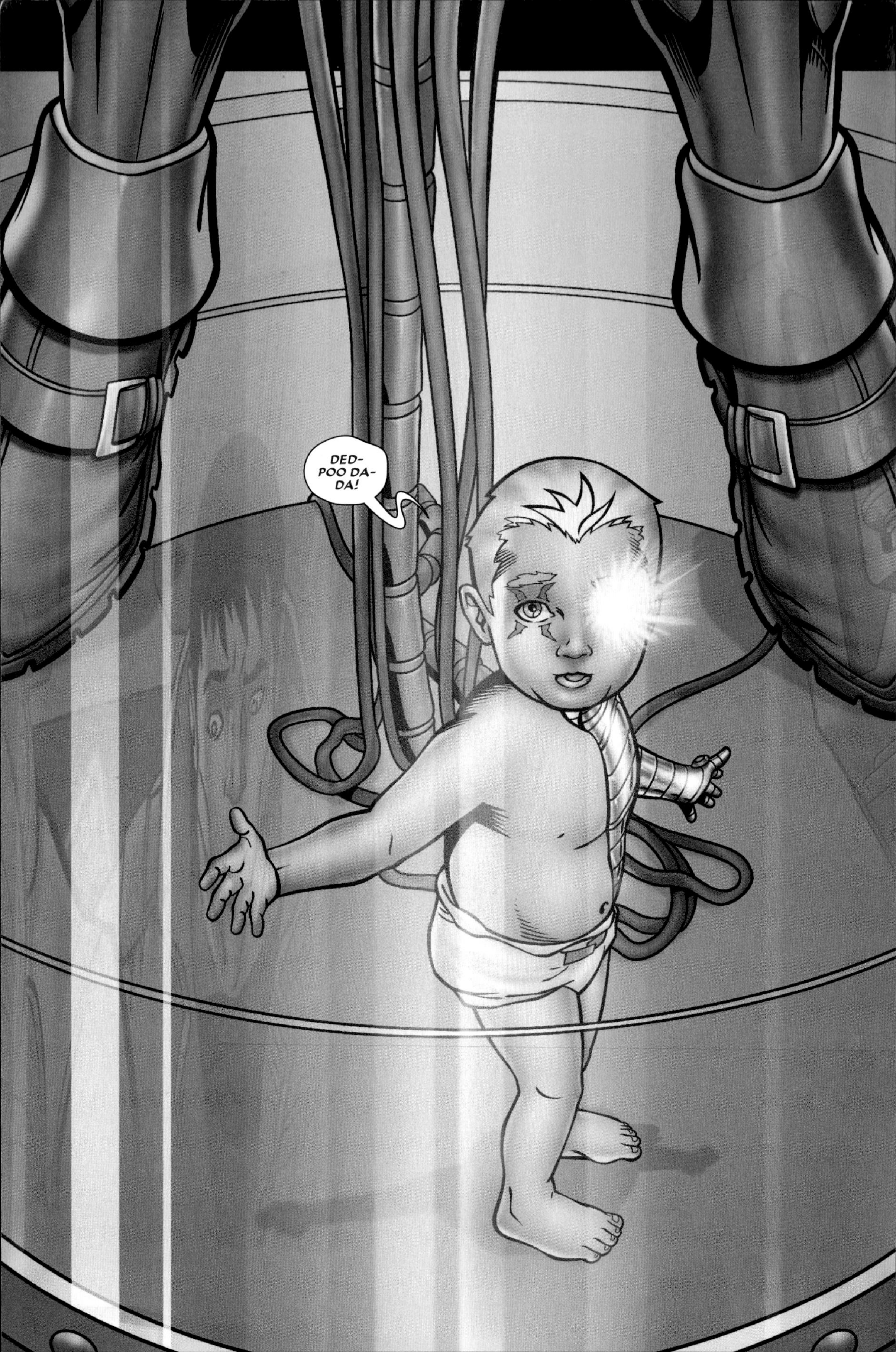
DED-POO DA-DA!

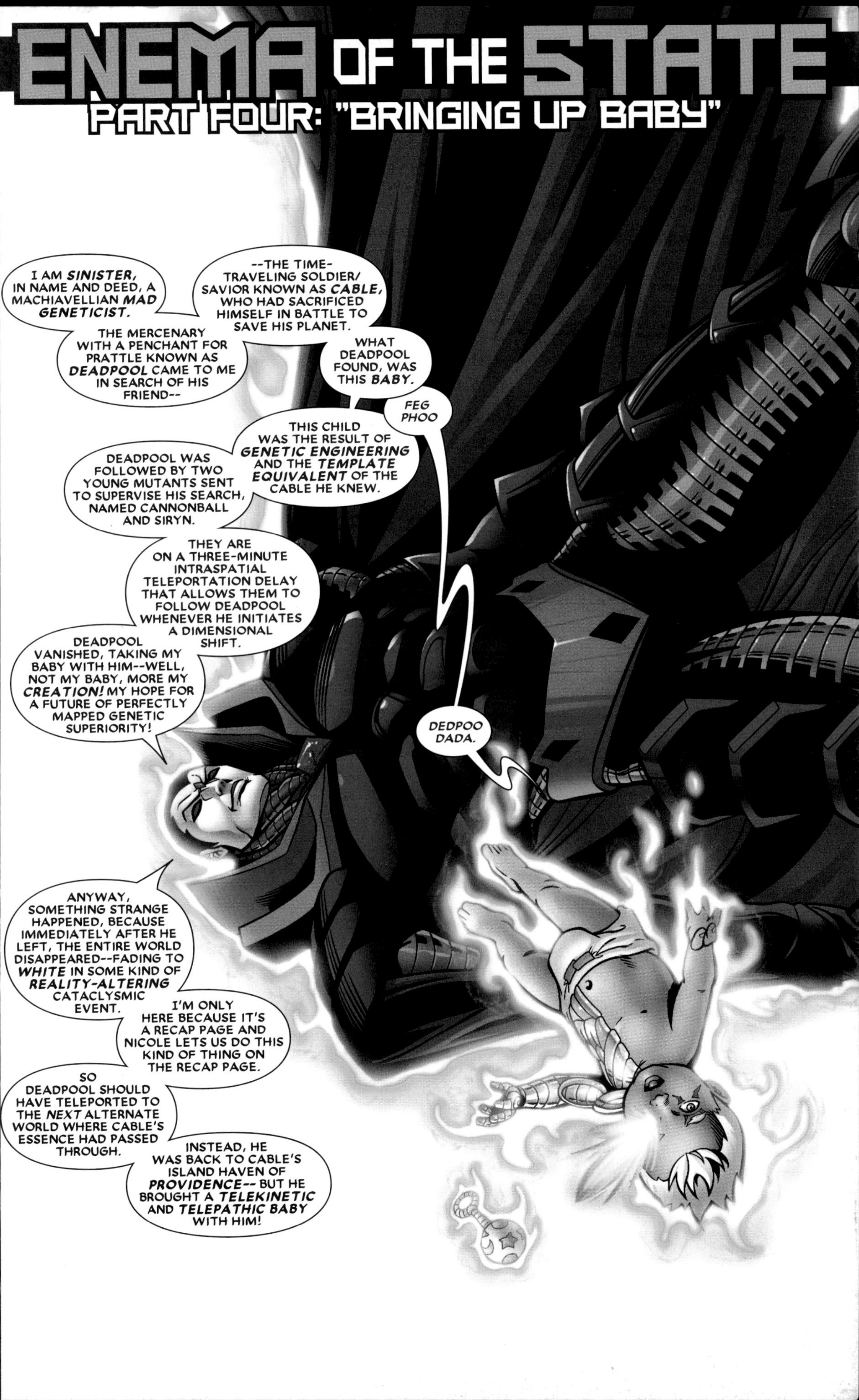

ENEMA OF THE STATE
PART FOUR: "BRINGING UP BABY"
I AM SINISTER, IN NAME AND DEED, A MACHIAVELLIAN MAD GENETICIST.
THE MERCENARY WITH A PENCHANT FOR PRATTLE KNOWN AS DEADPOOL CAME TO ME IN SEARCH OF HIS FRIEND--
--THE TIME-TRAVELING SOLDIER/ SAVIOR KNOWN AS CABLE, WHO HAD SACRIFICED HIMSELF IN BATTLE TO SAVE HIS PLANET.
WHAT DEADPOOL FOUND, WAS THIS BABY.
FEG PHOO
THIS CHILD WAS THE RESULT OF GENETIC ENGINEERING AND THE TEMPLATE EQUIVALENT OF THE CABLE HE KNEW.
DEADPOOL WAS FOLLOWED BY TWO YOUNG MUTANTS SENT TO SUPERVISE HIS SEARCH, NAMED CANNONBALL AND SIRYN.
THEY ARE ON A THREE-MINUTE INTRASPATIAL TELEPORTATION DELAY THAT ALLOWS THEM TO FOLLOW DEADPOOL WHENEVER HE INITIATES A DIMENSIONAL SHIFT.
DEADPOOL VANISHED, TAKING MY BABY WITH HIM--WELL, NOT MY BABY, MORE MY CREATION! MY HOPE FOR A FUTURE OF PERFECTLY MAPPED GENETIC SUPERIORITY!
DEDPOO DADA.
ANYWAY, SOMETHING STRANGE HAPPENED, BECAUSE IMMEDIATELY AFTER HE LEFT, THE ENTIRE WORLD DISAPPEARED--FADING TO WHITE IN SOME KIND OF REALITY-ALTERING CATACLYSMIC EVENT.
I'M ONLY HERE BECAUSE IT'S A RECAP PAGE AND NICOLE LETS US DO THIS KIND OF THING ON THE RECAP PAGE.
SO DEADPOOL SHOULD HAVE TELEPORTED TO THE NEXT ALTERNATE WORLD WHERE CABLE'S ESSENCE HAD PASSED THROUGH.
INSTEAD, HE WAS BACK TO CABLE'S ISLAND HAVEN OF PROVIDENCE-- BUT HE BROUGHT A TELEKINETIC AND TELEPATHIC BABY WITH HIM!

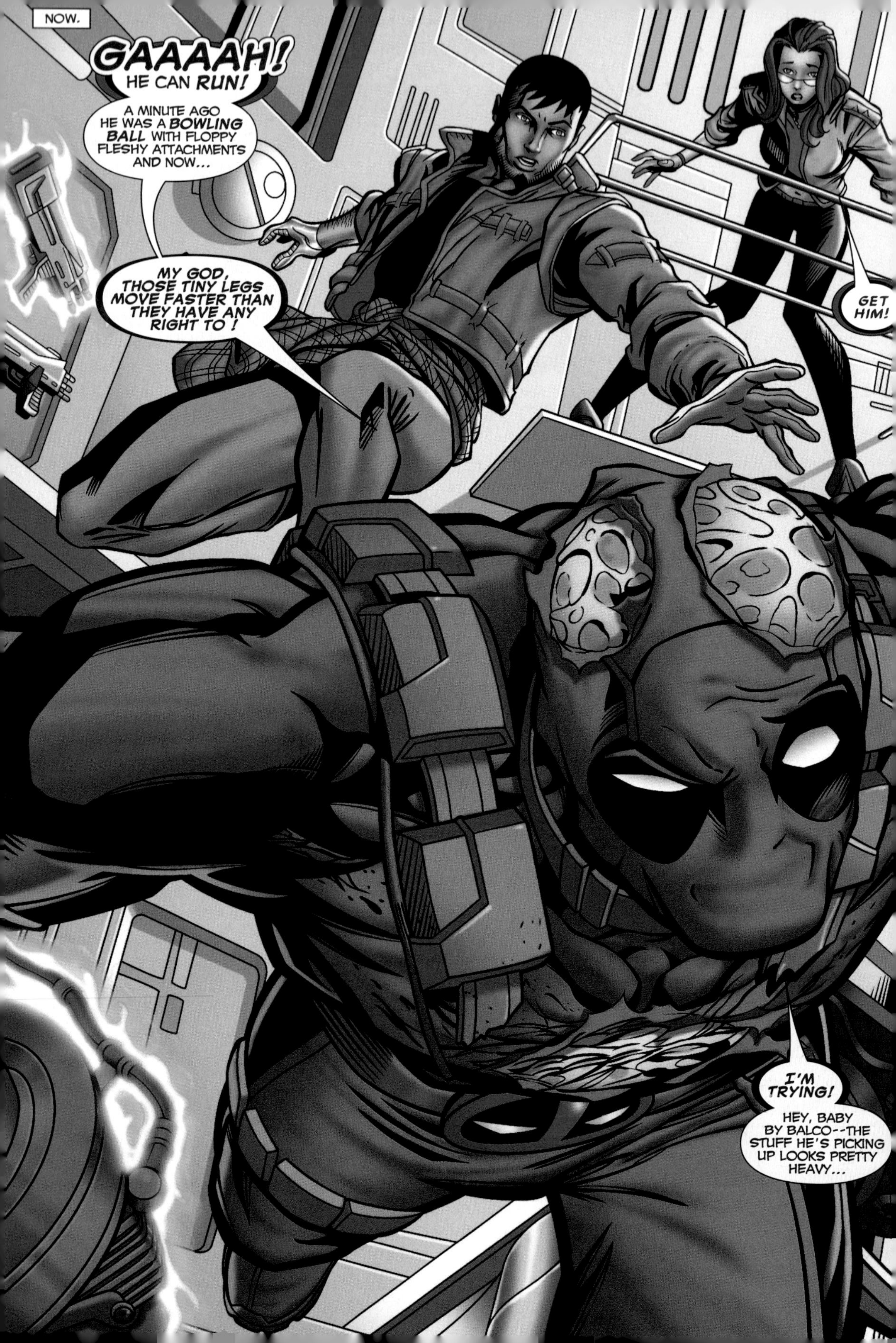
NOW.
GAAAAH! HE CAN RUN!
A MINUTE AGO HE WAS A BOWLING BALL WITH FLOPPY FLESHY ATTACHMENTS AND NOW...
MY GOD, THOSE TINY LEGS MOVE FASTER THAN THEY HAVE ANY RIGHT TO!
GET HIM!
I'M TRYING!
HEY, BABY BY BALCO--THE STUFF HE'S PICKING UP LOOKS PRETTY HEAVY...

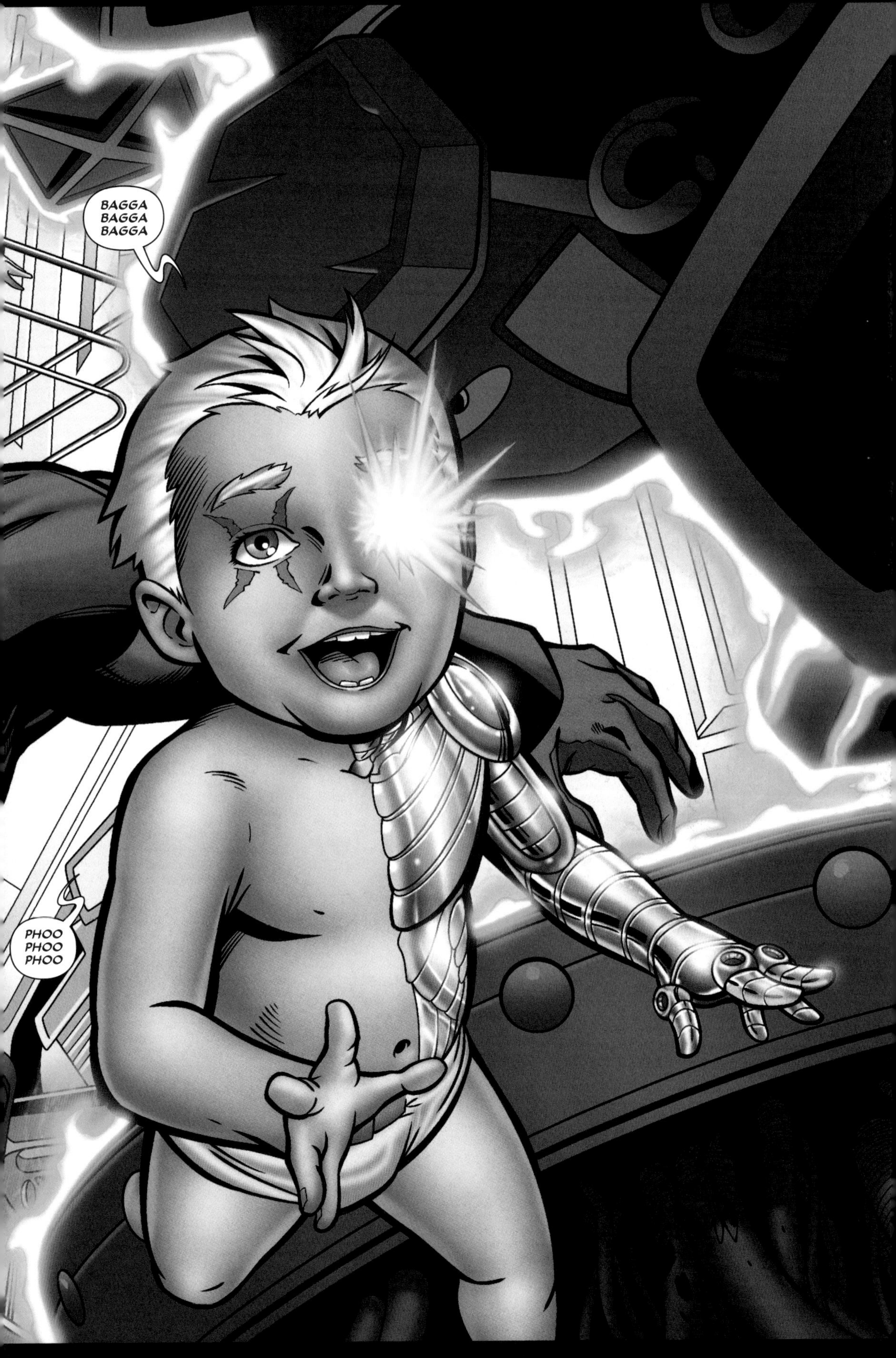
BAGGA BAGGA BAGGA
PHOO PHOO PHOO

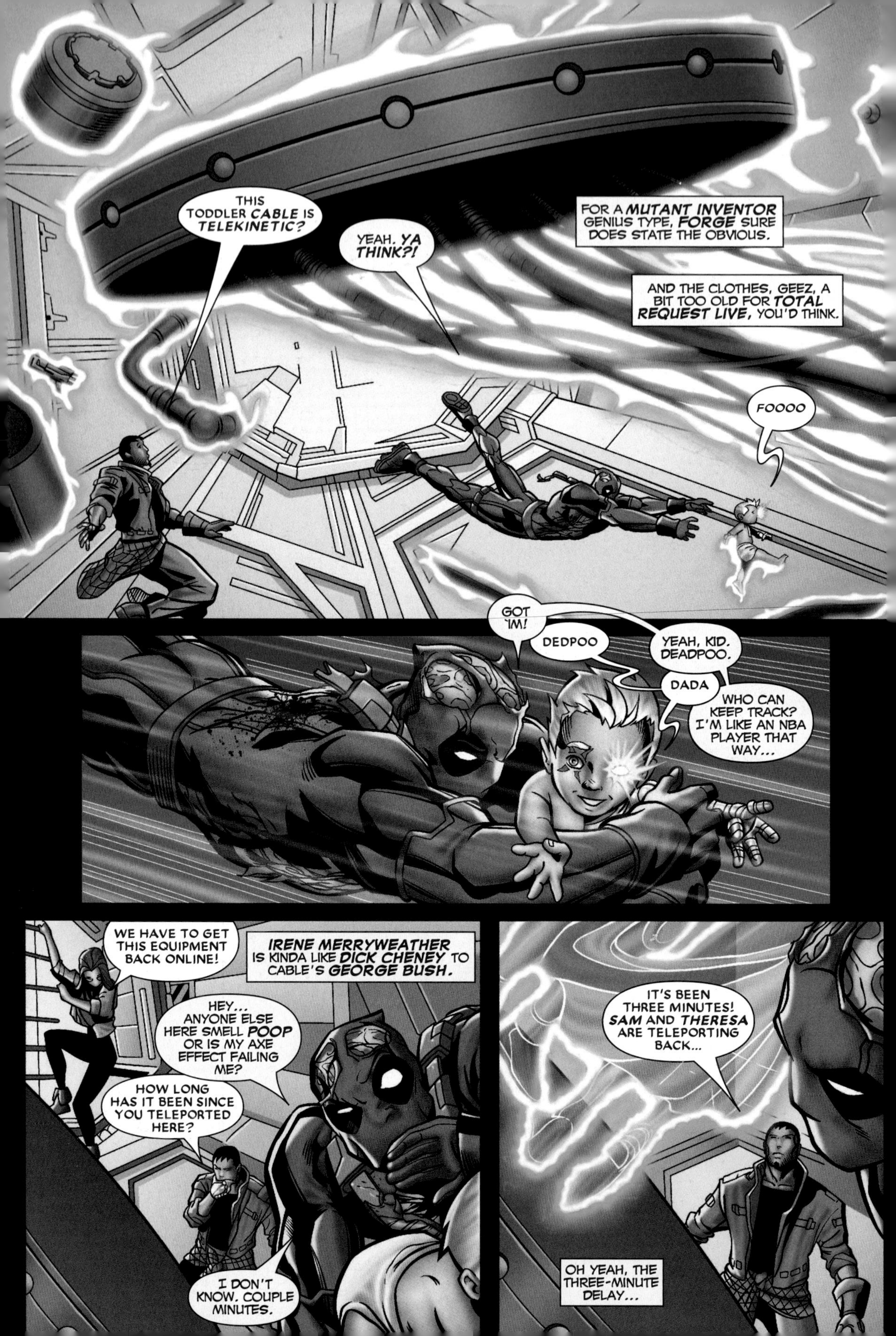
THIS TODDLER CABLE IS TELEKINETIC?
YEAH. YA THINK?!
FOR A MUTANT INVENTOR GENIUS TYPE, FORGE SURE DOES STATE THE OBVIOUS.
AND THE CLOTHES, GEEZ, A BIT TOO OLD FOR TOTAL REQUEST LIVE, YOU'D THINK.
FOOOO
GOT 'IM!
DEDPOO
YEAH, KID. DEADPOO.
DADA
WHO CAN KEEP TRACK? I'M LIKE AN NBA PLAYER THAT WAY...
WE HAVE TO GET THIS EQUIPMENT BACK ONLINE!
IRENE MERRYWEATHER IS KINDA LIKE DICK CHENEY TO CABLE'S GEORGE BUSH.
HEY... ANYONE ELSE HERE SMELL POOP OR IS MY AXE EFFECT FAILING ME?
HOW LONG HAS IT BEEN SINCE YOU TELEPORTED HERE?
I DON'T KNOW. COUPLE MINUTES.
IT'S BEEN THREE MINUTES! SAM AND THERESA ARE TELEPORTING BACK...
OH YEAH, THE THREE-MINUTE DELAY...

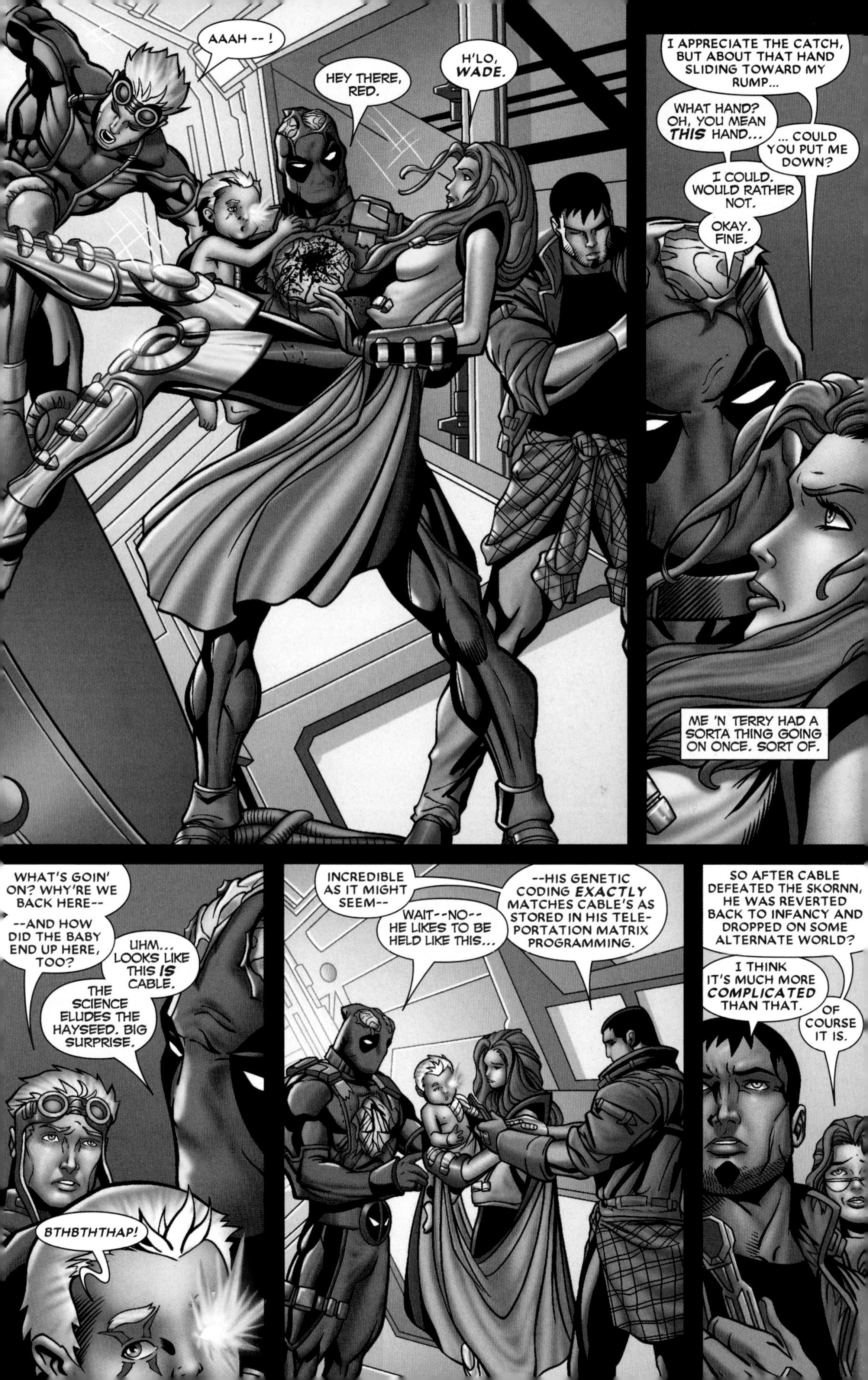
AAAH -- !
HEY THERE, RED.
H'LO, WADE.
I APPRECIATE THE CATCH, BUT ABOUT THAT HAND SLIDING TOWARD MY RUMP...
WHAT HAND? OH, YOU MEAN THIS HAND...
... COULD YOU PUT ME DOWN?
I COULD. WOULD RATHER NOT.
OKAY. FINE.
ME 'N TERRY HAD A SORTA THING GOING ON ONCE. SORT OF.
WHAT'S GOIN' ON? WHY'RE WE BACK HERE--
--AND HOW DID THE BABY END UP HERE, TOO?
UHM... LOOKS LIKE THIS IS CABLE.
THE SCIENCE ELUDES THE HAYSEED. BIG SURPRISE.
BTHBTHTHAP!
INCREDIBLE AS IT MIGHT SEEM--
WAIT--NO-- HE LIKES TO BE HELD LIKE THIS...
--HIS GENETIC CODING EXACTLY MATCHES CABLE'S AS STORED IN HIS TELE-PORTATION MATRIX PROGRAMMING.
SO AFTER CABLE DEFEATED THE SKORNN, HE WAS REVERTED BACK TO INFANCY AND DROPPED ON SOME ALTERNATE WORLD?
I THINK IT'S MUCH MORE COMPLICATED THAN THAT.
OF COURSE IT IS.

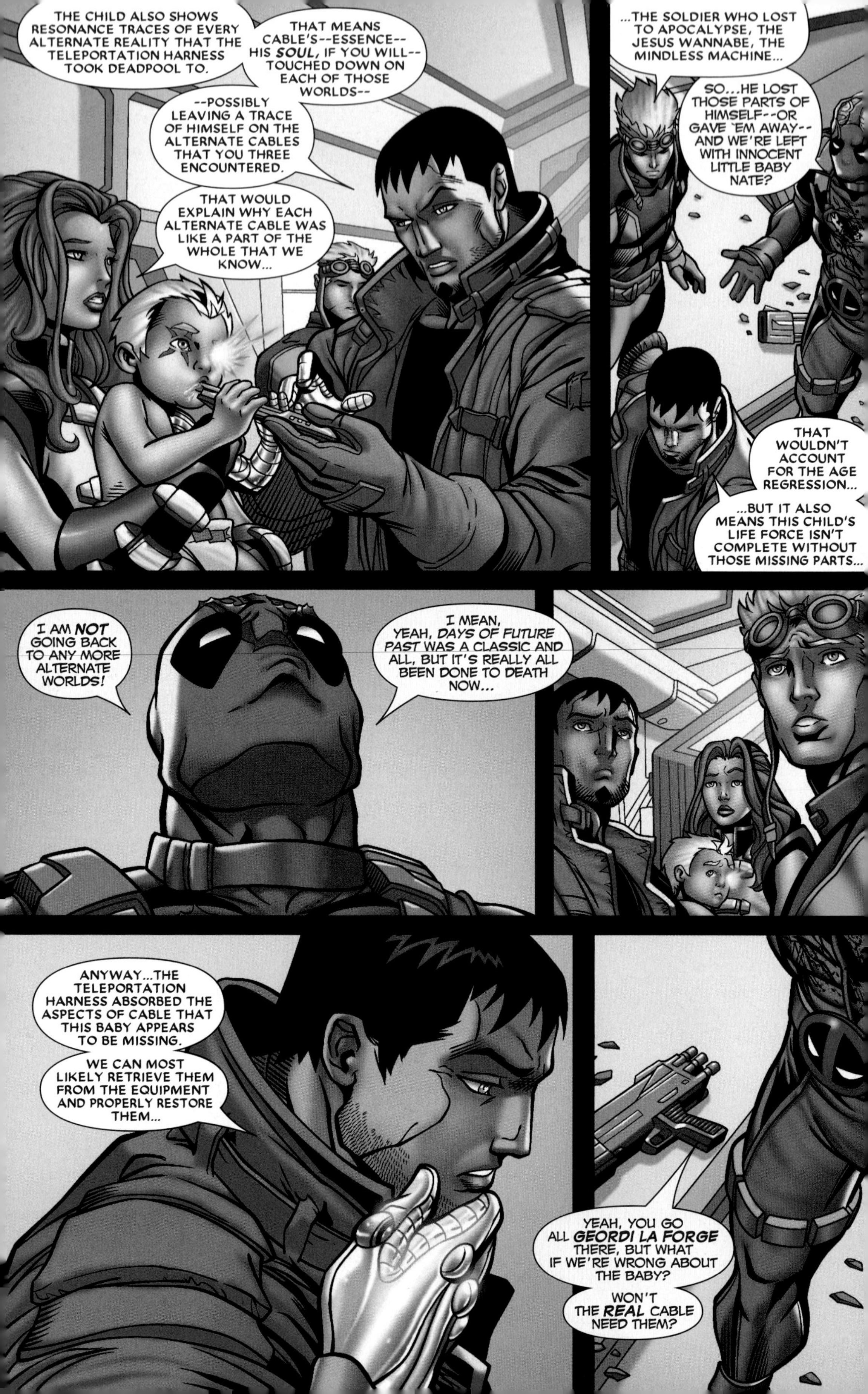
THE CHILD ALSO SHOWS RESONANCE TRACES OF EVERY ALTERNATE REALITY THAT THE TELEPORTATION HARNESS TOOK DEADPOOL TO.
THAT MEANS CABLE'S--ESSENCE--HIS SOUL, IF YOU WILL--TOUCHED DOWN ON EACH OF THOSE WORLDS--
--POSSIBLY LEAVING A TRACE OF HIMSELF ON THE ALTERNATE CABLES THAT YOU THREE ENCOUNTERED.
THAT WOULD EXPLAIN WHY EACH ALTERNATE CABLE WAS LIKE A PART OF THE WHOLE THAT WE KNOW...
...THE SOLDIER WHO LOST TO APOCALYPSE, THE JESUS WANNABE, THE MINDLESS MACHINE...
SO...HE LOST THOSE PARTS OF HIMSELF--OR GAVE 'EM AWAY--AND WE'RE LEFT WITH INNOCENT LITTLE BABY NATE?
THAT WOULDN'T ACCOUNT FOR THE AGE REGRESSION...
...BUT IT ALSO MEANS THIS CHILD'S LIFE FORCE ISN'T COMPLETE WITHOUT THOSE MISSING PARTS...
I AM NOT GOING BACK TO ANY MORE ALTERNATE WORLDS!
I MEAN, YEAH, DAYS OF FUTURE PAST WAS A CLASSIC AND ALL, BUT IT'S REALLY ALL BEEN DONE TO DEATH NOW...
ANYWAY...THE TELEPORTATION HARNESS ABSORBED THE ASPECTS OF CABLE THAT THIS BABY APPEARS TO BE MISSING.
WE CAN MOST LIKELY RETRIEVE THEM FROM THE EQUIPMENT AND PROPERLY RESTORE THEM...
YEAH, YOU GO ALL GEORDI LA FORGE THERE, BUT WHAT IF WE'RE WRONG ABOUT THE BABY?
WON'T THE REAL CABLE NEED THEM?

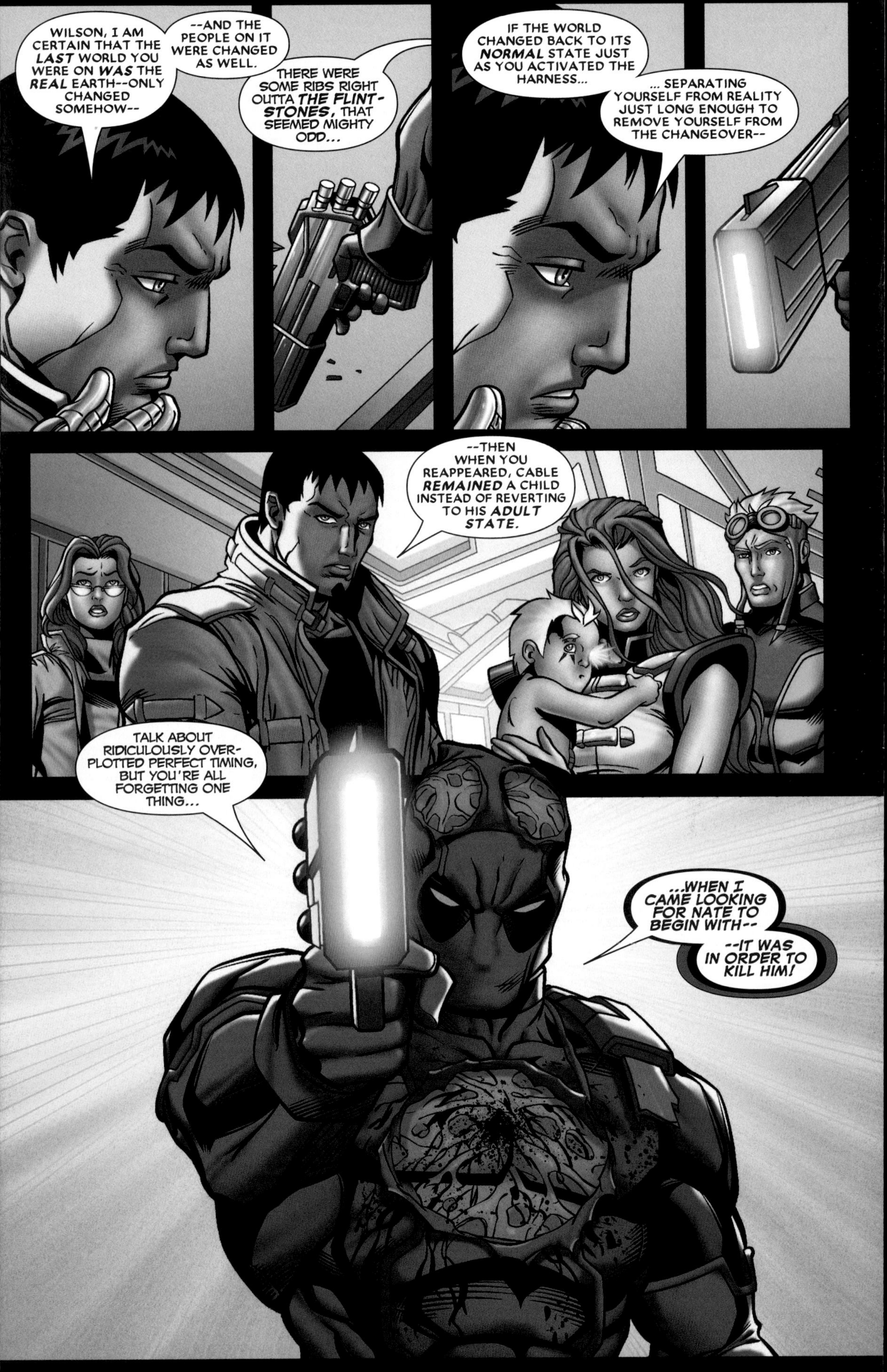
WILSON, I AM CERTAIN THAT THE LAST WORLD YOU WERE ON WAS THE REAL EARTH--ONLY CHANGED SOMEHOW--
--AND THE PEOPLE ON IT WERE CHANGED AS WELL.
THERE WERE SOME RIBS RIGHT OUTTA THE FLINT-STONES, THAT SEEMED MIGHTY ODD...
IF THE WORLD CHANGED BACK TO ITS NORMAL STATE JUST AS YOU ACTIVATED THE HARNESS...
... SEPARATING YOURSELF FROM REALITY JUST LONG ENOUGH TO REMOVE YOURSELF FROM THE CHANGEOVER--
--THEN WHEN YOU REAPPEARED, CABLE REMAINED A CHILD INSTEAD OF REVERTING TO HIS ADULT STATE.
TALK ABOUT RIDICULOUSLY OVER-PLOTTED PERFECT TIMING, BUT YOU'RE ALL FORGETTING ONE THING...
...WHEN I CAME LOOKING FOR NATE TO BEGIN WITH--
--IT WAS IN ORDER TO KILL HIM!

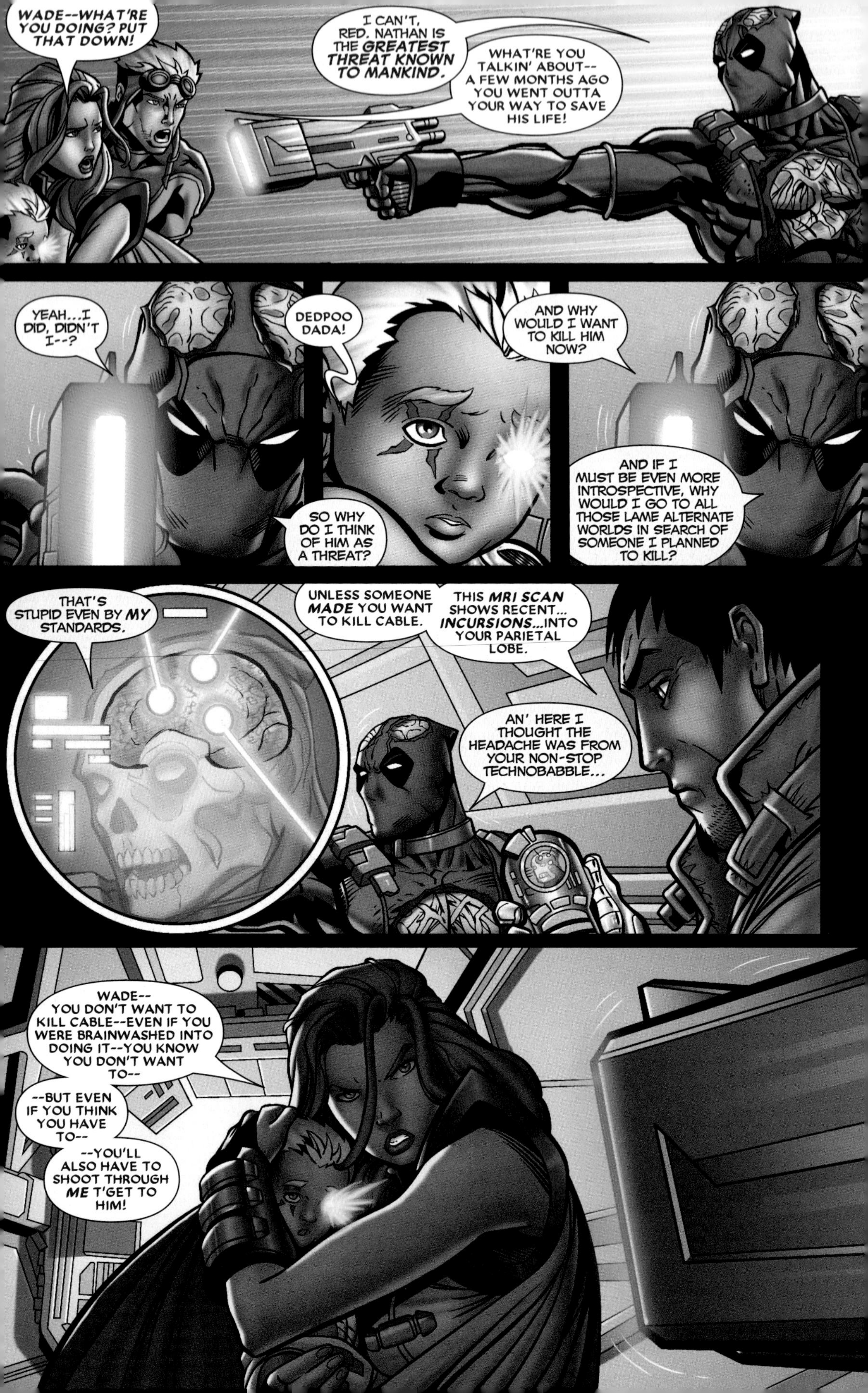
WADE--WHAT'RE YOU DOING? PUT THAT DOWN!
I CAN'T, RED. NATHAN IS THE GREATEST THREAT KNOWN TO MANKIND.
WHAT'RE YOU TALKIN' ABOUT-- A FEW MONTHS AGO YOU WENT OUTTA YOUR WAY TO SAVE HIS LIFE!
YEAH...I DID, DIDN'T I--?
SO WHY DO I THINK OF HIM AS A THREAT?
DEDPOO DADA!
AND WHY WOULD I WANT TO KILL HIM NOW?
AND IF I MUST BE EVEN MORE INTROSPECTIVE, WHY WOULD I GO TO ALL THOSE LAME ALTERNATE WORLDS IN SEARCH OF SOMEONE I PLANNED TO KILL?
THAT'S STUPID EVEN BY MY STANDARDS.
UNLESS SOMEONE MADE YOU WANT TO KILL CABLE.
THIS MRI SCAN SHOWS RECENT... INCURSIONS...INTO YOUR PARIETAL LOBE.
AN' HERE I THOUGHT THE HEADACHE WAS FROM YOUR NON-STOP TECHNOBABBLE...
WADE-- YOU DON'T WANT TO KILL CABLE--EVEN IF YOU WERE BRAINWASHED INTO DOING IT--YOU KNOW YOU DON'T WANT TO--
--BUT EVEN IF YOU THINK YOU HAVE TO--
--YOU'LL ALSO HAVE TO SHOOT THROUGH ME T'GET TO HIM!

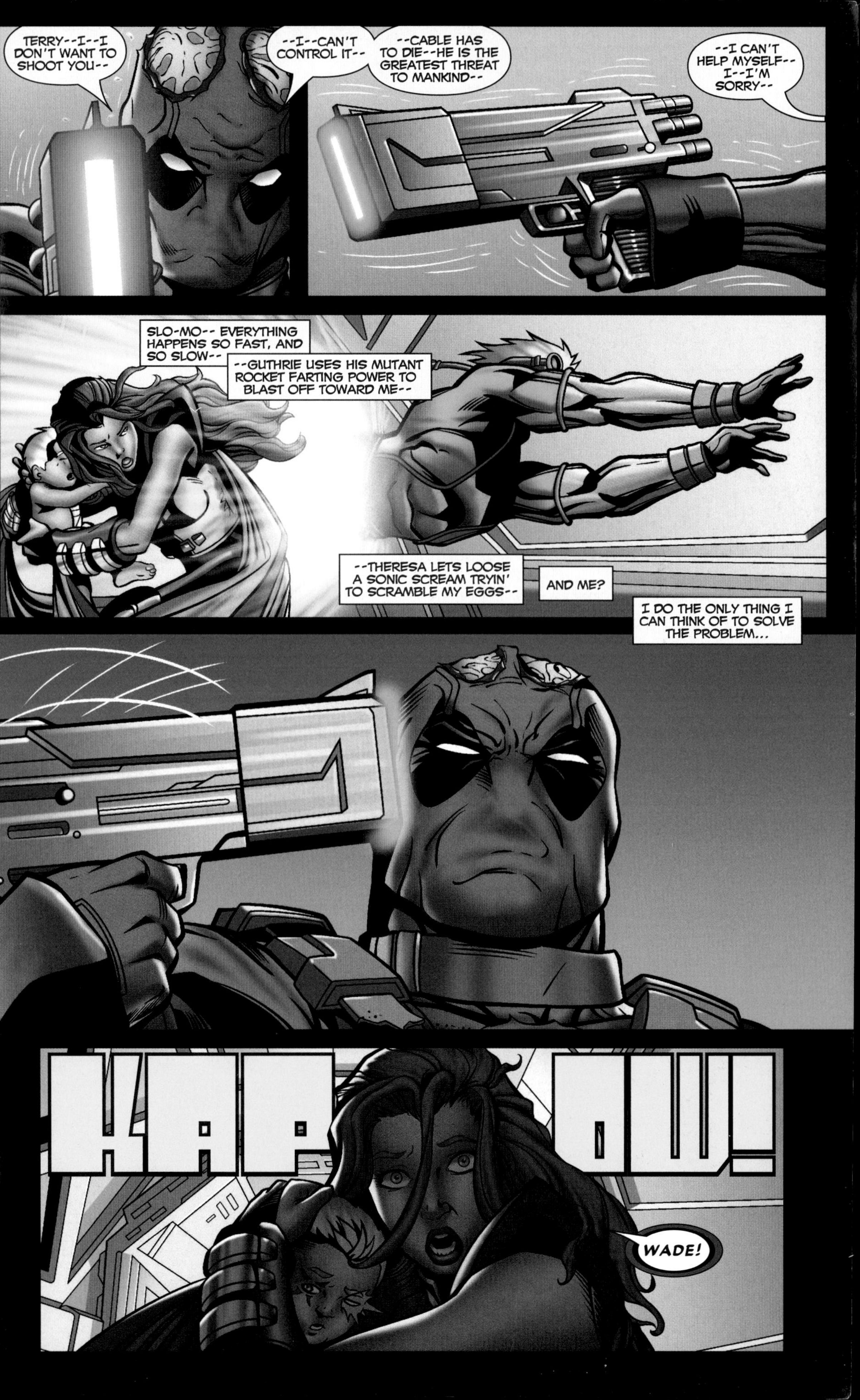
TERRY--I--I DON'T WANT TO SHOOT YOU--
--I--CAN'T CONTROL IT--
--CABLE HAS TO DIE--HE IS THE GREATEST THREAT TO MANKIND--
--I CAN'T HELP MYSELF-- I--I'M SORRY--
SLO-MO-- EVERYTHING HAPPENS SO FAST, AND SO SLOW--
--GUTHRIE USES HIS MUTANT ROCKET FARTING POWER TO BLAST OFF TOWARD ME--
--THERESA LETS LOOSE A SONIC SCREAM TRYIN' TO SCRAMBLE MY EGGS--
AND ME?
I DO THE ONLY THING I CAN THINK OF TO SOLVE THE PROBLEM...
KAP OW!
WADE!

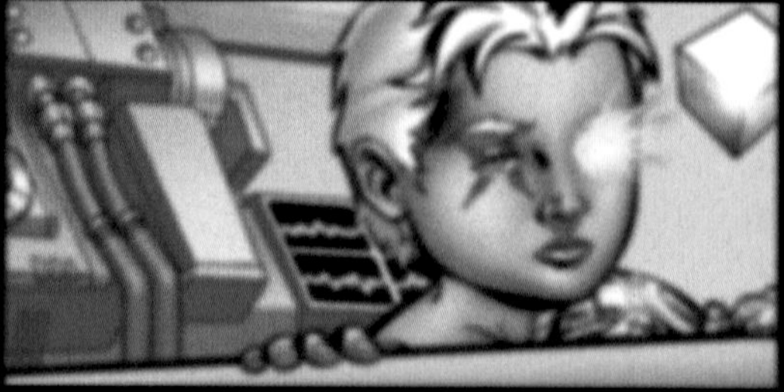

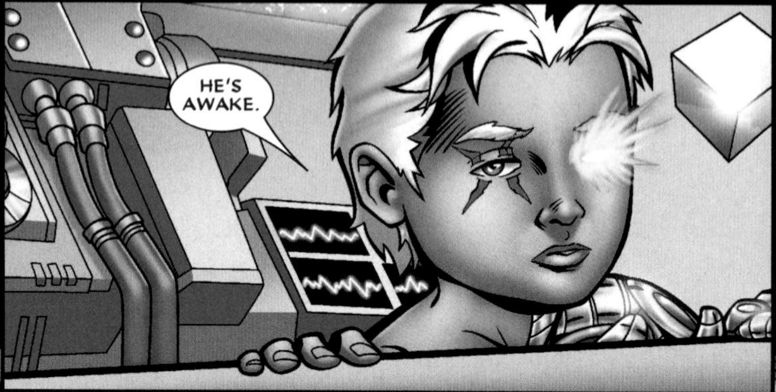
HE'S AWAKE.

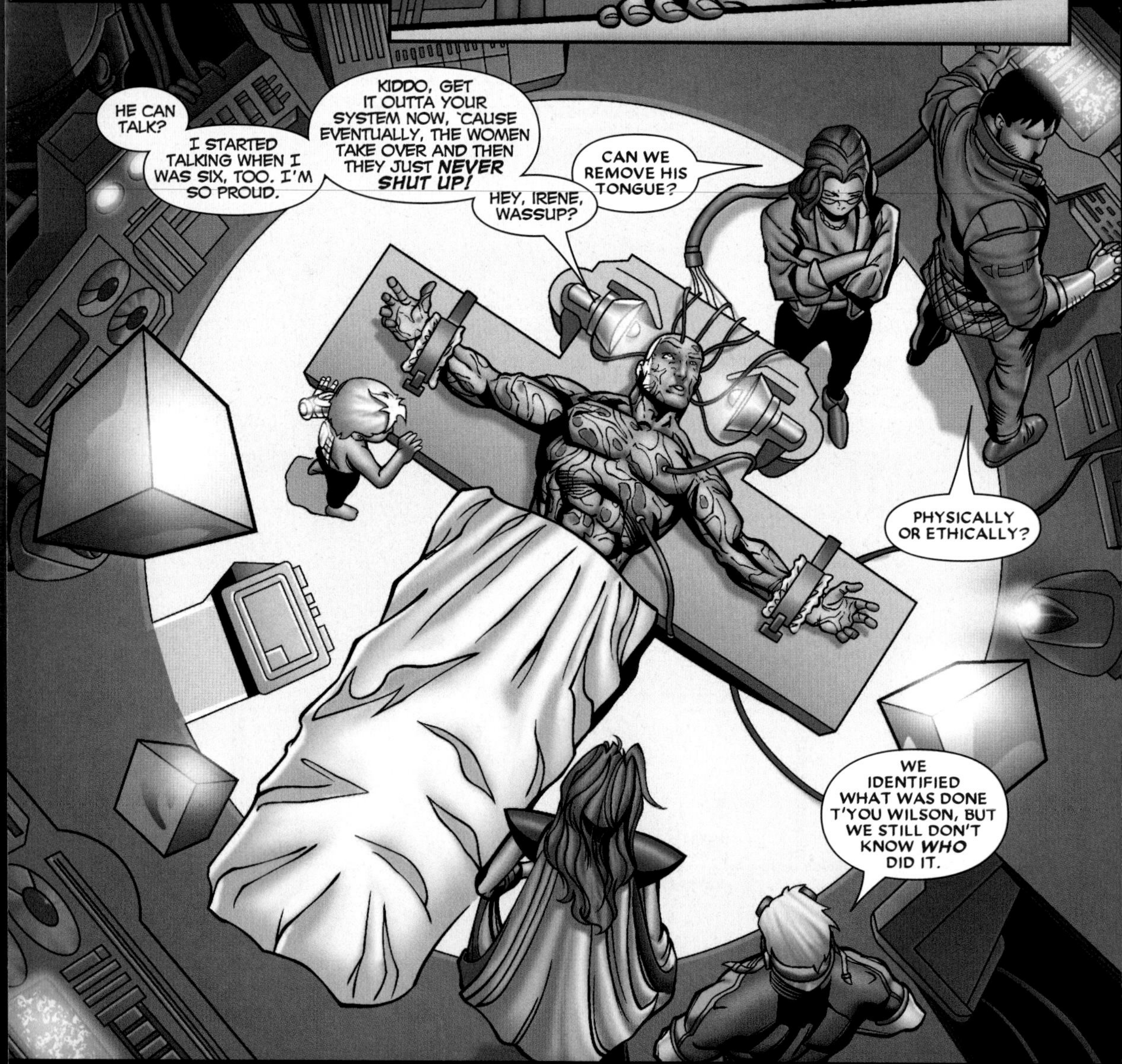
HE CAN TALK?
I STARTED TALKING WHEN I WAS SIX, TOO. I'M SO PROUD.
KIDDO, GET IT OUTTA YOUR SYSTEM NOW, 'CAUSE EVENTUALLY, THE WOMEN TAKE OVER AND THEN THEY JUST NEVER SHUT UP!
HEY, IRENE, WASSUP?
CAN WE REMOVE HIS TONGUE?
PHYSICALLY OR ETHICALLY?
WE IDENTIFIED WHAT WAS DONE T'YOU WILSON, BUT WE STILL DON'T KNOW WHO DID IT.

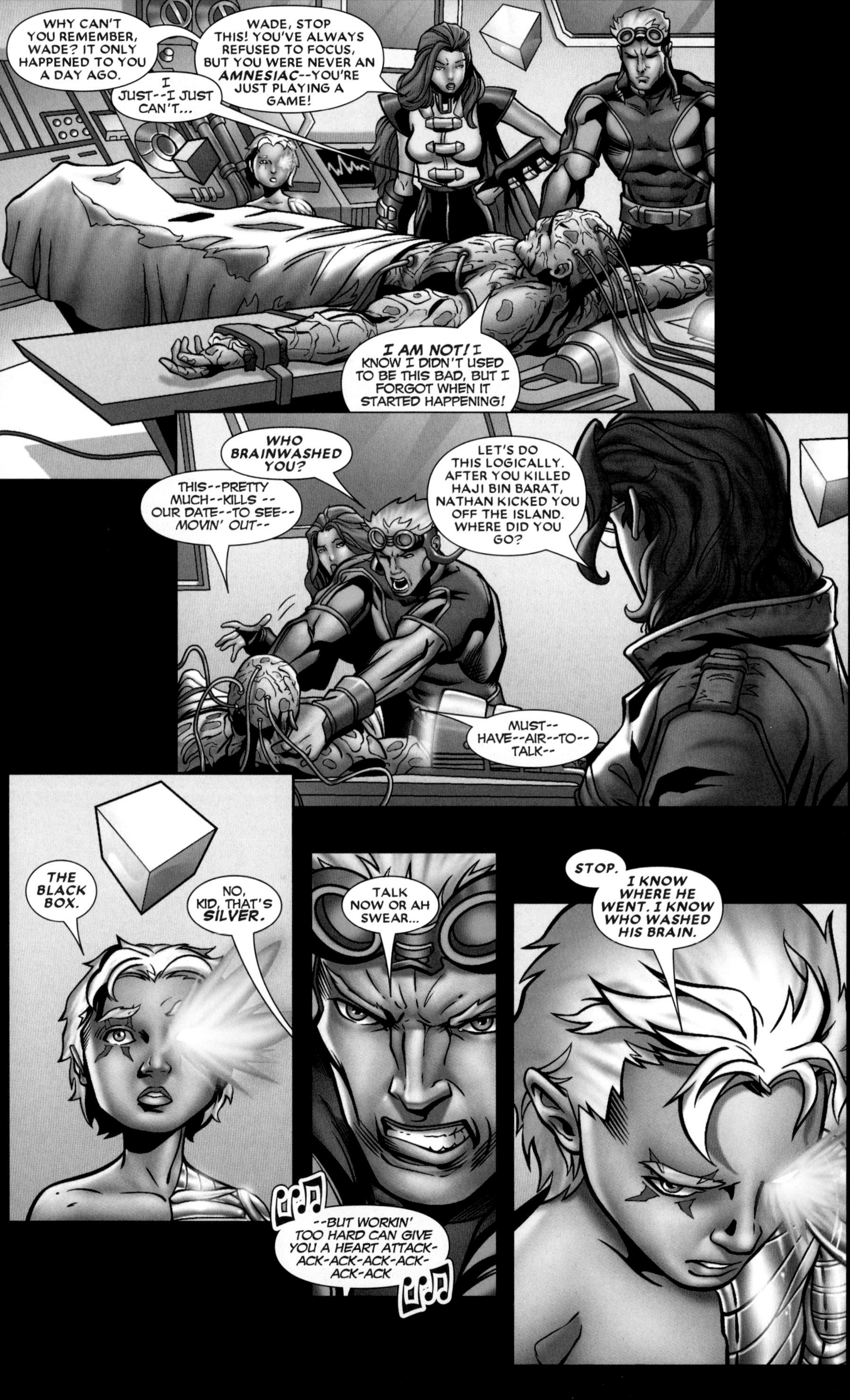
WHY CAN'T YOU REMEMBER, WADE? IT ONLY HAPPENED TO YOU A DAY AGO.
WADE, STOP THIS! YOU'VE ALWAYS REFUSED TO FOCUS, BUT YOU WERE NEVER AN AMNESIAC--YOU'RE JUST PLAYING A GAME!
I JUST--I JUST CAN'T...
I AM NOT! I KNOW I DIDN'T USED TO BE THIS BAD, BUT I FORGOT WHEN IT STARTED HAPPENING!
WHO BRAINWASHED YOU?
THIS--PRETTY MUCH--KILLS--OUR DATE--TO SEE--MOVIN' OUT--
LET'S DO THIS LOGICALLY. AFTER YOU KILLED HAJI BIN BARAT, NATHAN KICKED YOU OFF THE ISLAND. WHERE DID YOU GO?
MUST--HAVE--AIR--TO--TALK--
THE BLACK BOX.
NO, KID, THAT'S SILVER.
TALK NOW OR AH SWEAR...
--BUT WORKIN' TOO HARD CAN GIVE YOU A HEART ATTACK-ACK-ACK-ACK-ACK-ACK-ACK
STOP.
I KNOW WHERE HE WENT. I KNOW WHO WASHED HIS BRAIN.

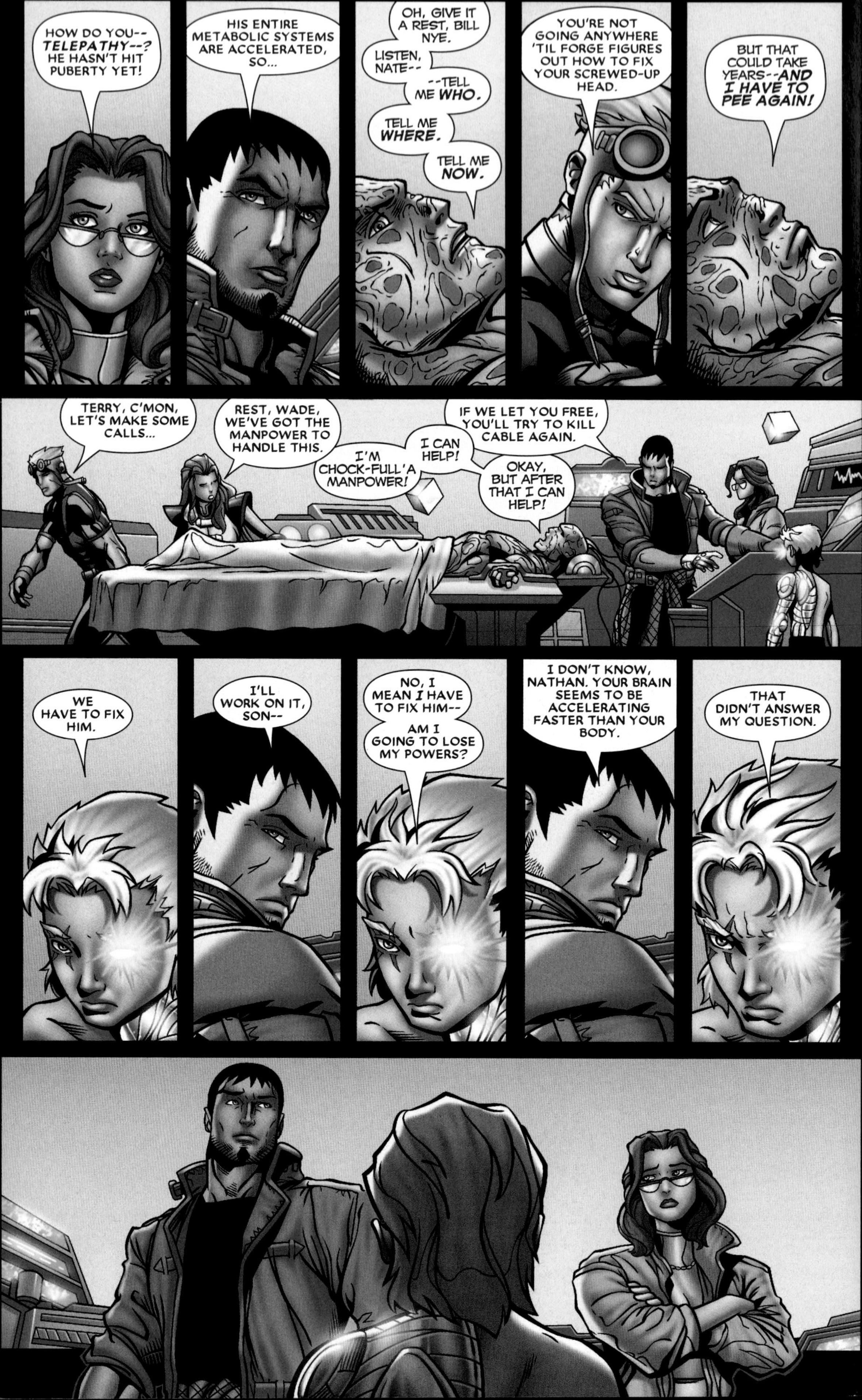
HOW DO YOU-- *TELEPATHY--?* HE HASN'T HIT PUBERTY YET!
HIS ENTIRE METABOLIC SYSTEMS ARE ACCELERATED, SO...
OH, GIVE IT A REST, BILL NYE.
LISTEN, NATE--
--TELL ME **WHO.**
TELL ME **WHERE.**
TELL ME **NOW.**
YOU'RE NOT GOING ANYWHERE 'TIL FORGE FIGURES OUT HOW TO FIX YOUR SCREWED-UP HEAD.
BUT THAT COULD TAKE YEARS--***AND I HAVE TO PEE AGAIN!***
TERRY, C'MON, LET'S MAKE SOME CALLS...
REST, WADE, WE'VE GOT THE MANPOWER TO HANDLE THIS.
I'M CHOCK-FULL'A MANPOWER!
I CAN HELP!
IF WE LET YOU FREE, YOU'LL TRY TO KILL CABLE AGAIN.
OKAY, BUT AFTER THAT I CAN HELP!
WE HAVE TO FIX HIM.
I'LL WORK ON IT, SON--
NO, I MEAN *I* HAVE TO FIX HIM--
AM I GOING TO LOSE MY POWERS?
I DON'T KNOW, NATHAN. YOUR BRAIN SEEMS TO BE ACCELERATING FASTER THAN YOUR BODY.
THAT DIDN'T ANSWER MY QUESTION.

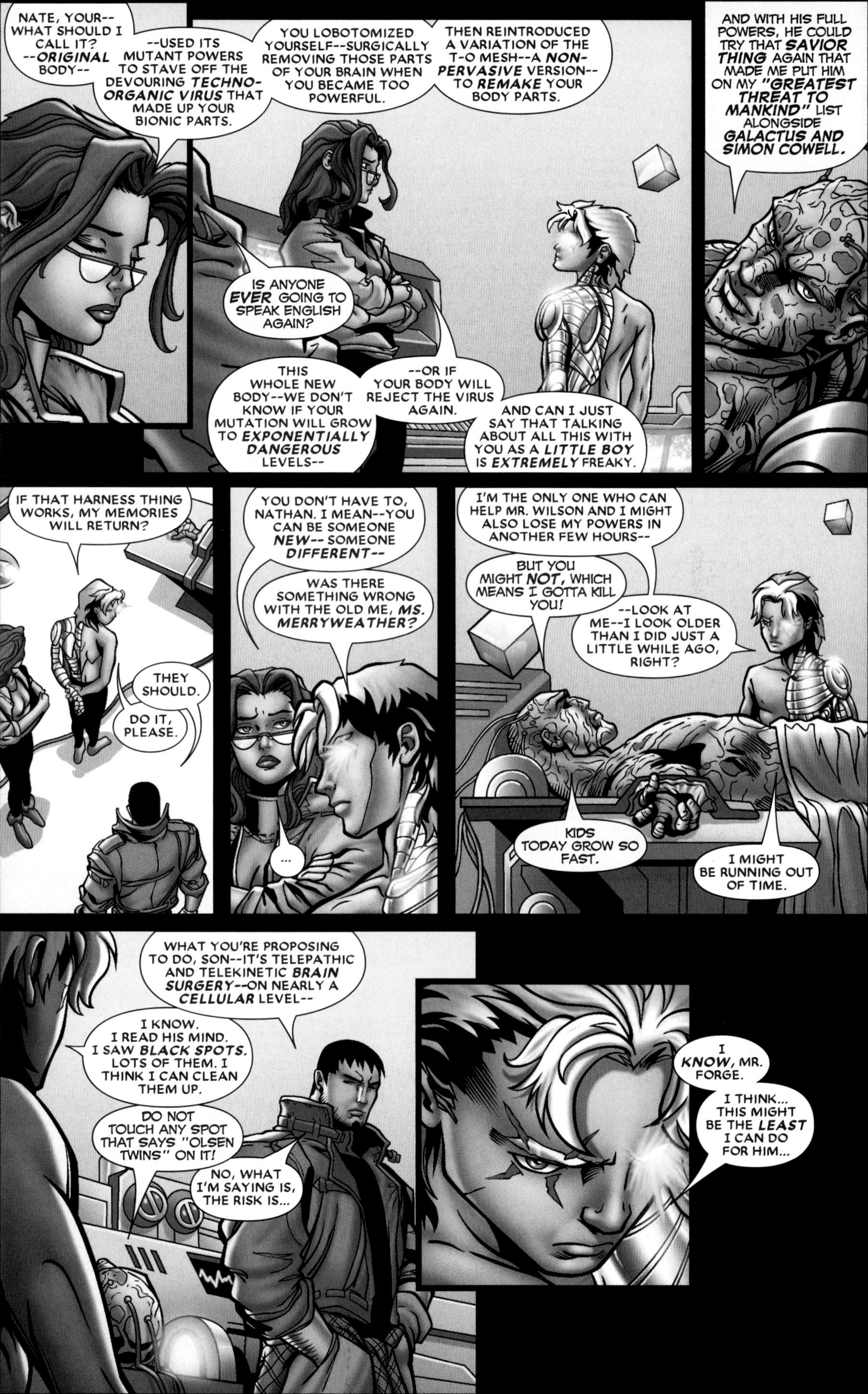

NATE, YOUR-- WHAT SHOULD I CALL IT? --ORIGINAL BODY--
--USED ITS MUTANT POWERS TO STAVE OFF THE DEVOURING TECHNO-ORGANIC VIRUS THAT MADE UP YOUR BIONIC PARTS.
YOU LOBOTOMIZED YOURSELF--SURGICALLY REMOVING THOSE PARTS OF YOUR BRAIN WHEN YOU BECAME TOO POWERFUL.
THEN REINTRODUCED A VARIATION OF THE T-O MESH--A NON-PERVASIVE VERSION--TO REMAKE YOUR BODY PARTS.
IS ANYONE EVER GOING TO SPEAK ENGLISH AGAIN?
THIS WHOLE NEW BODY--WE DON'T KNOW IF YOUR MUTATION WILL GROW TO EXPONENTIALLY DANGEROUS LEVELS--
--OR IF YOUR BODY WILL REJECT THE VIRUS AGAIN.
AND CAN I JUST SAY THAT TALKING ABOUT ALL THIS WITH YOU AS A LITTLE BOY IS EXTREMELY FREAKY.
AND WITH HIS FULL POWERS, HE COULD TRY THAT SAVIOR THING AGAIN THAT MADE ME PUT HIM ON MY "GREATEST THREAT TO MANKIND" LIST ALONGSIDE GALACTUS AND SIMON COWELL.
IF THAT HARNESS THING WORKS, MY MEMORIES WILL RETURN?
THEY SHOULD.
DO IT, PLEASE.
YOU DON'T HAVE TO, NATHAN. I MEAN--YOU CAN BE SOMEONE NEW-- SOMEONE DIFFERENT--
WAS THERE SOMETHING WRONG WITH THE OLD ME, MS. MERRYWEATHER?
...
I'M THE ONLY ONE WHO CAN HELP MR. WILSON AND I MIGHT ALSO LOSE MY POWERS IN ANOTHER FEW HOURS--
BUT YOU MIGHT NOT, WHICH MEANS I GOTTA KILL YOU!
--LOOK AT ME--I LOOK OLDER THAN I DID JUST A LITTLE WHILE AGO, RIGHT?
KIDS TODAY GROW SO FAST.
I MIGHT BE RUNNING OUT OF TIME.
WHAT YOU'RE PROPOSING TO DO, SON--IT'S TELEPATHIC AND TELEKINETIC BRAIN SURGERY--ON NEARLY A CELLULAR LEVEL--
I KNOW. I READ HIS MIND. I SAW BLACK SPOTS. LOTS OF THEM. I THINK I CAN CLEAN THEM UP.
DO NOT TOUCH ANY SPOT THAT SAYS "OLSEN TWINS" ON IT!
NO, WHAT I'M SAYING IS, THE RISK IS...
I KNOW, MR. FORGE.
I THINK... THIS MIGHT BE THE LEAST I CAN DO FOR HIM...

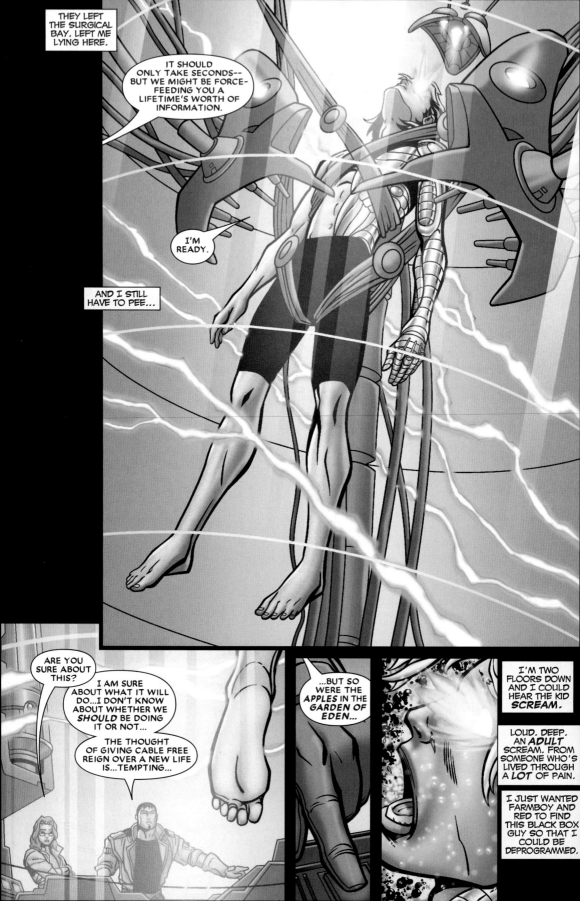

THEY LEFT THE SURGICAL BAY. LEFT ME LYING HERE.

IT SHOULD ONLY TAKE SECONDS-- BUT WE MIGHT BE FORCE-FEEDING YOU A LIFETIME'S WORTH OF INFORMATION.

I'M READY.

AND I STILL HAVE TO PEE...

ARE YOU SURE ABOUT THIS?

I AM SURE ABOUT WHAT IT WILL DO...I DON'T KNOW ABOUT WHETHER WE SHOULD BE DOING IT OR NOT...

THE THOUGHT OF GIVING CABLE FREE REIGN OVER A NEW LIFE IS...TEMPTING...

...BUT SO WERE THE APPLES IN THE GARDEN OF EDEN...

I'M TWO FLOORS DOWN AND I COULD HEAR THE KID SCREAM.

LOUD. DEEP. AN ADULT SCREAM. FROM SOMEONE WHO'S LIVED THROUGH A LOT OF PAIN.

I JUST WANTED FARMBOY AND RED TO FIND THIS BLACK BOX GUY SO THAT I COULD BE DEPROGRAMMED.

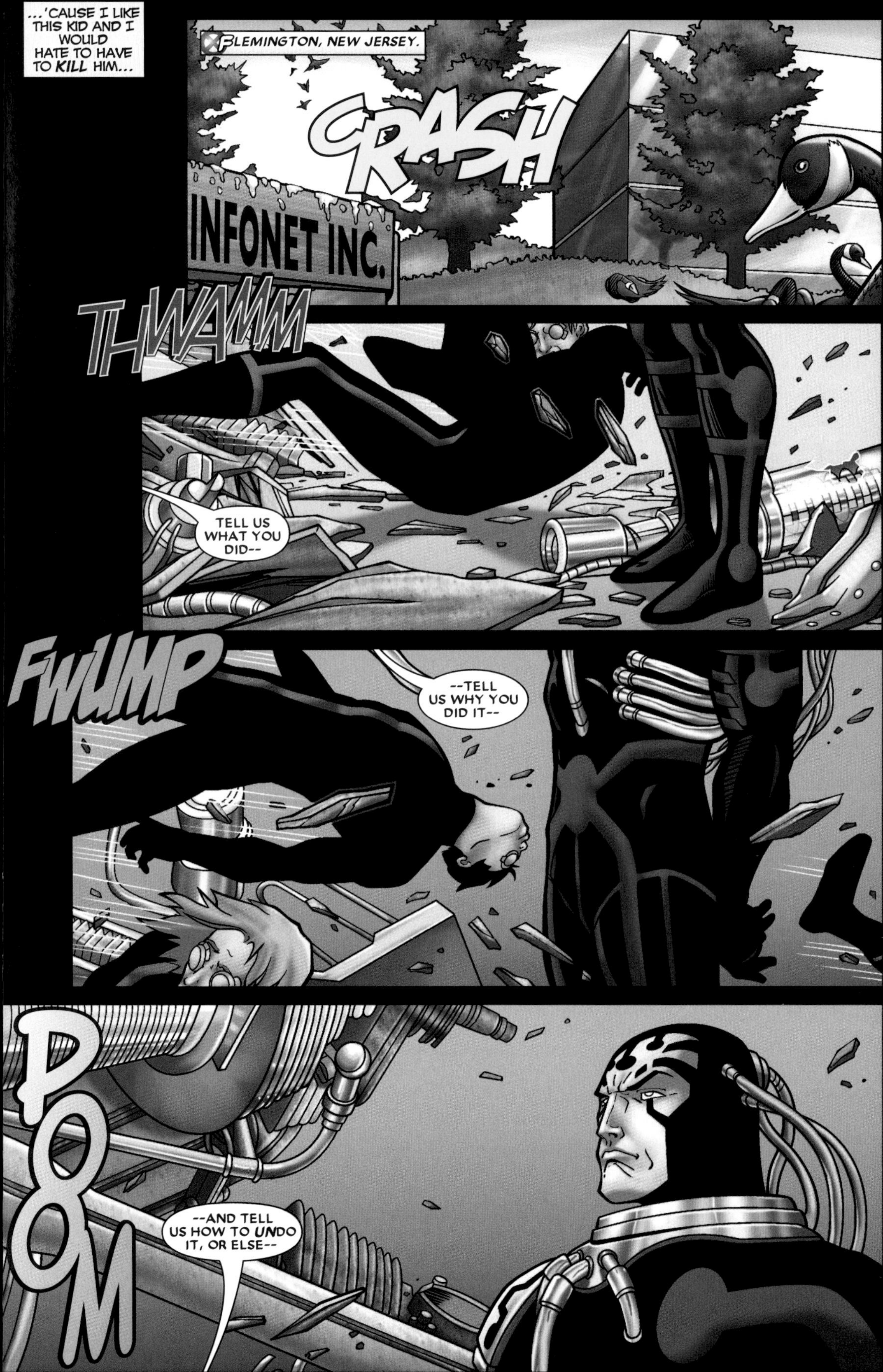
...'CAUSE I LIKE THIS KID AND I WOULD HATE TO HAVE TO KILL HIM...
BLEMINGTON, NEW JERSEY.
CRASH
INFONET INC.
THWAMM
TELL US WHAT YOU DID--
FWUMP
--TELL US WHY YOU DID IT--
POOM
--AND TELL US HOW TO UNDO IT, OR ELSE--

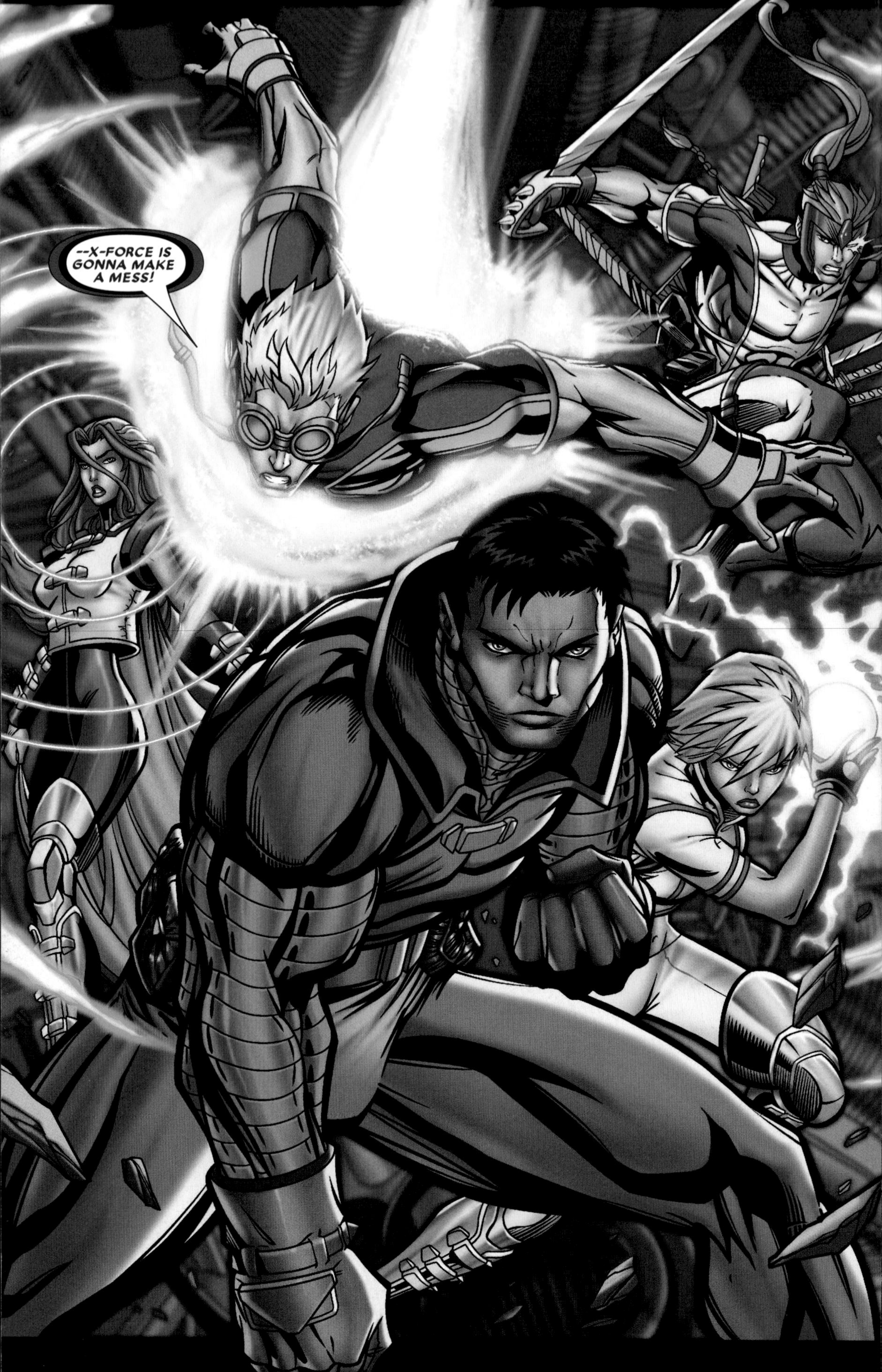
--X-FORCE IS GONNA MAKE A MESS!

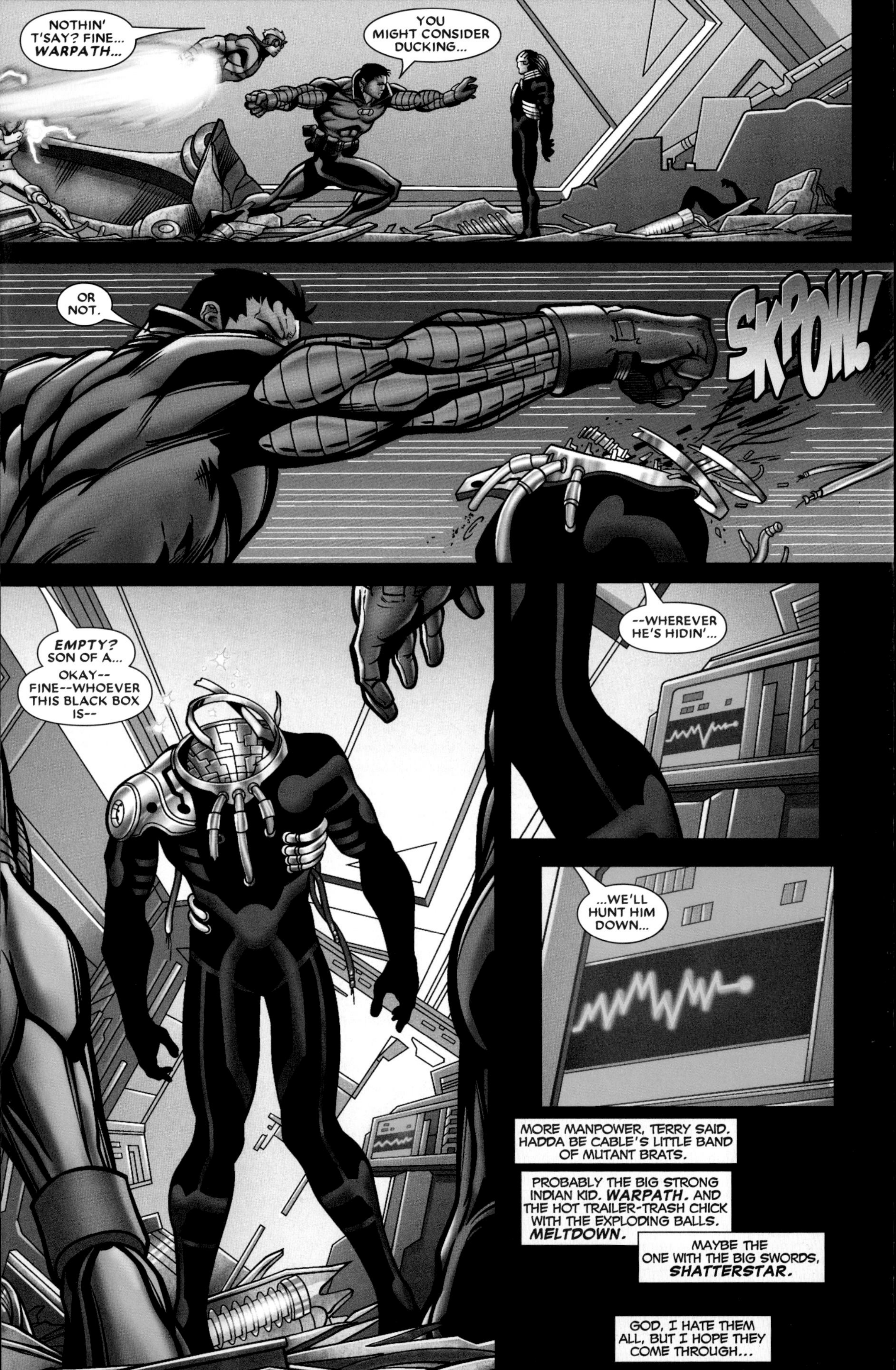
NOTHIN' T'SAY? FINE... WARPATH...
YOU MIGHT CONSIDER DUCKING...
OR NOT.
SKPOW!
EMPTY? SON OF A... OKAY-- FINE--WHOEVER THIS BLACK BOX IS--
--WHEREVER HE'S HIDIN'...
...WE'LL HUNT HIM DOWN...
MORE MANPOWER, TERRY SAID. HADDA BE CABLE'S LITTLE BAND OF MUTANT BRATS.
PROBABLY THE BIG STRONG INDIAN KID. WARPATH. AND THE HOT TRAILER-TRASH CHICK WITH THE EXPLODING BALLS. MELTDOWN.
MAYBE THE ONE WITH THE BIG SWORDS, SHATTERSTAR.
GOD, I HATE THEM ALL, BUT I HOPE THEY COME THROUGH...

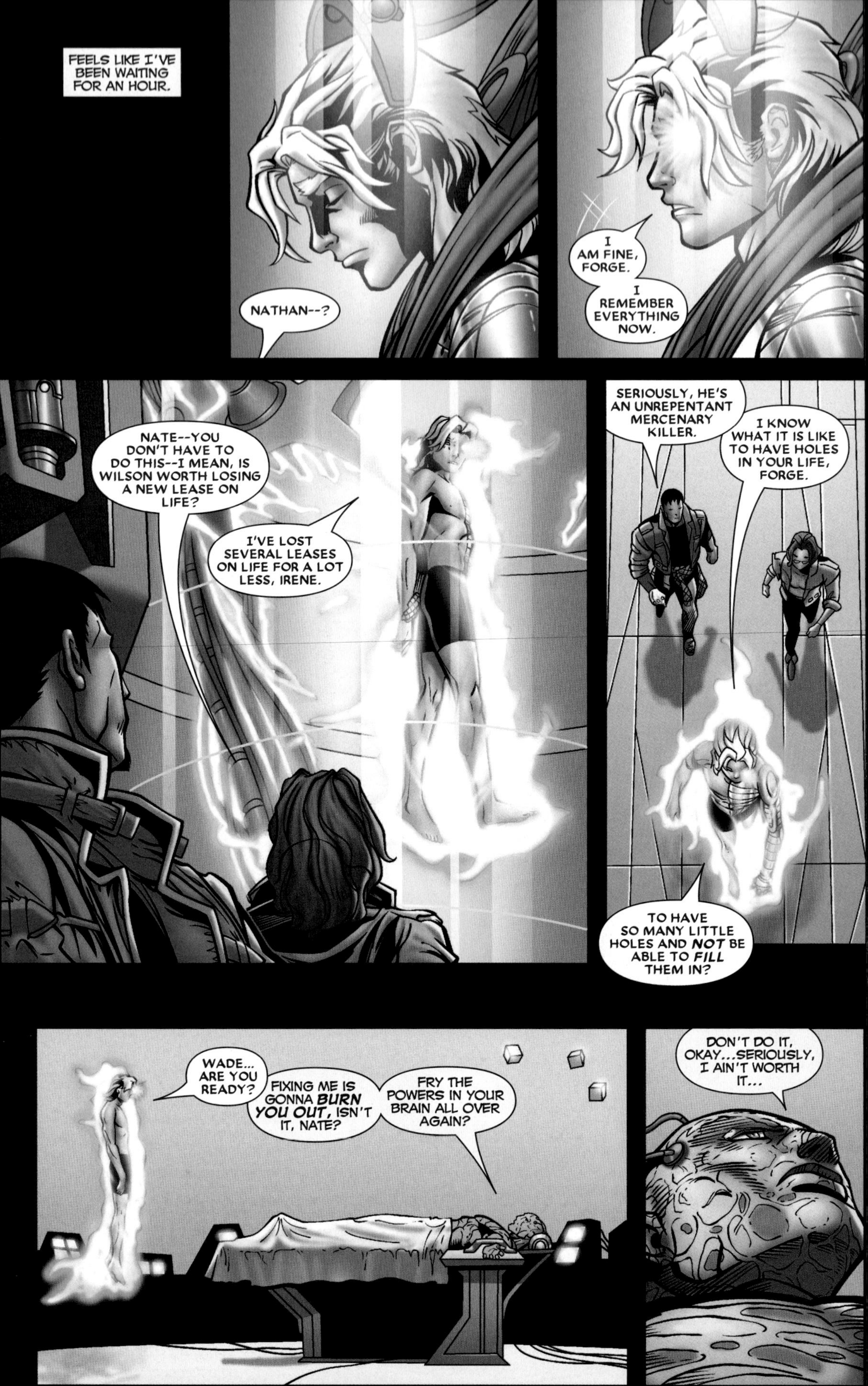
FEELS LIKE I'VE BEEN WAITING FOR AN HOUR.
NATHAN--?
I AM FINE, FORGE.
I REMEMBER EVERYTHING NOW.
NATE--YOU DON'T HAVE TO DO THIS--I MEAN, IS WILSON WORTH LOSING A NEW LEASE ON LIFE?
I'VE LOST SEVERAL LEASES ON LIFE FOR A LOT LESS, IRENE.
SERIOUSLY, HE'S AN UNREPENTANT MERCENARY KILLER.
I KNOW WHAT IT IS LIKE TO HAVE HOLES IN YOUR LIFE, FORGE.
TO HAVE SO MANY LITTLE HOLES AND NOT BE ABLE TO FILL THEM IN?
WADE... ARE YOU READY?
FIXING ME IS GONNA BURN YOU OUT, ISN'T IT, NATE?
FRY THE POWERS IN YOUR BRAIN ALL OVER AGAIN?
DON'T DO IT, OKAY...SERIOUSLY, I AIN'T WORTH IT...

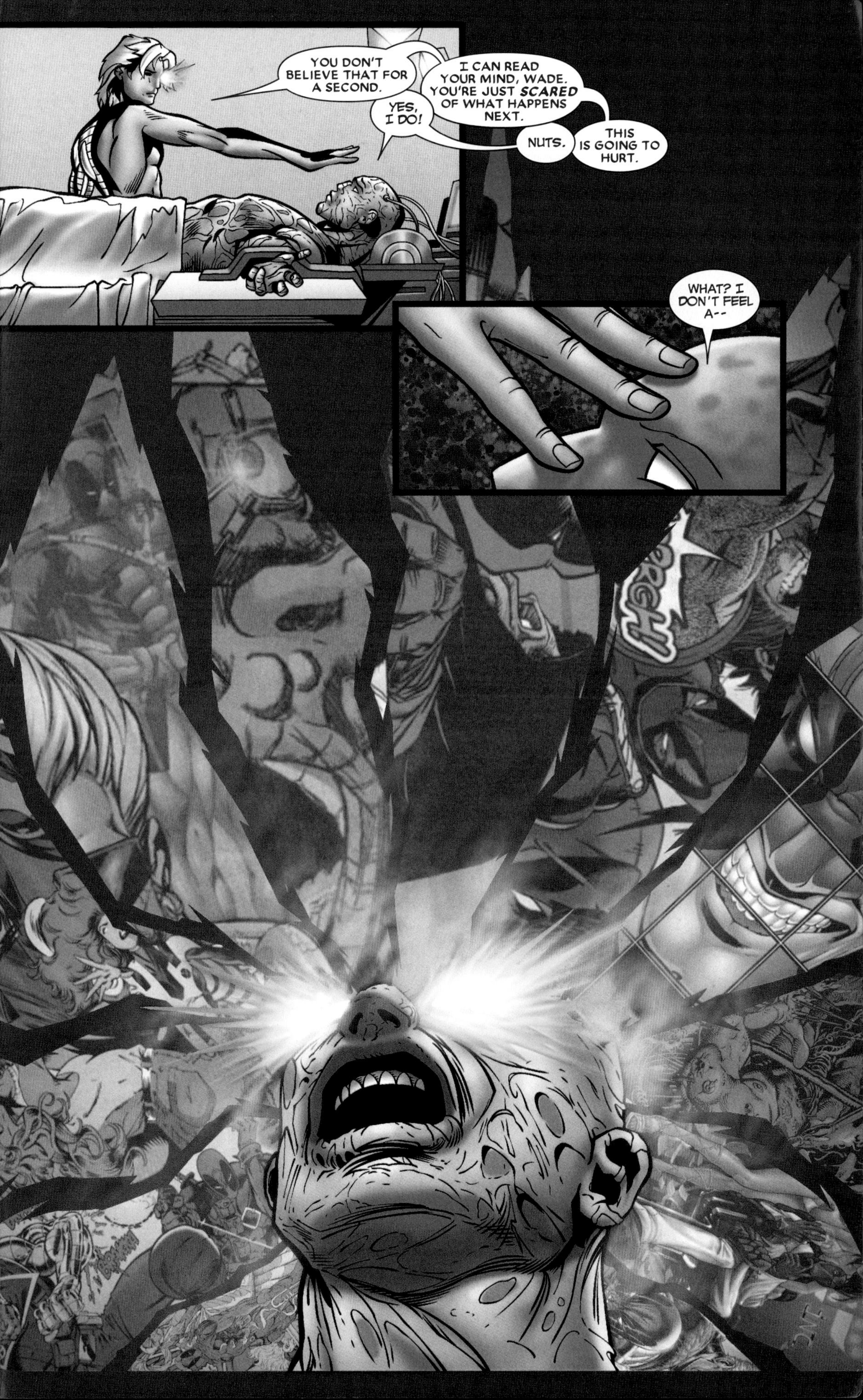
YOU DON'T BELIEVE THAT FOR A SECOND.
YES, I DO!
I CAN READ YOUR MIND, WADE. YOU'RE JUST SCARED OF WHAT HAPPENS NEXT.
NUTS.
THIS IS GOING TO HURT.
WHAT? I DON'T FEEL A--

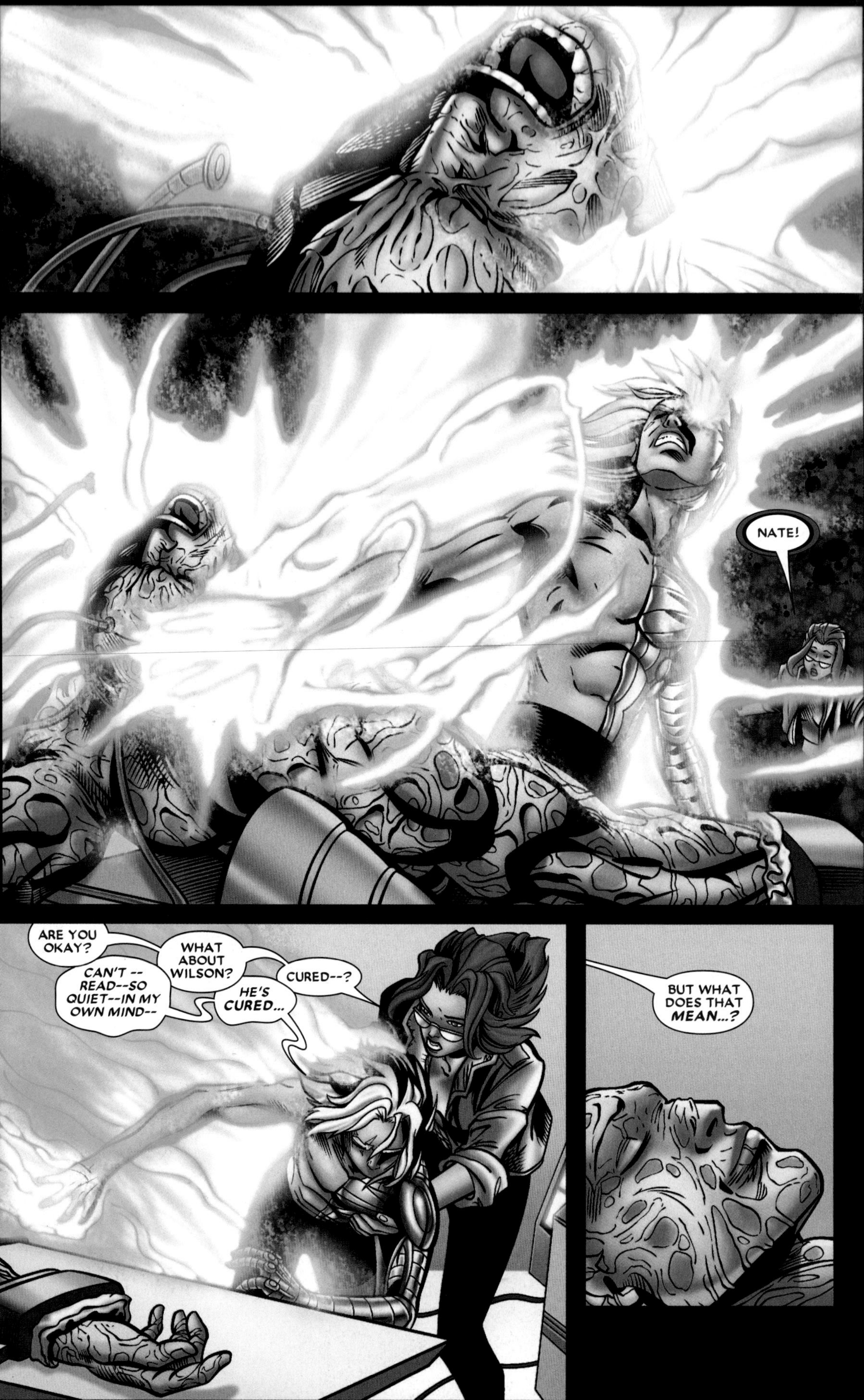
NATE!
ARE YOU OKAY?
WHAT ABOUT WILSON?
CAN'T -- READ--SO QUIET--IN MY OWN MIND--
HE'S CURED...
CURED--?
BUT WHAT DOES THAT MEAN...?

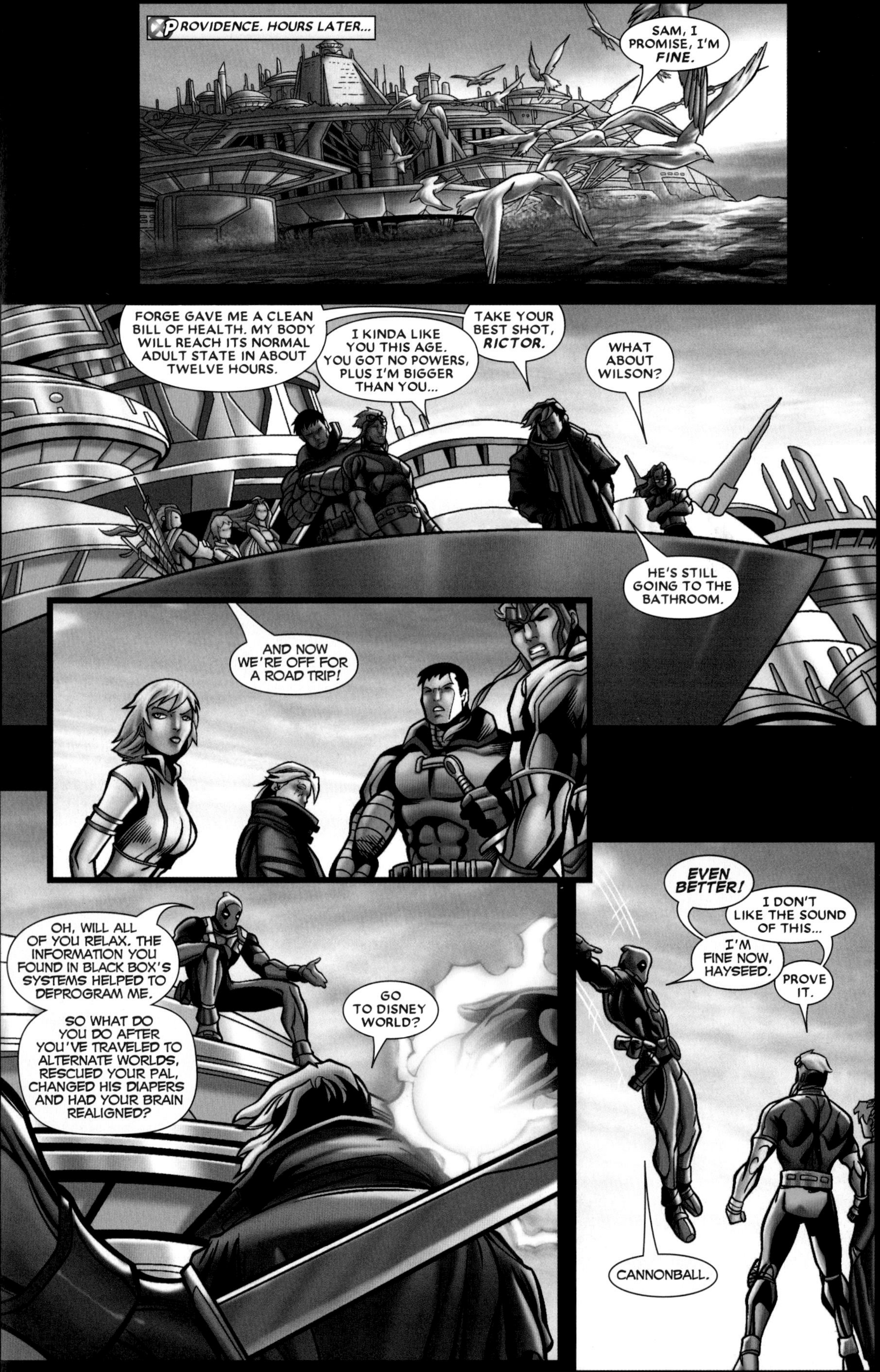
PROVIDENCE. HOURS LATER...
SAM, I PROMISE, I'M FINE.
FORGE GAVE ME A CLEAN BILL OF HEALTH. MY BODY WILL REACH ITS NORMAL ADULT STATE IN ABOUT TWELVE HOURS.
I KINDA LIKE YOU THIS AGE. YOU GOT NO POWERS, PLUS I'M BIGGER THAN YOU...
TAKE YOUR BEST SHOT, RICTOR.
WHAT ABOUT WILSON?
HE'S STILL GOING TO THE BATHROOM.
AND NOW WE'RE OFF FOR A ROAD TRIP!
OH, WILL ALL OF YOU RELAX. THE INFORMATION YOU FOUND IN BLACK BOX'S SYSTEMS HELPED TO DEPROGRAM ME.
SO WHAT DO YOU DO AFTER YOU'VE TRAVELED TO ALTERNATE WORLDS, RESCUED YOUR PAL, CHANGED HIS DIAPERS AND HAD YOUR BRAIN REALIGNED?
GO TO DISNEY WORLD?
EVEN BETTER!
I DON'T LIKE THE SOUND OF THIS...
I'M FINE NOW, HAYSEED.
PROVE IT.
CANNONBALL.

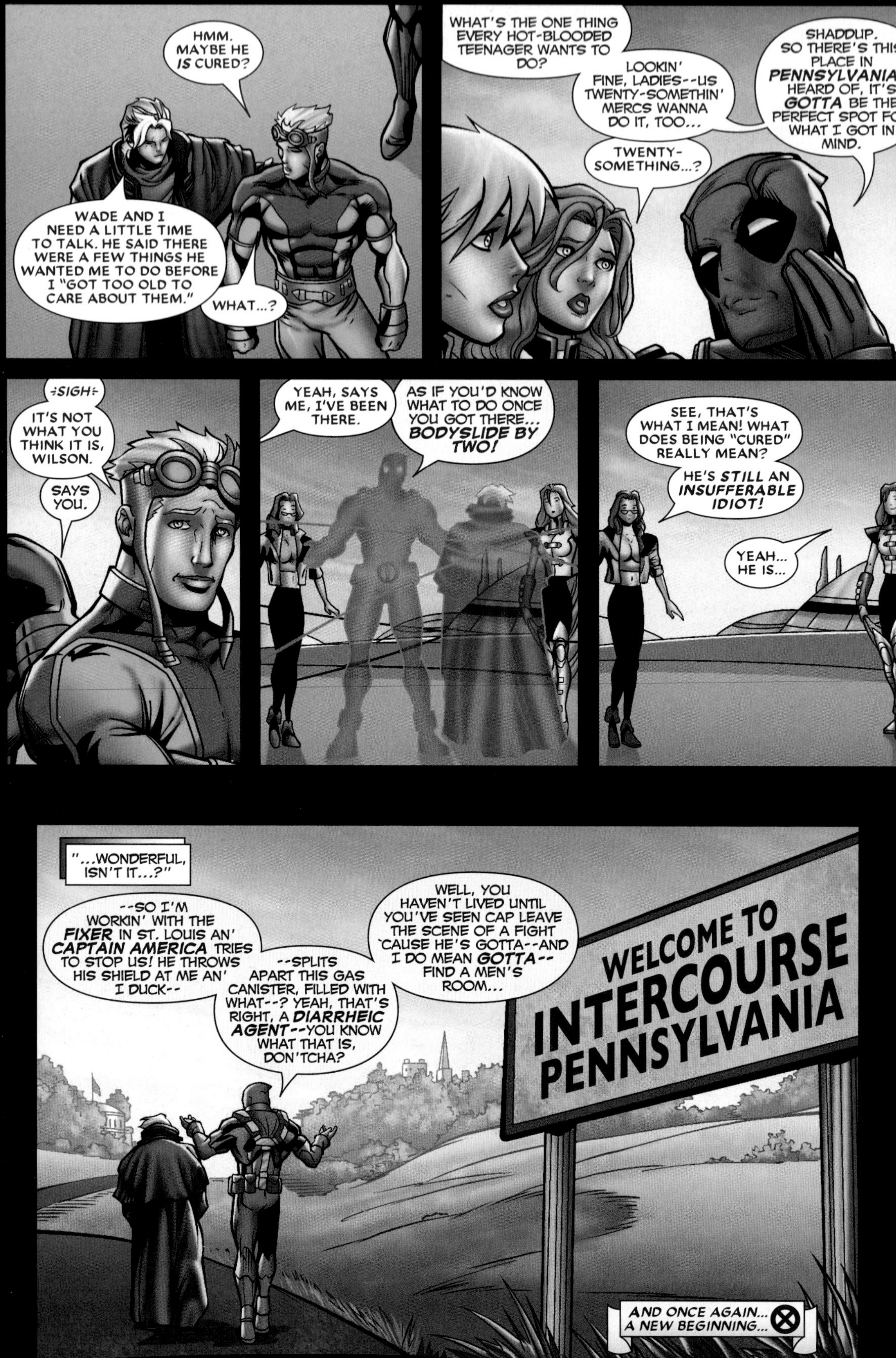

HMM. MAYBE HE *IS* CURED?
WADE AND I NEED A LITTLE TIME TO TALK. HE SAID THERE WERE A FEW THINGS HE WANTED ME TO DO BEFORE I "GOT TOO OLD TO CARE ABOUT THEM."
WHAT...?
WHAT'S THE ONE THING EVERY HOT-BLOODED TEENAGER WANTS TO DO?
LOOKIN' FINE, LADIES--US TWENTY-SOMETHIN' MERCS WANNA DO IT, TOO...
TWENTY-SOMETHING...?
SHADDUP. SO THERE'S THIS PLACE IN *PENNSYLVANIA* I HEARD OF, IT'S *GOTTA* BE THE PERFECT SPOT FOR WHAT I GOT IN MIND.
-SIGH-
IT'S NOT WHAT YOU THINK IT IS, WILSON.
SAYS YOU.
YEAH, SAYS ME, I'VE BEEN THERE.
AS IF YOU'D KNOW WHAT TO DO ONCE YOU GOT THERE... *BODYSLIDE BY TWO!*
SEE, THAT'S WHAT I MEAN! WHAT DOES BEING "CURED" REALLY MEAN?
HE'S *STILL* AN *INSUFFERABLE IDIOT!*
YEAH... HE IS...
"...WONDERFUL, ISN'T IT...?"
--SO I'M WORKIN' WITH THE *FIXER* IN ST. LOUIS AN' *CAPTAIN AMERICA* TRIES TO STOP US! HE THROWS HIS SHIELD AT ME AN' I DUCK--
--SPLITS APART THIS GAS CANISTER, FILLED WITH WHAT--? YEAH, THAT'S RIGHT, A *DIARRHEIC AGENT*--YOU KNOW WHAT THAT IS, DON'TCHA?
WELL, YOU HAVEN'T LIVED UNTIL YOU'VE SEEN CAP LEAVE THE SCENE OF A FIGHT 'CAUSE HE'S GOTTA--AND I DO MEAN *GOTTA*--FIND A MEN'S ROOM...
WELCOME TO INTERCOURSE PENNSYLVANIA
AND ONCE AGAIN... A NEW BEGINNING...

ISSUE #6

COVER PENCILS BY **PATRICK ZIRCHER**

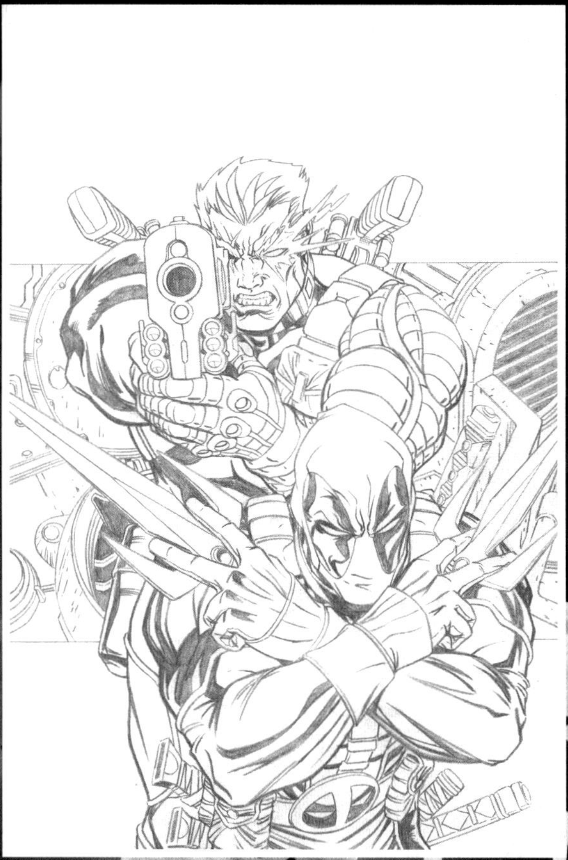

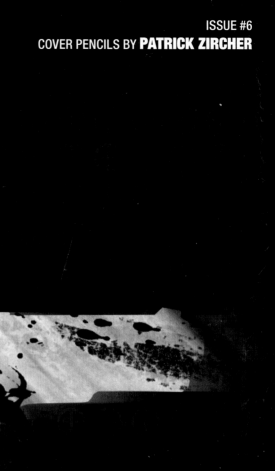

ISSUE #9

COVER SKETCH & PENCILS BY **PATRICK ZIRCHER**

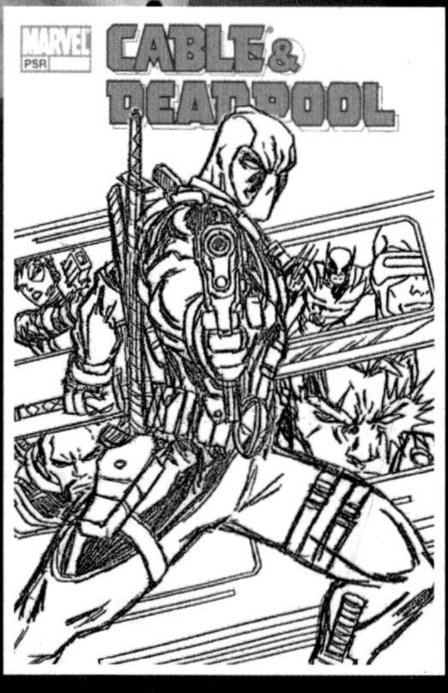
MARVEL
PSR
CABLE &
DEADPOOL

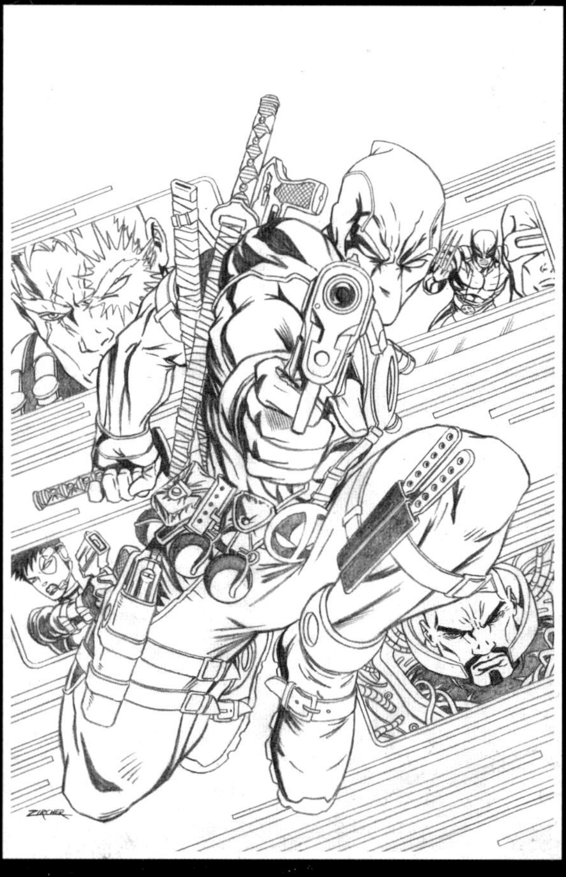
ZIRCHER

ISSUE #11

COVER SKETCH & PENCILS BY **PATRICK ZIRCHER**

INKS BY **M3TH**

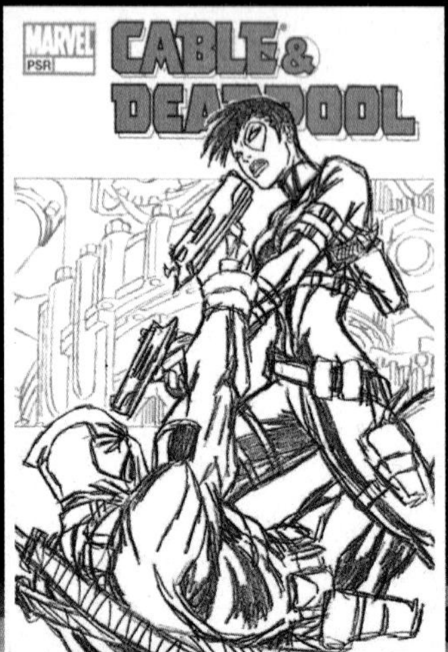
MARVEL
PSR

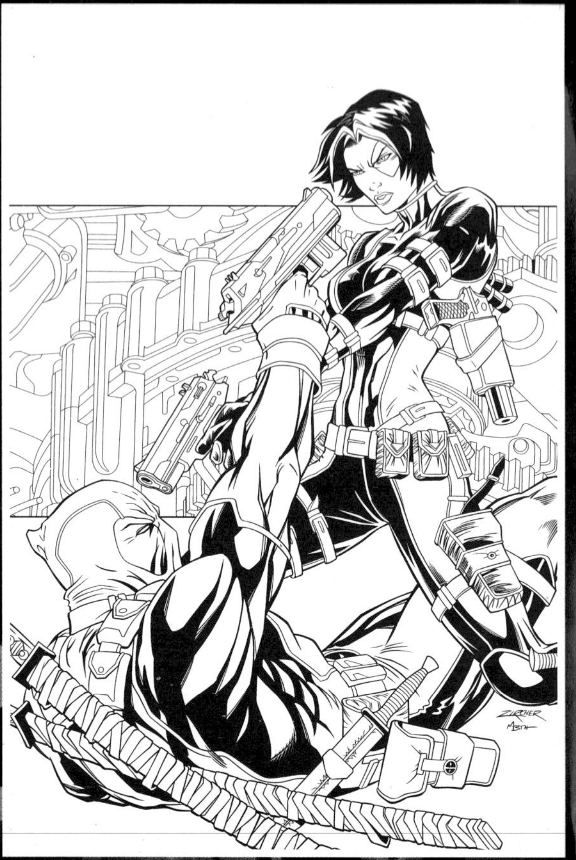

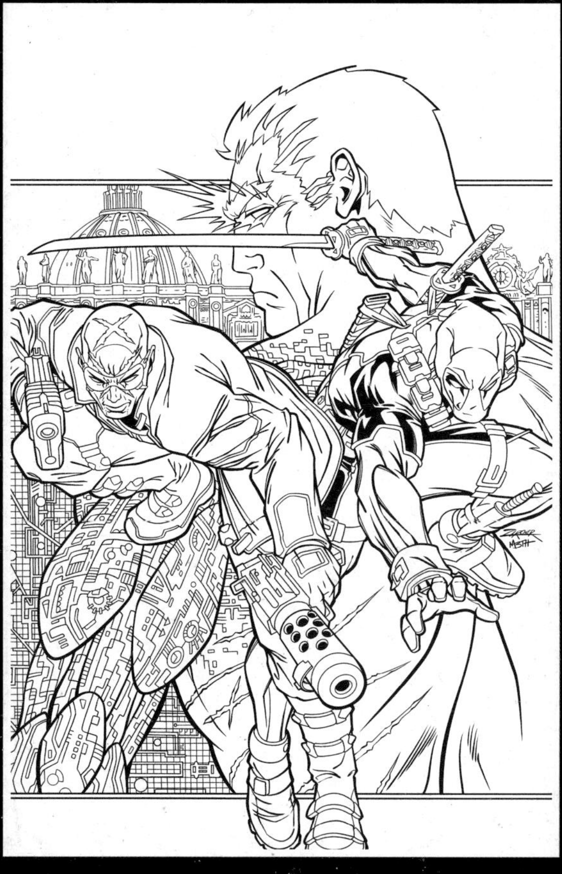

ISSUE #12

COVER SKETCH & PENCILS BY **PATRICK ZIRCHER**

INKS BY **M3TH**

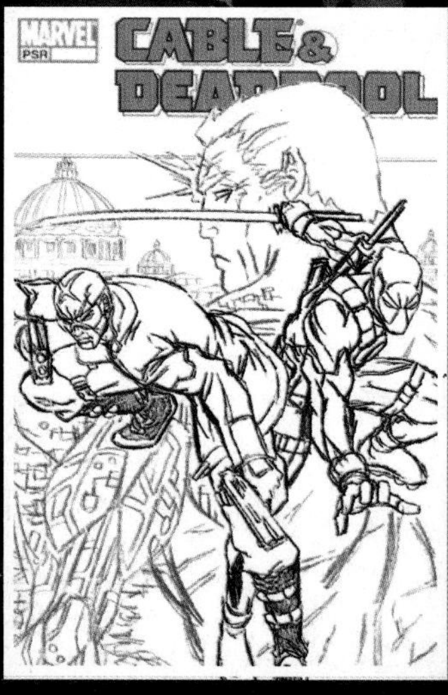
MARVEL
PSR